Sunset

The Western Garden Book

By the Editors of Sunset Books
and Sunset Magazine

Lane Publishing Co. • Menlo Park, California

The Western Garden Book has a companion—
Sunset's *Gardener's Answer Book*. This year-
round, easy-to-understand guide provides
practical answers to more than 400 specific
Western gardening questions.

Sunset Books
  Editor, David E. Clark
  Managing Editor, Elizabeth L. Hogan

Eleventh printing July 1987
(Updated December 1986)

Foreword

Welcome to the fourth edition of the *Sunset Western Garden Book.* This book serves those who garden in the western United States—from the coastal communities of California, Oregon, and Washington east through the hills, valleys, mountains, and deserts of Arizona, Nevada, Idaho, and Utah, to the mountains and plains of Montana, Wyoming, Colorado, and New Mexico.

This portion of the earth is indeed a special province. Its weather comes from the Pacific Ocean but is later modified by the many mountain ranges that subdivide western North America. The result is a gardening region like none other in the world. For the most part, our climates allow us to grow a wider array of plants and undertake a wider range of garden activity than is possible anywhere else.

The new *Sunset Western Garden Book* describes the several thousand plants that we can grow in the West, assigns them by numbers to the climates where they grow best, and tells you how to grow them. Climate maps and best-climate recommendations now include the tier of western states that was added to *Sunset Magazine's* circulation area in 1977— Montana, Wyoming, Colorado, and New Mexico.

Evolving out of several illustrious predecessors that go back as far as the early 1930's, this new edition brings a number of improvements. For the first time in the book's history, every one of the many hundreds of plant genera is illustrated. And a special plant selection guide (pages 97–160) contains not only a variety of plant listings and charts, but another first—color photographs of selected plants that do well in specific situations.

The latest thinking on use of water is reflected in this new edition. The West's great drought of 1975–1977 made us even more aware that our territory always will be subject to periodic dry years. As populations increase, water will become more and more treasured. Consequently, water requirements should be a part of almost all garden planning. In this new book, every permanent landscape plant in the Western Plant Encyclopedia is appraised for its drought tolerance (does it need a lot of water or a little?).

We at *Sunset* could not have written this book alone. The only way we could do it was to get answers from hundreds of garden experts all over the West. Our special thanks go to those whose names are listed on the next two pages.

We hope this book will make gardening more enjoyable for you than ever before.

Joseph F. Williamson
Garden Editor, *Sunset Magazine*

Staff

Editorial Director: Joseph F. Williamson
Garden Editor, *Sunset Magazine*

Book Editor: John R. Dunmire
Associate Editor, *Sunset Magazine*

Supervising Editor: Maureen Williams Zimmerman

Assistant Editor: Philip Edinger

Art Director: Roger Flanagan

Design: Joe di Chiarro

Illustrations: E. D. Bills, Mary Davey Burkhardt, Ireta Cooper

Climate Maps: Joe Seney

Special Consultants: Bob Cowden, Warren Jones, Glenn Park,
George Harmon Scott, Michael N. Smith,
Joseph A. Witt, Walter L. Doty,
Elsa Uppman Knoll

Staff Assistants: Rita Smith, Sherry Gellner, Peggy Kuhn Thompson,
Christine Barnes, Kathy Lefferts, Cornelia Fogle,
Barbara J. Braasch, Joan Erickson,
Julie Anne Gold, Joe Seals, Susan Warton,
John McCarthy, Colleen Hamilton,
Virginia Pribyl

Consultants

Pacific Northwest
Arthur L. Antonelli
Noble Bashor
Donald W. Berry
Wilbur L. Bluhm
Lloyd Bond
J. Harold Clarke
Jan de Graaff
Fred L. Delkin
Andrew A. Duncan
Chandler D. Fairbank
James Gossler
L. Keith Hellstrom
Harold T. Hopkins
Anton S. Horn
Wallace K. Huntington
Ray A. McNeilan
Grant E. Mitsch
Earl L. Phillips
Wallace M. Ruff
George Schenk
R. M. Snodgrass
Gilbert Sternes
D. J. Stevlingson

Charles Thurman
Paul Van Allen
Ted Van Veen
Mary Whiteley
Joseph A. Witt
Harriett G. Zorner

California and Nevada
William Aplin
David Armstrong
Robert Boddy
John Boething
Worth Brown
P. H. Brydon
Charles Burr
Philip E. Chandler
Francis Ching
B. D. Coate
Clifford Comstock
Al Condit
Ira J. Condit
Bob Cowden
Andre Cuenoud

A. G. Davids
Donald F. Dillon
Jocelyn Domela
Eckbo, Dean, Austin, and Williams
John Edwards
Clyde Elmore
Morgan Evans
Percy C. Everett
David Feathers
Bryan Fewer
Tokuji Furuta
Burr Garman
DeWayne E. Gilbert
Svend Gottschalk
George Haight
William A. Harvey
Ernest Hetherington
Barbara Joe Hoshizaki
Colin Jackson
Eric Johnson
William H. Jordan, Jr.
William Louis Kapranos
Myron W. Kimnach
Masaru Kimura

Table of Contents

More than 5,000 plants listed alphabetically according to botanical names. Common names are also listed for easy cross-reference.

The West's 24 Climate Zones

In this book's Western Plant Encyclopedia (beginning on page 161) and in Planting For a Purpose (pages 97 to 160) you will find climate zones assigned to almost every listed plant.

If you've been gardening for any time at all, you know why such climate assignments are necessary. The plants we grow in western gardens come from all parts of the world. Because of their greatly varied backgrounds, they differ immensely in their response to the different climates of the West. Many can't live through a cold winter. Others must have cold winters. Some can't perform well in coastal humidity; others depend on damp air—and so it goes. Many factors combine and interplay to establish climates. These factors combine in so many ways in the West that in this book we have identified two dozen different plant climate zones.

A plant climate zone is an area in which a common set of temperature ranges, humidity patterns, and other geographic and seasonal characteristics combine to allow certain plants to succeed and cause others to fail.

Remember, there's a difference between *weather* and *climate*. Weather is what is going on in the atmosphere outside your window at the moment you read this. Climate is the all-seasons accumulation of the effects of the weather that comes to your area.

Six important factors combine to make up western plant climate zones. Here they are:

1. Distance from the equator (latitude). Generally, the farther a spot is from the equator, the longer and colder are its winters. The number of hours of daylight increases in summer and decreases in winter as you progress from the equator toward the pole.

2. Elevation. High elevations mean longer and colder winters, and comparatively lower night temperatures all through the year.

3. Influence of the Pacific Ocean. Weather in the western United States comes almost completely from two sources—the Pacific Ocean is one of them. The more an area is dominated by the Pacific Ocean's weather, the moister is its atmosphere at all seasons, the milder its winters, the cooler its summers, and the more its rainfall is limited to fall, winter, and spring.

4. Influence of the continental air mass. This is the other major source of our weather in the West. The North American continent creates its own weather (quite different from that created by the ocean). The farther inland you live, the more the continental air mass influences your weather. The more such influence an area gets the colder are its winters, the hotter are its summers, and the more likely is its precipitation to come at any time of the year.

5. Mountains and hills. Our systems of hills and mountains act as barriers that determine whether areas beyond them will be influenced mostly by marine air or mostly by continental air—or, as happens in some places, by some of each. The Coast Ranges take some of the marine influence out of air that passes west-to-east across them. The marine influence that the Coast Ranges don't take out is effectively weakened or stopped by the lofty second barrier—the Sierra-Cascades and southern California's interior mountains. And beyond the mighty Rocky Mountains, the marine influence is virtually nil—here, arctic air plays a substantial role in the climate. In exactly the opposite order, first the Rockies, then the interior ranges, and then the Coast Ranges lessen or eliminate the westward influence of the continental air mass.

6. Local terrain. The five factors mentioned above operate at all seasons. Local terrain has its major effect on the cold air and frosts of fall, winter, and spring.

Warm air rises. Cold air sinks. Experienced gardeners understand the practical applications of these physical facts: they know that cold air flows (or moves or slides) downhill. If yours is a hillside garden—or even if your entire community is on a slanting plain that ultimately leads to lower ground in the next county—your garden will never be quite as cold in winter as will the gardens at the base of the hill, along the distant river, or at the lowest end of the sloping plain. The bands of a hillside or tilted valley floor from which cold air flows downhill are called *thermal belts*. The lowlands, valley centers, and river bottoms into which the cold air flows are called *cold-air basins*. Above the thermal belt, winter air can be so cold (because of the elevation influence mentioned above) that the temperature can be as low as in the cold basin at the base of the thermal belt, or even lower.

The 24 plant climate zones used in this book were mapped by drawing lines at certain latitudes (distances from the equator), drawing other lines representing the typical penetrations of marine and interior air, and drawing still more lines for elevations and the big, significant thermal belts and cold basins. The result was to define climate areas that are relatively constant within their boundaries.

In many cases, the lines that delineate the climates were plotted according to the success-failure records of certain indicator plants. Where such a plant succeeded regularly in one area and failed regularly in a nearby area, a climate line was drawn to separate the two.

Do not consider the lines on the maps as rigid. Only in a very few places in the West are the climate-controlling factors so consistent that we can draw a line on the ground with a stick and say "on this side of the line is climate X and on the other side, climate Y." Mostly, such a line would be nonsense. As the influences of the factors listed previously rise or fall, the lines shift gradually back and forth.

If your garden is well inside a climate zone's mapped boundaries, you can rest assured that your garden is in that zone without much qualification. But if you live near a dividing line, your climate can occasionally resemble the climate across the line.

Another point to consider is that conditions in your garden or neighborhood can create microclimates (little climates a few feet or a few hundred feet wide) that will be somewhat different from the general climate of your area. For example, a solid fence or row of dense evergreen trees at the bottom of a slope can trap cold air and cause colder night temperatures there. A south-facing wall will accumulate heat, creating a warm microclimate.

Also, there are many little thermal belts, hilltops, swales, canyons, and fog belt fingers that are too small to register on the maps. In such locations your climate may be *slightly* milder or *slightly* more severe than that of your neighbors half a mile away. But usually the change is no greater than to an adjacent climate.

Here is how to find the mapped climate zone for your area. First, look at the locator map on the opposite page. It tells you the page on which your state or your part of the state is mapped. Then turn to that page and on its map you will find your climate zone number.

The reference guides are county lines (dashed lines), state borders, and dots representing cities and towns. In larger towns and cities, the dot represents the city hall. The Los Angeles area map on pages 20 and 21, where county lines are few and cities are big, is further oriented by freeway routes. Communities shown on the maps are not necessarily the largest or most important. Many smaller towns are included because they happen to be on or near a transition line from one zone to another.

Descriptions of the 24 plant climate zones follow. In the chapter of this book called Planting For a Purpose and in the Western Plant Encyclopedia, climate adaptability is repeatedly indicated by two zone numbers connected by a dash (as Zones 4–9). This means that the plant is recommended for all the zones indicated from first to second number inclusive. In the descriptions that follow, temperatures are in degrees Fahrenheit.

SPECIAL ACKNOWLEDGMENT

The publishers of this book thank the many climatologists, bioclimatologists, meteorologists, and horticulturists who gave valuable assistance in making these climate maps. These experts are listed by name in the acknowledgments section in the opening pages of this book.

Special thanks go to the University of California Agricultural Extension Service for making available the map *California's Plantclimates,* from which most of the California climates shown on these pages were derived.

Zone 1 *Coldest Winters in the West*

Zones 1, 2, and 3 are the snowy parts of the West—the regions where snow falls and stays on the ground (a day, a week, or all winter) every winter. Of the three snowy-winter climates, Zone 1 is the coldest.

The extreme winter cold of Zone 1 can be caused by any or all of the three factors that can make cold winters: latitude (the farther north, the colder); influence of continental air mass (the more of it, the colder); and elevation (the higher, the colder). Most of Zone 1 in the Northwest and the Rocky Mountain states does indeed get its cold winter temperatures from all three contributing factors.

In this zone, the typical growing season (period between last frost in springtime and first frost in fall) lasts for not much longer than 100 days—although it may average as high as 180 days in some parts. In most Zone 1 places, frosts can occur on any day of the year.

Zone 2 *Second Coldest Climate—Soil Freezes in Winter*

Here, too, snow in winter is to be expected. The chief difference between Zone 2 and Zone 1 is that the record low temperatures and the average annual low temperatures are not as low as in Zone 1. And this makes a difference with many desirable garden plants.

In the northerly latitudes and interior areas where the continental air mass rules supreme, the difference between Zone 2 and Zone 1 is mostly one of elevation. Notice that some Zone 2 exists around Salt Lake City, along parts of the Snake River of Idaho, the Grande Ronde and Burnt rivers of Oregon, along the Columbia River and Spokane River in eastern Washington, and in the lakes region of the Idaho panhandle. In Colorado, Zone 2 is comprised of the river valleys of the western portion of the state and the low-elevation plains of the southeast corner of the state. Zone 2 makes up most of the high territory of New Mexico—only a small portion of the state is Zone 1. The Zone 2 that exists in California and Arizona is in higher elevations that are not as cold as the higher Zone 1.

During a 20-year period in Zone 2, annual low temperatures ranged from −3° to −34°F.

The growing season averages about 150 days. Some places can count on almost 200 frost free days in a row.

(Continued on page 13)

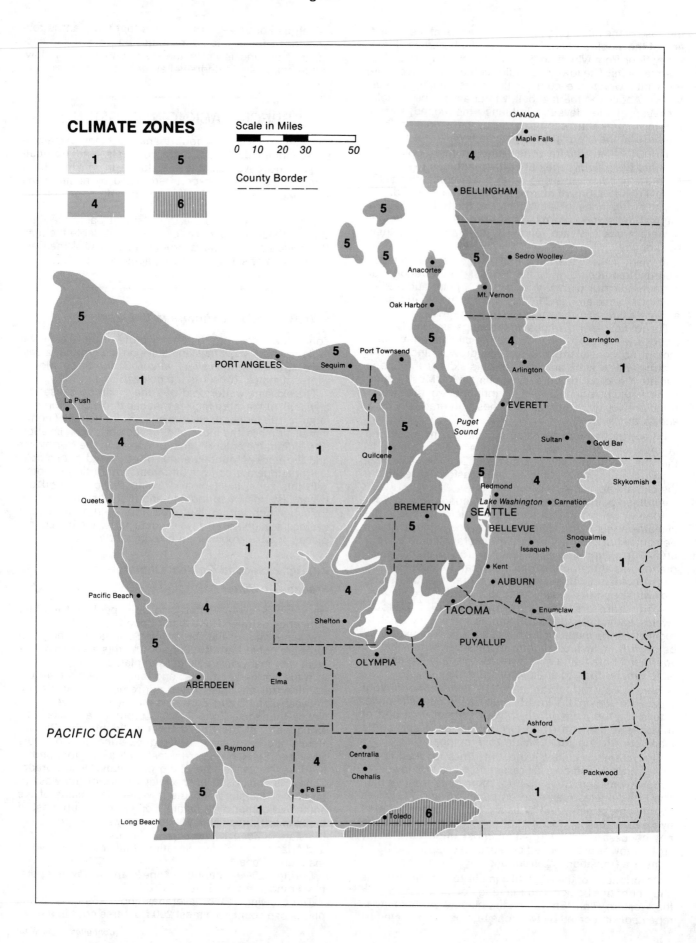

CLIMATE ZONES

Scale in Miles

County Border

1

4

5

6

CANADA

Maple Falls

4

1

BELLINGHAM

5

5

5

Sedro Woolley

5

Anacortes

5

Mt. Vernon

4

1

Darrington

Oak Harbor

Port Townsend

5

PORT ANGELES

Sequim

5

4

Arlington

1

La Push

4

EVERETT

Quilcene

1

Puget Sound

Sultan

Gold Bar

Skykomish

Queets

1

BREMERTON

5

Redmond

4

Lake Washington

Carnation

SEATTLE

BELLEVUE

Issaquah

Snoqualmie

1

Pacific Beach

4

Kent

AUBURN

4

Shelton

TACOMA

4

Enumclaw

5

PUYALLUP

5

5

OLYMPIA

ABERDEEN

Elma

4

Ashford

PACIFIC OCEAN

Raymond

Centralia

4

Chehalis

Packwood

5

Pe Ell

1

1

Toledo

6

Long Beach

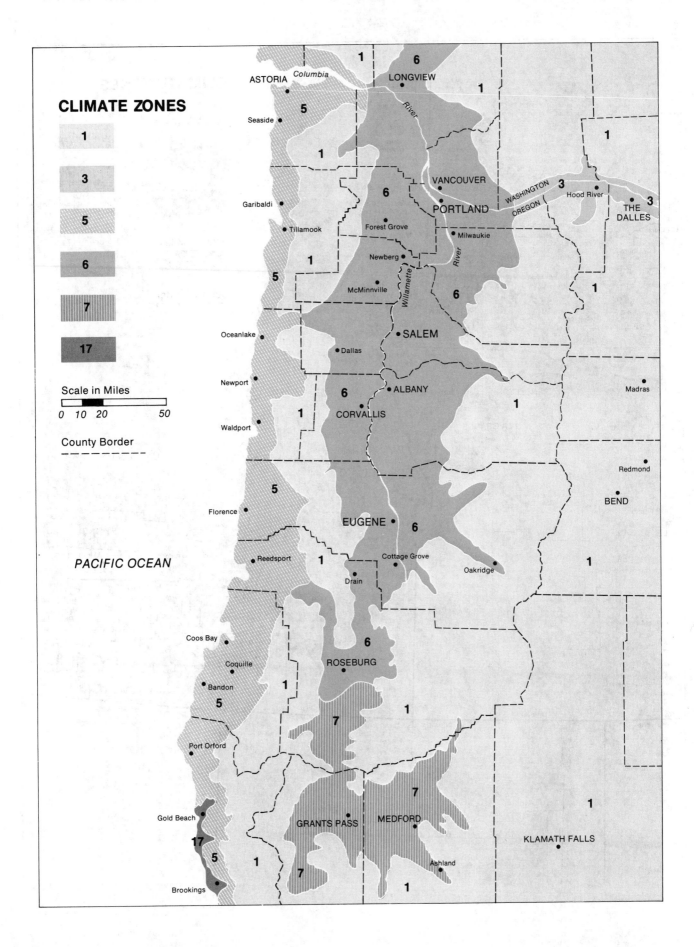

CLIMATE ZONES

1
3
5
6
7
17

Scale in Miles
0 10 20   50

County Border

PACIFIC OCEAN

1
6
5
ASTORIA *Columbia*
LONGVIEW
Seaside
1
VANCOUVER
1
PORTLAND
Garibaldi
WASHINGTON
OREGON
Hood River
3
THE DALLES
3
Tillamook
6
Forest Grove
Milwaukie
1
Newberg
River
5
McMinnville
Willamette
6
Oceanlake
SALEM
Dallas
1
Newport
6
ALBANY
Madras
Waldport
1
CORVALLIS
1
5
Florence
EUGENE
6
Redmond
BEND
Reedsport
1
Cottage Grove
Drain
Oakridge
1
Coos Bay
6
Coquille
ROSEBURG
Bandon
5
1
7
Port Orford
1
7
Gold Beach
17
5
GRANTS PASS
MEDFORD
1
1
KLAMATH FALLS
Ashland
Brookings
7
1

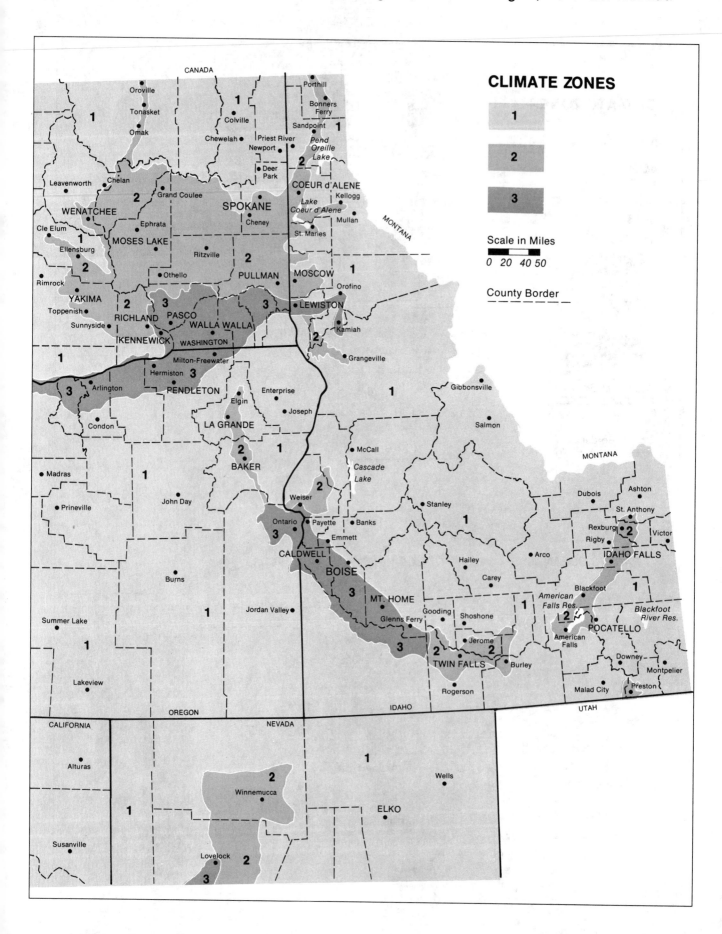

Zone 3 *Mildest of High-Elevation and Interior Climates*

East of the Cascades in the Northwest, the Zone 3 areas are the ones that often get called "banana belts". Of course, the only place you can grow the real, fruiting banana satisfactorily outdoors is in the tropics. But the "bananas" that the comparatively mild winter lows of Zone 3 allow gardeners to grow include such things as English boxwood and winter jasmine.

The portion of Zone 3 from Hood River to Lewiston is slightly lower in elevation than the surrounding Zone 2. This fact, combined with the influence of Pacific air that spills over the Cascades and through the Columbia Gorge, moderates most winters. Much planting is based on winter lows of 10° to 15°F. In an occasional winter, arctic air drops temperatures much lower. Such winters limit selection of broad-leafed evergreens.

Absolute cold is not so much the enemy here as drying winds that dehydrate plants growing in frozen soil. Wind protection, mulching, shade, and careful late autumn watering will help you grow many borderline evergreens.

In California the Zone 3 areas often happen to be the lowest parts of the high mountains—areas where many people keep gardens at cabins. The zone also includes the Reno area in Nevada.

Over a 20-year period, minimum temperatures in Zone 3 have ranged from 13° to −24°F.

Average growing season is about 160 days. In Walla Walla the season lasts almost 220 days.

Zone 4 *Interior, Cold-Winter Parts of Western Washington*

This is one of the smallest climate zones in the West. It is the region west of the Cascades that gets considerable influence from the Pacific Ocean and Puget Sound—but also is affected either by the continental air mass at times, or by higher elevation, or both. It touches salt water in Whatcom County and nowhere else, but in some higher spots it is in distant view of the ocean or the sound.

It differs from neighboring Zone 5 principally in greater frequency of extremely low winter temperatures, a shorter growing season, and considerably more rainfall.

The two Puget Sound climates (Zones 4 and 5) can be found in the same neighborhood, and their presence is behind much of the familiar northwestern talk about warm or cold gardens.

Some of the tenderer rhododendrons that Seattle grows will freeze here, as will some of the rarer shrubs from New Zealand and Chile. On the other hand, no zone grows better perennials and bulbs than Zone 4. People who like woodland plants and rock plants find this area a paradise.

Over a 20-year period, winter lows here ranged from 19° down to −7°F.

Zone 5 *Marine Influence–the Northwest Coast and Puget Sound*

The influence of mild ocean air brings relatively warm winters to this area, which is on the same latitude as Duluth, Minnesota, and Bangor, Maine. The climate is much like that of southern England, and the gardens in this area have benefited from England's long and

successful search for better and more varied garden plants. The region is one of the world's great centers of rhododendron culture and rock gardening.

Temperatures of 0°F. or lower are quite uncommon. Over a 20-year period, the minimum temperatures have ranged from 28° to 1°. The occasional big freeze when temperatures plummet to the vicinity of 0° does considerable damage if it comes very early or very late, when plants are not conditioned for such cold. These occasional big freezes should not serve as the gauge of hardiness; even native plants have been killed or injured by some of them. The growing season may run to 250 days in favored regions near salt water.

Many waterside areas show a very low heat accumulation in the summer. Those who want to grow heat-loving plants should pick out the hottest spots for them; a south wall or a west wall sheltered from cold winds will do. Select peach and tomato varieties with low heat needs.

Zone 6 *Willamette Valley–Partly Marine Influence, Partly Interior*

A somewhat longer growing season and warmer summers set the Willamette Valley climate off from the coast-Puget Sound climate (Zone 5). The Coast Range tempers the coastal winds and somewhat reduces the rainfall, but the climate of the valley is still essentially maritime much of the year, hence getting much less winter cold and less summer heat than areas east of the Cascades.

Average lows are similar to those of the coast-Puget Sound zone—even slightly colder in some places—but summer high temperatures average 5° to 9° warmer, warm enough to put sugar in the Elberta peaches and to speed growth of such evergreens as abelia and nandina. The long, mild growing season has made the Willamette Valley one of the West's great growing areas for nursery stock. Many of the West's (and the nation's) fruit and shade trees, deciduous shrubs, and broad-leafed evergreens started life here.

Any mention of the Willamette Valley must include roses and rhododendrons, both of which attain near-perfection here. Broad-leafed evergreens generally are at their clean, green best; choice rhododendrons, azaleas, and pieris grow as basic landscaping shrubs.

Zone 7 *Oregon's Rogue River Valley and California's Digger Pine Belt*

Zone 7 appears over quite a few thousand square miles in the regions west of the Sierra-Cascades. Because of the influence of latitude, this climate of similar character is found at low elevations in a valley in Oregon (the Rogue Valley) but at middle elevations in California (the low mountains, most of which can be identified by native Digger pines).

Hot summers and mild but pronounced winters give this area sharply defined seasons without severe winter cold or enervating humidity. The climate pleases the plants that require a marked seasonal pattern to do well—peony, iris, lilac, flowering cherry, for example. Deciduous fruit that require a marked seasonal pattern do well also; the region is noted for its pears, apples, peaches, and cherries.

Gardeners in a few spots in the Coast Ranges near San Francisco Bay will be surprised to find their gardens mapped in Zone 7, even though there isn't a Digger pine to be seen. These are hilltop and ridge-top areas that are too high (and hence too cold in winter) to be included with milder Zones 15 and 16.

For such a big area, it is of course impossible to state exact low temperatures. But at weather-recording stations in the Zone 7 area, the typical winter lows range from 23° to 9°F., the record lows from 15° to −1°.

Zone 8 *Cold-Air Basins (Low Spots) of California's Central Valley*

Only a shade of difference exists between Zone 8 and Zone 9, but it's an important difference—critical in some cases. Zone 9 is a thermal belt, meaning that cold air can flow from it to lower ground—and the lower ground is here in Zone 8. Citrus furnish the most meaningful illustration. Lemons, oranges, and grapefruit cannot be grown commercially in Zone 8 because winter nights can frequently be cold enough to injure or even kill the trees and the trees would need heating regularly. The same winter cold can damage many garden plants.

Zone 8 differs from Zone 14, which it joins near the latitudes of North Sacramento and Modesto, in that Zone 14 occasionally gets some marine influence.

Low temperatures in Zone 8 over a 20-year period have ranged from 29° to 13°F.

Certain features that Zone 8 and 9 share in common are described under Zone 9.

Zone 9 *Thermal Belts of California's Central Valley*

Repeating the example cited for Zone 8, the biggest readily apparent difference between 8 and 9 is that Zone 9 is a safer citrus climate. Most of the valley's commercial citrus crops are grown in Zone 9. The same distinction, thermal belt versus cold basin, is reflected in this book for certain species and varieties of hibiscus, melaleuca,

pittosporum, and other plants—recommended for Zone 9 but not for Zone 8.

Zones 8 and 9 have these features in common: summer daytime temperatures are high, sunshine is almost constant during the growing season, and growing seasons are long. Deciduous fruit and vegetables of nearly every kind thrive in these long, hot summers; winter cold is just adequate to satisfy dormancy requirements of the fruit trees. Fiercely cold, piercing north winds blow for several days at a time in winter—more distressing really to gardeners than to garden plants. Tule fogs (dense fogs that rise from the ground under certain peculiar weather conditions) come and stay for hours or days during winter. The fogs usually hug the ground at night and rise to 800 to 1,000 feet by afternoon. Heat-loving plants such as oleander and crape myrtle perform at their peak in Zones 8 and 9 (and 14). Plants that like summer coolness and humidity demand some fussing; careful gardeners accommodate them by providing shade and moisture.

In Zone 9, winter lows over a 20-year period have ranged from 28° to 18°F. Record lows have ranged from 21° to 15°.

Zone 10 *High Desert of Arizona and New Mexico*

This zone consists mostly of the 3,300 to 4,500-foot elevations in parts of Arizona and New Mexico. It also exists in southern Utah and southern Nevada. It has a definite winter season—from 75 to more than 100 nights each winter with temperatures below 32°F. In the representative towns of Albuquerque, Benson, and Douglas, average winter minimums range from 24° to 31° in December through February. Late frosts, with lows of 25° to 22°, are expected in April. Lowest temperature recorded is −17°.

Here the low winter temperatures give necessary chilling to make possible the growing of all of the deciduous fruit and the perennials that thrive in the coldest climates—lilacs, spiraea, and the like. The definite winter season calls for spring planting, followed by a spring-summer growing season (in neighboring Zones 12 and 13, most planting should be done in fall).

Distinguishing this climate from Zone 11 are more rainfall and less wind. Annual rainfall averages 12 inches, with half of that amount falling in July and August. In the eastern parts of Zone 10, summer's precipitation provides more water than winter's.

Zone 11 *Medium to High Desert of California and Southern Nevada*

In varying degrees, this climate has similarities to its two extremely different neighboring climates—the cold-winter Zones 1, 2, and 3 and the subtropical low desert, Zone 13.

It is characterized by wide swings in temperature, both between summer and winter and between day and night. Winter lows of 11° to 0°F. have occurred within the area. Highest summer temperatures recorded range from 111° to 117°. On the average, there are 110 days in the summer with temperatures above 90° and about 85 nights in winter with temperatures below 32°.

Hot summer days are followed by cool nights; freezing nights are often followed by 60° days.

The hazards of the climate are late spring frosts and desert winds. Wind protection greatly increases the chance of plant survival and the rate of plant growth.

(Continued on page 18)

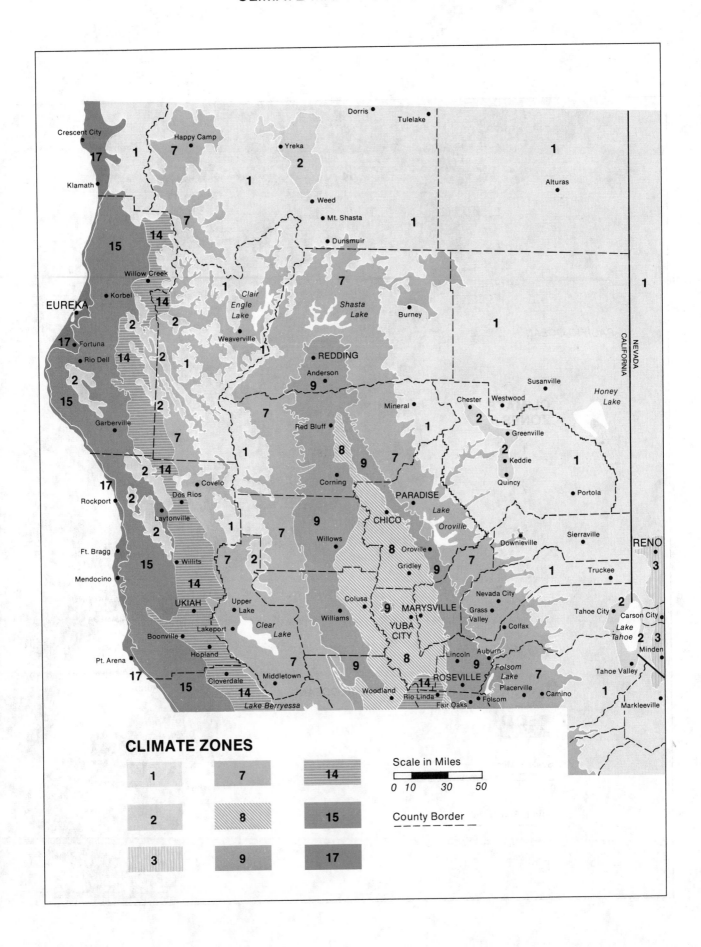

CLIMATE ZONES

1	7	14
2	8	15
3	9	17

Scale in Miles

0   10   30   50

County Border

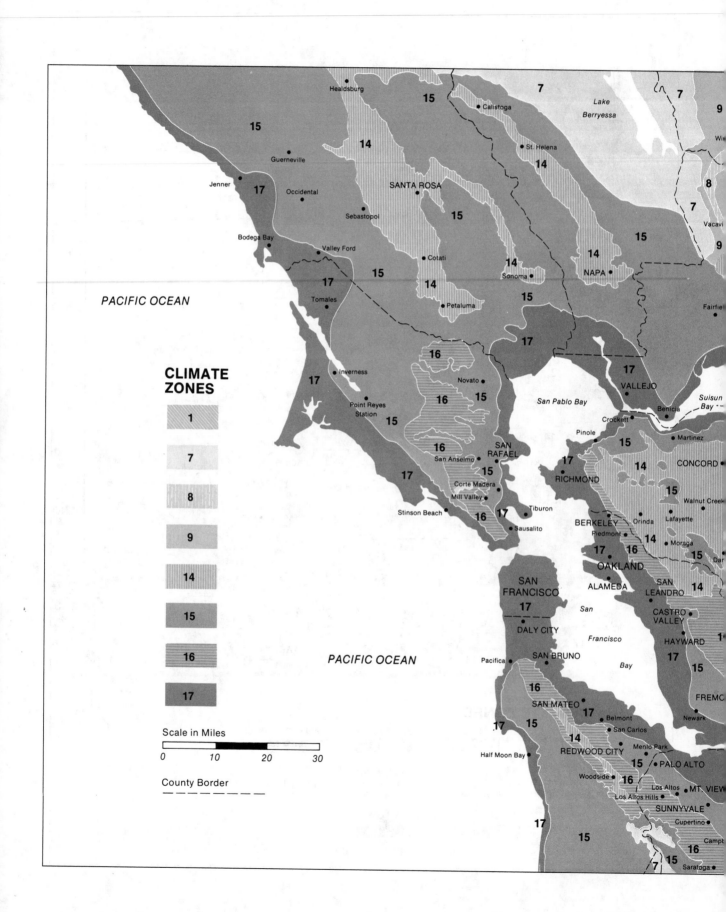

CLIMATE ZONES

	1
	7
	8
	9
	14
	15
	16
	17

Scale in Miles

0   10   20   30

County Border – – – – – – –

PACIFIC OCEAN

PACIFIC OCEAN

Healdsburg
15
7
Lake Berryessa
7
9
Calistoga
15
14
St. Helena
14
Wie
8
Guerneville
Jenner
17
Occidental
SANTA ROSA
14
7
Vacavi
Bodega Bay
Sebastopol
15
15
9
Valley Ford
15
14
NAPA
15
17
Cotati
Tomales
14
Sonoma
Petaluma
15
Fairfiel
Inverness
16
Novato
15
17
San Pablo Bay
Suisun Bay
Point Reyes Station
16
15
VALLEJO
17
Benicia
15
Crockett
Pinole
Martinez
San Anselmo
16
SAN RAFAEL
17
15
RICHMOND
14
CONCORD
Corte Madera
15
Walnut Creek
17
Mill Valley
Stinson Beach
16
Tiburon
BERKELEY
Orinda
Lafayette
Sausalito
17
Piedmont
14
Moraga
15
Dar
17
16
14
OAKLAND
SAN FRANCISCO
ALAMEDA
SAN LEANDRO
14
17
San
CASTRO VALLEY
DALY CITY
Francisco
HAYWARD
Pacifica
SAN BRUNO
Bay
17
15
16
FREMO
SAN MATEO
17
Belmont
Newark
17
15
San Carlos
14
Half Moon Bay
REDWOOD CITY
Menlo Park
15
PALO ALTO
Woodside
16
Los Altos
MT VIEW
Los Altos Hills
SUNNYVALE
Cupertino
Campt
17
15
16
7
15
Saratoga

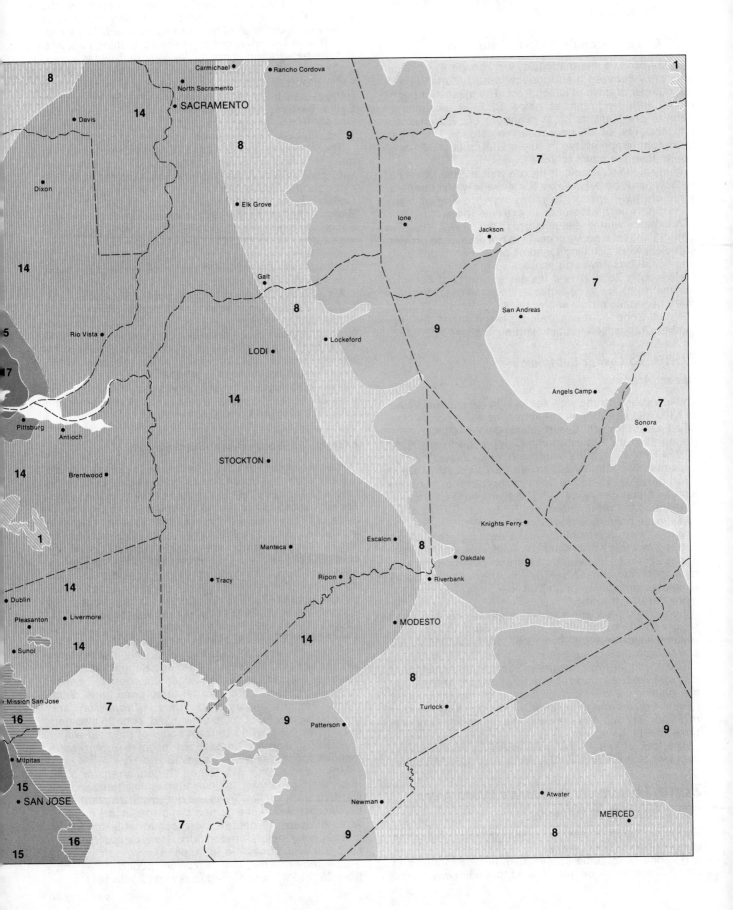

8

Carmichael ●

● Rancho Cordova

North Sacramento ●

14

● SACRAMENTO

● Davis

8

1

9

7

Dixon ●

● Elk Grove

14

Ione ●

Jackson ●

7

Galt ●

8

7

5

Rio Vista ●

LODI ●

● Lockeford

9

San Andreas ●

7

Pittsburg ●

Antioch ●

14

Angels Camp ●

7

14

Brentwood ●

STOCKTON ●

Sonora ●

1

Knights Ferry ●

Tracy ●

Manteca ●

Escalon ●

8

Oakdale ●

9

Dublin ●

14

Ripon ●

Riverbank ●

Pleasanton ●

● Livermore

● MODESTO

Sunol ●

14

14

8

Mission San Jose

7

Turlock ●

16

9

Patterson ●

9

Milpitas ●

15

● Atwater

● SAN JOSE

7

Newman ●

MERCED ●

16

9

8

15

Winter winds and bright sunlight may combine to kill normally hardy evergreen plants by desiccation, if winter soil moisture is not adequate.

Zone 12 *Arizona's Intermediate Desert*

This is Arizona's intermediate desert climate. The critical difference between it and the low desert (Zone 13) is in the number of days of killing frost. The mean number of nights with temperatures below 32°F. in localities of Zone 12 are: Tucson 22, Wickenburg 65. Extreme low temperatures of 6° have been recorded. The mean maximum temperatures in July and August are 5° or 6° cooler than the highs of Zone 13.

Many of the subtropicals that do well in Zone 13 are not reliably hardy here. However, the average winter temperatures are high enough to encourage growing of many such plants, with protection in extreme winters.

Although winter temperatures are lower than in Zone 13, the total hours of cold are not enough to provide sufficient winter chilling for some of the deciduous fruits and deciduous flowering shrubs.

Here as in Zone 13 and the eastern parts of Zone 10, summer rains are to be expected. In some cases they are more dependable than winter rains.

As in Zone 13, the growing season starts in September-October (often best planting season).

Zone 13 *Low or Subtropical Desert Areas*

The low desert, from below sea level in the Imperial Valley to 1,100 feet elevation in the Phoenix area, is rightly classified as subtropical desert. Mean daily maximum temperatures in the hottest month (July) range from 106° to 108°F. The winters are short and mild. Frosts can be expected from December 1 to February 15 but they are of short duration. There are rarely more than 6 to 10 nights with temperatures below 32°. The average minimum temperature in the winter months is 37°. However, lows of 19° to 13° have been recorded.

Winter lows and summer highs exclude some of the subtropicals grown in southern California's mild-winter Zones 22 to 24. However, numerous subtropicals with high heat requirements thrive in this climate. Some examples are dates, grapefruit, bauhinia, beaumontia, many cassias, thevetia.

Summer storms are a factor in gardening: the rains supply some soil moisture (but not enough to support a garden), and on many afternoons dense clouds shield plants from the hot sun.

The gardening year begins in September and October for most vegetables and annual flowers (corn and melons are planted in late winter). Growth of the fall-planted plants is slow through the short winter, picks up speed in mid-February and races through the increasing temperatures of March and April.

The lack of winter cold rules out fruit and flowering fruit with high chilling requirements, such as most apples.

Zone 14 *Northern California's Inland Areas with Some Ocean Influence*

This designation is used for similar climates that come about in two different ways:

(1) Zone 14 in some cases illustrates the moderating effect of marine air on inland areas that otherwise would be colder in winter and hotter in summer. The gap in northern California's Coast Ranges created by the Golden Gate and San Francisco and San Pablo bays allows considerable marine air to spill much farther inland than it can anywhere else. The same thing happens, but the penetration is not as deep, in the Salinas Valley.

(2) Zone 14 is also used to designate the cold-winter valley floors, canyons, and land-troughs in the Coast Ranges—all the way from Solvang and Santa Ynez in Santa Barbara County to Willow Creek in Humboldt County. These pockets are colder than the surrounding areas because cold air sinks.

These two kinds of Zone 14 are quite similar in maximum and minimum temperatures. The one measurement on which they differ in some degree is humidity. A good example can be seen in the lowland parts of Contra Costa County that lie east of the Oakland-Berkeley-El Cerrito hills as compared with Stockton and Sacramento on the floor of the Central Valley. Both areas are in Zone 14. In Stockton and Sacramento crape myrtles perform mightily. In the Contra Costa section they grow well enough but suffer from mildew because there is more moisture.

Are you in the drier or moister part of Zone 14?

If, on the map, your closest neighboring climate is one of the summer-dry ones—7, 8, 9, or 18—you can conclude that yours is the drier kind of Zone 14. But if Zone 15, 16, or 17 is your nearest neighbor, you are in one of the moister sections where crape myrtles and some other plants would be inclined to mildew.

Over a 20-year period, this area has had lows ranging from 26° to 16°F. Weather Bureau records show all-time lows here ranging from 20° down to 11°.

Zone 15 *North Coast Cold Winters*

"Coastal climate" as used here means the areas that are influenced by the ocean approximately 85 percent of the time and by inland air 15 percent of the time. Note that Zone 16 is also within the northern California coastal climate, but its winters are more mild because the areas are in thermal belts, as explained in the introduction on page 9. The cold-winter areas that make up Zone 15 are either in cold-air basins, or on hilltops above the thermal belts, or—as is the case north of Petaluma—in such northerly latitudes that plant performance dictates they be designated Zone 15. In Contra Costa, Napa, and Sonoma counties, Zone 15 exists on hills above the colder valley floors which are designated Zone 14.

In Zone 15 the finest climate for fuchsias begins. Lantanas may freeze but will recover quickly. Many plants recommended for Zone 15 are not suggested for 14 because they must have moister atmosphere, cooler summers, milder winters, or all three conditions. Such plants include canary bird flower (*Crotalaria*) and *Brunfelsia calycina*. On the other hand, Zone 15 also gets enough winter chilling to favor some of the cold-winter specialties such as herbaceous peonies (not recommended for milder-winter Zones 16 and 17).

Most of this zone, like 16 and 17, gets a regular afternoon wind in summer. It blows from early afternoon until shortly before sunset. Trees and dense shrubs planted on the windward side of a garden can disperse this nagging wind, making the garden more comfortable for plants and people. A neighborhood full of trees can successfully keep the wind above the rooftops.

Low temperatures over a 20-year period here range from 28° to 21°F. and record lows from 26° to 16°.

(Continued on page 24)

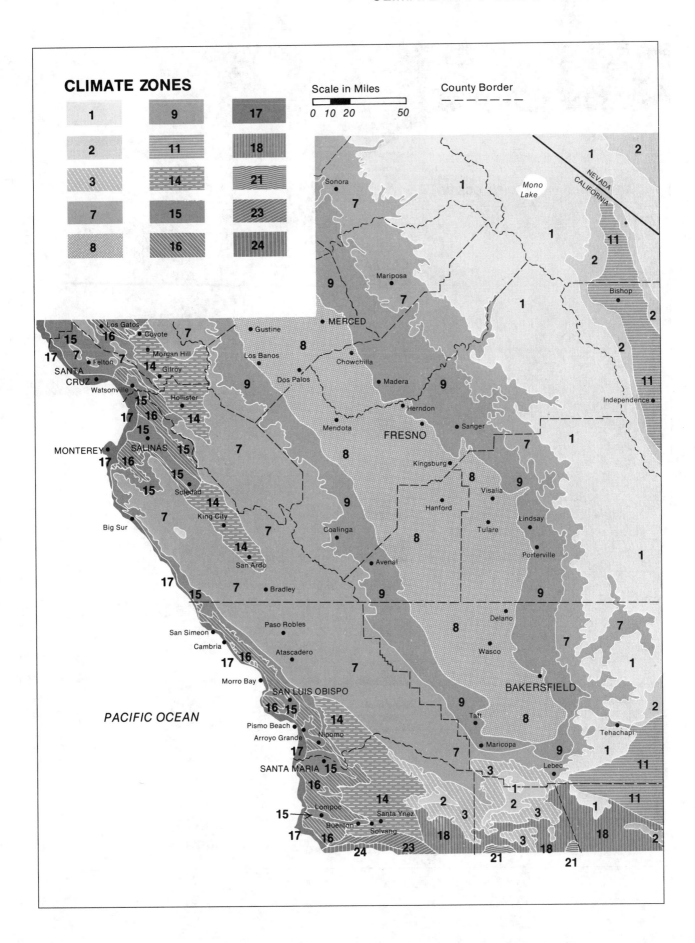

CLIMATE ZONES

1	9	17
2	11	18
3	14	21
7	15	23
8	16	24

Scale in Miles
0 10 20   50

County Border

NEVADA
CALIFORNIA

Mono Lake

Sonora
Mariposa
MERCED
Gustine
Los Gatos
Coyote
Morgan Hill
Gilroy
Los Banos
Dos Palos
Chowchilla
Madera
Herndon
Mendota
FRESNO
Sanger
Kingsburg
Visalia
Hanford
Tulare
Lindsay
Porterville
Felton
SANTA CRUZ
Watsonville
Hollister
MONTEREY
SALINAS
Soledad
King City
Big Sur
Coalinga
Avenal
Bradley
Paso Robles
San Simeon
Cambria
Atascadero
Morro Bay
SAN LUIS OBISPO
Pismo Beach
Arroyo Grande
Nipomo
SANTA MARIA
Lompoc
Buellton
Santa Ynez
Solvang
Bishop
Independence
Delano
Wasco
BAKERSFIELD
Taft
Maricopa
Lebec
Tehachapi
San Ardo

PACIFIC OCEAN

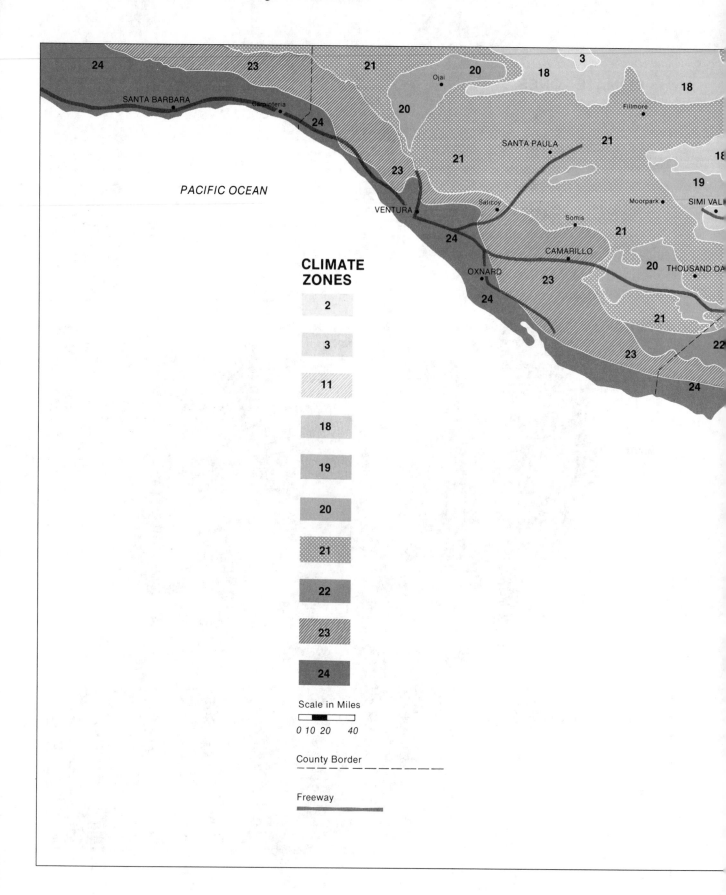

24

23

21

20

18

3

18

SANTA BARBARA

Ojai

Fillmore

Carpinteria

24

20

20

SANTA PAULA

21

18

PACIFIC OCEAN

21

23

19

VENTURA

Saticoy

Moorpark

SIMI VAL

Somis

**CLIMATE
ZONES**

24

21

CAMARILLO

OXNARD

20

THOUSAND OA

23

24

21

2	
3	
11	
18	
19	
20	
21	
22	
23	
24	

23

22

24

Scale in Miles

0 10 20   40

County Border — — — — —

Freeway

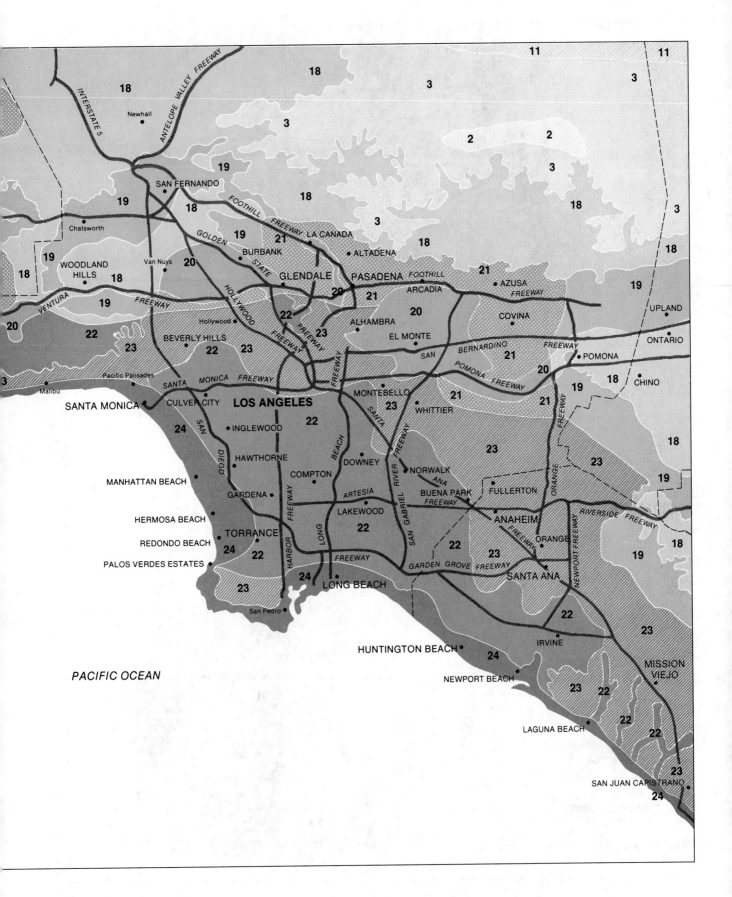

PACIFIC OCEAN

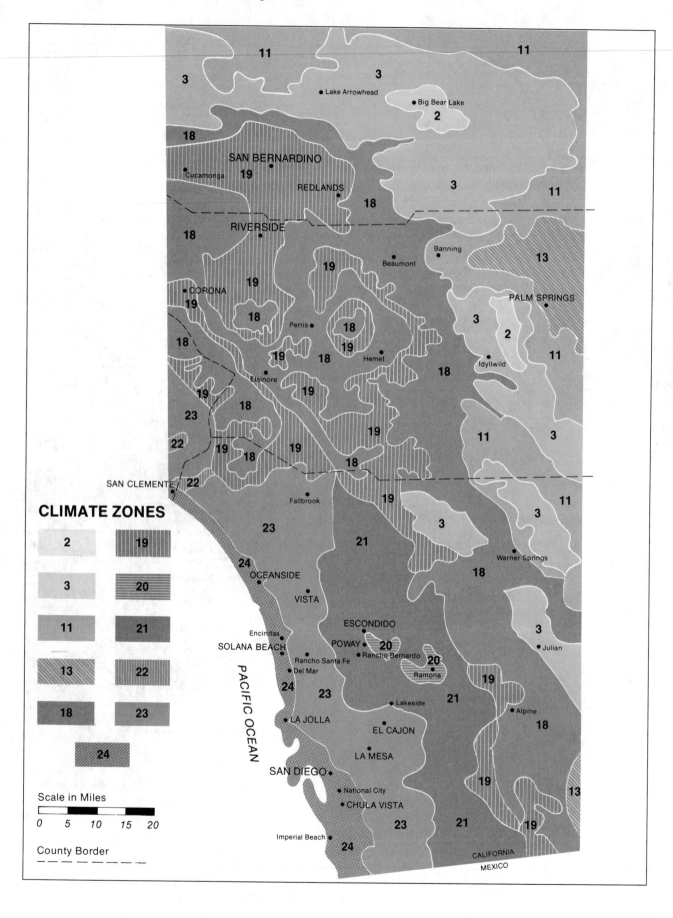

CLIMATE ZONES

Scale in Miles

0   5   10   15   20

County Border

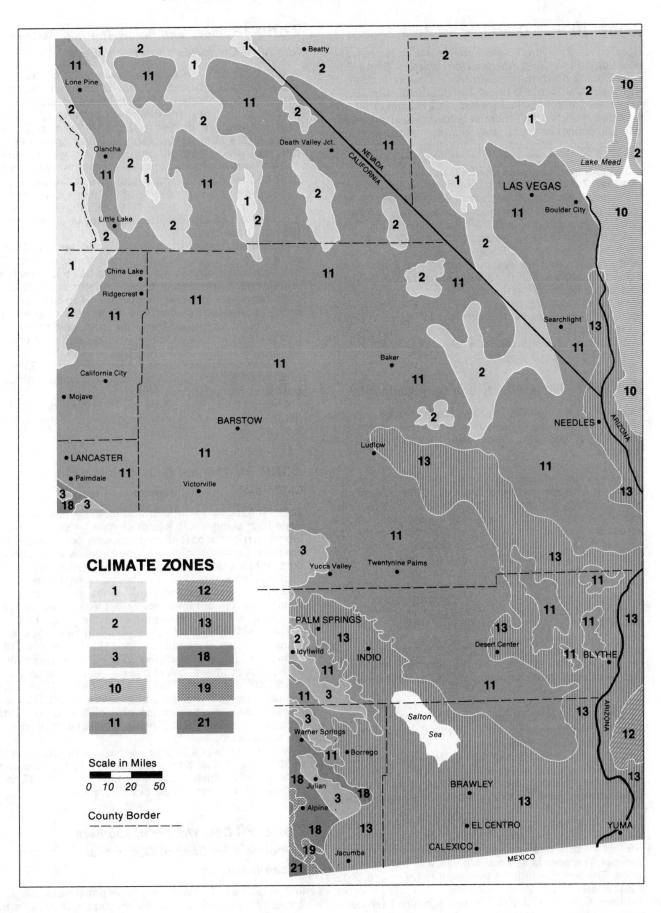

CLIMATE ZONES

1	12
2	13
3	18
10	19
11	21

Scale in Miles

0 10 20   50

County Border

Zone 16 *North Coast Thermal Belts*

Here's a much-favored climate that exists in patches and strips along the Coast Ranges from western Santa Barbara County north to northern Marin County. It's one of northern California's finest horticultural climates—especially for subtropical plants. The reason is that this climate consists of the thermal belts (slopes from which cold air drains) in the coastal area (dominated by ocean weather about 85 percent of the time and by inland weather about 15 percent). This climate gets more heat than maritime-dominated Zone 17 and has warmer winters than Zone 15. That's a happy combination.

Favored here but not favored in Zone 15 are such subtropical delights as princess flower (*Tibouchina*), *Eucalyptus citriodora*, and the hardiest avocados.

Some of the more favored portions of Zone 16, such as the hills of Oakland and Berkeley, practically never see a white frost. Very few weather recording stations are placed squarely within the indefinite borders of Zone 16. Those that do exist there show a typical range of winter lows over a 20-year period of 32° to 19°F. The lowest recorded temperatures at points within the zone range from 25° to 18°.

A summer afternoon wind is an integral part of this climate. Read about it under the Zone 15 heading.

Zone 17 *Marine Effects–Northern California*

This climate is dominated by the ocean about 98 percent of the time. In most cases you can see salt water from Zone 17; if you can't, you can probably hear the foghorns.

Garden plants here seldom suffer a frost of any consequence—in some areas of the zone frosts are unknown. The climatic features are cool, wet winters, and cool summers with frequent fog or wind. On most days and in most places the fog is not the sort that creeps across the ground and blots visibility; it tends, rather, to come in high and fast, interposing a cooling and humidifying blanket between the sun and the earth, reducing the intensity of the light and sunshine.

The result is a climate that favors fuchsias, rhododendrons, azaleas, hydrangeas, ferns, and begonias. Many plants that require shade elsewhere grow well here in full sun. Some heat-loving plants refuse to bloom because heat accumulation is too low (hibiscus, gardenia); many deciduous fruits do not find sufficient winter chill to set fruit; many citrus varieties lack the necessary heat.

Unless local features offer shelter from prevailing winds, the shoreline itself and the area immediately behind it are too gusty and too much subject to salt spray for any except the toughest, most tolerant plants. Beach gardens usually need all the help you can give them in the way of screens or windbreaks.

Behind the beaches and sea cliffs, local geography may reduce the fog cover, lessen the winds, and boost summer heat enough to create "banana belts"—areas in which you can grow the subtropicals that ordinarily sulk.

In a 20-year period the lowest winter temperatures in Zone 17 have ranged from 36° to 23°F. The lowest temperatures on record range from 30° to 20°. Of further interest in this heat-starved climate are the highs of summer. The normal summer highs are in the 60° to 75° range. The average highest temperature on record of 12 weather stations in Zone 17 is only 97°. In all the other northern California climates, average highest temperatures on record are in the 104° to 116° range.

Zone 18 *Above and Below Thermal Belts in Southern California's Interior Valleys*

Zones 18 and 19 are classified as interior climates. The major climate influence is that of the continental air mass; the ocean determines the climate no more than 15 percent of the time. The difference between 18 and 19 is that winters are colder in Zone 18 than in Zone 19 because the latter is favorably situated on slopes and hillsides where cold air drains off on winter nights. Zone 18 represents the cold-air basins beneath the air-drained thermal belts and the hilltops above them.

The high and low deserts of southern California are something else—see Zones 11 and 13. Zone 18 is generally west of the low deserts and lower in elevation than the high deserts.

Historically, many of the valley-floor parts of Zone 18 were once apricot, peach, apple, and walnut regions. The orchards have given way to homes, but the climate remains one that supplies enough winter chill for some plants that need it, while not becoming too cold for many of the hardier subtropicals. It is too hot, too cold, and too dry for fuchsias but, on the other hand, cold enough for tree peonies and many apple varieties, and mild enough for a number of avocado varieties.

Zone 18 never amounted to much for commercial citrus production (frosty nights called for too much heating) but citrus can be grown here.

Over a 20-year period, winter lows have ranged from 28° to 10°F. The all-time lows recorded in Zone 18 range from 22° to 7°.

Zone 19 *Thermal Belts Around Southern California's Interior Valleys*

This climate is as little influenced by the ocean as Zone 18, making it also a poor climate for such plants as fuchsias, rhododendrons, and tuberous begonias. But air drainage on winter nights generally takes away enough cold air to make winter lows much less severe here. Many sections of Zone 19 have always been prime citrus country—especially for those kinds that need extra summer heat in order to grow sweet fruit. Likewise, most avocados, and macadamia nuts, can be grown here.

The Western Plant Encyclopedia in this book cites many ornamental plants for Zone 19—but not for 18—because of the milder winters in Zone 19. Bougainvillea, bouvardia, bromelia, calocephalus, cape chestnut (*Calodendrum*), chorizema, several kinds of coral tree (*Erythrina*), leucocoryne, livistona palms, giant Burmese honeysuckle, myoporum, several of the more tender pittosporums, lady palm (*Rhapis excelsa*), and rondeletia are some examples.

Winter lows over a 20-year period have ranged from 27° to 22°F., and the all-time lows from 23° to 17°. These are considerably higher than in neighboring Zone 18, and that fact is what makes the big difference.

Zone 20 *Cold Winters in Southern California's Sections of Occasional Ocean Influence*

In Zones 20 and 21 the same relative pattern prevails as in Zones 18 and 19, in that the even-numbered zone is the climate made up of cold-air basins and hilltops and the

(Continued on page 29)

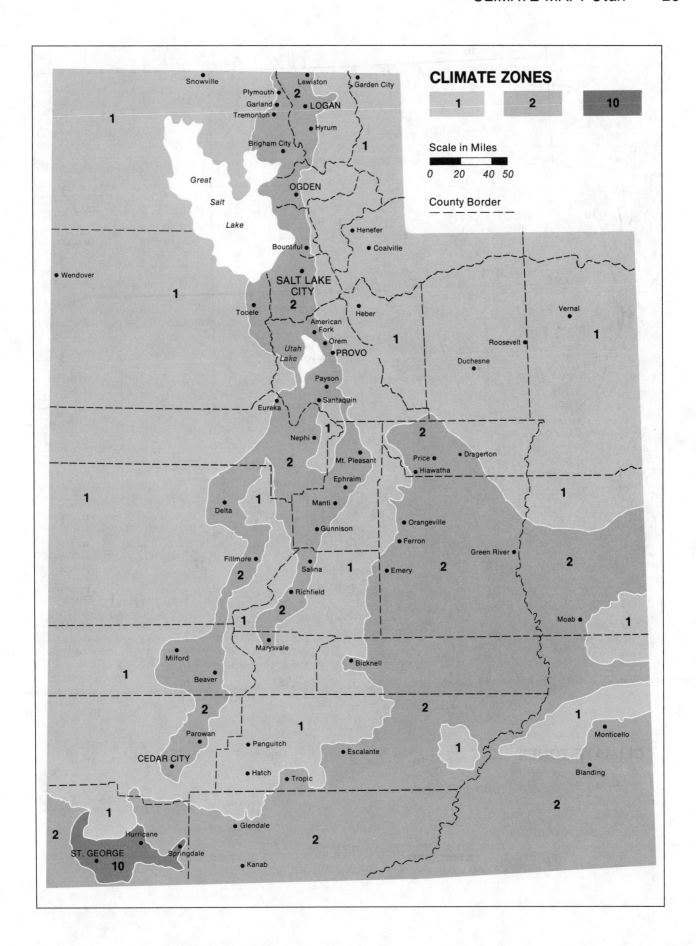

CLIMATE ZONES

| 1 | 2 | 10 |

Scale in Miles

0   20   40 50

County Border

Snowville

Lewiston

Garden City

Plymouth

Garland

2

Tremonton

LOGAN

Hyrum

Brigham City

1

Great

Salt

OGDEN

Lake

Henefer

Bountiful

Coalville

Wendover

SALT LAKE
CITY

1

Tooele

2

Heber

American
Fork

Vernal

Orem

Roosevelt

1

Utah
Lake

PROVO

Duchesne

Payson

Santaquin

Eureka

1

Nephi

Mt. Pleasant

2

Price

Dragerton

2

Ephraim

Hiawatha

1

Delta

Manti

1

Gunnison

Orangeville

Ferron

Fillmore

Salina

1

Emery

2

Green River

2

2

Richfield

2

Moab

1

Marysvale

Milford

Bicknell

1

Beaver

1

2

2

Parowan

1

Monticello

Panguitch

Escalante

1

CEDAR CITY

Hatch

Tropic

Blanding

2

Glendale

Hurricane

2

2

ST. GEORGE

Springdale

Kanab

10

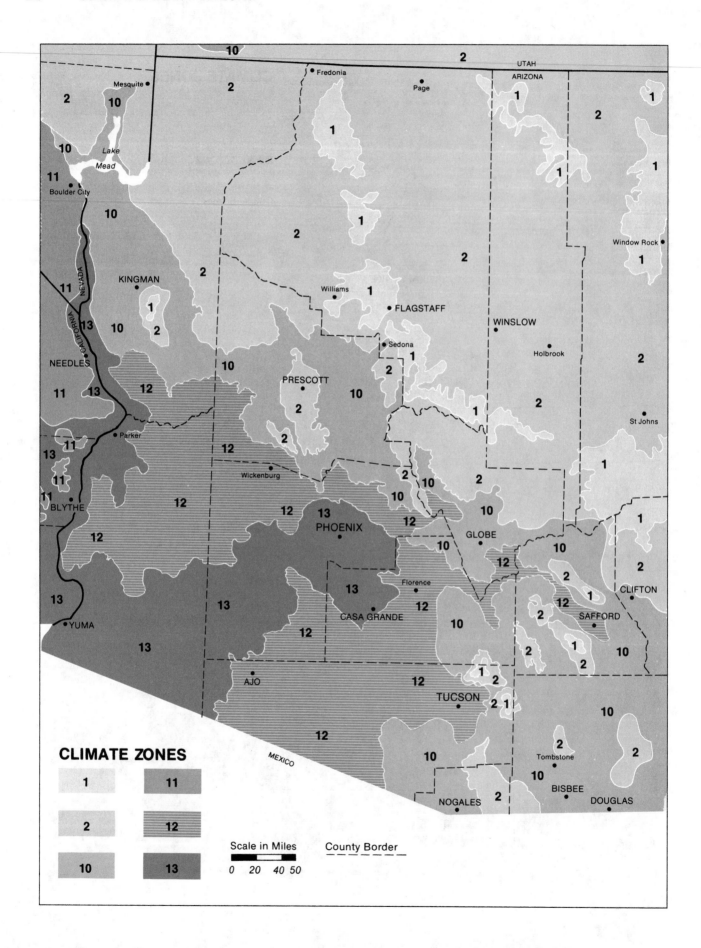

CLIMATE ZONES

1		11	
2		12	
10		13	

Scale in Miles

0   20   40 50

County Border

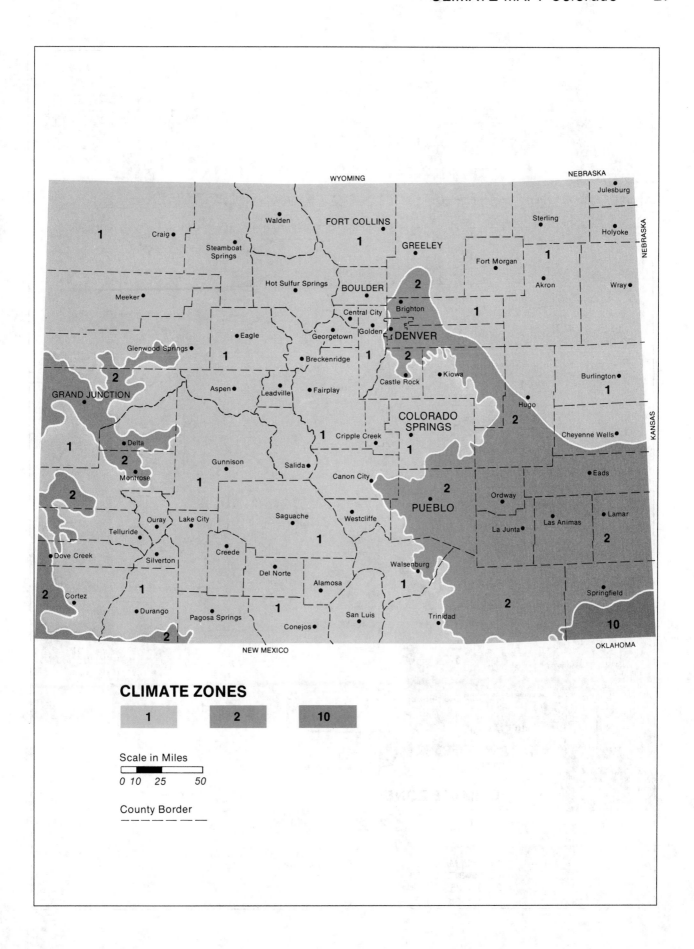

WYOMING

NEBRASKA

NEBRASKA

KANSAS

OKLAHOMA

NEW MEXICO

1   Craig

Walden

FORT COLLINS

Julesburg

Sterling

Holyoke

Steamboat
Springs

1

GREELEY

Fort Morgan

1

Akron

Wray

Meeker

Hot Sulfur Springs

BOULDER

2

Brighton

1

Glenwood Springs

Central City

Georgetown   Golden

DENVER

Eagle

1   Breckenridge

1

2

Burlington

1

2

GRAND JUNCTION

Aspen

Leadville   Fairplay

Castle Rock

Kiowa

COLORADO
SPRINGS

Hugo

2

1   Delta

2
Montrose

Gunnison

Cripple Creek

Salida

1

Cheyenne Wells

2   Canon City

1

Eads

2

Saguache

2
PUEBLO

Ordway

Las Animas

Lamar

2

Ouray   Lake City

Westcliffe

La Junta

Telluride

1

Dove Creek

Creede

Silverton

Del Norte

Walsenburg

1

Alamosa

1

2   Cortez

Durango   Pagosa Springs

1

San Luis

Trinidad

Springfield

Conejos

2

10

2

CLIMATE ZONES

| 1 | 2 | 10 |

Scale in Miles

0 10 25   50

County Border
- - - - - -

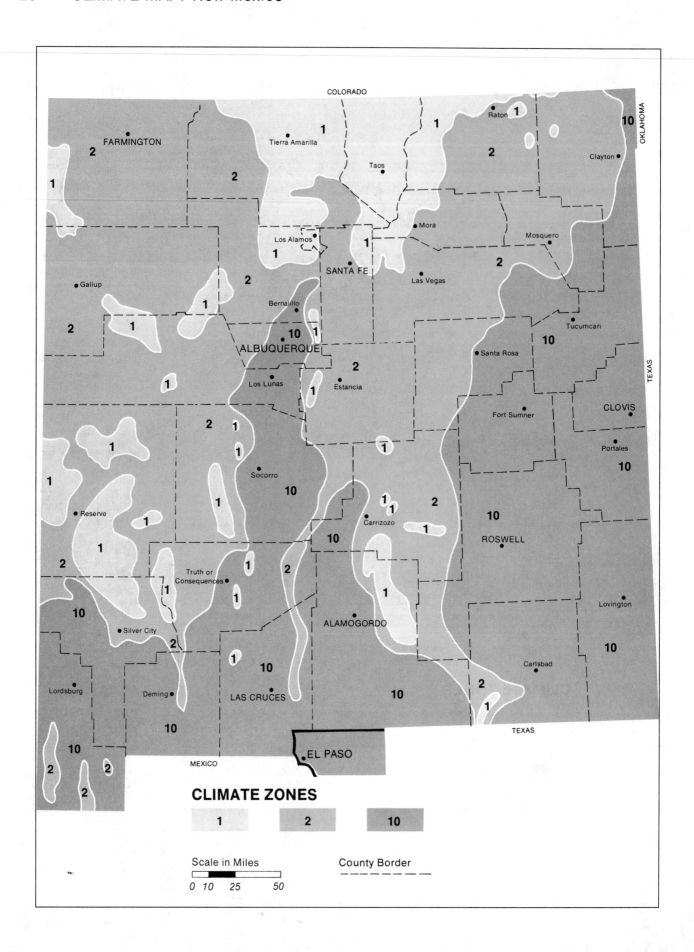

CLIMATE ZONES

| 1 | 2 | 10 |

Scale in Miles

0 10 25   50

County Border - - -

odd-numbered one comprises air-drained thermal belts. The difference is that Zones 20 and 21 get both coastal and interior weather. In these transitional areas, climate boundaries often move 20 miles in 24 hours with the movements of marine or interior weather.

Because of the greater ocean influence, this climate is better for plants that need moisture—fuchsias, tuberous begonias, and the like. The Los Angeles State and County Arboretum at Arcadia is in Zone 20 (bordering on Zone 21). The array of plants grown there gives some indication of the great choice available in this zone.

Winter lows over a 20-year period have ranged from 28° to 23°F. In recorded history, lows here have ranged from 21° to 14°.

Zone 21 *Thermal Belts in Southern California's Sections of Occasional Ocean Influence*

The description for Zone 20 tells of the interplay of weather influences in both Zone 20 and Zone 21. Your garden can be in ocean air or under a high ocean fog for one day and experience a mass of interior air (perhaps a drying Santa Ana wind from the desert) the next day. On the other hand, this Zone 21 is a thermal belt: cold air of winter nights drains off, making it possible to grow plants here that are too tender for Zone 20.

This area is fine citrus-growing country. Its mild winters favor a number of other tender items, because temperatures never dip very far below 30° here. Over a 20-year period, winter lows at the weather-recording stations in Zone 21 ranged from 36° to 23°F. Recorded lows have ranged from 27° to 17°.

This is the mildest zone (highest number) that gets adequate winter chilling for some plants (most forms of lilac, for instance).

Zone 22 *Cold-Winter Portions of Southern California's Coastal Climate*

Zone 22 is influenced by the ocean approximately 85 percent of the time and, further, is either a cold-air basin in winter or a hilltop above the air-drained slopes. It gets lower winter temperatures than neighboring Zone 23.

Actually, the winters are so mild here that winter lows are not of much significance, seldom below 28°F. The coldest temperatures generally are experienced in canyons and near canyon mouths where considerable cold air drainage may cause fairly heavy frost damage. The winter lows recorded range from 21° to 24°.

Gardeners who take advantage of building overhangs or the protection of tree branches can grow an impressive variety of subtropical plants—bananas, gingers, tree ferns, and the like. The lack of a pronounced chilling period during the winter limits the use of such deciduous woody plants as flowering cherry and lilac. Many herbaceous perennials from colder regions fail to thrive because winters are too warm for them to go dormant.

Zone 23 *Thermal Belts of Southern California's Coastal Climate*

Found here is one of the most favored gardening climates in North America for the growing of subtropical plants. It could be called the avocado belt, for this has always been southern California's best strip for growing that crop. Frosts don't amount to much (it's an air-drained thermal belt) and most of the time (approximately 85 percent) it is under the influence of the Pacific Ocean; only 15 percent of the time is the determining influence from the interior. A notorious portion of this 15 percent is on those days when hot and extremely drying Santa Ana winds blow down the hills and canyons from the mountains and deserts.

Zone 23 lacks either the necessary summer heat or the winter cold to grow successfully some items such as pears, most apples, most peaches. On the other hand, it enjoys more heat than the neighboring maritime climate, Zone 24. As an example of that difference, gardenias and oleanders are recommended for Zone 23 but not Zone 24.

In the temperature records books, most of Zone 23 fares pretty well as far as mildness is concerned. But severe winters have descended on some sections of Zone 23 at times, and the net result of this has been to make a surprising spread of low temperatures. Over a 20-year period, lows have ranged from 38° to 23°F. In recorded history, the lows have ranged from 28° to 23°.

Zone 24 *Marine Influence– Southern California Coast*

This is the climate along southern California's beaches that is almost completely dominated by the ocean. Where the beach runs along the base of high cliffs or palisades, Zone 24 extends only to the base of the precipice. But where hills are low or nonexistent, it runs inland several miles.

This is a mild marine climate (milder than northern California's maritime Zone 17), because below Point Conception the Pacific is comparatively warm. The winters are mild, the summers are cool and often of limited sunshine because of daily high fogs, and the air is seldom really dry. This is southern California's best fuchsia and tuberous begonia climate. Scores of less well-known plants from Chile, New Zealand, the Canary Islands, and the moister parts of South Africa do well here for the same reason—*Leucodendron argenteum* and *Corynocarpus laevigata* are examples. Very tender plants find a good home here, but they must be able to get along with only moderate summer heat. It's a climate in which gardens planted with certain kinds of plants can become jungles.

Areas of Zone 24 that are close to the mouths of canyons can suffer in winter from cold air that comes down the canyons on some winter nights. Several such canyons are big enough to be shown on the map—you will see them on the map along the coast south of Laguna Beach. Partly because of the unusually low temperatures created by this canyon action, the scope of winter lows in Zone 24 is broader than you might think. In a 20-year period, lows have ranged from 44° to 24°F. The all-time record lows range from 33° to 20°. This shows that there are some weather stations in Zone 24 that have never recorded a freezing temperature (32° or below).

The all-time high temperatures here are interesting in that they help define the total climate, but they aren't greatly significant in terms of plant growth. Average all-time high of weather stations in Zone 24 is 105°. Compare this to northern California's marine climate, Zone 17, which averages 97°, and to the average in some of southern California's inland climates—Zone 22 at 111°, Zone 20 at 114°, and Zone 18 at 115°.

Basic Planting and Care

How plants grow

Knowledge about how plants grow is an important key to becoming a successful gardener.

Green plants that grow in soil share certain characteristics with animals: both are composed of protoplasm (largely water and proteins); both have tissues of various kinds which serve various functions; both consume and store energy; and both are capable of reproducing themselves. But there is one significant difference: green plants are able to manufacture their own food from essentially inorganic materials.

The seed

A plant's life cycle typically begins with a seed (exceptions are the ferns, mosses, fungi, and algae, which develop from spores). Depending on its kind, a seed may be very large or of dustlike smallness, but each contains inside its protective coating an embryo plant and, in most cases, a supply of stored food (starch, proteins, oils) to start the embryo on its way. When germination conditions are favorable, the seed's stored food will launch the embryo plant into growth and sustain it until it is capable of manufacturing its own food.

Seeds sprout, or *germinate*, when given favorable conditions. Such conditions include moisture and a certain amount of warmth. In addition, some seeds have other special germination requirements: light or absence of light; a period of dormancy; very high or very low temperatures; weathering, exposure to acids, or grinding to soften and crack the seed coat. When germination occurs, the seed coat splits, a rootlet starts downward, and a sprout (*hypocotyl*)bearing seed leaves (*cotyledons*) makes its way toward the soil surface. Most garden plants have two seed leaves. Botanists refer to these plants collectively as *dicotyledons*, or "dicots" for short. But a number of familiar plants—grasses, corn, orchids, lilies, irises, palms—have only one cotyledon; these are classed as monocotyledons ("monocots"). All the conifers (pines, spruces, firs, etc.) and the cycads have many seed leaves.

The roots

The first single root sent down by the germinating seed soon begins to send out tiny white rootlets that draw in chemical substances needed for growth and the water to carry these substances to the aboveground part of the plant. If no moisture is available to a plant's roots, the plant dies. As a plant grows and matures, its roots take on different functions and a different appearance. The older portions grow a skinlike covering similar to bark. These larger, older roots act as vessels to transport water and nutrients to the rest of the plant, and sometimes serve as storage vessels for food. The entire root system anchors the plant in the soil.

Always found at the roots' ends are tender root tips. These contain a growing point that continually produces elongating cells that push the roots deeper and farther out in moist soil.

Immediately behind the root tip (or cap) is a zone of cells that produce single-celled root hairs. These very delicate root hairs perform the actual absorption of water and nutrients. Exposed to sunshine or dry air, the root hairs quickly shrivel and die. Therefore gardeners transplant as quickly as possible, without exposing roots to the air any more than is necessary. The loss of root hairs causes wilting in a new transplant; until roots grow a new set, they cannot meet the needs for water and food imposed by the leaves.

The stem

A woody dicotyledon can illustrate the complex internal system of plants. Between the cotyledons is the growth tip, which eventually elongates to form the stem. Growth buds develop along the stem and open to produce the first true leaves. The stem continues to elongate as the plant grows, producing additional buds. The end or *terminal* bud carries growth upward; side buds or *lateral* buds develop into leaves or, as the plant becomes larger, into branches.

If a terminal bud is removed or damaged, the side buds take over the growth of the branch. On the other hand, if the side buds are removed, energy is temporarily directed to the growth of the terminal bud. The gardener's art of "pinching" puts this growth characteristic to use by nipping off side buds to channel growth energy into the terminal, or removing terminal growth to promote growth of lateral buds into a more bushy plant. In some plants the buds may lie dormant in stem or bark for many years (*latent* buds), starting into growth only after pruning or injury removes the upper growth.

A primary function of the stem is to transmit water and nutrients absorbed by the root hairs to the growing points (buds, leaves, flowers) and to return to the roots the food (sugars) manufactured in the leaves. This exchange is carried on by a complex duct system of specialized cells that begins in the roots and leads to the growing points (see illustration to right). In the stems of most trees, shrubs, and herbaceous (soft-stemmed) plants, the tissues that make up the duct system are concentrated on either side of (or very near) the *cam-*

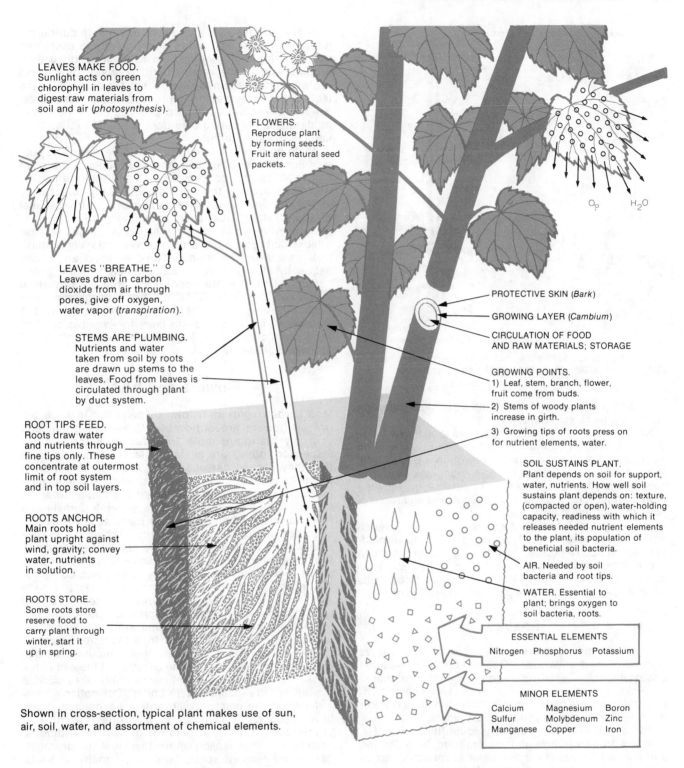

LEAVES MAKE FOOD.
Sunlight acts on green chlorophyll in leaves to digest raw materials from soil and air (*photosynthesis*).

FLOWERS.
Reproduce plant by forming seeds. Fruit are natural seed packets.

LEAVES "BREATHE."
Leaves draw in carbon dioxide from air through pores, give off oxygen, water vapor (*transpiration*).

STEMS ARE PLUMBING.
Nutrients and water taken from soil by roots are drawn up stems to the leaves. Food from leaves is circulated through plant by duct system.

ROOT TIPS FEED.
Roots draw water and nutrients through fine tips only. These concentrate at outermost limit of root system and in top soil layers.

ROOTS ANCHOR.
Main roots hold plant upright against wind, gravity; convey water, nutrients in solution.

ROOTS STORE.
Some roots store reserve food to carry plant through winter, start it up in spring.

$O_?$ H_2O

PROTECTIVE SKIN (*Bark*)

GROWING LAYER (*Cambium*)

CIRCULATION OF FOOD AND RAW MATERIALS; STORAGE

GROWING POINTS.
1) Leaf, stem, branch, flower, fruit come from buds.
2) Stems of woody plants increase in girth.
3) Growing tips of roots press on for nutrient elements, water.

SOIL SUSTAINS PLANT.
Plant depends on soil for support, water, nutrients. How well soil sustains plant depends on: texture, (compacted or open), water-holding capacity, readiness with which it releases needed nutrient elements to the plant, its population of beneficial soil bacteria.

AIR. Needed by soil bacteria and root tips.

WATER. Essential to plant; brings oxygen to soil bacteria, roots.

ESSENTIAL ELEMENTS
Nitrogen   Phosphorus   Potassium

MINOR ELEMENTS		
Calcium	Magnesium	Boron
Sulfur	Molybdenum	Zinc
Manganese	Copper	Iron

Shown in cross-section, typical plant makes use of sun, air, soil, water, and assortment of chemical elements.

bium—which is a layer of cells usually located just inside a plant's bark or "skin." This cambium layer produces the cells that constitute the duct system as well as the tissues that increase the girth of the plant. If plant ties or the wires that attach plant labels become too tight, they not only cut off the plant's circulation system but also interfere with the cambium layer that produces new cells for increasing girth. Unless these ties are loosened, the plant may be severely damaged or may die. This type of damage (usually referred to as *girdling*) is similar to damage caused by some fungi, insects, or animals.

Support of the plant is another important function of the stem. Many plants have quite rigid stems because the walls of their cells are stiffened by cellulose, lignin, and similar substances. In trees and shrubs, the interior dense heartwood serves solely as support, having outlived the functions of conductive or storage tissue. In some plants the stems are too long and thin to be held erect even by woody tissue. Vines have developed twining stems, tendrils, coiled leaf stalks, or adhesive disks to carry leaves and flowers up into the sunlight. Also, some annuals and perennials must be staked to keep from

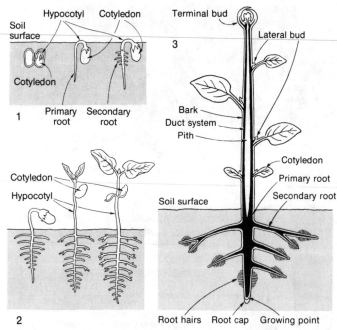

Germinating seed has primary root, hypocotyl, cotyledons.
Cotyledons sustain plant until true leaves, roots appear.

sprawling on the ground: their stems don't form enough woody tissue to stand upright.

A third function of the stem is to store food that will tide the plant through dormancy, start growth in spring, and help seeds develop. Food moves through a plant in the form of plant sugars; when stored it changes to starch. In spring when the plant is ready to resume growth, the stored starch changes back into sugar and again circulates through the plant.

Many familiar garden plants lack a woody branch structure but have, instead, underground stems or modified stems such as bulbs, rhizomes, corms, or tubers. In those specialized underground or modified stems is stored the food (starch) to carry the plant through its dormant period and provide push for new spring growth.

Leaves

The basic function of leaves is the manufacture of sugars and other carbohydrates. This manufacture—called *photosynthesis*—is carried out by the green material in the leaves known as *chlorophyll* which, with energy from sunlight, converts carbon dioxide from the air and water from the soil to carbohydrates and oxygen.

Photosynthesis requires large quantities of water, which is drawn up through the stem from the roots and into the leaf tissue. There the water encounters carbon dioxide which entered the leaf from the air through minute breathing pores (*stomata*) located most abundantly on the leaves' undersides. Since the interior leaf tissues must be moist but outside air frequently is dry, the stomata are able to close when necessary to prevent dehydration. The leaf is further protected against drying by an outer coat (*epidermis*) which may be waxy, resinous, hairy, or scaly.

In addition to allowing the inflow of carbon dioxide from the air, the stomata also permit the outflow of excess water vapor and oxygen which are by-products of the photosynthesis process.

Photosynthesis stops in deciduous plants during the dormant season, and slows down greatly in evergreen plants during their modified dormancy in cold weather. Simultaneously, the requirement for water drops, and roots no longer strain to keep up with the demands of the leaf system's manufacturing process. As a consequence, we are able to dig up most plants and move them with moderate safety during their dormant period (often from late fall to early spring).

Anything that interferes with photosynthesis and subsequent transfer of carbohydrates throughout the plant can have harmful consequences. Fertilizers are usually necessary because the soil may not supply consistently all the nutrients the plant needs to manufacture essential carbohydrates. Without an adequate nutrient supply, plant growth is poor or slow. Insect or fungus disease attacks that reduce leaf area, or severe midyear pruning, not only slow the manufacture of food and, consequently, slow growth, but also interfere with the plant's accumulation of winter food. Soot, grime, and dust on leaves can impede free air circulation through pores and reduce the amount of vital light available to the leaves. A smothering mat of leaves on a lawn, for example, can halt production of chlorophyll and cause grass to yellow and growth to cease.

Flowers and fruit

Most garden plants form flowers if permitted to do so, but not all flowers are noticeable. Some are green and scarcely distinguishable from leaves without close inspection; others are hidden by leaves or are so small that they escape detection. The majority of flowering plants bear *perfect* flowers in which male and female reproductive parts are both contained in a single flower. (In the minority are plants that have separate female and male flowers—either on the same plant, as in corn, or on separate plants, as in asparagus.) When the female flower parts are fertilized by male sexual cells (*pollen*), the flower produces a "fruit" of some sort that contains seeds. Some fruit become large, fleshy, and conspicuous, as the peach, tomato, banana, and apple; but many are simply dry, papery enclosures for the seeds. The seeds contained in the fruit reproduce the plant. The fruit—seed containers—of some kinds of plants are adapted to distribute seeds far from the parent plants.

The various flower parts and their functions are diagrammed and explained in the Glossary at the end of the book. The different ways that seed-setting takes place in the flower are explained there under "Pollination".

If left on the plant, flowers often are pollinated and form seeds. More plant energy then goes toward seed development than to vegetative growth or additional flowers. For that reason, more than just for neatness, gardeners remove spent flowers on many annuals, perennials, and some flowering shrubs.

In nature, the seedlings of any single kind of plant tend to vary to some degree. Isolation or carefully controlled breeding can assure uniform seedlings. Such work is done for you by growers when they select the seed that goes into seed packets or select the seed from which nursery plants are grown.

Although producing seeds is nature's primary method for starting new plants, many plants can be propagated by other methods and, in the nursery trade, usually are. These methods are collectively called *vegetative propagation* and are discussed on pages 37–44.

Soils and planting mixes

An understanding of your soil is perhaps the most important aspect of gardening. With that knowledge you will know how to water and fertilize your plants—in other words, how to care for them.

Soil is a mass of mineral particles mixed with living and dead organic matter, incorporating quantities of air and water. The size and form of the mineral particles chiefly determine the structure of the soil. Clay particles are the smallest, sand particles are the largest, and silt represents the intermediate size. Clay and sand give their names to two soil textures, while a combination of the three particle sizes forms loam soil.

Clay (also called adobe, gumbo, or just "heavy") soils are composed of microscopically small mineral particles. These tiny particles are flattened and fit closely together, so spaces between particles for air and water also are small. When clay soils get wet they dry out slowly because downward movement of water—*drainage*—is slow. However, the small particles of clay usually are well supplied with nutrients, and the slow drainage prevents loss of those nutrients by leaching.

Sandy soils have comparatively large particles that are rounded rather than flattened. The particle size and shape allow for much larger spaces between particles than clay soils have; consequently, sandy soils contain much soil air, drain well, and warm quickly. They also dry out quickly; the frequent watering that is necessary washes out valuable nutrients.

Loam soils are intermediate between the extremes of clay and sand. Their mineral composition is a mixture of clay, silt, and sand particles. The characteristics of loam soils are midway between those of clay and sand. Loam, then, is the "ideal" soil—draining well but not drying out too quickly, and having enough soil air for healthy root growth.

Organic soil amendments

Vital to the fertility of all soils—and especially to sand and clay—is organic matter, the decaying remains of once-living plants and animals. Organic soil amendments are what gardeners incorporate into their soil to improve or maintain the soil's texture and to encourage healthy root growth.

Organic soil amendments will improve aeration and drainage of clay soils. In a sandy soil, organic amendments help hold water and dissolved nutrients so the soil stays moist longer and can supply food for plants better. Decomposition of organic matter releases some nutrients, adding to soil fertility. Because organic matter is a desirable component of all soils, and because all organic materials are continually being decomposed by soil bacteria, even the best of soils will benefit from periodic application of organic amendments.

Organic soil amendments include such items as ground bark, peat moss, leaf mold, sawdust and wood shavings, manure, compost, and many other plant remains. The final product of the action by soil bacteria and other organisms on organic materials is *humus*, a soft material that helps bind together minute clay particles into larger crumbs, thereby improving aeration and drainage. Humus will also fill in pore spaces in sandy soils to help hold water and nutrients.

When you add organic amendments to your soil, be generous and mix them deeply and uniformly. For the most marked improvement, add a volume of amendment equal to 25 to 50 percent of the total soil volume in the cultivated area. Mix in thoroughly, either by spading and respading or by rotary tilling. The physical mixing will add some air to the soil, and the amendment will help to keep it there.

Organic amendment cautions

Organisms that break down organic materials require nitrogen. If they cannot get all the nitrogen they require from the organic material itself, they will take it from the soil, robbing roots of whatever nitrogen is available.

Most organic amendments you can buy at a nursery contain enough nitrogen to satisfy the soil bacteria; these amendments include peat moss, leaf mold, manure, and wood by-products such as ground bark that have been nitrogen fortified. Compost and various animal manures that are free from litter (sawdust, straw) also contain enough nitrogen, as do composted wood by-products. But with *raw* wood shavings, ground bark, straw, or manure with litter, you will need to add nitrogen. At first, use one pound of ammonium sulfate for each inch-deep layer of organic material spread over 100 square feet. In the second year, apply half as much ammonium sulfate as you used the first year; in the third and fourth years use one-fourth as much.

Nitrogen from decaying organic material isn't directly available to plants. It must be converted by soil organisms (fungi, molds, and bacteria) first into ammonia, then into nitrites, and finally into nitrates which can be absorbed by plant roots. The microorganisms that do this converting are actually plants themselves and need a certain amount of warmth, air, water, and nitrogen. Any soil amendments that improve aeration and water penetration will also improve the efficiency of soil organisms at their vital job of making nitrogen available.

Liberal use of organic matter can greatly lower soil *p*H (the acidity or alkalinity); where soil already is neutral or acid, this can result in a very acid soil. Having your soil tested yearly where acidity may be a problem will give you an indication of *p*H and, therefore, when you would need to take corrective measures.

Inorganic soil amendments

Mineral soil amendments may be useful in special cases but are no substitute for organic amendments, as they don't provide nourishment for soil microorganisms. Their best use comes as a supplement to organic materials.

The first group of mineral amendments includes perlite, pumice, and vermiculite. These amendments may improve the texture of clay soils and may help sandy soils by increasing their capacity to hold water and dissolved nutrients. Perlite and pumice are inert materials, like sand, but are water absorbent. They last considerably longer in the soil than vermiculite. Vermiculite has the ability to absorb nutrients as well as water, contributes some potassium and magnesium for plant growth, but breaks down faster than perlite or pumice. Because the cost of these mineral amendments is too great for large-scale use, their benefits are limited mostly to soils for small planting beds or containers.

The second group includes gypsum and lime, both of which will effect the same improvement on clay soils by causing the particles to group together into larger units or "crumbs" that will then have larger spaces between particle aggregates. This produces better aeration and drainage. Whether you use gypsum or lime depends upon the pH of your soil. For acid soils, lime is used; for neutral or alkaline soils, use gypsum. In general, alkaline soils are found in low-rainfall regions, acid soils where rainfall is plentiful. In addition to alteration of soil pH, lime is useful as a supplier of calcium; gypsum supplies both calcium and sulfur. Lime or gypsum may be used in regions such as parts of the Pacific Northwest where these minerals may be deficient. But before you consider using either gypsum or lime, ask your county agricultural agent for guidelines and possible recommendations of quantities to use.

Soil problems

Entirely satisfactory garden soils are rare indeed, and when they exist they usually represent careful preparation and careful management over several years. Some soil problems are quite obvious and easy to correct; others may require the assistance of professional help.

Alkalinity. Alkaline soil, common in light-rainfall areas, is soil that is high in calcium carbonate (lime) or certain other minerals such as sodium. Many plants grow well in moderately alkaline soil; others, notably camellias, rhododendrons, and azaleas, will not thrive there because the alkalinity causes particular elements necessary for their growth to be unavailable to the plants. Large-scale chemical treatment of highly alkaline soil is expensive and complex. A better bet is to plant in raised beds or containers, using a good prepared soil mix. Soils that are only slightly alkaline or nearly neutral will support many garden plants. They can be made to grow acid soil plants with liberal additions of peat moss, ground bark, or sawdust; fertilization with acid-type fertilizers; and periodic applications of chelates.

Deep watering can help lessen alkalinity, but remember that you need fast drainage if you water heavily.

Salinity. An excess of salts in the soil is a widespread problem in arid parts of the West. These salts may be naturally present in the soil or they may come from water (especially softened water, which has a high sodium content), from fertilizers and chemical amendments, and from manures with high salt content. Where these salts are not leached through the soil by high rainfall or deep irrigation, they reach high concentration in the root zone where they inhibit germination of seeds, stunt growth, and cause leaves to scorch and turn yellow or leaf margins to brown and wither (salt burn). Periodic and thorough leaching with water will lessen the salts content. To carry out this leaching, drainage must be good.

Acidity. Acid soil is at the opposite end of the scale from alkaline soil. It is most common in areas of heavy rainfall and is often associated with sandy soil and soils high in organic matter. Most plants grow well under mildly acid soil conditions, but intensely acid soils are undesirable. In the West, such soils are common in western Washington, western Oregon, and the north coast of California. Adding lime to such a soil should be undertaken only if a soil test indicates it is necessary. If acidity is a problem and lime is used to correct it, be sure to use fertilizers which do not have an acid reaction.

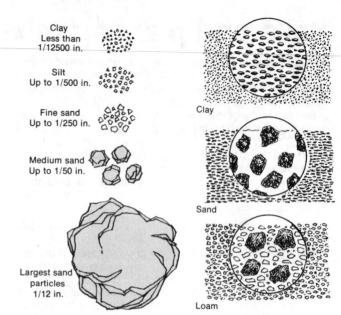

Clay
Less than
1/12500 in.

Silt
Up to 1/500 in.

Fine sand
Up to 1/250 in.

Medium sand
Up to 1/50 in.

Largest sand
particles
1/12 in.

Clay

Sand

Loam

Size of mineral particles determines texture of the soil. Loam, a mixture of different particles, is ideal.

Nutrient deficiency. If soil drains well, has ample water, is neither too acid nor too alkaline, and still fails to sustain plant growth well, it may be deficient in nutrients, most likely nitrogen. Fertilizers (see pages 52–55) are the quickest and easiest answer. Many complete fertilizers are available, and there are also formulations that provide any of the three basic elements—nitrogen, phosphorus, or potassium—individually. Manure and compost yield small quantities of nutrients, but are effective principally in building up the supply of organic material in the soil.

Soil analysis will reveal nutrient deficiencies as well as excess acidity or alkalinity. Commercial laboratories can perform such analyses. In some western states the agricultural extension service can analyze the soil. Soil testing kits for home use are available.

Chlorosis. A systemic condition in which a plant's newer leaves turn yellow, it is usually caused by a deficiency of iron (rarely, it results from lack of another mineral such as zinc). If the deficiency is mild, areas of yellow show up between the veins of the leaves, which remain a dark green. In severe or prolonged cases, the entire leaf turns yellow. Iron deficiency is only occasionally the result of a lack of iron in the soil; more frequently it is the result of some other substance (usually lime) making the iron unavailable to the plant. To correct chlorosis, treat the soil with iron sulfate or with iron chelate; the latter has the important ability to hold iron in a form that is available to plants. Follow label instructions carefully and avoid overdosing. Plants with serious iron shortages can also be treated with foliar sprays of iron.

Shallow soil (hardpan). A tight, impervious layer of soil can give trouble if it lies at or near the surface. Such a layer can be a natural formation—in the Southwest the commonest natural hardpan layer is called *caliche*—or it can be manmade. A common manmade hardpan occurs when builders spread out excavated subsoil over the surface, then compact it by driving trucks or other heavy equipment over it. If the subsoil has a clay content and is damp while construction is going on, it can take on brick-like hardness when it dries. A thin layer of topsoil conceals the problem without solving it. Roots cannot penetrate the hard layer, and water cannot drain through it. Planting holes become water tanks, and plants fail to grow. They may even die.

If the hardpan layer is thin and if your soil plot is accessible to heavy equipment, you may be able to improve or eliminate the problem by having the soil plowed to a depth of 12 inches or more. If this is impractical you can drill through it with a soil auger when planting. If the layer is too thick, a landscape architect can help you with a drainage system, which might involve sumps (side or bottom) or drain tiles. Or you can switch to raised bed and container gardening. If you want to improve the soil over large planting areas, dig up the area to a depth of 18 inches or so with heavy equipment, then add organic matter and thoroughly mix it in. As a beneficial extra step, you can then grow a crop of some heavy-rooting grass and, after it grows, rotary till it into the soil as additional organic material.

When one kind of soil overlies another, water movement across the dividing line (called an *interface*) is slowed or stopped. Water also fails to move upward across the interface by capillary action. If you must bring in additional soil to fill in low spots or to raise the level of your soil, don't add it as one single layer. Instead, add half the required new soil and mix it in thoroughly with existing soil by spading or rotary tilling. Then add the rest of the new soil to bring the level up to the desired height and thoroughly mix it in.

If you purchase topsoil, look for crumbly texture and try to determine whether or not it is saline (it shouldn't be). The soil should not contain potentially damaging herbicides. If it comes from good crop land, you can assume that salinity is low enough. Very fine-textured soils (clays and silts) should be avoided, as should soils that grew noxious weeds (Bermuda grass, wild morning glory, quack grass, nut grass, etc.). The best topsoil to purchase is the one which most closely approximates your existing soil.

Raised beds

If drainage is bad, consider building a raised bed in which you can prepare exactly a well-aerated rooting medium. Even if your soil is good you may find that the raised bed will highlight a spectacular planting, bring plants up to eye level, supply built-in seating, or interrupt the monotony of a flat garden or paved area. Walls may be of wood or masonry.

Compost

Well-made compost is a soft, crumbly, brownish or blackish substance resulting from decomposition of organic material. It has limited value as a nutrient source but great value as an organic soil amendment. Composting takes time, effort, and space in which to do it. But, if you have a ready supply of plant waste or a small garden that could be supplied by a continuously maintained compost pile, the time and effort might be well spent. Remember, though, that a poorly maintained compost pile will be slow to yield its reward and also may breed hordes of flies and give off an obnoxious odor.

In its simplest and least efficient form, composting consists of piling up grass clippings, leaves, and other garden debris plus vegetable kitchen refuse and permitting them to decompose. In 6 weeks to 6 months, depending on temperature, moisture and size of pieces of material, the compost will have broken down to the point that you can spade it back into your garden soil.

A better system for the average garden is to stack the material for composting to a height of 4 to 6 feet inside an enclosure that has openings in its sides for air to penetrate—a slatted bin or a wire mesh cylinder, for example. Turn the piled-up material once a week or more often to aerate the mass and to relocate pieces in various stages of decomposition (compost decomposes more rapidly in the heat and moisture of the pile's interior than on the outside). Thoroughly moisten the pile as needed; it should be about as wet as a squeezed-out sponge. If you add a few handfuls of complete fertilizer with every sizable load of raw material, the decomposition will proceed more rapidly.

A more sophisticated composting operation will have three receptacles: one for incoming raw material, one for material in the process of decomposition, and one for the finished product. If receptacles are placed side by side it will be simple to fork or shovel material from bin to bin.

Large, coarse pieces decompose slowly, so you should chop them up before adding to the pile or omit them altogether. A good mixture consists of green and dried materials in about equal proportions. The serious composter might consider purchasing a compost grinder that will chop up everything from leaves to thumb-thick branches into uniformly small fragments that will break down rapidly. These machines are a great aid to people who live beyond the service area of garbage collectors but who are prevented by ordinance from burning debris.

Propagating plants

When a gardener speaks of "propagation" he or she refers to all the ways of starting new plants. These methods range from the simplicity of planting seeds to the more complicated arts of budding and grafting. All except seed sowing are referred to as *vegetative propagation*; the resulting new plants will be identical to the plant from which the start came. Seeds, alone, differ in that respect: seedling plants may appear to be identical or nearly so, or they may vary considerably, but each seed is the new product of the union of two separate individuals. This mixture of parental characteristics is the chief factor in the breeding of new plants. Vegetative propagation makes it possible to maintain uniformity.

Plants from seeds

In nature, seeds are scattered from the seed-bearing plant. And scattering, or *broadcasting*, seeds is a method used for planting seeds of lawn grasses and sometimes of wildflowers. For most garden plants, however, seeds are sown more carefully in the open ground or in some sort of container.

Seeds in the open ground

Native wildflowers will make a reasonably good show if they are sown where they are to grow in time to catch fall rains, but they will do even better if the ground is cleared of weeds and grasses and prepared a bit by tilling and addition of some organic amendments. If you plan to broadcast seeds in drifts or patterned plantings, or if you wish to sow a broad area with tough, easy-to-grow plants such as sweet alyssum or California poppies, you can achieve a more even distribution by mixing the seed with several times its bulk of fine sand. After you have scattered the seeds or seed and sand mixture, rake lightly and water, then try to cover the area you have sown with a very thin mulch to prevent the soil from crusting and to hide the seeds from predators. (Be prepared, though, for a certain amount of loss to birds and sometimes rodents.)

Most garden annuals and vegetables also can be sown in place, but they will need more attention than broadcast wildflower seeds. Prepare the seedbed with care: fork, spade, or rotary till the area, working in soil amendments and a complete fertilizer (read the label to know how much to apply per 100 or 1,000 square feet). Rake smooth the prepared soil and moisten it well a few days before planting, if rains don't water it for you. If you plan to grow vegetables or annuals in rows, you can omit fertilizer at soil preparation time and apply it instead at seeding time in furrows 1 inch deeper than the seeds and 2 inches on either side of the seed row (again, follow label instructions for amount of seed per foot of row).

Align rows to take advantage of the sun's path; a north-south direction will give equal sunlight on both sides of the row. Follow seed packet instructions for spacing the rows. To plant the seeds, make a furrow that will be as deep as the planting depth specified on the seed packet. Use a hoe, rake, or stick to make the furrow, using a board as a straightedge or a taut string as a guideline if you want perfectly straight rows.

You will find seeds available for planting in three different forms: seeds in packets, pelletized seeds with each individual seed coated like a small pill for easy planting, and seed tapes in which seeds are properly spaced and imbedded in soil-degradable plastic—you just unroll the tape in the furrow and cover it with soil. In all cases you will find planting instructions on the seed, pellet, or tape package.

To sow seeds or seed pellets from packets, either tear off a small corner of the packet and tap the seeds out as you move the packet along the furrow, or pour a small quantity of seed into your palm, then lift pinches of seed between fingers and scatter them as evenly as possible in the furrow. When seedlings appear, remove excess plants (if necessary) so those you leave are spaced the distance apart that is recommended on the seed packet. Bare seeds scattered in furrows almost always come up so thickly that some thinning is required; pelletized seeds are easier to sow at the proper spacing, while seed tapes will do the spacing for you. If you wait too long to thin the seedlings, plants will develop poorly and will be more difficult to remove when you get around to thinning. Any weeds that sprout along with the intended plants should be removed when you thin—and afterward, too, if they continue to germinate. If you are careful you can quickly replant the surplus seedlings elsewhere.

Seeds in flats and containers

Many plants get off to a better start if sown in containers and later transplanted into place in the garden. Most nurseries stock seedling plants in flats or other containers ready for you to plant. By starting your own seedlings indoors or in a greenhouse—any location warmer than

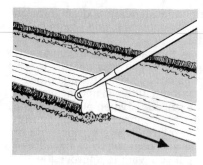

Hoe used with board makes straight furrows; run them north-south so new plants will receive even sunlight.

Sow seeds or seed pellets as evenly as possible in furrow dug to depth specified on seed packet.

Seed tapes have seeds already spaced—just unroll tape in furrow and cover it with prepared soil.

the out-of-doors, with adequate light—you can get a jump on the planting season by raising plants to set out at the earliest possible planting time in spring.

Almost anything that will hold soil and has provision for water to drain off will do for a seed-starting container. Your choice will depend on what you have available and how many seeds you have to plant. Plastic or wooden nursery flats will accommodate the largest number of seeds; other choices are clay or plastic pots, peat pots, aluminum foil pans (the sort sold for kitchen use), styrofoam or plastic cups, cut-down milk cartons, or shallow wooden boxes that you can make yourself. Remember to punch holes for drainage in the bottom of any container that will hold water; if you make your own wooden flats or boxes, leave about a ¼-inch space for drainage between boards that form the container's bottom. If you use containers that have held plants before, give them a thorough cleaning to avoid the possibility of infection by damping-off fungi which destroy seedlings (see page 66). A vigorous scrubbing followed by a few days of drying in the sun usually will suffice.

Unless you plan a large-scale seed planting operation, it will be easiest to buy a prepared mixture for starting the seeds. Nurseries carry a variety of such mediums; look for labels that say "potting soil." Prepared mixtures are ready to use immediately and usually have been sterilized, so carry no disease organisms. If you prefer, you can prepare your own mixture using about equal portions of potting soil, peat moss, and vermiculite or perlite; your objective is a soil that will drain easily yet still

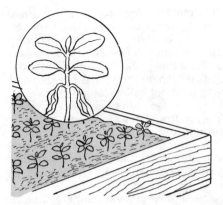

When seedlings have two sets of true leaves (left) they are ready to thin or transplant.To transplant, lift seedling carefully by leaves (center) and plant in individual container (right) until grown to garden-planting size.

retain moisture. You can use good garden soil in your seed planting mixture (equal parts soil, sand, and peat moss or ground bark) but such mixtures introduce the risk of damping-off fungi unless sterilized before use. Baking in the oven at 160° to 180° in a shallow pan for two hours will sterilize the soil (the odor is terrible), or you can fumigate the mixture with a commercial soil sterilant according to label directions.

Gently firm the mixture into the container and level it off about ¾ inch to 1 inch from the top of the container. If the mixture is powdery dry, water it and wait a day or two to plant. Very fine seeds can be broadcast over the surface and covered with sand; larger seeds can be planted in shallow furrows scratched into the surface or even poked in individually. Always remember that seeds should be covered no deeper than recommended on packet labels; a good general rule is to cover seeds to a depth equal to twice their diameter. Cover seeds with the proper amount of prepared mixture, press down gently but firmly, and then water. In order not to dislodge the seeds by direct watering, place the container in a tub, sink, or bucket containing a few inches of water. Enough water will be absorbed by the planting mix in the container within a few hours.

Thereafter, keep the seeding mixture moist but not soaking wet. One way is to place the container in a warm, protected spot out of direct sunlight and cover with a pane of glass to conserve moisture and a newspaper to exclude light. As soon as the first seedlings begin to appear (begin checking in about 3 days), remove the covering and give full light but not direct sun.

For slow-sprouting seeds or with plants whose seedlings develop slowly, you can sow seeds in pots, then tie a clear plastic bag around the pot. Place the pot where it receives good light but not direct sunlight. Air can get through the plastic, but water vapor cannot get out; seedlings will have enough water to complete germination without further watering. If you use this technique, be sure that your planting mixture is sterile and the container has not been used for planting before.

When the new seedlings have developed their second set of true leaves (see above), it will be time to transplant or thin them. If you don't need many plants, you will be able to thin them in place to give them enough elbow-room (1½ to 2 inches between them) to grow larger before you plant them out in the garden. But if you're going to want most of the plants that have germinated you will need to transplant them to larger containers for further growth to garden planting size. Preferably, transplant them into individual pots or cups; then when you

plant out in the garden they'll receive a minimum of root disturbance.

To do the first transplanting, fill a new container with moist planting mix; loosen the soil around the seedling plants (a kitchen fork is handy for this) and carefully lift out a seedling. Or lift a clump of seedlings and gently tease individual plants apart from the tangled mass of roots. Handle seedlings by their leaves to avoid bruising or crushing tender stems. Poke a hole with a pencil in the new container's planting mix, place the seedling in the hole, and firm the soil around it. Water the transplant right away. Do this for each seedling plant until they are all transplanted. Keep these plants out of direct sunlight for a few days until they have adjusted to the change.

In a few weeks to a month from the initial transplant, the seedlings should be ready to plant in the garden. During that month you can help their development by watering once with a half-strength liquid fertilizer solution or sprinkling lightly with a slow-acting fertilizer.

Division

If you grow clumping perennials, bulbs, or plants with rhizomes or tubers, you're bound to become involved with propagation sooner or later. To keep these plants healthy and vigorous, it's necessary to divide them periodically. Each year the typical perennial gains in girth by growing new roots and stems, usually around the outer perimeter of the previous year's growth. Eventually (usually in 2 to 4 years) these clumps get too big for their space in the garden. Also, growth can become weakened due to competition and crowding. When these conditions occur, it's time to divide the plant.

Each rooted segment or division is actually a plant in itself or is capable of becoming a new plant. If you divide an overgrown clump into separate parts you get many new plants. Division is a fast and inexpensive way of increasing your supply of favorite perennials. (Perennials that form a tap root and a single crown are best propagated by making cuttings of side branches or by sowing seeds.)

Most division is done in autumn or early spring, when plants are dormant. Fall is generally the best time to divide perennials that bloom in spring or early summer (in cold-winter regions, this must be done in *early* fall). After dividing, keep roots moist and plant them as soon as possible.

Deciduous and semideciduous perennials may be cut back to about 4 inches from the ground when you divide and transplant. Young, healthy foliage of evergreen perennials should not be cut back, but dead leaves should be removed.

Those bulbs that live over from year to year should be left undivided until flower production starts to fall off. Then dig (after foliage is thoroughly ripened) and pull the bulbs apart. Replant in well prepared soil, or store until appropriate planting time. Gladiolus, dahlias, and other similar plants are customarily dug up every year, divided, and stored until it's time to replant.

Cuttings

Most gardeners who have started new plants have tried cuttings from plant stems, roots, or leaves. From the propagator's standpoint, stem cuttings are of three types: softwood, semihardwood, and hardwood. These terms refer to the maturity of the wood.

Softwood and semihardwood cuttings

Softwood cuttings, which can be taken from spring until late summer during the active growing season, are the easiest and quickest rooting of stem cuttings. They are taken from soft, succulent new growth that has some flexibility but does break when bent sharply. Semihardwood cuttings are taken after the active growing season or after a growth flush, usually in summer or early fall when growth is firm enough to snap when the twig is bent sharply (if it just bends, the stem is too mature for satisfactory rooting).

In addition to deciduous and evergreen shrubs and trees, many herbaceous or evergreen perennials may be increased by softwood or semihardwood cuttings.

For both types of cutting, the procedures are the same. You'll have a better percentage of successful rootings if you start cuttings in a container of some sort—pot, can, flat or box, or cup. Be sure the container will drain water; if it has no drainage holes, poke or punch holes in its bottom so excess water will be able to drain out.

Choices of rooting medium are several, but all share one characteristic: they allow for easy water penetration and fast drainage. Pure sand (builder's sand or river sand) is the simplest medium but requires the most frequent watering. Better are half-and-half mixtures of sand and peat moss, perlite and peat moss, or perlite or vermiculite alone.

Fill the container with rooting medium and lightly firm it down so that the surface is just one inch below the container's top edge.

Take softwood or semihardwood cutting just below a leaf; strip off half the leaves; dip into rooting hormone; plant.

For the best cutting material, look for healthy, normal tip growth. Avoid spindly twigs or unusually fat shoots. With a sharp blade (shears or knife) cut a 4 to 5-inch-long stem, making the cut just below a leaf; remove all leaves on the lower half of the cutting. Dip the cut end into the rooting hormone powder, tap off the excess powder, and then insert the cutting to about half its length in the rooting medium you have readied. After you have finished one potful of cuttings, thoroughly water them.

Loss of water through the leaves that remain on the cuttings is the greatest threat to success with softwood and semihardwood cuttings. To minimize this, you can provide a greenhouse atmosphere—high humidity—for the cuttings while they are striking roots. A tried-and-true method is to invert a clear glass jar over a cutting, though with a large pot or flat full of cuttings this is impractical. Easiest of all is to place a plastic bag over the cuttings and container, then tie it around the container to confine humid air within the bag. Or if the container is small, place it in a plastic bag and tie the bag at the top. Ventilate any of these improvised greenhouses for a few minutes every day or two.

To provide high humidity for a cutting, invert a glass jar over it or tie a plastic bag around it.

Some softwood cuttings—fuchsias and impatiens, for example—root so easily that the glass jar or plastic bag is unnecessary. But whether the cuttings are covered or exposed, you should keep them out of direct sunlight during the rooting period.

When you see new growth forming on the cuttings you can be fairly sure that they have rooted. Wait a while until the rooted cuttings appear to be growing well, then move them into individual containers of potting soil (see pages 36–37) to further their development. Carefully loosen the rooting medium around each new plant so that you can remove it easily without tearing off new roots. Quickly transplant it into its individual container, water it, and move it to a spot where it will receive good light but no direct sun. After you see that new growth is continuing you can shift sun-loving plants to sunnier locations to prepare them for their ultimate places in the garden.

Hardwood cuttings

Hardwood cuttings are best made during the fall to spring dormant season from wood of the previous season's growth. Many deciduous shrubs and trees can be increased from cuttings taken during the dormant season. Deutzia, forsythia, grape, kolkwitzia, philadelphus, rose, and weigela are examples among well-known plants. Most nut and fruit trees and the large hardwood shade trees (beech, birch, maple, and oak, for example) will not root satisfactorily from cuttings without very special treatment, and are propagated by grafting or budding (see pages 41–44) or from seed.

Hardwood cuttings may take a longer time to root and start growth than softwood cuttings, so you will want to put your hardwood cuttings where they will remain undisturbed.

Best cuttings for this method are pencil-thick, 6 to 9 inches long, and with at least three leaf buds. Take them not from the tips of branches but from farther back on the stems. The top of each cutting should be cut just above a leaf bud, the bottom cut just below one. Be sure to cut stub that remains on plant back to a bud.

In all but the coldest Climate Zones (1, 2, and 3) you can set the cuttings out in the soil to root. Dig a trench that will accommodate the cuttings to half their length, put an inch of sand (builder's sand or river sand) in the bottom, set the base of each cutting on the sand, and fill in the trench with the garden soil mixed with some organic matter, perlite, or vermiculite. Water the cuttings

Plant hardwood cuttings in garden in most areas (left); in coldest climates, store over winter by burying (right) in shallow trenches or boxes of damp sawdust, peat, sand.

and be sure that the soil does not dry out later on. Dipping the ends of cuttings in a rooting hormone powder may help encourage root formation.

In Climate Zones 1, 2, and 3, you have a choice of several propagating methods. One is to take cuttings late in the dormant season, after much cold weather is past, and plant directly in the ground as described above. Or take the cuttings earlier, put them in a tightly sealed plastic bag, and place the bag in the refrigerator or in an unheated (but not freezing) room for the winter. When the coldest weather is past, plant out in the soil. A third option is to tie hardwood cuttings of each variety in separate bundles (labeled), and dig a trench in well-drained soil that will be deep enough to bury the bundles, laid on their sides, with 2 to 3 inches of soil. Place the bundles in the trench, cover with soil, and water them. Where the ground is likely to freeze, cover the buried cuttings with enough mulch to keep the ground from freezing. During the winter the lower ends of the cuttings will begin to form calluses from which roots will grow. When weather starts to warm as spring approaches, dig out the cuttings and plant them in the open ground or in containers where they will receive good light but no direct sun. Cuttings must be planted top side up; to be sure, make the top cut slanted, the bottom cut square.

Root cuttings

Any plant that will produce sprouts from the roots will grow from root cuttings. Familiar examples are Japanese anemone, Oriental poppy, trumpet creeper, blackberry, and raspberry. Actually, the roots you plant will show no visible growth buds; the buds develop after the root cutting is planted.

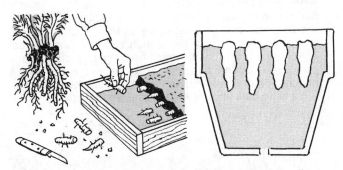

To make many root cuttings, set them horizontally in large flats; with a few cuttings, position them upright in a pot.

To make root cuttings, select roots 1/8 to 1/4 inch in diameter from vigorous plants and cut the roots into pieces 1 to 3 inches long. Fill a flat, box, or other shallow container (with drainage provided) to within an inch of its top with garden soil mixed by half with potting mix, sand, or perlite. Place the root cuttings on their sides on top of the soil. Cover them with 1/2 inch of additional soil mixture and water thoroughly; then place a pane of glass or piece of cardboard on top and set the container in the shade. Check every week for moisture and for sprouts and remove the covering when growth shows.

If you have only a few cuttings to root, place them upright in a pot of the rooting medium described above. The thickest end of the root cuttings should be upright, the tops of the cuttings just at soil level. Water the cuttings and place the pot in the shade, covered if you wish by glass or cardboard.

Leaf cuttings

Some plants will root successfully from a leaf or portion of a leaf. Begonias, African violets, various succulents, and sansevieria are among the more familiar plants that are propagated from leaves.

To multiply begonias, take a mature leaf, cut several of the main veins on the leaf's underside, and place the leaf flat on a moist rooting medium so that the cut veins are in contact with the soil. If necessary, hold the leaf in place with toothpicks. New plants will form on the leaf's upper surface above each cut.

With African violets, leave a bit of leaf stalk (1/4 inch to 2 inches) attached to the leaf; insert the leaf stalk into the rooting medium and steady the leaf with toothpicks. New plants will grow from the base of the leaf stalk.

Most succulents will send up new plants from the base of a leaf that touches soil—often from a leaf that has fallen onto the ground.

The long leaves of sansevieria may be cut into segments about 3 inches long; insert each segment (right side up) about an inch deep into the rooting medium. New plants will sprout from the base of each leaf section and can be transplanted.

Layering

The two layering methods—ground layering and air layering—tend to be slow to produce results, but with some hard-to-root plants you are more sure of success with layering than with cuttings. The reason that layering is more successful is that you don't remove the branch from the plant until it has formed roots.

Ground layering

Select a low-growing branch, about pencil size or slightly smaller, that can be bent easily to the ground. Make a notch halfway through the branch and just below a leaf joint about 8 to 12 inches back from the branch tip. Dust powdered rooting hormone onto the cut and insert a matchstick or small pebble into the cut to keep it open. Dig a wide hole about 4 inches deep so that you can bend the branch down into the hole, positioning the cut portion toward the bottom and bending the end of the branch up and out of the hole. Anchor the bent branch in the hole with a wire loop or rock, fill the hole with garden soil mixed with potting soil, peat moss, or other soil amendment, firm it in and water it. Tie the protruding end of the branch upright to a stake to help hold the layer in place.

Keep the soil around the layer moist, as you would for any cutting. In a few months to a year you should see new growth, indicating successful rooting, coming from the end of the branch you have tied upright. If not, carefully dig down to see if any roots have formed. Some plants may take two years or more to form roots. When you are sure roots have formed, you can cut the new plant from the parent plant, dig it up and move it to its intended location.

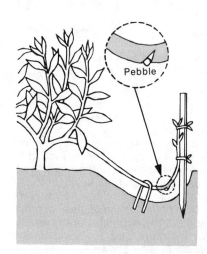 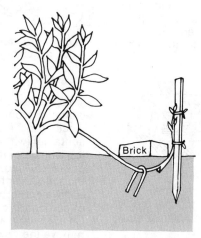 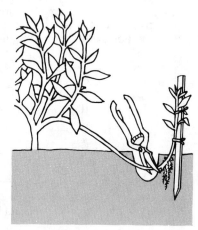

To ground layer, insert a pebble into a notch cut halfway through a low branch (left) and use a weight to anchor the branch underground (center). Dig underground and cut branch away from parent plant when new roots have formed (right).

Air layering

The principle of air layering is the same as the principle of ground layering; the difference is that air layering applies to branches higher on the plant. It is especially useful with some of the large house plants.

Select a branch from pencil size up to an inch in diameter. Below a leaf joint make either a slanting cut ⅓ through the stem, inserting a piece of matchstick to keep it spread apart, or remove a ring of bark about ¾ inch wide, scraping it down to the heartwood (the hard core of wood at the center of a stem or branch). Dust the cut lightly with rooting hormone powder, wrap the area with a generous handful of damp sphagnum moss, and enclose the moss with polyethylene plastic. Bind the plastic securely above and below the ball of moss with string, wire, or plastic ties.

If the rooting is successful, you'll see roots appearing in the sphagnum moss in several months. Then you can sever the newly rooted stem from the mother plant and pot it or plant it out on its own. At that time it usually is wise to reduce the number of leaves by half to prevent excessive transpiration while the newly independent plant is trying to get established. If no roots form, the branch will callus where it was cut and new bark will eventually grow over the cut area.

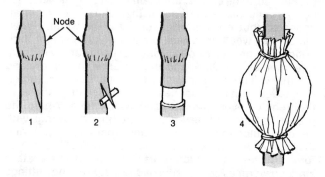

To air layer, work below a node (1) and make either a slanting cut (2) or remove a ring of bark (3). Dust with rooting hormone, wrap with moss, and enclose in plastic tied securely (4). Roots should appear in several months.

Budding and grafting

Anyone who has ever brought home from the nursery a bare-root rose plant or apple tree has benefited from the arts of budding and grafting. Relatively few home gardeners, however, have tried to propagate plants by either of these methods. Budding and grafting aren't really difficult, but they usually require some practice, a steady hand, and a few special tools.

Commercial propagators have very sound reasons for practicing budding and grafting. Either method uses much less tissue of the plant to be propagated than cuttings would. For plants in short supply—new rose varieties, for example—production is increased greatly by

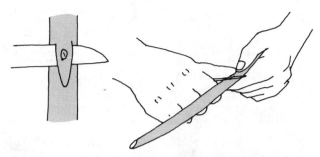

4) Slice under a strong bud on the budstick, starting ½ inch below the bud and finishing 1 inch above it. You must cut down into the wood a bit, not just under the layer of bark.

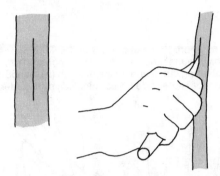

1) Budding begins by making a vertical cut 1 inch long in the stock branch, slicing down to the wood. Make cut at point where stock branch measures from ¼ to ½ inch in diameter.

5) Remove a shield shaped piece of bark with the bud by cutting about ¾ inch above the bud, slicing downward. Leave some of the wood attached to the back of the bud shield.

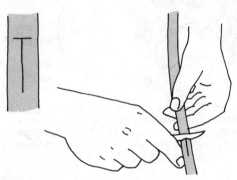

2) Make a horizontal cut through the bark, across the top of the vertical cut. The horizontal cut should circle about ⅓ the distance around the stock branch.

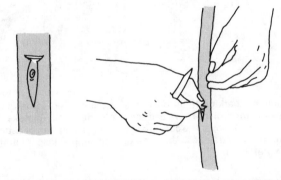

6) Push bud shield down into loosened bark flaps on the stock, being careful not to damage the bud. Top of the shield should match the top of the T-cut on the stock branch.

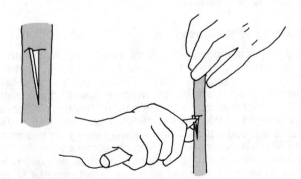

3) Gently pry up the corners where the cuts intersect. If the bark won't budge or it chips away, it is probably too early or too late in the season to do T-budding.

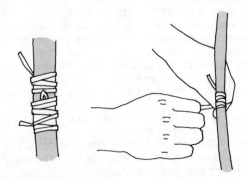

7) Bind the cut with plastic tape, leaving the bud exposed. (Don't use fabric tape; it won't stretch.) When the bud begins to grow, cut off the stem above the bud.

Bark Graft

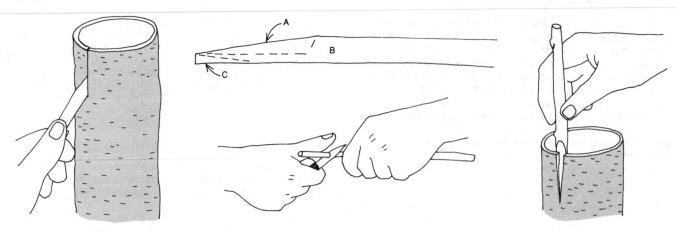

To begin bark graft, make a slit for each scion (left), slicing through stock bark to wood. You can place 3 or 4 scions on the stock. Do bark grafting in early spring, when bark pulls away from wood easily; take scions in winter and store them until spring. Trim scions (center) to fit into slits on stock.   Leave 3 or 4 buds on each scion. Make a slanting cut on inner side of scion (A). In addition, you can cut a ledge at top of inner slice (B; a difficult cut) to fit over stock, and also taper outer side (C) so scion can slide under one flap of the bark (right).

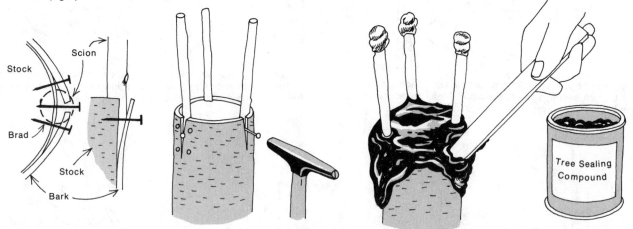

To complete bark graft, lift bark on stock and insert scion under one flap or down middle—whichever makes the snugger fit. Drive a wire brad through the bark and scion into the stock. To make the scion really secure, drive brads through the flaps on each side of the scion (left). Cover the cut surfaces with grafting wax or asphalt emulsion grafting compound (right). All scions may not grow, so start a few extra ones. Until new growth begins, inspect grafting wax for splits; rewax any you find. In hot areas, whitewash the entire grafted tree.

these methods. From a performance standpoint it makes sense to bud or graft plants to a rootstock that is known to grow well over much of the country. Many dwarf fruit trees, so much better adapted to the home garden than are full-sized versions, owe their reduced stature to rootstocks that dwarf the growth of normal-sized varieties grafted onto them. And the novelty offerings, such as three different apples on one tree, only come about through grafting. The standard or "tree" rose is another of these products, comprising three different varieties: one for the roots, another for the sturdy trunk, and a third for the bush on the top that provides the flowers you want.

Before you read the directions that follow, you'll have to learn a few terms of the trade:
• *stock* or *understock* is the name for the plant onto which you bud or graft; it supplies the root system (or trunk, or both) for the ultimate product;
• *scion* is the piece of stem that you graft onto the stock (the *bud* is the single growth bud that is placed into the stock in the budding process);

• *cambium* is the layer of cells that lies between the plant's bark and the woody core of a stem. It is the region in which growth takes place. Only when the cambium of the scion or bud unites with that of the stock will a graft or bud be successful.

Budding techniques

Budding accomplishes the same result as grafting but it is considerably easier to do and, for the novice, is more likely to be successful. You do it in summer and early fall, when plants are actively growing, by inserting a growth bud from one plant under the bark of another plant of a related kind. If you do the budding carefully and if the plants are compatible, the bud will unite with the stem into which it was inserted. Throughout fall and winter the bud will remain plump but dormant, then will begin to grow in spring when the surge of growth comes to all buds on the plant. At that time, cut off the stem to a point just above the growing bud that you inserted.

Roses and some other flowering shrubs are routinely

(Continued on page 44)

Whip Graft

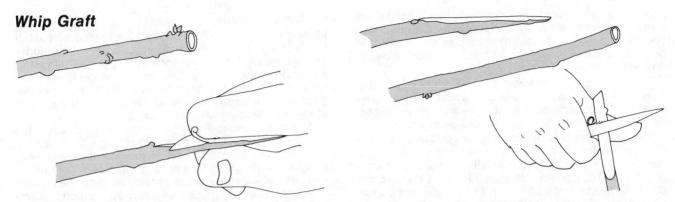

Whip graft begins with diagonal slice along stock, starting cut to right of a bud (left). Use a razor-sharp knife to cut an even diagonal, one thumb long. Trim the cut if necessary for an absolutely flat surface. Scion should be same diameter as stock. Compare buds (right) so when scion is cut to match stock, buds will point outward from tree, not inward. Then nick scion at beginning and end of cut so it will match the surface of cut on stock as closely as possible.

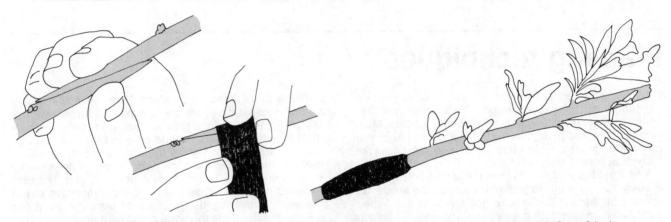

Place cut surface of scion against slice made on stock to check fit (left). Bark edges should meet all around. Cut a 6-inch length of plastic electrical tape and wrap it around joint from middle to end; overlap ½ inch. Wrap second length from middle to other end. Add 3 or 4 more layers of tape, winding it tightly (center). You can leave tape in place permanently if graft takes, or remove it in the third year. New shoots (right) show that cambium layer was matched properly.

Cleft Graft

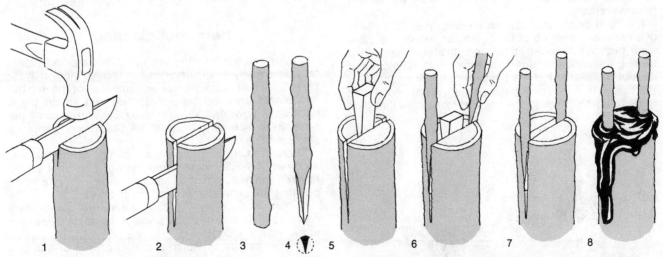

1 2 3 4 5 6 7 8

To make a cleft graft, prepare the stock by splitting it (1) several inches through a smooth straight-grained section so the split will be even (2). Take the scion (3) and shape one end into a long, gradually tapering wedge. The outside edge of the wedge should be slightly thicker than the inside (4). Hold the split in the stock open (5). Here (6) two scions are inserted into a stock, one at each end of the split. The scions must be carefully placed so the cambium layers match. After the scions are properly placed (7), cover the entire union with grafting wax (8).

propagated this way. The rootstock is a pencil-thick rooted cutting of a sort known to produce a good root system or a seedling plant of a species grown for that purpose; the bud is inserted into the rootstock close to the ground.

The T-bud is used with plants (roses, for example) that have thin bark; patch budding is employed on thick-barked plants such as walnuts, pecans, or avocados. Both methods work only if bark pulls away easily.

The stem from which you take the bud is called the *budstick*; it should be about the same diameter as the stock you are going to use. You will find the buds on the budstick at the base of leaf stalks. Remove the leaf, but don't cut off the leaf stalk; use it as a handle and also as an indicator: if, when the leaf stalk withers in a week or two after budding, the bud remains plump and green, then the operation has succeeded. But if the entire bud shield or patch (the bud together with its attached bit of bark and cambium) withers or turns dark, it has failed.

Grafting methods

Many different grafting methods have been devised, but all involve uniting a short length of stem—the scion—with the stock. The stock plant may be a pencil-slim seedling to be grafted near ground level or an old fruit tree to be grafted at the top of its trunk or on its major limbs. Illustrated on pages 42 and 43 are three of the simpler grafting methods: bark, whip, and cleft.

Whichever method you try, it is critical to align the cambium of scion to the cambium of stock. When that is done, the two cambiums will unite, the cuts callus over, and the scion will be ready to grow. Use a very sharp knife of high-quality steel for making all cuts; the cleaner the cuts the better chance for successful union of cambiums. All methods shown here call for cutting or sawing off the stock plant to the point where you wish to insert the scion. The tight union between stock and scion must be sealed off from air with some kind of sealing agent, usually grafting wax or plastic electrician's tape.

Planting techniques

Often busy gardeners forgo the pleasures of seed planting (under "Propagation," pages 35–37) and buy their annuals, vegetables, and perennials at the nursery. Many varieties of these plants, as well as some ground covers and hedge plants, are offered for sale in plastic packs, individual plastic pots, peat pots, or flats.

You'll get the best results from these small plants if you prepare the soil well, as you might for sowing seeds (described on page 36). If you're not ready to plant them right away, be sure your plants don't dry out while they're waiting to be planted; soil in small or shallow containers tends to dry quickly.

Plants in plastic packs, where each plant is in an individual cube of soil, are easy to remove by pushing up with your thumb on the bottom of a soil cube, lifting out the root ball with the other hand as soil is pushed up and out of its container. If there is a mat of interwoven roots at the bottom of the root ball, tear it off—the plant will benefit from its removal.

Plants in individual pots can be dislodged by slipping one hand over the top of the container, letting the plant stem protrude between index and middle fingers, then turning the container upside down so that the plant and its root ball slip out of the container into one hand.

If the plant is in a peat pot, you plant it pot and all and roots will grow through the pot. But make sure that peat

pots are moist before you plant them. Several minutes before transplanting, set the peat pots in a shallow container of water. A dry peat pot takes up moisture slowly from the soil, so roots may be slow in breaking through into the soil; this can stunt the plant's growth or cause roots within the peat pot to dry out completely. Also, be sure to cover the top of a peat pot with soil, because exposed peat will act as a wick to draw moisture out of the soil. If covering the peat would bury the plant too deeply, break off the top edge of the peat pot down to the plant's soil level or slightly below.

For plants in flats, a putty knife or spatula is a handy transplanting tool: separate the plants in the flat by cutting straight down around each one. Many gardeners prefer to gently separate individual plants out of flats with their fingers; you lose some soil this way, but you keep more roots on the plant. If you work quickly there will be little shock, and the loosened roots will grow out.

Bare-root planting

In winter and early spring you can find bare-root plants for sale in many retail nurseries and receive them at those times from mail order nurseries. Almost all of the deciduous plants are sold bare-root: fruit and shade trees, deciduous flowering shrubs, roses, cane fruit, some perennials, and perennial vegetables. Strawberry plants are also sold this way.

There are two valid reasons for getting out in the cold and wet of winter to buy and set out bare-root plants rather than waiting until spring, summer, or fall and planting the same plants from containers:

1) You save money. Typically, a bare-root plants costs only 40 to 70 percent of the price of the same plant later in the year in a container.

2) The manner in which a bare-root tree or shrub is planted makes it establish itself faster and often better than it would if set out later from a container.

The bare-root planting advantage is that when you set out a bare-root plant you can refill the planting hole with the native soil that you excavated when you dug the hole:

Plant taken from nursery flat or container should be set at the same soil level; press soil firmly around roots.

the roots will grow in only one kind of soil. In contrast, when you plant from a container you put two soils, usually with different composition and properties, in contact with each other—the soil mix in the container root ball, and the soil that you plant it in. Seldom are the two soils identical. With two different kinds of soil it may be difficult to get uniform water penetration into the total rooting area. Often container soil is more porous than the soil into which it is placed and will retain water too long before it can drain into garden soil. Some container soils have so much organic material (such as peat moss) that they have difficulty soaking up water if allowed to dry out. Roots may be slow to grow into native soil from the container mix, so that a deciduous plant from a container may take longer to establish than a bare-root plant.

For successful bare-root planting, the roots should be fresh and plump, not dry, withered, or half dead. If you have any doubts about freshness and plumpness of roots, soak them overnight in a bucket of water.

Dig the planting hole large enough to accommodate roots easily without cramping, bending, or cutting them to fit. But you should cut any broken roots back to healthy tissue. Set the plant out according to the bare-root planting illustrations (below), adjusting the plant's depth so that the old soil line (usually visible near the base of trunk or stems) will be at the surface level of soil surrounding the planting hole. Refill the hole about ¾ full with soil, firming it in around roots with your fingers, then thoroughly water the soil. Some settling may occur, and when it does it is relatively easy to readjust the planting level: grasp the base of the plant just above the roots and gently rock it from side to side while gently pulling up until you've regained the correct level (this is easy only when soil is saturated). Then add the remaining soil and water it.

After the initial watering when you plant, water bare-root plantings conservatively. Dormant plants need less water than actively growing ones, and if you keep the soil too wet new feeder roots may not form. Check soil periodically for moisture (using a trowel, fingers, soil sampling tube, or any pointed instrument) and water accordingly: if the root zone soil is damp, the plant doesn't need water. When weather turns warm and growth becomes active you will need to water more frequently. Make a soil ridge around the perimeter of the planting hole to create a basin for watering. The basin will insure that the water you apply will soak down through the plant's root zone. *Do not overwater*: check soil for moisture, as mentioned above, before watering. If hot, dry weather follows planting, shade the new plant at least until it begins to grow. And be patient; some bare-root trees and shrubs are slow to leaf out. Many will not do so until a few warm days break the plants' dormancy.

Planting balled and burlapped shrubs and trees

Balled and burlapped plants (often referred to simply as B and B) are dug with a ball of soil containing their roots, and the soil ball is then wrapped in burlap and tied up with twine to keep it intact. Plants sold this way have roots that won't survive bare-root transplanting: some deciduous shrubs and trees, evergreen shrubs such as rhododendrons and azaleas, and various conifers. Planting season varies by locality; appearance of B and B plants at the local nursery signifies that planting season has arrived.

Treat B and B plants carefully: don't use the trunk as a handle, and don't drop them because the root ball could shatter and expose the roots. Cradle the root ball well by supporting the bottom with one or both hands, if not too heavy. If a B and B plant is too heavy for one person to carry to its planting site, get a friend to help you carry it in a sling of canvas or stout burlap.

Many B and B plants are grown in clay or fairly heavy soil that will hold together well when plants are dug up and burlapped. At times, this soil will be denser than the garden soil. When this occurs the problem is that the clay soil around the plant's roots absorbs water more slowly than the lighter garden soil around it. The result can be that your B and B plant is dry even though your garden soil may be moist. You can remedy this situation by adjusting planting techniques and subsequent watering.

Dig a planting hole twice as wide as the root ball and about 6 inches deeper. If your soil is light to medium (and the B and B soil is heavier), incorporate peat moss, ground bark, nitrogen-fortified sawdust, or similar organic amendments (but not animal manures). Add one shovelful of organic amendment to three of soil to the soil you will return to the hole (backfill soil). This will improve the water retention of the backfill soil, creating a transition zone of soil.

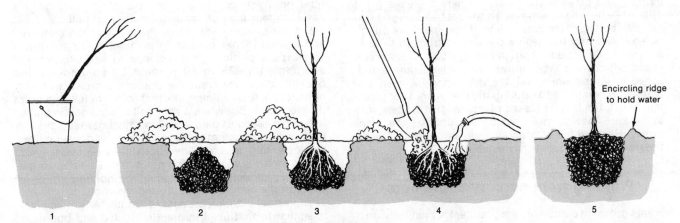

Encircling ridge to hold water

Soak bare-root plant overnight in a bucket of water (1). Form cone of soil (2) in hole large enough to fit roots easily. Spread roots evenly over cone of soil. (3). Add soil gradually, firming as added (4); soak deeply. Form watering basin (5).

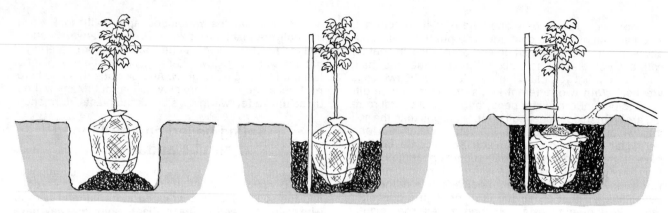

Set balled and burlapped plant (left) on mound of backfill soil so top of ball is 2 inches above soil surface. If necessary, anchor the stake securely in ground (center). Tie trunk to stake, fill with soil, firm, and flood watering basin (right).

Shovel slightly more than 6 inches of backfill soil into the hole and lower the B and B plant into it. The top of the root ball will be an inch or two higher than the surface of the surrounding soil, but the inevitable settling as you plant and water will bring the ball down to the proper level (just slightly higher than the surrounding soil). Fill the hole half full with backfill soil, firming it with a stick or your fingers. If you are setting out a B and B plant in a windy location, you should stake it at this point in the planting process. The round root ball can act like a ball and socket joint as the wind buffets the plant; such shifting of the root ball will break new roots that are growing out of the root ball into your garden soil. Drive the stake firmly into the soil beneath the planting hole and alongside the root ball, on the side of the plant from which the prevailing winds blow.

After any necessary staking, fill the hole to within 3 to 4 inches from the top, untie the twine that holds burlap around the trunk and spread the burlap open. Water the plant thoroughly, then add backfill soil to the level of soil around the planting hole. Make a ring of mounded soil around the hole's perimeter to form a watering basin and water the last soil you added.

During the first couple of years after planting, pay close attention to watering—especially if the root ball soil is heavier than your garden soil. Keep the surrounding garden soil moist (but never continually soggy) so that roots will grow out of the root ball into the surrounding soil as fast as possible and the original root ball will not dry out. *Note*: If a soil ball does become dry, the ball will shrink, harden, and actually shed water. Where there's a great difference between garden soil and root ball soil, you can achieve better water penetration if you carefully punch holes in the root ball with a pointed instrument ¼ to ½ inch wide. Or use a root irrigator (page 52). After several years, when roots have grown out and become established in your garden soil, the difference between soil types won't matter. Also, during the first years after planting, check the ties on staked plants at least twice a year to be sure they do not become too tight as the plant grows. Remove the staking as soon as possible—when the plant has its roots firmly established.

Planting from nursery containers

Plants grown in containers are popular for many reasons: most broad-leafed evergreen shrubs and trees—the West's landscaping specialties—are offered only in cans;

plants in cans are available at all seasons for planting when the gardener is ready to use them; they come in a variety of sizes and prices; they are easy to transport; and they do not require immediate planting after purchase. You can buy a container plant in bloom or in fruit and know exactly what color or variety you're getting.

When shopping for container-grown plants, look for plants that have a generally healthy, vigorous appearance and good foliage. The root system should be unencumbered—not tangled or constricted by the plant's own roots. Two signs of a rootbound condition are roots protruding above the soil level and roots growing through the container's drainage holes. Additional indicators of crowded roots are: plants that are unusually large for the size of their containers; unusually leggy plants; and dead twigs or branches.

Nurseries sell plants in a variety of containers—metal cans (1 gallon and 5 gallon are standard sizes), plastic "cans" and pots, fiber pots, and even wooden boxes for large specimen shrubs and trees. With straight-sided metal cans, have the cans slit down each side. The best time to cut cans is just before you plant, but you may prefer to have cans cut at the nursery before taking plants home. Handle cut edges with care. If planting is delayed, keep the plants in a cool place and water often enough to keep roots moist (water gently so that you don't wash out soil). With tapered metal cans and plastic "cans" and pots, you can easily knock the plants out of their containers; sharp taps on the bottom and sides will loosen the root ball so the plant will slide out easily. With fiber pots you can also knock the plants out, but it's easier to tear the pots away from the root ball.

Dig the planting hole twice the width of the container and several inches deeper. In planting container-grown stock it's a particularly good idea to add organic soil amendments—25 to 50 percent by volume—to the backfill soil. Many container plants are grown in a very light, loose, fast-draining mix that favors quick, even root development. But when a root ball of light soil is placed in heavier (denser) garden soil, as most garden soils are, roots will be reluctant to move out into the denser garden soil, resulting in a shallow-rooted, slow-growing plant that is highly subject to drying out. Also, the denser garden soil may act as a "container" by holding too much water in the very light soil around the roots.

The actual planting process for container-grown plants is similar to that used in planting balled and burlapped plants. With container-grown plants, though, you get a chance to see some of the root system; you should take a

Remove plant from container (1); check the root system. If root bound, gently loosen roots at sides, bottom (2). Set on backfill soil, fill ¾ of hole with soil, firm it, and water (3). Add remaining soil, water, make watering basin (4).

look at it before you fill in the soil. If roots are crowded or coiled on the surface, straighten, loosen, and cut them with your fingers, a stick, or a knife. If the root ball is dense or compacted, it is a good idea to loosen the mass so that roots will be encouraged to reach out into the garden soil. Make several vertical cuts into the root ball with a knife, then gently loosen roots at the sides and bottom of the root ball.

Place enough amended backfill soil in the bottom of the hole to position the top of the plant's root ball about an inch above the surrounding grade. Fill in around the root ball with backfill soil, firming it in with your fingers, until the hole is about ¾ full. Then water thoroughly to settle the plant and eliminate any air pockets in the soil (check to see that the top of the root ball is slightly above soil grade). Finish filling in the hole. Make a ring of mounded earth around the hole's perimeter to form a watering basin, and then thoroughly water.

Transplanting a shrub or small tree

A time may come when you may need or want to move a shrub or small tree from one place to another. With expert care you can do this at any time of year, but with most plants you'll be more assured of success if you transplant in cool weather while the plant is dormant or semidormant (tropical plants transplant best after soil has warmed up in spring). The inevitable loss of some roots is not as critical during a plant's dormant season.

Dormant deciduous plants such as roses can be moved bare-root. Prepare the new planting hole before you dig up the plant to be moved; that way you can accomplish the operation as quickly as possible so roots will not dry out.

To move evergreen plants (both broad-leafed and conifers) or deciduous ones that are in leaf, dig them with soil around the roots. The bigger the plant, the more difficult and time consuming transplanting becomes. If you plan ahead, you can prepare the plant for moving by partially root pruning it several months to a year in advance of actual transplanting. Mark a circle around the plant that is ten times (or larger, if practical) the diameter of the plant's trunk at ground level. Then, with a sharp spade cut around the circle to the spade's depth. This will encourage the plant to grow a new set of feeder roots where you root pruned; and the shock of losing the roots you cut will be minimized by leaving the plant undisturbed for a period of time. When you do transplant, dig outside the circle made by root pruning so the majority of roots the plant depends upon will be in the root ball.

Several days before the move, thoroughly soak the soil around the plant so that digging will be easy and the root ball will hold together. Prepare a planting hole as described under "Planting balled and burlapped shrubs

and trees" (pages 45–46). Particularly if you are about to move an evergreen plant, you would be wise first to spray the foliage with an antidesiccant spray. The spray will cut down water loss through the plant's tissues during the months the new roots will be forming.

Begin the transplant operation by digging a trench around the plant just outside the circle you cut if you root pruned months earlier, or around the drip line if you did not root prune. Dig this trench as deep as the root ball is wide, and a spade's width wide (or more) for easier work. When the trench is completed you're ready to secure the root ball.

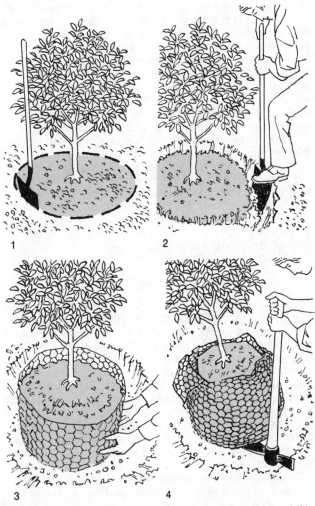

Prepare plant for moving by pruning roots with spade (top left) several months ahead. Dig a trench outside the root-pruning circle (top right). Wrap root ball with chicken wire (left) and cut under root ball (right).

Burlap is the traditional material for wrapping a root ball, but chicken wire is easier to use and purchase. Use small mesh wire (1 inch or less) and encircle the root ball tightly, securing the cut ends by wrapping cut wires together or by threading them together with a length of wire. Tighten the wire further as shown in the illustration (page 47), then slice under the root ball with a spade. In heavier soils, the wire should help keep the bottom soil intact as you lift or lever the root ball out of the ground. For sandier soils that tend to break up, slide a piece of chicken wire under the root ball and lift the mass from beneath with this wire. Replant as described for balled and burlapped plants on pages 45–46.

Small plants will require correspondingly small root balls, so with these you may be able to eliminate the wiring process. Any plant whose root ball you can carry in a shovel or in both hands may not need wiring

Of course, some very large shrubs and trees are beyond your capacity—your hand tools couldn't do the digging job adequately and the root ball would be too heavy for you to lift. The answer in this case is to hire the job out to a landscape contractor.

Watering your garden

Western gardeners—except those living in California's north coast fog belt and in the area north of the Siskiyous and west of the Cascades—work in a climate characterized by low rainfall, a long dry season, or both. This means that well over half of the West's gardening population spends a good part of each year watering plants.

This annual routine is increasingly affected by the continuing rise in the West's population while, at the same time, the overall western water supply remains virtually fixed: more and more people are putting demands on a finite amount of water. Superimposed on this pattern is the unpredictable but recurring drought year in which so little rain falls during the "wet season" that watersheds and reservoirs are not filled to capacity to meet needs during the following dry months. Obviously, water management will be a continually increasing challenge.

There are two ways in which this challenge can be met. Westerners with established gardens can alter their watering practices to conserve water while still maintaining their gardens. For those about to start a garden from scratch—or about to revamp an established one—the wisest approach will be to choose landscape materials from among the many plants that, after they become established, don't require continuous watering to survive the hot, dry months (see pages 148–151).

Basic water knowledge

"How often shall I water it?" is perhaps the question most frequently asked by the novice gardener. No question is quite so difficult to answer. The variable factors involved are many and complex: the needs of the particular plant, its age, the season, the weather (temperature, humidity, and amount of wind), the nature of the soil (and the water), the method of application. To ignore these factors and water by calendar or clock may subject your garden to drought or drowning. To say "Give a plant as much water as it needs for healthy growth" is not really an answer. But this much we can say: frequent light sprinkling and frequent heavy soaking alike are bad. *Water thoroughly—and infrequently.*

To understand this advice, it helps to know how water and soil interact, and what roots need for good health.

Shallow watering = shallow roots

Roots develop and grow in the presence of water, air, and nutrients. Except for naturally shallow-rooted plants (rhododendrons and azaleas, for example), plants will root throughout the depth at which these essentials are found. If only the top foot of soil is kept well watered, roots will develop in the top foot. Even lawn grasses, generally considered shallow rooted, can run roots from 10 to 24 inches deep. If shallow watering keeps the roots near the surface, plants will be open to severe damage if you go away for a long weekend and the weather turns hot, drying the top inches of soil: there will be no deep reserves of water to tap, and no roots to tap them even if reserves were there.

Water thoroughly

A little water wets only a little soil. You can't dampen soil to any depth by watering it lightly. You can have a damp soil only by wetting it thoroughly, then letting it partially dry out. Water moves down through the soil by progressively wetting soil particles. When a particle has acquired its clinging film of water, every additional drop becomes "free" water, free to move down and wet lower particles. And it does move *down*; there is little lateral movement of water within the soil (though there is greater lateral movement in heavy soil than in sandy soil). It is important to wet a plant's entire root zone. Keep this in mind when building basins or ditches. A small basin around the trunk of a tree will tend to keep the roots inside a small area. Water put into a ditch 6 inches or more from a row of plants may not water the entire root area; try to soak every square inch of root area.

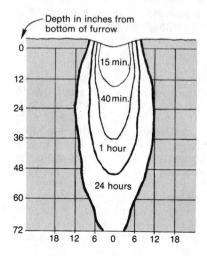

Water moves downward in the soil; there is little lateral movement of water.

Water absorption

When you soak your soil, you are wetting each layer of soil, as the water moves downward through it, to a condition known as *field capacity*. In this condition, each soil particle holds the maximum amount of water film it can against the pull of gravity, and the amount of air space in the soil is low. As plant roots and evaporation draw water from the soil, the films of water become thinner and more space is gained for soil air. When the film becomes so thin that its molecular attraction to the soil particle is stronger than the root tips' ability to extract it, the plant will wilt even though some water remains in the soil. During the stages in which soil dries from field capacity to wilting point, all the plant has sufficient water for healthy growth.

Field capacity varies by soil type. Clay soils with many fine particles hold more water than sandy soils with fewer, coarser particles. Loamy soils, with a mixture of particle sizes, have an intermediate field capacity.

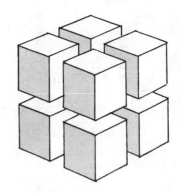

Eight 1-foot cubes have 48 square feet of surface area to which water can adhere.

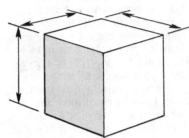

Though it has same outside dimension as above, this 2-foot cube has less surface area to which water can adhere—only 24 square feet.

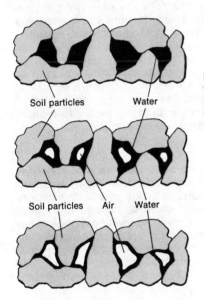

Progression of drying from field capacity (top) shows the changing amounts of water and air in soil.

Soil particles   Water

Soil particles   Air   Water

3 to 4 inches are dry, and especially if it is during the growing season, you probably will need to water.

In winter when the days are short and the nights are long, and the sun is low on the horizon (diminishing light intensity and lowering plant water use), plants in leaf can exist for days or weeks on much less water than they demand in summer.

How to apply water

Particular techniques or aids to conserve water are covered on pages 51–52 under "Watering to conserve water." Here, we discuss application fundamentals.

Watering frequency

To maintain a healthy air-water ratio for plant roots, you shouldn't keep your garden constantly at field capacity. Water deeply but not too often (depending, of course, upon the factors that influence rate of soil drying). If damp soil continues low in oxygen long enough, root development and nutrient absorption are both reduced so that plant growth is slowed. Also, harmful organisms proliferate, producing toxic substances. Plants vary in their ability to resist these unfavorable conditions, but all plants (except water plants) require soil air.

If temperature, humidity, wind, and day length never varied you could water your garden according to a calendar schedule. Weather conditions, however, will upset such a schedule at least part of the time. Under the influence of a hot, dry wind, plants use water so rapidly that shallow-rooted ones sometimes cannot absorb water from the soil fast enough to prevent wilting. In such weather you need to water more frequently than a timed schedule would suggest. Conversely, when coolness or humidity prevail you should water less frequently. The one watering frequency rule that can be applied safely to all types of soil and climate is this: test the soil. If the top

Sprinkling

The simplest way to apply water evenly over a large surface is by sprinkling; sprinkling produces artificial rainfall. Many plants, especially the shade-loving ones that like a cool, humid atmosphere, thrive with overhead sprinkling. Plants benefit by having dust rinsed from their leaves; sprinkling discourages certain pests, especially spider mites.

On the negative side, sprinkling can waste water. Wind can carry off a certain amount of water before it reaches the ground, and water sprinkled or running off onto pavement is literally thrown away. In areas where humidity is high, some foliage diseases (mildew and rust, for example) will be encouraged, though you can minimize the risk by sprinkling early in the morning so that leaves will dry quickly as the day warms. Another potential drawback to sprinkling is that some plants with weak stems or heavy flowers will bend and possibly break under a heavy load of water.

You can determine how long to leave sprinklers running by making a few simple calculations. One inch of rain will penetrate about 12 inches in sandy soil, about 7 inches in loam, and perhaps 4 to 5 inches in clay. Therefore, if you want to water to a depth of 12 inches you

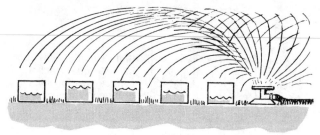

You can test the "rainfall" from sprinklers by spacing containers at regular intervals and timing when they fill.

would need about an inch of "rain" in sandy soil, 2½ inches in clay. Next, find out how long it takes your sprinkler to produce 1 inch of moisture. Place a number of shallow containers at regular intervals in a line running out from the sprinkler. Turn on the water and note the time it takes to fill the containers to 1 inch. This also will demonstrate the efficiency of your sprinkler, as the "rainfall" pattern will be more or less irregular (some containers will fill to the 1 inch level faster than others) depending on the kind of sprinkler you use. When you know how long it takes your sprinkler to discharge an inch of water, just multiply this time interval by the number of inches you want. The result equals the length of time to leave the sprinklers on.

To compensate for the sprinkler's irregular distribution, you should overlap the areas covered as you move the sprinkler.

Portable sprinklers that you attach to the end of a hose are handy to use and can do the job well if you determine a sprinkler's water distribution pattern and overlap settings to provide uniform coverage. Permanently installed underground sprinkling systems will save you the time and labor of setting and moving hoses and can be more efficient than hose-end sprinklers if you make sure the water pattern covers only the plants you want to water.

Runoff may occur in some soils that are unable to absorb water as fast as sprinklers deliver it. Inadequate water penetration results even though you've run the sprinklers long enough. On a clay soil, the penetration can be so slow that more than 50 percent of the water is lost by runoff if the ground slopes just slightly. Without exaggerating, you could easily sprinkle on 6 inches of water and only 3 would enter the soil.

There are several ways to overcome this condition. You can have the soil aerated with an aerator that removes *plugs* of soil—but it's not a certain cure. Spiking soil is generally not desirable because the spikes are likely to compact the soil around the holes they drive.

The best method is to adjust your sprinkling procedure. For one thing, you can slow down the delivery rate so the soil absorbs the delivered water. Select a sprinkler that delivers water more slowly. Sprinkler heads vary greatly in their rates of application—not only from one type of head to another, but even among different models of one style. Look for a sprinkler that delivers fewer gallons per minute than your present sprinkler. The other choice is to run the sprinklers at full rate until runoff starts, shut them off for a half hour, then repeat the process once more.

A very good solution to the water-runs-off-the-surface problem is to remove the plants from the bed (or tear out the old lawn) and condition the soil to a 9-inch depth (as deep as you can make a rotary tiller penetrate). Thoroughly incorporate into the soil an amendment

equal to 25 to 50 percent of the total volume of soil being treated. This method is described in the soils chapter on page 35. A heavy soil conditioned in this fashion will take water much faster than it did before it was conditioned and will hold the water longer, all the while keeping more soil air among the roots. After the conditioning job is completed, replace the plants or install a new lawn.

In terms of water frugality, the most practical solution to water running down slopes is to remove the plants that are there (especially if they are lawn grasses or dichondra) and replace them either with an inert ground cover—gravel, rocks, or the like—or with carefully planted drought-tolerant plants that can function on the amount of water that can penetrate before runoff occurs. The best way to enhance water penetration around shrubs and wide-spreading ground cover plants is to build an irrigation basin around each plant.

When water is scarce, sprinkling can still be efficient and economical if done properly. This applies whether you have a sprinkler system or just a sprinkler at the end of a hose. Sprinkling is best done in early morning (especially in high humidity areas, to minimize foliage diseases) or at night—when it is windless, cool, and pressure is best—making sure you put water only onto soil that has roots in it. Check sprinkler systems to be sure they are not wasting water by getting water onto paving or barren ground, spreading water unevenly, or making geysers or bubbles instead of even spray. Always time a sprinkling to last no longer than necessary to moisten root systems of the plants you're watering.

Soaking

Flooding or soaking is an effective means of supplying sufficient water to the large and deep root systems of large shrubs or trees. Surround each plant with a depression that extends a short distance beyond the plant's branch spread, or make a basin by forming a ridge of soil several inches high encircling the plant at the edge of its branch spread. (Follow the latter procedure for shallow-rooted plants such as rhododendrons, azaleas, and camellias, rather than scooping out soil beneath the plants.) To water, simply fill the basin *slowly* and leave water on until the basin fills up. Around large and deep-rooted trees, make the basins about 6 inches deep.

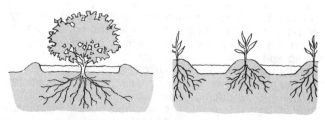

Watering basins (left) and furrows between rows (right) contain water while it soaks into the ground.

To soak smaller plants, tie a piece of burlap over the hose end or attach a manufactured water bubbler or force-breaker, turn on the hose and let the water flow out gently. Move the hose end from place to place as soil becomes thoroughly wet. To soak large areas, use a canvas or plastic soaker hose that permits water to escape slowly along its entire length. A drip irrigation setup (page 52) will enable you to soak widely spaced plants with no water waste and no hose moving.

If you grow vegetables or flowers in rows, the furrow between rows takes the place of the basin around individual plants. Broad, shallow furrows are generally better than deep narrow ones: there is less danger to roots in scooping out shallow furrows, and less likelihood that roots will be exposed by a strong flow of water. And a wide furrow will assure soaking of a wide root area (remember that water in soil moves primarily downward, not laterally). Try to do furrowing before root systems of plants in rows have developed and spread; if you wait too long you may damage roots when you furrow.

Soil soakers were the forerunners of drip irrigation and still are particularly useful if you need to water plants set out in rows. Attached to a hose end, these long tubes of canvas (or of perforated or porous plastic) seep or sprinkle water along their entire length. You also can water trees and shrubs with a soaker by placing it in a circle around the plant, following the branch spead.

Just position the soaker, attach the hose, and turn on the water for a slow and steady delivery. Plastic tubes perforated with tiny holes were originally meant for sprinkling, but turned with holes to the ground they function as soakers without any water loss from wind evaporation. As with drip irrigation systems, you will need to leave soakers on longer than you would a sprinkler.

Canvas or plastic soaker hose has outlets along entire length, waters long beds without washing the soil out.

Watering to conserve water

The only gardens that can make it from one rainy season to another without water are those that contain nothing but established drought-tolerant plants. All other plants need water in the dry season. Faced with the prospect of water shortage and increasing water costs, you should know how to apply water most economically.

Lawns consume water

All-year green lawns are alien and water-demanding in the arid-summer parts of western America. Lawns exist naturally east of the Mississippi and in northern Europe where precipitation comes (usually) every month of the year. Dichondra and most lawn grasses require great amounts of water; if they don't receive it, they die. When water is short in western America, one of the wisest economies is to remove a water-consuming lawn or not to include it in a new landscaping plan.

When to water—and when to hold back

Plants that are supposed to live for only a season or for a year or two will need water through dry months. To main-

tain a good appearance, many ground covers also will need regular watering. And the shallow-rooted garden favorites such as azaleas, rhododendrons, and heathers will perish if their water supply is cut off. But beyond those categories are some woody plant species that have been spoiled for years by well-meaning gardeners—shrubs and trees that could get from one rainy season to the next, after they are established, with no watering at all. For example, look at the trees and shrubs that survive with no irrigation in abandoned gardens and along country roads, and those that survive, often with infrequent watering, along freeways and in some parks and playgrounds. When water is scarce, think twice before you water any tree or shrub that has been in the ground for more than two years. Try extending the time between waterings for as long as the plants look presentable.

Usually you can tell by a plant's leaves that it is beginning to become desperate for water. Most leaves will exhibit a dullness or loss of reflective quality, or inward rolling edges, just before they wilt. Wilted leaves, of course, are a sure tipoff, but getting to that stage is hard on a plant and you must be right there to supply water soon after wilting if the plant is to survive. In many cases when an unwatered shrub or tree drops some of its leaves, but doesn't wilt or even turn dull, it is simply employing natural means for surviving a drought. When regular water is supplied again, new leaves will grow.

Some plants, aside from those already mentioned, can't do without water during the dry season. Among these are lawn trees that have grown dependent on summer watering (particularly if their root systems extend only to the depth of the average lawn watering) and plants native to cool climates (Monterey pines, for example) growing in hot inland gardens.

Mulches conserve water

A mulch placed over the ground occupied by a plant's roots will keep the soil beneath cool and moist longer than the soil would be if exposed to hot sun and drying wind. Mulched plants, then, will be able to go longer between waterings than unmulched ones. Many materials

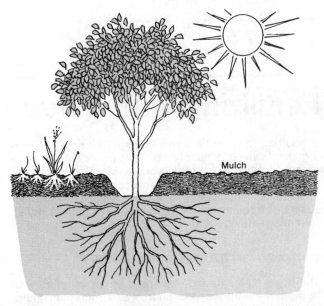

Mulch keeps root zone cool and moist even in hot weather; weed roots are anchored poorly, easy to pull out of mulch.

have been tried and proven effective as mulches: compost, animal manures, ground bark, leaves, sawdust, straw, hoed or pulled weeds, processing by-products (grape and apple pomace, cottonseed hulls, rice hulls), even old newspapers. Rocks and gravel will also do the job. Plastic film will reduce water loss but may also have adverse effects on soil and roots beneath—it's best for strawberries and other low-growing row crops.

Conservation through planting location

Another method of saving water is to place all plants that require summer watering in sites protected from drying winds and out of direct sunlight. Soil on north-facing slopes, in shaded areas, or in spots in the lee of hedges, screens, windbreaks, or buildings will dry out more slowly than soil in exposed areas. Plants in such locations will need less water than they would require if planted in the open.

Drip irrigation

You can cut your water use by 20 to 50 percent with drip irrigation. You put together your own system from any number of manufactured components, all of which, no matter how complex, simply deliver small amounts of water to individual plants through a network of narrow tubes or porous tubing. No water is wasted by wind evaporation or spilling on pavement or bare ground. A drip system can be on or below the ground; you can keep

Two versions of drip irrigation: spray emitters (top) can be turned so that water sprinkles plant; a network of narrow tubes (bottom) can irrigate hard-to-reach plants individually.

it in place from year to year for watering trees, shrubs, hedges, and ground covers, or you may prefer to remove it after each season of watering annuals or vegetables.

Drip irrigation systems deliver water slowly so that it will soak each plant's root area. You use less water than by sprinkling, but it takes a longer time to apply the needed amount of water. And it will not be as successful in sandy soil in which the very limited lateral spread of slowly delivered water may not moisten enough area.

Hand watering

This, the oldest method of water application, is effective but is the most time-consuming and most boring. Many people tire of the task before they have given the plants enough water. You have to use a low volume of water that will soak in rather than run off, and hold the hose long enough to moisten the plant's root system—about half an hour for a small tree, 3 minutes for a knee-high shrub.

Root irrigators

On sloping ground a sure way to get water efficiently to tree and shrub roots without runoff is with a deep root

Subsoil irrigator puts water right where the roots can use it. A refinement of root irrigator mixes fertilizer from a cartridge with water.

irrigator. In appearance—and effect—it is a hose-end giant hypodermic needle. Attach the manufactured implement to the hose, insert it into the root zone of tree or shrub, and turn on the valve; water is emitted through the holes near the tip, 12 to 18 inches below ground.

Fertilizing your garden

In addition to light, air, water, and space for roots, growing plants need a supply of nutrients—elements necessary to carry out their life processes. Some of these nutrients, the so-called trace elements, are needed in infinitesimal quantities and are usually present in most soils. But three major elements may have to be supplied for consistently good growth.

The basic nutrients

The three elements that may have to be supplied with fertilizer are nitrogen, phosphorus, and potassium. In unimproved soils, nitrogen comes primarily from decomposing organic material, which is generally in very short

supply in western soils, especially in the drier regions. Nitrogen is used in large quantities by plants; it is also easily lost by the leaching action of rainfall or irrigation, and is eagerly used up by soil organisms. As a result, nitrogen must be added to the soil from time to time if good growth is to be expected. Phosphorus and potassium are present in the mineral particles in most soils, but they become available to plants so slowly that supplementary feedings are often advisable.

Nitrogen

The first percentage listed on a fertilizer label's analysis applies to nitrogen. In the natural course of events (with no fertilizer added), nitrogen that comes into the soil as dead plant or animal material must undergo several chemical changes before it becomes available to a plant's roots (see "Organic amendments" on page 33). Fertilizers can supply a greater amount of nitrogen more quickly than can the remains donated by nature.

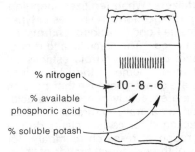

Fertilizer labels show what percentages of the three primary nutrients are inside.

% nitrogen
% available phosphoric acid
% soluble potash

10 - 8 - 6

If a fertilizer's label says that all or most of the nitrogen contained is in the *nitrate* or *nitric* form, you are assured that the fertilizer will be fast acting and that the nitrogen will be released quickly. On the other hand, if most of the nitrogen is *ammonic* or *organic*, the nitrogen release will not be quite as fast but should be more sustained once it starts. Of the latter two, ammonic nitrogen will cause a considerably faster response than organic nitrogen.

To prevent nitrogen from leaching through the soil quickly, consider using a slow release fertilizer that is effective for three months to a year (see page 54).

Nitrogen's fast response is more noticeable and significant in lawn grasses than in most other plants, though it applies to all. It is easy to burn a lawn by putting on too much nitrogen, since lawns are made up of thousands of tiny plants growing together. A high concentration of nitrogen quickly reaches the dense mat of grass surface roots, whereas shrub and tree roots grow deeper and are more wide spreading.

Nitrogen is most active in the young, tender parts of plant tissue, such as tips of shoots, buds, and opening leaves. If there's a deficiency of nitrogen, only the growing tips will function properly. Older leaves may turn yellow, die, and drop off.

Sources of nitrogen. Nitrogen is not present in the minute particles of mineral soil from which plants derive their phosphorus, potassium, and other mineral elements. All nitrogen must come from other sources: the air, organic matter, or fertilizers. Nitrogen from the air enters the soil via rainfall or is extracted from soil air by specialized nitrogen-fixing bacteria that live on the roots of certain plants.

Carbon-nitrogen ratio. If the organic matter you add to the soil is high in carbon compared to nitrogen, soil organisms working to digest the high carbon material may compete with plants for the limited amounts of nitrogen available in the soil. For this reason, the high carbon (high cellulose) soil conditioners such as sawdust, wood shavings, ground bark, and straw require special handling. One choice is to shop for and buy those materials in fortified form (with nitrogen already added to the material so that the organisms of decomposition will not "take" any nitrogen from the soil). If you get unfortified material, you should mix a nitrogen fertilizer with it; directions are on page 33.

Phosphorus

The second percentage in a fertilizer label's analysis indicates how much available phosphoric acid the mixture contains. The mineral or clay particles that contain phosphorus ions release them reluctantly to the microscopic film of water (soil solution) that surrounds the soil particles. As the root tips grow into contact with the soil solution, they absorb the phosphorus that the solution is holding in available form. This reduces the concentration of phosphorus ions in the soil solution around the root tips, making the remaining phosphorus insufficient to meet the plant's needs. Then more phosphorus is released from the soil particles to the solution.

The root grows into fresh areas of soil solution, repeating the process. During periods of rapid growth, the phosphorus absorption and renewal cycle around a soil particle takes place constantly. If the concentration of phosphorus in the soil solution is too low, or if the rate of renewal is too slow, plant growth is retarded.

Phosphorus moves slowly. The phosphoric acid from fertilizer ionizes in the soil to form other phosphate compounds, some of which plants can use, some of which are so insoluble that plants cannot use them. This process is called "fixation" and can be a problem in highly acid soils. If your soil is acid, you may have to raise its available phosphorus level to a point where the fixing power has been satisfied.

The most effective way to apply a fertilizer containing phosphorus is to concentrate the phosphates where roots can get at them. When you plant a new tree or shrub, dig in superphosphate or a complete fertilizer that contains phosphorus as well as nitrogen and potash. Thoroughly mix as much as label directions specify into what you estimate will be the root area for a few years to come. The same advice would apply to planting of perennials and annual plants. For seed planting, place the fertilizer beside the seed rows, a couple of inches to one side and a couple of inches below the seed level (following fertilizer label directions for amount per foot of row).

The least effective ways of applying phosphorus (though the only methods for established plantings) are to broadcast and mix it lightly into the soil surface or to spray a solution on the soil.

Potassium

The third percentage on a fertilizer label's analysis represents potassium. This element is described in various ways: "available or soluble potash," "water soluble potash," or "water soluble potash from muriate or tankage." Plants remove from the soil more potassium than any other nutrients except nitrogen and calcium.

Potassium in the soil exists in several forms. One form is soluble in water; other forms are insoluble. Most of the natural soil potassium is not available to plants even though it may be abundant. About one percent of the total soil potassium acts as an important reservoir, called *exchangeable* potassium. Derived from minerals or fertilizers or crop residues, exchangeable potassium is not soluble or free to move with soil water until modified by a slow weathering process. However, roots can pick up exchangeable potassium directly from the clay or humus particles without that element actually entering the soil solution. When you add fertilizer containing soluble potassium to the soil, a transfer occurs from solution to exchangeable potassium.

Calcium, magnesium, sulfur

Some fertilizers contain these elements, others do not. Although these elements are important, they are usually present in the soil in adequate supply. One exception worth noting is the sulfur deficiency in many soils of the high rainfall areas of the Pacific Northwest. There, sulfur can be readily leached away, just as nitrogen is. Additional sulfur is applied regularly to annual crops and lawns for optimum performance. Calcium and sulfur often get into the soil in other kinds of garden products: lime (calcium), lime-sulfur fungicide and soil conditioner (calcium and sulfur), gypsum (calcium and sulfur), superphosphate (some sulfur in addition to the phosphates), and soil sulfur used for acidifying alkaline soils.

What they do. Calcium is a highly essential plant nutrient. It plays a fundamental part in cell manufacture and growth—most roots must have some calcium right at the growing tips. In the cells of green leaves, every chlorophyll molecule has an atom of magnesium as its central part. Sulfur acts hand in hand with nitrogen in making new protoplasm for plant cells; it is just as essential as nitrogen but its deficiency in the soil is not so widespread.

Iron, zinc, manganese

If soil is highly alkaline, as some soils are in low-rainfall areas, plants may not be able to absorb enough iron, zinc, and manganese. If you live in such an area, you probably know of the need for these minor elements. Nurseries and garden stores sell products you can put on the soil or spray on the leaves to correct the deficiency. Some of these products are *chelated*, meaning that the iron, zinc, or manganese is in a form that can be used by the roots, and is not susceptible to the fixing that makes the native iron, zinc, or manganese unavailable.

What they do. Iron is essential to chlorophyll formation. Manganese and zinc seem to function as catalysts or "triggers" in the utilization of other nutrients.

Types of fertilizers

A visit to a nursery will reveal a sometimes bewildering selection of fertilizers. You'll find fertilizers for a variety of specified uses and with differing formulas; there are granular types packaged in cartons and sacks and liquid ones in bottles. When you understand the basic types of fertilizers, though, the confusion will clear and you can select for your particular needs.

Complete fertilizer. Any fertilizer that contains all three of the primary nutrient elements—nitrogen, phosphorus, and potassium—is called a complete fertilizer. These primary nutrient elements are known by their chemical symbols N, P, and K respectively, but gardeners and agriculturists generally think of them by another abbreviation: three numbers in a row on a fertilizer package representing the percentages of N, P, and K in that fertilizer.

Some fertilizer manufacturers put their product's N, P, and K percentages in big numbers on the label, right under the product name, like this: 10-8-6. Without looking at the fine print under *Guaranteed Analysis* (always listed somewhere on a fertilizer label), you can tell that the fertilizer contains 10 percent total nitrogen, 8 percent phosphoric acid, and 6 percent water soluble potash.

There are many different fertilizer analyses on the market, but even when the analysis is the same on two different products, the formula by which one manufacturer arrived at his analysis can differ from the others (see explanation of different types of nitrogen on page 53).

The higher the numbers in the analysis, the "stronger" or more concentrated is the fertilizer (a 22-6-4 formula contains twice as much nitrogen as does an 11-6-4 fertilizer). The higher the concentration (of N especially) the less you apply at one time.

Special purpose fertilizers. When fertilizer shopping, you will find fertilizers packaged for certain uses or types of plants, such as "Camellia Food," "Rhododendron and Azalea Food," or "Rose Food." The camellia and rhododendron-azalea fertilizers belong to an old established group—the acid plant foods. Some of the compounds used in these fertilizers are chosen because they have an acid reaction, so they are especially beneficial to acid-loving plants where soil is naturally neutral or alkaline. The other fertilizers packaged for certain plants do not have as valid a background of research (compare, for example, the NPK ratios of three different brands of "rose foods").

Another special group of fertilizers contains just one of the three major elements. These fertilizers are for use in cases where only one of the elements is known to be deficient, usually following a soil test.

Also available are fertilizers that contain two of the three elements: N and P, N and K, or P and K.

Slow release fertilizers. These fertilizers are specially manufactured to release their nitrogen, in particular, at a steady rate over a much longer period than the average complete fertilizer. One type is a urea-formaldehyde resin that breaks down slowly in the soil. Another is a mixture of metal ammonium phosphates which dissolve very slowly in soil water. A third is a granule coated with plastic which, when moist, permits fertilizer to diffuse slowly until surrounding soil has absorbed an adequate amount. Then diffusion stops until more fertilizer is needed.

Organic fertilizers. The word "organic" simply means that the nutrients contained in the product are derived solely from the remains, part of the remains, or a by-product of a once-living organism. (Urea is a *synthetic* organic fertilizer—an organic substance manufactured from inorganic materials.) Cottonseed meal, blood meal, bone meal, hoof and horn meal, and all manures are examples of organic fertilizers. Most of these products packaged as fertilizers (manure usually excepted) will have their NPK ratios stated on the package labels. Most are high in just one of the three major nutrients and low or zero in the other two, although you may find some fortified with nitrogen, phosphorus, and potash for a higher analysis. In general (again, manure excepted) the organics release their nutrients over a fairly long period; the potential drawback is that they may not release enough of their principal nutrient at a time to give the plant what it needs for best growth. Because they depend on soil organisms to break them down to release their nutrients, most organic fertilizers are effective only when soil is moist and soil temperature is warm enough for the soil organisms to be active.

Manure is a complete fertilizer, but low in the amounts of N, P, and K it can supply. Manures vary in their nutrient content according to the animal source and what the animal had been eating, but an NPK ratio of 1-1-1 is typical. Rather than as nutrient suppliers, manures find their best use as mulches or as soil conditioners.

Fertilizers with insecticides, herbicides. Some fertilizers are prepared in combination with insecticides, weed killers, or both. In principle, one application will feed plants, give systemic protection against certain pests, and kill or prevent weed growth. Read label directions and cautions carefully to determine potential usefulness.

Liquid fertilizers. The most widely sold fertilizers are the solid types—granular or pelletized—that you apply to the soil surface or mix into the soil. But liquid fertilizers have certain attributes that recommend their use:
• they are easy to use, especially on container plants;
• there is no risk of burning a plant as long as you follow label directions for dilution;
• the nutrients, in solution, are available to plant roots immediately.
They are less practical than the solids for large-scale use because of their greater cost and because they must be reapplied more often (their nutrients in solution leach through the root zone more rapidly).

Liquid fertilizers come in a variety of different formulations, including complete formulas and special types that offer just one or two of the major elements. All are made to be diluted with water: some are concentrated liquids themselves, others are powder or pellets. Growers of container plants often use liquid fertilizers at half the recommended dilution twice as frequently as recommendations suggest so that plants receive a more steady supply of nutrients.

Timing a feeding

When you realize what can happen in 12 months to the fertilizer you apply at any one time, you see why just one annual application may not be adequate. The nitrogen that isn't used by plants can be leached out by watering and used up by soil organisms. The phosphorus may have been just enough to satisfy the other soil minerals that "fix" it, leaving the roots to get what soil phosphorus they can. The soluble potassium may be used up rapidly, creating a hard pull on what exchangeable potassium exists in the soil.

If a fertilizer carries no instructions on its label for repeat application, use these suggestions as a guide:
• Feed roses with label-recommended amounts as a new year's growth begins and as each bloom period ends.
• Feed azaleas, camellias, and most rhododendrons (some varieties are unusually sensitive to fertilizers) immediately after bloom and again monthly until August.
• Feed begonias, fuchsias, and other lush, full summertime flower producers every month with label-recommended amounts or once every 10 days to 2 weeks with no more than half the recommended amount.

Suggestions for fertilizing annuals appear on page 78; vegetables take approximately the same care.

Pest control

Several kinds of creatures can damage cultivated plants. This section describes the most notable plant damagers and ways to reduce their damage. Garden pests are presented in two groups: first are the insects, mites, snails, and slugs; next are the warm-blooded creatures that may eat or damage garden plants — rodents, deer, and birds.

A third group, the nematodes, deserve special mention. They are too small to see and the damage they do is hard to assess. When plants fail to thrive for no particular reason, suspect these minute worms. Most attack roots, causing distortion which hinders the plant's ability to utilize available food and water. The only chemical control is soil sterilization before planting. Most nursery plants are free of nematodes; gift plants from friends' gardens or flea markets may not be. Encourage good soil structure and composition by digging in plenty of humus; ensuing microbial action may limit nematode spread. Above all, use resistant plants when possible: for example, Nemaguard rootstock for fruit trees.

On those occasions when some kind of creature does damage to a plant, your action choices range from doing nothing (giving nature a chance to work) to restraints (washing plants or physically destroying the damagers) to biological controls (improving the balance of nature's own control system) to chemical controls.

Of all the species of insects in the United States and Canada, only about one percent have common names—and man seems to give common names only to creatures that are his friends or foes. The other 99 percent of insects participate in the local ecosystem without any publicity at all.

Some large insects eat some smaller ones, while other small ones kill large insects by spending their early lives inside the bodies or eggs of their hosts. Also, a number of viruses, bacteria, and fungi cause insects and mites to die. And, of course, spiders, lizards, toads, birds, and some larger animals also feed upon insects and mites.

In general, when any kind of living creature damages a plant in your garden, figure that nature's controls probably have become unbalanced temporarily. In a diversified garden, plant-damaging insects and mites are kept in check by nature most of the time.

Because of this natural system of checks and balances in a garden, it makes sense to weigh which control—physical, chemical, or biological—will take care of a specific plant damager with least risk of destroying harmless or helpful creatures. The physical or biological controls may take more time and trouble than spraying or dusting, but a chemical may kill more things than necessary. For effective and safe control, read labels carefully before applying any pesticide to plants or soil.

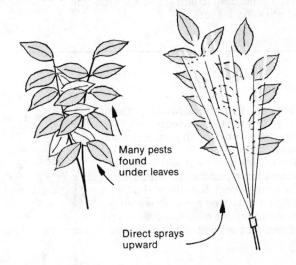

Many pests found under leaves

Direct sprays upward

Ways to control garden pests

Physical Controls require no further explanation.

Live Controls are living organisms that are raised and sold by commercial firms. The organisms usually come with accompanying directions about time and place of release.

Aphytis wasps. Parasites of scale.

Cryptolaemus beetles. Predators of mealybugs.

Encarsia wasps. Tiny wasps parasitic to whiteflies.

Lacewings, lacewing larvae. Insects, the larvae of which eat aphids, cabbage worms and loopers, corn earworms, geranium budworms, mites, and mealybugs.

Mite-eating mites (Phytoseiulus persimilis). Non-sucking and non-damaging mites that eat the pest mites.

Trichogramma wasps. Parasitic wasps that destroy the eggs of cabbage worms and loopers, corn earworms, and geranium budworms.

Packaged controls carry one or more active ingredients. New chemical controls enter the market from time to time, and existing controls are sometimes removed if research turns up any possibility of hazard to health or the environment.

Allethrin is allied to pyrethrins. See *Pyrethrins.*

Bacillus thuringiensis. Contains bacteria that destroy digestive processes of caterpillars; it is harmless otherwise. Caterpillars stop eating but remain on the plant, moving slowly until they starve to death. Sold as Thuricide, Dipel, and Biotrol.

Baygon. An insecticide used to kill earwigs.

Cygon. See *Systemics.*

Diazinon is a broad-spectrum killer of many kinds of insects and mites (unfortunately including parasites and predators). It is reasonably safe to use on edible crops (read label for required timing before harvest).

Disyston. See *Systemics.*

Dursban. A chlorinated hydrocarbon that kills soil insects.

Dusting sulfur. Finely ground sulfur mixed with clay, talc, and gypsum. Use in cool weather.

Kelthane. Kills mites. Usually in multi-ingredient products.

Malathion. This bad-smelling compound is relatively safe if used according to label directions. Effective on sucking and chewing insects.

Mesurol. Controls snails and slugs. Unfortunately kills earthworms and insects, too.

Metaldehyde. In bait form kills snails and slugs. When fresh, it is toxic to dogs.

Meta-systox-R. See *Systemics.*

Methoxychlor. A chlorinated hydrocarbon that kills many kinds of insects.

Nicotine sulfate. Like pyrethrins and rotenone, it's a botanical (made from a plant). It carries a skull-and-crossbones.

Oil spray kills tiny insects by smothering or acts as a carrier for malathion or diazinon.

Orthene. See *Systemics.*

Pyrethrins. Some made from daisy flowers, some synthesized. They give quick knockdown of insects but do not last long.

Rotenone is made from certain plant roots. It is more toxic than pyrethrins and is stronger. If it gets in water, it kills fish.

Ryania has a plant origin. It is a stomach poison for caterpillars and relatively nontoxic to higher animals.

Sevin. Reasonably safe to use, it is a champion at killing chewing insects, but at a cost: it kills honeybees and numerous parasites and predators. Use it only if a chewing insect is doing serious damage to your plants. Mites usually build up following use of sevin—that's why it is often packaged as a mixture with kelthane or sulfur.

SBP-1382. Synthetic pyrethrins. See *Pyrethrins.*

Sulfur. See *Dusting sulfur.*

Systemics: cygon, disyston, meta-systox-R, orthene. They poison a plant's juices, killing creatures that feed on the plant. They have some hazards (read labels carefully). From the viewpoint of your garden's ecosystem, they are probably the least troublesome chemicals. They do not kill beneficial or harmless insects that happen to land on a treated leaf. They poison only those insects that pierce the plant's skin and suck quantities of its juices.

Thiodan. Common name for endosulfan, an insecticide effective against many insects, including whiteflies, and mites.

Zectran has been useful in snail and slug control, but not always easy to find.

Aphids

Aphids are those soft, round, pinhead to matchhead-sized insects that huddle together on new shoots, buds, and leaves.

If you look closely at aphid colonies, you may learn worthwhile things about how their world functions. For one thing, if most of the aphids have wings, it means they are either about to leave or have just arrived. For another, in a garden's insect-spider community, the aphid seems to be meat and potatoes for many.

One choice then is just to wash aphids off with water from the hose or with soapy water from some kind of spray device (the soap kills some of the ones that hold on).

Also make sure that ants aren't indirectly responsible for the aphids. Ants frighten away the many parasites and predators of aphids.

To keep ants out of trees and shrubs, spray diazinon on

the ground beneath or generously spread a band of manufactured ant-barrier sticky material around the base of each trunk. Don't be stingy. Buy the ant barrier by the bucket or by the tube, and apply a layer 3 inches wide and 1 inch deep. Once or twice a year, crease and stir it to keep it sticky.

Another option is to buy lacewing eggs or larvae. Release the larvae on the aphid plants. They will (according to plan) eat the aphids. When the lacewings run out of aphids and other insects, they will need protein of some kind to sustain themselves. Flower pollen is very good for that purpose. Or you can spray on a commercially made protein substance called wheast.

Adult ladybird beetles (ladybugs) sold as aphid controllers are rarely successful. Whether ladybird beetles choose to remain around your garden is up to them. Usually they leave. The same goes for praying mantises, but mantises have an additional fault—they can eat each other and honeybees, too.

You can spray or dust plants with the substances listed below under "Packaged controls."

Physical controls: *water jet, wash off with soap solution*

Live controls: *lacewings*

Packaged controls: *diazinon, disyston, malathion, meta-systox-R, nicotine sulfate, orthene, or pyrethrins*

Cabbage Root Maggots

Starting in April, a specific kind of fly lays eggs in the soil around the bases of cruciferous plants (cabbages, Brussels sprouts, radishes, rutabagas, turnips, mustard—even stock and sweet alyssum). Larvae that hatch move to the roots, feed on them and either destroy them for use (as with radishes) or make the plants collapse.

Where climate allows, the best control is to plant susceptible crops in fall, so they mature before the maggots can cause significant damage.

At midyear try setting out large nursery-started plants. They seem less susceptible than younger plants.

Nothing else seems to work well. Flat collars of tarpaper placed tightly around the stem supposedly repel the flies or prevent them from laying eggs, but they aren't foolproof. A sheet of plastic film over the ground is good in theory, but flies often get through the spaces around the plant stems.

If you've lost crops to cabbage root maggots in the past, do some studying of diazinon-product labels. There are seedling treatments with diazinon dusts for radishes, and pre-planting soil treatments and post-planting drench treatments with liquids for the other susceptibles.

Physical controls: *plastic ground cover, tarpaper collars*

Live controls: *none*

Packaged controls: *diazinon*

Cabbage Worms, Cabbage Loopers

Many vegetable gardeners confuse these two because of their similar names, diets, and habits. Both feed in vegetable gardens from spring through summer.

Cabbage worm

Holes in leaves could be made by these, or by earwigs, slugs, or snails. Green droppings in the leaves are a clue that the pests are cabbage worms or cabbage loopers. To make sure—and to tell which one might be responsible—examine the plants for larvae during day or night. Cabbage worms are velvety green, and fat; cabbage loopers are striped measuring worms.

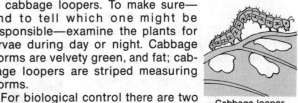

Cabbage looper

For biological control there are two living creatures that you can buy and release: lacewing larvae eat small cabbage worms or loopers, and *Trichogramma* wasps destroy the eggs the adults lay.

Physical controls: *handpicking*

Live controls: *lacewings,* Trichogramma *wasps*

Packaged controls: Bacillus thuringiensis *and sevin; also, pyrethrins, rotenone for cabbage worms*

Codling Moths

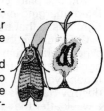

Worms in apples and pears are the larvae of codling moths. They first appear from March to June—earlier in the south, later in the north.

The moths lay eggs on leaves and twigs; the larvae that hatch move into embryo fruit and grow with them. One control consists of coating the surfaces of the fruity parts in early spring with any of several poisons that will kill the larvae.

The female moth after mating lays abundant eggs singly for 2 or 3 weeks if the weather is cool, but usually more quickly. Eggs need at least 5 days to hatch. Spraying should coincide with maximum egg hatch to kill young larvae before they enter the fruit.

You can determine if trees have a codling moth problem by monitoring moth population with pheromone traps. The female moth releases a pheromone (scented hormone) which attracts mates. Duplicating this attraction, a pheromone trap lures the male to his death. Using one trap per fruit tree and beginning at blossom time, record the number of new moths in the trap each week. When the weekly moth catch is lower than the previous week's, total the number of moths caught in the last 3 or 4-week period. If the total catch per trap is less than 20, no spray is needed. If the total catch is greater than 20 and it has been warmer than 65°F. on the previous 3 days, spray immediately. If the total catch is greater than 20 and the weather has been cool, delay spraying for a week. The count-spray procedure should be repeated about mid-June and early August.

Chemicals such as diazinon and methoxychlor can control this insect. However, these poisons kill the bees that the blossoms attract and also open the tree to invasion by the first insects or mites to appear after the product breaks down.

Physical controls: *none*
Live controls: *none*
Packaged controls: *Diazinon, methoxychlor*

Corn Earworms, Geranium Budworms

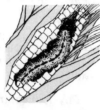

Four of the worst troublemakers are really two brother *Heliothis* caterpillars. The corn earworm and cotton boll-worm are the same larvae under different aliases; and the tobacco budworm (the main threat to California's geranium blossoms after mid-July) also doubles as "that little green worm that eats petunias."

Both of these are larvae of night-flying moths. During the period when the moon is full, its bright light seems to distract the moths—they stop mating and laying eggs. This means that for about a week after a full moon, your corn will be less bothered.

However, right after that, moths start mating at an increased rate. By the time of the new moon, young larvae are very numerous. Each such cyclic population gets bigger. By later summer, corn earworms are real trouble about 2 weeks after a full moon.

You can plant corn early in March or April to avoid the later-emerging moths. Look also for corn varieties with tight husks that help keep out worms.

Chemical and biological controls work best when you synchronize them with the breeding cycle. Since most egg-laying occurs during the first week after the full moon, you can release trichogramma wasps then to destroy *Heliothis* eggs. Or release lacewing larvae about a week after the full moon to eat young *Heliothis* larvae.

A puff of sevin dust at the tip of each corn ear, just as the silk emerges, will stop corn earworms. Repeat the dusting each week until silks begin to turn brown. You can also apply sevin or diazinon to petunia flowers or geranium leaves each week if they show serious tobacco budworm damage. When tobacco budworms are inside the buds, chemicals can't reach them. Break off and destroy flower clusters that have holes in them.

Physical controls: *handpicking, mineral oil on cornsilks*
Live controls: *lacewings,* Trichogramma *wasps*
Packaged controls: Bacillus thuringiensis *on tomatoes and geraniums; diazinon, disyston, meta-systox-R, orthene, sevin; sevin dust on cornsilks*

See explanation of controls on page 56.

Cutworms, Armyworms

A large group of variously patterned and colored, hairless larvae of night-flying moths make up the diverse group called cutworms. They all feed by night; most hide in holes in the ground during the day. Some live their full larval lives in lawns, hiding in holes beneath grass or dichondra by day, coming up at night and chewing on the turf.

The variegated cutworm, a common one, will eat leaves but also cuts holes into tomatoes, beans, and similar edible above-ground parts of vegetables. A common cutworm trick is to bite off brand-new seedlings during the night, a habit it shares with sowbugs, pillbugs, and earwigs.

The creatures called armyworms are closely related to cutworms, but they feed in daytime and operate in great numbers together—hence the name.

If you find cutworms on your plants at night (or armyworms during the day) destruction by hand is the most effective control. The chemical controls aren't sure-fire; they are sevin (hard on honeybees if nectar-bearing flowers are present), orthene, or diazinon.

Physical controls: *handpicking*
Live controls: *none*
Packaged controls: *diazinon, orthene, sevin*

Earwigs

Earwigs' prime food is decaying organic material. That's why a compost pile so often looks like an earwig convention. Earwigs also eat plant tissue, especially flowers, tasty leaves, and fruit. In an earwig neighborhood it's wise to put a compost pile as far as possible from the vegetable garden and fruit trees.

Sometimes you see earwigs in daytime, but they are most active at night. When dawn comes, they scurry back into tight, cozy places. A practical and widely used control is to put rolled-up newspapers or rolled-up pieces of cardboard out in the garden in the evening and then in the morning gather them up and destroy them. Or, try a commercial earwig bait with baygon in it.

Physical controls: *rolled-up newspapers or cardboard set out at night and collected in the morning*
Live controls: *none*
Packaged controls: *bait containing baygon*

Flea Beetles

These creatures are shiny black, pinhead sized, and jump like fleas. They rasp the soft leaf tissue on dichondra, making lawns brown and withered. Meanwhile, the young (larvae) feed underground on dichondra roots, causing ultimate wilting and collapse of the plants whether rasped by adults or not. The dichondra leaves become dry nubbins.

If you see any of this, act at once with chemicals. There are no known biological controls for flea beetles. Get some diazinon or dursban and apply it just on dichondra according to label instructions. Apply a follow-up treatment within a month.

Physical controls: *none*

Live controls: *none*

Packaged controls: *diazinon, dursban*

Grasshoppers

In areas where grasshoppers occur in large numbers, they lay their eggs in the soil in natural, uncultivated fields year after year. Eggs are laid in the fall and begin hatching from March to early June, depending on temperature and climate.

The newly hatched grasshopper, called a nymph or hopper, resembles the adult but is smaller and lacks wings. Nymphs or hoppers feed voraciously on plant tissues, sometimes stripping entire areas bare. When hoppers reach maturity, they fly out and find new feeding areas.

If you see just a few grasshoppers, learn to live with their minor damage. Or pick slower-moving adults, throw them to the ground to daze them, and step on them. This control is effective if the problem isn't severe and you are persistent. If you think grasshoppers are breeding in your garden, cultivate all areas to break up egg sacs. Birds, especially sparrows, consume many newly hatched grasshoppers.

When grasshoppers arrive in droves, chemicals may be your only successful control method.

Physical controls: *cultivate breeding grounds; handpick when they are sluggish*

Live controls: *none*

Packaged controls: *diazinon, dursban, malathion, sevin*

Mealybugs

These are closely related to scale insects but differ in looks—there's a white, cottony covering over the body, and the body tapers toward the tail. Also unlike scale, adult mealybugs move around.

Mealybugs also resemble woolly aphids. You can tell the difference by scraping off the fuzz—if it's a mealybug, you'll find an alligator-shaped body inside.

There are many parasites and predators of mealybugs. Mealybugs are much worse on house plants than on garden plants because the predators and parasites can't get in the house.

From commercial insectaries, you can buy cartons of a predator beetle called *Cryptolaemus* to release in trees and shrubs that have mealybugs. Lacewing larvae also eat mealybugs.

If your plants become weak from mealybug feeding or too coated with honeydew, spray with one of the packaged controls listed below. Repeat in three to four weeks.

Physical controls: *none*

Live controls: Cryptolaemus *beetles, lacewing larvae*

Packaged controls: *diazinon, malathion, orthene*

Mites

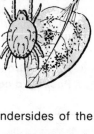

To the naked eye, mites look like specks of red, yellow, or green dust. Actually, they are tiny spider relatives (they have eight legs). Mites damage outdoor plants much more in the interior climates than on the coast, but they are significant everywhere.

Mites stipple little yellowish spots on tops of leaves by sucking plant juices. Sometimes you see webbing on the undersides of the leaves or on the ground.

Dust from the air that settles on leaves seems to encourage mites. Keeping plants washed with a hose is a good way of keeping mite populations low. However, once a plant has a bad mite infestation, don't count on washing it off. Some mites hang on tenaciously, and the hose pressure can strip leaves before it washes them away.

By the time the leaves are very spotted and the webbing very noticeable, applying any kind of control would probably waste time and money. The mites are ready to leave the plant by then.

If you have a plant that gets mites every year, you might wisely put a chemical on it to kill the mites before they reach maturity. Use dusting sulfur (if air temperature is under 90°F.), orthene, or kelthane. Be sure to cover undersides of leaves and repeat the application in 10 days.

From commercial insectaries you can buy packages of live mites that don't suck plant juices but do eat other kinds of mites. Lacewing larvae also eat mites.

Physical controls: *keep plants washed*

Live controls: *lacewing larvae, mite-eating mites (*Phytoseiulus persimilis*)*

Packaged controls: *dusting sulfur, kelthane, orthene*

Oak Moth

The pale brown California oak moth (*Phryganidia californica*) can damage oaks in Zones 7 to 9 and 14 to 24. Twice a year, a tan to gray moth with a 1-inch wing span lays eggs in the oak trees; the larvae hatch about 12 days later. They grow slowly, eating oak leaf tissue all the while, ultimately becoming 1¼-inch-long worms with olive green bodies, black and yellow stripes on back and sides.

Eggs laid in October and November produce a brood that chews leaves April to June. The second brood produces larvae that chew in September or October.

The time for decision—to spray or not to spray—comes when the worms enlarge to the point that you can see their green droppings (and maybe even hear them fall). If the droppings create an inconvenience—falling onto people, walks, patios, cars—have the tree sprayed. (It takes a commercial, high-pressure rig to reach the top of a big oak tree.) But if the droppings pose no nuisance, you can let the infestation go without putting your tree into jeopardy. In the wild (where nobody sprays) occasional big infestations completely defoliate oak trees but the trees come back the next year. Wait as long as possible before having an oak sprayed for worms because natural predators or parasites may come along and quickly kill off all but a very few of the worms without your doing a thing. That happens frequently.

Your tree man can spray with *Bacillus thuringiensis*, effective only on larvae of the age that eat voraciously; sevin, which brings results on larvae of any age, but unfortunately kills honeybees too; or orthene.

Physical controls: *none*

Live controls: *none*

Packaged controls: Bacillus thuringiensis, *orthene, sevin*

Pillbugs, Sowbugs

They have seven pairs of legs and sectioned shells, which make them isopods. Pillbugs roll up into black balls about the size of a large pea. Sowbugs are gray, not as rounded, and can't roll up tight. Both have always been around gardens, playing nuisance-or-nothing roles. But at times some observant gardeners witness them eating 1 or 2-day-old seedlings, or the skins of melons, cucumbers, and squash.

Mulching and composting encourage pillbugs and sowbugs because organic matter is their main food. They'll probably come to an area if you sprout seeds near a compost pile or use lots of compost in soil where you sprout seedlings. When that happens, some experts say, the sowbugs or pillbugs may eat infant seedlings.

If chemical controls seem necessary, use a sowbug-earwig bait containing baygon or drench seedbed soil with a pyrethrin and rotenone spray.

Physical controls: *none*

Live controls: *none*

Packaged controls: *bait containing baygon; pyrethrin and rotenone spray to drench seedbed soil*

Scale Insects

As an adult the scale insect lives under a stationary waxy shell that sticks to the plant. It lays its eggs in there. When the eggs hatch, the young crawl out and go elsewhere on the plant to establish themselves as mature fixed lumps or flat slivers. A tiny filament mouth part runs from the underside of the creature into the plant tissue. Through it the creature sucks plant juices, devitalizing the plant. Meanwhile, most kinds of scale insects exude a sticky substance that molds and darkens leaves.

Parasites and predators of scale insects have been more extensively studied than those of most other garden plant damagers. Available from commercial insectaries are *Aphytis* wasps that parasitize red scale and other armored forms. But mostly the creatures that eat and live upon scale insects exist naturally in and around garden plants.

In California, the parasites and predators that help destroy scale insects are inhibited by dust and ants. Wash plants off frequently.

See explanation of controls on page 56.

To kill crawler scale—the young that look like tiny moving specks of a different color than the adults—spray in spring with orthene, malathion, or diazinon. To kill the adults in winter, spray deciduous plants with oil spray, oil plus malathion, or oil plus diazinon.

Physical controls: *wash plants frequently*

Live controls: Aphytis *wasps*

Packaged controls: *diazinon, malathion, or orthene in spring; oil spray, oil plus malathion, or oil plus diazinon in winter on deciduous plants*

Slugs, Snails

Slugs and snails are similar creatures—a slug is just a snail without a shell to hide in. Both destroy many plants by biting tissue with rasping mouths underneath their bodies. Both hide by day and feed at night (or sometimes during very gray, damp days).

Controls for the two creatures are the same except that hand picking is quite easy with snails—you just grab them by their shells. With slugs, there is no shell to grab.

In Europe, where California's most common snails came from (they were imported deliberately), man is a natural predator, and as a result snails are seldom a garden pest there. Europeans go out at night or after a rain to collect them for dinner.

About a dozen other creatures occasionally feed upon snails and slugs, including opossums (nocturnal themselves). In some parts of Southern California there exists an introduced kind of snail that eats European brown snails more often than it eats vegetation.

The best control for slugs and snails has remained the same since the 1930s: manufactured bait containing metaldehyde. You throw it on the ground around plants that the creatures eat. If you use pellets, scatter them sparingly, not in piles.

Metaldehyde has one drawback—dogs tend to eat it and get sick or perhaps even die. Find a way to keep your dog away from metaldehyde for at least three or four days after treatment; by then it will have lost its toxicity for dogs. Never apply it in the presence of dogs; they might believe they are being fed with it.

A product called mesurol is effective but not as specific as metaldehyde; it also kills earthworms and insects. Zectran has been useful, when available.

Physical controls: *handpicking*

Live controls: *none*

Packaged controls: *mesurol, metaldehyde bait, zectran*

Strawberry Root Weevils

Strawberry root weevils and about 14 related species damage plants in two ways. As beetles (adults) they start feeding as soon as they emerge in spring, making square-cornered notches in leaf edges on rhododendrons, azaleas, viburnums, primulas, and other plants—usually the most expensive ones.

Then later in summer the gray or black beetles walk considerable distances, laying eggs loosely on the soil or in folds of leaves. The eggs hatch and white or pinkish larvae burrow into soil, eating tender roots as they go.

Root weevils have always been difficult or impossible to control. By drenching soil with sevin, diazinon, or orthene you can perhaps protect the shallower roots. Or you can spray tops of plants with the same chemicals to protect foliage, but the treatment may not be effective.

Physical controls: *none*   **Live controls:** *none*

Packaged controls: *diazinon, orthene, sevin*

Tent Caterpillars

They start in early spring as tiny worms in small colonies, and by June grow into black and orange worms 2 to 3 inches long. They forage out of webby tents spun on branches.

In June the caterpillars leave their branches, move to protected places, and pupate (turn into cocoons). Ten days after pupation, moths emerge, fly about, and lay bands of eggs around branches of trees. Those eggs will hatch next spring.

Nature gives you built-in controls: in spring, some flies lay eggs on the caterpillars' heads. The eggs hatch into tiny larvae that begin feeding on the caterpillars' nonessential organs. When the fly larvae are ready to pupate, they finally eat the essential organs and then exit from the dying caterpillars. Viruses also kill the caterpillars.

If tent caterpillars survive all of this and threaten your tree, you can cut the colonies off and throw them away, or spray just the tents with a product containing one of the packaged controls listed below.

Physical controls: *cut off colonies and discard*

Live controls: *none*

Packaged controls: *spray tents with* Bacillus thuringiensis, *diazinon, malathion, orthene, pyrethrins, rotenone, or sevin*

Thrips

Often, the presence of thrips doesn't affect a garden significantly. At certain times you can shake thrips out of any blossom—do it over white paper so you can see the speck-sized insects.

These casually present thrips can be good to have around. They serve as food for certain insect predators who later may do something nice for your plants. But when thrips get numerous, trouble comes on the plants that they favor (especially those with white or pastel blossoms). Flowers and leaves don't open normally; they look twisted or stuck together and discolored. If you look closely, you'll see fecal spotting and the thrips' mouth-damage trademark: strips of seersucker puckerings in the flower or leaf tissue. Enough puckerings make a massive distortion.

If thrips become too troublesome, spray the affected plants with one of the packaged controls listed below.

Physical controls: *none*   **Live controls:** *none*

Packaged controls: *malathion, meta-systox-R, orthene*

Whiteflies

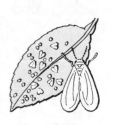

They're little (1/8 inch) white things that fly up from plants when brushed or touched, then return to the interior of the plant. Turn a leaf on the plant over and you see even more: winged adults, stationary pupae and nymphs that suck plant juices and exude a sticky substance, and (with sharp eyes or a hand lens) tiny eggs and freshly hatched, mobile young.

It may strain your belief, but nature keeps whiteflies in check better than anything man has devised. A number of wasps lay eggs in whitefly nymphs and pupae; the wasp larvae hatch there and kill their hosts.

A gardener who sprays too soon can make matters worse by killing parasitizing wasps. The result is an explosion of whiteflies. So if you can see just a few whiteflies, don't spray them.

Two mechanical methods—vacuuming and singeing with a burning-newspaper torch—work only on the flying adults. Jar the main stem of the plant, making as many adults fly as possible, and then either suck them up or fry them in mid-air.

Colored cards (bright orange–yellow seems to work best) smeared with a transparent, sticky insect–catching material can be tried. The color attracts the adults and the sticky substance entraps them.

A few devotees of the shoofly plant (*Nicandra physalodes*) claim that it keeps whiteflies away from nearby plants.

As a biological control, you can buy eggs of *Encarsia* (a whitefly-killing wasp) and place them among your infested plants.

If the whiteflies become too numerous and plants become debilitated and sticky, spray with a liquid dishwashing soap solution (one tablespoon to a gallon of water). Or spray with one of the packaged controls listed below.

Physical controls: *bright orange–yellow card smeared with sticky material; soap or detergent solution; vacuum cleaner; newspaper torch*

Live controls: Encarsia *wasps, shoofly plant*

Packaged controls: *cygon, diazinon, disyston, malathion, meta-systox-R, methoxychlor, orthene, pyrethrin and allethrin, SBP-1382, thiodan*

Gophers, Deer, and Other Plant Damagers

Damage done by creatures other than insects is one of the most frustrating things a gardener has to deal with. A number of animals and birds can cause damage in your garden. Fortunately there are some things you can do to foil them.

Gophers

Gophers are serious garden pests in many areas of the West. They feed on roots and bulbs from an elaborate system of tunnels usually 6 to 18 inches below the surface, and even eat the tops of some plants. First sign of their presence is often a mound of fresh, finely pulverized soil in lawn or flower bed. This soil is a by-product of burrowing operations, and it is brought to the surface through short side runs opening off the main burrow.

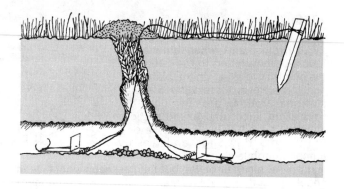

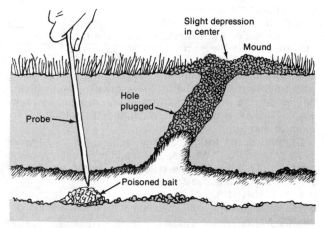

Two Macabee gopher traps in main run (top) attach to stake. Or use probe to locate run (bottom), drop in poisoned bait.

You may find a hole in this mound or (more often) you will find a plug of earth blocking the exit. Trapping is the most widely used and generally most successful control method. Avoid the tempation to place a single trap down a hole you can see from the surface. Instead dig down to the main horizontal runway from which the surface hole comes. If you are using a Macabee trap (most popular), place two of them in each runway, one on either side of your excavation. Attach each trap to a stake on the surface with chain or wire.

Plug the hole with folded carrot tops, fresh green grass, or some other fresh, tender greens; their scent attracts the gophers. Next, place a board or soil over the greens and the top of the hole to block all light. Check traps frequently and clear tunnels if the gopher has pushed soil into the traps. Be persistent; a wily gopher may avoid getting trapped on your first tries.

You can also try poisoned bait, as described for moles.

If you live near orchards or open fields and suffer frequent invasions by gophers, protect your young plants by lining planting holes with chicken wire or other fine-meshed (one inch or smaller) hardware cloth.

Moles

Some moles are insectivorous; others eat plants as well as bugs and worms. Regardless of their feeding habits, their tunnels cause trouble by disfiguring lawns, heaving up seedlings, and severing tender roots. Evidences are ridges of raised and cracked soil above feeder runs and little conical mounds of soil pushed up from below.

Again, trapping is the most efficient control method. Set traps carefully. The harpoon-type trap is the easiest

to set because you don't have to dig into the runway; the trap is positioned above the soil. Another effective trap that must be set into the mole run has scissors action.

Poison bait is sometimes effective, too. Probe for the deep burrows with a metal rod or sharpened stick, then insert bait and gently close the hole.

Voles, field mice

These small rodents multiply with astonishing rapidity when not controlled by their natural predators—owls, snakes, weasels, cats—and can become serious pests. Though they live in abandoned gopher and mole burrows they feed principally on above-ground portions of plants.

Some people have succeeded in trapping voles and field mice in mouse traps, rat traps, and box traps. Try baiting traps with walnut meats securely attached with thread or a rubber band. Poisoned grain bait also can provide effective control. In general, these animals' skill at concealment and rapid breeding make control difficult. An adept professional exterminator can quickly wipe them out.

Rabbits

In rural gardens and in suburban fringe areas that border on undeveloped countryside, rabbits can be anything from minor nuisances to serious damagers. If hungry enough, rabbits will eat nearly anything within reach, seeking out vegetables, juicy young shoots, and succulent growth; they also will nibble lawn grass, summer flowers, all sorts of shrubs, and tree bark. During winter in snowy country, rabbits often gnaw on tree bark exposed above the soil line. The only sure method of excluding rabbits from your garden is to fence them out. Good security will be provided by a 2-foot-high fence of chicken wire or other wire mesh, the mesh no larger than 1½ inches. But essential to success of a fence is its extension 6 inches underground. Rabbits may ultimately burrow beneath the 6-inch underground extension, but if you check periodically you usually can notice their holes before the rabbits have succeeded in tunneling completely under the fence. To counteract possible damage to trees, encircle trunks with a wire mesh cylinder 2 feet high; bury its base 2 to 3 inches in the soil and stake it.

Commercial rabbit repellents have worked for some gardeners and not for others. Most of the sprays repel by coating plants with a substance that tastes bad to the rabbit. This eliminates the sprays' use on edible (to humans) plants, and means that repellents must be applied again as new growth is produced.

Deer

Though they're pleasant to see, deer can ruin the looks of a garden in a very short time. You can try putting chicken wire cages around young plants; these cages will keep other nibblers away, too. Commercial repellents work *if* you spray frequently enough to keep new growth well covered and to replace what rain or sprinkling remove. Some people have success repelling deer with blood meal; they sprinkle it on the ground around plantings or hang little cloth bags filled with it around the garden. Blood meal often works, and it furnishes fertilizer to the garden as it dissolves, but it smells bad when wet and dogs are attracted to it. Six-foot fences usually keep deer out on level ground, but some deer can clear 7 or even 8 feet. A horizontal outrigger extension on a fence makes it harder for a deer to jump it. For a list of deer-resistant plants, turn to page 125.

Birds

Most gardeners consider birds as friends rather than enemies, but certain birds at certain times can be nuisances, eating tender seedlings, transplants, fruits, nuts, and berries. Reflectors and fluttering objects may reduce damage. However, the only across-the-board solution to garden-plundering birds is screen or netting. You can buy nylon or plastic netting in rolls from 4½ to 13 feet wide and up to 200 feet long.

Broad-mesh netting (¾ inch) is the most popular for trees, since it lets air, water, and sunlight in easily. Enclose fruit trees with nets two or three weeks before fruit ripens. Tie nets off where the lowest branches leave the trunk. Remove net at harvest time.

Fine-mesh screen and nylon netting are the most popular for covering rows of sprouting seedlings and maturing vegetables—birds can't get their beaks through them. Tent the material over the rows with stakes and string for support.

Plant disease control

Knowing about plant diseases helps not only to recognize them, but also points the way to their control. Some plant diseases are caused by the deficiency of one or more essential nutrients, by the inability of plants to utilize such nutrients, by poor drainage, or by excess salts in the soil. Most diseases, however, are caused by bacteria, viruses, or fungi.

Bacterial diseases

Bacteria are microscopic single-celled plants that are unable to manufacture their own food, as do green plants; those which cause plant diseases must obtain their nutrients from other plants.

Fireblight. This disease is caused by bacteria that survive in blighted twigs and cankers. When a flowering shoot of a pear, apple, crabapple, pyracantha, cotoneaster, quince, hawthorn, or toyon suddenly wilts and looks as though it were scorched by fire, it has fireblight. During moist weather in early spring the bacteria are carried to the blossoms by bees, flies, and other insects. The infection progresses down the shoot into the bark of larger limbs where dark sunken cankers form.

You can do two things to control fireblight. Protect blossoms from infection by spraying at 4 or 5-day intervals through the blossoming period with a weak streptomycin or fixed copper spray. Also, prune out and burn the diseased twigs and branches. Make cuts at least 6 inches below the infected area. After each cut, sterilize the pruning tools and the cut surface with disinfectant— rubbing alcohol or a 5 percent solution of household bleach (but be sure to wash bleach off the tool or it will corrode the metal). Where the problem is persistent, it would be better to grow non-susceptible plants.

Cherry "dead bud." This bacterial blight disfigures both fruiting and flowering cherries in the Northwest. First symptom is dying buds on spurs in early spring, as the disease starts in a tree's lower limbs and moves up. Both flower buds and leaf buds can be affected. Spray once in October and again as soon as possible after January. Use copper hydroxide at 6 pounds per 100 gallons of water, with highly refined petroleum oil. Bordeaux mixture is also effective if you mix fresh ingredients just before use and agitate while spraying.

Pseudomonas. Prevalent during wet springs in the Pacific Northwest, this disease causes dieback of smaller twigs in plums, prunes, cherries, apricots, peaches, pears, and other fruit trees. For the home gardener, control is not practical; subsequent new growth will hide dead twigs.

Virus diseases

Ultramicroscopic virus particles are capable of infecting plants and reproducing in them at the expense of the host. Insects and man carry viruses from plant to plant.

Virus diseases are a serious threat to many agricultural crops such as tomatoes, sugar beets, beans, citrus, and sugar cane. In the home garden, virus damage is seen in many forms. In some cases, such as rose mosaic, it does not reduce the growth of the plant. The most common symptom is a mottled area on leaves or a stunting and general yellowing of the foliage. Viruses produce abnormalities in growth, variegation of foliage, or "breaking" (color distortion) of blossoms.

There is no cure at this time for a virus-infected plant. However, you can reduce chances of a virus entering the plant by controlling the insects that carry the virus. Aphids are most efficient in spreading different kinds of viruses; leafhoppers, thrips, and whiteflies can be culprits too. Also, man does a fair job of spreading these diseases by propagating infected plants from cuttings, by budding or grafting, by pruning and pinching diseased plants, and by smoking or handling tobacco while working around plants (this can spread tobacco viruses).

Fungus diseases

Certain many-celled, branching, threadlike plants called fungi obtain their food parasitically from green plants, causing diseases in the process. Many of these fungi produce great numbers of tiny reproductive bodies called spores. These can be carried by wind or water to other plants where they germinate to produce another group of fungus threads. Fungus diseases are among the most widespread of plant disorders; fortunately most are controllable by sanitation, dusts, and sprays.

Powdery mildew. This disease appears as a white or gray, powdery or mealy coating on leaves, tender stems,

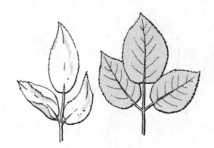

Signs of mildew problem are white powdery or mealy growth and distortion of leaves.

and flower buds. Powdery mildew spores are unique in that they can cause infection in the absence of free moisture. Plants are most susceptible under conditions of high humidity, crowding, poor air circulation, and more shade (less sun) than the plant needs. Powdery mildew occurs even in desert climates because of an increase in humidity (and lower temperature) at night—especially when air circulation is poor.

Rust. This disease usually appears first on the underside of leaves. Yellow orange colored pustules or wartlike formations mature and eventually burst. Spores are spread by wind and splashing water. Upper leaf surfaces may show mottled and yellowish areas in corresponding position to the rust pustules. Generally the development of rust is favored by moisture (rain, dew, or fog), cool nights, and fairly warm days. Rust survives the winter on living plants and on dead leaves. Winter cleanup will reduce infestation.

Lower surface of a snapdragon leaf (right) shows rust symptoms—orange spots in clusters.

Leaf spot, leaf blight, scab, anthracnose, shot hole. Red, brown, or yellow spots on leaves and stems are common on a number of plants. In some cases the spots drop out, leaving a "shot hole" condition. The spores of fungi causing these diseases are airborne or waterborne. The source of the disease is generally in plant refuse, dead leaves, or fruit. Thorough garden cleanup is important to reduce infection.

The fungi flourish in wet spring weather with warm temperatures and also in rainy summer weather. Therefore, these diseases are far less serious in low rainfall areas than west of the Cascades in Oregon and Wash-

Attack of shot hole fungus has left its very distinctive marks on this infected leaf.

ington and along the foggy coast of northern California. Black spot on roses, for example, is practically unknown in areas of limited rainfall.

Recommended spraying for scab in heavy rainfall areas: just before the flower buds open, spray with dormant spray of lime sulfur. When blossoms show pink, and again when ¾ of blossom petals have fallen, spray with wettable sulfur.

Scab disfigures fruit, causes leaf drop in affected plants.

The anthracnose fungi infect leaves and tender shoots as they emerge in the spring. On older leaves the infection produces large irregular brown blotches, and leaves fall earlier than they should. These fungi also cause twig die-back and canker on small branches. These blighted twigs and cankers are the source of infection the following spring. Spread of fungus spores depends on rain or dripping fogs. The disease is most severe in wet springs and is checked by dry weather. To control it, prune infected twigs and branches; also, see chart for correct sprays to use.

Peach leaf curl. This disease also infects nectarines and almonds. You can recognize it when new leaves thicken and pucker along the midrib, causing curling. The curled leaves may be tinged with red or yellow and they fall prematurely. New leaves then arise from dormant buds.

Peach leaf curl distorts the leaves, can weaken the tree.

The fungus overwinters on the bark and twigs of these trees and on old, infected leaves; it develops most rapidly during cool, moist spring weather. Control peach leaf curl by spraying or brushing the entire tree with lime sulfur or Bordeaux mixture after leaves drop in the fall and again just before flower buds open in the spring.

Dutch elm disease. This disease (DED) slowly spread across the United States and in the early 1970s it reached the West.

Control for leaf and stem diseases

Of the three kinds of diseases of leaves, stems, and flowers discussed on pages 63 to 66, the fungi are the most controllable. Fireblight, a bacterial disease, is controllable by chemicals and it, too, is charted with the fungus diseases.

All of the chemicals listed in the chart should be available, individually or in mixtures, in small packages in your nursery or garden center. Remember that new and better controls may become available, and that older ones may be taken off the market. Always follow label directions for mixing and applying the chemicals. Also, use a product only on the plants mentioned on the label.

*Best results only when fresh ingredients are mixed together immediately before use and the mixture agitated continually while spraying.

Common or coined name of active ingredient and formulation / Disease	Acti-dione (Cycloheximide) wettable powder	Benomyl wettable powder	Bordeaux* water suspension of copper and lime	Captan dust or wettable powder	Ferbam dust or wettable powder	Fixed copper dust or liquid	Folpet (Phaltan) dust or wettable powder	Lime sulfur liquid	Karathane dust, liquid, or wettable powder	Streptomycin wettable powder	Sulfur dust or wettable powder	Thiram dust or wettable powder	Zineb (Dithane Z-78) dust or wettable powder
Anthracnose		•	•	•	•	•	•	•				•	•
Damping off			•							•		•	•
Fireblight		•				•							•
Leaf spot		•	•	•		•				•		•	
Peach leaf curl			•					•					•
Powdery mildew	•	•					•	•	•		•		
Scab		•		•	•	•	•					•	
Shot hole		•	•	•	•	•							•
Rust							•						•

DED is spread by the elm bark beetle. Beetle larvae overwinter in dead and dying elm trees, and as young beetles emerge in the spring the sticky disease spores stick to their bodies. The disease also spreads from infected to healthy trees by natural root grafting.

The beetles spread the disease when they migrate to healthy elms to feed. The fungus spores anchor in feeding wounds where some begin to grow; others spread throughout the tree and progressively clog conductive tissues. First, the foliage on infected trees wilts due to lack of water. Next, leaves turn yellow from lack of nutrients (a condition called chlorosis). The leaves eventually fall off, and finally the tree dies.

If you have an elm and suspect that it has DED, call your county agricultural agent and report the symptoms. Someone there will advise you on the best control method.

Soil-borne diseases

These infect plants through their roots, which are often severely damaged before symptoms show aboveground.

Verticillium wilt. This is one of the most widespread and destructive plant diseases—especially in California. The fungus that causes the disease can survive in the soil for years. Rotation (the growing of nonsusceptible plants on the infected soil for long periods) will not starve out this fungus, but will reduce disease losses.

The fungus invades and plugs the water-conducting tissues in the roots. A common symptom is a wilt on one side of the plant. Leaves yellow, then turn brown and die upward from the base of the plant or branch; affected branches of woody plants die. If you cut one of these branches, you will find that the sapwood (outer layer of tissue in a stem or branch) is usually discolored—frequently olive green, dark brown, or black. Development of the fungus is favored by a cool, moist soil in spring. Wilting of foliage may not show until days are sunny and warm and the plant is under water stress (leaves transpiring water faster than roots can take it in).

No spray is effective since the fungus attacks through the root system. The disease can be controlled for shallow-rooted plants by hiring a commercial applicator firm to fumigate the soil with chloropicrin (tear gas) or methyl bromide before planting or replanting (don't handle these toxic materials yourself). However, fumigation has not been successful with deep-rooted shrubs and trees. Planting wilt-resistant varieties will help reduce infection.

Mildly affected plants often recover from an attack. You can aid recovery by deep but infrequent irrigation. If a plant has been neglected, add fertilizer to stimulate new root growth. Shrubs and trees in lush vegetative growth should not be fertilized after disease appears.

Soil where highly susceptible crops have been grown, such as tomatoes, potatoes, cotton, strawberries, and various melons, is frequently infected.

Resistant or immune plants include: apple, *Arctostaphylos* (manzanita), *Asparagus*, bamboo, beans, *Buxus* (boxwood), *Ceanothus*, *Citrus*, conifers, corn, *Eucalyptus*, ferns, figs, grasses, *Liquidambar, Morus* (mulberry), *Nerium* (oleander), pear, *Pyracantha, Quercus* (oak), strawberries (certain varieties), tomatoes (certain varieties), *Umbellularia californica,* and walnut.

Texas root rot. A damaging and widespread disease in the semiarid Southwest from California's Imperial and Coachella valleys eastward, it is caused by a fungus that destroys the outer portion of the roots, thus cutting off the water supply to the upper parts of the plant. The first sign of the disease is a sudden wilting of the leaves. When this happens at least 50 percent of the root system has been damaged.

This fungus is favored by a highly alkaline soil that contains very little organic matter. Fortunately the fungus does not compete well with other soil-inhabiting organisms. Therefore, control measures are aimed at lessening alkalinity by adding sulfur and increasing the population of organisms that are antagonistic to the fungus by adding organic matter that decomposes rapidly, such as manure and fir sawdust.

You can attempt to save a damaged tree in this way: drill holes 2 to 3 feet deep and spaced 3 feet apart in a wide band around the drip line of the tree. Fill holes with a mix of organic matter (manure or sawdust) and soil. If you use manure only, don't go higher than 10 percent of the mix. If you use sawdust, make a mix of 1 part sawdust to 5 parts of soil. To a cubic yard of mix add 5 pounds of sulfur and 1 pound of ammonium sulfate. You'll get quicker action in lowering the pH by using iron sulfate or combining 4 pounds of sulfur and 2 pounds of iron sulfate. Blend the mix well and fill holes. Water deeply.

Since the root system is damaged, decrease the aboveground growth by pruning back and thinning to remove half the foliage.

When setting out trees and shrubs in Texas root rot areas, dig a broad deep hole and backfill around the roots with a mix of about 20 percent organic matter (10 percent if it's manure) and 80 percent soil. Add sulfur, iron, and ammonium sulfate.

Root rots—water molds. The diseases caused by the water mold fungi are so much a part of western gardening that they are seldom mentioned as diseases. However, they are indirectly referred to in practically all of the advice given on soil preparation and watering. When you read about *touchy plants, infrequent but deep watering, sharp drainage, well-drained soil, good aeration, and keeping a plant on the dry side,* frequently the advice is meant to avoid water molds.

Free water (excess water that fills all the air spaces in the soil) causes death to plant roots by suffocation. But water can pass through the soil continuously without root damage if it carries air with it. The damage from "overwatering" is, in almost all cases, not caused by water itself but by the destruction of roots by water molds, fungi which thrive when free water stands too long around roots, especially when soil is warm. Improving soil drainage (pages 33–35) helps.

Damping off. The most conspicuous type of "damping off" occurs when seedlings develop a stem rot near the soil surface and fall over. Another type rots the seedling before it emerges from the soil, or causes seed to decay before sprouting. A third (often called sore shin) girdles the seedling, which may remain alive and standing for a while. These damping off diseases are most serious in nursery operations, agriculture, and floriculture, but they can plague home gardeners, too. Professional horticulturists practice careful sanitation and sterilize their soil mixes.

A home gardener can do three things to reduce the occurrence of damping off: 1) buy seeds that have been treated with a fungicide or dust them with one before planting; 2) provide good air circulation and ventilation, especially indoors, to keep tops of seedlings dry and standing moisture to a minimum; 3) use an inert material rather than garden soil to sow seeds or root cuttings—sphagnum moss, vermiculite, perlite, pumice, sand, and sterilized commercial mix are all possibilities. These are safe, at least the first time they are used.

Controlling weeds

Weed control is more than mere garden housekeeping. A weed-free garden is not only more attractive than a weedy one, but healthier as well. Weeds compete with garden plants for water, nutrients, and space. Control consists basically of preventing weed growth and mechanical destruction of weeds. Occasionally, but not often, you may have to kill them by chemical means.

Home gardeners can plant ground covers, annuals, and vegetables close together to shade out weeds, thereby preventing them from growing at all. Most mulches retard weed growth, too. If some weeds do come up you can pull, hoe, or cultivate.

Hand pulling is sometimes necessary, as when weeds

are growing among choice, shallow-rooted plants such as cyclamen, rhododendrons, and azaleas. Where damage to surface roots is not a risk, hoeing and cultivating give good control and, in roughing up the soil surface and breaking the crust, give better aeration and water penetration. Many tools are available for various types of weeds and plantings; common garden hoes and cultivating forks in a variety of sizes are useful for working among row crops, little garden plants, and shrubs. Scuffle hoes (flat-bladed, disk type, or U-shaped) are easier to use in close quarters or under spreading plants. You push and pull them, and they cut weeds on either kind of stroke without digging into roots of desirable plants.

For larger areas (orchards, roadsides, vacant lots), rotary tilling or disking is effective, especially where there are no summer rains to germinate late weed crops. They not only knock down weeds but also incorporate them into the soil, where they decay to form humus.

If you keep an eye out for small weeds and destroy them when you first see them, your garden should be neat and you'll never have to struggle with large weeds. So, become acquainted with the wide variety of hoes and cultivators your garden center carries; many of them are fun to use and the end result is a weed-free garden.

Chemical weed killers come into our lives mostly as overflow from agriculture and institutional landscape maintenance work. In those endeavors, chemicals are used to reduce time spent hoeing, hand pulling, or cultivating large fields. Using chemicals in a home garden risks damaging valuable plants. If you feel you must use chemical weed killers, be very careful with them. Some can be used in established plantings (read product label for cautions) to control specific weeds, while others will destroy all vegetation. Chemicals that are applied to the soil to kill weed seeds before or as they germinate are the pre-emergence controls. Liquids that you spray or sprinkle on the undesired plants are the contact killers. A third category, translocated chemicals, contain an active ingredient which is absorbed by the plant and interferes with its metabolism, causing the plant's death. *Always follow label directions exactly* and be careful not to let the chemicals come in contact with anything but the weeds you're trying to kill. Some weed killers are so persistent that traces remain in a sprayer even after rinsing. Read label instructions carefully.

Chemical weed killers

Chemical	Effect	Comments	Chemical	Effect	Comments
Amino triazole	Kills poison oak and other woody perennials; annuals.	Will also kill or damage desirable grasses and ornamentals.	**Eptam (EPTC)**	Grass control around shrubs and trees.	Work into soil.
Ammate	Kills annual and woody vegetation (poison oak).	Respraying probably necessary. Clean sprayer thoroughly after use.	**Fortified diesel, stove, or weed oils**	Destroys top growth of all the vegetation it contacts.	May smell oily for several days.
Cacodylic acid	Kills all top growth. Best on young weeds.	Won't kill perennial plants.	**Glyphosate**	Controls poison oak, grasses (including Bermuda grass), most weeds.	Apply to plants in active growth.
Casoron	Kills weeds around roses and other selected woody ornamentals.	Work into soil or water in.	**Prometon**	Kills all top growth, prevents seed germination for a season or more.	Medium-term control of all vegetation. Often mixed with pentachlorophenol.
Cyanamid	Temporary soil sterilant (used before turf is planted).	After application wait 24 to 30 days before planting turf.	**Simazine**	Kills seedlings on germination. Many special uses.	Granules often used for weed control in orchards, vineyards.
Dacthal	Kills grass in established plantings.	Destroys germinating seeds.	**Trifluralin**	Controls annual weeds in established plantings.	Work into soil or water in.
Dalapon	Controls grasses.	Don't irrigate for 24 hours after applying.	**Vapam**	A soil fumigant that kills many seeds before they sprout.	Don't breathe fumes or get the material on your shoes.
Diphenamid	Controls grasses, some other weeds, in ground covers, dichondra lawns.	Spray on established ground covers. Repeat sprays probably needed.			

Pruning

Pruning is both a skill and an art. The skill is in making proper cuts that will heal well. The art is in making cuts in the right places so that the plant will develop its potential beauty or produce an optimum crop.

No matter how much or how little pruning you do on an established plant, the objective is to modify the growth of the plant. The modification can be done for any of the following reasons, singly or in combination:

• to maintain plant health by removing dead, diseased, or injured wood;
• to control or direct growth;
• to increase quality or yield of flowers or fruit.

You never should have to cut back a plant continually to keep it in bounds. A plant that seems to require such treatment was the wrong choice for its garden location; the repeated cutting back only destroys the plant's natural beauty. Exceptions are formal hedges, espaliered fruit trees, topiary, and pollarding (see Glossary).

Some of the tools used in pruning are illustrated on pages 93–94.

Plant growth and pruning know-how

To understand how to approach the pruning of any plant, you need to know how growth occurs. And since all growth originates in *buds*, they are the first plant parts for you to consider.

The *terminal growth bud* develops at the end of a stem or branch. This bud causes the stem to grow in length.

Lateral buds grow along the sides of stems. These buds are responsible for producing the side or lateral growth that creates a plant's bushiness.

In some plants, there may be *latent buds*—buds that lie dormant beneath the bark. These will grow after pruning or injury removes the actively growing part of the stem.

During the season of active growth, terminal buds draw plant energy to themselves and grow, adding length to the stems. But if any growing terminal bud is cut or nipped off, elongation of the stem or branch ceases and growth is stimulated in the lateral buds below the bud you removed. The flow of plant energy to a terminal growth bud is caused by hormones called auxins that are produced within the bud. When you remove the bud, one or more of the buds below it will begin to produce auxins and will take over and draw plant energy. All the kinds of pruning cuts, including pinching, should be made just above some growth—a growth bud, stem, or branch. For explanations of how to make proper cuts, see "Pruning cuts" on page 69.

Pinching. The first opportunity you have to control or direct plant growth is to remove—to pinch out—new growth before it elongates into stems. This is especially useful with young plants that you want to make bushier. For example, you can pinch out all the terminal buds on every branch of a young fuchsia plant. This will force growth from buds that are at the leaf bases along the stems, creating perhaps two, three, or four new side branches instead of just one lengthening branch. When this happens all over the plant, you get all-over growth.

Conversely, if you want a plant to gain height, keep side growth pinched back so the terminal bud on the main stem continues to elongate.

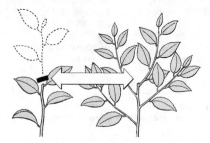

Removing the terminal shoot or bud (pinching) activates the buds below into strong growth.

Heading back. This sort of pruning—also called cutting back—takes advantage of the same growth principle as pinching: that growth elongates in one direction until it is stopped. The difference is that in heading back you cut off lengths of stem already grown rather than removing growth before it forms stems. In heading back, you cut stems down to promising side branches or to lateral buds that will grow in the directions you want. The annual ritual of rose pruning probably is the most familiar example of heading back.

Heading back may be done for a variety of reasons: to remove weak or unproductive wood; to encourage growth in the direction you want it to take (or prevent growth from continuing in the wrong direction); to stimulate flower or fruit production by encouraging growth of wood that will produce either; to prevent wind or snow damage to extra long or heavy branches; and sometimes as part of a program to revitalize an old plant.

In heading back you come to grips with pruning as an artistic exercise, since you will be making decisions about which growth to remove and which to leave, thereby controlling and directing a plant's growth. For some general guidelines, refer to "Pruning to shape" on page 70.

Terminal bud

Lateral bud

Lateral bud

Leaf

Latent bud

Terminal bud

During the season of active growth, terminal buds draw plant energy to themselves and grow, adding length to

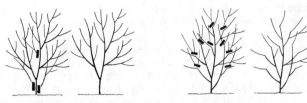

Thinning (left) opens up and simplifies the plant structure. Heading back (right) reduces size, encourages fullness.

Thinning. Think of thinning as the extreme of heading back; instead of removing parts of stems you remove entire stems, limbs, or branches. Reasons for thinning are essentially the same as for heading back. It usually accomplishes the opening up of a plant by simplification of its structure; removal of old and unproductive growth, weak or excess growth, or limbs that are growing in directions that detract from the plant's attractiveness. Again, a familiar example is rose pruning—removing entire canes to the plant's base.

Shearing. This is the only form of pruning that could be called indiscriminate. You ignore all advice that tells you to cut just above growing points and, instead, clip the surface of densely foliaged plants. Shearing maintains formal hedges and topiary work; the plants that normally are used for these purposes have buds and branches so close together on their stems that every cut is close to a growing point. See drawings below for basic hedge trimming guidelines.

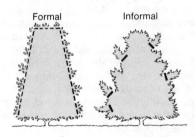

Shear hedges so sides slope in somewhat at top. If hedge flares out at top, lower leaves, branches won't get enough light.

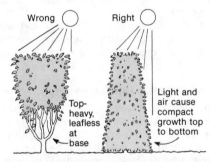

Formal hedges must be sheared regularly; informal hedges need an occasional shaping by cutting back or pinching to keep bushy, in bounds.

Pruning cuts

After you understand how to approach a pruning job, you need to know how to make good pruning cuts. The first lesson is: never leave a stub. Or to put it another way, always make a cut just above some sort of growth (a bud or a stem). To understand why this advice is given, think of a stem or branch as a conveying tube for water and plant nutrients. If you cut a branch some distance beyond its uppermost remaining growing part, you leave nothing in the stub itself to maintain growth; there is no reason for water and nutrients to enter it. The stub, no longer a part of the plant's active metabolism, withers and dies. Then, decay can work into the plant through the dead stub.

There is a right way to make pruning cuts and several wrong ways, as the illustrations (below) show. You want to avoid leaving stubs and you also want to avoid undercutting the bud or branch. Best cuts, as illustrated, place the lowest part of the cut directly opposite and slightly above the upper side of the bud or branch to which you are cutting back.

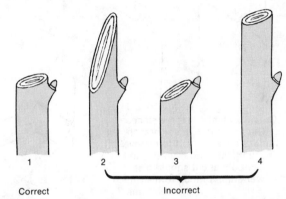

Correct pruning cut (left) has lowest point even with the top of growth bud, slants upward at a 45° angle.

When you make cuts with shears, be sure that they are sharp. Ragged edges on a pruning cut heal more slowly than clean cuts. Use shears that are strong enough for the job. If you can't get them to cut easily through a branch, the shears are too small, too dull, or both. Switch to a stronger pair of shears or use a pruning saw instead. With hook and blade pruning shears, remember to place the blade, not the hook, on the side toward the plant. As the drawings (below) show, if the hook is on the side toward the plant, you will leave a small stub.

Pruning saws come in handy when you need to cut limbs that are too thick for shears or loppers and when a

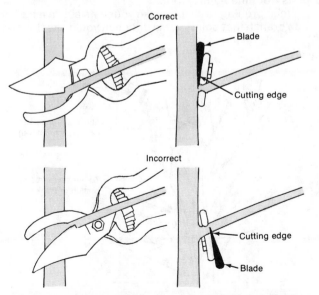

Hold pruning shears with the blade closest to growth that will remain; stub results when you reverse the shear position.

plant's growth won't allow your hand and the shears to get into position to make a good cut. Large limbs are heavy, and if you cut down through one with a single cut it's likely to split or tear before the cut is finished (possibly splitting farther back than you intended). To cut a large limb without this happening, make it a three-part operation as illustrated (below).

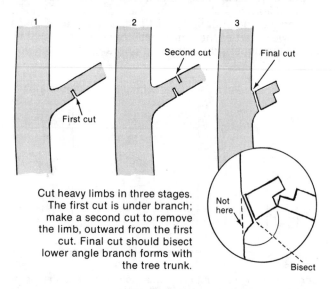

Cut heavy limbs in three stages. The first cut is under branch; make a second cut to remove the limb, outward from the first cut. Final cut should bisect lower angle branch forms with the tree trunk.

Pruning to shape

"To shape" is another concept in which the artistic side of pruning comes forward in determining *your* concept of what the right shape of a particular plant should be. Every plant has a "natural" shape; its growth tends to conform to a natural pattern, whether round, gumdrop shaped, wide spreading, vase shaped, or arching. Observe what a plant's natural shape is and then prune the plant in a manner that will allow the natural form to continue to develop. Remove excess growth that obscures the basic pattern or any errant growth that departs from the natural form.

When pruning to shape, make your cuts above a bud or side branch that points in the direction you'd like the new

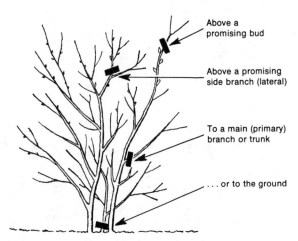

Above a promising bud

Above a promising side branch (lateral)

To a main (primary) branch or trunk

. . . or to the ground

Enhance a plant's natural growth pattern by pruning it to shape; use the techniques detailed on the previous pages.

growth to take. If you have no preference for the branch's direction, remember that generally it is better for a new branch to grow toward an open space than toward another branch. Also, it is generally better for growth to be directed toward the outside of the plant rather than toward its interior. Try to eliminate branches that cross and touch one another. Crossing branches can suffer injury by rubbing together and are usually unattractive, especially in deciduous plants out of leaf.

Special kinds of pruning

The general information already presented will guide you through most ordinary pruning situations, but for particular types of plants or for particular landscape situations there are additional guidelines.

Pruning for flower production

Flowering shrubs will bloom either from new growth or from old wood, depending on the plant species. Before you prune a flowering shrub, determine which sort of growth bears flowers so that you avoid inadvertently cutting out stems that would give you a flower display.

Most spring-flowering shrubs bloom from wood they formed during the year before. Wait until they have finished flowering before pruning these plants (or do some pruning by taking cut flowers while they are in bud or bloom); growth that the shrubs make after flowering will provide blooms for the next year.

Most summer-flowering shrubs bloom on growth they made during the spring of the same year. These are the shrubs you can prune during the winter dormant season without sacrificing bloom.

Some shrubs bloom twice, first from old wood in the spring, later on new growth in summer. The critical clue is seeing whether the first flowers come on old or new growth.

Pruning for specific landscape uses

Many plants are adaptable enough to do landscape jobs not conventionally associated with them. Many sprawling shrubs or vines (climbing roses, *Bougainvillea,* and *Xylosma,* for instance) can easily be made into good ground covers by suppressing vertical growth and pegging down horizontal branches (use pieces of wire bent into hairpin shapes). California pepper, ordinarily considered a tree, makes a very fine clipped hedge. Sturdily upright Japanese black pine may be trained to cascade.

If your planting space is narrow, consider training an espalier against a wall or fence (see pages 124–125). Espaliers need sturdy supports and frequent tying, pinching, and pruning. The essential operations are directing branches where you want them and suppressing other branches that interfere with the desired effect.

Standards, a popular novelty, are plants shaped to resemble small trees. Sometimes the crown portion of the "tree" is grafted onto the "trunk"; in other cases careful pruning develops the tree form. Even vines can be staked and pruned, or trained over wire and wood forms to become standards.

Pollarding and pleaching are specialized growth training methods. Pollarding is used to keep naturally spreading trees in bounds — yearly drastic cutting eventually forms large knobby stubs from which long shoots grow each spring. Pleaching involves interweaving branches together to form a hedge or arbor, resulting in a neat, rather formal pattern.

Pruning conifers

These evergreens fall into two broad classes: those with branches radiating out from the trunk in whorls and those that sprout branches in a random fashion. Spruce, fir, and most pines are examples of the whorl type; arborvitae, hemlock, juniper, and taxus (yew) are examples of random-branching conifers. Conifers normally don't require pruning. But if a conifer must be pruned, it will respond well if you follow a few rules. You should selectively prune back to another branch or bud on the whorl-branching types; generally, you can shear the random-branching plants.

On the whorl-branching types, you can induce branching and thicken the tip growth by pinching back the *candles* (lighter colored new growth) about halfway.

Avoid damaging the central *leader* (the central vertical stem) on conifers unless you want to limit the height. If the central leader is damaged, you can stake one of the next lower branches vertically and train it as a new leader.

You can either slightly shorten a branch or take it off altogether. When shortening a branch don't cut below the last green growth; if you do, most species won't develop new growth from the remaining bare wood.

When some conifers grow to within a foot or so of the size you desire, cut back the new growth so that about 1 inch of it remains. This will produce enough small side branchlets to make full, dense foliage. Once this bushy growth forms at the ends of the branches, you can hold the plant to a small size year after year by shortening new growth that develops and cutting out wild shoots.

When a conifer has been damaged by cold or breakage, you may have to remove entire limbs. If this happens, it's almost impossible to restore its natural shape. But you can often make the most of this situation by trimming or training the damaged plant into an unusual sculptural form.

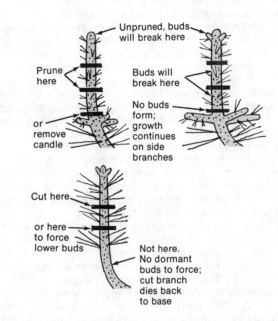

Prune whorl-branching conifers back to a branch or bud.

Trees

No distinct line separates a tree from a shrub. There are trees that reach a mature 15 feet, but some shrubs reach up to 20 feet. And some of these shrubs will serve as small trees, particularly if the lower branches are removed. Safest to say, then, is that a tree is a large, woody plant that you can stand under.

Think of a tree as having one or several trunks topped by a foliage canopy. Some trees assume that aspect readily; others go through a prolonged, shrubby youth during which they maintain branches down to ground level. In time, though, most become high enough to walk under.

Tips for selecting a tree

Because trees are the largest plants in the landscape, it is natural that they should require more years to reach mature height, or even to begin to fulfill your expectations, than other garden plants do. That fact underscores the importance of selecting just the right trees for your needs and desires. Fifteen years, for example, is a long time to wait before discovering that you've made a poor choice.

Whether you're setting out to select one free-standing tree, a grove of trees, or many trees of one kind to line out as a windbreak, realize that each kind of tree has its own virtues and limitations.

Consider these six points:

• *Climate adaptability.* First be sure that any tree you consider is noted as being successful in your western climate zone (see climate zone maps on pages 8–29). This will save you the disappointment and expense of planting one that will freeze over winter, fail for lack of enough winter cold, or succumb to the excesses of some western summers.

• *Garden adaptability.* If a tree will grow in your climate zone, read its cultural requirements and decide how well your garden can satisfy them. Don't plant a moisture-loving tree if you can't meet its water needs, even though with water it would grow splendidly in your area. In the same vein, you wouldn't want to plant a wind-sensitive tree where it would be constantly buffeted, or locate a shade-preferring type in total sun.

• *Growth rate.* Different trees grow at different rates, from racehorse fast to a snail-like slowness and all degrees between. This speed, or lack of it, can be a critical factor when you are choosing a tree to solve some garden problems. If, for example, you need a tree to screen hot sun from south-facing windows, or to block an objectionable view, you may want one that will grow fast to do the job in a hurry. On the other hand, if you are choosing a tree only for the beauty of its flowers—a deciduous magnolia, for example—you may be willing to wait a number of years before the plant assumes tree proportions. Many fast-growing trees tend to be shorter lived than slower-growing ones and are more likely to have brittle wood that is subject to storm damage (see "Longevity," on next page).

• *Root system.* A tree with a network of greedy surface roots is a poor candidate for sharing a lawn or garden area; the tree will take most of the water and nutrients. But the same tree planted at the garden's edge or along a country drive may be outstanding. Some trees grow surface roots that can lift and crack nearby pavement, a point to check out if you're choosing a tree for patio, entryway, or parking strip. And still others have roots that invade and clog sewer lines in their vicinity.

• *Maintenance.* Notice the words "messy" or "litter" in a tree's description. Those words may refer to foliage, flower, or fruit drop; and to you they may spell work if the litter gathers in a place that you want to keep neat, such as a lawn or a patio. But the same tree may pose no problem if grown toward the back of a garden or in a naturalistic setting where litter can remain where it falls.

If your region receives regular high winds or consistent annual snowfall, note the trees described as having weak or brittle wood or weak crotches. If you plant one of those, be prepared for remedial pruning to repair storm damage. And be aware that the tree's beauty may be ruined by the necessary removal of damaged limbs. Wherever heavy storms can be expected, shallow-rooted kinds with dense foliage are more likely to be uprooted when winds are high and soil soaked.

• *Pest, disease problems.* Some trees may be plagued by particular insects or diseases in part of the region to which they are adapted. Often damage may be trivial; but if the action of a particular pest or disease will spoil your enjoyment of a tree (or compel you to wage eternal battle) you would be wise to plant a less troublesome one.

• *Longevity.* There are trees you can plant for your grandchildren to enjoy, and others that will grow quickly but slide into unattractive old age while your garden is still maturing. The short-lived trees are not less desirable because of their life span, but they should be planted only where their removal won't be a blow to your overall garden design. Many attractive flowering trees will run their course in about 20 years but can be replaced by another of the same kind to fill the gap again within a few years. But if you want to screen out the neighboring high rise for a long time, look for a tree that's likely to last as long as you will.

Planting and caring for young trees

After you select a tree that seems promising for your garden, you can further ensure its success by the way you plant it and care for it.

Some trees are sold with roots bare (no soil) from late fall through early spring (dormant season). Many of these trees plus others are sold in containers or as balled-and-burlapped plants all year. Planting guidelines for all three types of nursery stock appear on pages 44–47.

Even drought-tolerant trees will need routine watering for the first one or two years after planting; their roots need that time to grow large enough to carry the tree through dry periods. For all trees, then, follow a regular watering schedule during the first several years. See water advice on pages 48–52 for indications of how often you might water, based upon your climate and soil type.

A newly planted tree's trunk benefits from protection during at least the first year after planting. Drying winds, scorching sun, winter freezes (in some zones), and physical damage by chewing dogs, scratching cats, and careless lawn mowers can injure tender bark, sometimes producing anything from growth setback to death. As a simple precaution, wrap the trunk with burlap (loosely tied) or a manufactured tree trunk wrapping. If chewing

Protect newly planted tree by wrapping the trunk with tree tape or burlap (left) or encircling with cylinder of woven wire (right).

animals are likely to be a problem, you can also encircle the lower portion of trunk with a cylinder of woven wire.

Whenever you encircle a trunk or limb with a nonexpandable material (for staking or for protection) be sure to check the tie several times each growing season. Before you might expect it, a tree can grow enough that the tie will constrict the trunk to the point of permanently damaging it.

If possible, it is better to leave a newly planted tree unstaked; the trunk will strengthen and thicken faster without additional support. But often a new tree will be top-heavy enough to topple in a strong wind if it's not supported. For such trees, staking as shown in the diagram (below) has proven best in University of California experiments. This technique permits some flexibility in wind—the flexibility helping to promote a stronger trunk—but not so much that the tree would fall or tilt.

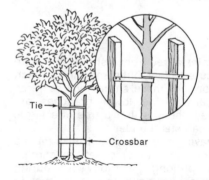

Staking holds a tree upright but leaves it flexible. Crossbar at the bottom braces two stakes; tie (looped around the trunk just below the branches) lets the tree bend a bit in the wind.

Tie

Crossbar

Young trees increase in trunk girth faster if lower branches are allowed to remain on the trunk for several years. On such trees, leave the lower trunk branches on. Cut them back only if they show signs of growing at the expense of higher branches that you intend for the tree's permanent framework. Then in three to five years you can remove the unwanted lower branches from the trunk.

• *Deciduous trees for summer shade:*

Albizia julibrissin	Morus alba
Fraxinus velutina 'Modesto'	Pistacia chinensis
	Platanus acerifolia
Gleditsia triacanthos inermis	Quercus coccinea
	Zelkova serrata

• *Evergreen trees for all-year shade:*

Cinnamomum camphora	Magnolia grandiflora
Eucalyptus cornuta	Pittosporum undulatum
Ficus macrophylla	Quercus ilex
Ficus rubiginosa	Schinus terebinthifolius

Shrubs

Shrubs range from ankle-height Lilliputians to multi-stemmed Gullivers you can actually walk under. Forms run from spreading to upright, stiff to vinelike. Many produce colorful flowers, fruit, or both, but some do neither to a conspicuous degree. Among the latter type are the familiar junipers, yews, and other conifer relatives. On the other hand, roses, camellias, and rhododendrons have been cultivated so long for their beautiful blossoms that one automatically thinks of them as "flowers" in the same sense as petunias and marigolds, yet they are indisputably shrubby.

Shrubs are *woody* plants that usually increase in size by growing new wood from older wood as well as by extending new stems from the plant's base. Unless specially trained, a shrub will have several to many stems that rise from ground level or close to it (in contrast to the typical tree that grows a single trunk, rising from the ground, and branches out higher up).

Whether a foot-high shrublet or a 15-foot shrub-tree, a shrub is planted to occupy a more or less permanent place in the garden. This permanence is perhaps a shrub's greatest virtue: after planting you can expect years of enjoyment with no more effort than routine garden care plus occasional shaping or guidance. That is not to say you must never move or discard a shrub. But it means that you have no *need* to replant each year, as with annuals, or periodically dig up and rejuvenate as with perennials.

Choosing a shrub

In times past, most homeowners sought out bulky shrubs for "foundation plantings," to provide transition from house to garden by hiding the unattractive high house foundation. But with the disappearance of high foundations in many modern homes, shrubs have taken on new landscape lives. Because they encompass such a diversity of size, shape, and appearance, shrubs naturally can perform a great range of landscape functions well. In fact, it would be no trick at all to plant a garden with nothing but shrubs in variety and achieve an ever-changing, always interesting landscape.

Some shrubs grow slowly, taking many years to achieve the beauty of maturity; their attractiveness makes them worth waiting for, but wait you must. Others can be found that will grow rapidly to a satisfying size and beauty but will pass into a less attractive old age (or even just die) in 10 to 15 years. The wise garden planner can take advantage of both sorts. While the slower shrubs are building their bulk and character, the faster but less permanent sorts can fill in the blank spaces with their own worthwhile forms and colors; when the fast-maturing ones begin to go downhill, the slower sorts will be well on their way to filling their intended roles. And the fast-growing but short-lived ones can always be counted on to function in the manner of long-term perennials whenever there is garden space for them.

When you set out to choose shrubs for your garden, don't be guided solely by flashy color or sentimental attachment. Also keep in mind the following basic points:

• *Adaptability.* No shrub will satisfy you unless it is suited to your climate, your garden soil, and the environment your garden provides. First, then, be sure that the shrubs you're considering are recommended for your western climate zone. Next check the plant description to determine whether your garden can meet the plant's additional requirements. You may have to face the fact that the lilacs of your childhood just won't make it where you are now. It's better to have a beautiful memory rather than a disappointing reality.

• *Plant size.* If you have a space for a 4 by 4-foot plant but install one that will reach 12 feet in all directions, you're bound to be unhappy in time. The too-large plant will overbalance the landscape and crowd its neighbors. Then you'll probably feel compelled to cut it back to fit, usually destroying much of its natural beauty and possibly interfering with its potential flower or fruit display. Remember that the most attractive shrubs (except those intended for topiary or formally sheared hedges) are those that are allowed to reach their natural size without severe restriction. Choose, then, according to the space you have available.

• *Growth rate.* Hand in hand with knowledge of a plant's ultimate size should go the realization of how fast it will get there. Slow growth is the price you will have to pay for some of the most desirable shrubs, so place those plants where their slowness will be no detriment to your plans. A slow-growing windbreak or view screen, for example, will only be a source of great frustration as it inches its way upward; fast shrubs selected for these purposes obviously would provide satisfaction much sooner.

• *Texture.* The individual leaf texture, as well as the texture of many leaves in mass, varies almost as much as do the shrubs themselves—from the minute needles and scales of junipers or tiny boxwood leaves to the foot-and-a-half fans of Japanese aralias. Shiny, dull, hairy or fuzzy, smooth, quilted—these qualities of individual leaf texture combined with size and shape of leaf give a plant its character. You can do much to highlight a shrub's inherent beauty if you consider how its foliage texture will relate to that of its neighboring plants, plus how its texture would relate to any structure it is to complement. Many bold-leafed plants of different kinds grouped together fight with one another for visual dominance; the effect is assertive but confused, and no one plant is displayed to full advantage. Conversely, a variety of finely textured, small-leafed shrubs together produces an indistinct landscape where nothing is highlighted. If you capitalize on *differences* in texture—whether large leaves against small (or vice versa) or fine-textured foliage against broad and stiff—the beauty of the individual plants will have a chance to show off.

Planting shrubs

Nurseries sell shrubs in containers, in bare root form during the dormant season, and sometimes balled and burlapped. Full planting instructions for all three sorts appear under "Planting techniques" on pages 44–47.

• *These shrubs have edible fruit:*

Blueberry	Kumquat (see *Citrus*)
Carissa grandiflora	Peach (genetic dwarfs)
Currant	Psidium
Feijoa sellowiana	Punica granatum

• *Shrubs that have bold or tropical-appearing foliage:*

Aralia
Dombeya
Eriobotrya deflexa
Fatsia japonica
Ficus lyrata
Mahonia bealei
Mahonia lomariifolia

Melianthus major
Philodendron
  (arborescent types)
Schefflera
Trevesia
Tupidanthus calyptratus
Yucca

• *Deciduous shrubs with attractive branches in winter:*

Amelanchier
Cornus alba 'Sibirica'
Cornus sanguinea
Cornus stolonifera
Chaenomeles 'Contorta'
Corylopsis
Corylus avellana 'Contorta'

Euonymus alata
Kolkwitzia amabilis
Rosa sericea
  pteracantha
Salix purpurea
Vaccinium parvifolium

Perennials

Perennials are as diverse an assortment of plants as you'll find under one collective heading, yet they have this in common: none are actually woody as shrubs are, but all do live from year to year as annuals do not. Typically, a perennial has one blooming season each year, from as brief as a week to more than a month long. After blooming the plant may put on new growth for the next year; it might die down and virtually disappear until the time is right, some months later, for growth to resume; or it may retain much the same appearance throughout the year. Some perennials store away reserve food for the next season in specialized underground tissues such as corms, tubers, rhizomes, fleshy roots, and bulbs; these plants are a cohesive enough group that they are discussed separately under "Bulbs" on pages 75–77.

Many of the popular perennials are grown for flower beauty, and any attractive foliage is just an added bonus. A smaller group of perennials — artemisias, for example—are grown for foliage alone, the flowers being inconsequential or even a liability. Some perennials have evergreen foliage and are attractive throughout the year.

Garden use

At one time perennials were considered plants to be grouped together in the perennial border, a garden fashion legacy from Edwardian England. Without question, perennial borders can be beautiful, but they require careful planning and a great deal of maintenance. More and more, perennials are being evaluated on individual rather than collective merits and used as individuals combined with other kinds of plants in the landscape.

Like annuals, perennials provide color masses but differ in that they will bloom several years in a row without having to be dug up and replanted. In that respect they fall between annuals and flowering shrubs: more permanent than annuals, less permanent than flowering shrubs. In fact, their semipermanence is one distinct selling point. You can leave perennials in place for several years with little maintenance beyond annual cleanup, some fertilizing, and routine watering; but if you want to change the landscape they are easy to dig up and replant—much more so than the average flowering shrub.

Planting and care

Most perennials give top performance in good soil. Because you expect them to remain in place for several years after planting, it pays to prepare the soil well before you set them out. Dig liberal amounts of organic material into the soil; use about 25 percent by volume of amend-

ments such as ground bark, peat moss, compost, or aged manure. At the same time you can incorporate a fertilizer that is high in phosophorus and potash into the area to be planted. If you can, prepare the soil at least a few weeks prior to planting so that soil will have a chance to settle.

Care of established perennials

Most perennials begin their yearly growth cycle in spring, following winter dormancy, and will benefit from application of a complete fertilizer at that time. Use a fertilizer with a moderate amount of nitrogen—5-10-10 or 6-10-4, for example. Fertilizer marketed as "bulb food" will be suitable. The fertilizer will provide a boost to get the plants going through the bloom season. Then just after flowering, give plants another application of fertilizer so they will put on good growth that will produce the next year's flowers. Use amounts of fertilizer specified on the product label.

Routine watering during the growth and bloom period will satisfy most perennials except those noted in the Western Plant Encyclopedia as preferring dry or unusually wet soil.

After flowering has finished, it is a good idea to remove the old blossoms to prevent the plant's energy from going into seed production. Remove only old flowers and stems; leave most of the foliage for the time being, because the leaves will help the plant manufacture food to store for the next year's growth.

Later in the season (usually in fall) when old leaves and flower stalks have dried, you should clean up the perennial plantings. Removing dead growth minimizes the carry-over from year to year of certain diseases and eliminates hiding and breeding places for various insects, snails, and slugs.

Where winters are cold, many gardeners routinely mulch their perennials to protect them from alternate freezing and thawing. Where soil is reliably frozen all winter and a good snow cover is virtually guaranteed, mulching is not as necessary because plants will remain dormant until spring finally arrives. But where cold snowy days can trade back and forth with sunny and warmer ones during a winter, a mulch will ensure that plants stay cold and inactive. After the ground first freezes, apply a lightweight mulch that won't pack down into a sodden mass. Straw is one popular choice; evergreen boughs are good where available.

Digging, dividing, and replanting

Some perennials—peonies, for example—will thrive almost indefinitely in one location. But more typically a perennial will grow into such a thick clump that performance declines because plants are crowded. When plants become crowded, dig the clump during its dormant period (sometime after bloom season), separate it into individual plants or smaller clumps, and replant in soil that you have prepared by adding organic matter and fertilizer (see "Division" on pages 37–38). If you plan to replant in the same soil, heel-in (see Glossary) the perennials you will replant while you get the soil into shape. Set the divisions in a shady location, their roots covered with sand, sawdust, ground bark—any material that you can moisten to keep roots moist and plump but which will not remain saturated.

- *Perennials that are grown for foliage:*

Alocasia	Aspidistra elatior
Artemisia	Gunnera
Artichoke	Hosta
Asarum caudatum	Phormium tenax
Asparagus (ornamental)	

- *Tall-growing perennials for background, accent:*

Aster novae-angliae	Hibiscus moscheutos
Delphinium elatum	Kniphofia uvaria
Eremurus	Romneya coulteri
Helianthus	Solidago

Bulbs and bulblike plants

Bulbs are a very specialized group of perennial plants. Whether true bulbs or other bulblike plants, they all hold a reserve of nutrients in a thickened underground storage organ. This reserve makes the bulb you purchase in fall an almost sure thing for spring bloom: all the nutrients the plant needs to complete its life cycle are in storage, waiting for the right combination of moisture and soil temperature to trigger the cycle's beginning.

By popular usage, a number of plants other than true bulbs are called "bulbs" (see page 77); true bulbs, corms, tubers, tuberous roots, and rhizomes share many characteristics and requirements that permit generalization.

Planting

The bulb you purchase from a nursery or commercial specialist may be a sure first-season performer, but performance in subsequent years will depend on the care you give it. This care begins with the soil.

Most bulbs prefer soil that drains well yet is water retentive. These requirements may sound mutually exclusive, but they are not. Water should pass through the soil so it doesn't remain saturated, yet enough water should stay in the soil to keep roots healthy (see "Soils," page 33). You achieve this balance by adding organic matter to your soil; organic matter will improve drainage in a heavy soil, but will increase water retention in sand. Soil that will grow good annuals should work well.

In planting true bulbs and most corms, the rule of thumb says to dig a hole about three times as deep as the bulb's greatest diameter. (To determine planting depths for the other "bulbs," see individual plant descriptions in the Western Plant Encyclopedia in the back of the book.) A tablespoonful of bone meal or superphosphate mixed into the bottom of the planting hole will help the bulb replenish its nutrient supply after flowering. If you will be planting many bulbs in one bed, it may be easier to dig a trench or to excavate the bed to the desirable planting depth than to dig numerous individual holes. When all the bulbs are set in place and covered with soil, soak the area thoroughly. In some regions the initial watering, in addition to rain, will supply sufficient moisture for the bulbs until their leaves poke above the soil surface. However, if you live in an arid climate or have an unusually dry winter, you will have to give the bulbs periodic soakings throughout the winter and into the blooming season. Summer flowering bulbs will require watering at least until they finish blooming.

The roots of bulbs grow deep in the soil—deeper than the depth at which you planted— so that water, to do them any good, must penetrate deep enough to reach the roots. (See "Watering" on pages 48–52 for more specific advice on watering practices.) A mulch will help conserve soil moisture and in hot, dry regions will also hold down soil temperature. It will also continue to suppress weeds after the bulb foliage has disappeared.

After flowering

After a bulb has finished flowering, its supply of stored nutrients is depleted. To perform well the next year it must replenish the supply. For that reason it is vital to leave the foliage on the plant, even if it begins to look unsightly, until it has yellowed and can be pulled off easily. The foliage continues to manufacture food for the plant (see "How plants grow," page 32); cutting it off prematurely amounts to cutting off next year's blossoms—or at least reducing their quantity and quality.

Also to encourage the next year's flowering, apply a complete fertilizer. Some nurseries carry "bulb food" with the proper nutrient formulation. The same fertilizer you use after bloom should be applied again in spring just as the bulbs begin their growth spurt.

Container culture

Most bulbs are quite easy to grow in containers, and containers give you great flexibility in changing garden color schemes and flower placement. Not only can you change

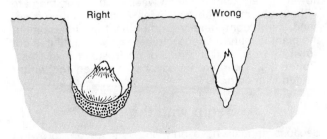

Plant bulbs in U-shaped holes or trenches, in contact with soil containing some bone meal or superphosphate.

the scene by shifting pots of blooming bulbs; you also can take them off-stage when bloom is finished.

A number of bulbs will grow permanently in containers with occasional repotting and soil rejuvenation plus applications of fertilizer (see list). The general advice under "Container gardening" (pages 79–81) plus tips under individual descriptions in the Western Plant Encyclopedia will cover their container culture over a long period of time.

In addition, many favorite spring flowering sorts—daffodils, tulips, crocuses, Dutch irises, hyacinths, scillas, and freesias—will give a good show in pots for their first bloom season, after which you can plant them out in their intended garden spots.

For spring flowering bulbs, a suitable container soil mixture contains equal parts good garden soil (loam), coarse sand, and organic matter such as peat moss, leaf mold, compost, or ground bark. Select top quality bulbs for container culture; they will give the best flower display and will recuperate most quickly when planted out in the garden after their season in containers.

Plant spring flowering bulbs so that they nearly touch one another, their tips level with the soil surface (which should be about one inch below the container's rim to facilitate watering). Small bulbs—crocuses and scillas, for example—should be planted slightly deeper, with tips just beneath the soil. Water thoroughly after you have filled soil in around the bulbs.

Since you aren't planting these bulbs in the cool soil depths they prefer, you must somehow make up for this deficiency. The objective is to give the bulbs a good winter chill without freezing them. Where winters are cool (Climate Zones 1–7), placing the pots full of bulbs in an unheated room or burying them to the pots' rims in soil covered with mulch on the north side of a house may be sufficient. Where winters are warm (Climate Zones 8–24), you can choose from among these options to give bulbs the winter chill they prefer:
• Bury pots in a foot-deep trench and cover with 6 to 8 inches of moist wood shavings, sawdust, sand, peat moss, or even earth.

• Place pots in a shaded cold frame and bury as above.
• Set pots in a deep basket or box, cover as above, and put pots in the coolest (shadiest) garden spot; keep covering moist to maintain coolness.

After 8 to 10 weeks, uncover (carefully) a pot or two and check for signs of growth—roots emerging from the drainage hole or shoots breaking through the potting soil. When you see such signs, lift pots from their trench, basket, or cold frame and bring into a shaded location without direct sunlight. If shoots are already showing they will be white or palest green; leave these pots in the shady spot until the shoots begin to take on a normal green color, then move into the chosen garden location.

When potted bulbs have finished blooming, continue watering and fertilizing until foliage turns yellow. When foliage has browned you can remove bulbs from the pots and plant them out in the garden. Bloom the following spring usually will not be up to par but should return to normal in the following years, given good soil and some fertilizer.

• *Favorite bulbs for naturalizing:*

Brodiaea	Cyclamen
Chionodoxa	Leucojum
Colchicum autumnale	Muscari
Convallaria majalis	Narcissus
Crocus	Scilla

• *Tall-growing bulbs for background, accent:*

Agapanthus orientalis	Iris pseudacorus
Canna	Iris (Spuria hybrids)
Dahlia	Lilium (some hybrids)
Fritillaria imperialis	Watsonia
Gladiolus	Zantedeschia aethiopica

• *These bulbs will grow permanently in containers:*

Achimenes	Hippeastrum
Begonia (tuberous)	Oxalis
Caladium bicolor	Sinningia speciosa
Clivia miniata	Vallota speciosa
Haemanthus katharinae	Veltheimia viridifolia

Annuals

Think of annuals as the real workhorses of the garden. Their lives are short— within one growing season they germinate from seed, grow and bloom, form seeds, die—but that brief lifetime is almost incredibly productive. The majority of flowering shrubs and perennials have one flowering period during a few weeks of the year, then are without bloom for the remainder. Annuals, on the other hand, can bloom literally for months, from the moment the plant is mature enough to bear flowers until it is cut down by frost. And in areas of no frosts or mild frosts (Zones 8–24) certain annuals can brighten the winter garden with color.

Begin with the soil

Because annuals have only one year (or one growing season) in which to perform, you have to make certain provisions for them in advance. Soil preparation is the most important factor in successful annual growing. Unlike trees, shrubs, and some perennials, around which you can continue to improve soil for years while they are in the ground, annuals must make do with the soil they are planted in during their months in your garden.

Essential soil properties are good drainage and porosity. Organic soil amendments such as ground bark, peat moss, aged animal manures, and compost dug into the soil prior to planting will help create a good environment for annual roots. They will improve moisture retention, help prevent rapid leaching of nutrients, and improve soil structure so that roots will grow freely. Whether you plan to sow seeds or set out small plants, first refer to soil preparation advice on pages 35–36 under "Seeds in the open ground."

If you can, prepare your soil a month or more in advance of the time you intend to sow seeds or set out plants. Advance preparation gives soil time to "mellow"

"Bulb" types defined

The word "bulb" is used in everyday language to cover several different types of plants; all of them have swollen or thickened storage organs which produce leaves, stems, flowers, and roots. The accompanying drawings show the various "bulbs" and clarify the differences between them.

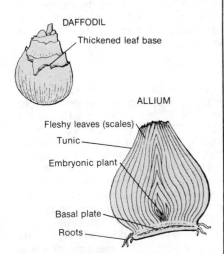

DAFFODIL
- Thickened leaf base

ALLIUM
- Fleshy leaves (scales)
- Tunic
- Embryonic plant
- Basal plate
- Roots

TRUE BULB. *Short underground stem (on solid basal plate) surrounded by fleshy leaves (scales) that protect, store food for use by embryonic plant. Outer scales dry, form papery covering (tunic).*

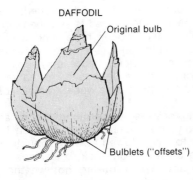

DAFFODIL
- Original bulb
- Bulblets ("offsets")

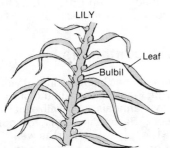

LILY
- Leaf
- Bulbil

BULBLET *(often called "offset"). The new bulb is formed from a lateral bud on the basal plate. The old bulb may die or, like daffodils, keep coming back each year; bulblets can be separated and replanted. Bulbils are small bulbs produced in axils of leaves, flowers, stems.*

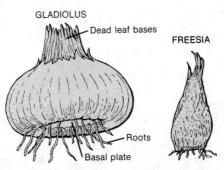

GLADIOLUS
- Dead leaf bases

FREESIA
- Roots
- Basal plate

CORM. *Swollen underground portions of stem—usually broader than high—covered with one or more dead leaf bases; has basal plate. Food storage is in the solid tissue. New corms formed from axillary buds on top of old corm during growing season.*

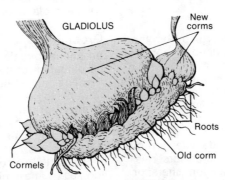

GLADIOLUS
- New corms
- Roots
- Old corm
- Cormels

CORMEL. *While one to several big new corms are forming, smaller ones (cormels) are also being produced from the axillary buds on top of the old corm. The cormels will take two to three years to bloom, while larger corms will blossom the following year.*

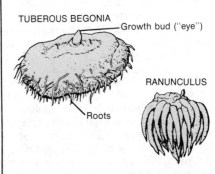

TUBEROUS BEGONIA
- Growth bud ("eye")
- Roots

RANUNCULUS

TUBER. *Short, fat, underground stem is for food storage; it is either flattened, rounded, or irregular. Does not creep like a rhizome. Usually knobby with growth buds (eyes)—each a scalelike leaf with bud in its axil. Divide large tubers like rhizomes.*

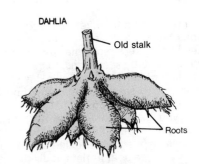

DAHLIA
- Old stalk
- Roots

TUBEROUS ROOTS. *Actually roots (not stems), with thickened food storage structures. They do not bear growth buds as do tubers, but can be divided in the same way as rhizomes and tubers—cut sections with part of old stem base attached. Growth buds are in old stem.*

RHIZOME. *A thickened stem for food storage that grows horizontally along or under the surface of the soil. Foliage, roots, and flower stalks grow from buds on the rhizome. Cut sections of the rhizome with growth buds for new plants.*

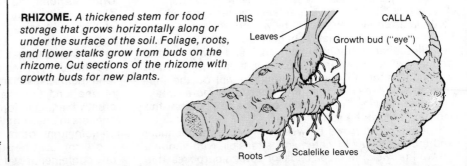

IRIS
- Leaves
- Roots
- Scalelike leaves

CALLA
- Growth bud ("eye")

after addition of amendments and gives the gardener a chance to eliminate many weeds that will germinate before the annuals are set out.

Time the planting

In the mild-winter zones (8 to 24) there are two principal times of year for planting annuals: early spring for those that bloom in late spring, summer, and fall; and late summer or fall for the winter and early spring bloomers. Gardeners in cold-winter zones have only the early spring planting time. Both planting times share moderately cool weather and will proceed into the sort of weather that favors development of annuals.

The summer flowering annuals need to establish roots before really warm days come along to hasten growth. If planted when weather is already warm or even hot, annuals will form flowers while still young and before roots are established; the result is stunted plants that rarely attain full size or productivity. You gain no advantage by setting out plants too early, either. Annuals planted too early run the risk of frost damage, or will simply sit there in cold soil and atmosphere without growing until the days begin to get longer and warmer.

Winter-blooming annuals should be set out while days are still warm enough for good plant growth but nights are lengthening. Winter annuals set out while days are longer than nights may perish or rush to maturity as stunted, poorly established plants.

How to plant

Annuals begin their year as seedlings emerging from the soil. Many gardeners prefer to sow their own annual seeds for the simple pleasure it brings, to try out new strains sold by seed firms, to get a jump on the season by starting plants indoors while it is still too cold outside to plant, or to save money. You'll find guidelines for seed sowing on pages 35–37.

If you have neither time nor desire to raise annuals from seed, you'll find it easy to buy a wide selection of popular types and varieties already started at nurseries. They may be sold in flats, individual small containers, or in small group containers. Handling of these plants is discussed on pages 46–47.

Care after planting

For any annual, the secret to success after planting is to keep plants growing steadily. The key activities which help plants grow are watering, feeding, and grooming.

Watering, alone, assures steady growth if you attend to it faithfully. The objective is to keep water supplied before plants show they need it by wilting, yet not to over-water (soggy soil restricts root development). Let the top inch (less than an inch for very small and newly planted annuals) of soil dry before you water, then apply enough water to penetrate deeply. Sprinkling will do the job, though spray may topple the taller and more weak-stemmed flowers. Try to sprinkle in the early part of the morning before the sun is high.

Irrigation in furrows between rows is an economical and thorough way to water, and is feasible with annuals grown in rows or in block beds for cutting purposes. It is sometimes possible to hoe up a shallow dike around a small bed of annuals and irrigate by flooding. Probably the easiest way to water is by hand-held hose, but to avoid stooping, washing out young plants, or messy splashing, use a water breaker or bubbler (one of several devices to break the force of water issuing from a hose) mounted on a suitable straight or curved extension.

But no matter how you water, a mulch of some sort of organic material will prolong intervals between waterings by preventing soil from drying as rapidly as it would if no mulch were covering it. In addition, mulches will prevent the soil surface from crusting, so that water and air penetration will improve.

Fertilizers

If you mixed a fertilizer into the soil before you set out your annuals, you probably supplied enough nutrients to last the plants at least half their growing season. An application of complete fertilizer after bloom is underway will tide them through their season in the cold-winter zones. Where winters are warmer, another application in late summer could be advantageous. If you did not add fertilizer to your soil before planting annuals, give them an application of a complete fertilizer (with higher percentage of nitrogen) about a month after planting, then follow with a second (and possibly third) application. Timed release fertilizers release their nitrogen, in particular, over a much longer period than the average complete fertilizer, so they don't have to be applied as often.

Liquid fertilizers may be convenient if you don't have a large planting. Monthly applications of regular-strength dilution or applications every 2 weeks at half strength will keep plants growing steadily.

Grooming

An annual plant's life objective is to produce seeds for perpetuation of the species. Once seed is set, the plant hardens into maturity and produces fewer and fewer flowers. To keep bloom coming all season long, you have to interrupt nature's seed producing process by removing old blossoms before they can begin seed formation. This grooming need be no more than a weekly removal of faded blooms.

Ordinarily, removing flowers will prolong bloom as long as you have given your annuals regular attention. If, however, they appear to have slowed flower production and begun hardening off too soon, look to any one of these factors: inadequate water during hot weather, depletion of nutrients, or cold or even frosty nights that signal to the plant the end of a growing season.

Annuals in containers

Until this point, the assumption has been made that you'll plant annuals in the ground. Planting them in the ground still is traditional, but most annuals also will excel as splashy container subjects. Basic directions for container plants (pages 79–81) apply to annuals as well.

Either in pots and tubs or in hanging baskets, annuals lend themselves to mass plantings. You can group plants of one kind together for real color impact or let your creative imagination run wild by combining different annuals in one container. There are no real guidelines for combinations other than personal preference and trial and error. Just be sure that all annuals you combine in one container are supposed to bloom at the same time of year; otherwise the mass effect will be diminished and the later-flowering ones will probably not develop well.

- *Short annuals for foreground planting:*

Ageratum houstonianum
Catharanthus roseus (dwarf varieties)
Celosia (dwarf varieties)
Lobelia erinus
Lobularia maritima
Nemesia strumosa 'Nana Compacta'
Petunia hybrida (dwarf strains)
Phlox drummondii (dwarf strains)
Portulaca
Salvia splendens (dwarf varieties)
Tagetes (dwarf strains)
Verbena
Viola wittrockiana
Zinnia (dwarf strains)

- *Twenty all-time favorite annuals:*

Aster (Callistephus)
Bachelor's button (Centaurea cyanus)
Calendula
Cockscomb (Celosia)
Coreopsis
Cosmos
Impatiens
Lobelia
Marigold (Tagetes)
Nasturtium (Tropaeolum)
Pansy (Viola wittrockiana)
Petunia
Phlox
Rose moss (Portulaca)
Scabiosa
Scarlet sage (Salvia splendens)
Snapdragon (Antirrhinum)
Stock (Matthiola)
Sweet alyssum (Lobularia maritima)
Zinnia

Container gardening indoors and out

Generally speaking, container plants require more attention than plants growing in the ground but their potential advantages may outweigh the extra care demanded. For the gardener with only a balcony or a paved patio, plants in containers are the only way to have a garden at all. And even when a garden is available, container plants can be skillfully used to provide seasonal flowers that you bring on stage when colorful and remove to an unobtrusive area when bloom is over. Container culture offers you a chance to enjoy plants that aren't entirely suited to your garden conditions. You can grow acid-soil plants in regions where native soil is alkaline, and plants that demand fast drainage when your garden soil is clay. Plants too tender for your winter temperatures can be moved to shelter when cold weather comes.

The extra attention container plants need can be expressed in three categories: soil preparation, watering, and fertilizing.

Soil mixes for containers

Container plants need a soil that is porous and well-drained, yet moisture retentive. Roots must be able to grow easily throughout the soil, drainage must be fast enough that roots aren't suffocated in soggy soil, and the soil should retain enough moisture that you won't have to water the plants constantly.

Even the best garden soils fail to satisfy container soil requirements. In containers, garden soil inevitably forms a dense mass that roots can't penetrate easily, and it remains soggy for too long after watering.

Consequently, "potting mixes" have long been favored for container plants. Originally, the gardener formulated his own potting mix from garden soil, organic matter, and perhaps sand. Now, the task is simpler: you can go to a nursery or garden supply center and buy prepared potting mixes that you can use right out of the bag. The formulations may differ somewhat from brand to brand, but all ensure porosity, good drainage, and moisture retention.

Only if you plan a large-scale potting operation might the prepared potting mixes be impractical because of cost. If this is the case—or if you simply prefer to do it yourself—you can formulate your own potting mixture. There are countless possible formulations, but all have this in common: they are a combination of organic material (peat moss, bark, leaf mold, compost, etc.) and mineral matter (soil, sand, vermiculite, or perlite) combined in proportions to yield the desired porosity, drainage, and moisture retention. A tried-and-true basic mix consists of 2 parts good garden soil (but not a heavy clay soil), 1 part perlite (or 1 part river or builder's sand if no perlite is available), and 1 part peat moss or other form of organic matter. For the popular plants that prefer acid soil—rhododendrons and azaleas, camellias, heathers—use a mix that contains at least half organic matter (peat moss, leaf mold, or finely ground bark).

If you understand its limitations, a good medium you mix yourself for container plants is the U.C. Mix developed at the University of California. It contains no soil, so there is less danger from soil-borne fungi or bacteria; but it is so porous that it will dry out more rapidly than the average mix. The porosity allows nutrients to leach through quickly, necessitating frequent fertilizer applications. The U.C. Mix in any of its variations contains fine sand combined with peat moss, sawdust, or ground bark. Similar in purpose are the Cornell mixes, which employ peat moss and fine vermiculite and which are especially useful where light weight is essential. Instructions may be found in *Gardening in Containers* (Lane Publishing Co., Menlo Park, CA); and, in more detail, in *Plantation Propagation*, by Hudson Hartman and Dale Kester (Prentice-Hall, Inc., Englewood Cliffs, NJ).

Watering

Water container plants not according to a calendar schedule, but according to what your inspection of the soil indicates. Unlike plants in the ground that can survive some drought because their roots penetrate deep into the soil, container plants have dense and compact root systems that are wholly dependent for moisture on you and rainfall. In hot, dry, windy weather you may need to water actively growing plants more than once a day; when weather is cool, still, and overcast, or if plants are semidormant, you may get by with weekly (or even less frequent) watering. Test the soil with your fingers: if it's dry beneath the surface, it's time to water. To water thoroughly, be sure to apply water on the entire soil surface until you see it flowing out the drainage holes. This will guarantee moistening the entire soil mass, and also will prevent any potentially harmful salts from accumulating in the soil.

Note: If water comes out the drainage hole too fast, check to see if water is just running down the inside of the container and not moistening the soil. If the root ball has become too dry it can shrink away from the sides of the container; if that happens, water will run around the root ball without penetrating it. To correct the problem, set the container in a tub of water and soak the plant until bubbles stop rising. If that isn't practical, cork the container's drainage holes and then water the plant; remove corks after the soil is soaked.

Fertilizing

Heavy and thorough watering leaches out plant nutrients from container soils, so regular fertilizer applications are required for best plant growth. Use either liquid or dry fertilizers according to label directions. The slow-release, dry fertilizers release nutrients steadily over a period of time, so don't need to be applied as often as other fertilizers. With fertilizers, except for slow-release types, light and frequent applications will give best results. But let the plant, not a fixed schedule, be your guide. Observe its growth rate, bloom period, season of new growth production, and dormant season; then give fertilizer only at the times of year the plant needs it for growth and bloom.

Transplanting

Shift plants to larger containers when their root systems fill the containers in which they are growing; usually the first sign of this is roots protruding from drainage holes. Generally speaking, container plants should be shifted to

a slightly larger container rather than to a much larger one, since you want to keep the soil mass fairly well filled with roots (unused soil in a container can stagnate and become a haven for potentially harmful organisms). With fast-growing plants you can safely shift to a definitely larger container. And you can always put a number of small plants in a larger container; their combined root systems will occupy the total soil mass. A general guideline when moving plants to larger containers is to select a new container that will allow an inch or two of fresh soil on all sides of the root mass. If the plant's root ball appears compacted, cut it vertically with a sharp knife to encourage roots to move out into new soil in the larger container. Make at least four equally spaced cuts about ¼ to 1 inch deep, depending on root ball size.

If you have an older plant in a large container and want to maintain it in good health in that container indefinitely, you can periodically root-prune the plant. During the plant's dormant period gently turn the plant out of its container, shave off an inch or two of the outer root mass on all sides and on the bottom with a sharp knife, then replant in the same container with fresh soil mix around the outside and underneath.

To keep plant in same container, shave off an inch or two of root mass, replant in container with some fresh soil added, and water well.

House plants

Plants that you keep indoors require the same attention to soil preparation, watering, and fertilizer application as outlined for container plants in general. Container soil for house plants, however, should be composed entirely of sterile materials, as are the prepared potting soil mixes and all U.C. Mixes (page 79). If you include garden soil, sterilize it with heat or a chemical soil sterilizer. Potentially harmful organisms in garden soils pose a great threat to plant health when confined with the roots in a limited soil mass and in the warmth and low light level of a home. Be sure to plant in containers that have holes or spaces for water to drain through.

Plants in the home usually receive their only light through a window, so care in plant placement is needed. Give them good *light* but avoid the searing sun that comes through south and west windows. In those exposures, set plants back from the windows or moderate sunlight with thin curtains. Plants that make a big flower display generally require more light than plants you grow for foliage alone.

Cut into the root ball (1) of a pot-bound plant to loosen soil mass. Move plant into a new container, allowing inch or two of fresh soil all around (2). Firm the soil (3) and water (4).

Low humidity is the bane of most house plants, and low humidity goes hand-in-hand with heated rooms. Best places for plants are the cooler spots around the house (but areas with adequate light); the higher humidity in bathrooms and kitchens favors growth. Avoid at all costs locating plants near hot air registers.

Rain water is best for house plants, but few people have the time or inclination to collect it and rely, instead, on water that flows from the tap. Usually tap water is satisfactory unless it contains quantities of harmful salts or is artificially softened with sodium. If your house water is softened, draw your water for house plants from an outside tap. If you are compelled to use softened water or water that contains alkaline salts, give your house plants complete leachings about once a month. Thoroughly flush water through the soil several times, or set the plant in the sink and let a trickle of water run through all the soil for a while.

- *Trees that can be grown in containers:*

Abies	Franklinia alatamaha
Acer circinatum	Ginkgo biloba
Acer japonicum	Lagerstroemia indica
Acer palmatum	Laurus nobilis
Amelanchier	Parrotia persica
Araucaria heterophylla	Picea
Camellia reticulata	Podocarpus
Citrus (many)	Prunus subhirtella
Crataegus phaenopyrum	pendula
Eriobotrya deflexa	Punica granatum
Fagus sylvatica varieties	Pyrus kawakamii
Ficus benjamina	Sesbania tripetii
Ficus elastica	Stewartia
Ficus retusa	

- *Some favorite plants for bonsai training:*

Abies	Ginkgo biloba
Acer buergeranum	Juniperus chinensis
Acer palmatum	sargentii
Buxus microphylla	Juniperus scopulorum
japonica	Pinus albicaulis
Camellia sasanqua	Pinus monophylla
Celtis	Pinus parviflora
Chaenomeles 'Contorta'	Pinus thunbergiana
Chamaecyparis	Pyracantha
Cotoneaster conspicuus	Sciadopitys verticillata
Cotoneaster dammeri	Taxus
Cotoneaster microphyllus	Ulmus parvifolia
Fagus sylvatica	Zelkova serrata

- *Flowering plants to grow in hanging baskets:*

Abelia floribunda	Lobelia erinus
Abutilon	Nemesia strumosa
megapotamicum	Oscularia deltoides
Achimenes	Osteospermum
Begonia (tuberous)	fruticosum
Browallia speciosa	Pelargonium peltatum
Camellia sasanqua	Petunia
Campanula (trailing	Polygonum capitatum
kinds)	Rhipsalidopsis gaertneri
Convolvulus	Rosmarinus officinalis
mauritanicus	'Prostratus'
Epiphyllum	Schlumbergera bridgesii
Fuchsia	Sedum sieboldii
Hoya	Sollya heterophylla
Ipomoea	Streptosolen jamesonii
Kalanchoe uniflora	Thunbergia
Lampranthus spectabilis	Vinca
Lantana montevidensis	

Vegetables

Raising your own vegetables can be fun, fulfilling, and economical. But for the experience to be all three, you will need to invest some time in planning and, afterward, in maintenance.

Before you take a shovel to the soil, stop to evaluate your needs. How many people do you hope to feed from your vegetable plot? It is all too easy to overplant, then work too hard to maintain a garden that ends up producing many more vegetables than you can use.

Consider what vegetables you really like and make your planting choices from them. Especially if you have a limited area in which to plant a garden, raise just the sorts that will give you a satisfactory return from the space they occupy. Melons, some squashes, and corn, for example, require large land areas relative to the amount of edible material they produce; beans, tomatoes, and zucchini, on the other hand, can overwhelm you with their bounty from a postage-stamp plot.

Planting the garden

As soon as you know which vegetables you're going to plant, you're ready to prepare the garden. Be sure to choose a sunny location away from the root competition of trees or shrubs. Then work the soil, adding organic matter, as described under "Annuals" on pages 76–79.

In planting vegetables, you usually have two options: planting seeds or setting out young plants sold by many nurseries. Seed planting is far more economical if you compute price per plant, but for a small garden the purchase of young plants will not represent any great outlay. Realize that the earliest crops usually will come on plants set out as early as possible in the growing season (see "Time the planting," page 78). Seeds started indoors just before the ground has warmed up enough in spring to start a garden will be ready to plant out at the very beginning of the growing season; nurseries often have young plants available at the earliest possible planting date. Full seed planting information appears on pages 35–37.

Warm-season or cool-season vegetables?

A distinct difference in heat requirements for growth separates warm-season from cool-season vegetables and determines which of each are best adapted to your particular climate.

Warm-season vegetables, the summer crops, need both soil warmth to germinate and long days and high temperatures (or short days and early heat)— without significant cooling at night—to form and ripen fruit. With nearly all of these vegetables, the fruit is the object of the harvest rather than the leaves, roots, or stems. The basic need of warm-weather vegetables is enough growing heat, both to keep growth moving without stopping and to ripen the crops.

Cool-season vegetables grow steadily at average temperatures 10 to 15 degrees below those needed by warm-season crops. Many of them—cabbage, for example—will endure some frost. But the most important difference between warm and cool-season vegetables is that you do not grow cool-season ones for their fruit or seeds: most of them are leaf and root crops. The few that break this rule are peas and broad beans (grown for edible seeds) and artichokes, broccoli, and cauliflower (they

Plant these vegetables for SUMMER-FALL harvest

Plant	Planted as	Planting time by climate zone 1–3	4–7	8, 9	10, 11	12, 13	14–17	18, 19	20, 21	22–24	Approx. days to harvest
Beans (lima)	Seeds*	June	May-June	Apr.-June	May-July	July-Aug.	Apr.-July	Mar.-Aug.	Mar.-Aug.	Mar.-Aug.	65–95**
Beans (snap)	Seeds*	June	May-June	Apr.-June	May-June	July-Aug.	Apr.-July	Mar.-Aug.	Mar.-Aug.	Mar.-Aug.	50–70**
Beets	Seeds*	May-June	Apr.-June	Apr.-June	Mar.-May	Sept.	Apr.-Sept.	Apr.-Sept.	Apr.-Sept.	Apr.-Sept.	46–65
Broccoli	Plants	Apr.-June	Apr.-May	Mar.&Aug.	Apr.-July	Sept.	Mar.&Aug.				50–90
Brussels sprouts	Plants	May-June	Mar.-May	Aug.	July-Aug.						80–90
Cabbage	Plants	May-June	Mar.-May	Jan.–Feb.	Mar.-May	Sept.					60–120
Carrots	Seeds	May-July	May-July	May-June	Mar.-May Aug.-Sept.	Sept.	Mar.-Apr. Sept.	Mar.-Aug.	Mar.-Aug.	Mar.-Aug.	65–75
Cauliflower	Plants	May-June	Mar.-May	July–Aug.	Mar.-May	Sept.					60–100
Celery	Plants	June-July	May		May-June						100–135
Chard	Seeds	Mar.-June	Mar.-June	Mar.-Apr. Aug.	July-Sept.	Sept.	Aug.-Sept.	Aug.-Oct.	Aug.-Oct.	Aug.-Oct.	45–60
Corn	Seeds	June	May-June	May-June	May-July	Mar.-Apr.	Mar.-July	Mar.-July	Mar.-July	Mar.-July	60–90**
Cucumbers	Seeds	Mid May-June	May-June	May-June	May-June	Aug.-Sept.	Apr.-June	Mar.-July	Mar.-July	Mar.-July	55–65
Eggplant	Plants	Mid May-June	May-June	May-June	May-June	Apr.-May	Apr.-June	Mar.-June	Mar.-June	Mar.-June	65–80
Endive	Seeds	Apr.-June	Apr.-May	Apr.-May		Sept.	Mar.-Apr.	Apr.-June	Apr.-June	Apr.-June	65–90
Kohlrabi	Seeds	Apr.-May	Apr.-May	Apr.-May		Sept.	Mar.-Apr.				55–65
Lettuce	Seeds*	Mar.-Aug.	Mar.-Apr. Aug.	Mar.-Apr. Aug.	July-Aug.	Sept.– Nov.	Mar. Aug.-Sept.	Sept.	Sept.	Apr. & Sept.	40–95**
Melons	Seeds	May-June	May-June	May-June	May-June	Apr.-June	Apr.-June	Apr.-July	Apr.-July	June-July	80–95
Onions (bunching)	Seeds*	Apr.-May	Apr.-May	Mar.-Apr. Sept.	Apr.	Sept.	Mar.-Apr. Sept.				60–75
Onions (bulbing)	Sets, Seeds	Apr.-May Mar.	Mar.-May Mar.	Feb.-Apr. Nov.-Feb.		Oct.-Apr. Nov.-Feb.	Oct.-Apr. Feb.-Mar.	Oct.-Apr. Nov.-Feb.	Oct.-Apr. Nov.-Feb.	Oct.-Apr. Nov.-Feb.	100–120 130–180

*For continuous crop, sow seeds at 2–3 week intervals.
**Depends on variety planted.

produce edible flowers). Success with cool-season crops depends on bringing plants to maturity in the kind of weather that favors vegetative growth rather than flowering. In general, you plant in very early spring so the crop will mature before summer heat settles in, or in late summer so that the crop matures during fall or even winter. In Zones 12 to 24 many cool-season vegetables can be planted in fall to harvest either in winter or early spring.

In summary, vegetables are easy to grow. But if you are to achieve greatest success, remember this one fact: the minute a vegetable plant stops growing, it is in trouble. Keeping them growing steadily and rapidly is the key to a bountiful harvest.

Plant	Planted as	Planting time by climate zone									Approx. days to harvest
		1–3	4–7	8, 9	10, 11	12, 13	14–17	18, 19	20, 21	22–24	
Parsley	Seeds	Apr.–May	Apr.–May	Apr.–May	May-June		Apr.–June	Apr.–June	Apr.–June	Apr.–June	70–90
Parsnip	Seeds	Apr.–May	Apr.–May	Apr.–May	Mar.–Apr.		Apr.–May	Mar.–May	Mar.–May	Mar.–May	100–120
Peas	Seeds	Mid Feb.–May	Mid Feb.–May	Feb.–Apr. Sept.	July-Aug.	Aug.-Sept.	Mar.–Apr. Sept.	Sept.	Sept.	Sept.	60–70
Peppers	Plants	May	May	May-June	May-June	Mar.–May	Mar.–June	Mar.–July	Mar.–July	June-July	60–80
Potatoes	Sets	May	Apr.–May	Dec.–Mar.	Mar.–July	Nov.–Jan.	Mar. June	Mar.–Apr.	Mar.–May	Mar.–May	90–105
Pumpkins	Seeds	June	June	Apr.–June	May-June	Apr.–Aug.	Apr.–June	Apr.–June	Apr.–June	Apr.–June	100–120
Radishes	Seeds*	Apr.–June	Apr.–June	Mar.–May Sept.-Oct.	July-Sept.	Sept.-Oct.	Mar.–May Sept.-Oct.	May-Oct.	May-Oct.	May-Oct.	20–50**
Rutabagas	Seeds	Apr.–May	Mar.	Mar.	Mar.		Mar.				90
Spinach	Seeds*	Apr.–May	Apr.–May	Apr.–May	July-Aug.	Sept.-Oct.	May	Sept.	Sept.	Sept.	40–50
Squash	Seeds	May-June	Apr.–June	Mar. June	May-July	May-Aug.	Mar.–June	Mar.–July	Mar.–July	Mar.–July	50–60
Tomatoes	Plants	May-early June	May-June	Apr.–July	May-June	Mar.	Apr.–July	Apr.–July	Apr.–July	June-July	55–90**
Turnips	Seeds*	Apr.–May	Mar.–May	Mar.–May		Aug.-Sept.	Mar.–Apr.	Apr.-Sept.	Apr.-Sept.	Apr.-Sept.	35–60

Plant these vegetables for WINTER-SPRING harvest

Plant	Planted as	Planting time by climate zones									Approx. days to harvest
		1-3	4–7	8, 9	10, 11	12, 13	14–17	18, 19	20, 21	22–24	
Artichokes	Plants or roots			Sept.-May			Oct.-May	Oct.-May	Oct.-May	Oct.-May	1 year
Asparagus	Roots	Apr.–May	Apr.	Nov.-Mar.	Feb.-Apr.		Nov.-Mar.	Oct.-Feb.	Oct.-Feb.	Oct.-Feb.	2 years
Beets	Seeds*					Oct.-Mar.		Oct.-Mar.	Oct.-Mar.	Oct.-Mar.	46–65
Broccoli	Plants					Oct.-Dec.	Sept.-Feb.	Oct.-Feb.	Oct.-Feb.	Oct.-Feb.	50–90

*For continuous crop, sow seeds at 2–3 week intervals.
**Depends on variety planted.

(Continued on next page)

Plant these vegetables for WINTER-SPRING harvest

Plant	Planted as	Planting time by climate zone									Approx. days to harvest
		1–3	4–7	8, 9	10, 11	12, 13	14–17	18, 19	20, 21	22–24	
Brussels sprouts	Plants			Aug.–Oct.		Sept.–Dec.	Sept.–Oct.	Oct.–Feb.	Oct.–Feb.	Oct.–Feb.	80–90
Cabbage	Plants			July		Oct.–Dec.	Sept.–Oct.	Oct.–Jan.	Oct.–Jan.	Oct.–Jan.	60–120
Carrots	Seeds*					Oct.–Mar.	Oct. Mar.–June	Sept.–Feb.	Sept.–Feb.	Sept.–Feb.	65–75
Cauliflower	Plants			Aug.–Nov.		Oct.–Dec.	Sept.–Oct.	Sept.–Feb.	Sept.–Feb.	Sept.–Feb.	60–100
Celery	Plants			June–Aug.		Aug.–Oct.	Sept.	Aug.–Oct.	Aug.–Oct.	Aug.–Oct.	100–135
Chard	Seeds				Feb.–Apr.	Oct.–Mar.	Mar.	Oct.–Mar.	Oct.–Mar.	Oct.–Mar.	45–60
Cucumbers	Seeds					Dec.–Mar.					55–65
Eggplant	Plants					Feb.–Mar.					65–80
Endive	Seeds				Feb.–Mar.	Oct.–Feb.		Oct.–Jan.	Oct.–Jan.	Oct.–Jan.	65–90
Kohlrabi	Seeds				Feb.–Mar.	Oct.–Feb.		Oct.–Jan.	Oct.–Jan.	Oct.–Jan.	55–65
Lettuce	Seeds*				Feb.–Mar.	Oct.–Apr.	Sept.–Mar.	Oct.–Mar.	Oct.–Mar.	Oct.–Mar.	40–95**
Melons	Seeds					Feb.–Mar.					80–95
Onions (bunching)	Seeds				Feb.–Mar.	Oct.–Feb.	Oct.–Feb.	Oct.–Jan.	Oct.–Jan.	Oct.–Jan.	60–75
Onions (bulbing)	Sets				Nov.–Apr.	Nov.–Feb.					100–120
Parsley	Seeds					Sept.–Jan.		Oct.–Jan.	Oct.–Jan.	Oct.–Jan.	70–90
Parsnip	Seeds					Sept.–Jan.		Jan.	Jan.	Jan.	100–120
Peas	Seeds				Feb.–Mar.	Oct.–Mar.	Oct.	Oct.–Jan.	Oct.–Jan.	Oct.–Jan.	60–70
Peppers	Plants					Feb.					60–80
Potato	Sets					July–Aug.	Feb.–Mar.		July–Aug.	July–Aug.	90–105
Radishes	Seeds*			Mar.–Apr.	Mar.–Apr.	Nov.–Apr.	Mar.–Apr.	Nov.–Apr.	Nov.–Apr.	Nov.–Apr.	20–50**
Rhubarb	Roots	Mar.–Apr.	Mar.–Apr.		Mar.–Apr.		Jan.	Nov.–Feb.	Nov.–Feb.	Nov.–Feb.	1 year
Rutabagas	Seeds					Sept.–Feb.	Sept.–Oct.	Oct.–Nov.	Oct.–Nov.	Oct.–Nov.	90 days
Spinach	Seeds*				Feb.–Mar.	Nov.–Mar.	Sept.–Nov.	Oct.–Feb.	Oct.–Feb.	Oct.–Feb.	40–50
Squash	Seeds					Dec.–Mar.					50–60
Tomatoes	Plants					Jan.–Mar.					55–90
Turnips	Seeds*				Mar.	Oct.–Mar.	Sept.–Oct.	Oct.–Mar.	Oct.–Mar.	Oct.–Mar.	35–60

*For continuous crop, sow seeds at 2–3 week intervals.
**Depends on variety planted.

Lawns

The irrigated, mowed lawn became a basic part of landscaping for the arid West during the early part of the twentieth century when dams, pipelines, and electric pumps began to make water abundant. In the years since, the lawn has established a firm emotional hold on Western garden tradition, with little thought given by gardeners to a lawn's great need for water. Now, in the last quarter of the century, an increasing population has caught up to the water supply. And with the new need for water frugality come hard-boiled realities about lawns: Kentucky bluegrass, ryegrass, fine-leafed fescues, and bentgrasses need a *great* amount of water—more per square foot than any other kind of garden plant.

One alternative to the water-demanding grass lawn is a ground covering of gravel, brick, or other inert material. Or, you can use any of the drought-tolerant ground covers that take no foot traffic, such as juniper, ivy, and baccharis. But for homeowners who must have a lawn (nothing else serves as well for games, picnics, bare feet, somersaults) there are drought-tolerant grasses in addition to the familiar types that require frequent irrigation.

The various lawn plants are described in the Western Plant Encyclopedia, beginning on page 161; see the listing under Grasses (page 314) for names of individual types. Ground cover choices are charted on pages 112–114, and the plants are described in the Encyclopedia. No matter which route you choose—lawn or ground cover—you will have to plan for installation and subsequent maintenance; and you may find that your choice will be determined largely by the installation and maintenance requirements. To generalize: lawns, even of drought-tolerant grasses, need the greatest amount of labor if the result is to be a good lawn. Soil should be carefully prepared, planting should not be undertaken carelessly, and routine maintenance involves mowing, watering, and applications of fertilizer.

Less demanding of labor and less expensive are most herbaceous ground covers that root as they spread or increase from clumps. They should have soil prepared as carefully as for lawns, and they will need regular water and, for best appearance, fertilizer. But they need no regular mowing—perhaps only an occasional mowing to rejuvenate them.

Simplest to plant and care for are the shrubby ground covers. Most are sold in small pots or gallon containers and are planted as described under "Planting techniques" (pages 44–47). Maintenance during early years will consist of watering and weed removal between plants; a drip irrigation setup can simplify watering, while a mulch over the entire area will eliminate most weeds and make for easy pulling of those that do grow. A number of ground cover shrubs will thrive, after they're established, with little or no water between rainy seasons—an important consideration whenever water is in short supply.

Lawn grasses

For those parts of the West that continue to have bounteous water available, this book contains references to the high water consumers: bluegrass, ryegrass, fine-leafed fescues, and bentgrass. But for the gardener with limited water available, it also describes over a dozen kinds of mowable turf that can live and stay green through the dry season with waterings only once every 12 to 30 days.

Your choice of lawn grass depends on your climate. There are two basic kinds of grasses—cool-season and subtropical—and each has its own part of the West.

Cool-season grasses withstand winter cold but most types languish in hot, dry summers. They are best adapted to the Northwest, to regions where marine influence tempers summer heat, and to the Rocky Mountain area where they can get plenty of water.

Subtropical grasses, unlike the cool-season types, grow vigorously during hot weather and go dormant in cool or cold winters. But even in their brown or straw-colored winter phase they keep up a thick carpet that keeps mud from being tracked into the house. If their winter brownness is offensive, they can either be dyed green or overseeded with certain annual cool-season grasses that will provide green during mild winters.

Drought-tolerant grasses divide themselves between the previous two groups:
• Certain ones are among the hardy, cool-season grasses that you grow from seeds sown in October. Most will stay green all year.
• Others belong to the group of warm-season grasses that you start in spring from stolons, sprigs, plugs, or sod. All of these turn brown in winter.

Cool-season grasses

Lawns of these grasses are started from seeds. The seeds are sold either in blends of several different grasses or as individual types. Lawns made of a single grass type will be the most uniform in appearance, giving you the maximum expression of whatever character you desire (fine texture or toughness, for example). Chief disadvantage to one-type lawns is that they could be wiped out if that one grass were susceptible to a pest or disease in your area or sensitive to local environmental conditions. A blend of several kinds of grasses is safer. Even though the makeup of the mature lawn may dwindle to one, two, or three kinds, these will be the kinds that do best under your lawn's conditions of soil, climate, and maintenance practices.

Buy your seed primarily on the basis of the kind of lawn you want, secondarily on the cost required to cover your area rather than the cost per pound. Choice, fine-leafed blends contain many more seeds per pound than do coarse, fast-growing blends; therefore, seed of fine-textured grasses will cover a greater area per pound.

In general, the grasses that stand up to drought and can be started from seed in the fall look more coarse than the familiar Kentucky bluegrass. There are two basic kinds: the tall fescues that are used mostly at low elevations (they can't take cold winters), and several specialties of the Rocky Mountains and high plains that are almost untried in milder winter regions.

Subtropical grasses

The better subtropical grasses are grown from stolons, sprigs, plugs, or sod. Common Bermuda, U-3 Bermuda, and *Zoysia japonica* may be available in seed form, but seeding is unsatisfactory and the seeds are not widely offered. The hybrid Bermudas and St. Augustine grass cover quickly from runners, while the zoysias are relatively slow. All can crowd out broad-leafed weeds. Hybrid Bermudas require frequent, close mowing, and frequent attention to thatch removal.

Soil preparation

A good lawn begins with a good environment for roots: uniform soil texture to a depth of 8 to 12 inches (or more), easily permeable by water and roots, well furnished with nutrients, and neither too acid nor too alkaline.

The most practical time to install a built-in watering system is when you're planting a new lawn. Underground drip irrigation— soft plastic tubes buried beneath the turf—can reduce the amount of water you put on your lawn. The tubes work by capillary action, eliminating surface sprinkler heads. (For more information on watering alternatives, see pages 48–52.)

If you're replacing a dead lawn, remove the old sod first. Digging existing sod into the soil makes for poor rooting, erratic water penetration, and irregular settling. Use a power-driven lawn edger (more satisfactory than a power sod cutter) to make parallel slices a spade's width apart across the lawn; then push a sharp spade under the sod and between the slice marks to peel the old sod from the soil beneath. If you must then add topsoil to raise the grade, buy the best you can find and blend it carefully with existing soil to avoid an "interface," a plane where two unlike soils meet.

Soil pH. Overly acid soils typically are found in high-rainfall regions, while highly alkaline soils are associated with arid lands. But before you do any guesswork and tampering with the acidity or alkalinity of your soil, have the soil tested. County agricultural agents can recommend laboratories for such testing, or the index to your telephone book's yellow pages may have an entry for soil testing. In some areas the county agricultural agencies will do soil tests. If tests indicate a highly acid soil (pH below 5.5), add lime (calcium carbonate is best) at the rate of 50 to 75 pounds per 1,000 square feet. Apply it with a spreader, for even distribution, to dry soil, being careful to keep lime away from roots of acid-loving plants. If the pH is above 8.0 (highly alkaline), add iron sulfate at 20 pounds per 1,000 square feet or soil sulfur at 10 pounds per 1,000 square feet. Iron sulfate is fast acting and will supply iron which is lacking in high pH soils. A pH higher than 8.5 may indicate an alkaline soil problem caused by excessive sodium. Consult your county agricultural agent or a commercial soil laboratory for assistance in correction of this type of soil problem.

Thoroughly incorporate any of these pH correction materials into the top 6 inches of soil.

Organic soil amendments. Few soils are naturally capable of taking up water easily (no runoff) and holding it so that watering intervals can be lengthened during a long dry season. To get this kind of soil, add and blend in organic soil amendments to supply air spaces in the soil and improve water penetration.

Nitrogen-stabilized soil amendments derived from sawdust and ground bark are available at most garden supply stores. These products are the simplest and safest to use, although more costly than untreated raw materials. Use plenty—30 to 50 percent by volume. Three inches of amendment mixed with the top 6 inches of soil makes a 33 percent mix. If you use raw sawdust or bark, provide

extra nitrogen to take care of the needs of soil organisms that work to decompose them. Mix in 55 pounds of ammonium sulfate or 35 pounds of ammonium nitrate for each 1,000 square feet of sawdust or bark laid 3 inches deep. Or use calcium cyanamid (25 pounds per 1,000 square feet) before blending in amendments. This material will kill weed seeds during its decomposition and will leave behind sufficient nitrogen to feed soil organisms and the young grass. If you use cyanamid at this stage, be sure to follow it up with another application to the finished seedbed. When adding nitrogen to raw materials to hasten their breakdown, it is necessary to keep the seedbed moist for at least 30 days prior to seeding. Failure to do so will produce a temporary salinity which could be harmful to germination and subsequent growth.

Blend in the amendment and nutrients thoroughly with a rotary tiller, making repeated passes until the mixture is completely uniform.

Mix nutrients into rooting area. Although you can't possibly add enough nitrogen to last the life of your lawn, you should add enough to sustain the grass right after it sprouts. This can be added along with organic materials, or it can be spread on the finished seedbed. You should add phosphorus during the preparatory stages; tilling it in is the only way to get it into the rooting area. Before cultivating, add 40 pounds of single superphosphate. In some areas of the West, especially where rainfall is high, you might need potash. Check with your county agricultural agent or other local expert. If you need it, cultivate in 10 pounds of muriate of potash per 1,000 square feet. This is a good time to add iron in the form of sulfate or chelate to avoid problems of iron-deficiency chlorosis. Use 5 to 10 pounds of iron sulfate per 1,000 square feet, being careful to avoid scattering any on concrete, which it will stain red. Follow label directions for chelates.

1) Add materials necessary to correct pH, the soil amendments, and nutrients (commercial fertilizer) to the seedbed.

2) Thoroughly incorporate materials into the soil. A rotary tiller makes the job much easier.

3) Rake or pull out weeds, rocks; make sure the seedbed is as free of obstruction as possible.

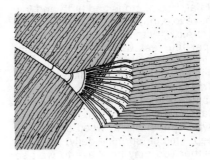

8) Rake in seed lightly to assure good contact with the seedbed and a high sprouting rate.

4) Rake or drag the seedbed to establish level, smooth out soil, and reveal high and low spots.

9) Apply a mulch of damp peat moss or sawdust; make the mulch $\frac{1}{8}$ to $\frac{3}{16}$ of an inch deep.

5) After raking and leveling, firm the seedbed with a full roller, making passes in two directions.

10) Keep mulch or seedbed dark with moisture until the grass is up. Sprinkle gently—don't wash the seeds out.

6) If not done previously, spread a commercial fertilizer over the area according to the label directions; blend in.

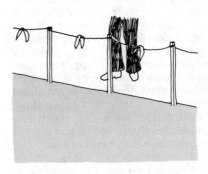

11) Keep a barrier around the area until 8 weeks after the first mowing. Grass must "knit."

7) Sow lawn seed by hand or with a mechanical seeder (see 6). A still, windless day is best for sowing.

12) Beginning a week after the grass is up, you can pull the weeds. Don't use weed sprays yet.

Smoothing the seedbed. Rake and drag the seedbed until it is smooth and flat, free of clods and high and low spots. Usually you'll have to conform to surrounding paving, but if you have a choice, try to have a slight pitch—a fall of 6 to 12 inches per 100 feet will give better drainage. After raking and leveling, firm the seedbed with a full roller, making passes in two directions. If rolling turns up low spots, rake or drag and roll again. If you're using cyanamid, spread 35 pounds per 1,000 square feet evenly over the finished surface. Rake it lightly into the top ¼ to ½ inch of seedbed, where most of the weed seeds are. Soak the area and keep it moist (sprinkle daily) for 24 to 30 days. In warm weather you may not have to wait so long; sow a few radish seeds, which will sprout in a few days. If they begin to form true leaves, soil is safe for grass seed.

Sowing the seed. Cool-season grasses may be sown almost any month of the year in mild climates and from spring through fall in colder areas, but fall and spring are usually best. Fall seeding reduces danger of heat injury, but allow 6 weeks of 50° to 70°F. weather for grass to get a good start before heavy frosts come and soils turn cold. Fall seeding saves water, since fall and winter rains help germinate the seed and establish the roots. Spring seeding gives grass a long growing season in which to get established. On the other hand, late spring and summer heat will require frequent hand watering during germination and careful irrigation later. And weeds will be plentiful.

Pick a windless day for sowing, and sow seed as evenly as possible. A spreader or mechanical seeder will help here. After sowing, rake in seed very lightly to insure contact with seedbed. If you expect hot, dry weather or drying winds, it's a good idea to put down a thin, moisture-holding mulch. Use ⅛ to ³⁄₁₆ inch of peat moss or screened, aged sawdust. To keep peat moss from blowing away (and to overcome its reluctance, when dry, to take up water), soak, knead, and pulverize it. After mulching, roll with an empty roller to press seed into contact with soil.

Water thoroughly, taking care not to wash out seed, then keep seedbed dark with moisture until all the grass is up. This may mean watering half an hour each day (sometimes 2 or 3 times a day) for up to three weeks if your seed mixture contains slow-germinating varieties. Hand sprinkling is best, although a well-designed underground system may do the job without flooding or washouts. Mow for the first time when grass blades are about 2 inches high, or when they begin to take on a noticeable curvature. Mow bent grasses when they reach one inch. Be sure mower blades are sharp, and let sod dry out enough so that mower wheels will not skid or tear.

The drought-tolerant, cool-season grasses deviate somewhat in their post-sowing needs. Their particular mowing and watering requirements are mentioned under their individual entries in the Western Plant Encyclopedia (see the Grasses entry on page 314 for a summary of the various types).

Sod, sprigs, stolons, plugs. Western turf farms offer ready-made (almost) lawns in the form of sod. Using sod is expensive compared with seeding, but the labor involved is much less and the saving in time is considerable. Prepare a seedbed as previously described, but work for a surface about ¾ inch lower than the surrounding paving. Spread a layer of complete fertilizer (same amount as label calls for on new lawns), then unroll delivered sod on prepared seedbed. Lay strips parallel, with strip ends staggered as in a bricklayer's running bond

pattern. Press end of each strip closely against the end of the last strip laid. Roll with a half-full roller, then water carefully until roots have penetrated deeply into the prepared seedbed.

Prepare seedbed, then lay sod strips so joints at ends of the strips are staggered.

In sprigging (widely used to establish hybrid Bermudas and some bents), prepare seedbed as for sowing. Presoak seedbed so that it will be damp when you plant sprigs, then let it dry out to good working consistency. Make a series of parallel trenches 3 inches deep and 10 inches apart. Lay sprigs or stolons (either from plastic bags or freshly torn from flats or sod) in trenches and press soil back into trenches. Keep moist until they root and begin to grow.

Cleated roller turns soil over stolons (runners) after they are broadcast on the seedbed.

You can broadcast stolons over prepared seedbed at the rate of 3 to 5 bushels per 1,000 square feet. Roll with a half-filled roller, then mulch with ½ inch of top-grade topsoil, peat moss, sawdust, or ground bark. Roll again, water thoroughly, and keep moist until grass takes root and begins to grow.

You can cut and lift plugs from flats of grass with a special plugging tool. Plant these in holes in the seedbed prepared by the same planting tool. Space 12 to 15 inches apart.

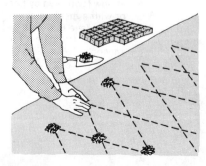

Flat-grown grasses can be turned out of flat, cut apart easily. Space plugs evenly.

Garden maintenance

The phrase "garden maintenance" can imply something a little different to each gardener, depending upon the sort of garden and, therefore, on what must be "maintained." To the person who grows many annual flowers or a large vegetable garden, maintenance will involve yearly digging and replenishing of the soil for those plants. The gardener with fruit trees or deciduous shrubs sees yearly pruning as a maintenance item.

Any gardener who tries to grow plants not perfectly adapted to his area must follow additional maintenance procedures; these are discussed under "Climate modification" on pages 94–96.

For any maintenance work, you are likely to need tools. Here, then, are presented the many gardeners' helpers and the uses for which they are intended.

Tools of the trade

Whether garden maintenance is pleasant exercise or just hard work depends, in part, on having the right tools to accomplish the tasks at hand. This doesn't mean that you have to buy a multitude of tools for your outdoor work; it suggests that you should own precisely the tools needed to accomplish the routine work in your garden.

When you shop for a hand tool, test the feel of it in your hand before you buy. Length and style of handle, for example, partly determine how comfortable a tool will be for you to use. It pays to buy the best quality available even though this will mean a greater initial expense: a high quality tool will give you more years of service for its cost than will a cheaper model.

Shovels and spades

These are the tools for digging holes and trenches and for transplanting. Many styles are available, each designed for a particular purpose. Choice of handle length, D-handle or straight, is personal; choose the one that will be the most comfortable in the type of work you intend to do. For working the soil (as opposed to simply digging), see "Spading forks" (page 90).

Long handle, round point (1, 2). A versatile tool for digging and scooping. The round-point irrigation shovel pictured below **(1)** has a straight shank, which gives it more strength and adapts better to digging planting holes or ditches with vertical sides.

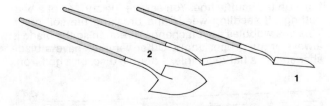

Long handle, square point (3). For leveling areas for patios and walks, squaring off the bottoms of ditches,

and shoveling snow. When shoveling dirt or gravel, this shovel is especially handy when you get toward the bottom of the pile.

D-handle shovels (4). For jobs such as moving soil, sand, gravel, and for picking up litter. Round-point and square-point models are available.

Square-end spade (5). For edging, digging, and cultivating. It can be used with a chopping motion to break up earth clods. This tool is easy to use; you have a choice of a long handle or the shorter D-handle.

Garden shovel (6). Somewhat smaller and lighter than the regular round-point shovel. Use it for digging holes, cultivating, and edging.

Transplanting spade (7). A favorite with gardeners for transplanting shrubs and moving perennials.

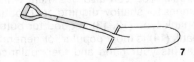

Scoop shovel (8). For moving sawdust, manure, and other light materials. Serves as a garden dust pan for collecting litter.

Spading forks

These are the tools to use for breaking up the soil, digging in rocky, clayey, or heavy soil, and digging out plants when you want to sever as few roots as possible.

Long-handled spading fork (9). Long handle gives good leverage when you are working in hard soil. Breaks up adobe clods better than a spade.

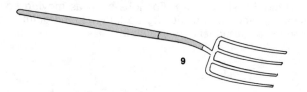

Short-handled fork (10). You have a choice of a number of models. Tines range from 7 to 11 inches long; weight also varies. Generally, short-handled spading forks work best for cultivating crowded planting beds or for lifting clumps of perennials without damaging tubers, rhizomes, or a plant's fleshy or thickly matted system of roots.

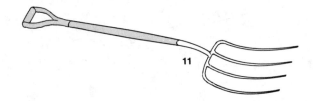

Barn or manure fork (11). Not for spading; use for moving garden prunings, long weeds, manure, and other materials that hang together. Also good for turning over layers of compost.

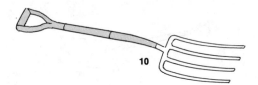

Trowels

Use trowels to plant bulbs, annuals, vegetables, and small perennials. You can also use them while on your hands and knees for shallow digging or uprooting weeds. A straight shank type **(12, 13)** is good for bulb planting; the drop shank **(14)** is most popular for general use. Pick a trowel that fits your hand and feels balanced. Buy a

sturdy one: working in hard soil will bend and soon break the shanks on all except the best quality trowels.

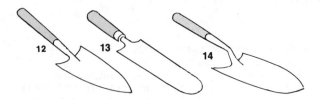

Hoes

There are hoes for many different garden jobs, from cultivating to digging furrows to destroying weeds.

Garden hoes (15, 16, 17). The 6-inch-wide hoe **(15)** is the most commonly used. Other types have a 2½-inch-wide blade **(16)** for light jobs in narrow spots or an 8-inch-wide blade for driveways and walks. Some special kinds possess names that suggest their use: planter hoe, cotton hoe, square-top onion hoe. The latter **(17)**, also called a strawberry hoe, has a blade 7 inches wide and about 1¾ inches high; use it around shallow-rooted plants. To be effective, a hoe should be sharpened each time you take it into the garden. On hard cutting jobs, resharpen about every 2 hours.

Hoes with the conventional design of those illustrated below employ flat front edges to cut weeds off at ground level and sharp corners to work like a small pick. Get a hoe that is light enough to be wielded for an hour or two at a time.

When hoeing weeds with a conventional hoe, advance forward at the unhoed weeds as you work rather than backing into them and trampling them before they are hoed. Hold the hoe so the blade is at about a 30° angle to the ground and work with a smooth, horizontal movement, drawing it back toward you so that weeds are deposited in a straight line. Don't chop downward, because chopping jars your arms and shoulders needlessly, makes an uneven surface, and may cut roots of desirable plants.

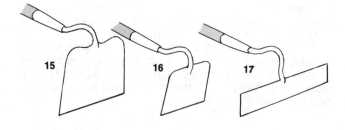

Push-pull weeder-cultivator (18). One of many variations on the scuffle hoe. You scrape the surface of a bed, cutting off seedling weeds and breaking the soil crust. This one wobbles as you change direction so the blade is always at the proper angle. Other varieties have a blade shaped like a flat rectangle, a double disc, or a golf iron.

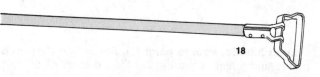

Warren hoe (19). For cultivating between plants or for making furrows. You make the furrow with the pointed end, sow seed, then turn the hoe over and use the "ears" to pull the soil over the seed.

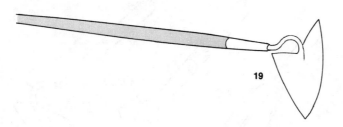

Weeding hoe (20). Hoe on one side, weed puller on the other side.

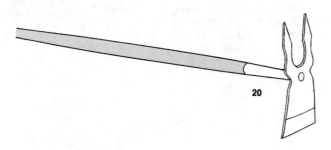

Grape hoe or eye hoe (21). Wide blade smashes through hard, root-filled soil. Use it to cut bushy weeds, invasive tree roots, spreading ground cover.

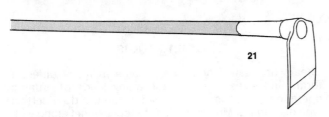

Rakes

Use rakes to smooth seedbeds, gather up debris, and aid in renewing lawns.

Level-head rake (22). Flat top used to level seed beds and break up earth clods.

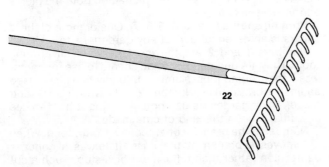

Metal bow rake (23). Good tool for leveling soil or gravel and breaking up earth clods. The bow acts as a shock absorber, giving the rake springy, resilient action.

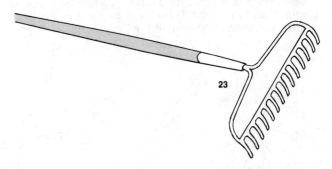

Lawn rakes (24, 25). Indispensable for raking lawn clippings, leaves, and other light matter on both paved and natural surface. You have a wide selection to choose from. Some are made of metal, others of bamboo or plastic; some are fan shaped, others rectangular.

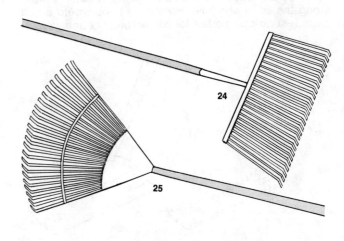

Self-cleaning rake (26). This rake, heavier than the other types, is for clearing out lawn thatch and severing long surface runners of certain lawn grasses. You don't lift it from the ground: the pull stroke gathers debris toward the operator, the push stroke clears material from the blades.

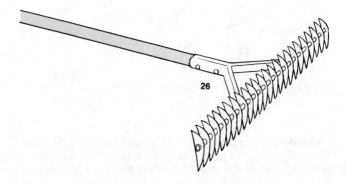

Special tools

In addition to the standard garden maintenance tools, a number of other pieces can be highly useful for particular jobs.

Cultivators (27). Good for breaking up hard soil around plants. They won't qualify for deep cultivating. For best results, combine chopping and pulling motions.

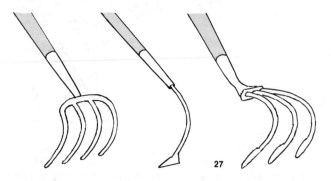

Weed and grass cutters (28). Weed cutter is used for rugged weeds and grasses in uncultivated garden areas. It removes top growth but not weed roots, unless you use blade as a chopper. Grass cutter helps in cutting grass along the edge of a lawn. Swing it as you would a golf club. Test various models for correct balance and weight.

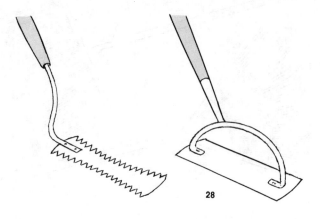

Asparagus or dandelion weeders (29). For lifting out tap-rooted weeds in the garden and for weeding in such tight places as between steppingstones in a path. These tools are useful, too, for small cultivating jobs.

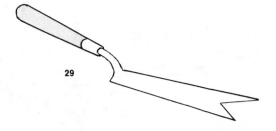

Small hand cultivators and hoes (30). For close-up kneeling or sitting jobs or for planting on a hillside. The working end of these cultivators is the same shape and design as that of regular-sized tools, but they are smaller, with palm-sized handles.

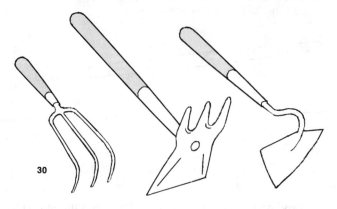

Pick mattock (31). This is two tools in one. The sharp pick is handy for loosening compacted or rocky soil that is difficult to penetrate with a spading fork or shovel; it will also break up asphalt. Wide mattock blade cuts through root-filled soil.

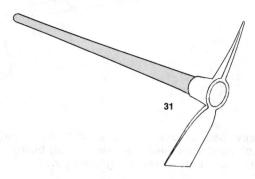

Pruning tools

Shears and saws for pruning come in many different forms and sizes to match the many kinds of pruning operations; each implement is designed to do a certain type of pruning. Most home gardeners can get along with just three basic implements: 1) hand shears for routine cutting of spent flowers, twigs, and small branches; 2) hand loppers for cutting finger-sized limbs; and 3) a pruning saw for removal of larger limbs or for branch removal where shears or loppers can't fit easily to give a proper cut.

If you attempt to use just one kind of pruning instrument for many types of plant cutting, you're bound to make bad cuts at times—often damaging both the plants and the misused tool.

Pruning shears (1, 2, 3, 4, 5, 6, 7). One or more of these shears is an essential part of any gardener's tool kit.

Numbers **1** and **2** are the most basic of all pruning tools. They are one-hand pruning shears to use for countless light pruning jobs. Number **1** cuts with a steel blade against a brass anvil. Number **2** cuts with a hook and blade. Many gardeners use both and find it hard to see any difference in the kind of cuts made.

Number **3**, the branch cutter, comes from Japan. When it removes a branch at the base, it leaves a concave depression rather than a flush cut or a stub. Such a cut can heal very fast. Bonsai experts like to prune with it.

Number **4**, a pair of flower shears, has blades designed to cut and hold flower stems.

Number **5** comes in many models. These are fruit shears, used commonly to cut stems of fruit that don't break off—such as lemons and grapes. Sharp blade crosses over sharp blade. The same cutting method is employed in other one-hand specialty pruning shears that look like this one.

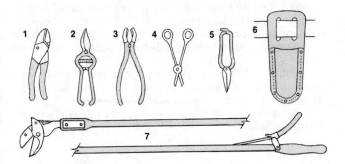

Number **6** is a leather scabbard with belt slots in the top flap. You can hang one of them on your hip and put your pruning shears in it.

Number **7** is an extension pruner with blade and anvil cutter at one end of a 4-foot, lightweight pole, and a squeeze handle to work it on the other end. Use it for cutting flowers and doing other light pruning beyond arm's reach.

Lopping shears (8, 9). Use these wherever added leverage of long handles will give you more cutting strength than you get from one-hand shears and wherever the long handles can help you reach farther.

Number **8** is the hook and blade style. The hook holds the branch while the blade slices through it. Number **9** is the blade and anvil type. A sharp steel blade cuts against a flat plate or anvil of brass.

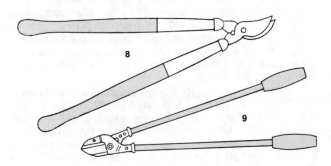

Hedge shears (10, 11, 12, 13). Hand-operated hedge shears are used by gardeners with not enough hedge to make an electric trimmer worthwhile and by others who believe that they can do a better job manually than with an electric trimmer.

Numbers **10** and **11** are similar except that number **10** has a shock absorber between the blade butts to absorb the jar when the blades come together.

Number **12** has longer handles (20 inches long instead of 10 inches) for trimming tall hedges. If you are 5 feet, 5 inches tall you can clip as high as 8½ feet with this one.

Most hedge shears have one blade serrated and notched. The notch holds bigger twigs for non-slip cuts.

Number **13** is a cordless battery powered hedge trimmer. This device will do the same job as hand tools in less time.

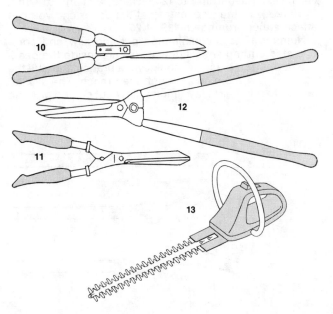

Pruning saws (14, 15, 16, 17). You should never try to force pruning shears through a branch. If shears won't cut a branch easily, use a pruning saw.

Pruning saws are designed to cut quickly through fresh, green, wet wood. Many of them, such as the curved types represented by numbers **14** and **16**, are also designed to fit into close quarters. Curved pruning saws have teeth made in such a way that they cut on the pull stroke. Straight saws cut on the push stroke. This makes the curved ones especially useful for doing overhead work. The curved blade on saw number **14** folds into the handle for carrying and storage. A hole at the base of the blade, exposed when folded, makes it possible to hang the saw, with a clip, from your belt. The curved blade on saw number **16** is broader and has fewer points to the inch, suiting it to heavier work than number **14**.

Number **17**, a straight saw, has 6 points to the inch (more than number **16** and fewer than number **14**) and it's designed for the heaviest pruning work. Saw number **15** is one of several utility saws for pruning and for cutting up logs. Some have a full bow frame. This model has a triangular bow frame. The acute-angled end goes away from you and pushes overhanging branches out of the way as you cut.

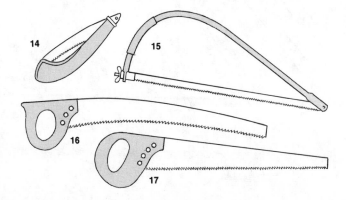

Pole pruners and pole saws (18, 19, 20). You need one of these devices to cut or saw branches high overhead.

Number **18** is a telescoping lightweight metal tube that can be extended from 6 to 12 feet (and, with an extra unit, to 18 feet). To the wooden cap at the upper end you can attach either pruning unit **19** or **20**.

Number **19** is a combination pruning saw and cord-operated cutting shears (the shears are inside the beak-like hook). You place the hook over a branch and pull the cord to draw the blade through the branch. The saw attached to number **19** is a regular draw-cut curved pruning saw.

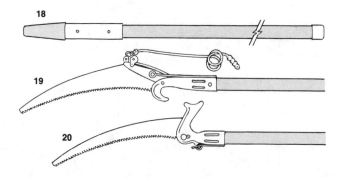

Number **20**, another attachment for the telescoping pole, is just a saw. The hook at the base of the saw pulls off dead branches; the little horn on the outer end of the hook pushes branches and raises ropes.

Instead of a telescoping metal tube, similar units use a series of wooden poles that lock together to make any length up to 18 feet. If, in your pruning, there is any chance of contacting electric lines overhead, the wooden units offer the only safe choice.

Lawn shears (21, 22, 23, 24, 25). With the heaviest of these **(21)**, you can stand up to cut the edges of lawns

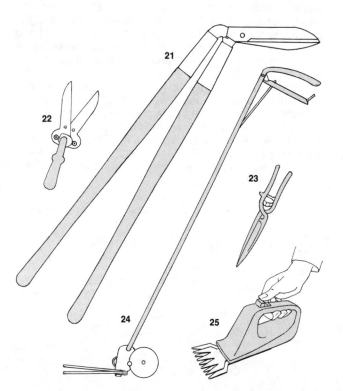

(you can cut right into the sod) and the edges of thick, spreading ground covers such as ivy and vinca. The other lawn shears **(22, 23, 24)** are meant only for shearing grass and will not do a satisfactory cutting job on garden plants. They cut grass by action of one steel blade slicing across another.

Number **22** operates by vertical squeezing action; one handle is over the other. (There is another form, in which one blade remains in a fixed position while the other slices across it. The harder you squeeze on its vertical handles the more tension you apply to its blades, thereby forcing a cut through tough grass stems and stolons.)

Number **23** operates by horizontal action; handles are on the same plane as the blades, but offset so you don't bruise your knuckles.

Number **24** has grass shears on wheels at the base of a 3-foot handle so you can wheel it along, squeezing the handle to clip grass from a stand-up position.

Number **25** is a cordless electric grass shears with rechargeable battery.

Climate modification

Many gardeners restrict their planting choices to those plants that will comfortably endure the weather of their area in all four seasons. Others, tempted by the lure of the exotic or willing to give special attention to favorite plants that require it for survival, will find themselves needing to know about frost protection, winter cover, or how to provide additional humidity during the growing season. And for those gardeners who want to outwit the weather completely, there is the greenhouse.

Protection from occasional frosts

Protecting plants from cold weather is second nature to gardeners in regions where winter means snow and zero temperatures (Zones 1–3 in this book). In mild-winter regions where frosts and occasional hard freezes occur (Zones 4–24), gardeners are not so winter conscious. They grow many semihardy and tender plants, and frequently several winters will pass with no damage. Then along comes a winter with temperatures just a few degrees lower, and those tender plants are killed—unless they are protected.

There are a number of things you can do to minimize frost and freeze damage. First, build your basic landscaping—shade trees, screening and foundation plantings, hedges—with thoroughly hardy plants. Use more tender plants as fillers, as summertime display plants, in borders, or in areas of secondary interest; plant them in sheltered sites (entryways, courtyards); or grow them in containers and move them to sheltered sites when the weather turns cold.

Next, learn your garden microclimates; find which areas are warm, which cool. Most dangerous to tender plants are stretches of open ground exposed to the sky on all sides, particularly to the *north* sky. Plants in hollows or in low, enclosed areas where cold air is held motionless are also in danger. Safest areas for tender plants are under overhanging eaves (best protection), lath structures, or evergreen tree branches. Slopes from which cold air drains freely are safer than valley or canyon floors. South-facing walls absorb much heat during the day and radiate it at night, warming nearby plants. The warmest location of all is a south-facing wall with an overhang. Not only does it give maximum protection against frost, in cool-summer climates it also supplies the heat necessary to stimulate bud, blossom, and fruit in heat-loving plants such as bougainvillea, hibiscus, fig, and evergreen magnolia.

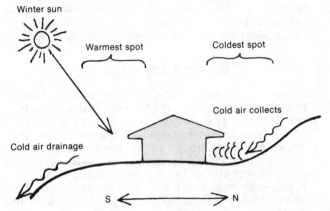

Take advantage of garden microclimates to grow plants which require varying conditions. Hills and hollows, points of the compass, and structures influence microclimates.

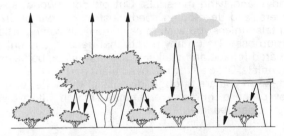

Arrows represent heat loss. Plants exposed to open, cloudless sky—especially the north sky—are more subject to frost damage than ones grown under trees or overhangs.

Conditioning plants and soil for frosts. Feed and water while plants are growing fastest in late spring and early summer. Taper off nitrogen feeding in late summer to discourage production of new growth that would not have time to mature before cold weather hits.

Actively growing plants are more susceptible to cold than dormant or semidormant plants. Reducing water will help harden growth, but soil around plants should be moist at the onset of the frost season; moist soil holds and releases more heat than dry soil.

Some hardy plants have early blossoms that are damaged by spring frosts. Try to delay bloom of deciduous magnolias and some early rhododendrons beyond the time of heavy frosts by planting them with a north exposure or in the shade of high-branching deciduous trees.

Be especially watchful for frosts early in fall or in spring after growth is underway; these are much more damaging than frosts which come while plants are semidormant. The signs are still air (tree branches motionless, smoke goes straight up); absence of cloud cover (stars easily visible, very bright); low humidity (windshield, grass dry); and low temperature (45°F. or less at 10 P.M.). If you notice these signs at bedtime, take steps to get tender container plants under shelter of porch roof, eaves, or garage, and to erect shelters over tender plants in the ground. Burlap or plastic film over stakes or frames will

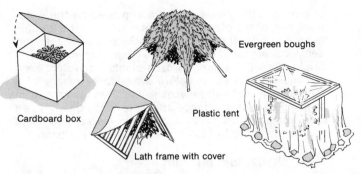

These simple homemade devices can save a choice plant from a sudden fall or early spring frost.

do the job. Make sure that the covering material does not touch the plant, and uncover the plant during daytime.

After a frost. If plants have been damaged by frost, don't hurry to prune them. Premature trimming may stimulate new, tender growth that will be nipped by later frosts. And you may cut out more than necessary, mistaking still-alive growth for dead. Wait until new growth begins in spring, then remove only wood which is clearly dead.

Winter-long protection in severe climates

In high elevations where soil freezes hard and temperatures drop below zero, gardeners do not grow tender plants. But many gardeners do grow roses, and a few attempt broad-leafed evergreens—boxwood, euonymus, holly, pieris, and rhododendrons. All of these plants will need help to get through such winters alive.

With roses, which are basically deciduous, your aim is to keep roots and bud union (at the very least) alive, and to preserve as many live canes as possible. In regions that regularly get down to 15°F. or lower, wait until a couple of hard freezes have hit, then tie rose canes together and mound soil to 12 inches high over bud union and base of canes. After soil mounds freeze, cover mounds with straw or secure cut evergreen boughs so that they cover mounds and canes; you want to keep mounds and canes consistently cold, rather than leaving them exposed to repeated freezing and thawing (and the drying action of winter winds). Even better is a cylinder of wire mesh or tar paper to encircle each bush after you have mounded it; fill the cylinders with straw or other loose material for insulation. Early spring weather often brings warm days alternating with freezing ones, so remove protection cautiously and gradually as garden soil starts to thaw. Protect tree and climbing roses with a thick insulation of cornstalks or straw wrapped in burlap around the canes. Tree roses are especially vulnerable because the bud union, from which grows the rose you want, is about 3 feet in the air, exposed to the elements. Simplest protection is to grow these roses as container plants and take them into the shelter of a greenhouse, garage, cold porch, or basement to wait out winter. For both climbers and tree roses, you also can dig up roots on one side of the plant, tip the plant over so that it lies on the ground (or in a shallow trench), then cover canes and exposed roots with soil. Remove soil gradually in spring as ground thaws, then bring plants back to upright position and replant the exposed roots.

Some broad-leafed evergreens will survive fairly low temperatures but succumb to windburn and sunburn when low temperatures, strong sun, and cold, drying winds combine forces. Protect these plants with shelters of burlap, lath, sheets of plywood placed on the windward side of the plant, or evergreen boughs stuck in the ground around the plant like shocks of corn. Best garden location for these plants is a spot where winter's bright sun will not strike frozen plants. Above all, keep soil moist and keep moisture available by means of a thick mulch that will prevent soil in the root area from freezing. Greatest damage comes to these plants when they transpire water through their leaves and can't replace moisture because water in the soil is frozen.

Heat, shade, and humidity

These three subjects are bound together very closely. In plant descriptions, you frequently see such recommendations as "Grow in sun near coast, part or full shade inland." This tells what to do for shade-loving plants. These plants, mostly native to forest floors, have shallow roots that seldom penetrate beneath the surface layer of leaf mold. They use much water during growth and bloom (tuberous begonias, fuchsias, azaleas), but their leaves are not adapted to store water (as succulent plants do) or to resist evaporation in warm, dry, windy weather (as many waxy or leathery-leafed plants do). In hot sun, in very dry weather, or in warm windy weather, they lose water faster than they can take it up; sunburn, wilting, or withering results.

To grow shade plants successfully, keep direct sunlight down, humidity up. If you live near the ocean, fog cover and natural humidity may be enough (but even here you'll need to furnish shelter against strong, constant winds). Farther inland place your shade plants under shelter of high-branching trees, under lath structures, or on the north or east sides of buildings, walls, or fences. Protect from drying winds by fences, louvers, or windbreak plantings. Wind protection helps keep humidity high by reducing air motion; humidity also is increased by mulching (a coarse, moist mulch will evaporate a considerable amount of water into the air), and by watering often. When temperatures are really high or humidity exceptionally low, water with special diligence and supplement surface irrigation with sprinkling or misting. (This last may not be practical where water contains large amounts of salts that could damage foliage.)

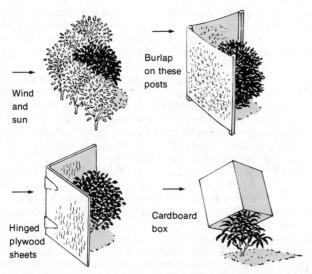

Keep freezing wind and drying sun from damaging broad-leafed evergreens with shelters like these.

Protect newly set plants from strong sun and wind with temporary shelters. These can be as simple as a shingle lean-to placed on the sunny side of the plant or a small newspaper pup tent held down at the edges by a few handfuls of soil. Or they can be as elaborate as lath or burlap panels supported above the plants on low stakes. The object is to keep strong sun and wind from the young plants until the roots are able to do an efficient job of taking water from the soil to meet the plants' needs.

Garden sanitation

Occasional cleanups keep a garden healthy as well as attractive. Plant debris around the garden affords a damp, cool breeding ground for slugs, snails, and several kinds of insects. Lumber stacked on the ground also supplies a feeding ground for termites and a breeding place for rodents; try to keep it on racks against a seldom-seen stretch of fence or outbuilding wall.

If you keep pots and other plant containers on bare ground, move them occasionally so you can look for and exterminate slugs, snails, and their pearly eggs that might be hiding there. At the same time, probe the container drainage holes for more eggs and creatures.

Once in a while, when you go out to look around the garden carry a bucket, pruning shears (a scabbard is handy), and tying materials. Cut off dead wood, spent flowers, and developing seed clusters or fruit of ornamentals (unless you wish to save them for some particular purpose). Tie up any plants that need it, and cut off withered foliage and stalks of spent annuals, bulbs, and perennials. Drop all the removed plant parts in the bucket and, when you are through, dispose of them. Performing a few of these chores several times a month will save you major cleanups later.

Greenhouses

The ultimate climate modification comes when you grow plants in a greenhouse. In these glass or plastic structures you have the opportunity to exercise complete control, if you wish, over temperature, humidity, and even day length. Not every gardener will feel the need for a growing environment where the climatic factors are so completely regulated, but many have discovered the usefulness of a greenhouse for these purposes:
• Wintering plants that are too tender for the normal winter low temperatures in the garden.
• Starting seeds of annuals and vegetables early so that plants can be set out in the garden as soon as weather permits.
• Starting cuttings and seeds that require the growth stimuli a greenhouse can provide.
• Raising vegetables and flowers out of season (particularly when outside conditions are too cold), or maturing them earlier than would be normal if planted outdoors.
• Growing specialty plants (orchids and tropical plants, for example) that could not be grown outdoors because temperature, humidity, or both are not favorable to the particular plants.

A greenhouse may be a simple lean-to constructed of plastic, a small bay window attachment on a house window, or a more elaborate separate structure with precise controls for regulation of heat, humidity, ventilation, and water. The size and style of greenhouse you choose will be dictated by your needs and the cost of construction; the variations are numerous.

Planting for a Purpose —a Plant Selection Guide

The thousands of plants described in the Western Plant Encyclopedia (beginning on page 161) comprise an almost infinitely varied assortment of sizes, shapes, textures, and colors. They can ornament gardens from breezy seashores to simmering deserts, from subtropical balminess to alpine chill.

The pleasure of choosing from this rich assortment is available to anyone with a sense of adventure and a bit of earth, be it window box or acreage. But such abundance sometimes can lead to bewilderment— the following pages are designed to help you avoid confusion. The lists of plants will help you focus your choices on your needs, whether you want proven plants for specific landscape functions, for special effects, or specialized plants for solving garden problems.

The greater part of all western gardens originate at the nursery or garden center. The lists and charts in this section are designed to help make your nursery shopping simpler.

Trees for garden and patio

Patio trees are generally small, as trees go, and are also good-looking at close range. Many have showy displays of flowers, fruit, or both; some have striking fall foliage color or unusually decorative bark. All are "well-mannered": root systems are not likely to crack pavement or greedily take water and nutrients from neighboring plants; branches do not shed annoying quantities of leaves or drop messy fruit to litter or stain patio surfaces.

All patio trees also qualify as fine candidates for garden planting, but the garden trees list contains additional kinds that are worthy even though they may fall short of patio qualifications. Some are too large or dense for most patio situations but can provide needed height or pools of shade in the landscape. Others may shed leaves or fruit that would require frequent cleanup on a patio, but can be absorbed into garden plantings.

For more detailed guidelines on choosing trees, read the "Trees" section on pages 71 and 72.

Canopy of leaves shelters patio

Tree branches overhead screen sun, fill patio with dappled light. This Chinese scholar tree *(Sophora japonica)* is complemented by bright red L-shaped bench, Oriental feeling of other plants in the patio.

DECIDUOUS

NAME OF PLANT	CLIMATE ZONES	GARDEN	PATIO
Acer buergeranum	4–9, 14–17, 20, 21		●
Acer capillipes	1–9, 14–24	●	
Acer circinatum	1–6, 14–17		●
Acer davidii	1–6, 15–17, 20, 21	●	●
Acer ginnala	1–9, 14–16	●	●
Acer griseum	1–9, 14–21	●	●
Acer palmatum	1–9, 14–24	●	●
Albizia julibrissin	2–23	●	●
Amelanchier	1–6	●	●
Bauhinia blakeana	19, 21, 23		●
Bauhinia variegata	13, 18–23	●	●
Betula	Varies	●	
Calodendrum capense	19, 21–24	●	
Carpinus	1–9, 14–17	●	
Celtis	Varies	●	
Cercidiphyllum japonicum	1–6, 14–16, 18–20	●	
Cercidium	10–14, 18–20	●	●
Cercis	Varies	●	●
Chilopsis linearis	11–13, 18–21	●	●
Chionanthus	Varies	●	●
Cladrastis lutea	1–9, 14–16	●	
Cornus florida	1–9, 14–16	●	●
Cornus kousa	3–9, 14, 15, 18, 19	●	●
Crataegus	1–11, 14–17	●	●
Davidia involucrata	4–9, 14–21	●	
Erythrina	Varies	●	
Filbert	2–7	●	
Firmiana simplex	5, 6, 8, 9, 12–24	●	●
Franklinia alatamaha	2–6, 14–17	●	●
Fraxinus holotricha	4–24	●	
Fraxinus velutina	8, 9, 10–24	●	
Ginkgo biloba	1–9, 14–24	●	
Gleditsia triacanthos	1–16, 18–20	●	
Gymnocladus dioica	1–3, 7–10, 12–16, 18–21	●	
Halesia	2–9, 14–24	●	●
Idesia polycarpa	4–9, 14–17, 19–24	●	
Jacaranda mimosifolia	13, 15–24	●	●
Koelreuteria	Varies	●	●
Laburnum	1–10, 14–17	●	●
Lagerstroemia indica	7–9, 12–14, 18–21	●	●
Liquidambar	Varies	●	●
Liriodendron tulipifera	1–10, 14–23	●	
Magnolia (many species)	Varies	●	●
Malus	1–11, 14–21	●	●
Morus alba	All	●	
Nyssa sylvatica	3–10, 14–21	●	
Oxydendrum arboreum	3–9, 14–17	●	●
Parkinsonia aculeata	11–17	●	
Parrotia persica	4–6, 15–21	●	●
Persimmon	Varies	●	●
Pistacia chinensis	8–16, 18–23	●	
Prosopis glandulosa torreyana	8–14	●	
Prunus mume	2–9, 12–22	●	●
Prunus, flowering cherry	4–6, 15–17	●	●
Prunus, flowering peach	2–24	●	●
Prunus, flowering plum	Varies	●	●
Punica granatum	7–24	●	●
Pyrus	Varies	●	●
Quercus coccinea	All	●	
Quercus douglasii	All	●	
Quercus garryana	4–6, 15–17	●	
Quercus kelloggii	5–7, 15, 16, 18–21	●	
Quercus palustris	All	●	
Quercus phellos	1–4, 6–16, 18–21	●	
Quince	All	●	●
Robinia ambigua 'Idahoensis'	All	●	
Robinia hispida macrophylla	All	●	
Robinia pseudoacacia	All	●	
Sapium sebiferum	8, 9, 12, 14–16, 18–21	●	●
Sophora japonica	All	●	
Sorbus aucuparia	1–10, 14–17	●	●
Stewartia	4–6, 14–17, 20, 21	●	●
Styrax	3–10, 14–21	●	●
Tabebuia	15, 16, 20–24	●	●
Tilia cordata	1–17	●	●
Tilia euchlora	1–17	●	
Tipuana tipu	12–16, 18–24	●	●
Vitex agnus-castus	4–24	●	●
Zelkova serrata	3–21	●	
Zizyphus jujuba	7–16, 18–24	●	●

EVERGREEN

NAME OF PLANT	CLIMATE ZONES	GARDEN	PATIO
Acacia baileyana	7–9, 13–24	●	
Acacia pendula	13–24	●	
Acacia podalyriifolia	8, 9, 13–24		●
Acer oblongum	8–10, 12, 14–24	●	
Acer paxii	8, 9, 14–24	●	●
Acmena smithii	15–17, 19–24	●	●
Agonis	15–17, 20–24	●	●
Arbutus unedo	4–24	●	●
Bauhinia forficata	9, 12–23		●
Brugmansia	16–24		●
Callistemon citrinus	8, 9, 12–24	●	●
Callistemon viminalis	8, 9, 12–24	●	●
Cassia leptophylla	21–24	●	●
Castanospermum australe	18–22	●	
Ceanothus 'Ray Hartman'	4–7, 14–24	●	
Citrus	8, 9, 12–24		●
Clethra arborea	15–17, 21–24		●
Cocculus laurifolius	8, 9, 12–20	●	●
Cornus capitata	8, 9, 14–20	●	●
Crinodendron patagua	14–24	●	●
Cupaniopsis anacardioides	16, 17, 19–24	●	
Dodonaea viscosa	7–9, 12–24	●	●
Drimys winteri	8, 9, 14–24	●	
Eriobotrya deflexa	8–24	●	●
Eriobotrya japonica	4–24	●	●
Eucalyptus calophylla	8–24	●	
Eucalyptus erythrocorys	8–24	●	
Eucalyptus ficifolia	8–24	●	●
Eucalyptus forrestiana	8–24	●	
Eucalyptus leucoxylon macrocarpa 'Rosea'	8–24	●	●
Eucalyptus macrandra	8–24	●	●

(Continued on page 101)

Isolating an attractive plant draws attention to its special beauty. Without the distraction of nearby plantings, this silk tree *(Albizia julibrissin)* assumes center stage.

Choose a distinctive tree for a garden focal point

A flowering garden tree shows up well in front of green street trees. Unsurpassed summer flower show from a small tree adorns this crape myrtle *(Lagerstroemia indica)*.

EVERGREEN (Cont'd.)

NAME OF PLANT	CLIMATE ZONES	GARDEN	PATIO
Eucalyptus nicholii	8–24	●	
Eucalyptus pauciflora	8–24	●	
Eucalyptus polyanthemos	8–24	●	
Eucalyptus pulchella	8–24	●	
Eucalyptus torquata	8–24	●	●
Ficus benjamina	13, 23, 24	●	●
Ficus microcarpa	9, 15–24		
Ficus rubiginosa	18–24		
Hakea laurina	9, 12–17, 19–24		●
Harpephyllum caffrum	17, 19, 21–24	●	
Heteromeles arbutifolia	5–24	●	●
Hoheria populnea	4–6, 15–17, 21–24	●	
Hymenosporum	8, 9, 14–23		
Ilex (many species)	Varies	●	
Lagunaria patersonii	13, 15–24	●	
Laurus nobilis	5–9, 12–24		●
Leptospermum laevigatum	14–24		●
Leptospermum petersonii	14–24		●
Ligustrum lucidum	5, 6, 8–24	●	●
Lysiloma thornberi	10, 12–24	●	●
Macadamia	9, 16, 17, 19–24	●	●
Magnolia (many species)	Varies	●	●
Maytenus boaria	8, 9, 14–21	●	●
Melaleuca ericifolia	9, 12–24	●	●
Melaleuca quinquenervia	9, 13, 16, 17, 20–24	●	●
Melaleuca styphelioides	9, 13–24	●	●
Metrosideros	Varies	●	●
Michelia doltsopa	14–24	●	●
Nerium oleander	8–16, 18–23	●	●
Olea europaea (if fruit prevented)	8, 9, 11–24	●	●
Olmediella betschlerana	9, 14–24	●	●
Osmanthus fragrans	8, 9, 12–24	●	●
Palms	Varies	●	●

NAME OF PLANT	CLIMATE ZONES	GARDEN	PATIO
Photinia fraseri	4–24		●
Pinus contorta	1–9, 14–17	●	
Pinus densiflora	4–9, 14–17	●	
Pinus nigra	1–12, 14–17	●	
Pinus wallichiana	4–9, 14–17	●	
Pittosporum eugenioides	9, 14–17, 19–22		●
Pittosporum phillyraeoides	9, 12–24		●
Pittosporum rhombifolium	12–24	●	●
Pittosporum tenuifolium	9, 14–17, 19–24	●	●
Pittosporum tobira	8–24		●
Pittosporum undulatum	16, 17, 21–24		●
Pittosporum viridiflorum	15–17, 20–24		●
Podocarpus gracilior	8, 9, 13–24	●	●
Podocarpus macrophyllus	4–9, 12–24	●	●
Prunus caroliniana	7–24	●	
Prunus ilicifolia	7–9, 12–24	●	
Prunus lusitanica	4–9, 14–24	●	
Prunus lyonii	7–9, 12–24	●	
Pyrus	Varies	●	●
Quercus ilex	4–24	●	
Quercus suber	8–16, 18–23	●	
Rhus lancea	8, 9, 12–24		●
Schefflera	21–24		●
Schinus terebinthifolius	15–17, 19–24	●	●
Sequoia sempervirens	4–9, 14–24	●	●
Sophora secundiflora	8–16, 18–24	●	
Stenocarpus sinuatus	16, 17, 20–24	●	●
Thevetia thevetioides	22–24	●	●
Tristania conferta	19–24	●	
Tristania laurina	19–24		●
Tsuga canadensis	3–7, 17	●	●
Tupidanthus calyptratus	19–24	●	●
Umbellularia californica	4–10, 12–24	●	●
Xylosma congestum	8–24	●	●

Where garden and patio meet . . . a tree can define the boundary

At the point of transition between garden, patio, and planting bed, this small *Magnolia soulangiana* (often called tulip tree) displays profusion of pink blossoms. Ivy ground cover protects root zone from foot traffic and soil compaction.

Hedge and screen plants offer a kaleidoscope of seasonal changes. Coppery red leaves on
Photinia fraseri are not a fall feature—they come as new growth just after spring flower show.

*Photinias through
two seasons*

Decked out in spring flower display is closely related
Chinese photinia *(Photinia serrulata)*.

Hedges, screens, backgrounds, and barriers

All plants in this list are well-foliaged from the ground up, able to provide a dense separation or screen in your landscape. Some are only knee-high shrublets good for edging a walk or path; at the other extreme are shrubby trees that, grouped closely, can block an objectionable view or direct the eye to a garden focal point. Those plants indicated as good for barriers are either impenetrably dense, armed with thorns, or both.

Singled out with this symbol (••) are the plants that will tolerate shearing into formal hedges; those with a single dot (•) are best as informal hedges.

DECIDUOUS

NAME OF PLANT	CLIMATE ZONES	HEDGE	SCREEN	BACKGROUND	BARRIER
Atriplex lentiformis	7–14, 18, 19	•			
Berberis	1–11, 14–17	•	•	•	•
Blueberry	4–6	•			
Caesalpinia pulcherrima	12–16, 18–23		•		
Callicarpa bodinieri giraldii	1–6	•			
Caragana arborescens	1–21	•			
Carpinus betulus	3–9, 14–17	••	•		
Chaenomeles	1–21	•			•
Crataegus monogyna	1–11, 14–17	••	•	•	•
Elaeagnus angustifolia	1–3, 7–14, 18, 19	•	•	•	•
Fouquieria splendens	10–13, 18–20	•	•		•
Ligustrum	Varies	••	•		
Liquidambar styraciflua	1–9, 14–24		•		
Lonicera	Varies	•	•	•	
Maclura pomifera	All	•		•	•
Rhamnus frangula 'Columnaris'	1–7, 10–13	••	•	•	
Rosa eglanteria	All	•	•		•
Rosa hugonis	All	•	•		
Rosa rugosa	All	•			•
Rosa (Floribunda, Grandiflora, Polyantha hybrids)	All	•			•
Salix purpurea 'Gracilis'	All	•		•	
Viburnum opulus 'Nanum'	1–9, 14–24	•			
Weigela	1–11, 14–17			•	•

EVERGREEN

NAME OF PLANT	CLIMATE ZONES	HEDGE	SCREEN	BACKGROUND	BARRIER
Abelia grandiflora	5–24	•	•		
Bamboo (many)	Varies	•	•	•	•
Berberis	1–11, 14–17	•		•	•
Buxus	Varies	••			
Callistemon citrinus	8, 9, 12–24	••	•	•	
Callistemon salignus	8, 9, 12–24	••	•	•	
Calocedrus decurrens	1–12, 14–24		•	•	
Camellia japonica and C. sasanqua	4–9, 14–24	•	•	•	
Carissa	22–24	••	•		•
Ceratonia siliqua	9, 13–16, 18–24	•	•	•	
Chamaecyparis lawsoniana (several)	4–6, 15–17	•	•	•	
Choisya ternata	7–9, 12–17	•	•		
Cocculus laurifolius	8, 9, 12–24		•	•	

(Continued on next page)

Flowers are a welcome feature on plants grown as screens. A fast-growing, undemanding shrub for hedge, screen, and even windbreak is *Callistemon citrinus* (lemon bottlebrush). Bursts of red blooms appear throughout the year.

Barrier shrubs are most effective when they have thorns; they may also have attractive flowers and fruit. This is *Berberis darwinii*, a 5–10-foot arching plant.

You can screen with blossoms or separate with spiny branches

EVERGREEN (Cont'd.)

NAME OF PLANT	CLIMATE ZONES	HEDGE	SCREEN	BACKGROUND	BARRIER
Corynocarpus laevigata	16, 17, 23, 24	●	●	●	
Cotoneaster (some)	Varies	●	●	●	
Crassula argentea	16, 17, 22–24	●			
Cupressocyparis leylandii	3–24		●	●	
Cupressus forbesii	8–14, 18–20	●●	●	●	
Cupressus glabra	5, 8–24	●●	●	●	
Dodonaea viscosa	7–9, 12–24	●	●	●	
Elaeagnus	Varies	●●	●		
Erica (some)	Varies		●	●	
Escallonia	4–9, 14–17, 20–24	●●	●	●	
Eucalyptus globulus 'Compacta'	8–24		●		
Eucalyptus gunnii	8–24		●		

NAME OF PLANT	CLIMATE ZONES	HEDGE	SCREEN	BACKGROUND	BARRIER
Eucalyptus lehmannii	8–24		●		
Eucalyptus platypus	8–24		●		
Eucalyptus spathulata	8–24		●		
Eucalyptus stellulata	8–24		●		
Eugenia uniflora	21–24	●			
Euonymus fortunei 'Sarcoxie'	1–17	●●			
Euonymus japonica	5–20	●●	●		
Euonymus kiautschovica	1–13	●●	●		
Feijoa sellowiana	7–9, 12–24	●	●		
Ficus benjamina	13, 23, 24	●	●		
Gardenia jasminoides	7–9, 12–16, 18–23	●			
Garrya elliptica	5–9, 14–21	●	●		

●● Formal hedge
● Informal hedge

(Continued on page 106)

Strategic plantings create visual barriers

Sometimes a solid wall of foliage is unnecessary; here, a few plants give adequate separation. Medium-height bamboos serve as graceful screens or hedges. Clumping kinds of bamboo have less invasive roots.

*Try a low-growing,
low-maintenance hedge
to border a walk*

Sometimes a hedge merely defines
a pathway or prevents traffic onto a lawn.
Admirable for this use is *Hebe buxifolia*.

EVERGREEN (Cont'd.)

NAME OF PLANT	CLIMATE ZONES	HEDGE	SCREEN	BACKGROUND	BARRIER
Grevillea robusta	8, 9, 12–24	•	•		
Grevillea rosmarinifolia	8, 9, 12–24	•			
Grewia occidentalis	8, 9, 14–24	•	•		
Griselinia	9, 15–17, 20–24		•		
Hakea suaveolens	9, 12–17, 19–24			•	•
Hebe buxifolia	14–24	•			
Heteromeles arbutifolia	5–24			•	•

NAME OF PLANT	CLIMATE ZONES	HEDGE	SCREEN	BACKGROUND	BARRIER
Hibiscus rosa-sinensis	9, 12, 13, 15, 16, 19–24		•		
Hypericum beanii	4–24	•			
Ilex	Varies	••	•	•	•
Itea ilicifolia	4–24		•		
Juniperus (shrub types)	All				•
Juniperus (columnar types)	All	••	•	•	•

EVERGREEN (Cont'd.)

NAME OF PLANT	CLIMATE ZONES	HEDGE	SCREEN	BACKGROUND	BARRIER
Kochia	All	•			
Lagunaria patersonii	13, 15–24		•		
Lantana	See Encyclopedia	•			
Larrea tridentata	10–13, 19	•	•		
Laurus nobilis	5–9, 12–24	••	•	•	
Leptospermum	14–24	••	•		
Leucophyllum frutescens	7–24	•			
Ligustrum	Varies	••	•		
Lonicera (shrub type)	Varies	•	•		
Lysiloma thornberi	10, 12–24			•	
Mahonia aquifolium	1–21	•	•		•
Mahonia nevinii	8–24	•	•		•
Melaleuca armillaris	9, 12–24	••	•		•
Melaleuca hypericifolia	9, 12–24	••	•		
Melaleuca nesophylla	9, 13, 16–24	••	•		
Murraya paniculata	21–24	•			
Myrica californica	4–6, 14–17, 20–24	••	•	•	
Myrsine africana	8, 9, 14–24	••			
Myrtus communis	8–24	••	•		
Nandina domestica	5–24	•	•		
Nerium oleander	8–16, 18–23	•	•	•	
Olmediella betschlerana	9, 14–24	•	•	•	•
Osmanthus fragrans	8, 9, 12–24	•	•	•	
Osmanthus heterophyllus	3–10, 14–24	•	•	•	
Osmarea burkwoodii	4–9, 14–17	•			
Pernettya mucronata	4–7, 14–17	•			
Photinia	Varies	•	•	•	
Pittosporum eugenioides	9, 14–17, 19–22	••	•	•	
Pittosporum tenuifolium	9, 14–17, 19–24	••	•	•	
Pittosporum tobira	8–24			•	
Pittosporum undulatum	16, 17, 21–24			•	•
Pittosporum viridiflorum	15–17, 20–24			•	
Platycladus orientalis	All	•	•		
Podocarpus	Varies	•	•	•	
Portulacaria afra	13, 16, 17, 22–24	•	•		
Prunus caroliniana	7–24	••	•	•	
Prunus ilicifolia	7–9, 12–24	••	•	•	
Prunus laurocerasus	4–9, 14–24	••	•	•	
Prunus lusitanica	4–9, 14–24	••	•	•	
Prunus lyonii	7–9, 12–24	••	•	•	
Pseudotsuga menziesii	1–10, 14–17		•	•	
Psidium littorale	9, 14–24	•	•		
Pyracantha	Varies	•	•	•	•
Quillaja saponaria	8, 9, 14–24	•		•	
Raphiolepis	8–10, 12–24	•		•	
Rhamnus alaternus	4–24	••	•	•	
Rhamnus crocea ilicifolia	7–16, 18–21			•	
Rhus integrifolia	15–17, 20–24	••	•	•	
Rhus lancea	8, 9, 12–24	••	•	•	
Rhus laurina	20–24	••	•		
Rhus ovata	7–24	••	•	•	
Ribes speciosum	8, 9, 14–24				•
Rosmarinus officinalis	4–24	••			
Sedum dendroideum praealtum	8, 9, 12, 14–24	•			
Sequoia sempervirens	4–9, 14–24	•	•	•	
Simmondsia chinensis	10–13, 19–24	••			
Syzygium paniculatum	16, 17, 19–24	••	•	•	
Taxus	3–9, 14–24	••	•	•	
Tecoma stans	12, 13, 21–24			•	
Tecomaria capensis	12, 13, 16, 18–24	•			
Ternstroemia gymnanthera	4–9, 12–24	•			
Teucrium	Varies	••	•		
Thevetia	Varies			•	
Thuja	Varies	••	•	•	
Tsuga canadensis	3–7, 17	••	•	•	
Tsuga heterophylla	1–7, 14–17	••	•	•	
Umbellularia californica	4–10, 12–24	•	•	•	
Viburnum cinnamomifolium	5–9, 14–24	•		•	
Viburnum odoratissimum	8, 9, 14–24			•	
Viburnum suspensum	8–10, 13–24	•	•	•	
Viburnum tinus	14–23	•	•		
Xylosma congestum	8–24	••	•	•	

•• Formal hedge
• Informal hedge

Plants to use for windbreaks

Where a wind blows from a predictable direction daily or almost daily through certain seasons, the best plan is to lift the wind gradually. If you have space, do it with as many as five rows of shrubs and trees with rows sixteen feet apart. If space is limited, use a row of shrubs on the windward side and trees inside. Even if space allows only one row, some bushy trees will help moderate wind.

TREES

Evergreen

NAME OF PLANT	CLIMATE ZONES
Acacia melanoxylon	8, 9, 13–24
Calocedrus decurrens	1–12, 14–24
Casuarina stricta	8, 9, 12–24
Chamaecyparis lawsoniana	4–6, 15–17
Cupressocyparis leylandii	3–24
Cupressus glabra	5, 8–24
Cupressus macrocarpa	17
Eucalyptus camaldulensis	8, 9, 12–24
Eucalyptus cinerea	8, 9, 12–24
Eucalyptus cladocalyx	15–17, 19–24
Eucalyptus cornuta	15–17, 19–24
Eucalyptus erythronema	9, 14–24
Eucalyptus ficifolia	16, 17, 21–24
Eucalyptus globulus	14–17, 19–24
Eucalyptus globulus 'Compacta'	14–17, 19–24
Eucalyptus gunnii	5, 6, 8, 9, 14–24
Eucalyptus lehmannii	16, 17, 21–24
Eucalyptus leucoxylon	8, 9, 14–24
Eucalyptus melliodora	15–24
Eucalyptus microtheca	8–24
Eucalyptus niphophila	5, 9, 14–24

NAME OF PLANT	CLIMATE ZONES
Eucalyptus robusta	8, 9, 12–24
Eucalyptus rudis	8, 9, 12–24
Eucalyptus spathulata	15–17, 19–24
Lagunaria patersonii	13, 15–24
Ligustrum lucidum	5, 6, 8–24
Picea abies	1–6, 14–17
Pinus canariensis	8–11, 14–24
Pinus contorta	1–9, 14–17
Pinus halepensis	8–24
Pinus muricata	8, 9, 14–17, 22–24
Pinus nigra	1–12, 14–17
Pinus radiata	8, 9, 14–24
Pinus sylvestris	1–9, 14–17
Pinus torreyana	8, 9, 14–24
Pittosporum (all but P. phillyraeoides)	Varies
Pseudotsuga menziesii	1–10, 14–17
Schinus molle	8, 9, 12–24
Sequoia sempervirens	4–9, 14–24
Tamarix aphylla	10–13
Thuja plicata	1–9, 14–24

Deciduous

NAME OF PLANT	CLIMATE ZONES
Broussonetia papyrifera	3–24
Elaeagnus angustifolia	1–3, 7–14, 18, 19
Maclura pomifera	All
Populus alba 'Pyramidalis'	All

NAME OF PLANT	CLIMATE ZONES
Populus nigra 'Italica'	All
Prosopis glandulosa torreyana	8–14
Tamarix	Varies
Ulmus pumila	All

SHRUBS

Evergreen

NAME OF PLANT	CLIMATE ZONES
Acacia cyclopis	8, 9, 13–24
Acacia verticillata	14–24
Bambusa oldhamii	16–24
Cortaderia selloana	4–24
Dodonaea viscosa	7–9, 12–24
Elaeagnus pungens	4–24
Escallonia	4–9, 14–17, 20–24
Eucalyptus grossa	9, 14–24
*Eucalyptus platypus	9, 14–24
Eucalyptus tetraptera	9, 14–24
Griselinia littoralis	9, 15–17, 20–24
*Hakea suaveolens	9, 12–17, 19–24
*Juniperus (columnar shrubs)	All
Lavatera assurgentiflora	14–24
*Leptospermum laevigatum	14–24

NAME OF PLANT	CLIMATE ZONES
Ligustrum japonicum 'Texanum'	4–24
*Melaleuca	Varies
*Myoporum laetum	8, 9, 14–17, 19–24
Nerium oleander	8–16, 18–23
*Pittosporum (all but P. napaulense)	Varies
*Prunus caroliniana	7–24
*Prunus laurocerasus	4–9, 14–24
*Prunus lyonii	7–9, 12–24
Pyracantha (tall growing ones)	Varies
*Rhamnus alaternus	4–24
*Taxus baccata 'Stricta'	3–9, 14–24
*Taxus cuspidata	3–9, 14–24
*Taxus media	3–9, 14–24
Tecomaria capensis	12, 13, 16, 18–24
*Thuja occidentalis	2–9, 15–17, 21–24

*Can become small tree.

SHRUBS (Cont'd.)

Deciduous

NAME OF PLANT	CLIMATE ZONES	NAME OF PLANT	CLIMATE ZONES
Atriplex lentiformis	7–14, 18, 19	Syringa vulgaris	1–11
*Caragana arborescens	1–21	*Tamarix	All
Lonicera tatarica	1–9, 14–21		

*Can become small tree.

Effective windbreaks stretch and flex in the wind

Avoid plants with brittle wood; their branches can snap off in a high wind. Nearly indestructible pampas grass (*Cortaderia selloana*) takes wind in stride, as well as desert heat, coastal salt spray, poor soil, and drought. Do not confuse with its lookalike *C. jubata*, a serious weed (see page 254.)

Fast-growing plants

In the case of a shrub, tree, or vine, "fast" means that it will grow rapidly enough (both in height and width) to begin assuming its mature landscape role in one to four years. For annuals and perennials, "fast" means that it will reach an impressive size within a year.

Not all fast growers, however, are fault free. Some grow quickly but soon slide into an unattractive old age. These are best planted for quick effect at the same time as you plant slower growing, choicer plants; then remove the fast ones when they lose their beauty, by which time the slower plants will have grown large enough to be presentable. As a double-check on possible surprises (good or bad) that any one of these fast growers may hold in store for you, read the description of the plant in the Western Plant Encyclopedia (beginning on page 161). Some plants simply grow fast under almost any conditions; others definitely need certain growing conditions and care to grow with racehorse speed.

TREES

NAME OF PLANT	CLIMATE ZONES	NAME OF PLANT	CLIMATE ZONES
Acacia	Varies	Liriodendron tulipifera	1–10, 14–23
Acer saccharinum	1–9, 14–24	Maclura pomifera	All
Ailanthus altissima	All	Magnolia veitchii	4–9, 14–24
Albizia distachya	15–17, 22–24	Melaleuca	Varies
Alnus rhombifolia	1–9, 14–21	Metasequoia glyptostroboides	3–9, 14–24
Betula nigra	All	Morus alba	All
Callistemon citrinus	8, 9, 12–24	Myoporum laetum	8, 9, 14–17, 19–24
Cassia excelsa	12, 13, 19–24	Olmediella betschlerana	9, 14–24
Casuarina	8–9, 12–24	Parkinsonia aculeata	11–24
Catalpa	All	Paulownia tomentosa	All
Cedrus deodara	2–12, 14–24	Phyllostachys bambusoides	4–24
Cercidium	10–14, 18–20	Pinus	Varies
Chilopsis linearis	11–13, 18–21	Platanus	Varies
Chorisia speciosa	15–24	Populus	Varies
Cupressocyparis leylandii	3–24	Pterocarya stenoptera	5–24
Cupressus forbesii	8–14, 18–20	Quercus rubra	1–12, 14–24
Cupressus glabra	5, 8–24	Robinia pseudoacacia	All
Eriobotrya japonica	4–24	Salix	Varies
Eucalyptus	Varies	Sapium sebiferum	8, 9, 12, 14–16, 18–21
Fraxinus ornus	3–9, 14–17	Schinus molle	8, 9, 12–24
Fraxinus quadrangulata	1–6	Sequoia sempervirens	4–9, 14–24
Fraxinus uhdei	9, 12–24	Sequoiadendron giganteum	All
Gleditsia triacanthos	1–16, 18–20	Taxodium mucronatum	5, 6, 8–10, 12–24
Grevillea robusta	8, 9, 12–24	Tecoma	12, 13, 21–24
Harpephyllum caffrum	17, 19, 21–24	Tipuana tipu	12–16, 18–24
Hoheria populnea	4–6, 15–17, 21–24	Ulmus parvifolia	8, 9, 12–24
Ligustrum lucidum	5, 6, 8–24		

SHRUBS

NAME OF PLANT	CLIMATE ZONES
Abutilon	13.15–24
Acacia	Varies
Baccharis pilularis	5–11, 14–24
Buddleia davidii	1–9, 12–24
Caesalpinia	Varies
Callistemon	8, 9, 12–24
Caragana arborescens	1–21
Ceanothus	4–7, 14–24
Cestrum	Varies
Chamelaucium uncinatum	8, 9, 12–24
Choisya ternata	7–9, 12–24
Chorizema	15–17, 19–24
Cistus	4–9, 12–24
Convolvulus cneorum	7–9,.12–24
Cornus stolonifera	1–9, 14–21
Cotoneaster lacteus	4–24
Crotalaria agatiflora	13, 15–24
Cytisus	Varies
Dodonea viscosa	7–9, 12–24
Dombeya	21–24
Duranta	Varies
Elaeagnus	Varies
Eriobotrya deflexa	8–24
Escallonia	4–9, 14–17, 20–24
Eucalyptus	Varies
Forsythia intermedia	2–11, 14–16, 18, 19
Fremontodendron	7–24
Fuchsia	Varies
Gamolepis chrysanthemoides	8, 9, 13–24

NAME OF PLANT	CLIMATE ZONES
Grewia occidentalis	8, 9, 14–24
Griselinia littoralis	9, 15–17, 20–24
Hakea suaveolens	9, 12–17, 19–24
Hebe	Varies
Hibiscus	Varies
Hydrangea	Varies
Hypericum calycinum	2–24
Ilex 'Nellie Stevens'	4–9, 14–24
Lantana	See Encyclopedia
Lavatera assurgentiflora	14–24
Ligustrum japonicum	4–24
Melaleuca	Varies
Melianthus major	8, 9, 12–24
Nerium oleander	8–16, 18–23
Philadelphus	Varies
Prunus laurocerasus	4–9, 14–24
Pyracantha coccinea	All
Rhamnus alaternus	4–24
Rhus (some)	Varies
Rosa	Varies
Salix	Varies
Sesbania tripetii	7–9, 12–16, 18–23
Solanum rantonnetii	15–24
Sparmannia africana	17, 21–24
Spartium junceum	5–9, 11–24
Tamarix	Varies
Thevetia	Varies
Tibouchina urvilleana	16, 17, 21–24
Weigela florida	1–11, 14–17

PERENNIALS, ANNUALS

NAME OF PLANT	CLIMATE ZONES
Acanthus mollis	4–24
Ajuga reptans	All
Carpobrotus	12–24
Chrysanthemum frutescens	All
Colocasia esculenta	13, 16–22
Cortaderia selloana	4–24
Cyperus papyrus	8, 9, 12–24
Ensete	17, 19–24
Euryops	14–17, 19–24

NAME OF PLANT	CLIMATE ZONES
Felicia amelloides	8, 9, 13–24
Lavatera trimestris	All
Musa	Varies
Philodendron	Varies
Phormium tenax	7–24
Ricinus communis	All
Romneya coulteri	5–10, 12–24
Saxifraga rosacea	1–7, 14–17

Ground covers and lawn substitutes

The best-known ground cover is lawn (see pages 85–88), and it is unsurpassed as a surface to walk and play upon. But where foot traffic is not important or not wanted, many other ground cover plants can offer much of a lawn's neatness and uniformity with considerably less maintenance. Choices of ground covers run the gamut of foliage textures and colors, and many are noted for production of colorful flowers. Pattern plantings can be made, using different ground covers to contrast pleasantly with one another. Most ground covers function as barriers in the landscape, rather than as the green bridge between areas a lawn provides. A few, however, will tolerate foot traffic.

Combine ground covers for a new effect

Several different ground covers give a variety of sizes and textures. Highest, at right, are two forms of prostrate juniper. Closest to house is white-flowered star jasmine (*Trachelospermum jasminoides*). Along driveway is low mat of *Vinca minor*.

SHRUBS

NAME OF PLANT	CLIMATE ZONES	NAME OF PLANT	CLIMATE ZONES
Abelia grandiflora 'Prostrata'	5–24	Ceanothus gloriosus	See Encyclopedia
Arctostaphylos edmundsii	6–9, 14–24	Ceanothus griseus horizontalis	Varies
Arctostaphylos hookeri	6–9, 14–24	Ceanothus maritimus	4–7, 14–24
Arctostaphylos hookeri 'Monterey Carpet'	6–9, 14–24	Chorizema ilicifolium	15–17, 19–24
Arctostaphylos media	4–9, 14–24	Cistus salvifolius	7–9, 12–24
Arctostaphylos pumila	17	Coprosma kirkii	8, 9, 14–17, 21–24
Arctostaphylos uva-ursi	1–9, 14–24	Cornus canadensis	1–7
*Ardisia japonica	5, 6, 15–17	Correa pulchella	14–24
Atriplex semibaccata	8, 9, 12–24	Cotoneaster (some)	Varies
Baccharis pilularis	5–11, 14–24	Cytisus kewensis	4–6, 16, 17
Bamboo (some)	Varies	*Daphne blagayana	4–6
Calluna vulgaris (some)	2–6, 15–17	Erica (some)	Varies
*Camellia sasanqua (some)	4–9, 14–24	*Gaultheria ovatifolia	4–7, 14–17
Carissa grandiflora (some)	12, 13, 16–24		

*Will grow in shade.

SHRUBS (Cont'd.)

NAME OF PLANT	CLIMATE ZONES
*Gaultheria procumbens	2–7, 14–17
Genista lydia	4–6, 14–17
Genista sagittalis	2–9, 11–22
Hebe menziesii	14–24
*Hypericum calycinum	2–24
Hypericum coris	4–24
Juniperus (ground cover forms)	All
Lantana montevidensis	8–10, 12–17, 23, 24
Leptospermum scoparium 'Horizontalis'	14–24
Leptospermum scoparium 'Waerengi'	14–24
Leucothoe fontanesiana	4–7, 15–17
*Lysimachia	1–9, 14–24
*Mahonia nervosa	2–9, 14–17
*Mahonia repens	1–21
*Muehlenbeckia	Varies
Myoporum parvifolium	14–16, 18–24
*Nandina domestica 'Harbour Dwarf'	5–24

NAME OF PLANT	CLIMATE ZONES
*Pachysandra terminalis	1–10, 14–21
Paxistima canbyi	1–10, 14–21
Pyracantha 'Santa Cruz'	4–24
Pyracantha 'Walderi'	4–24
Raphiolepis (some)	8–10, 12–24
Ribes viburnifolium	8, 9, 14–24
Rosmarinus officinalis 'Collingwood Ingram'	4–24
Rosmarinus officinalis 'Lockwood de Forest'	4–24
Rosmarinus officinalis 'Prostratus'	4–24
*Ruscus hypoglossum	4–24
*Sarcococca hookerana humilis	4–9, 14–24
*Taxus baccata 'Repandens'	3–9, 14–24
Teucrium chamaedrys	All
*Vaccinium vitis-idaea	2–7, 14–17

VINES

NAME OF PLANT	CLIMATE ZONES
Bougainvillea	Varies
*Cissus	Varies
*Euonymus fortunei & varieties	1–17
*Fatshedera lizei	4–10, 12–24
Gelsemium sempervirens	8–24
Hardenbergia	Varies
*Hedera	Varies
Hibbertia scandens	16, 17, 21–24
Jasminum nitidum	12, 13, 16, 19–21
Jasminum polyanthum	9, 12–24
Lonicera japonica	2–24

NAME OF PLANT	CLIMATE ZONES
*Muehlenbeckia axillaris	3–9, 14–24
Passiflora	Varies
Pyrostegia venusta	13, 16, 21–24
*Rhoicissus capensis	16, 17, 21–24
Rosa banksiae	4–24
Rosa bracteata 'Mermaid'	4–24
Sollya heterophylla	8, 9, 14–24
Tetrastigma	13, 17, 20–24
Thunbergia gregorii	21–24
Trachelospermum	Varies

PERENNIALS

NAME OF PLANT	CLIMATE ZONES
Acaena	4–9, 14–24
Achillea tomentosa	All
*Aegopodium podagraria	1–7
*Ajuga reptans	All
Arabis	Varies
Arctotheca calendula	8, 9, 13–24
Arctotis	7–9, 14–24
*Asarum caudatum	4–6, 14–17, 21
Asparagus densiflorus 'Sprengeri'	12–24
*Brunnera macrophylla	All
Calocephalus brownii	16, 17, 19, 21–24
*Campanula	All
Carpobrotus	12–24
Cephalophyllum 'Red Spike'	8, 9, 11–24
Cerastium tomentosum	All
Ceratostigma plumbaginoides	2–9, 14–24
*Convallaria majalis	1–7, 14–20
Convolvulus mauritanicus	4–9, 12–24
Coronilla varia	All
*Crassula multicava	16, 17, 22–24
*Cymbalaria muralis	3–24
Delosperma 'Alba'	12–24
Drosanthemum	14–24
Dryas	1–6
*Duchesnea indica	All
*Epimedium	1–9, 14–17
Erigeron karvinskianus	8, 9, 12–24
Festuca ovina glauca	All

NAME OF PLANT	CLIMATE ZONES
*Fragaria chiloensis	4–24
*Galax urceolata	1–6
Gazania	8–24
Halimium	7–9, 12–24
Helianthemum	All
*Heterocentron elegans	17, 21–24
Iberis sempervirens	All
Lampranthus	14–24
*Liriope spicata	All
Lotus berthelotii	9, 15–24
*Lysimachia nummularia	1–9, 14–24
Malephora	Varies
*Mentha	Varies
*Myosotis	All
Nepeta faassenii	All
*Ophiopogon japonicus	5–10, 12–24
Oscularia	15–24
Osteospermum fruticosum	8, 9, 14–24
*Oxalis oregana	4–9, 14–24
Pelargonium peltatum	8, 9, 12–24
*Pellaea viridis	14–17, 19–24
Polygonum capitatum	8, 9, 12–24
Polygonum cuspidatum compactum	All
Polygonum vaccinifolium	4–7
Potentilla cinerea	1–17
Potentilla tabernaemontanii	All
Santolina	All
Saponaria ocymoides	All

*Will grow in shade.

(Continued on next page)

PERENNIALS (Cont'd.)

NAME OF PLANT	CLIMATE ZONES
Saxifraga rosacea	1–7, 14–17
*Saxifraga stolonifera	4–9, 14–24
*Saxifraga umbrosa	1–7, 14–17
Sedum (many)	Varies
*Soleirolia soleirolii	8–24
Thymus	All
*Tolmiea menziesii	5–9, 12–24

NAME OF PLANT	CLIMATE ZONES
*Tradescantia fluminensis	12–24
*Vancouveria	Varies
Verbena	Varies
Vinca	Varies
Viola hederacea	8, 9, 14–24
Viola odorata	All

WALK-ON LAWN SUBSTITUTES

NAME OF PLANT	CLIMATE ZONES
Chamaemelum nobile	All
*Cotula squalida	4–9, 14–24
Dichondra micrantha	8, 9, 12–24
Hippocrepis comosa	8–24

NAME OF PLANT	CLIMATE ZONES
Mazus reptans	1–7, 14–24
Phyla nodiflora	8–24
Sagina subulata	1–11, 14–24
Zoysia tenuifolia	8, 9, 12–24

*Will grow in shade.

*Instead of a lawn—
a carpet of flowers*

A number of ground covers have attractive blossoms. Generous winter color here comes from fast-growing *Osteospermum fruticosum*, a good 12-inch-high ground cover for sunny locations.

Plants for indoor arrangements

The enjoyment of many plants can be extended by cutting them for display indoors. Usually the first that come to mind are fresh flowers; one of the lists below contains flowering plants with blossoms that will last well when cut and placed in water. But even longer-lasting enjoyment can be had from arrangements of dried flowers, dried seed capsules, fresh or dry foliage—plants for long-lasting arrangements are also listed.

DRIED FLOWERS

NAME OF PLANT	KIND	CLIMATE ZONES
Acanthus mollis	Perennial	4–24
Achillea	Perennial	All
Allium	Perennial	Varies
Artichoke	Perennial	8, 9, 14–24
Briza maxima	Annual	All
Carthamus tinctorius	Annual	All
Catananche caerulea	Perennial	All
Celosia	Annual	All
Echinops exaltatus	Perennial	All
Eriogonum	Perennial, annual	Varies

NAME OF PLANT	KIND	CLIMATE ZONES
Eryngium	Perennial	All
Gomphrena globosa	Annual	All
Helichrysum bracteatum	Annual	All
Helipterum roseum	Annual	All
Limonium	Perennial, annual	Varies
Moluccella laevis	Annual	All
Protea	Shrub	16, 17, 21–24
Xeranthemum annuum	Annual	All

FRESH FLOWERS

Achillea
Allium
Anemone
Antirrhinum majus
Artichoke
Baptisia australis
Billbergia
Bulbinella floribunda
Camellia japonica
Carthamus tinctorius
Catananche caerulea
Celosia
Centaurea cyanus
Centaurea moschata
Chamelaucium uncinatum
Chrysanthemum (most)
Coreopsis (most)
Cosmos
Cymbidium
Cyperus papyrus
Delphinium
Dianthus caryophyllus
Echinops exaltatus
Eryngium
Eucalyptus megacornuta
Eucalyptus orpetii
Francoa ramosa
Freesia
Gaillardia
Gerbera jamesonii
Geum
Gladiolus
Helichrysum bracteatum
Heliopsis helianthoides
  scabra

Helleborus
Hemerocallis
Iris (many)
Kniphofia uvaria
Lathyrus odoratus
Leucocoryne ixioides
Limonium
Lychnis coeli-rosa
Matthiola incana
Moluccella laevis
Narcissus
Nicotiana alata
Ornithogalum
Paeonia (herbaceous)
Papaver orientale
Physostegia virginiana
Protea
Ranunculus
Rosa
Rudbeckia
Salix caprea
Salix discolor
Salix gracilistyla
Salpiglossis sinuata
Stokesia laevis
Syringa vulgaris
Tagetes
Tritonia
Trollius
Tulbaghia fragrans
Tulipa
Watsonia
Zantedeschia

FOLIAGE

Acacia (some)
Eucalyptus perriniana
Eucalyptus polyanthemos
Eucalyptus pulverulenta
Galax urceolata
Gaultheria shallon
Leucodendron argenteum
Macadamia
Magnolia grandiflora

Marrubium vulgare
Myrsine africana
Ruscus
Sciadopitys verticillata
Senecio greyi
Sequoia sempervirens
Stranvaesia davidiana
Vaccinium ovatum

DRIED SEED CAPSULES

Ailanthus altissima
Baptisia australis
Belamcanda chinensis
Brachychiton
Cedrela
Celastrus
Cimicifuga
Clematis
Coix lacryma-jobi
Corn, Ornamental
Eucalyptus megacornuta

Gourd
Iris foetidissima
Jacaranda mimosifolia
Koelreuteria
Lunaria annua
Magnolia grandiflora
Nelumbo
Nigella damascena
Physalis alkekengi
Platanus
Ruta graveolens

Good choices for rock gardens

Small or tiny shrubs, miniature bulbous plants, annuals and perennials that form low tufts of leaves or creeping mats of foliage—these are the sorts listed here for planting in rock gardens. Classic European rock gardens and Alpine landscapes can be re-created in cool Pacific Northwest gardens; but to put together the same effect in southern California will call for a different assortment of plants. Read carefully the climate zone adaptations and the individual plant descriptions in the Western Plant Encyclopedia (beginning on page 161).

*Seasonal effects spark
basic rock garden plantings*

Wisely chosen rock garden plants transform a slope into a tapestry of flower and foliage colors and textures, interesting at all times of year. Grouped around plum-colored Japanese maple (*Acer palmatum*) are azaleas, dianthus, and rockrose (*Cistus*) in various shades of pink; yellow broom (*Genista*) and sunrose (*Helianthemum*); and an apricot-colored sunrose.

TREES

NAME OF PLANT	CLIMATE ZONES	NAME OF PLANT	CLIMATE ZONES
Abies balsamea 'Nana'	3–7, 15–17	Pinus edulis	See Encyclopedia section
Acer palmatum	1–9, 14–24	Pinus monophylla	See Encyclopedia section
Pinus albicaulis	See Encyclopedia section	Pinus mugo mugo	See Encyclopedia section
Pinus contorta latifolia	See Encyclopedia section	Pinus strobus 'Nana'	See Encyclopedia section
Pinus densiflora 'Umbraculifera'	See Encyclopedia section		

SHRUBS AND SHRUBLETS

NAME OF PLANT	CLIMATE ZONES
Andromeda polifolia	All
Azalea (rhododendron)	Varies
Berberis stenophylla 'Corallina Compacta'	1–11, 14–17
Calluna vulgaris (some)	2–6, 15–17
Calocephalus brownii	16, 17, 19, 21–24
Chamaecyparis (some)	Varies
Cistus	7–9, 12–24
Daboecia (some)	Varies
Daphne (some)	Varies
Erica (some)	Varies
Gaultheria (most species)	Varies
Genista (some)	Varies
Halimiocistus sahucii	4–24
Halimium	7–9, 12–24
Hebe cupressoides 'Nana'	14–24

NAME OF PLANT	CLIMATE ZONES
Helianthemum nummularium	All
Hypericum coris	4–24
Jasminum parkeri	9, 12–24
Juniperus	All
Myoporum debile	15–17, 19–24
Penstemon rupicola	1–7
Pimelea prostrata	4–7, 14–17
Polygala chamaebuxus	4–6
Potentilla cinerea	1–17
Rhododendron chryseum	4–6, 14, 17
Rhododendron impeditum	4–6, 14, 17
Rhododendron keiskei	4–6, 14, 17
Rhododendron moupinense	4–6, 14, 17
Rhododendron pemakoense	4–6, 14, 17
Spiraea bullata	1–11, 14–21
Teucrium	All

PERENNIALS

NAME OF PLANT	CLIMATE ZONES
Acaena	4–9, 14–24
Achillea tomentosa	All
Aethionema	1–9
Ajuga genevensis	All
Alyssum	All
Anacyclus depressus	All
Anagallis monelli linifolia	All
Androsace	1–6, 14–17
Anemone pulsatilla	1–6, 15–17
Arabis	Varies
Arenaria	2–9, 14–24
Armeria	All
Aubrieta deltoidea	1–9, 14–21
Campanula	Varies
Cerastium tomentosum	All
Crassula lactea	16, 17, 22–24
Crassula schmidtii	16, 17, 22–24
Dianthus (smallest)	All
Dryas	1–6
Echeveria (many)	Varies
Erigeron	Varies
Eriogonum	Varies
Erodium chamaedryoides	7–9, 14–24
Erysimum kotschyanum	1–11, 14–21
Euphorbia myrsinites	All
Gazania (clumping sorts)	8–24
Gentiana	1–6, 14–17
Geranium	Varies
Graptopetalum	8–24
Gypsophila repens	1–11, 14–16, 18–21
Herniaria glabra	All
Heuchera	Varies

NAME OF PLANT	CLIMATE ZONES
Iberis sempervirens	All
Iris cristata	4–9, 14–24
Iris, Pacific Coast	4–24
Iris tectorum	4–9, 14–24
Kalanchoe beharensis	21–24
Leontopodium alpinum	1–9, 14–24
Lewisia	1–7
Lithodora diffusa	5–7, 14–17
Mazus reptans	1–7, 14–24
Oenothera missouriensis	All
Onosma tauricum	1–9, 14–17
Origanum dictamnus	8–24
Oxalis adenophylla	4–9, 14–24
Oxalis hirta	8, 9, 14–24
Papaver burseri	All
Penstemon davidsonii	1–7
Phlox divaricata	1–17
Phlox nivalis	4–7
Phlox subulata	1–17
Polemonium reptans	1–11, 14–17
Primula (most)	Varies
Raoulia australis	7–9, 13–24
Saxifraga	Varies
Sedum (many)	Varies
Sempervivum	All
Silene acaulis	1–11, 14–16, 18–21
Thymus	All
Veronica	All

BULBS

NAME OF PLANT	CLIMATE ZONES
Allium ostrowskianum 'Zwanenburg'	All
Crocus	All
Cyclamen	Varies
Freesia	8, 9, 12–24
Fritillaria (most species)	1–7, 15–17
Galanthus	1–9, 14–17
Iris reticulata	All
Leucocoryne ixioides	13, 16, 19, 21–24
Milla biflora	13, 16–24

NAME OF PLANT	CLIMATE ZONES
Muscari	All
Narcissus (smaller species)	All
Sparaxis	9, 13–24
Sternbergia lutea	All
Tritonia	9, 13–24
Tulipa (species, not hybrids)	See Encyclopedia
Zephyranthes	1–9, 14–24

Fragrant plants

A garden's fragrance can be as memorable as its appearance; years later the scent of a particular blossom or leaf can evoke recollection of past experience. Notably aromatic plants are presented here in two groups: those with perfumed flowers, and plants in which fragrance comes from foliage.

Flower fragrance usually is most pronounced on warm and humid days, least noticeable when weather is dry and hot. Many of the aromatic foliage plants release more scent when foliage is moistened, bruised, or brushed against as you walk past. Notice that many of these scented foliage plants also are culinary herbs.

TREES

NAME OF PLANT	CLIMATE ZONES	FLOWERS	FOLIAGE
Calocedrus decurrens	1–12, 14–24		•
Caragana arborescens	1–21	•	•
Cinnamomum	Varies	•	•
Citrus	8, 9, 12–24	•	
Cryptocarya rubra	14–17, 20–24		•
Cupressus	Varies		•
Dalea spinosa	11–13	•	
Drimys winteri	8, 9, 14–24	•	
Eucalyptus (many)	8–24		•
Hymenosporum flavum	8, 9, 14–23,	•	
Idesia polycarpa	4–9, 14–17, 19–24	•	
Laurus nobilis	5–9, 12–24		•
Magnolia grandiflora	4–12, 14–24	•	
Malus	1–11, 14–21	•	

NAME OF PLANT	CLIMATE ZONES	FLOWERS	FOLIAGE
Michelia	Varies	•	
Pinus	See Encyclopedia section		•
Pittosporum eugeniodes	9, 14–17, 19–22	•	
Pittosporum undulatum	16, 17, 21–24	•	
Pittosporum viridiflorum	15–17, 20–24	•	
Prunus blireiana	2–12, 14–22	•	
Robinia pseudoacacia	All	•	
Thuja	Varies		•
Tilia	Varies	•	
Umbellularia californica	4–10, 12–24		•
Vitex agnus-castus	4–24		•

SHRUBS

NAME OF PLANT	CLIMATE ZONES	FLOWERS	FOLIAGE
Acacia (several)	Varies	•	
Aloysia triphylla	9, 10, 14–24		•
Artemisia	All		•
Azara (some)	Varies	•	
Boronia megastigma	15–17, 20–24	•	
Bouvardia longiflora 'Albatross'	12, 13, 16, 17, 19–24	•	
Brugmansia candida	16–24	•	
Buddleia	Varies	•	
Calycanthus floridus	1–9, 14–22	•	
Carissa grandiflora	22–24	•	
Cestrum nocturnum	13, 16–24	•	
Cestrum parqui	13–24	•	
Chimonanthus praecox	4–9, 14–17	•	
Choisya ternata	4–9, 12–24	•	
Cistus	7–9, 12–24		•
Citrus	8, 9, 12–24	•	
Clerodendrum bungei	5–9, 12–24	•	
Clethra	Varies	•	
Coleonema	7–9, 14–24		•
Corylopsis	4–7, 15–17	•	
Cytisus	Varies	•	
Daphne	Varies	•	

NAME OF PLANT	CLIMATE ZONES	FLOWERS	FOLIAGE
Elaeagnus	Varies	•	
Escallonia (some)	4–9, 14–17, 20–24		•
Gardenia	Varies	•	
Hamamelis mollis	4–7, 15–17	•	
Jasminum	Varies	•	
Juniperus	Varies		•
Lavandula angustifolia	4–24	•	•
Lonicera	Varies	•	
Michelia figo	9, 14–24	•	
Murraya paniculata	21–24	•	
Myrica	4–7		•
Myrtus communis	8–24		•
Origanum	Varies		•
Osmanthus	Varies	•	
Osmarea burkwoodii	4–9, 14–17	•	
Philadelphus (most)	Varies	•	
Pittosporum napaulense	15–17, 20–24	•	
Pittosporum tobira	4–24	•	
Plumeria	Varies	•	
Raphiolepis 'Majestic Beauty'	8–10, 12–24	•	

SHRUBS (Cont'd.)

NAME OF PLANT	CLIMATE ZONES	FLOWERS	FOLIAGE
Rhododendron 'Else Frye'	See Ency-cylopedia section	●	
Rhododendron 'Fragrantissimum'	See Ency-clopedia section	●	
Rhus aromatica	1–3, 10		●
Ribes viburnifolium	8, 9, 14–24		●
Rosa (many)	All	●	

NAME OF PLANT	CLIMATE ZONES	FLOWERS	FOLIAGE
Rosmarinus	4–24		●
Salvia	Varies		●
Sarcococca	4–9, 14–24	●	
Spartium junceum	5–9, 11–24	●	
Syringa vulgaris	1–12, 14–16, 18–22	●	
Ternstroemia gymnanthera	4–9, 12–24	●	
Viburnum (many)	Varies	●	

VINES

NAME OF PLANT	CLIMATE ZONES	FLOWERS	FOLIAGE
Anredera cordifolia	4–24	●	
Beaumontia grandiflora	12, 13, 16–17 21–24	●	
Clematis armandii	4–9, 12–24	●	
Distictis laxiflora	16, 22–24	●	
Ipomoea alba	See Ency-clopedia section	●	
Jasminum	Varies	●	

NAME OF PLANT	CLIMATE ZONES	FLOWERS	FOLIAGE
Lonicera	Varies	●	
Mandevilla laxa	4–9, 14–21	●	
Passiflora alatocaerulea	5–9, 12–24	●	
Stephanotis floribunda	23, 24	●	
Trachelospermum	Varies	●	
Wisteria	All	●	

PERENNIALS, ANNUALS, BULBS

NAME OF PLANT	CLIMATE ZONES	FLOWERS	FOLIAGE
Achillea	All		●
Alpinia zerumbet	22–24	●	
Amaryllis belladonna	4–24	●	
Anethum graveolens	All		●
Anthemis	All		●
Chamaemelum nobile	All		●
Cheiranthus cheiri	4–6, 14–17 22, 23	●	
Chrysanthemum balsamita	All		●
Convallaria majalis	1–7, 14–20	●	
Crinum	12–24	●	
Crocus chrysanthus	All	●	
Dianthus	All	●	
Dictamnus albus	1–9		●
Foeniculum vulgare	All		●
Freesia	8, 9, 12–24	●	
Galium odoratum	1–6, 15–17		●
Hedychium	17, 22–24	●	
Heliotropium arborescens	8–24	●	
Hemerocallis lilio-asphodelus	All	●	
Hesperis matronalis	All	●	
Hosta plantaginea	1–10, 12–21	●	
Hyacinthus	All	●	
Hymenocallis	5, 6, 8, 9, 14–24	●	
Hyssopus officinalis	All		●
Iberis amara	All	●	
Iris (bearded)	All	●	

NAME OF PLANT	CLIMATE ZONES	FLOWERS	FOLIAGE
Lathyrus odoratus	All	●	
Leucocoryne ixioides	13, 16, 19, 21–24	●	
Lilium	All	●	
Lobularia maritima	10–24	●	
Marrubium vulgare	All		●
Matthiola	All	●	
Melissa officinalis	All		●
Mentha	Varies		●
Milla biflora	13, 16–24	●	
Monarda	All		●
Narcissus (many)	All	●	
Nelumbo	All	●	
Nepeta	All		●
Nicotiana	All	●	
Odontoglossum pulchellum	23, 24	●	
Paeonia	Varies	●	
Pelargonium (several)	8, 9, 12–24		●
Polianthes tuberosa	24	●	
Primula alpicola	1–6, 17	●	
Reseda odorata	All	●	
Ruta graveolens	All		●
Salvia	Varies		●
Satureja	Varies		●
Tanacetum vulgare	All		●
Thymus	All		●
Tropaeolum majus	See Ency-clopedia section	●	
Viola odorata	All	●	

Vines and vinelike plants

A vine is a more or less flexible shrub that doesn't stop growing in height or length (depending on whether you grow it vertically or horizontally). Most need some sort of support if they are to be anything more than a sprawling mass or a ground cover. But therein lies their usefulness: with their ability to "wander" and their willingness to be guided, they can find employment as decorative garden frosting, emphasizers (or maskers) of architectural lines, or as purely utilitarian sun, wind, or view screens.

Despite the familiar phrase, "a clinging vine," not all vines cling in the same manner—some don't cling at all. Vines fall into four general climbing types.

1) *Twining*. New growth twists or spirals as it grows. Nearly all will twist around other growth, new or old, on itself (and on nearby plants as well), requiring some thinning out and guidance. Nearly all have too small a turn to encircle a large post; the best support is a cord or wire.

2) *Tendrils*. Specialized growths along the stems reach out and wrap around whatever is handy—wire or rope, another stem of the vine, or another plant. Tendrils grow out straight until they make contact, then they contract into a spiral spring.

3) *Clinging*. Special growths along stems attach to a flat surface and hold on. Some clingers have tendrils with suction cup discs at the ends; others have hooklike claws or tips on tendrils that hook into small irregularities or crevices of a flat surface. Still another sort is equipped with small roots along the stems; these roots cling fast even to vertical surfaces.

4) *Must be tied*. These vines have no means of attachment, must be tied to a support. Some of these plants—jasmine and climbing roses, for example—tend to produce new growth toward the shaded side of their stems, so that when tied to a trellis the new growth tends to weave through the older. Others, such as *Fatshedera lizei*, are naturally sprawling and somewhat shrubby but will grow reasonably flat as long as you tie and train them.

EVERGREEN

NAME OF PLANT	CLIMATE ZONES	HOW IT CLIMBS	GROWTH RATE	FLOWERS	SUITED TO SHADE
Anemopaegma chamberlaynii	15–17, 19, 21–24	Tendrils	Medium	●	
Antigonon leptopus	12, 13, 18–21	Tendrils	Fast	●	
Beaumontia grandiflora	12, 13, 16–17, 21–24	Twining	Fast	●	
Bougainvillea	Varies	Must be tied	Fast	●	
Cissus	Varies	Tendrils	Medium		●
Clematis armandii	4–9, 12–24	Tendrils	Fast	●	●
Clerodendrum thomsoniae	22–24	Twining	Slow	●	
Clytostoma callistegioides	9, 13–24	Tendrils	Fast	●	●
Distictis	Varies	Tendrils	Medium fast	●	●
Euonymus fortunei	1–17	Clinging	Medium		●
Fatshedera lizei	4–10, 12–24	Must be tied	Medium		●
Ficus pumila	8–24	Clinging	Medium fast		●
Gelsemium sempervirens	8–24	Twining	Medium	●	
Hardenbergia comptoniana	15–24	Twining	Medium	●	●
Hardenbergia violacea	9–24	Twining	Fast	●	
Hedera canariensis	8, 9, 12–24	Clinging	Fast		●

Vines with masses of blossoms can give a seasonal face lift to buildings. Japanese wisteria (*Wisteria floribunda*) reliably provides lavish early spring flower display in all zones. Drifts of fallen petals look lovely, are easy to sweep up.

Vines soften architectural lines

For mild-winter climates there is a wealth of spectacular tropical and subtropical vines. This is *Mandevilla* 'Alice du Pont'.

EVERGREEN (Cont'd.)

NAME OF PLANT	CLIMATE ZONES	HOW IT CLIMBS	GROWTH RATE	FLOWERS	SUITED TO SHADE
Hedera helix	All	Clinging	Fast		●
Hibbertia scandens	16, 17, 21–24	Twining	Fast	●	●
Hoya carnosa	15–24	Clinging, must be tied	Slow	●	●

(Continued on next page)

EVERGREEN (Cont'd.)

NAME OF PLANT	CLIMATE ZONES	HOW IT CLIMBS	GROWTH RATE	FLOWERS	SUITED TO SHADE
Jasminum grandiflorum	9, 12–24	Must be tied	Fast	●	●
Jasminum nitidum	12, 13, 16, 19–21	Must be tied	Medium	●	●
Jasminum officinale	12–24	Twining	Fast	●	●
Jasminum polyanthum	9, 12–24	Twining	Fast	●	
Kadsura japonica	7–9, 14–22	Twining	Fast		●
Lapageria rosea	5, 6, 15–17, 23, 24	Twining	Slow	●	●
Lonicera hildebrandiana	9, 14–17, 19–24	Twining	Fast	●	●
Lonicera japonica	2–24	Twining	Fast	●	●
Lonicera sempervirens	3–24	Twining	Medium	●	●
Macfadyena unguis-cati	8–24	Tendrils	Medium fast	●	
Mandevilla 'Alice du Pont'	21–24	Twining	Medium	●	●
Mina lobata	20–24	Twining	Fast	●	
Muehlenbeckia complexa	8, 9, 14–24	Twining	Fast		●
Pandorea	16–24	Twining	Fast	●	●
Passiflora	Varies	Tendrils	Fast	●	
Polygonum aubertii	8, 9, 13–24	Twining	Fast	●	
Pyrostegia venusta	13, 16, 21–24	Tendrils	Fast	●	●
Rhoicissus capensis	16, 17, 21–24	Tendrils	Slow		●
Rosa (climbing sorts)	Varies	Must be tied	Medium	●	
Senecio confusus	16–24	Twining	Fast	●	
Senecio mikanioides	14–24	Twining	Fast	●	
Solandra maxima	17, 21–24	Must be tied	Fast	●	
Solanum jasminoides	8, 9, 12–24	Twining	Fast	●	●
Stephanotis floribunda	23, 24	Twining	Medium	●	●
Stigmaphyllon ciliatum	19–24	Twining	Fast	●	●
Tecomaria capensis	12, 13, 16, 18–24	Must be tied	Fast	●	
Tetrastigma	13, 17, 20–24	Tendrils	Fast		
Thunbergia	Varies	Twining	Fast	●	
Trachelospermum	Varies	Twining	Medium	●	●

DECIDUOUS

NAME OF PLANT	CLIMATE ZONES	HOW IT CLIMBS	GROWTH RATE	FLOWERS	SUITED TO SHADE
Actinidia chinensis	4–9, 14–24	Twining, must be tied	Fast	●	●
Actinidia kolomikta	4–9, 15–17	Twining	Fast		●
Akebia quinata	All	Twining	Fast	●	●
Ampelopsis brevipedunculata	All	Tendrils, twining	Fast		●

Vines spill downward as well as climb

Vines can climb up over one side of a wall, then tumble downward on the opposite side. Vibrantly colorful *Bougainvillea* will produce summer flower display in mild-winter, warm-summer zones. In addition to red, pink, white, purple, orange, and yellow varieties are also available.

DECIDUOUS (Cont'd.)

NAME OF PLANT	CLIMATE ZONES	HOW IT CLIMBS	GROWTH RATE	FLOWERS	SUITED TO SHADE
Anredera cordifolia	4–24	Twining	Fast	●	
Antigonon leptopus	12, 13, 18–21	Tendrils	Fast	●	
Aristolochia durior	All	Twining	Fast	●	●
Campsis	Varies	Clinging	Fast	●	
Celastrus	See Encyclopedia	Twining	Fast		●
Clematis (all but C. armandii)	Varies	Twining	Fast	●	
Grape	All	Tendrils	Fast		
Humulus lupulus	All	Twining	Fast		
Hydrangea anomala	1–21	Clinging	Slow	●	●
Lonicera heckrottii	2–24	Twining	Fast	●	●
Mandevilla laxa	4–9, 14–21	Twining	Medium fast	●	
Parthenocissus	Varies	Tendrils, clinging	Fast		●
Polygonum aubertii	1–7, 10–12	Twining	Fast	●	
Polygonum baldschuanicum	All	Twining	Fast	●	
Rosa (climbing sorts)	Varies	Must be tied	Medium	●	
Solanum wendlandii	16, 21–24	Twining	Fast	●	
Vigna caracalla	12–24	Twining	Fast	●	
Wisteria	All	Twining	Fast	●	●

ANNUALS

NAME OF PLANT	CLIMATE ZONES	HOW IT CLIMBS	GROWTH RATE	FLOWERS	SUITED TO SHADE
Bean, scarlet runner	All	Twining	Fast	●	
Cobaea scandens	All	Tendrils	Fast	●	
Ipomoea	Varies	Twining	Fast	●	
Lathyrus odoratus	All	Tendrils	Fast	●	

Plants for espaliers

The classic espalier is a fruit tree trained so that its branches grow in a flat plane, often in a rigid candelabra arrangement. With this method of training against a sunny wall, crops could be raised early or in marginally warm regions. In today's landscape the practice of espaliering has expanded to include purely ornamental plants trained against walls and fences both in the traditional formal arrangement and in irregular patterns determined by a plant's natural growth habits. Espaliers are well-suited to the narrow planting space between a walk and wall, and against any wall or fence where you want a tracery of branches, foliage, or flowers. The plants listed below are among the easiest to train as espaliers because their growth tends toward arrangement in flat surfaces, and is strong enough to be self-supporting yet flexible enough to be guided without breaking easily.

Use an espalier
to lend interest to a fence

Tying, pinching, and pruning are steps in training an espalier. *Pyracantha* is one of the easiest plants to train as an espalier and offers two seasons of color: in the spring, white flowers; in the autumn, red berries.

NAME OF PLANT	CLIMATE ZONES
Abutilon	13, 15–24
Acer circinatum	1–6, 14–17
Apple	Varies
Apricot	Varies
Azalea (rhododendron)	Varies
Bauhinia punctata	13, 18–23
Calliandra haematocephala	22–24
Callistemon	8, 9, 12–24
Camellia (some)	4–9, 14–24
Carissa grandiflora 'Fancy'	22–24

NAME OF PLANT	CLIMATE ZONES
Cestrum (some)	Varies
Citrus	Varies
Clianthus puniceus	8, 9, 14–24
Cocculus laurifolius	8, 9, 12–24
Coprosma repens	15–17, 21–24
Cotoneaster 'Hybridus Pendulus'	4–24
Cotoneaster lacteus	4–24
Elaeagnus (evergreen ones)	Varies
Eriobotrya deflexa	8–14

NAME OF PLANT	CLIMATE ZONES
Eriobotrya japonica	4–24
Escallonia exoniensis	4–9, 14–17, 20–24
Eucalyptus caesia	8–24
Eucalyptus orbifolia	8–24
Eucalyptus rhodantha	8–24
Euonymus fortunei (some)	1–17
Feijoa sellowiana	7–9, 12–24
Ficus auriculata	20–24
Ficus benjamina	13, 23, 24
Fig, Edible	4–9, 12–24
Gardenia	Varies
Grewia occidentalis	8, 9, 14–24
Griselinia	9, 15–17, 20–24
Hibiscus rosa-sinensis	9, 12, 13, 15, 16, 19–24
Ilex altaclarensis 'Wilsonii'	3–24
Ilex cornuta 'Burfordii'	4–24
Iochroma cyaneum	16, 17, 19–24
Itea ilicifolia	4–24
Juniperus chinensis 'Torulosa'	All
Laburnum watereri	1–10, 14–17
Magnolia grandiflora	4–12, 14–24
Malus	1–11, 14–21
Michelia figo	9, 14–24
Nectarine	Varies
Ochna serrulata	14–24

NAME OF PLANT	CLIMATE ZONES
Osmanthus fragrans	8, 9, 12–24
Peach	Varies
Pear	Varies
Photinia fraseri	4–24
Plum	Varies
Podocarpus gracilior	8, 9, 13–24
Podocarpus macrophyllus	4–9, 12–24
Prunus (deciduous)	Varies
Pyracantha	Varies
Pyrus kawakamii	8, 9, 12–24
Rhododendron 'Else Frye'	See Encyclopedia section
Rhododendron 'Fragrantissimum'	See Encyclopedia section
Rhus integrifolia	15–17, 20–24
Rhus laurina	20–24
Rhus ovata	7–24
Sarcococca ruscifolia	4–9, 14–24
Sophora secundiflora	8–16, 18–24
Tecomaria capensis	12, 13, 16, 18–24
Viburnum burkwoodii	1–9, 14–24
Viburnum macrocephalum macrocephalum	1–9, 14–24
Viburnum plicatum	1–9, 14–24
Xylosma congestum	8–24

Deerproof (or close to it)

Browsing deer are charming to watch, but they can do considerable damage to plants in country areas and in suburban fringe gardens. Various ways to discourage or repel deer and protect plants from them are presented on page 62. A sufficiently hungry deer will find almost any plant palatable—the list below contains plants that deer *usually* shun.

NAME OF PLANT	KIND	CLIMATE ZONES
Agapanthus	Perennial	7–9, 12–24
Agave	Perennial	Varies
Aloe	Perennial	8, 9, 12–24
*Arbutus unedo	Shrub	4–24
Artemisia tridentata	Perennial	All
Artichoke	Perennial	8, 9, 14–24
Bamboo	Perennial	Varies
Buddleia davidii	Shrub	1–9, 12–24
Buxus	Shrub	Varies
Calendula	Annual	All
Calycanthus occidentalis	Shrub	4–9, 14–22
Chamaerops humilis	Shrub	5–24
Choisya ternata	Shrub	7–9, 12–17
Cistus	Shrub	8, 9, 12–24
Coprosma repens	Shrub	15–17, 21–24
Correa	Shrub	14–24
*Cotinus coggygria	Shrub	All
Cytisus scoparius	Shrub	4–9, 14–22
Daphne	Shrub	Varies
Digitalis	Perennial	All
Echium fastuosum	Perennial	14–24
Ferns	Perennial	Varies
Gelsemium sempervirens	Vine	8–24
Hedera helix	Vine	All
Helleborus	Perennial	Varies
Hypericum	Shrub	4–24
Iris	Bulb	Varies
Jasminum	Shrub, vine	Varies
Juniperus	Shrub	All
Kerria japonica	Shrub	1–21

NAME OF PLANT	KIND	CLIMATE ZONES
Kniphofia uvaria	Perennial	1–9, 14–24
Lantana	Shrub	8–10, 12–17, 23, 24
Leucojum	Bulb	Varies
Lupinus	Annual, perennial	Varies
Mahonia	Shrub	Varies
Melianthus major	Shrub	8, 9, 12–24
*Myrica californica	Shrub	4–6, 14–17, 20–24
Narcissus	Bulb	All
*Nerium oleander	Shrub	8–16, 18–23
Papaver orientale	Perennial	1–17
Papaver rhoeas	Annual	All
Phormium tenax	Perennial	7–24
*Prunus caroliniana	Shrub	7–24
Rhododendron (not azaleas)	Shrub	Varies
Rhus ovata	Shrub	7–24
Romneya coulteri	Perennial	5–10, 12–24
Rosmarinus officinalis	Shrub	4–24
Rudbeckia hirta	Perennial	All
Solanum jasminoides	Vine	8, 9, 12–24
Solanum wendlandii	Vine	16, 21–24
Spartium junceum	Shrub	5–9, 11–24
*Syzygium paniculatum	Shrub	16, 17, 19–24
Tecomaria capensis	Vine	12, 13, 16, 18–24
Teucrium fruticans	Shrub	4–24
Tulipa	Bulb	All
Zantedeschia	Rhizome	5, 6, 8, 9, 14–24
Zauschneria	Perennial	4–10, 12–24
Zinnia	Annual	All

*Can become small tree.

Plants that attract birds

If you like to have birds in your garden, you can include some of these plants in your landscaping. Remember, though, that if your attempt to lure birds succeeds, you probably won't get full enjoyment from plants that produce enticing fruit: birds will eat the fruit just when they become colorful.

Most plants whose flowers are listed as attractants are ones that hummingbirds visit in their search for flower nectar.

FRUIT

Trees

NAME OF PLANT	CLIMATE ZONES	NAME OF PLANT	CLIMATE ZONES
Amelanchier laevis	1–6	Malus	1–11, 14–21
Arbutus	Varies	Morus	Varies
Carpinus caroliniana	1–9, 14–17	Persimmon	Varies
Celtis	Varies	Prunus	Varies
Cornus	Varies	Sambucus	Varies
Crataegus	1–11, 14–17	Schinus	Varies
Eriobotrya japonica	4–24	Sorbus	1–10, 14–17
Fig, Edible	4–9, 12–24		

Shrubs

NAME OF PLANT	CLIMATE ZONES	NAME OF PLANT	CLIMATE ZONES
*Arbutus unedo	4–24	Lantana	8–10, 12–17, 23, 24
Arctostaphylos	Varies	Ligustrum	Varies
Aronia arbutifolia	1–7	Lonicera	Varies
Blackberry	Varies	Mahonia	Varies
Callicarpa	1–6	*Myrica	Varies
Carissa grandiflora	22–24	*Photinia	Varies
Cestrum	Varies	*Prunus	Varies
Cornus	Varies	Pyracantha	Varies
Cotoneaster	Varies	* Rhamnus purshiana	1–9, 14–17
Elaeagnus	Varies	Rhus laurina	20–24
Euonymus	Varies	Ribes	Varies
Garrya	Varies	Rosa multiflora	All
Gaultheria	4–7, 14–17	Rubus deliciosus	1–5, 10
Grape	Varies	Symphoricarpos	Varies
*Heteromeles arbutifolia	5–24	Vaccinium	Varies
*Ilex	Varies	Viburnum	Varies

*Can become small tree.

Perennials, Vines

NAME OF PLANT	CLIMATE ZONES	NAME OF PLANT	CLIMATE ZONES
Ampelopsis brevipedunculata	All	Lonicera	Varies
Duchesnea indica	All	Parthenocissus	Varies
Fragaria	4–24		

SEEDS

Trees

Abies	Larix
Alnus	Picea
Betula	Pinus
Cercidium	Quercus
Fagus sylvatica	Ulmus

Shrubs, Perennials, Annuals

Ageratum houstonianum	Lonicera
Atriplex	Rosmarinus officinalis
Coreopsis	Solidago
Cosmos	Tagetes
Helianthus annuus	

FLOWERS

Trees

NAME OF PLANT	CLIMATE ZONES
Acacia	Varies
Albizia	Varies
Cercidium	10–14, 18–20

NAME OF PLANT	CLIMATE ZONES
Eriobotrya	Varies
Eucalyptus platypus	14–24
Melia azedarach	6, 8–24

Shrubs

NAME OF PLANT	CLIMATE ZONES
Abutilon	13, 15–24
Acacia	Varies
Buddleia	Varies
Caesalpinia gilliesii	8–16, 18–23
Callistemon citrinus	8, 9, 12–24
Ceanothus	4–7, 14–24
Cestrum	Varies
Chaenomeles	1–21
Chilopsis linearis	11–13, 18–21
Feijoa sellowiana	7–9, 12–24
Fuchsia	Varies
Grevillea lanigera	15–24
Holodiscus discolor	1–7, 14–17
Justicia brandegeana	12, 13, 15–17, 21–24
Lonicera	Varies
Melaleuca	Varies
Ribes	Varies
Rosmarinus	4–24
Weigela	1–11, 14–17

Perennials, Vines

NAME OF PLANT	CLIMATE ZONES
Alcea rosea	All
Aloe	8, 9, 12–24
Aquilegia	All
Delphinium	Varies
Digitalis	All
Heuchera	Varies
Impatiens	Varies
Kniphofia uvaria	1–9, 14–24
Lobelia cardinalis	1–7, 13–17
Lonicera	Varies
Mimulus	Varies
Monarda didyma	All
Nicotiana	All
Penstemon	Varies
Phlox	Varies
Tecomaria capensis	12–16, 18–24
Zauschneria	4–10, 12–24

These plants draw bees

Some flowers are particularly appealing to bees and will invariably attract them when in bloom. If you like the sound of busy bees on a warm day, you can draw them to your garden by planting these flowers. On the other hand, if you wish to minimize the presence of bees in your garden, you'd be wise to omit such plants from your landscape. The following plants are noted for being special favorites of bees.

TREES

Acacia	Eucalyptus (especially
Avocado	E. ficifolia, E. melliodora)
Citrus	Gleditsia triacanthos
Crataegus	Schinus terebinthifolius
Eriobotrya japonica	Sorbus aucuparia
	Tilia cordata

PERENNIALS, VINES

Centaurea cineraria	Phyla nodiflora
Eriogonum	Polygonum capitatum
Gladiolus	Salvia officinalis
Ice Plants	Satureja montana
Lavandula angustifolia	Thymus
Lobularia maritima	Wisteria
Lonicera japonica 'Halliana'	

SHRUBS

Abelia	Escallonia
Acacia	Feijoa sellowiana
Artemisia	*Heteromeles arbutifolia
Buddleia	Ligustrum
*Callistemon citrinus	*Murraya paniculata
Calluna vulgaris	Pyracantha
Ceanothus	Rosmarinus officinalis
Choisya ternata	*Syzygium
Cotoneaster	Teucrium chamaedrys
Echium	Trachelospermum jasminoides
Erica	

*Can become small tree.

Sow a spring bouquet

A combination planting of varieties that bloom at the same time makes a garden-bed flower arrangement. White marguerites (*Chrysanthemum frutescens*), yellow daffodils (*Narcissus*), orange California poppies (*Eschscholzia*), and blue Dutch iris usher in the spring flower parade.

Showy flowers by season

Most gardeners eagerly anticipate the flowering of plants in their gardens—
whether this means a grandiose display of rhododendrons or a single potful of
crocuses. Flowers provide changing interest throughout the year. Gathered
here are the most widely grown color producers, listed under the seasons in which they flower.

SPRING

Vines

NAME OF PLANT	CLIMATE ZONES	YELLOW-ORANGE	RED-PINK	BLUE-PURPLE	WHITE	MULTICOLORS
Bougainvillea	Varies	•	•	•	•	
Clematis	Varies	•	•	•	•	
Distictis buccinatoria	8, 9, 14–24		•			
Hibbertia scandens	16, 17, 21–24	•				
Jasminum	Varies	•	•		•	
Lonicera	Varies	•	•			
Solandra maxima	17, 21–24	•				
Solanum jasminoides	8, 9, 14–24			•	•	
Wisteria	All		•	•	•	

Perennials

NAME OF PLANT	CLIMATE ZONES	Y	R	B	W	M
Aethionema	1–9		•			
Aquilegia	All	•	•	•	•	
Arabis	Varies		•		•	
Arctotis	7–9, 14–24	•	•	•	•	•
Aster	All		•	•	•	
Aubrieta deltoidea	1–9, 14–21		•	•		
Aurinia saxatilis	All	•				
Bellis perennis	All		•		•	
Bergenia	1–9, 14–24		•		•	
Billbergia	16–24		•	•	•	
Campanula	Varies		•	•	•	
Convallaria majalis	1–7, 14–20				•	
Cymbidium	See Encyclopedia	•	•	•	•	•
Cynoglossum amabile	All			•	•	
Delphinium	Varies		•	•	•	
Dianthus	All	•	•	•	•	
Dicentra spectabilis	1–9, 14–24		•			
Digitalis	All	•		•	•	
Heliotropium arborescens	8–24			•	•	
Helleborus	Varies		•	•	•	
Heuchera sanguinea	All		•		•	
Iberis sempervirens	All				•	
Kniphofia uvaria	1–9, 14–24	•	•		•	
Osteospermum	8, 9, 14–24	•		•	•	
Paeonia (herbaceous)	1–11, 14–16		•		•	
Papaver orientale	1–17	•	•		•	
Phlox subulata	1–17		•	•	•	
Primula malacoides	14–24		•	•	•	
Primula polyantha	1–9, 12–24	•	•	•	•	
Saxifraga	Varies		•	•	•	
Senecio hybridus	16, 17, 22–24		•	•	•	•
Viola cornuta	All	•	•	•	•	•
Viola odorata	All		•	•	•	•

Shrubs

NAME OF PLANT	CLIMATE ZONES	YELLOW-ORANGE	RED-PINK	BLUE-PURPLE	WHITE	MULTICOLORS
Abutilon hybridum	13, 15–24	•	•		•	
Acacia	Varies	•				
Azalea (see Rhododendron)	Varies	•	•	•	•	
Callistemon	8, 9, 12–24		•	•	•	
Camellia	4, 9, 14–24		•			
Ceanothus	Varies			•	•	
Choisya ternata	4–9, 12–24				•	
Cistus	4–9, 12–24		•		•	
Deutzia	1–11, 14–17		•		•	
Erythrina	Varies		•			
Forsythia	2–11, 14–16, 18, 19	•				
Fremontodendron	7–24	•				
Gamolepis chrysanthemoides	8, 9, 13–24	•				
Hibbertia cuneiformis	13, 15–24	•				
Jasminum	Varies	•			•	
Kolkwitzia amabilis	1–11, 14–20		•			
Leptospermum	14–24		•		•	
Melaleuca	Varies		•	•	•	
Philadelphus	Varies				•	
Raphiolepis	4–10, 12–24		•		•	
Rhododendron	Varies	•	•	•	•	
Rosa	All	•	•	•	•	•
Spiraea	1–11, 14–21		•		•	
Syringa	Varies		•	•	•	
Weigela	1–11, 14–17	•	•		•	

Annuals

NAME OF PLANT	CLIMATE ZONES	Y	R	B	W	M
Antirrhinum majus	All	•	•		•	•
Calendula officinalis	All	•	•			
Centaurea cyanus	All		•	•	•	
Clarkia	All		•	•	•	
Consolida ambigua	All		•	•	•	
Dianthus barbatus	All		•		•	
Dimorphotheca	All	•				
Eschscholzia californica	All	•	•		•	
Lathyrus odoratus	All		•	•	•	
Lobularia maritima	10–24		•		•	
Lupinus nanus	8, 9, 14–24		•	•	•	
Matthiola incana	All		•	•	•	•
Mimulus hybridus	All	•				•
Myosotis sylvatica	All			•	•	
Nemesia strumosa	All	•	•	•	•	
Papaver rhoeas	All		•		•	
Viola wittrockiana	All	•	•	•	•	

(Continued on next page)

SPRING (Cont'd.)

Trees

NAME OF PLANT	CLIMATE ZONES	YELLOW-ORANGE	RED-PINK	BLUE-PURPLE	WHITE	MULTICOLORS
Acacia	Varies	●				
Aesculus carnea	1–9, 14–17		●			
Bauhinia	Varies		●	●	●	
Catalpa	All				●	
Cornus	Varies		●			
Crataegus	1–11, 14–17		●			
Erythrina	Varies	●	●			
Laburnum	1–10, 14–17	●				
Leptospermum	14–24		●		●	
Magnolia	Varies	●	●	●	●	
Malus	1–11, 14–21		●			
Melaleuca	Varies		●	●	●	
Paulownia tomentosa	All			●		
Prunus (flowering types)	Varies		●		●	
Tabebuia chrysotricha	15, 16, 20–24	●				

Bulbs and Bulblike Plants

NAME OF PLANT	CLIMATE ZONES	YELLOW-ORANGE	RED-PINK	BLUE-PURPLE	WHITE	MULTICOLORS
Anemone coronaria	All		●	●	●	
Babiana	4–24		●	●	●	
Clivia miniata	15–17, 19–24	●	●			
Crocus	All	●		●	●	●
Cyclamen	Varies		●		●	
Dietes	8, 9, 13–24	●			●	●
Freesia	8, 9, 12–24	●	●	●	●	●
Fritillaria	1–7, 15–17	●	●			●
Gladiolus	All	●	●	●	●	●
Hippeastrum	12, 13, 19, 21–24	●	●		●	
Hyacinthus orientalis	All		●	●	●	
Iris	Varies	●	●	●	●	●
Ixia maculata	5–24	●	●		●	
Muscari	All			●	●	
Narcissus	All	●			●	
Ranunculus	All	●	●		●	●
Sparaxis tricolor	9, 13–24	●	●	●	●	●
Tulipa	All	●	●	●	●	●
Watsonia	4–9, 14–24		●		●	
Zantedeschia	5, 6, 8, 9, 14–24	●	●		●	

SUMMER

Trees

NAME OF PLANT	CLIMATE ZONES	Y	R	B	W	M
Albizia julibrissin	2–23		●			
Calodendrum capense	19, 21–24		●			
Catalpa	All				●	
Erythrina humeana	12, 13, 20–24		●			
Eucalyptus ficifolia	15–17, 22–24		●			
Jacaranda mimosifolia	13, 15–24			●		
Lagerstroemia indica	7–9, 12–14, 18–21		●			
Magnolia grandiflora	4–12, 14–24				●	
Melaleuca	Varies		●	●	●	

Bulbs and Bulblike Plants

NAME OF PLANT	CLIMATE ZONES	Y	R	B	W	M
Agapanthus	7–9, 12–24			●	●	
Amaryllis belladonna	4–24		●			
Begonia tuberhybrida	5, 17, 24	●	●		●	
Canna	All	●	●			
Cyclamen purpurascens	1–9, 14–24		●			
Dahlia	All	●	●	●	●	●
Dietes	8, 9, 13–24	●			●	●
Gladiolus	All	●	●	●	●	●
Hemerocallis	All	●	●			●
Lilium	All	●	●		●	
Tigridia pavonia	All	●	●		●	

Perennials

NAME OF PLANT	CLIMATE ZONES	Y	R	B	W	M
Achillea	All	●			●	
Aquilegia	All	●	●	●	●	
Arctotis	7–9, 14–24	●	●	●	●	●
Aster	All		●	●	●	
Astilbe	2–7, 14–17		●		●	
Begonia, fibrous	Varies		●		●	
Bellis perennis	All		●		●	
Calceolaria integrifolia	14–24	●				
Campanula	Varies			●	●	
Catharanthus roseus	All		●		●	
Ceratostigma plumbaginoides	2–9, 14–24			●		
Chrysanthemum frutescens	All	●			●	
C. maximum	All				●	
C. parthenium	All	●			●	
Coreopsis grandiflora	All	●				
Delphinium	Varies		●	●	●	
Dianthus	All	●	●		●	
Digitalis	All	●	●	●	●	

NAME OF PLANT	CLIMATE ZONES	Y	R	B	W	M
Echinops exaltatus	All			●		
Gaillardia grandiflora	All	●	●			
Gazania	8–24	●	●			●
Gerbera jamesonii	8, 9, 12–24	●	●			
Heliotropium arborescens	8–24			●	●	
Heuchera sanguinea	All		●		●	
Kniphofia uvaria	1–9, 14–24	●	●			
Limonium	Varies			●	●	
Lobelia cardinalis	1–7, 13–17		●			
Mirabilis jalapa	4–24	●	●		●	
Osteospermum	8, 9, 14–24		●	●	●	
Pelargonium domesticum	8, 9, 12–24		●		●	
Pelargonium hortorum	8, 9, 12–24		●		●	
Penstemon gloxinioides	All		●		●	
Phlox paniculata	1–14, 18–21		●		●	
Platycodon grandiflorus	All			●	●	
Romneya coulteri	5–10, 12–24				●	
Rudbeckia hirta	All	●				

(Continued on page 133)

Feature summer's bounty in raised beds and containers

Easily moved containers and raised beds full of specially mixed soil hold a lavish flower display. Marigolds in variety provide dominant yellow and orange notes in this summer scene. Lavender accent is *Ageratum houstonianum*, while white flowers are double Shasta daisies (*Chrysanthemum maximum*), single feverfew (*Chrysanthemum parthenium*), and small clumps of sweet alyssum (*Lobularia maritima*).

Plan flower color at tree height, shrub level, and low to the ground

Color at several heights relieves garden monotony. Cool summer effect comes from blue *Agapanthus*, pink petunias and fibrous begonias (in shadiest area), white Shasta daisies (*Chrysanthemum maximum*) against backdrop of large *Nerium oleander*.

Throughout fall, Sasanqua camellias bring white, all shades of pink, and red to the landscape. Numerous flowers can make a show for months.

When leaves start to drop, bright flowers revive the garden

Containers brimming with flowers can be moved onstage when most showy, offstage as they fade. Popular favorite among fall flowers, chrysanthemums come in many shapes and sizes; shown on a *Sunset* patio are just a few of those available.

SUMMER (Cont'd.)

Annuals

NAME OF PLANT	CLIMATE ZONES	YELLOW-ORANGE	RED-PINK	BLUE-PURPLE	WHITE	MULTICOLORS
Ageratum houstonianum	All			●		
Amaranthus	All		●			
Antirrhinum majus	All	●	●		●	
Calendula officinalis	All	●	●			
Callistephus chinensis	All		●	●	●	
Celosia	All	●	●			
Centaurea cyanus	All		●	●	●	
Clarkia	All	●	●			
Coreopsis tinctoria	All	●	●			
Cosmos	All	●	●			
Dianthus barbatus	All		●		●	
Gaillardia pulchella	All	●	●			
Gypsophila elegans	All				●	
Helianthus annuus	All	●				
Helichrysum bracteatum	All	●	●			
Impatiens wallerana	All	●	●		●	
Ipomoea (most)	All		●	●	●	
Lathyrus odoratus	All		●	●	●	
Limonium (some)	All			●		
Linum grandiflorum 'Rubrum'	All		●			
Lobelia erinus	All		●	●	●	
Lobularia maritima	10–24		●	●	●	
Mimulus hybridus	All	●				
Nicotiana	All		●		●	
Papaver rhoeas	All	●	●		●	
Petunia	All	●	●	●	●	
Phlox drummondii	All	●	●			
Portulaca	All	●	●			
Salvia splendens	All		●	●		
Scabiosa atropurpurea	All		●	●		
Tagetes	All					●
Thunbergia alata	All	●			●	
Tropaeolum majus	All	●	●			
Verbena (most)	All		●	●	●	
Zinnia	All	●	●	●	●	●

Vines

NAME OF PLANT	CLIMATE ZONES	YELLOW-ORANGE	RED-PINK	BLUE-PURPLE	WHITE	MULTICOLORS
Antigonon leptopus	12, 13, 18–21		●			
Bean, Scarlet Runner	All		●			
Bougainvillea	Varies	●	●	●	●	
Clematis	Varies	●	●	●	●	
Cobaea scandens	All			●	●	
Hibbertia scandens	16, 17, 21–24	●				
Jasminum	Varies	●			●	
Lonicera (some)	Varies	●	●		●	
Mandevilla	Varies		●			
Passiflora	Varies		●	●	●	
Polygonum aubertii	All				●	
Trachelospermum jasminoides	8–24				●	

Shrubs

NAME OF PLANT	CLIMATE ZONES	Y	R	B	W	M
Abutilon megapotamicum	13, 15–24	●	●			
Brunfelsia	13–17, 20–24			●	●	
Callistemon	8, 9, 12–24		●	●		
Erythrina (some)	Varies		●			
Fuchsia	Varies		●	●	●	●
Hibiscus mutabilis	4–24		●		●	
Hibiscus rosa-sinensis	9, 12, 13, 15–16, 19–24	●	●		●	
Hibiscus syriacus	1–21		●	●	●	
Hydrangea macrophylla	2–24		●	●	●	
Jasminum	Varies	●			●	
Justicia carnea	8, 9, 13–24		●			
Lagerstroemia indica	7–14, 18–21		●		●	
Melaleuca	Varies		●		●	
Nerium oleander	8–16, 18–23	●	●		●	
Philadelphus	Varies				●	
Tibouchina urvilleana	16, 17, 21–24			●		

FALL

Trees

NAME OF PLANT	CLIMATE ZONES	Y	R	B	W	M
Bauhinia blakeana	19, 21, 23		●			
Erythrina humeana	12, 13, 20–24		●			
Magnolia grandiflora	4–12, 14–24				●	
Melaleuca	Varies		●	●	●	

Shrubs

NAME OF PLANT	CLIMATE ZONES	Y	R	B	W	M
Brugmansia	16–24				●	
Callistemon	8, 9, 12–24		●		●	
Camellia sasanqua	4, 9, 14–24		●		●	
Cleyera japonica	4–6, 8, 9, 14–24				●	
Erythrina humeana	12, 13, 20–24		●			
Fuchsia magellanica	2–9, 14–24		●	●		
Gamolepis chrysanthemoides	8, 9, 13–24	●				
Hydrangea macrophylla	2–24		●	●	●	
Jasminum	Varies	●			●	
Melaleuca (some)	Varies		●	●	●	
Nerium oleander	8–16, 18–23	●	●		●	

Perennials

NAME OF PLANT	CLIMATE ZONES	Y	R	B	W	M
Anemone hybrida	All		●		●	
Anthemis tinctoria	All	●				
Arctotis	7–9, 14–24	●	●	●	●	●
Aster	All		●	●	●	
Begonia, fibrous	Varies		●		●	
Calceolaria integrifolia	14–24	●				
Campanula	Varies			●	●	
Catharanthus roseus	All		●		●	
Ceratostigma plumbaginoides	2–9, 14–24			●		
Chrysanthemum frutescens	All	●	●		●	
C. maximum	All				●	
C. morifolium	All	●	●	●	●	●
Delphinium	Varies			●	●	
Digitalis	All		●		●	
Echinops exaltatus	All			●		
Gaillardia grandiflora	All	●	●			
Gerbera jamesonii	8, 9, 12–24	●	●		●	
Osteospermum	8, 9, 14–24		●	●	●	
Sedum spectabile	All		●			
Solidago	All	●				
Stokesia laevis	1–9, 12–24			●	●	

(Continued on next page)

FALL (Cont'd.)

Bulbs and Bulblike Plants

NAME OF PLANT	CLIMATE ZONES	YELLOW-ORANGE	RED-PINK	BLUE-PURPLE	WHITE	MULTICOLORS
Begonia tuberhybrida	5, 17, 24	•	•		•	
Canna	All	•	•		•	
Colchicum autumnale	1–9, 15–24		•	•	•	
Cyclamen (hardy)	1–9, 14–24		•	•	•	

NAME OF PLANT	CLIMATE ZONES	YELLOW-ORANGE	RED-PINK	BLUE-PURPLE	WHITE	MULTICOLORS
Dietes	8, 9, 13–24	•			•	
Lycoris	Varies	•	•			
Schizostylis coccinea	5–9, 14–24		•			
Zephyranthes	1–9, 14–24	•	•		•	

Annuals

NAME OF PLANT	CLIMATE ZONES	Y	R	B	W	M
Ageratum houstonianum	All			•		
Calendula officinalis	All	•				
Helianthus	All	•				
Lobularia maritima	10–24			•	•	•

Vines

NAME OF PLANT	CLIMATE ZONE	Y	R	B	W	M
Clematis	Varies	•	•	•	•	
Distictis buccinatoria	8, 9, 14–24		•			
Hibbertia scandens	16, 17, 21–24	•				
Mandevilla	Varies		•			

WINTER

Trees

NAME OF PLANT	CLIMATE ZONES	Y	R	B	W	M
Acacia	Varies	•				
Bauhinia variegata	13, 18–23		•	•		
Erythrina	Varies	•	•		•	
Melaleuca	Varies		•	•	•	

Shrubs

NAME OF PLANT	CLIMATE ZONES	Y	R	B	W	M
Acacia	Varies	•				
Camellia	4–9, 14–24		•		•	
Chaenomeles	1–21		•		•	
Chamelaucium uncinatum	8, 9, 12–24		•			
Erythrina	Varies	•	•			
Euphorbia pulcherrima	16–24		•		•	
Forsythia	2–11, 14–16, 18, 19	•				
Jasminum mesnyi	4–24	•				
Lampranthus	15–24	•	•	•	•	
Melaleuca	Varies		•	•	•	

Perennials

NAME OF PLANT	CLIMATE ZONES	Y	R	B	W	M
Arctotis	7–9, 14–24	•	•	•	•	•
Bergenia crassifolia	1–9, 14–24		•		•	
Cymbidium	See Encyclopedia	•	•		•	
Helleborus	Varies			•	•	
Euryops pectinatus	14–17, 19–24	•				
Osteospermum	8, 9, 14–24		•	•	•	
Primula polyantha	1–10, 12–24	•	•	•	•	•
Senecio hybridus	16, 17, 22–24		•	•	•	•
Strelitzia reginae	9, 12–24	•		•		•
Tulbaghia fragrans	13–24		•	•		

Bulbs and Bulblike Plants

NAME OF PLANT	CLIMATE ZONES	Y	R	B	W	M
Clivia miniata	15–17, 19–24	•	•			
Crocus	All	•	•	•	•	•
Cyclamen	Varies		•		•	
Eranthis hyemalis	1–9, 14–17	•				
Iris unguicularis	5–24			•		

Hardy perennials promise dependable winter color

Dwellers in mild-winter climates can enjoy flower color the year around. All the colors of the rainbow can be found in *Primula polyantha*, a wildly colorful winter-blooming perennial.

WINTER (Cont'd.)

Annuals

NAME OF PLANT	CLIMATE ZONES	YELLOW-ORANGE	RED-PINK	BLUE-PURPLE	WHITE	MULTICOLORS
Antirrhinum majus	All	●	●		●	
Calendula officinalis	All	●				
Centaurea cyanus	All		●	●	●	
Dimorphotheca	All	●				
Linaria maroccana	10–13	●	●	●		
Lobularia maritima	10–24		●	●	●	

NAME OF PLANT	CLIMATE ZONES	YELLOW-ORANGE	RED-PINK	BLUE-PURPLE	WHITE	MULTICOLORS
Matthiola incana	8, 9, 12–24	●	●	●	●	
Papaver nudicaule	All	●	●		●	
Primula malacoides	12–24		●	●	●	
Viola cornuta	All	●	●	●	●	●
Viola wittrockiana	All	●	●	●	●	●

A single flowering tree can add welcome color in mild winters. Many acacias burst into winter bloom with clusters of fluffy yellow or cream-colored flowers covering the branches.

Splash color into the winter landscape with flowering trees and shrubs

Some flowering shrubs blossom well before foliage sprouts. Flowering quince (*Chaenomeles*) covers itself with blossoms in late winter before leaves appear. Salmon pink is the most typical color, but varieties are available with flowers of white, various shades of pink, and red.

Autumn foliage color

Plants change leaf color in fall in varying degrees, depending on the nature of the plant and the kind of climate it grows in (generally the change is less noticeable in mild-winter areas than in cold-winter regions). The plants grouped below make an autumnal foliage change that will attract attention; many are worth planting for that reason alone.

TREES

NAME OF PLANT	CLIMATE ZONES
Acer (many)	Varies
Amelanchier	1–6
Betula occidentalis	1–3, 10
Betula pendula	1–11, 14–24
Cercidiphyllum japonicum	1–6, 14–16, 18–20
Cercis	Varies
Cladrastis lutea	1–9, 14–16
Cornus	Varies
Crataegus	1–11, 14–17
Fagus sylvatica	1–9, 14–24
Franklinia alatamaha	2–6, 15–17
Fraxinus (deciduous species)	Varies
Ginkgo biloba	1–9, 14–24
Gleditsia triacanthos	1–16, 18–20
Gymnocladus dioica	1–3, 7–10, 12–16, 18–21
Halesia	2–9, 14–24
Hamamelis mollis	4–7, 15–17
Koelreuteria bipinnata	8–24
Lagerstroemia indica	4–9, 12–14, 18–21
Larix	Varies
Liquidambar	Varies
Liriodendron tulipifera	1–10, 14–23

NAME OF PLANT	CLIMATE ZONES
Malus	1–11, 14–21
Nyssa sylvatica	3–10, 14–21
Oxydendrum arboreum	3–9, 14–17
Pear	1–11, 14–16, 18
Persimmon	Varies
Pistacia chinensis	8–16, 18–23
Populus	Varies
Prunus (deciduous)	Varies
Pyrus (deciduous)	Varies
Quercus coccinea	All
Quercus kelloggii	5, 6, 7, 15, 16, 18–21
Quercus palustris	All
Quercus phellos	1–4, 6–16, 18–21
Quercus rubra	1–12, 14–24
Salix	Varies
Sapium sebiferum	8, 9, 12, 14–16, 18–21
Sassafras albidum	4–6, 10, 12, 14–17
Sorbus aucuparia	1–10, 14–17
Styrax japonicus	3–10, 14–21
Taxodium distichum	1–9, 14–24
Zelkova serrata	3–21

SHRUBS

NAME OF PLANT	CLIMATE ZONES
Amelanchier	1–6
Aronia arbutifolia	1–7
Berberis thunbergii	1–11, 14–17
Blueberry	2–9, 14–17
Cercis	Varies
Cornus	Varies
*Cotinus coggygria	All
Cotoneaster divaricatus	All
Cotoneaster horizontalis	1–11, 14–24
Crataegus	1–11, 14–17
Cryptomeria japonica 'Elegans'	4–9, 14–24
Enkianthus	2–9, 14–21
Euonymus alata	1–9, 14–16
Fothergilla	3–9, 14–17
Hamamelis virginiana	1–9, 14–16, 18–21
Hydrangea quercifolia	1–22
Kerria japonica	1–21
Lagerstroemia indica	4–9, 12–14, 18–21

NAME OF PLANT	CLIMATE ZONES
*Magnolia salicifolia	2–9, 14–21
*Malus (some)	1–11, 14–21
Nandina domestica	5–24
*Parrotia persica	4–6, 15–21
Photinia villosa	1–6
*Punica granatum	7–24
*Rhamnus purshiana	1–9, 14–17
Rhododendron molle	4–6, 15–17
*Rhododendron quinquefolium	4–6, 15–17
Rhododendron schlippenbachii	4–6, 15–17
*Rhus glabra	1–10, 14–17
*Rhus typhina	1–10, 14–17
Salix	Varies
Spiraea (several)	1–11, 14–21
Stachyurus praecox	4–6, 14–17
*Stewartia	4–6, 14–17, 20, 21
Viburnum (many)	Varies

*Can become small tree.

PERENNIALS, ANNUALS, VINES

NAME OF PLANT	CLIMATE ZONES
Kochia scoparia trichophylla	All
Parthenocissus	All

NAME OF PLANT	CLIMATE ZONES
Saxifraga rosacea	1–7, 14–17
Sedum sieboldii	All

Reliably bringing eastern fall color to western gardens is brilliant sweet gum (*Liquidambar*). Leaves color best when trees are in full sun and well-drained soil.

Some trees turn color even in the warmest autumns

Holding its leaves for a long period before shedding them, the maidenhair tree (*Ginkgo biloba*) becomes luminous yellow every autumn.

Colorful fruits and berries

These plants offer garden color in the form of colorful fruit or seed capsules. Some give this color in addition to flower display; others give it as a surprise following an inconspicuous blossoming.

Profusely fruiting tree demands little or no maintenance

Of the many colorful fruiting shrubs, the cotoneasters rank high among those that perform consistently and with little maintenance. This is *Cotoneaster lactea.*

TREES

NAME OF PLANT	CLIMATE ZONES
Acmena smithii	15–17, 19–24
Citrus	Varies
Cornus nuttallii	2–9, 14–20
Crataegus	1–11, 14–17
Ilex	Varies
Koelreuteria	Varies

NAME OF PLANT	CLIMATE ZONES
Malus	1–11, 14–21
Persimmon	Varies
Pittosporum rhombifolium	12–24
Schinus	Varies
Sorbus	Varies
Syzygium paniculatum	16, 17, 19–24

PERENNIALS, VINES

NAME OF PLANT	CLIMATES ZONES
Ampelopsis brevipedunculata	All
Arum italicum	4–6, 8–24
Celastrus	All

NAME OF PLANT	CLIMATE ZONES
Dianella tasmanica	8, 9, 14–24
Kadsura japonica	7–9, 14–22
Ophiopogon jaburan	5–10, 12–24

SHRUBS

NAME OF PLANT	CLIMATE ZONES
Aronia arbutifolia	1–7
*Arbutus unedo	4–24
Berberis darwinii	1–11, 14–17
Berberis thunbergii	1–11, 14–17
Berberis wilsonae	1–11, 14–17
Callicarpa	1–6
Carissa grandiflora	22–24
Cestrum	Varies
*Clerodendrum trichotomum	15–17, 20–24
*Cornus kousa	3–9, 14, 15, 18, 19
*Cornus mas	1–6
Corokia	4–24
*Corylus	1–9, 14–20
Cotoneaster	Varies
Duranta	Varies
Elaeagnus	Varies
Euonymus alata	1–9, 14–16
Euonymus fortunei 'Vegeta', 'Carrierei',	1–17
Euonymus kiautschovica	1–13
*Heteromeles arbutifolia	5–24

NAME OF PLANT	CLIMATE ZONES
Ilex	Varies
Kolkwitzia amabilis	1–11, 14–20
Lonicera (most shrubby types)	Varies
Malus	1–11, 14–21
Nandina domestica	5–24
Pernettya mucronata	4–7, 15–17
*Photinia serrulata	4–16, 18–22
Photinia villosa	1–6
*Punica granatum	5–24
Pyracantha	Varies
Raphiolepis	8–10, 12–24
Sarcococca ruscifolia	4–9, 14–24
Skimmia	4–9, 14–22
Solanum pseudo-capsicum	23, 24
*Stranvaesia davidiana	4–11, 14–17
Symphoricarpos	Varies
*Taxus	3–9, 14–24
Ugni molinae	14–24
Vaccinium	Varies
Viburnum (many)	Varies

*Can become small tree.

Sometimes fruit is edible as well as colorful

Most often thought of only as edible, citrus fruits are indisputably showy on the tree.

Many attractive fruits are edible, though not necessarily tasty. The strawberry tree, *(Arbutus unedo)* gets its name from appearance and texture of fruit rather than its flavor. Fruits and flowers appear in fall and winter.

Leaf variegation adds close-up novelty

Plants with dark leaves—often bronze or purple—add an unusual note to a garden. This one, *Dodonaea viscosa* 'Purpurea', is one of the most widely adapted and versatile.

From a distance, variegated foliage often looks like sun dappling. Closer, you can see subdued variegation typical of *Pittosporum tobira* 'Variegata', a useful 5-foot shrub for sun or shade.

Foliage doesn't have to be green

Cool gray foliage softens the effect of bright flowers. The accent plant shown here is *Senecio cineraria*, commonly called dusty miller. Behind it are hen and chicks (*Echeveria elegans*), basket of gold (*Aurinia saxatilis*), white marguerite (*Chrysanthemum frutescens*), cushion bush (*Calocephalus brownii*), forget-me-not (*Myosotis sylvatica*), Italian bellflower (*Campanula isophylla*), and calendulas.

Plants with colored foliage

Not all color comes from flowers or fruit. Here are candidates for long-term garden exclamation points via colored leaves: gray, red or bronze, yellow, blue, and variegated. They can be used to enliven the basic green of other garden foliage, in combinations with one another (such as gray and red), and to complement flower colors in season.

GRAY

Trees

NAME OF PLANT	CLIMATE ZONES
Cupressus glabra	5, 8–24
Eucalyptus baueriana	8, 9, 12–24
Eucalyptus caesia	16, 17, 21–24
Eucalyptus globulus 'Compacta'	14–24
Eucalyptus kruseana	16, 17, 21–24
Eucalyptus leucoxylon	8, 9, 12–24
Eucalyptus macrocarpa	8, 9, 12–24
Eucalyptus pulverulenta	8, 9, 12–24
Eucalyptus rhodantha	8, 9, 12–24
Juniperus scopulorum (some)	All

Shrubs

NAME OF PLANT	CLIMATE ZONES
Artemisia	All
Atriplex	Varies
Convolvulus cneorum	7–9, 12–24
Elaeagnus 'Coral Silver'	All
Juniperus (some)	All
Leucodendron argenteum	17, 20–24
Leucophyllum frutescens	7–24
Mahonia nevinii	8–24
Pimelea prostrata	4–7, 14–17
Salvia leucophylla	10–24
Santolina chamaecyparissus	All
Teucrium fruticans	4–24
Zauschneria cana	4–10, 12–24

Perennials, Annuals

NAME OF PLANT	CLIMATE ZONES
Achillea	All
Artemisia	All
Artichoke	8, 9, 14–24
Calocephalus brownii	16, 17, 19, 21–24
Centaurea	8–24
Cerastium tomentosum	All
Cotyledon orbiculata	Varies
Dudleya	16, 17, 21–24
Echeveria (many)	Varies
Euryops	14–17, 19–24

NAME OF PLANT	CLIMATE ZONES
Graptopetalum	8–24
Kalanchoe beharensis	21–24
Lavandula (most)	Varies
Leontopodium alpinum	1–9, 14–24
Lotus berthelotii	9, 15–24
Lychnis coronaria (annual)	All
Saxifraga burserana	1–7, 14–17
Senecio cineraria	All
Senecio vira-vira	All
Stachys byzantina	All

BRONZE, RED

Trees

NAME OF PLANT	CLIMATE ZONES
Acer palmatum (some)	1–9, 14–24
Acer platanoides (some)	1–9, 14–17
Cercis canadensis 'Forest Pansy'	1–3, 7–20
Cordyline australis 'Atropurpurea'	5, 8–11, 14–24
Corylus maxima 'Purpurea'	1–9, 14–20
Cotinus coggygria (some)	All
Fagus sylvatica (some)	1–9, 14–24
Prunus blireiana	2–12, 14–22
Prunus cerasifera (some)	2–22

Shrubs

NAME OF PLANT	CLIMATE ZONES
Acalypha wilkesiana	21–23
Acokanthera	21, 23, 24
Cordyline terminalis (some)	21–24
Corylus avellana 'Fusco-Rubra'	1–9, 14–20
Dodonaea viscosa 'Purpurea', 'Saratoga'	7–9, 12–24
Iresine herbstii	22–24
Prunus cistena	2–12, 14–22
Pseudopanax crassifolius	16, 17, 21–24

Perennials

NAME OF PLANT	CLIMATE ZONES
Aechmea hybrids	22–24
Aeonium arboreum 'Atropurpureum'	15–17, 20–24
Ajuga reptans varieties	All
Astilbe 'Fanal'	2–7, 14–17
Caladium bicolor varieties	Varies
Canna (some)	All

NAME OF PLANT	CLIMATE ZONES
Crassula corymbulosa	16, 17, 22–24
Kalanchoe laciniata	17, 21–24
Pennisetum setaceum 'Cupreum'	All
Phormium tenax varieties	7–24
Sedum spathulifolium 'Purpureum'	All
Sedum spurium 'Dragon's Blood'	All

(Continued on next page)

YELLOW, GOLDEN

Shrubs, Perennials

NAME OF PLANT	CLIMATE ZONES
Chamaecyparis lawsoniana (some)	4–6, 15–17
Chrysanthemum parthenium 'Aureum'	All
Juniperus (several)	All
Ligustrum vicaryi	All
Platycladus orientalis (several)	All
Taxus baccata (several)	1–9, 14–24
Thuja occidentalis 'Rheingold'	1–9, 15–17, 21–24

Trees

NAME OF PLANT	CLIMATE ZONES
Acer japonicum 'Aureum'	1–6, 14–16
Chamaecyparis lawsoniana (some varieties)	4–6, 15–17
Gleditsia triacanthos 'Sunburst'	1–16, 18–20
Robinia pseudoacacia 'Frisia'	All
Thuja plicata 'Aurea'	1–9, 14–24

BLUE

Trees

NAME OF PLANT	CLIMATE ZONES
Chamaecyparis lawsoniana (some)	4–6, 15–17
Cunninghamia lanceolata 'Glauca'	4–6, 14–21
Eucalyptus niphophila	8–24
Juniperus deppeana pachyphlaea	All
Juniperus occidentalis	All
Picea pungens (some)	1–6, 15–17

Shrubs, Perennials

NAME OF PLANT	CLIMATE ZONES
Chamaecyparis lawsoniana (some)	4–6, 15–17
Eucalyptus macrocarpa	8–24
Eucalyptus rhodantha	8–24
Festuca ovina 'Glauca'	All

VARIEGATED

Shrubs

NAME OF PLANT
Aucuba japonica (several)
Buxus sempervirens 'Aureo-Variegata'
Coprosma repens 'Variegata', 'Argentea'
Cotoneaster horizontalis 'Variegatus'
Daphne odora (some)
Elaeagnus pungens (some)
Euonymus (some)
Fatsia japonica 'Variegata'
Griselinia littoralis 'Variegata'
Griselinia lucida 'Variegata'
Hydrangea macrophylla 'Tricolor'
Ilex (various)
Juniperus (various)
Leucothoe fontanesiana 'Rainbow'
Ligustrum ovalifolium 'Aureum'
Myrtus communis 'Compacta Variegata', 'Variegata'
Osmanthus heterophyllus 'Variegatus'
Pieris japonica 'Variegata'
Pittosporum tobira 'Variegata'
Rhamnus alaternus 'Variegata'
Salvia officinalis 'Tricolor'
Taxus baccata 'Stricta Variegata'
Viburnum tinus 'Variegatum'
Weigela florida 'Variegata'

Perennials, Annuals

NAME OF PLANT
Aegopodium podagraria 'Variegatum'
Aloe saponaria
Aloe variegata
Arabis caucasica 'Variegata'
Caladium bicolor
Coleus hybridus
Euphorbia marginata
Hosta (various)
Ligularia tussilaginea 'Aureo-maculata'
Liriope muscari 'Silvery Sunproof', 'Variegata'
Pachysandra terminalis 'Variegata'
Pelargonium hortorum (several)
Phormium tenax 'Variegatum'
Portulacaria afra 'Foliis Variegatis' and 'Variegata'
Sansevieria trifasciata
Sedum sieboldii 'Variegatis'
Thymus citriodorus 'Argenteus'
Thymus (several)
Tradescantia fluminensis 'Variegata'
Tulbaghia violacea varieties
Vinca major (variegated form)
Yucca aloifolia 'Variegata'
Yucca gloriosa (variegated form)
Zantedeschia albomaculata
Zantedeschia elliottiana

Trees

NAME OF PLANT	CLIMATE ZONES
Acer negundo 'Variegatum'	1–10, 12–24
Cornus florida 'Welchii'	1–9, 14–16
Cornus nuttallii 'Goldspot'	2–9, 14–20
Fagus sylvatica 'Tricolor'	1–9, 14–24
Ilex (various)	Varies

Vines

NAME OF PLANT	CLIMATE ZONES
Actinidia kolomikta	4–9, 15–17
Euonymus fortunei (some)	1–17
Fatshedera lizei 'Variegata'	4–10, 12–24
Hedera (some)	Varies
Lonicera japonica 'Aureo-reticulata'	2–24

Shade-tolerant plants

Shade, whether cast by overhanging trees, north-facing walls, or a patio over-head, is characterized by lower light intensity and cooler atmosphere than nearby sunny locations. Many plants that thrive on sunlight and warmth fail to perform under the different environment that shade provides. In these lists are trees, shrubs, vines, perennials, and annuals that tolerate shade; many *prefer* it.

*Cool, shady
garden refreshes
on a hot day*

Out of the hot sun, shade-loving companions in summer patio are pink *Impatiens wallerana*, lighter pink fuchsias in hanging baskets, several ferns, and gray green, hanging donkey tail sedum (*Sedum morganianum*).

TREES

NAME OF PLANT	CLIMATE ZONES
Acer circinatum	1–6, 14–17
Acer palmatum	1–9, 14–24
Arbutus unedo	4–24
Corynocarpus laevigata	16, 17, 23, 24
Ficus	Varies
Ilex	Varies
Laurus nobilis	5–9, 12–24
Lithocarpus densiflorus	4–7, 14–24
Olmediella betschlerana	9, 14–24

NAME OF PLANT	CLIMATE ZONES
Palms	Varies
Podocarpus	Varies
Pseudopanax lessonii	17, 20–24
Schefflera	Varies
Stenocarpus sinuatus	16, 17, 20–24
Strelitzia nicolai	22–24
Tree Ferns	Varies
Tupidanthus calyptratus	19–24
Umbellularia californica	4–10, 12–24

VINES

NAME OF PLANT	CLIMATE ZONES
Cissus	Varies
Fatshedera lizei	4–10, 12–24
Hedera	Varies
Hoya carnosa	15–24

NAME OF PLANT	CLIMATE ZONES
Monstera deliciosa	21–24
Parthenocissus	All
Rhoicissus capensis	16, 17, 21–24
Trachelospermum jasminoides	8–24

(Continued on next page)

SHRUBS

NAME OF PLANT	CLIMATE ZONES
Abutilon	13, 15–24
Ardişia japonica	5, 6, 15–17
Aucuba japonica	4–11, 14–23
Azalea (see Rhododendron)	Varies
Azara	Varies
Brunfelsia pauciflora calycina	13–17, 20–24
Buxus	Varies
Calycanthus	Varies
Camellia	4–9, 14–24
Cantua buxifolia	16–24
Carpenteria californica	5–9, 14–24
Cleyera japonica	4–6, 8, 9, 14–24
Cocculus laurifolius	8, 9, 12–24
Coffea arabica	21–24
Coprosma repens	15–17, 21–24
Cordyline stricta	16, 17, 20–24
Cycads	Varies
Daphne odora	4–9, 14–24
Dizygotheca elegantissima	16, 17, 22–24
Enkianthus	2–9, 14–21
Euonymus fortunei	1–17
Fatsia japonica	4–9, 13–24
Fuchsia	Varies
Gardenia jasminoides	7–9, 12–16, 18–23
Gaultheria	Varies
Griselinia lucida	9, 15–17, 20–24
Hydrangea	Varies
Ilex	Varies

NAME OF PLANT	CLIMATE ZONES
Itea ilicifolia	4–24
Juniperus	All
Kalmia	1–7, 16, 17
Kalmiopsis leachiana	4–6, 14–17
Laurus nobilis	5–9, 12–24
Leucothoe	Varies
Loropetalum chinense	6–9, 14–24
Mahonia nervosa	2–9, 14–17
Nandina domestica	5–24
Olmediella betschlerana	9, 14–24
Osmanthus	Varies
Pernettya mucronata	4–7, 15–17,
Philodendron selloum	8, 9, 12–24
Pieris	Varies
Pittosporum	Varies
Rhamnus purshiana	1–9, 14–17
Rhapis	Varies
Rhododendron	Varies
Ruscus	4–24
Sarcococca	4–9, 14–24
Skimmia	4–9, 14–22
Stachyurus praecox	4–6, 14–17
Symphoricarpos	Varies
Taxus	3–9, 14–24
Ternstroemia gymnanthera	4–9, 12–24
Vaccinium	Varies
Viburnum davidii	4–9, 14–24
Viburnum suspensum	8–10, 13–24

PERENNIALS, BULBS, ANNUALS

NAME OF PLANT	CLIMATE ZONES
Acanthus mollis	4–24
Aconitum	1–9, 14–21
Aegopodium podagraria	1–7
Ajuga	All
Alpinia zerumbet	15–17, 22–24
Anemone hybrids	All
Aquilegia	All
Arum	4–6, 8–24
Asarum caudatum	4–6, 14–17, 21
Aspidistra elatior	4–9, 12–24
Astilbe	2–7, 14–17
Begonia	Varies
Bergenia	1–9, 14–24
Billbergia	16–24
Browallia	All
Caladium bicolor	12, 13, 16, 17, 22–24
Calceolaria crenatiflora	14–24
Calceolaria 'John Innes'	All
Campanula	Varies
Clivia miniata	15–17, 19–24
Coleus hybridus	See Encyclopedia
Colocasia esculenta	13, 16–22
Convallaria majalis	1–7, 14–20
Cotula squalida	4–9, 14–24
Crassula	8, 9, 12–24
Cymbalaria muralis	3–24
Cymbidium	See Encyclopedia section
Dianella tasmanica	8, 9, 14–24
Dicentra	1–9, 14–24
Digitalis	All
Doronicum	1–6, 15–17
Duchesnea indica	All
Epigaea repens	1–7
Epimedium	1–9, 14–17

NAME OF PLANT	CLIMATE ZONES
Erythronium	1–7, 15–17
Ferns	Varies
Galax urceolata	1–6
Haemanthus katharinae	See Encyclopedia
Hedychium	17, 22–24
Helleborus	Varies
Hepatica	1–11, 14–16
Heterocentron elegans	17, 21–24
Hosta	1–10, 12–21
Impatiens oliveri	15–17, 21–24
Impatiens wallerana	All
Iris, crested	Varies
Iris foetidissima	All
Kalanchoe beharensis	21–24
Ligularia tussilaginea	4–10, 14–24
Lilium	All
Liriope	5–10, 12–24
Lysimachia nummularia	1–9, 14–24
Meconopsis betonicifolia	1–7, 17
Mertensia	1–21
Mimulus hybridus	All
Monarda	All
Myosotis	All
Narcissus	All
Ophiopogon	5–10, 12–24
Oxalis oregana	4–9, 14–24
Pachysandra terminalis	1–10, 14–21
Phlox divaricata	1–17
Polemonium	1–11, 14–17
Polygonatum multiflorum	1–7, 15–17
Primula	Varies
Pulmonaria	1–9, 14–17
Ranunculus repens 'Pleniflorus'	All
Rehmannia elata	7–10, 12–24
Rohdea japonica	4–9, 14–24

PERENNIALS, BULBS, ANNUALS (Cont'd.)

NAME OF PLANT	CLIMATE ZONES	NAME OF PLANT	CLIMATE ZONES
Sanguinaria canadensis	1–6	Strelitzia	Varies
Sansevieria	13–24	Streptocarpus	17, 22–24
Saxifraga stolonifera	4–9, 14–24	Thalictrum	All
Saxifraga umbrosa	1–7, 14–17	Tolmiea menziesii	5–9, 12–24
Schizanthus pinnatus	1–6, 15–17, 21–24	Tradescantia	Varies
Scilla	All	Trillium	Varies
Sedum morganianum	13–17, 18–24	Trollius	All
Senecio hybridus	All	Vancouveria	Varies
Shortia	1–7	Vinca	Varies
Sinningia speciosa	See Encyclopedia	Viola	All
Smilacina racemosa	1–7, 15–17	Zantedeschia	5, 6, 8, 9, 14–24
Soleirolia soleirolii	8–24		

Shade-adapted plants like this don't need bright sunshine to flower. Reigning queens of cool-climate shaded gardens are the many varieties of fuchsia. You have a choice of upright shrubby types for planting beds or trailing sorts to put in hanging containers.

Vivid flowers light up shady garden spots

A large planting of one kind of shade-tolerant plant can give a lavish effect. Cinerarias (*Senecio hybridus*) bring bright colors to shady gardens as early as late winter in mildest climates.

Heat-resistant plants for south and west exposures

One of the most taxing garden locations is the south or west-facing wall or fence, against which the sun shines for most of the day or during the hottest part of it. It is an especially tough group of plants that can grow under conditions of intense solar heat plus heat reflected from a fence or wall. Here are the most successful and widely available of such plants.

Some plants thrive even in intense heat

For quick color in hot locations, turn to summer annuals such as zinnias, marigolds *(Tagetes)*, and China asters *(Callistephus)* until more permanent plants listed below become established.

NAME OF PLANT	KIND	CLIMATE ZONES
Antigonon	Vine	12, 13, 18–21
Bamboo	Perennials	Varies
Bauhinia punctata	Shrub	13, 18–23
Beaumontia grandiflora	Vine	12, 13, 16–17, 21–24
Bougainvillea	Vine	See Encyclopedia
Caesalpinia	Shrub, tree	Varies
Calliandra	Shrub	Varies
Callistemon	Shrub	8, 9, 12–24
Citrus	Shrub, tree	Varies
Coprosma kirkii	Shrub	8, 9, 14–17, 21–24
Cotoneaster horizontalis perpusillus	Shrub	1–11, 14–24
Dais cotinifolia	Shrub, tree	16–24
Distictis buccinatoria	Vine	8, 9, 14–24
Elaeagnus	Shrub	Varies
Exochorda macrantha	Shrub	7–9, 14–18
Fig, edible	Tree	4–9, 12–24
Gamolepis chrysanthemoides	Shrub	8, 9, 13–24
Grevillea	Shrub	Varies
Grewia occidentalis	Shrub, tree	8, 9, 14–24
Hibbertia scandens	Vine	16, 17, 21–24
Hibiscus rosa-sinensis	Shrub	9, 12, 13, 15, 16, 19–24

NAME OF PLANT	KIND	CLIMATE ZONES
Juniperus	Shrub, tree	All
Lantana	Shrub	Varies
Ligustrum ovalifolium	Shrub	4–24
Lonicera hildebrandiana	Vine	9, 14–17, 19–24
Macfadyena unguis-cati	Vine	8–24
Magnolia grandiflora	Tree	4–12, 14–24
Malus	Tree	1–11, 14–21
Nerium oleander	Shrub	8–16, 18–23
Olea europaea	Tree	8, 9, 11–24
Photinia fraseri	Shrub	4–24
Pittosporum	Shrub, tree	Varies
Prunus caroliniana	Shrub, tree	7–24
Punica granatum	Shrub	7–24
Pyracantha	Shrub	Varies
Pyrostegia venusta	Vine	13, 16, 21–24
Pyrus	Tree	Varies
Rosa (climbing)	Vine	Varies
Solandra maxima	Vine	17, 21–24
Tecomaria capensis	Vine	12, 13, 16, 18–24
Thevetia peruviana	Tree	12–14, 21–24
Thunbergia grandiflora	Vine	16, 21–24
Wisteria	Vine	All
Xylosma congestum	Shrub	8–24
Yucca	Shrub, tree	Varies

Plants that grow in wet soil

Water must pass through the root area quickly or plants will suffer from lack of oxygen (see "Watering frequency" on page 49). Even so, some plants grow very well in wet soils where excess water limits but does not exclude oxygen. Some of these plants are listed below. Don't expect heroic swamp tolerance; most of these plants simply offer better than average performance under poor drainage conditions. Check their descriptions in the Western Plant Encyclopedia (beginning on page 161) for degree of moisture tolerance for each.

TREES

NAME OF PLANT	CLIMATE ZONES
Acer rubrum	1–7, 14–17
Alnus species	Varies
Betula	Varies
Casuarina	8–9, 12–24
Clethra arborea	15–17, 21–24
Eucalyptus citriodora	16, 17, 21–24
Eucalyptus erythrocorys	16, 17, 21–24
Fraxinus latifolia	4–24
Fraxinus pennsylvanica	1–6
Liquidambar styraciflua	1–9, 14–24
Magnolia grandiflora	4–12, 14–24
Magnolia virginiana	4–9, 14–24
Melaleuca quinquenervia	9, 13, 16, 17, 20–24
Myoporum laetum	8, 9, 14–17, 19–24

NAME OF PLANT	CLIMATE ZONES
Nyssa sylvatica	3–10, 14–21
Pear	1–11, 14–16, 18
Picea sitchensis	4–6, 14–17
Platanus	Varies
Populus	Varies
Pterocarya stenoptera	5–24
Quercus bicolor	1–3, 10
Salix	Varies
Sambucus caerulea	1–17
Sambucus-callicarpa	4–7, 14–17
Sequoia sempervirens	4–9, 14–24
Taxodium	Varies
Thuja occidentalis	1–9, 15–17, 21–24
Umbellularia californica	4–10, 12–24

SHRUBS

NAME OF PLANT	CLIMATE ZONES
Aronia arbutifolia	1–7
Calycanthus	Varies
Clethra alnifolia	2–6
Cornus stolonifera	1–9, 14–21
Gaultheria shallon	4–7, 14–17
Kalmia microphylla	1–7, 16, 17

NAME OF PLANT	CLIMATE ZONES
Myrica	Varies
Salix	Varies
Thuja occidentalis varieties	2–9, 15–17, 21–24
Vaccinium	Varies
Zenobia pulverulenta	4–7, 14–17

PERENNIALS

NAME OF PLANT	CLIMATE ZONES
Aconitum	1–9, 14–21
Alocasia	22–24
Arundo donax	All
Aster novae-angliae	All
Astilbe	2–7, 14–17
Bambusa (most; see Bamboo)	Varies
Caltha palustris	All
Colocasia esculenta	Varies
Cortaderia selloana	4–24
Cyperus	8, 9, 12–24
Eichhornia crassipes	8, 9, 13–24
Equisetum hyemale	All
Ferns (many)	Varies
Galium odoratum	1–6, 15–17
Hibiscus moscheutos	1–21
Iris ensata	All
Iris, Louisiana hybrids	2–24
Iris pseudacorus	All

NAME OF PLANT	CLIMATE ZONES
Iris sibirica	All
Lobelia cardinalis	1–7, 13–17
Lysimachia nummularia	1–9, 14–24
Lythrum salicaria	All
Mentha	Varies
Mimulus	Varies
Monarda didyma	All
Myosotis scorpioides	All
Phyllostachys (most; see Bamboo)	Varies
Primula (sections Candelabra, Sikkimensis)	Varies
Sanguinaria canadensis	1–6
Sisyrinchium californicum	4–24
Soleirolia soleirolii	8–24
Tolmiea menziesii	5–9, 12–24
Trollius	All
Zantedeschia	5, 6, 8, 9, 14–24

Simple and good-looking landscape with plants requiring little water: lavender-flowered *Limonium perezii* and ground cover of *Baccharis pilularis*.

*You can use
basic landscaping plants
that get by
with little water*

Two outstanding drought tolerant low shrubs or shrubby ground covers form pleasant garden association. Gray leaves and yellow flowers belong to *Santolina chamaecyparissus*; bright green foliage in foreground is *Rosmarinus officinalis* 'Prostratus', which features blue flowers in late winter.

Drought tolerant plants

Much of the West is characterized by a short annual rainy season followed by many dry months in which plants receive no water unless you deliberately apply it. And in periodically recurring drought years, in which rainfall is far below normal, water available for gardens may be severely limited or completely nonexistent. Fortunately, there are numerous fine plants that will thrive with little or no water during the normal dry season once they are established in the garden. Here are some proven performers.

TREES

NAME OF PLANT	CLIMATE ZONES	NAME OF PLANT	CLIMATE ZONES
Acacia (many)	Varies	Melia azedarach	6, 8–24
Aesculus californica	4–7, 14–19	Olea europaea	8, 9, 11–24
Ailanthus altissima	All	Parkinsonia aculeata	11–24
Albizia julibrissin	2–23	Pinus (many)	Varies
Brahea armata	12–17, 19–24	Pistacia	Varies
Casuarina	8–9, 12–24	Populus fremontii	7–24
Cedrus deodara	2–12, 14–24	Quercus (many)	Varies
Celtis	Varies	Rhus lancea	8, 9, 12–24
Ceratonia siliqua	9, 13–16, 18–24	Robinia	All
Cercidium	10–14, 18–20	Schinus molle	8, 9, 12–24
Eriobotrya japonica	4–24	Schinus terebinthifolius	13, 14, 15–17, 19–24
Eucalyptus (most)	Varies	Sequoiadendron giganteum	3–24
Fig, Edible	4–9, 12–24	Tilia tomentosa	1–21
Geijera parviflora	8, 9, 13–24	Tristania conferta	19–24
Grevillea	Varies	Ulmus pumila	1–3, 10, 11
Koelreuteria paniculata	2–21	Walnut	Varies
Lyonothamnus floribundus	15–17, 19–24	Zizyphus jujuba	7–16, 18–24
Maclura pomifera	All		

SHRUBS

NAME OF PLANT	CLIMATE ZONES	NAME OF PLANT	CLIMATE ZONES
Acacia (many)	Varies	Fallugia paradoxa	2–23
*Arbutus unedo	4–24	Fremontodendron	7–24
Arctostaphylos	Varies	Garrya	Varies
Artemisia	All	Genista	Varies
Atriplex	Varies	Grevillea	Varies
Baccharis pilularis	5–11, 14–24	*Hakea	9, 12–17, 19–24
Caesalpinia gilliesii	8–16, 18–23	*Heteromeles arbutifolia	5–24
*Callistemon citrinus	8, 9, 12–24	Hypericum calycinum	4–24
*Caragana arborescens	1–21	*Lagerstroemia indica	4–9, 12–14, 18–21
Cassia artemisioides	8, 9, 12–16, 18–23	Lantana	8–10, 12–17, 23, 24
Catha edulis	13, 16–24	Lavandula	Varies
Ceanothus	Varies	Lavatera assurgentiflora	14–24
*Cercis occidentalis	2–24	Leucophyllum frutescens	7–24
*Cercocarpus	Varies	*Lysiloma thornberi	10, 12–24
*Chamaerops humilis	5–24	Mahonia	Varies
Chamaelaucium uncinatum	8, 9, 12–24	*Melaleuca (most species)	Varies
Cistus	7–9, 12–24	Myoporum debile	15–17, 19–24
Convolvulus cneorum	7–9, 12–24	*Nerium oleander	8–16, 18–23
Coprosma kirkii	8, 9, 14–17, 21–24	*Photinia serrulata	4–16, 18–22
*Cotinus coggygria	All	*Pinus edulis	See Encyclopedia section
Cotoneaster	Varies	*Pinus monophylla	See Encyclopedia section
Crassula argentea	8, 9, 12–15, 17–24	*Pittosporum	Varies
Crassula falcata	8, 9, 12–15, 17–24	Plumbago auriculata	8, 9, 12–24
*Cupressus glabra	5, 8–24	Portulacaria afra	13, 16, 17, 22–24
Cytisus	Varies	*Prosopis glandulosa torreyana	8–14,
*Dalea spinosa	11–13		
Dendromecon	5–8, 14–24	*Prunus caroliniana	7–24
*Dodonaea viscosa	7–9, 12–24	*Prunus ilicifolia	7–9, 12–24
Echium	Varies	*Prunus lyoni	7–9, 12–24
Elaeagnus	Varies	*Punica granatum	7–24
Escallonia	4–9, 14–17, 20–24		

*Can become small tree.

(Continued on next page)

Non-thirsty plants can blossom beautifully

Many drought resistant plants make fine flower displays. Fragile beauty of Matilija poppy flower (*Romneya coulteri*) contrasts with plant's rugged, drought resistant constitution.

SHRUBS (Cont'd.)

NAME OF PLANT	CLIMATE ZONES
Pyracantha	Varies
*Rhamnus alaternus	4–24
Rhamnus californica	4–24
*Rhamnus crocea ilicifolia	7–16, 18–21
Rhus ovata	7–24
Rosa rugosa	All
Rosmarinus	4–24
Salvia clevelandii	10–24
Salvia leucantha	10–24

NAME OF PLANT	CLIMATE ZONES
Santolina chamaecyparissus	All
Simmondsia chinensis	10–13, 19–24
Sollya heterophylla	8, 9, 14–24
Spartium junceum	5–9, 11–24
*Tamarix	Varies
Taxus	3–9, 14–24
Teucrium	Varies
Trichostema lanatum	14–24
*Xylosma congestum	8–24

*Can become small tree.

PERENNIALS, BULBS, ANNUALS

NAME OF PLANT	CLIMATE ZONES
Achillea	All
Agave	Varies
Aloe arborescens	8, 9, 12–24
Amaryllis belladonna	4–24
Anacyclus depressus	All
Arctotheca calendula	8, 9, 13–24
Baccharis pilularis	5–11, 14–24
Baptisia australis	All
Carpobrotus	12–24
Centranthus ruber	7–9, 14–24
Cleome spinosa	All
Coreopsis	Varies
Cortaderia selloana	4–24
Dietes vegeta	8, 9, 13–24
Dudleya brittonii	16, 17, 21–24
Echeveria (most)	Varies
Eriogonum	Varies
Euphorbia (most)	Varies
Euryops	14–17, 19–24
Gaillardia	All
Hippocrepis comosa	8–24
Iris, bearded	All
Iris, Pacific Coast natives	Varies

NAME OF PLANT	CLIMATE ZONES
Kniphofia uvaria	1–9, 14–24
Leonotis leonurus	8–24
Leucocoryne ixioides	13, 16, 19, 21–24
Liatris	1–3, 7–10, 14–24
Limonium perezii	13, 16, 17, 20–24
Linum	All
Marrubium vulgare	All
Mimulus	7–9, 14–24
Narcissus	All
Oenothera berlandieri	All
Pennisetum setaceum	All
Phlomis fruticosa	All
Phormium	7–24
Polygonum cuspidatum compactum	All
Portulaca grandiflora	All
Puya berteroniana	9, 13–17, 19–24
Romneya coulteri	5–10, 12–24
Sedum (many)	Varies
Sisyrinchium bellum	4–24
Tithonia rotundifolia	All
Verbena	Varies
Yucca (most)	Varies
Zauschneria	4–10, 12–24

VINES

NAME OF PLANT	CLIMATE ZONES	NAME OF PLANT	CLIMATE ZONES
Bougainvillea	12, 13, 15–17, 19, 21–24	Tecomaria capensis	12, 13, 16, 18–24
Cissus trifoliata	12, 13	Wisteria	All

Versatile succulents store water in leaves, stems, roots

This versatile group of plants looks attractive throughout the year on minimal water. Sample of succulents includes tubbed jade plant (*Crassula argentea*), gray green *Dudleya brittonii* in pot, small-leafed *Portulacaria afra* at left foreground, red-flowered *Crassula falcata*, and fuzzy rosettes of *Echeveria* 'Doris Taylor'.

Plants to use near swimming pools

Plants chosen to landscape swimming pool areas must meet two requirements. They should not be bristly, prickly, sharp, or thorny so as to annoy or injure pool users. They also should be as litter-free as possible, and what litter they produce should be large enough to be removed by hand from the pool rather than passing into the pool's filter. The following plants will meet these specifications.

Plants nearest pool should produce minimal amount of litter for filter (or pool owner) to remove. Dominant plants are bright gazanias; red flowers in clusters atop stems belong to *Aloe saponaria*.

*Practical poolside plants—
riotously colorful
or restfully green*

SHRUBS

NAME OF PLANT	CLIMATE ZONES
Camellia	4–9, 14–24
Crassula argentea	16, 17, 22–24
Fatsia japonica	4–9, 13–24
Griselinia	9, 15–17, 20–24
Juniperus	All

NAME OF PLANT	CLIMATE ZONES
Pittosporum tobira 'Wheeler's Dwarf'	8–24
Raphiolepis	8–10, 14–24
Sparmannia africana	17, 21–24
Ternstroemia gymnanthera	4–9, 12–24
Viburnum davidii	4–9, 14–24

TREES

NAME OF PLANT	CLIMATE ZONES
Cordyline	Varies
Cupaniopsis	16, 17, 19–24
Dracaena	Varies
Ensete	13, 15–24
Ficus auriculata	20–24
Ficus lyrata	22–24
Firmiana simplex	5, 6, 8, 9, 12–24
Montanoa arborescens	16, 17, 20–24

NAME OF PLANT	CLIMATE ZONES
Musa	Varies
Palms	Varies
Schefflera	Varies
Stenocarpus sinuatus	16, 17, 20–24
Strelitzia	22–24
Tree Ferns	Varies
Trevesia	21–24
Tupidanthus calyptratus	19–24

VINES

NAME OF PLANT	CLIMATE ZONES
Beaumontia grandiflora	12, 13, 16, 17, 21–24
Cissus	Varies
Fatshedera lizei	4–10, 12–24

NAME OF PLANT	CLIMATE ZONES
Solandra maxima	15–24
Tetrastigma	13, 17, 20–24

PERENNIALS

NAME OF PLANT	CLIMATE ZONES
Agapanthus	7–9, 12–24
Agave attenuata	20–24
Aloe saponaria	8, 9, 12–24
Alpinia zerumbet	15–17, 22–24
Artichoke	8, 9, 14–24
Aspidistra elatior	4–9, 12–24
Canna	All
Clivia miniata	15–17, 19–24
Colocasia esculenta	See Encyclopedia
Cyperus	8, 9, 12–24
Dianella tasmanica	8, 9, 14–24
Dietes	8, 9, 13–24
Gazania	8–24

NAME OF PLANT	CLIMATE ZONES
Hedychium	17, 22–24
Hemerocallis	All
Kniphofia uvaria	1–9, 14–24
Liriope	Varies
Ophiopogon	5–10, 12–24
Philodendron (treelike types)	Varies
Phormium	7–24
Sedum	Varies
Strelitzia	22–24
Succulents	Varies
Yucca	Varies
Zoysia tenuifolia	8–24

Attractive all year round, various junipers are principal planting around this naturalistic pool.
Clumps with swordlike leaves, white flowers are *Dietes vegeta*.

Plants for hillsides and erosion control

Hillsides generally offer a less hospitable plant environment than do level gardens. Soil may be shallow, poor, or—where the bank is the result of a grading cut—virtually nonexistent. Hillsides also are more difficult to water thoroughly unless you form watering basins around each new plant so that water will soak in rather than run off. Fortunately, there are numerous plants that will cope successfully with less-than-ideal conditions and provide good-looking cover for slopes. In addition, those plants starred (*) have dense, strong root systems that will help prevent soil erosion.

SHRUBS

NAME OF PLANT	CLIMATE ZONES
Abelia	Varies
Acacia cultriformis	13–24
Acacia cyanophylla	13–24
Acacia longifolia	8, 9, 14–24
Arctostaphylos densiflora	7–9, 14–21
Arctostaphylos edmundsii	6–9, 14–24
Arctostaphylos hookeri	6–9, 14–24
Arctostaphylos uva-ursi	1–9, 14–24
Atriplex	Varies
Baccharis pilularis	5–11, 14–24
Bamboo (some)	Varies
Callistemon phoeniceus 'Prostrata'	8, 9, 12–24
Calluna (some)	2–6, 15–17
Carissa grandiflora (some)	12, 13, 16–21
*Ceanothus (many)	Varies
Cercis occidentalis	2–24
Chaenomeles	1–21
Chamelaucium uncinatum	8, 9, 12–24
Chorizema	15–17, 19–24
*Cistus	Varies
Coleonema	7–9, 14–24
Convolvulus cneorum	7–9, 12–24
*Coprosma kirkii	8, 9, 14–17, 21–24
Correa	14–21
*Cotoneaster (many)	Varies
Cytisus kewensis	4–6, 16, 17
Daboecia azorica	8, 9, 14–24
Daboecia cantabrica	3–9, 14–24
Dendromecon	5–8, 14–24
*Echium fastuosum	14–24
Elaeagnus	Varies
Erica (some)	Varies
*Eriogonum fasciculatum	8, 9, 14–24
Eucalyptus (some)	Varies
*Fallugia paradoxa	2–23
Forsythia suspensa	2–11, 14–16, 18, 19
Fremontodendron	7–24
Gaultheria shallon	4–7, 14–17

NAME OF PLANT	CLIMATE ZONES
Genista (some)	Varies
Grevillea lanigera	15–24
Grewia occidentalis	8, 9, 14–24
Halimiocistus	4–24
Halimium	7–9, 12–24
Heteromeles arbutifolia	5–24
*Hypericum calycinum	2–24
*Jasminum mesnyi	4–24
*Jasminum nudiflorum	3–21
*Juniperus (ground covers)	All
Lagerstroemia indica (shrub types)	7–14
*Lantana	8–10, 12–17, 23, 24
Lonicera pileata	2–9, 14–24
*Mahonia repens	1–21
Myoporum debile	15–17, 19–24
Philadelphus mexicanus	8, 9, 14–24
Plumbago auriculata	8, 9, 12–24
Prunus laurocerasus 'Zabeliana'	3–9, 14–21
Pyracantha 'Santa Cruz'	4–24
Pyracantha 'Walderi'	4–24
*Rhamnus crocea ilicifolia	7–16, 18–21
*Rhus aromatica	1–3, 10
*Rhus integrifolia	15–17, 20–24
*Rhus laurina	20–24
*Rhus trilobata	1–3, 10
*Ribes viburnifolium	8, 9, 14–24
*Rosa multiflora	All
*Rosa rugosa	All
*Rosmarinus officinalis	4–24
Santolina	All
Solanum rantonnetii	15–24
Sollya heterophylla	8, 9, 14–24
Sophora secundiflora	8–16, 18–24
*Symphoricarpos	Varies
Taxus baccata 'Repandens'	3–9, 14–24
Trichostema lanatum	14–24
Westringia rosmariniformis	15–17, 19–24
Xylosma congestum	8–24

*Will control erosion.

VINES

NAME OF PLANT	CLIMATE ZONES
Bougainvillea	12, 13, 15–17, 19, 21–24
*Cissus antarctica	13, 16–24
*Cissus hypoglauca	13–24
*Euonymus fortunei (prostrate forms)	1–17
*Hedera	Varies
Ipomoea acuminata	8, 9, 12–24
Lathyrus latifolius	All
*Lonicera japonica	2–24
*Parthenocissus quinquefolia	All
Passiflora	Varies

NAME OF PLANT	CLIMATE ZONES
Polygonum aubertii	All
*Rhoicissus capensis	16, 17, 21–24
*Rosa banksiae	4–24
Senecio confusus	13, 16–24
Solandra maxima	17, 21–24
Tecomaria capensis	12, 13, 16, 18–24
*Tetrastigma voinieranum	13, 17, 20–24
*Trachelospermum jasminoides	8–24
Tropaeolum majus	All
*Vinca	Varies

*Will control erosion.

PERENNIALS

NAME OF PLANT	CLIMATE ZONES
Arctotheca calendula	8, 9, 13–24
*Bamboo (some)	Varies
Centranthus ruber	7–9, 14–24
Cerastium tomentosum	All
Convolvulus cneorum	7–9, 12–24
Convolvulus mauritanicus	4–9, 12–24
*Coronilla varia	All
Delosperma 'Alba'	12–24
*Drosanthemum floribundum	14–24
Gazania rigens leucolaena	8–24
Hemerocallis	All

NAME OF PLANT	CLIMATE ZONES
Hippocrepis comosa	8–24
Lampranthus	15–24
*Malephora	Varies
Osteospermum fruticosum	8, 9, 14–24
Pelargonium peltatum	15–17, 22–24
Phlomis fruticosa	All
*Polygonum cuspidatum compactum	All
Polygonum vaccinifolium	4–7
*Romneya coulteri	5–10, 12–24
Salvia (some)	Varies
Sedum	Varies

*Will control erosion.

*Mix colors, textures
of hillside plants*

As long as plants have roughly the same requirements, you can combine varieties to add interest to a hillside. Frothy, multi-colored sea of different heathers (*Erica*) thrives in cool-summer region on well-drained slope.

Where oak root fungus is present in the soil

Oak root fungus (*Armillaria*) infects the soil in many parts of the world, but for various reasons it is more of a problem in California than elsewhere in the West. The fungus organism sustains itself on buried wood, mostly dead roots, but it also gets into the tissues of living plants—often it kills them. Some plants resist this fungus infection; gardeners in armillaria-infested neighborhoods can play it safe by planting known resistant plants such as these.

TREES

NAME OF PLANT	CLIMATE ZONES
Abies concolor	1–9, 14–24
Acacia longifolia	8, 9, 14–24
Acer macrophyllum	4–17
Acer palmatum	1–9, 14–24
Ailanthus altissima	All
Arbutus menziesii	3–7, 14–19
Avocado	Varies
Brachychiton populneus	12–24
Broussonetia papyrifera	3–24
Carya illinoensis	4–9, 10, 12–16, 18–23
Castanea sativa	2–9, 14–17
Catalpa bignonioides	All
Celtis occidentalis	All
Ceratonia siliqua	9, 13–16, 18–24
Cercis occidentalis	2–24
Cercis siliquastrum	2–19
Crabapple, Flowering	1–11, 14–21
Cryptomeria japonica	4–9, 14–24
Elaeagnus angustifolia	1–3, 7–14, 18, 19
Eucalyptus camaldulensis	8–24
Fig, 'Kadota'	4–9, 12–24
Fig, 'Mission'	4–9, 12–24
Fraxinus uhdei	9, 12–24
Fraxinus velutina 'Modesto'	3–24
Ginkgo biloba	1–9, 14–24
Ilex aquifolium	4–9, 14–24
Ilex opaca	2–9, 15, 16, 19–23
Jacaranda mimosifolia	13, 15–24

NAME OF PLANT	CLIMATE ZONES
Liquidambar orientalis	5–9, 14–24
Liquidambar styraciflua	1–9, 14–24
Liriodendron tulipifera	1–10, 14–23
Macadamia	9, 16, 17, 19–24
Maclura pomifera	All
Magnolia	Varies
Maytenus boaria	8, 9, 14–21
Melaleuca styphelioides	9, 13–24
Metasequoia glyptostroboides	3–9, 14–24
Pear	1–11, 14–16, 18
Persimmon	Varies
Pinus canariensis	5–24
Pinus nigra	All
Pinus patula	5–24
Pinus radiata	7–9, 14–24
Pinus torreyana	5–24
Pistacia chinensis	8–16, 18–23
Pittosporum rhombifolium	12–24
Plum, Japanese	Varies
Prunus cerasifera	2–22
Pseudotsuga menziesii	1–10, 14–17
Pyrus calleryana	2–9, 14–21
Quillaja saponaria	8, 9, 14–24
Sapium sebiferum	8, 9, 12, 14–16, 18–21
Sequoia sempervirens	4–9, 14–24
Sophora japonica	All
Ulmus parvifolia	8, 9, 12–24
Walnut, California Black (Juglans hindsii)	5–9, 14–20

SHRUBS

NAME OF PLANT	CLIMATE ZONES
Acacia verticillata	14–24
Brugmansia suaveolens	16–24
Buxus sempervirens	3–6, 15–17
Calycanthus occidentalis	4–9, 14–22
Carpenteria californica	5–9, 14–24
Clerodendrum bungei	5–9, 12–24
Cotinus coggygria	All
Exochorda racemosa	3–9, 14–18
Hibiscus syriacus	1–21
Ilex aquipernyi	4–9, 14–24
Lonicera nitida	4–9, 14–24

NAME OF PLANT	CLIMATE ZONES
Mahonia aquifolium	1–21
Mahonia nevinii	8–24
Myrica pensylvanica	4–7
Nandina domestica	5–24
Phlomis fruticosa	All
Prunus caroliniana	7–24
Prunus ilicifolia	7–9, 12–24
Prunus lyonii	7–9, 12–24
Psidium littorale	9, 15–24
Vitex agnus-castus	4–24

Seacoast plantings

Salt-laden winds, fog and humid air, sandy soil, and low sun intensity are among the special conditions seacoast gardens impose on plants. These conditions prevail whether you have a cool north coastal garden or a subtropical location in Zone 24. For gardens directly or largely influenced by the ocean, these plants are proven performers.

Rugged, salt-resistant plants can bloom brilliantly

A seacoast trademark, dazzlingly brilliant ice plants (these are *Lampranthus*) thrive on salt air, sandy soil.

TREES

NAME OF PLANT	CLIMATE ZONES	NAME OF PLANT	CLIMATE ZONES
Albizia distachya	15–17, 22–24	Ficus rubiginosa	18–24
Casuarina stricta	8–9, 12–24	Melaleuca quinquenervia	9, 13, 16, 17, 20–24
Cordyline australis	5, 8–11, 14–24	Metrosideros	Varies
Cordyline indivisa	16, 17, 20–24	Myoporum laetum	8, 9, 14–17, 19–24
Cupaniopsis	16, 17, 19–24	Pinus (several)	Varies
Cupressus macrocarpa	17	Quercus ilex	4–24
Eucalyptus (several)	Varies	Vitex lucens	16, 17, 22–24

SHRUBS

NAME OF PLANT	CLIMATE ZONES	NAME OF PLANT	CLIMATE ZONES
Acacia longifolia	8, 9, 14–24	Euonymus japonica	5–20
Acacia verticillata	14–24	Genista	Varies
Acokanthera	21, 23, 24	Griselinia	9, 15–17, 20–24
*Arbutus unedo	4–24	*Hakea	9, 12–17, 19–24
Atriplex	Varies	Halimium	7–9, 12–24
Calothamnus	8–9, 12–24	Hebe	14–24
Carissa	22–24	Juniperus	All
Cistus	7–9, 12–24	*Lagunaria patersonii	13, 15–24
Coprosma	Varies	Lavatera assurgentiflora	14–24
Corokia cotoneaster	4–24	Leptospermum	14–24
Cytisus	Varies	*Leucodendron argenteum	17, 20–24
*Dodonaea viscosa	7–9, 12–24	Lonicera nitida	4–9, 14–24
Echium	Varies	Lonicera pileata	2–9, 14–24
Elaeagnus	Varies	Melaleuca (most species)	Varies
Escallonia	4–9, 14–17, 20–24	*Myoporum (some)	Varies

*Can become small tree.

(Continued on next page)

Tall trees protect garden from ocean

Even right at the beach you can have a garden if you choose appropriate plants. These trees are *Melaleuca quinquenervia*.

SHRUBS (Cont'd.)

NAME OF PLANT	CLIMATE ZONES
Myrica	Varies
*Pittosporum crassifolium	9, 14–17, 19–24
Raphiolepis	8–10, 14–24
*Rhamnus alaternus	4–24
Rhus integrifolia	15–17, 20–24

*Can become small tree.

NAME OF PLANT	CLIMATE ZONES
Rosa rugosa	All
Rosmarinus officinalis	4–24
Spartium junceum	5–9, 11–24
Tamarix	Varies
Westringia rosmariniformis	15–17, 19–24

PERENNIALS, ANNUALS

NAME OF PLANT	CLIMATE ZONES
Aloe arborescens	8, 9, 12–24
Aurinia saxatilis	All
Calocephalus brownii	16, 17, 19, 21–24
Centaurea cyanus	All
Cerastium tomentosum	All
Chrysanthemum carinatum	All
Chrysanthemum frutescens	All
Cortaderia selloana	4–24
Erigeron glaucus	4–6, 15–17, 22–24
Erigeron speciosus	All

NAME OF PLANT	CLIMATE ZONES
Eriogonum	Varies
Eschscholzia californica	All
Euryops	14–17, 19–24
Felicia amelloides	8, 9, 13–24
Impatiens oliveri	15–17, 21–24
Lavandula angustifolia	4–24
Limonium perezii	13, 16, 17, 20–24
Lonas annua	All
Phormium	7–24
Santolina chamaecyparissus	All

GROUND COVERS, VINES

NAME OF PLANT	CLIMATE ZONES
Abronia	5, 17, 24
Arctostaphylos uva-ursi	1–9, 14–24
Arctotheca calendula	8, 9, 13–24
Atriplex semibaccata	8, 9, 12–24
Baccharis pilularis	5–11, 14–24
Carissa (some)	22–24
Carpobrotus	12–24
Ceanothus gloriosus	Varies
Ceanothus griseus	Varies

NAME OF PLANT	CLIMATE ZONES
Delosperma	12–24
Drosanthemum	14–24
Juniperus conferta	All
Lampranthus	14–24
Muehlenbeckia complexa	8, 9, 14–24
Osteospermum fruticosum	8, 9, 14–24
Polygonum aubertii	All
Solandra maxima	17, 21–24
Tecomaria capensis	12, 13, 16, 18–24

Flower garden flourishes by the sea

In a hollow created by strategic planting of Canary Island broom (*Cytisus canariensis*) and Monterey cypress (*Cupressus macrocarpa*), cutting garden thrives. Rugged flowers include California poppies (*Eschscholzia californica*), basket of gold (*Aurinia saxatilis*), geraniums, calendulas, cornflowers (*Centaurea cyanus*), and blue marguerites (*Felicia amelloides*). At right is yellow-flowered perennial *Euryops pectinatus*.

Plants with low fuel volume

Fire risk is high where native brush and woodland encounter dwellings. No plant will stop a fire, but homeowners can lower the risk by removing highly combustible brush from around the home, introducing low-growing plants with potentially high water content and low fuel volume, irrigating new plantings as needed, and grooming to prevent build-up of potential fuel. Here are suggested plants:

TREES, SHRUBS

Callistemon	Prunus lyonii
Ceratonia siliqua	Rhamnus alaternus
Cistus	Rhus (evergreen types)
Heteromeles arbutifolia	Schinus molle
Myoporum	Schinus terebinthifolius
Nerium oleander (dwarf kinds)	Teucrium chamaedrys

PERENNIALS, VINES

Achillea	Ice plants
Agave	Osteospermum fruticosum
Aloe	Pelargonium peltatum
Arctotheca calendula	Portulacaria afra
Artemisia (low growing kinds)	Potentilla tabernaemontanii
Atriplex (some)	Santolina
Campsis	Senecio cineraria
Convolvulus cneorum	Solanum jasminoides
Gazania	Yucca (trunkless kinds)

Some poor risks for smoggy areas

Air pollution adversely influences plants as well as humans. In plants, the effects will range from poor appearance to poor performance, or both. To the home gardener, damage to plants by polluted air is disconcerting, but the damage can be critical to commercial growers of vegetables and flowers. Consequently, most research into air pollution damage has been conducted to establish susceptibility of crop plants; the results have catalogued the most susceptible rather than the most resistant.

At present, the plants most tolerant of different types of air pollution reveal themselves by good to excellent performance in smoggy areas. In the absence of scientifically established resistance, this implied resistance is your best guide. Look around in gardens, along highways. Ask a reputable local nurseryman to suggest plants that have demonstrated good performance locally. Plants propagated in polluted areas for the nursery trade are likely to be among the more resistant.

These fruit, vegetable, and ornamental plants are especially susceptible to smog damage, sometimes so much so that their commercial production is risky.

EDIBLE CROPS

Almond	Grape
Apple	Lettuce (head and romaine)
Apricot	Nectarine
Avocado	Onion
Beans	Parsley
Broccoli	Peach
Cantaloupe	Pepper
Carrot	Plum
Cherry	Prune
Citrus	Radish
Corn	Spinach
Cucumber	Tomato
Fig	

ORNAMENTALS

Acer (maple)	Morus (mulberry)
Adiantum (maidenhair fern)	Orchids
Antirrhinum (snapdragon)	Petunia hybrida
Calendula officinalis	Philadelphus (mock orange)
Catalpa	Philodendron
Chrysanthemum	Pinus (many)
Coleus blumei	Platanus (plane tree, sycamore)
Cyclamen	Rhododendron (including azaleas)
Dianthus caryophyllus (carnation)	Senecio hybridus (cineraria)
Liquidambar (sweet gum)	Viola (violet, pansy)
Matthiola (stock)	Zinnia

Occasionally technical words are used; these are defined in the Gardeners' Language Glossary at the end of the book.

Western Plant Encyclopedia

The plant descriptions in this encyclopedia appear in alphabetical order under each plant's scientific name, except for common fruits and vegetables, which are described under their common names (apple, tomato). If you know only a plant's common name, look for it in its alphabetical place, where you will find a cross-reference to the scientific name. Scientific names listed are based on *Hortus Third* (New York: Macmillan Publishing Company, 1976). Some of these names will be unfamiliar, but they represent the latest research and their use will make it easier for plant people everywhere to speak a common language. For the convenience of plant shoppers, former and perhaps more familiar scientific names are listed as cross-references.

At the head of a description, a plant's common name appears in capital letters in a lighter typeface than its scientific name. Directly after the common name (if there is one), you will find a word or two telling what kind of plant it is, such as tree or bulb.

A statement of climate adaptability is given for each plant except summer annuals and some house plants. "All Zones" means the plant is recommended for the entire West. Other than that, zones are indicated by numbers, which are explained and mapped on pages 8 to 29. Where two zone numbers are joined by a dash, as in "Zones 1–6, 15–17," the plant is recommended for the zones specified and all the zones between them. Microclimates are explained on pages 9 and 94–95. Any garden may contain favored sites where plants of borderline hardiness stand a fairly good chance of survival.

The drawings are intended to give you a general idea of the appearance of one member of a particular group of plants. Often you can assume that other closely related plants look like it; read through the descriptions of other plants in the same group to make sure.

All plants described are sold in the West or have been sold here within recent years. Many that are rare are so described; many others are common in some areas, rare in others. If you can't find a plant that you want, inquire at your best local nursery. They may be able to order the plant for you or suggest a specialist grower. Joining a horticultural society or volunteering for work at an arboretum or botanical garden can put you in touch with rare plants and their growers.

Sample Entry:

Scientific name (genus and species) or common name of familiar fruit or vegetable.

Former scientific names.

FATSIA japonica *(Aralia sieboldii, A. japonica)*. JAPANESE ARALIA. Evergreen shrub. Zones 4–9, 13–24.

Common name.

Climate adaptability.

Type of plant.

AARON'S BEARD. See *Hypericum calycinum.*

ABELIA. Evergreen, partially evergreen, or deciduous shrubs. Graceful arching branches densely clothed with oval leaves about ½–1½ in. long, usually quite glossy; the new growth bronzy. Tubular or bell-like flowers in clusters at ends of branches or among the leaves; blossoms small but generous enough to be showy mostly during the summer and early fall months. When blooms drop, they usually leave purplish or copper-colored sepals which continue color into the fall months. Leaves also may take on bronzy tints in fall.

Abelia grandiflora

To keep abelias' graceful form, prune them selectively; don't shear. The more stems you cut to the ground in winter or early spring, the more open and arching will be next year's growth. Plants grow and flower best in sun, but they will take some shade. Abelias are adaptable and useful in shrub borders, as space dividers and visual barriers, near house walls; lower kinds are good bank or ground covers. Need average watering.

A. floribunda. MEXICAN ABELIA. Evergreen. Zones 8, 9, 12–24. Severely damaged at 20°F. Usually 3–6 ft. tall, sometimes 10 ft. Arching stems are reddish and downy or hairy. Pendulous tubular flowers, 1½ in. long, reddish purple, single or in clusters. Usually summer blooming, but often in full bloom in January. Partial shade in hot-summer areas.

A. grandiflora. GLOSSY ABELIA. Evergreen to partially deciduous. Zones 5–24. Hybrid of two species from China. Best known and most popular of the abelias. Grows to 8 ft. high or more. Spreads to 5 ft. or more. Flowers white or faintly tinged pink, June-October.

A. g. 'Edward Goucher' (*A. gaucheri*). Like *A. grandiflora*, evergreen in milder climates to nearly deciduous at 15°F. Lower growing (to 3–5 ft.) and lacier than *A. grandiflora*. Small lilac pink flowers with orange throats make a showy display June-October.

At 0°F. both freeze to the ground but usually recover to bloom the same year, making graceful border plants 10–15 in. tall.

A. g. 'Prostrata'. Occasionally partially deciduous even in mildest climates. Low-growing (1½–2 ft.), spreading variety useful as ground cover, bank planting, low foreground shrub. For massing, set 3–4 ft. apart.

A. g. 'Sherwoodii'. Smaller than *A. grandiflora*, more spreading; grows 3–4 ft. tall, 5 ft. wide.

ABELIOPHYLLUM distichum. WHITE FORSYTHIA. Deciduous shrub. Native to Korea. Zones 3–6. Not a forsythia but resembles it in growth habit and profusion of bloom in February—but in dazzling white. Lower and slower growing than most forsythias, to 3–4 ft. and as wide. Leaves bluish green, opposite, 1–2 in. long. Attractive purple buds in fall and winter on brown or black new wood. Buds open pink, flowers quickly turn white. Fragrant. Budded branches will bloom in winter when brought indoors. Easy to grow in sun or light shade. Routine garden care. Prune in bloom or immediately after. Cut some of the oldest branches at base to keep new flowering wood coming.

Abeliophyllum distichum

ABIES. FIR. Evergreen trees. In nature are tall, erect, symmetrical trees with uniformly spaced branch whorls. Look for large cones held erect; they shatter after ripening, leaving a spiky stalk. Most (but not all) native firs are high mountain plants which grow best in or near their natural environment. They grow slowly if at all in hot, dry, windy areas at low elevations.

Abies concolor

Christmas tree farms grow native firs for cutting, and nurseries in the Northwest and northern California grow a few species for the living Christmas tree trade. Licensed collectors in the Northwest dig picturesque, contorted firs at high elevations near timberline and market them through nurseries as "alpine conifers." Use these in rock gardens; small specimens are good container or bonsai subjects. Birds attracted by fir seeds.

Abies concolor

Firs from some other parts of the world do well in warm, dry climates.

A. amabilis. SILVER FIR, CASCADE FIR. Zones 1–7, 15–17. Native southern Alaska south through Coast Ranges and Cascades of Washington and Oregon. Tall tree in the wilds, smaller (20–50 ft.) in lowland gardens in the Pacific Northwest. Dark green leaves, silvery beneath, curve upward along the branches. Give it room to grow.

A. balsamea. BALSAM FIR. Zones 3–7, 15–17. Native to eastern American mountains. Only the dwarf variety 'Nana' is occasionally sold in the West. Interesting rock garden subject. Slow growing, dense, dark green cushion; partial shade, ample water.

A. bracteata (*A. venusta*). SANTA LUCIA FIR, BRISTLECONE FIR. Zones 8, 9, 14–21. From steep, rocky slopes on the seaward side of the Santa Lucia Mountains, Monterey County, California. A tall tree (70 ft. in 50 years), with spreading (15–20 ft.) lower branches, and slender steeplelike crown. Its stiff needles, 1½–2½ in. long, have unusually sharp points; dark green above, white lines beneath. Roundish cones are unique—about 4 in. long, with a long, slender, pointed bract on each cone scale. Exceptionally heat and drought tolerant.

A. concolor. WHITE FIR. Zones 1–9, 14–24. Native to mountains of southern Oregon, California, southern Rocky Mountains, Baja California. One of the big five in timber belt of the Sierra Nevada, along with ponderosa pine, sugar pine, incense cedar, and Douglas fir. It's one of the popular Christmas trees and one of the most commonly grown native firs in western gardens.

Large, very symmetrical tree in its native range and in the Northwest. Slower growing in California gardens; best as container plant in southern California. Bluish green, 1–2-in.-long needles. Variety 'Candicans' has blue white foliage.

A. grandis. LOWLAND FIR, GRAND FIR. Zones 1–9, 14–17. From British Columbia inland to Montana, southward to Sonoma County, California. In California it grows near the ocean along Highway 1.

Under this fir, many Northwest gardeners live and garden successfully; they prune it high. It's one of the largest firs, reaching to 300 ft.; lower in cultivation. Handsome, deep green, 1–1½-in.-long needles, glossy above, white lines beneath; in two rows along branches.

A. koreana. KOREAN FIR. Zones 3–9, 14–24. Native to Korea. Slow-growing, compact, pyramidal tree seldom over 30 ft. Shining, green, short needles. Sets cones on young, small trees. Variety 'Aurea' is even slower, smaller; gold green foliage.

A. lasiocarpa. ALPINE FIR. Zones 1–9, 14–17. Native to Alaska, south through the high Cascades of Washington and Oregon; nearly throughout the Rocky Mountains. Narrow, steeple shaped tree 60–90 ft. in good soil in moist areas. Bluish green, 1–1½-in.-long needles.

Best known in gardens as an "alpine conifer" dug near timberline and sold in nurseries. Extremely slow growing in California gardens. Allow 15–20-ft. spread in Northwest gardens as it usually doesn't hold its narrow shape in cultivation.

A. l. arizonica. CORK FIR. Zones 1–9, 14–17. Native to San Francisco Peaks, Arizona, at 8,500 ft. elevation. Has interesting creamy white, thick, corky bark. Very handsome as a youngster. Good bonsai.

A. magnifica. RED FIR. Zones 1–7. Native to the mountains of southern Oregon, California's Sierra Nevada south to Kern County, and the Coast Ranges south to Lake County. Tall, stately tree with symmetrical, horizontal, rather short branches. New growth silvery gray. Mature, 1-in.-long needles blue green, curve upward on upper limbs, in two rows on lower branches.

The "silver tip" of California cut Christmas tree trade is red fir. Hard to grow at low elevations.

A. nordmanniana. NORDMANN FIR. Zones 1–11, 14–24. Native to the Caucasus, Asia Minor, Greece. Vigorous, densely foliaged fir 30–50 ft. tall in cultivation and 20 ft. wide. Shining dark green, ¾–1½-in.-long needles, with whitish bands beneath, densely cover branches.

More adaptable to California gardens than native firs. Give it adequate water. Will submit to long-term container growing.

A. pinsapo. SPANISH FIR. Zones 5–11, 14–24. Native to Spain. Very slow growing, to 25 ft. in 40 years. In southern California, good dwarf effect for years. Dense symmetrical form; it's sometimes taken for a spruce. Stiff, deep green, ½–¾-in.-long needles uniformly around branches. There is a blue gray variety, 'Glauca'.

A. procera (*A. nobilis*). NOBLE FIR. Zones 1–7, 15–17. Native to the Siskiyou Mountains of California, north in the mountains of Oregon and Washington. Grown in Northwest nurseries as live Christmas trees. Similar to California's red fir in appearance. Grows 90–200 ft. high in wilds, almost as high in Northwest gardens. Short stiff branches, blue green, 1-in.-long needles. Large cones with extended bracts as in *A. bracteata*.

ABRONIA. SAND VERBENA. Zones 5, 17, 24. Not a true verbena. Oval to roundish, very thick, fleshy leaves. Small, tubular, fragrant flowers in headlike clusters. The first two species are naturally suited for holding sand in beach gardens. They are not hardy in severe climates.

*Abronia
latifolia*

A. latifolia. YELLOW SAND VERBENA. Perennial. Native to seacoast, British Columbia to Santa Barbara. Under ideal conditions plants form leafy mats up to 3 ft. across. Thick leaves 1½ in. long and as wide. The whole plant is gummy enough so that it may become incrusted with sand or dust. Bright yellow flowers from May-October. Sow seed in flats, in pots, or in light, well-drained, sandy soil. Scraping or peeling off the papery covering that encloses the seed should facilitate germination.

A. umbellata. PINK SAND VERBENA. Perennial. Native to coasts, British Columbia to Baja California. Creeping, rather slender, fleshy, often reddish stems 1 ft. or more long. Leaves 1–2 in. long, not quite as wide. Flowers rosy pink, bloom almost throughout year. Grow as *A. latifolia*.

A. villosa. Resembles *A. umbellata* but plant is hairy, somewhat sticky, and is an annual. Desert native that thrives in heat, drought. Like other abronias, seeds hard to find.

ABUTILON. FLOWERING MAPLE, CHINESE BELLFLOWER, CHINESE LANTERN. Evergreen viny shrubs. Zones 13, 15–24. Mostly native to South America. Rapid growing; planted primarily for the pleasure provided by flowers. Coarse and rangy growth; avoid by pinching out branch tips.

Can be trained as standards or espaliers, but best as loose, informal espalier. Abutilon enjoys moist soil. Partial shade inland, full sun on coast. Will not bloom in deep shade. In cold climates it can be used as container plant indoors in winter, out on terrace in summer. Gets whitefly and scale insects. Control both with malathion or light oil spray.

*Abutilon
hybridum*

A. hybridum. Upright arching growth to 8–10 ft., and spreading as wide. Broad maplelike leaves. Drooping bell-like flowers in white, yellow, pink, and red. Main blooming season from April-June. White and yellow forms seem to bloom almost continuously. The best-known flowering maple.

A. megapotamicum. Vigorous growth to 10 ft. and as wide. Leaves are arrowlike, 1½–3 in. long. Flowers resembling red and yellow lanterns gaily decorate the long rangy branches, May-September. This vine-shrub is more graceful in detail than in entirety, but can be trained to an interesting pattern. Good hanging basket plant. 'Marianne' has superior form; 'Variegata' has leaves mottled with yellow.

A. pictum 'Thompsonii'. Similar to *A. hybridum,* but foliage strikingly variegated with creamy yellow. Pale orange bells veined with red.

ABYSSINIAN BANANA. See *Ensete ventricosum*.

ABYSSINIAN SWORD LILY. See *Gladiolus callianthus*.

ACACIA. Evergreen shrubs and trees. Native to tropics and warm temperate regions all over the world, particularly Australia.

The first acacias came into California gardens a few years after the discovery of gold. More than 80 species have been tested in the past 100 years. Of these, some 20 species now serve, beautifully and functionally, in California and Arizona landscapes. Several are fountains of clear yellow flowers in January-February. Some are

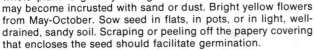
*Acacia
baileyana*

(Continued on page 165)

Acacia

NAME	ZONES	HEIGHT	SPREAD	LEAVES	FLOWERS	COMMENTS
Acacia armata KANGAROO THORN	13–24	10–15 ft.	10–12 ft.	Light green, waxy, 1-in.-long leaves on thorny branches.	Yellow, single ¼-in.-wide balls. Feb.-Mar.	Blooms when young. Used as pot plant in cold areas. Grown as shrub barrier in California. Thorniness makes it real barrier.
A. baileyana BAILEY ACACIA (Often called MIMOSA as cut flowers.)	7–9, 13–24. Borderline Zone 6.	20–30 ft.	20–40 ft.	Feathery, finely cut, blue gray.	Yellow, in clusters. Fragrant. Profuse in Jan.-Feb.	Most commonly planted and one of hardiest. Wonderful tree on banks when grown as multitrunked tree-shrub.
A. b. 'Purpurea' PURPLE-LEAF ACACIA	8, 9, 14–24	20–30 ft.	20–30 ft.	Same, except for lavender to purple new growth.	Same.	Cut back to encourage new growth, prolong foliage color.
A. constricta MESCAT ACACIA	10–24	10–18 ft.	To 18 ft.	Tiny, feathery.	Yellow, fragrant.	Spiny shrub native to Arizona, New Mexico, Texas, Mexico.
A. cultriformis KNIFE ACACIA	13–24	10–15 ft.	10–15 ft.	Silvery gray, shaped like 1-in.-long paring knife blades stuck into stems.	Yellow, in clusters. March.	Naturally a multistemmed tree. Barrier or screen. Useful on banks, slopes.

(Continued on next page)

NAME	ZONES	HEIGHT	SPREAD	LEAVES	FLOWERS	COMMENTS
A. cyanophylla BLUE-LEAF WATTLE	13–24	20–30 ft.	15–20 ft.	Narrow, 6–12 in. long, bluish.	Nearly orange balls in clusters. Heavy bloom in Mar., Apr.	Screen for privacy against wind, dust. Multitrunked tree-shrub on banks, hillsides. Long branches droop gracefully when laden with flowers.
A. cyclopis	8, 9, 13–24	10–15 ft.	15–20 ft.	Dark green, narrow, to 3½ in. long.	Bright yellow, single or clustered; inconspicuous. Spring.	Screening plant along highways. Very drought resistant. Good for hedges. Unusual seeds—black with red rings.
A. dealbata (*A. decurrens dealbata*)	8, 9, 14–24. Borderline Zone 6.	To 50 ft.	40-50 ft.	Feathery, silvery gray.	Similar to *A. baileyana*	Twigs and young branches also silvery gray; attractive. Very fast growing.
A. decora GRACEFUL WATTLE	13–24	6–8 ft.	6–8 ft.	Rather narrow, 2 in. long, curved, bluish.	Yellow balls in 2-in.-long clusters. Mass display in spring.	Screening. Can be used as trimmed hedge 5 ft. high. Drought resistant.
A. decurrens (*A. decurrens mollis*) (Plants offered are often the similar *A. mearnsii.*) GREEN WATTLE	8, 9, 14–24. Borderline Zone 6.	To 50 ft.	40–50 ft.	Feathery, dark green.	Yellow, in clusters. Feb.-Mar.	Longer lived than *A. baileyana*; takes more wind and water. Leaves larger, but still finely cut. Looks almost pinelike in groves.
A. farnesiana SWEET ACACIA (Some plants sold under this name are *A. smallii.*)	8, 9, 10–24	To 20 ft.	15–25 ft.	Deciduous. Feathery, finely divided. Branches thorny.	Deep yellow, fragrant, single balls. Jan.-Apr., and longer.	Does well in alkaline soils of low and high deserts where temperatures do not drop below 15°F. A valuable tree or screen in Arizona.
A. longifolia (Often sold as *A. latifolia.*) SYDNEY GOLDEN WATTLE	8, 9, 14–24	To 20 ft.	To 20 ft.	Bright green, 3–6 in. long.	Golden yellow in loose 2½-in.-long spikes along branches in late winter, early spring.	Usually big, rounded, billowy shrub. Very fast growing; very tolerant. Used as road screening against dust, headlights. Good soil binder near beach (winds make it prostrate).
A. melanoxylon BLACKWOOD ACACIA, BLACK ACACIA	8, 9, 13–24	To 40 ft.	To 20 ft.	Dark green, 2–4 in. long.	Creamy to straw color, in short clusters. Mar.-Apr.	Fast upright grower. The one acacia that always succeeds in California's Central Valley. A troublemaker in confined situations.
A. pendula WEEPING ACACIA, WEEPING MYALL	13–24	To 25 ft.	To 15 ft.	Blue gray, to 4 in. long, on long weeping branches.	Yellow, in pairs or clusters. Blooms erratically in Apr., May.	Beautiful weeping tree. Perfect for cascading from behind wall. Interesting structural form as mature individual. Makes graceful espalier.
A. podalyriifolia PEARL ACACIA	8, 9, 13–24	10–20 ft.	12–15 ft.	Roundish, 1½ in. long, silvery gray, soft and satiny to touch.	Light yellow, fluffy, in long clusters. Nov.-Mar.	Shrub or can be trained as rounded, open-headed tree. Excellent for patio use. Good winter color; earliest to bloom (November in San Diego).
A. redolens (*A. ongerup*)	8, 9, 12–24	1–2 ft.	15 ft.	Narrow, gray green, leathery.	Puffy yellow balls, spring.	Ground cover for banks, large areas of poor soil. Endures drought, heat. 'Ongerup' and *A. melanoxylon* 'Ongerup' similar or identical.
A. retinodes (Often sold as *A. floribunda.*) WATER WATTLE, FLORIBUNDA ACACIA	8, 9, 13–24. Borderline Zones 5, 6.	To 20 ft.	To 20 ft.	Yellow green, to 5 in. long.	Yellow, small heads in clusters. Blooms most of year near coast.	Quick screen. Less dense than *A. longifolia*. Tends to get leggy. The only acacia with chance of survival in Seattle if mild winters come four in a row.
A. saligna WILLOW ACACIA	14–24	10–20 ft.	15–25 ft.	Dark green, to 8 in. long.	Yellow, showy, large, in clusters. Profuse in March.	Graceful weeping habit. Fast growth. Reaches good flowering size in 3–4 years from seed.
A. subporosa BOWER WATTLE, RIVER WATTLE	13–24	20–40 ft.	18–20 ft.	Narrow, drooping.	Paired yellow puffs, spring.	Graceful weeping big shrub, small tree. Needs water, good drainage.
A. verticillata	14–24	To 15 ft.	To 15 ft.	Dark green, needle-like leaves, ¾ in. long, in whorls. Looks like an airy conifer.	Pale yellow in 1-in.-long spikes. Apr.-May.	Good low hedge in wind. Unpruned, it develops open form with many spreading, twisting trunks. Sheared, it grows dense and full. Good at beach; resists oak root fungus.

quite fragrant when in bloom. Many decorate and protect hillsides, banks, freeway landscapes. Some serve well in beach plantings. Attractive to birds.

Though there are hundreds of species, most nurseries sell only a few. You can easily grow your own from seed you collect or order from a specialist. Sow individually in peat pots and set out pot and all when well established.

The acacias differ widely in foliage and growth habit. Some have feathery, much divided leaves; others have flattened leaf stalks that fulfill the function of leaves.

Whether a larger-growing species of acacia is a shrub or tree depends on how it is pruned in youth. Remove the lead shoot and it grows as a shrub; remove the lower branches and it grows treelike. Stake the tree types until they are deeply anchored. Deep infrequent watering will discourage surface rooting and give plants better anchorage.

Prune large trees to open interiors, reducing dieback of shaded branches and preventing damage by wind. Thin by removing branches entirely to the trunk.

All acacias are relatively short-lived—20–30 years. But if a tree grows to 20 ft. high in 3 years, the short life can be accepted.

Many acacias become chlorotic where water is bad and salts accumulate, as do many other plants in such soil.

The blackwood acacia (*A. melanoxylon*) has aggressive roots, lifts sidewalks, splits easily, suckers. In shallow soil or where roots compete, it is a bad actor. Yet in the right place it is a well-behaved, beautiful tree. It is vigorous and dependable under difficult conditions of poor soil, wind, and drought.

Acacia melanoxylon

ACAENA. SHEEP BUR. Perennials. Zones 4–9, 14–24. The two New Zealand natives described below are plants that form large, loose mats of attractive gray green or pale green leaves that are divided into leaflets. Grow from seed or divisions in spring. Rather slow to establish. Plant 6–12 in. apart in sun or part shade. They burn in hot sun. Need ample water. Use in areas where a gray green, loose, fine-textured mat is wanted—beside paths, under not too shady trees, or in rock gardens. Can take some foot traffic. Remove burs, which look messy and stick to clothing or to pets.

A. buchananii. Has dense, silky, whitish green leaves with 11–13 round, small leaflets with scallop-toothed edges.

A. microphylla. NEW ZEALAND BUR. Has 7–13 pale green leaflets that are similar to above but larger and almost without hairs.

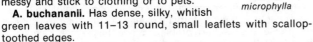

Acaena microphylla

ACALYPHA. Evergreen tropical shrubs. Zones 21–23. Both species described below are quite tender. One of them can be used as an annual.

A. hispida. CHENILLE PLANT. Native to the East Indies. Needs tropical climate. Best grown in plastic-covered outdoor rooms. Control size by pinching and pruning; can grow to a bulky 10 ft. Leaves heavy, broad to 8 in., rich green. Flowers hang in 18-in.-long clusters resembling tassels of crimson chenille. Blooms most heavily in June; scattered bloom throughout year. With heavy pruning, a good house plant.

A. wilkesiana (*A. tricolor*). COPPER LEAF. Native to South Pacific islands. Foliage more colorful than many flowers. Used as an annual, substituting for flowers from September to frost. Leaves to 8 in., bronzy green mottled with shades of red and purple; or red with crimson and bronze; or green, edged with crim-

Acalypha hispida

son, stippled with orange and red. In a warm, sheltered spot, it can grow as a shrub to 6 ft. or more if winter appearance is not important. Best in container with fast draining soil mix, kept slightly dry through winter.

ACANTHUS mollis. BEAR'S BREECH. Perennial. Zones 4–24. Native to southern Europe. Fast growing, spreading plant with basal clusters of handsome, deeply lobed and cut, shining, dark green leaves to 2 ft. long. Rigid 1½-ft. spikes of tubular whitish, lilac, or rose flowers with green or purplish spiny bracts top 2–3-ft. stems. Blooms late spring or early summer. Variety 'Latifolius' has larger leaves, is hardier.

Requires light shade but will take sun in coastal areas. Cut back after flowering. If you grow it for the foliage alone, cut off flower stalks before they bloom. Bait for slugs and snails. Divide clumps between October and March. Plant where it can be confined. Roots travel underground, make plant difficult to eradicate. Effective with bamboo, large-leafed ferns. Best in moist, shady situations, but will also grow in dry, sunny areas—even in parking strips.

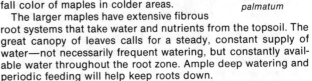

Acanthus mollis

ACER. MAPLE. Deciduous or evergreen trees or large shrubs. When you talk of maples, you're talking about many trees—large and medium-sized deciduous shade trees, smaller evergreen and deciduous trees, and dainty, picturesque shrub-trees. In general, maples are highly favored in the Pacific Northwest, in the intermountain areas, and to a lesser extent in northern California, but, with a few exceptions are not adapted to southern California or the Southwest's desert areas. Practically all maples in southern California show marginal leaf burn after mid-June and lack the fall color of maples in colder areas.

Acer palmatum

The larger maples have extensive fibrous root systems that take water and nutrients from the topsoil. The great canopy of leaves calls for a steady, constant supply of water—not necessarily frequent watering, but constantly available water throughout the root zone. Ample deep watering and periodic feeding will help keep roots down.

A. buergeranum. TRIDENT MAPLE. Deciduous tree. Zones 4–9, 14–17, 20, 21. Native to China, Japan. Grows 20–25 ft. high. Roundish crown of 3-in.-wide, glossy, 3-lobed leaves that are pale beneath. Fall color usually red, varies to orange or yellow. Low spreading growth; stake and prune to make it branch high. A decorative, useful patio tree. A favorite bonsai subject.

A. campestre. HEDGE MAPLE. Deciduous tree. Zones 1–9, 14. Native to Europe, western Asia. Slow growing to 70 ft., seldom over 30 ft. in cultivation. Forms especially dense, compact, rounded head in the Northwest, thinner in California. Leaves 3–5 lobed, 2–4 in. wide, dull green above; turn yellow in fall. Rated high in the Northwest.

A. capillipes. Deciduous tree. Zones 1–9, 14–24. Native to Japan. Moderate growth rate to 30 ft. Young branches red, turning brown with white stripes with age. Young leaves red, leaf stalks and midribs red. Leaves, shallowly 3 lobed, 3–5 in. long, turn scarlet in fall.

A. cappadocicum. COLISEUM MAPLE. Deciduous tree. Zones 1–6. Native to western Asia. Known here in its variety 'Rubrum', RED COLISEUM MAPLE. Grows to 35 ft.; forms compact rounded crown. Leaves 5–7 lobed, 5½ in. wide. Bright red spring foliage turns rich, dark green.

A. circinatum. VINE MAPLE. Deciduous shrub or small tree. Zones 1–6, 14–17. Native to moist woods, stream banks in coastal mountains of British Columbia south to northern California. Crooked, sprawling, and vinelike in the forest shade, with many stems from the base, or single-trunked small tree 5–35 ft. high in full sun. Leaves 5–11 lobed, 2–6 in. wide and as long;

light green turning orange, scarlet, or yellow in the fall; new spring foliage usually has reddish tints. Tiny reddish purple flowers in clusters, April-May, followed by paired winged fruit which look like little red bow ties among the green leaves. One of the most airy and delicate western natives. The rare variety 'Monroe' has finely cut leaves.

Let it go untrimmed to make natural bowers, ideal settings for ferns and woodland flowers. Use under a canopy of tall conifers where its blazing fall color is brilliant contrast. Can be espaliered against shady side of a wall. Its contorted leafless branches make an intricate pattern in winter. Loses its vinelike characteristics in open situations. Select in fall to get best forms for autumn color.

A. davidii. DAVID'S MAPLE. Deciduous tree. Zones 1–6, 15–17, 20, 21. Native to central China. This 20–35-ft.-high maple is distinctive on several counts. Bark is shining green striped with silvery white, particularly effective in winter. Leaves are glossy green, oval or lobed, 2–7 in. long, 1½–4 in. wide, each embossed with deep veins. New foliage bronze tinted turning to bright yellow, red orange, and purple in fall. Greenish yellow flowers, in clusters, showy in April or May.

Acer davidii

A. ginnala. AMUR MAPLE. Deciduous shrub or small tree. Zones 1–9, 14–16. Native to Manchuria, north China, Japan. To 20 ft. high. Three-lobed, toothed leaves to 3 in. long, 2 in. wide. Striking red fall color. Clusters of small yellowish flowers fragrant in early spring; followed by handsome bright red, winged fruit. Comes into its own in the coldest areas of the West. Grown as staked, trained single tree or multiple-trunked tall shrub.

A. glabrum. ROCKY MOUNTAIN MAPLE. Deciduous shrub or small tree. Zones 1–3, 10. Leaves 3–5 lobed or divided into 3 leaflets, 2–5 in. wide, on dark red twigs. Fruit tinged red. Fall foliage yellow. Multitrunked clumps may be only 6 ft. tall or up to 30 ft. under ideal conditions. Needs well-drained soil and ample moisture.

A. griseum. PAPERBARK MAPLE. Deciduous tree. Zones 1–9, 14–21. Native to China. Grows to 25 ft. or higher with narrow to rounded crown. In winter it makes a striking silhouette with bare branches angling out and up from main trunk and reddish bark peeling away in paper-thin sheets. Late to leaf out in spring, leaves are divided into 3 coarsely toothed leaflets 1½–2½ in. long, dark green above, silvery below. Inconspicuous red flowers in spring develop into showy winged seeds. Foliage turns brilliant red in fall.

A. japonicum. FULLMOON MAPLE. Deciduous shrub or small tree. Zones 1–6, 14–16. Native to Japan. To 20–30 ft. Nearly round 2–5-in.-long leaves cut into 7–11 lobes. Practically unknown in western gardens, but two varieties are obtainable. Both are small, slow growing, best placed as shrubs.

A. j. 'Aconitifolium'. FERNLEAF FULLMOON MAPLE. Has leaves deeply cut, almost to the leaf stalk, with each lobe cut and toothed. Fine fall color where adapted.

A. j. 'Aureum'. GOLDEN FULLMOON MAPLE. Leaves open pale gold in spring and remain a pale chartreuse yellow all summer.

A. macrophyllum. BIGLEAF MAPLE. Deciduous tree. Zones 4–17. Native to streambanks, moist canyons, Alaska to foothills of California. Broad-topped, dense shade tree 30–95 ft. high—too big for a small garden or a street tree. Large 3–5-lobed leaves, 6–15 in. wide; sometimes bigger on young, vigorous sapling growth; medium green turning yellow in fall. Small greenish yellow flowers in drooping clusters, April-May, followed by clusters of paired winged seeds which look rather like tawny drooping butterflies. Yellow fall color spectacular in cool areas. Resistant to oak root fungus.

Acer macrophyllum

A. morrisonense. FORMOSAN MAPLE, MT. MORRISON MAPLE. Deciduous tree. Zones 4–6, 15–17. Native to Taiwan (Formosa). Fast, upright growth rounding with age; probably 30–40 ft. Greenish bark striped white. New growth red in early spring, fall foliage red. Summer foliage light green, red leaf stalks; leaves 3 lobed, 5 in. long, 4 in. wide. Needs ample water, good soil; not

for areas where summers are hot, dry, and windy.

A. negundo. BOX ELDER. Deciduous tree. Zones 1–10, 12–24. Native to most of U.S. Where you can grow other maples of your choice this is a weed tree of many faults—seeds readily, hosts box elder bugs, suckers badly, subject to breakage. Fast growing to 60 ft., usually less. Leaves divided into 3–5 (or 7–9) oval, 2–5-in.-long leaflets with toothed margins; yellow in fall.

A. n. 'Variegatum'. VARIEGATED BOX ELDER. Not as large or weedy as the species. Combination of green and creamy white leaves stands out in any situation. Large pendant clusters of white fruit are spectacular. Highly regarded in the Northwest; occasionally planted in northern California.

A. oblongum. EVERGREEN MAPLE. Evergreen or partially evergreen tree. Zones 8–10, 12, 14–24. Native to the Himalayas and China. To 20–25 ft. high, spreads almost as wide; branches tend to sweep outward and upward. Slender, shiny, deep green leaves, no lobes. New growth attractive bronzy pink in spring. Loses all leaves in sharp cold.

A. o. biauritum. See *A. paxii.*

A. palmatum. JAPANESE MAPLE. Deciduous shrub or tree. Zones 1–9, 14–24. Native to Japan and Korea. Slow growing to 20 ft.; normally many stemmed. Most airy and delicate of all maples. Leaves 2–4 in. long, deeply cut into 5–9 toothed lobes. All year interest: young spring growth is glowing red; summer's leaves are soft green; foliage turns scarlet, orange, or yellow in fall months; slender leafless branches in greens and reds provide winter pattern. Resists oak root fungus.

Grafted garden varieties are popular (the list below includes only the best known of dozens available), but common seedlings have uncommon grace and usefulness. They are more rugged, faster growing, more drought tolerant, and stand more sun and wind than named forms. Maples thrive everywhere in the Northwest (where they make good small street trees). They can be grown with success in California if given shelter from hot, dry, or constant winds. Filtered shade is best but full sun is satisfactory. In California consider the local soil and water; wherever azaleas are difficult and suffer from salt buildup in the soil, Japanese maples will show burn on leaf edges. Give same watering treatment as azaleas—flood occasionally to leach out salts.

Used effectively on north and east walls, in patios and entryways, as small lawn tree. Attractive in groves (like birches) as woodland planting; set out plants of different sizes and spacings for natural effects. Seen under oaks, as background for ferns and azaleas, alongside pools. Invaluable in tubs and for bonsai. Since it is inclined to grow in planed surfaces, pruning to accentuate this growth habit is easy. Prune to plane downward when given a water foreground.

The grafted garden forms are usually smaller than seedlings, more weeping and spreading, brighter in foliage color, and more finely cut in leaf. In California it seems that the finer the cut leaf the greater the leaf burn problem. Since these kinds make good tub plants, it's easy to give them special placement and watering attention. Some of the best are:

'Atropurpureum'. RED JAPANESE MAPLE. Purplish or bronze to bronzy green leaves, brighter in sun. Holds color all summer.

'Bloodgood'. Vigorous, upright growth to 15 ft. Deep red spring and summer foliage, scarlet in fall. Bark blackish red.

'Bonfire'. Orange pink spring and fall foliage; twisted trunk, short branches, drooping branchlets.

'Burgundy Lace'. Leaves more deeply cut than 'Atropurpureum'; branchlets bright green.

'Butterfly'. Small (to 7 ft.) shrub with small bluish green leaves edged in white. Cut out growth that reverts to plain green.

'Crimson Queen'. Small, shrubby, with finely cut leaves that hold color all summer, turn scarlet before dropping off in fall.

'Dissectum' ('Dissectum Viridis'). LACELEAF JAPANESE MAPLE. Small shrub with drooping branches, green bark; pale green, finely dissected leaves turn gold in autumn.

'Ever Red' ('Dissectum Atropurpureum'). Small mounding shrub with weeping branches. Finely dissected, purple tinged, lacy foliage turns crimson in fall.

'Garnet'. Similar to 'Crimson Queen' and 'Ever Red'; somewhat more vigorous grower.

'Heptalobum Osakazuki'. Vigorous (to 10 ft. or more) plant with large green leaves that turn fiery scarlet in autumn.

'Koshimino' ('Sessilifolium'). Upright, narrowish to 12 ft. Small leaves without leaf stalks sit right on branches. Green leaves turn red in fall.

'Linearilobum' ('Scolopendriifolium'). To 8 ft., with green leaves divided into extremely long, narrow segments. Fall color yellow.

'Ornatum' ('Dissectum Atropurpureum'). RED LACE-LEAF JAPANESE MAPLE. Like 'Dissectum', but with red leaves turning brighter red in autumn.

'Oshio Beni'. Like 'Atropurpureum' but more vigorous; makes long, arching branches.

'Roseo-marginatum'. Small. Pale green leaves are edged with pink. Cut out growth that reverts to green.

'Sango Kaku' ('Senkaki'). Vigorous, upright, treelike. Fall foliage yellow, tinted rose. Twigs, branches striking coral red.

A. paxii (*A. oblongum biauritum*). Zones 8, 9, 14–24. Evergreen tree to 30 ft. Leaves usually 3 lobed, occasionally oval or mitten shaped. Slow growth; compact head of dense foliage.

A. platanoides. NORWAY MAPLE. Deciduous tree. Zones 1–9, 14–17. Native to Europe, western Asia. Broad-crowned, densely foliaged tree to 50–60 ft. Leaves 5 lobed, 3–5 in. wide, deep green above, paler beneath; turn yellow in fall. Showy clusters of small, greenish yellow flowers in early spring. Very adaptable, tolerating many soil and climate conditions, but poor in southern California and desert. Once a widely recommended street tree but now objected to where aphids cause honeydew drip and sooty mold. Voracious root system deep down and at surface also a problem. Among the horticultural varieties here are some of the best (purple-leafed forms perform poorly in alkaline soils unless soil is conditioned):

'Almira'. Dwarfish, informal globe to 16 ft.

'Cavalier'. Compact, round headed, to 30 ft.

'Cleveland' and 'Cleveland II'. Shapely, compact, well-formed trees about 50 ft. tall.

'Columnare'. Slower grower, narrower form than the species.

'Crimson King'. Holds purple foliage color until leaves drop. Slower growing than the species. Fine in Northwest and California foothills.

'Drummondii'. Leaves are edged with silvery white; unusual and striking.

'Emerald Queen'. Quick grower with good form.

'Faassen's Black'. Pyramidal in shape, with dark purple leaves.

'Globe'. Slow growing with dense, round crown; eventual height 20–25 ft.

'Green Lace'. Finely cut, dark green leaves; moderate growth rate to 40 ft.

'Miller's Superform'. Exceptionally tall and fast growing.

'Royal Red Leaf'. Another good red or purple-leafed form.

'Schwedler' or 'Schwedleri'. Purplish red leaves in spring turn to dark bronzy green, gold in autumn.

'Summer Shade'. Fast growing variety especially adapted to hot-summer climates.

A. pseudoplatanus. SYCAMORE MAPLE. Deciduous tree. Zones 1–9, 14–20. Native to Europe, western Asia. Moderate growth to 40 ft. or more. Leaves 3–5 in. wide, 5 lobed, thick, prominently veined, dark green above, pale below. No particular fall color. The variety 'Atropurpureum' has leaves that are rich purple underneath.

A. rubrum. SCARLET MAPLE, RED MAPLE. Deciduous tree. Zones 1–9, 14–17. Native to eastern U.S. Fairly fast growth to 40 ft. or more with 20-ft. spread. Faster than Norway or sycamore maples. Presents red twigs, branchlets, buds, and quite showy flowers. Fruit dull red. Leaves 2–4 in. long, 3–5 lobed, shining green above, pale beneath, furnish brilliant scarlet in frosty areas.

Acer rubrum

Rates high in Pacific Northwest where several selected forms are available. Needs ample moisture in Zone 14.

'Armstrong' and 'Armstrong II'. Tall, very narrow trees with good red fall color.

'Bowhall'. Tall, narrow, cone shaped, with orange red foliage color in fall.

'Columnare'. Tall, broadly columnar.

'Gerling'. Broadly pyramidal, to 35 ft. with 20-ft. spread.

'October Glory'. Tall, round-headed tree; last to color in fall.

'Red Sunset'. Colors earlier than 'October Glory'.

'Scanlon Red'. Compact, conical, to 35 ft. with 16-ft. spread; brilliant orange, umber, and red in fall.

'Schlesingeri'. Tall, broad, fast, regular; orange red fall color.

'Shade King'. Very fast grower to 50 ft. Pale green foliage turns bright red in fall.

A. saccharinum. SILVER MAPLE. Deciduous tree. Zones 1–9, 14–24. Native to eastern U.S. Grows fast to 40–100 ft. with equal spread. Open form, with semipendulous branches; casts fairly open shade. Bark silvery gray except on oldest wood. Leaves 3–6 in. wide, 5 lobed, light green above, silvery beneath. In Northwest, fall color is a mixture of scarlet, orange, and yellow—often in same leaf.

You pay a penalty for the advantage of fast growth. Weak wood and narrow crotch angles make it break easily. Many rate it least desirable of maples. Unusually susceptible to aphids and cottony scale. Suffers from chlorosis in alkaline soils.

A. s. 'Wieri' (*A. s.* 'Laciniatum'). WIER MAPLE. CUTLEAF SILVER MAPLE. Same as species except leaves are much more finely cut; makes open shade.

A. saccharum. SUGAR MAPLE. Deciduous tree. Zones 1–10, 14–20. From eastern U.S.; in the Northeast it's source of maple sugar. Moderate growth to 60 ft. and more. Stout branches with upward sweep form fairly compact crown. Leaves 3–6 in. wide, 3–5 lobed, green above, pale below. Spectacular fall color in cold-winter areas—yellow and orange to deep red and scarlet. The variety 'Cutleaf' has leaves divided into narrow segments, casts less dense shade. 'Green Mountain' is most drought resistant variety.

A. s. grandidentatum (*A. grandidentatum*). WASATCH MAPLE, BIG-TOOTH MAPLE, ROCKY MOUNTAIN SUGAR MAPLE. Leaves 3–5 lobed with large blunt teeth. Shrubby to tree of 20–30 ft. Fall color brilliant tones of yellow, orange, rose red. In nature, plant of canyons and streamsides. In gardens, requires well-drained soil on dry side.

A. truncatum. Deciduous tree. Zones 1, 4–9, 14–23. Native to China. Grows fairly rapidly to 25 ft. Like a small Norway maple with more deeply lobed leaves to 4 in. wide. Expanding leaves a purplish red, summer leaves green, autumn leaves dark purplish red. A good lawn or patio tree.

ACHILLEA. YARROW. Perennials. All Zones. Yarrows are among the most carefree and generously blooming perennials for summer and early fall, several being equally useful in the garden or as cut flowers (cut and dry taller kinds for winter bouquets). Leaves are gray or green, bitter-aromatic, usually finely divided (some with toothed edges). Flower heads usually in flattish clusters. Yarrows thrive in sun, need only routine care—moderate watering (but can endure much drought once established), cutting back after bloom, dividing when clumps get crowded. Fire retardant.

Achillea
tomentosa

A. ageratifolia. GREEK YARROW. Native to Balkan region. Low mats of silvery leaves, toothed or nearly smooth edged. White flower clusters ½–1 in. across on stems 4–10 in. tall.

A. clavennae (often sold as *A. argentea*). SILVERY YARROW. Mats of silvery gray, silky leaves that are lobed somewhat like chrysanthemum leaves. Flat-topped loose clusters of ½–¾-in.-wide, ivory white flower heads on 5–10-in.-high stems. Combines beautifully with *Festuca ovina glauca,* yellow sunroses (*Helianthemum*), creeping yellow-flowered sedums.

A. filipendulina. FERNLEAF YARROW. Native to the Orient. Tall, erect plants 4–5 ft. high with deep green, fernlike leaves. Bright yellow flower heads in large flat-topped clusters. Dry or fresh, they are good for flower arrangements. Several horticultural varieties available: 'Gold Plate', a tall plant, has flower clusters up to 6 in. wide; and 'Coronation Gold', to about 3 ft., also has large flower clusters. Combine these tall yarrows in borders with clumps of delphiniums, red-hot poker, and Shasta daisies.

A. millefolium. COMMON YARROW, MILFOIL. It may spread a bit or grow erect to 3 ft. Narrow, fernlike leaves on 3-ft.-high stems are green or gray green. White flower clusters grow on long stems. *A. m.* 'Rosea' has rosy flower heads. One of the more successful garden varieties is 'Fire King'. It grows to about 3 ft., has gray foliage and dark reddish flowers, and is good for dry, hot situations. 'Cerise Queen' has brighter red flowers.

A. ptarmica. Erect plant up to 2 ft. high. Narrow leaves with finely toothed edges. White flower heads in rather open, flattish clusters. 'The Pearl' has double flowers.

A. taygetea. Native to the Levant. Grows to 18 in. Gray green divided leaves 3–4 in. long. Dense clusters of bright yellow flower heads fade to primrose yellow—excellent contrast in color shades until time to shear off the old stalks. Good cut flowers.

A. tomentosa. WOOLLY YARROW. Native to Europe and the Orient. Makes a flat spreading mat of fernlike, deep green, hairy leaves. Golden flower heads in flat clusters top 6–10-in. stems in summer. 'Primrose Beauty' has pale yellow flowers; 'King George' has cream flowers. A good edging and a neat ground cover for sunny or partly shaded small areas; used in rock gardens. Shear off dead flowers to leave attractive green mat of low-growing foliage.

ACHIMENES. Tender perennial with very small, irregular, conelike rhizomes. Native to tropical America. Related to African violet and gloxinia, requires similar treatment. Plants 12–24 in. high, some trailing. Slender stems; roundish, crisp, bright to dark green, hairy leaves. Flaring tubular flowers 1–3 in. across, pink, blue, lavender, orchid, purple.

Achimenes

Grow as house plant, in greenhouse or lathhouse, or in patio protected from direct sun and wind. Plant rhizomes March-April, placing ½–1 in. deep in moist peat moss and sand. Keep in light shade at 60°F. with even moisture. When 3 in. high, set 6–12 plants in 6–7-in. fern pot or hanging basket. Soil mix: equal parts peat moss, perlite, leaf mold. In fall, cure and dry rhizomes; store in cool dry place over winter; repot in spring.

ACIDANTHERA bicolor. See *Gladiolus callianthus.*

ACMENA smithii (*Eugenia smithii*). LILLY-PILLY TREE. Evergreen large shrub or small tree. Zones 15–17, 19–24. Australia. Big feature is its dramatic show of clusters of white, lavender, or lavender pink ¼–½-in.-wide edible berries in winter; they last a long time. If trained, can make tree to 10–25 ft. high. Awkward in growth unless trained. Shiny, pinkish green to green, 3-in.-long leaves. Many small white flowers in clusters at branch tips. Takes normal good garden care but is at its best with deep, rich soil and ample water.

Acmena smithii

ACOELORRHAPHE wrightii (*Paurotis wrightii*). Palm. Outdoors Zones 19–24; house plant anywhere. Native to Florida, West Indies. Fan palm with several slender trunks that grow stiffly and somewhat slowly to 10–15 ft. Leaves 2–3 ft. across, green above, silvery below. Very hardy (to 20°F.) but somewhat difficult to establish. Does best in partial shade with ample feeding and plenty of water. Subject to chlorosis; prepare soil carefully with organic amendments and iron where salts in soil or water are a problem. Treat with iron if leaves go yellow green. Large plants are among the most beautiful of palms but are rare, expensive. Slow from seed to multitrunk phase; supply available in nurseries may improve.

Acoelorrhaphe wrightii

ACOKANTHERA. Evergreen shrub. Zones 21, 23, 24. Native of South Africa. Distinguished, rather slow growing, to 10 ft. and as wide (keep them smaller and more dense by cutting back long branches and removing weak ones). Most admired for leaf color—glossy dark green to deep plum purple—against a very dark brown framework of stems and branches. Flowers, white or tinged pink and very fragrant, appear throughout the year with the big show in early spring. They are followed by blackish purple, olive-sized fruit which are very poisonous (fruit can be avoided by removing flowers as they fade).

Acokanthera oblongifolia

Especially tolerant of wind and salt. Best in full sun. Need plenty of water in summer. Useful in hedges, foundation plantings, and as an espalier.

A. oblongifolia (*A. spectabilis*). AFRICAN WINTERSWEET. Narrow leaves, 3–5 in. long. Flowers about 1 in. long. Many plants sold under this name belong to the next species.

A. oppositifolia (*A. venenata*). BUSHMAN'S POISON. Flowers smaller than above. Leaves broader, relatively shorter, tinged red, purplish, or bronze.

ACONITUM. ACONITE, MONKSHOOD. Perennial. Zones 1–9, 14–21. Leaves in basal clusters usually divided into lobes. Flowers shaped like hoods or helmets, along tall spikes. Caution: all parts of the plant are poisonous. Monkshood has a definite place in rich soil under trees, at the back of flower beds, or even at the edge of a shaded bog garden. Substitute for delphinium in shade. Combines effectively with ferns, thalictrum, Japanese anemone, astilbe, hosta, and francoa.

Aconitum napellus

Difficult to establish in warm, dry climates. Needs ample moisture; should never dry out. Sow seeds in spring, or late summer and early fall, for bloom the following year. Divide clumps in early spring or late fall, or leave undivided for years. Goes completely dormant in winter; mark site.

A. carmichaelii (*A. fischeri*). Native to central China. Densely leafy stems 2–4 ft. high. Leaves leathery, dark green, lobed and coarsely toothed. Deep purple blue flowers form in dense branching clusters 4–8 in. long. Blooms in fall. Variety 'Wilsonii' grows 6–8 ft. high, has more open flower cluster 10–18 in. long.

A. napellus. GARDEN MONKSHOOD. Native to Europe. Upright leafy plants 2–5 ft. high. Leaves 2–5 in. wide, divided into narrow lobes. Flowers usually blue or violet, in spikelike clusters.

ACORUS gramineus. Perennial. All Zones. Native to Japan, northern Asia. Related to callas, but fans of grasslike leaves more nearly resemble miniature tufts of iris. Flowers are inconspicuous. Two varieties are better known than species: 'Pusillus' is tiny, with leaves seldom more than 1 in. long. It is used in planting miniature landscapes and dish gardens. 'Variegatus', with leaves to 18 in. long, ¼ in. wide, can be planted in bog gardens or at edge of pool. 'Variegatus' is also useful in dry landscapes—collections of grasses, bamboos, or sword-leafed plants among gravel and boulders; has white-edged leaves.

Acorus gramineus

ACROCARPUS fraxinifolius. PINK CEDAR. Deciduous to nearly evergreen tree native to India, Burma. Zones 21–24. In spite of common name, not a cedar but a relative of the cassias. In climate zones indicated it fills a definite need for a tall-growing, slen-

Acrocarpus fraxinifolius

der tree. Has a clean, green trunk and striking foliage—long, 2-ft.-wide leaves are divided into many leaflets; red on expanding, leaves turn green at maturity. Small scarlet blossoms in dense clusters bloom in great profusion on bare branches in late winter, early spring. Only does its best where protected from strong winds. Although successful street plantings exist, plant has never been common; nurseries fail to follow up on early sales with continuing supply of plants. A fast grower.

Acrocarpus fraxinifolius

ACROCOMIA. GRU-GRU PALM. Slow growing feather palms from Mexico, West Indies, South America. Long, black spines grow on the single or multiple trunks. Fruit sweet and edible. Needs ample water.

A. mexicana. Zone 24. Mexican palm 15–20 ft. tall, with olive to dark green 8–12-ft. feather leaves on mature plants. Takes little or no frost.

A. totai. Zones 23, 24. Native to Paraguay, Argentina. To 20 ft., with 6–9-ft.-long, medium to dark green feather leaves. Hardier than the former.

Acrocomia mexicana

ACTINIDIA. Deciduous vines. Native to east Asia. Handsome foliage. Plant in rich soil. Give ample water and feed often. Supply sturdy supports for them to twine upon— such as a trellis, arbor, or patio overhead. Or you can train them to cover walls and fences; guide and tie vines to the support as necessary. Thin occasionally to shape or to control pattern.

A. arguta. HARDY KIWI. Zones 1–9, 14–24. Much like *A. chinensis* but with smaller leaves, flowers; fruit 1–1½ in. long, fuzzless (eat skin and all). Female varieties 'Ananasnaja' and 'Hood River' need male for pollen. Winter chill requirement not determined.

Actinidia chinensis

A. deliciosa (*A. chinensis*). KIWI, CHINESE GOOSEBERRY VINE. Zones 4–9, 14–24. Twines and leans to 30 ft. if not curbed. Leaves 5–8 in. long, roundish, rich dark green above, velvety white below. New growth often has rich red fuzz. Flowers (May) 1–1½ in. wide, opening creamy and fading buff. Fruit egg-sized, roughly egg shaped, covered with brown fuzz. Green flesh edible and delicious, with hints of melon, strawberry, banana. Although single plants are ornamental, you need a male and female plant for fruit. The best female (fruiting) varieties are 'Chico' and 'Hayward' (similar, possibly identical varieties); 'Vincent' needs little winter chill, is good variety for mildest winter climates.

A. kolomikta. Zones 4–9, 15–17. Rapid growth to 15 ft. or more to produce a wondrous foliage mass made up of heart shaped, 3–5-in.-long, variegated leaves. Some leaves all white, some green splashed with white, others have rose, pink, or even red variegation.

ADENIUM obesum. Shrub, usually grown in container indoors. Can be kept outdoors in Zones 23–24. Twisted branches grow from huge, fleshy, half-buried trunk or rootstock. Leaves sparse; plant leafless for long periods. Clustered saucer shaped blossoms are deep pink, 2 in. or more across. Cannot take frost or winter chill and cold soil. Needs heat, light, good drainage, infrequent watering in summer, even less in winter—in short, plant for careful enthusiasts and collectors. In bloom,

Adenium obesum

extremely showy; in eastern tropical Africa, where it is native, it is known as desert rose or desert azalea. Milky sap is poisonous.

ADIANTUM. MAIDENHAIR FERN. Mostly native to tropics; some are western natives. Stems are thin, wiry, and dark. Fronds finely cut, the leaflets mostly fan shaped, bright green, thin textured. Plants need shade, steady moisture, and a soil rich in organic matter. Leaves of even hardy varieties die back in hard frosts. Kinds listed as tender or indoor plants sometimes succeed in sheltered places or lanais in mild winter areas. Protect from snails and slugs.

Adiantum pedatum

A. capillus-veneris. SOUTHERN MAIDENHAIR. Zones 5–9, 14–24. Native to North America. To 18 in. tall, fronds twice divided but not forked. Needs leaf mold or peat moss.

A. hispidulum. ROSY MAIDENHAIR. Tropics of Asia, Africa. Indoor or greenhouse plant. To 12 in. tall. Young fronds rosy brown, turning medium green, shaped somewhat like five-finger fern.

A. pedatum. FIVE-FINGER FERN, WESTERN MAIDENHAIR. Zones 1–9, 14–21. North America. Fronds fork to make a fingerlike pattern atop slender 1–2½-ft. stems. General effect airy and fresh; excellent in containers or shaded ground beds.

A. peruvianum. SILVER DOLLAR MAIDENHAIR. Peru. Indoor or greenhouse plant. To 18 in. or more in height. Segments of leaves quite large, to 2 in. wide.

A. raddianum (*A. cuneatum, A. decorum*). Brazil. Tender fern for indoors or greenhouse. Fronds cut 3–4 times, 15–18 in. long. Many named varieties differing in texture and compactness. Grow in pots; move outdoors to a sheltered, shaded patio in summer. Varieties commonly sold are 'Fritz-Luthii', 'Gracillimum' (most finely cut), and 'Pacific Maid'.

A. tenerum. (Plant sold as *A. t.* 'Wrightii' is similar or identical.) New World tropics. Indoors or greenhouse. Long, broad fronds arch gracefully, are finely divided into many deeply cut segments ½–¾ in. wide.

ADROMISCHUS. Succulents. Zones 15–24; indoor plants anywhere. Native to South Africa. Short-stemmed plants grown for their fleshy, often interestingly marked leaves; flowers not important. All need sun, warmth, and good drainage, but leaves will burn in full summer desert sun.

Adromischus festivus

A. cristatus. Leaves fleshy, to 2 in. long, 1 in. wide, light green. Leaf tips are squared off and have a wavy margin.

A. festivus. PLOVER EGGS. Leaves fleshy, somewhat flattened, gray green with purplish mottling.

AECHMEA. Bromeliads. Outdoors Zones 22–24. Elsewhere, greenhouse or indoor plants. In the frost free areas, grow in pots, in hanging baskets, or in moss fastened in crotches of trees—always in shaded places with good air circulation. Indoors or outdoors, soil should be fast draining but moisture retentive. Apply water every week or two into cups within leaves. Put water on soil when it's really dry to the touch. Bromeliad specialists list dozens of species and varieties, and new hybrids appear frequently.

Aechmea fasciata

A. chantinii. Rosettes of leaves 1–3 ft. long, green to gray green banded with silver or darker green. Tall flower clusters have orange, pink, or red bracts, yellow and red flowers; white or blue fruit.

A. fasciata. Gray green leaves, cross banded with silvery white. From the center grows a cluster of rosy pink flower bracts in which nestle pale blue flowers that change to deep rose.

(Continued on next page)

'Silver King' has unusually silvery leaves; leaves of 'Marginata' are edged with creamy white bands.

A. 'Foster's Favorite'. Hybrid with bright wine red, lacquered leaves about 1 ft. long. Drooping spikelike clusters of coral red and blue flowers. 'Royal Wine', another hybrid, forms an open rosette of somewhat leathery, glossy, light green leaves, burgundy red beneath. Orange to blue flowers in drooping clusters.

A. fulgens. Green leaves, dusted with gray, 12–16 in. long, 2–3 in. wide. Flower cluster usually above the leaves; blossoms red, blue, and blue violet. Variety *discolor* has brownish red or violet red leaves, usually faintly striped. Many hybrids.

A. pectinata. Stiff rosettes up to 3 ft.; leaves to 3 in. Broad, strongly marked pink or red at bloom time. Flowers whitish and green.

A. weilbachii. Shining leaves make rosettes 2–3 ft. wide. Leaf color green or suffused with red tones. Dull red flower stalk 1½ ft. tall has orange red berries, tipped lilac.

AEGOPODIUM podagraria. BISHOP'S WEED, GOUT-WEED. Deciduous perennial. Zones 1–7. Very vigorous ground cover best in semishade or shade with moderate water. Many light green, divided leaves make a low (6 in.) dense mass; leaflets are ½–3 in. long. To keep it low and even, mow it 2 or 3 times a year. Spreads by creeping underground rootstocks, may become invasive; best if contained behind underground barrier of wood, concrete, or heavy tarpaper.

A. p. 'Variegatum'. The most widely planted form; leaflets are edged white, giving luminous effect in shade. Pull plants that revert to solid green leaves.

*Aegopodium
podagraria
'Variegatum'*

AEONIUM. Succulents. Zones 15–17, 20–24. Among the most useful succulents for decorative effects, in pots or in the ground. Especially good in full sun near ocean; part shade inland.

A. arboreum. Branched stems to 3 ft. tall, each branch with a 6–8-in.-wide rosette of light green, lightly fringed, fleshy leaves. Yellow flowers in long clusters. Variety 'Atropurpureum' has dark purple rosettes, is more striking and more widely grown than the green one. Rosettes of 'Zwartkop' are nearly black.

A. decorum. Bushy rounded plants to 10 in., the many branches ending in 2-in. rosettes. Fleshy leaves tinted reddish, red edges. Neat, compact. Pink flowers.

A. floribundum. Hybrid between *A. simsii* and *A. spathulatum*. Makes a 1-ft. cushion with 2–3-in. rosettes of medium green, fleshy leaves streaked with darker green. Abundant yellow flowers in spring.

A. haworthii. Free branching, shrubby, to 2 ft., with blue green, red-edged rosettes 2–3 in. wide. White flowers.

A. 'Pseudotabulaeforme'. Smooth, flat, light green rosettes to 10 in. wide. Makes offsets freely.

A. simsii (*A. caespitosum*). Low, dense, spreading, very leafy, 6 in. tall. Bright green rosettes of leaves. Yellow flowers.

A. urbicum. "Dinner platter" rosettes to 8–10 in. wide. Long, narrow, light green leaves, loosely arranged, have reddish edges. Similar plants may be sold under the same name.

*Aeonium
arboreum*

AESCHYNANTHUS (*Trichosporum*). Trailing indoor plants and greenhouse plants. Related to African violets but you wouldn't guess it. Shining leaves usually in pairs along stems. Bright tubular flowers. Good in hanging pots. Need high temperatures, high humidity, and much light. Plant in loose, open, fibrous potting mix.

A. 'Black Pagoda'. Has dark green leaves marbled with blackish purple, good display

*Aeschynanthus
radicans*

of clustered deep orange flowers at the branch tips.

A. marmoratus. ZEBRA BASKET VINE. Grown for its green leaves mottled with maroon rather than for its inconspicuous greenish flowers.

A. pulcher. Resembles *A. radicans*, but has greenish, shorter flower tubes.

A. radicans (*A. lobbianus*). LIPSTICK PLANT. Tubular red 2-in. flowers emerge from tubular, purplish black flower tubes like lipsticks from their cases.

A speciosus. Bright yellow and orange flowers up to 4 in. long.

A. splendidus. Yellow orange to orange 4-in. flowers in clusters of 6–20 at ends of trailing stems.

AESCULUS. HORSECHESTNUT. Deciduous trees or large shrubs. Leaves are divided fanwise into large toothed leaflets. Flowers, in long, dense, showy clusters at the ends of branches, attract hummingbirds. Fruit is a leathery capsule enclosing glossy seeds.

A. californica. CALIFORNIA BUCKEYE. Zones 4–7, 14–19. Native to dry slopes and canyons below 4,000 ft. elevation in Coast Ranges and Sierra Nevada foothills.

Shrublike or small tree, often with several stems to 10–20 ft. or more high. New foliage pale apple green; mature leaves have 5–7 rich green, 3–6-in.-long leaflets. Striking sight in April or May when fragrant, creamy flower plumes make it a giant candelabrum. Large, pear shaped fruit, with green covering splitting to reveal large, brown, shiny seeds, are favorites for fall flower arrangements.

*Aesculus
carnea*

In drought conditions it drops its leaves very early—by July—but if given plenty of water will hold them until fall. After leaf drop, presents interesting silhouette—silvery trunk, branches, branchlets. Needs room; it's very wide-spreading.

A. carnea. RED HORSECHESTNUT. Zones 1–9, 14–17. Origin: hybrid between *A. hippocastanum* and *A. pavia*. To 40 ft. high and 30 ft. wide. Round-headed with large dark green leaves divided fanwise into 5 leaflets; casts dense shade. In April–May the tree wears hundreds of 8-in.-long plumes of soft pink to red flowers. 'Briotii' has rosy crimson flowers; 'O'Neill' has flowers of bright red. These smaller horsechestnuts are easy to accommodate in small gardens. Needs summer water.

A. hippocastanum. COMMON HORSECHESTNUT. Zones 1–9, 14–17. To 60 ft. high with a 40-ft. spread; bulky, densely foliaged tree giving heavy shade. Needs summer water. Leaves divided fanwise into 5–7-toothed, 4–10-in.-long leaflets. Spectacular in spring with its ivory flowers with pink markings in 12-in.-long plumes. Invasive roots can break up walks. Seeds are slightly toxic. 'Baumannii' has double flowers, sets no seeds.

AETHIONEMA. STONECRESS. Perennials. Zones 1–9. Native to Mediterranean region and Asia Minor. Choice little shrublets, attractive in or out of bloom, best adapted to colder climates, and a favorite among rock gardeners. Need full sun, grow best in a light porous soil with considerable lime. Bloom late spring to summer. When flowering stops, cut back dead flower stems.

A. schistosum. Erect, unbranched stems 5–10 in. high, densely clothed with narrow, slate blue, ½-in.-long leaves. Flowers rose, petals about ¼ in. long, fragrant.

A. warleyense (*A. 'Warley Rose'*). A hybrid, forms a neat, compact plant to 8 in. high. Pink flowers in dense clusters. Widely used; only one planted to any extent in warmer climates.

*Aethionema
warleyense*

AFRICAN BOXWOOD. See *Myrsine africana*.

AFRICAN CORN LILY. See *Ixia maculata*.

AFRICAN DAISY. See *Arctotis, Dimorphotheca, Osteospermum.*

AFRICAN IRIS. See *Dietes.*

AFRICAN LINDEN. See *Sparmannia africana.*

AFRICAN RED ALDER. See *Cunonia capensis.*

AFRICAN VIOLET. See *Saintpaulia.*

AFRICAN WINTERSWEET. See *Acokanthera oblongifolia.*

AGAPANTHUS. LILY-OF-THE-NILE. Evergreen or deciduous perennials with thick rootstocks and fleshy roots. Outdoor plants in Zones 7–9, 12–24; indoor/outdoor tub or pot plants where winters are cold.

Agapanthus orientalis

Adaptable. Grow in full sun or as little as 3 hours sun a day. Best in loamy soil but will grow in heavy soils. Thrives with ample water during growing season but established plants can endure drought. Divide infrequently; every 5 or 6 years is usually sufficient. In cold-winter areas lift and store over winter, replant in spring. Superb container plant. Good near pools.

A. africanus. (Often sold as *A. umbellatus*). Evergreen. Leaves shorter, narrower than those of *A. orientalis*; flower stalks shorter (to 1½ ft. tall), fewer flowered (20–50 to the cluster). Blue flowers midsummer to early fall.

A. inapertus. Deciduous. Deep blue tubular flowers droop from a 4–5 ft. stalk.

A. orientalis. (Often sold as *A. africanus, A. umbellatus*). Evergreen. Most commonly planted. Broad, arching leaves in big clumps. Stems to 4–5 ft. tall bear up to 100 blue flowers. There are white ('Albus'), double ('Flore Pleno'), and giant blue varieties.

A. 'Peter Pan'. Evergreen. Outstanding free-blooming dwarf variety. Foliage clumps are 8–12 in. tall; clustered blue flowers top 12–18-in. stems.

A. 'Queen Anne'. Evergreen. Foliage clump 12–15 in. tall; leaves narrow. Flower stalks 2 ft. tall; flowers medium blue over a long summer season.

A. 'Rancho White'. Evergreen. Foliage clump 1–1½ ft. tall; leaves broad. Flower stalks 1½–2 ft. tall carry heavy clusters of white flowers. Also known as 'Dwarf White' and 'Rancho'. 'Peter Pan Albus' is similar or identical.

AGAPETES serpens (*Pentapterygium serpens*). Evergreen shrub. Zones 15–17, 23, 24, or greenhouse. Arching, drooping branches to 3 ft. or more rise from a swollen, tuberlike base. Narrow leaves ½–1 in. long crowd in two rows along branches. Lanternlike, inch-long flowers, red marked with deeper red chevrons, hang under the branches in spring. A blueberry relative, it needs acid planting mix, some shade, and liberal watering. Odd, showy hanging basket plant. Also attractive planted above retaining wall or on high bank where viewers can see stripings on flowers. Native to moderate elevations in Himalayas, it merits trial in mildest Northwest gardens.

Agapetes serpens

AGATHAEA coelestis. See *Felicia amelloides.*

AGATHIS robusta. QUEENSLAND KAURI. Evergreen tree. Zones 15, 16, 20–23. Here's a dramatic strong skyline tree. Handsome in youth in containers. Moderate growth to an eventual 75 ft. in 80 years. Typically nar-

Agathis robusta

row and columnar. Open spaces between clumped branches present a striking layered effect. Leaves, light green to pinkish copper in new growth, then dark green, are broad, leathery, 2–4 in. long, and exceptionally glossy. The foliage mass shines in the sun, sparkles in the rain, and ripples brightly in the breeze. A moisture loving tree—be generous with water and fertilizer. Sometimes confused with *Podocarpus nagi* in nurseries. Rare.

Agathis robusta

AGAVE. Succulents, mostly gigantic, with large clumps of fleshy, strap shaped leaves. The flower clusters are big, but not colorful. After flowering, which may take years, the foliage clump dies, usually leaving behind suckers which make new plants. Drought resistant; they shrivel from serious drought but plump up again when watered or rained on. Fire retardant.

Agave attenuata

A. americana. CENTURY PLANT. Zones 12–24. Leaves to 6 ft. long, with hooked spines along the edge and a wicked spine at the tip, blue green in color. Be sure you really want one before planting it. The bulk and spines make it formidable to remove. After 10 years or more the plant makes a branched flower stalk 15–40 ft. high with yellowish green flowers. There are several varieties with yellow or white striped leaves.

A. attenuata. Zones 20–24. Leaves 2½ ft. long, soft green or gray green, fleshy, somewhat translucent, no spines. Makes clumps to 5 ft. across; older plants develop a stout trunk to 5 ft. tall. Greenish yellow flowers dense on arching spikes, to 12–14 ft. long. Will take poor soil but is best in rich soil with ample water. Protect from frost and hot sun. Statuesque container plant. Good near ocean or pool.

A. deserti. Zones 12–24. Small clumping plant with especially attractive yellow flowers.

A. victoriae-reginae. Zones 12, 13, 15–17, 21–24. Clumps only a foot or so across. The many dark green leaves are 6 in. long, 2 in. wide, stiff, thick, with narrow white lines. Slow growing, it will stand in pot or ground 20 years before flowering (greenish flowers on tall stalks), then dying.

A. vilmoriniana (*A. mayoensis*). OCTOPUS AGAVE. Zones 12–24. Pale green or yellowish green rosettes up to 3 ft. wide. Leaves 3–4 in. wide, fleshy, deeply channeled above, with a single long spine at the end. Arching, twisted leaves give plant look of an octopus or huge spider. Very handsome in containers.

AGERATUM houstonianum. FLOSS FLOWER. Annual. All Zones, if planting times followed. Reliable favorite for summer and fall color in borders and containers. The lavender blue-flowered varieties combine with flowers of almost any color or shape. Leaves roundish, usually heart shaped at the base, soft green, and hairy. Tiny lavender blue, white, or pink tassel-like flowers in dense clusters. Dwarf varieties make excellent edgings, or pattern plantings with other low-growing annuals.

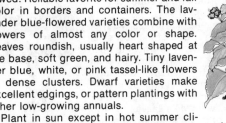
Ageratum houstonianum

Plant in sun except in hot summer climates where filtered shade is beneficial; rich, moist soil best. In mild-winter areas, plant in late summer for fall color. Easy to transplant, even when in bloom. Effective combinations: lavender blue ageratum with salmon pink annual phlox, Madagascar periwinkle (*Catharanthus,* formerly known as *Vinca rosea*) in pink shades, or dwarf yellow marigolds.

Dwarf lavender blue varieties (4–6 in. tall) include 'Blue Angel', 'Blue Blazer', 'Blue Cap', and 'Midget Blue'. 'Royal Blazer' is a dwarf deep purple blue. Slightly taller (9–12 in.) lavender blues are 'Biscay', 'Blue Chip', and 'Blue Mink'. Light pink 'Pinkie' and white 'Summer Snow' are in the 9–12 in. range.

AGLAOMORPHA. Tropical epiphytic ferns. Zones 15–17, 19–24. Grown in hanging baskets, on plaques, rarely in the ground. Well-established plants can take an occasional very light frost but do best in a humid, sheltered environment. Fronds resemble coarse conventional ferns but often broaden toward the base into brown shieldlike organs that recall shields of staghorn ferns (*Platycerium*).

A. coronans (*Polypodium coronans*). Plant has 2–4-ft.-long fronds.

A. heracleum (*Polypodium heracleum*). Fronds are 3–6 ft. long.

Aglaomorpha coronans

AGLAONEMA. Perennials. Tropical plants valued mostly for their ornamental foliage, and usually grown in greenhouses or as indoor plants. Flowers resemble small, greenish white callas. Among the best plants for poorly lighted situations. Need a rich, porous potting mix; thrive with lots of water but will get along with small amounts. Cut stems will grow a long time in a glass of water. Exudation from leaf tips, especially of *A. modestum*, spots wood finishes, as on table tops.

Aglaonema modestum

A. commutatum. Grows to 2 ft. Leaves to 6 in. long, 2 in. across, deep green, marked on veins with pale green. Flowers followed by inch-long clusters of yellow to red berries. *A. c. maculatum,* with many gray green irregular stripes on leaves, is the commonest. 'Pseudobracteatum', 1–2 ft. tall, has white leafstalks and deep green leaves marked with pale green and creamy yellow. 'Treubii' has narrow leaves heavily marked with silvery gray.

A. costatum. Slow growing, low plant with broad, deep green leaves spotted white and a broad white stripe along the midrib. *A. c.* 'Foxii' is similar or identical.

A. crispum (*A. roebelenii*). Robust plant with leathery leaves to 10 in. long, 5 in. wide, dark green with pale green markings. Sometimes sold as *A.* 'Pewter'.

A. 'Malay Beauty' (Also known as *A.* 'Pewter'). Resembles *A. c.* 'Pseudobracteatum' but with paler cream variegation.

A. modestum (Often sold as *A. simplex*). CHINESE EVERGREEN. A serviceable, easily grown plant, in time forming substantial clumps with several stems 2–3 ft. high. Leaves shiny dark green, to 18 in. long, 5 in. across.

A. 'Silver King' and **'Silver Queen'.** Both are heavy producers of narrow, dark green leaves strongly marked with silver. Both grow to 2 ft. 'Silver King' has larger leaves than 'Silver Queen'.

AGONIS. Evergreen tree. Zones 15–17, 20–24. Native to Australia.

A. flexuosa. PEPPERMINT TREE, AUSTRALIAN WILLOW MYRTLE. One of the best small trees for California gardens where temperatures stay above 27°F. Will freeze to the ground at 25°F.; in the Sacramento Valley, it has come back from the stump. Spreading, medium fast growing to 25–35 ft., or a big shrub. Narrow, willowlike leaves to 6 in. long densely clothe the weeping branches. Leaves smell like peppermint when crushed. Small white flowers carried abundantly in June. Use it in a lawn, trained as an espalier, or as a tub plant. Very tolerant of soil types, watering practices.

Agonis flexuosa

A. juniperina. JUNIPER MYRTLE. More open, finer textured than *A. flexuosa,* but grows to about the same height. Narrow, ¼–½-in.-long leaves are soft green. Bears fluffy white flower clusters, summer to November. Same climate adaptability as *A. flexuosa*. Especially lovely with junipers and other needle-leafed plants.

AGROPYRON. WHEATGRASS. Zones 1–3, 10. Basically pasture grasses, two kinds of wheatgrass make reasonably attractive lawns in Rocky Mountains and high plains. They can survive with 8–18 in. of rainfall per year, but when planted close and mowed at 2 in. they should be soaked to 18–20 in. every 30 days. Plant 2 lbs. per 1,000 sq. ft.

A. cristatum. CRESTED WHEATGRASS. Bunching rather than sod-forming grass. Fairway strain, used for low-maintenance, low-irrigation lawns is shorter, denser, and finer than common kind.

A. smithii. WESTERN WHEATGRASS. Forms sod, but slowly. Tolerates great heat, cold, moderate alkali.

Agropyron smithii

AGROSTIS. BENT, BENT GRASS. Lawn grasses. All Zones. All except redtop make beautiful velvety lawns under proper conditions and with constant care. They need frequent close mowing, frequent feeding, occasional topdressing, and much water. In hot weather they succumb to fungus diseases. In San Francisco Bay Area bent grasses (planted intentionally or distributed by birds) tend to dominate bluegrasses and fescues. Best putting greens are of bent grass.

A. gigantea. REDTOP. Coarser than other bents, not generally used in lawns. Has been used as quick-sprouting nurse grass in mixtures or for winter overseeding of Bermuda or other winter-dormant grasses.

Agrostis stolonifera

A. stolonifera. CREEPING BENT. Premium lawn, but requires most care, including frequent mowing to ½ in. tall with special mower. Seed-grown strains include Emerald, Penncross, and Seaside. In some areas you can buy sprigs or sod of choice varieties named Congressional and Old Orchard.

A. tenuis. COLONIAL BENT. More erect than creeping bent, somewhat easier to care for, but still fussy. Astoria and Highland are best known strains, with the latter tougher, hardier, more disease resistant. Mow at ¾ in.

AILANTHUS altissima (*A. glandulosa*). TREE-OF-HEAVEN. Deciduous tree. All Zones. Native to China. Planted a century ago in California's gold country where it now runs wild. Fast growth to 50 ft. Leaves 1–3 ft. long are divided into 13–25 leaflets 3–5 in. long. Inconspicuous greenish flowers are usually followed by handsome clusters of red brown, winged fruit in late summer and fall; great for dried arrangements. Often condemned as a weed tree because it suckers profusely and self-seeds, but it must be praised for its ability to create beauty and shade under adverse conditions—drought, hot winds, extreme air pollution, and every type of difficult soil.

Ailanthus altissima

AIR PLANT. See *Kalanchoe pinnata*.

AJUGA. CARPET BUGLE. Perennial. All Zones. One species is a rock garden plant; the others, better known, are ground covers.

A. genevensis. Rock garden plant 5–14 in. high, no runners. Grayish hairy stems and coarse-toothed leaves to 3 in. long. Flowers in blue spikes; there are rose and white forms. Full sun.

A. pyramidalis. Erect plants 2–10 in.

Ajuga reptans

high; do not spread by runners. Stems, with long grayish hairs, have many roundish 1½–4-in.-long leaves. Violet blue flowers are not obvious among the large leaves. Variety 'Metallica Crispa' has reddish brown leaves with a metallic glint.

A. reptans. The popular ground cover ajuga. Fast growing, spreads by runners and makes a mat of dark green leaves that grow 2–3 in. wide in full sun, 3–4 in. wide in part shade. Bears mostly blue flowers in 4–6-in.-high spikes. Many varieties are available; some are sold under several names.

All the varieties of *A. reptans* (listed below) make thick carpets of lustrous leaves, enhanced from spring to early summer with spikes of showy flowers. Plant in spring or early fall 6–12 in. apart, 18 in. for the big ones. Full sun to part shade; those with bronze or metallic tints keep color best in full sun. Feed in spring or late summer. Water every 7–10 days in summer. Mow or trim off old flower spikes. Subject to root-knot nematodes; also subject to rot and fungus diseases where drainage or air circulation is poor.

Varieties listed below as giant and jungle ajugas are sold under many names: green ones as 'Crispa' and purplish or bronzy ones as 'Metallica Crispa', 'Bronze Ripple', or 'Rubra'. (These are not the same as *A. pyramidalis* 'Metallica Crispa'.) All have blue flowers.

'Burgundy Lace'. Variety of *A. reptans* with reddish purple foliage variegated with white and pink.

'Giant Bronze'. Deep metallic bronze leaves larger, more vigorous, and crisper than those of *A. reptans*. To 6 in. tall in sun, 9 in. tall in shade.

'Giant Green'. Like 'Giant Bronze' except leaves are bright green.

'Jungle Bronze'. Large, rounded, wavy-edged leaves of bronzy tone, in clumps; tall growing; flowers on 8–10-in.-high spikes.

'Jungle Green'. Largest-leafed ajuga—rounded, crisp edged, and green. Less mounding than 'Jungle Bronze'.

'Purpurea'. (Often sold as 'Atropurpurea'.) Similar to *A. reptans* but with bronze or purple tint in leaves. Leaves often slightly larger.

'Variegata'. Leaves edged and splotched with creamy yellow. Flowers blue.

AKEBIA quinata. FIVELEAF AKEBIA. Deciduous vine, evergreen in mild winters. All Zones. Native to Japan, China, and Korea. Twines to 15–20 ft. Grows fast in mild regions, slower where winters are cold. Dainty leaves on 3–5-in. stalks, each divided into 5 deep green leaflets 2–3 in. long, notched at tip. Its clusters of quaint dull purple flowers in spring are more a surprise than a show. The edible fruit, if produced, looks like a thick, 2½–4-in.-long, purplish sausage.

Akebia quinata

Plant in sun or shade. Give it support to climb on and keep it under control. Benefits from annual pruning. Recovers quickly when cut to the ground. When grown on post or column, and you want a tracery effect, prune out all but 2 or 3 basal stems.

A. trifoliata. THREELEAF AKEBIA. Like the above, but with 3 instead of 5 leaflets.

ALASKA YELLOW CEDAR. See *Chamaecyparis nootkatensis.*

ALBIZIA (formerly *Albizzia*). Deciduous to semievergreen trees. Birds are attracted to flowers.

A. distachya (*A. lophantha*). PLUME ALBIZIA. Semievergreen. Zones 15–17, 22–24. Native to Australia. Not as hardy as the better-known *A. julibrissin*. In California coastal areas it often naturalizes. Drought tolerant; will grow in pure sand at beach. Many mass plantings in Golden Gate Park, San Francisco. Fast growing to 20 ft.

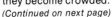
Albizia julibrissin

Foliage is dark velvety green compared to the light yellowish green of *A. julibrissin*, but also fernlike. The flowers in late spring are greenish yellow in fluffy, 2-in.-long spikes. Best as a temporary screening at beach while slower permanent planting develops. Gets tacky-looking inland.

Albizia julibrissin

A. julibrissin. SILK TREE (this is the MIMOSA of eastern U.S.). Deciduous. Zones 2–23. Native to Asia from Iran to Japan. Rapid growth to 40 ft. with wider spread. Can be headed back to make a 10–20-ft. umbrella. Pink fluffy flowers like pincushions on ferny-leafed branches in summer. Light-sensitive leaves fold at night. The variety 'Rosea' has richer pink flowers and is considered hardier.

Does best with high summer heat. One of the three best sellers in inland valleys of southern California. Attractive in both high and low deserts of the Southwest. It's sufficiently hardy in the mild areas of the Pacific Northwest. With ample water grows fast; on skimpy irrigation usually survives, but grows slowly, looks yellowish.

It's an excellent small shade tree with unique flat-topped shape making a true canopy for a patio. Because of its undulating form and flowers held above the foliage, silk tree is especially beautiful when viewed from above—from a deck or hilltop. Somewhat of a problem to get started as a high-headed tree. Must be staked and trained by rubbing out buds which start too low. Best planted from containers established at least one year; bare-root plants need skillful planting, watering.

It is most attractive in its natural growth habit—a multiple-stemmed tree. Filtered shade permits growth of lawn and shrubs beneath it. However, for patio use, litter of fallen leaves, flowers, and pods must be considered.

ALCEA rosea (*Althaea rosea*). HOLLYHOCK. Biennial or short-lived perennial. All Zones. This old-fashioned favorite has its place against a fence or wall or at the back of a border. Old single varieties can reach 9 ft.; newer strains and selections are shorter. Big, rough, roundish heart shaped leaves more or less lobed; single, semi-double, or double flowers 3–6 in. wide in white, pink, rose, red, purple, creamy yellow, apricot. Summer bloom. Chater's Double is a fine perennial strain; 6-ft. spires have 5–6-in. flowers. So-called annual strains bloom first year from seed sown in early spring; Summer Carnival strain is 5–6 ft. tall with double 4-in. flowers; Majorette strain 2½ ft. with 3–4-in. flowers. Rust resistant 'Silver Puffs' resembles Majorette in size, has silvery pink bloom. Destroy rust infected leaves as soon as disease appears. Bait to protect from snails and slugs.

Alcea rosea

ALDER. See *Alnus.*

ALDER BUCKTHORN. See *Rhamnus frangula.*

ALEXANDRA PALM. See *Archontophoenix alexandrae.*

ALGERIAN IVY. See *Hedera canariensis.*

ALLIUM. ORNAMENTAL ALLIUM. Bulbs. All Zones except as noted below. About 500 species, all from the Northern Hemisphere, many from mountains of the West. Relatives of the edible onion, peerless as cut flowers (fresh or dried) and useful in borders; smaller kinds are effective in rock gardens. Most ornamental alliums are hardy, sun loving, easy to grow. Thrive in deep, rich, sandy loam; need ample moisture when growing. Plant bulbs in fall. Lift and divide only after they become crowded.

Allium giganteum

(Continued on next page)

Alliums bear small flowers in compact or loose roundish clusters at ends of leafless stems 6 in.-5 ft. or more tall. Many are delightfully fragrant; those with onion odor must be bruised or cut to give it off. Flowers in shades of pink, rose, violet, red, blue, yellow, to white. Bloom from late spring through summer.

A. aflatunense. Round clusters of lilac flowers on stems 2½–5 ft. tall. Resembles *A. giganteum* but with smaller (2–3 in.) flower clusters; blooms late May.

A. albopilosum. See *A. christophii*.

A. atropurpureum. Stems to 2½ ft. tall carry 2-in. clusters of dark purple to nearly black flowers.

A. caeruleum (*A. azureum*). BLUE ALLIUM. Cornflower blue flowers in dense round clusters 2 in. across on 1 ft. stems, June.

A. cepa. See Onion.

A. christophii (*A. albopilosum*). STAR OF PERSIA. Distinct, with very large clusters, 6–12 in. across, of lavender to deep lilac, starlike flowers with metallic sheen; June bloom. Stems 12–15 in. tall. Leaves to 18 in. long, white and hairy beneath. Dried flower cluster looks like elegant ornament.

A. giganteum. GIANT ALLIUM. Spectacular ball-like clusters of bright lilac flowers on stems 5 ft. or more tall. Leaves 1½ ft. long, 2 in. wide. July bloom.

A. karataviense. TURKESTAN ALLIUM. Large, dense, round flower clusters vary from pinkish to beige to reddish lilac, bloom in May. Broad, flat, recurving leaves, 2–5 in. across.

A. moly. GOLDEN GARLIC. Bright, shining yellow flowers in open clusters on 9–18-in.-high stems; June bloom. Flat leaves 2 in. wide, almost as long as flower stems.

A. narcissiflorum. Foot-tall stems with loose clusters of ½-in. bell shaped bright rose flowers.

A. neapolitanum. Spreading clusters of large white flowers on 12-in. stems; bloom in May. Leaves 1 in. wide. Variety 'Grandiflorum' is larger and earlier. A form of 'Grandiflorum' listed as 'Cowanii' is considered superior. Grown commercially as cut flowers; pot plant in cold climates.

A. ostrowskianum (*A. oreophilum ostrowskianum*). Large, loose clusters of rose-colored flowers in June on 8–12-in. stems; 2–3 narrow, gray green, leaves. Variety 'Zwanenburg' has deep carmine red flowers, 6-in. stems. Rock gardens, cutting.

A. porrum. See Leek.

A. pulchellum. Tight clusters of red purple flowers on 2-ft. stems.

A. rosenbachianum. Similar to *A. giganteum* but slightly smaller, blooms earlier.

A. sativum. See Garlic.

A. schoenoprasum. See Chives.

A. scorodoprasum. See Giant Garlic.

A. sphaerocephalum. DRUMSTICKS, ROUND-HEADED GARLIC. Tight, dense, spherical red purple flower clusters on 2-ft. stems. Spreads freely.

A. tuberosum. CHINESE CHIVES, GARLIC CHIVES, ORIENTAL GARLIC. Spreads by tuberous rootstocks and by seeds. Clumps of gray green, flat leaves ¼ in. wide, 1 ft. or less long. Abundance of 1–1½-ft.-tall stalks bear clusters of white flowers in summer. Flowers have scent of violets, are excellent for fresh or dry arrangements. Leaves have mild garlic flavor, are useful in salads, cooked dishes. Grow like chives. Dormant in winter.

A. unifolium. California native with extremely handsome, satiny lavender pink flowers on 1–2-ft. stems; June bloom.

ALLOPLECTUS nummularia (*Hypocyrta nummularia*). GOLDFISH PLANT. Related to African violet and has similar cultural needs. Foot-long arching branches closely set with shiny oval or roundish leaves to 2½ in. long. Flowers about 1 in. long, orange, puffy and roundish, pinched at tip into pursed mouth like that of goldfish.

With ample warmth and humidity, plant will bloom the year around. Easy to root from tip cuttings; stems may root when in contact with damp soil mix. Because of arching, trailing growth, best in hanging pot or basket.

Alloplectus nummularia

ALLSPICE, CAROLINA. See *Calycanthus floridus*.

ALMOND. Deciduous tree. For ornamental relatives, see *Prunus*. Zones 8–10, 12, 14–16, 19–21. Almonds as trees are nearly as hardy as peaches, but as nut producers they are more exacting in climate adaptation. Zones listed are for best nut production. Frost during the trees' early blooming period cuts the crop, and if they escape that a late (April) frost will destroy small fruit that are forming. Nuts will not develop properly in areas with cool summers and high humidity. To experiment in areas where frost is a hazard, choose late-blooming varieties.

Almond

Tree grows to 20–30 ft. high, erect when young, spreading and dome shaped in age. Leaves 3–5 in. long, pale green with gray tinge. Flowers 1–2 in. across, palest pink or white. Fruit looks like a leathery, flattened, undersized green peach. The hull splits to reveal the pit, which is the almond that you harvest.

Harvest almonds when hulls split. At this stage, you may need to knock nuts from trees or pick them off ground. Remove leathery hull and spread hulled nuts in sun for day or two to dry. To test for adequate dryness shake nuts—kernels should rattle in shells. Store dried hulls indoors.

Almonds do well in any type of soil except heavy, poorly drained soil, where they are subject to root rot. Need deep soil—at least 6 ft. Will exist on less water than most fruit trees. Water deeply but infrequently. They need spraying to control mites which cause premature yellowing and falling of leaves. Trees can be weakened or eventually killed by mites. Brown rot makes fruit rot and harden; it also attacks twigs, killing them back and forming cankers on main trunk and branches.

Two varieties must be planted for pollination. (If you don't have room, plant 2 or 3 in one hole.) These are the varieties you may find in nurseries:

'Carmel'. A regular heavy bearer of small nuts with good flavor. Pollenizes 'Nonpareil' and 'Texas' ('Mission').

'Hall' ('Hall's Hardy'). Hard-shell nut of good size and quality. Pink bloom comes late—an advantage in late frost regions. Tree hardy as a peach. Partially self-fertile, but better with 'Jordanolo' or 'Texas' ('Mission') as pollenizers.

'Jordanolo'. High quality nut, but subject to bud failure in areas of extreme summer heat. 'Ne Plus Ultra' and 'Nonpareil' are pollenizers.

'Kapareil'. Small, soft-shell nuts. Pollenizer for 'Nonpareil'.

'Ne Plus Ultra'. Large kernels in attractive soft shells. Pollenizer for 'Nonpareil'.

'Nonpareil'. Best all-around variety. Easily shelled by hand. Some bud failure in very hot-summer regions. Pollenize with 'Jordanolo', 'Ne Plus Ultra', 'Kapareil'.

'Texas' ('Mission'). Small, semihard-shelled nut. Regular, heavy producer. Late bloomer, one of safest for cold-winter, late frost areas. Use 'Nonpareil' or 'Hall' as pollenizers.

ALMOND, FLOWERING. See *Prunus*.

ALNUS. ALDER. Deciduous trees. Moisture loving; of remarkably rapid growth. All give interesting display of tassel-like greenish yellow male flower catkins (in clusters) before leaves. Female flowers develop into small woody cones that decorate bare branches in winter; these delight flower arrangers. Seeds attract birds. Roots are invasive—less troublesome if deep watering practices are followed.

A. cordata. ITALIAN ALDER. Zones 8, 9, 14–24. Native to Italy, Corsica. Young growth vertical; older trees to 40 ft., spreading to 25 ft. Heart shaped, 4-in. leaves, glossy rich green above, paler beneath.

Alnus rhombifolia

Short deciduous period. More restrained than *A. rhombifolia*. Favored in Southwest, except high desert.

A. glutinosa. BLACK ALDER. Zones 1–10, 14–24. Native to Europe, North Africa, Asia. Not as fast as *A. rhombifolia*. Probably best as multistemmed tree. Grows to 70 ft. Roundish, 2–4-in., coarsely toothed leaves, dark lustrous green. Makes dense mass from ground up. Good for screen.

A. oregona (*A. rubra*). RED ALDER. Zones 4–6, 15–17. Native to stream banks and marshy places. Most common alder of lowlands in Pacific Northwest. Ranges from Alaska south to Santa Cruz County, California; rarely found more than 10 miles from coast in California. Grows to 90 ft. high but usually 45–50 ft. Attractive light gray, smooth bark. Dark green, 2–4-in. leaves, rusty hairy beneath; coarsely toothed margins are rolled under. Can take surprising amount of brackish water and is useful wherever underground water is somewhat saline. Generally disliked in Northwest because it's a favorite of tent caterpillars.

A. rhombifolia. WHITE ALDER. Zones 1–9, 14–21. Native along streams throughout most of California's foothills except along coast; mountains of Oregon, Washington, north to British Columbia, east to Idaho. Very fast growing to 50–90 ft., with 40-ft. spread. Very heat and wind tolerant. Spreading or ascending branches often pendulous at tips. Coarsely toothed, 2½–4½-in. leaves dark green above, paler green beneath. In its native areas, it's susceptible to tent caterpillars.

ALOCASIA. ELEPHANT'S EAR. Perennials. Outdoors in Zones 22–24; indoor/outdoor plants anywhere. Native to tropical Asia. Handsome, lush plants for tropical effects. Flowers resemble those of calla (*Zantedeschia*). Plant in filtered sunlight in wind protected places. Provide ample organic matter in soil, lots of water, light, frequent feedings. Tropical plant specialists sell many kinds with ornamental leaves in coppery and purplish tones, often with striking white veins.

Alocasia macrorrhiza

A. macrorrhiza. Evergreen at 29°F.; loses leaves at lower temperatures but comes back in spring if frosts not too severe. Large arrow shaped leaves to 2 ft. or longer on stalks to 5 ft. tall. Makes dome shaped plant 4 ft. across. Tiny flowers on spike surrounded by greenish white bract. Reddish fruit forms on spike much like corn on the cob.

A. odora. Similar to above, but not quite so hardy. Flowers fragrant.

ALOE. Succulents of lily family. Zones 8, 9, 12–24. Form clumps of fleshy pointed leaves and branched or unbranched clusters of orange, yellow, cream, or red flowers. Most are South African. Showy, easy, drought tolerant, they rate among southern California's most valuable ornamentals. Most kinds make outstanding container plants. Some species in bloom every month. Biggest show February-September.

Aloe arborescens

Range from 6-in. miniatures to trees. Leaves may be green or gray green, and are often strikingly banded or streaked with contrasting colors. Aloes grow easily in well-drained soil in reasonably frost-free areas. Sun or light shade in hot-summer areas. Where winters are cooler, grow in pots and shelter from frosts. Aloes listed here are only a few of the more widely available ones; specialists in succulents have dozens on their lists.

A. arborescens. TREE ALOE. Older clumps may reach 18 ft. Branching stems carry big clumps of gray green, spiny-edged leaves. Flowers (December-February) in long, spiky clusters, bright vermilion to clear yellow. Stands drought, sun, salt spray. Tolerates shade. Foliage damaged at 29°F., but plants have survived 17°F.

A. aristata. Dwarf species for pots, edging, ground covers. Reaches 8–12 in. height and spread. Rosettes densely packed with 4-in.-long, ¾-in.-wide leaves ending in whiplike threads.

Flowers orange red in 12–18-in-tall clusters, winter.

A. bainesii. Tree of slow growth with heavy, forking trunk and branches. Rosettes of 2–3-ft. leaves, spikes of rose pink flowers on 1½–2-ft. stalks. Used for stately, sculpturesque pattern in landscape. Hard to find in nurseries.

A. barbadensis (*A. vera*). MEDICINAL ALOE, BARBADOS ALOE. Clustering rosettes of narrow, fleshy, stiffly upright leaves 1–2 ft. long. Yellow flowers in dense spike atop 3-ft. stalk. Favorite folk medicine plant used to treat burns, bites, inflammation, and host of other ills. One of best for Zones 12, 13. Survives without extra water, but needs some to look good.

A. brevifolia. Makes low clumps of blunt, thick, gray green, spiny-edged leaves 3 in. long. Clusters of red flowers, 20 in. tall, intermittent all year.

A. ciliaris. Climbing, sprawling with pencil-thick stems to 10 ft. long. Leaves small, thick, soft green. Long-stalked 3–6-in. flower clusters with 20–30 scarlet, green or yellow-tipped flowers, intermittent all year. Takes some shade, little frost.

A. distans. JEWELED ALOE. Running, rooting, branching stems make clumps of 6-in. fleshy blue green leaves with scattered whitish spots and white teeth along edges. Forked flower stems 1½–2 ft. tall carry clusters of red flowers.

A. ferox. Tree type. Thick, 15-ft. trunk carries rosettes of very spiny, dull green, 2½-ft.-long leaves. Glowing scarlet flower clusters like large candelabra.

A. humilis. Tight clumps of 4-in.-long, ¾-in.-wide fiercely tooth-edged leaves. Flowers red, on stalks 10–16 in. tall.

A. marlothii. When small, use in pots or dish gardens. When mature, a tree type with 2½-ft.-long, spiny leaves and red flowers in large candelabra.

A. nobilis. Dark green leaves edged with small hooked teeth grow in rosettes to 12 in. across and about as tall. Clustered orange red flowers appear on 2-ft. stalks in June, last for 6 weeks. Good container subject—takes limited root space.

A. saponaria. Short-stemmed, broad clumps. Broad, thick, 8-in.-long leaves variegated with white spots. Clumps spread rapidly and may become bound together—take up too-thick clumps and separate them. Branched flower stalk 18–30 in. tall. Orange red to shrimp pink flowers over long period.

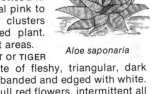

A. striata. CORAL ALOE. Leaves broad, 20 in. long, spineless, gray green, with narrow pinkish red edge. They grow in rosettes 2 ft. wide on short trunk. Brilliant coral pink to orange flowers in branched clusters February-May. Handsome, tailored plant. Keep it from hottest sun in desert areas.

Aloe saponaria

A. variegata. PARTRIDGE-BREAST OF TIGER ALOE. Foot-high triangular rosette of fleshy, triangular, dark green, 5-in.-long leaves strikingly banded and edged with white. Loose flower clusters of pink to dull red flowers, intermittent all year.

A. vera. See *A. barbadensis.*

ALOYSIA triphylla (*Lippia citriodora*). LEMON VERBENA. Deciduous or partially evergreen herb-shrub. Zones 9, 10, 14–24. Borderline hardy as far north as Seattle if planted against warm wall. It is the herb that grew like a gangling shrub in grandmother's garden. Prized for its lemon-scented leaves. Used in potpourri, iced drinks; leaf put in bottom of jar when making apple jelly. Legginess is natural state of this plant; it ranges up to 6 ft. or more. Narrow leaves to 3 in. long are arranged in whorls of 3 or 4 along branches. Bears open clusters of very small lilac or whitish flowers in summer. By pinch-pruning you can shape to give interesting tracery against wall. Or let it grow among lower plants to hide its legginess. Full sun, good drainage, average water.

Aloysia triphylla

ALPINE LAUREL. See *Kalmia microphylla.*

ALPINE TOTARA. See *Podocarpus nivalis.*

ALPINIA. Perennials with rhizomes. Evergreen in Zones 22–24, die down in winter in Zones 15-17. Roots hardy to about 15°F. Give lightly shaded, wind-free exposure, good soil. In order to bloom, must be established at least 2 years, must have lots of water. Remove flowered canes yearly.

A. sanderae. VARIEGATED GINGER. To 3–4 ft. tall, with 8-in.-long leaves striped with white. Rarely flowers. Good in containers.

A. zerumbet *(A. nutans, A. speciosa).* SHELL GINGER, SHELL FLOWER. Native to tropical Asia and Polynesia. Grandest of gingers, best all year appearance. To 8–9 ft. tall. Leaves shiny, 2 ft. long, 5 in. wide, with distinct parallel veins; grow on stems that are maroon at maturity. Waxy white or pinkish, shell-like, fragrant flowers marked red, purple, brown, in pendant clusters on arching stems in late summer.

Alpinia zerumbet

ALSOPHILA australis, A. cooperi. See *Sphaeropteris.*

ALSTROEMERIA. Perennials. Zones 5–9, 14–24. South American natives. Leafy stems 2–5 ft. tall, topped with broad loose clusters of azalealike flowers in beautiful colors—orange, yellow, shades of pink, rose, red, lilac, creamy white to white; many are streaked and speckled with darker colors. Masses of color in borders from May to midsummer. Long-lasting cut flowers.

Alstroemeria aurantiaca

Nurseries differ as to what names they sell them by, but you're sure to get vibrant colors whether you buy them as Chilean hybrids, Ligtu hybrids, or just plain alstroemeria. These spread freely by roots and seeds. Tops wither after bloom (flowerless shoots dry up even sooner); remove developing seeds if you want to limit their spread.

A few nurseries offer 3–4-ft.-high PERUVIAN LILY *(A. aurantiaca)* which has orange yellow flowers spotted with brown, and a pure yellow form, 'Lutea.'

Best in cool, moist, deep, sandy to medium loam. Plant roots in fall; if you buy alstroemeria in gallon cans, you can plant it out any time in mild-winter climates. Set roots 6–8 in. deep, 12 in. apart; handle brittle roots gently. Leave clumps undisturbed for many years because they reestablish slowly after transplanting. Alstroemerias are easy from seed sown where plants are to grow or sown in individual pots for transplanting. Sow in fall, winter, or earliest spring. All are hardy in cold-winter climates if planted at proper depth and kept mulched in winter. Give them ample water in spring and summer; taper off in late summer, fall. Partial shade in warm-summer areas; sun along coast.

ALTERNANTHERA ficoidea (often sold as *A. bettzickiana*). Perennial grown in most Zones as annual for colorful foliage, which somewhat resembles that of coleus. Plants grow 6–12 in. tall and should be planted 4–10 in. apart for colorful effect. Plant in full sun; where winters are cold, plant only after soil warms up. Average water. Keep low and compact by shearing. Grow from cuttings. 'Aurea Nana' is low grower with yellow-splotched foliage. 'Bettzickiana' has spoon shaped leaves with red and yellow markings. 'Magnifica' is red bronze dwarf. 'Parrot Feather' and 'Versicolor' have broad green leaves with yellow markings and pink veins.

Alternanthera ficoidea 'Bettzickiana'

ALTHAEA rosea. See *Alcea rosea.*

ALUMINUM PLANT. See *Pilea cadierei.*

ALUMROOT. See *Heuchera.*

ALYOGYNE huegelii *(Hibiscus huegelii).* BLUE HIBISCUS. Evergreen shrub. Zones 15–17, 20–24. Upright growth to 5–8 ft. Foliage deeply cut, dark green, rough textured. Flowers 4–5 in. across, lilac blue with glossy petals. Blooms off and on throughout year; individual flowers last 2–3 days. Hardy to about 23°F. Pinch or prune occasionally to keep it compact. Best in dry, warm location, full sun. Variable from seed. 'Santa Cruz' is good deep blue selection. 'Monterey Bay' is even bluer.

Alyogyne huegelii

ALYSSUM. Perennials. All Zones. Mostly native to Mediterranean region. Mounding plants or shrublets that brighten spring borders and rock gardens with their cheerful bloom. Best in full sun or just a little shade. Fairly drought tolerant.

A. montanum. Stems up to 8 in. high; leaves gray, hairy (denser on underside); flowers yellow, fragrant, in dense short clusters.

A. saxatile. See *Aurinia.*

A. wulfenianum. Prostrate and trailing, with fleshy, silvery leaves and sheets of pale yellow flowers.

Alyssum montanum

ALYSSUM, SWEET. See *Lobularia.*

AMARACUS dictamnus. See *Origanum dictamnus.*

AMARANTHUS. AMARANTH. Annuals. All Zones. Coarse, sometimes weedy plants; a few ornamental kinds grown for their brightly colored foliage or flowers. Grow in full sun or part shade; give average soil and water. Sow early summer—soil temperature must be above 70°F. for germination.

A. caudatus. LOVE-LIES-BLEEDING, TASSEL FLOWER. Sturdy, branching plant 3–8 ft. high; leaves 2–10 in. long, ½–4 in. wide; flowers red, in drooping, tassel-like clusters. Curiosity rather than pretty plant.

A. hybridus erythrostachys. PRINCE'S FEATHER. To 5 ft. high with leaves 1–6 in. long, ½–3 in. wide, usually reddish. Flowers red or brownish red in many-branched clusters.

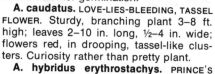

Amaranthus caudatus

A. tricolor. JOSEPH'S COAT. Branching plant 1–4 ft. high. Leaves 2½–6 in. long, 2–4 in. wide, blotched in shades of red and green. Newer selections such as 'Early Splendor', 'Flaming Fountain', and 'Molten Fire' are masses of yellow to scarlet foliage at tops of main stems and principal branches.

AMARCRINUM memoria-corsii (A. 'Howardii'). Bulb. Hybrid between *Crinum moorei* and belladonna lily *(Amaryllis belladonna).* Blooms outdoors in summer and fall in California; also pot plant. Flowering stems to 4 ft. carry very large clusters of soft pink, funnel shaped, very fragrant, long-lasting flowers resembling belladonna lily. Sun or partial shade, ample water. With year-round water, plant stays evergreen in mild climates. If no water is available, it simply endures until water comes, then starts growth and bloom. Scarce in nurseries; get offset bulbs from a friend. Be

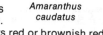

Amarcrinum memoria-corsii

especially careful to protect from snails, slugs, which can make ragged ruins out of the tropical-looking foliage fountains.

AMARYLLIS belladonna (*Brunsvigia rosea*). BELLADONNA LILY, NAKED LADY. Bulb. Zones 4–24. Hardy in mild-winter areas; needs protected south exposure and warm, dry summer to bloom in western Oregon and Washington. Native to South Africa. Bold straplike leaves in clumps 2–3 ft. across in fall and winter; dormant late spring and early summer. In August, clusters of 4–12 trumpet shaped, rosy pink, fragrant flowers bloom on top of bare, reddish brown stalks 2–3 ft. tall. Will grow in almost any soil; drought resistant, very long lived. Plant right after bloom; set bulb top even with ground level. Lift and divide clumps infrequently; may not bloom for several years if disturbed at wrong time. For plants with common name AMARYLLIS, see *Hippeastrum*.

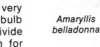
Amaryllis belladonna

A. hallii. See *Lycoris squamigera*.

AMELANCHIER laevis. SHADBUSH, SHADBLOW, SERVICE (often pronounced "sarvis") BERRY. Deciduous small tree. Zones 1–6. Narrow upright growth to 30–35 ft. Drooping clusters of white flowers in spring precede purplish young foliage that turns to deep green. Dark blue edible fruit in early summer are very popular with birds. Yellow and red foliage color in fall. Roots not aggressive, shade not heavy. Plant against dark background to show off form, flowers, fall color. Give it sun, ordinary good soil, moderate water.

Amelanchier laevis

AMERICAN SWEET GUM. See *Liquidambar styraciflua*.

AMETHYST FLOWER. See *Browallia*.

AMPELOPSIS brevipedunculata. BLUEBERRY CLIMBER. Deciduous vine. All Zones. Strong rampant climber with twining tendrils. To 20 ft. Large, handsome, 3-lobed, 2½–5-in.-wide leaves are dark green. In warm climates it turns red and partially drops its leaves; more leaves come out and redden and drop all winter. Many clusters of small grapelike berries turn from greenish ivory to brilliant metallic blue in late summer and fall. Sun or shade. Average water. Needs strong support. Superb on concrete and rock walls, or to shade arbors. Attracts birds.

Boston ivy and Virginia creeper, formerly included in genus *Ampelopsis*, are now placed under genus *Parthenocissus* because, unlike *Ampelopsis*, both have disks at ends of their tendrils.

Ampelopsis brevipedunculata

AMUR CHOKECHERRY. See *Prunus maackii*.

ANACYCLUS depressus. Perennial. All Zones. Slowly forms dense, spreading mat somewhat like chamomile. Grayish leaves finely divided; single daisylike flowers to 2 in. across; white ray-type petals are red on reverse side; yellow center discs. Blossoms in summer. Good in sunny, dry, hot rock gardens. Generally hardy, but may freeze in extremely severe winters or rot in cold, wet, heavy soil.

Anacyclus depressus

ANAGALLIS. PIMPERNEL. Annuals or perennials. All Zones. Two species sometimes seen, one a weed. Like warm soil, full sun, much or little water; less aggressive kinds attractive in rock gardens with sunroses (*Helianthemum*), sedums, snow-in-summer (*Cerastium*).

A. arvensis. SCARLET PIMPERNEL. Annual. Low-growing weed with ¼-in. flowers of brick red. *A. a. caerulea* has somewhat larger flowers of deep, pure blue and is attractive enough to plant.

A. monelli. Perennial or biennial to 18 in., with ¾-in. flowers of bright blue. *A. m.* 'Phillipsii' is compact 12-in.-tall selection; *A. m. linifolia* has narrower leaves.

Anagallis monelli linifolia

ANCHUSA. Annuals, biennials, or perennials. All Zones. Related to forget-me-not (*Myosotis*), but larger and showier, anchusas are worth growing for vibrant blue color. Prefer sun, dry soil.

A. azurea (*A. italica*). Perennial. All Zones. Coarse, loose spreading, 3–5 ft. tall. Leaves 6 in. or longer, covered with stiff bristly hairs. Clusters of bright blue blossoms ½–¾ in. across bloom in summer and fall. Horticultural forms include 'Dropmore', gentian blue; 'Opal', sky blue; and 'Loddon Royalist' (more recent), bearing rich blue flowers. Not for small areas. Once established, difficult to eradicate.

Anchusa capensis

A. capensis. CAPE FORGET-ME-NOT, SUMMER FORGET-ME-NOT. Zones 7–24. Native of South Africa. Hairy annual or biennial, 1½ ft. high; leaves narrow, to 5 in. long, ½ in. wide. Flowers bright blue, white throated, ¼ in. across, in clusters 2 in. long. Use for vivid clean blue in summer borders with marigolds, petunias.

ANDROMEDA polifolia. BOG ROSEMARY. Evergreen shrublet. All Zones. Not adapted in areas with alkaline soil or water. Grows to 12 in., spreading by creeping rootstocks. Leathery narrow leaves, somewhat like rosemary, 1½ in. long, gray green above, gray beneath. Bears attractive clusters of pale pink, ¼-in. globe shaped flowers at tip of branches in April. Sun or part shade; ample water. Choice rock garden plant in Zones 4–6 where it combines well with other acid-loving plants. Inconsistent in northern California. Varieties 'Nana' and 'Nana Compacta' are lower growing and more compact.

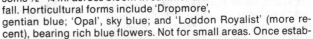
Andromeda polifolia

A. floribunda, A. japonica. See *Pieris floribunda, P. japonica*.

A. speciosa. See *Zenobia pulverulenta*.

ANDROSACE. ROCK-JASMINE. Perennials. Most used Zones 1–6, 14–17. Choice rock garden miniatures grown mostly by alpine plant specialists. All types require sun, moderate watering, perfect drainage, best adapted to gravelly banks in rock gardens. Protect from more aggressive rockery plants such as alyssum, arabis, aubrieta. Rarely succeed in warm-winter areas.

A. lanuginosa. Trailing plant forms mats 3 ft. across. Silvery leaves to ¾ in. long, covered with silky white hairs. Pink flowers in dense clusters on 2-in. stems. *A. l. leichtlinii* has white flowers with crimson eyes.

Androsace lanuginosa

A. primuloides. Trailing, forms 4-in.-long runners. Leaves ½–2 in. long in rosettes covered with silvery hairs. Flowers pink, to ½ in. across, in clusters on 5-in. stems.

A. sarmentosa. Spreads by runners. Leaves to 1½ in. long, in rosettes, covered with silvery hairs when young. Flowers rose colored, ¼ in. across, in clusters on stems 5 in. tall. Variety *chumbyi* forms dense clump, has woolly leaves.

ANEMONE. WINDFLOWER, ANEMONE. Perennials with tuberous or fibrous roots. All Zones (but see notes under *A. fulgens* below). A rich and varied group of plants ranging in size from alpine rock garden miniatures to tall Japanese anemones grown in borders; bloom extends from very early spring to fall, depending on species. First three species described below (*A. blanda, A. coronaria, A. fulgens*) happen to be anemones you can grow from tubers. Directions for planting all of them are given in the three paragraphs that follow description of *A. fulgens.* The other two species at the end are treated as hardy perennials.

Anemone blanda

A. blanda. Zones 1–9, 14–23. Stems rise 2–8 in. from tuberous roots. Finely divided leaves covered with soft hairs. In spring, one sky blue flower 1–1½ in. across on each stem. Often confused with *A. apennina,* which has more pointed leaf segments. Grow with and among Japanese maples, azaleas, and other light shrubbery. Associate with miniature daffodils, tulips, scillas; or grow in pots. New selections have larger (2 in.) flowers on larger (10–12 in.) plants. 'Blue Star' is blue, 'Pink Star' pink, 'Radar' purplish red, and 'White Splendor' is white.

Anemone coronaria

A. coronaria. POPPY-FLOWERED ANEMONE. All Zones. Common large-flowered, showy anemone valued for cutting and for spectacular color in spring borders. Finely divided green leaves. Flowers red, blue, and white, 1½–2½ in. across, borne singly on 6–18-in. stems. Tuberous rooted. Popular strains include: De Caen, with single flowers in mixed colors, also named varieties in separate colors; St. Brigid, with double or semidouble flowers in mixed and separate colors.

A. fulgens. SCARLET WINDFLOWER. Zones 1–9, 14–24. To 1 ft. from tuberous roots. Leaves entirely or slightly divided. Flowers 2½ in. across, brilliant scarlet with black stamens. St. Bavo strain comes in unusual color range that includes pink and rusty coral. Effective in rock garden pockets, borders, containers, and for cut flowers.

All three kinds perform best in position with some shade every day. Set out tubers October to November.

In cold-winter areas, wait until spring to set out *A. coronaria* and *A. fulgens;* or if planted in November, mulch with 6–8 in. of leaf mold or peat moss after first hard frost. Rake off thick mulches after hard frosts have passed.

Plant 1–2 in. deep, 8–12 in. apart, in rich, light, well-drained garden loam, or start in flats of damp sand; set out in garden when leaves are few inches tall. Protect from birds until leaves toughen. In warmer climates, some soak tubers of poppy-flowered anemones for a few hours before planting. In high-rainfall areas excess moisture induces rot.

A. hybrida (*A. japonica, A. hupehensis japonica*). JAPANESE ANEMONE. All Zones. A long-lived, fibrous-rooted perennial indispensable for fall color in partial shade. Graceful branching stems 2–4 ft. high rise from clump of dark green, soft-hairy, 3–5-lobed leaves. Flowers semidouble, white, silvery pink, or rose. Many named varieties available. Slow to establish, but once started spreads readily if roots not disturbed. Mulch in fall where winters are extremely severe. Increase by divisions in fall or early spring, or root cuttings in spring. May need staking. Effective in clumps in front of tall shrubbery, along fences or walls, or under high-branching trees.

Anemone hybrida

A. pulsatilla. EUROPEAN PASQUE FLOWER. Zones 1–6, 15–17.

Attractive alpine plant forming clumps, 9–12 in. high. Fernlike silky-hairy leaves, 4–6 in. long, appearing after flowers. Blossoms bell shaped, to 2½ in. across, blue to reddish purple, with golden stamens, appearing in April and May. Handsome seed clusters like feathery, smoky gray pompons. This hardy plant best adapted to cool moist climates, rarely succeeds in warm dry areas. Sun or partial shade. Sow seeds or make divisions in spring. Choice and distinctive in borders or rock gardens.

ANEMOPAEGMA chamberlaynii (*Bignonia chamberlaynii*). YELLOW TRUMPET VINE. Evergreen vine. Full sun or partial shade, average water. Zones 15–17, 19, 21–24. Climbs by unbranched tendrils. Leaves divided into two leaflets to 7 in. long. Flowers yellow, trumpet shaped, 3 in. long, in clusters longer than the leaves. Summer blooming. Often confused with *Macfadyena (Doxantha) unguis-cati; Anemopaegma* has larger leaflets (7 in. against 2 in.), paler yellow flowers with purple or white markings in the throat, and unbranched tendrils that coil instead of branched tendrils with little hooks (like cat's claws) at the end. *Anemopaegma* needs something to cling to; *Macfadyena* can fasten itself to nearly any surface, clinging by its claws.

Anemopaegma chamberlaynii

ANETHUM graveolens. DILL. Annual herb. All Zones. To 3–4 ft. Soft, feathery leaves; umbrellalike 6-in.-wide clusters of small yellow flowers. Seeds and leaves have pungent fragrance. Sow seed where plants are to be grown, in full sun. Thin seedlings to 18 in. apart. Sow seed several times during spring and summer for constant supply. Use seeds in pickling and vinegar; fresh or dried leaves on lamb chops, in salads, stews, sauces. Sprouts and grows better in spring than summer. An easy way to grow it in a casual garden is to let a few plants go to seed. Seedlings appear here and there at odd times and can be pulled and chopped as "dill weed."

Anethum graveolens

ANGELICA archangelica. ANGELICA. Biennial. All Zones. To 6 ft. Tropical-looking plant with divided and toothed, yellow green leaves 2–3 ft. long. Greenish white flowers in large umbrellalike clusters. Grow in moist, rich, slightly acid soil in part shade. Cut flowers before buds open to prolong plant's life. Propagate from seed sown as soon as ripe in fall. Use to flavor wines; hollow stems may be candied.

Angelica archangelica

ANGELICA TREE. See *Aralia spinosa.*

ANGEL'S HAIR. See *Artemisia schmidtiana.*

ANGEL'S TEARS. See *Narcissus triandrus, Soleirolia soleirolii.*

ANGOPHORA costata (*A. lanceolata*). GUM MYRTLE. Evergreen tree. Zones 16, 17, 21–24. Native to eastern Australia. Highly praised by those who have used it and seen it. Mature tree in Pasadena 40–50 ft. high and almost as broad.

Beautiful smooth trunk in tones of cream, rose, and mauve. Has thick, glossy, 3–5-in.-long, eucalyptuslike leaves with a prominent midrib. New growth is shiny red turning to rich green. White flowers are

Angophora costata

carried in clusters at branch ends in summer, followed by fruit with spiny prickles. Appears to adapt to variety of soils, watering treatments. As tough and tolerant as its eucalyptus relatives. Skyline tree where it has room.

ANIGOZANTHOS. KANGAROO PAW. Evergreen perennials. Zones 12, 13, 15–24, hardy to about 25°F. Native to open eucalyptus forests in western Australia. From thick rootstocks grow clumps of dark green, smooth swordlike leaves to 3 ft. or taller. Striking tubular flowers curved at tips like kangaroo paws (tips split into 6 segments) in red, purple, green, or yellow in woolly one-sided spikes on 3–6-ft. stems. Flowers attract hummingbirds. Intriguing in flower, otherwise not outstanding. Bloom from late spring to fall, if spent flowering spikes cut to ground. Light sandy soil, or heavier soil with good drainage and careful watering; sunny exposure.

Anigozanthos flavidus

A. flavidus (A. flavida). Branching stems to 5 ft. Tubular, curved, hairy flowers 1–1½ in. long, yellow green tinged with red. Variations occur, with colors ranging from deep rust red to pure yellow, with many shades of orange and buff between. Heavy flower producer.

A. manglesii. Unbranched green stems to 3 ft., thickly covered with red hairs. Flowers brilliant deep green, red at base, woolly on outside, 3 in. long.

ANISACANTHUS thurberi. DESERT HONEY-SUCKLE. Evergreen or deciduous shrub. Zones 8–13, 18, 19. Native to Arizona, New Mexico, Texas, northern Mexico. In mild-winter areas grows to 3–5 ft. with stout branches. Looks best when treated as perennial, cut to ground in winter either by frost or by pruning shears. Plant in sun. Drought tolerant. Valued for its long season of color—spring and summer. Tubular, 1½-in.-long yellow orange flowers in spikes; light green 1½–2-in.-long, leaves ½ in. wide. Plants sold under this name may be *Justicia leonardii;* these have leaves to 6 in. long and bright red flowers.

Anisacanthus thurberi

ANISE. See *Pimpinella anisum.*

ANNONA cherimola. CHERIMOYA. Briefly deciduous large shrub or small tree. Zones 21–24. Hardy to about 25°F. Ample water. Grows fast first 3–4 years, then slows to make 15-ft. tree with 15–20-ft. spread. After tree has developed for 4 or 5 years, prune annually to produce bearing wood. Leaves dull green above, velvety-hairy beneath, 4–10 in. long; leaves drop in late spring. Thick, fleshy, 1-in., brownish or yellow hairy flowers begin opening about time of leaf fall and continue forming for 3–4 months; give a fruity fragrance; pleasant near terrace.

Annona cherimola

Large green fruit weigh ½–1½ lbs. Skin of most varieties looks like short overlapping leaves; some show knobby warts. Pick when fruit turns to yellowish green, then store in refrigerator until skin turns brownish green to brown. Skin is tender and thin. Handle fruit carefully. Creamy white flesh contains large black seeds. Flesh is almost custardlike; eat it with a spoon. Flavor is bland, with suggestion of bananas, pineapples, or nectarines. Serve chilled.

ANNUAL MALLOW. See *Lavatera trimestris.*

ANREDERA cordifolia *(Boussingaultia basselloides, B. gracilis pseudo-basel-loides).* MADEIRA VINE. Perennial vine. Zones 4–24. In Zones 4–10, treat as you would dahlias: dig in fall and store tubers over winter. Heart shaped green leaves 1–3 in. long. Fragrant white flowers in foot-long spikes in late summer, fall. Climbs by twining; may reach 20 ft. in one season. Sun; average water. Small tubers form where leaves join stems. Old-fashioned plant useful for summer screening of decks or other sitting areas. Can run rampant in mildest coastal climate.

Anredera cordifolia

ANTHEMIS. Evergreen perennials. All Zones. Aromatic foliage, especially when bruised. Leaves divided into many segments. Flowers daisylike or buttonlike.

A. nobilis. See *Chamaemelum.*

A. tinctoria. GOLDEN MARGUERITE. Erect, shrubby. Grows to 2–3 ft. Angular stems. Light green leaves with broader divisions than *A. nobilis.* Golden yellow, daisylike flowers to 2 in. across bloom in summer and fall. Plant in full sun. Average water.

Anthemis tinctoria

Grow from seed, stem cuttings, or divisions in fall or spring. Summer border plant. Varieties are: 'Beauty of Grallagh', golden orange flowers; 'E. C. Buxton', white with yellow centers; 'Kelwayi', golden yellow flowers; 'Moonlight', soft, pale yellow.

ANTHRISCUS cerefolium. CHERVIL. Annual culinary herb. All Zones. Grows 1–2 ft. Finely cut, fernlike leaves resembling parsley; white flowers. Use fresh or dried same as parsley; flavor milder than parsley. Grow from seed in raised bed near kitchen door, in box near barbecue, or in vegetable garden. Part shade best, ordinary garden soil, moisture. Goes to seed quickly in hot weather. Keep flower clusters cut to encourage vegetative growth.

Anthriscus cerefolium

ANTHURIUM. Perennial greenhouse or house plants. Native to tropical American jungles. Exotic anthuriums with lustrous flower bracts in vivid red, luscious pinks, or white, and handsome dark green leaves are no more difficult to grow as house plants than are some orchids.

The higher humidity, the better. Anthurium leaves lose shiny texture and may die if humidity drops below 50 percent for more than a few days. Keep pots on trays of moist gravel, in bathroom, or under polyethylene cover. Sponge or spray leaves several times daily. For good bloom, plant by window with good light but no direct sun. Generally grow best in 80°–90°F. temperatures, but will get along in normal house temperature (low 70s). Growth stops below 65°F, damaged below 50°F. Protect from drafts. Pot anthuriums in coarse porous mix of leaf mold, sandy soil, and shredded osmunda. Give mild feeding every 4 weeks.

Anthurium andraeanum

A. andraeanum. Dark green oblong leaves to 1 ft. long and 6 in. wide, heart shaped at base. Flower bracts spreading, heart shaped, to 6 in. long, surrounding yellow, callalike flower spike. Flower bracts in shades of red, rose, pink, and white shine as though lacquered. Bloom more or less continuously—plant may have 4–6 flowers during the year. Flowers last 6 weeks on plant, 4 weeks after cut.

A. crystallinum. Leaves up to 1½ ft. long, 1 ft. wide are deep green with striking white veining. Flowers unexciting, with small, narrow, greenish bracts. Many similar anthuriums exist in florist trade; plants offered as *A. crystallinum* may be *A. clarinervium*, *A. magnificum*, or some other species.

A. scherzeranum. Slow growing, compact plant to 2 ft. Dark green leaves 8 in. long, 2 in. wide. Flower bracts broad, 3 in. long, deep red varying to rose, salmon, white. Yellow flower spikes spirally coiled. Easier to handle than *A. andraeanum* and often thrives under ordinary good house plant conditions.

ANTIGONON leptopus. ROSA DE MONTANA, QUEEN'S WREATH, CORAL VINE (must have been loved by many to earn so many nice common names). Deciduous vine, evergreen in warmest winter areas. Zones 12, 13, 18–21. Native to Mexico. Revels in high summer heat, sun, ample water. Fast growing, climbing by tendrils to 40 ft. Foliage, of dark green, 3–5-in.-long, heart shaped or arrow shaped leaves, is open and airy. Small rose pink flowers to 1½ in. long are carried in long trailing sprays from midsummer to fall. In cold winters leaves fall and most of top dies. Recovers quickly. Treat as perennial. Where winter temperatures drop below 25°F. protect roots with mulch. There is a white variety, 'Album'.

Antigonon leptopus

A wonderful vine in the low deserts of California and Arizona. In those climates it can grow without irrigation, but it may die back to ground in summer. Elsewhere give it hottest spot in garden. Let it shade patio or terrace; drape its foliage and blossom sprays along eaves, fence, or garden wall.

ANTIRRHINUM majus. SNAPDRAGON. Perennial usually treated as annual. All Zones. Among best flowers for sunny borders and cutting, reaching greatest perfection in spring and early summer—in winter and spring in warm-winter, hot-summer regions. Individual flower of basic snapdragon has 5 lobes, which are divided into unequal upper and lower "jaws"; slight pinch at side of flower will make dragon open his jaws. Later developments include double flowers; the bell shaped flower, with round, open flowers; and the azalea shaped flower, which is a doubled bellflower.

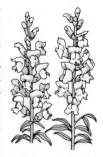

Antirrhinum majus

Snapping snapdragons in tall (30–36 in.) range include Ginger Snaps, Pinnacle, Rocket, Sentinel, Tetra (Super Tetra, Giant Tetra), and Topper strains. Double Supreme strain grows to 30 in. Intermediate strains (12–20 in.) are Carioca, Coronette, Hit Parade, Majestic, Promenade, and Sprite. Dwarfs (6–8 in.) are Floral Carpet, Magic Carpet, and Tom Thumb.

Bell-flowered or penstemon-flowered strains are Bright Butterflies and Wedding Bells (30 in.), Little Darling (12–15 in.), and Pixie (6–8 in.). Azalea-flowered strains are Madame Butterfly (30 in.) and Sweetheart (12 in.).

Sow seed in flats from late summer to early spring for later transplanting, or buy flat-grown plants at nursery. Set out plants in early fall in mild-winter areas, spring in colder sections. If snapdragons set out in early fall reach bud stage before night temperatures drop below 50°F., they will start blooming in winter and continue until weather gets hot. Rust is most serious handicap; start with rust resistant varieties and keep plants in vigorous growth, watered and fed regularly. Avoid overhead watering, which helps spread rust spores, but don't let plants go dry. If necessary, change snapdragon planting locations from one year to another in order to avoid rust.

Valuable cut flowers. Tall and intermediate forms are splendid vertical accents in borders with delphinium, iris, daylily, peach-leafed bluebell, Oriental poppy. Dwarf kinds effective as edgings, in rock gardens, raised beds, or pots.

APACHE PLUME. See *Fallugia paradoxa*.

APHELANDRA squarrosa. Evergreen house plant. Native to Mexico, South America. Popular for leaves and flowers. Large, 8–12-in.-long, dark green leaves strikingly veined with white. Yellow flowers tipped with green, and waxy, golden yellow flower bracts make colorful upright spikes at tips of stems. Variety 'Louisae' is best known, but newer varieties 'Apollo White' and 'Dania' are more compact and show more white venation. To make plants bushy, cut stems back to one or two pairs of leaves after flowering. Give plant routine house plant culture. Place it where it gets morning (or filtered) sun. Occasionally used outdoors in protected spots in southern California gardens.

Aphelandra squarrosa

APONOGETON distachyus. CAPE PONDWEED, WATER HAWTHORN. Aquatic plant. All Zones. Native to South Africa. Like miniature water lily, it produces floating leaves from submerged tuber. Leaves are long and narrow; ⅓-in.-long white fragrant flowers stand above water in two-branched cluster. In hot-summer climates, blooms in cool weather and is dormant in hottest weather; where winters are cold, blooms in summer and is dormant in winter. Same culture as waterlily (*Nymphaea*); will bloom in considerable shade.

Aponogeton distachyus

APPLE. Deciduous fruit tree. For ornamental relatives see *Malus*. Most widely adapted deciduous fruit. It is grown in every western climate except low deserts of California and Arizona. Mild winters of the low desert and the marine and coastal climates of southern California do not provide enough winter cold for most standard varieties. Since nursery customers often insist on most popular varieties they see on fruit stands, varieties are sold in areas unfavorable to best performance. Often, in southern California, Phoenix, Tucson, nurseries offer varieties for customers who live in nearby higher elevations. For this reason, the apple chart indicates where some varieties perform best, as well as where they are sold.

Apple

Varieties that need pollenizer to set fruit are noted on chart. All others are self-fruitful or partially self-fruitful. If a pollenizing variety grows in your neighborhood, you need not plant one yourself.

If you have a tree that is not bearing, graft branch of another variety onto it; or place fresh flower bouquets from another variety (in can of water) at base of tree. Don't use 'Gravenstein' or 'Winesap' to pollinate other self-unfruitful varieties.

The apple needs sun and has moderate water requirements. Don't crowd it into partially shaded places. To have more than one variety in limited space, buy multiple-variety trees or dwarf trees.

Multiple-variety trees have 3–5 varieties grafted onto single trunk and rootstock; they may be standard, dwarf, or semidwarf. You get not only variety but also pollination, if needed.

In selecting varieties remember that all good apples are not red. Skin color is not an indicator of quality or taste. Red varieties are widely sold only because red apples have sales appeal. Make sure that eye appeal alone or slight preference of taste or name doesn't dictate your selection of a difficult-to-grow variety. For example: if to your taste 'Golden Delicious' and 'Red Delicious' are nearly equal, consider differences in growing them. 'Golden Delicious' produces fruit without pollenizer and comes into bearing earlier. It keeps well, while 'Red Delicious' becomes mealy if not stored at 50°F. or lower. And, it can be used for cooking while 'Red Delicious' is strictly an eating apple.

The apple tree will need much care if you want perfect fruit. However, as an ornamental tree it has more character, better form, and longer life than most deciduous fruit trees. It does best in deep soil but gets by in many imperfect situations, including heavy soils. To prevent wormy apples and other damage from insects and disease it is generally necessary to follow a spray program. See "Codling moths" on pages 57–58.

DWARF AND SPUR APPLES

True dwarf apples (usually 5–6 ft. in height and spread and seldom over 8 ft.) are made by grafting standard apple varieties on a dwarf rootstock named M (or EM) 9. Such trees take up little room and are easy to care for; on the other hand, their root systems are shallow, and trees require support, good soil, and extra care in feeding and watering. M 26 rootstock produces somewhat larger, but still dwarf, trees that need staking during their early years. 'Garden Delicious' and 'Homesweet' are genetic dwarfs—naturally slow growing, small trees that are grafted on ordinary apple understock. Other genetic dwarfs may be expected in time.

Semidwarf trees are larger than true dwarfs but smaller than standard trees. They bear bigger crops than dwarfs and take up less space than standards. Many commercial orchards get high yields by using semidwarf trees and planting them close together. Semidwarf rootstocks reduce tree size by approximately the following factors: trees on M 7A and MM 106 are about half normal size, on MM 111 and EM 2 about ⅔ size, and MM 104 about ¾ normal size.

Rarely, growers offer trees dwarfed by double-working—grafting piece of M 9 trunk on vigorous rootstock, then grafting bearing variety on this "interstock." The resulting dwarf is somewhat larger than a true dwarf tree and has much more vigorous roots.

Apples bear flowers and fruit on spurs, short branches which grow from 2-year or older wood. Spurs normally begin to appear only after tree has grown in place from 3–5 years. On spur-type apples, spurs form earlier (in 2 years from planting) and grow closer together on shorter branches, giving more apples per foot of branch. Spur apples are natural or genetic semidwarfs about ⅔ size of normal apple tree when grafted on ordinary rootstocks. They can be further dwarfed by grafting onto dwarfing rootstocks; M 7A and M 26 give smallest trees, MM 106 and MM 111 somewhat larger ones.

TRAINING AND PRUNING APPLE TREES

Careful early training and some annual pruning and shaping are necessary to make apple trees manageable in size, healthy, and productive. Most home and orchard apples grow on vase shaped trees—broad, spreading, with three (sometimes more) main scaffold branches arising from trunk 30–36 in. tall. These branches should not arise at the same point; select ones that are evenly spaced around trunk and at least 8 or 9 in. apart. As tree grows, prune out crossing branches and over-vigorous branches growing toward center of tree.

Spur apples and apples on semidwarfing rootstocks are often trained as central-leader or pyramidal trees. Side branches grow outward from central trunk to form symmetrical pyramid, with tiers of branches that grow shorter toward top of plant. Keep branches from growing directly above and close to lower branches; upper ones will shade lower ones out. Keep side branches from outgrowing the leader and secondary side branches from outstripping primary branches. If branches grow at a narrow angle to leader, spread them to a 45° angle by heavy wire or wood-and-nail spreaders.

Dwarf trees can grow as pyramids, as single-stem trees with fruiting spurs along main trunk, or as espaliers tied to wood or wire frames, fences, or other supports.

Apples produce fruit from spurs—short branches which remain productive for up to 20 years. Pruning of mature trees consists of removing weak, dead, or poorly placed branches and twigs to encourage development of strong new growth and to permit sunlight to reach into tree, where it will encourage spur growth and discourage mildew.

Apple

VARIETY	CLIMATE ADAPTATION	RIPENING DATE	FRUIT	REMARKS
'Arkansas Black'	Zones 1–3, 10–11.	October, November.	Medium sized. Dark, deep red. Hard-crisp.	'Arkansas Black Spur' is spurred variation.
'Astrachan' ('Red Astrachan')	Zones 7–9, 14–22.	Early July.	Medium sized, irregular shape. Red striped or yellow. Juicy and tart. Good eating, excellent cooking.	Early ripening makes it good in California's interior valleys. More red in 'Red Astrachan'; yellow often called 'White Astrachan'.
'Bellflower'	Best in Zones 14–16, 18–22.	September.	Medium to large. Greenish to yellow. Semifirm, fine texture, good quality.	Big, spreading form makes good shade tree.
'Beverly Hills'	Zones 18–24. One of best for southern California coast.	Early.	Small to medium, yellow, splashed and striped red. Tender, somewhat tart. Excellent quality. Somewhat resembles 'McIntosh'.	Definitely for cool areas. Will not develop good quality in hot interiors.
'Buckley Giant'	Zones 4–6.	Midseason.	Medium to large, yellow with red striping. Moderately firm, fleshy, fine texture. Not juicy.	Like 'Gravenstein', but lacks the flavor. Resists many diseases, bears well west of the Cascades.
'Chehalis'	Zones 4–6.	Mid-September to early October.	Large, yellow green. Soft, but bakes well. Mild flavor, melting flesh; good in salads.	Like 'Golden Delicious' but resists scab in western Washington, Oregon.
'Cortland'	Zones 1–6.	Fall.	Medium sized, pale red, fine texture, mild flavor.	Related to 'McIntosh' but lacking its quality. Can be too soft when ripe.

(Continued on next page)

VARIETY	CLIMATE ADAPTATION	RIPENING DATE	FRUIT	REMARKS
'Criterion'	Zones 6, 7, 15, 16.	Late midseason.	Large, bright yellow with pink blush on one cheek, pointed shape of 'Delicious'.	Firm, sweet, juicy. Use for dessert and cooking. Not common.
'Delicious' ('Red Delicious')	Sold wherever apples will grow. Best in Zones 2–7.	Midseason to late.	Everybody recognizes pointed blossom end with 5 knobs. Color varies with strain and garden climate; best where days are bright and warm, nights cool.	Many strains that vary in ripening season, depth and uniformity of coloring. Standards include 'Classic', 'Early Red One', 'Nured Royal', 'Red King Delta', 'Sharp Red', 'Starkrimson', 'Starking Full Red', 'Topred', 'Spurred', 'Crimson Spur', 'Oregon Spur Red', 'Red King Oregon Spur', 'Redspur', 'Spured Royal', 'Wellspur'. Needs pollenizers.
'Earliblaze'	Zones 1–3, 7, 15, 16.	Mid-August.	Medium to large, round, greenish yellow heavily striped and blushed red. Flesh white, crisp.	Excellent cooking apple; sweet enough for dessert.
'Early Crimson'	Zones 8, 9, 14–17.	Late June, early July.	Large red apple with white flesh; good dessert quality.	One of the earliest apples. Keeps well after harvest.
'Galer'	Zones 1–3, 6, 7.	Late midseason.	Medium sized, yellow striped red. Mild, sweet flavor.	Good keeping variety for home orchard.
'Garden Delicious'	Zones 1–3, 6–9, 14–20.	Late summer.	Medium to large golden green, red blush.	Genetic dwarf not over 4–6 ft. tall, 6–8 ft. wide.
'Golden Delicious' ('Yellow Delicious')	Most widely adapted variety. Try anywhere except Zones 12, 13.	Midseason to late.	Clear yellow; similar in shape to 'Delicious', with less prominent knobs. Highly aromatic, crisp, excellent eating and cooking.	Not yellow-colored 'Red Delicious'; different taste, habit. Spurred types available: 'Goldspur', 'Yelospur'. 'Prime Gold' is rust-resistant variety.
'Gordon'	Zones 18–24	July-October	Large, greenish yellow blushed red. Sweet-tart. Long blooming, bearing periods.	Tree vigorous, upright, semidwarf. Many closely spaced spurs.
'Granny Smith'	Zones 6–9, 14–16.	Late August, mid-September; much later in cool-summer areas.	Large, bright to yellowish green, firm fleshed, tart.	Australian favorite now growing here. Stores well, makes good pies, sauce.
'Gravenstein'	Widely sold Zones 4–11, 14–24. Best in 15–17.	Early to midseason.	Brilliantly red striped over deep yellow. Crisp, aromatic, juicy. Excellent eating; applesauce with character.	Justly famous variety of California's north coast apple district. 'Red Gravenstein' is more highly colored. Needs pollenizer.
'Holland'	Zones 20–24.	Early to mid-October.	Very large. Dark strawberry red skin. Firm, smooth, juicy.	Bears at early age.
'Idared'	Zones 4–6, 15–17.	October.	Bright red apple with firm white flesh, tart at picking time.	Stores well and flavor sweetens in storage. Early, annual heavy bearer.
'Jonathan'	Sold everywhere. Best Zones 2–7.	Early fall. Midseason.	Medium to large, round-oblong. High-colored red. Juicy, moderately tart, crackling crisp, sprightly.	All-purpose apple. Subject to mildew. 'Nured Jonathan' and 'Valnur Red Jonathan' color earlier than parent.
'July Golden'	Sold, adaptable Zones 7–9, 14–16.	Early summer.	Bright yellow, with crisp, firm flesh.	Resembles 'Golden Delicious', but ripens 1½ months earlier.
'King'	Zones 4,5.	Midseason to late.	Large, waxy yellow with red striping. Crisp and sweet. Good for baking or eating. Keeps very well.	Large sturdy tree to 30–35 ft. Needs pollenizer.
'Lodi'	Zones 1–6, 8, 9.	Early.	Large, pale yellow, crisp and tart.	Resembles 'Transparent', but larger, firmer, less mealy.
'Macoun'	Zones 1–7, 15, 16.	Mid-October.	Medium sized, red striped on green ground. Sweet, crisp, juicy. Tasty for dessert and cooking.	Large, upright trees fairly resistant to mildew, scab. Thin for good fruit size.
'McIntosh' ('Red McIntosh')	Zones 4, 6, 11, 12.	Late midseason.	Medium to large. Bright red, nearly round. Snowy white, tender flesh. Tart, excellent.	Excellent apple for garden if good care given. 'Double Red McIntosh' and 'Nured McIntosh' have high color. 'Early McIntosh' and 'Milton McIntosh' ripen earlier. Spurred variety is 'Morspur McIntosh'.
'Melrose'	Zones 1–7, 15, 16.	Late October.	Medium to large, roundish, red striped deeper red. Flesh white, mildly subacid, aromatic.	Cross between 'Jonathan' and 'Delicious'. Exceptional storage, good dessert apple. Somewhat mildew resistant.

VARIETY	CLIMATE ADAPTATION	RIPENING DATE	FRUIT	REMARKS
'Mutsu'	Zones 4–9, 15, 16.	Late October.	Large, greenish yellow to yellow blushed red. Flesh white, coarse, somewhat more tart than 'Golden Delicious'.	Good dessert and cooking apple with long storage life. Tree exceptionally large and vigorous. Needs pollenizer.
'Newtown Pippin' ('Yellow Newtown', 'Yellow Pippin')	Zones 1–11, 13–22.	Late.	Large, green. Crisp and tart, fair eating, excellent cooking.	Large, vigorous tree.
'Northern Spy' ('Red Spy')	Zones 1–3, 6. Best in cold-winter areas.	Late.	Large, red. Tender, fine-grained flesh. Apple epicure's delight for sprightly flavor.	Slow to reach bearing age. Needs pollenizer.
'Pacific Pride'	Zones 4–6.	Midseason. Earlier than 'King'.	Large, striped red over yellow. Juicy, firm, crisp, tart. High quality apple for eating and cooking.	Vigorous and productive. Resembles 'King' and 'Gravenstein'.
'Pettingill'	Zones 23, 24.	Midseason to late.	Large, red-blushed green to red, thick skinned. Firm, white, tasty, moderately acid flesh.	Large, upright, productive tree with very low chilling requirement. Regular bearer.
'Regent'	Zones 1–3, 6, 7.	Late.	Medium sized, oblong, yellow with bright red stripes. Flesh white, crisp, juicy, somewhat more acid than 'Delicious'.	Vigorous; bears heavily on young trees.
'Red Fireside'	Zones 1–3, 6, 7.	Late.	Large, striped dark red over medium red. Flesh yellowish, juicy, mildly acid, excellent dessert quality.	Tree vigorous, very hardy.
'Red June'	Zones 5–7, high elevations in California.	Early.	Red with yellow suffusion. Tart, tender flesh.	Good early pie and sauce apple.
'Red Melba'	Zones 6, 7, 15, 16.	Summer.	Pale green blushed red to all-over red. Medium to large. Crisp, white flesh.	Tree productive, bears young.
'Rome Beauty' ('Red Rome')	Zones 3–7, 10, 11.	Late midseason.	Large, round, smooth, red. Greenish white flesh. Mediocre fresh. Outstanding baking apple.	Early bearer. 'Red Rome' is all-over red kind most frequently sold. 'Barkley Red Rome' is another all-over red.
'Spartan'	Zones 4–7, 15, 16.	Midseason to late.	Small to medium, dark red with purplish bloom. Crisp flesh, excellent flavor.	Equals 'McIntosh' in flavor. Tree habit good; heavy bearing necessitates thinning.
'Spitzenberg' ('Esopus Spitzenberg')	Zones 1–3, 6.	Late.	Medium to large, red dotted yellow. Crisp, fine grained, tangy, spicy.	Old favorite, best in cold-winter areas.
'Stayman Winesap' (and 'Winesap')	Zones 1–7, 10, 11.	Latest.	Medium to large, round. Lively flavor. Fine grained, firm, juicy. 'Stayman Winesap' is large, red with green and russet dots. 'Winesap' is smaller, entirely red.	Old-timers that remain top favorites. Most 'Winesap' trees sold at nurseries are really 'Stayman Winesap'. 'Red Winesap', 'Red Stayman', 'Nured Winesap', 'Spur Winesap', and 'Van Well Winesap' are also sold.
'Summerred' ('Early Summerred')	Zones 4–7, 15, 16.	Late August.	Medium sized, bright red; tart and good chiefly for cooking until fully ripe, then good dessert quality too.	Consistent annual bearer for western Oregon and Washington. Goes over-ripe too fast in hot-summer climates.
'Transparent' ('Yellow Transparent')	Zones 1–9, 14, 15, 19, 20.	Early.	Medium to large, greenish or whitish yellow, lightly blushed on one side. Tender, tart; good for cooking.	Ripens mid-June to mid-July in Sacramento Valley. Doesn't keep.
'Tydeman's Red' ('Tydeman's Early Worcester')	Zones 4–7, 15, 16.	Late August, early September.	Medium, round, bright red. Resembles 'McIntosh'. Good for cooking, tart but good eating.	Long, sprawling branches need control; tip-prune to encourage branching or grow as espalier.
'Valmore'	Zones 8, 9, 18–24.	August.	Large, red blushed yellow. Flesh yellowish white, aromatic, good for cooking, eating.	Will fruit in warm areas with little winter chill.
'Wealthy' ('Red Wealthy', 'Double Red Wealthy')	Zones 1–3, 6, 7.	Midseason.	Large, rough, red. Flesh white veined pink, firm, tart, juicy. Good cooking variety, satisfactory dessert quality.	Cold-hardy tree that tends to alternate bearing.
'Winter Pearmain' ('White Winter Pearmain')	Zones 20–24.	Midseason.	Medium to large. Pale greenish yellow skin with pink blush. Excellent flavor, tender flesh, fine grained. All-purpose.	Performs better than standard cold-winter varieties in southern California. Needs pollenizer.
'Winter Banana'	Zones 4–9, 14–24.	Midseason.	Large, attractive, pale yellow blushed pink, waxy finish. Tender, tangy, distinctive aroma.	One of few standard varieties that will accept mild winters. Needs pollenizer. There is a 'Spur Winter Banana'.

APRICOT. Deciduous fruit tree. For ornamental relatives, see *Prunus.* Apricots can be grown throughout the West, with these limitations: because they bloom early in the season they will not fruit in regions with late frosts; in cool, humid coastal areas, tree and fruit are unusually subject to brown rot and blight; in mild-winter areas of southern California, choose varieties with low chilling requirements. Apricots are good choice as dual-purpose fruit and shade tree. Easy to maintain. Your county agent or farm advisor can give you a local timetable and directions for spraying apricots (essential dates: during dormant season, before and after flowering, and at red-bud stage). To get big apricots, do this: in midspring, thin excess fruit off branches leaving 2–4 in. between individual apricots. Can be trained as espalier.

Apricot

Apricots bear most fruit on short fruit spurs which form on last year's growth and remain fruitful for about 4 years. Pruning should be directed toward conserving enough new growth (which will produce spurs) to replace old exhausted spurs which should be cut out.

Here's a list of varieties sold at nurseries. Many are available on dwarf and semidwarf rootstocks. Varieties that need a pollenizer are so indicated.

'Aprigold'. Zones 2, 3, 5–9, 12–16, 18–23. Good quality, full-sized fruit. Genetic (natural) dwarf 4–6 ft. tall, 6–8 ft. wide.

'Autumn Royal'. Zones 2, 3, 5–9, 12–16, 18–23. Resembles 'Royal' but ripens fruit in September; only autumn-ripening apricot tree.

'Blenril'. Zones 2, 3, 5, 6. Like 'Royal' in quality. Needs pollenizer (any variety except 'Riland').

'Chinese' ('Mormon'). Zones 1–3, 5, 6. Late bloom, hardy tree; good production in late-frost and cold-winter regions.

'Early Gold'. ('Early Golden'. 'Earligold'). Zones 8–12, 14–23. Early fruiting variety that needs little winter chill.

'Floragold'. Zones 2, 3, 5–16, 18–23. Early ripening full-sized fruit grows on genetic (natural) semidwarf tree (about half size of normal apricot tree).

'Golden Amber'. Zones 2, 3, 5–9, 12–16, 18–23. Resembles 'Royal', but tree blooms over month-long period, fruit ripens over similar period from mid-June to mid-July.

'Goldrich'. Zones 2, 3, 5, 6. Good quality fruit on hardy, cold-resistant tree. Needs pollinizing.

'King'. Zones 8–9, 12–16, 14–23. Early ripening, very large, very highly colored. Hard to pollinate; 'Perfection' does best job.

'Moongold'. Zones 1–3. Plum-sized, golden, sweet, sprightly fruit. Developed for coldest-winter climates.

'Moorpark'. Zones 2, 3, 5–11, 14–16. Very large fruit, fine flavor. Color develops unevenly. Good home dessert or drying variety, poor canner.

'Newcastle'. Zones 10–12, 20–23. Good southern California variety; needs little winter chilling.

'Nugget'. Zones 18–23. Large fruit with good flavor and color. Low chilling requirement. Ripens very early, before extreme summer heat.

'Perfection' ('Goldbeck'). Zones 2, 3, 5–9, 12–16, 18–23. Fruit very large but flavor only mediocre. Chilling requirement low, tree hardy. Needs pollenizer (any variety except 'Reeves').

'Redsweet'. Zones 12–16, 18–23. Highly colored, very early-ripening fruit. Needs early-blooming pollenizer ('Nugget' or 'Perfection').

'Reeves'. Zones 12, 13, 18–24. Medium-sized yellow orange fruit. Ripens early. Needs pollenizer. Largely supplanted by newer varieties.

'Riland'. Zones 2, 3, 5, 6. Early-ripening, highly colored, roundish fruit. Needs pollenizer.

'Rival'. Zones 2, 3, 5, 6. Large, oval orange fruit blushed red. Needs early-flowering pollenizer ('Perfection').

'Royal'. 'Blenheim'. Zones 2, 3, 5–16, 18–23. Regardless of how labeled in nurseries these are either two identical varieties or one variety under two names. Standard variety in California's apricot regions. Good for canning or drying.

'Royalty'. Zones 2, 3, 5–9, 12–23. Extra-large fruit on heavy, wind resistant spurs. Early bearing.

'Snowball'. Zones 14–16, 18–23. Early ripening; white skin with pink blush, white flesh.

'Southern Giant'. Zones 8–9, 14–24. Fine quality fruit with very low chilling requirement.

'Sun-Glow'. Zones 2, 3, 5, 6. Highly colored, early fruit. Hardy tree with extra-hardy fruit buds.

'Sungold'. Zones 1–3. Plum-sized, slightly flattened bright orange, sweet, mild fruit. Developed for coldest winter climates.

'Tilton'. Zones 1–3, 5–8, 10, 11, 18, 20. Higher chilling requirement than 'Royal', but less subject to brown rot and sunburn.

'Valnur'. Zones 2, 3, 5, 6. Very early, medium-large fruit. Good pollenizer.

'Wenatchee' ('Wenatchee Moorpark'). Zones 2, 3, 5, 6. Large fruit, excellent flavor.

APTENIA cordifolia (*Mesembryanthemum cordifolium*). Shrubby perennial. Zones 17, 21–24. Sun. Needs little water. Ice plant relative with trailing stems to 2 ft. long and profusion of inch-wide heart shaped or oval bright green, fleshy leaves. Purplish red inch-wide ice plant flowers in spring and summer. Though fleshy, looks less like ice plant than most. Use as trailer in rock garden, on slope or wall, or in hanging pot. *A. c.* 'Variegata' has white-bordered leaves.

Aptenia cordifolia

AQUILEGIA. COLUMBINE. Perennials. All Zones. Columbines have fairylike, woodland quality with their lacy foliage and beautifully posed flowers in exquisite pastels, deeper shades, or white. Erect, branching, from 2 in. to 4 ft. high. Fresh green divided leaves reminiscent of maidenhair fern. Bloom in spring, early summer. Flowers to 3 in. across; erect or nodding, often with sepals and petals in contrasting colors; usually have backward-projecting, nectar-bearing spurs. Some kinds have large flowers and very long spurs; these have airier look than short-spurred kinds or double-flowered strains, although the latter make bolder color mass. Tall (2–3 ft.), long-spurred strains are Long-Spurred Champion, McKana Giants, McKana Improved, Mrs. Scott Elliott, and Teicheriana. Tall F₁ hybrid strain called Spring Song has nearly double flowers, and Double Flowered Mix is completely double.

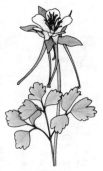

Aquilegia McKana Giant

Short-growing strains for rock garden or foreground plantings are Biedermeier (10–12 in.), Dragonfly (12 in., with long-spurred flowers), and Fairyland (18 in., with short-spurred single and double flowers in blue, purple, rose, and white). Named varieties in separate colors are available.

All columbines are hardy and tolerate filtered shade but will take full sunlight, especially along coast. Cut back old stems for second crop of flowers; leave some seed if you want plants to self-sow. All kinds of columbines attract hummingbirds. Subject to leaf miners, aphids, and red spider mites but usually require only routine care, water. Replace old plants about every 3 years.

A. alpina. ALPINE COLUMBINE. Native of the Alps. Grows 12–16 in. high. Flowers blue, to 2 in. across, with straight or curved spurs 1 in. long.

A. caerulea. ROCKY MOUNTAIN COLUMBINE. To 1½–3 ft. high. Flowers erect, 2 in. or more across, blue and white. Spurs straight or spreading, to 2 in. long. State flower of Colorado. This species hybridized with *A. chrysantha* and others to produce many long-spurred hybrids. Best in filtered shade and moist soil.

A. chrysantha. GOLDEN or GOLDEN-SPURRED COLUMBINE. Native to Arizona, New Mexico, and adjacent Mexico. Large, much branched plant to 3–4 ft. One of showiest species. Leaflets densely covered with soft hairs beneath. Flowers erect, 1½–3 in.

across, clear yellow; spurs slender, 2–2½ in. long.

A. formosa. WESTERN COLUMBINE. Native Utah and California to Alaska. Grows 1½–3 ft. high. Flowers nodding, 1½–2 in. across, red and yellow; spurs stout and straight, red. Good in woodland garden; allow to form seeds which are relished by song sparrows, juncos, and other small birds. *A. f. truncata* is sometimes sold as *A. californica;* it is tall columbine with red spurs, orange petals, and yellow sepals.

A. longissima. Native to southwest Texas and northern Mexico. Plant 2½–3 ft. tall. Similar to *A. chrysantha.* Flowers numerous, erect, pale yellow; spurs very narrow, drooping, 4–6 in. long.

A. vulgaris. EUROPEAN COLUMBINE. Naturalized in eastern U.S. Grows to 1–2½ ft. Flowers nodding, up to 2 in. across, blue, purple, or white; short, knobby spurs about ¾ in. long.

ARABIS. ROCKCRESS. Perennials. All Zones, except as noted. Low-growing, spreading plants for edgings, rock gardens, ground covers, pattern plantings. All kinds have attractive year-round foliage and clusters of white, pink, or rose purple flowers in spring. Sun. Moderate water.

Arabis caucasica

A. alpina. MOUNTAIN ROCKCRESS. Zones 1–7. Low tufted plant, rough-hairy, with leafy stems 4–10 in. high and basal leaves in clusters. White flowers in dense, short clusters. Variety 'Rosea', 6 in. high, has pink flowers; 'Variegata' has variegated leaves. Quite often plants sold as *A. alpina* really are *A. caucasica.*

A. blepharophylla. CALIFORNIA ROCKCRESS, ROSE CRESS. Zones 5, 6, 15–17. Native to rocky hillsides and ridges near sea, Marin County to Monterey County, California. Tufted perennial 4–8 in. high. Basal leaves 1–2¾ in. long. Rose purple flowers, fragrant, ½–¾ in. wide, in short dense clusters. Blooms March and April. Rock plant in nature, equally adapted to well-drained spot in rock garden. Also good container plant.

A. caucasica. (*A. albida*). WALL ROCKCRESS. Native Mediterranean region to Iran. Dependable old favorite. Forms mat of gray leaves to 6 in. high. White ½-in. flowers almost cover plants in early spring. Excellent ground cover and base planting for spring-flowering bulbs such as daffodils and paper-white narcissus. Companion for *Aurinia saxatilis* and aubrieta.

A. c. 'Variegata'. Has gray leaves with creamy white margins. 'Floreplena' has double flowers; 'Rosabella' and 'Pink Charm' have pink blooms. Latter two are popular rock garden plants in colder climates. Start plants from cuttings or sow seeds in spring or fall. Provide some shade in hot dry areas. Short lived where winters are warm.

A. sturii. Dense fist-sized cushions of small bright green leaves eventually grow into small mats. Clusters of white flowers on 2–3-in. stems in early spring. Some consider it one of 50 finest rock garden plants.

ARALIA. Deciduous shrub trees. Zones 2–24. Striking bold-leafed plants that may eventually grow to 25–30 ft. under ideal conditions. Often shrublike, especially in colder areas where it may grow as multi-stemmed (because of suckering habit) shrub to 10 ft. Branches are nearly vertical or slightly spreading, usually very spiny. Huge leaves, clustered at ends of branches, are divided into many leaflets; have effective pattern value. White flowers may be small but in such large, branched clusters they are showy in midsummer; followed by purplish berrylike fruit.

Not good near swimming pools because of spines; even leaf stalks are sometimes prickly. Protect plants from wind to avoid burning foliage. Sun or light shade, moderate water.

Aralia chinensis

A. chinensis. CHINESE ANGELICA. Less prickly than *A. spinosa.* Leaves 2–3 ft. long, divided into 2–6-in.-long, toothed leaflets

without stalks. Flower clusters grow to 1–2 ft. wide.

A. elata. JAPANESE ANGELICA TREE. Native to northeast Asia. Similar to *A. chinensis* but leaflets are narrower, have fewer teeth. *A. e.* 'Variegata' has leaflets strikingly bordered with creamy white.

A. elegantissima. See *Dizygotheca.*

A. papyrifera. See *Tetrapanax.*

A. sieboldii. JAPANESE ARALIA. See *Fatsia.*

A. spinosa. DEVIL'S WALKING STICK, HERCULES' CLUB, ANGELICA TREE. Native to eastern U.S. Like other two aralias but much more spiny; branches look more clublike. Leaves 3–4 ft. long, divided into 2–3-in.-long stalked, finely toothed leaflets. Branched flower clusters are huge, 3–4 ft. wide.

ARAUCARIA. Evergreen trees. These strange-looking conifers provide definite silhouette with their evenly spread tiers of stiff branches. Prominent skyline trees in many parks and old estates in California. Most have stiff, closely overlapping, dark to bright green leaves. In age they bear large, spiny, 10–15-lb. cones that fall with a crash—these are not trees to sit under.

Araucaria heterophylla

All do well in wide range of soils with adequate drainage and abundance of moisture. They become so towering that they should be given park space. Can serve well as skyline trees. They thrive in containers for several years, even in desert areas.

A. araucana (*A. imbricata*). MONKEY PUZZLE TREE. Zones 4–9, 14–24. Native to Chile. Arboreal oddity with heavy, spreading branches and ropelike branchlets closely set with sharp-pointed dark green leaves. Hardiest of araucarias. Slow growing in youth, it eventually reaches 70–90 ft. Hardy west of Cascades in Northwest.

A. bidwillii. BUNYA-BUNYA. Zones 7–9, 12–24. Native to Australia. Probably most widely planted araucaria both in coastal and valley areas of California. Moderate growth to 80 ft.; broadly rounded crown supplies dense shade. Two kinds of leaves: juvenile are glossy, rather narrow, ¾–2 in. long, stiff, more or less spreading in 2 rows; mature leaves are oval, ½ in. long, rather

Araucaria araucana

woody, spirally arranged and overlapping along branches. Unusual but very tough and low-light-tolerant house plant.

A. cunninghamii. HOOP PINE. Zones 17, 21–24. Native to Australia. Unusual silhouette of long horizontal or upswept branches with foliage tufted at tips. Eventual height: 100 ft. Juvenile leaves needlelike and flattened, ½ in. long, with spiny recurved points; adult leaves broader, overlapping, and points incurved.

A. heterophylla. (*A. excelsa*). NORFOLK ISLAND PINE. Zones 17, 21–24. Moderate growth rate to 100 ft., of pyramidal shape. Juvenile leaves rather narrow, ½ in. long, curved and with sharp point; mature leaves somewhat triangular and densely overlapping. Can be held in containers for many years—outdoors in mild climates, house plant anywhere. Good container plant for shaded entryways. Also can be used as indoor Christmas tree.

ARAUJIA sericifera. WHITE BLADDER FLOWER. Evergreen or partially deciduous vine. Zones 8, 9, 14–24. Native to Brazil. Woody vine that sometimes pops up spontaneously in gardens from wind borne, silky-tufted seeds. Becomes weedy, massive tangle in year or two. Leaves tend to drop at base. Twines 20–30 ft. in one season. Leaves 2–4 in. long, glossy dark green above, whitish beneath. White or pinkish bell-shaped flowers, 1–1½ in. wide, followed by long, flat, leathery fruit. Not first-

Araujia sericifera

class vine. Used for quick temporary screen in poor soil, windy places. Sun or partial shade, much or little water.

ARBORVITAE. See *Thuja, Platycladus.*

ARBUTUS. Evergreen trees and shrub-trees. One is western native, other is Mediterranean shrub-tree of wide adaptability. Resistant to oak root fungus.

A. 'Marina'. Evergreen tree to 40 ft., usually less. Zones 8, 9, 14–24. Hybrid of uncertain parentage. Resembles *A. unedo* but has larger leaves, rosy pink flowers in the fall. Good garden substitute for madrone.

A. menziesii. MADRONE, MADROÑO. Evergreen tree or large shrub. Zones 3–7, 14–19. Native from British Columbia to southern California in Coast Ranges, occasionally in middle elevations of Sierra Nevada. Mature height varies—20–100 ft. Forms broad, round head almost as wide as tall. In groves, plants are more slender.

Arbutus unedo

Main feature is smooth, reddish brown bark that peels in thin flakes. Leathery 3–6-in.-long leaves are shiny dark green on top, dull gray green beneath. In spring, large clusters of white to pinkish, bell shaped flowers at branch ends. These are followed in early fall by clusters of brilliant red and orange rough-coated berries that remain on tree most of winter if birds don't get them.

If you live in madrone country and have a tree in your garden, treasure it. It is exacting in requirements in gardens outside of its native area. Must have fast drainage and nonalkaline water. Water just enough to keep plants going until they are established, and then give only infrequent and deep watering.

A. unedo. STRAWBERRY TREE. Evergreen shrub-tree. Zones 4–24. Native to southern Europe, Ireland. Damaged in severe winters in Zones 4–7, but worth risk. Remarkably good performance in both climate and soil extremes from desert (in shade) to seashore. Needs little water once established; tolerates much water if planted in well-drained soil.

Slow to moderate growth to 8–35 ft. with equal spread. Normally has basal suckers, stem sprouts. Can be pruned, not sheared, to make open-crowned tree. Or, plant several and leave unpruned to make screen. Trunk and branches have rich red brown, shreddy bark; tend to become somewhat twisted and gnarled in age. Dark green, handsome, red-stemmed leaves are oblong and 2–3 in. long. Clusters of small white or greenish white, urn shaped flowers and red and yellow, ¾-in. round fruit, somewhat strawberrylike in texture, appear at the same time in fall and winter; fruit edible but mealy and nearly tasteless.

A. u. 'Compacta' is a smaller shrub, but still larger than *A. u.* 'Elfin King', a picturesque, contorted true dwarf form not over 5 ft. tall at 10 years of age; it flowers and fruits nearly continuously. 'Elfin King' is splendid container plant or show plant for small entry garden.

ARCHONTOPHOENIX. Palms. Outdoors in Zones 21–24, house plant anywhere. Called BANGALOW or PICCABEEN palms in Australia. They grow to 50 ft. or more, with 10–15-ft. spread. Handsome, stately, difficult to transplant when large. Where winds are strong, plant in lee of buildings to prevent damage. Young trees can't take frost; mature plants may stand 28°F. They tolerate shade and can grow many years grouped under tall trees. Moderate water requirements. Old leaves shed cleanly, leaving smooth green trunks. Feathery leaves on mature trees 8–10 ft. long, green above, gray green beneath.

Archontophoenix cunninghamiana

A. alexandrae. ALEXANDRA PALM. Trunk enlarged toward base.

A. cunninghamiana (*Seaforthia elegans*). KING PALM. Commoner than the above. Trunk not prominently enlarged at base.

Clustered amethyst flowers are handsome. Highly recommended for nearly frost free areas.

ARCTOSTAPHYLOS. MANZANITA. Evergreen shrubs. Large group of western natives ranging in size from creepers to full-sized shrubs to small trees. Waxy, bell-like flowers and fruit like tiny apples. Most are characterized by (and admired for) crooked branches with smooth red to purple bark. Shrubs attract birds.

Arctostaphylos densiflora

Low-growing ground cover manzanitas do best in loose soils that drain rapidly. They tolerate heavier soils. Taller ground covers, especially those that spread by rooting branches, and most shrub and tree forms, *must* have loose, well-drained soil.

First summer after planting, water every 4–7 days, depending on weather. Established plants in warm-summer areas generally thrive on once-a-month watering in well-drained soil; less frequently in heavy soils. You may be able to stretch intervals to once or twice a summer. Control growth by frequent pinching during growing season. Plants feeble in heavy shade.

Blooming season is not noted in following list unless it differs from general February-March-April sequence.

A. bakeri 'Louis Edmunds'. Zones 4–9, 14–17. Upright shrub to 5–6 ft. tall. Gray green foliage. Pink flowers in hanging clusters. Good garden tolerance.

A. columbiana. HAIRY MANZANITA. Zones 4–6, 15–17. Native to low coastal mountains, central California to British Columbia. Form propagated and sold in northwestern nurseries is called 'Oregon Hybrid'. Low-growing compact shrub with reddish bark, gray green leaves 3 in. long, white flowers, and red-cheeked summer fruit. Useful plant tough enough for highway landscaping in western Oregon and Washington.

A. densiflora. VINE HILL MANZANITA. Zones 7–9, 14–21. Native to Sonoma County, California. All varieties except 'Sentinel' grow low and spreading; outer branches take root when they touch soil. Main stems slender and crooked. Bark of trunks and branches smooth, reddish black. Leaves light or dark green, glossy, small, in ½–1 in. range. Flowers white or pink. In bank planting, low types do best on east or northeast-facing slopes, in loose soil with good drainage.

A. d. 'Harmony'. Very similar to 'Howard McMinn' (below) but somewhat taller and broader. Less well known, but considered best form by some specialists.

A. d. 'Howard McMinn'. Grows in mound 5–6 ft. (usually much less) and spreads as much as 7 ft. in 5 years. If tip-pruned after flowering, plant becomes dense as sheared Kurume azalea. (Don't prune tips of prostrate branches.) Flowers whitish pink.

A. d. 'Sentinel'. An upright form to 6 ft. or more and spreading to 8 ft. Light green downy leaves. Full sun. Can be trained as small tree by selecting dominant stem or stems and removing others. Sensitive to salt burn, root rots.

A. edmundsii. LITTLE SUR MANZANITA. Zones 6–9, 14–24. Low-growing manzanitas from Monterey County, California, coast. Three varieties are grown from cuttings: 'Danville' is 4–24 in. tall to 12 ft. wide, with roundish light green inch-long leaves on red stems and pink flowers in December and January; 'Carmel Sur' has exceptionally good form—gray green neat-looking foliage, soft pink flowers; is fast growing, very garden tolerant. 'Little Sur' has dense, flat growth, bronzy new growth, pointed leaves with reddish margins, slow growth rate, and soft pink flowers in March-April. Good hillside planting.

A. 'Emerald Carpet'. Zones 6–9, 14–24. Dense, uniform carpet 9–14 in. tall, mounding slightly higher after many years. Leaves roundish oval, ½ in. long, bright green in hottest, driest weather. Small pink flowers in March-April, not showy. In hot interior valleys needs deep irrigation every 2–3 weeks. One of greenest, most uniform manzanitas.

A. franciscana. Zones 6–9, 14–24. Lower growing (to 2½ ft.), spreading slowly to 7 ft. (in 15 years). Native to San Francisco and nearly extinct there.

A. hookeri. MONTEREY MANZANITA. Zones 6–9, 14–24. Native to

Monterey Peninsula. Slow growing to form dense mounds 1½–4 ft. high, spreading to 6 ft. and more. Oval ¾-in.-long, bright green glossy leaves. Flowers white to pinkish; fruit bright red, shiny; bark red brown, smooth. Good on hillsides.

A. h. 'Monterey Carpet'. Compact growth to make 12-in.-high ground cover spreading by rooting branches to 12 ft.

A. h. 'Wayside'. Taller growing to 4 ft. while spreading to 8 ft. and more. Trailing branches take root. May be slow to fill in; eventually dense, attractive mound.

A. manzanita. COMMON MANZANITA. Tall shrub or treelike shrub. Zones 2–9, 14–24. Native to inner Coast Ranges, Sierra Nevada foothills. Widely adapted. Grows 6–20 ft. high, spreads 4–10 ft. wide. Crooked picturesque branching habit; purplish red bark. Shiny bright green to dull green, broadly oval leaves, ¾–1½ in. long. Flowers white to pink in open drooping clusters. Fruit white turning to deep red.

A. m. 'Dr. Hurd'. Treelike form to 15 ft. tall, as wide or wider. Mahogany bark; large, light green leaves; white flowers January–March. Good garden tolerance; subject to salt burn.

A. media. Zones 4–9, 14–24. May be a natural hybrid of *A. uva-ursi* and *A. columbiana*. As far as gardener is concerned it's a higher growing *A. uva-ursi* (to 2 ft.) with brighter red branches and leathery dark green leaves. Spreads faster than *A. uva-ursi*.

A. nummularia. FORT BRAGG MANZANITA. Zones 14–24. Low-growing (6–18 in., rarely taller), densely foliaged shrub with small bright green leaves, small white flowers. Attractive, but considered difficult outside its native north coastal California forests. Needs good drainage, acid soil, and shade except near coast.

A. pumila. DUNE MANZANITA. Zone 17. Native to dunes around Monterey Bay, California. Spreading, prostrate habit, to 1–2½ ft. high. Roots freely where branches touch ground. Leaves dull green, narrowish, ½–1 in. long. Short dense clusters of small white to pink flowers. Good ground cover in sandy or well-drained soil near coast.

A. stanfordiana. STANFORD MANZANITA. Zones 4–9, 14–17. Native to California's Lake, Mendocino, Napa, and Sonoma counties. Wide climate range. Soil adaptation very poor. Must have rapid drainage to avoid root rot. Spreading shrub to 3–7 ft. high (and as wide) with smooth reddish brown bark, glossy deep green leaves 1–1¾ in. long. Flowers pink in open clusters. Fruit red to red brown. Relaxed and graceful manzanita. Selected forms, propagated by cuttings, are:

A. s. 'Fred Oehler'. Parent plant is 4 ft. high, 6 ft. wide. Produces good crop of pink flowers in pendulous clusters.

A. s. 'Louis Edmunds'. See *A. bakeri* 'Louis Edmunds'.

A. s. 'Trinity'. Similar to *A. stanfordiana* but has reddish purple flowers.

A. 'Sunset'. Zones 6–9, 14–24. Natural hybrid between *A. hookeri* and *A. pajaroensis* from Monterey County, California. New foliage coppery red, turning bright green. Makes mound 4–5 ft. tall by 4–6 ft. wide. Pinkish white flowers in March–April.

A. uva-ursi. BEARBERRY, KINNIKINNICK. Zones 1–9, 14–24. Native from San Mateo County, California, north to Alaska. Also widespread in other northern latitudes. Long a popular ground cover in Pacific Northwest and intermountain areas. Prostrate, spreading and rooting as it creeps to 15 ft. wide; bright glossy green, leathery leaves to 1 in., turning red in winter. Flowers white or pinkish. Fruit bright red or pink. A most useful plant in Northwest: for slopes too steep for lawn, as trailing mat atop wall, combining with mugho pines, yews. Slowness in starting causes weed problems. Mulch with peat moss or sawdust to keep down weeds, and keep soil moist for root growth and rooting of branches. Good on hillsides, near coast.

A. u. 'Alaska'. Flat grower with small round dark green leaves.

A. u. 'Massachusetts'. Like the above, small-leafed, flat-growing variety. Good resistance to leaf spot and leaf gall in Northwest.

A. u. 'Point Reyes'. Dark green leaves are closely set along branches. More tolerant of heat and drought than *A. u.* 'Radiant'.

A. u. 'Radiant'. Leaves lighter green than *A. u.* 'Point Reyes', more widely spaced. Heavy crop of large bright red fruit in autumn, lasting into winter; sometimes fails to fruit if pollinating insects not active at bloom time.

ARCTOTHECA calendula. CAPE WEED. Evergreen perennial. Zones 8, 9, 13–24. Rapid running ground cover, less than 1 ft. tall, with yellow daisy flowers 2 in. across most of year, peaking March through June. Gray green, deeply divided leaves. Full sun; not fussy about soil or irrigation practices. Needs little water once established. Space 18 in. apart for fast cover. Some frost damage in high 20s, but quick recovery. Not for small areas; good on hillsides.

Arctotheca calendula

ARCTOTIS. AFRICAN DAISY. Annuals and perennials, the latter usually grown as annuals but hardy Zones 7–9, 14–24. "African daisy" can refer to any of several plants; names and identities of the plants are often confused, even by seedsmen and nurserymen. African daisies in *Arctotis* have lobed leaves that are rough, hairy, or woolly; their flower heads usually have contrasting ring of color around central eye. African daisies in *Dimorphotheca* (common for winter mass flower color) are annuals with smooth green foliage and flowers in the yellow-orange-salmon range, or white. Trailing ground cover African daisies and woody, shrubby white, yellow or purple African daisies are *Osteospermum*. All do best with full sun and light soil; need little water except when in active growth.

Arctotis acaulis

A. acaulis. Perennial. Spreading, stemless clumps of leaves; flower heads to 3½ in. wide on 6-in.-long stalks are yellow with purplish black centers.

A. breviscapa. Annual, somewhat smaller than *A. acaulis,* with orange yellow, brown-centered flowers.

A. hybrids. Most garden plants are hybrids 12–18 in. tall. Three-inch flowers come in white, pink, red, purplish, cream, yellow, and orange, usually with dark ring around nearly black eye spot. In mild climates plants make growth in winter and early spring, bloom from spring into early summer, with scattered bloom later. They will self-sow, but tend to revert to orange. You can perpetuate colors you like by taking cuttings. Plants survive as perennials in mildest climates, but bloom best in their first year. Strains offered include Giant Mixed and T. & M. Hybrids. The recent Venidio-Arctotis hybrids are broad (3 ft. or more), mounding perennials with a longer bloom season and somewhat larger flowers. They are easily propagated, but still rare.

A. stoechadifolia grandis. Bushy annual to 2 ft., with gray green, slightly hairy leaves and 3-in. white daisies in which yellow ring surrounds deep blue central eye.

ARDISIA. Evergreen shrubs or shrublets.

A. crenata *(A. crenulata, A. crispa).* Usually grown indoors. Most familiar as 18-in. single-stemmed pot plant. In large tub it can reach 4 ft. with nearly equal spread. In spring, spirelike clusters of tiny (¼ in.) white or pinkish flowers are carried above shiny, wavy-edged, 3-in.-long leaves. Flowers are followed by brilliant scarlet fruit in autumn and usually through winter. Routine house plant care.

Ardisia japonica

A. japonica. Zones 5, 6, 15–17. Low shrub that spreads as ground cover by rhizomes to produce succession of upright branches 6–18 in. high. Leathery bright green leaves (4 in. long) are clustered at tips of branches. White, ¼-in. flowers, 2–6 in cluster, appear in fall, followed by small (¼ in.), round, bright red fruit that last into winter. Makes quality ground cover in shade. Needs ample water.

ARECA lutescens. See *Chrysalidocarpus lutescens.*

ARECASTRUM romanzoffianum. (Often sold as *Cocos plumosa*.) QUEEN PALM. Zones 12, 13, 15–17, 19–24. South America. Exceptionally straight trunk to 50 ft. tall, arching, bright green, glossy feather-type leaves 10–15 ft. long are subject to breakage in high wind. Fast grower, responding quickly to water and fertilizer. Very subject to mites; wash frequently. Damaged at 25°F., but has recovered from 16°F. freeze.

Arecastrum romanzoffianum

ARENARIA. SANDWORT. Perennial ground covers. Zones 2–9, 14–24. Low evergreen plants carpet ground with dense mats of mosslike foliage, have small white flowers in late spring and summer. They are often used as lawn substitutes, between stepping stones, or for velvety green patches in rock gardens. Can be invasive, hard to eradicate in well-watered gardens.

Arenaria montana

    A. balearica. CORSICAN SANDWORT. Forms dense mat to 3 in. high. Leaves oval, thick, glossy, to ⅛ in. long. Grows best in shade with lots of water. Adapted to planting in small areas such as carpet at base of container-grown tree.

    A. montana. It grows 2–4 in. high with weak stems up to 1 ft. long usually covered with soft hairs. Leaves grayish, ½–¾ in. long. White flowers, 1 in. across, profuse in June. Good plant to let trail over sunny rock or tumble over low wall. Moderate water requirements.

    A. verna (*A. caespitosa*). See *Sagina subulata*.

ARGEMONE. PRICKLY POPPY. Annuals or biennials. All Zones. Prickly leafed and prickly stemmed plants with large, showy poppy flowers. Native to desert or dry areas Wyoming to Mexico and west to California. Grow easily from seed sown where plants are to bloom, or from seed sown in pots for gentle transplanting. Need sun and good drainage. Bloom mostly in summer. To 3 ft. Extremely drought tolerant.

Argemone mexicana

    A. intermedia. See *A. polyanthemos*.

    A. mexicana. Annual. Yellow to orange flowers.

    A. platyceras. Annual. White flowers. Commonest kind.

    A. polyanthemos (*A. intermedia*). Annual or biennial. White flowers.

ARISTOLOCHIA. Deciduous or evergreen vines. Curiously shaped flowers in rather sober colors resemble curved pipes with flared bowls.

    A. californica. CALIFORNIA DUTCHMAN'S PIPE. Deciduous. Zones 7–9, 14–24. Native to coast ranges and Sierra Nevada foothills of northern California. Will cover 8 by 12-ft. screen with some training, or climb by long thin shoots 10–16 ft. into nearby tree. Flower display before leaves, late January to April. Pendulous, 1-in.-long flowers are cream colored with red purple veins at maturity. Bright green, heart shaped leaves

Aristolochia elegans

to 5 in. long. Grows from seed or from rooted shoots around base of vine. Interesting and useful where many less hardy vines would freeze. Accepts any soil, but needs partial shade and ample moisture.

    A. durior. DUTCHMAN'S PIPE. Deciduous. All Zones. Native to eastern United States. Will cover 15 by 20 ft. in one season. Easily grown from seed. Large, 6–14-in.-long, kidney shaped, deep green glossy leaves are carried in shinglelike pattern to form dense cover on trellis. Flowers, with yellowish green 3-in. curved tube, flare into 3 brownish purple lobes about 1 in. wide. Bloom in June and July, almost hidden by leaves. Thrives in full

sun or heavy shade. No special care. Generous feeding and watering will speed growth. Cut back in winter if too heavy. Short lived in warm-winter areas. Will not stand strong winds.

    A. elegans. CALICO FLOWER. Outdoors in Zones 23–24; house or greenhouse plant elsewhere. Twining evergreen vine to 6 ft. or more. Wiry, slender stems, heart shaped leaves 3 in. long. Whitish buds shaped like little pelicans open to 3-in.-wide heart shaped flowers of deep purple veined creamy white. Needs rich soil, moisture, partial shade.

ARMERIA. THRIFT, SEA PINK. Hardy evergreen perennials. All Zones. Narrow stiff leaves grow in compact tufts or basal rosettes; small white, pink, rose or red flowers in dense globular heads from early spring to late fall. Sturdy, dependable plants for edging walks or borders and for tidy mounds in rock gardens, raised beds. Attractive in containers. Need full sun; not fussy about water if drainage is excellent. Shear flowers after bloom. Feed once a year with slow-acting fertilizer. Propagate by divisions or from seeds in spring or fall.

Armeria maritima

    A. juniperifolia (*A. caespitosa*). Native to mountains of Spain. Stiff, needle shaped leaves ½ in. long in low, extremely compact rosettes. Flowers rose pink or white in dense, round clusters on 2-in. stems. This little mountain native is very touchy about drainage; apply mulch of fine gravel around plants to prevent basal stem rot, especially in summer.

    A. maritima (*Statice armeria, Armeria vulgaris*). COMMON THRIFT. Tufted mounds spreading to 1 ft. with 6-in.-long stiff, grasslike leaves. Small white to rose pink flowers in tight, round clusters at top of 6–10-in. stalks. Blooms almost all year along coast; flowers profusely in spring in other areas.

ARONIA arbutifolia. RED CHOKEBERRY. Deciduous shrub. Zones 1–7. Native to eastern United States. Hardy to −10°F. Noteworthy for long season of bright red foliage and fruit in autumn. Large, openly branched, upright to 6–10 ft. or more. Leaves, narrow ovals generally about 3 in. long and half as wide, are dark green above, gray and feltlike beneath. Small ½-in. flowers, white or pink tinged, in 2-in. clusters, April or May, followed by clusters of brilliant red, ¼-in. berrylike fruit. These

Aronia arbutifolia

ripen to blend with red foliage in September and hang on after leaves have fallen, attract birds. Variety 'Brilliantissima' has exceptionally good berry color.

    Any soil. Full sun. Tolerates heavy clay. Grows in swamps in native area. Use in shrubbery border, at edge of woodland, but keep in mind that it spreads and shoots up suckers freely.

ARTEMISIA. Evergreen or deciduous shrubs or woody perennials. All Zones. Several species are valuable for interesting leaf patterns and silvery gray or white aromatic foliage; others are aromatic herbs. Plant in full sun. Drought resistant. Keep on dry side. Divide in spring and fall. Most kinds excellent for use in mixed border where white or silvery leaves soften harsh reds or oranges, and blend beautifully with blues, lavenders, and pinks.

    A. abrotanum. SOUTHERNWOOD, OLD MAN. Deciduous shrub. To 3–5 ft. Beautiful lemon-scented, green, feathery foliage; yellowish white flower heads. Use for pleasantly scented foliage in shrub border. Hang sprigs in closet to discourage moths. Burn

Artemisia dracunculus

a few leaves on stove to kill cooking odors.

A. absinthium. COMMON WORMWOOD. Deciduous shrub. To 2–4 ft. Silvery gray, finely divided leaves with bitter taste but pungent odor. Minute yellow flowers. Keep pruned to get better shaped plant. Divide every 3 years. Background shrub. Good gray feature in flower border, particularly fine with delphiniums. Leaves used to flavor wine, season poultry, also for medicinal uses.

A. caucasica. SILVER SPREADER. Evergreen shrublet 3–6 in. tall, spreading to 2 ft. in width. Silky, silvery green foliage; small yellow flowers. Bank or ground cover. Needs good drainage, requires little, if any, summer water. Takes extremes of heat and cold, is fire resistant. Plant 1–2 ft. apart.

Artemisia abrotanum

A. dracunculus. FRENCH TARRAGON, TRUE TARRAGON. Perennial. To 1–2 ft.; spreads slowly by creeping rhizomes. Creeping habit. Shiny dark green, narrow leaves—very aromatic. Woody stems. Flowers greenish white in branched clusters. Dies to ground in winter. Attractive container plant. Cut sprigs in June for seasoning vinegar. Use fresh or dried leaves to season salads, egg and cheese dishes, fish. Divide plant every 3 or 4 years to keep it vigorous. Propagate by divisions or by cuttings. Plants grown from seed are not true culinary tarragon.

A. frigida. FRINGED WORMWOOD. Perennial. To 1–1½ ft. with white, finely cut leaves. Small yellow flowers in late August. Young plants compact. Cut back when they become rangy.

A. lactiflora. WHITE MUGWORT. Border perennial. Tall straight column to 4–5 ft. One of few artemisias with attractive flowers: creamy white in large, branched, 18-in. sprays, August-September. Leaves dark green with broad, tooth-edged lobes.

A. ludoviciana albula (*A. albula*). SILVER KING ARTEMISIA. Bushy perennial. To 2–3½ ft., with slender spreading branches. Silvery white 2-in. leaves, the lower ones with 3–5 lobes, upper ones narrow, unlobed. Cut foliage useful in arrangements.

A. pontica. ROMAN WORMWOOD. Shrub. To 4 ft. Feathery, silver gray leaves. Heads of whitish yellow, nodding flowers in long, open, branched clusters. Leaves used in sachets.

A. pycnocephala. SANDHILL SAGE. Shrubby perennial. Native to beaches of northern California. Erect, rounded, somewhat spreading; 1–2 ft. tall. Soft, silvery white or gray leaves, crowded, divided into narrow lobes. Very small yellow flowers. Remove flower spikes as they open to keep plants compact. Becomes unkempt with age. Replace every 2 years.

A. schmidtiana. ANGEL'S HAIR. Perennial. Forms dome, 2 ft. high and 1 ft. wide, of woolly, silvery white, finely cut leaves. Flowers insignificant. Variety 'Silver Mound' is 12 in. high.

A. stellerana. BEACH WORMWOOD, OLD WOMAN, DUSTY MILLER. Woody perennial. Dense, silvery gray plant to 2½ ft. with 1–4-in. lobed leaves. Hardier than *Senecio cineraria* (another dusty miller), this artemisia is often used in its place in colder climates. Yellow flowers in spikelike clusters.

A. tridentata. BIG SAGEBRUSH. Evergreen shrub. Native to Great Basin region of the West. Grows 1½–15 ft. high. Many branches. Hairy gray leaves about ¾ in. long. Narrow, usually 3-toothed at tip, very aromatic. Insignificant flowers. This is sagebrush that gives pungent sage fragrance for which western deserts are known. Of limited landscape use, but grows easily in any sunny, well-drained situation.

ARTICHOKE. Perennial vegetable with landscape value. Grow as dependable perennial crop in Zones 8, 9, 14–24. Anywhere else, plant in spring when offered and hope for the best—you'll get foliage, maybe flowers, and a crop if you're lucky. A big ferny-looking plant with irregular, somewhat fountainlike form—to 4 ft. high, 6–8 ft. wide. Leaves are silvery green. Big flower buds form at tops of stalks: they are the artichokes you cook and eat. If not cut, buds open into spectacular purple blue,

Artichoke

6-in. thistlelike flowers which can be cut for arrangements.

In California's cool-summer coast (Zone 17), where it is grown commercially, artichoke can be both handsome ornamental plant and a producer of fine, tender artichokes from September to May or all year. In climate Zones 8, 9, 14–16, 18–24 plant grows luxuriantly at least from spring through fall, and edible buds come as extra dividend in early summer only. In colder winter climates artichoke is rarity and must be protected through winter to keep roots and shoots alive. Useful near swimming pools.

Plant dormant roots or plants from containers in winter or early spring, setting root shanks vertically with buds or shoots just above soil line. Space plants 4–6 ft. apart in full sun. After growth starts, water thoroughly once a week, wetting entire root system. If grown only for ornamental value, can tolerate much drought, going dormant in summer heat. Spray to control aphids; after buds start to form use just strong jet sprays of water to blast off aphids (no insecticides then). Bait to control snails and slugs. For gopher control, plant in raised beds with wire-mesh bottoms or in large containers. Harvest buds while they are still tight and plump. Cut off old stalks near ground level when leaves begin to yellow. In cold-winter areas, cut tops to 12 in. in fall, tie them over root crown and mulch heavily to protect from frost.

ARTILLERY PLANT. See *Pilea microphylla*.

ARUM. Perennials with tuberous roots. Zones 4–6, 8–24. Arrow shaped or heart shaped leaves. Curious callalike blossoms on short stalks. Flower bract half encloses thick fleshy spike which bears tiny flowers. Require shade, rich soil, ample moisture. Use in flower borders where hardy; as indoor plants in cold-winter climates.

A. cornutum. See *Sauromatum*.

A. italicum. ITALIAN ARUM. Arrow shaped leaves, 8 in. long and broad, veined with white. Very short stem; white or greenish white (sometimes purple spotted) flowers in spring and early summer; bract first stands erect, then folds over and conceals short yellow spike. Dense clusters of bright red fruit follow. These last long after leaves have faded and are the most conspicuous feature of the plant. They resemble small, bright red ears of shucked corn.

Arum italicum

A. palaestinum. BLACK CALLA. Leaves 6–8 in. long. Also has arrow shaped flower bract about same length, greenish outside, blackish purple within, curved back, revealing the blackish purple spike; spring and early summer.

A. pictum. Light green, heart shaped, 10-in.-long leaves on 10-in. stalks appear in spring. Flower bract is violet, green at base. Spike purplish black.

ARUNDINARIA. See *Bamboo*.

ARUNDO donax. GIANT REED. Perennial. All Zones. One of largest grasses, planted for bold effects in garden fringe areas or by watersides. Also planted in hot-summer climates as quick windbreak or erosion control. Often called a bamboo. Strong, somewhat woody stems, 6–20 ft. high. Leaves to 2 ft. long, flat, 3 in. wide. Flowers in rather narrow, erect clusters to 2 ft. high. *A. d.* 'Versicolor' (*A. d.* 'Variegata') has white or yellowish-striped leaves. Needs rich moist soil. Protect roots with mulch in cold-winter areas. Cut out dead stems and thin occasionally to get look-through quality. Extremely invasive; plant only where you can control it. Can become a pest in irrigation ditches. Stems have some value as plant stakes.

Arundo donax

ASARUM caudatum. WILD GINGER. Perennial. Zones 4–6, 14–17, 21. Native to woods of Coast Range, mainly in redwood belt from Santa Cruz Mountains to Del Norte County, north to British Columbia. Remarkably handsome ground cover for shade, forming a lush, lustrous dark green carpet of heart shaped leaves 2–7 in. across, 7–10 in. high. Flowers reddish brown, bell shaped with long tails, produced close to ground under leaves; bloom in spring.

Asarum caudatum

Grows in average soil with heavy watering but spreads faster, is more luxuriant in rich soil with ample humus. Start from divisions or from container-grown plants. Protect from slugs and snails.

ASCLEPIAS. Perennials or shrubs. Milkweeds are best known representatives. Just a few are grown as garden plants. Full sun, average soil and water.

A. fruticosa *(Gomphocarpus fruticosus)* and **A. physocarpa** *(G. physocarpus)*. SWAN PLANT, GOOSE PLANT. Zones 14–24. Shrubby perennials. These two very similar plants sometimes volunteer in gardens. Plants are occasionally sold for fat, puffy, pale green inflated seed pods with curving stems like swans' necks. Fruit have covering of soft, fleshy prickles. Stripped of leaves and dried, stems make striking arrangements. Plants are narrowly upright, 3–6 ft. tall, and the many stems are clothed with gray green, willowlike leaves. Flowers are not showy.

Asclepias fruticosa

A. tuberosa. BUTTERFLY WEED. All Zones in conditions noted below. Many stems to 3 ft. rise every year from perennial root. Broad clusters of bright orange flowers appear in midsummer, attract swarms of butterflies. Hardy anywhere, prefers good drainage and little summer water. Native to eastern U.S.

ASH. See *Fraxinus*.

ASH, MOUNTAIN. See *Sorbus*.

ASPARAGUS, EDIBLE. Perennial vegetable. All Zones. One of most permanent and dependable of home garden vegetables. Plants take 2–3 years to come into full production, but then furnish delicious spears every spring for 10–15 years. They take up considerable space, but do so in the grand manner, tall, feathery, graceful plants being highly ornamental. Use asparagus along sunny fence or as background for flowers or vegetables.

Edible Asparagus

Seeds grow into strong young plants in one season (sow in spring), but roots are far more widely used. Set out seedlings or roots (not wilted, no smaller than man's hand) in fall or winter (mild climates), or early spring (cold winters). Make trenches 1 ft. wide and 8–10 in. deep. Space trenches 4–6 ft. apart. Heap loose, manure-enriched soil at bottom of trenches and soak. Set roots so that tops are 6–8 in. below surface. Space them 12 in. apart. Spread roots out evenly. Cover with 2 in. of soil and water again.

As young plants grow, gradually fill in trench, taking care not to cover growing tips. Soak deeply whenever soil begins to dry out at root depth. Don't harvest any spears the first year; object at this time is to build big root mass. When plants turn brown in late fall or early winter, cut stems to ground. In cold-winter areas permit dead stalks to stand until spring; they will help trap and hold snow, which will furnish protection to root crowns.

The following spring you can cut your first spears; cut only for 4–6 weeks, or until appearance of thin spears indicates that roots are nearing exhaustion. Then permit plants to grow. Cultivate, feed, and irrigate heavily. The third year you should be able to cut spears for 8–10 weeks. Spears are ready to cut when they are 5–8 in. long. Thrust knife down at 45° angle to soil; flat cutting may injure adjacent developing spears. If asparagus beetle appears during cutting season, control with rotenone or (carefully noting label precautions) malathion. After cutting season spray with any all-purpose insecticide. Use bait to control snails and slugs; sevin, dibrom, or diazinon for earwigs or cutworms.

ASPARAGUS, ORNAMENTAL. Perennials. Outdoors in Zones 12–24, house plant anywhere. There are about 150 kinds of asparagus besides edible one—all members of lily family. Best known of ornamental kinds is the fern asparagus (*A. setaceus*) which is not a fern. Although valued mostly for their handsome foliage of unusual textural quality, some have small but fragrant flowers and colorful berries. Green foliage sprays are made up of what looks like leaves (needlelike or broader). Actually they are short branches called cladodes. True leaves are inconspicuous dry scales.

Asparagus densiflorus 'Sprengeri'

Most ornamental asparagus look greenest in part shade, but thrive in sun near coast. Leaves turn yellow in dense shade. Plant in well-drained soil to which peat moss or ground bark has been added. Because of fleshy roots, can withstand some drought, but grow better with ample water. Feed in spring with complete fertilizer. Trim out old shoots to make room for new growth. Will survive light frosts but may be killed to ground by severe cold. Frosted plants often come back from roots.

A. asparagoides. SMILAX ASPARAGUS. Much-branched vine with spineless stems to 20 ft. or more. Leaves to 1 in. long, sharp pointed, stiffish, glossy grass green. Small fragrant white flowers in spring, followed by blue berries. Often seen in older gardens, foliage sprays prized for table decoration. If it gets little water, plant dies back in summer, coming back from roots with fall rains. Self-sows readily. Becomes tangled mass unless trained. Variety 'Myrtifolius', commonly called baby smilax, is more graceful form, with smaller leaves.

A. crispus (often sold as *A. scandens* 'Deflexus'). BASKET ASPARAGUS. Airy, graceful plant for hanging baskets. Drooping, zigzag stems have bright green, 3–angled leaves in whorls of three.

A. densiflorus 'Myers' (*A. myersii*). MYERS ASPARAGUS. Plants send up several to many stiffly upright stems to 2 ft. or more—they are densely clothed with needlelike deep green leaves. Plants have fluffy look. Good in containers. A little less hardy than Sprenger asparagus.

A. d. 'Sprengeri' (*A. sprengeri*). SPRENGER ASPARAGUS. Arching or drooping stems 3–6 ft. long. Shiny, bright green needlelike leaves, 1 in. long, in bundles. Bright red berries. Popular for hanging baskets or containers, indoors and out. Train on trellis; climbs by means of small hooked prickles. Used as billowy ground cover where temperatures stay above 24°F. Takes full sun as well as part shade; grows in ordinary or even poor soil. Will tolerate dryness of indoors but needs bright light. Form sold as *A. d.* 'Sprengeri Compacta' or *A. sarmentosus* 'Compacta' is denser with shorter stems.

A. falcatus. SICKLE-THORN ASPARAGUS. Derives common name from curved thorns along stems by which it climbs to 40 ft. in its native area (in gardens usually grows to 10 ft.). Leaves 2–3 in. long in clusters of 3–5 at ends of branches. Tiny, white fragrant flowers in loose clusters. Brown berries. Rapid growing. Excellent foliage mass to cover fence or wall, or provide shade for a pergola or lathhouse. Foliage resembles that of *Podocarpus macrophyllus*.

A. meyeri. See *A. densiflorus* 'Myers'.
A. officinalis. See Asparagus, edible.
A. plumosus. See *A. setaceus*.
A retrofractus. Erect, shrubby, slightly climbing, very tender. Slender, silvery gray stems grow slowly to 8–10 ft. high. Leaves

threadlike, 1-in. long, in fluffy, rich green tufts. Clusters of small white flowers. Handsome in containers; useful in flower arrangements. Cut foliage lasts 10 days out of water, several weeks in water.

A. sarmentosus. See *A. densiflorus* 'Sprengeri Compacta'.

A. scandens. BASKET ASPARAGUS. Slender branching vine climbing to 6 ft. Deep green needlelike leaves on zigzag, drooping stems. Greenish white flowers ⅛ in. long. Scarlet berries.

A. scandens 'Deflexus'. See *A. crispus*.

A. setaceus (*A. plumosus*). FERN ASPARAGUS. Sometimes called emerald feather. Branching woody vine climbs by wiry, spiny stems to 10–20 ft. Tiny threadlike leaves form dark green feathery sprays that resemble fern fronds. Tiny white flowers. Berries purple black. Dense, fine-textured foliage mass useful as screen against walls, fences. Florists use foliage as fillers in bouquets; holds up better than delicate ferns. Dwarf variety 'Nanus' is good in containers. 'Pyramidalis' has upswept, windblown look, is less vigorous than common fern asparagus.

A. sprengeri. See *A. densiflorus* 'Sprengeri'.

ASPEN. See *Populus*.

ASPEN DAISY. See *Erigeron speciosus macranthus*.

ASPERULA odorata. See *Galium odoratum*.

ASPIDISTRA elatior (*A. lurida*). CAST-IRON PLANT. Evergreen perennial. Zones 4–9, 12–24, also house plant. Sturdy, long-lived foliage plant remarkable for its ability to thrive under conditions unacceptable to most kinds of plants. Leaf blades 1–2½ ft. long, 3–4 in. wide, tough, glossy dark green and arching, with distinct parallel veins— each blade supported by a 6–8-in.-long grooved leaf stalk. Inconspicuous brownish flowers bloom in spring close to ground. Although extremely tolerant, re-

Aspidistra elatior

quiring minimal care, aspidistra grows best in porous soil enriched with organic matter, and responds to feeding in spring and summer. Will grow in dark, shaded areas (under decks or stairs) anywhere as well as in filtered sun— except in Zones 12 and 13 where it takes full shade only. Keep leaves dust free and glossy by hosing them off, or clean with soft brush or cloth. Average water best; tolerates some drought.

Variegated form (*A. elatior* 'Variegata') has leaves striped with white, loses its variegation if planted in too rich soil.

ASPIDIUM capense. See *Rumohra adiantiformis*.

ASPLENIUM. Ferns. Widespread and variable group. Need shade, liberal watering.

A. bulbiferum. MOTHER FERN. Outdoors Zones 14 (protected), 15–17, 20–24; house plant elsewhere. From New Zealand. Graceful, very finely cut light green fronds to 4 ft. tall. Fronds produce plantlets which can be removed and planted. Heavy or medium shade. Hardy to 26°F. Watch for snails and slugs.

Asplenium bulbiferum

A. daucifolium (*A. viviparum*). House plant. Similar to *A. bulbiferum* but smaller (to 2 ft.), with more finely divided fronds. Also makes plantlets.

A. nidus (*A. nidus-avis*). BIRD'S NEST FERN. House plant. Tender fern with showy, apple green, undivided fronds to 4 ft. long, 8 in. wide, growing upright in cluster. Striking foliage plant; best as container plant to be grown indoors in winter, on shady patio in summer. One snail or slug can ruin a frond.

Asplenium nidus

ASTER. Perennials. All Zones. (For the common annual or China aster, sold in flats at nurseries, see *Callistephus*). There are over 600 species of true asters, ranging from alpine kinds forming compact mounds 6 in. high to open-branching plants 6 ft. tall. Flowers are white or shades of blue, red, pink, lavender, or purple, mostly with yellow centers. Most asters bloom in summer and fall; some hybrids start flowering in spring. Taller asters are

Aster frikartii

invaluable for abundant color in large borders or among shrubs. Large sprays effective in arrangements. Compact dwarf or cushion types make tidy edgings, mounds of color in rock gardens, good container plants.

Plant in full sun. Adapted to most soils. Need routine care, although more luxuriant in fertile soil with regular watering. Resistant to insects and diseases, except for mildew on leaves in late fall. Strong-growing asters have invasive roots, need control. Divide clumps yearly in late fall or early spring. Replant vigorous young divisions from outside of clump; discard old center. Divide smaller, tufted, less vigorously growing kinds every 2 years.

A. alpinus. Mounding plant 6–12 in. tall. Leaves ½–5 in. long, mostly in basal tuft. Several stems grow from basal clump and each carries one violet blue flower 1½–2 in. across; May-June bloom. Best in cold-winter areas.

A. amellus. ITALIAN ASTER. Sturdy, drought resistant, hairy plant to 2 ft. Branching stems with violet, yellow-centered flowers 2 in. across.

A. dumosus. BUSHY ASTER. To 2–3 ft. Narrow leaves 3 in. long. Blue or white flowers ½ in. across. Widely used in developing lower-growing varieties, commonly called dwarf Michaelmas daisies, invaluable as low border plants.

A. frikartii. One of the finest, most useful and widely adapted perennials. Hybrids between *A. amellus* (see above) and *A. thomsonii*, a hairy leafed, lilac-flowered, 3-ft. species native to the Himalayas. Abundant, lavender to violet blue, fragrant single flowers, 2½ in. across. Open spreading growth to 2 ft. high. Blooms May to October—almost all year in mild-winter areas if dead flowers are removed regularly. Best variety is 'Wonder of Stafa'.

A. fruticosus. See *Felicia fruticosa*.

A. novae-angliae. NEW ENGLAND ASTER. Stout-stemmed plant to 3-5 ft. with hairy leaves to 5 in. long. Flowers deep purple, 2 in. across. Good in wet areas.

A. novi-belgii. NEW YORK ASTER. To 3 ft., similar to New England aster, but with smooth leaves. Full clusters of bright blue violet flowers.

Michaelmas daisy is the name applied to hybrids of *A. novae-angliae* and *A. novi-belgii*. They are tall (3–4 ft.), graceful, branching plants. Many horticultural varieties with flowers in white, pale to deep pink, rose, red, and many shades of blue, violet, and purple.

Oregon-Pacific asters, hybrids between a dwarf species native to the West and some well-known Michaelmas daisies, are splendid garden plants. Dwarf, intermediate, taller forms range in height from under 12–30 in. Compact, floriferous, blooming late spring to fall. Many named varieties available in white, blue, lavender, purple, rose, pink, cream.

A. yunnanensis 'Napsbury'. An improved garden variety of this Chinese species. Leaves dark green in basal tufts. Stems to 18 in., each bearing single lavender blue, orange-centered flower. Blooms in summer.

ASTILBE. FALSE SPIRAEA, MEADOW SWEET. Perennials. Zones 2–7, 14–17 (short lived in Zones 8, 9, 18–24). Valued for light, airy quality of plumelike flower clusters and attractive foliage, ability to provide color from May through July. Leaves divided, with toothed or cut leaflets; leaves in some species simply lobed with cut margins. Small white, pink, or red flowers in grace-

Astilbe Hybrid

ful, branching clusters held on slender, wiry stems from 6 in.-3 ft. or higher.

Most astilbes sold in nurseries are hybrids. There are many varieties, but most nurseries stock only a few. Some of best are: 'Avalanche', 24 in., white flowers; 'Betsy Cuperus', 30 in., pale pink flowers; 'Deutschland', 24 in., creamy white flowers; 'Fanal', 24 in., bronzy foliage, garnet red flowers; 'Glow', 24 in., ruby red flowers; 'Rheinland', 24 in., bright pink flowers; 'Straussenfeder', 30 in., drooping, arching, coral pink flowers.

Plant in sun or shade depending on light intensity of climate zone. Needs cool, moist soil, rich in humus. Cut back after flowering. Divide clumps every 4–5 years. Combine in shade gardens with columbine, meadow rue, plantain lily, bergenia; in sunnier situations with peonies, delphiniums, iris. Often planted at edge of pools. Good in pots and tubs.

A. chinensis 'Pumila'. Low mats of leaves make 4-in.-deep ground cover. In summer, lilac pink flower clusters to 12–15 in.

ATHEL TREE. See *Tamarix aphylla.*

ATHYRIUM filix-femina. LADY FERN. Zones 1-9, 14-24. Grows to 4 ft. or more in rich, damp soil in shade. Rootstock rises up to make short trunk in older plants. Vertical effect, narrow at bottom, spreading broadly at top. Thin fronds, very finely cut, bright green, semievergreen in mildest areas but deciduous in repeated frosts. Good choice for woodland or streamside garden. Invasive and may choke out choicer plants.

Athyrium filix-femina

ATRIPLEX. SALTBUSH. Evergreen or deciduous shrubs. Unusually tolerant of direct seashore conditions or highly alkaline desert soils. Saltbushes are mostly grown for their gray or silvery foliage; flowers and seeds attract birds. Many species useful as fire-resistant plants on arid hillsides of California. Plants char but come back. Because of their fire resistance, drought tolerance, and erosion control, new kinds are likely to appear in desert nurseries.

Atriplex hymenelytra

A. canescens. FOUR-WING SALTBUSH. Evergreen. Zones 2–24. Native throughout much of arid section of West. Fire resistant. Dense growth 3–6 ft. high, spreading to 4–8 ft. Narrow gray leaves ½–2 in. long. Mass plantings, clipped and unclipped hedges. Space plants 4 ft. apart.

A. hymenelytra. DESERT HOLLY. Evergreen (everwhitish). Zones 3, 7-14, 18, 19. Native to deserts of southern California, western Arizona, southern Nevada, southwestern Utah. Compact shrub 1–3 ft. high with whitish branches and silvery, deeply toothed roundish leaves, to 1½ in. long. Has Christmas holly look—in white. Much used for decorations. Outside its native range, soil drainage must be very fast. Water heavily only during blooming period—February-May; some summer water if drainage fast. Short lived.

A. lentiformis. QUAIL BUSH. Deciduous. Zones 7-14, 18, 19. Native to alkali wastes in California valleys and deserts and east to Nevada, Utah, and New Mexico. Densely branched, sometimes spiny shrub, 3–10 ft. high, 6–12 ft. wide. Oval bluish gray leaves ½–2 in. long. Useful as hedge or windbreak where salt-tolerant plants are needed.

A. l. breweri. BREWER SALTBUSH. Almost evergreen. Zones 8, 9, 14–24. Native to California coast south of San Francisco Bay, inland to Riverside County. Fire resistant. Like quail bush but not spiny. Grows 5–7 ft. high, 6–8 ft. wide; can be hedge sheared. Useful gray plant on ocean front. Will grow in reclaimed marine soil. Plant 4–6 ft. apart for solid cover.

A. semibaccata. AUSTRALIAN SALTBUSH. Evergreen. Zones 8, 9, 12–24. Fire resistant. Excellent gray green ground cover to 12 in., spreading to 1–6 ft. and more. Forms dense mat of ½–1½-in.-long leaves. Deep rooted. Plant 3 ft. apart for solid cover.

AUBRIETA deltoidea. COMMON AUBRIETA. Perennial. Zones 1–9, 14–21. Native from east Mediterranean region to Iran. Low spreading, mat-forming perennial—familiar sight in Northwest and high-elevation rock gardens where it is often seen in bloom in early spring, with basket-of-gold alyssum, rock-cress (Arabis), perennial candytuft (Iberis), and Phlox subulata. Ideal for chinks in dry stone walls or between patio flagstones. Grows 2–6 in. high, 12–18 in. across. Small gray green leaves with a few teeth at top. Tiny rose to deep red, pale to deep lilac, or purple flowers. In the Rockies, at least half a dozen named varieties are sold.

Aubrieta deltoidea

Plant in full sun except in hot sections, where light shade is recommended. Needs water before and during bloom. Takes some drought later on. After bloom, shear off flowers before they set seed. Don't cut back more than half—always keep some foliage. After trimming, topdress with mixture of gritty soil and bone meal. Sow seeds in late spring for blooms the following spring. Difficult to divide clumps; make cuttings late summer.

AUCUBA japonica. JAPANESE AUCUBA. Evergreen shrub. Zones 4–24. Native from Himalayas to Japan. Important shrub to western gardeners. Performs well in deep shade. Seedlings vary in leaf form and variegations; many varieties offered. Standard green-leafed aucuba grows at moderate rate to 6–10 (sometimes 15) ft. and almost as wide. Can be kept lower by pruning. Buxom shrub, densely clothed with polished, dark green leaves 3–8 in. long, 1½–3 in. wide, edges toothed.

Aucuba japonica

Minute, dark maroon flowers in March are followed by clusters of bright red, ¾-in. berries from October to February. Both sexes must be planted to insure fruit crop.

Green-leafed varieties are: 'Longifolia' ('Salicifolia'), narrow willowlike leaves (female); 'Nana', dwarf female form to about 3 ft.; 'Serratifolia', long leaves, coarsely toothed edges (female).

Variegated-leafed varieties (usually slower growing) are: 'Crotonifolia' (male), leaves heavily spotted or splashed with white and gold; 'Fructu Albo' (female), leaves variegated with white, berries pale pinkish buff; 'Picturata' ('Aureo-maculata') (female), leaves centered with golden yellow, edged with dark green dotted yellow; 'Sulphur' (female), green leaves with broad yellow edge; 'Variegata', or gold dust plant (male or female), dark green leaves spotted with yellow (best known aucuba).

Tolerant of wide range of soil, but will grow better and look better if poor or heavy soils are improved. Requires shade from hot sun, accepts deep shade. Tolerates low light level under trees, competes successfully with tree roots. Gets mealybug and mites. Prune to control height or form by cutting back to a leaf joint (node). Drought tolerant once established.

All aucubas make choice tub plants for shady patio or in the house. Use variegated forms to light up dark corners. Associate with ferns, hydrangeas.

AURICULA. See *Primula auricula.*

AURINIA saxatilis (*Alyssum saxatile*). BASKET-OF-GOLD. Perennial. All Zones. Stems 8–12 in. high; leaves gray, 2–5 in. long. Dense clusters of tiny golden yellow flowers in spring and early summer. Use as foreground plant in borders, in rock gardens, atop walls. Full sun or light shade, moderate water. Shear lightly (not more than half) right after bloom. Generally hardy, but may be killed in extremely cold winters. Self-sows readily. Varieties include 'Citrina' ('Lutea'), with pale yellow flowers; 'Compacta', dwarf, tight growing; 'Plena' ('Flore

Aurinia saxatilis

Pleno'), double flowered; 'Silver Queen', compact, with pale yellow flowers.

AUSTRALIAN BLUEBELL CREEPER. See *Sollya heterophylla.*

AUSTRALIAN FLAME TREE. See *Brachychiton acerifolius.*

AUSTRALIAN FUCHSIA. See *Correa.*

AUSTRALIAN TEA TREE. See *Leptospermum laevigatum.*

AUSTRALIAN TREE FERN. See *Sphaeropteris cooperi.*

AUSTRALIAN WILLOW. See *Geijera parviflora.*

AUSTRIAN BRIER. See *Rosa foetida.*

AVOCADO. Evergreen trees. Two races of avocados are grown in California— Mexican and Guatemalan. (Widely planted 'Fuerte' is thought to be hybrid of the two.) Guatemalan varieties find ideal climate protected from direct wind in Zones 19, 21, 23, and 24. Mexican varieties—smaller and less attractive fruit—are hardier and grow in Zones 9, 16–24. Although avocados are hardy to 20°–24°F., flowers form in winter and temperatures much below freezing destroy crop. Resist oak root fungus.

Avocado

Avocados tend to bear crops in cycles, producing heavy crop one year and light one the next. (Light crop is generally enough for homeowner.) Consistent bearing varieties are noted below.

When using in landscape, remember that most varieties will grow to 30 ft. and spread wider (tree size can be controlled by pruning). Tree should have best of protection from winds. It drops leaves quite heavily all year. Wide-spreading branches with heavy foliage make dense shade beneath—good garden area for potted plants that need shade. St. Augustine grass will grow beneath avocado trees.

The all-important factor in growing avocados is good drainage. High water table in winter rainy season is often fatal, even in well-drained soils. Build wide basin for watering, let fallen leaves build up there to provide mulch. Most roots are in top 2 ft. of soil, so water lightly and frequently enough to keep that layer moist but not wet (fast drainage is important). Give heavy irrigation every third or fourth time to wash out any excess accumulated salts. This will minimize salt burn. Fertilize lightly. Control chlorosis with iron sulfate or iron chelate.

Fruit of all varieties on following list have thin, pliable, smooth skin—except those otherwise noted.

'Bacon'. Mexican. Zones 9, 16, 17, 19–24. Upright grower. Medium-sized green fruit of good quality, November-March. Regular annual crop. Produces when young.

'Duke'. Mexican. Zones 16–22. Large tree. Medium to large green fruit, September-November.

'Fuerte'. Hybrid. Zones 20–24. Large tree; best known avocado. Early flowers subject to frost in borderline areas. Medium green fruit of high quality, November–June.

'Gwen'. Guatemalan. Zones 19–24. Tree to 20 ft. tall, narrow. Black-skinned fruit ripens February to November.

'Hass'. Guatemalan. Zones 16, 17, 19, 21, 23, 24. Large spreading tree. Medium to large dark purple (almost black) fruit, April-October. Pebbly skin, thick but pliable.

'Jim'. Mexican. Zones 19–24. Upright growth. Medium fruit with thin green skin. Bears young and regularly, October-January.

'Mexicola'. Mexican. Zones 9, 16–22. Good garden avocado but fruit too small for commercial market. Probably hardiest. Consistent bearer of small, dark purple fruit with thin, tender skin, and outstanding nutty flavor, August-October.

'Pinkerton'. Guatemalan. Zones 19–24. Large tree with heavy annual production of large green fruit. Main crop January–April.

'Reed'. Guatemalan. Zones 21–24. Slender upright grower. Medium to large, round, rough-skinned fruit. Bears most years, July–September.

'Rincon'. Guatemalan. Zones 19-24. Low-growing tree. Small, green fruit with large seed, ripens January–April. Smooth skin, medium thick, pliable.

'Whitsell'. Guatemalan. Zones 19–24. Tree 10–12 ft. tall. Large black-skinned fruit February to November. Tends to bear in alternate seasons.

'Wurtz'. (Often sold as 'Dwarf', 'Littlecado', and 'Minicado'.) Guatemalan. Small tree (8–10 ft. tall), with slender weeping branches. Medium-sized green fruit in summer; bears young, but not an annual bearer. For small garden or large containers.

'Zutano'. Mexican. Zone 9, 19–24. Upright grower. Pear shaped fruits, 'Fuerte' size, green, good quality, October–February. In southern California, tends to get "end spot" (brown scaly area at tip of fruit).

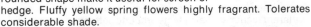

AZALEA. See *Rhododendron.*

AZARA. Evergreen shrubs. Most appreciated in Zones 14–17. Best known species is *A. microphylla*. Its flat-branching habit, and neatly arranged leaves make it natural for espaliers or as free-standing silhouettes against walls. Other three species are quite different, but all four have sweetly fragrant yellow flowers that smell like chocolate to some, vanilla to others.

Azara microphylla

All azaras need protection from hot afternoon sun. All need fast draining soil, ample water, and regular fertilizing.

A. dentata. Zones 15–17. Large shrub or small tree to 15 ft. Inch-wide, toothed, rounded shiny leaves. Dense branching, rounded shape make it useful for screen or hedge. Fluffy yellow spring flowers highly fragrant. Tolerates considerable shade.

A. lanceolata. LANCELEAF AZARA. Zones 15–17. Large spreading shrub to 20 ft. Equal to *A. microphylla* in pattern value but with much larger leaves, more lush effect. Leaves mostly 2½ in. long, rather narrow. Foliage bright yellowish green. April flowers pale yellow, in short clusters.

A. microphylla. BOXLEAF AZARA. Zones 5–9, 14–24. Slow growing when small, fast when established; to 12–18 ft., spreading 8–12 ft. When old, treelike to 30 ft.

Arching branches spread fanlike to give definite two-dimensional effect. May become leggy and awkward unless controlled by tipping young branches. Shiny dark green leaves, roundish, ½–¾ in. long. Flowers yellow, fragrant, in short clusters from February to March.

A. petiolaris (*A. gilliesii*). Zones 15–17. Large shrub to 15–20 ft., but easily trained into single-stemmed tree. Deep green, lustrous, oval to roundish leaves, 1½–3 in. long, look somewhat like holly leaves and hang from branches like aspen. Nodding, 1-in.-long clusters of bright yellow, tiny flowers February-March.

AZTEC LILY. See *Sprekelia formosissima.*

BABIANA. BABOON FLOWER. Corms. With care, outdoors in Zones 4–24. Native to South Africa. Spikes of freesialike flowers in blue, lavender, red, cream, and white bloom in March (California) to June (Northwest). Leaves are strongly ribbed, usually hairy, set edgewise to stem. Full sun or very light shade. Plant corms 4 in. deep, 3 in. apart. Plant along border edge, paths, in rock gardens; also in deep pots. Ample water during growth, less after leaves turn yellow. In mild climates leave in

Babiana stricta

ground several years, but never in cold, wet, heavy ground. In coldest areas, lift, store corms like gladiolus.

B. rubrocyanea. Spikes to 5–6 in. with 6 or 7 flowers to a spike. Bottom half of each flower deep red, upper half royal blue.

B. stricta. Very attractive. Royal blue flowers on 1-ft. stems. Leaves 6 in. high. Varieties in purple, lavender, white, and blue-and-white.

BABOON FLOWER. See *Babiana*.

BABY BLUE EYES. See *Nemophila menziesii*.

BABY'S BREATH. See *Gypsophila paniculata*.

BABY SNAPDRAGON. See *Linaria maroccana*.

BABY'S TEARS. See *Soleirolia soleirolii*.

BACCHARIS. Shrubs of daisy family, but lacking showy bloom. Some are useful landscape plants in difficult growing conditions.

B. pilularis. COYOTE BRUSH, DWARF CHAPARRAL BROOM. Zones 5–11, 14–24. Native to California coast, Sonoma to Monterey counties. Remarkable climate and soil adaptation. Thriving in almost swampy situation or without summer water along coast. Most dependable of all ground covers in California's high desert.

Makes dense, rather billowy mat of bright green, 8–24 in. high and spreading to 6 ft. or more. Small, ½-in., toothed leaves are closely set on many branches.

Baccharis pilularis

Very valuable, very dependable bank cover for minimum maintenance areas in sun. Needs pruning once a year before new growth starts. Cut out old arching branches and thin to rejuvenate. Flowers are of no interest; male and female borne on different plants. Female plants produce cottony seeds which can make a mess as they blow about. Plants available in most nurseries are cutting-grown from male plants. 'Twin Peaks' ('Twin Peaks #2') has small, dark green leaves and moderate growth rate. 'Pigeon Point' has larger, lighter green leaves, grows faster (9 ft. wide in 4 years).

B. sarothroides. DESERT BROOM. Zones 10–12. Nearly leafless, but with bright green branches through year. Grows 6–7 ft. tall, but can be clipped to 2 or 3 ft. Female plants covered with cottony fluff of seeds in late fall and winter. Can take good or poor drainage. Useful for erosion control, replanting disturbed land, or natural landscape in desert regions.

BACHELOR'S BUTTON. See *Centaurea cyanus*.

BALD CYPRESS. See *Taxodium distichum*.

BALLOON FLOWER. See *Platycodon grandiflorum*.

BALSAM. See *Impatiens balsamina*.

BAMBOO. Giant grasses with woody stems divided into sections called internodes by obvious joints called nodes. Upper nodes produce buds which develop into branches; these, in larger bamboos, divide into secondary branches which bear leaves. Bamboos spread by underground stems (rhizomes) which, like aboveground stems, are jointed and carry buds. Manner in which rhizomes grow explains difference between running and clump bamboos.

Bambusa glaucescens

In running bamboos (*Arundinaria, Chimonobambusa, Phyllostachys, Pseudosasa, Sasa, Semiarundinaria,* and *Shibataea*), underground stems grow rapidly to varying distances from parent plant before sending up new vertical stems. These bamboos eventually form large patches or groves unless spread is curbed. They are generally fairly hardy bamboos from temperate regions in China and Japan.

Bambusa oldhamii

In clump bamboos (*Bambusa, Sinarundinaria, Yushania*), underground stems grow only a short distance before sending up new stems. These form clumps that expand slowly around their edges. Most are tropical or subtropical.

Plant container-grown bamboos at any time of year. Best time to propagate from existing clumps is just before growth begins in spring; divide hardy kinds in March or early April, tropical ones in May or early June. (Transplanting at other times is possible, but risk of losing divisions is high in summer heat or winter chill and wet soil.) Cut or saw out divisions with roots and at least 3 connected stems. If divisions are large, cut back tops to balance loss of roots and rhizomes. Foliage may wilt or wither, but canes (stems) will send out new foliage.

Phyllostachys aurea

Rhizome cuttings are another means of propagation. In clumping bamboos this cutting consists of rooted base of culm or cane; in running bamboos it is a foot-long length of rhizome with roots and buds. Plant in rich mix with ample organic material added.

Mature bamboos make phenomenally fast growth during their brief growth period; stems of giant kinds can grow several feet a day. Stems of all bamboos have already attained their maximum diameter when they poke through ground; they reach their maximum height usually within a month. Many do become increasingly leafy in subsequent years, but not taller. Plants are evergreen, but there is considerable dropping of older leaves; old plantings develop nearly weedproof mulch of dead leaves. Individual canes live for

Phyllostachys nigra

several years, but eventually die and should be cut out.

Don't expect bamboos to grow phenomenally fast the first year after transplanting. Giant timber bamboo, for example, needs 3–5 years to build up rhizome system capable of supporting timber-sized stems that grow several feet a day. Growth during early years will be less impressive. To get fast growth and great size, water frequently and feed once a month with high-nitrogen or lawn fertilizer; to restrict size and spread, water and feed less. Plants, once established, tolerate considerable drought, but rhizomes will not spread into dry soil (or into water). The accompanying chart lists two heights for each bamboo. Controlled Height means average height under dry conditions with little feeding, or with rhizome spread controlled by barriers. Uncontrolled Height refers to plants growing under best conditions and unconfined by barriers.

Disregard rule of never buying rootbound plants in the case of bamboo. The more crowded it is in the container, the faster its growth when planted out. Both running and clumping types grow well when roots are confined. Spread of running kinds can be controlled by planting in stout boxes, above or in ground. In large areas, control with soil barriers of 18-in.-deep strips of galvanized sheet metal or poured concrete, or by planting in bottomless oil drums or long flue tiles. You can limit lateral spread by running a spade to its full depth around circumference of clump. New shoots are tender and break off easily; they do not resprout. Another way to limit spread of large running

(Continued on page 197)

Bamboo

(*Synonyms* refers to alternate names under which these bamboos may be sold. For explanation of Controlled and Uncontrolled Height, see facing page; for Roman numerals I, II, III, and IV, see page 197.

NAME	SYNONYMS	CONTROLLED HEIGHT (UNCONTROLLED HEIGHT) AND GROWTH HABIT	STEM DIAMETER	HARD-INESS	COMMENTS (GROWTH HABIT, CHARACTERISTICS, USES)
Arundinaria disticha DWARF FERNLEAF BAMBOO	*Sasa disticha, Pleioblastus distichus.*	1–2 ft. (2–3 ft.) Running.	⅛ in.	10°F.	I. Delicate in appearance. Tiny, two-ranked ferny leaves. Rampant; cut back to ground if rank or stemmy.
A. humilis	*Sasa humilis.*	1–2 ft. (2–4 ft.). Running.	⅛ in.	0°F.	I. Graceful, arching stems. Aggressive spreader, good erosion control; deep ground cover in confined areas.
A. pygmaea	*Sasa pygmaea.*	½–1 ft. (1–1½ ft.). Running.	⅛ in.	0°F.	I. Aggressive spreader; good bank holder and erosion control. Can be mowed every few years to keep it from growing stemmy and unattractive.
A. simonii SIMON BAMBOO, MEDAKE	*Pleioblastus simonii.*	10 ft. (20 ft.) Running.	1½ in.	0°F.	III. Vertical growth pattern, moderate spreader. Screens, hedges; garden stakes.
A. s. variegata		10 ft. (20 ft.) Running.	1½ in.	0°F.	III. Like above, but some leaves have white striping.
A. variegata DWARF WHITESTRIPE BAMBOO	*Sasa variegata, S. fortunei.*	1–2 ft. (2–3 ft.) Running.	¼ in.	0°F.	I. Fast spreader; curb rhizomes. Use in tubs or as deep ground cover. Sun or light shade.
A. viridistriata	*A. auricoma.*	1–2 ft. (2½ ft.) Running.	¼ in.	0°F.	I. Leaves 8 in. long, 1½ in. wide are strikingly variegated green and gold.
Bambusa beecheyana BEECHEY BAMBOO	*Sinocalamus beecheyanus.*	12–20 ft. (20–40 ft.) Clump.	4–5 in.	20°F.	IV. Stems arch strongly for broad, graceful effect. Tropical looking. Scarce.
B. glaucescens	*B. multiplex, B. argentea.*	8–10 ft. (15–25 ft.) Clump.	1½ in.	15°F.	II. Branches from base to top. Dense growth. Hedges, screens. Less common than its varieties described below.
B. g. 'Alphonse Karr' ALPHONSE KARR BAMBOO	*B. verticillata.*	8–10 ft. (15–35 ft.) Clump.	½–1 in.	15°F.	II. Similar to above, but stems are brilliantly striped green on yellow. New stems pinkish and green.
B. g. 'Fernleaf' FERNLEAF BAMBOO	*B. nana, B. disticha.*	6–10 ft. (10–20 ft.) Clump.	½ in.	15°F.	II. Closely spaced leaves, 10-20 to twig, give ferny look. Loses this look, grows coarser with rich soil, ample water.
B. g. 'Golden Goddess' GOLDEN GODDESS BAMBOO	Sometimes sold as *B. falcata.*	6–8 ft. (6–10 ft.) Clump.	½ in.	15°F.	II. Graceful dense, arching growth. Good container or screen plant. Give tops room to spread.
B. g. riviereorum CHINESE GODDESS BAMBOO		4–6 ft. (6–8 ft.) Clump.	¼ in.	15°F.	II. Solid stems arch gracefully. Tiny leaves in lacy, ferny sprays.
B. g. 'Silverstripe'		20 ft. (40 ft.) Clump.	1½ in.	15°F.	II. Most vigorous of hedge bamboo varieties. Leaves have white stripes; occasional white stripes on stems.
B. oldhamii OLDHAM BAMBOO, CLUMPING GIANT TIMBER BAMBOO	*Sinocalamus oldhamii, Dendrocalamus latiflorus.*	15–25 ft. (20–40 ft.) Clump.	3 in.	20°F.	IV. Densely foliaged, erect clumps make it good plant for big, dense screens. Or use single plant for imposing vertical mass. Commonest big bamboo in southern California.
B. tuldoides PUNTING POLE BAMBOO	*B. thouarsii.*	15–20 ft. (20–40 ft.) Clump.	2 in.	20°F.	IV. Prolific producer of slender, erect stems. Best as single plant.
B. ventricosa BUDDHA'S BELLY BAMBOO		3–6 ft. (15–30 ft.) Clump.	2 in.	20°F.	II or IV. Stays small, produces swollen stems that give it its name only when confined in tubs or grown in poor, dryish soil. Otherwise a giant bamboo with straight stems.
Chimonobambusa falcata	*Arundinaria falcata, Bambusa falcata.*	6–10 ft. (20 ft.) Clump.	½–¾ in.	20°F.	II. Rare, attractive bamboo with bluish powdery young stems, velvety ring at joints. Needs shade, withers in hot sun.

(Continued on next page)

NAME	SYNONYMS	CONTROLLED HEIGHT (UNCONTROLLED HEIGHT) AND GROWTH HABIT	STEM DIAMETER	HARD-INESS	COMMENTS (GROWTH HABIT, CHARACTERISTICS, USES)
C. marmorea MARBLED BAMBOO (sometimes sold as "dwarf black bamboo")	*Arundinaria marmorea.*	2–4 ft. (4–6 ft.) Running.	¼ in.	20°F.	III. New stem sheaths marbled cream and purplish. Older stems nearly black. Densely leafy; makes first-class hedge plant if roots are curbed.
C. quadrangularis SQUARE-STEM BAMBOO	*Bambusa quadrangularis.*	10–15 ft. (20–30 ft.) Running.	1 in.	15°F.	III. Squarish stems have prominent joints, carry heavy whorls of branches. Valued for vertical effect.
Phyllostachys aurea GOLDEN BAMBOO		6–10 ft. (10–20 ft.) Running.	2 in.	0°F.	III. Erect, stiff stems, usually with crowded joints at base—good identifying mark. Dense foliage makes it good screen or hedge. Can take much drought, but looks better with ample water. Good in tubs.
P. aureosulcata YELLOW GROOVE BAMBOO		12–15 ft. (15–25 ft.) Running.	1½ in.	−20°F.	III. Like more slender, more open golden bamboo. Young stems green with pronounced yellowish groove. Hardiest bamboo.
P. bambusoides GIANT TIMBER BAMBOO, JAPANESE TIMBER BAMBOO	*P. reticulata.*	15–35 ft. (25–45 ft.) Running.	6 in.	0°F.	IV. Once commonest of large, hardy timber bamboos. Most perished during blooming period in 1960s–1970s. New plants from seed will eventually become available. Makes beautiful groves if lowest branches are trimmed off.
P. b. 'Castillon'	*P. castillonis.*	10–15 ft. (15–20 ft.) Running.	2 in.	0°F.	III. Yellow stems show green stripe above each branch cluster. Bloomed in 1960s, now virtually extinct; a few plants reported recovering.
P. meyeri		10–20 ft. (20–30 ft.) Running.	2 in.	−4°F.	III. Somewhat like golden bamboo, but lacks crowded basal joints. Hardy to cold.
P. nigra BLACK BAMBOO		4–8 ft. (10–15 ft.) Running.	1½ in.	5°F.	III. New stems green, turning black in second year (rarely olive green dotted black). Best in afternoon shade where summers are hot.
P. pubescens MOSO BAMBOO	*P. edulis.*	20–40 ft. (40–60 ft.) Running.	8 in.	5°F.	IV. Largest of running timber bamboos. Gray green, heavy stems; small feathery foliage. Rare and hard to establish.
Pseudosasa japonica METAKE, ARROW BAMBOO	*Arundinaria japonica.*	6–10 ft. (10–18 ft.) Running.	¾ in.	0°F.	III. Stiffly erect stems with one branch at each joint. Leaves large, with long pointed tails. Rampant thick hedge in mild winter climates; slow spreader where winters are cold, making dense, erect clumps.
Sasa palmata PALMATE BAMBOO	Sometimes sold as *S. senanensis.*	4–5 ft. (8–12 ft.) Running.	⅜ in.	0°F.	In class by itself. Grows bigger in Zones 4–6 and 15–17 than in 18–24. Broad, handsome leaves (to 15 in. long by 4 in. wide) spread fingerlike from stem and branch tips. Rampant spreader; curb it.
S. tessellata	*Arundinaria ragamowskii.*	2–3 ft. (3–6 ft.) Running.	¼ in.	0°F.	Resembles *S. palmata*, but much lower growth, much longer leaves (to 2 ft.). Slow spreader, best in shade. Rare.
S. veitchii		2–3 ft. Running.	¼ in.	0°F.	I. Rampant spreader with large (7 in. by 1 in.) dark green leaves that turn whitish buff all around edges in autumn for variegated effect. Appropriate in Japanese gardens if curbed.
Semiarundinaria fastuosa NARIHIRA BAMBOO		8–10 ft. (12–25 ft.) Running.	1¼ in.	−4°F.	II or III. Rigidly upright growth. Slow spreader easily kept to a clump. Planted closely makes tall, narrow dense hedge or windbreak.
Shibataea kumasaca		2–3 ft. (5–6 ft.) Running.	¼ in.	10°F.	III. Slow spreading, makes compact clumps of unbamboolike appearance. Leaves are short and broad (4 in. long, 1 in. wide), distinctly stalked. Needs acid soil.

NAME	SYNONYMS	CONTROLLED HEIGHT (UNCONTROLLED HEIGHT) AND GROWTH HABIT	STEM DIAMETER	HARD-INESS	COMMENTS (GROWTH HABIT, CHARACTERISTICS, USES)
Sinarundinaria murielae		6–8 ft. (15 ft.) Clump.	½ in.	0°F.	III. Remarkable as fairly hardy clumping bamboo. Light, airy, graceful narrow clump arching and drooping at top.
S. nitida		6–8 ft. (15–20 ft.) Clump.	¾ in.	0°F.	III. Resembles *S. murielae* but has greenish purple stems that mature to deep purplish black. Needs shade to look its best. Rare.
Yushania aztecorum	*Arthrostylidium longifolium.*	8–10 ft. (20 ft.) Clump.	½ in.	20°F.	III. Extremely narrow leaves (6 in. by ⅛ in.) give lacy look. Foliage masses bend nearly to ground. Rare.

bamboos: dig foot-deep trench around plant and sever any rhizomes that grow into it; trench will fill with loose mulch of bamboo leaves. Sift through leaves with gloved hands to find roving rhizomes.

Scale, mealybug, and aphids are occasionally found on bamboo but seldom do any harm; if they secrete honeydew in bothersome amounts, spray with malathion.

The chart classes each bamboo by habit of growth, which, of course, determines its use in the garden. In **Group I** are the dwarf or low-growing ground cover types. These can be used for erosion control or (carefully confined in a long section of flue tile) as small clumps for border or rock garden. **Group II** includes clump bamboos with fountainlike habit of growth. These have widest use in landscaping. They require no more space than average strong-growing shrub. Clipped, they make hedges or screens that won't spread much into surrounding soil; unclipped, they may be lined up as informal screens or grown singly to show off their graceful form.

Bamboos in **Group III** are running bamboos of moderate size and more or less vertical growth. Use them as screens, hedges, or (curbed) alone. **Group IV** includes the giants. Use running kinds for groves, oriental effects on grand scale. Clumping kinds have tropical look, especially if used with broad-leafed tropical plants. All may be thinned and clipped to show off stems. Thin clumps or groves by cutting out old or dead stems at base.

Some of the smaller bamboos bloom on some of their stalks every year and continue to grow. Some bloom partially and at erratic intervals. Some have never been known to bloom. Others bloom heavily, set seed, and die. Giant timber bamboo (*Phyllostachys bambusoides*) and other species of *Phyllostachys* bloom at rare intervals of 30–60 years, produce flowers for a long period, and become enfeebled. They may recover very slowly or die. There is evidence that very heavy feeding and watering may speed their recovery.

Not recommended for year-round indoor culture, but container-grown plants can spend extended periods indoors in cool, bright rooms. Revive plants by taking them outdoors, but avoid sudden changes in temperature, light.

There are several ways to eliminate unwanted bamboo. Digging it out with mattock and spade is sometimes difficult, but is surest. Rhizomes are generally not deep, but they may be widespread. Remove them all or regrowth will occur. Starve out roots by cutting off all shoots before they exceed 2 feet in height; repeat as needed—probably many times over the course of a year. Contact foliage sprays that kill leaves have the same effect as removing stems. Translocation weed killers that move through leaves to roots are effective. You can paint weed killer on fresh new sprouts with a paint brush. Soil fumigation will kill plants. Repeat treatment may be necessary with any chemical treatment. Avoid injury to foliage or roots of desirable plants.

BAMBURANTA. See *Ctenanthe compressa, Hybophrynium braunianum.*

BAMBUSA. See Bamboo.

BANANA. See *Musa, Ensete.*

BANANA SHRUB. See *Michelia figo.*

BAPTISIA australis. FALSE INDIGO, WILD INDIGO. Perennial. All Zones. Native to eastern and southern U.S. Somewhat like bush lupine in habit, 3–6 ft. tall, with bluish green, deeply cut leaves. Spikes of small indigo blue, sweet pea shaped blooms in early summer, followed by inflated seed pods—both interesting in arrangements. Full sun, ordinary soil. Tap rooted, stands drought. Cut back spent flowers for repeat bloom. Specialists carry seed.

Baptisia australis

BARBADOS PRIDE. See *Caesalpinia pulcherrima.*

BARBERRY. See *Berberis.*

BARREL CACTUS. See *Echinocactus, Ferocactus.*

BASEBALL PLANT. See *Euphorbia obesa.*

BASIL. See *Ocimum.*

BASKET FLOWER. See *Hymenocallis narcissiflora.*

BASKET-OF-GOLD. See *Aurinia saxatilis.*

BASSWOOD. See *Tilia americana.*

BAUHINIA. Evergreen or deciduous trees or half-climbing shrubs. These flamboyant flowering plants have very special place in Hawaii, mild-winter areas of California, and Arizona. They vary greatly by species and climate vagaries. Common to all garden bauhinias are twin "leaves" (actually twin lobes). Need sun, warmth, moderate water.

B. blakeana. HONG KONG ORCHID TREE. Partially deciduous for short period. Zones 19, 21, 23. Native to southern China. Its flowers, shaped like some orchids, range from cranberry maroon through rose, purple, to orchid pink, often in same blossoms. They are much larger (5½–6 in. wide) than those of other bauhinias; unlike others, they appear in autumn and early winter. Gray green leaves tend to drop off around bloom time but not completely. Umbrella-type growth habit; to 20 ft. high.

Bauhinia forficata

B. forficata. (Often sold as *B. corniculata* or *B. candicans.*) Evergreen to deciduous large shrub or tree. Zones 9, 12–23. Native to Brazil. Probably hardiest bauhinia. Creamy white flowers to 3 in. wide, with narrow petals in spring and through summer. Deep green leaves, more pointed lobes than others. Grows to 20 ft., often with twisting, leaning trunk, picturesque angled branches. Short sharp thorns at branch joints. Good canopy patio tree. In hot dry weather blooms tend to shrivel during day. Avoid by giving it some afternoon shade.

B. punctata *(B. galpinii).* RED BAUHINIA. Evergreen to semideciduous shrub. Zones 13, 18–23. Native to South and tropical Africa. Brick red to orange flowers, spectacular as bougainvillea where adapted. Sprawling, half climbing with 15-ft. spread. Best as espalier on warm wall. With hard pruning can make splendid flowering bonsai for large pot or box.

B. variegata. (Commonly sold as *B. purpurea.*) PURPLE ORCHID TREE. Partially to wholly deciduous. Zones 13, 18–23. Native to India, China. Most frequently planted. Hardy to 22°F. Spectacular street trees where spring weather is warm and stays warm. Wonderful show of light pink to orchid purple, broad petaled, 2–3-in.-wide flowers usually January to April. Light green, broadly lobed leaves generally drop in midwinter. Produces huge crop of beans after blooming; messy looking. Trim them off if you wish—trimming brings new growth earlier. Inclined to grow as shrub with multiple stems. Staked and pruned, it becomes attractive tree 20–35 ft. high.

B. v. 'Candida'. WHITE ORCHID TREE. Has white flowers, otherwise like *B. variegata*.

BAY. See *Laurus, Umbellularia californica.*

BAYBERRY. See *Myrica pensylvanica.*

BEACH ASTER. See *Erigeron glaucus.*

BEACH WORMWOOD. See *Artemisia stellerana.*

BEAD PLANT. See *Nertera granadensis.*

BEAN, BROAD. Also called "fava" or "horse bean." This bean (actually a giant vetch) was known in ancient and medieval times; it is a Mediterranean plant, while all other familiar beans are New World plants. It is an annual of bushy growth to 2–4 ft. See climate restrictions below. Best known in coastal climates. You can cook and eat immature pods like sugar-podded peas; prepare immature and mature seeds in same way as green or dry limas.

Unlike true beans, this is cool-season plant. In cold-winter areas plant as early in spring as soil can be worked. In mild coastal climates, plant in fall for late winter or early spring ripening. Matures in 120–150 days, depending on temperature. Plant seeds 1 in. deep at 4–5-in. intervals and thin to 8–10 in. apart in rows. Space rows 18–30 in. apart. Spray or dust for aphids.

Fava Bean

Most people eat fava beans with safety; a very few (principally of Mediterranean ancestry) have a genetic enzyme deficiency that can cause severe reactions to the beans and even the pollen.

BEAN, DRY. Annual. Same culture as bush form of snap bean. Let beans remain on bush until pods turn dry or begin to shatter, thresh them from hulls, dry, store to be soaked and cooked later. 'Pinto', 'Red Kidney', and 'White Marrowfat' are this kind.

Dry Bean

BEAN, LIMA. Annual. Like snap or string beans (which they resemble), limas come either in bush or vine (pole) form. They develop slower than string beans, bush types requiring 65–75 days, pole kinds 78–95 days; and they do not produce as reliably in extremely dry, hot weather. They must be shelled before cooking—a tedious chore, but worth it if you like fresh limas. Among bush types 'Burpee's Improved Bush', 'Henderson Bush', and 'Fordhook 242' are outstanding; the last two are especially useful in hot-summer areas. 'Prizetaker' and 'King of the Garden' are fine large-seeded climbing forms; 'Small White Lima' or 'Sieva' is usually grown for drying, but it gives heavy yields of green shelled beans. Culture is same as for snap beans.

Lima Bean

BEAN, SCARLET RUNNER. Annual twining vines. Showy and ornamental with bright scarlet flowers in slender clusters, and with bright green leaves divided into 3 roundish, 3–5-in.-long leaflets. Use to cover fences, arbors, outbuildings; for quick shade on porches, summer cottages.

Flowers are followed by flattened, very dark green pods which are edible and tasty when young, but which toughen as they reach full size. Beans can be shelled from older pods for cooking like green limas. Culture is same as for snap beans.

Scarlet Runner Bean

BEAN, SNAP. Annual. The snap (or string, or green) bean is most widely planted and most useful for home gardens of all the kinds of beans. These have tender, fleshy pods with little fiber. They may be green, yellow (wax beans), or purple ('Royalty'). Purple kinds turn green in cooking. Plants grow as self-supporting bushes or as climbing vines (pole beans). Bush types bear earlier, but vines are more productive. Varieties are too numerous to discuss. Plants resemble scarlet runner bean, but white or purple flowers are not showy.

Snap Bean

Plant seeds as soon as soil is warm, in full sun and good soil. These seeds must push heavy seed leaves through soil, so see that it is reasonably loose and open. Plant seeds of bush types an inch deep and 1–3 in. apart in rows, with 2–3 ft. between rows. Pole beans can be managed in a number of ways: set 3 or 4 poles in the ground and tie together at top in wigwam fashion; or set single poles 3 or 4 ft. apart and sow 6 or 8 beans around each, thinning to 3 or 4 strongest seedlings; or insert poles 1 or 2 ft. apart in rows and sow seeds as you would bush beans; or sow along sunny wall, fence, or trellis and train vines on web of light string supported by wire or heavy twine. Moisten ground thoroughly before planting; do not water again until seedlings have emerged.

Once growth starts, keep soil moist. Occasional deep soaking is preferable to frequent light sprinklings which may encourage mildew. Feed after plants are in active growth and again when pods start to form. Pods are ready in 50–70 days, according to variety. Pick every 5–7 days; if pods mature, plants will stop bearing. Control aphids and diabrotica (spotted cucumber beetle) with rotenone or all-purpose vegetable garden dust. Check whiteflies with malathion spray, following precautions on label concerning harvest date.

BEARBERRY. See *Arctostaphylos uva-ursi.*

BEARD TONGUE. See *Penstemon.*

BEAR'S BREECH. See *Acanthus mollis.*

BEAR'S FOOT FERN. See *Humata tyermannii.*

BEAUCARNEA recurvata. PONYTAIL, BOT-
TLE PALM. Succulent shrub or tree. House
plant anywhere, hardy Zones 13, 16–24 (but
note cautions below). Base of stem is
greatly swollen; in young plants it resembles big onion sitting on soil. On old trees
in ground it can be woody mass several feet
across. Trunk is at first single, later sparsely
branched. Leaves cluster at ends of
branches in dense tufts; arching and
drooping, they measure 3 ft. or more in
length, ¾ inch wide. Very old trees may
produce inconspicuous clusters of creamy
white flowers.

Outdoors give them sun, well-drained
soil, and infrequent deep watering. They do
exceptionally well as house plants when
given good light and not overwatered. Ma-
ture plants have endured temperatures to 18°F.; young plants in
containers freeze to death in the low 20s. Plants moved from
indoors to permanent garden locations outdoors should have
gradually increasing exposure to sun and low temperatures to
make the transition.

*Beaucarnea
recurvata*

BEAUMONTIA grandiflora. HERALD'S TRUM-
PET, EASTER LILY VINE. Evergreen vine.
Zones 12, 13, 16–17, 21–24. Climbs by arching, semitwining branches to as much as 30
ft., and spreads as wide. Large, dark green,
6–9-in., oval to roundish leaves, smooth
and shiny above, slightly downy beneath,
furnish lush tropical look. From April until
September it carries fragrant, trumpet
shaped, 5-in.-long, white, green-veined
flowers which look like Easter lilies.

Needs deep, rich soil, ample water, and
heavy feeding. Prune after flowering to
keep it in scale, but preserve good propor-
tion of 2 and 3-year-old wood. Flowers are not borne on new
growth. Makes big espalier on warm wall, sheltered from wind.
Or train along eaves of house; give it a sturdy support. Good
near swimming pools. Hardy to 28°F.

*Beaumontia
grandiflora*

BEAUTYBERRY. See *Callicarpa bodinieri giraldii.*

BEAUTY BUSH. See *Kolkwitzia amabilis.*

BEE BALM. See *Monarda.*

BEECH. See *Fagus.*

BEEFWOOD. See *Casuarina.*

BEET. Biennial grown as annual. To have
fresh beets throughout summer, plant
seeds in short rows at monthly intervals,
starting as soon as soil can be worked in
spring. Best in sun; where summers are
very hot, plant to mature before or after extreme summer heat. Cover seeds with ¼ in.
of compost, sand, or vermiculite to prevent
caking. Sow seeds 1 in. apart; thin to 2 in.
while plants are small, using thinnings—
tops and roots—for food. To keep roots
tender, water frequently in dry weather.
Feed plants at 3–4 week intervals for
speedy growth. Begin harvesting when
beets are 1 in. wide; complete harvesting

Beet

before beets exceed 3 in.—larger ones are woody.

Round red varieties include 'Detroit Dark Red' and 'Crosby's
Egyptian' (old favorites) and many newer varieties. Novelties include 'Cylindra' and 'Forma Nova' (long cylindrical roots); there
are golden yellow and white varieties.

BEGONIA. Perennials, sometimes shrubby,
grown for textured, multicolored foliage,
saucer-sized flowers, and/or lacy clusters
of smaller flowers. Outdoors, most grow
best in pots in the ground, or in hanging
baskets in filtered shade with rich, porous,
fast-draining soil, consistent but light feeding, and enough water to keep soil moist
but not soggy. Most thrive as indoor plants,
in greenhouse, or under lath. Some prefer
terrarium conditions. Almost all require at
least moderate humidity. (During hot, dry
summers, misting may be necessary.)

Most can be propagated easily from leaf,
stem, or rhizome cuttings. They also grow
from dust-fine seed. Of the many hundreds
of species and varieties, relatively few are
sold widely. In the list below, you'll find the
most widely grown begonias. Enthusiasts obtain others from
specialty dealers, at American Begonia Society sales, and from
the ABS seed fund.

*Begonia
tuberhybrida*

The society classifies begonias by grouping them according
to growth habit, which coincidentally groups them by their care
needs. The following list uses a version of the society's classifications to replace such outdated misnomers as "fibrous,"
"tuberous-rooted," and "wax begonias."

Cane-type begonias. They get their name from their stems,
whict grow tall and woody with prominent bamboolike joints.
The group includes so-called "angel-wing" begonias. Plants are
erect with multiple stems, some reaching 5 ft. or more under the
right conditions. Most bloom profusely with large clusters of
white, pink, orange, or red flowers early spring through autumn.
Some are everblooming. When roots fill 4-inch pots, plants can
be placed in large containers or in the ground where they will
get plenty of light, some sun, and no wind. They may require
staking or a trellis. Protect from heavy frosts. Old canes that
have grown barren should be pruned to 2 leaf joints in early
spring to stimulate new growth.

B. 'Irene Nuss' (often sold as 'Irene Ness'). Fragrant coral pink
flowers in drooping clusters from April to December. Leaves
large, dark green.

B. 'Lucerna' ('Corallina de Lucerna', sometimes sold as
'Lucerne'). Tall plant with rose red flowers in spring and summer
and silver-spotted leaves. Easy to grow.

B. 'Sophie Cecile'. Clusters of rose-pink flowers in spring and
summer are profuse on this favorite with large, deeply cut,
glossy green leaves splashed with silver.

B. 'Orange Rubra'. Clusters of orange flowers on 4-ft.-tall
plant with silver-dotted green leaves.

Hiemalis begonias. Some called "Rieger begonias." These
profuse bloomers make outstanding house plants. The numerous flowers average about 2 in. across and appear over a long
season that includes winter. When plants are well grown, green
leaves and stems are all but invisible underneath a blanket of
bloom. Give these bushy, compact plants plenty of light in
winter. In summer, keep out of hot noonday sun. Water
thoroughly when top inch of soil is dry. Don't sprinkle leaves. If
powdery mildew appears, control with benomyl. Plant may get
rangy, an indication of approaching dormancy. In this case, cut
stems to 4-in. stubs.

Rex begonias. Bold, multicolored leaves make these probably
the most striking of all foliage begonias. While many named
varieties are grown by collectors, easier-to-find unnamed seedling plants are almost equally decorative. The leaves grow from a
rhizome, a usually creeping kind of stem. See Rhizomatous begonias for care. In addition, rex begonias should get high humidity (at least 50 percent) to do their best. Provide it by misting with
a spray bottle, placing pot on wet pebbles in a tray, or keeping

(Continued on next page)

plants in greenhouse. When rhizome grows too far past edge of pot for your taste, either repot into slightly larger container or cut off rhizome end inside pot edge. Old rhizome will branch and grow new leaves. Make rhizome cuttings of the piece you remove and root in mixture of half peat moss-half perlite.

B. 'Helen Teupel'. Bronze red and silver-green leaves. Flowers are light pink.

B. 'Merry Christmas'. Green and rose-red leaves have silver highlights. Sold widely, but finicky about water and humidity.

Rex begonia

Rhizomatous begonias. Like rex begonias, these grow from a rhizome, a usually creeping stem-type structure at or near soil level. Although some have handsome flowers, they are grown primarily for foliage, which varies in color and texture among species and varieties. The group includes so-called "star begonias," named for their leaf shape. Rhizomatous begonias perform well as house plants when given bright light through a window and watered only when the top inch or so of soil is dry. Plant them in wide, shallow pots. They flower from winter through summer, the season varying among specific plants. White to pink flowers appear in clusters on erect stems above the foliage. Rhizomes will grow over edge and eventually form ball shaped plant. Leave or, if you wish, cut rhizomes back to the pot. The old rhizome will branch and grow new leaves. Root the pieces of rhizome in a medium of half peat moss-half perlite.

B. bowerae. Tiny, deep green leaves with black "stitching" on edges. Profuse with shell-pink blooms January through March.

B. 'Cleopatra' ('Maphil'). Popular, easily grown "star begonia" with star-shaped leaves marked brown with chartreuse veins. Red undersides. Pink flowers profuse in winter and early spring.

B. 'Erythrophylla'. BEEFSTEAK BEGONIA. Widely grown plant with dark green, roundish leaves. Undersides deep red. Plant can grow to several feet across. Flowers pink. Variety 'Helix' has spiraled leaves. Variety 'Bunchii' has lettuce like frills and ruffles on leaf edges.

B. 'Freddie'. Old favorite as a house plant, this large-leafed variety is coppery-green with red undersides. Tall sprays of pink flowers appear nearly year-round.

B. 'Joe Hayden'. Small leaves satiny dark green with red undersides. Winter flowers are red.

B. masoniana. IRON CROSS BEGONIA. Large puckered leaves known for chocolate brown pattern resembling Maltese cross on green background. Flowers insignificant.

Semperflorens begonias. BEDDING BEGONIAS. These tough plants used to be called "wax begonias." Grown in garden beds or containers as if annuals, they produce lots of small flowers spring through fall in a white-through-red range. In mild climates, can overwinter, live for years. Foliage can be green, red, bronze, or variegated. Very useful western garden plant. Thrives in full sun along coast. Prefers broken shade inland, but dark-foliaged kinds will take sun if well watered. F_1 hybrid strains (Butterfly, Cinderella, Glamour) are more uniform, sun tolerant, and large flowered—as much as 3 in. across.

B. 'Calla King' and **B. 'Calla Lily'.** Varieties with variegated green and white leaves. First has pink-and-white flowers, second red flowers.

B. 'Charm'. Large green leaves splotched with gold markings. Pink flowers. Easy to grow. Makes good hanging basket.

Shrublike begonias. This large class is marked by multiple stems which are soft and green rather than bamboolike as in the cane-type group. They are grown both for foliage and flowers. Leaves are very interesting—some are heavily textured; others grow white or red "hairs"; and still others develop a soft, feltlike coating. Most grow upright and bushy, but others are less erect and make suitable hanging basket subjects. Flowers in shades of pink, red, white, and peach can come anytime depending on species or variety. Care consists of repotting into larger container as the plant outgrows its pot. Some shrub like begonias can get very large—as tall as 8 ft. They require ample moisture—water when soil begins to dry on surface. Prune to shape; pinch tips to encourage branching.

B. foliosa. Inch-long leaves packed tightly on twiggy plant give fernlike look. Stems arch or droop to 3 ft. Flowers are small, white to red.

B. 'Medora'. This old favorite has small wavy green leaves with silver spots on many long stems. Pink flowers appear spring through fall.

B. 'Richmondensis'. Exceeds 2 ft. tall with arching stems that contain shiny, crisp leaves deep green with red undersides. Salmon pink flowers develop from darker buds. Big and sturdy. Good for narrow space with limited light.

Trailing or climbing begonias. These have stems that trail or climb depending on how you train them. They are suited to hanging basket culture or planting in the ground where well protected.

B. 'Ellen Dee'. Green foliage, orange flowers.

B. solananthera. Glossy, light green leaves, fragrant white flowers with red centers.

Tuberous begonias. Among the best-known in the West are these magnificent large-flowered hybrids that grow from a tuber. Types range from ones with a few upright stems and saucer-sized flowers to multistemmed hanging basket types covered with flowers. Except for some rare types, they are summer and fall-blooming in almost any flower color except blue. Buy dormant tubers in early February, the bigger the better. Place in shallow flats and barely cover with coarse organic matter such as leaf mold. Water regularly and keep in broken shade or under lights indoors. As each plant reaches 3 in. high, repot into 8–10-in. pot with rich, humusy, fast-draining soil mix. For upright types, insert a stake or two at that time, being careful not to pierce the tuber. Water to keep soil moist, but not soggy. If leaves yellow, you are overwatering. Fertilize weekly with quarter-strength high-nitrogen fertilizer until mid-May, when you should switch to a program alternating bloom fertilizer with complete fertilizer. Grow in filtered shade, such as under lath or in the open with eastern exposure. For best bloom, mist with water several times a day unless you live in foggy coastal area. Watch for fuzzy white spots on leaves which signal powdery mildew. Control with karathane; prevent with benomyl. In fall, when leaves begin to yellow and wilt, reduce watering. When stems have fallen off the plant on their own, lift the tuber, shake the dirt off, dry it in the sun for 3 days, and store in cool, dry place with its label until spring, when little pink buds will become visible. Then begin the process over. In April and May, you can buy small seedling plants and plant them directly in pots.

Pacific strain. Upright plants have large flowers in shades of white, pink, red, yellow, peach. Flower shapes resemble roses or carnations, are ruffled or have petal edges of contrasting color. Hanging basket plants are profuse with smaller flowers in same color range. Pinching produces more branches and flowers.

Multiflora begonias. Bushy, compact plants 12–18 in. tall. Profuse bloom in carmine, scarlet, orange, yellow, apricot, salmon, pink. Includes **B. 'Nonstop'.**

Bertinii hybrids. Similar in form to multifloras with flowers of pink, red, coral orange. Good in Southern California.

BELAMCANDA chinensis. BLACKBERRY LILY. Perennial with rhizome. All Zones. Common name derives from cluster of shining black seeds exposed when capsules split. Sword shaped, irislike leaves 1 in. wide. Flowers 1½–2 in. across, orange dotted with red, on 2–3-ft. branching stems; bloom over long period in August, September. Sun or part shade, average water. Plant rhizomes 1 in. deep in porous soil. Effective in clumps in border. Seed capsules make unique arrangements.

Belamcanda chinensis

BELLADONNA LILY. See *Amaryllis belladonna*.

BELLFLOWER. See *Campanula*.

BELL-FRUITED MALLEE. See *Eucalyptus preissiana*.

BELLIS perennis. ENGLISH DAISY. Perennial, often treated as an annual for winter-spring bloom in hot-summer areas. All Zones. Native to Europe and Mediterranean region. The original English daisies are the kind you often see growing in lawns. Plump, fully double ones sold in nurseries are horticultural varieties. Rosettes of dark green leaves 1–2 in. long. Pink, rose, red, or white double flowers on 3–6-in. stems, in spring, early summer. Meadow plant; needs good soil, much moisture, light shade in warm areas, full sun near coast. Edging or low bedding plant; effective with spring bulbs.

Bellis perennis

BELLS-OF-IRELAND. See *Moluccella laevis.*

BELOPERONE. See *Justicia.*

BENT, BENT GRASS. See *Agrostis.*

BERBERIS. BARBERRY. Deciduous and evergreen shrubs. Zones 1–11, 14–17. Approximate hardiness for each species, deciduous and evergreen, is given in descriptions below. Ability of barberries, especially the deciduous species, to take punishment in climate and soil extremes makes them worth attention in all "hard" climates. Barberries require no more than ordinary garden care. Give sun or light shade, average water. Vigorous growers can take a lot of cutting back for growth renewal. Left to their own ways, some of the inner branches die and plant becomes ratty. In list below, details on time of bloom, flower color, and spines are omitted unless plant differs from typical—yellow flowers in spring and spiny branches.

Berberis darwinii

B. buxifolia. MAGELLAN BARBERRY. Evergreen. Hardy to 0°F. Rather rigid upright growth to 6 ft., and as wide. Leaves small, leathery, to 1 in. long. Flowers orange yellow. Berries dark purple, 1 or 2 at each leaf cluster.

B. b. nana. To 1½ ft. high and 2 ft. wide. Use as traffic regulator or where yellow bloom in evergreen is important. (There is an even lower-growing variety, 'Pygmaea'.)

B. chenaultii. Evergreen. Hardy to 0°F. Slow-growing, low (to 4 ft.), with arching branches. Leaves dark green, spine toothed, 1–1½ in. long. Flowers bright yellow. Low barrier hedge, foreground planting.

B. darwinii. DARWIN BARBERRY. Evergreen. Hardy to 10°F. Showiest barberry. Fountainlike growth to 5–10 ft. high and 4–7 ft. wide. Leaves small (1 in.), crisp, dark green, hollylike. Orange yellow flowers are so thick along branches that it's difficult to see foliage. Berries dark blue and numerous—popular with birds. Wonderful as background for Oregon grape (*Mahonia aquifolium*). Spreads by underground runners.

B. gladwynensis 'William Penn'. Evergreen, partially deciduous around 0°–10°F. Resembles *B. julianae* in size and general effect, but with broader, glossier leaves; faster growing. Good show of bright yellow flowers.

B. irwinii (*B. stenophylla irwinii*). Hybrid. Evergreen. Hardy to 0°F. Graceful fountainlike growth habit to 18 in. high. Attractive dark green foliage of narrow 1-in.-long leaves.

B. julianae. WINTERGREEN BARBERRY. Evergreen or semi-deciduous. Hardy to 0°F., but foliage damaged by winter cold. Dense, upright, to 6 ft., with slightly angled branches. Very leathery, spiny-toothed, 3-in.-long, dark green leaves. Fruit bluish black. Reddish fall color. One of thorniest—formidable as barrier hedge.

B. mentorensis. Hybrid. Evergreen to about −5°F. Semi-deciduous to deciduous in colder weather. Hardy to −20°F. Stands hot dry weather. Rather compact growth to 7 ft. and as wide. Easy to maintain as hedge at any height. Leaves dark

green, 1 in. long, beautiful red fall color in cold climates. Berries dull dark red.

B. stenophylla. ROSEMARY BARBERRY. Evergreen garden hybrids. Hardy to 0°F. Leaves narrow, ½–1 in. long, with inrolled edges, spiny tip. Of many varieties, best known are 'Corallina Compacta', coral barberry, 18 in. tall, with nodding clusters of bright orange flowers. Rock garden, foreground.

B. thunbergii. JAPANESE BARBERRY. Deciduous. Hardy to −20°F. Graceful growth habit with slender, arching, spiny branches, usually to 4–6 ft. tall with equal spread, if not sheared. Densely foliaged with roundish, ½–1½-in.-long leaves, deep green above, paler beneath, turning to yellow, orange, and red before they fall. Beadlike, bright red berries stud branches in fall and through winter. Hedge, barrier planting, or single shrub.

B. t. 'Atropurpurea'. RED-LEAF JAPANESE BARBERRY. Foliage bronzy red to purplish red all summer. Must have sun to develop color.

B. t. 'Aurea'. Bright golden yellow foliage, best in full sun. Will tolerate light shade. Slow-growing to 18–24 in.

B. t. 'Crimson Pygmy' (*B. t.* 'Atropurpurea Nana'). Hardy to −10°F. Selected miniature form, generally less than 1½ ft. high and 2½ ft. wide as 10-yr.-old. Mature leaves bronzy blood red, new leaves bright red. Must have sun to develop color.

B. t. 'Kobold'. Extra-dwarf bright green variety of Japanese barberry. Like 'Crimson Pygmy' in habit but fuller, rounder.

B. t. 'Rose Glow'. New foliage marbled bronzy red and pinkish white, deepening to rose and bronze. Colors best in full sun or lightest shade.

B. verruculosa. WARTY BARBERRY. Evergreen. Hardy to 0°F. Neat tailored shrub with informal elegance. Can reach 3–4 ft. tall, but can be held to 18 in. without becoming clumpy. Perky, glossy dark green, 1-in.-long leaves are whitish beneath. In fall and winter a red leaf develops as highlight here and there in green foliage. Berries black with purplish bloom. Very choice and easy to use on banks, in foreground of shrubbery, or in front of leggy rhododendrons or azaleas.

B. wilsoniae. WILSON BARBERRY. Deciduous to nearly evergreen in mild climates. Hardy to 5°F. Moderate growth to 6 ft. high and as wide, but can be held to 3–4 ft. hedge. Fine-textured foliage, with light green, roundish, ½–1 in. leaves. Small yellow flowers in dense clusters. Beautiful coral to salmon red berries. Handsome barrier hedge.

BERCKMAN DWARF ARBORVITAE. See *Platycladus orientalis.*

BERGENIA. Perennials. Evergreen except in coldest areas. Zones 1–9, 14–24. Member of saxifrage family, native to Himalayas and mountains of China. Thick rootstocks; large, glossy green leaves. Thick leafless stalks, 12–18 in. high, bear graceful nodding clusters of small white, pink, or rose flowers. Ornamental foliage an all-year asset. Strong, substantial textural quality in borders, under trees, as bold-patterned ground cover. Effective with ferns, hellebores, hostas, as foreground planting for *Fatsia japonica*, aucubas, rhododendrons.

Bergenia crassifolia

Best performance in partial shade but will take full sun in cool coastal climates. *B. cordifolia* and *B. crassifolia* endure neglect, poor soil, cold, but respond to good soil, regular watering, grooming. Established plants in shade fairly drought tolerant. Cut back yearly to prevent legginess. Divide crowded clumps, replant vigorous divisions. Bait for snails and slugs.

B. ciliata (*B. ligulata*). Choicest, most elegant. To 1 ft. Lustrous, light green leaves to 12 in. long and wide; smooth on edges but fringed with soft hairs; young leaves bronzy. Flowers white, rose, or purplish, bloom late spring, summer. Slightly tender; leaves burn in severe frost.

B. cordifolia. HEARTLEAF BERGENIA. Leaves glossy, roundish, heart shaped at base, with wavy-toothed edges. Spring-blooming rose or lilac flowers in pendulous clusters partially hidden by large leaves. Plant grows to 20 in.

B. crassifolia. WINTER-BLOOMING BERGENIA. Best known. Leaves dark green, 8 in. or more across, slightly toothed, and wavy on edges. Flowers rose, lilac, or purple, in dense clusters on erect stems standing well above leaves. Plants 20 in. high. Blooms January, February.

B. hybrids. With searching, connoisseurs may find named hybrids like 'Ballawley' (purple crimson flowers, 9-in. leaves); 'Evening Glow' and 'Sunningdale' (magenta flowers, maroon winter foliage); or 'Silver Light' (white flowers, hardier than *B. ciliata*).

BERMUDA, BERMUDA GRASS. See *Cynodon*.

BERMUDA BUTTERCUP. See *Oxalis pes-caprae*.

BETHLEHEM SAGE. See *Pulmonaria saccharata*.

BETULA. BIRCH. Deciduous trees. The white-barked European white birch has relatives that resemble it in graceful habit and in the small-scale, finely toothed leaves, but which vary in size and bark color. All birches need ample water at all times and a regular feeding program. All are susceptible to aphids that drip honeydew and for that reason are not trees for a patio or to park a car under. Generally too greedy for lawns. Poor tolerance of drought. On all birches, small conelike fruit hang on branches through the winter.

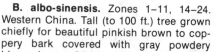

Betula pendula

B. albo-sinensis. Zones 1–11, 14–24. Western China. Tall (to 100 ft.) tree grown chiefly for beautiful pinkish brown to coppery bark covered with gray powdery bloom. Leaves 3 in. long. Variety *B. a.-s. septentrionalis* has flaking bark that is orange to orange brown. Rare.

B. jacquemontii. Zones 3–11, 14–17. Northern India. Tall narrow tree with brilliant white bark.

B. nigra. RIVER BIRCH, RED BIRCH. All Zones. Native to eastern half of the United States. Very fast growth in first years. Eventually to 50–90 ft. Pyramidal form. Trunk often forks near ground, but tree can be trained to single stem. Young bark is pinkish, very smooth and shining. On older trees it flakes and curls in cinnamon brown to blackish sheets. Diamond shaped leaves, 1–3 in. long, are bright glossy green above, silvery below. Needs ample moisture.

B. occidentalis (*B. fontinalis*). Zones 1–3, 10. Large shrub or clumping small tree to 12–15 ft. Bark smooth, shiny, cinnamon brown. Leaves 2 in. long, turning pale clear yellow in fall. A native streamside tree, it likes moisture but needs good drainage as well.

B. papyrifera. CANOE BIRCH, PAPER BIRCH. Zones 1–6. Native to northern part of North America. Similar to European white birch but tree is taller (to 100 ft.), more open, less weeping. Trunk creamy white. Bark peels off in papery layers. Leaves are larger (to 4 in. long), more sparsely borne.

B. pendula. EUROPEAN WHITE BIRCH. Zones 1–11, 14–24. Native from Europe to Asia Minor. Probably most frequently planted deciduous tree in West. Delicate and lacy. Upright branching with weeping side branches. Average mature tree 30–40 ft. high, spreading to half its height. Bark on twigs and young branches is golden brown. Bark on trunk and main limbs becomes white, marked with black clefts; oldest bark at base is blackish gray. Rich green glossy leaves to 2½ in. long, diamond shaped, with slender tapered point. Often sold as weeping birch, although trees vary somewhat in habit, and young trees show little inclination to weep.

European white birch has many uses. Its form and color are enhanced by dark background of pines. Dramatic when nightlighted. Lends itself to planting in grove formation, some single, some grouped. Trees of unequal sizes and planted with unequal spacing look more natural. Trees grown in clumps of several trunks are available.

B. p. 'Dalecarlica' (*B. pendula* 'Laciniata'). CUTLEAF WEEPING BIRCH. Leaves deeply cut. Branches strongly weeping; graceful open tree. Weeping forms are more affected by dry hot weather than species. Foliage shows stress by late summer.

B. p. 'Fastigiata' (*B. alba* 'Fastigiata'). PYRAMIDAL WHITE BIRCH. Branches upright; habit somewhat like Lombardy poplar. Excellent screening tree.

B. p. 'Purpurea' (*B. alba* 'Purpurea'). PURPLE BIRCH. Twigs purple black. New foliage rich purple maroon, fading to purplish green in summer; striking effect against white bark. Best in cool to cold climates.

B. p. 'Trost's Dwarf'. True 3 ft. by 3 ft. dwarf for bonsai, container, rock garden. Needs excellent drainage.

B. p. 'Youngii'. YOUNG'S WEEPING BIRCH. Slender branches hang straight down. Form like weeping mulberry, but tree is more graceful. Decorative display tree. Trunk must be staked to desired height. Same climate limitations as *B. p.* 'Dalecarlica'.

BEVERLY HILLS ARBORVITAE. See *Platycladus orientalis* 'Beverleyensis'.

BIGNONIA. TRUMPET VINE. Botanists have reclassified plants formerly called *Bignonia,* so that the trumpet vines you knew as *Bignonia* are now placed under other names. Many are still sold under the old names. Since most gardeners still compare one ''bignonia'' with another when making their selections, we list them below and give the names under which they are described:

B. chamberlaynii. See *Anemopaegma chamberlaynii*.
B. cherere. See *Distictis buccinatoria*.
B. chinensis. See *Campsis grandiflora*.
B. jasminoides. See *Pandorea jasminoides*.
B. radicans. See *Campsis radicans*.
B. speciosa. See *Clytostoma callistegioides*.
B. tweediana. See *Macfadyena unguis-cati*.
B. venusta. See *Pyrostegia venusta*.
B. violacea. See *Clytostoma callistegioides*.

BIG SAGEBRUSH. See *Artemisia tridentata*.

BIG TREE. See *Sequoiadendron giganteum*.

BILLBERGIA. Evergreen perennials. Zones 16–24. Indoor/outdoor plants anywhere. Relative of pineapple, native to Brazil, where the plants grow as epiphytes on trees. Stiff, spiny-toothed leaves in basal clusters. Showy bracts and tubular flowers in drooping clusters. Usually grown in containers for display indoors or on patios. In southern California, often grown on limbs of trees or on bark slabs, with roots wrapped in sphagnum moss and leaf mold; as an easy ground cover under trees; or in borders. Excellent cut flowers.

Billbergia nutans

Best in filtered shade. Pot in light porous mixture of sand, ground bark, or leaf mold. Need little water in winter when growth is slow, large amounts during active growth in warm weather. Usually hold water in funnel-like center of leaf rosette which acts as reservoir. When grown as house plants, give plenty of light and sun. Increase by cutting off suckers from base of plant. Specialists in bromeliads list dozens of varieties.

B. nutans. QUEEN'S TEARS. Most commonly grown. Spiny green leaves to 1½ ft. long. Long spikes of rosy red bracts and drooping flowers with green petals edged deep blue. Vigorous.

B. pyramidalis. Leaves to 3 ft. long, 2½ in. wide, with spiny-toothed margins. Flowers with red, violet-tipped petals and bright red bracts in dense spikes 4 in. long.

B. sanderana. Leaves leathery, to 1 ft. long, spiny toothed, dotted with white. Loose, nodding, 10-in.-long clusters of flowers with blue petals, yellowish green at the base; sepals tipped with blue, bracts rose-colored.

BIRCH. See *Betula.*

BIRCH BARK CHERRY. See *Prunus serrula.*

BIRD OF PARADISE. See *Strelitzia.*

BIRD OF PARADISE BUSH. See *Caesalpinia gilliesii.*

BIRD'S-EYE BUSH. See *Ochna serrulata.*

BIRD'S-EYES. See *Gilia tricolor.*

BIRD'S FOOT FERN. See *Pellaea mucronata.*

BIRD'S FOOT TREFOIL. See *Lotus corniculatus.*

BIRD'S NEST FERN. See *Asplenium nidus.*

BISHOP'S HAT. See *Epimedium grandiflorum.*

BISHOP'S WEED. See *Aegopodium podagraria.*

BITTERROOT. See *Lewisia rediviva.*

BITTERSWEET. See *Celastrus.*

BLACKBERRY. For ornamental relatives see *Rubus.* The West has its own special kinds of blackberries. Most are trailing types as compared to the hardy, upright, stiff-caned kinds of the Midwest and East. The wild blackberry of the Pacific Northwest and northern California has contributed its rich sprightly flavor to several varieties. Each has its own pattern of climate adaptation. Leaves divided fanwise, often with thorny stalks and midribs.

Blackberry

All blackberries require a deep soil, full sun, and ample water through growing season. Trailing types are best grown on some kind of trellis.

Pruning must follow growth habit. Roots are perennial but canes are biennial, appearing and growing one year, flowering and fruiting the second. Where grown on trellis, train only 1-year-old canes on trellis, and remove all canes that have fruited in August after harvest (cut canes to the ground). Train canes of current season (growing beneath trellis) on trellis and prune to 6–8 ft. Thin out all but 12–16 canes. These will produce side branches during remainder of growing season. Cut side branches back to 12 in. in early spring. With new spring growth, small branches grow from the side branches. These bear fruit.

Thin out semiupright varieties to 4–8 canes, prune at 5–6 ft., and spread fanwise on trellis. Upright varieties need no trellis but are easier to handle tied to a wire about 2½ ft. above ground. Select 3 or 4 canes and tip them at 2½–3 ft. to force side growth. Tie where canes cross wire.

Red-berry mite (mostly in the 'Himalaya' and 'Evergreen' varieties), spider mites, and whitefly are sometimes a problem. To control, spray in winter and again as buds are about to break, with a dormant spray containing lime sulfur. Spray with malathion as leaves unfold and again a month later.

Fertilize established plantings with commercial fertilizer according to manufacturer's label. In Northwest, feed at blossom time. Best results in California if you split yearly amount into 3 applications: before new growth starts, again in midspring, and again in midsummer. Keep down weeds. Pull out suckers. Above all, don't let plants get away from you.

These varieties are available in western nurseries (all are trailing types except where noted otherwise):

'Boysen' and 'Thornless Boysen'. All Zones. Not reliably hardy in Zone 1 but come through winter if canes are left on ground and covered with snow or with straw mulch. Popular for high yield and flavor—eaten fresh, cooked, or frozen. Berries are reddish, large (1¼ in. long, 1 in. thick), soft, sweet-tart, delightful aroma. Berries carry dusty bloom, are not shiny.

'Cascade'. Best in Zones 4–6, 16, 17. Some grown 20–24. Not adapted 9–13. Not reliably hardy Zones 1–3. Berries bright, deep red, almost black (red when cooked) about 1 in long, ½ in. thick, with classic wild blackberry flavor. Tender and very juicy; a poor shipper but an excellent garden variety.

'Evergreen' and 'Thornless Evergreen'. Strong canes, semierect growth. This is *the* commercial blackberry in Zones 4–6. Not reliably hardy Zones 1–3. Grown in Zones 15–17 where quantity is important. Bushes vigorous with heavy crops of large (1½ in. long, ¾ in. thick), exceptionally firm, black sweet berries. Seeds large.

'Himalaya'. Seldom sold but has escaped and grows wild wherever adapted. Can be prodigious, spreading pest. Grown in Zones 14–17 for long harvest season—mid-July to October. Extremely vigorous, semierect canes grow 20–30 ft. in one season. Berries shiny jet black, medium (1 in. long, ¾ in. thick). Seeds medium large.

'Logan' and 'Thornless Logan'. Same climate adaptation as 'Boysen' berry. Berries (1¼ in. long, ¾ in. thick) are light reddish, not darkening when ripe, with fine hairs that dull its color. Flavor tarter than 'Boysen'; excellent for canning and pies.

'Marion'. Similar to 'Olallie' in berry size and quality but better adapted Zones 4–6. Climate adaptation same as 'Cascade'.

'Nectar'. Identical to 'Boysen'.

'Olallie'. Better adapted in California than in its Oregon homeland. Zones 7–9, 14–24. Berries large (1½ in. long, ¾ in. thick), shiny black, firm, sweeter than 'Cascade' but with some wild blackberry sprightliness.

'Smoothstem'. Zones 4–9, 14–17. Semierect canes 8–10 ft. long. Fruit large, blunt, jet black. Productive; poor shipper but good home variety. Thornless.

'Tay' or 'Tayberry'. Zones 4–9, 14–17. Hybrid between blackberry and raspberry. Long, trailing, thorny vines. Heavy bearer of mild-flavored dark red to purple-black 1½-in. fruit earlier than other blackberries.

'Thornfree'. Zones 4–9, 14–17. Semierect thornless canes 7–8 ft. long. Tart shiny black berries are medium large. Heavy bearing.

'Young' and 'Thornless Young'. Climate adaptation similar to 'Boysen' berry, but not as productive in all climates. Berry same size and color as 'Boysen' but shiny and somewhat sweeter.

BLACKBERRY LILY. See *Belamcanda chinensis.*

BLACK CALLA. See *Arum palaestinum.*

BLACK-EYED SUSAN. See *Rudbeckia hirta.*

BLACK-EYED SUSAN VINE. See *Thunbergia alata.*

BLACK SALLY. See *Eucalyptus stellulata.*

BLACK SNAKEROOT. See *Cimicifuga racemosa.*

BLANKET FLOWER. See *Gaillardia grandiflora.*

BLAZING STAR. See *Mentzelia.*

BLECHNUM *(Lomaria).* Evergreen ferns of symmetrical, formal appearance.

B. brasiliense. Zones 19, 21–24. Dwarf tree fern reaching only 4 ft. in height. Nearly erect fronds in compact clusters. Variety 'Crispum' has elegantly ruffled fronds, reddish when young. Shade, ample water.

B. gibbum. Zones 19, 21–24. Dwarf tree fern with wide-spreading crown of fronds atop slender trunk eventually 3 ft. high.

Blechnum spicant

(Continued on next page)

'Moorei' has wider, more leathery leaflets, is more attractive in winter. Needs moist soil and shade, but avoid overhead water.

B. penna-marina. Zones 15–17, 20–24; with protection Zones 4–6. Spreads slowly to make patches of refined 4–8 in. fronds in cool, moist, sheltered places or can be used as house plant.

B. spicant. DEER FERN, DEER TONGUE FERN. Zones 1–9, 14–24. Native to northern California and Northwest. Produces fronds of 2 kinds: sterile fronds are narrow, dark glossy green, spreading or angled, 1–3 ft. tall; fertile fronds are stiffly erect, very narrow, with narrow, widely spaced leaflets. Deep shade, moisture, woodsy soil. Difficult in southern California's mild winters.

Blechnum brasiliense

BLEEDING HEART. See *Dicentra.*

BLETILLA striata (*B. hyacinthina*). CHINESE GROUND ORCHID. All Zones except in conditions noted below. A terrestrial orchid native to China and Japan. Lavender, cattleya shaped, 1–2-in. flowers produced, up to a dozen on 1½–2-ft. stem, for about 6 weeks beginning in May or June. Pale green, plaited leaves, 3–6 to plant. *B. s.* 'Alba' is white-flowered form.

Bletilla striata

Plant the tuberlike roots outdoors in fall in all but coldest areas of West for spring and early summer bloom. Hardy to about 20°F. (to 10°F. if roots are protected). Dies back to ground each winter. Mulch with straw in cold climates. In time will develop large clumps if grown in light shade and in a moist soil, rich in humus. Can be divided in early spring before growth starts, but don't do it too often; blooms best when crowded.

Locate plants (potted or in ground) under high-branching trees or under lath.

BLISTER CRESS. See *Erysimum.*

BLOOD-LEAF. See *Iresine herbstii.*

BLOOD LILY. See *Haemanthus katharinae.*

BLOOD-RED TRUMPET VINE. See *Distictis buccinatoria.*

BLOODROOT. See *Sanguinaria canadensis.*

BLUE ANGEL TEARS. See *Lindernia grandiflora.*

BLUEBEARD. See *Caryopteris.*

BLUEBELL. See *Endymion, Scilla.*

BLUEBERRY. For ornamental relatives see *Vaccinium.* Deciduous shrub. Best in Zones 4–6. Hardy in Zones 2, 3 but needs special acid soil preparation there. Grown successfully in northern California coastal area (Zone 17) and by gardeners willing to give them special attention in Zones 7–9, 14–16. Native to eastern U.S. Blueberries thrive under conditions that suit rhododendrons and azaleas, to which they are related. They need sun and cool, moist, acid soil that drains well. In California, if soil is at all alkaline, grow them in straight peat moss or ground bark.

Blueberries contribute more than fruit to garden. They are handsome plants for

Blueberry

hedge or shrub border. Most varieties are upright growers to 6 ft. or more; a few are rather sprawling and under 5 ft. Leaves, to 3 in. long, bronze in new growth, then dark green, turning scarlet or yellow in fall. Flowers tiny, white to pinkish, urn shaped, in spring. Fruit very decorative in summer. Plant 3 ft. apart as informal hedge; in larger plantings, as shrubs, space 4–5 ft. apart.

Plant two varieties for better pollination. Shallow roots benefit from 4–6-in.-thick mulch of sawdust, ground bark, or the like. Water frequently. Use acid-forming fertilizers. In California you may need to use iron sulfate or iron chelate to correct chlorosis.

Prune to prevent overbearing. Plants shape themselves, but often produce so many fruit buds that fruit is undersized and growth of plants slows down. Keep first-year plants from bearing by stripping off flowers. On older plants, cut back ends of twigs to point where fruit buds are widely spaced. Or, simply remove some of oldest branches each year. Remove all weak shoots.

The following varieties have proved themselves in home gardens. Choose for long harvest season. Plant at least 2 for each season ("early" means ripening early to mid-June; "mid-season" means early to mid-July; "late" means late July into August). Allow 2 plants for each member of your family. Although all varieties are sold in Northwest and northern California, growers especially recommend for California: 'Berkeley', 'Bluecrop', 'Dixi', 'Earli-blue', 'Jersey'.

'Atlantic'. Late. Sprawling habit. Light blue, large berry.

'Berkeley'. Midseason to late. Open, spreading, tall. Very large light blue berries.

'Bluecrop'. Midseason. Erect, tall growth. Large berries. Excellent flavor. Attractive shrub.

'Blueray'. Midseason. Vigorous, tall. Large, highly flavored, crisp berries. Attractive shrub.

'Collins'. Early to midseason. Erect, attractive bush. Small clusters of large, very tasty fruit.

'Concord'. Midseason. Upright to spreading growth. Attractive. Large berry of tart flavor until fully ripe.

'Coville'. Late. Tall, open, spreading. Unusually large leaves. Very attractive. Long clusters of very large light blue berries.

'Dixi'. Late. Not attractive plant—tall and open. Needs heavy pruning. Berries, among largest and tastiest, are medium blue, firm and sweet.

'Earliblue'. Early to midseason. Tall, erect. Large heavy leaves. Large berries of excellent flavor.

'Ivanhoe'. Early to midseason. Very large dark blue berries—firm, crisp, tart.

'Jersey'. Midseason to late. Tall, erect growing. Large, light blue berries. Very bland. Yellow fall and winter color.

'Pemberton'. Very vigorous, tall. Berries large, dark blue, of good dessert quality.

'Rancocas'. Early to midseason. Tall, erect, open arching habit. Excellent shrub. Leaves smaller than most. Needs heavy pruning. Berries mild and sweet. Dependable old-timer.

'Rubel'. Early to late. Erect, tall growth. Berries firm and tart. Needs pruning to produce large berries.

'Stanley'. Early to midseason. Erect, medium tall. Attractive foliage. One of tastiest—firm, aromatic berries with spicy flavor.

'Weymouth'. Very early. Ripens all berries quickly. Erect, medium height. Large dark blue berries of fair quality, lack aroma.

BLUEBERRY CLIMBER. See *Ampelopsis brevipedunculata.*

BLUE BLOSSOM. See *Ceanothus thyrsiflorus.*

BLUE CROWN PASSION FLOWER. See *Passiflora caerulea.*

BLUE DAWN FLOWER. See *Ipomoea acuminata.*

BLUE DICKS. See *Dichelostemma pulchellum.*

BLUE DRACAENA. See *Cordyline indivisa.*

BLUE-EYED GRASS. See *Sisyrinchium bellum.*

BLUE FESCUE. See *Festuca ovina glauca.*

BLUE GINGER. See *Dichorisandra thyrsiflora.*

BLUE GRAMA GRASS. See *Bouteloua gracilis.*

BLUEGRASS. See *Poa.*

BLUE GUM. See *Eucalyptus globulus.*

BLUE HIBISCUS. See *Alyogyne huegelii.*

BLUE LACE FLOWER. See *Trachymene coerulea.*

BLUE MARGUERITE. See *Felicia amelloides.*

BLUE MIST. See *Caryopteris clandonensis.*

BLUE SHIMPAKU. See *Juniperus chinensis* 'Blaauw'.

BLUE SPIRAEA. See *Caryopteris incana.*

BLUE STAR CREEPER. See *Laurentia fluviatilis.*

BLUE THIMBLE FLOWER. See *Gilia capitata.*

BOG ROSEMARY. See *Andromeda polifolia.*

BOKHARA FLEECEFLOWER. See *Polygonum baldschuanicum.*

BO-TREE. See *Ficus religiosa.*

BORAGE. See *Borago officinalis.*

BORAGO officinalis. BORAGE. Annual herb. All Zones. Grows 1–3 ft. high. Leaves bristly, gray green, to as long as 4–6 in.; edible, tastes like cucumbers. Blue, saucer shaped, nodding flowers in leafy clusters on branched stems. Sun or shade, medium watering, tolerates poor soil. Grows large, needs lots of room. Seeds itself freely but doesn't transplant easily. Good drought resistant ground cover, soil binder. Use small tender leaves in salads, pickling, or cooked as greens. Flowers make attractive garnish, also good cut flower.

Borago officinalis

BORONIA. Evergreen shrubs. Small shrubs from Australia. Plants have wispy look from finely divided leaves; leaflets needlelike. Attractive but relatively short-lived. They need sun or light shade, well-drained, slightly acid sandy or light loamy soil, and careful watering; they can never go completely dry or stay wet at root for any length of time and survive.

    B. denticulata. Zones 15–17. Grows 3–4 ft. high. Fragrant narrow leaves. Starlike light pink flowers. Easier to grow than the other two.

    B. elatior. PINK BORONIA, TALL BORONIA. Zones 15–17. Grows to 4–6 ft. Clouds of ¼-in. bell shaped pink to rose flowers in spring. Cut back severely after flowering.

    B. megastigma. BROWN BORONIA. Zones 15–17, 20–24. Only 1–2 ft. tall, with nodding ½-in. bell shaped flowers, brown lined with yellow. Powerful, pleasant fragrance combines freesia, orange

Boronia megastigma

blossom, and other fragrances; blooms February-March. Count on replacing it every 2 or 3 years from seed or cuttings. Will last longer if grown in light mix in containers.

BOSTON FERN. See *Nephrolepis exaltata* 'Bostoniensis'.

BOSTON IVY. See *Parthenocissus tricuspidata.*

BOTTLEBRUSH. See *Callistemon, Melaleuca.*

BOTTLE PALM. See *Beaucarnea recurvata.*

BOTTLE TREE. See *Brachychiton populneus.*

BOUGAINVILLEA. Evergreen shrubby vines. Reliably hardy in nearest we have to tropical climate—Zones 22–24. Yet widely and satisfyingly grown in Zones 12, 13, 15–17, 19, 21. Low-growing shrubby types in full bloom in gallon can and adaptable to container growing, have widened their use even into Zones 5, 6 of Northwest. There they are used on terrace or patio as summer annual or moved into protected area over winter. Where frost is expected, vines should be given protected warm wall or warmest spot in garden. If vines get by first winter or two they will be big enough to take winter damage and recover. In any case, flower production comes so quickly that replacement is not a real deterrent.

Bougainvillea 'San Diego Red'

    Bougainvilleas' vibrant colors come not from the small inconspicuous flowers, but from the 3 large bracts that surround them. Vines make dense cover of medium-sized medium-green leaves. Vigor and growth habit vary by species and variety. Plant in sun, or light shade in hottest areas—in early spring (after frosts) to give longest possible growing time before next frost.

    Caution: Bougainvillea roots don't knit soil together in firm root ball in container, and roots are highly sensitive to disturbance. If you knock plant from container roughly, you may fatally damage roots. For plastic container, cut out bottom, place container in planting hole, then cut container from top to bottom and remove sides; fill in with soil. For metal container, poke 6–8 holes in sides and bottom of can before setting it in hole. Fill in around can with soil; metal will rust.

    Supply sturdy supports and keep shoots tied up so that they won't whip in wind, and so strong gusts won't shred leaves against sharp thorns along stems.

    Fertilize in spring and summer. Water normally while plants are growing fast, then ease off temporarily in midsummer to promote better flowering. Don't be afraid to prune—to renew plant, shape, or direct growth. Prune heavily in spring after frost. On wall-grown plants, nip back long stems during growing season to produce more flowering wood. Shrubby kinds or heavily pruned plants make good self-supporting container shrubs for terrace or patio. Without support and with token corrective pruning, bougainvillea can make broad, sprawling shrub, bank and ground cover, or hanging basket plant.

    Double-flowering kinds can look messy because they hold faded flowers for a long time.

    All of the following are tall-growing vines except those noted as shrubs.

    'Afterglow'. Yellow orange; heavy bloom. Open growth, sparse foliage.

    'Barbara Karst'. Bright red in sun, bluish crimson in shade; blooms young and for long period. Vigorous growth. Likes heat of desert. Fast comeback after frost.

    'Betty Hendry' ('Indian Maid'). Basically red, but with touches of yellow and purple. Blooms young and for a long period.

    B. brasiliensis. See *B. spectabilis.*

    'Brilliant Variegated'. Spreading, mounding shrub. Leaves variegated with gray green and silver. Brick red flowers. Often used in hanging baskets, pots.

(Continued on next page)

'California Gold' ('Sunset'). Close to pale yellow. Blooms young.

'Cherry Blossom'. Double-flowered rose pink with white to pale green centers.

'Crimson Jewel'. Vigorous shrubby, sprawly plant. Good in containers, as shrub, sunny bank cover. Lower growth, better color than 'Temple Fire'. Heavy bloom, long season.

'Crimson Lake'. See 'Mrs. Butt'.

'Hawaii' ('Raspberry Ice'). Shrubby, mounding, spreading. Leaves have golden yellow margins. New leaves tinged red. Flowers red. Good hanging basket plant. Regardless of its tropical name, it's one of the hardiest.

'Isabel Greensmith'. Flowers variously described as orange, red orange, or red with yellow tinting.

'Jamaica White'. Bracts white, veined light green. Blooms young. Moderately vigorous.

'James Walker'. Big reddish purple flowers on big vine.

'La Jolla'. Bright red bracts, compact, shrubby habit. Good shrub, container plant.

'Lavender Queen'. An improved B. spectabilis, with bigger bracts, heavier bloom.

'Manila Red'. Many rows of magenta red bracts make heavy clusters of double-looking bloom.

'Mary Palmer's Enchantment'. Very vigorous, large-growing vine with pure white bracts.

'Mrs. Butt' ('Crimson Lake'). Old-fashioned variety with good crimson color. Needs lots of heat for bloom. Moderately vigorous.

'Orange King'. Bronzy orange. Open growth. Needs long summer, no frost.

'Pink Tiara'. Abundant pale pink to rose flowers over long season.

'Raspberry Ice'. See 'Hawaii'.

'Rosea'. Large rose red bracts on large vine.

'Rosenka'. Can be held to shrub proportions if occasional wild shoot is pruned out. Gold flowers age pink.

'San Diego Red' ('San Diego', 'Scarlett O'Hara'). One of best on all counts: large, deep green leaves that hold well in cold winters; deep red bracts over long season; hardiness equal to old-fashioned purple kind. Vigorous, high climbing. Can be trained to tree form by staking and pruning.

'Southern Rose'. Lavender rose to pink.

B. spectabilis (B. brasiliensis). Hardy and vigorous. Blooms well in cool summers. Purple flowers. Best for Zones 16, 17.

'Tahitian Maid'. Extra rows of bracts give double effect to blush pink clusters.

'Temple Fire'. Shrublike growth to 4 ft. high, 6 ft. wide. Partially deciduous. Bronze red.

'Texas Dawn'. Choice, vigorous pink. Purplish pink bracts in large sprays.

'White Madonna'. Pure white bracts.

BOULDER RASPBERRY. See *Rubus deliciosus*.

BOUSSINGAULTIA. See *Anredera*.

BOUTELOUA gracilis. BLUE GRAMA GRASS. Pasture grass used for low-maintenance, low-water-use lawns in sunny, arid, alkaline regions of Rocky Mountains and high plains. Hardy throughout this area, but little tested elsewhere. Bunching rather than sod forming, it nevertheless makes fair lawn if sown at 1 lb. per 1,000 sq. ft. Sow in fall to take advantage of winter rain, snow. Water to depth of 12 in. while it is becoming established; thereafter it can get along with virtually no irrigation. Mow at 1½ in.

*Bouteloua
gracilis*

BOUVARDIA. Evergreen shrubs. Native to Arizona, New Mexico, Mexico, and Central America. Loose, often straggling growth habit. Showy clusters of tubular flowers

(fragrant in one species). The fragrant one is the most tender and looks poorest after flowers are gone. The non-fragrant red-flowered types are hardier, easier.

B. glaberrima. Zones 8–10, 14–24. Native to mountain canyons in southern Arizona, New Mexico. To 3 ft. tall, shrubby but dying back at tops in cold weather. Smooth green leaves 1–3 in. long. Clustered inch-long tubular red (rarely pink or white) flowers. Tolerates drought, likes part shade.

*Bouvardia
longiflora*

B. longiflora 'Albatross' (*B. humboldtii* 'Albatross'). Zones 12, 13, 16, 17, 19–24. The fragrant one. Snow-white, 3-in.-long tubular flowers in loose clusters on a weak-stemmed shrub, 2–3 ft. high with paired 2-in. leaves. They appear at almost any time. Pinch out stem tips to make bushier. Cut back flowering branches from time to time to stimulate new growth. Grow in tubs or boxes in rich, fast draining soil mix. Ample water.

B. ternifolia (*B. jacquinii*). Zones 8–10, 14–24. A 6-ft.-tall shrub with 2-in. leaves in whorls of 3 or 4. Red, 1-in.-long, tubular flowers in loose clusters at ends of branches. Selected forms are pink, rose, coral, red. Same requirements as *B. glaberrima*.

BOWER VINE. See *Pandorea jasminoides*.

BOWSTRING HEMP. See *Sansevieria*.

BOX, BOXWOOD. See *Buxus*.

BOX ELDER. See *Acer negundo*.

BOYSENBERRY. See Blackberry.

BRACHYCHITON (*Sterculia*). Evergreen to partly or wholly deciduous trees. Native to Australia. All have woody, canoe shaped fruits that delight flower arrangers, but are merely litter to some gardeners. Drought tolerant.

B. acerifolius (*Sterculia acerifolia*). FLAME TREE, AUSTRALIAN FLAME TREE. Deciduous for brief period. Zones 16–21, 23. When at its best, a most spectacular red-flowering tree. Hardy to 25°F. To 60 ft. or more. Strong, heavy, smooth trunk, usually green. Leaves are handsome, glossy, bright green 10-in.-wide fans, deeply lobed. Showiest flowering season usually May to June. Tree wholly or partially covered with

*Brachychiton
populneus*

great clusters of small, ¾-in., tubular, red or orange red bells. Leaves drop before flowers appear in portion of tree that blooms.

B. populneus (*Sterculia diversifolia*). BOTTLE TREE. Evergreen. Zones 12–24. Moderate growth to 30–50 ft., 30-ft. spread. Common name from very heavy trunk, broad at base, tapering quickly. Leaves (2–3 in. long) give general effect of poplar. They shimmer in breeze like aspen's. Cluster of small, bell shaped, white flowers in May and June noticeable close up. The 2½–3-in. woody fruit that follow are noticeable in litter they produce. Appreciated in low and intermediate deserts, where frequently used as screens or high, wide windbreaks. Very susceptible to Texas root rot.

BRACHYCOME iberidifolia. SWAN RIVER DAISY. Annual. All Zones. Native to western Australia. Charming plant producing myriad daisylike flowers, 1 in. across, in blue, rose, white, and bicolors. Blooms in late spring and early summer. Small narrow divided leaves. Sow seed in broad masses where plants are to grow. Sun. Effective under light-foliaged deciduous trees, as ground cover in bulb beds, or in rock gar-

*Brachycome
iberidifolia*

dens. Another effective use is in mixed plantings of annuals in large flower pots, window boxes, raised planting beds.

BRACHYSEMA lanceolatum. SCIMITAR SHRUB, SWAN RIVER PEA SHRUB. Evergreen. Zones 8, 9, 12–24. Earns its common names and place in gardens by its unusual flowers. They are bright red, sweet pea shaped, but with inch-long pairs of petals (keels) shaped like a scimitar. Never makes great show of flowers, but it's rarely out of bloom. To 3 ft. or more, loosely formed, erect in growth, spreading in age. Leaves narrow, to 4 in. long, dark green above, silvery beneath. Prune by thinning out old straggly stems. Best in full sun, with fast drainage, in sandy soil. Takes drought. Don't pamper. Go light with fertilizers.

Brachysema lanceolatum

BRACKEN. See *Pteridium aquilinum*.

BRAHEA *(Erythea).* Palms. These fan palms from Mexico are somewhat like the more familiar washingtonias in appearance, but with important differences. All tolerate drought.

B. armata. MEXICAN BLUE PALM. Zones 12–17, 19–24. Grows slowly to 40 ft., top spreading 6–8 ft. Leaves silvery blue, almost white. Conspicuous creamy flowers. Hardy to 18°F. and takes drought, heat, and wind.

B. brandegeei. SAN JOSE HESPER PALM. Zones 19, 21–24. Slow grower with slender flexible trunk. Eventually tall; reaches 125 ft. in its native Baja California. Trunk sheds leaves when old. When leaf stalks are trimmed, they often leave spiral pattern. Three-ft. leaves are light gray green. Hardy to 26°F.

B. edulis. GUADALUPE PALM. Zones 13–24. From Guadalupe Island off Baja California. Like *B. armata* but leaves are light green, flowers less conspicuous. Old leaves drop, leaving the naked, elephant hide trunk ringed with scars. Slow grower to 30 ft., stout trunked. Hardy to below 20°F. and takes beach and desert conditions.

B. elegans. FRANCESCHI PALM. Zones 13–17, 19–24. Slowest growing of erytheas; develops a trunk very slowly and reaches only 15 ft. Leaves gray green. From northern Mexico; hardy to 22°F.

Brahea armata

BRAKE. See *Pteris*.

BRAMBLE. See *Rubus*.

BRASSAIA actinophylla. See *Schefflera actinophylla*.

BRASSAVOLA. Epiphytic orchids native to tropical America. House or greenhouse plants. Large, spiderlike, white or greenish white flowers with narrow sepals and petals and large lip. Flowers grow singly or in short-stemmed clusters. Tough, leathery leaves grow from small pseudobulbs. Plants similar to laelias. Grow in any orchid soil mix. Need 60°–65°F. night temperature, 5°–10°F. higher in day. Water liberally and give plenty of sun during growing season. Reduce humidity during dormant period.

B. cucullata. Fragrant, 2-in. flowers in summer or fall. Grasslike leaves to 12 in. long with pseudobulb included. Unlike many orchids this one will produce flower stems from the same pseudobulb for several years in succession. Hardy enough to grow outdoors through winter in warm climate areas in southern California.

Brassavola nodosa

B. digbyana *(Laelia digbyana).* Fragrant 4–6-in. flowers notable for huge, fringed, white to cream lip. Petals pale green tinted lavender. Summer bloom. Tough, leathery, gray green leaves. Transmits big fringed lip to its hybrids and is famous orchid parent.

B. nodosa. LADY-OF-THE-NIGHT. In fall 3-in. flowers appear, 2–6 on a stem; sweetly fragrant at night. Fleshy, 6-in.-long leaves. Hardy outdoors in winter where temperatures are mild. Grows best in hanging containers.

BRAZILIAN FLAME BUSH. See *Calliandra tweedii*.

BRAZILIAN PLUME FLOWER. See *Justicia carnea*.

BRAZILIAN SKY FLOWER. See *Duranta stenostachya*.

BREATH OF HEAVEN. See *Coleonema* and *Diosma*.

BRIDAL VEIL. See *Tripogandra multiflora*.

BRIDAL VEIL BROOM. See *Genista monosperma*.

BRIMEURA amethystina *(Hyacinthus amethystinus).* Bulb. All Zones. Bulbs, leaf rosettes exactly resemble small hyacinths. For rock gardens or naturalizing. Flowers in spring on 6–8-in.-tall stems topped with a loose spike of clear blue bells with paler blue streaks. Plant in mid to late autumn, 2 in. deep, 3 in. apart. Mulch in areas where winters are very cold.

Brimeura amethystina

BRIZA maxima. RATTLESNAKE GRASS, QUAKING GRASS. Annual. All Zones. Native to Mediterranean region. Ornamental grass of delicate, graceful form used effectively in dry arrangements and bouquets. Grows 1–2 ft. high. Leaves to 6 in. long; ¼ in. wide. Clusters of nodding, seed-bearing spikelets ½ in. or more long, papery and straw-colored when dry, dangle on thread-like stems. Spikelets resemble rattlesnake rattles. Scatter seed where plants are to grow; thin seedlings to 1 ft. apart. Often grows wild along roadsides, in fields.

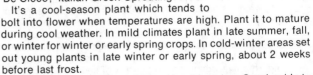

Briza maxima

BRISBANE BOX. See *Tristania conferta*.

BROCCOLI. Biennials grown as annuals. All Zones in conditions noted below. Best all-round cole crop (cabbage and its close relatives) for home gardener; bears over long season, is not difficult to grow. Grows to 4 ft. and has branching habit. Central stalk bears cluster of green flower buds that may reach 6 in. in diameter. When central cluster is removed, side branches will lengthen and produce smaller clusters. Good varieties are 'Calabrese', 'Cleopatra', 'De Cicco', 'Italian Green Sprouting'.

It's a cool-season plant which tends to bolt into flower when temperatures are high. Plant it to mature during cool weather. In mild climates plant in late summer, fall, or winter for winter or early spring crops. In cold-winter areas set out young plants in late winter or early spring, about 2 weeks before last frost.

Young plants resist frost, but not hard freezing. Good guide to planting time is appearance of young plants in nurseries. You can raise young plants from seed sown 4–6 weeks ahead of planting time, but even one pack of seed will produce far more

Broccoli

plants than even the largest home garden could handle, so save surplus seed for later plantings. A dozen plants at each planting will supply a family.

Sun. Space plants 18–24 in. apart in rows and leave 3 ft. between rows. Keep plants growing vigorously with regular deep irrigation and one or two feedings of commercial fertilizer before heads start to form. Cut heads before clustered buds begin to open. Include 5 or 6 in. of edible stalk and leaves. Control aphids and cabbage worm with malathion *before heads form,* or use all-purpose vegetable dust.

BRODIAEA. Corms. All Zones (but note conditions below). Many are natives of the Pacific Coast where they bloom in sunny fields and meadows, spring and early summer. Few grasslike leaves, and clusters of funnel shaped or tubular, ½–2-in.-long flowers atop the stem. In nature often found in adobe soil, where it rains heavily in winter and early spring, and corms completely dry out in summer. Best with similar conditions in gardens (no dry season watering). Where plants must take summer watering, plant in sandy or gritty soil. Plant corms 2–3 in. deep. In cold-winter areas, grow in containers or protect from freezing and thawing by mulch.

Brodiaea elegans

Brodiaea includes many plants now listed under different names. Cross-references below will guide you to appropriate entries under *Dichelostemma* and *Triteleia*.

B. capitata. See *Dichelostemma pulchellum*.
B. grandiflora. See *B. coronaria* below. Another plant known by same name is *Triteleia grandiflora*.
B. coronaria. (*B. grandiflora*). HARVEST BRODIAEA. Clusters of dark blue inch-long flowers on 6–10-in stem. Late spring, early summer bloom.
B. elegans (often seen as *B. grandiflora* or *B. coronaria*). HARVEST BRODIAEA. Similar to *B. coronaria*, but taller (to 16 in.).
B. hyacinthina. See *Triteleia hyacinthina*.
B. ida-maia. See *Dichelostemma ida-maia*.
B. ixioides. See *Triteleia ixioides*.
B. lactea. See *Triteleia hyacinthina*.
B. laxa. See *Triteleia laxa*.
B. lilacina. See *Triteleia hyacinthina lilacina*.
B. lutea. See *Triteleia ixioides*.
B. minor. Dark blue flowers on stems that may be 3 or 4 in. long, rarely 12 in.
B. peduncularis. See *Triteleia peduncularis*.
B. 'Queen Fabiola'. See *Triteleia* 'Queen Fabiola'.
B. tubergenii. See *Triteleia tubergenii*.
B. uniflora. See *Ipheion uniflorum*.

BROMELIAD. Any plant belonging to the bromelia or pineapple family (Bromeliaceae) is a bromeliad. Most bromeliads are stemless perennials with clustered leaves and with showy flowers in simple or branched clusters. Leaves of many kinds are handsomely marked, and the flower clusters gain beauty from colorful bracts.

In most areas of the West bromeliads are considered choice house plants. Kinds most often grown indoors were, in their native homes, epiphytes: plants that perch on trees or rocks and gain their sustenance from rain and from whatever leaf mold gathers around their roots. These often have cupped leaf bases that hold water between rains. In mildest areas of the West many of these epiphytes grow well in sheltered places out of doors.

Fanciers often fasten them to tree branches, packing sphagnum moss around the roots to hold moisture and encourage root growth. More often they are grown in pots of loose, fast draining, highly organic growing mix. Feed lightly but frequently, and keep central cups filled with water.

A few bromeliads (*Puya* is the best known) are desert plants that resemble yuccas and thrive in the same conditions.

BROMELIA balansae. HEART OF FLAME. Bromeliad. Zones 19–24. Pineapple relative. Forms impressive cluster of 30–50 arching leaves, saw toothed, glossy dark green above, whitish beneath. To 4 ft. tall, 4–6 ft. across. Center leaves turn bright scarlet in spring or early summer. From this center rises stalk bearing spike of rose-colored flowers margined with white. Needs warm nights to perform satisfactorily. Almost any soil if drainage is good. Grows best in sun, in porous soil with plenty of organic matter. Water occasionally, feed lightly once or twice in summer.

Bromelia balansae

BRONZE DRACAENA. See *Cordyline australis* 'Atropurpurea'.

BROOM. See *Cytisus, Genista, Spartium*.

BROUSSONETIA papyrifera. (Has been sold as *Morus papyrifera*.) PAPER MULBERRY. Deciduous tree. Zones 3–24. Valuable as shade tree where soil and climate limit choice. Takes stony, sterile, or alkaline soils, strong winds, desert heat, drought. Hardy in all but coldest areas. Moderate growth to 50 ft. with dense, broad crown to 40 ft. across. Smooth gray bark. Heart shaped, 4–8-in., rough leaves, gray, hairy beneath; edges toothed, often lobed when young. Male flowers, catkins; female, rounded heads. Suckering habit can be problem in highly cultivated gardens. Seldom suckers in desert. Good in rough bank plantings. Common name comes from inner bark, used for making paper and Polynesian tapa cloth.

Broussonetia papyrifera

BROWALLIA. AMETHYST FLOWER. Annuals, sometimes living over as perennials. All Zones in conditions noted below. Choice plant for connoisseur of blue flowers. Bears one-sided clusters of lobelialike blooms ½–2 in. long and just as wide in brilliant blue, violet, or white; blue flowers are more striking because of contrasting white eye or throat. Flowers profusely in warm shade or filtered sunlight. Graceful in hanging basket or pots. Fine cut flower.

Browallia speciosa

Sow seeds in early spring for summer bloom, in fall for winter color indoors or in greenhouses. Plants need warmth, regular moisture. Can lift vigorous plants in fall, cut back and pot; new growth will produce flowers through winter in warm location. Rarely sold as plants in nurseries; get seeds from specialists.

B. americana. Branching, 1–2 ft. high, roundish leaves. Violet or blue flowers ½ in. long, ½ in. across, borne among leaves. 'Sapphire', dwarf compact variety, dark blue with white eye, very free blooming. This species and its variety often listed in catalogs as *B. elata* and *B. elata* 'Sapphire'.
B. speciosa. Lives over as perennial in mild-winter climates. Sprawling, to 1–2 ft. high. Flowers dark purple above, pale lilac beneath, 1½–2 in. across. 'Blue Bells Improved', lavender blue, grows 10 in. tall, needs no pinching to make it branch. 'Marine Bells' has deep indigo flowers. 'Silver Bells' has white flowers.

BRUGMANSIA (*Datura*). Evergreen shrubs. Zones 16–24. Related to the annual or perennial jimsonweeds or thorn apples (*Datura*). All kinds sold have tubular flowers and are known as "angel's trumpet." Flowers and seeds poisonous if eaten.

All are large shrubs that can be trained as small trees. Garden care is same for all: plant in wind-sheltered location in sun or

Brugmansia candida

shade. Give ample water during growth and bloom season. Expect frost damage and unattractive winter appearance. Prune in early spring after last frost. Cut back branchlets to 1 or 2 buds. (Tubbed plants can be wintered indoors with a little light and very little water.)

Large of leaf and flower, they are dominating shrubs and should be brought into garden with that in mind. White-flowered angel's trumpet is showy in moonlight.

B. arborea. Plants usually offered under this name are either one of the two white-flowered species described below. The true *B. arborea* has less impressive flowers.

B. candida. Native to Peru. Fast and rank growing with soft, pulpy growth to 10–15 ft. (6 ft. or more in one season). Dull green large leaves in the 8–12 in.-range. The heavy white trumpets, single or double, 8 in. or more long, are fragrant especially at night. They appear in summer and fall, often as late as November or December in warm, sheltered gardens.

B. sanguinea. Native to Peru. Fast growing to 12–15 ft. Leaves bright green to 8 in. long. Trumpets, orange red with yellow veinings, about 10 in. long, hang straight down bell fashion from new growth. Rare.

B. suaveolens. Native to Brazil. Similar to *B. candida,* except leaves and flowers are somewhat larger and flowers less fragrant. Some observers see it as bushier and wider spreading. As with *B. candida,* white flowers are veined with green.

BRUNFELSIA pauciflora calycina (*B. calycina*). Evergreen shrubs. Zones 13–17, 20–24. In all but warmest locations they will lose most of their foliage for short period. Upright or spreading, to about 3 ft. Oval, 3–4-in.-long leaves dark green above, pale green below. Tubular, rich dark purple flowers flare to 2 in. wide, several in a cluster, spring, early summer.

Brunfelsia pauciflora 'Floribunda'

The handsome brunfelsias deserve extra attention. Give them soil mix that's rich, well-drained, on acid side. Need iron in Zone 13 to prevent chlorosis. Protect from full sun for very best in foliage and flower. Need constant supply of water and food through growing season. Prune in spring to remove scraggly growth and to shape. Use where you can admire spectacular flower show. Grow well in containers.

B. p. 'Eximia' (*B. c. eximia*). This is somewhat dwarfed, compact version of the following, more widely planted variety. Flowers are a bit smaller but more generously produced.

B. p. 'Floribunda'. YESTERDAY-TODAY-AND-TOMORROW. Earns its common name by quick color change of blossoms—purple ("yesterday"), lavender ("today"), white ("tomorrow"). Flowers profusely displayed all over plant. In partial shade, will reach 10 ft. or more with several stems from base. (May be held to 3 ft. by pruning.)

B. p. 'Macrantha' (*B. floribunda* 'Lindeniana', *B. grandiflora*). Differs markedly from above. The most tender. More slender growing; larger leaves, often 8 in. long, 2½ in. wide. Flowers 2–4 in. across, are deep purple with lavender zone bordering white throat. Lack marked change of color and bloom off and on through year. Treat with iron if foliage yellows.

BRUNNERA macrophylla. BRUNNERA. Perennial. All Zones. Charming in filtered shade in warm areas, sun or light shade on coast. In spring, airy clusters of tiny, clear blue forget-me-not flowers with yellow centers. Dark green, heart shaped leaves 3–6 in. across. To 18-in. high. There is a rare variety with white-edged leaves. Uses: Informal ground cover under high-branching deciduous trees; among spring-flowering shrubs such as forsythia, deciduous magnolias; filler between newly planted evergreen shrubs. Once established, self-sows

Brunnera macrophylla

freely. Planted seeds often difficult to germinate (try freezing them before sowing). Increase by dividing clumps in fall.

BRUNSVIGIA rosea. See *Amaryllis belladonna*.

BRUSH CHERRY, AUSTRALIAN BRUSH CHERRY. See *Syzygium paniculatum*.

BRUSSELS SPROUTS. Annual. All Zones except in conditions noted below. A cabbage relative of unusual appearance. Mature plant has crown of fairly large leaves and its tall stem is completely covered with tiny sprouts. Fairly easy to grow where summers are not too hot, long, or dry. 'Jade Cross Hybrid' is easiest to grow and most heat tolerant; 'Long Island Improved' ('Catskill') is standard market variety. You may have to grow your own from seed. Sow outdoors or in flats in April, transplant young plants in June or early July to sunny place where they will grow and bear in fall. In mild climates plant in fall or winter for winter and spring use.

Brussels sprouts

Treat it the same as broccoli. When big leaves start to turn yellow, begin picking. Snap off little sprouts from bottom first—best when slightly smaller than golf ball. Leave little sprouts on upper stem to mature. After picking, remove only leaves below harvested sprouts. Stalks continue to produce over long period; single plant will yield from 50–100 sprouts.

BUCHLOE dactyloides. BUFFALO GRASS. Pasture grass often used as low-maintenance, drought-tolerant lawn in Rocky Mountains and high plains. Slow to sprout and fill in, it spreads rapidly by surface runners once established and makes matted, reasonably dense turf that takes hard wear and looks fairly good with very little summer water. Needs sun. Gray green from late spring to hard frost, straw-colored through late fall and winter. Runners can invade surrounding garden beds.

Buchloe dactyloides

Given minimum water it grows to about 4 in. tall and requires little or no mowing. More water will mean higher growth, some mowing. Sow 2 lbs. per 1,000 sq. ft. Soak occasionally to 12 in. while grass is getting started. You can start from sod; in spring plant 4-in.-wide plugs 3–4 ft. apart on prepared soil; cover should be complete in two seasons.

BUCKEYE. See *Aesculus californica*.

BUCKTHORN. See *Rhamnus cathartica*.

BUCKWHEAT. See *Eriogonum*.

BUDDLEIA. BUTTERFLY BUSH. Evergreen or deciduous shrubs or small trees. Many species known; all have some charm either of flower color or fragrance, but only two species are readily available. Sun or light shade, average water.

B. alternifolia. FOUNTAIN BUTTERFLY BUSH. Deciduous shrub or small tree. All Zones. It can reach 12 ft. or more, with arching, willowlike branches rather thinly clothed with 1–4-in.-long leaves, dark dull green above, gray-hairy beneath. Blooms in spring from the previous year's growth, the small clusters of mildly fragrant lilac purple flowers carried in profusion to make sweeping wands of color. Tolerant of many soils, doing especially well in

Buddleia davidii

poor, dry gravels. Prune after bloom by removing some of oldest wood down to within few inches of ground. Or train up into small single or multiple-trunked tree. So trained it somewhat resembles a small weeping willow.

B. davidii. COMMON BUTTERFLY BUSH, SUMMER LILAC. Deciduous or semievergreen shrub. Zones 1–9, 12–24. Makes fast, rank growth each spring and summer to 3, 4, or even 10 ft. Leaves tapering, 4–12 in. long, dark green above, white felted beneath. In midsummer small fragrant flowers (lilac with orange eye) appear in dense, arching, spikelike, slender clusters 6–12 in. or more long, at branch ends. Smaller clusters appear at ends of side branches. Butterflies often visit flowers.

Vigorous, it grows like a weed. Needs good drainage and enough water to maintain growth, but little else. In cold climates the soft wood freezes nearly to ground but roots hardy. Whether plants are deciduous in cold-winter areas or semievergreen in mild winters, for best appearance cut plants back to within a few inches of ground—do this after fall flowering in Zones 4–9, 12–24; or in spring in Zones 1–3, 10, 11. Susceptible to pests, especially red spider mites in hot dry areas.

Many varieties are obtainable, differing mostly in flower colors which include pink, lilac, blue, purple, and white.

BUFFALO GRASS. See *Buchloe dactyloides.*

BUGBANE. See *Cimicifuga.*

BULBINELLA floribunda (*B. robusta, B. setosa*). Perennial, tuberous rootstock. Zones 14–24. Native to South Africa. Valuable for winter color, forming large clump of 20–26-in., narrow, floppy leaves topped in January-February with 4-in.-long spikes of clear yellow flowers. Similar to poker plant (*Kniphofia*) but spikes are shorter, less pointed, and individual flowers are bell shaped, not tubular. Splendid cut flower. Low-maintenance borders—makes colonies in rather short time. Sun; part shade

Bulbinella floribunda

in hot-summer areas. Any soil, if well-drained. Ample water in winter, spring; keep on dry side in summer. Pull off old dry foliage after bloom. Divide crowded clumps. Easy from seed sown in spring.

BULL BAY. See *Magnolia grandiflora.*

BUNCHBERRY. See *Cornus canadensis.*

BUNNY EARS. See *Opuntia microdasys.*

BUNYA-BUNYA. See *Araucaria bidwillii.*

BURK RED CEDAR. See *Juniperus virginiana* 'Burkii'.

BURMESE PLUMBAGO. See *Ceratostigma griffithii.*

BURRO TAIL. See *Sedum morganianum.*

BUSH ANEMONE. See *Carpenteria californica.*

BUSHMAN'S POISON. See *Acokanthera oppositifolia.*

BUSH MORNING GLORY. See *Convolvulus cneorum.*

BUSH POPPY. See *Dendromecon.*

BUSHY YATE. See *Eucalyptus lehmannii.*

BUSY LIZZIE. See *Impatiens wallerana.*

BUTCHER'S BROOM. See *Ruscus aculeatus.*

BUTIA capitata. PINDO PALM. Zones 7–9, 12–24. Native to Brazil, Uruguay, Argentina. Slow-growing, very hardy palm to 10–20 ft. Trunk heavy, strongly patterned with stubs of old leaves: attractive if these are trimmed to same length. Feathery leaves—gray green, arching. Very small flowers, yellow to red. Hardy to 15°F. Slow growth. Sun or light shade, average water.

Butia capitata

BUTTERFLY BUSH. See *Buddleia.*

BUTTERFLY FLOWER. See *Schizanthus pinnatus.*

BUTTERFLY ORCHID. See *Oncidium papilio.*

BUTTERFLY WEED. *Asclepias tuberosa.*

BUTTERNUT. See *Juglans cinerea* under Walnut.

BUTTONWOOD. See *Platanus occidentalis.*

BUXUS. BOXWOOD, BOX. Evergreen shrubs, small trees. Widely used for edging and hedging. When not clipped, most grow soft and billowing. All grow in full sun or shade. All are easy where adapted and therefore often neglected. Extra care with watering, feeding, and spraying in summer for mites and scale will pay off in better color and greater vigor. Flowers quite inconspicuous.

Buxus microphylla japonica

B. harlandii. Zones 8–24. The boxwood sold by this name in California, commonly called Korean boxwood, does not fit description of the true species *B. harlandii* and differs from both Japanese boxwood and true Korean boxwood. Leaves are narrower and brighter green than those of Japanese boxwood and plant appears better suited to colder areas of California, with greener winter color.

B. microphylla. This species is rarely planted. Its widely planted varieties include:

B. m. japonica. JAPANESE BOXWOOD. Zones 8–24. Hardy to 0°F. but poor winter appearance in cold areas. It takes California's dry heat and alkaline soil that rule out English boxwood. Compact foliage (small, ⅓–1 in. round-tipped leaves) is lively bright green in summer, turns brown or bronze in winter in many areas. Grows slowly to 4–6 ft. if not pruned, then is a pleasing informal green shrub. Most often clipped as low or medium hedge or shaped into globes, tiers, pyramids in containers. Can be held to 6-in. height as a hedge or border edging.

B. m. j. 'Compacta'. Extra-dwarf plant with tiny leaves. Slow growing, good rock garden plant.

B. m. j. 'Green Beauty'. Hardier than common Japanese boxwood (to −10°F.), holds its deep green color in coldest weather and is considerably greener than *B. m. japonica* in summer heat.

B. m. j. 'Richardii'. Hardy to 0°F. Zones 4–24. Tall growing (6 ft. or more), more vigorous than Japanese boxwood. Leaves deeper green, larger, and usually notched at tip.

B. m. koreana. KOREAN BOXWOOD. All Zones. Hardy to −18°F. Slower and lower growing than Japanese boxwood. Leaves smaller, ¼–½ in. This should not be confused with "Korean boxwood" or "*Buxus harlandii*" commonly sold in California. *B. m. koreana* is noted for its hardiness and will live where others freeze out. It is slower growing and smaller in leaf than the plant sold as *B. harlandii.*

B. sempervirens. COMMON BOXWOOD, ENGLISH BOXWOOD. Zones 3–6, 15–17. Dies out in alkaline soils, hot-summer areas. Dwarf form *B. s.* 'Suffruticosa' is best known; the taller-growing varieties are used in Northwest. Species will grow to height of

15–20 ft. with equal spread. Dense foliage of medium-sized, lustrous, dark green, oval leaves.

B. s. 'Arborescens'. Slow. Becomes beautiful small tree to 18 ft. More open than *B. sempervirens.*

B. s. 'Aureo-variegata'. Leaves yellow or marked with yellow.

B. s. 'Inglis'. Densely branched, cone shaped shrub with dark green foliage. Holds color well in winter. Hardy to −20°F.

B. s. 'Rotundifolia'. Dwarf, slow growing plant with nearly round leaves.

B. s. 'Suffruticosa'. TRUE DWARF BOXWOOD. Slower growing than others, to 4–5 ft. but generally clipped lower. Small leaves, dense form and texture. There's a silver-edged variegated form.

CABBAGE. For ornamental relatives see Cabbage, Flowering. Annual or biennial grown as annual. All Zones in conditions noted below. There are early varieties that mature in 7–8 weeks from transplanting into garden and late varieties that require 3–4 months. In addition to green cabbage you can also get red and curly leafed (Savoy) varieties. To avoid overproduction, set out a few plants every week or two or

Cabbage

plant both early and late kinds. Time plantings so heads will form either before or after hot summer months. In cold-winter areas, set out late varieties in midsummer for late fall and early winter crops. In mild-winter areas plant in fall or winter. To avoid pest buildup, plant in different site each year. Sow seeds ½ in. deep about 6 weeks before planting-out time. Transplant to rich moist soil, spacing plants 24–30 in. apart. Give frequent light applications of nitrogen fertilizer and never let plants wilt. Mulch helps maintain soil moisture and coolness. Best in sun; tolerates light shade in hot climates. Control aphids with soapy water spray, rotenone, or malathion. Control green cabbage worm with vegetable dust, *Bacillus thuringiensis,* or rotenone. Light frost doesn't hurt cabbage, but harvest and store before heavy freezes occur.

CABBAGE, FLOWERING. Annual or biennial grown as annual. All Zones in conditions noted below. Flowering cabbage and flowering kale are grown for their highly ornamental, highly colored leaf rosettes, which look like giant peonies in deep blue green marbled and edged with white, cream, rose, or purple. Kale differs from cabbage in being slightly looser in the head, fringier at leaf edges. It appreciates same soil, care, and timing as conventional cabbage, and its 10-in. "flowers" are spectacular in cool-season garden, either in open ground beds 15–18 in. apart, potted singly in 8-in. pots, or potted several plants

Flowering Cabbage

to a large container. Colors are strongest after first frosts touch plants. Single rosette cut and placed on spike holder in bowl makes striking harvest arrangement. Foliage edible cooked or raw, just like ordinary cabbage or kale.

CABBAGE PALM. See *Sabal palmetto.*

CACTUS. Large family of succulent plants. (See Succulent.) Generally leafless, they have stems modified into cylinders, pads, or joints which store water in times of drought. Thick skin reduces evaporation, and most species have spines to protect plants against browsing animals. Flowers are usually large and brightly colored; fruit may also be colorful, and a few are edible.

All (with one doubtful exception) are native to the Americas. Here they grow from Canada to Argentina, from sea level into high mountains, in deserts or in dripping jungles. Many are native to drier parts of the West.

They range in height from few inches to 50 ft. Larger species are used to create desert landscapes. Smaller species are grown in pots or, if sufficiently hardy, in rock gardens. Many are easy, showy house or greenhouse plants. Large cactuses for land-

scaping require full sun, well-drained soil. Water newly planted cactuses very little; roots are subject to rot before they begin active growth. In 4–6 weeks, when new roots are active, water thoroughly, then let soil dry before watering again. Reduce watering in fall to allow plants to go dormant. Feed monthly in spring, summer. For some larger kinds for garden use see: *Carnegiea, Cephalocereus, Cereus, Echinocactus, Espostoa, Ferocactus, Lemaireocereus, Opuntia.*

Smaller cactuses for pot or rock garden culture usually have interesting form and brightly colored flowers. Feed and water plants well during warm weather for good display; taper off on fertilizer to encourage winter dormancy. Use fast draining soil mix. See *Chamaecereus, Coryphantha, Echinopsis, Gymnocalycium, Lobivia, Lobivopsis, Mammillaria.*

Showiest in flower are jungle cactuses that grow as epiphytes on trees or rocks. These need rich soil with much humus, frequent feeding and watering, partial shade, and protection from frost. Grow in lath house or greenhouse, or handle as outdoor/indoor plants. See *Epiphyllum, Rhipsalidopsis, Schlumbergera.*

CAESALPINIA (*Poinciana*). Evergreen and deciduous shrubs, small trees. (Tropical royal poinciana is *Delonix regia.*) These members of pea family grow quickly and easily in hot sun with light, well-drained soil and infrequent, deep watering.

C. gilliesii (*Poinciana gilliesii*). BIRD OF PARADISE BUSH. Deciduous or evergreen shrub or small tree. Zones 8–16, 18–23. Occasionally seen Zones 6, 7. Tough, interesting, fast growing to 10 ft., with finely cut, filmy foliage on rather open, angular branch structure. Drops leaves in cold winters. Blooms all summer; clusters of yellow flowers adorned with protruding, bright red, 4–5 in.-long stamens. Flowers attract hummingbirds.

Caesalpinia gilliesii

C. pulcherrima (*Poinciana pulcherrima*). DWARF POINCIANA, BARBADOS PRIDE. Deciduous shrub. Zones 12–16, 18–23. Fast, dense growth to 10 ft. tall, 10 ft. wide. Dark green leaves with many ¾-in.-long leaflets. Blooms throughout warm weather; flowers orange or red (rarely yellow), clustered, with long red stamens. May be evergreen in mild winters. Useful for quick screening. Freezes to ground in colder areas but rebounds quickly in spring. Even if it doesn't freeze back, you can cut it back to ground in early spring to make more compact mound.

CAJEPUT TREE. See *Melaleuca quinquenervia.*

CALADIUM bicolor. FANCY-LEAFED CALADIUM. Tuberous-rooted perennial. Best adapted Zones 23, 24; in protected gardens Zones 12, 13, 16, 17, 22; elsewhere as indoor or greenhouse plant in winter, outdoors in summer. Native to tropical America.

Not grown for flowers. Instead, entire show comes from large arrow shaped, long-stalked, almost translucent leaves colored in bands and blotches of red, rose, pink, white, silver, bronze, and green. Most varieties sold in nurseries derived from *C.*

Caladium bicolor

bicolor, 2 ft., occasionally to 4 ft. Because caladiums need warm shade, daytime temperature of 70°F, best adapted as summer pot plant in sheltered patios or plunged in borders. Combine with ferns, coleus, alocasias, colocasias, and tuberous begonias.

Same pot culture as tuberous begonias. Start tubers indoors in March, outdoors in May. Pot in mix of equal parts coarse sand, leaf mold, ground bark or peat moss. Use 5-in. pot for 2½-in. tuber, 7-in. pot for 1 larger or 2 smaller tubers. Fill pot halfway with mix, stir in heaping teaspoon of fish meal. Add 1 in. mix, set tuber with knobby side up, cover with 2 in. of mix. Water thoroughly.

(Continued on next page)

To plant in ground, replace top 6 in. of existing soil with same mix as for pots. Place 1 tablespoon of fish meal in bottom of each hole; proceed as described above. Keep soil moist, not wet. Provide more moisture as leaves develop. Syringe overhead every day or two during active growth. Feed with liquid fish fertilizer once a week, starting when leaves appear. Bait for slugs and snails. Gradually withhold water when leaves start to die down. In about a month, lift tubers, remove most of soil, dry in semishade for 10 days. Dust tubers with insecticide-fungicide preparation; store for winter in dry peat moss or vermiculite at temperature between 50–60°F.

C. esculentum. See *Colocasia.*

CALAMONDIN. See *Citrus.*

CALATHEA. Indoor or greenhouse plants. Native to tropical America or Africa. Calatheas are usually called marantas, to which they are closely related and from which they differ only in technical aspects. Interesting plants for indoor decoration in winter, outdoor use in summer. Ornamental leaves, beautifully marked in various shades of green, white, and pink, arranged in basal tufts. Flowers of most are inconspicuous and of no consequence. Need

Calathea zebrina

warm atmosphere (not under 55°F.) and shade, although good light necessary for rich leaf color. Porous soil mix, perfect drainage; stagnant conditions harmful. Wet leaves frequently. Repot as often as necessary to avoid rootbound condition.

C. crocata. ETERNAL FLAME. Leaves 6 in long, 1–1½ in. wide. dark green above, purple beneath. Two-in. spikes of bright orange flower bracts look like little torches. Clump has several shoots; each shoot dies after blooming, but new ones appear to keep up the show. Variable performance as house plant; subject to mites in low humidity. Does better in greenhouse.

C. lancifolia (usually sold as *C. insignis*). Long (12–18 in.), narrow wavy-edged leaves are yellow green banded with dark olive green.

C. insignis. Striking, 3–7 ft. in native jungle, lower in cultivation, with 12–18-in.-long, yellow green leaves striped olive green.

C. louisae. To 3 ft., with foot-long dark green leaves heavily feathered with gray green along midrib.

C. makoyana. Showy, 2–4 ft. high. Leaves with areas of olive green or cream above; pink blotches beneath. Silver featherings on rest of upper surface, with corresponding cream-colored area underneath.

C. ornata. Sturdy, 1½–3 ft. high. Leaves 2–3 ft. long, rich green above, purplish red beneath. Juvenile leaves usually pink striped between veins; intermediate foliage striped white. Variety 'Roseo-lineata' has pink and white stripes at angle to midrib.

C. zebrina. ZEBRA PLANT. Compact, 1–3 ft. high. Elliptic leaves 1–2 ft. long, almost half as wide, velvety green with alternating bars of pale yellow green and olive green extending outward from midrib; purplish red underneath.

CALCEOLARIA. Perennials. Native Mexico to Chile. Loose clusters of small pouchlike or slipperlike flowers, usually yellow, sometimes red bronze, or spotted with red or orange brown, in spring and summer. Plants much branched, often woody stemmed and shrubby, 8 in.–6 ft. high, with dark green, crinkly leaves.

C. crenatiflora. Zones 14–24 as bedding plant or pot plant for outdoor use in shade; house plant elsewhere. Usually grown from seed sown in spring or summer in light porous soil, with plants ready for final potting or planting out in fall. Average water. This is florist's calceolaria, with masses of inch-long yellow to velvety red-spotted and marbled flowers. Can reach 2½ ft.; most popular strains are

Calceolaria integrifolia

Multiflora Nana and Multiflora, lower growing—9–15 in. Usually discarded after flowering but sometimes lives over. Strain called Anytime tolerates high temperatures better than other strains.

C. integrifolia. Zones 14–24. Shrubby plant 1½–6 ft. high. Leaves about 3 in. long and 1 in. wide. Clusters of yellow to red brown, unspotted flowers ½ in. across. Will grow in full sun, take heat, light frost. Average water. Borders, pots, hanging baskets. Best bloom when rootbound. Good cut flower. Variety 'Golden Nugget' most commonly sold; vigorous, 18–24 in., clear golden yellow flowers spring to fall. 'Russet' and 'Kentish Hero' have orange red to brown flowers.

C. 'John Innes'. All Zones. Bedding and rock garden plant to 8 in. high, with 3-in.-long leaves and large, golden yellow, purple-spotted flowers in June, July. Spreading growth habit in some instances; stems tend to take root in contact with soil. Needs rich moist soil and shade.

CALENDULA officinalis. CALENDULA, POT MARIGOLD. Annual. All Zones in conditions noted below. Sure, easy color from late fall through spring in mild-winter areas; spring to midsummer in colder climates. Besides familiar orange and bright yellow double, daisylike blooms 2½–4½ in. across, calendulas come in more subtle shades of apricot, persimmon, cream, and soft yellow. Pacific Beauty strain one of best. Plants somewhat branching, 1–2 ft. high. Leaves are long, narrow, round on ends, slightly sticky, and aromatic. Plants effective in masses of single colors in borders, parking strips, along drives, in containers. Long-lasting cut flowers.

Calendula officinalis

Sow seed in place or in flats in late summer or early fall in mild-winter climates; spring elsewhere. Or buy seedlings at nurseries. Needs sun. Adapts to most soils, ample or little water, if drainage is fast. Remove spent flowers to prolong bloom. Although an excellent pot plant, the common name is actually derived from the plant's earlier use as a "pot herb"—a vegetable to be used in the cooking pot.

CALICO BUSH. See *Kalmia latifolia.*

CALICO FLOWER. See *Aristolochia elegans.*

CALIFORNIA BAY. See *Umbellularia californica.*

CALIFORNIA FAN PALM. See *Washingtonia filifera.*

CALIFORNIA FUCHSIA. See *Zauschneria.*

CALIFORNIA GERANIUM. See *Senecio petasitis.*

CALIFORNIA HOLLY. See *Heteromeles arbutifolia.*

CALIFORNIA HOLLY GRAPE. See *Mahonia pinnata.*

CALIFORNIA INDIAN PINK. See *Silene californica.*

CALIFORNIA LAUREL. See *Umbellularia californica.*

CALIFORNIA NUTMEG. See *Torreya californica.*

CALIFORNIA PITCHER PLANT. See *Darlingtonia californica.*

CALIFORNIA POPPY. See *Eschscholzia californica.*

CALLA. See *Zantedeschia.*

CALLIANDRA. Evergreen shrubs. Group of 250 or more species represented here by a flame bush, a pink powder puff, and fairy dusters. All are showy, spreading shrubs that need sun and warmth.

C. californica. Zones 10–24. Similar to *C. eriophylla* except foliage is more luxuriant. Blooms through warm part of year if given some supplemental summer water.

C. eriophylla. FAIRY DUSTER, FALSE MESQUITE. Zones 10–24. Native to Imperial and eastern San Diego counties, California, east to Texas; and Baja California. Open growing to 3 ft., spreading 4–5 ft. Leaves

Calliandra tweedii

finely cut into tiny leaflets. Flower clusters show pink to red stamens in fluffy balls to 1½ in. across, February or March. Very drought resistant.

C. haematocephala (*C. inaequilatera*). PINK POWDER PUFF. Zones 22–24. Native to Bolivia. Grows fast to 10 ft. or more, equal spread. Its beauty has carried it into less kind areas than Zones 22–24: into 13, 16–21 where it is given special protection of overhang or warm sunny wall. (In form, it's natural espalier.) Foliage not as feathery as *C. tweedii*. Leaflets longer, broader and darker green; glossy copper when new, turning to dark metallic green. Big powder puffs (2–3 in. across) of silky stamens, watermelon pink, are produced October-March. There is a rare white-flowered form. Needs plenty of water and light soil.

C. tweedii (often sold as *C. guildingii*). TRINIDAD FLAME BUSH, BRAZILIAN FLAME BUSH. Best in Zones 22–24; satisfactory 15–21; freezes back but recovers in Zones 7–9, 12–14.

Graceful, picturesque structure to 6–8 ft. tall, 5–8 ft. wide. Leaves, lacy and fernlike, divided into many tiny leaflets, scarcely hide branches. At branch ends flower clusters show as bright crimson pompons, February to fall. Not fussy about soil. Once established it's quite drought resistant. Prune to thin and also to retain interesting branch pattern.

CALLICARPA bodinieri giraldii (*C. giraldiana*). BEAUTYBERRY. Deciduous shrub. Zones 1–6. This species seems to be the only one in cultivation in the West. To 6–10 ft., with gracefully recurving branches. Leaves narrow, to 4 in. long, something like peach leaves in form; turn pink to purple before falling. Small lilac flowers in 1-in.-wide clusters followed by small violet purple fruit that last well into fall. Freezes to ground in cold winters, comes back quickly from stump sprouts. Sun, average water.

Callicarpa bodinieri giraldii

CALLIOPSIS. See *Coreopsis tinctoria*.

CALLISIA. House plants or indoor/outdoor plants for hanging pots. They look like, and are related to, wandering Jews (*Tradescantia* and *Zebrina*). For care, see *Tradescantia* description.

C. elegans. Stems spread or reach upward instead of drooping, usually much less than maximum of 2 ft. Leaves thick, semisucculent, 3 in. long by 1 in. wide, dark olive green above with white pinstripes running lengthwise, purple underneath. Small flowers, not often seen.

C. fragrans. Leaves to 10 in. long make big rosettes that resemble loose-knit hens and chicks (*Echeveria*). Long runners produce miniatures of parent at tips. Makes massive hanging basket plant that is impressive rather than attractive. Branched clusters of fragrant flowers seldom produced. Offsets can be detached and set in shallow trays of water, the rosettes resting on pebbles or other support. They will root and grow for several months with no further attention, tolerating low light, dryness.

Callisia elegans

C. repens. This creeping, trailing plant is often sold as *Tradescantia* or as 'Little Jewel'. Closely spaced, thick, fleshy, shiny bright green leaves an inch long or less make it attractive hanging pot plant. Small flowers bloom infrequently.

CALLISTEMON. BOTTLEBRUSH. Evergreen shrubs or trees. Zones 8, 9, 12–24, but borderline—often severely damaged— at 20°F. Native to Australia. Colorful flowers in dense spikes or round clusters consisting principally of long, bristlelike stamens—hence name, bottlebrush. Flowers followed by woody capsules that persist for years and sometimes look like bands of beads pressed into bark. Thrive in full sun. Drought tolerant but grow best in moist, well-drained soils. Generally tolerant of saline-alkaline soils but sometimes suffer

Callistemon citrinus

from chlorosis. Fast growing, easy to train. Quick wall cover as informal espaliers. Several can be trained as small trees. Some can be used in formal clipped hedges or as informal screens or windbreaks. A few can be trained as ground covers.

Many kinds are being sold under names whose identification is uncertain. Closely related to melaleuca, and some plants sold as *Callistemon* may be melaleucas.

C. citrinus (*C. lanceolatus*). LEMON BOTTLEBRUSH. Best-selling bottlebrush, most tolerant of heat, cold, and most adverse soils (can be troubled with chlorosis in Zones 12 and 13). Massive shrub to 10–15 ft., but with staking and pruning in youth easily trained into narrowish, round-headed 20–25-ft. tree. Nurseries offer it as shrub, espalier, or tree. Narrow, 3-in.-long leaves coppery colored in new growth, then vivid green. Bright red, 6-in.-long brushes appear in cycles throughout year. Hummingbirds love flowers.

Variable plant when grown from seed. Cutting-grown selections with good flower size and color are *C. c.* 'Improved' and *C. c.* 'Splendens'. *C. c.* 'Compacta' is smaller (4 ft. by 4 ft. at 3 years), with smaller spikes. *C. c.* 'Jeffersii' is smaller (to 6 ft. tall, 4 ft. wide), stiffer in branching, with narrower, shorter leaves, and reddish purple flowers fading to lavender.

C. cupressifolius. The plant sold under this name may be a melaleuca or variety of some other species of *Callistemon*. Shrubby, 4–5 ft. high, 4–6 ft. wide. Growth is spreading, with drooping branchlets. Foliage gray green; new foliage pink. Red flower clusters to 3 in. long in June-July.

C. 'Jeffersii'. See *C. citrinus* 'Jeffersii'.

C. linearis. NARROW-LEAFED BOTTLEBRUSH. Shrubby, 6–8 ft. tall (sometimes to 15 ft.), 5 ft. wide, with narrow, 2–5-in.-long leaves. Bright crimson brushes 5 in. long in summer.

C. pachyphyllus viridis. Stiff-branched, spreading shrub to 6–7 ft. Leaves nearly as narrow and stiff as pine needles. Flower spikes are bright apple green against dark green foliage.

C. phoeniceus. FIERY BOTTLEBRUSH. Shrub 6–8 ft. high, similar to *C. citrinus*, but stiffer growing, more densely foliated. Light green to gray leaves 4 in. long. Flower brushes to 4 in. long, rich red; blooms in spring, again in fall. *C. p.* 'Prostratus' is interesting plant with floppy stems that grow with contours of ground.

C. rigidus. STIFF BOTTLEBRUSH. Erect, sparse, rigid shrub or small tree to 20 ft. with 10-ft. spread. Leaves sharp pointed, gray green (sometimes purplish). Red flower brushes 2½–4½ in. long, spring and summer. Seed capsules prominent. Least graceful bottlebrush, but drought tolerant.

C. 'Rosea'. Plants sold under this name are similar to *C. citrinus* 'Jeffersii' but taller and have rose pink flowers.

C. salignus. WHITE BOTTLEBRUSH. Shrub or tree to 20–25 ft. Dense crown of foliage. New growth bright pink to copper. Willowy leaves 2–3 in. long. Flowers pale yellow to creamy in 1½–3-in. clusters. Train as small shade tree or plant 4–5 ft. apart as hedge.

C. viminalis. WEEPING BOTTLEBRUSH. Shrub or small tree with pendulous branches. Fast growing to 20–30 ft. with 15-ft. spread. Leaves narrow, light green, 6 in. long. Bright red brushes May-July, and

Callistemon viminalis

scattered bloom throughout the year. Needs ample water. Not for windy, dry areas. May be damaged by cold some winters in Zones 12 and 13. As tree, needs staking, thinning of surplus branches to prevent tangled, topheavy growth. Inclined toward sparseness because leaves tend to grow only at ends of long, hanging branches. 'Captain Cook' is dwarf variety useful as border or low hedge or screen plant. 'McCaskillii' is denser in habit than others, more vigorous, and better in flower color and form. Variety sold as 'Dwarf' resembles 'McCaskillii'.

Callistemon viminalis

CALLISTEPHUS chinensis. CHINA ASTER. Annual. All Zones in conditions noted below. Splendid cut flower and effective bedding plant when well-grown and free of disease. Plants 1–3 ft. high, some kinds branching, others (developed mainly for florists) with strong stems and no sideshoots. Leaves deeply toothed or lobed. Summer is bloom season. Many different flower forms: quilled, curled, incurved, ribbonlike, or interlaced rays; some with crested centers; varieties offered as pompon, peony flowered, anemone flowered, ostrich feather. Colors range from white to pastel pinks, rose pink, lavender, lavender blue, violet, purple, crimson, wine, and scarlet.

Callistephus chinensis

Plant in rich loamy or sandy soil in full sun. Sow seed in place after frosts or set out plants from flats. Keep growth steady; sudden checks in growth are harmful. Subject to aster yellows, virus disease carried by leafhoppers. Remove and burn infected plants. Spray or dust to control leafhoppers. All but wilt-resistant types are subject to aster wilt or stem rot, caused by parasitic fungus which lives in soil and is transmitted through roots into plants. Overwatering produces ideal condition for diseases, especially in heavy soil. Never plant in same location in successive years.

CALLUNA vulgaris. SCOTCH HEATHER. Evergreen shrub. Zones 2–6, 15–17. This, the true and only Scotch heather, has crowded, tiny, scalelike dark green leaves and one-sided spikes of bell shaped rosy pink flowers. Garden varieties (far more common than wild kind) include dwarf ground cover and rock garden plants 2–4 in. tall and robust 2–3-footers. Flower colors include white, pale to deep pink, lavender, and purple. Foliage can vary to paler and deeper greens, yellow, chartreuse, gray, or russet, often changing color in winter. Most bloom in mid to late summer; a few bloom into late fall. To prune, shear off faded flowers and branch tips immediately after bloom (with latest varieties, delay pruning until March).

Calluna vulgaris

They thrive in full sun (light shade in hot interior valleys) in sandy, peaty, fast draining soil. In Northwest, where they are best adapted, they require little or no fertilizing. Where watering must be frequent, light feeding with acid plant food in February or March and again in June encourages good growth, bloom.

Lower kinds make good rock garden or ground cover plants; taller varieties make good backgrounds for lower kinds and are attractive cut flowers. Good hobby plants, they come in stimulating variety of colors and textures; by carefully choosing varieties you can have bloom from June-November. Combine them with heaths (*Erica*) for year-round bloom, or use with other acid-soil plants (rhododendron, pieris, huckleberry) for contrasting texture. Here are a few of the scores of varieties obtainable from specialists:

'Alba Plena'. Loose, medium-green mound to 12 in. Double white flowers Aug.-Sept. Fast growing.

'Aurea'. Spreading, twiggy, 8–12 in. plant with gold foliage turning russet in winter. Sparse purple bloom Aug.-Sept.

'Aureafolia'. Upright, to 18–24 in. Chartreuse foliage, tinged gold in summer. White flowers Aug.–Sept.

'County Wicklow'. Mounding, 9–18 in., medium green. Pink double flowers from white buds Aug.-Oct.

'Dainty Bess'. Tiny gray-foliaged mat 2–4 in. tall. Lavender flowers Aug.-Sept.; shapes itself to rocks, crevices.

'David Eason'. Spreading mound, 12–18 in. Light green foliage; reddish purple flowers Oct.-Nov.

'Else Frye'. Erect plant to 24 in. Medium-green foliage; double white flowers July-Aug.

'Foxii Nana'. Small mound to 6 in. Dark green foliage; purple flowers Aug.-Sept. A dwarf pincushion.

'Goldsworth Crimson'. Mounding, 18–24 in. Dark or smoky green foliage; crimson flowers Oct.-Nov.

'H. E. Beale'. Loose mound to 2 ft. Dark green foliage; soft pink double flowers Aug.-Oct. Long spikes good for cutting.

'J. H. Hamilton'. Prostrate, bushy, to 9 in. Deep green foliage; profuse double pink bloom Aug.-Sept.

'Mair's Variety'. Erect, 2–3 ft. Medium green foliage; white flowers July-Sept. Easy to grow, good background.

'Mrs. Pat'. Bushy, to 8 in. Light green foliage; new growth pink. Light purple flowers July-Sept.

'Mrs. Ronald Gray'. Creeping mound, to 3 in. Dark green foliage; reddish purple Aug.-Sept. Excellent ground cover.

'Mullion'. Tight mound to 9 in. Dark green foliage, rosy purple flowers Aug.-Sept. Fine ground cover.

'Nana'. Low, spreading, to 4 in. Dark green foliage; purple flowers July-Sept. Often called carpet heather.

'Nana Compacta'. Tight mound to 4 in. Medium green. Purple flowers July-Sept. Pincushion heather for rockery.

'Roma'. Compact, to 9 in. Dark green foliage; deep pink flowers Aug.-Oct.

'Searlei'. Bushy, 12–18 in. Yellow green feathery foliage. White flowers Aug.-Oct.

'Tib'. Rounded, bushy, to 12–18 in. Medium-green foliage; deepest rosy purple double flowers Aug.-Sept.

CALOCEDRUS decurrens (*Libocedrus decurrens*). INCENSE CEDAR. Evergreen tree. Zones 1–12, 14–24. Native to mountains of southern Oregon, California, western Nevada; northern Baja California. Unlike most of its native associates—white fir, Douglas fir, sugar pine—it adapts to many western climates. Symmetrical tree to 75–90 ft. with dense, narrow, pyramidal crown; trunk with reddish brown bark. Rich green foliage in flat sprays. Tree gives pungent fragrance to garden in warm weather. Small, yellowish brown to reddish brown cones which, when open, look like ducks' bills.

Calocedrus decurrens

Although slow-growing at first, once established it may grow 2 ft. per year. Deep but infrequent watering in youth will make it unusually drought tolerant when mature. Takes blazing summer heat. Tolerates poor soils. Good tree to make green wall, high screen, windbreak. Common on the Yosemite Valley floor, this tree has been seen by millions.

CALOCEPHALUS brownii. CUSHION BUSH. Evergreen shrubby perennial. Zones 16, 17, 19, 21–24. Best adapted Zones 17, 24. Native to Australia, Tasmania. An unusual mounding plant, silvery white throughout; at its best when buffeted by winds and exposed to salt air and spray. Wiry branching stems; tiny threadlike leaves, 1/8 in. long, pressed tightly against slender stems.

Calocephalus brownii

Grows 3 ft. tall, equally broad. Flower heads button shaped, ½ in. across, in clusters. Stunning high ground cover or rock garden plant. Effective in large planters with succulents. Fresh or dried foliage attractive in arrangements. Full sun, sandy or gravelly soil, fast drainage. Sensitive to excess water, severe cold. Cut out dead wood on older plants.

Calocephalus brownii

CALOCHORTUS. Corms. All Zones. Western natives, most numerous in California. Of most interest to hobbyists willing to devote more than ordinary care to beautiful group of plants. It's best to plant kinds native to your area or similar climate. All kinds should be kept moist in spring, allowed to go dry in summer. Can grow in cans or boxes; plunge in garden in fall, lift after bloom to dry out in summer. In colder climates, mulch plantings to protect from alternate freezing and thawing, remove mulch in spring; or grow indoors in pots.

Calochortus venustus

Flower forms divide into 3 groups: globe tulips or fairy lanterns have 3–5 nodding flowers to a stalk, and petals turn inward to form globe. Star tulips have erect, cup shaped flowers, often with tips of petals rolled outwards; some have long straight hairs on inner flower surfaces and are called cat's ears or pussy ears. Most striking are mariposa lilies, whose erect, branching, 10–24-in. stems hold big, colorful, cup shaped flowers. Leaves scanty, long, grasslike. Here are kinds most often available for sale:

C. albus. WHITE GLOBE LILY, FAIRY LANTERN. Sierra foothills, Coast Range. Two-ft. stems; white 1¼-in. flowers March-May.

C. amabilis. GOLDEN FAIRY LANTERN. North Coast Range. Stems 15 in. tall; flowers 1¼ in. long, deep yellow often tinged brown, March-May.

C. amoenus. PURPLE GLOBE TULIP. Sierra foothills. Rosy purple lanterns 1¼-in. long; 8–16-in. stems; April-June.

C. clavatus. Sierra Nevada foothills. Mariposa lily with yellow flowers sometimes marked brownish red, 2–3 in. wide on stems to 3 ft. Blooms April-June.

C. luteus (*C. luteus citrinus*). Coast Range or Sierra Nevada foothills. Yellow 2½-in. mariposa lilies on 1–1½ ft. stems April-June. For plant often sold as *C. l. oculatus,* see *C. vestae.*

C. maweanus. See *C. tolmiei.*

C. nudus. SIERRA STAR TULIP. Mountains of northern California. Flowers white to lavender, 1–1½ in. wide, on 4–10 in. stems.

C. nuttallii. SEGO LILY. Eastern Montana to northern California, south to New Mexico and Arizona. State flower of Utah. Flowers white, marked lilac or purple, 2–3 in. wide; stems 1½ ft. tall. Early summer bloom.

C. splendens. LILAC MARIPOSA. Coast Range, northern California to Baja California. Deep lilac 2-in. flowers, sometimes with purple centers, on 1–2 ft. stems. Early summer bloom.

C. tolmiei (*C. maweanus*). CAT'S EARS, PUSSY EARS. Mountains of Washington, Oregon, northern California. White to cream flowers often tinged pinkish or purplish, 1½ in. wide, fringed and furry on inner surfaces. Weak stems to 16 in. Spring blooming.

C. uniflorus (*C. lilacinus*). STAR TULIP. Northern California coast and Coast Range. Lilac flowers 1 in. long, 1½ in. wide on 4 in. stems. Spring.

C. venustus. WHITE MARIPOSA LILY. Central, southern California Coast Range, southern Sierra Nevada foothills. Flowers 3–3½ in. wide, white or yellow to purple, dark red, often with peacock eye at base of petals. Stems 10 in., often much more, in height. Color forms include 'Eldorado' (white with red eye) and 'Roseus' (white and rose). May-July bloom.

C. vestae (*C. luteus oculatus*). Northern California Coast Range. White through pink and lilac to rose, with red brown peacock eye in center banded in yellow. Most common forms are lilac with dark center and rose with dark eye. Flowers 1½ in. wide on 1–1½ ft. stems in late spring, early summer.

CALODENDRUM capense. CAPE CHESTNUT. Briefly deciduous tree. Zones 19, 21–24; worth risking Zones 15, 16. Native to South Africa. Broad crowned, 25–40 ft. Noteworthy for profuse display of spikes of rosy lilac, 1½-in.-long flowers, whole cluster measuring 10–12 in. high by as much across and extending well above foliage like candelabra. Blooms generally from May into July. Seldom flowers when young. Slow-growing. Leaves are light to medium green, oval shaped, to 6 in. Time of flowering and deciduous period varies by location and season. Plant it out of prevailing wind. Average water requirement.

Calodendrum capense

CALONYCTION aculeatum. See *Ipomoea alba.*

CALOTHAMNUS. NET BUSH. Evergreen shrubs. Native to western Australia. Zones 8–9, 12–24. Related to bottle brush (*Callistemon*) and probably adapted to same climates. Fairly drought resistant, take sun, heat, wind, salt breeze, and poor soil if it drains well (expect root rot if drainage is poor). Needlelike leaves densely clothe rather spreading branches. Flowers, somewhat resembling one-sided bottle brushes, grow along branches, rather close to wood. Sporadic bloom throughout year.

Calothamnus quadrifidus

Prune hard after flowering to keep plants from getting straggly. Generally not attractive in age, showing more wood than foliage.

Of many species introduced, the following are being grown by nurseries:

C. quadrifidus. Grows to 6–8 ft. high. Dark green leaves, ½–1 in. long. Short clusters of dark red flowers.

C. villosus (*C. villosus prostratus*). To 4 ft. Soft-hairy, ½-in.-long leaves. Long, deep red flower clusters.

CALTHA palustris. MARSH-MARIGOLD. Perennial. All Zones. Native to eastern U.S. Bog or marsh plant well-adapted to edges of pools, ponds, streams, other moist situations. With sufficient water, can be grown in borders, but must not dry out in summer. Sun or shade. Good with bog irises, moisture loving ferns. To 2 ft., lush green leaves 2–7 in. across; vivid yellow flowers are 2 in. across, in clusters. Increase by divisions or sow seed in boggy soil.

Caltha palustris

CALYCANTHUS. Deciduous shrubs, represented in western gardens by a western and eastern native. Average water needs.

C. floridus. CAROLINA ALLSPICE. Hardy Zones 1–9, 14–22. Native Virginia to Florida. Grows to 10 ft., spreading 5–8 ft., stiffly branched. Leaves oval to 5 in., glossy dark green above, grayish green beneath. Flowers, 2 in. wide, maroon brown, with strawberrylike fragrance, carried at ends of leafy branchlets in May-July, depending on climate and exposure. They are followed by brownish pear shaped capsules fragrant when crushed. Grows in shade or sun, any soil. Rare.

Calycanthus occidentalis

C. occidentalis. SPICE BUSH. Zones 4–9, 14–22. Native along streams, moist slopes, California Coast Range, Sierra Nevada foothills. To 4–12 ft. high. Leaves 2–6 in. long, 1–2 in. wide, bright green, turning yellow in fall. Flowers reddish brown to 2 in. across, like small water lilies, appear April-August depending on climate. Both flowers and bruised leaves have fragrance of old wine barrel. Takes sun or part shade and ordinary garden care. Can be trained into multistemmed small tree.

CALYPSO bulbosa. Terrestrial orchid. Zones 4–6, 15–17. Native to northern hemisphere and fairly common in heavily forested areas of Northwest, where it grows on decayed logs or in leaf mold. Needs shade, moist (not constantly wet) soil.

Solitary, pendant, pink flowers an inch or more across with brown spots in lines, and purple and yellow markings in pouchlike lip. Flower stalk to 9 in. tall; solitary roundish leaf 3 in. across. Grow in leaf mold or forest duff and protect from birds and slugs. Will take subzero temperatures.

Calypso bulbosa

CAMASS. See *Camassia*.

CAMASSIA. CAMASS. Bulbs. Zones 1–9, 14–17. Most species native to moist meadows, marshes, fields in northern California and Northwest. Plant in moist situation, fairly heavy soil, where bulbs can remain undisturbed for many years. Set bulbs 4 in. deep, 6 in. apart. To avoid premature rooting, plant after weather cools in fall. Need lots of water while growing. Grasslike basal leaves dry quickly after late spring-early summer bloom.

C. cusickii. Dense clusters of pale blue flowers on stems 2–3 ft. tall.

C. leichtlinii. Large handsome clusters of creamy white flowers on stems 2–4 ft. tall. *C. l. suksdorfii* is attractive blue variety. 'Alba' has whiter flowers than species, and 'Plena' has double greenish yellow blooms.

C. quamash (*C. esculenta*). Loose clusters of deep blue flowers on 1–2 ft. stems; flowers of 'Orion' are deeper blue, those of 'San Juan Form' still deeper blue.

Camassia quamash

CAMELLIA. Evergreen shrubs and small trees. Zones 4–9, 14–24. Native to eastern and southern Asia. There are over 3,000 named kinds, and range in color, size, and form is remarkable. But camellia breeding is still in its infancy, and what is yet to come stirs the imagination—blue and purple camellias, yellow and orange camellias, fragrant camellias, all are possible.

In these few pages we treat briefly the cultural requirements of camellias and describe some of the lesser known species as well as the widely distributed old favorites and new varieties. Where a certain type of camellia has a specific cultural need, that need is given in the description. General cultural requirements appear below.

Camellias need well-drained soil rich in organic material. Never plant camellias so trunk base is below soil line, and never permit soil to wash over and cover this base. Keep roots cool with 2-in.-thick mulch.

Camellias make outstanding container plants—especially in wooden tubs and half-barrels. As a general rule, plant gallon-can camellias into 12–14-in.-wide tubs, 5-gallon ones into 16–18-in. tubs. Fill with a planting mix containing 50 percent or more organic material.

Camellias thrive and bloom best when sheltered from strong hot sun and drying winds. Tall old plants in old gardens prove that camellias can thrive in full sun when mature enough to have roots shaded by heavy canopy of leaves. Established (more than 3 years old and vigorous) plants can survive on natural rainfall. Young plants will grow better and have more attractive flowers if grown under partial shade of tall trees, under lath cover, or on north side of a building.

Some species and varieties are more sun tolerant than others; a few, like *C. japonica* 'Lotus', need shade. If your water is high in salts and if you irrigate your camellias, leach accumulated salts with deep soaking—twice in summer—to dissolve harmful salts and carry them deep below the root zone.

Fertilize with a commercial acid plant food. Generally, time to feed is in weeks and months following bloom; read fertilizer label for complete instructions. Don't use more than called for. Better to cut amounts in half and feed twice as frequently. Don't feed sick plant. Poor drainage, water or soil with excess salts are the main trouble causers. Best cure is to move plant into above-ground bed of straight ground bark or peat moss until it recovers.

Scorched or yellowed areas in center of leaves are usually due to sunburn. Burned leaf edges, excessive leaf drop, or corky spots usually indicate over-fertilizing. Yellow leaves with green veins are signs of chlorosis. Check drainage, leach, treat with iron or iron chelates.

One disease may be serious: camellia petal blight. Flowers rapidly turn ugly brown. Browning at edges of petals (especially whites and pale pinks) may be caused by sun or wind, but if brown rapidly runs into center of flower, suspect petal blight. Sanitation is the best control. Pick up and burn (or place in covered garbage can) all fallen flowers and petals, and pick off all infected flowers from plants; encourage neighbors to do the same. Remove mulch (if you use one), haul it away, and replace with fresh one; a deep mulch (4–5 in.) helps keep spores of fungus from reaching the air. Spraying ground under plants with PCNB several weeks before flowers open will lessen chance of infection; benomyl will prevent infestation if present on flowers when spores alight.

Some flower bud dropping may be natural phenomenon; many camellias set more buds than they can open. Some bud drop can be caused by overwatering, more by underwatering, especially during summer. It can also be caused by spells of very low humidity.

Some varieties bear too many flowers. To get nicest display from them, remove buds in midsummer like this: from branch-end clusters, remove all but one or two round flower buds (leaf buds are slender); along stems, remove enough to leave single flower bud for each 2–4 in. of branch.

Prune right after flowering or during summer and fall. Remove dead or weak wood and thin when growth is so dense that flowers have no room to open properly. Prune at will to get form you want. Shorten lower branches to encourage upright growth. Lanky shrubs can be fattened by cutting back top growth. Make cut just above scar that terminates previous year's growth (it is usually slightly thickened, somewhat rough area where bark texture and color change slightly). A cut just above this point will usually force 3 or 4 dormant buds into growth.

C. granthamiana. Many plants are rare in nature. This one is as rare as can be; only one specimen has ever been found in the wilds, and that not until 1955.

It becomes a big shrub or small tree of rather open growth with leathery, heavily veined and crinkled glossy leaves 2–6 in. long. Flowers large (to 6 in. or more across), white, single, often with fluted or folded ("rabbit-ear") petals and centered with heavy tuft of bright yellow stamens. Flowers open in October, November, and December from large, brown, scaly, silky-haired buds. A cross between this one and *C. reticulata* produced 'China Lady', which looks like big pink *C. granthamiana*. This species has been the parent of several other remarkable seedling camellias.

C. hiemalis. Includes number of varieties formerly listed as Sasanquas but differing in their later and longer bloom and heavier-textured flowers. Four good examples:

'Chansonette'. Vigorous spreading growth. Large, bright pink, formal double flowers with frilled petals.

'Shishi-Gashira'. One of most useful and ornamental shrubs. Low growing with arching branches that in time pile up tier on tier to make compact, dark green, glossy-leafed plant. Leaves rather small for camellia, giving medium-fine foliage texture. Flowers rose red, semidouble to double, 2–2½ in. wide, heavily borne over long season—October to March in good year. Full sun or shade.

Camellia hiemalis

'Showa-No-Sakae'. Faster growing, more open than 'Shishi-Gashira'; willowy, arching branches. Semidouble to double flowers of soft pink, occasionally marked with white. Try this as espalier or in hanging basket.

'Showa Supreme' is very similar, but has somewhat larger flowers of peony form.

Higo camellias. These camellias, bred for 200 years in Japan but only now attracting attention in the U.S., are probably varieties of *C. japonica*. They are generally compact plants with dense, heavy foliage and thick-petaled single flowers with broad, full brush of stamens in the center. In ideal Higo camellia, mass of stamens should be at least half the diameter of flower. Colors include white, pink, red, and variegated. Many named varieties are already available in this country, and more are likely to appear.

C. japonica. This to most gardeners is *the* camellia. Naturally a large shrub or small tree, but variable in size, growth rate, and habit. Hundred-year-old plants in California are over 20 ft. high and equally wide, and larger plants exist, but most gardeners can consider camellias 6-12-ft. shrubs. Many are lower growing.

Here are 16 varieties that are old standbys with western gardeners. Easily obtainable, inexpensive, and handsome even in comparison with some of the newest introductions, they are plants for the beginner—but not only for the beginner.

In the list, season of bloom is noted by "E," "M," or "L." In California "early" means October-January; "midseason," January-March; "late," March-May. In the Northwest, it's December-February for "early"; March and April, "midseason"; May, "late."

Also, flower size is noted for each variety. A "very large" flower is over 5 in. across. "Large" is 4–5 in., "medium large" 3½–4 in., "medium" 3–3½ in., "small" 2½–3 in., "miniature" 2½ in. or less.

'Adolphe Audusson'. M. Very large, dark red, semidouble flowers, heavily borne on a medium-sized, symmetrical, vigorous shrub. Hardy. 'Adolphe Audusson Variegated' is identical, but heavily marbled white on red.

'Alba Plena'. E. Brought from China in 1792, and still a favorite large, white, formal double. Slow bushy growth. Early bloom a disadvantage in cold or rainy areas. Protect flowers from rain and wind.

'Berenice Boddy'. M. Medium semidouble, light pink with deeper shading. Vigorous upright growth. One of most cold-hardy of camellias.

'Debutante'. E-M. Medium large, peony-form flowers of light pink. Profusely blooming. Vigorous upright growth.

'Donckelarii'. M. Red marbled white; amount of marbling varies, even on same plant. Large semidouble flowers. Slow bushy growth. Hardy.

'Elegans' ('Chandler'). Also known as 'Chandleri Elegans' and 'Francine'. E-M. Very large anemone-form camellia with rose pink petals and smaller petals called petaloids, the latter often marked white. Slow growth and spreading, arching branches make it a natural for espalier. Stake to provide height, and don't remove main shoot; it may be very slow to resume upward growth. A hundred-year-old-plus variety that remains a favorite. Its offspring resemble it in every way except flower color: 'C. M. Wilson', pale pink; 'Shiro Chan', white, sometimes faintly marked with pink; and 'Elegans (Chandler) Variegated', heavily marbled rose pink and white.

'Finlandia'. E-M. Medium large semidouble with swirled and fluted petals. Medium, compact growth. Similar are 'Finlandia Blush', with pale pink flowers; 'Finlandia Red', a salmon red; and 'Finlandia Variegated', with white flowers streaked crimson. All freely blooming.

'Glen 40' ('Coquetti'). M-L. Large formal double of deep red. One of best reds for corsages. Slow, compact upright growth. Handsome even out of flower. Hardy; very good in containers.

'Herme' ('Jordan's Pride'). M. Medium large, semidouble flowers are pink, irregularly bordered white and streaked deep pink. Sometimes has all solid pink flowers on certain branches. Free blooming, dependable.

'Kumasaka'. M-L. Medium large, rose form to peony form, rose pink. Vigorous, compact, upright growth and remarkably heavy flower production make it choice landscape plant. Hardy. Takes morning sun.

'Magnoliaeflora'. M. Medium semidouble flowers of pale pink. Many blossoms, good cut flower. Medium grower of compact yet spreading form. Hardy.

'Mathotiana'. M-L. Very large rose form to formal double of deep crimson, sometimes with purplish cast. Vigorous upright grower. Takes cold and stands up well in hot summer areas.

(Continued on next page)

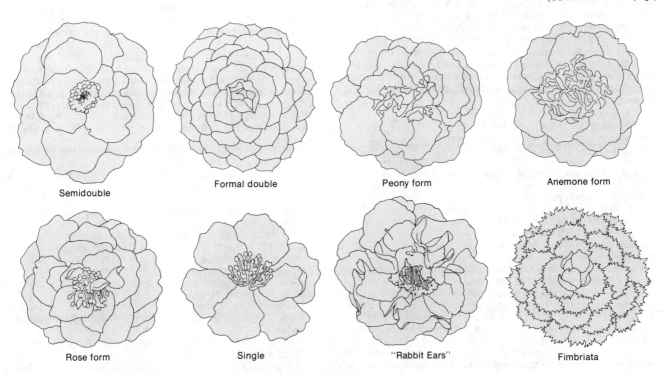

Semidouble   Formal double   Peony form   Anemone form

Rose form   Single   "Rabbit Ears"   Fimbriata

Flower forms of *Camellia japonica*; formal double is the most familiar, but others are gaining in popularity.

Does not grow very well along the southern California coast.

'Mrs. Charles Cobb'. M. Large semidouble to peony-form flowers in deep red. Freely flowering. Compact plant with dense foliage. Best in warmer areas.

'Prince Eugene Napoleon' ('Pope Pius IX'). M. A cherry red, medium large formal double. Medium, compact, upright growth.

'Purity'. L. White, medium-sized rose form to formal double, usually showing a few stamens. Vigorous upright plant. Late bloom often escapes rain damage.

'Ville de Nantes'. M-L. Large semidouble flowers of deep red blotched white. Petals pleated and fringed. Slow bushy growth.

The preceding 16 are the old classics in the camellia world. The following, all introduced since 1950, may supplant them in time:

'Betty Sheffield Supreme'. M. Unique flower markings: petals white with deep pink to red border. Form variable, from semidouble through peony form to formal double. Large flowers on medium, compact shrubs.

'Carter's Sunburst'. E-L. Large to very large pale pink flowers striped deeper pink. Semidouble to peony form to formal double flowers on medium, compact plants.

'Drama Girl'. M. Huge, semidouble flowers of deep salmon rose pink. Vigorous, open, pendulous growth.

'Guilio Nuccio'. M. Coral rose, very large semidouble flowers with inner petals fluted in "rabbit-ear" effect. Unusual depth and substance. Vigorous upright growth. This variety is considered by many to be the world's finest camellia. Variegated, fringed forms are available.

'Kramer's Supreme'. M. Very large, deep peony-form full flowers of deep clear red. Slightly fragrant. Unusually vigorous, compact, and upright. Takes some sun.

'Mrs. D. W. Davis'. M. Spectacular, very large, somewhat cup shaped flowers of palest blush pink open from egg-sized buds. Vigorous, upright, compact plant with very handsome broad leaves.

'Nuccio's Gem'. E-M. Medium to large full formal double, white. Strong, full, upright grower.

'Reg Ragland'. E-L. Large, semidouble red flowers with smaller, upright center petals surrounding mass of yellow stamens. Medium, compact growth.

'Swan Lake'. M-L. Very large, white, formal double to peony-form flower. Vigorous upright growth.

'Tiffany'. M-L. Very large, warm pink flowers. Rose form to loose, irregular semidouble. Vigorous, upright shrub.

'Tomorrow'. E-M. Very large semidouble to peony-form flower of strawberry red. Vigorous, open, somewhat pendulous growth.

C. lutchuensis. Limber-branched shrub to 10 ft. with tiny (1½ in. long, ½ in. wide) leaves and profusion of tiny white flowers with strong, pleasant fragrance. Is being used as parent to introduce fragrance to larger camellias. Long pliant branches make it an easily trained espalier.

C. reticulata. Some of the biggest and most spectacular camellia flowers occur in this species, and likely as not they appear on some of the lankiest and least graceful plants.

Plants differ somewhat according to variety, but generally speaking, they are rather gaunt and open shrubs which eventually become trees of considerable size—possibly 35 or 50 ft. tall. For gardens, consider them 10-ft.-tall shrubs, 8 ft. wide.

Camellia reticulata

Leaves also variable, tend to be dull green, leathery, and strongly net-veined.

Culture is quite similar to that of other camellias, except that the plants seem intolerant of heavy pruning. This, added to their natural lankiness and size, makes them difficult to place in garden. They are at their best in light shade of old oaks, where they should stand alone with plenty of room to develop. They are good container subjects while young, but are not handsome out of bloom. They develop better form and heavier foliage in open ground. In Zones 4–6 grow them in containers so you can move them into winter protection, or plant beneath overhang or near wall for protection.

Best known varieties have very large, semidouble flowers with the inner petals deeply fluted and curled. These inner petals give great depth to flower. All bloom from January to May in California, March through May in Northwest. Best varieties for garden use are these:

'Buddha'. Rose pink flower of very large size; inner petals unusually erect and wavy. Gaunt, open; fast growth.

'Butterfly Wings'. Loose, semidouble, of great size (reported up to 9 in. across), rose pink; petals broad and wavy. Growth open, rather narrow.

'Captain Rawes'. Reddish rose pink semidouble flowers of large size. Vigorous bushy plant with good foliage. Hardiest of Reticulatas.

'Chang's Temple'. True variety is large, open-centered, deep rose flower, with center petals notched and fluted. 'Cornelian' (see below) is sometimes sold as 'Chang's Temple'.

'Cornelian'. Rosy pink to red heavily variegated with white. Large, deep, irregular peony-form flowers with wavy petals. Vigorous plant with big leaves usually marked with white. This variety is often sold as 'Chang's Temple' (see above) or as 'Lion Head'. The true 'Lion Head' is not in American gardens.

'Crimson Robe'. Very large, bright red, semidouble flowers. Petals firm textured and wavy. Vigorous plant of better appearance than most Reticulatas.

'Purple Gown'. Large, purplish red, peony-form to formal double flowers. Compact plant with best growth habit and foliage in the group.

'Shot Silk'. Large, loose, semidouble flowers of brilliant pink with iridescent finish that sparkles in sunlight. Fast, rather open growth.

'Tali Queen'. Very large, deep reddish pink flowers of loose semidouble form with heavily crinkled petals. Plant form and foliage very good. This plant is often sold as 'Noble Pearl'; true 'Noble Pearl' is not available in this country.

C. rusticana. SNOW CAMELLIA. A race of small-flowered camellias from a cold and extremely snowy part of Japan. Flowers may be white, pink, or red, and single to double in form. Plants tend to be spreading and branches are remarkably supple. They are not any hardier than *C. japonica* and are generally considered to be a subspecies—*C. j. rusticana.*

C. saluenensis. Shrub of densely leafy growth to 10–15 ft. tall. Leaves elliptic, rather narrow, pointed, thick textured, 1½–2½ in. long and half as wide. Flowers are bell shaped, rather small, and vary in color from white to fairly deep pink. Flowering is in early spring. Not of great value in itself, it has brought floriferousness, hardiness, and graceful appearance to a large group of its hybrids.

C. sasanqua. Sasanquas are useful broad-leafed evergreens for espaliers, ground covers, informal hedges, screening, containers, and bonsai. They vary in form from upright and densely bushy to spreading and vinelike. Leaves dark green, shiny, 1½–3½ in. long, a third as wide. Flowers very heavily produced in autumn and early winter, short-lived, rather flimsy, but so numerous that plants make a show for months. Some are lightly fragrant.

Most Sasanquas tolerate much sun, and some thrive in full hot sun if soil is right and watering ample. They take drought very well. The Sasanquas are perfectly hardy in camellia areas of Pacific Northwest, but flowers are too often damaged by fall and winter rains and frost to call them successful.

'Apple Blossom'. Single white flowers blushed with pink, from pink buds. Spreading plant.

'Cleopatra'. Rose pink, semidouble, with narrow, curving petals. Growth is erect, fairly compact. Takes clipping well.

'Hana Jiman'. Large semidouble flowers white, edged pink. Fast, open growth; good espalier.

'Jean May'. Large double shell pink. Compact, upright grower with exceptionally glossy foliage.

'Mine-No-Yuki' ('White Doves'). Large, white, peony-form double. Drops many buds. Spreading, willowy growth; effective espalier.

'Momozono-Nishiki'. Large semidouble flowers are rose, shaded white. Twisted petals.

'Narumigata'. Large, single cupped, white flowers, tinged pink.

'Setsugekka'. Large, white, semidouble flowers with fluted petals. Considerable substance to flowers; cut sprays hold well.

in water. Shrub's growth is upright and rather bushy.

'Sparkling Burgundy'. Large peony-form flowers of ruby rose. Vigorous upright growth. Excellent espalier.

'Tanya'. Deep rose pink single flowers. Tolerates much sun. Good ground cover.

'White Frills'. Semidouble, frilled white flowers on a spreading, willowy plant. Outstanding in Zones 23, 24.

'Yuletide'. Profusion of small, single, bright red flowers on dense, compact, upright plant. Late fall, winter bloom.

C. sinensis *(Thea sinensis)*. TEA. Here the tea plant grows as dense round shrub to 15 ft. with leathery dull dark green leaves to 5 in. long. Flowers are white, small (1½ in. across), and fragrant; autumn. Takes well to pruning. Tea can be grown in California but has never been a major crop for economic reasons.

C. vernalis. Certain camellias once classed as Sasanquas have been placed here because they bloom later than Sasanquas, are denser in growth, shinier in leaf, and have firmer-textured flowers. They are generally sold as Sasanquas. Best known varieties are:

'Dawn'. Single to semidouble small white flowers blushed pink. Dense, upright shrub of unusual hardiness.

'Hiryu'. Deep red, small, rose form, double. Dense, upright plant.

Hybrid camellias. The term as used here refers to camellias which are hybrids between two or more species. Several hundred of these hybrids have been introduced, and a few are available with a little looking. The first wave of hybridizing utilized *C. japonica* and *C. saluenensis;* this cross gave plants resembling *C. japonica* in foliage of generally good garden form and with a profusion of medium-sized flowers. Although some of these are still around, the big effort now is in crosses involving *C. reticulata.* These hybrids are more spectacular in flower and should be considered separately. (The S-M-L code for flower size and bloom season is explained under *C. japonica*.)

Hybrids involving *C. saluenensis* or other small-flowered species and varieties:

'Donation'. M. Large, semidouble flowers of orchid pink borne all along stems. Blooms young and heavily, on vigorous, upright, compact plant with slightly pendulous branches. Quite cold and sun resistant. Appreciates a little shade in hot dry areas. There is a variegated form.

'E. G. Waterhouse'. M-L. Medium, full, formal double of excellent form. Light pink flowers heavily produced on vigorous, upright shrub.

'Fragrant Pink'. M. Cross between *C. j. rusticana* and *C. lutchuensis* has small, deep pink, loose peony-form flowers on spreading bush. Flowers very fragrant.

'Pink Bouquet'. M. Medium to large, light rose pink semidouble flowers on vigorous, upright plant. Long, profuse bloom; good landscape plant.

'J. C. Williams'. E-L. Medium-sized, single, cup shaped flowers

of phlox pink over very long season. Vigorous upright shrub with rather pendulous branches.

Hybrids involving *C. reticulata:*

'Aztec'. E-L. Very large semidouble to peony form of deep rose red. Vigorous, upright, open growth.

'Flower Girl'. E-M. Large to very large, semidouble to peony-form flowers of bright pink. Vigorous upright growth. Profuse flowering and small leaves come from its Sasanqua parent, big flowers from its Reticulata ancestor.

'Francie L'. M-L. Very large semidouble flowers with upright, wavy petals. Deep rose pink.

'Howard Asper'. M-L. Very large peony-form flower; medium salmon pink. Large, spreading plant with big, broad, heavy leaves.

'Leonard Messel'. M-L. Large rose pink semidouble flower on a loose-branching, upright shrub. Bred in England.

'Mandalay Queen'. M-L. Very large, semidouble, rose pink flowers with fluted petals. Fast, upright, open growth.

'Valentine Day'. M. Large to very large salmon pink, formal double flowers. Fast, upright grower.

'Valley Knudsen'. M-L. Large to very large deep orchid pink semidouble to loose peony form. Compact upright growth.

CAMPANULA. BELLFLOWER. Mostly perennial, some biennial, a few annual. All Zones, but see Uses–Remarks in chart below. Majority best adapted in Zones 1–7, but several thrive in Zones 8, 9, 14–24. Vast and varied group (nearly 300 species) including creeping or tufted miniatures, trailers, and erect kinds 1–6 ft. tall. Flowers generally bell shaped, but some star shaped, cup shaped, or round and flat. Usually blue, lavender, violet, purple, or white; some pink. Bloom period from spring to fall.

Campanula isophylla

Uses for campanulas are as varied as the plants. Gemlike miniatures deserve special settings—close-up situations in rock gardens, niches in dry walls, in raised beds, or containers. Trailing kinds are ideal for hanging pots or baskets, wall crevices; vigorous spreading growers serve well as ground covers. Upright growers are valuable in borders, for cutting, occasionally in containers.

In general, campanulas grow best in good, readily drained soil that's kept moist through the dry months; plant in filtered shade in warmer climates, full sun near coast. Exceptions are noted in chart. Most species fairly easy to grow from seed sown in flats in spring or early summer, transplanted to garden in fall for bloom the following year; also increased by cuttings or divisions. Divide clumps in fall every 3–4 years; some may need yearly division. Low-growing kinds especially attractive to snails, slugs.

Campanula

NAME	GROWTH HABIT, SIZE	FOLIAGE	FLOWERS	USES-REMARKS
Campanula barbata Short-lived perennial or biennial	Clumps of erect stems 4–18 in. high.	Leaves mostly at base of stem, 2–5 in. long, narrow, hairy.	Bell shaped, lilac blue, bearded inside, 1 in. long, nodding, few near top of each stem. Summer.	Foreground in borders, rock gardens. Tap rooted and needs good drainage. White forms may appear from seed.
C. carpatica (*C. turbinata*) TUSSOCK BELLFLOWER Perennial	Compact leafy tufts, stems branching and spreading. Usually about 8 in. tall, may reach 12–18 in.	Leaves smooth, bright green, wavy, toothed, 1–1½ in. long.	Open bell or cup shaped, blue, or white, 1–2 in. across, single and erect on stems above foliage. Blooms late spring.	Rock garden, foreground in borders, edging. Variable in flower size and color. 'Blue Carpet' and 'White Carpet' good dwarf varieties. Easy from seed; increase named varieties from cuttings.
C. elatines garganica (*C. garganica*) Perennial	Low (3–6 in. high) with outward spreading stems.	Small, gray or green sharply toothed, heart shaped leaves.	Flat, star shaped, violet blue, borne few or singly at tops of stems. June to fall.	Rock gardens. Usually sold as *C. garganica*. Somewhat like a miniature, prostrate *C. poscharskyana*.

(Continued on next page)

NAME	GROWTH HABIT, SIZE	FOLIAGE	FLOWERS	USES-REMARKS
C. fragilis Perennial	Vinelike trailing flower stems 12–16 in long. Dies back to a tight basal rosette of leaves.	Glossy oval leaves 1 in. across.	Star shaped, blue with white centers, 1½ in. across, in leaf joints at ends of branches. Late summer and fall.	Choice spots in rock gardens or walls. Hanging containers. A plant for collectors, specialists.
C. glomerata Perennial	Upright, with erect side branches to 1–2 ft.	Basal leaves broad, wavy edged. Stem leaves broad, toothed. Both somewhat hairy.	Narrow, bell shaped, flaring at the mouth, 1 in. long, blue violet, tightly clustered at tops of stems. June-July.	For shaded borders or large rock gardens. Plants have proportionately more foliage than flowers. Seed-grown strains Superba and Alba are deepest purple and white respectively.
C. isophylla ITALIAN BELLFLOWER, STAR OF BETHLEHEM Perennial	Trailing or hanging stems to 2 ft. long.	Leaves heart shaped, light green, toothed, 1–1½ in. long and wide.	Pale blue, star shaped, 1 in. wide, profuse in late summer and fall. Variety 'Alba' most popular, has white flowers, larger than the above. Variety 'Mayi', gray, soft hairy leaves, large lavender blue flowers.	Hanging baskets, wall pots, on top of walls, rock garden. Choice ground cover for small areas on slopes, in mild-winter climates. Filtered shade. Hardy San Francisco and south; in southern California, best near coast; indoor/outdoor plant in cold-winter areas.
C. lactiflora Perennial	Erect, branching, leafy, 3½–5 ft. tall.	Oblong, pointed, toothed leaves 2–3 in. long.	Broadly bell shaped to star shaped, 1 in. long, white to pale blue in drooping clusters at ends of branches, June-September.	Rear of borders in sun or partial shade. Quite drought resistant. Endures even dry shade and is long-lived.
C. medium CANTERBURY BELL, CUP-AND-SAUCER Biennial or annual	Sturdy, hairy, leafy, with erect stems 2½–4 ft. tall.	Basal leaves 6–10 in., stem leaves 3–5 in., wavy margined.	Bell shaped, urn shaped, 1–2 in. across, single or double, held upright in long, loose open clusters. Purple, violet, blue, lavender, pink, white, May-July.	Sow seed in May-June for bloom next year, or set out plants from nursery 15–18 in. apart. Good for cutting. 'Calycanthema', commonly called cup-and-saucer, very popular. Annual variety with bell shaped flowers (not cup-and-saucer) blooms in 6 months from seed.
C. persicifolia PEACH LEAFED BLUEBELL Perennial	Strong-growing, slender, erect stems 2–3 ft. tall. Plants leafy at base.	Basal leaves smooth edged, green, 4–8 in. long. Stem leaves 2–4 in. long, shaped like leaves of peach tree.	Open, cup shaped, about 1 in. across, held erect on short side shoots on sturdy stems. Blue, pink, or white. June-August.	Choice plant for borders. Easy from seed sown in late spring. 'Telham Beauty', old but still popular, has 3-in. blue flowers. 'Blue Gardenia' and 'White Pearl' have double flowers.
C. portenschlagiana (C. muralis) DALMATIAN BELLFLOWER Perennial	Low, leafy, mounding mats 4–7 in. high.	Roundish, heart shaped, deep-green leaves with deeply toothed, slightly wavy edges.	Flaring bell shaped, to 1 in. across, violet blue, 2–3 flowers on each semierect stem. May-August, sometimes blooming again in fall.	Fine plant for edging or as small-scale ground cover. In warm regions best in partial shade. Spreads moderately fast, is sturdy, permanent, and not invasive. Easily increased by dividing.
C. poscharskyana SERBIAN BELLFLOWER Perennial	Spreading, much branching, leafy, with semiupright flowering stems 1 or more ft. tall.	Long heart shaped, irregularly toothed, slightly hairy leaves 1–3½ in. long, ¾–3 in. wide.	Star shaped, ½–1 in. across, blue lilac or lavender, spring to early summer.	Very vigorous. Shaded border near pools, shaded rock gardens, with fuchsias and begonias. Stands some drought; takes sun near coast. Small area ground cover.
C. pyramidalis CHIMNEY BELLFLOWER Biennial or short-lived perennial	Sturdy upright stems, unbranched or branched at base, 4–6 ft. tall.	Leaves nearly heart shaped, about 2 in. long, with long stalks.	Flat, saucer shaped blue or white flowers, over 1 in. long, in dense spikes. July-September.	For back of perennial borders or for bays in big shrubbery borders, or in containers. Stake early to keep stems straight. In cold-winter climates, mulch around plants.
C. rapunculoides ROVER BELLFLOWER Perennial	Clumps of long-stemmed leaves send up 3 ft. spires of blue purple bells.	Medium green, large, heart shaped at base.	Funnel shaped flowers 1 in. long. Sometimes pale blue or white.	Tough, invasive plant, useful in difficult soils, climates. Don't plant near delicate subjects.
C. rotundifolia BLUEBELL OF SCOTLAND, HAREBELL Perennial	Upright or spreading, simple or much branched, 6–20 in. tall.	Leaves green or sometimes slight grayish. Basal leaves roundish, long stalked, 1 in. across. Stem leaves grasslike, 2–3 in. long. May dry up before blooming time.	Broad bell shaped, bright blue, 1 in. across, 1 or a few nodding in open clusters. July-August.	Flower color variable, sometimes in lavender, purple, or white shades. Rock gardens, borders, naturalized under deciduous trees. Self-sows in favorable situations.

CAMPHOR TREE. See *Cinnamomum camphora.*

CAMPSIS. TRUMPET CREEPER, TRUMPET VINE. Deciduous vines. Vigorous climbers that cling to wood, brick, and stucco surfaces with aerial rootlets. Old plants sometimes become topheavy and pull away from supporting surface unless thinned. Will spread through garden and into neighbor's by suckering roots. If you try to dig suckers up, any piece of root left will grow another plant. Can be trained as big shrub, flowering hedge if branches are shortened after first year's growth. Use for large-scale effects—quick summer screen. All produce open arching sprays of trumpet shaped flowers in August-September. Sun, average water.

Campsis radicans

   C. **grandiflora** (*Bignonia chinensis*). CHINESE TRUMPET CREEPER. Zones 2-12, 14-21. Not as vigorous, large, or hardy as American native, but with slightly larger, more open scarlet flowers. Leaves divided into 7-9 leaflets, 2½ in. long.
   C. **radicans** (*Bignonia radicans*). COMMON TRUMPET CREEPER. Zones 1-21. Native to eastern United States. Most used in cold-winter areas. Deep freeze will kill to ground but new stems grow quickly. Leaves divided into 9-11, 2½-in.-long, toothed leaflets. Flowers are 3-in.-long orange tubes with scarlet lobes that flare to 2 in. wide, grow 6-12 in cluster. Grows fast to 40 ft. or more, bursting with health and vigor. There is a rare yellow flowering variety 'Flava'.
   C. **tagliabuana.** All Zones. Hybrid between the two other species. 'Mme. Galen', best known variety, has attractive salmon red flowers.

CANARY BIRD BUSH. See *Crotalaria agatiflora.*

CANARY BIRD FLOWER. See *Tropaeolum peregrinum.*

CANDLE BUSH. See *Cassia alata.*

CANDLE LARKSPUR. See *Delphinium elatum.*

CANDOLLEA cuneiformis. See *Hibbertia cuneiformis.*

CANDYTUFT. See *Iberis.*

CANNA. Tuberous rootstocks. All Zones. Best adapted to warm-summer climates. You should lift and store the roots over winter in Zones 1-3. Native to tropics and subtropics. An old favorite that can add tropical touch in right place. Large, rich green to bronzy red leaves resemble those of banana or ti plants. Flowers reminiscent of ginger lilies (*Hedychium*) bloom on 3-6-ft. stalks in summer, fall. A dozen or more varieties available, in varying sizes and shapes in white, ivory, shades of yellow, orange, pink, apricot, coral, salmon, and red. Bicolors include 'Cleopatra' with flowers strikingly streaked and spotted red on yellow. Low-growing strains are Grand Opera (26 in.), Pfitzer's Dwarf (30-36 in.), and Seven Dwarfs (18 in.); grow the last from seeds.

Canna

   Needs full sun. Most effective in groups of single colors against plain background. Grow in borders, near poolside (with good drainage), in large pots or tubs on terrace or patio. Leaves useful in arrangements; cut flowers do not keep well. Plant rootstocks in spring after frosts, in rich loose soil. Set 5 in. deep, 10 in. apart. Water heavily during flowering season; remove faded flowers after bloom. After all flower clusters have bloomed, cut stalk to ground.

CANTALOUPE. See Melon.

CANTERBURY BELL. See *Campanula medium.*

CANTUA buxifolia. MAGIC FLOWER, SACRED FLOWER OF THE INCAS. Evergreen shrub. Zones 16-24. Native of Peru, Bolivia and northern Chile. Scraggly open growth to 6-10 ft. Small leaves 1-in. or less in length. Magnificent blossoms come sporadically through year; 4-in. tubular rose or cerise red flowers with yellow stripes appear in terminal clusters, arching branches with their weight.

   Give it light soil in partial shade. Drought tolerant. Needs support of stake or trellis. Young plants effective in hanging baskets. Or grow in tub and hide plant when it's out of bloom. Prune after flowering.

Cantua buxifolia

CAPE CHESTNUT. See *Calodendrum capense.*

CAPE COWSLIP. See *Lachenalia.*

CAPE FORGET-ME-NOT. See *Anchusa capensis.*

CAPE FUCHSIA. See *Phygelius capensis.*

CAPE HONEYSUCKLE. See *Tecomaria capensis*

CAPE MARIGOLD. See *Dimorphotheca, Osteospermum.*

CAPE PONDWEED. See *Aponogeton distachyus.*

CAPE PRIMROSE. See *Streptocarpus.*

CAPE WEED. See *Arctotheca calendula.*

CARAGANA arborescens. SIBERIAN PEA-SHRUB. Deciduous shrub or small tree. Zones 1-21. Native to Siberia, Manchuria. Fast growing to 20 ft., with 15-ft. spread, often with spiny twigs. Fragrant flowers in spring resemble yellow sweet peas. Leaves 1½-3 in. long, divided into 4-6 pairs of roundish, bright green, ½-in. leaflets. Useful where choice is limited by extremes in cold, heat, sun, drought. Nearly indestructible in mountains or desert. Use as windbreak, clipped hedge, cover for wildlife, attractive small tree.

Caragana arborescens

CARAWAY. See *Carum carvi.*

CARDINAL CLIMBER. See *Ipomoea quamoclit.*

CARDINAL FLOWER. See *Lobelia cardinalis.*

CARDOON. Perennial. Zones 8, 9, 14-24. Vegetable closely related to artichoke, but grown for edible leaf stalks rather than for flower buds. For climate, soil, and other requirements see Artichoke. To prepare leaves for harvest, blanch them by gathering them together, tying them up, and wrapping with paper to exclude light. Allow month's blanching before harvest. To cook, cut heavy leaf midribs into 3-4-in. lengths, parboil until tender, then fry; or serve

Cardoon

boiled with butter or other sauce.

As ornamental, makes large (to 8 ft. or more), striking, gray green plant that naturalizes in mild-winter climates. Size, spininess rule it out in small gardens. Purple artichoke flowers attractive cut and dried. Can escape and become weed.

CARICA. Evergreen. One type is a relatively hardy (to 28°F.) ornamental plant or tree; the other is the typical fruiting tree. Grow in sun or light shade with ample water.

C. papaya. PAPAYA. Outdoors in Zones 21, 23, 24; or a greenhouse plant. To 20 ft. tall (or more). Native to tropical America. Key to success is to live in the right place—where there's soil warmth in winter. More are lost to root rot in cold, wet, late winter and spring soil than to frosts. Grow on south slope or south side of house where winter sun hits soil—and the more reflected heat at that season the better.

Carica pubescens

Grow 3–5 in a group. Need male and female trees for fruit production. Papaya grows as a straight trunk, topped by crown of broad (to 2 ft.), fanlike, deeply lobed leaves on 2-ft.-long stems. To get most fun and fruit, don't attempt to grow it as permanent tree. Inconspicuous cream-colored flowers. It bears fruit when young. Keep a few plants coming along each year and destroy old ones. Give plants ample water and fertilizer in warm weather.

C. pubescens (*C. candamarcensis*). MOUNTAIN PAPAYA. Zones 21–24. Native to mountains of Colombia and Ecuador. Generally grown as a shrub though it resembles a many-trunked, upright tree to 10–12 ft. Foliage borne in dense clusters at tops of trunks. Elaborately lobed, 12–13-in.-wide leaves are fanlike, veined, sandpapery, dark green above, lighter below. Inconspicuous flowers, cream-colored. Fruit is small (3–4 in.), barely edible.

CARISSA. Evergreen shrubs. Their rightful climates are Zones 22–24; however so many find carissa appealing that they are grown far beyond safe limits (Zones 12, 13, 16–21). Excellent in ocean wind, salt spray. Easy to grow. Accept variety of soils, exposures. Fairly drought tolerant near coast; need water in hot inland summers. Bloom and fruit best in full sun but will take fairly heavy shade. Prune to control erratic growth.

Carissa grandiflora

C. edulis. Native to Africa. Differs from widely grown *C. grandiflora* in several ways. Shrubby or somewhat vinelike to 10 ft. (Will grow to 30 ft. high and as wide.) Foliage of small (to 2 in.) glossy, bright green, red-tinged leaves. Bears large clusters of pure white fragrant flowers, opening from pink buds. Cherry-sized fruit changes from green to red to purplish black as it ripens.

C. grandiflora. NATAL PLUM. Native to South Africa. Fast growing, strong, upright, rounding shrub of rather loose habit to 5–7 ft. (occasionally to 18 ft.). Lustrous, leathery, rich green, 3-in., oval leaves. Spines along branches and at end of each twig. White flowers, almost as fragrant as star jasmine and of same 5-petal star shape but larger (to 2 in. wide), appear throughout year, followed by red, plum shaped (1–2 in.) fruit. Flowers, green and ripe fruit often appear together. Fruit varies in sweetness, but generally has quality of rather sweet cranberry and makes good sauce. You can eat them fresh; harvest when scarlet. Use as screen or hedge. Prune heavily for formal hedges, lightly for informal screen. Strong growth, spines discourage trespassers.

If you grow Natal plum outside Zones 22–24, give it same favorite spot you'd give bougainvillea—warm south or west-facing wall, preferably with overhang to keep off frost. It may also be grown as an indoor plant in good light.

C. g. 'Boxwood Beauty'. Exceptionally compact growth to 2 ft. and as wide. Deep green leaves, like a large-leafed boxwood. Excellent for hedging and shaping. No thorns.

C. g. 'Fancy'. Upright grower to 6 ft. Unusually large fruit, good show of flowers. Use as lightly pruned screen.

C. g. 'Green Carpet'. Low growing to 1–1½ ft. and flat, spreading to 4 ft. and more. Leaves smaller than *C. grandiflora*. Excellent ground cover.

C. g. 'Horizontalis'. To 1½–2 ft., spreading, trailing. Dense foliage.

C. g. 'Prostrata'. Vigorous, to about 2 ft. and spreading. Good ground cover. Prune out any growth that tends toward upright. Can be trained as espalier.

C. g. 'Ruby Point'. Upright grower to 6 ft. New leaves hold their red coloring through the growing season.

C. g. 'Tomlinson'. Dwarf, compact growth to 2–2½ ft. high, 3 ft. wide. Shiny mahogany-tinted foliage, large flowers, wine-colored fruit. No thorns. Slow growing. Tub plant, foundation plantings.

C. g. 'Tuttle' (*C. g.* 'Nana Compacta Tuttlei'). To 2–3 ft. high, 3–5 ft. wide. Compact, dense foliage. Heavy producer of flowers and fruit. Used as ground cover.

CARMEL CREEPER. See *Ceanothus griseus horizontalis*.

CARNATION. See *Dianthus caryophyllus*.

CARNEGIEA gigantea. SAGUARO. Giant cactus. Zones 12, 13, 18–21. Native to northern Mexico, Arizona, California. Columnar and branching, with prominent ribs that give it fluted appearance. Grows very slowly to 50 ft. Spines light brown, ½–3 in. long.

Carnegiea gigantea

Flowers on mature plants are single, white, and grow to 4–5 in. long, May. Night blooming. State flower of Arizona. Oval, edible fruit splits open to show red pulp within; sometimes mistaken for flowers. Slow enough to stay pot size or garden size for many years.

CAROB. See *Ceratonia siliqua*.

CAROLINA ALLSPICE. See *Calycanthus floridus*.

CAROLINA JESSAMINE. See *Gelsemium*.

CAROLINA LAUREL CHERRY. See *Prunus caroliniana*.

CARPENTERIA californica. BUSH ANEMONE. Evergreen shrub. Zones 5–9, 14–24. Native to California, localized in Sierra Nevada foothills between Kings and San Joaquin rivers in Fresno County. Slow growing to 3–6 ft. with many stems arising from base. Older bark light-colored and peeling, new shoots purplish. Leaves thick, narrow, dark green above and whitish beneath, 2–4½ in. long. Flowers, white, anemonelike, 1½–3 in. wide, opening May-August, are slightly and pleasantly fragrant. Resistant to oak root fungus.

Carpenteria californica

This attractive native with rather formal look accepts ordinary garden conditions. Grows in shade or sun, but looks best in light shade. Takes much drought once established. Inspect new growth occasionally and wash off aphids that could disfigure plants. Spray as new leaves form. Prune after flowering to restrain growth or shape.

CARPET BUGLE. See *Ajuga*.

CARPINUS. HORNBEAM. Deciduous trees. Hardy, well-behaved, relatively small shade trees. Long life and good habits as street trees (not recommended for southern California and desert). Ordinary garden watering. Retain leaves well into winter. Fruit, small hard nutlets in leaflike bracts, are carried in attractive drooping clusters.

C. betulus. EUROPEAN HORNBEAM. Zones 3–9, 14–17. Moderate growth to 40 ft. Dense pyramidal form, eventually becoming broad with drooping outer branches. Dark green leaves, 2–5 in. long and toothed. Fall color yellow or dark red in cold winters. Fruit clusters to 5 in. long. Subject to scale insect infestations. Can be clipped into hedge or screen. Variety 'Fastigiata' is narrow column in youth, dense pyramid in maturity; it is the variety commonly sold. 'Quercifolia' has oaklike leaves.

Carpinus betulus

C. caroliniana. AMERICAN HORNBEAM. Zones 1–9, 14–17. Native from Florida to Texas, north to Virginia, southern Illinois. Moderate growth to 25–30 ft., round-headed. Bark is smooth and gray. Dark green leaves, 1–3 in. long, edges toothed. In fall leaves turn mottled yellow and red. Fruit clusters 1½–4 in. long.

CARPOBROTUS. ICE PLANT, SEA FIG, HOTTENTOT FIG. Succulent perennials or subshrubs. Zones 12–24. Coarse-leafed, trailing plants useful for covering sunny banks, in binding loose sand at beach, for covering seldom watered marginal areas. Not affected by diseases, insects, or smog—even fairly resistant to fires. Fast growing, easy to increase by cuttings set 1½–2 ft. apart.

Carpobrotus chilensis

C. chilensis *(Mesembryanthemum aequilaterale)*. Native along coast, Oregon to Baja California. The straight 3-sided fleshy leaves are 2 in. long; flowers lightly fragrant, rosy purple. Summer bloom.

C. edulis *(Mesembryanthemum edule)*. From South Africa. Leaves curved, 4–5 in. long. Flowers pale yellow to rose. Fruit edible, but not very good.

CARRION FLOWER. See *Stapelia*.

CARROT. Biennial grown as annual. All Zones in conditions noted below. The variety to plant depends on the soil condition: carrots reach smooth perfection only in good-textured soil free of stones and clods. Grow in sun. Maintain even soil moisture: alternate dry and wet conditions cause split roots. Plant long market kinds only if you can give them a foot of this ideal, light soil. If you can provide only a few inches, plant shorter, stockier varieties such as 'Nantes Half Long', 'Chantenay' or 'Burpee's Goldinhart'.

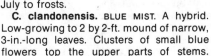

Carrot

Sow thickly in rows at least 12 in. apart. Soil should be fine enough for root development and loose enough so crusting can't check sprouting of seeds. If crust should form, keep soil soft by sprinkling. Too much nitrogen or a lot of manure will make excessive top growth and cause forking of roots.

Make successive plantings when first planting is up and growing; in cold-winter climates make last sowing 70 days before anticipated killing frost. When tops are 2 in. high thin plants to 1½ in. apart, and thin again if roots begin to crowd. Tiny carrots removed in thinnings are good butter steamed. After first thinning, apply narrow band of commercial fertilizer 2 in. out from the row. Begin harvest when carrots reach finger size. In mild-winter climates, carrots store well in the ground; dig as needed. Diseases and pests not a problem in most home gardens.

CARROT WOOD. See *Cupaniopsis anacardioides*.

CARTHAMUS tinctorius. SAFFLOWER, FALSE SAFFRON. Annual. All Zones in conditions noted below. A relative of the thistles that is ornamental as well as economically useful. Erect spiny-leafed stems, 1–3 ft. tall, branching above, bearing orange yellow flower heads above leafy bracts; inner bracts are spiny. Durable cut flower, fresh or dried. (An ornamental spineless safflower is also available.) Grown commercially for oil extracted from the seeds. The dried flowers from the flower heads have been used for seasoning in place of true saffron, which they strongly resemble in color and flavor. Sow seeds in place in spring after frosts. Full sun. Once established, plants need little water.

Carthamus tinctorius

CARUM carvi. CARAWAY. Biennial herb. All Zones in conditions noted below. Mound of carrotlike leaves, 1–2 ft. high, first year. Umbrellalike clusters of white flowers rise above foliage second year. Plant dies after seeds ripen in midsummer. Start from seed sown in place in fall or spring. Thrives in well-drained soil in full sun. Average water. Thin seedlings to 18 in. Use dried seeds for flavoring pickles, vegetables, cookies, rye bread.

Carum carvi

CARYA illinoensis *(Carya pecan)*. PECAN. Deciduous tree. Zones 7–9, 12–16, 18–23 as ornamental; Zones 8–9, 12–14, 18–20 to produce good nut crop. Grows as a tree (crop doubtful) in Zones 4–6, 10. Native to southern and central U.S. Graceful shapely tree to 70 ft. tall and wide. Foliage like English walnut but prettier, with more (11–17) leaflets that are narrower and longer (4–7 in.); foliage pattern finer textured, shade lighter. Resistant to oak root fungus.

Carya illinoensis

Needs deep (6–10 ft.), well-drained soils. Won't stand salinity. In zinc-deficient desert soils, prevent (or cure) pecan rosette (abormal clumps of twigs) with zinc sulfate sprays or soil treatment. Needs occasional deep watering in hot-summer climates. Prune to shape or to remove dead wood. Select varieties by climate: 'F. W. Anderson' (self-fertile), good for San Joaquin Valley; 'Mahan' (self-fertile) thrives in low desert; 'Western Schley' fruits over wide range of climates, needs pollenizer. 'Wichita' is good pollenizer for 'Western Schley', bears good nuts very young. 'Barton', 'Burkett', 'Choctaw', 'Mohawk', 'Stuart', 'Success' also sold. Of these, 'Burkett' needs pollenizer.

CARYOPTERIS. BLUEBEARD. Deciduous shrubs. Zones 1–7, 14–17. Valued for contribution of cool blue to flower border from August to frost. Generally grown as shrubby perennial. If not frozen back in winter, cut it back nearly to ground in spring. Light soil. Full sun. Takes considerable drought. If you cut it back after each wave of bloom, it may flower repeatedly July to frosts.

Caryopteris clandonensis

C. clandonensis. BLUE MIST. A hybrid. Low-growing to 2 by 2-ft. mound of narrow, 3-in.-long leaves. Clusters of small blue flowers top the upper parts of stems. Selected forms, 'Azure' and 'Heavenly Blue', both have deep blue flowers.

C. incana *(C. mastacanthus)*. COMMON BLUEBEARD, BLUE

SPIRAEA. Taller growing than above, to 3–4 ft., with lavender blue flowers.

CARYOTA. FISHTAIL PALM. Outdoors in Zones 23, 24, house plant anywhere. Feather palms with finely divided leaves, the leaflets flattened and split at the tips like fish tails. Tender. Come from southeast Asia, where they grow in full sun. In California they need partial shade, protected site. Indoors, give them as much light as possible.

C. mitis. CLUSTERED FISHTAIL PALM. Slow grower to 20–25 ft. Basal offshoots eventually form clustered trunks. Foliage light green. Very tender, and thrives only in ideal environment. Not for novices.

Caryota ochlandra

C. ochlandra. CANTON FISHTAIL PALM. Probably eventually 25 ft. tall. Medium dark green leaves. Hardiest of the caryotas, it has survived to 26°F.

C. urens. FISHTAIL WINE PALM. Single-stemmed palm to 100 ft. in Asia, to 15–20 ft. here with careful protection. If temperatures go below 32°F., it's certain to die. Dark green leaves.

CASCARA sagrada. See *Rhamnus purshiana.*

CASHMERE BOUQUET. See *Clerodendrum bungei.*

CASIMIROA edulis. WHITE SAPOTE. Evergreen, or erratically behaves as deciduous tree. Zones 15, 16, 22–24. Beautiful tropical tree that will withstand more cold than most avocados, and seems to do well wherever lemons are grown. To 50 ft. Keep it to almost any height by pinching out terminal bud if wide umbrella type is wanted. Prune off lower branches. Luxuriant glossy green leaves divided fanwise into 3–7 oval, 3–5-in.-long leaflets.

Casimiroa edulis

Tree bears heavy crop of 3–4-in., round fruits, pale green to yellow. Flavor is described in many ways—similar to peach but more bland, banana only sweeter, ripe pear in rich syrup, custard with banana-peach flavor. Consistency of papaya. Fruit ripens August through November. Overripe fruit becomes slightly bitter. Pick when firm ripe; allow yellowish flesh to become mellow and sweet. Mature tree may produce several hundred pounds of fruit, far more than any one family can use. Cleanup becomes a chore. Plant where dropping fruit can be raked up, or get lost in ground cover. Goes deciduous for short time, when hit by frost or in June when the tree "moults" or becomes completely bare for brief period.

Not particular about soil; needs ample water and consistent feeding. Budded trees give best fruit, and are grown in limited quantities. 'Coleman', 'Pike', 'Wilson', and 'Suebelle' are all good varieties.

CASSIA. SENNA. Evergreen, partially evergreen, or deciduous shrubs, trees. For southern California and Arizona, a great reservoir of landscaping materials from many lands. Yellow or golden are the words for cassia. Flowers on the different kinds are yellow, egg-yolk yellow, bright yellow, deep yellow, gold. As a group, cassias bloom better and live longer in fast draining soil with infrequent but deep watering. Some of the tree forms, *C. excelsa* and *C. leptophylla,* grow in lawns where drainage is fast. All need sun.

Cassia artemisioides

In the following list of kinds, flowering dates are approximate. Many will bloom almost any time or scatter bloom over a long period.

C. alata. CANDLE BUSH. Deciduous shrub 8–12 ft., and spreading wider. Zone 23. Native to tropics. Golden yellow flowers (1 in. wide) in big spikelike clusters, November-January. Leaves of 12–28 leaflets, 2½ in. long. Prune hard after bloom.

C. artemisioides. FEATHERY CASSIA. Evergreen shrub. Zones 8, 9, 12–16, 18–23. Native to Australia. Attractive, light and airy structure to 3–5 ft. Leaves divided into 6–8 gray, 1-in.-long, needlelike leaflets. Flowers (¾ in.) sulfur yellow, 5–8 in a cluster, January-April, often into summer. Prune lightly after flowering to eliminate heavy setting of seed. Drought resistant.

C. bicapsularis. Evergreen shrub to 10 ft. Zones 13, 22–24. Native to tropics. Recovers after killed to ground by frost. Yellow ½-in.-wide flowers in spikelike clusters, from October-February if not cut short by frost. Prune severely after flowering. Leaflets roundish, rather thick, 6–10 to a leaf.

C. corymbosa. FLOWERY SENNA. Large evergreen shrub to 10 ft. Zones 13, 21–24; naturalized here and there in Santa Barbara. Native to Argentina. Yellow flowers in rounded clusters, spring to fall. Dark green leaves with 6 narrow, oblong, 1–2 in. leaflets. Prune severely after flowering. (For small garden, less rank-growing *C. tomentosa* is better.)

C. didymobotrya. (Also sold as *C. nairobensis.*) Evergreen shrub. Zones 13, 22–24; often escapes, naturalizes. Native to east Africa. Rangy grower to 10 ft. Leaflets 2 in. long, 8–16 pairs per leaf. Yellow, 1½-in.-wide flowers in upright, dense clusters (to 12 in.), December-April. Thrives in heat. Stands some drought when established. Smelly but attractive plant for large wild gardens.

C. excelsa *(C. carnaval).* **CROWN OF GOLD TREE.** Partially evergreen tree. Zones 12, 13, 19–24. Native to Argentina. Grows fast to 25–30 ft. Leaves divided into 10–20 pairs of 1-in.-long leaflets. Large bright yellow flowers in 12–16-in.-long clusters, late summer, early fall. Prune hard after flowering. Needs moisture in growing season.

Cassia excelsa

C. leptophylla. GOLD MEDALLION TREE. Near-evergreen tree. Zones 21–24. Native to Brazil. Most shapely and graceful of the cassias. Fast growing to 20–25 ft.; open headed, low spreading, tending to weep. Leaves with up to 12 pairs of narrow leaflets. Deep yellow flowers to 3 in. wide, in 6–8-in.-long spikes through July-August with scattered blooms April-May.

C. multijuga. Evergreen tree. Zones 22–24. Native to Brazil. Heavy-foliaged, much branched tree to 15–20 ft. Somewhat brittle. Yellow, 2-in.-wide flowers in clusters in late summer and fall. Leaves have 18–40 pairs of rather narrow leaflets that grow to length of ¾ in.

C. splendida. GOLDEN WONDER SENNA. Evergreen shrub. Zones 12, 13, 21–24. Native to Brazil. This name has been applied to a number of cassias of varying growth habits. Those in Los Angeles State and County Arboretum are 10–12 ft. high, and about as wide.

Orange yellow flowers (1½ in. wide) in loose clusters at branch ends, November-January. Other plantings of cassias with this name, with bright yellow flowers, are strongly horizontal in branch pattern, 5–8 ft. high, spreading to 12 ft. wide. All need to be severely pruned after flowering.

C. sturtii. Evergreen shrub. Zones 12–14. Native to Australia. Leaves with 2–5 pairs of narrow inch-long leaflets. Bushy 3–6-ft. gray green shrub with clustered bright yellow flowers. Longer bloom than *C. artemisioides,* neater plant.

C. surattensis *(C. glauca).* Evergreen shrub. Zones 19–24. Grows fast to 6–8 ft., and spreads wider. Bright yellow flowers (¾ in. wide) in small clusters at branch ends, nearly the year around. Roundish, 1½-in.-long leaflets, 12–20 to each leaf. Does not need to be pruned heavily. This shrub is one of best for small gardens.

C. tomentosa. WOOLLY SENNA. Evergreen shrub. Zones 13, 17, 22–24. Native to Mexico and South America. Vigorous, rank growth to 8 ft. (or 12–15 ft.). Leaves divided into 12–16 leaflets 2½ in. long that are green above, white hairy beneath. Deep yellow flowers in upright clusters at ends of branches in winter, early spring. Prune hard after flowering.

CASTANEA. CHESTNUT. Deciduous trees. Zones 2–9, 14–17. The American chestnut *(C. dentata)* is nearing extinction as result of a fungus disease. However, two other chestnuts are available in the West. They have handsome dark to bright green foliage. Creamy white small flowers in long (about 8–10 in.), slim catkins make quite a display in June or July. The large edible nuts are enclosed in prickly bur. Wonderful

Castanea mollissima

dense shade trees where there is space to accommodate them, such as large country places. Need occasional deep watering.

C. mollissima. CHINESE CHESTNUT. Native to China, Korea. Grows to 60 ft. with rounded crown that may spread to 40 ft. Leaves 3–7 in. long, with coarsely toothed edges. Most nursery trees are grown from seeds, not cuttings, hence the nuts are variable, but generally of good quality. Single trees bear lightly or not at all. Plant two or more to insure cross-pollination and you'll get a substantial crop. Intolerant of alkaline soil conditions.

C. sativa. SPANISH CHESTNUT. Native to southern Europe, north Africa, western Asia. Larger, broader tree than Chinese chestnut. Can reach 100 ft. in height with greater spread, but usually a 40–60-ft. tree in gardens. Leaves 4–9 in. long, with sharply toothed edges. Produces large chestnuts of excellent quality; these are the ones usually sold in markets. Size, litter, and disagreeable odor of pollen make it a tree for wide open spaces. Resistant to oak root fungus.

CASTANOSPERMUM australe. MORETON BAY CHESTNUT. Evergreen tree. Zones 18–22. Native to Australia. Beautiful in foliage; spectacular in flower. To 50–60 ft. tall, nearly as wide. Large leaves, dark shiny green, are divided into 11–15 leaflets about 1½ by 5 in. Flowers are bright red and yellow, produced in stiff spikes about 8 in. long. They grow from twigs, branches, and main trunk in summer. Seeds like chestnuts are edible when roasted. Moderate water requirements.

Castanospermum australe

CAST-IRON PLANT. See *Aspidistra elatior*.

CASTOR BEAN. See *Ricinus communis*.

CASUARINA. BEEFWOOD, SHE-OAK. Evergreen trees. Zones 8, 9, 12–24. Native mostly to Australia. Sometimes called Australian pine. Slight resemblance to a pine, and fruits look like woody cones, but it's not a pine. Long, thin, jointed, green branches with inconspicuous true leaves look like long pine needles. Tolerates many tough conditions, dry or wet soil, salinity, heat, wind. Particularly used in desert areas. Hardy to 15°F. In desert, it is often confused with Athel tamarisk *(Tamarix aphylla)* because of similar foliage. Distinctive difference: casuarinas produce woody, conelike fruit.

Casuarina stricta

C. cunninghamiana. RIVER SHE-OAK. Tallest and largest. To 70 ft. Finest texture, with dark green branches.

C. equisetifolia. HORSETAIL TREE. Fast grower to 40–60 ft., 20-ft. wide. Has pendulous gray green branches. Plant sold under this name may be *C. cunninghamiana* or hybrid between it and *C. glauca*.

C. stricta. MOUNTAIN or DROOPING SHE-OAK, COAST BEEFWOOD. Fast grower to 20–35 ft. Darkest green foliage and largest cones (1 in.). Makes beautiful silhouette against sky. Properly watered and shaped, is attractive street tree. Good at seashore.

CATALINA CHERRY. See *Prunus lyonii*.

CATALINA IRONWOOD. See *Lyonothamnus floribundus*.

CATALINA PERFUME. See *Ribes viburnifolium*.

CATALPA. Deciduous trees. All Zones. One of the few truly hardy deciduous trees that can compete in flower and leaf with subtropicals of southern California. Large upright clusters of trumpet shaped, 2-in.-wide flowers, pure white, striped and marked with yellow and soft brown, displayed in late spring and summer above bold, large, heart shaped leaves. Flowers are followed by long, bean shaped seed capsules sometimes called Indian beans or Indian stogies.

Catalpa speciosa

Unusually well-adapted to extremes of heat and cold, and to soils throughout the West. Moderate water. Where winds are strong, should be planted in lee of taller trees or buildings to protect leaves from wind damage. Some gardeners object to litter of fallen flowers in summer, and seed capsules in autumn. Plants need attention to shaping while young, seldom develop a well-established dominant shoot. Shorten side branches as the tree grows. When branching begins at the desired height, remove lower branches.

C. bignonioides. COMMON CATALPA, INDIAN BEAN. Native to southeastern United States. Generally smaller than *C. speciosa*, 20–50 ft. according to climate or soil, with somewhat smaller spread. Leaves 5–8 in. long, often in whorls, give odd odor when crushed. The variety 'Aurea' has yellow leaves. Resistant to oak root fungus.

C. b. 'Nana'. (Almost always sold as *C. bungei*.) UMBRELLA CATALPA. A dense globe form usually grafted high on *C. bignonioides*. It never blooms. Cut it back to keep it in scale.

C. erubescens 'Purpurea'. Young leaves and branchlets of this catalpa are deep blackish purple, turning purple-toned green in summer.

C. speciosa. WESTERN CATALPA. Native southern Illinois to Arkansas. A round-headed, 40–70-ft. tree. Leaves 6–12 in. long; no odor when crushed. Flowers fewer in cluster than *C. bignonioides*. Most widely distributed in the West. Early training and pruning will give tall trunk and umbrella shaped crown.

CATANANCHE caerulea. CUPID'S DART. Perennial. All Zones. Sturdy, free-flowering plant for summer borders and arrangements. Leaves gray green, 8–12 in. long, mostly at base of stem. Lavender blue, 2-in. flower heads reminiscent of cornflowers are surrounded by strawlike shining bracts. Stems 2 ft. tall. Flowers may be dried for use in bouquets. Remove faded flowers to prolong bloom. Plant in full sun; drought resistant. 'Alba' is a white variety.

Catananche caerulea

CATHA edulis. KHAT. Evergreen shrub. Zones 13, 16–24. Valued for all-year foliage beauty. Bronzy green, shiny, oval, 2–4-in.-long, slightly toothed leaves take on reddish tints through fall and winter. Grown as spreading shrub to 8 ft. Old plants in parks more than 20 ft. Pinch or prune to keep compact. Effective as espalier. Red stems and bark add interest. Medium-sized leaves make good transition between large leaves such as loquat and small-scale foliage. Very small white flowers. Needs fast drainage but not rich soil. Does well in poor soil, dry situations, or coastal winds.

Catha edulis

CATHARANTHUS roseus (*Vinca rosea*). MADAGASCAR PERIWINKLE. Perennial, usually grown as annual. All Zones in conditions noted below. Invaluable for summer-fall color in hot climates. Showiest summer flower in desert gardens. Glossy leaves 1–3 in. long cover bushy plant 1–2 ft. high. Phloxlike flowers 1½ in. wide in pure white, white with rose or red eye, blush pink, or bright rose. The Little series grows a compact 8–10 in. Creeping strains, including the Carpet series, grow 4–8 in. tall, 18 in. wide. Will bloom first season from seed

Catharanthus roseus

sown early indoors, in greenhouse or coldframe. Nurseries sell plants in flats in late spring. Plant in full sun or partial shade. Requires little water, ordinary soil. Self-sows readily.

Continues to flower after zinnias and marigolds have gone, up until Thanksgiving if weather stays mild. Lives over in frostless areas, but may look ragged in winter. In coastal areas, blooms in late summer after heat builds up.

CATMINT. See *Nepeta faassenii*.

CATNIP. See *Nepeta cataria*.

CAT'S CLAW. See *Macfadyena unguis-cati*.

CAT'S EARS. See *Calochortus tolmiei*.

CATTLEYA. Epiphytic orchids. Native to tropical America. Most popular and best known of orchids. For house and greenhouse primarily. Showy flowers are used extensively for corsages.

Species, varieties, and hybrids are too numerous to list here. All have pseudo-bulbs 1–3 in. thick bearing leathery leaves, and 1–4 or more flowers on stem. Plants range from a few inches to 2 ft. or more in height. Commercial growers offer plants with wide range of flower colors: lavender and purple; white; semi-albas (white with colored lip); novelties—yellow, orange, red, green, bronze—many of which are crosses between *Cattleya* and other gen-

Cattleya

era. Newest hybrid forms are the miniature cattleyas and the bifoliates or multifloras. The latter are standard-sized plants with leaves in pairs. These plants produce large clusters of 3–5-in. flowers and, best of all, many bloom more than once a year.

All cattleyas grow best in greenhouse where temperature, humidity, and light can be readily controlled. However, you can also grow them as house plants. Main requirements: (1) warm temperature (60°F. at night, 10°F. or higher during the day); (2) relatively high humidity—50–60 percent or better; (3) good light—20–40 percent of outside light with protection from hot midday sun. (Color of orchid foliage should be light green and leaves should be erect. When light intensity is too low, leaves turn dark green and new growth becomes soft.) Also see Orchid.

Ceanothus

SPECIES OR VARIETY	SIZE	FOLIAGE	FLOWERS	COMMENTS
Ceanothus 'Blue Buttons'	8–10 ft. tall, 12–15 ft. wide.	Shiny green, textured, ¼-in. leaves.	Medium lavender in large clusters.	Purple-tinged younger stems add to its attractiveness. Gradually takes on form of small live oak.
C. 'Concha'	6–7 ft. tall. 6–8 ft. wide.	Densely clad with dark green 1-in. leaves.	Dark blue 1-in. flower clusters.	One of the best. 'Consuelo' similar, but without reddish flower buds.
C. 'Dark Star'	5–6 ft. tall, 8–10 ft. wide.	Tiny, dark green, ¼-in. leaves.	Dark cobalt blue 1½-in. clusters.	Similar to 'Julia Phelps', maybe better. Deerproof.
C. 'Far Horizon'	4–6 ft. tall, 6–10 ft. wide.	Glossy, deep green, 1½-in leaves.	Dark blue 2½–3-in. flower clusters.	Very bushy and dense.
C. 'Frosty Blue'	6–9 ft. tall, 8–10 ft. wide.	Dark green ½-in. leaves. Dense.	Deep blue, frosted 2½–3-in. spikes.	Flowers shimmer with white. Sturdy stems. Can be shaped as small tree.
C. 'Gentian Plume'	10–20 ft. tall, 12–20 ft. wide.	Dark green 2½-in. leaves.	Dark blue 10-in. flower spikes.	Leggy when young; pinching helps. If stems get so long that plants "fall apart," prune them.
C. gloriosus POINT REYES CEANOTHUS	12–18 in. tall, 12–16 ft. wide.	Dark green, oval, 1-in. leaves, tough and spiny.	Mostly light blue 1-in. clusters.	Much used in Zones 4–6. Does not do well in summer heat of Zones 7, 14, 18–21.
C. gloriosus 'Anchor Bay'	12–18 in. tall, 6–8 ft. wide.	Very dense.	Somewhat deeper blue than above.	Dense foliage holds down weeds.
C. gloriosus exaltatus 'Emily Brown'	2–3 ft. tall, 8–12 ft. wide.	Dark green, hollylike, 1-in. leaves.	Dark violet blue 1-in. clusters.	Stands heavy soil, water near coast.
C. gloriosus porrectus	3–4 ft. tall, 6–8 ft. wide.	Dark green, hollylike, ½-in. leaves.	Medium dark blue 1-in. clusters.	Dense growth but sparse bloom.
C. griseus horizontalis CARMEL CREEPER	18–30 in. tall, 5–15 ft. wide.	Glossy, oval, 2-in., bright green leaves.	Light blue 1-in. clusters.	Some sold under this name may be 'Hurricane Point'. Sometimes winter-damaged in Zones 4–7, 14.
C. griseus horizontalis 'Hurricane Point'	2–3 ft. tall, to 36 ft. wide.	Glossy, oval, 2-in. leaves.	Pale blue 1-in. clusters.	Very fast, somewhat rank grower. Deer love this and the other forms of C. griseus.

CAULIFLOWER. Annual or biennial grown as annual. All Zones in conditions noted below. Related to broccoli and cabbage with similar cultural requirements, but more difficult to grow. Easiest in cool, humid coastal regions; where summers are dry and hot, grow it to harvest well before or well after midsummer. Home gardeners usually plant one of the several 'Snowball' varieties, or 'Burpee's Dry Weather'. An unusual variety is 'Purple Head', which has large plants with heads of deep purple color, turning green in cooking, and flavor somewhat intermediate between cauliflower and broccoli.

Cauliflower

Grow cauliflower like broccoli. Start with small plants. Space them 18–20 in. apart in rows 36 in. apart. Be sure to keep plants actively growing; any check during transplanting or later growth is likely to cause premature setting of undersized heads. When heads first appear, tie up the large leaves around them to keep them white. ('Purple Head' does not need this treatment.) Harvest as soon as it reaches full size.

CEANOTHUS. WILD LILAC. Mostly evergreen shrubs, small trees, or ground covers. Zones 4–7, 14–24. In colder zones stay with varieties locally tested and sold. Some species grow in eastern U.S., Rocky Mountains, the Northwest, and Mexico, but most are native to California. They range in flower color from white through all shades

Ceanothus griseus horizontalis

of blue to deep violet blue. They all flower in spring, mostly in March or April. In descriptions on chart, time of flowering is not indicated unless it is unusual.

Ceanothus sometimes get aphids and whitefly, but these are easy to control. As a group, ceanothus plants don't live very long—5–10 years is typical.

Almost all ceanothus can succumb to root rot caused by water mold organisms. In the wild, this doesn't happen because the plants grow on rocky slopes and generally go without water all summer. But in the garden it's a major factor. If possible, plant ceanothus beyond reach of sprinklers, and water them by hose through the first dry season only. In subsequent years they can grow on whatever water they get during the rainy season or from the subsoil during the dry season.

Ceanothus griseus horizontalis

Ceanothus gloriosus   *Ceanothus 'Ray Hartman'*

SPECIES OR VARIETY	SIZE	FOLIAGE	FLOWERS	COMMENTS
C. griseus horizontalis 'Yankee Point'	3–5 ft. tall, 8–10 ft. wide.	Glossy, dark green, 1½-in. leaves.	Medium blue 1-in. clusters.	One of best ground-covering kinds. Looks refined.
C. griseus 'Louis Edmunds'	5–6 ft. tall, 9–20 ft. wide.	Bright glossy green 1-in. leaves.	Medium sea blue 1-in. clusters.	Stands heavy soil, water.
C. griseus 'Santa Ana'	4–5 ft. tall, 10–15 ft. wide.	Rich, dark green, ½-in. leaves.	Dark midnight blue 1-in. clusters.	Small leaves, somewhat brushy stems, but beautiful flowers.
C. hearstiorum	6-in. tall, 6–8 ft. wide.	Bumpy 1½-in. leaves.	Medium blue 1-in. clusters.	One of flattest, but lets in weeds. Spreads from center like a star. Variable performance; not dependable.
C. impressus SANTA BARBARA CEANOTHUS	6–9 ft. tall, 10–15 ft. wide.	Dense mass of dark green ½-in. leaves.	Lovely dark blue 1-in. clusters.	Temperamental; does best near coast.
C. impressus 'Puget Blue'	4–6 ft. tall, 7–9 ft. wide.	Dark green ½-in. leaves.	Deep blue 1-in. clusters.	Does well in heavy soil. Not reliably hardy in Zones 4–7.
C. 'Joyce Coulter'	2–5 ft. tall, 10–12 ft. wide.	Medium green 1-in. leaves.	Medium blue 3–5-in. spikes.	Grows as mound rather than ground cover.
C. 'Julia Phelps'	4½–7 ft. tall, 7–9 ft. wide.	Small, dark green, ½-in. leaves.	Dark indigo blue 1-in. clusters.	One of best colors, best bloomers.
C. maritimus	1–3 ft. tall, 3–8 ft. wide.	Blue green to grayish ½-in. leaves—typically gray or white beneath.	White to pale lavender ½-in. clusters.	Height and color vary a lot.
C. 'Mountain Haze'	6–8 ft. tall, 8–10 ft. wide.	Glossy, medium green, roundish 1-in. leaves.	Medium blue 3–4-in. spikes.	Fast grower.
C. 'Owlswood Blue'	8–10 ft. tall, 10–12 ft. wide.	Dark green, oval, 2½-in. leaves.	Dark blue 4–6-in. flower spikes.	
C. 'Ray Hartman'	12–20 ft. tall, 15–20 ft. wide.	Big, dark green, 2–3-in. leaves.	Medium blue 3–5-in. spikes.	Can be trained as small tree.
C. rigidus 'Snowball'	6 ft. tall, 12–16 ft. wide.	Dark green ½-in. leaves.	White puffs ¾-in. wide.	Handsome, dense, mounding.
C. 'Sierra Blue'	10–12 ft. tall, 8–10 ft. wide.	Glossy, medium green, 1½-in leaves.	Bright medium blue 6–8-in. spikes.	Very fast grower; weedy first few years.

(Continued on next page)

SPECIES OR VARIETY	SIZE	FOLIAGE	FLOWERS	COMMENTS
C. thyrsiflorus BLUE BLOSSOM	6–21 ft. tall, 8–30 ft. wide.	Medium green, glossy leaves to 2 in.	Light to dark blue 3-in. flower spikes.	One of the hardiest evergreen ceanothus. Variety 'Skylark' ('Frades' Selection') has very dark blue flowers, blooms very late, grows exceptionally compact.
C. thyrsiflorus 'Millerton Point'	10–12 ft. tall, 12–14 ft. wide.	Medium green, narrow, 2-in. leaves.	White 3-in. flower spikes.	
C. thyrsiflorus 'Snow Flurry'	6–10 ft. tall, 8–12 ft. wide.	Rich green 2-in. leaves.	Pure white and profuse.	

CEDAR. See *Cedrus.*

CEDAR, WESTERN RED. See *Thuja plicata.*

CEDAR OF LEBANON. See *Cedrus libani.*

CEDRELA. Deciduous or evergreen trees. Flower in spring. Leaves divided into many leaflets, somewhat like tree of heaven (*Ailanthus*). Water needs average.

C. fissilis. Evergreen in tropical areas, deciduous in mildest California climates. Zones 16, 17, 22–24. Native to Central and South America. Smooth-trunked, round-headed tree grows to 50 ft. or more. Beautiful old street trees in Santa Barbara. Yellowish, velvety flowers in dense drooping clusters followed by star shaped, woody capsules containing winged seeds; much prized for dry arrangements.

C. sinensis. Deciduous. Zones 2–9, 14–24. Native to China. Slow to medium growth to 50 ft. White flowers in long, pendulous clusters, April and May, followed by capsules similar to above. Prized for beauty of new growth—tinted in shades of cream, soft pink, and rose. Suckers freely.

Cedrela sinensis

CEDRUS. CEDAR. Evergreen trees. These conifers are the true cedars, and among most widely grown conifers in the West. Cedars bear needles in tufted clusters. Cone scales, like those of firs, fall from tree, leaving a spiky core behind. Male catkins produce prodigious amounts of pollen that may cover you with yellow dust on a windy day. All are deep rooted, drought tolerant once established.

C. atlantica. ATLAS CEDAR. Zones 2–23. Native to Algeria. Slow to moderate growth to 60 ft. and more. Open, angular growth in youth. Branches usually get too long and heavy on young trees unless tips are pinched out or cut back. In Zones 4–7, at any age branches tend to break in heavy snows. Growth naturally less open with age. Less spreading than other true cedars, but still needs 30-ft. circle. Needles, less than 1 in. long, are bluish green. Varieties: *C. a.* 'Aurea', leaves with yellowish tint; *C. a.* 'Glauca', silvery blue; *C. a.* 'Pendula', branches droop vertically. Untrained, spreading, informally branching plants are sold as "rustics."

C. brevifolia. CYPRUS (or CYPRIAN) CEDAR. Zones 5–24. Resembles *C. libani* (see below) but is smaller tree (to 50 ft.), with shorter needles (¼–½ in.) and smaller cones. Rare. Sometimes considered variety

Cedrus atlantica

Cedrus deodara

of *C. libani.* Very slow growing. Native to island of Cyprus.

C. deodara. DEODAR CEDAR. Zones 2–12, 14–24. Native to the Himalayas. Fast growing to 80 ft. with 40-ft. spread at ground level. Lower branches sweep down to ground, then upwards. Upper branches openly spaced, graceful. Nodding tip identifies it in skyline. Softer, lighter texture than other cedars. Planted as living Christmas tree in small lawn, it soon overpowers area. However, you can control spread of tree by cutting new growth of side branches halfway back in late spring. This pruning also makes tree more dense. Very drought resistant once established.

Although deodars sold by nurseries are very similar in form, many variations occur in a group of seedlings—from scarecrows to compact low shrubs. These variations are propagated by cuttings or grafting: 'Aurea', with yellow new foliage turning golden green in summer; 'Descanso Dwarf' ('Compacta'), a slow growing form reaching 15 ft. in 20 years; and 'Pendula' ('Prostrata'), which grows flat on ground or will drape over rock or wall. Deodar cedar can be pruned to grow as spreading low or high shrub. Annual late spring pruning will keep it in the shape you want.

C. libani. CEDAR OF LEBANON. Zones 2–24. Native to Asia Minor. To 80 ft., but slow growing—to 15 ft. in 15 years. Variable in growth habit. Usually a dense, narrow pyramid in youth. Needles, less than 1 in. long, are brightest green of the cedars in young trees, dark gray green in old trees. Spreads picturesquely as it matures to become majestic skyline tree with long horizontal arms and irregular crown. Rather scarce and expensive because of time to reach salable size. Routine garden care. No pruning needed. 'Sargentii' or 'Pendula Sargentii' is slow grower with short trunk and crowded, weeping branches; choice container or rock garden plant.

CELASTRUS. BITTERSWEET. Deciduous vines. Hardy all zones, best 1–7 where winters are cold. Grown principally for clusters of handsome fruit, yellow to orange capsules which split open to display brilliant red-coated seeds inside. Branches bearing fruit are much prized for indoor arrangements. Since birds seem uninterested in fruit, display is prolonged into winter.

Celastrus scandens

Vigorous and twining with ropelike branches. Need support. Will become tangled mass of intertwining branches unless pruned continuously. Cut out fruiting branches in winter; pinch out tips of vigorous branches in summer. Routine feeding, watering.

C. orbiculatus. To 30–40 ft. Leaves roundish, toothed, to 4 in. Fruit on short side shoots is partially obscured until leaves fall.

C. rosthornianus (*C. loeseneri*). CHINESE BITTERSWEET. To 20 ft. with dark green oval leaves to 5 in. long. Fruit heavily borne all along branches.

C. scandens. AMERICAN BITTERSWEET. Native to eastern U.S. To 10–20 ft. Leaves very light green, oval, toothed, to 4 in. Fruit in scattered dense clusters is held above leaves, looks showy before foliage falls. Male and female flowers on different plants. To get fruit, plant one male plant with the female plants.

CELERIAC. Biennial grown as annual. All
Zones in conditions noted for celery below.
A form of celery grown for its large
rounded, edible roots rather than for its leaf
stalks. Usually displayed in markets as
"celery root."

These roots are peeled and cooked or
used raw in salads. Growth requirements
are same as for celery. Plants should grow
6–8 in. apart in rows spaced 18–24 in.
apart. Harvest when roots are 3 in. across
or larger—in about 120 days. 'Giant
Prague' is the recommended variety.

Celeriac

CELERY. Biennial grown as annual. All
Zones in conditions noted below. Plant
seeds in flats in early spring. Where winters
are mild, start in summer and grow as
winter crop. Seedlings are slow to reach
planting size (save time by purchasing
seedlings). Plant seedlings 6 in. apart in
rows 24 in. apart. Enrich planting soil with
fertilizer. Soak ground around plants
thoroughly and often. Every 2 or 3 weeks
apply liquid fertilizer with irrigation water.
Work some soil up around plants as they
grow to keep them upright and whiten
stalks. Or blanch by setting bottomless milk
carton, tar paper cylinder, or similar device over plants to
exclude light from stalks (leaves must have sunlight). Or use
unblanched (green). Bait to control snails and slugs; use Bordeaux solution or maneb to control blight.

Celery

CELERY ROOT. See *Celeriac.*

CELOSIA. COCKSCOMB, CHINESE WOOL-
FLOWER. Annuals. All Zones in conditions
noted below. Grow best in hot-summer
climates, including desert. Richly colored
tropical plants, some with flower clusters in
bizarre shapes. Although attractive in cut
arrangements with other flowers, in gardens celosias are most effective by themselves. Cut blooms can be dried for winter
bouquets. Sow seed in place in late spring
or early summer, or set out plants from
flats. Succeed with little summer water in
Zones 4–9, 14–24. Need full sun.

Cockscombs are derived from a silvery
white-flowered species, *C. argentea,* which
has narrow leaves 2 in. or more long. There
are two kinds. One group has plumy flower clusters (plume
cockscomb), often sold as *C.* 'Plumosa'. Some of these, like
Chinese woolflower (sometimes sold as *C.* 'Childsii') have plumy
flower clusters that look like tangled masses of yarn. Flowers
come in brilliant colors of pink, orange red, crimson, gold. You
can get forms that grow 2½–3 ft. high or dwarf, more compact
varieties. The latter, with their heavily branched plumes, grow to
about 1 ft. high.

The other group is the crested cockscombs (often sold as *C.*
'Cristata')—velvety fan shaped flower clusters, often much contorted and fluted. Flowers are yellow, orange, crimson, purple,
and red. Tall kinds grow to 3 ft., dwarf varieties to 10 in. high.

Celosia cristata

CELTIS. HACKBERRY. Deciduous trees.
Related to elm and similar to them in most
details, but smaller. All have virtue of deep
rooting; old trees in narrow planting strips
expand in trunk diameter and nearly fill
strips—but without a surface root or any
sign of heaving the sidewalk or curb. Bare-
root plants, especially in larger sizes, sometimes fail to leaf out. Safer to buy in con-

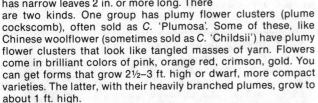
Celtis occidentalis

tainers. Or try for small-sized bare-root
trees with big root systems. Stake well in
windy locations, at least until tree is well-
established. When established will take
desert heat, wind, much drought, and
alkaline soil.

Street or lawn trees, overhead shade,

Celtis occidentalis

even near buildings or paving. All have inconspicuous flowers.
Especially good in windy places. Only pest of note seems to be
aphids occasionally. In Zones 1–3, 10–13, insects cause leaf gall
on hackberry trees. Attractive to birds.

C. australis. EUROPEAN HACKBERRY. Zones 8–16, 18–20. Moderate grower to 40 ft. in 14–15 years. In youth, branches are more
upright than other hackberries. Never as widespreading as
common hackberry. Dark green leaves 2–5 in. long, more
coarsely toothed and more sharply pointed than common
hackberry. Has shorter deciduous period than common
hackberry.

C. occidentalis. COMMON HACKBERRY. All Zones. Native to
eastern U.S. Grows to form rounded crown 50 ft. or more high,
and nearly as wide. Branches are spreading and sometimes
pendulous. Leaves oval, bright green, 2–5 in. long, finely
toothed on edges. Tree does not leaf out until April or later. In
Zones 10–13, it lives longer than and is superior to commonly
planted so-called Chinese elm (correctly the Siberian elm—
Ulmus pumila). Resistant to oak root fungus.

C. pallida. DESERT HACKBERRY, GRANJENO. Shrub or small tree
to 18 ft. Zones 10–13. Evergreen (deciduous in cold-winter
areas). Dense spiny growth; leaves 1 in. or less in length. Small
orange berries. Useful in desert regions as honey source, bird
food, erosion control, screen or barrier planting.

C. reticulata (*C. douglasii*). WESTERN HACKBERRY. Zones 1–3,
10–12. Native to eastern Washington and through intermountain
area to Utah, and in desert mountains of Arizona and southern
California. Worthwhile ornamental tree in that area. Grows to
25–30 ft. high with similar spread. Has somewhat pendulous
branches. Oval leaves to 2½ in. long, margins toothed, pale beneath, strongly veined. Tiny red or brown berries eaten by birds.

C. sinensis. CHINESE HACKBERRY, YUNNAN HACKBERRY. Zones
8–16, 18–20. Similar in growth habit to common hackberry, but
smaller. Leaves to 4 in. long, smoother and glossier than other
hackberries, and have scallop-toothed edges.

CENTAUREA. Annuals and perennials.
Perennial kinds hardy Zones 8–24. Out of
some 500 species, only dozen or so widely
cultivated. Of these, annuals (cornflower
and sweet sultan) grown mainly for cut
flowers; perennial kinds used principally
for soft, silvery white or gray foliage. All
centaureas relatively easy to grow, need
full sun, perform best in light, neutral soils;
add lime to acid soils. Sow seed of annuals
in spring or fall. Set out plants of perennial

Centaurea cineraria

kinds from cans or flats any time, preferably spring or fall; also
sow seed, make cuttings in summer. Moderate water users but
see *C. gymnocarpa.*

C. cineraria (*C. candidissima*). DUSTY MILLER. (This common
name applied to many plants with whitish foliage. Also see
Senecio cineraria.) Compact perennial to 1 ft. or more, velvety
white leaves, strap shaped, with broad roundish lobes, mostly in
basal clump. Solitary 1-in. flower heads (purple, occasionally
yellow) in summer. Trim back after flowering. Most popular of
dusty millers in California. Attracts bees.

C. cyanus. CORNFLOWER, BACHELOR'S BUTTON. Annual, 1–2½
ft., branching if given sufficient space. Narrow, gray green
leaves, 2–3 in. long. Flower heads 1–1½ in. across, blue, pink,
rose, wine red, and white. Blue varieties are traditional favorites
for boutonnieres. 'Jubilee Gem', bushy, compact, 1-ft. tall, deep
blue flowers; Polka Dot strain has all cornflower colors on 16-in.
plants. Sow seed in early spring in cold-winter areas, late
summer-fall where winters are mild.

C. gymnocarpa. VELVET CENTAUREA. (Often called dusty
miller.) Perennial. 1–3-ft., white feltlike leaves, somewhat

resembling *C. cineraria* but leaves more finely divided. Usually 2 or 3 purple flower heads at ends of leafy branches. Trim plants after bloom. Drought tolerant.

C. moschata. SWEET SULTAN. Annual. Erect, branching at base, to 2 ft., Imperialis strain to 3 ft. Green deeply toothed leaves; thistlelike, 2-in. flower heads mostly in shades of lilac through rose, sometimes white or yellow; musklike fragrance. Sow seed directly on soil in spring or set out as transplants. Needs lots of heat; no overhead water. Splendid cut flower.

CENTIPEDE PLANT. See *Homalocladium platycladum.*

CENTRANTHUS ruber (*Valeriana rubra*). JUPITER'S BEARD, RED VALERIAN. Perennial. Zones 7–9, 14–24. Rank, invasive, and much maligned. Used correctly, it's hard to beat for long, showy bloom in difficult situations. Very drought tolerant. Bushy, to 3 ft. high. Bluish green leaves 4 in. long. Small deep crimson to pale pink flowers about ½ in. long, in dense terminal clusters. Blooms late spring, early summer. Variety 'Albus' is white.

Centranthus ruber

Use in fringe areas of garden, on rough slopes, banks, walls, streetside areas far from hose. Naturalized in many parts of West. White variety especially attractive with large beds of daylilies. Good cut flower. Plant in sun or partial shade. Will grow in poor dry soil, accepts almost any condition except damp shade. Self-sows prolifically because of small dandelionlike parachutes on seeds. Cut off old flowering stems to shape plant and prolong bloom.

CENTURY PLANT. See *Agave americana.*

CEPHALOCEREUS senilis. OLD MAN CACTUS. Zones 21–24. Native to Mexico. Slender columnar cactus of slow growth to eventual 40 ft., usually much less. Covered with long, grayish white hairs. Yellow 1½-in. spines. Old plants have 2-in.-long, rose-colored flowers in April. Night blooming. Protect from hard frosts. Good pot plant; older plants striking in cactus garden. Indoors give it south light.

*Cephalocereus
senilis*

CEPHALOPHYLLUM 'Red Spike'. Often sold as *Cylindrophyllum speciosum.* RED SPIKE ICE PLANT. Succulent perennial. Zones 8, 9, 11–24. Clumping plant 3–5 in. high, slowly spreading to 15–18 in. wide. Spiky, bronzy red leaves point straight up. Bright cerise red, 2-in.-wide flowers in winter, with scattering of bloom at other seasons. Needs sun, tolerates drought.

*Cephalophyllum
'Red Spike'*

Plant 6–12 in. apart for ground cover. Water infrequently during summer in Zones 11–13 to avoid damping off. Can be fire retardant; draws bees.

CEPHALOTAXUS. PLUM YEW. Evergreen trees or shrubs. Zones 4–9, 14–17. Related to yews (*Taxus*), differing in larger, brighter green needles and in larger fruit that resemble small green or brown plums (female plants only). They grow slowly, tolerate shade (require it where summers are hot), and like acid to neutral soil, average water.

C. fortunei. CHINESE PLUM YEW. Big shrub or small tree 10 ft. tall (rarely more) with soft needlelike leaves up to 3½ in. long, ⅛ in. wide.

C. harringtonia. Spreading shrub or small tree with needles

*Cephalotaxus
harringtonia*

1–2½ in. long. The variety 'Fastigiata' is only one available in the West; it resembles Irish yew, because it is narrow and erect.

CERASTIUM tomentosum. SNOW-IN-SUMMER. Perennial. All Zones. Low-growing plant that performs equally well in mild and cold climates, coastal or desert areas. Spreading dense tufty mats of silvery gray, ¾-in.-long leaves. Snowy-white masses of flowers, ½–¾ in. across, in early summer. Plant grows to about 6–8 in. high, spreads 2–3 ft. in 1 year.

*Cerastium
tomentosum*

Use as ground cover on sunny bank or on level ground. (Avoid extensive planting in prominent situations; not as long-lived as some ground covers.) Effective in patterns with other low perennials; in rock gardens; cascading from top of walls; edging paths or driveways; between stepping stones or bulbs; as filler between low shrubs.

Plant in full sun, or light shade in warmest areas. Any soil as long as drainage is good: standing water causes root rot. Set divisions or plants 12–18 in. apart, or sow seeds. Once established, needs only occasional watering; for fast growth, water regularly and feed 2 or 3 times a year. Shear off faded flower clusters. May look a bit shabby in cold winters, but revives rapidly in spring. Divide in fall or early spring.

CERATONIA siliqua. CAROB, ST. JOHN'S BREAD. Evergreen large shrub or tree. Zones 9, 13–16, 18–24. Native to eastern Mediterranean region. Allowed to grow naturally, it maintains bushy form with branches to ground, often multistemmed. Use this way as big hedge, informal or trimmed. Trained as tree, with lower branches removed, it grows at moderate rate to become dense, round-headed, to 30–40 ft., and as wide. Will reach 20 ft. in 10 years. As street tree, it needs more than normal space as roots will break sidewalks.

Ceratonia siliqua

Foliage is unusually dense, dark green with a sparkle. Individual leaves are divided into 4–10 round leaflets averaging about 2 in. long. Small red flowers in spring. Female trees offer problem of pod pick-up. Flattened dark brown leathery pods, 1 ft. long, grow abundantly. Rich in sugar, the pods are milled to a fine powder and sold in health food stores as substitute for chocolate.

Give young trees winter protection first year or two. Hardy to 18°F. Although often given summer watering, the carob is subject to root crown rot and should be watered infrequently and deeply. Once established, needs no summer water. Resistant to oak root fungus and fire damage.

CERATOSTIGMA. Technically evergreen or semievergreen subshrubs or perennials, but all best treated as perennials, cutting back each winter regardless of frost. Valued for rich deep blue, phloxlike flowers in clusters, summer to late fall when garden needs cool blues. Tolerant of varying soils, water schedules, sun or part shade.

*Ceratostigma
plumbaginoides*

C. griffithii. BURMESE PLUMBAGO. Zones 4–9, 14–24. Similar to *C. willmottianum* (see below) in hardiness and appearance, but more compact and lower growing (2½–3 ft.). Displays its brilliant blue flowers somewhat later, from July into late fall.

C. plumbaginoides. (Often sold as *Plumbago larpentae.*) DWARF PLUMBAGO. Zones 2–9, 14–24. A perennial wiry-stemmed ground cover 6–12 in. high. In loose soil and where growing season is long, spreads rapidly by underground stems, eventually covering large areas. Bronzy green to dark green leaves, 3 in. long, turn reddish brown with frosts. Intense blue (½ in. wide) flowers from July until first frosts. When plants show signs of aging, remove old crowns, replace with rooted stems.

C. willmottianum. CHINESE PLUMBAGO. Zones 4–9, 14–24. Grows as airy mass of wiry stems to 2–4 ft. high and equally wide. Deep green leaves, roundish to oval, 2 in. long; turn yellow or red and drop quickly after frost. Bright blue, ½-in.-wide flowers, June-November. In colder winters stems die back to ground and are replaced by new ones. In milder winters stems survive and should be cut back hard in early spring.

For the pale blue-flowered Cape plumbago, see *Plumbago auriculata.*

CERATOZAMIA mexicana. Cycad. Zones 21–24. Related to *Cycas revoluta,* similar in appearance. Trunk usually a foot high, 4–6 ft. in great age, a foot thick. Very slow in growth. Leaves in whorl, 3–6 ft. long, divided featherwise into 15–20 pairs of foot-long, inch-wide leaflets. Striking in containers or protected place in open ground. Part shade. Protect from frosts. Give ample water.

Ceratozamia mexicana

CERCIDIPHYLLUM japonicum. KATSURA TREE. Deciduous tree. Zones 1–6; under high branching trees in Zones 14–16, 18–20. Native to Japan. A tree of many virtues where adapted. Light and dainty branch and leaf pattern. Foliage, always fresh looking, shows tints of red throughout growing season. Beautifully colored in brilliant red or yellow in fall, especially if watered infrequently at end of summer.

Rather slow growing, eventually to 40 ft. or more. Varying growth habits: some have single trunk; most have multiple trunks angled upward and outward. Nearly round, 2–4-in. leaves neatly spaced in pairs along arching branches. Mature leaves are dark blue green above, grayish beneath. Flowers inconspicuous.

Needs special protection from hot sun and dry winds and needs plenty of moisture during growing season in interior climates.

Cercidiphyllum japonicum

CERCIDIUM. PALO VERDE. Deciduous trees. Zones 10–14, 18–20. The common name palo verde covers four desert trees—Mexican palo verde (see *Parkinsonia*), blue palo verde, littleleaf palo verde and Sonoran palo verde. All attract birds.

C. floridum (*C. torreyanum*). BLUE PALO VERDE. Native to deserts of southern California, Arizona, Sonora, Baja California. It belongs to and beautifies desert and the garden oases that have been planted there. In gardens, grows fast to 30 ft. and as wide. In spring, 2–4½-in.-long clusters of small bright yellow flowers almost hide the branches. When out of bloom, shows intricate pattern of blue green, spiny branches, branchlets, and leaf stalks. Leaves have 1–3 pairs of smooth, tiny leaflets, and are shed early, leaving bluish green leaf stalks for lightly filtered shade.

Will survive much drought, but is denser, more attractive, and grows faster with water and fertilizer.

C. microphyllum. LITTLELEAF PALO VERDE, FOOTHILLS PALO VERDE. Native to eastern San Bernardino County, California; Arizona; Sonora; Baja California. Similar to blue palo verde, except bark and leaves (with 4–12 pairs of hairy leaflets) are yellowish green, and flowers paler yellow in 1-in.-long clusters.

C. praecox. SONORAN PALO VERDE. Native to Sonora and Baja California. The handsomest palo verde in form and trunk color (lime green). Develops beautiful umbrella top. To 10–15 ft. high.

Cercidium floridum

CERCIS. REDBUD. Deciduous shrubs or trees. Five redbuds are grown in the West: two western natives, an eastern native, one from Europe, one from China. Early spring flowers are sweet pea shaped, small, in clusters; where adapted are borne in great profusion on bare twigs, branches, sometimes even on main trunk. Attractive broad rounded leaves are heart shaped at base. All give fall color with first frosts. Flowers are followed by clusters of flat pods. Average water needs (except drought tolerant *C. occidentalis*).

Cercis occidentalis

C. canadensis. EASTERN REDBUD. Zones 1–3, 7–20. Native of eastern U.S. Largest and fastest of available species where adapted. To 25–35 ft. tall. Most apt to take tree form. Round headed but with horizontally tiered branches in age. Rich green, 3–6-in.-long leaves have pointed tips. Small (½ in. long) rosy pink flowers clothe bare brown branches in early spring.

Garden varieties include: 'Alba' ('White Texas'), white flowers, choice; 'Forest Pansy', purple foliage and reddish branches; 'Oklahoma', wine red flowers; 'Plena' ('Flame'), double flowers like rosebuds; 'Rubye Atkinson', pure pink flowers.

C. chinensis. CHINESE REDBUD. Zones 4–20. Native to China, Japan. Seen mostly as light, open shrub to 10–12 ft. Clusters (3–5 in. long) are deep rose, almost rosy purple. Leaves sometimes glossier and brighter green than *C. canadensis,* with transparent line around the edge. Spectacular in high deserts of Arizona.

C. occidentalis. WESTERN REDBUD. Zones 2–24. Native to California, Arizona, Utah, but predominantly in California foothills below 4,000 ft.

A shrub or small tree 10–18 ft. in height and spread. Usually grows several trunks from base. All-year interest. In spring it delivers 3-week brilliant display of magenta flowers, ½ in. long. Summer foliage of handsome blue green, 3-in. leaves, notched or rounded at tip; interspersed are brilliant magenta newly forming seed pods. In fall whole plant turns light yellow or red. In winter, bare branches in picturesque pattern hold reddish brown seed pods.

Excellent for dry, seldom watered banks. Water regularly in first year or two to speed growth. Profuse flower production only where winter temperatures drop to 28°F. or lower. Resistant to oak root fungus.

C. reniformis. Zones 2–9, 14–24. Native to Southwest. Leaves leathery, blue green, 2–3 in. wide, with rounded or notched tips. Flowers as in *C. canadensis;* variety 'Alba', with white flowers, is sold in West.

C. siliquastrum. JUDAS TREE. Zones 2–19. Native to Europe and western Asia. Generally of shrubby habit to 25 ft., occasionally a taller, slender tree with single trunk. Flowers are purplish rose, ½ in. long. Large 3–5-in. leaves, deeply heart shaped at base, rounded or notched at tip. Occasionally damaged by late frosts in Northwest. Can be grown in soil where oak root fungus (*Armillaria*) is present.

CERCOCARPUS. MOUNTAIN MAHOGANY. Evergreen or deciduous tall shrubs or small trees. Natives of western mountains and foothills. Very drought tolerant. Several have a most attractive open structure and branching pattern. Distinguished in fall by long-lasting small fruit topped by a long, twisted, feathery, tail-like plume that sparkles in sunlight. Sun or light shade. About 20 kinds are native to the West, but these three are most widespread:

C. betuloides. Zones 6–24. Evergreen, native to dry slopes and foothills, below 6,000 ft. elevation, southwestern Oregon, California, northern Baja California. Called hardtack, mountain ironwood, sweet brush. Generally a shrub 5–12 ft. high. Can form small tree to 20 ft. with wide-spreading

Cercocarpus betuloides

crown of arching branches. Wedge shaped, ½–1-in. leaves clustered on short spurs, dark green above, pale beneath, feather veined with toothed edges.

C. ledifolius. CURL-LEAF MOUNTAIN MAHOGANY. All Zones. Evergreen, native to dry mountain slopes, 4,000–9,000 ft. elevation, throughout the western states from eastern slopes of Sierra-Cascades divide to Rockies. In warmer western part of its range about the same size as *C. betuloides;* in highest, coldest part of the range very slow growing and an excellent hedge or small tree of character. Leaves leathery, ½–1 in. long, resinous, dark green above, white below, with inrolled edges.

C. montanus. All Zones, most useful 1–2, 10. Deciduous shrub usually 4–6 ft. tall and as wide, rarely to 8–9 ft. Leaves 1–2 in. long, white underneath. Useful in dry places, coldest climates.

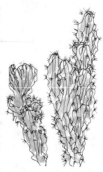

CEREUS peruvianus. Cactus. Zones 16, 17, 21–24. Tall, branching, treelike cactus eventually reaching 30–50 ft. Striking bluish green, especially when young; ribbed with scattered spines. Flowers white, 6–7 in. long, 5 in. across, in June. Night blooming. Variety 'Monstrosus' is smaller, slower growing, with ribs irregularly broken up into knobs and crests. Striking outline; effective in large containers. Protect from hard frosts.

Cereus peruvianus 'Monstrosus'

CEROPEGIA woodii. ROSARY VINE. Succulent. Outdoors in Zones 21–24, house plant anywhere. From South Africa. Little vine with hanging or trailing thin stems growing from tuberous base. Leaves in pairs, heart shaped, thick and succulent, ⅔ in. long, dark green marbled white. Little tubers that form on stems can be used to start new plants. Flowers small, dull pink or purplish, not showy but interesting in structure. Best in pots; stems may trail in thin curtain or be trained on small trellis. Give some shade and regular watering.

Ceropegia woodii

Other ceropegias are available from specialists: some are shrubby, some vining, some stiffly succulent, but all have similarly fascinating flower structure.

CESTRUM. Evergreen shrubs. Native to American tropics. All the kinds have showy, tubular flowers. Flowers and fruit attract birds. Fast growing, inclined to be rangy and top-heavy unless consistently pruned. Best in warm sheltered spot in part shade. Feed and water generously. Add organic soil amendments before planting. Nip back consistently for compactness and cut back severely after flowering or fruiting. In climates specified below, plants may freeze back in heavy frosts but recover quickly.

Cestrum elegans

C. aurantiacum. ORANGE CESTRUM. Zones 16, 17, 21–24. Native to Guatemala. Rare and handsome. To 8 ft. Brilliant show: clusters of 1-in.-long orange flowers late spring, summer, followed by white berries. Deep green, oval, 4-in. leaves. Tall growing; best used as vine or espalier.

C. elegans (*C. purpureum*). RED CESTRUM. Zones 13, 17, 19-24 Shrub or semiclimber to 10 ft. high or higher, with arching branches, deep green 4-in. leaves. Masses of purplish red, 1-in.-long flowers in spring and summer; scattered bloom throughout year, followed by red berries. Good espalier.

C. nocturnum. NIGHT JESSAMINE. Zones 13, 16–24. Native to West Indies. Evergreen shrub to 12 ft. with 4–8-in.-long leaves and clusters of creamy white flowers in summer, white berries. Powerfully fragrant at night. Too powerful for some people.

C. parqui. WILLOW-LEAFED JESSAMINE. Zones 13–24. Native to

Chile. To 6–10 ft. tall with many branches from base. Dense foliage of willowlike leaves, 3–6 in. long. Flowers, greenish yellow, 1 in. long, in clusters, summer. Berries dark violet brown. Not as attractive as other species in form, flowers, or fruit but its perfume is potent. Leaves blacken in light frost. Best used where winter appearance is unimportant. In cold-winter areas, protect roots with mulch and use as perennial.

CHAENOMELES. (Some formerly called *Cydonia.*) FLOWERING QUINCE. Deciduous shrubs. Zones 1–21. Flowering quinces are among first shrubs to bloom each year. As early as January you can take a budded stem or two indoors, place it in water in warm window and watch buds break into bloom. The plants themselves are picturesque, practically indestructible shrubs of varying growth habit. Leaves shiny green, red tinged when young. Branches are attractive when out of leaf—strong in line with an Oriental feeling. Some grow to 10 ft. and spread wider; some are compact and low growing. Most are thorny; a few are thornless. Some of them bear small quincelike fruit. All are useful grown as hedges and barriers.

Chaenomeles

All are easy to grow in sun with average garden watering. Tolerant of extremes in cold and heat, light to heavy soil. May suffer from chlorosis in alkaline soils (use iron chelate or iron sulfate). May bloom reluctantly in warm-winter areas. Prune any time to shape, limit growth, or gain special effects. Good time to prune is in bud and bloom season. (Use cut branches for indoor arrangements.) New growth that follows will bear next year's flowers. Flowers attract birds.

In the following list of choice varieties we have noted, in addition to color, the height. Those noted as tall are in the 6-ft. and more class; low varieties are in the 2–3-ft. range. Flower color is given for each. All are garden hybrids; specialists can furnish even more varieties.

'Apple Blossom'. Tall. White and pink.
'Cameo'. Low, compact. Double, soft apricot pink.
'Contorta'. Low. White to pink; twisted branches. Good as bonsai.
'Corallina'. ('Coral Glow'). Tall. Reddish orange.
'Coral Sea'. Tall. Large, coral pink.
'Enchantress'. Tall. Large, shell pink.
'Falconet Charlot'. Tall, thornless. Double salmon pink.
'Hollandia'. Tall. Large red flowers, reblooms in fall.
'Jet Trail'. Low. Pure white.
'Nivalis'. Tall. Large, pure white.
'Pink Beauty'. Tall. Purplish pink.
'Pink Lady'. Low. Rose pink blooms from deeper colored buds.
'Red Ruffles'. Tall. Almost thornless. Large, ruffled, red.
'Snow'. Tall. Large, pure white.
'Stanford Red'. Low, almost thornless. Tomato red.
'Texas Scarlet'. Low. Tomato red.
'Toyo Nishiki'. Tall. Pink, white, pink and white, solid red all on same branch.

CHAIN FERN. See *Woodwardia.*

CHAMAECEREUS sylvestri. PEANUT CACTUS. Zones 16, 17, 19-24. Native to Argentina. Dwarf cactus with cylindrical, ribbed, spiny, 2–3-in. joints that fall off easily and root just as easily. Likes sun, average water during growth and bloom cycle. Profusely blooming in spring and early summer; even tiny rooted joints bloom. Flowers bright scarlet, almost 3 in. long. Great favorite with children.

Chamaecereus sylvestri

CHAMAECYPARIS. FALSE CYPRESS. Evergreen trees, shrubs, and shrublets. All produce cones ½ in. long. Take average water.

Many varieties, but all sold are forms of five kinds—two western natives, one from the eastern U.S., and two from Japan. These are the basic five (they and their many varieties are charted for size, shape, texture, and performance):

C. lawsoniana. An important timber tree in coastal Oregon (also native to extreme northern California). It and its varieties are probably the most adaptable in mild western climates. Its yellow-leafed varieties seem to burn in California. Best in Zones 4–6. Foliage burns in dry cold or hot sun in Zones 2, 3. Good performance in Zones 15–17 and poor to satisfactory in Zones 7–9, 14, 18–21 (best in partial shade there). Can be used as hedge, screen, or background plant.

C. nootkatensis. The hardy timber tree of Alaska and moun-

Chamaecyparis lawsoniana

tains of Oregon and Washington. It and its varieties do not thrive in cold dry winds or high summer heat. Use in Zones 4–6, 15–17.

C. obtusa. Japanese species of tree best known for its dwarf and compact varieties. Best adapted Zones 4–6, 15–17.

C. pisifera. Japanese species of tree with many forms. Best adapted Zones 4–6, 15–17; will grow in favored sites Zones 1–3.

C. thyoides. Eastern American tree represented by a few garden varieties. Zones as for *C. pisifera.*

Chamaecyparis is rich source of bonsai material. For this use, there are many interesting dwarf forms and climate restrictions are less limiting; container-grown plants can be sheltered against extreme cold and wind in cold frame or similar shelter. The variety list here is not exhaustive; new varieties appear nearly every year. In purchasing, be aware that many of these garden varieties are very similar and are frequently mislabeled.

In growing chamaecyparis, be sure to provide fast drainage. They are susceptible to root rot in heavy, slow draining soils. Many forms develop dead foliage on the inner parts. Some of this is normal aging; an excess may indicate too much shade or spider mite infestation. A strong jet from hose will clear out most of the mites and the dead foliage as well.

Chamaecyparis

SPECIES OR VARIETY	HEIGHT	SPREAD	COLOR	FORM, TEXTURE	REMARKS
Chamaecyparis lawsoniana PORT ORFORD CEDAR, LAWSON CYPRESS	To 60 ft. or higher.	To 30 ft. at base.	Blue green, variable.	Pyramidal or columnar form with lacy, drooping, flat foliage sprays and conical crown.	Can be planted as close as 3 ft. apart without becoming thin or straggly, and topped at 10 ft. or more for windbreak or sun screen.
C. l. 'Allumii' SCARAB CYPRESS, BLUE LAWSON CYPRESS	To 30 ft.	Narrow.	Blue green, new foliage metallic blue.	Compact, narrow pyramidal form. Scalelike leaves are carried in regular vertical planes.	A widely adapted, slow growing tree. Planted 2–3 ft. apart makes narrow, formal hedge.
C. l. 'Azurea'	To 6 ft.	To 3 ft.	Silvery gray blue.	Broad pyramidal form. Soft-textured, drooping branches.	Avoid crowding for shapely plants.
C. l. 'Ellwoodii' ELLWOOD CYPRESS	Slowly to 6 or 8 ft., higher with age.	To 2 or 3 ft.	Silvery blue.	Dense, compact columnar form. Light textured with soft, prickly, needlelike leaves.	One of most widely planted and widely adapted trees. 'Ellwoodii Improved' is slower growing, bluer.
C. l. 'Fletcheri' FLETCHER CYPRESS	6–8 ft., higher with age.	To 3 or 4 ft.	Blue gray; purplish or brown in winter.	Dense pyramidal form. Soft, prickly foliage.	Somewhat like "Ellwoodii" but taller, broader, and faster growing.
C. l. 'Forsteckensis' (*C. l.* 'Forsteckiana') FORSTECK CYPRESS	4 ft.	To 6 ft.	Dark green.	Dense, compact form. Mosslike texture; densely tufted branches.	A rock garden or container plant. Makes a dense, informal hedge.
C. l. 'Lutea' GOLDEN LAWSON CYPRESS	To 30 ft. or more.,	To 10 or 12 ft.	New growth yellow, old growth blue gray.	Soft fronds.	Probably best of the taller yellow false cypresses. Susceptible to sunburn.
C. l. 'Minima Glauca' LITTLE BLUE CYPRESS	To 3 ft.	To 2½ ft.	Blue green.	Compact, nearly globular form. Dense foliage; soft texture.	A shrub well-suited for pots, boxes, rock gardens, low uniform landscape plantings.
C. l. 'Nidiformis' *C. nidiformis, C. l.* 'Nestoides' *C. nidifera* BIRD NEST CYPRESS	To 5 ft. or more in 10 years.	3–5 ft.	Dark green.	Spreading, flat-topped form with outward spraying branches, often with depressed "nest" in center of top.	Good for informal screening, hedge, as showy isolated plant. 'Grandi' ('Tamariscifolia') similar, with bluish foliage.
C. l. 'Stewartii' STEWART GOLDEN CYPRESS	To 30 ft.	10–12 ft. at 18-ft. height.	New growth yellow, old growth dark green.	Upright, slender, pyramidal form. Soft texture; drooping branchlets.	Handsome and widely planted. Needs room for good growth. Used in parks, public playgrounds.
C. l. 'Wisselii' WISSEL CYPRESS	To 15 or 18 ft., higher in 15–20 years.	4–5 ft.	Dark blue green.	Slender, upright form with twisted foliage; irregular branches, somewhat like those of *Juniperus chinensis* 'Torulosa'.	Subject to insects and diseases, especially in hot, dry climates. Keep sprayed for red spider mites.

(Continued on next page)

SPECIES OR VARIETY	HEIGHT	SPREAD	COLOR	FORM, TEXTURE	REMARKS
C. nootkatensis NOOTKA CYPRESS, ALASKA YELLOW CEDAR	80 ft.	20-30 ft.	Bluish green.	Pyramidal form, with dense, fine-textured foliage. Often has pendulous branches. Coarser than Lawson cypress.	Slow growing, it will stand greater cold and poorer soil than Lawson cypress, though latter can probably stand more heat.
C. nootkatensis 'Compacta'	To 3 or 5 ft.	To 2 or 2½ ft.	Blue green.	Narrow, pyramidal form.	Handsome in containers—a miniature tree rather than shrub.
C. n. 'Pendula'	10 ft. in 10 years, eventually 30 ft.	3–10 ft.	Yellowish green.	Weeping branch tips, nodding top.	Like C. nootkatensis, takes damp soil conditions better than Lawson cypress.
C. obtusa HINOKI FALSE CYPRESS	40–50 ft., higher with great age.	15–30 ft.	Dark glossy green.	Spreading, irregular, open form.	Very slow growing and suited principally to a large Oriental garden. Splendid bonsai subject. Prune to shape.
C. o. 'Aurea' GOLDEN HINOKI CYPRESS	30–40 ft.	10–15 ft.	Dark green. Young growth is golden.	Foliage is bunched, flattened in horizontal plane.	Slow growing. For Oriental garden, woodland edge. Color hard to blend. Useful with dark greens. Subject to sunburn.
C. o. 'Crippsii' CRIPPS GOLDEN CYPRESS	To 30 ft. Can be kept smaller.	To 10 ft.	Yellow when young. Later dark green.	Somewhat open, pyramidal habit.	Use for line and pattern in Oriental gardens or against fence, screen, wall. Can be pruned attractively by spacing branches at various levels.
C. o. 'Filicoides' FERNSPRAY CYPRESS	To 15 ft.	To 6 ft.	Medium green.	Dense foliage; branchlets short, crowded, frondlike.	Slow growing, with gracefully curved limbs. For Oriental gardens, entryways, large planting boxes.
C. o. 'Gracilis' (Often sold as C. obtusa). SLENDER HINOKI CYPRESS	Slow to 20 ft.	4–5 ft.	Very dark, glossy green.	Slender, somewhat weeping form. Soft and dense, with nodding top and branch ends.	Choice plant that is slow to outgrow its place. Good entryway plant or container subject.
C. o. 'Kosteri'	To 30 in. in 10 years.	30 in.	Dark glossy green.	Like a dwarfer, denser C. o. 'Nana Gracilis'.	One of best for rock garden, small container, Japanese garden.
C. o. 'Lycopodioides' CLUB-MOSS CYPRESS	Slow to 3 ft.	3 ft.	Dark green.	Branchlets short, irregular, crowded or bunched.	Unusual plant for close-range viewing. Rock garden or container.
C. o. 'Nana' DWARF HINOKI CYPRESS	Very slow to 3 ft.	2 ft. or more	Dark green.	Dense foliage in flat, stratified planes.	A 60-year-old plant may be 3 ft. tall, 2 ft. across. Rock gardens, mass plantings on slopes.
C. o. 'Nana Aurea' GOLDEN DWARF HINOKI CYPRESS	To 4 ft.	To 3 ft.	New foliage yellow. Old foliage dark green.	Dense foliage in flat-sided sprays.	Useful where touch of yellow is needed; Oriental and rock gardens.
C. o. 'Nana Gracilis' (Usually sold as C. o. 'Nana') DWARF HINOKI CYPRESS	To 4 ft.	To 3 ft.	Dark green.	Dense foliage; flattened, cupped fronds.	Most commonly used dwarf hinoki cypress; Oriental and rock gardens.
C. o. 'Sanderi' (C. o. 'Ericoides')	4-6 ft.	4-6 ft.	Gray green, purple brown in winter.	Fluffy, needlelike rather than scalelike foliage.	Winter color interest; grows scraggly with age.
C. o. 'Torulosa' (C. o. 'Coralliformis')	To 3 ft.	3 ft.	Dark green. Red-tinted twigs.	Twisted, threadlike branches.	Slow growing; rock gardens, bonsai containers.
C. pisifera (Retinispora pisifera) SAWARA FALSE CYPRESS	20–30 ft. or more.	To 20 ft.	Dark green above, lighter beneath.	Spine-tipped, scalelike leaves; rather loose, open growth.	Good in large Oriental gardens. Prune heavily to force new growth, hide dead foliage on inner branches.
C. p. 'Cyano-Viridis' (C. p. 'Boulevard')	Rather slow to 5–8 ft.	3–4 ft.	Light, silvery blue green.	Good, dense form; soft, fine-textured, fluffy-looking foliage.	Good for color and texture contrast with other evergreens.
C. p. 'Filifera' THREAD CYPRESS, THREADBRANCH CYPRESS	To 8 ft. or higher.	To 6 ft.	Dark green.	Loose mound, attractive when young. Too open in old age. Weeping, threadlike twigs.	Oriental and rock gardens. Contrast with dense, solid shrubs. Prune to keep in bounds. C. p. 'Filifera Aurea', GOLDEN THREAD CYPRESS, has yellow foliage.
C. p. 'Plumosa' PLUME FALSE CYPRESS	20–30 ft.	10–12 ft.	Bright green.	Upright branches, compact, cone shaped. Short, soft needles. Frondlike, feathery twig structure.	Carefully pruned, a big shrub. Unpruned, a tree. Slow growing at first.

SPECIES OR VARIETY	HEIGHT	SPREAD	COLOR	FORM, TEXTURE	REMARKS
C. p. 'Plumosa Aurea'	20–30 ft.	10–12 ft.	New growth golden yellow; old growth green.	As C. p. 'Plumosa'.	Prune hard by pinching tips to restrain growth, promote density. Like variety 'Plumosa', tends to lose lower branches as it ages.
C. p. 'Snow'	To 5 ft. in 10 years.	5 ft.	Gray green, sprays tipped white.	Eventually like 'Squarrosa' in form, texture.	Striking color, good form. Needs protection against sun, strong wind.
C. p. 'Squarrosa' MOSS CYPRESS	20–30 ft. or much higher.	10–30 ft.	Silvery gray green.	Soft, feathery, with long, needlelike leaves.	Attractive while young. As it ages, thin it out for greater character, picturesqueness. Big background plantings, massive yet soft-textured area cover.
C. p. 'Squarrosa Minima' (C. p. 'Pygmaea', C. p. 'Squarrosa Pygmaea')	Dwarf (see remarks.)	(See remarks.)	Gray green to dark green depending on form.	Sharp-pointed leaves.	Several forms go under this name. One is a very compact, very slow growing globe form to 6 by 6 in. in 5 years, with dark green, very short needles. Another is gray green, lacy foliaged, grows to 18 in. high and spreads much wider.
C. p. 'Squarrosa Veitchii'	To 20 or 30 ft.	10–30 ft.	Blue green.	Lighter, airier than variety 'Squarrosa'.	An improvement in color and texture over variety 'Squarrosa'.
C. thyoides WHITE CEDAR	To 90 ft.	20–25 ft.	Light green to gray green. Turns bronzy in winter.	Narrow, tall, cone shaped tree.	Needs soil moisture, winter chill for good growth.
C. t. 'Andelyensis'	To 3 ft. at 10 years, eventually 10 ft.	1 ft. at 10 years, eventually 3 ft.	Gray green.	Dense cone.	Used as miniature columnar evergreen in bonsai, rock gardens.

CHAMAEDOREA. Palms. House plants, outdoors Zones 16, 17, 22–24. Small shade-tolerant feather type. Generally slow growing, they are good in containers indoors or on shaded patio. All need ample water along with good drainage. Some have single trunks, others clustered trunks. Leaves variable in shape. Some have decorative orange seeds.

C. cataractarum. Single-stemmed palm growing slowly to 4–5 ft.; trunk speckled. Older plants take some frost.

Chamaedorea elegans

C. costaricana. Develops fairly fast into bamboolike clumps of 8–10-ft. trunks if well-fed and liberally watered. Good pot palm; will eventually need good-sized container. Lacy, feathery leaves 3–4 ft. long.

C. elegans. (Widely sold as *Neanthe bella*.) Often called parlor palm, the best indoor chamaedorea, tolerating crowded roots, poor light. Single-stemmed; grows very slowly to eventual 3–4 ft. Douse potted plants with water occasionally; feed regularly. Groom by removing old leaf stalks. Repot every 2–3 years, carefully washing off old soil and replacing with good potting mix. Effective potted 3 or more to container.

C. ernesti-augustii. Slow growing to 5 ft., with dark green, fishtail shaped leaves. Needs shade and protected location.

C. erumpens. Cluster forming, bamboolike dwarf with drooping leaves. Slow grower to 4–5 ft. Needs shade or part shade, no frost.

C. geonomiformis. Fine palm for pots. Grows slowly to 4 ft. Broad oblong leaves are not feathery, but are deeply split at tips like fishtails.

C. glaucifolia. Slow to 8 ft. or more, with fine-textured, feathery leaves, 4–6 ft. long, with bluish green tint on both sides (most marked on underside).

C. klotzschiana. Single-trunk palm of slow growth to 4–5 ft. Handsome, dark green, feathery leaves. Hardy to 28°F.

C. microspadix. Cluster palm with slender, ringed stems to 8 ft. Feathery leaves. One of hardier kinds; it takes very light frost.

C. radicalis. Slow growing, single-stemmed plant to 4 ft. tall. Strong-patterned dark green leaves. Interesting, colorful seed

formation. Hardiest of chamaedoreas; will take temperatures down to a range of 22°–28°F.

C. seifrizii. Cluster palm of dense, compact growth to 8–10 ft. Feathery leaves with narrow leaflets. Takes 28°F. and can be used outdoors in protected areas in part shade. Needs ample moisture.

C. tenella. Single trunk to 3–4 ft. Dark bluish green leaves are exceptionally strong, large, broad, undivided but deeply cleft at ends.

C. tepejilote. Single trunk ringed with swollen joints like bamboo. Moderate growth to 10 ft.; leaves 4 ft. long, feathery. Grows well in frost-protected, shady areas inland.

CHAMAEMELUM nobile *(Anthemis nobilis).* CHAMOMILE. Evergreen perennial. All Zones. Forms soft-textured, spreading, 3–12-in. mat of light bright green, finely cut, aromatic leaves. Most commonly grown form has summer-blooming flower heads resembling small yellow buttons; some forms have little daisylike flower heads. Makes lawn substitute if mowed or sheared occasionally. Also used between stepping stones. Plant divisions 12 in. apart in full sun or very light shade. Water moderately. Chamomile tea is made from dried flower heads, but sweeter, more flavorful tea comes from flowers of *Matricaria recutita (M. chamomilla)*.

Chamaemelum nobile

CHAMAEROPS humilis. MEDITERRANEAN FAN PALM. Zones 4–24. Probably hardiest palm; has survived 6°F. Clumps develop slowly from offshoots, curve to height of 20 ft., may be 20 ft. wide. Growth extremely slow in Portland, Seattle. Leaves green to bluish green. Versatile: Use in containers, mass under trees, use for impenetrable

Chamaerops humilis

hedge. Drought and wind resistant. Feed and water in summer to speed growth.

CHAMELAUCIUM uncinatum. (Sometimes sold as *C. ciliatum*.) GERALDTON WAXFLOWER. Evergreen shrub. Zones 8, 9, 12–24. Native to Australia. Bright green needlelike leaves and showy sprays of winter-blooming, pale pink or rosy ½-in. flowers are cherished for flower arrangements of long lasting beauty. Light and airy, loose and sprawling, fast growth to 6–8 ft., or, when staked, to 10–12 ft. with equal spread. Looks somewhat like loose-growing heather. Very old plants have interesting twisted trunks and shaggy bark.

Chamaelaucium uncinatum

Plant on sunny dry bank or in cutting garden in fast draining soil and water deeply but infrequently in summer. Or combine with plants that don't require regular summer watering such as *Cassia artemisioides* or rosemary. Prune freely for arrangements or cut back after flowering. Seedling plants vary. Select in bloom to get color you want. Variety 'Vista' has large pink flowers.

CHAMOMILE. See *Chamaemelum nobile*, *Matricaria recutita*.

CHAPARRAL BROOM. See *Baccharis pilularis*.

CHARD. See Swiss Chard.

CHASMANTHIUM latifolium (*Uniola latifolia*). SEA OATS, BAMBOO GRASS. Perennial. All Zones. Ornamental grass making broad clumps of broad, bamboolike leaves topped with arching flowering stems, 2–5 ft. tall, carrying showers of silvery green flower spikelets that resemble flattened clusters of oats (or flattened armadillos). Flowering stems dry to an attractive greenish straw color and are attractive in dried arrangements. Clumps broaden slowly and are not aggressive like bamboo. Leaves turn brown in winter and plants should be cut back near the ground. Give full sun in cool-climate areas, partial shade where summers are hot. Happy in average soil with average garden watering. Divide clumps when overgrown and bloom drops off. Stake if flowering stems sprawl too far.

Chasmanthium latifolium

CHASTE TREE. See *Vitex*.

CHAYOTE. Vine with edible fruit, climbing by tendrils. Related to squash. Perennial in Zones 14–16, 19–24, annual elsewhere. Vine and leaves resemble those of squash. Flowers inconspicuous. Fruit is principal crop. It is green or yellow green, irregularly oval, grooved, and contains large seed surrounded by meaty solid flesh. Both meat and seed, when boiled or baked have flavor somewhat like squash. Well-grown plant should produce 200 or more fruit. Fruit measure 3–8 in. long.

Chayote

Needs full sun; warm, rich soil; ample water; and fence or trellis to climb. Buy fruit at store in fall, allow to sprout, plant whole fruit edgewise, sprouted end at lowest point, narrow end exposed. If shoot is long, cut it back to 1–2 in. Plant 2 or more

vines to assure pollination. Plant in February or March; in area where roots might freeze, plant in 5-gallon can or tub and store plant until after frost. Plants can produce 20–30 ft. of vine in first year, 40–50 ft. in second. Tops die down in frost. Bloom starts when day-length shortens in fall; fruit are ready in a month.

CHECKERBERRY. See *Gaultheria procumbens*.

CHECKERED LILY. See *Fritillaria meleagris*.

CHECKER LILY. See *Fritillaria lanceolata*.

CHEIRANTHUS allionii. See *Erysimum hieraciifolium*.

CHEIRANTHUS cheiri. WALLFLOWER. Perennial or biennial. Zones 4–6, 14–17, 22, 23. Old-timers esteemed for sweet fragrance and rich colors of flowers that bloom in spring and early summer. Erect bushy plants to 1–2½ ft.; narrow bright green leaves 3 in. long. Flowers ½ in. across, in velvety tones of yellow, orange, brown, red, pink, rose, burgundy, in dense clusters at tops of leafy stems. Excellent with tulips in yellow, orange, or lilac shades; or beneath lilacs, which bloom at same time.

Cheiranthus cheiri

Locate in full sun, or in light shade where spring sun is bright. Likes moist soil. Plant in mounded or raised beds to provide best possible drainage. Sow seeds in spring for bloom following year, or set out nursery transplants in fall or early spring. Young plants need long period to develop vegetative growth.

CHENILLE PLANT. See *Acalypha hispida*.

CHERIMOYA. See *Annona cherimola*.

CHERRY. Here we consider the sweet cherries, sour cherries, and Duke cherries (hybrids between sweet and sour cherries). All require well-drained soil and regular deep watering.

Fruiting Cherry

SWEET CHERRIES

Most seen at markets and most widely known in the West. Trees 30–35 ft. tall, as broad in some varieties. They are at their best in deep well-drained soil in Zones 2, 6, 7, 14, 15. They have high chilling requirement (need many winter hours at below 45°F. temperature), and therefore are not adapted to mild-winter areas of southern California or low desert.

Two trees are needed to produce fruit, and second tree must be chosen with care. No combination of these will produce fruit: 'Bing', 'Lambert', 'Royal Ann'. These varieties will pollinize any other cherry: 'Black Tartarian', 'Corum', 'Deacon', 'Republican', 'Sam', and 'Van'. However, because 'Lambert' blooms late, it is pollinized best by 'Republican'.

'Garden Bing' and 'Stella' are self-fertile.

Fruiting spurs are long lived, do not need to be renewed by pruning. Prune trees only to maintain good structure and shape. Fruit appear in late spring in warm areas, early summer in Northwest.

Birds everywhere like sweet cherries. Protect with manufactured netting over tree.

For control of brown rot and blossom blight, spray with a copper spray just as leaves fall in autumn, with insecticide-miticide in spring before buds open, and with fungicide when first blooms appear and weekly during bloom for control of brown rot and blossom blight.

Varieties:

'Berryessa'. Resembles 'Royal Ann', but larger, less tendency to make double fruit in hot weather.

'Bing'. Top quality. Large, dark red, meaty, fruit of fine flavor. Midseason.

'Black Tartarian'. Smaller than 'Bing', purplish black, firm, sweet fruit. Ripens early.

'Chinook', Resembles 'Bing', ripens 4–10 days earlier.

'Corum'. Light-colored fruit with colorless juice, flesh whitish. Excellent flavor. Ripens 7 days before 'Royal Ann'.

'Deacon'. Large tree. Large to medium-sized firm black fruit. Sweet pleasant flavor. Ripens 7 days earlier than 'Bing'.

'Early Burlat'. Ripens 2 weeks ahead of 'Bing', comparable with it in appearance, flavor.

'Garden Bing'. Genetic (natural) dwarf 5–6 ft. tall. Slow growing. Sweet black fruit. Self-fertile.

'Hardy Giant'. Dark red fruit resembles 'Bing'. Good pollinizer, especially for 'Lambert'.

'Jubilee'. Resembles 'Bing', but fruit larger with fewer double fruit.

'Kansas Sweet' ('Hansen'). Large red cherry with semisweet flavor. Late ripening.

'Lambert'. Large, vigorous tree, less spreading than 'Bing' and 'Royal Ann'. Very large, black, late ripening fruit, very firm. Flavor more sprightly than 'Bing'.

'Mona'. Resembles 'Black Tartarian' but larger. Very early ripening.

'Rainier'. Has yellow skin with pink blush; ripens a few days before 'Bing'.

'Republican' ('Black Republican', 'Black Oregon'). Large spreading tree. Purplish black, small round fruit, dark juice, tender, crisp. Good flavor. Late season.

'Royal Ann' ('Napoleon'). Large, spreading tree, very productive. Light yellow fruit with pink blush, tender, crisp. Sprightly flavored. Midseason.

'Sam'. Vigorous dense tree. Large, firm black fruit. Excellent flavor.

'Stella'. Dark red fruit like 'Lambert'; ripens a few days later. Self-fertile and good pollinizer for other cherries.

'Sunset'. Very late dark red cherry; late ripening lessens danger of cracking in late spring rains.

'Van'. Heavy-bearing tree. Black shiny fruit, firmer and slightly smaller than 'Bing'. Good flavor. Ripens earlier than 'Bing' in Northwest, right with it in California.

SOUR CHERRIES

Sour cherry is a spreading, irregular growing, garden-sized tree to 20 ft. You can prune to increase irregularity if you want ornamental tree, or force more regular, upright pattern by pruning out drooping side branches. Sour cherries are self-fruitful, and are reasonably good pollinizers for sweet cherries. 'Montmorency' and 'Early Richmond' are preferred varieties with small, bright red, soft, juicy, sweet-tart fruit. 'English Morello' is darker, with more tart fruit and red juice. 'Meteor' has fruit like 'Montmorency', but smaller tree. 'North Star', with red to dark red skin, yellow sour flesh, is small, very hardy tree.

DUKE CHERRIES

Trees are somewhat larger than sour cherries. Climate adaptation same as sweet cherries. Duke cherries are self-fruitful. Their fruit have shape and color of sweet cherries; flavor, texture of sour cherries. They are uncommon in the West, but make good home orchard trees.

Varieties: 'May Duke', medium-sized, early, dark red. 'Late Duke', large, light red fruit ripening in July.

CHERRY, FLOWERING. See *Prunus.*

CHERRY PLUM. See *Prunus cerasifera.*

CHERVIL. See *Anthriscus cerefolium.*

CHESTNUT. See *Castanea.*

CHICORY. All Zones, but difficult in hot-summer areas. Botanically known as *Cichorium intybus.* Dried ground roots can be roasted and used as substitute for coffee. Wild form grows as 3–6 ft. perennial roadside weed in much of West and is recognized by its pretty sky blue flowers. Grown for its leaves, known as chicory, endive, or curly endive; or for its bleached sprouts, known as Belgian or French endive, endive hearts, or witloof ("white leaf"). For culture, see Endive.

Chicory

Radicchio is the name given to a number of red-leafed chicories grown for salads. 'Rossa de Verona' or 'Rouge de Verone' is the best known. It makes lettucelike heads that color to a deep rosy red as weather grows cold in autumn or winter. Slight bitterness lessens as color deepens. Sow in early summer to mature in cold weather.

CHILEAN BELLFLOWER. See *Lapageria rosea.*

CHILEAN GUAVA. See *Ugni molinae.*

CHILEAN JASMINE. See *Mandevilla laxa.*

CHILEAN WINE PALM. See *Jubaea chilensis.*

CHILOPSIS linearis. DESERT WILLOW. Deciduous large shrub or small tree. Zones 11–13, 18–21. Native to desert washes and stream beds below 5,000 ft.

Open and airy when trained as small tree. Grows fast (to 3 ft. in a season) at first, then slows down, levels off at about 25 ft. In age, develops shaggy bark and twisting trunks somewhat like Australian tea tree (*Leptospermum laevigatum*). Drops leaves early, holds a heavy crop of catalpalike fruit through winter, and can look shaggy. But pruning can make it most handsome.

Long, narrow 2–5-in. leaves. Flowers look somewhat like catalpa's, trumpet shaped with crimped lobes—pink, white, rose, or lavender, marked with purple. Flower color varies among seedlings. Nurseries select most colorful. Flowers appear in spring and often through fall, borne first year from gallon cans; attract birds. Easy to propagate from hardwood cuttings.

Chilopsis linearis

CHIMING BELLS. See *Mertensia ciliata.*

CHIMONANTHUS praecox (*C. fragrans, Meratia praecox*). WINTERSWEET. Deciduous shrub. Zones 4–7 (where it blooms February-March), 8, 9, 14–17 (where it blooms December-May). Native to China and Japan. Needs some winter cold.

Tall, open, growing slowly to 10–15 ft. high and 6–8 ft. wide, having many basal stems. Keep lower by pruning while in flower. Or prune as small tree by removing excess stems. Leaves medium green, tapering, 3–6 in. long and half as wide. Flowers on leafless stems, 1 in. across, outer sepals pale yellow, inner sepals chocolate-colored, smaller. Plant where its winter fragrance can be enjoyed. Some possible locations: near a much-used service entrance or path, near a bedroom window. In hot-summer areas it grows best if shaded from afternoon sun. Needs occasional deep watering in summer.

Chimonanthus praecox

CHIMONOBAMBUSA. See *Bamboo.*

CHINA ASTER. See *Callistephus chinensis.*

CHINABERRY. See *Melia azedarach.*

CHINA FIR. See *Cunninghamia lanceolata.*

CHIN CACTUS. See *Gymnocalycium.*

CHINCHERINCHEE. See *Ornithogalum thyrsoides.*

CHINESE ANGELICA. See *Aralia chinensis.*

CHINESE BELLFLOWER. See *Abutilon.*

CHINESE CABBAGE. Biennial grown as annual. All Zones in conditions noted below. Makes head somewhat looser than usual cabbage; sometimes called "celery cabbage." More delicate flavor than cabbage in salads or cooked. There are two kinds: *pe-tsai,* with tall narrow heads, and *wong bok,* with short broad heads. Favored pe-tsai variety is 'Michihli'; wong bok varieties include 'Springtime', 'Summertime', and 'Wintertime' (early to late maturing). Definitely cool-season crop; very prone to bolt to seed in hot weather, or in long days of spring and early summer. Plant seeds directly in open ground in July in Zones 1–6, 10, 11; in August or September in other areas. Sow seeds thinly in rows 24–30 in. apart and thin plants to 18–24 in. apart. Heads should be ready in 70–80 days.

Chinese Cabbage

CHINESE CHIVES. See *Allium tuberosum.*

CHINESE EVERGREEN. See *Aglaonema modestum.*

CHINESE FLAME TREE. See *Koelreuteria bipinnata.*

CHINESE FORGET-ME-NOT. See *Cynoglossum amabile.*

CHINESE FOUNTAIN PALM. See *Livistona chinensis.*

CHINESE GOOSEBERRY VINE. See *Actinidia chinensis.*

CHINESE GROUND ORCHID. See *Bletilla striata.*

CHINESE HOUSES. See *Collinsia heterophylla.*

CHINESE JUJUBE. See *Ziziphus jujuba.*

CHINESE LANTERN. See *Abutilon.*

CHINESE LANTERN PLANT. See *Physalis alkekengi.*

CHINESE PARASOL TREE. See *Firmiana simplex.*

CHINESE PARSLEY. See *Coriandrum sativum.*

CHINESE PLUMBAGO. See *Ceratostigma willmottianum.*

CHINESE REDBUD. See *Cercis chinensis.*

CHINESE SCHOLAR TREE. See *Sophora japonica.*

CHINESE SWEET GUM. See *Liquidambar formosana.*

CHINESE TALLOW TREE. See *Sapium sebiferum.*

CHINESE WINGNUT. See *Pterocarya stenoptera.*

CHINESE WOOLFLOWER. See *Celosia.*

CHIONANTHUS. FRINGE TREE. Deciduous trees. Earn common name from narrow, fringelike, white petals. These flowers are borne in impressive, ample lacy clusters. There are male and female trees. If both are present, female plants produce fruit like small dark olives in clusters. Male trees have larger flowers. Broad leaves turn deep yellow in fall. Water requirement moderate.

C. retusus. CHINESE FRINGE TREE. Zones 2–9, 14–24. Generally smaller growing than *C. virginicus*—to 20 ft. Leaves 2–4 in. long. Flower clusters to 4 in. long; blooms in June and July. In bloom, it's a magnificent tree, something like tremendous white lilac.

C. virginicus. FRINGE TREE. Zones 1–6, 15–17. Native Pennsylvania to Florida and Texas. Grows to 30 ft. where well-adapted. Leaves and flower clusters twice size of *C. retusus,* and it blooms earlier (May). Fragrant. In Zones 1–6 it is lucky to reach 12 ft. in 10 years, and is best used as very slow growing, airy shrub (it blooms profusely when only 2–3 ft. tall). Flowers are more greenish than white there, and it is one of last deciduous plants to leaf out in spring.

Chionanthus retusus

Chionanthus virginicus

CHIONODOXA. GLORY-OF-THE-SNOW. Bulbs. Zones 1–7, 14, 17–20. Native to alpine meadows in Asia Minor. Charming small bulbous plants 4–6 in. high; among first to bloom in spring. Narrow basal leaves, 2 or 3 to each flower stalk. Blue or white, short, tubular, open flowers in loose spikes. Plant bulbs 3 in. deep in September or October in half shade; keep moist. Under favorable conditions plants self-sow freely.

C. luciliae. Most generally available. About 10 brilliant blue, white-centered, starlike flowers on 6-in. stalks. Variety 'Alba' offers larger white flowers; 'Gigantea' has larger leaves, larger flowers of violet blue with white throat.

C. sardensis. Deep true gentian blue flowers with very small white eye.

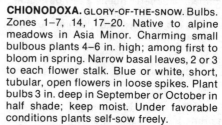
Chionodoxa luciliae

CHIRANTHODENDRON pentadactylon (*C. platanoides*). MONKEY HAND TREE. Evergreen tree. Zones 16, 17, 20–24. Fast growing to 40–50 ft. with spread of 20–30 ft. Leaves 8–10 in. long, shaped like sycamore, medium green with rusty underside. Odd flowers somewhat resemble waxy, deep red, smallish tulips, covered on outside with soft fuzz. Projecting from flower is fantastic structure that resembles tiny red hand, complete with fingernails. Blooms appear from March-October; borne toward ends of branches, leaves almost cover them. Tree has survived temperatures in low 20s.

Continual leaf-drop in summer and strong surface rooting rules it out as patio or street tree. Best in deep soil with infrequent but deep watering.

Chiranthodendron pentadactylon

CHIVES. Small, clump-forming, perennial onion (*Allium*) relative. For garlic chives see *Allium*. All Zones in conditions noted below. Its leaves are grasslike in general appearance, but are round and hollow in cross-section. Clumps may reach 2 ft. in height but are usually shorter. Cloverlike spring flowers are in clusters atop thin stems and are rose purple. Plant is pretty enough to use as edging for sunny or lightly shaded flower border or herb garden. Does best in moist, fairly rich soil. May be increased by divisions or grown from seed. Evergreen (or nearly so) in mild regions, goes dormant where winters are severe, but small divisions may be potted in rich soil and grown on kitchen window sill. Chop or snip leaves into salads, cream cheese, cottage cheese, egg dishes, gravies and soups for delicate onionlike flavor, and as pretty garnish.

Chives

Garlic Chives

CHLOROPHYTUM. Lily relatives with small white or greenish flowers in long clusters and clumps of attractive evergreen foliage.

C. bichetii. House plant. Slow-growing, eventually 8–10 in. tall, 18 in. across. Leaves dark green with white stripes, shorter and relatively broader than those of spider plant (below), gracefully recurved. Small white flowers on 8-in. stalks. Does not make runners. Light to heavy shade; water only when dry, and feed occasionally to maintain good leaf color.

C. comosum (often sold as *C. capense*) SPIDER PLANT. Evergreen perennial. House plant; outdoor ground cover in Zones 15–17, 19–24. Native to Africa. Shade loving plant forms 1–3-ft.-high clumps of soft curving leaves like long broad grass blades. 'Variegatum' and 'Vittatum', striped white, are popular. Flowers white, ½ in. long, in loose leafy-tipped spikes standing above foliage. Greatest attraction: miniature duplicates of mother plant, complete with root, at end of curved stems (as with strawberry plant offsets); these offsets can be cut off, potted individually. Excellent, easily grown house plant for fully lighted window, greenhouse. Ground cover or hanging basket plant in partial shade.

Chlorophytum comosum

CHOISYA ternata. MEXICAN ORANGE. Evergreen shrub. Borderline Zones 4–6; good in 7–9, 12–17; good but often suffers from pests and soil problems in Zones 18–24. Hardy to 15°F. Rapid growing to 6–8 ft. high and as wide. Lustrous yellow green leaves held toward end of branches are divided into fans of 3 leaflets (to 3 in. long); fans give shrub dense, massive look but with highlights and shadows. Clusters of fragrant white flowers, somewhat like small orange blossoms, open in very early spring and bloom continuously into April, intermittently through summer. Attractive to bees.

Choisya ternata

Use as attractive informal hedge or screen. Mass to fill large spaces. Prune throughout growing season to shape and thin out branches, forcing replacement wood from inside plant. Cut freely for decoration when in bloom.

Grows in full sun in cool-summer areas; elsewhere in light shade. Gets straggly and bears few flowers when in too much shade. It's touchy about soil conditions. Difficult in alkaline soils or where water is high in salts. Under such conditions, prepare special soil mix as for azaleas. Subject to root rot and crown rot

if drainage is not fast. Water infrequently but deeply. Subject to damage from sucking insects and mites.

CHOKECHERRY. See *Prunus virginiana.*

CHORISIA. FLOSS SILK TREE. Evergreen to briefly deciduous trees with heavy trunks studded with thick, heavy spines. Native to South America. Young trunks are green, becoming gray with age. Leaves divided into leaflets like fingers of a hand; leaves fall during autumn flowering or whenever winter temperatures drop below 27°F. Reduce water in late summer (on blooming-sized trees) to encourage more flowers.

Chorisia speciosa

Flowers large and showy, somewhat resembling narrow-petaled hibiscus. Fast drainage and controlled watering are keys to success. Water established trees once a month.

C. insignis. WHITE FLOSS SILK TREE. Zones 19–24. To 50 ft. tall. Flowers white to pale yellow, 5–6 in. across. Blooms fall into winter; flowering stopped by frost.

C. speciosa. Zones 15–24. Grows 3–5 ft. a year for first few years, then slowly to 30–60 ft. Flowers pink, purplish rose, or burgundy. Two grafted kinds are obtainable: 'Los Angeles Beautiful' has wine red flowers; 'Majestic Beauty', rich pink.

CHORIZEMA. FLAME PEA. Evergreen shrubs. Zones 15–17, 19–24. Native to Australia. Hardy to about 24°F. All three species present riotous, gaudy display of blended orange and purplish red flowers resembling sweet peas in clusters, February–June. Fast growing with slender graceful branches.

Chorizema cordatum

Take sun but flower color is more intense in part shade. Average water requirements. Left to go their own way, they are attractive spilling over wall, on banks, in containers, hanging baskets. Pruned, pinched, and cut back severely after flowering, they make compact 2-ft. shrubs for ground cover, edging, or flower border. Source of late winter color.

C. cordatum. (Sometimes erroneously sold as *C. ilicifolium*.) HEART-LEAF FLAME PEA. Grows 3–5 ft. high, sometimes more under ideal conditions. Dark green leaves 1–2 in. long, with small prickly teeth along the edges.

C. ilicifolium. HOLLY FLAME PEA. Low spreading shrub 2–3 ft. high. Oval, ¾–1-in. leaves similar to *C. cordatum* but edges are wavy and have deep prickly teeth; vaguely resemble holly leaves.

C. varium. BUSH FLAME PEA. More compact growth habit, to 3 ft.; branches and leaves are hairy.

CHRISTMAS BERRY. See *Heteromeles arbutifolia.*

CHRISTMAS CACTUS. See *Schlumbergera bridgesii.*

CHRISTMAS ROSE. See *Helleborus niger.*

CHRYSALIDOCARPUS lutescens. (Often sold as *Areca lutescens.*) Zone 24; can grow in pots or in shady sheltered spot in frost free areas, Zone 23. House plant anywhere. Clumping feather palm of slow growth to 10–15 feet. Graceful plant with smooth trunks and yellowish green leaves. Takes sun near coast; average water. Gets spider mites when grown indoors. Tricky to maintain, but a lovely palm.

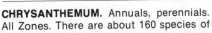
Chrysalidocarpus lutescens

CHRYSANTHEMUM. Annuals, perennials. All Zones. There are about 160 species of chrysanthemum, mostly native to China, Japan, and Europe. Included are some of most popular and useful of garden plants—top favorite being *C. morifolium*, whose modern descendants are known as florists' chrysanthemums. But there are many other worthwhile species in cultivation, capable of producing summer and fall color in borders, containers, or (widest use) as cut flowers. Water during dry spells.

Chrysanthemum morifolium

C. arcticum. ARCTIC CHRYSANTHEMUM. Very hardy autumn-blooming perennial, forming clump with stems 6–12 in. high. Spoon shaped leaves, usually 3-lobed, 1–3 in. long, leathery in texture. White or pinkish flower heads 1–2 in. across. From this species have been developed group of hybrids known as Northland daisies with single flowers 3 in. or more across, in shades of pink, rose, rosy purple, and yellow. *C. arcticum* itself is primarily rock garden plant. Taller growing varieties serve best in borders.

C. balsamita. COSTMARY. Weedy 2–4 ft. perennial with sweet-scented foliage that justifies its presence in herb garden (use leaves in salads and in sachets). If leggy stems are cut back, fragrant gray green basal leaves with tiny scalloped margins can make herb garden edging. Divide clumps and reset divisions in late summer or fall.

Chrysanthemum balsamita

C. carinatum. SUMMER CHRYSANTHEMUM, TRICOLOR CHRYSANTHEMUM. Summer and fall-blooming annual, growing 1–3 ft. high, about 3 ft. wide. In mild-winter climates blooms winter and spring. Deeply cut foliage; showy, single, daisylike, 2-in.-wide flower heads in purple, orange, scarlet, salmon, rose, yellow and white, with contrasting bands around dark center. Satisfactory, long-lasting cut flowers. Sow seeds in spring either in flats or in open ground. Where winters are mild, sow in fall. Court Jesters is an excellent strain. Full sun. Light or heavy soil; grows wild in sand dunes along sections of southern California coast.

C. coccineum (*Pyrethrum roseum*). PAINTED DAISY, PYRETHRUM. Bushy perennial to 2–3 ft. with very finely divided, bright green leaves and single, daisylike, long-stemmed flowers in pink, red, and white. Also available in double and anemone-flowered forms. Starts blooming in April in mild-winter climates, in May or June in colder areas; if cut back, blooms again in late summer. Excellent for cutting, borders; combine with *Campanula persicifolia*, columbine, delphinium, dianthus. Best in full sun. Needs summer heat to perform well. Divide clumps or sow seeds in spring; double forms do not always come true from seed—they may revert to single flowers.

C. frutescens. MARGUERITE, PARIS DAISY. Zones 14–24. Short-lived perennial grown as annual in cold climates. Bright green, coarsely divided leaves; abundant daisylike flowers, 1½–2½ in. across, in white, yellow, or pink. 'Snow White', double anemone type, has pure white flowers, more restrained growth habit; 'White Lady' and 'Pink Lady' have buttonlike flower heads; 'Silver Leaf' has gray green leaves and masses of white flowers that are much smaller than those of regular marguerite.

Chrysanthemum frutescens

Group of selections from New Zealand show wide range of flower form and color: 'First Love', lilac pink, with anemone (cushion) centers; 'Flirtation', single pink with yellow center; 'Golden Anniversary', white single with yellow cushion center; 'Honeymoon', large single yellow with yellow eye; 'June Bride', rose pink single with pink cushion center; 'Puppy Love', prolific, small pale pink flowers with cushion centers; 'Silver Anniversary', white double flowers, finely cut silvery green foliage.

All kinds, but particularly familiar white and yellow margue-

rites, are splendid for containers and for quick effects in borders, mass displays in new gardens.

Small plants set out in spring will grow 4 ft. across by summer. In buying plants, avoid large vigorous-looking ones with large leaves—they will bloom sparsely. Also avoid plants showing signs of fasciation (flattening or widening of stems) near crown.

Plant in full sun, light soil. Grow exceptionally well near coast; with sufficient water and good drainage, also succeed inland, but may freeze in cold winters. For continued bloom, prune lightly at frequent intervals. Do not prune older plants severely—they seldom produce new growth from hardened wood. Replace every 2–3 years with new plants. Few pests, although subject to leaf miner, to thrips (which reduce flower size and quality), and—on old plants—to root galls and nematodes.

C. maximum. SHASTA DAISY. Hardy, sturdy perennial, valuable for summer and fall bloom in all climates. Original 2–4-ft.-tall Shasta daisy with its coarse leathery leaves and white, gold-centered flower heads 2–4 in. across has been largely superseded by varieties with larger, better formed, longer-blooming flowers. They are available in single, double, quilled, and shaggy-flowered forms. All are white, but two show touch of yellow. Some bloom May-October. Shasta daisies are splendid in borders and cut arrangements. Cut blooms may be dyed by plunging freshly cut stems into water containing household dye or food coloring.

Following are some of the varieties available in nurseries:

'Esther Read', most popular double white, longest bloom; 'Marconi', large frilly double; 'Aglaya', similar to 'Marconi', longest blooming season; 'Alaska', big old-fashioned single; 'Horace Read', 4-in. wide, dahlialike flower; 'Majestic', large yellow-centered flower; 'Thomas Killin', 6-in.-wide (largest) yellow-centered flower.

'Cobham's Gold' has distinctive flowers in yellow-tinted, off white shade. 'Canarybird', another yellow, is dwarf, with attractive dark green foliage.

Most popular varieties for cut flowers are 'Esther Read', 'Majestic', 'Aglaya', and 'Thomas Killin'.

Shasta daisies are easy from seed. Catalogues offer many strains, including Roggli Super Giant (single) and Diener's Strain (double). 'Marconi' (double), also available in seed, nearly always blooms double. 'Silver Princess' (also called 'Little Princess' and 'Little Miss Muffet') is 12–15-in. dwarf single.

Set out divisions of Shasta daisies in fall or early spring, container-grown plants at any time. Thrive in fairly rich, moist, well-drained soil. Prefer sun, but do well in partial shade in hot-summer climates; double-flowered kinds hold up better in very light shade. In coldest regions mulch around plants, but do not smother foliage. Divide clumps every 2–3 years in early spring (or in fall in mild-winter areas). Shasta daisies generally easy to grow, but have a few problems. Disease called "gall" causes root crown to split into many weak, poorly rooted growing points that soon die. Dig and burn affected plants. Sterilize soil before planting in same spot. Bait to control snails and slugs.

Shasta daisies in well-drained soils can take plenty of water, especially before and during bloom; at this time apply liquid fertilizer to encourage large flowers. Also cut old flowers to prolong bloom.

C. morifolium. FLORISTS' CHRYSANTHEMUM. The most useful of all autumn-blooming perennials for borders, containers, and cutting, and the most versatile and varied of all chrysanthemum species, available in many flower forms, colors, plant and flower sizes, and growth habits. Colors include yellow, red, pink, orange, bronze, purple, lavender, and multi-colors. Following are flower forms as designated by chrysanthemum hobbyists:

Anemone. One or more rows of rays with large raised center disk or cushion, same color as rays or different. (Disbud for very large flowers.)

Brush. Narrow, rolled rays give brush or soft cactus dahlia effect.

Decorative. Long, broad rays overlap in shingle effect to give broad, full flower.

Incurve. Big double flowers with broad rays curving upward and inward.

Irregular curve. Like above, but with looser, more softly curving rays.

Laciniated. Fully double, with rays fringed and cut at tips in carnation effect.

Pompon. Globular, neat, compact flowers with flat, fluted, or quilled rays. Usually small, they can reach 5 in. with disbudding.

Quill. Long, narrow rolled rays; like spider, but less droopy.

Reflex. Big double flowers with rays that curl in, out, and sideways, creating shaggy effect.

Semidouble. Somewhat like single or daisy, but with 2, 3, or 4 rows of rays around a yellow center.

Single or *daisy.* Single row of rays around a yellow center. May be large or small, with broad or narrow rays.

Spider. Long, curling, tubular rays ending in fish-hook curved tips.

Spoon. Tubular rays flatten at tip to make little disks, sometimes in colors that contrast with body of flower.

It's easy to grow chrysanthemums, not so easy to grow prize-winning chrysanthemums. The latter need more water, feeding, pinching, pruning, grooming, and pest control than most perennials.

Plant in good, well-drained garden soil improved by organic matter and a complete fertilizer dug in 2 or 3 weeks before planting. In most areas chrysanthemums do best in full sun; in hot climates provide shade from afternoon sun. Don't plant near large trees or hedges with invasive roots.

Set out young plants (rooted cuttings or vigorous, single-stem divisions) in early spring. When dividing clumps, take divisions from outside; discard woody centers. Water deeply at intervals determined by your soil structure—frequently in porous soils, less frequently in heavy soils. Too little water causes woody stems and loss of lower leaves; overwatering causes leaves first to turn yellow, then blacken and drop. Stems are attacked by borers in desert areas. Aphids are the only notable pest in all areas. Good way to avoid them is to feed plants with systemic insecticide/fertilizer combination.

Feed plants in ground 2 or 3 times during the growing season; make last application with low-nitrogen fertilizer not less than 2 weeks before bloom.

Sturdy plants and big flowers are result of frequent pinching, which should begin at planting time with removal of tip of new plant. Lateral shoots will form; select 1–4 of these for continued growth. Continue this pinching all summer, nipping top pair of leaves on every shoot that reaches 5 in. in length. On some early-blooming cushion varieties, or in coldest regions, pinching should be stopped earlier. Stake plants to keep them upright. To produce huge blooms, remove all flower buds except for 1 or 2 in each cluster—this is called *disbudding.*

Pot culture: Pot rooted cuttings in February, March, or April, using porous, fibrous, moisture-holding planting mix. Move plants on to larger pots as growth requires—don't let them become rootbound. Pinch as directed above, and stake as required. Plants need water every day in warm weather; every other day when cool. Feed with liquid fertilizer every 7–10 days until buds show color.

Care after bloom: Cut back plants to within 8 in. of ground. Check or renew labels. When soils are heavy and likely to remain wet in winter, dig clumps with soil intact, and set on top of ground in inconspicuous place. Cover with sand or sawdust if you wish. Take cuttings from early to late spring (up until May for some varieties); or when shoots are 3–4 in. long. As new shoots develop, you can make additional cuttings. In cold-winter areas, store in coldframe or mulch with light, noncompacting material like excelsior.

Off season, potted chrysanthemums: Florists and stores sell potted chrysanthemums in bloom every day of the year, even though by nature a chrysanthemum blooms in late summer or fall. Growers force these plants to bloom out of season by subjecting them to artificial day lengths, using lights and dark cloths. You can plunge the potted flowering plants right into a garden bed or border as an immediate (but expensive) display of chrysanthemums. Or you can enjoy them in the house while flowers remain fresh, and then plant them out. Either way, they will not bloom again at the same off-season time the next year. Instead, they will revert to nature and commence once again to bloom in fall.

Cut off flowers when they fade, leaving stems about 6–8 in.

long. Remove soil clump from pot and break apart the several individual plants that were grown in the pot. Plant these individual plants. When new growth shows from the roots, cut off remainder of old flower stems.

C. multicaule. Annual. Broad-rayed buttery yellow daisies 2½ in. across rise above mats of bright green fleshy foliage 6–8 in. wide. Blooms best in cool weather; usually sold in fall, winter, early spring from flats or pots. Plants may live over a second year in cool coastal climates. Give them sun, average soil, water.

C. paludosum. Annual, sometimes living over for a second bloom season. Flowers look something like miniature Shasta daisies. White daisy flower heads 1–1½ in. wide appear on 8–10 in. stems above dark green, deeply toothed leaves. For care, see *C. multicaule* above.

C. parthenium. FEVERFEW. Compact, leafy, aggressive perennial, once favored in Victorian gardens. The old-fashioned single, white-flowered forms self-sow freely, grow as weeds in some areas. Leaves have strong odor, offensive to some. Named varieties vary in height from 1–3 ft. 'Golden Ball' has bright yellow flower heads and no rays; 'Silver Ball' is completely double with only the white rays showing. In 'Aureum', commonly sold in flats as 'Golden Feather', chartreuse-colored foliage is principal attraction. Sow seeds in spring for bloom by midsummer, or divide in fall or spring (in cold climates). Can also grow from cuttings. Full sun or light shade.

CHRYSOLARIX amabilis, C. kaempferi. See *Pseudolarix kaempferi.*

CHUPAROSA. See *Justicia californica.*

CIBOTIUM. Tree ferns. One fairly common, one quite rare.

Cibotium glaucum

C. glaucum. (Usually sold as *C. chamissoi.*) HAWAIIAN TREE FERN. Zones 17, 24. Grows to 6 ft. high, 8 ft. wide, and has feathery, golden green fronds (apple green if shaded). Bare trunks imported from Hawaii; these trunks can be potted up in loose, fast draining soil rich in organic material. If temperatures and humidity are kept high, and soil is not too wet, plants will root and grow. Give good light, but not hot sun; average water. Leaf crowns can become very broad. Hardy to 32°F.

C. schiedei. MEXICAN TREE FERN. Zones 16, 17, 21–24. Can reach 15 ft. tall with wide-spreading, lacy, arching and drooping, chartreuse fronds. Hardy to 24°F. when mature. Shade. Rare.

CIDER GUM. See *Eucalyptus gunnii.*

CIGAR PLANT. See *Cuphea ignea.*

CILANTRO. See *Coriandrum sativum.*

CIMICIFUGA. BUGBANE. Perennials. Zones 1–7, 17. Stately, upright, slim spikes of small white flowers grow from clumps of shiny, dark green leaves divided into many 1½–3-in.-long, deeply toothed leaflets. Flowers late summer to fall. Handsome among large ferns in woodland garden. Best in partial shade, rich, well-drained, moist soil. Will take considerable sun with ample water. Clumps can remain undisturbed for many years. Divide in fall or (in cold areas) in early spring before growth starts. Dried seed clusters useful in flower arrangements.

Cimicifuga racemosa

C. racemosa. BLACK SNAKEROOT. Native to eastern U.S. Flower spikes grow to 7 ft.

C. simplex. KAMCHATKA BUGBANE. Flower spikes to 3–5 ft.

CINERARIA. See *Senecio hybridus.*

CINNAMOMUM. Evergreen trees. Slow to moderate growing, eventually reaching considerable size. Both species have aromatic leaves that smell like camphor when crushed. Good for large lawns but competitive root system makes them poor choice for garden beds. Thrive in hot-summer areas where winter temperatures stay above 20°F.

Not much bothered by pests, but subject to a root rot—verticillium wilt. Symptoms: wilting and dying of twigs, branches, entire center of tree, or entire tree. Wood in twigs or branches shows brownish discoloration. No cure is known; cut out damaged branches. Fertilize trees with nitrogen fertilizer and water deeply. Trees often outgrow it. Most susceptible after wet winters or in poorly drained soils.

Cinnamomum camphora

C. camphora. CAMPHOR TREE. Zones 8, 9, 12–24. Native to China, Japan. A delight to the eye in every season. In winter foliage is shiny yellow green. Beautiful in rain when trunks look black. In early spring new foliage may be pink, red, or bronze, depending on tree. Usually strong structure, heavy trunk, and heavy upright spreading limbs. Grows slowly to 50 ft. or more with wider spread. Leaves 2½–5 in. long. Drops leaves quite heavily in March but fairly clean otherwise. Clusters of tiny fragrant yellow flowers in profusion in May, followed by small blackish fruits.

C. glanduliferum. NEPAL CAMPHOR TREE. Zones 15–17, 19–24. Native to Himalayas. Differs in having larger, richer green, more leathery leaves. Apparently faster growing than the common camphor tree, more upright in branching habit, and slightly more tender.

CINQUEFOIL. See *Potentilla.*

CISSUS. Evergreen vines distinguished for their foliage. Most climb by tendrils. Related to Virginia creeper, Boston ivy, and grape. Easy to grow. Not fussy about soil, water, or fertilizer. Flowers inconspicuous. Useful near swimming pools.

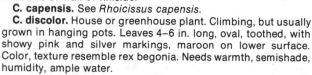

Cissus antarctica

C. antarctica. KANGAROO TREEBINE. Zones 16–24. Native to Australia. Vigorous once established. To 10 ft. A graceful vine. Medium green shiny leaves, 2–3½ in. long and almost as wide, toothed edges. Good tub plant indoors or out, in sun or shade, for climbing up or tumbling down, for trellis or wall or hillside.

C. capensis. See *Rhoicissus capensis.*

C. discolor. House or greenhouse plant. Climbing, but usually grown in hanging pots. Leaves 4–6 in. long, oval, toothed, with showy pink and silver markings, maroon on lower surface. Color, texture resemble rex begonia. Needs warmth, semishade, humidity, ample water.

C. hypoglauca. Zones 13–24. Native to Australia. Rapid growth to 15 ft. in one season. Eventually 30–50 ft. tall. Leaves highly polished, divided into 5 roundish, leathery leaflets 3 in. long; foliage strong in texture with bronzy color tones. New growth covered with rust-colored fuzz. Use in same way as *C. antarctica*. Makes good bank cover in sun or light shade, will control erosion.

C. quadrangula (*C. quadrangularis*). House or greenhouse plant. Succulent vine, usually grown in hanging basket. Generally leafless, with fleshy, jointed, thick, 4-angled or winged stems that climb or trail several feet. Occasional leaves oval or 3 lobed, 2 in. long. Odd rather than pretty, but easy in good light, good drainage.

C. rhombifolia. GRAPE IVY. Zones 13, 15, 16, 21–24 (needs all-year warmth). Native to South America. To 20 ft. Beautiful dark green foliage. Leaves divided into diamond shaped leaflets 1–4

in. long, with sharp-toothed edges; show bronze overtones because of reddish hairs on veins beneath. Widely used indoors. Outdoors it grows to good size and can be trained on trellis, pergola, or driftwood branches. Grows in sun or fairly deep shade, tolerating low light intensity indoors. The variety 'Mandaiana' is more upright and compact, with larger, more substantial leaflets. 'Ellen Danica' has its leaflets shallowly lobed like an oak leaf; it is more compact grower than grape ivy, with darker green, less lustrous leaves.

C. striata. Zones 13–24. Native to South America. In effect a miniature Virginia creeper, with small leaves divided into 3–5 leaflets, each 1–3 in. long, leathery. Stems reddish. To 19 ft. Use to make long traceries against plain surfaces, as ground or wall cover, or to spill over wall. Sun or shade. Useful and beautiful.

C. trifoliata. Zones 12, 13. Hardy deciduous vine with small almost succulent leaves, ivy shaped, 1–2 in. wide. Very fast growing. Good on trellis or rough wall or scrambling over rocks. Looks woodsy and cool even though it's quite drought resistant.

C. voinieriana. See *Tetrastigma.*
C. vomerensis. See *Tetrastigma.*

CISTUS. ROCKROSE. Evergreen shrubs. Borderline in Zones 4–6; satisfactory in Zones 7–9, 12–15, 18–22; best in Zones 16, 17, 23, 24. Native to Mediterranean region. Hardy to 15°F. Producers of showy spring flowers, rockroses are also sun loving, fast growing, drought resistant, recommended for planting in fire hazard areas, tolerant of poor dry soil. Will take cold ocean winds, salt spray, or desert heat. Rockroses should have well-drained soil if they are to be watered frequently. To keep plants vigorous and neat, cut out a few old stems from time to time. Tip-pinch young plants to thicken growth, or give a light overall shearing to new growth.

Cistus purpureus

When planting in area that will be neglected—no water once plant is established—don't plant rootbound plants. Cut circling roots and spread out the mass so plant will have chance to root down to lower soil levels.

Use as dry-bank cover, massed by themselves, or interplanted with ceanothus, wild buckwheat, or sunroses (*Helianthemum*). Taller kinds make good informal screens or low dividers. Useful in big rock gardens, in rough areas along drives and roads, or for sunny wild areas. They can control erosion.

C. corbariensis. See *C. hybridus.*
C. 'Doris Hibberson'. Compact, to 3 ft. tall and as wide. Gray green foliage. Leaves 1–2 in. long, oval. Clear pink, 3-in.-wide flowers with crinkled silky petals in June, July. Flower color blends with other colors better than commonly grown *C. purpureus*.

C. hybridus (*C. corbariensis*). WHITE ROCKROSE. Spreading growth to 2–5 ft. high and almost as wide. Leaves to 2 in. long, gray green, crinkly, fragrant on warm days. Flowers 1½ in. across, white with yellow centers, in late spring. Widely grown.

C. incanus (*C. villosus*). Bushy plant 3–5 ft. tall and equally wide. Oval 1-3-in.-long leaves densely covered with down. Flowers purplish pink, 2–2½ in. across, in late spring and early summer. Used in fire hazard areas. *C. i. creticus* (*C. creticus*) is similar, but with wavy-edged leaves.

C. ladanifer (*C. ladaniferus maculatus*). CRIMSON-SPOT ROCKROSE. Compact, to 3–5 ft. high, with equal spread. Leaves to 4 in. long, dark green above, lighter green beneath, fragrant. Large, 3-in.-wide, white flowers with dark crimson spot at base of each petal, June-July.

C. purpureus. ORCHID ROCKROSE. Compact grower to 4 ft. and equally wide, often lower and wider where constant ocean winds keep plants low. Leaves 1–2 in. long, dark green above, gray hairy beneath. Reddish purple, 3-in.-wide flowers with red spot at base of each petal, June-July. Very fine where cool winds and salt spray limit choice of plants.

C. salviifolius. (Usually sold as *C. villosus* 'Prostratus'.) SAGELEAF ROCKROSE. Wide-spreading shrub to 2 ft. high and 6 ft.

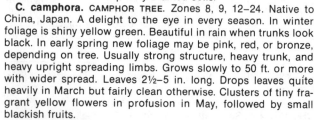

across. Leaves light gray green, about 1 in. long, crinkly, veined, crisp looking. Flowers 1½ in. wide, white with yellow spots at base of petals, very profuse in late spring. Good bank or ground cover for rough situations.

C. villosus. See *C. incanus.*
C. villosus 'Prostratus'. See *C. salviifolius.*

CITRON. See *Citrus.*

CITRUS. Evergreen trees and shrubs highly valued for fruit and as landscaping plants. Most can be grown outdoors in Zones 8, 9, 12–24; indoor/outdoor container plants anywhere. As landscaping plants, they offer attractive form and glossy deep green foliage all year, fragrant flowers, and decorative fruit in season. As producers of quality fruit, varieties must be selected according to two considerations: total amount of heat available through fruit developing period (need varies according to type) and winter cold they will get. Choice and use is also determined by whether plants are standard trees or dwarfs. Citrus flowers draw bees.

Orange

Heat requirements. Lemons and limes need the least heat, and will produce usable fruit in cool-summer areas (where winter temperatures are not too low). 'Valencia' orange has higher heat requirement and greater frost tolerance. Navel oranges need even more heat. But their fruit development period is shorter than 'Valencia' and a tree will produce palatable fruit between winter frosts if summer heat is high. Navel, therefore, is a good selection for Zones 8, 9, 12, 13. Mandarin oranges (tangerine group) need high heat for top flavor. Grapefruit develops full flavor only in areas of prolonged high heat.

Hardiness. Citrus of one kind or another are grown in every Arizona and California climate where winter temperatures do not fall much below 20°F. From least hardy to hardiest they rank generally in this order: 'Mexican' lime (28°F.), limequat, grapefruit, regular lemon, tangelo and tangor, 'Bearss' lime, sweet orange, most mandarin oranges (tangerines), 'Rangpur' lime and 'Meyer' lemon, 'Owari' mandarin, sour orange, kumquat, calamondin (20°F.).

Standard or dwarf. Most standard citrus trees grow to 20–30 ft. high and almost as wide. Dwarfs (grown on dwarfing rootstock) become 4–10-ft. shrubs or small trees of equal beauty and greater landscaping utility. They can be located more easily than standards in garden warm spots and, in containers, they can be easily protected from frost and placed in wind-protected warm spots for extra heat. Some 30 varieties of citrus are available on dwarf rootstocks.

Drainage. First requirement is fast drainage. If soil drains slowly, don't attempt to plant citrus in it regardless of how you condition planting soil. In poorly drained soil, plant above soil level in raised beds or by mounding up soil around plant. Drainage in average soil, and water retention in very light soil, will be improved by digging in a 4–6 in. layer of peat moss, sawdust, or ground bark to depth of 12 in.

Watering. Citrus needs moist soil, but never free-standing water. It needs air in the soil. Danger from overwatering is greatest in clay soil where air spaces are minute. In soil with proper drainage, water newly planted trees almost as frequently as trees in containers—twice a week in normal summer weather, more frequently during hot spell. Water established trees every other week. In clay soils, space watering intervals so top part of soil dries between irrigations. Don't let tree reach wilting point.

If you build basins, make them wider than spread of branches. Citrus roots extend out twice as far as the distance from the trunk to branch ends. Keep trunk dry by starting basin 6 in. or more from trunk. When you water, put on enough to wet entire root zone (that is, wet to depth of 4 ft.).

Mulching. Since citrus roots grow near surface as well as deeper, a mulch over soil is beneficial. Use a 2–3-in.-deep layer of sawdust or the like, or large pebbles or gravel.

Fertilizing. Universities recommend from 1½–2 lbs. of actual nitrogen for mature trees each year (to get pounds of "actual nitrogen", multiply percentage of total nitrogen, as stated on label, times weight of fertilizer). It's best to apply ⅓ in late winter, ⅓ in June, and ⅓ in August. Spread fertilizer beneath and well beyond branch spread of tree, and water in deeply. Use a high nitrogen formula.

Citrus may suffer from iron chlorosis or zinc deficiency. Iron chlorosis (yellowing leaves with dark green veins) may also be caused by excess water, so check your irrigation practice. Treat with chelated iron or iron sulfate. Zinc deficiency shows up as a yellowish blotch or mottle between leaf veins. Control with zinc foliar sprays. Commercial products are available as sprays containing both iron chelates and zinc.

Pests and diseases. Citrus can get aphids, mites, scale insects, and mealybugs. If their natural enemies fail to clear them up, and if jets of water fail to keep them in check, spray with chemicals listed for those creatures in the "Pest control" chapter (pages 55–63). If scale remains troublesome, spray with light oil in early spring. Bait or spray for snails and slugs whenever necessary, especially during warm-night spells of winter and spring.

The few fungus ailments of citrus occur in poorly drained soil. Water molds, causing root rot, show up in yellowing and dropping foliage. Best control is to correct your watering schedule.

Brown rot gummosis usually occurs in older trees at base of trunk. Keep base of trunk dry; trim and clean the oozing wounds, removing decayed bark to a point where discolored wood does not show. Paint areas with Bordeaux paste mixture.

Sunburn. Citrus bark sunburns in hot-sun areas. Trunks should be wrapped (commercial paper trunk band is available). When exposing trunks or limbs by heavy pruning, protect bark with whitewash or cold-water paint. Common cold-water wall paint in tan or brown, similar to bark color, is satisfactory.

Pruning. Commercial trees are allowed to carry branches right to ground. Production is heaviest on lower branches. Growers prune only to remove twiggy growth and weak branches or, in young plant, to nip back wild growth and balance plant. You can prune garden trees to shape as desired; espaliers of citrus are traditional. Lemons and sour oranges are often planted close and pruned as hedges. Many citrus are thorny. Pruners and pickers should wear gloves and long sleeves.

Citrus in containers. Daily watering may be necessary in hot weather. Containers should have diameter of at least 18 in.

Citrus indoors. Gardeners in cold-winter, warm-summer areas can store plants indoors for winter protection. A cool greenhouse is best, but a basement area with good bright light is satisfactory. Use very little water.

GRAPEFRUIT

'Marsh' seedless. The West's main commercial type. Large light yellow fruit. Ripens 18 months after bloom—late November to June in desert areas. Needs highest, most prolonged summer heat for top quality. Even out of best climate it's a beautiful tree. Standard tree grows to 30 ft. or more; on dwarf rootstock, less than half as high. Large glossy leaves.

'Oro Blanco'. Large, light yellow fruit with thick skin. Yellow flesh has grapefruit flavor but is sweeter, less astringent. Extends season in Southern California, bearing November to February ('Marsh' November to February in the same region).

'Ruby' ('Redblush', 'Ruby Red'). Pink grapefruit. Red-blushed skin and pinkish flesh. Does not color well except in desert.

LEMONS

"Eureka'. The standard lemon of markets. Bears throughout year. Not as vigorous as 'Lisbon' lemon. Somewhat open growth, branches with few thorns. As a dwarf, it's dense with large dark leaves. New growth is bronzy purple. Height 20 ft.; less as dwarf.

'Improved Meyer'. By law, this strain replaced the old-friend variety 'Meyer' in 1978. 'Improved Meyer' supposedly has more resistance to infection and virus diseases. Other than that, it should be like the

Lemon

original. Fruit is quite different from commercial lemon—rounder, thin skinned, more orange-colored. Tangy aroma, very juicy, but less acid than standard lemon. Bears fruit all year round, at early age. Tree is not a dwarf on its own roots. Will grow to 12 ft. with a 15-ft. spread. On dwarf rootstock it's half that size.

'Lisbon'. Vigorous growth, thorny, upright, denser than 'Eureka', to 20–25 ft. Can be trimmed up into highly decorative small tree. Fruit practically identical to 'Eureka'. Ripens mostly in fall, but some ripening all year. More resistant to cold than 'Eureka' and better adapted to high heat. Best lemon for Arizona.

'Ponderosa'. A novelty. Bears huge, rough lemons with thick coarse skin. Two lb. fruit not unusual. Mild lemon flavor. Bears at early age, frequently in gallon-can size. Main crop winter with some fruit through year. Tree angular-branched, open; large leaves widely spaced. To 8–10 ft.; dwarf size, 4–6 ft.

'Villa Franca'. Generally similar to 'Eureka' but tree is larger, more vigorous, and has denser foliage and thornier branches. Fruit is similar to 'Eureka'. Sold in Arizona to grow in Zones 12 and 13; not common in California.

LIMES

'Bearss'. Best lime for California gardens. Succeeds where the orange is successful. Tree is quite angular and open when young but forms dense round crown to 15–20 ft. when mature. Half that size on dwarf rootstock. It's thorny and inclined to drop many leaves in winter. Young fruit green, light yellow when ripe, almost size of lemon. When fully ripe it is especially juicy. Seedless. Main crop winter to late spring, some fruit all year.

'Mexican'. The standard bartender's lime—small, green to yellow green. Grow it in Zones 21–23. Grows to 12–15 ft. with upright twiggy branches.

LIMEQUAT

'Eustis'. Hybrid of 'Mexican' lime and kumquat. Fruit is jumbo olive in shape and size, light yellow when ripe. Produces lime flavoring in regions too frosty for true limes. Rind edible. Flavor and aroma of lime. Ripens late fall and winter. Some fruit all year. Tree is shrublike, angular-branching, twiggy, and rather open. Dwarf plant excellent in container.

MANDARIN ORANGES (Tangerines)

'Clementine'. Algerian tangerine. Fruit a little larger than 'Dancy', fewer seeds, ripens November-December. Fruit remains on tree, juicy and sweet, for months. Grows to 12 ft., semiopen with vertical, spreading, somewhat willowy branches. Seems to develop full flavor in areas too cool for a good 'Dancy'. 'Clementine' usually bears light crops unless planted with another variety for pollination.

'Dancy'. The standard tangerine in markets before Christmas. Fruit smaller and seedier than other mandarins. Best flavor in Zones 12 and 13 but good on the coast in Zones 21–23. Ripens December-January. Holds well on tree. Upright tree with erect branches. Dwarf tree handsome in container or as espalier.

'Fairchild'. Hybrid between 'Clementine' mandarin and 'Orlando' tangelo. Medium-sized deep orange fruit peels easily, is juicy and tasty, has many seeds. Ripens November-December. Small compact tree bears every year. Good in Zones 12, 13. Needs another variety nearby for pollination.

'Fremont'. Hybrid between 'Clementine' and an Oriental mandarin called Ponkan. Medium-sized bright orange fruit ripens December-January. Flavor good. Tree tends to bear in alternate years; thin fruit when number on tree is unusually heavy. Good in Zones 12, 13.

'Honey'. Hybrid between 'King' and 'Willow' mandarin. Small seedy fruit with rich and sweet flavor. Tends to bear heavily in alternate years. Vigorous tree.

'Kara'. Hybrid between 'King' and 'Owari'. Fruit large (2½ in.) for mandarin. Tart-sweet, aromatic flavor when ripened in warm interior climates. Ripens January and February in Zones 12, 13; March to May and June in Zones 8, 9, 14, 15, 18–23. May be very seedy or nearly seedless some seasons. Tree form resembles 'Owari'. Spreading, often drooping branches with large leaves.

Grows to a rounded 15–20 ft. Half that size as dwarf.

'Kinnow'. Hybrid between 'King' and 'Willow' mandarin. Medium-sized fruit has rich, aromatic flavor. Stores well on tree. Ripens January to May. Handsomely shaped tree—columnar, dense, very symmetrical to 20 ft. (dwarf will reach 10 ft.). Densely foliaged with slender leaves. Good in any citrus climate.

'Owari'. Owari Satsuma. Source of imported canned mandarins. Sweet delicate flavor, nearly seedless, medium to large fruit. Loose skin. Earliest mandarin to ripen—October to Christmas. Gets overripe soon if left on tree, but keeps well in cool storage. Standard trees are spreading, to 10–15 ft. high. Dwarf trees can be used as 6-ft. shrubs. Open, angular growth in early age; then more compact. Not suited to desert.

'Wilking'. From same parents as 'Honey' and 'Kinnow'. Small to medium-sized fruit with relatively thin rind; very juicy with rich distinctive flavor. Fruit stores well on tree. Tends to bear heavily in alternate years. Tree is rounded, medium height, and nearly thornless.

ORANGES

The commercial oranges of the West are typified by the 'Washington' navel and the 'Valencia'. Listed here are first 'Washington' and the other navel varieties, then 'Valencia' and its counterparts, and finally the other lesser known oranges.

'Washington' navel. Widely adapted except desert regions; best in warm interiors. Standard tree is 20–25 ft. globe. On dwarf stock it becomes 8-ft. mound. Bears December-February.

'Robertson' navel. Variant of 'Washington' navel. Fruit identical but earlier by 2–3 weeks. Tends to carry fruit in clusters. Tree generally smaller in size than 'Washington'. Has same climate adaptation. Dwarf trees produce amazing amount of fruit.

'Skaggs Bonanza'. Another variant of 'Washington'. Fruit colors and ripens earlier; tree comes into bearing younger. Very heavy bearing.

'Summernavel'. Fruit much like 'Washington'. Sometimes fails to color as well, but flavor is good. Later ripening—well into summer months. Tree is more openly branched with much larger leaves than 'Washington'. A dwarf tree will cover area bigger than 8 ft. square quite rapidly.

At some seasons navel oranges are subject to split navels. This generally occurs when weather conditions favor fast fruit development and seems unrelated to culture. However, it's best to keep tree in even growth by avoiding excess fertilizer. Watch leaf color: yellowish leaves are signs of nitrogen need; dark green lush leaves with burning tips or edges indicate too much nitrogen.

'Valencia'. The juice orange of stores. Most widely planted orange in the world, widely adapted in California. Poor risk in Arizona; if planted there, select a warm location or provide some protection to fruit, which must winter on tree. One of "Arizona Sweets" (see below) would be safer selection. Fruit matures in summer and stores on tree for months, improving in sweetness. Tree vigorous and fuller growing than 'Washington' navel, both as standard and dwarf.

'Seedless Valencia'. Variant of 'Valencia'. Fruit size, quality, and season are same. May not bear as prolifically.

"Arizona Sweets". These are a group of varieties grown in Arizona. 'Diller', 'Hamlin', 'Marrs', and 'Pineapple' are the principal ones.

'Diller'. Small to medium-sized oranges with few seeds, high quality juice. Ripen November-December (before heavy frost). Vigorous, large, dense tree with large leaves.

'Hamlin'. Similar to 'Diller', with medium-sized fruits, not as hardy.

'Marrs'. Early-ripening, tasty, low-acid fruit on a naturally semidwarf tree. Bears young.

'Pineapple'. Early-ripening fruit of medium size, excellent flavor.

'Shamouti'. Originated in Palestine and considered there to be finest orange. Large, seedless, no navel. Not a commercial orange in California because not sufficiently superior to 'Washington' navel. Grown on dwarf rootstock for home gardeners because of beauty in form and foliage. It's wider than tall. Leaves larger than navel. Heavy crop of fruit in early spring.

'Tarocco'. Red or red suffused pulp, pink to red juice. Color varies. The less heat, the more color. Good quality in cooler areas. Ripens late spring. Tree is very vigorous, open growing with long, willowy, vinelike branches. Dwarf tree makes ideal espalier. Other blood oranges are 'Moro', with orange skin and deep purple red flesh; and 'Sanguinelli', with red skin and purple red flesh.

'Trovita'. Originated from seedling of 'Washington' navel. About navel size with thin skin, but without navel. Ripens in early spring. Apparently requires less heat than other sweet oranges and develops good quality fruit near —not on—coast. Nevertheless it tolerates heat well enough to pass as one of the "Arizona Sweets." Dwarf tree has 'Washington' navel look with handsome dark green leaves.

KUMQUAT *(Fortunella)*

Very hardy. May not flower or fruit in cold-winter citrus climates, but always worthwhile for form and foliage. Leaves bright green, 3 in. long, oval, pointed. White flowers have rich orange blossom perfume. Edible rind is sweet, flesh tart. Fruit used in marmalade, jelly; is candied, preserved whole. Expect regular fruit production only in warm-summer areas. Plant size variable when grown on its own roots—from 6–25 ft. On dwarf rootstock, a compact, dense shrub-tree to 4 ft. Admirably suited, in pots or tubs, for patio or garden.

F. crassifolia. MEIWA KUMQUAT. Fruit round; larger, somewhat sweeter than Nagami. Tree less hardy.

F. margarita. NAGAMI KUMQUAT. Fruit oval, bright orange, about 1 in. in diameter.

SOUR-ACID MANDARIN ORANGES

Calamondin. Fruit looks like small (¾–1½ in.) orange. Hundreds hang from tall (8–10 ft. even as dwarf), columnar plant. Most attractive in containers. Flesh is tender, juicy, sour, with a few small seeds. Primary use is as an ornamental; not a fruit to eat fresh. Skin and flesh good in marmalades.

'Otaheite' orange. Natural dwarf only a few feet tall. Usually grown indoors as decorative pot plant. Not true orange. Will bear very young. Fruit is orange to reddish orange, small, round, rough skinned, insipid in flavor. About as hardy as lemon.

'Rangpur' lime. Probably not lime at all. Fruit looks and peels like a mandarin, does not have lime taste. Less acid than lemon but with other flavors that make it a rich interesting base for ades and mixed drinks. Good landscape tree, vigorous, sturdy, bushy. Fast growth to 15 ft. and as wide (as dwarf, to 8 ft.) Dense when pruned, open otherwise. Fruit colorful as ornaments, hang on tree throughout year. Has wide climate tolerance.

TANGELOS

'Minneola'. Hybrid of 'Dancy' tangerine and grapefruit. Fruit is bright orange red, smooth, large. Flavor similar to tangerine. Few seeds. Ripens February to March. Stores well on tree for 2 months. Tree is not as large or dense as grapefruit. Leaves 3½–5 in. long and pointed. Thrives in all citrus districts.

'Orlando'. Fruit medium large, like flattened orange. Rind is orange, adheres to orange-colored flesh. Very juicy, mildly sweet, matures early in season. Tree is similar to 'Minneola' but with distinctively cupped leaves. Less vigorous and more cold resistant than 'Minneola'.

'Sampson'. Hybrid of tangerine and grapefruit, but fruit more like small grapefruit with orange red pulp. Best for juice and marmalades. Ripens February-April. Standard tree is vigorous, fast, to 30 ft. Form similar to grapefruit. Most decorative as dwarf tree. Dark green, oval, 2–3-in. leaves; golden fruit in winter. Best in Zones 14–16, 20–23. Subject to sunburn in desert areas.

TANGORS

'Dweet'. Hybrid of orange and tangerine. Fruit is egg shaped with neck, and as large as 'Valencia' orange. Skin is tight. Seedy, but packed with rich juice. Ripens May-August. Dwarf tree to 8 ft. is moderately branched and rather open. Fruit at end of branches bends them down. Susceptible to sunburn, defoliation, dieback. Unsatisfactory in desert areas. Best in Zones 14, 18–23.

'Temple'. Tangerine-orange hybrid (a tangor). High quality fruit in Zone 13. Flat, deep bright orange; loose skin, easily peeled. Pulp more tender than sweet, orange, juicy, of "different" good flavor. Ripens in early spring. Tree spreads wider than high, to 12 ft. high, bushy and thorny. To a wide 6 ft. on dwarf stock. Leaves are similar to mandarin, smaller and narrower than orange.

MISCELLANEOUS

Sour orange, Seville orange. *(Citrus aurantium.)* Zones 8, 9, 12–14, 18–21. Make large hedges, street trees, lawn trees. Fragrant flowers. Spectacular orange red, 3-in. fruits in clusters. Fruit is bitter and makes excellent bitter marmalade. Tree grows to 20–30 ft. with 15–20-ft. spread, dense foliage. Plant 6–10 ft. apart for tall screen; 3–4 ft., (prune heavily) for hedge.

'Bouquet'. Bouquet orange. 'Bouquet des Fleurs'. Another very hardy sour orange for Zones 8, 9, 12–14, 18–21. Big shrub or small tree to 8–10 ft. Graceful foliage, dark green. Used as hedge or windbreak. Flowers unusually large and extremely fragrant. Fruit small, bitter, used only in marmalades.

'Chinotto' orange (often sold as myrtle-leaf orange). Smaller in all dimensions than other sour oranges. Dense, bushy, round headed, with closely set, small, almost myrtlelike leaves. Very slow growing to 7–10 ft. Formal appearance, often rounded high on stem and clipped. Ideal tub plant. Fruit ornamental, small, round, bright orange; used in Europe for candying.

'Etrog' citron. Attractive foliage. Fruit is small, oblong, yellow, fragrant and unusually lumpy on the surface. Peel used in candying.

CLADRASTIS lutea. YELLOW WOOD. Deciduous tree. Zones 1–9, 14–16. Native to Kentucky, Tennessee, and North Carolina. Slow growing to 30–35 ft. with broad, rounded head half as wide as tree is high. Divided 8–12-in.-wide leaves look somewhat like English walnut, bright green in summer, brilliant yellow in fall.

May not flower until 10 years old, and may skip bloom some years, but spectacular when it does bloom. In May or early June it produces long (6–10 in.) clusters of white flowers (like wisteria's), very fragrant. Blooms followed by flat, 3–4-in.-long seed pods. Useful and attractive as terrace, patio, or lawn tree even if it never blooms. Average water and soil.

Cladrastis lutea

Prune when young to shorten side branches. Remove lower branches entirely when tree has height you want.

CLARKIA (includes *Godetia*). Annuals. All Zones in conditions noted below. Native to western South and North America, especially numerous in California. They grow in the cool season, bloom in spring and early summer. Attractive in mixed borders or in mass displays, alone or with love-in-a-mist (*Nigella*), cornflower, violas, sweet alyssum. Cut branches keep for several days; cut when top bud opens—others open successively.

Clarkia amoena

Sow seeds in place in fall (in mild-winter areas) or spring. Seedlings difficult to transplant but volunteer seedlings grow very well. Keep soil moist during and after germination, and until flowering. Best in sandy soil without added fertilizer. Sun.

C. amoena (*Godetia amoena, G. grandiflora*). GODETIA, FAREWELL-TO-SPRING. Native California to British Columbia. Two wild forms: coarse-stemmed and sprawling, 4–5 in. high; slender stemmed, 1½–2½ ft. high. Tapered leaves, ½–2 in. long. On both forms, upright buds open into cup shaped, slightly flaring, pink or lavender flowers, 2 in. across, usually blotched or penciled crimson. Although seeds of named varieties are sold in England and rarely in United States, strains of mixed colors are easy to find. Dwarf Gem grows 10 in. tall; Tall Upright reaches 2–3 ft.

C. concinna. RED-RIBBONS. Native to California. To 18 in. tall. Deep pink to lavender flowers with 3-lobed, fan shaped petals. Leaves rounded, ½–2 in. long. May be found in wildflower seed mixes.

C. pulchella. Native to Pacific Northwest. Slender, upright, reddish stemmed, mostly unbranched, 1–1½ ft. high. Leaves narrow, 1–2 in. long, sparse. Flowers single, with 4 petals tapered to clawlike base, 3-lobed at tip; semidouble and dwarf forms. Some garden clarkias probably hybrids between *C. pulchella* and *C. unguiculata.*

C. unguiculata *(C. elegans).* CLARKIA, MOUNTAIN GARLAND. Erect, 1–4 ft. with reddish stems; leaves 1–1¾ in. long; flowers 1 in. across, rose, purple, white; varieties with double white, orange, salmon, crimson, purple, rose, pink, and creamy yellow flowers. Double-flowered kinds are ones usually sold in seed packets.

CLEMATIS. Most of the 200-odd species are deciduous vines; exceptions are the evergreen *C. armandii,* and a few interesting free-standing or sprawling perennials or small shrubs. All have attractive flowers and most are spectacular. The flowers are followed by fluffy clusters of seeds with tails, often quite effective in flower arrangements. Leaves of deciduous kinds are dark green, usually divided into leaflets; leaf stalks twist and curl to hold plant to its support. Although the deciduous clematis are hardy in all western climates and are enjoyed in most, they perform best in

Clematis armandii

Pacific Northwest (Zones 1–6) and in coastal northern California (Zones 15–17).

Clematis are not demanding, but their few specific requirements should be met. Plant vine types next to trellis, tree trunk, or open framework for stems to grow on. Plant so that roots are cool while tops are in full sun. Give them rich, loose, fast draining soil; add generous quantities of peat moss, ground bark, and the like. Where soils are strongly acid, add lime. Where soils tend to be neutral or alkaline, add bone meal. Unlike most plants, clematis should be planted deep. Set top of root ball 2 in. below soil surface and cover with soil.

To provide cool area for roots, add mulch; or place large flat rock over soil; or plant shallow-rooted ground cover over the root area; or plant in shade of small shrub or evergreen vine and stake so the top can catch sun. Put in support when planting and tie up stems at once. Stems are easily broken. Protect with wire netting if child or dog traffic is heavy. Clematis need constant moisture and nutrients to make their great rush of growth. Fertilize every month in growing season.

In the list of species and hybrids that follows we have noted the type of pruning each should receive to give its best flower crop. Since there are many kinds not included in the list and more will be sold in nurseries by hybrid name only, here's how to let common sense guide your pruning: time of flowering dictates time and kind of pruning. Kinds that bloom in summer only are blooming on wood produced in spring. To get this new wood, cut back after flowering in late fall and early spring as buds swell. Cut to within 6–12 in. of ground, or to 2–3 buds, for first 2 or 3 years. Cut older plants to 2 ft. or less. *C. jackmanii* is typical of this group. For convenience in pruning instructions, we call this method "J" (for *C. jackmanii*).

Kinds that bloom in spring and again in summer are blooming on old wood in spring, new wood in summer. Make the fall or early spring pruning a light corrective one and prune flowered portions immediately after bloom in spring. We call this pruning method "L" (for *C. lanuginosa*).

Kinds that bloom in spring only are blooming on wood of previous year. Cut back in spring after flowering to restrict sprawl and tangle. Preserve framework of main branches.

To sum it up: If you don't know which type you have, watch it for a year to see when it blooms (in spring only, in summer only, or both) and prune accordingly.

Cut flowers choice for indoors (float in bowl). Burn cut stems

with match to make flowers last longer. Unless otherwise specified, flowers are 4–6 in. across.

C. armandii. EVERGREEN CLEMATIS. Hardy Zones 4–9, 12–24 but best adapted Zones 4–6, 15–17. Native to China. Leaves burn at tips badly where soil or water contain excess salts. Fast growing to 20 ft. Leaves divided into 3 glossy dark green leaflets, 3–5 in. long; they droop downward to create strongly textured pattern. Glistening white, 2½-in.-wide, fragrant flowers in large, branched clusters in March-April.

Slow to start, races when established. Needs constant pruning after flowering to prevent tangling and build-up of dead thatch on inner parts of vine. Keep and tie up stems you want, and cut out all others. Frequent pinching will hold foliage to eye level.

Train along fence tops or rails, roof gables. Allow to climb tall trees. Trained on substantial frame, makes privacy screen if not allowed to become bare at base.

There is a light pink flowered form, *C. a.* 'Hendersoni Rubra'.

C. chrysocoma. Deciduous vine. Native to western China. To 6–8 ft. or more in height and fairly open. Young branches, leaves, and flower stalks covered with yellow down. Flowers long stalked, white, shaded pink, 2 in. wide, in clusters from old wood in spring, with later flowers following from new wood. Will take considerable shade. Pruning: "L."

C. davidiana. See *C. heracleifolia davidiana.*

C. dioscoreifolia *(C. paniculata).* SWEET AUTUMN CLEMATIS. Native to Japan. Tall, vigorous, forming billowy masses of small (1 in. wide), creamy white, fragrant flowers in late summer and fall. Leaves, dark green, glossy, divided into 3–5 oval, 1–2½-in.-long leaflets. After bloom or in early spring, prune year's growth to 1 or 2 buds. Good privacy screen, arbor cover.

C. 'Duchess of Edinburgh'. Fully double white flowers in early spring, again in summer. Pruning: "L."

C. 'Ernest Markham'. One of best reds. Grows like *C. jackmanii.* Pruning: "J."

C. 'Gypsy Queen'. Flowers deep violet with wine crimson tints, summer and fall. Pruning: "J."

C. 'Hagley Hybrid' ('Pink Chiffon'). Deep shell pink flowers. Pruning: "J."

C. heracleifolia davidiana *(C. davidiana).* Native to China. Half-woody perennial to 4 ft. high. Deep green leaves divided into 3 broad oval, 3–6-in.-long leaflets. Dense clusters of 1-in.-long tubular, medium to deep blue fragrant flowers July-August. Use in perennial or shrub border. Pruning: "J."

C. integrifolia. Native to Europe and Asia. Semishrubby perennial to 3 ft. with dark green, undivided 2–4-in.-long leaves and nodding, urn shaped, 1½-in.-long blue flowers in June-July. Prune after bloom.

C. jackmanii. Series of hybrids between forms of *C. lanuginosa* and *C. viticella.* All are vigorous plants of rapid growth to 10 ft. or more in one season. The best known of the older large-flowered hybrids is known simply as *C. jackmanii.* It has profusion of 4–5-in., rich purple flowers with 4 sepals. Blooms heavily June-July on. Later hybrids have larger flowers with more sepals, but none has as many flowers. *C. j.* 'Comtesse de Bouchaud' has silvery rose pink flowers, *C. j.* 'Mme. Edouard Andre' purplish red. All flower on new wood; all do best with severe pruning in early spring as buds begin to swell. Freezes to ground in cold winter areas. Pruning: "J."

C. lanuginosa. Native to China. A parent of many of the finest large-flowered hybrids. Grows only to about 6–9 ft. but produces magnificent display of large (6 in.) lilac to white flowers in May-July. Best known for its variety *C. l.* 'Candida', with 8-in. white flowers and light yellow stamens. Blooms on new and old wood. In favorable climates will bloom in March-April. Prune only to remove dead or weak growth in early spring. Then after first flush of flowers, cut back flowered portions promptly for another crop later in the summer. Pruning: "L."

C. lawsoniana. Thought to be hybrid of *C. lanuginosa* and *C. patens.* To 6–10 ft. Large (6–9 in.) flowers, rosy purple and dark veined. Its best known form is *C. l.* 'Henryi' with tremendous 8-in. flowers, white with dark stamens, June-August. Pruning: "L."

C. 'Lord Neville'. Flowers rich deep blue, sepal edges crimped. Pruning: "L."

C. macropetala. DOWNY CLEMATIS. Native to China, Siberia. Variable in size, may be 6–30 ft. high. In early spring, produces

4-in. lavender to powder blue flowers that have appearance of doubleness; they look like ballet skirts. They are followed by showy bronzy pink and silvery tailed seed clusters. *C. m.* 'Markhamii' has lavender pink flowers. Prune lightly in February to remove weak shoots and limit vigorous growth to sound wood.

C. 'Mme. Baron-Veillard'. Vigorous plant of *C. jackmanii* type. Medium-sized 5-in. flowers of warm lilac rose. Pruning: "J."

C. montana. ANEMONE CLEMATIS. Native to Himalayas, China. Vigorous to 20 ft. or more. Extremely hardy, easy to grow. Massive display in early spring of 2–2½-in. anemonelike flowers, opening white, turning pink. Flowers on old wood, so can be heavily thinned or pruned immediately after flowering to rejuvenate or reduce size.

C. m. rubens. To 15–25 ft. Foliage is bronzy green, new growth crimson. Fragrant flowers, rose red changing to pink, are carried throughout vine fabric.

C. m. 'Tetrarose'. Considered more vigorous than *C. m.* 'Rubens'.

Clematis montana

C. 'Mrs. Cholmondeley' (pronounced "Chumley"). Vigorous vine of *C. jackmanii* type. Lavender blue flowers with long, pointed sepals. Pruning: "J."

C. 'Nelly Moser'. Mauve sepals marked by dark red stripe in center of each. Pruning: "L."

C. paniculata. See *C. dioscoreifolia.*

C. 'Prins Hendrik'. Big flowers of near azure blue with ruffled sepals. Pruning: "L."

C. 'Ramona'. Lavender blue; classic for planting with yellow or coppery climbing roses. Pruning: "L."

Clematis 'Nelly Moser'

C. tangutica. GOLDEN CLEMATIS. Native to Mongolia, northern China. To 10–15 ft. high, with gray green, finely divided foliage. Bright yellow, 2–4-in., nodding, lantern shaped flowers in great profusion from July to fall. They are followed by handsome silvery-tailed seed clusters. Prune like *C. dioscoreifolia.* Uncommon.

C. texensis. SCARLET CLEMATIS. Native to Texas. Fast growing to 6–10 ft. Dense bluish green foliage. Flowers bright scarlet, urn shaped to 1 in. long, in July-August. Has not done well in Seattle, but flourishes in Reno. More tolerant of dry soils than most clematis. Pruning: "J."

C. 'The President'. Deep purple blue with dark stamens. Pruning: "L."

C. viticella. Native to southern Europe, western Asia. To 12–15 ft. Purple or rose purple, 2-in. flowers, June-August. Very hardy. Better known is variety 'Betty Balfour', with much larger, deep velvety purple flowers. Pruning: "J."

CLEOME spinosa. SPIDER FLOWER. Summer annual. Shrubby, branching plant topped in late summer and fall with many open, fluffy clusters of pink or white flowers with extremely long protruding stamens. Slender seed capsules follow blossoms. Short strong spines on stems; lower leaves divided, upper ones undivided. Leaves and stems have clammy feeling to the touch and strong, but not unpleasant, odor. Plants grow 4–6 ft. tall, 4–5 ft. wide; especially vigorous in warm, dry inland areas. Grow in background, as summer hedge, against walls or fences, in large containers, or naturalize in fringe areas of garden. Flowers and dry capsules useful in arrangements.

Cleome spinosa

Sow seed in place in full sun; they sprout rapidly in warm soil. Keep plants on dry side or they will become too rank. A number of varieties can be grown from seed. In most cases color is indicated by variety name: 'Cherry Queen', 'Mauve Queen', 'Pink Queen', 'Purple Queen', 'Rose Queen', and 'Ruby Queen'. 'Helen Campbell' is snow white.

CLERODENDRUM. GLORYBOWER. Evergreen and deciduous; shrubs, trees, or vinelike shrubs. Some outdoor; some houseplants. Average water.

C. bungei (*C. foetidum*). CASHMERE BOUQUET. Evergreen shrub. Zones 5–9, 12–24. Native to China. Rapid growing to 6 ft. tall; soft wooded. Prune severely in spring and pinch back through growing season to make 2–3-ft. compact shrub. Spreads by suckers, eventually forming thicket if not restrained. Big leaves (to 12 in.), broadly oval with toothed edges, dark green above, with rusty fuzz beneath; ill smelling when crushed. Delightfully fragrant flowers in summer: ¾ in. wide, rosy red, in large (to 8 in.) loose clusters. Plant in part shade where its appearance, except in flowering season, is not important. It is resistant to oak root fungus.

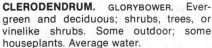
Clerodendrum thomsoniae

C. fragrans pleniflorum. Evergreen to partly deciduous shrub. Zones 8, 9, 12–24. Coarse shrub spreading freely by root suckers unless confined. To 5–8 ft. (much less in containers), with 10-in.-leaves like those of *C. bungei.* Flowers pale pink, double, in broad clusters that resemble florist's hydrangea; they have sweet, clean fragrance. Shade.

C. thomsoniae (*C. balfouri*). BLEEDING HEART GLORYBOWER. Evergreen shrubby vine. Zones: Outdoors in most protected spots of 22–24; elsewhere indoor/outdoor pot plant. Native to west Africa. Leaves oval, 4–7 in. long, dark green, shiny, distinctly ribbed. Flowers are study in color contrast—scarlet 1-in. tubes surrounded by large (¾ in. long) white calyx; carried in flattish 5-in.-wide clusters August-October. Will flower in 6-in. pot. Does well as indoor/outdoor tubbed vine. Can grow to 6 ft. or more if left untrimmed. Give support for twining. Needs rich, loose soil mix, plenty of water with good drainage. Prune after flowering.

C. trichotomum. HARLEQUIN GLORYBOWER. Deciduous shrub-tree. May freeze to ground in Zones 5, 6 and come back from roots; adapted Zones 15–17, 20–24. Native to Japan. Grows with many stems from base to 10–15 ft. or more. Leaves oval, to 5 in. long, dark green, soft, hairy. Fragrant clusters of white tubular flowers almost twice as long as prominent, fleshy, ½-in.-long scarlet calyces. Late summer bloom. Calyces hang on and contrast pleasingly with turquoise or blue green metallic-looking fruit. Variety *fargesii,* from China, is somewhat hardier, smaller, has smooth leaves and green calyces that later turn pink. Grow in sun or partial shade. Routine care. Give room to spread at top and plant under it to hide its legginess.

CLETHRA. Deciduous shrub and evergreen tree. Distinctive plants with definite climate and soil preferences.

C. alnifolia. SUMMERSWEET, SWEET PEPPERBUSH. Deciduous shrub. Zones 2–6. Native to eastern U.S. To 10 ft. high with thin strong branches forming vertical pattern. Spreads slowly by suckers into broad clumps. Dark green leaves, 2–4 in. long, half as wide, have toothed edges. Leafs out very late, in mid-May. Blooms in late summer. Each branch tip carries several 4–6-in.-long spires of tiny gleaming white flowers, spicily perfumed. Grows best in soils where rhododendrons thrive. Full sun in cool gardens, some shade where summers are warm. *C. a.* 'Pinkspire' has deep pink flowers, *C. a.* 'Rosea', pale pink.

Clethra arborea

C. arborea. LILY-OF-THE-VALLEY TREE. Evergreen tree. Zones 15–17, 21–24. Native to Madeira. (For another lily-of-the-valley tree, see *Crinodendron.*) Beautiful small tree. Grows at moderate rate to 20 ft., rather stiffly upright with 10-ft. spread. Densely clothed with glossy, bronzy green, 4-in.-long leaves. White flowers in upright branched clusters resemble lily-of-the-valley, even to their fragrance. They appear in late summer.

Leaf tips burn with frost, but plant comes back from old wood or from roots when damaged.

(Continued on next page)

Easy to grow in soils where azaleas or rhododendrons thrive. Where salts build up, condition soil with peat moss or ground bark and make sure drainage is fast. Needs abundant moisture. If necessary, spray for red spider mites in summer.

CLEYERA japonica *(Eurya ochnacea).* Evergreen shrub. Zones 4–6, 8, 9, 14–24. Native to Japan and southeast Asia. Handsome foliage shrub related to camellia. Similar in character to ternstroemia. Grows at moderate rate to 15 ft. tall and as wide with graceful, spreading, arching branches. Leaves of new growth are beautiful deep brownish red. Mature leaves, 3–6 in. long, are glossy dark green with reddish midrib. Small clusters of fragrant, creamy white flowers in September-October are followed by small, dark red puffy berries which last through winter. Flowers and berries are attractive but not showy, don't form on young plants. 'Tricolor' *(C. fortunei)* has yellow and rose variegation on its foliage. Same soil and care as camellias.

Cleyera japonica

CLIANTHUS puniceus. PARROT-BEAK. Evergreen shrublike vine. Zones 8, 9, 14–24. Native to New Zealand. Moderate growth to 12 ft. Foliage hangs gracefully in open pattern made up of sprays of glistening, dark green, 3–6-in. leaves divided into many narrow leaflets. Flowers rose scarlet (rarely pink or white), sweet pea shaped, with 3-in. parrot-beak keels swung downward between leaves. June blooming. Pods that follow are 3 in. long. Full sun on coast; part shade inland. Train as espalier or on support to bring out full beauty of leaves and flowers. Routine garden care with ample water through blooming season. If soil is heavy, mix in organic soil amendment. Watch for snails and spider mites.

Clianthus puniceus

CLIFF-BRAKE. See *Pellaea.*

CLIFF ROSE. See *Cowania mexicana stansburiana.*

CLIMBING FERN. See *Lygodium japonicum.*

CLIMBING LILY. See *Gloriosa rothschildiana.*

CLIVIA miniata. KAFFIR LILY. Evergreen perennial with tuberous roots. Zones 13–17, 19–24. Native to South Africa. Striking member of amaryllis family with brilliant clusters of orange, funnel shaped flowers rising from dense clumps of dark green, strap shaped 1½-ft.-long leaves. Blooming period is December to April; most bloom March-April. Ornamental red berries follow flowers. French and Belgian hybrids have yellow to deep red orange blooms on thick, rigid stalks, and very wide, dark green leaves.

Clivia miniata

In frostless areas or well-protected parts of garden, clivias are handsome in shaded borders with ferns, azaleas, other shade plants. Superb in containers; grow indoors in cold climates. For best growth, clivia needs ample light, no direct sun. Plant with top of tuber just above soil line. Let clumps grow undisturbed for years. Plants growing in containers bloom best when roots are crowded, plants well fed.

CLOVE PINK. See *Dianthus caryophyllus.*

CLOVER. See *Trifolium.*

CLYTOSTOMA callistegioides *(Bignonia violacea, B. speciosa).* VIOLET TRUMPET VINE. Evergreen. Permanent in Zones 9, 13–24; perennial elsewhere. Tops hardy to 20°F.; roots to 10°F. Strong growing, will clamber over anything by tendrils. Needs support on walls. Extended terminal shoots hang down in curtain effect. Leaves divided into 2 glossy dark green leaflets with wavy margins. Violet lavender or pale purple trumpet flowers 3 in. long and nearly as wide at the top, in sprays at end of shoots, late spring to fall. Full sun or shade, average water. Prune in late winter to discipline growth, prevent tangling. At other times of year, remove unwanted long runners and spent flower spikes.

Clytostoma callistegioides

COARSE-FLOWERED MALLEE. See *Eucalyptus grossa.*

COBAEA scandens. CUP-AND-SAUCER VINE. Tender perennial grown as annual in all zones. Native of Mexico. Extremely vigorous growth to 25 ft. Flowers bell shaped, first greenish, then violet or rose purple; also white-flowered form. Called cup-and-saucer-vine because 2-in.-long cup of petals sits in large green saucerlike calyx. Leaves divided into 2 or 3 pairs of oval, 4-in. leaflets. At ends of leaves are curling tendrils that enable vine to climb rough surfaces without support.

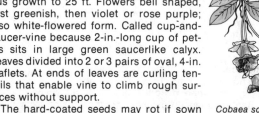
Cobaea scandens

The hard-coated seeds may rot if sown out of doors in cool weather. Start seeds indoors in 4-in. pots; notch seeds with knife and press edgewise into moistened potting mix. Barely cover seed. Keep moist but not wet, and transplant to warm, sunny location when weather warms up. Blooms first year from seed. In mild winters it lives from year to year, eventually reaching more than 40 ft. in length and blooming heavily from May until October. When growing it near the coast, plant out of ocean wind.

COBRA LILY. See *Darlingtonia californica.*

COBWEB HOUSELEEK. See *Sempervivum arachnoideum.*

COCCULUS laurifolius. Evergreen shrub or small tree. Zones 8, 9, 12–24. Native to Himalayas. Slow at first then moderately fast to 25 ft. or more. Can be kept lower by pruning or trained as espalier. Usually multistemmed shrub with arching spreading growth as wide as high. Staked and trained as tree, it takes on umbrella shape. Leaves shiny, leathery, oblong to 6 in., with 3 strongly marked veins running from base to tip. Will grow in sun or dense shade; likes moisture; tolerates many soil types. Useful as screen or background plant.

Cocculus laurifolius

COCKSCOMB. See *Celosia.*

COCKSPUR CORAL TREE. See *Erythrina crista-galli.*

COCKSPUR THORN. See *Crataegus crus-galli.*

COCOS plumosa. See *Arecastrum romanzoffianum.*

CODIAEUM variegatum. CROTON. Green-house or house plant, outdoor annual in Zone 24. Grown principally for coloring of large, leathery, glossy leaves, which may be green, yellow, red, purple, bronze, pink, or almost any combination of these. Leaves may be oval, lance shaped, or very narrow; straight edged or lobed. Dozens of named forms combine these differing features. Can reach 6 ft. or more, but is usually seen as single-stemmed plant 6–24 in. tall. It performs best in a warm, bright, humid greenhouse.

Codiaeum variegatum

COELOGYNE. Epiphytic orchids. Native to the eastern hemisphere. Close to five dozen species varying widely in growth habit, but most are not sold. Grow like cattleyas: regular feeding during the growing season, partial shade. Osmunda, firmly packed, is one of the best potting media for these orchids. To prevent rot, keep water out of new growth where flower cluster forms. Greenhouse plants.

Coelogyne cristata

C. cristata. Probably most popular species in collections. Light green 1–3-in. pseudobulbs topped by 6–9-in. leaves. Large, showy 3–4-in. white flowers with yellow throats; 3–8 pendulous flowers to a stem. Bloom in winter to spring. Can be grown outdoors all winter in mildest climate areas. Keep plant on dry side once growth has matured—October or November—until after flowers have faded. Slight shriveling of pseudobulbs will not be harmful.

COFFEA arabica. COFFEE. House or patio plant (outdoor shrub Zones 21–24). Native to east Africa. The coffee tree of commerce is sold as a handsome container plant for patio, lanai, and large well-lit rooms. Must be protected from frosts.

It's an upright shrub to 15 ft. with evenly spaced tiers of branches, clothed with shining, dark green oval leaves to 6 in. long. Small, ¾-in., white fragrant flowers are clustered near leaf bases. They are followed by ½-in. fruit that start green and finally turn purple or red. Each contains 2 seeds—coffee beans. Grow in container, using same soil mixes and culture as for camellias. Needs shade outdoors.

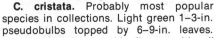
Coffea arabica

COFFEEBERRY. See *Rhamnus californica.*

COFFEE FERN. See *Pellaea andromedifolia.*

COIX lacryma-jobi. JOB'S TEARS. Perennial grass grown as annual in colder climates. A curiosity grown for its ornamental "beads." Loose growing with smooth, prominently jointed stems to 6 ft. Leaves to 2 ft. long, 1½ in. wide, sword shaped. Outside covering of female flower hardens as seed ripens; becomes shining pearly white, gray, or violet bead ¼–1½ in. across. String beads in bracelets, rosaries, other articles. Cut stems for winter arrangements before seeds dry and shatter. Sun or shade; ordinary soil.

COLCHICUM autumnale. MEADOW SAFFRON. Corm. Zones 1–9, 14–24. Mediterranean plant of lily family; sometimes called autumn crocus, but not a true crocus. Shin-

Coix lacryma-jobi

ing, brown-skinned, thick-scaled corms send up clusters of long-tubed, flaring, lavender pink, rose purple, or white flowers to 4 in. across in late summer, whether corms are sitting in dish on window sill or planted in soil. When planted out, broad 6–12-in.-long leaves show in spring and then die long before flower cluster rises from ground. Best planted in sun in average soil where they need not be disturbed oftener than every 3 years or so. Corms available during brief dormant period in July-August.

Colchicum autumnale

The two best varieties are 'The Giant', single lavender, and 'Waterlily', double violet. Plant with tips 3–4 in. under soil surface. To plant in bowls, set upright on 1–2 in. of pebbles, or in special fiber sold for this purpose, and fill with water to base of corm.

COLEONEMA and DIOSMA. BREATH OF HEAVEN. Evergreen shrubs. Zones 7–9, 14–24. Native to South Africa. Filmy and delicate character with slender branches and narrow, heathlike leaves, fragrant when brushed or bruised. Flowers tiny, freely carried over long season in winter and spring, with scattered bloom to be expected at any time. You will find them in nurseries under either name, *Coleonema* or *Diosma.* Actually, your choice amounts to a white or a pink-flowering breath of heaven.

Plant in light soil and full sun. They can take some shade, but are likely to grow rather taller there than expected. Fast drainage is a must. Average water; don't

Coleonema pulchrum

overwater. To control size and promote compactness, shear lightly after main bloom is over. For even more filmy look, thin out some interior stems.

Good on banks or hillsides, along paths where you can break off and bruise a twig to enjoy foliage fragrance. Frequently used next to buildings, though a little wispy for such use.

C. album. (Almost universally sold as either *Diosma reevesii,* or *D. alba.*) WHITE BREATH OF HEAVEN. Grows to 5 ft. or more and as wide. White flowers.

C. pulchrum. PINK BREATH OF HEAVEN, PINK DIOSMA. (Often sold as *Diosma pulchra.*) Grows usually to 5 ft., occasionally to 10 ft. Flowers pink.

Diosma ericoides. BREATH OF HEAVEN. Introduced into California in 1890. However, most plants sold under this name now are *Coleonema album.* Has similar form and white flowers.

COLEUS hybridus (often sold as *C. blumei*). COLEUS. Perennial treated as annual, winter greenhouse or house plant. Native to tropics. Grown for brilliantly colored leaves; blue flower spikes are attractive, but spoil shape of plant and are best pinched out in bud. Leaves may be 3–6 in. long in large-leafed strains (18–24 in. tall); 1–1½ in. long in newer dwarf (12 in.) strains. Colors include green, chartreuse,

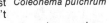
Coleus hybridus

yellow, buff, salmon, orange, red, purple, and brown, often with many colors on single leaf.

Giant Exhibition and Oriental Splendor are large-leafed strains. Carefree is dwarf, self-branching, and its 1–1½-in. leaves are deeply lobed and ruffled. Salicifolius has crowded, long narrow leaves resembling foot-high feather duster. Named cutting-grown varieties exist, but most plants are grown from seed.

Useful for summer borders and as outdoor/indoor container and hanging basket plants. Plant from flats or pots in spring. Easy from seed sown indoors or, with protection, out of doors in warm weather. Easy from cuttings, which root in water as well as other rooting media. Best in strong, indirect light or thin shade—color less vivid in too much shade or too much sun.

(Continued on next page)

Needs warmth, rich, loose well-drained soil, ample water. Feed regularly with high-nitrogen fertilizer. Pinch stems repeatedly to encourage branching and compact habit; remove flower buds to keep plant growing vigorously.

COLLARDS. See Kale.

COLLINSIA heterophylla *(C. bicolor).* CHINESE HOUSES. Annual. Native to California. Rather uncommon spring to early summer blooming plant with snapdragon-like flowers to 1 in. long, held in tiers at top of 1–2-ft.-tall, somewhat hairy stems; upper lip of flower white, lower one rose or violet. Leaves oblong, to 2 in. long. Gives light, dainty effect in front of borders, scattered under deciduous trees, or as ground cover for bulbs. Sow seed in place in fall or spring in rich, moist soil. Self-sows under favorable conditions.

Collinsia heterophylla

COLOCASIA esculenta *(Caladium esculentum).* TARO, ELEPHANT'S EAR. Perennial with tuberous roots. Evergreen only in Zones 23, 24 (tops freeze at 30°F.); grows as herbaceous perennial in Zones 13, 16–22 where tubers may be left in ground; in Zones 1–12, 14, 15, grow in containers or lift and store tubers over winter. Native to tropical Asia and Polynesia. Fast growing to 6 ft. Mammoth, heart shaped, gray green leaves add lush effect to any tropical planting within one season. Flowers resembling giant callas, seldom seen. Effective with tree ferns, araliads, ginger, strelitzia. Handsome in large tub, raised beds. Useful near swimming pools.

Thrives in warm filtered shade with protection from wind, which tears leaves. Plant tubers in spring in rich moist soil. Give lots of water, feed lightly once a month in growing season.

Colocasia esculenta

COLONIAL BENT. See *Agrostis tenuis.*

COLORADO REDTWIG. See *Cornus stolonifera coloradensis.*

COLUMBINE. See *Aquilegia.*

COLUMNEA. House plants. Some shrubby, but most arching or trailing with attractive foliage and showy flowers in shades of red, orange, and yellow. Related to African violets though they don't look it; but do require similar care although they prefer slightly cooler temperatures and aren't as touchy about water. Paired, shiny leaves; flowers are long tubes with flared mouths.

There are many named varieties, all good looking, and many species from Central and South America. Easiest to find is:

C. 'Stavanger'. NORSE FIRE PLANT. Trailing stems can reach several feet if plant is grown in hanging basket. Neat pairs of rounded, shiny leaves, ½ inch across; 3–4-in.-long red flowers.

Columnea 'Stavanger'

COMAROSTAPHYLIS diversifolia. SUMMER HOLLY. Evergreen shrub or small tree. Zones 7–9, 14–24. Native to coastal southern California and Baja California. It's handsome, deserves to be used more. Related to manzanita. Rather formal growth to 6 ft. as shrub, 18 ft. as small tree. Gray bark.

Comarostaphylis diversifolia

Leathery 1–3-in.-long leaves, shiny dark green above, white hairy beneath, margins inrolled. (Variety *planifolia* has flat leaves.) Small, white manzanitalike flowers in April-May, followed by clusters of red, warty berries similar to those of madrone. Adaptable to many situations, but grows best in half shade with some moisture, good drainage.

Comarostaphylis diversifolia

COMFREY. See *Symphytum officinale.*

COMPASS BARREL CACTUS. See *Ferocactus acanthodes.*

CONFEDERATE ROSE. See *Hibiscus mutabilis.*

CONSOLIDA ambigua *(Delphinium ajacis).* LARKSPUR, ANNUAL DELPHINIUM. All Zones. Native to southern Europe. Upright, 1–5 ft. tall, with deeply cut leaves, spikes densely set with 1–1½-in.-wide flowers (most are double) in white and shades of blue, lilac, pink, rose, salmon, carmine, and blue-and-white bicolor. Best bloom in cooler spring and early summer months. Giant Imperial strain, many 4–5-ft. vertical stalks compactly placed. Regal strain, 4–5 ft., base-branching stems, large flowers similar to perennial delphiniums, in thick spikes. Super Imperial strain, base branching; large flowers in 18-in., cone shaped spikes. Steeplechase, base branching, biggest double flowers, 4–5-ft. spikes; heat resistant. Sow seed where plants are to grow; fall planting is best except in heavy, slow draining soils. Cover seed with ⅛ in. soil; thin plants to avoid crowding, get maximum flower size.

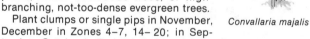

Consolida ambigua

CONVALLARIA majalis. LILY-OF-THE-VALLEY. Perennial grown from pip (upright small rootstock). Zones 1–7, 14–20. Small, fragrant, drooping, waxy, white, bell shaped, spring-blooming flowers on 6–8-in. stems rising above 2 broad basal leaves. Ground cover in partial shade; carpet between camellias, rhododendrons, pieris, under deciduous trees, or high-branching, not-too-dense evergreen trees.

Plant clumps or single pips in November, December in Zones 4–7, 14–20; in September, October in Zones 1–3. Give rich soil with ample humus. Average water. Set clumps 1–2 ft. apart, single pips 4–5 in. apart, 1½ in. deep. Cover yearly with leaf mold, peat moss, or ground bark. Large, prechilled forcing pips, available in December, January (even in mild-climate areas) can be potted for bloom indoors. After bloom, plunge pots in ground in cool shaded area. When dormant, either remove plants from pots and plant in garden, or wash soil off pips, place in plastic bags, and store in vegetable compartment of refrigerator until December or January; at this time, either pot (as before, for bloom indoors), or plant out in permanent spot in garden.

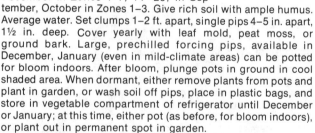

Convallaria majalis

CONVOLVULUS. Evergreen shrub, evergreen perennial, and annual. All have funnel shaped flowers much like morning glories. In fact, common vining morning glories *(Ipomoea)* are sometimes sold as *Convolvulus.*

C. cneorum. BUSH MORNING GLORY. Evergreen shrub. Marginal Zones 5, 6; best Zones 7–9, 12–24. Native to southern Europe. Rapid growing to 2–4 ft. and as wide. Smooth-as-silk, silvery gray, lance shaped leaves 1–2½ in. long. White or pink-

Convolvulus cneorum

tinted morning glories with yellow throats open from pink buds, May-September. Compact and fully flowered if grown in full sun; looser habit with flowers more closed in light shade. Give it light soil and fast drainage. Avoid planting where it will get frequent sprinklings. Prune severely to renew plant; can get leggy if left alone. Fire retardant if flourishing.

C. mauritanicus. GROUND MORNING GLORY. Evergreen perennial. Zones 4–9, 12–24. Native to Africa. Grows 1–2 ft. high with branches trailing to 3 ft. or more wide. Soft, hairy, gray green roundish leaves ½–1½ in. long. Flowers lavender blue, 1–2 in. wide, June-November. Grows well in light gravelly soil with good drainage, but will take clay soil if not over watered. Full sun. Tends to become woody; prevent by trimming in late winter. Use on dry banks as ground cover (plant 3 ft. apart), or group with helianthemum or cerastium.

C. tricolor. DWARF MORNING GLORY. Summer annual. Native to southern Europe. Bushy, branching, somewhat trailing plants to 1 ft. high and 2 ft. wide. Small, narrow leaves. Flowers, 1½ in. across, variable in color but usually blue with yellow throat. Nick tough seed coats with knife and plant in place when soil has warmed up. Needs sun and warmth; blooms best when kept on dry side. Use as edging, against low trellis, or at top of wall.

COPPER LEAF. See *Acalypha wilkesiana*.

COPROSMA. Evergreen shrubs. Native to New Zealand. Drought tolerant once established.

C. 'Coppershine'. Zones 8, 9, 14–17, 21–24. Rounded shrub to 6 ft. with equal spread; fast growing while young. Leaves 1–1¾ in. long, half as wide, leathery, polished bright green heavily shaded coppery brown; new growth even more heavily tinted, and entire plant bright copper in winter. Good medium-sized hedge, screen.

C. kirkii. Zones 8, 9, 14–17, 21–24. Spreading shrub to 2–3-ft. high or nearly prostrate, with long, straight stems slanting outward from base. Leaves, closely set on stems, are yellow green, small, narrow (½–1 in. long). Tolerant of sun or partial shade, and grows in wide range of soils. Prune regularly to keep plants dense. Tough, medium-height ground cover or bank cover. Tolerates sea wind, salt spray. Will control erosion.

Coprosma repens

C. pumila. Zones 8, 9, 14–24. Spreading, mounding shrub to 2–2½ ft. tall, eventually 8 ft. wide. Leaves bright shining green, roundish oval, to ¾ in. long. Plant 2–2½ ft. apart for ground cover in 3 years. Prune out upwardly growing branches. Tolerates most soils, much drought or heavy watering. 'Verde Vista' is best cutting-grown selection.

C. repens *(C. baueri)*. MIRROR PLANT. Zones 15–17, 21–24. Rapid growth to 10 ft. with 6-ft. spread. Open, straggly shrub if neglected but beautiful plant when cared for. You can't imagine shinier, glossier leaves: they're dark to light green, 3 in. long, oval or oblong. Inconspicuous greenish or white flowers often followed by small yellow or orange fruit. Variety 'Variegata' has leaves blotched with yellowish green. Variety 'Argentea' is blotched with white.

Two prunings a year will keep it dense and at any height desired. Where shrub receives ocean wind, no pruning necessary. Except in beach areas, give it part shade; water generously. Use as hedge, screen, wall shrub, informal espalier.

CORAL BELLS. See *Heuchera sanguinea*.

CORAL BERRY. See *Symphoricarpos orbiculatus*.

CORAL GUM. See *Eucalyptus torquata*.

CORAL TREE. See *Erythrina*.

CORAL VINE. See *Antigonon leptopus*.

CORDYLINE. Evergreen palmlike shrubs or trees. (Often sold as *Dracaena;* for true *Dracaena,* see that entry.) Woody plants with swordlike leaves, related to yuccas and agaves, but usually ranked with palms in nurseries and in landscape. Like moisture. Good next to swimming pools.

C. australis *(Dracaena australis)*. Zones 5, 8–11, 14–24. In youth, fountain of 3-ft.-long, narrow (2–5 in. wide), swordlike leaves. Upper leaves erect; lower leaves arch and droop. In maturity, 20–30-ft. tree, branching high on trunk, rather stiff like Joshua tree. Fragrant tiny ¼-in. flowers in late spring are carried in long, branching clusters.

Cordyline australis

For more graceful plant, cut back when young to force multiple trunks. Or plant in clumps of 6–8. Cut a few each year back to ground until all develop multiple trunks. Hardiest of cordylines, to 15°F. or lower. Takes almost any soil but grows fastest in soil deep enough for big carrotlike root. Drought tolerant. Used for tropical effects; with boulders and gravel for desert look; patio or terrace where there's room for its strong character. Useful near seashore.

C. a. 'Atropurpurea'. BRONZE DRACAENA. Like the above, but with bronzy red foliage. Slower growth. Combine with gray or warm yellowish green to bring out color.

C. indivisa. BLUE DRACAENA. Zones 16, 17, 20–24. Trunk to 25 ft., topped with crown of rather stiff, huge (6 ft. long, 6 in. wide) leaves. White flowers in 4-ft.-long clusters. Plant in groups of varying heights. Hardy to 26° F. Tolerates drought and seaside conditions.

C. stricta. Zones 16, 17, 20–24. Slender stems clustered at base or branching low with branches quite erect. Swordlike 2-ft.-long leaves are dark green with hint of purple. Lavender flowers in large branched clusters, very decorative in spring. Will grow to 15 ft., but can be kept lower by cutting tall canes to ground. New canes replace them. Stick long cuttings in ground; will root quickly. Hardy to 26°F. Needs shade except near coast. Takes desert heat with ample water in shade. Fine container plant indoors or out; good for tall tropical-looking background in narrow, shaded areas, in lanais, or in side gardens.

C. terminalis. TI. Outdoors Zones 21–24, house plant elsewhere. Plants are usually started from "logs"—sections of stem imported from Hawaii. Lay short lengths in peat moss-sand mixture, covering about ½ their diameter. Keep moist. When shoots grow out and root, cut them off and pot them. Take ordinary indoor care; tolerate low light intensity. Plant has many named forms with red, yellow, or variegated leaves. White foot-long flower clusters. Outdoors in Hawaii, it's 10-ft. plant with 30-in.-long, 5-in.-wide leaves; usually much smaller when grown indoors. Outdoors in southern California, reaches 6–8 ft. in special locations where soil stays warm and frost does not form.

COREOPSIS. Annuals and perennials. Easily grown members of sunflower family yielding profusion of yellow, orange, maroon, or reddish flowers from late spring to fall. Remove old flowers from all types to prolong bloom. Both annual and perennial kinds are easy to propagate—annuals from seed sown in place (full sun) or in flats, perennials from seed or division of root crown. Tend to self-sow; seeds attract birds. Established plants can thrive on very little water.

Coreposis tinctoria

C. auriculata 'Nana'. Perennial. Evergreen to semievergreen in Zones 17–24; deciduous elsewhere. Makes 5–6-in.-high mat of 2–5-in.-long leaves. Under ideal conditions it will spread by stolons to form 2-ft.-broad clump in a year. Flower heads bright orange yellow, 1–2½ in. wide, rise well above foliage mat. Long and profuse blooming season from spring to fall if you remove flowers as they fade. Best used in foreground of taller plants, in border, or as edging. Can be used in larger areas. Keep faded flowers removed with lawn mower set at 2–3 in.

C. gigantea. Perennial. Zones 16, 17, 21–24. Native to coastal southern California, Baja California. Thick succulent trunks 3 ft. tall (rarely 10 ft.) hold a few branches tipped with clusters of fernlike leaves. Clusters of 3-in. yellow daisies appear in spring. Showy in seaside plant collection; rarely sold in nurseries.

C. grandiflora. COREOPSIS. Perennial. All Zones. One–2 ft. high, spreading to 3 ft. with narrow, dark green 3–5 lobed-leaves. Large bright yellow flowers, 2½–3 in. across, on long slender stems high above foliage, bloom all summer. Variety 'Sunburst' has large, semidouble flowers.

C. lanceolata. COREOPSIS. Perennial. All Zones. One–2 ft. high. Leaves somewhat hairy, narrow, mostly in tuft near base. Flower heads 1½–2 in. across, yellow, on pale green stems. Some lower stem leaves have a few lobes. When well-established will persist year after year. Excellent cut flower.

C. maritima. Perennial. Zones 14–24. Native to coast of southern California. Sometimes called sea dahlia. Grows 1–3 ft. high from tuberous tap root. Stems hollow. Leaves somewhat succulent, divided into very narrow lobes. Clear yellow flower heads 2½–4 inches across on 9–12-in.-long stems, bloom in spring. Borders, naturalizing, striking cut flowers.

C. tinctoria. ANNUAL COREOPSIS, CALLIOPSIS. Annual. All Zones. Slender, upright, 1½–3 ft. tall with wiry stems; much like cosmos in growth habit. Leaves and stems smooth. Flowers similar to perennial coreopsis, in yellow, orange, maroon, bronze, and reddish, banded with contrasting colors; purple brown centers. Dwarf and double varieties. Sow seed in place in full sun and dryish soil.

C. verticillata. Perennial. Zones 14–24. Plant is 2½–3 ft. tall, half as broad. Many erect or slightly leaning stems carry many whorls of finely divided, very narrow leaves. At top are 2-in. bright yellow daisies, freely borne over long summer and autumn season. One of the most tolerant of drought, neglect.

CORIANDER. See *Coriandrum sativum.*

CORIANDRUM sativum. CORIANDER, CHINESE PARSLEY, CILANTRO. Annual herb. All Zones in conditions noted below. Grows 12–15 in. high. Delicate fernlike foliage; flat clusters of pinkish white flowers. Aromatic seeds crushed before use in seasoning sausage, beans, stews, cookies, wines. Young leaves used in salads, soups, poultry recipes, and variety of Mexican and Chinese dishes. Grow in good, well-drained soil, full sun. Start from seed (including coriander seed sold in grocery stores); grows quickly, self-sows.

Coriandrum sativum

CORN. Annual. All Zones in conditions noted below. Sweet corn is the one cereal crop that home gardeners are likely to grow; it requires considerable space, but is still well worth growing. In picked corn, sugar changes to starch very quickly, and only by rushing ears from garden direct to boiling water can you capture full sweetness. Corn needs heat, but suitable early hybrid varieties will grow even in cool-summer areas of Northwest.

Corn is widely adapted but grows best in deep, rich soils; good drainage is important. Give full sun. Sow seed 2 weeks after average date of last frost, and make 3 or 4 more plantings at 2-week intervals; or plant early, midseason, and late varieties. Plant corn in blocks of short rows rather than stringing out single long rows; pollination is by wind, and unless good supply of pollen falls on silks, ears will be poorly filled. Don't plant popcorn near sweet corn; pollen of one kind can affect characteristics of other. For the same reason, some

Sweet Corn

supersweet varieties have to be grown at a distance from other varieties. Plant either in rows 3 ft. apart and thin seedlings to stand 12 in. apart, or plant in "hills" (actually clumps) 3 ft. apart each way. Place 6 or 7 seeds in each hill and thin to 3 strongest plants. Give plants ample water and one feeding when stalks are 7–8 in. tall. Make certain that you apply good deep watering that thoroughly wets entire root zone just as tassel emerges from stalk; repeat again when silk forms. Don't remove suckers that appear. Check carefully when ears are plump and silk has withered; pull back husks and try popping a grain with your thumb. Generally, corn is ready to eat 3 weeks after silks first appear. Kernels should squirt milky juice; watery juice means that corn is immature. Doughy consistency indicates overmaturity. Overage sweet corn is no better than market sweet corn.

Corn earworm is principal insect pest. Control it by spraying or dusting sevin directly on silk clusters when silks first become visible or squirt silks with mixture of 1 teaspoon malathion in ½ pint mineral oil, about ½ teaspoon of it onto each cluster of silks, using medicine dropper or oil can. Make 3–4 applications at 3–4-day intervals.

Ornamental Corn

Ornamental corn. Annual. Some kinds of corn are grown for beauty of shelled ears rather than for eating qualities. Calico, Indian, Squaw, or rainbow corn are among names given to strains which have brightly colored grains—red, brown, blue, gray, black, yellow, or many mixtures of these colors. Grow like sweet corn, but permit ears to get fully ripe; silks will be withered, husks turning straw color, and kernels firm. Cut with 1½ in. of stalk below ear, pull back husks (but leave attached to ears), and dry thoroughly. Grow well away from late sweet corn; pollen can affect flavor of the latter. *Zea mays japonica* includes several kinds of corn grown for ornamental foliage; one occasionally sold is 'Gracilis', a dwarf corn with bright green leaves striped white.

Popcorn. Annual. Grow and harvest popcorn just like ornamental corn described above. When ears are thoroughly dry, rub kernels off cobs and store in dry place. White and yellow popcorn resemble other corn in appearance. Strawberry popcorn, grown either for popping or for its ornamental value, has stubby, fat ears packed with red strawberrylike kernels.

Popcorn

CORNELIAN CHERRY. See *Cornus mas.*

CORNFLOWER. See *Centaurea cyanus.*

CORN PLANT. See *Dracaena fragrans.*

CORNUS. DOGWOOD. Deciduous (except where noted) shrubs or trees (one's a ground cover perennial). All offer attractive foliage and flowers; some are spectacular in fruit and winter bark. Need ample water.

C. alba. TATARIAN DOGWOOD. Shrub. Zones 1–9, 14–24. In cold-winter areas its blood red, bare twigs are colorful against snow. Upright to about 10 ft. high and spreads wide, eventually producing thicket of many stems. Branches densely clothed with 2½–5-in.-long leaves, to 2½ in. wide, deep rich green above, lighter beneath; red in fall. Fragrant, creamy white small flowers in 1–2-in.-wide, flattish clusters in April, May. Bluish white to whitish small fruit. Variety 'Argenteo-marginata' (*C. 'Elegantissima'*) has showy green and white leaves on red stems. Best in shade.

Cornus florida

C. a. 'Sibirica'. SIBERIAN DOGWOOD. Less rampant than species, it grows to about 7 ft. high with 5-ft. spread. Gleaming coral red branches in winter. Tolerates shade.

With both plants, new wood is brightest, so cut back in spring to force new growth.

C. alternifolia. PAGODA DOGWOOD. Shrub or small tree. Zones 1–6. Multitrunked, to 20 ft. high with strong horizontal branching pattern for winter silhouette. Light green leaves turn red in fall. Small, clustered creamy flowers in spring are not showy. Blue black fruit follow. Tolerates shade.

C. canadensis. BUNCHBERRY. Deciduous carpet plant. Zones 1–7. Difficult but possible in Zones 8, 9, 14–16. Native northern California to Alaska and eastward. It's difficult to believe this 6–9-in. perennial is related to dogwoods when you see it under trees by lakes and streams in Northwest. Creeping rootstocks send up stems topped by whorls of 4–6 oval or roundish, 1–2-in.-long leaves; deep rich green, they turn yellow in fall, die down in winter.

Flowers in May or June—small, compact cluster of tiny flowers surrounded by usually 4 oval, ½–¾-in.-long, pure white bracts. Clusters of small, shiny, bright red fruit in August and September.

For cool, moist climates, in acid soil with generous amounts of humus or rotten wood. Considered hard to establish, but when transplanted with piece of rotten log with bark attached, it establishes readily.

C. capitata. EVERGREEN DOGWOOD. Big shrub or small tree. Zones 8, 9, 14–20. From Himalayas. Hardy to 15°F. Not reliably evergreen in cold weather. Often in mild winters it loses half its leaves. Moderate growth to 20–30 ft. high and eventually an equal spread. Green to grayish green, 2–4-in.-long by ¾–1¾ in.-wide leaves; some turn red or purplish in fall.

Unless grown from cuttings trees don't flower until about 8 or 10 years old, but when they do they are delightful. Small flower cluster is surrounded by 4–6 creamy to pale yellow, 1½–2-in.-long bracts in May and June. Large, fleshy, reddish purple fruit in October and November can be litter problem. Birds may clean up some fruit.

C. controversa. GIANT DOGWOOD. Tree. Zones 3–9, 14, 18, 19. From the Orient. Hardy to 5°F. Leaves, flowers, and fruit like big shrubby dogwoods, but grows rapidly into magnificent 40–60-ft. tree with picturesque horizontal branches; luxuriant 3–6-in.-long oval leaves, 2–3 in. wide, are dark green above, silvery green beneath; glowing red in fall. Creamy white flowers are not spectacular, but so abundant in May they give good show. They form in fluffy, flattish clusters 3–7 in. wide. Shiny, bluish black, ½-in.-wide fruit ripen in August and September; enjoyed by birds.

Locate plants in full sun for most flowers and best autumn color. Keep soil moist.

C. 'Eddie's White Wonder'. Tree. Zones 2–9, 14–20. Hybrid between *C. florida* and *C. nuttallii;* taller, more erect than former, twiggier than latter. Blooms May, with 4 or 5-bracted flower clusters. Easier to transplant than western native *C. nuttallii*.

C. florida. FLOWERING DOGWOOD, EASTERN DOGWOOD. Tree. Zones 1–9, 14–16. Sometimes succeeds in southern California if given azalea conditions. Native to eastern U.S. To 20 ft. high. Most commonly planted of flowering dogwoods in Northwest and mountain areas where it's easy to grow and much a part of spring flower display. Generally performs best in high shade; screen from western sun.

In form, it somewhat resembles our western native, *C. nuttallii*, with its horizontal branching pattern. But gray twigs at branch ends tend to be upright. It usually has shorter trunk. Small flower clusters are surrounded by 4 roundish, 2–4-in.-wide, white bracts with notched tips. Flowers almost cover tree in May before leaves expand. Oval, 2–6-in.-long by 2½-in.-wide leaves bright green above, lighter beneath; turn glowing red before they fall. Clusters of small oval scarlet fruit last into winter or until birds eat them.

C. f. 'Cherokee Chief'. Deep rosy red flower bracts that are paler at base.

C. f. 'Cherokee Princess'. Gives unusually heavy display of white blooms.

C. f. 'Cloud Nine'. Blooms young and heavily. Tolerates south-

ern California heat and lack of winter chill better than other varieties. Blooms better in cold climates than other kinds of *C. florida*.

C. f. 'Pendula'. Drooping branches give it weeping look.

C. f. 'Rainbow'. Leaves strongly marked bright yellow on green. Heavy bloomer, large bracts.

C. f. 'Rubra'. Long-time favorite for its pink or rose flower bracts.

C. f. 'Welchii'. TRICOLOR DOGWOOD. Best known for its variegated, 4-in.-long leaves of creamy white, pink, deep rose, and green throughout spring and summer; turn deep rose to almost red in fall. Rather inconspicuous pinkish to white flower bracts are not profuse. Does best with some shade.

C. kousa. KOUSA DOGWOOD. Big shrub or small tree. Zones 3–9, 14, 15, 18, 19. Native to Japan and Korea. Later blooming than other flowering dogwoods—in June and July. Big multistemmed shrub, or (with training) small tree to 20 ft. or higher. Delicate limb structure and spreading, dense horizontal growth habit. Lustrous, medium green leaves, 4 in. long, have rusty brown hairs at base of veins on undersurface. Yellow and scarlet fall color.

Flowers along tops of branches show above leaves. Creamy white, slender-pointed, 2–3-in.-long, rather narrow bracts surround flower cluster; turn pink along edges. In October, red fruit hang below branches like big strawberries.

Cornus kousa

C. k. chinensis. Native to China, has larger leaves and larger flower bracts.

C. mas. CORNELIAN CHERRY. Shrub or tree. Zones 1–6. Native to southern Europe and Orient. One of earliest dogwoods to bloom, it shows mass of clustered small yellow blossoms on bare twigs in February and March. It's usually an airy, twiggy shrub but can be trained as 15–20-ft. small tree. Oval leaves, 2–4 in. long, shiny green turning to yellow; some forms turn red in fall. Autumn color is enhanced by clusters of bright scarlet, ¾-in.-long fruit which hang on from September until birds get them. Fruit edible; is used in making preserves. Withstands sub-zero temperatures. Tolerates alkaline soils.

C. nuttallii. PACIFIC DOGWOOD, WESTERN DOGWOOD. Tree. Zones 2–9, 14–20. Native to Pacific Northwest and northern California. One of our most spectacular natives when it wears its gleaming white flower bracts on bare branches in April or May. Often there's a second flowering with leaves in September. Unfortunately, it's not as easy to grow in gardens as Eastern dogwood *(C. florida)*. It reacts unfavorably to routine garden watering, fertilizing, pruning. Injury to its tender bark provides entrance for insects and diseases. But if you give plants exceptionally good drainage, infrequent summer watering, and plant under high-branching trees so bark will not sunburn, you have a chance of success.

Where adapted, this tree will grow to 50 ft. or more high with 20-ft. spread. It may grow one trunk or several. Gray-barked branches grow in pleasing horizontal pattern, attractive in winter. Oval, 3–5-in.-long leaves are rich green above, grayish green beneath; they turn to beautiful yellows, pinks, and reds in fall. The 4–8 flower bracts are 2–3 in. long, roundish, rounded or pointed, white or tinged with pink. Decorative red to orange red fruit in buttonlike clusters form in fall.

C. n. 'Colrigo Giant' (often sold as 'Corigo Giant'). Low-branching but erect habit, vigorous, heavy trunked, with profusion of 6-in. flower heads. Named for Columbia River Gorge, where parent plant was found.

C. n. 'Goldspot'. Leaves splashed with creamy yellow. Flowers when only 2 ft. tall. Bracts are larger than species. Long, 2-month flowering season, often with some fall bloom.

C. sanguinea. BLOODTWIG DOGWOOD. Shrub. Zones 1–7. Big show comes in fall with dark blood red foliage, and in winter with purplish to dark red bare twigs and branches. Prune severely in spring to produce new branches and twigs for winter color. Grows as big multistemmed shrub to 12 ft. high, about 8 ft. wide. Dark green leaves 1½–3 in. long. June flowers are greenish white in 2-in.-wide clusters. Black fruit.

C. stolonifera (*C. sericea*). REDTWIG DOGWOOD. RED-OSIER DOGWOOD. Shrub. Zones 1–9, 14–21. Native to moist places, northern California to Alaska and eastward. Another dogwood with brilliant show of red fall color and bright red winter twigs. Not only thrives in coldest mountain areas of West, but throughout California—even intermediate valleys of southern California if given frequent watering. Grows rapidly as big multistemmed shrub to 15 ft. or more high. Spreads widely by creeping underground stems and rooting branches. Tolerates shade. To control, cut off with a spade roots that have gone too far. Cut off branches that touch ground. Small creamy white flowers in 2-in.-wide clusters appear among leaves (oval, 1½–2½ in. long, fresh deep green) throughout summer and into fall. Fruit are white or bluish.

C. s. baileyi. Grows 6–8 ft. tall; exceptionally bright red twigs in winter. *C. s. coloradensis,* COLORADO REDTWIG, is shorter (5–6 ft.) and twigs are not so bright a red.

C. s. 'Flaviramea'. YELLOWTWIG DOGWOOD. Has yellow twigs and branches.

C. s. 'Kelseyi' (*C. s. 'Nana'*). Dwarf seldom over 18 in. tall. Bright red stems.

COROKIA cotoneaster. Evergreen shrub. Zones 4–24. Native to New Zealand. Slow growing to 10 ft., but usually seen as 2-4 ft. plant in container. Intricate branch pattern made up of many slim, contorted, interlaced, nearly black branches. Sparse foliage; leaves ¾ in. long, dark glossy green above, white underneath. Tiny starlike ½-in. yellow flowers in spring followed by small orange fruit (on older plants). Sun or part shade, average water. Tolerates alkaline soil, seaside conditions. Thrives in container with fast draining mix. Night lighting from beneath emphasizes bizarre quality of branch pattern.

Corokia cotoneaster

CORONILLA varia. CROWN VETCH. Perennial. All Zones. Relative to peas, beans, and clovers. Creeping roots and rhizomes make it tenacious ground cover with straggling stems to 2 ft. Leaves made up of 11–25 oval leaflets ½–¾ in. long. Lavender pink flowers in 1-in. clusters soon become bundles of brown, slender, fingerlike seedpods. Goes dormant and looks ratty during coldest weather. Tolerates shade; thrives in full sun. In spring, mow it, feed and water several times, and it will make lush green summer cover. Too invasive and rank for flower beds. Use for covering cut banks and remote places, controlling erosion. Once established, difficult to eliminate. Variety 'Penngift' is widely sold in cold-winter climates.

Coronilla varia

CORREA. AUSTRALIAN FUCHSIA. Evergreen shrubs. Successful in Zones 5, 6 when winters aren't too cold (hardy to about 20°F.); generally successful Zones 14–24. Flower form may suggest fuchsia, but in all other ways *Correa* are far from fuchsialike. Low to medium height, usually dense and spreading. Leaves small (to 1 in.), roundish, densely felted underneath, and give gray or gray green effect that contrasts subtly with other grays and distinctly with dark greens. All (except summer-flowering *C. alba*) are valued for their long winter-flowering season, normally from November-April. Flowers small, ½–¾ in., individually handsome but not showy; hang down along branches like small bells.

Correa pulchella

Must have fast draining soil. Do well in poor, even rocky soil. Easy to kill with kindness—overwatering and overfeeding.

Use as ground covers on banks or slopes. Attractive in large containers placed where flowers can be enjoyed close up. Generally thought to do best in full sun in coastal areas, partial shade inland, but many can be seen in full sun, all climates. Should not get reflected heat from wall or paving.

C. alba. To 4 ft. with arching branches. White flowers bloom in summer.

C. backhousiana. (Often sold as *C. magnifica.*) More successful in southern California than *C. pulchella.* Growth habit upright and rather sprawling to 4–5 ft. and as wide. Flowers chartreuse.

C. harrisii. To 2½ ft. high and more compact than other correas. Flowers beautiful clear red.

C. pulchella. Most widely grown correa in northern California. To 2–2½ ft. high and spreads to as much as 8 ft. Leaves green above, gray green below. Light pink flowers.

CORTADERIA selloana. PAMPAS GRASS. Evergreen giant ornamental grass. Zones 4–24. Root hardy but deciduous in Zones 2–3. Native to Argentina. Very fast growing in rich soil in mild climates; from gallon can size to 8 ft. in one season. Established, may reach 20 ft. in height. A fountain of saw toothed, grassy leaves above which, in late summer, rise long stalks bearing white to chamois or pink 1–3-ft. flower plumes.

Cortaderia selloana

Will grow in any soil from driest to wettest, acid to alkaline. Takes hot dry winds of deserts and fog winds of coast. Its willingness to grow under rough conditions gives it value in large bank planting and as first line of defense in wide windbreak. But sheer bulk of plant can become problem in small gardens, and it's not easy to reduce in size. Roots and stems are tough and woody, and leaf edges are like sharp saws. One way to keep it under control is to burn it to the ground periodically.

Note: A similar grass, *C. jubata,* can become serious weed in areas where winters are mild. It seeds itself freely and resists summer drought well enough to crowd out many native plants. It looks enough like pampas grass to tempt amateur flower arrangers to gather plumes; seeds from these might establish plants in the neighborhood. Best bet is to grub out volunteer pampas grass seedlings as soon as they appear.

CORYDALIS. Perennials. Zones 4–9, 14–24. Handsome clumps of dainty divided leaves similar to bleeding heart (to which it is closely related) or maidenhair fern. Clusters of small spurred flowers, usually yellow. Plant in partial shade, rich moist soil. Effective in rock crevices, in open woodland, near pool or streamside. Combine with ferns, columbine, bleeding heart, primroses. Divide clumps or sow seeds in spring or fall. Plants self-sow in garden.

Corydalis lutea

C. cheilanthifolia. Hardy Chinese native, 8-10 in. high with fernlike green foliage. Clusters of yellow, ½-in.-long flowers in May and June.

C. lutea. Native to southern Europe. To 15 in. tall. Masses of gray green foliage on many stems. Golden yellow, ¾-in.-long, short-spurred flowers throughout summer.

CORYLOPSIS. WINTER HAZEL. Deciduous shrubs. Zones 4–7, 15–17. Valued for show of soft yellow, fragrant flowers that come on bare branches in March or earlier. New leaves that follow bloom are often tinged pink, then bright green; roundish, somewhat resembling hazelnut (filbert) leaves. Slow growing to 8–10 ft. and as wide. Make rather open structure with attractive delicate branching pattern.

Plant in sheltered location in sun or par-

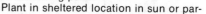

Corylopsis spicata

tial shade. Average water. Need same type soil as rhododendrons. Use in shrub border, edge of woodland.

C. pauciflora. BUTTERCUP WINTER HAZEL. Flowers are primrose yellow, ¾ in., bell shaped, in drooping clusters of 2 or 3. Leaves 1–3 in. long, with sharply toothed edges.

C. spicata. SPIKE WINTER HAZEL. Flowers are pale yellow, ½ in., bell shaped in 1½-in.-long drooping clusters of 6–12. Leaves to 4 in. long with toothed edges.

CORYLUS. FILBERT, HAZELNUT. Deciduous shrubs or small trees. Zones 1–9, 14–20. Although mostly thought of as producing edible nuts (see Filbert) the following types are grown as ornamentals; one is western native. Average water unless noted otherwise below.

C. avellana. EUROPEAN FILBERT. Not as widely grown as its two varieties described below; shrub 10–15 ft. high and as wide. Leaves broad, roundish, 3–4 in. long; turn yellow in fall. Ornamental greenish yellow male flower catkins hang on all winter, turn yellow in earliest spring before leaves appear. Roundish nuts of good flavor enclosed by 2 irregularly lobed bracts.

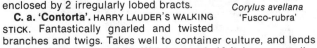

Corylus avellana
'Fusco-rubra'

C. a. 'Contorta'. HARRY LAUDER'S WALKING STICK. Fantastically gnarled and twisted branches and twigs. Takes well to container culture, and lends itself to display as curiosity. Will grow to 8–10 ft. Leaves smaller than species.

C. a. 'Fusco-rubra' (*C. a.* 'Atropurpurea'). Identical to species except for its handsome purple leaf color.

C. cornuta californica. WESTERN HAZELNUT. Native to damp slopes below 7,000 ft. elevation, north Coast Range and Sierra Nevada of California, north to B.C. Grows as open, spreading multistemmed shrub 5–12 ft. high. Roundish, somewhat hairy leaves, 1½–3 in. long, with coarsely toothed edges; turn bright yellow in fall. Like *C. avellana,* male flower catkins decorative. Nuts small, kernel flavorful; enveloped in leafy husk with long drawn-out beak.

C. maxima. See *Filbert.*

C. m. 'Purpurea'. Makes handsome, well-structured, small tree to 20 ft., or suckering shrub to 12–15 ft. Roundish leaves 2–6 in. long, dark purple in spring and summer. Burns quite badly in southern California hot-summer areas.

CORYNOCARPUS laevigata. NEW ZEALAND LAUREL. Evergreen shrub or small tree. Good in Zones 16, 23; best in Zones 17, 24. Handsome, upright, growing 20–40 ft. high. Beautiful dark green, very glossy, leathery leaves, oblong to 7 in. by 2 in. wide. Flowers noticeable but of no importance—tiny, whitish, in 3–8-in.-long upright clusters. Fruit orange, oblong, 1 in. long, extremely poisonous.

Easy to grow in sun or part shade. Requires moist conditions. Good in containers. Slow growing; keeps attractive form for years. Use as screen or large hedge, background. Good in sheltered areas, entryways, under overhangs.

Corynocarpus laevigata

CORYPHANTHA vivipara. (Usually sold as *Mammillaria vivipara.*) Little cactus. All Zones. Native Alberta to north Texas. Has single or clustered globular, 2-in. bodies covered with little knobs which bear white spines. Flowers purple, showy, to 2 in. long. One of hardiest forms of cactus, taking temperatures far below zero. Grow plant in full sun; it will tolerate much to little water in growing season.

Coryphantha vivipara

COSMOS. Annuals. All Zones in conditions noted below. Native to tropical America, mostly Mexico. Showy summer and fall-blooming plants, open and branching in habit, with bright green divided leaves and daisylike flowers in many colors and forms (single, double, crested, and frilled). Heights vary from 2½–8 ft. Give mass color in borders, background, or as filler among shrubs. Useful in arrangements if flowers are cut when freshly opened and placed immediately in deep cool water. Sow seed in open ground from spring to summer, or set out transplants from flats. Plant in full sun in not too rich soil. Drought resistant. Self-sow freely, attract birds.

Cosmos bipinnatus

C. bipinnatus. Flowers in white and shades of pink, rose, lavender, purple, or crimson, with tufted yellow centers. Heights up to 8 ft. Modern improved cosmos include Sensation strain, 3–6 ft. tall and earlier to come into bloom than old-fashioned tall kinds. Sensation varieties are 'Dazzler' (crimson) and 'Radiance' (rose with red center); white and pink are also available. 'Candystripe' has smaller (3 in.) white and rose flowers; blooms even earlier on smaller plants.

C. sulphureus. YELLOW COSMOS. Grows to 7 ft., with yellow or golden yellow flowers with yellow centers. Tends to become weedy looking at end of season. Klondike strain is earlier blooming, semidwarf (2–3 ft. tall), floriferous. Semidouble flower heads are 2 in. across. Colors range from yellow to bright red. Dwarf Klondike strain is only 18 in. tall.

COSTA RICAN HOLLY. See *Olmediella betschlerana.*

COSTA RICAN NIGHTSHADE. See *Solanum wendlandii.*

COSTMARY. See *Chrysanthemum balsamita.*

COTINUS coggygria (*Rhus cotinus*). SMOKE TREE. Deciduous tree. All Zones, especially valuable in 1–3, 10, 11. (For another smoke tree, see *Dalea spinosa.*) Unusual shrub tree creating broad, urn shaped mass usually as wide as high—eventually to 25 ft. Roundish leaves 1½–3 in. long, bluish green in summer; turn yellow to orange red in fall. Dramatic puffs of purple to lavender "smoke" come from large, loose clusters of fading flowers. As tiny greenish blossoms fade, stalks of sterile flowers elongate and become clothed with purple fuzzy hairs. Grow in full sun.

Cotinus coggygria

C. c. 'Purpureus' has purple leaves which gradually turn to green, and richer purple smoke puffs. *C. c.* 'Royal Purple' retains purple leaves through the summer.

At its best under stress in poor or rocky soil. When grown in highly cultivated gardens, must have fast drainage and infrequent watering to avoid root rot. Resistant to oak root fungus.

COTONEASTER. Evergreen, semideciduous, and deciduous shrubs. They range from ground covers to stiffly upright, small shrubs, to tall-growing (20 ft.) shrubs of fountainlike growth with graceful arching branches. All grow vigorously and thrive with little or no maintenance. In fact they look better and produce better crops of fall and winter berries if planted on dry slopes—where they will control erosion—or in poor soil rather than rich moist garden soil. All do best in full sun. Spring bloom; flowers white or pinkish, resembling tiny single roses, pretty because of their abundance but not showy.

Cotoneaster lacteus

(Continued on page 258)

Cotoneaster

SPECIES OR VARIETY	HARDINESS	SIZE, HABIT	LEAVES	FRUIT	USES, COMMENTS
Cotoneaster acutifolius PEKING COTONEASTER	Deciduous. All Zones, best 1–3.	To 10 ft. tall, nearly as wide.	Glossy green when mature, 1–2 in. long. Turn orange red in fall.	Black, ⅜ in. long.	Useful as 10 ft. screen or 3–5 ft. hedge in coldest, most difficult climates. Tolerates part shade.
C. adpressus CREEPING COTONEASTER	Deciduous. All Zones.	Slow growing, eventually to 1 ft. with 6-ft. spread.	Dark green, nearly smooth, to ½ in. long. Reddish fall color.	Good show of ¼-in. bright red fruit.	Bank or ground cover. Will follow contours of ground or rocks, drape down wall. Tolerates part shade.
C. a. praecox (C. praecox)	Deciduous. All Zones.	More vigorous than species; to 1–1½ ft. high and spreading.	Oval, to 1 in. long, with wavy margins. Maroon red fall color.	Fruit larger than species—to ½ in., bright red.	Same as C. adpressus.
C. apiculatus CRANBERRY COTONEASTER	Deciduous. All Zones.	To 4 ft. high and spreading wider. Growth similar to C. horizontalis.	Roundish, less than ½ in. long, shiny bright green above. Maroon red fall color.	Large (cranberry-sized) bright red fruit in clusters.	Hedge, background. Berries color early, hold long. 'Nana' is dwarf form—very attractive in rock gardens and mound plantings. 'Tom Thumb' even smaller (to 4–5 in. tall). Tolerates part shade.
C. buxifolius (Often sold as C. glaucophylla, C. pannosa, or C. pannosa nana)	Semi-evergreen or evergreen. Zones 4–24.	1–2 ft. and spreading or to 6 ft. and stiffly arching.	Tiny, oval, dull green above, with white or tan fuzz underneath. Overall look gray.	Deep, bright red fruit borne singly on short branch-lets.	Mislabeled in nursery trade. Taller plants sold as C. glaucophyllus, shorter as C. pannosa nana. Good contrast with dark green.
C. congestus (C. microphylla glacialis)	Evergreen. Zones 2–24.	Grows 8 in. a year to an eventual 3 ft.; dense, rounded form with branches curving downward.	Small (⅓ in.), rounded, dark green above, whitish underneath.	Fruit small (¼ in.), bright red.	Rock hugging, attractive in containers, foreground. Equally good Zone 2 and desert. 'Likiang' is especially fine variety.
C. conspicuus WINTERGREEN COTONEASTER	Evergreen. Zones 3–24.	Arching branches. Resembles C. microphyllus but taller, to 4–6 ft.	Small (¼ in.), oval, narrow, dark green above, paler below.	Bright red ⅜-in. fruit in profusion.	Not much grown; its variety (below) widely grown.
C. c. decorus NECKLACE COTONEASTER	Evergreen. Zones 3–24.	Almost pros-trate. Grows with short rigid branches from main stems.	Same as C. conspicuus.	Same as C. conspicuus.	Ground cover, containers, rock gardens.
C. dammeri (C. humifusus) BEARBERRY COTONEASTER	Evergreen. All Zones.	Prostrate branches to 10 ft. long, 3–6 in. tall; branches root freely, grow fast.	Oval, 1 in. long, bright green above, whitish below. C. dammeri radicans has blunt, often notched leaves.	Fruit ½ in. across, brilliant red, showy.	Ground cover in sun or part shade, cascades over wall or rocks. 'Coral Beauty' has coral fruit, 'Royal Beauty' deep red fruit. 'Skogsholmen' is a little taller (12–18 in.), looser in growth habit, faster (2 ft. a year spread), a little stiffer in branching, hardy Zones 3–24. See 'Lowfast' for another fast, lower growing (to 12 in.) ground cover for Zones 4–24.
C. divaricatus SPREADING COTONEASTER	Deciduous. All Zones.	To 6 ft. high with many stiff branches spreading out from center.	Oval, ¾ in. long, dark green above, pale beneath, thickly set on branches. Turns orange to red in fall.	Great show of ⅓-in.-long, egg shaped red fruit.	Use as boundary, informal hedge or screen, or large bank planting.
C. franchetii	Evergreen. Zones 2–14.	Fountainlike, arching growth to 10 ft. or more. In poor soil with little water, to 5–6 ft.	Thickish, oval, to 1¼ in. long. Downy when young, dull green when mature. Reddish fall color.	Fruit orange red, ⅓ in. long, in clusters.	Attractive as tree-shrub or multistemmed small tree. Not plant to shear or clip.

SPECIES OR VARIETY	HARDINESS	SIZE, HABIT	LEAVES	FRUIT	USES, COMMENTS
C. glaucophyllus	See *C. buxifolius*.				
C. henryanus	Semi-evergreen. Zones 4–24.	Arching, spreading growth to 8–12 ft.	Large (to 5 in.) narrow, willowlike, deeply veined, green above, tawny, hairy beneath.	Fruit showy, red, in dense clusters.	Useful for Christmas greens as fruit is long lasting. Beautiful as individual shrub-tree.
C. horizontalis ROCK COTONEASTER	Deciduous, but out of leaf very short time. Zones 1–11, 14–24.	Low growing (2–3 ft.), wide spreading (to 15 ft.) with stiffly angled branches; single-plane secondary branching in flat herring-bone pattern.	Small (½ in. or less) roundish, glossy bright green above, pale beneath. Hold late, turn orange and red before falling.	Shiny bright red fruit make fine display.	Give it room to spread; don't plant where branch ends must be pruned. Bank cover, filler, low traffic barrier. *C. h. perpusillus* is flatter, more compact, with ¼-in. leaves. 'Robustus' is larger in leaf and fruit, taller. 'Variegatus' has leaves edged with white.
C. 'Hybridus Pendulus' (C. 'Pendula')	Evergreen or semi-deciduous. Zones 4–24.	To 6 ft., spreading wider. Vertical main branches, curving weeping branches.	Deep green, to 2 in. long. Closely set on branches.	Red, ¼-in. diameter.	Use singly in border or as espalier. Often grafted high on treelike under-stock to make small, spreading, weeping patio tree.
C. integerrimus. (C. vulgaris)	Deciduous. All Zones.	Slender, erect, 3–6 ft. tall, spreading at top.	Oval to roundish, 1–2 in. long, dull green.	Red, long lasting, ¼-in. diameter.	Useful shrub in coldest climates.
C. lacteus (C. parneyi) PARNEY COTONEASTER, RED CLUSTERBERRY	Evergreen. Zones 4–24.	Arching growth to 6–8 ft. or more. Foliage growth to base of plant.	Leathery, to 2 in. long, heavily veined, deep green above, white, hairy beneath.	Long-lasting red fruit in clusters 2–3 in. wide.	Use for screen or clip into formal hedge. Can be quite invasive. Effective as espalier or in container. Cut sprays valued for arrangements. Holds fruit well into spring.
C. 'Lowfast'	Evergreen. Zones 4–24.	Very vigorous, prostrate, rooting from trailing branches; to 12 in. high and spreading to 10–15 ft.	Oval, ¾ in. long, dark green above, gray green beneath; somewhat like *C. dammeri* but not as closely set along branches.	Red fruit.	Fast ground cover; spreads as much as 2 ft. a year. Other uses same as *C. dammeri*.
C. microphyllus ROCKSPRAY COTONEASTER	Evergreen. Zones 2–9, 14–24.	Main branches usually trailing and rooting, secondary branches upright; 2–3 ft. tall, spreading 6 ft. or more.	Very small (⅓ in.), dark green above, gray and hairy on lower surface.	Rosy red, ¼ in. across, but seeming larger contrasted with tiny leaves.	Good bank cover if not overfed and over-watered. Prune out upright branches or not, depending on desired effect. Use in big rock gardens, above walls. 'Cooperi' is especially small in leaf. 'Emerald Spray' has good resistance to fireblight.
C. m. cochleatus	Evergreen. Hardy to −5°. Zone 1 (with protection), 2–6, 14–24.	More prostrate, more compact than *C. microphyllus*.	Like *C. microphyllus*, but broader toward leaf tips.	As in *C. microphyllus*.	Molds its growth to contours of ground or rock. Best of *C. microphyllus* group as ground cover.
C. m. thymifolius	Evergreen. Hardy to −5°. Zones 2–9, 14–24.	More compact than *C. microphyllus*, but with stiff, upright branches.	Narrower than *C. microphyllus*, rolled under at edges.	As in *C. microphyllus* but somewhat smaller, sometimes in clusters.	Like other varieties, may tend to become woody, with foliage at ends of stems. Prune to thin and shorten.
C. multiflorus	Deciduous. All Zones.	Spreading shrub 6–8 ft. tall or small tree with arching branches 10-12 ft. tall.	Oval to nearly round, to 2½ in. long, 1½ in. wide. Dark and smooth above, pale beneath.	Clustered red fruit ¼-⅜ in. long.	Clustered white flowers fairly showy in spring. Big shrub for screening.

(Continued on next page)

SPECIES OR VARIETY	HARDINESS	SIZE, HABIT	LEAVES	FRUIT	USES, COMMENTS
C. pannosus and **C. pannosus 'Nanus'**	See *C. buxifolius.*				
C. parneyi	See *C. lacteus.*				
C. salicifolius WILLOWLEAF COTONEASTER	Evergreen or semi-evergreen. Zones 4–24.	Vigorous upright growth to 15 ft. high, arching branches spreading to 15–18 ft.	Narrow, willowlike (1–3½ in. long), wrinkled dark green above, grayish green beneath. *C. s. floccosus* has leaves glossy green above.	Bright red fruit ¼ in. wide, borne in 2-in. clusters.	Useful for big-scale screening, backgrounds. Or use as single or multistemmed small tree. Can be invasive.
C. s. 'Herbstfeuer' ('Autumn Fire')	Same as *C. salicifolius.*	Prostrate, to 6 in. high, spreading to 8 ft.	Same as *C. salicifolius.*	Same as *C. salicifolius.*	Plant 4–6 ft. apart for bank, ground cover.
C. s. 'Repens' (*C. s.* 'Repandens')	Same as *C. salicifolius.*	Trailing or weeping branches with eventual 8-ft. spread.	Like those of *C. salicifolius* but somewhat narrower.	Same as *C. salicifolius.*	Effective in hanging pot, grafted high on treelike stem as small weeping tree, or arching over slope.
C. watereri	Evergreen Zones 4–7, 14–17. Deciduous Zones 2–3.	Vigorous, erect, then arching, to 15–20 ft. tall and as wide.	Dark green, 4–5 in. long.	Unusually large dark red fruit in large clusters.	Group of garden hybrids. 'John Waterer' is often trained as short or tall standard tree. 'Cornubia' carries heavy crop of the largest fruit in entire group.

Sudden wilting and blackening of twigs or branches indicates fireblight, a bacterial disease. Cut out and destroy damaged wood, making cuts well below damaged tissue and sterilizing pruning tools between each cut with household disinfectant.

While some medium and tall growers can be sheared, they look best when allowed to maintain natural fountain shapes. Prune only to enhance graceful arch of branches. Keep medium growers looking young by pruning out portion of oldest wood each year. Prune ground covers to remove dead or awkward branches. Give flat growers room to spread. Don't plant near walk or drive where branch ends will need shearing. Stubbed branches unattractive.

Cotoneaster buxifolius

Cotoneaster horizontalis

COTTONWOOD. See *Populus.*

COTULA squalida. NEW ZEALAND BRASS BUTTONS. Evergreen perennial. Zones 4–9, 14–24. Grows only a few in. high but branches creep to 1 ft. or more. Leaves are soft, hairy, fernlike, bronzy green. Flowers are like yellow brass buttons about ¼-in. across. Calyxlike bracts below heads fit tightly against "buttons." Can be used as ground cover in full sun to medium shade. Give average water. Can be increased by planting divisions.

Cotula squalida

COTYLEDON. Succulents. Various sizes and appearances. Easily grown from cuttings and handsome in containers, raised beds, or open ground beds. Grow in full sun but best in light shade; plants are drought tolerant.

C. orbiculata. Zones 16, 17, 21–24. Shrubby, compact, to 3 ft. tall. Opposing pairs of fleshy leaves are 2–3 in. long, rounded, gray green to nearly white, narrowly edged red. Green-leafed forms are available. Flower stems rise above plant and carry clusters of orange, bell shaped, drooping flowers in summer. Good landscaping shrub in mild climates and well-drained soils. Splendid container plant.

Cotyledon orbiculata

C. undulata. Zones 17, 23, 24. Striking 18-in. plant with broad, thick leaves thickly dusted with pure white powder. Leaf edges wavy. Flowers (spring and early summer) orange, drooping, clustered. Overhead watering washes off powder.

COWANIA mexicana stansburiana. CLIFF ROSE. Evergreen shrub. Zones 1–3, 10–13. Native to California's Mojave Desert, Nevada, Arizona, Utah, Colorado, New Mexico, and Mexico. Much branched, straggly shrub to 6 ft. high and as wide. Tiny, ½-in. deeply toothed leaves. Flowers like ½-in.-wide miniature single roses, creamy or sulfur yellow, rarely white, in April-June. Its moment of glory comes following bloom when many very tiny fruit with their long plumy tails soften shrub to feathery haze. Pruning and infrequent watering will make it acceptable subject in desert gardens.

Cowania mexicana stansburiana

COWBERRY. See *Vaccinium vitis-idaea.*

COW ITCH TREE. See *Lagunaria patersonii.*

COWSLIP. See *Primula veris.*

COYOTE BRUSH. See *Baccharis pilularis.*

CRABAPPLE. Deciduous fruit tree. Crabapple is a small, usually tart apple. Many kinds are valued more for their springtime flowers than for their fruit. These are flowering crabapples, described under *Malus.* Crabapple varieties grown mostly for fruit (used for jelly making and pickling) are infrequently sold at western nurseries. Of several that may be sold, most popular is 'Transcendent', yellow apple to 2 in. wide, with red cheeks. Ripens in late summer. Zones 1–9, 11–21. For culture, see Apple.

Crabapple

CRAB CACTUS. See *Schlumbergera truncata.*

CRANBERRY BUSH. See *Viburnum trilobum.*

CRANESBILL. See *Geranium, Erodium chamaedryoides.*

CRAPE MYRTLE. See *Lagerstroemia indica.*

CRASSULA. Succulents. Zones 16, 17, 22–24; with overhead protection Zones 8, 9, 12–15, 18–21; house plants anywhere. Mostly from South Africa. Most soils, sun or shade; drought tolerant. Flowers, as described for various species below, can be counted on only when plants grown outdoors in some sunshine.

Crassula argentea

    C. arborescens. A shrubby, heavy-branched plant very like jade plant, but with gray green, red-edged, red-dotted leaves. Flowers (usually seen only on old plants) white, fading pink, star shaped. Good change of pace from jade plant; smaller and slower growing.
    C. argentea. (Sometimes sold as *C. portulacea.*) JADE PLANT. Top-notch house plant, large container plant, landscaping shrub in mildest climates. Stout trunk, sturdy limbs even on small plants—and plant will stay small in small container. Can reach 9 ft. in time, but is usually less. Leaves are thick, oblong, fleshy pads 1–2 in. long, glossy bright green, sometimes with red-tinged edges. Clusters of pink, star shaped flowers form in profusion, November–April. Good near swimming pools. Can be grown as hedge.
    C. corymbulosa. Low-growing, 6–30 in., slightly branched with rosettes of long, triangular, fleshy leaves. These are dark red when plant is grown in full sun and in poor soil. Very small white flowers.
    C. falcata. Full grown plants reach 4 ft., with equal spread. Leaves fleshy, sickle shaped, gray green, vertically arranged in opposite rows on stems. Dense, branched clusters of scarlet flowers late summer.
    C. lactea. Spreading, semishrubby plant 12–24 in. tall. Fleshy dark green leaves, white flowers in 4–6-in. clusters, October-December. Grows in shade—even dense shade. Fine rock garden plant.
    C. lycopodioides. Leafy, branching, erect stems to foot high, closely packed with tiny green leaves in 4 rows; effect is that of braided watch chain or of some strange green coral. Very small greenish flowers. Easy and useful in miniature and dish gardens.

Crassula falcata

    C. 'Morgan's Pink'. Fine miniature hybrid. Densely packed, fleshy leaves in tight cluster to 4 in. tall. Big brushlike clusters of pink flowers are nearly as big as the plant. Spring bloom.
    C. multicava. Dark green, spreading ground cover or hanging plant. Light pink mosquitolike flowers in loose clusters late winter, spring, Rampant grower in sun or shade, in any soil.
    C. pyramidalis. Interesting oddity to 3–4 in. high; flat, triangu-

lar leaves closely packed in 4 rows give plant squarish cross section. Flowers are insignificant.
    C. schmidtii. Mat-forming, spreading plant to 4 in. tall with long, slender, rich green leaves. Winter-spring flowers small, heavily borne, clustered, dark rose or purplish. Good pot or rock garden plant.
    C. tetragona. Upright plants with treelike habit, 1-2 ft. high. Leaves narrow, an inch long. Flowers white. Widely used in dish gardens to suggest miniature pine trees.

CRATAEGUS. HAWTHORN. Deciduous trees. Zones 1–11, 14–17. These trees, members of rose family, are known for their pretty spring flowers and showy fruit in summer, fall. Keep aphids in check. Fireblight makes entire branches die back quickly. Cut out blighted branches well below dead part; wash pruning tools with disinfectant between each cut. Attract bees, birds.
    Hawthorns have thorny branches and need some pruning to thin out excess twiggy growth. Grow plants on dry side to avoid rank, succulent growth.

Crataegus laevigata

    C. ambigua. RUSSIAN HAWTHORN. Moderate growth to 15–25 ft. with vase form, twisting branches for attractive silhouette. Leaves small (to 2½ in. long), deeply cut. White flowers, heavy crop of small red fruit. Extremely winter hardy.
    C. 'Autumn Glory'. Hybrid origin. Vigorous growth to 25 ft. with 15-ft. spread. Twiggy, dense. Dark green leaves similar to *C. laevigata* but more leathery. Clusters of single white flowers in spring. Very large, glossy, bright red fruit, autumn into winter. Type most susceptible to fireblight.
    C. crus-galli. COCKSPUR THORN. Wide-spreading tree to 30 ft. Stiff thorns to 3 in. long. Smooth, glossy, dark green, toothed leaves. White flowers. Dull orange red fruit. Good red and yellow fall color.
    C. laevigata. ENGLISH HAWTHORN. Native to Europe and North Africa. Moderate growth to 18–25 ft. with 15–20-ft. spread. Leaves similar to *C. monogyna* but lobes are toothed. Best known through its varieties: 'Paul's Scarlet', clusters of double rose to red flowers; 'Double White'; 'Double Pink'. Doubles set little fruit. 'Crimson Cloud' ('Superba') has bright red single flowers with white centers, bright red fruit.
    C. lavallei *(C. carrierei).* CARRIERE HAWTHORN. Hybrid origin. To 25 ft. with 15–20-ft. spread. More erect and open branching with less twiggy growth than other hawthorns. Very handsome. Leaves dark green, leathery, 2–4 in. long, toothed; turn bronze red after first sharp frost and hang on well into winter. White flowers in spring followed by loose clusters of very large orange to red fruit that persist all winter. Fruit is messy on walks, patios.
    C. mollis. DOWNY HAWTHORN. Big broad tree to 30 ft. with look of mature apple tree. Leaves to 4 in. long, lobed, toothed, covered with down. Flowers white, 1 in. wide. Red fruit are 1 in. across and are also downy; they don't last on tree as long as those of other species, but have value in jelly making.
    C. monogyna. Native to Europe, North Africa, and western Asia. Classic hawthorn of English countryside for hedges and boundary plantings. Represented in western nurseries by variety 'Stricta'. Narrow growth habit to 30 ft. tall and 8 ft. wide. Plant 5 ft. apart for dense narrow screen or barrier. Leaves 2 in. long, with 3–7, deep, smooth-edged lobes. Flowers white. Fruit are small, red, in clusters, rather difficult to see.
    C. oxyacantha. See *C. laevigata.*
    C. phaenopyrum *(C. cordata).* WASHINGTON THORN. Native to southeastern United States. Moderate growth to 25 ft. with 20-ft. spread. Light and open limb structure. Glossy leaves 2–3 in. long with 3–5 sharp-pointed lobes (like some maples); foliage turns beautiful orange and red in fall. Small white flowers in broad clusters in late spring or early summer. Shiny Chinese red fruit in autumn hang on well into winter. More graceful and delicate than other hawthorns, and preferred street or lawn tree. Least susceptible to fireblight.
    C. pinnatifida. Native to northeastern Asia. To 20 ft. high, 10–12 ft. wide. Leaves lobed like those of *C. laevigata* but big-

ger and thicker; they turn red in fall. Tree habit is more open and upright than *C. laevigata*. Flowers white, ¾-in. wide in 3-in. clusters. Fruit slightly smaller than those of *C. lavallei*.

C. 'Toba'. Canadian hybrid of great cold tolerance. To 20 ft. Leaves similar to *C. lavallei*. White flowers age to pink. Sets few large fruit.

C. viridis. GREEN HAWTHORN. Moderate growth to 25–30 ft., with broad, spreading crown. Leaves yellowish in fall, not showy. Clustered white flowers followed by red fruit.

CREAM BUSH. See *Holodiscus discolor*.

CREEPING BUTTERCUP. See *Ranunculus repens* 'Pleniflorus'.

CREEPING BENT. See *Agrostis stolonifera*.

CREEPING CHARLIE. See *Pilea nummulariifolia*.

CREEPING JENNIE. See *Lysimachia nummularia*.

CREEPING ST. JOHNSWORT. See *Hypericum calycinum*.

CREEPING ZINNIA. See *Sanvitalia procumbens*.

CREOSOTE BUSH. See *Larrea tridentata*.

CRESS, GARDEN. Summer annual. It is sometimes called PEPPER GRASS. Flavor resembles watercress. Easy to grow as long as weather is cool. Sow seed as early in spring as possible. Plant in rich, moist soil. Make rows 1 ft. apart, thin plants to 3 in. apart. Eat thinnings. Make successive sowings every 2 weeks up to middle of May. Cress matures fast. To 10–12 in. high. Where frosts are mild, sow through fall and winter. Try growing garden cress in shallow pots of soil or planting mix in sunny kitchen window. It sprouts in a few days; can be harvested (with scissors) in 2–3 weeks. Or grow it by sprinkling seeds on pads of wet cheesecloth; keep damp until harvest in 2 weeks.

Garden Cress

CRETE DITTANY. See *Origanum dictamnus*.

CRIMSON FLAG. See *Schizostylis coccinea*.

CRINODENDRON patagua (*C. dependens, Tricuspidaria dependens*). LILY-OF-THE-VALLEY TREE. Evergreen tree. Zones 14–24. Native to Chile. (For another lily-of-the-valley tree, see *Clethra*.) Somewhat like evergreen oak in general appearance; sometimes called flowering oak. Grows at moderate rate to 25 ft. and almost as wide, with upright branching and a rounded crown. Leaves 2½ in. long, ½–1 in. wide, dark green above, gray green beneath with irregularly toothed edges.

In June and July, sometimes into October, it wears hundreds of ¾-in.-long, white, bell shaped flowers. These are followed by numerous attractive cream and red seed capsules which drop and can be messy on paving. Tends to grow shrublike, or some branches turn down while others stick up. Early staking and pruning important. Prune out brushy growth toward center; remove branches that tend to hang down.

Does well in wet spots and thrives on lawn watering. In lawn, water deeply once a month to discourage surface rooting.

Crinum powellii

CRINUM. Bulbs. Zones 23, 24; or in sheltered, sunny garden situations Zones 12–22; other areas in containers. Distinguish from near relative amaryllis by crinum's long slender flower tube that is longer than flower segments. Long-stalked cluster of lily shaped, 4–6-in.-long, fragrant flowers rises in spring or summer from persistent clump of long, strap shaped or sword shaped leaves. Bulbs large, rather slender, tapering to stemlike neck; thick fleshy roots. Bulbs generally available (from specialists) all year, but spring, fall planting preferred.

Plant in sun or a little shade. Provide soil with plenty of humus; set bulbs 6 in. under surface; give ample water, space to develop. Divide infrequently. Bait for snails. In colder sections, mulch heavily in winter; or in containers, move into frostproof place.

C. moorei. Large bulbs with 6–8 in. diameter, and stemlike neck 12 in. or more long. Long, thin, wavy-edged, bright green leaves. Bell shaped pinkish red flowers.

C. powellii. Resembles *C. moorei*, one of its parents, having dark rose-colored flowers. 'Alba' is good pure white form.

Crocosmia crocosmiiflora

CROCOSMIA. Corms. Zones 5–24, but need sheltered location and winter mulch in colder zones. Native to tropical and South Africa. Formerly called tritonia, and related to freesia, ixia, sparaxis. Sword shaped leaves in basal clumps. Small orange, red, yellow flowers bloom in summer on branched stems. Useful for splashes of garden color and for cutting. Plant in full sun near coast and in coastal valleys, part shade inland. Drought tolerant plants.

C. crocosmiiflora (*Tritonia crocosmiiflora*). MONTBRETIA. A favorite for generations, montbretias can still be seen in older gardens where they have spread freely, as though native, producing orange crimson flowers 1½–2 in. across on 3–4-ft. stems. Sword shaped leaves to 3 ft., ½–1 in. broad. Many named forms once common; now little grown. Good for naturalizing on slopes or in fringe areas.

C. masoniorum. From South Africa. Leaves 2½ ft. long, 2 in. wide. Flowers flaming orange to orange scarlet, 1½ in. across, in dense, one-sided clusters on 2½–3-ft. stems which arch over at top. Buds open slowly from base to tip of clusters and old flowers drop cleanly. Flowers last 2 weeks when cut.

Crocosmia masoniorum

CROCUS. Corms. All Zones, but most species best adapted to colder climates. Leaves are basal and grasslike—often with silvery midrib—and appear before, with, or after flowers, depending on species. Flowers with long stemlike tubes and flaring or cup shaped petals are 3–6 in. long; short (true) stems are hidden underground.

Most crocus bloom in earliest spring or late winter, but some species bloom August-November, flowers rising from bare earth weeks or days after planting. All thrive in sun or light shade; mass them for best effect. Attractive in rock gardens, between stepping stones, in containers. Set corms 2–3 in. deep in light, porous soil. Protect from gophers. Divide every 3–4 years.

Crocus vernus

C. ancyrensis. Flowers golden yellow, small, very early.

C. angustifolius. (Formerly *C. susianus.*) CLOTH OF GOLD CROCUS. Orange gold, starlike flowers, with dark brown center stripe. January-February bloom, March in cold climates.

C. chrysanthus. Orange yellow, sweet scented. Hybrids and selections from plant range from white and cream through the yellow and blues, often marked with deeper color. Usually even more freely flowering than Dutch crocus, but with smaller flowers. Spring bloom. Popular varieties are: 'Blue Pearl', palest blue; 'Cream Beauty', pale yellow; 'E. P. Bowles', yellow with purple featherings; 'Lady-killer', outside purple edged white, inside white feathered purple; 'Princess Beatrix', blue with yellow center; and 'Snow Bunting', pure white.

C. imperati. Bright lilac inside, buff veined purple outside, saucer shaped. Early spring.

C. kotschyanus. (Formerly *C. zonatus.*) Pinkish lavender or lilac. September bloom.

C. sativus. SAFFRON CROCUS. Lilac. Orange red stigma is true saffron of commerce. Interesting rather than showy. Autumn.

C. sieberi. Delicate lavender blue with golden throat. One of earliest.

C. speciosus. Showy blue violet flowers in October. Lavender and mauve varieties available. Fast increase by seed and division. Showiest autumn-flowering crocus.

C. tomasinianus. Slender buds, star shaped silvery lavender blue flowers, sometimes with dark blotch at tips of segments. Very early—January or February in milder climates.

C. vernus. DUTCH CROCUS. Familiar crocus in shades of white, yellow, lavender, and purple, often penciled and streaked. February-April (depending on climate). Most vigorous crocus, and only one widely sold in all areas. A favorite for forcing into early bloom in pots.

CROSSANDRA infundibuliformis. Evergreen greenhouse or house plant. Native to India. Grow it in 4–5-in. pot as 1–1½-ft. plant. Its glossy, very dark green, gardenialike leaves are attractive all year, and short, full spikes of scarlet orange or coral orange flowers are showy for long period in summer. Grow in warmest spot with good light, as with African violet. Give average water and feed with liquid fertilizer once a month. Buy plants from florist or nurseryman, or raise from seed. Blooms in 6–9 months from seed.

Crossandra infundibuliformis

CROTALARIA agatiflora. CANARY BIRD BUSH. Evergreen shrub. Zones 13, 15–24. Native to east Africa. Recovers quickly after frost damage. Fast, rank growth to 12 ft. and as wide unless frequently pruned (which it should be). Common name is well-earned. Unique, 1½-in. flowers are strung along flower spike (to 14 in. long) like so many chartreuse birds. Heaviest bloom in summer or fall but in frost free areas blooms intermittently for 10 months. Foliage is pleasing gray green, with leaves divided into 3-in.-long leaflets.

Yellow green flowers harmonize with most colors. Try with red geraniums, zinnias, coral tree *(Erythrina),* or with other yellow-flowered shrubs for long succession of bloom. Will grow in almost any soil, in either sun or part shade, average water. Prune 2 or 3 times a year to correct open, weak-stemmed growth, condense and improve outline, and keep growth within bounds.

Crotalaria agatiflora

CROTON. See *Codiaeum variegatum.*

CROWN IMPERIAL. See *Fritillaria imperialis.*

CROWN OF GOLD TREE. See *Cassia excelsa.*

CROWN-OF-THORNS. See *Euphorbia milii.*

CROWN PINK. See *Lychnis coronaria.*

CROWN VETCH. See *Coronilla varia.*

CRYPTANTHUS zonatus. Perennial used as house plant; outdoors Zones 17, 23, 24. Native to Brazil. Bromeliad (pineapple relative) grown for showy leaves—in spreading, low-growing clusters to 18 in. wide, usually less. Individual leaves wavy, dark brownish red, banded crosswise with green, brown, or white. Unimportant little white flowers grow among leaves. Pot in equal parts coarse sand, ground bark or peat moss, and shredded osmunda. Shade, average water.

Cryptanthus zonatus

CRYPTOCARYA rubra. Evergreen tree. Zones 14–17, 20–24. Native to Chile. Slow to moderate growth to 30–40 ft. Dense, slightly spreading crown. Distinguished by its rich brown bark and beautiful coppery red new foliage. The 2–3-in.-long roundish leaves, thick in texture, mature to very glossy dark green above, bluish green beneath; spicily fragrant when crushed. Stake and prune unless multiple trunk is desired. Occasional frost damage in Zones 14–16. Needs moderate watering.

Cryptocarya rubra

CRYPTOMERIA japonica. JAPANESE CRYPTOMERIA. Evergreen tree. Zones 4–9, 14–24. Graceful conifer, fast growing (3–4 ft. a year) in youth. Eventually skyline tree with straight columnar trunk; thin red brown bark peeling in strips. Foliage soft bright green to bluish green in growing season, brownish purple in cold weather. Branches, slightly pendulous, are clothed with short, ½–1-in.-long, needlelike leaves. Roundish red brown cones ¾–1 in. wide. Deep soil, ample water (except in Zones 5, 17, 24). Resists oak root fungus.

C. j. 'Elegans'. PLUME CEDAR, PLUME CRYPTOMERIA. Quite unlike species. Feathery, grayish green, soft-textured foliage. Turns rich coppery red or purplish in winter. Grows slowly into broad-based, dense pyramid, 20–25 ft. high. For Oriental effect, prune out some branches to give tiered look. Give it space to show it off.

C. j. 'Lobbii Nana' *(C. j. 'Lobbii').* Upright, dwarf, very slow to 4 ft. Foliage dark green.

C. j. 'Pygmaea' *(C. j. 'Nana').* DWARF CRYPTOMERIA. Bushy dwarf 1½–2 ft. high, 2½ ft. wide. Dark green needlelike leaves, twisted branches.

C. j. 'Vilmoriniana'. Slow growing dwarf to about 1–2 ft. Fluffy gray green summer foliage turns bronze during late fall and winter. Rock garden or container plant.

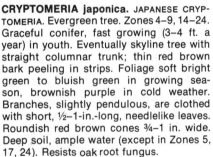

Cryptomeria japonica

CTENANTHE. House plants; foliage plants for patio containers or gardens in Zones 23, 24. Leaves are big feature. They may be short stalked along stem or long stalked and rise from base only. Insignificant white flowers form under bracts in spikes at ends of branches. Use with other tropical foliage plants such as philodendron, alocasia, tree ferns. Plant in partial shade in rich moist soil, feed with liquid fertilizer.

C. 'Burle Marx'. Grows to 15 in. Leaves gray green above, feathered with dark green; maroon underneath. Leaf stalks ma-

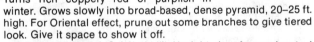

Ctenanthe compressa

roon. Tender; best grown as house plant, even in mild Zones 23, 24.

C. compressa. (Often sold as *Bamburanta arnoldiana*.) BAMBURANTA. Plants to 2–3 ft. high. Leathery leaves are oblong, lopsided, to about 15 in. long, waxy green on top, gray green beneath, held at angle on top of wiry stems.

C. oppenheimiana. GIANT BAMBURANTA. Compact, branching, 3–5 ft. high. Narrow leathery leaves, dark green banded with silver above, purple beneath, set at angle on downy stalks. *C. o.* 'Tricolor' has showy cream patches with its other colors.

CTENITIS pentangularis. Fern. Zones 17, 21–24. Native to New Zealand. This low-growing fern makes dense clumps of triangular, finely cut fronds. Will take moderately dry conditions and temperatures down to 26°F.

Ctenitis pentangularis

CUCUMBER. All Zones in conditions noted below. Vines need at least 25 sq. ft. per hill, but you can grow vines on fence or trellis to conserve space. A warm-weather, sun-requiring vegetable needing warm soil to sprout seeds and warmth for pollination. Principal types are long, smooth, green, slicing cucumbers; small, numerous pickling cucumbers; and roundish, yellow, mild-flavored lemon cucumbers. Novelties include Oriental varieties (long, slim, very mild), Armenian cucumber (actually long, curving, pale green, ribbed melon with cucumber look and mild cucumber flavor), and English greenhouse cucumber. English greenhouse cucumbers must be grown in greenhouse to avoid pollination by bees, with subsequent loss of form and flavor; well-grown, are mildest of all cucumbers.

Cucumber

Plant seeds in sunny spot 1 or 2 weeks after average date of last frost and keep soil evenly moist. To grow cucumbers on trellis, plant seeds 1 in. deep and 1–3 ft. apart and permit main stem to reach top of support. Pick while young to insure continued production.

CUCUMBER TREE. See *Magnolia acuminata*.

CUNNINGHAMIA lanceolata. CHINA FIR. Evergreen tree. Zones 4–6, 14–21. Native to China. Picturesque conifer with heavy trunk, stout whorled branches, and drooping branchlets. Grows moderately to 30 ft. with 20-ft. spread. Stiff needlelike leaves 1½–2½ in. long, sharp pointed, green above, whitish beneath. Brown cones (1–2 in.) interesting, but not profuse. Among palest of needled evergreens in spring and summer; turns red bronze in cold winters. Needs protection from hot dry wind in summer and cold winds in winter. Requires average water. Becomes less attractive as it ages. Prune out dead branchlets.

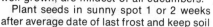
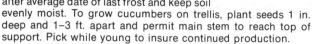

Cunninghamia lanceolata

C. l. 'Glauca' is more widely grown and hardier than *C. lanceolata*. Its foliage is striking gray blue.

CUNONIA capensis. AFRICAN RED ALDER. Evergreen large shrub or small tree. Zones 9, 12–24. Native to South Africa. Small tree with single or multiple trunks, or large shrub.

Slow to moderate growth to 25–35 ft. as tree. Good large tub plant. Foliage effective at close range. Twigs are wine red and new growth bronzy red, turning dark green.

Cunonia capensis

Leaves divided into 5–9 narrowish, toothed leaflets 3 in. long, 1 in. wide. Dense spiky clusters of small white flowers, late summer. Hardy to 20°F. Severely damaged at 16°F. Average water.

CUP-AND-SAUCER. See *Campanula medium*.

CUP-AND-SAUCER VINE. See *Cobaea scandens*.

CUPANIOPSIS anacardioides (*Cupania anacardioides*). CARROT WOOD, TUCKEROO. Evergreen tree. Zones 16, 17, 19–24. Native to Australia. Slow to moderate growth to 30 ft. high, 20-ft. spread. Open-branching in youth, becoming dense with age. Leaves made up of 6–10 leathery, 4-in.-long leaflets. Somewhat resembles carob, but neater, more delicate and airy. Gives heavy dense shade. Clean, handsome patio, lawn, or street tree. Flowers are inconspicuous. Prune to enhance structure, remove excess branches. Interesting as multistemmed tree. Deep rooting. Tolerates poorly drained soil; needs average water. Mature trees hardy to 22°F.; young trees more tender. Stands salt wind on coast or dry hot wind inland. Good near swimming pools.

Cupaniopsis anacardioides

CUP FLOWER. See *Nierembergia*.

CUPHEA. Shrubby perennials or dwarf shrubs. Outdoors all year in Zones 16, 17, 21-24; summer bedding or indoor/outdoor pot plant elsewhere. Native Mexico and Guatemala. Interesting for summer color in small beds, as formal edging for border, along paths. Take ordinary soil, sun or part shade (potted plants best in light shade); lots of moisture. Pinch tips for compact growth; cut back older plants severely in late fall or early spring. Easy from cuttings.

C. hyssopifolia. FALSE HEATHER. Compact shrublet 6 in.–2 ft. with flexible, leafy branchlets. Leaves evergreen, ½–¾ in. long, very narrow. Tiny summer flowers in pink, purple, or white are scarcely half as long as leaves. White form most useful.

Cuphea ignea

C. ignea. CIGAR PLANT. Leafy, compact, 1 ft. high and wide. Leaves narrow, dark green, 1–1½ in. long. Flowers tubular, ¾ in. long, bright red with dark ring at end and white tip (hence name cigar plant); blooms summer and fall.

CUPID'S DART. See *Catananche caerulea*.

CUP-OF-GOLD-VINE. See *Solandra maxima*.

CUPRESSOCYPARIS leylandii. Evergreen tree. Zones 3–24. Hybrid between *Chamaecyparis nootkatensis* and *Cupressus macrocarpa*. Grows extremely fast (from cuttings to 15–20 ft. in 5 years). Most planted as quick screening. However, some 10-year-old plantings have become open and floppy with age. Long, slender, upright branches of flattened, gray green foliage sprays give youthful tree narrow pyramidal form. Produces small cones composed of scales. Accepts wide variety of soil and climate, average water, strong wind; in warm-summer climates loses stiff, upright habit and is subject to coryneum canker.

Cupressocyparis leylandii

'Naylor's Blue' has grayish blue foliage; 'Castlewellan' has golden yellow new growth and a narrow, erect habit.

CUPRESSUS. CYPRESS. Evergreen trees. These coniferous trees have tiny scalelike leaves closely set on cordlike branches and interesting golfball-sized globular cones made up of shield shaped scales. All are drought tolerant once established.

C. forbesii. TECATE CYPRESS. Zones 8–14, 18–20. Native to Santa Ana Mountains, Orange Co., and mountains of San Diego Co., California. Grows as low-branching tree to 20 ft., with cherry red bark and green foliage. Very fast growing—in fact it may get too top heavy for size of root system. Needs to be kept on dry side for wind resistance. Useful as hedge or screen.

Cupressus glabra

C. glabra. (Often sold as *C. arizonica*.) SMOOTH ARIZONA CYPRESS. Grown in Zones 5, 8–24 but at its best in high desert and hot interiors, where it's valued as fast-growing windbreak tree, tall screen. Native to central Arizona. Unusually drought resistant when established. Seedlings vary in form and foliage color. Usually to 40 ft., spreading to 20 ft. Smooth, cherry red bark, with green to blue green to gray foliage. If you want uniformity in growth habit and color, look for selected forms: *C. g.* 'Gareei', rich, silvery, blue green foliage; *C. g.* 'Pyramidalis', compact and symmetrical.

C. macrocarpa. MONTEREY CYPRESS. Zone 17. Native to California's Monterey Peninsula. Beautiful tree to 40 ft. or more, with rich bright green foliage. Narrow and pyramidal in youth, spreading and picturesque in age or in windy coastal conditions. Away from cool coastal winds is very subject to coryneum canker fungus, for which there is no cure. Look for foliage that first turns yellow, then deep reddish brown, and falls off slowly. Destroy infected trees. Fast-growing windbreak tree in coastal conditions.

Cupressus sempervirens

C. sempervirens. ITALIAN CYPRESS. Zones 4–24; best in 8–15, 18–20. Native to southern Europe, western Asia. Species itself, with horizontal branches and dark green foliage, is seldom sold. *C. s.* 'Stricta' (*C. s.* 'Fastigiata'), COLUMNAR ITALIAN CYPRESS, and *C. s.* 'Glauca', BLUE ITALIAN CYPRESS (really blue green) are classic Mediterranean cypresses. They grow eventually into dense, narrow, columnar trees to 60 ft. *C. s.* 'Golden Pillar' (pyramidal) and 'Swane's Golden' (narrowly columnar) have golden yellow new growth.

CURRANT. For ornamental relatives see *Ribes*. Deciduous shrub. Best in Zones 1–6, 17, but grown in all Zones except where irrigation water or soil is high in sodium. Grow in shade in hot-summer areas, full sun in coastal areas. Average water. Many-stemmed shrub to 3-5 ft. high and equally broad, depending on vigor and variety. Attractive foliage of lobed and toothed leaves to 3 in. wide.

Currant

Flowers, yellowish in drooping clusters, are followed by clusters of red or white fruit in early summer. Leaves drop rather early in fall. Currants bear at base of year-old wood and on spurs on 2 and 3-year wood. Prune so that you keep balance of 1, 2, and 3-year canes; prune out older canes and weak growth. 'Red Lake', 'Perfection', and 'Cherry' are preferred varieties.

In some areas it is illegal to plant currants, which might be hosts to white pine blister rust. Ask nurseryman or county agent about your area's requirements.

CUSHION BUSH. See *Calocephalus brownii*.

CUSHION PINK. See *Silene acaulis*.

CUSSONIA spicata. SPIKED CABBAGE TREE. Evergreen tree. Zones 16, 17, 19–24. Native to South Africa. Known chiefly for its lobed, toothed, and cut leaves—something like giant dark green snowflakes. Leaves grow on 6–10-in. stalks, are 4–7 in. long, divided into 5–9 leaflets. Foliage displayed on 10–20 ft., smooth-trunked tree, with branches in rounded crown. Under best conditions, tree blooms: small flowers, yellowish, in dense spikes 3–9 in. long, stand above leaves. Hardy to about 20°F. Full sun, much summer water (with fast drainage).

Cussonia spicata

CUTLEAF or FERNLEAF ELDER. See *Sambucus canadensis* 'Laciniata'.

CYANOTIS. Evergreen perennials used as house plants. Related to wandering Jews (*Tradescantia* and *Zebrina*), they resemble them but have shorter stems, fleshier, more succulent leaves, and noticeable covering of soft "fur." Give them fairly rich, loose planting mix, moderate water, and bright light. Reduce watering in dull winter weather. Propagate by cuttings.

Cyanotis somaliensis

C. kewensis. TEDDY BEAR. Leaves 1–1½ in. long, coated with brown "fur." Small 3-petaled flowers are purplish red.

C. somaliensis. PUSSY-EARS. Stems somewhat longer than above (to 9-10 in.), leaves covered with white "fur," flowers blue.

CYCAD. Member of Cycadales, an order of slow-growing evergreen plants with large, firm, palmlike or fernlike leaves, and fruit borne in cones. Most people think of them as kind of palm.

Most are native to tropical regions; some are subtropical, and some of these are hardy enough to grow out of doors in mild-winter climates. Extremely long lived. Average water. All are choice house plants—tough leaves, slow growth, and smallish root system make them adapted to pot culture indoors.

Most common one is *Cycas revoluta* (see next entry). For others, see *Ceratozamia* and *Dioon*.

CYCAS revoluta. SAGO PALM. Cycad. Zones 8–24. In youth (2–3 feet high), they have airy, lacy appearance of ferns. With age (grow very slowly to as high as 10 ft.) they look more like palms than ferns. But they are neither—they are primitive, cone-bearing plants related to conifers. From central point at top of single trunk (sometimes several trunks), featherlike leaves grow out in rosettes. Leaves 2–3 ft. long (larger on very old plants), divided into many narrow, leathery, dark glossy green segments. Makes offsets (new plants attached to parent).

Cycas revoluta

Choice container or bonsai plant; useful for tropical look. Tough, tolerant house or patio plant that looks best in partial shade. Average water. Hardiest (to 15°F.), most widely grown cycad.

CYCLAMEN. Tuberous-rooted perennials. Grown for pretty white, pink, rose, or red flowers that resemble shooting stars. Attractive leaves in basal clumps. Zones and uses for large-flowered florists' cyclamen (*C. persicum*) are given under that name.

All other types are small flowered, hardy, best adapted Zones 1–9, 14–24. They bloom as described in listing below, and all lose leaves during part of year. Leaves may appear before or with flowers. Use hardy types in rock gardens, in naturalized

Cyclamen persicum

clumps under trees, as carpets under camellias, rhododendrons, and large, noninvasive ferns. Or grow them in pots out of direct sun.

All kinds of cyclamen grow best in fairly rich, porous soil with lots of humus. Plant tubers 6–10 in. apart, cover with ½ in. soil (except florists', in which upper half of tuber should protrude above soil level). Best planting time is dormant period, June-August. (Except for *C. persicum,* which is always sold as a potted plant rather than a tuber and is available at most seasons, although most are sold in the late fall or during the winter-spring blooming period.) Keep soil moist; topdress annually with light application of potting soil with complete fertilizer added, being careful not to cover top of tuber. Do not cultivate around roots.

Cyclamen grow readily from seed; small-flowered hardy species take several years to bloom. Florists' cyclamen blooms in about 15–18 months and frequently self-sows when growing in favorable location.

C. atkinsii. Crimson flowers on 4–6-in. stems; deep green, silvery mottled leaves. Also pink, white varieties. January-March.

C. cilicium. Pale pink, purple-blotched, fragrant flowers on 2–6-in. stems, mottled leaves. September-January. There is white-flowered variety, 'Album'.

C. coum. Deep crimson rose flowers on 4–6-in. stems; round, deep green leaves. White, pink varieties. Bloom January to March.

C. europaeum. See *C. purpurascens.*

C. hederifolium (*C. neapolitanum*). Rose pink flowers on 3–4-in. stem, August-September. Large light green leaves marbled silver and white. Also white variety. One of easiest and most vigorous, very reliable in cold-winter climates. Set corms a foot apart.

C. persicum. FLORISTS' CYCLAMEN. Potted plant all areas; outdoors Zones 16–24. Blooms late fall to spring: crimson, red, salmon, purple, or white, on 6–8-in.-tall stems. Leaves kidney shaped, dark green. Good choice for color in places occupied by tuberous begonias in summer. Must have shade in warm summer climates.

C. purpurascens (*C. europaeum*). Distinctly fragrant crimson flowers, July-August, on 5–6-in. stem. Bright green leaves mottled silvery white; almost evergreen.

C. repandum. Bright crimson flowers on 5–6-in. stem, long narrow petals; rich green ivy shaped leaves, marbled silver, toothed on edges. Spring.

CYCLOPHORUS. See *Pyrrosia.*

CYDONIA. See *Chaenomeles.*

CYDONIA oblonga. See Quince, Fruiting.

CYLINDROPHYLLUM. See *Cephalophyllum.*

CYMBALARIA. Small creeping perennial plants. Zones 3–24. Related to snapdragons. Unshowy, they have their uses as small-scale ground covers in cool, shady places or as decorations for terrarium or hanging basket. In ground, can be invasive.

C. aequitriloba. Inch-deep mat that looks like small-scale dichondra. Leaves have slight lobes (3–5). Purple snapdragon shaped flowers are pretty but too tiny to make a show. Shade, good soil, ample water. Use as moss substitute.

C. muralis (*Linaria cymbalaria*). KENILWORTH IVY. Perennial usually growing as annual. Dainty creeper which may appear uninvited in shadier parts of garden, sometimes even sprouting in chinks of stone or brick wall. Trailing stems root at joints. Leaves 1 in. wide or less, smooth, with 3–7 toothlike lobes. Small lilac blue flowers carried singly on stalks a little longer than leaves.

Cymbalaria muralis

CYMBIDIUM. Terrestrial orchids. Native to high altitudes in southeast Asia, where rainfall is heavy and nights cool. Very popular because of their relatively easy culture.

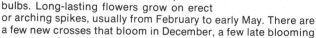
Miniature *Cymbidium*

Except in frost free areas, grow plants in containers in lathhouse, greenhouse, or under overhang or high-branching tree. For added enjoyment bring indoors when in flower. Excellent cut flower.

Long, narrow, grasslike foliage forms sheath around short, stout, oval pseudobulbs. Long-lasting flowers grow on erect or arching spikes, usually from February to early May. There are a few new crosses that bloom in December, a few late blooming ones to prolong flowering period.

Flower best if given as much light as possible without burning foliage. In general, plants do well with 50 percent shade—under plastic cloth shading or under lath. Let leaf color be your guide: plants with yellow green leaves generally flower best; dark green foliage denotes too much shade. (Shade plants during flowering period to prolong bloom life, keep flowers from fading.)

Plants prefer 45°–55° F. night temperature rising to as much as 80°–90°F. during day. They'll stand temperatures as low as 28°F. for short time only; therefore, where there's danger of harder frosts, protect plants with covering of polyethylene film. Flower spikes are more tender than other plant tissues.

Keep potting medium moist during period new growth is developing and maturing—usually March-September. In winter water just enough to keep bulbs from shriveling. On hot summer days syringe foliage early in day.

Good soil mix for cymbidiums is 2 parts redwood bark or sawdust, 2 parts peat moss, 1 part sand. Add 4-in. pot of complete fertilizer to each wheelbarrow of mix. Ready-blended mixes are excellent. Whatever the medium, it should drain fast and still retain moisture.

Feed with complete liquid fertilizer high in nitrogen every 10 days to 2 weeks, January-July. Use low nitrogen fertilizer August-December.

Transplant potted plants when bulbs fill pots. When dividing plants keep minimum of 3 healthy bulbs (with foliage) in each division. Dust cuts with sulfur or paint them with tree seal to discourage rot. Watch for slugs and snails at all times.

Most cymbidium growers list only hybrids in their catalogs—large-flowered varieties with white, pink, yellow, green, or bronze blooms. Most have yellow throat, dark red markings on lip. Large-flowered forms produce dozen or more 4½-5-in. flowers per stem. Miniature varieties, about quarter size of large flowered forms, are popular for their size, free blooming qualities, flower color.

CYNODON dactylon. BERMUDA GRASS, BERMUDA. Lawn grass. Subtropical fine-textured grass that spreads rapidly by surface and underground runners. Tolerates heat, needs less water than most lawn grasses, and looks good if well maintained. It turns brown in winter; some varieties stay green longer than others, and most stay green longer if well fed. Bermuda grass can be overseeded with cool-season grasses or dyed green for winter color. Needs sun and should be cut low; ½ in. is desirable. Needs thatching—removal of matted layer of old stems and stolons beneath the leaves—to look its best.

Cynodon dactylon

Common Bermuda is good minimum-maintenance lawn for large area. Needs feeding, careful and frequent mowing to remove seed spikes. Roots invade shrubbery and flower beds if not carefully confined. Can become extremely difficult to eradicate. Plant from hulled seed or sprigs.

Hybrid Bermudas are finer in texture and better in color than common kind. They crowd out common Bermuda in time but are harder to overseed with rye, bluegrass, or red fescue. Help them stay green in winter by feeding in September and October and by removing thatch, which insulates grass from warm soil. Useful in areas with short dormant season. Grow from sprigs (stolons), plugs, or sod.

'Santa Ana'. Deep green, coarse, holds color late, smog resistant. Takes hard wear.

'Tifgreen'. Fine textured, deep blue green, dense. Few seed spikes, sterile seeds. Takes close mowing, preferred for putting greens. Outstanding for home lawns.

'Tifway'. Low growth, fine texture, stiff blades, dark green, dense, wear resistant. Slow to start. Sterile (no seeds).

'Tifdwarf'. Extremely low and dense; takes very close mowing. Slower to establish than others, but slower to spread where it's not wanted. Useful as small-scale ground cover on banks, among rocks, near garden steps.

'U-3'. Finer textured than common, but with obvious and unattractive seed spikes. Very tough. Grow from sprigs; not dependable from seed, tending to revert to mixture of many types. Not up to other hybrids in quality.

CYNOGLOSSUM. Biennials, usually treated as annuals; perennials. Bedding, border, or wild garden plants with blue, white, or pink flowers like forget-me-nots.

C. amabile. CHINESE FORGET-ME-NOT. Biennial grown as annual. All Zones. Plant is 1½–2 ft. tall. Leaves grayish green, soft, hairy, lance shaped. Loose sprays of rich blue, pink, or white flowers, larger than forget-me-nots, appear in spring, into summer where weather is cool. 'Firmament', widely available, most popular variety, has rich blue flowers on compact, 18-in.-high plants. Combine with snapdragons, godetias, candytuft, clarkia, violas; especially effective with white, yellow, pink, salmon or coral flowers.

Cynoglossum amabile

Blooms first year from seed sown (preferably where plants are to grow) in fall or early spring. Hardy except in most severe winters. Sun, regular watering.

C. grande. WESTERN HOUND'S TONGUE. Perennial. Zones 4–9, 14–24. Native to Coast Range and Sierra Nevada slopes below 4,000 ft. Blooms March-June. Flowers blue, ⅓–½ in. across, white in center. Plants 1–2½ ft. tall, die back in summer to heavy underground root. Needs woodsy site with cool soil and little or no summer water. Leaves hairy, mostly basal, spreading, 6–12 in. long.

CYPERUS. Perennials. Zones 8, 9, 12–24 as outdoor plant. Sedges—grasslike plants distinguished from true grasses by 3-angled, solid stems and very different flowering parts. Valued for striking form, interesting silhouette or shadow pattern.

Most cyperus are bog plants by nature; they grow in rich, moist soil or with roots submerged in water—sun or shade. Groom plants by removing dead or broken stems; divide and replant vigorous ones when clump becomes too large, saving smaller, outside divisions and discarding overgrown centers. In cold climates, pot up divisions, keep over winter as house plants.

Cyperus papyrus

C. albostriatus (C. diffusus). Resembles C. alternifolius (below), but tends to be shorter (to 20 in.), with broader leaves and more lush, soft appearance. Vigorous, invasive, best used in contained space.

C. alternifolius. UMBRELLA PLANT. Narrow, firm, spreading leaves arranged like ribs of umbrella at tops of 2–4-ft. stems. Flowers in dry greenish brown clusters. Dwarf form is C. a. 'Gracilis' (C. a. 'Nanus'). Grows in or out of water. Effective near pools, in pots, planters; or in dry stream beds or small rock gardens. Self-sows. Can become weedy. Can take over a small pool.

C. isocladus (C. haspan). DWARF PAPYRUS. Flowers and long thin leaves combine to make filmy brown and green clusters on

slender stems about 18 in. high. Sink in pots in water gardens where slender leafless stems will not lose delicately shaped design among larger and coarser plants. Use in Oriental gardens.

C. papyrus. PAPYRUS. Tall, graceful, dark green stems 6–10 ft. high. Clusters of green threadlike parts to 18 in. long, longer than small leaves at base of cluster. Will grow quickly in 2 in. of water in shallow pool or can be potted and placed on bricks or inverted pot in deeper water. Protect from strong wind. Also grows well in rich, moist soil out of water. Used by flower arrangers for novel effects.

CYPHOMANDRA betacea. TREE TOMATO. Evergreen or partially evergreen shrub. Zones 16, 17, 22–24; with overhead protection in 14, 15, 18–21; elsewhere indoor/outdoor or greenhouse. Fast growth to 10–12 ft. Treelike habit.

Leaves 4–10 in. long, pointed oval. Summer and fall flowers small, pinkish. Winter fruit is red, 2–3 in. long, egg shaped, edible, with acid, slightly tomatolike flavor. If you find the fruit too tart, try stewing it with a little sugar, as the Australians do. Grow from seed like tomato. Shelter from frost and spray to control sucking insects. Give average water, sun or part shade.

Cyphomandra betacea

CYPRESS. See Cupressus. True cypresses are all Cupressus; many plants erroneously called cypress will be found under Chamaecyparis.

CYPRESS VINE. See Ipomoea quamoclit.

CYPRIPEDIUM. LADY'S SLIPPER, MOCCASIN FLOWER. See also Paphiopedilum. Terrestrial orchids. Zones 1–8, 14, 15. Native to northern hemisphere, two to the West. Short stem with pair of leaves near ground or long stem with many leaves along stem. Flowers, on straight stems well above foliage, have pouchlike lip. All like moist but well-drained neutral to slightly acid soil rich in humus. Plant in cool spot which receives filtered sun. Use in woodland setting with ferns and native wildflowers.

C. acaule. PINK LADY SLIPPER. Native to eastern U.S. Rose pink flower, one to stem in May and June. Stem to 10 in. tall. Two oval, 6–9-in.-long leaves flat to ground. Needs cold winters, and acid, leafy soil to thrive.

Cypripedium reginae

C. calceolus pubescens. YELLOW LADY SLIPPER. Native to eastern U.S. Yellow flowers, 1–3 to a stem, have twisted sepals, bloom in May and June. Oval, hairy leaves. Height: 1–2 ft. Needs cold winters to thrive.

C. californicum. Native to boggy areas of northern California, southern Oregon. Small, greenish yellow to brown sepals, yellow petals, pouch white to pinkish, spotted with brown. Often as many as a dozen flowers to a leafy stem in summer. Leaves oval, to 6 in. long. Plant varies in height from 12–18 in. Oval leaves. Plant it and let it alone—dislikes root disturbance.

C. montanum. Grows in clumps in forests below 5,000 ft. in California, north to British Columbia, east to Wyoming. In summer, 1–3 fragrant flowers with purplish brown sepals and petals, and white pouch veined purple. Grows 1–2 ft. high. Hairy 4–6-in.-long leaves. Difficult to grow outside its native regions.

C. reginae. SHOWY LADY SLIPPER. Native to eastern U.S. In June, 1–3 flowers with white sepals and petals, rose pink pouch. Grows 2 ft. or more high. Oval leaves. Needs cold winters to thrive.

CYPRUS (OR CYPRIAN) CEDAR. See Cedrus brevifolia.

CYRTANTHUS mackenii. Bulb. Zones 23, 24, or sheltered situations in Zones 16–22, elsewhere container plant. South African native. Foot-long, narrow (⅓ in. wide) leaves have somewhat wavy edges. Tubular, curved, 2-in.-long white flowers nod in loose clusters at ends of stems. Blooms in spring. There are also cream and yellow flowered forms and hybrids in coral, orange, and red shades. Plants are actively growing throughout year; produce numerous offsets. Grow them in well-drained acid soil; keep soil moist. Grow in partial shade. If grown in pots, you'll need to repot them annually.

Cyrtanthus mackenii

CYRTOMIUM falcatum. HOLLYFERN. Zones 16, 17, 22–24. Coarse-textured but handsome fern 2–3 ft. tall, sometimes more. Leaflets large, dark green, glossy, leathery. Takes indoor conditions well and thrives outside in milder areas. Ample water. Hardy to 25°F. Take care not to plant too deeply. Forms with fringed leaflets available.

Cyrtomium falcatum

CYTISUS. BROOM. Most widely planted brooms belong here, but look for Spanish broom under *Spartium,* other choice shrubs under *Genista.* Deciduous or evergreen shrubs (many nearly leafless, but with green or gray stems). Sweet pealike flowers, often fragrant. Drought tolerant—so much so that they have become weeds in northern California and northwestern park and range lands—but better looking with a little summer water. They need sun and good drainage, tolerate wind, seashore conditions, and rocky, infertile soil. Where soil is highly alkaline, give them iron sulfate. Prune after bloom to keep to reasonable size and form, lessen production of unsightly seed pods.

C. battandieri. ATLAS BROOM. Semievergreen or deciduous. Zones 5, 6. Fast growth to 12–15 ft. high and as wide. Can be trained as small tree. Leaves divided into 3 roundish leaflets to 3½ in. long, to 1½ in. wide, covered with silvery, silky hairs. Fragrant, clear yellow flowers in spikelike (5-in.) clusters at branch ends, June-September.

Cytisus battandieri

C. canariensis (*Genista canariensis*). CANARY ISLAND BROOM. Evergreen. Zones 8, 9, 12–24. Damaged at 15°F. but recovers quickly. Many-branched, upright shrub to 6–8 ft. high, 5–6 ft. wide. Bright green leaves divided into ½-in. leaflets. Bright yellow, fragrant flowers in short clusters at ends of branches, spring and summer. Genista of florists. Grows like weed and spreads by seedlings.

C. kewensis. KEW BROOM. Dwarf shrublet. Best in Zones 4–6; less vigorous but satisfactory in 16, 17. Low, less than 1 ft. high, spreading with trailing branches to 4 ft. or more. Creamy white, ½-in. flowers in April-May. Tiny leaves. Branches will cascade in open pattern over wall or steep bank. One of best prostrate forms.

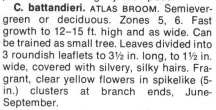

Cytisus racemosus

C. lydia. See *Genista lydia.*

C. praecox. WARMINSTER BROOM. Zones 2-9, 12-22. Deciduous. Compact growth with many slender stems to 3-5 ft. high and 4-6 ft. wide. Mounding mass of pale yellow to creamy white flowers March-April in south, April-May, north. Small leaves that fall early. Effective as informal screen or hedge, along drives, paths, garden steps. 'Allgold', slightly taller, has bright yellow flowers;

'Hollandia', pink ones. 'Moonlight', formerly considered *C. praecox* variety, is now thought to be form of *C. scoparius.*

C. purgans. PROVENCE BROOM. Zones 4–6. Deciduous. Dense mounding growth to 3 ft. high with equal spread. Silky, hairy leaves roundish, ¼–½ in. long. Fragrant chrome yellow flowers. May-July.

C. racemosus (*Genista racemosa;* often mistakenly sold as *G. fragrans*). Evergreen. Zones 7–9, 11–24. Similar in growth habit to *C. canariensis,* but with larger leaflets and longer, looser spikes of yellow, fragrant flowers in late spring. Naturalizes where adapted.

C. scoparius. SCOTCH BROOM. Evergreen. Zones 4–9, 14–22. This one has given all brooms a bad name. Has spread like weed over thousands of acres of open land in northern California and Northwest. Upright growing mass of wandlike green stems (often leafless or nearly so) may reach 10 ft. Golden yellow (¾-in.) flowers, spring and early summer.

Much less aggressive are lower growing, more colorful forms. Most of these grow 5–8 ft. tall: 'Burkwoodii', red touched yellow; 'Carla', pink and crimson lined white; 'Lilac Time', lilac pink, compact; 'Lord Lambourne', scarlet and cream; 'Moonlight', pale yellow, compact; 'Pomona', orange and apricot; 'St. Mary's', white; 'San Francisco' and 'Stanford', red.

DABOECIA. Small evergreen shrubs of heather family. Give them acid, fast draining soil and partial shade, except near coast where they can tolerate full sun. Most useful on hillsides, in rock or wild gardens. Water-dependent but less so than rhododendrons and azaleas.

D. azorica. Zones 8, 9, 14–24. Mounds to 6–10 in. Closely set, bright green leaves ¼ in. long, broader than other heaths and heathers. Egg shaped, rosy red flowers ½ in. long on spikelike clusters, April-May, occasionally in fall.

D. cantabrica. Zones 3–9, 14–24. Erect stems make slightly spreading plant 1½–2 ft. tall. Leaves larger than *D. azorica.* Pinkish purple, ½-in. egg shaped flowers in narrow 3–5-in. clusters, June-October (April in warmer areas). Cut back in fall to keep compact. 'Alba' has white flowers, 'Praegerae' pure pink, and 'Rosea' deep pink bloom.

Daboecia cantabrica

DAFFODIL. See *Narcissus.*

DAHLBERG DAISY. See *Dyssodia tenuiloba.*

DAHLIA. Perennials grown from tuberous roots. All Zones. Native to Mexico, Guatemala. Except for tree dahlia (*D. imperialis*) described at end of this section, dahlias are represented today exclusively by hybrids and strains, hundreds of them. Through centuries of hybridizing and selection, these bush and bedding dahlias have become tremendously diversified with numerous flower types in all colors but true blue. Sketches illustrate type based on flower form as classified by American Dahlia Society.

Dahlia hybrid

Bush and bedding plant dahlias grow from 15 in. to over 6 ft. high. Taller bush forms make summer hedges, screens, fillers among shrubs; lower kinds give mass color in borders and containers. Modern dahlias with strong stems, long-lasting blooms that face outward or upward, and substantial attractive foliage have become useful as cut flowers. Leaves are generally divided into many large, deep green leaflets.

Planting. Most dahlias are started from tubers. Plant them after frost is past and soil is warm. Full sun; light afternoon shade in hottest areas. Several weeks before planting, dig soil 1 ft. deep, work in ground bark, composted redwood sawdust, or

peat moss; also add coarse sand to heavy soils.

Make holes 1 ft. deep and 3 ft. apart for most varieties; space largest kinds 4–5 ft.; smaller ones 1–2 ft. If you use fertilizer at planting time, thoroughly incorporate ¼ cup of complete fertilizer in bottom of hole, then add 4 in. of plain soil. Drive 5-ft. stake into hole, place tuber horizontally with eye pointing toward stake and 2 in. from it. Cover tuber with 3 in. of soil. Water thoroughly if no rains expected. As shoots grow, gradually fill hole with soil.

Plant seeds of tall dahlias early indoors; transplant seedlings to garden position after frosts are over. Following fall and thereafter, dig and store tubers as described below. Sow seed of dwarf dahlias in place after soil is warm; or buy and plant started seedlings from nursery. Lift dwarf dahlia tubers in climates where ground freezes in winter; elsewhere they can remain permanently in place.

Thinning, pinching. On tall-growing types, thin to strongest shoot or 2 shoots (you can make cuttings of removed shoots). When remaining shoots have 3 sets of leaves, pinch off tips just above top set; 2 side shoots develop from each pair of leaves. For large flowers, remove all but terminal buds on side shoots. Smaller flowering dahlias such as miniatures, pompons, singles, or dwarfs need only first pinching.

Watering. Start watering regularly after shoots are above ground. Throughout active growth, keep soil moist to depth of 1 ft. Dahlias planted in enriched soil don't need additional food. If soil lacks nutrients, side dress plants with fertilizer high in phosphates and potash when first flower buds appear. Avoid high-nitrogen fertilizers: they result in soft growth, weak stems, tubers liable to rot in storage. Mulch to keep down weeds, eliminate cultivating which may injure feeder roots.

Cut flowers. Pick nearly mature flowers in early morning or evening. Place cut stems immediately in 2–3 in. of hot water; let stand in gradually cooling water for several hours or overnight.

Lifting, storing. After tops turn yellow or are frosted, cut stalks to 4 in. above ground. Dig around plant 1 ft. from center, carefully pry up clump with spading fork, shake off loose soil, let clump dry in sun for several hours. From that point, follow either of two methods:

(1) Divide clumps immediately (as described under method 2 below). This saves storage space. Freshly dug tubers are easy to cut; it is easy to recognize eyes or growth buds at this time. Dust cut surfaces with sulfur to prevent rot, bury tubers in sand, sawdust, or vermiculite, and store through winter in cool dry place.

(2) Leave clumps intact, cover them with dry sand, sawdust, peat moss, perlite, or vermiculite; store in cool (40°–45°F.) dry place. There is less danger of shrinking with this storage method. About 2–4 weeks before planting in spring, separate tubers by cutting from stalk with sharp knife; leave 1 in. of stalk attached to each tuber, which must have eye or bud in order to produce new plant. Place tubers in moist sand to encourage development of sprouts.

D. imperialis. TREE DAHLIA. Zones 4–6, 8, 9, 14–24. A 10–20-ft. multistemmed tree grows each year from permanent roots, produces 4–8-in. lavender daisy-type flowers with yellow centers, at branch ends in late fall. Leaves composed of many leaflets. Frosts kill tops completely; cut back to ground afterward. If it bloomed longer or remained evergreen, would be valued landscape plant, but annual live-and-die cycle relegates it to tall novelty class. Seldom sold in nurseries. Grow from cuttings

taken near tops of stems (or from side shoots) in fall; root in containers of moist sand kept in protected place over winter. Or dig root clump and divide in fall. Full sun or half shade. *D. excelsa, D. maxonii* are similar.

DAIS cotinifolia. POMPON TREE. Briefly deciduous. Zones 16–24. Native to South Africa. Worthwhile flowering shrub or small tree, somewhat like crape myrtle in size and shape. Slow to 12 ft. with 10-ft. spread. Flower clusters resemble 1½-in. balls of pink shredded coconut; carried at ends of twigs in June and July. Flowers remain after fading and are then rather unsightly. Bluish green leaves to 2½-in. long drop in sharp frosts. By nature a multitrunked shrub-tree, it looks best trained to single trunk. Unusually tolerant of heat. Will stand reflected light and heat of pavement and walls. Needs sun, average soil and watering.

Dais cotinifolia

DAISY TREE. See *Montanoa.*

DALEA spinosa. SMOKE TREE. Deciduous. Zones 11–13. Native to desert washes below 1,500 ft. in southern California, Arizona, Baja California. The few small leaves drop early. When out of leaf, its intricate network of gray spiny branches resembles cloud of smoke. Good show of fragrant violet blue flowers, April-June (flower branches make choice dry arrangements).

Useful in natural desert gardens. Seems happy at edge of irrigation. Usually grows to 12 ft., but with water in summer grows in bursts to as much as 30 ft. Easily grown from seed sown in warm weather. Sow in place or in small container and plant out.

Dalea spinosa

DAME'S ROCKET. See *Hesperis matronalis.*

DANCING LADY. See *Oncidium varicosum.*

DANDELION *(Taraxacum officinale).* Perennial. It's a weed in lawns and flower beds but it can also be a cultivated edible-leaf crop. All Zones. Seeds sold in packets. Cultivated forms have been selected for larger and thicker leaves than those on common weed form.

Tie leaves together to bleach interiors and eat like endive. Add tender leaves to mixed green salads, or boil thick leaves as "greens."

Cultivated
Dandelion

DAPHNE. Evergreen and deciduous shrubs. Of many kinds, three are widely

Informal decorative

Formal decorative

Cactus

Semicactus

Single

Collarette

Ball

Anemone

Pompon

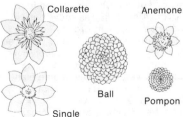

Decorative and cactus dahlias reach impressive sizes; many reach or exceed 1 ft. in diameter. Other kinds shown are equally good for cutting, are easier to arrange.

grown in West and most of others are choice rock garden subjects with limited distribution in nursery trade.

Although some daphnes are easier to grow than others, all require fast draining soil and careful hand with summer watering. They are far more temperamental in California than in Northwest.

D. blagayana. Evergreen. Zones 4–6. Spreading, almost prostrate (to 6 in. high), rooting along trailing branches. Oval leaves 1–1½ in. long, half as wide. Fragrant white flowers at ends of leafy twigs from March through April. Use in rock gardens or as small-area ground cover in part shade.

Daphne odora 'Marginata'

D. burkwoodii. Evergreen or semievergreen to deciduous. Zones 3–6, 14–17. Erect, compact growth to 3–4 ft. with closely set narrow leaves and numerous small clusters of fragrant white (fading pink) flowers around branch ends in late spring and again in late summer. Sun or light shade. Use in shrub borders, woodland edge, foundation planting.

D. b. 'Somerset'. Similar to above but larger plants (4–5 ft.) and deeper pink flowers, May-June.

D. cneorum. GARLAND DAPHNE. Evergreen. Zones 2–9, 14–17. Matting and spreading; less than 1 ft. high and 3 ft. wide. Good container plant. Trailing branches covered with narrow, 1-in.-long, dark green leaves. Clusters of fragrant rosy pink flowers in April and May. Choice rock garden plant; give it partial shade in warm areas, full sun in cool-summer areas. After bloom, topdress with mix of peat moss and sand to keep roots cool and induce additional rooting of trailing stems.

D. c. 'Ruby Glow'. Has larger flower clusters and deeper color than above. Repeats bloom in late summer and early fall.

D. collina. Evergreen. Zones 15–17; 5 and 6 with protection; 14 in partial shade. Neat dense mound to 2 ft. high and wide. Small (2 in. long) dark green leaves, paler beneath. Fragrant deep rose flowers in clusters at branch tips in April-May. Sometimes repeats bloom in summer and fall.

D. c. neapolitana. Variety is smaller growing, more open and spreading, and perhaps easier to grow.

D. genkwa. LILAC DAPHNE. Deciduous. Best in Zones 4–6, 16, 17. Erect open growth to 3–4 ft. high and as wide. Before leaves expand, clusters of lilac blue, scentless flowers wreathe branches, making foot-long blossom wands. White fruit follow flowers. Leaves are oval, 2 in. long. Use in rock garden, shrub border. Full sun or partial shade.

D. laureola. SPURGE LAUREL. Evergreen. Zones 4–6. Best in woodland plantings. Erect growth to 4 ft. high, 3 ft. wide. Glossy dark green leaves, 2–3 in. long. Stalkless clusters of yellow green flowers nestled among leaves are faintly fragrant. December-April. Will take heavy shade.

D. mantensiana. Evergreen. Zones 4–6, 15–17. Grows slowly to 1½ ft., spreading to 3 ft. Clusters of perfumed purple flowers tip branches May-June and often through summer. Densely branched and well-foliaged, it can be used in same way as low-growing azaleas. Leaves narrow, to 1¼ in. long.

D. mezereum. FEBRUARY DAPHNE. Deciduous. Zones 1–7, 14–17. Rather gawky, stiffly twigged, erect growth to 4 ft. with roundish 2–3-in.-long, thin leaves. Should be planted in groups. Sun to partial shade. Fragrant, reddish purple flowers in short stalkless clusters are carried along branches before leaves come out in February and continue until April. May go dormant by late July or August. Clusters of red fruit follow.

D. m. 'Alba'. Same as above but with white flowers, yellow fruit, and not as rangy in growth.

D. odora. WINTER DAPHNE. Evergreen. Zones 4–9, 14–24. So much loved, so prized for its pervasive, pre-spring fragrance that it continues to be widely planted in spite of its unpredictable behavior. Very neat, handsome plant usually to about 4 ft. high and spreading wider; occasionally grows 8-10 ft. high. Rather narrow 3-in.-long leaves are thick and glossy. Flowers—pink to deep red on outside with creamy pink throats—appear in nosegay clusters at ends of branches, February-March.

Other varieties of *D. odora* are: 'Alba', plain green leaves and pure white flowers; 'Alba Marginata', leaves edged with yellow and white flowers; 'Rose Queen', larger clusters of pink flowers.

D. odora needs much air around its roots—a porous soil. Otherwise, water molds attack. Dig planting hole twice as wide as root ball and 1½ times as deep. Refill with 1 part soil, 1 part fine sand, 2 parts ground bark. To create ideal drainage: before refilling hole, drill through bottom until you hit a better-draining soil layer. Refill that chimney with mixture, too. Set top of root ball higher than soil surface. Fill containers with same mix.

In Zones 18–24, transplanting an existing *D. odora* often fails; digging cuts roots, plant suffers, water molds get at it. Transplanting works in Zones 4–9, 14–17.

Plant this daphne where it can get at least 3 hours of shade a day. If possible, shade soil around roots with living ground cover. A pH of 7.0 is right for it (important in Zones 4–6). Feed right after bloom with complete fertilizer but not acid plant food.

During dry season, water as infrequently as plant will allow. Little or no water in summer increases flowering next spring and helps prevent death from water molds.

Shape plants by cutting at bloom season; cut flowering twigs back to good bud, small shoot, or large branch.

D. o. 'Marginata'. More widely grown than species. Leaves are edged with band of yellow.

D. retusa. Evergreen. Zones 5, 6, 15–17. Sturdy, compact growth to 1–2 ft. high and as broad. Leaves to 3 in. long; tips broad, sometimes notched. Lilac-scented flowers in 3-in. clusters, white tinged with pink or rose, in May-June, are followed by red fruit. Combines well with dwarf rhododendrons. Takes sun (but not reflected heat) and partial shade.

DARLINGTONIA californica. CALIFORNIA PITCHER PLANT, COBRA LILY. Novelty perennial. Zones 4–7, 14–17. Native to bogs in mountains of northern California and Oregon. Grow in containers in sunny spot indoors or in greenhouse. Interesting for its unusual leaves and habit of digesting insects. Plant makes clumps of 1–2-ft., tubelike, yellow green, veiny leaves, hooded at top. Hood has translucent spots. At mouth opening are 2 flared lobes, often reddish in color. Insects are lured into this leafy trap by sticky glands. Once insects are inside, downward pointing hairs prevent escape. Insects fall to base of leaf, decay, and when they are in a soluble state they become protein food absorbed by plant's cells.

Darlingtonia californica

Striking flowers, nodding at ends of 2½–4-ft. stems, appear April-June. Long, slender, pale green sepals, shorter dark purple petals. Blooms followed by mahogany brown seed capsules.

Pot in live sphagnum moss; keep moist at all times. Water overhead. Dry fertilizer, saline water are harmful. Collected plants are packaged and sold in a few nurseries and specialty shops, generally from October through June. They rarely thrive beyond a season or two.

DATE PALM. See *Phoenix*.

DATURA. For cultivated plants known as *Datura*, see *Brugmansia*.

DAUBENTONIA tripetii. See *Sesbania tripetii*.

DAVALLIA trichomanoides. SQUIRREL'S FOOT FERN. Outdoors in Zones 17, 23, 24; elsewhere, indoor or greenhouse plant. Very finely divided fronds to 12 in. long, 6 in. wide, rise from light reddish brown, furry rhizomes (like squirrel's feet) that creep over soil surface. Can be used in mild-winter areas (hardy to 30°F.) as small-scale ground cover in partly shaded areas. Best use in any climate is as hanging basket plant. Use light, fast draining soil mix.

Davallia trichomanoides

Needs less water than other ferns. Feed occasionally. (For similar fern, see *Humata*.)

Davallia trichomanoides

DAVIDIA involucrata. DOVE TREE. Deciduous. Zones 4–9, 14–21. Native to China. Tree to 35 ft. in Pacific Northwest (higher in California), with rounded crown and strong branching pattern. Has clean look in and out of leaf. When it flowers in May general effect is that of white doves resting among green leaves—or as some say, like handkerchiefs drying on branches.

Leaves are vivid green, 3–6 in. long, roundish to heart shaped. Small, clustered, red-anthered flowers are carried between two large, unequal, white or creamy white bracts; one 6 in. long, other about 4 in. Fruit brown, about size of golf ball; hang on tree well into winter.

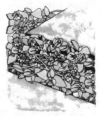

Davidia involucrata

In Zones 7–9, 14, 18–21, give it partial or afternoon shade. Average water. Plant it by itself; it should not compete with other flowering trees. Nice in front of dark conifers where vivid green and white stand out.

DAWN REDWOOD. See *Metasequoia glyptostroboides*.

DAYLILY. See *Hemerocallis*.

DEAD NETTLE. See *Lamium maculatum*.

DEER FERN. See *Blechnum spicant*.

DEERHORN CEDAR. See *Thujopsis dolabrata*.

DEER TONGUE FERN. See *Blechnum spicant*.

DELOSPERMA 'Alba'. WHITE TRAILING ICE PLANT. Succulent perennial. Zones 12–24. Dwarf, spreading, rooting freely from stems. Good ground cover and bank cover. Small fleshy leaves of good green color. Small white flowers are not showy. Set in sun 1 ft. apart for quick cover. Give just enough water to keep plants looking lively; in some climates, no summer watering is needed. Good near seashore; can be fire retardant. Draws bees.

Delosperma 'Alba'

D. nubigenum. All Zones. Unique among ice plants in being hardy in cold-winter climates. Fleshy cylindrical bright green leaves turn red in fall, green up again in spring. Bright golden yellow flowers 1–1½ in. wide blanket plants in spring. Effective rock garden plant in mountain climates.

DELPHINIUM. Perennials, some short lived and treated as annuals. Most people associate delphiniums with blue flowers, but color range also includes shades of red, pink, lavender, purple, white, and yellow; attracts birds. Leaves are lobed or fanlike, variously cut and divided. Taller hybrids offer rich colors in elegant spirelike form. All kinds are effective in borders and make good cut flowers. Lower-growing kinds serve well as container plants. For annual delphiniums (LARKSPURS) see *Consolida*.

All kinds are easy to grow from seed. Sow fresh seed in flats of light soil mix in July-August in mild-winter areas; set out transplants in October for bloom in late spring and early summer. (In mild-winter climates, most perennial forms are short lived, often treated as annuals.) In cold climates, refrigerate summer-harvested seed in airtight containers until

Delphinium elatum

time to sow. Sow seed in March-April, set out transplants in June-July for first bloom by September (and more bloom the following summer).

Delphiniums need full sun, rich porous soil, regular watering, and fertilizing. Improve poor or heavy soils by blending in soil conditioners. Add lime to strongly acid soils. Work small handful of bonemeal or superphosphate into bottom of each hole before setting out plant. Be careful not to cover root crown.

Here is how to grow close-to-perfection plants: when new shoots develop in spring, remove all but 2 or 3 strongest and apply complete fertilizer alongside plants. Bait for slugs and snails. Stake flower stalks early. After bloom, cut back flower spikes, leaving foliage at bottom; after new shoots are several inches high, cut old stalks to ground; fertilize to encourage good second bloom in late summer, early fall.

D. ajacis. See *Consolida*.

D. belladonna. Sturdy, bushy perennial. Zones 1–9, 14–24. To 3–4 ft.; deeply cut leaves; short stemmed, airy flower clusters. Varieties: 'Belladonna', light blue; 'Bellamosum', dark blue; 'Casa Blanca', white; 'Cliveden Beauty', deep turquoise blue. All have flowers 1½–2 in. across, are longer lived than tall hybrids listed under *D. elatum*, following.

D. cardinale. SCARLET LARKSPUR. Perennial. Zones 14–24. Native to California coastal mountains, Monterey County south. Erect stems grow 3–6 ft. from deep, thick, woody roots. Leaves 3–9 in. wide, with deep narrow lobes. Flowers 1 in. across, with scarlet calyx and spur and yellow, scarlet-tipped petals; May-June bloom. Sow seed early for first-year bloom.

D. elatum. CANDLE DELPHINIUM, CANDLE LARKSPUR. Perennial. Zones 1–9, 14–24. This 3–6-ft. Siberian species, with small dark or dull purple flowers, together with *D. cheilanthum* and others, is parent of modern tall-growing delphinium strains such as spectacular Pacific strain.

Pacific strain delphinium hybrids (also called Giant Pacific, Pacific Hybrids, and Pacific Coast hybrids) grow up to 8 ft., come in selected color series such as 'Summer Skies', light blue; 'Blue Bird', medium blue; 'Blue Jay', medium to dark blue; 'Galahad', clear white with white "bee" center; 'Percival', white with black bee; also in other purple, lavender, pink named varieties.

The Dwarf Giant Pacific 'Blue Fountains'—to 24 in. high—comes in a mixture of blue shades, some with dark blue bees.

Other series have flowers in shades of lilac pink to deep raspberry rose, clear lilac, lavender, royal purple, and darkest violet. Wrexham strain, tall growing with large spikes, was developed in England.

D. grandiflorum (*D. chinense*). CHINESE or BOUQUET DELPHINIUM. Short-lived perennial treated as biennial or annual. All Zones. Bushy, branching, 1 ft. tall or less. Varieties include 'Dwarf Blue Mirror', 1 ft., upfacing flowers of deep blue; and 'Tom Thumb', 8 in. tall, with pure gentian blue flowers.

D. nudicaule. SCARLET LARKSPUR. Perennial. Zones 5–7, 14–24. Native of northern California, southwestern Oregon. Slender plant 1–3 ft. Leaves long stalked, mostly basal, broadly divided. Flowers few, long spurred, red. Sun or half shade; best in woodland situation.

DENDROBIUM. Epiphytic orchid. Native to east and southeast Asia. Distributed over wide range of climates; many species differ in cultural needs.

D. nobile hybrids are best for novice. They vary from white through pink to rosy purple in color. Leathery leaves 5–6 in. long. Flowers grow in clusters all along well-ripened stems. Well-grown plants may have hundreds of 3-in. flowers. Grow under same conditions as cattleyas until new growth matures in fall. Then move them into cool, bright greenhouse with little water and no feeding. Resume normal cattleya treatment after flower buds form. Splendid orchids for greenhouse, they seldom get enough light to bloom well in living rooms or sun porches.

Dendrobium nobile

DENDROCALAMUS. See *Bamboo*.

DENDROMECON. BUSH POPPY. Evergreen shrubs. Zones 5–8, 14–24. Has been grown as south-wall shrub in Zone 5. Both species give showy display of bright yellow, 2-in.-wide, poppylike flowers. Sun loving. Thrive in dry, well-drained soil. Use on banks, roadsides, with other native shrubs.

D. harfordii *(D. rigida harfordii)*. ISLAND BUSH POPPY. Native to Santa Cruz and Santa Rosa Islands off coast of southern California. Rounded or spreading large shrub or small tree to 20 ft. Leaves deep green, to 3 in. long, half as wide. Free flowering April-July and scattered bloom throughout year. Prune to thin or shape after bloom.

Dendromecon harfordii

D. rigida. BUSH POPPY. Native to dry chaparral in lower elevations in California. Untidy growing wild. Freely branched shrub 2–8 ft. with shredding, yellowish gray or white bark. Thick, veiny, gray green leaves 1–4 in. long. Flowers March-June. Prune back to 2 ft. after flowering.

DEODAR CEDAR. See *Cedrus deodara*.

DESERT BROOM. See *Baccharis sarothroides*.

DESERT CANDLE. See *Eremurus*.

DESERT GUM. See *Eucalyptus rudis*.

DESERT HOLLY. See *Atriplex hymenelytra*.

DESERT HONEYSUCKLE. See *Anisacanthus thurberi*.

DESERT IRONWOOD. See *Olneya tesota*.

DESERT OLIVE. See *Forestiera neomexicana*.

DESERT WILLOW. See *Chilopsis linearis*.

DEUTZIA. Deciduous flowering shrubs. Zones 1–11, 14–17. They are best used among evergreens where they can make a show when in flower, blend back in with other greenery during rest of year. Their May flowering coincides with that of late spring bulbs—tulips and Dutch iris.

Plant in sun or light shade. Prune after flowering. With low or medium-growing kinds, cut to ground some of oldest stems every other year. Prune tall-growing kinds severely by cutting back wood that has flowered. Cut to outward-facing side branches. Need average garden water.

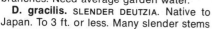

Deutzia rosea

D. gracilis. SLENDER DEUTZIA. Native to Japan. To 3 ft. or less. Many slender stems arch gracefully to 3 ft. and spread to 5 ft. Bright green, 2½-in.-long leaves with sharply toothed edges. Clusters of snowy white flowers cover branches.

D. lemoinei. Hybrid. Neat, compact shrub to 6 ft. high. Leaves, 1–4 in. long, have finely toothed edges. White flowers, tinged pinkish or purplish outside, in large broad clusters.

D. rosea. Hybrid. Low-growing shrub (to 3–4 ft.), with finely toothed, 1–3-in.-long leaves. Flowers pinkish outside, white inside, in short clusters.

D. scabra. Native to Japan, China. This plant and its varieties are robust shrubs 7–10 ft. tall. Leaves oval, 3 in. long, dull green, roughish to touch, with scallop-toothed edges. May-June flowers white or pinkish in narrow upright clusters. *D. s.* 'Pride of Rochester', best known, bears large clusters of small, double, frilled flowers, rosy purple outside.

DEVIL'S BACKBONE. See *Pedilanthus tithymaloides*.

DEVIL'S WALKING STICK. See *Aralia spinosa*.

DIANELLA tasmanica. Perennial. Zones 8, 9, 14–24. Fibrous-rooted plant with sturdy, swordlike leaves to 4–5 ft. Small, pale blue, summer-blooming flowers in loose clusters on straight, slender stalks, followed by glistening turquoise blue berries lasting 2 or more months. Grow in partial shade, or full sun along coast. Provide rich, porous soil and routine feeding. They need ample water to fruit well, but tolerate drought once established. Attractive near swimming pools.

Dianella tasmanica

DIANTHUS. PINK. Perennials, biennials, annuals. All Zones. Over 300 species, many with high garden value, and extremely large number of hybrids. Most kinds form attractive evergreen mats or tufts of grasslike green, gray green, blue green, or blue gray leaves. Single or double flowers in white and shades of pink, rose, red, yellow, and orange bloom in spring or summer, sometimes until frost. Many have rich spicy fragrance.

Among dianthus are appealing border favorites such as cottage pink and sweet William, highly prized cut flowers such as carnation or clove pink, and rock garden miniatures.

Dianthus caryophyllus

All kinds of dianthus thrive in full sun (light afternoon shade in hot areas), and in light, fast draining soil. Carnations, sweet William, and cottage pinks need fairly rich soil; rock garden or alpine types require gritty growing medium, with added lime if soil is acid. Avoid overwatering. Shear off faded blooms. Sow seed of annual kinds in flats or directly in garden. Propagate perennial kinds by cuttings made from tips of growing shoots, or by division, layers, or seed.

Carnations and sweet William are subject to rust and fusarium wilt. Control rust by spraying foliage weekly with benlate; remove and destroy plants infected by wilt. Replant only in clean or sterilized soil. Take cuttings only from disease-free plants.

D. barbatus. SWEET WILLIAM. Vigorous biennial often grown as annual. Sturdy stems 10–20 in. high; leaves are flat, light to dark green, 1½–3 in. long. Dense clusters of white, pink, rose, red, purplish, or bicolored flowers, about ½ in. across, set among leafy bracts; not very fragrant. Sow seed in late spring for bloom following year. Double-flowered and dwarf (8–10 in. tall) strains are obtainable from seed. Wee Willie (4 in.) and Summer Beauty strains bloom in summer from early spring sowing.

D. caryophyllus. CARNATION, CLOVE PINK. Perennial. There are two distinct categories of carnations: florist and border types. Both have double flowers, bluish green leaves, and branching, leafy stems often becoming woody at base.

Border carnations. Bushier, more compact than florist type, 12–14 in. high. Flowers 2–2½ in. wide, fragrant, borne in profusion. Enfant de Nice strain has blooms in red, rose, salmon, white. Dwarf Fragrance mixture comes in similar colors. Effective as shrub border edgings, in mixed flower border, and in containers. New hybrid carnations grown from seed are usually treated as annuals, but often live over. 'Juliet' makes compact, foot-tall clumps with long production of 2½-in. scarlet flowers. Pixie Delight strain is similar, but includes full range of carnation colors. Knight series has strong stems, blooms in 5 months from seed.

Florist carnations. Grown commercially in greenhouses, outdoors in gardens in mild-winter areas. Greenhouse-grown plants reach 4 ft., have fragrant flowers 3 in. wide in many colors—white, pink and red shades, orange, purple, yellow, and variegated. For large flowers, leave only terminal bloom on each stem and pinch out all other buds down to fifth joint, below which new flowering stems will develop. Stake to prevent sprawling. Start with strong cuttings taken from most vigorous plants of selected named varieties. Sturdy plants conceal supports, look quite tidy.

D. chinensis. CHINESE PINK, RAINBOW PINK. Biennial or short-lived perennial; most varieties grown as annuals. Erect, 6–30 in. high, stems branching only at top. Stem leaves narrow, 1–3 in. long, ½ in. wide, hairy on margins. Basal leaves usually gone by flowering time. Flowers about 1 in. across, rose lilac with deeper colored eye; lack fragrance. Modern strains are compact (1 ft. tall or less) domes covered with bright flowers in white, pink, red, and all variations and combinations of these colors. 'Queen of Hearts' is choice scarlet, and Magic Charms includes entire color range. Petals on some are deeply fringed, on others, smooth edged. Some flowers have intricately marked eyes. Sow directly in ground in spring, in full sun, for summer bloom. Pick off faded flowers with their bases to prolong bloom.

D. deltoides. MAIDEN PINK. Hardy perennial forming loose mats. Flowering stems 8–12 in. high with short leaves. Flowers about ¾ in. across, borne at end of forked stems; petals sharp toothed, light or dark rose to purple or white, spotted with lighter colors. Blooms in summer, sometimes again in fall. Named varieties are: 'Vampire', deep red; 'Zing', bright scarlet; 'Zing Rose', rose red. These bloom in a few weeks from seed but are hardy perennials.

D. gratianopolitanus (*D. caesius*). CHEDDAR PINK. Perennial. Neat, compact mounds of blue gray foliage on weak, branching stems up to 12 in. long. Flowering stems erect, 3–12 in. high. Very fragrant pink blooms with toothed petals. May–June.

D. 'Little Joe'. Perennial. Irresistible little plant forming clump of deep blue gray foliage 4–6 in. high and about 6 in. across. Crimson red single flowers bloom from May to November if dead blooms are removed. Especially effective with rock garden campanulas.

D. plumarius. COTTAGE PINK. Perennial. Charming, almost legendary plant, cultivated for hundreds of years, used in developing many hybrids. Typically has loosely matted gray green foliage. Flowering stems 10–18 in. tall; flowers spicily fragrant, single or double, with petals more or less fringed, rose, pink, or white with dark centers. Highly prized are old laced pinks, with spicily fragrant white flowers in which each petal is outlined in red or pink. Blooms from June to October. Indispensable edging for borders, or peony or rose beds. Perfect in small arrangements and old-fashioned bouquets.

D. 'Rose Bowl'. Perennial. Gray green, very narrow leaves form tight mat 2–3 in. high. Richly fragrant, cerise rose flowers 1 in. across on 6-in. stems. Blooms almost continuously if spent blooms are removed regularly.

D. 'Tiny Rubies'. Perennial. Tufts of gray foliage to 3 in. high, spreading to 4 in. Small, double, fragrant ruby red flowers in early summer. This and other dwarf kinds of dianthus are among longest lived and most attractive rock garden subjects and small-scale ground covers, with fresh-looking foliage at all seasons.

DIASCIA. TWINSPUR. Annual, perennial. South African natives with rich salmon to coral pink flowers, each with 2 prominent spurs on back. Flowers in spikelike clusters at ends of stems. Use in rock gardens, borders, pots.

D. barberae. Annual. All zones. Slender stems 6–12 in. tall. Sow seed directly in ground in full sun, partial shade in hot summer areas.

D. cordata. Perennial. Zones 7–9, 14–24. Low green mat with 10-in. sprays of salmon pink. Summer blooming.

D. 'Ruby Field'. Perennial. Similar to *D. cordata*, with longer bloom season.

D. rigescens. Perennial. Zones 7–9, 14–24. Sprawling stems make 2-ft.-wide clumps, turn up at ends to display 6–8-in. spikes of rich pink. Spring and summer bloom. Cut out old stems to groom.

Diascia barberae

DICENTRA. BLEEDING HEART. Perennials. Zones 1–9, 14–24. Short lived in mild-winter areas. Graceful, divided, fernlike foliage. Dainty flowers, usually heart shaped, pink, rose, or white on leafless stems. Most kinds need shade, combine handsomely with ferns, begonias, primroses, fuchsias, bergenias, hellebores. In general, dicentras need rich, light, moist, porous soil. Never let water stand around roots. Since foliage dies down in winter, mark clumps to avoid digging into roots in dormant season.

Dicentra spectabilis

D. chrysantha. GOLDEN EARDROPS. Native to inner Coast Ranges and Sierra Nevada foothills of California. Erect perennial with sparse, blue gray, divided leaves on stout hollow stems 4–5 ft. high. Flowers golden yellow, short spurred, held upright in large clusters. Requires warmth, good drainage, not-too-rich soil. Has deep tap root, needs no water during flowering in spring and summer. Seed available from wildflower specialists.

D. eximia. FRINGED BLEEDING HEART. Native of northeastern U.S. Forms tidy, nonspreading clumps 12–18 in. high. Leaves blue gray, at base of plant, more finely divided than those of western bleeding heart. Flowers, deep rose pink with short rounded spurs, bloom May–August. Cut back in July or August for second growth and sometimes repeat bloom. Variety 'Alba' has white flowers. 'Bountiful' has deep blue green foliage and fuchsia-red flowers.

D. formosa. WESTERN BLEEDING HEART. Native to moist woods along Pacific Coast. Leafless flower stalks 8–18 in. high, with clusters of pendulous pale or deep rose flowers on reddish stems April–June. Blue green foliage. Variety 'Sweetheart', beautiful white flowers, light green leaves, blooms May–October. *D. f. oregana*, native of Siskiyou Mountains in southern Oregon and northern California, grows about 8 in. high, has translucent blue green leaves, cream-colored flowers with rosy-tipped petals; in its best climates, it spreads aggressively.

D. 'Luxuriant'. Hybrid of *D. eximia* and *D. peregrina*. Extremely vigorous. Dark blue green foliage. Flowers as dark as those of *D. eximia* 'Bountiful', even in full sun. Foliage mass 10 in. tall, flower spikes 18–20 in. high.

D. spectabilis. COMMON BLEEDING HEART. Native of Japan. Old garden favorite, showiest of bleeding hearts. Leafy-stemmed plants 2–3 ft. high. Leaves soft green, largest of all dicentras. Rose pink, pendulous, heart shaped flowers, 1 in. or more long, with white petals protruding, borne on one side of arching stems; bloom in late spring. Beautiful with maidenhair ferns and in arrangements with tulips and lilacs. In Southwest, can sometimes establish bleeding heart permanently in cool moist spot in foothill canyons, but usual practice is to plant or pot up new roots each year and discard plants in early summer after blooming. These dormant roots—fleshy and sometimes even woody—are available in late fall, winter, and earliest spring. Plant as soon as they become available in your area.

DICHELOSTEMMA. Corms. All Zones. Western natives usually sold as species of *Brodiaea,* and still considered brodiaeas by many botanists. See *Brodiaea* for culture. All have few narrow grassy leaves.

D. ida-maia (*Brevoortia* or *Brodiaea ida-maia*). FIRECRACKER FLOWER. Clusters of 6–20 or more pendulous, tubular, scarlet flowers tipped green. Blooms May–July. To 3 ft. Good summer-dry woodland plant. Takes some shade.

D. pulchellum (*D. capitatum, B. capitata*). BLUE DICKS, WILD HYACINTH. Deep blue or violet blue flowers in tight headlike cluster surrounded with purplish bracts. Blooms March–May. To 2 ft. Thrives in poor soils, summer-baked locations. One of prettiest spring flowers for sunny banks.

Dichelostemma ida-maia

DICHONDRA micrantha (often sold as *D. carolinensis* or *D. repens*). DICHONDRA. Perennial lawn plant or ground cover plant. Zones 8, 9, 12–24. Ground-hugging plant that spreads by rooting surface runners. Small round leaves look like miniature water lily pads. In shade and with heavy feeding and watering it can grow to 6 in. tall and needs frequent mowing. In sun and in areas subject to foot traffic—as between stepping stones—it stays low and seldom, if ever, needs mowing.

Dichondra micrantha

To plant, prepare soil as for a lawn. Sow seed in April or May. Two lbs. per 1,000 sq. ft. will give fast coverage (lesser amounts bring slower coverage with increased weed problems). Or plant from plugs cut from flats of dichondra. Place 1-in.-square or (preferably) 2-in.-square pieces at 6–12-in. intervals. Be sure runners on plugs are at soil level or slightly below.

Dichondra requires ample fertilizer and water to look its best. Dichondra flea beetle can devastate lawn. First signs are browning leaves with engraved lines where tissue has been gnawed. Control at once with diazinon.

DICHORISANDRA. Perennials usually grown as house plants. Relatives of wandering Jews (*Tradescantia* and *Zebrina*). Like them in foliage (although leaves are much larger), but have erect fleshy stems rising from fleshy rootstocks, flowers in dense clusters. They need rich house plant soil mix, ample water and feeding during warm weather. They slow down or even go dormant in cool, dull weather and need partial drying off at that time.

D. reginae. To 2 ft. Leaves to 6 in. long, purple beneath, dark green marked with silver above. Blue flowers in dense spikes at ends of stems. Showy plant; subject to leaf burn if overfed or overwatered. Don't discard if top dies; new stems often appear from roots.

Dichorisandra reginae

D. thyrsiflora. BLUE GINGER. To 3 ft. in 8-in. pot, much more in open ground or large tub. Stems erect, occasionally with branch or two. Deep green leaves to 6 in. or more. In greenhouse or other favorable situation may produce 6-in.-long, narrow clusters of bright blue flowers.

DICKSONIA. Tree ferns. Hardy, slow-growing, from southern hemisphere. See Ferns for culture.

D. antarctica. TASMANIAN TREE FERN. Zones 8, 9, 14–17, 19–24. Native to southeastern Australia, Tasmania. Hardiest of tree ferns; well-established plants tolerate 20°F. Thick, red brown fuzzy trunks grow slowly to 15 ft. Out from top of trunk grow many arching 3–6-ft. fronds; mature fronds are darker green than either Hawaiian tree fern (*Cibotium*) or Australian tree fern (*Sphaeropteris*).

Dicksonia antarctica

D. squarrosa. Zones 17, 23, 24. Native to New Zealand. Slender, dark trunk to eventual 20 ft., but slow. Flat crown of 8-ft.-long, stiff, leathery fronds. Much less frequently grown than *D. antarctica*.

DICTAMNUS albus. GAS PLANT, FRAXINELLA. Perennial. Zones 1–9. Sturdy, long lived, extremely permanent in colder climates. Once established needs little care. Forms clumps 2½–4 ft. high. Strong lemony odor when rubbed or brushed against. Attractive, glossy, olive green leaves with 9–11 leaflets 1–3 in. long. Spike-like clusters of white flowers about 1 in. long with prominent greenish stamens, June-July. There are varieties with pink and rosy purple flowers and darker green leaves, growing taller and more robust than species. Never common, but worth looking for or growing from seed (a slow process).

Effective in borders; combine white-flowered kind with yellow daylily, Siberian iris, taller campanulas. Good cut flower. Plant in sun or part shade in good soil. Average water. Divide infrequently; divisions take 2–3 years before making a show. Propagate from seed sown in fall or spring or from root cuttings in spring. Common name, gas plant, derives from this phenomenon: if lighted match is held near flowers on warm, still evenings, volatile oil exuded from glands on that part of plant will ignite and burn briefly.

Dictamnus albus

DIDISCUS coeruleus. See *Trachymene coerulea*.

DIEFFENBACHIA. DUMB CANE. Evergreen indoor foliage plant (you can move it into sheltered patio or lanai in summer). Striking variegated leaves. Colors vary from dark green to yellow green and chartreuse, with variegations in white or pale cream. Small plants generally have single stems; older plants may develop multiple stems. Flowers—like odd, narrow callas—form on mature plants. Common name reflects fact that acrid sap will burn mouth and throat, and may paralyze vocal cords.

Give ample north light; turn occasionally, and water only when soil surface feels dry. If plant gets leggy, air-layer it or root cuttings in water. Old, leggy plants, cut back to 6 in. from soil line, usually resprout with multiple stems. Repot when roots begin pushing plant up in pot.

Dieffenbachia amoena

Once repotted, plant usually sends out new basal shoots. Potting soil should drain freely. Feed bimonthly in spring and summer with half-strength liquid fertilizer. Underfed, underwatered plants show amazingly strong hold on life, recovering from severe wilting when better conditions come. They will not withstand constant overwatering, and sudden change from low to high light level will sunburn leaves.

D. amoena. To 6 ft. or higher. Broad, dark green, 18-in.-long leaves marked with narrow, white, slanting stripes on either side of midrib.

D. 'Exotica'. More compact with smaller leaves than others. Leaves have dull green edges and much creamy white variegation. Midrib is creamy white.

D. maculata (*D. picta*). To 6 ft. or higher. Wide, oval green leaves, 10 in. or more in length, have greenish white dots and patches.

D. m. 'Rudolph Roehrs'. To 6 ft., with 10-in. leaves of pale chartreuse, blotched with ivory and edged with green.

D. m. 'Superba'. Foliage thicker and slightly more durable than species; more creamy white dots and patches.

DIERAMA. FAIRY WAND. Corms. Zones 4–24. Native to South Africa. Swordlike 2-ft. leaves; slender, tough, arching stems 4–7 ft. tall, topped with pendulous, bell shaped, mauve, purple, or white flowers. Effective against background of dark green shrubs or at edge of pool where graceful form can be displayed. Plant in sun, moist soil. When dividing clumps, include several corms in each division.

D. pendulum. Flowers white, lavender pink, or mauve, 1 in. long, March or April.

D. pulcherrimum. Leaves very stiff. Flowers bright purple to almost white, 1½ in. long, May, June.

Dierama pulcherrimum

DIETES *(Moraea)*. FORTNIGHT LILY, AFRICAN IRIS. Evergreen perennials growing from rhizomes. Zones 8, 9, 13–24. Clumps of narrow, stiff irislike leaves that grow fan shaped. Flowers like miniature Japanese iris appear on branched stalks throughout spring, summer, and fall, sometimes well into winter in mild areas. Each flower lasts only a day, but is quickly replaced by another. Bloom bursts seem to come at 2-week intervals—hence the name fortnight lily. Break off forming seed pods to increase flower production and prevent volunteer plants. Effective near swimming pools.

Dietes vegeta

Give plants of *Dietes* full sun or light shade in any fairly good soil. Established plants tolerate drought but bloom more freely with regular watering. Divide overgrown clumps in autumn or winter. *Moraea* differs from *Dietes* because corms are dormant for part of the year.

D. bicolor. To 2 ft. Flowers light yellow with maroon blotches, about 2 in. wide. Cut flower stems to ground after blossoms fade.

D. vegeta *(D. iridioides, Moraea iridioides)*. To 4 ft., with 3-in.-wide waxy white flowers with orange and brown blotch, purple stippling. 'Johnsonii' is robust variety with large leaves and flowers. Break off old blossoms individually to prevent self-sowing and prolong bloom, but don't cut off long, branching flower stems. These last from year to year. Instead cut back to lower leaf joint near base of plant. Excellent in permanent landscape plantings with pebbles, rocks, substantial shrubs. Very drought resistant.

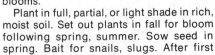

DIGITALIS. FOXGLOVE. Biennials or perennials. All Zones. Erect plants 2–8 ft. high with tubular flowers shaped like fingers of glove in purple, yellow, white, pastels. Bloom May–September. Hairy, gray green leaves grow in clumps at base of plant. Use foxgloves for vertical display among shrubs, or with ferns, taller campanulas, meadow rue. Hummingbirds like foxglove blooms.

Digitalis purpurea

Plant in full, partial, or light shade in rich, moist soil. Set out plants in fall for bloom following spring, summer. Sow seed in spring. Bait for snails, slugs. After first flowering cut main spike; side shoots develop, bloom until September. Plants self-sow freely.

D. ferruginea. RUSTY FOXGLOVE. Biennial or perennial with very leafy stems to 6 ft. Leaves deeply veined. Flowers ¾–1¼ in. long, yellowish, netted with rusty red, in long dense spikes.

D. grandiflora *(D. ambigua)*. YELLOW FOXGLOVE. Biennial or perennial. Hairy-leafed plant 2–3 ft. high. Toothed leaves wrap around stem. Large flowers, 2–3 in. long, yellowish marked with brown.

D. mertonensis. True perennial with spikes of odd yet attractive coppery rose, 2–3 ft. tall. Though hybrid between two species, it comes true from seed.

D. purpurea. COMMON FOXGLOVE. Biennial, sometimes perennial. Naturalizes in shaded places. Variable, appears in many garden forms. Bold, erect, to 4 ft. or more high. Clumps of large, rough, woolly, light green leaves; stem leaves short stalked, becoming smaller toward top of plant; these leaves are source of digitalis, valued but highly poisonous medicinal drug. Flowers 2–3 in. long, pendulous, purple, spotted on lower, paler side, borne in one-sided, 1–2-ft.-long spikes. Several garden strains: Excelsior, 5 ft., has fuller spikes, with flowers more horizontally held to show off interior spotting; Foxy, 3 ft., performs as annual, blooming in 5 months from seed; Gloxiniiflora, 4 ft., has flowers that are individually larger and open wider than common foxglove; Monstrosa, 3 ft., has topmost flower of each spike open or bowl shaped and 3 in. wide; Shirley is tall (6 ft.), robust strain in full range of colors. Volunteer foxglove seedlings are frequently white.

DILL. See *Anethum graveolens*.

DIMORPHOTHECA. CAPE MARIGOLD, AFRICAN DAISY. (For other plants known as African daisy, see *Arctotis, Osteospermum*.) Annuals. All Zones. Gay, free-blooming, daisy-flowered plants, unsurpassed for winter and spring color in dry warm-winter areas. Not as well-adapted in cool, moist coastal climate. Broadcast seed in late summer or early fall where plants are to grow. Best in light soil; moderate watering. Need full sun; flowers close when shaded, during heavy overcast, and at night. Use in broad masses as ground cover, in borders, parking strips, along rural roadsides, as filler among low shrubs.

Dimorphotheca sinuata

D. barberae. See *Osteospermum*.

D. ecklonis. See *Osteospermum*.

D. fruticosa. See *Osteospermum*.

D. pluvialis *(D. annua)*. Branched stems 4–16 in. high. Leaves to 3½ in. long, 1 in. wide, coarsely toothed. Flower heads 1–2 in. across; rays white above, violet or purple beneath; yellow center. Variety 'Glistening White', dwarf form, flower heads 4 in. across, is especially desirable.

D. sinuata. (Usually sold as D. 'Aurantiaca'.) Best known of annual African daisies. Plants 4–12 in. high. Leaves narrow, 2–3 in. long, with a few teeth or shallow indentations. Flower heads 1½ in. across, with orange yellow rays, sometimes deep violet at base, yellow center. Hybrids between this species and D. pluvialis in white and shades of yellow, orange, apricot, salmon, often with contrasting dark centers.

Excellent for winter-spring color in Zones 10–13: reseeds yearly. Needs some supplemental water October-March if winter rains don't come. Leave area dry over summer.

DIOON. Cycads. In general, resemble *Cycas revoluta* and take same culture. Dioons are more tender and less frequently sold.

Dioon edule

D. edule. Zones 13, 17, 19–24. Very slow. Eventually forms cylindrical trunk 6–10 in. wide, 3 ft. high. Leaves spreading, slightly arching, 3–5 ft. long, made of many leaflets toothed at tip or smooth edged. Leaves dusty blue green, soft, feathery on young plants; darker green, more rigid, hard, shiny on mature plants.

D. spinulosum. Zones 21–24. Slow growth to 12 ft. Leaves to 5 ft. long, with up to 100 narrow, spine toothed, dark green 6–8-in.-long leaflets. Protect from frosts.

DIOSMA. See *Coleonema* and *Diosma*.

DIOSPYROS. See *Persimmon*.

DIPLACUS. See *Mimulus*.

DIPLADENIA amoena, D. splendens. See *Mandevilla* 'Alice du Pont'.

DIPLOPAPPUS fruticosus. See *Felicia fruticosa*.

Distictis buccinatoria

DISTICTIS. Evergreen vines. Climb by tendrils and have trumpet shaped flowers. To 20–30 ft. tall. Hardy to 24°F. Sun or part shade.

D. buccinatoria *(Bignonia cherere, Phaedranthus buccinatorius)*. BLOOD-RED TRUMPET VINE. Zones 8, 9, 14–24. Leaves have 2 oblong to oval leaflets 2–4 in. long. Clusters of 4-in.-long trumpet shaped flowers stand out well from vine. Color is orange red fading to bluish red, with yellow throat. Flowers appear in bursts throughout year when weather warms. Effective on fence, high wall, arbor. Prune yearly to keep under control. Give protected site in interior valleys. Feed and water young plants generously until established.

D. laxiflora *(D. lactiflora, D. cinerea).* VANILLA TRUMPET VINE. Zones 16, 22–24. Native to Mexico. More restrained than most trumpet vines and requires less pruning. Leaves, with 2–3 deep green, oblong (2½ in. long) leaflets, make attractive pattern all year. The 3½-in.-long, vanilla scented trumpets, at first violet, fading to lavender and white, appear in generous clusters throughout warmer months, sometimes giving 8 months of bloom. Average water.

D. 'Rivers'. (Sometimes labeled *D. riversii.*) ROYAL TRUMPET VINE. Zones 16, 22–24. Plants sold under this name have larger leaves and flowers than other kinds. Much more vigorous with substantial glossy deep green leaves giving them better winter appearance. Purple trumpets (to 5 in.) marked orange inside. Average water.

Distictis 'Rivers'

DIZYGOTHECA elegantissima. (Often sold as *Aralia elegantissima.*) THREADLEAF FALSE ARALIA. House plant (juvenile stage); evergreen garden shrub (mature form) for Zones 16, 17, 22–24. Leaves on juvenile plants are lacy—divided like fans into very narrow (⅜ in.), 4–9-in.-long leaflets with notched edges—dark shiny green above, reddish beneath. As plants mature, leaves become bigger with coarsely notched leaflets to 12 in. long and 3 in. wide. Rarely flowers as house plant.

As house plant, give it ample light but no direct sunshine. Needs fast draining, moisture retentive soil mix (waterlogged or dry soil will make leaves drop). Feed monthly. Subject to pests indoors, not outdoors.

In mild climates, plant in sheltered areas. Can become 5–12-ft. shrub or small tree. As single plant, makes lacy pattern against wall. Attractive seen through translucent glass or plastic panel.

Dizygotheca elegantissima

DODECATHEON. SHOOTING STAR. Perennial. All Zones—hardiness varies with species. Mostly native to West. Spring flowers somewhat like small cyclamen, few to many in cluster on leafless stem, varying from a few in. to 2 ft. tall. Colors of many species range from white to pink, lavender, or magenta. Pale green leaves in basal rosettes dry up in summer heat. Needs porous, rich, well-drained soil, ample water while growing or blooming. Let soil dry out after bloom.

Collector's items, rarely available in nurseries. Buy seed from native plant seed specialists or gather from wild plants (with owner's permission). Grow species that are native to your area; not all are hardy everywhere.

Dodecatheon hendersonii

DODONAEA viscosa. HOP BUSH, HOPSEED BUSH. Evergreen shrub. Zones 7–9, 12–24. Native to Arizona and elsewhere in warmer parts of the world. Fast growing, with many upright stems to 12–15 ft. high, spreading almost as wide (can be trained to tree form by cutting out all but single stem). Willow-like green leaves to 4 in. long.

Most popular variety is 'Purpurea', PURPLE HOP BUSH, selected form with rich bronzy green leaves that turn deeper in win-

Dodonaea viscosa

ter. Seedlings vary much in color. Variety 'Saratoga' (grown from cuttings) is uniformly rich purple in color. Plant purple-leafed kinds in full sun to retain rich coloration; will turn green in shade.

Can be pruned as hedge or espalier, or planted 6–8 ft. apart and left unpruned to become big informal screen. Probably its biggest asset is its wide cultural tolerance. It takes any kind of soil, ocean winds, dry desert heat. It's quite drought resistant when established, but will also take ample water (grows well in flower beds).

Clusters of flowers are insignificant. Creamy to pinkish winged fruit attractive in late summer.

Dodonaea viscosa

DOG-TOOTH VIOLET. See *Erythronium dens-canis.*

DOGWOOD. See *Cornus.*

DOLICHOS. Perennial twining vines which produce dense cover of light green leaves divided like fans into 3 leaflets. Give average watering.

D. lablab. HYACINTH BEAN. Perennial vine usually grown as annual. All Zones in conditions noted below. Fast to 10 ft. Broad, oval leaflets to 3–6 in. long. Sweet pealike purple or white flowers in loose clusters on long stems stand out from foliage. Flowers followed by velvety, beanlike pods to 2½ in. long. Grow plants like string beans. Quick screening. Sun.

D. lignosus. AUSTRALIAN PEA VINE. Zones 16, 17, 21–24. Somewhat woody vine with small triangular 1½-in.-long leaflets and small white or rose purple flowers clustered at ends of long stalks. Evergreen in mild winters. Grow from seed and train on trellis or frame for summer screen. Grows to 10 ft. or more. Sun.

Dolichos lablab

DOMBEYA. Evergreen shrubs. Zones 21–24. Tender to frost, but make quick comebacks. They have big, tropical-looking, toothed leaves and large, dense, hydrangealike flower clusters that droop from branches. Dombeyas need only sun, warmth, reasonably good soil, and ample water. Faded flower clusters hang on and look untidy unless removed. Can be espaliered or trained over arbors to display flowers. Mix with trees for jungle background.

D. cayeuxii. PINK BALL DOMBEYA. To 10 ft. Pink flowers in dense, heavy, drooping clusters. Winter bloom.

D. wallichii. To 30 ft., but usually seen as big, rounded shrub 12–15 ft. high, with big leaves to 6–10 in. long and as wide. Big ball shaped flower clusters in coral pink to red. Blooms late August into winter.

Dombeya cayeuxii

DONKEY TAIL. See *Sedum morganianum.*

DORONICUM. LEOPARDS BANE. Perennials. Zones 1–7, 14–17. Showy, bright yellow daisylike flowers on long stems rise from mounds of dense, dark green, usually heart shaped leaves. Blooms in early spring. Grow in partial shade, good soil. Divide clumps every 2–3 years; young plants bloom best. Average water.

Use in groups under high-branching deciduous trees; combine with white, pur-

Doronicum cordatum

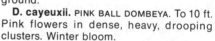

ple, or lavender tulips, blue violas, forget-me-nots; use in front of purple lilacs; or with hellebores at edge of woodland or shade border. Good cut flower.

D. cordatum *(D. caucasicum)*. Stem 1–1½ ft. high. Flower heads 2 in. across, borne singly on 1–1½-ft. stems. Increases by stolons. Variety 'Magnificum' more robust, with larger flowers; 'Finesse' has 3-in. flowers.

D. plantagineum. PLANTAIN LEOPARDS BANE. Early blooming, rather coarse, with tuberous rhizomes. Stout stems 2–5 ft. tall. Flowers 2–4 in. across, few to a stem. Best in wild garden.

DOROTHEANTHUS bellidiformis. LIVINGSTONE DAISY. Succulent annual. All Zones. Ice plant, but unlike most others, an annual. Useful and pretty temporary carpeter in poor, dry soil, full sun. Trailing, a few inches high, with fleshy leaves of bright green and daisylike 2-in. flowers in white, pink, orange, red. Sow seed in warm weather. Comes into bloom quickly. Fire resistant if well watered. Draws bees.

Dorotheanthus bellidiformis

DORYANTHES palmeri. SPEAR LILY. Enormous succulent. Zones 15–17, 19–24. Native to Australia. Gigantic cluster of 100 or so leaves which may reach 8 ft. in length by 6 in. wide. Flower stalk 6–9 ft. high; clustered flowers crimson, white within. Summer bloom. Striking in big gardens. Grow as you would century plant, but requires more water to look good, and will tolerate more shade. Also striking subject for patio containers. *D. excelsa,* sometimes offered, has taller flower spikes (to 18 ft.), shorter leaves.

Doryanthes palmeri

DOUBLE WEEPING CHERRY. See *Prunus subhirtella* 'Yae-shidare-higan'.

DOUGLAS FIR. See *Pseudotsuga menziesii*.

DOVE TREE. See *Davidia involucrata*.

DOXANTHA unguis-cati. See *Macfadyena unguis-cati*.

DRACAENA. (For other plants often called dracaena, see *Cordyline*.) Evergreen plants (small palmlike trees). Essentially foliage plants, grown in house or on lanais—certain kinds can be grown outdoors as noted below. Some show graceful fountain forms with broad, curved, ribbon leaves, occasionally striped with chartreuse or white. Some have very stiff, swordlike leaves. Almost never flower as house plants. Fairly drought resistant. In containers, water only when top ½–1 in. is dry. Outdoors take sun, indoors take shade.

Dracaena draco

D. australis. See *Cordyline australis*.

D. deremensis. Outdoors, out of wind, in Zones 24; otherwise, house plant. Native to tropical Africa. Most commonly sold is variety 'Warneckii'. Erect, slow growing, but eventually 15 ft. tall. Long, 2-ft. leaves, 2 in. wide, rich green, striped white and gray. Others are: 'Bausei', green with white center stripe; 'Longii', with broader white center stripe; and 'Janet Craig', with broad, dark green leaves. Compact versions of 'Janet Craig' and 'Warneckii' exist.

D. draco. DRAGON TREE. Outdoors in Zones 16, 17, 21–24; house plant anywhere.

Dracaena marginata

Native to Canary Islands. Stout trunk with upward-reaching or spreading branches topped by clusters of heavy, 2-ft.-long, sword shaped leaves. Grows slowly to 20 ft. high and as wide. Makes odd but interesting silhouette. Clusters of greenish white flowers form at branch ends. After blossoms drop, stemmy clusters remain. Trim them off to keep plants neat.

D. fragrans. CORNPLANT. Outdoors, out of wind, in Zones 21, 23, 24; other than that, house plant. Native to west Africa. Upright, eventually to 20 ft. high, but slow growing. Heavy, ribbonlike, blue green leaves to 3 ft. long, 4 in. wide. (Typical plant in 8-in. pot will bear leaves about 18 in. long.) Tolerates darker position in house than other dracaenas. Variety 'Massangeana' has broad yellow stripe in center of leaf. Other striped varieties are 'Lindenii' and 'Victoriae'.

D. marginata. Outdoors, out of wind, Zones 21, 23, 24. House plant anywhere. Slender, erect, smooth gray stems to eventual 12 ft. carry chevron markings where old leaves have fallen. Stems topped by crowns of narrow leathery leaves to 2 ft. long, ½ in. wide. Leaves are deep glossy green with narrow margin of purplish red. Very easy, very popular. If plant grows too tall, cut off crown and re-root it. New crowns will appear on old stem. 'Tricolor' or 'Candy Cane' adds narrow gold stripe to green and red.

D. surculosa *(D. godseffiana)*. House plant. Native to west Africa. Slow grower, smaller than other dracaenas. Slender erect or spreading stems set with pairs or trios of 5-in.-long, 2-in.-wide, dark green leaves spotted with white. 'Kelleri' and 'Florida Beauty' are more heavily spotted.

D. sanderana. Outdoors, out of wind, Zones 21, 23, 24; or house plant anywhere. Native to west Africa. Neat and upright, to a possible 6–10 ft., somewhat resembling young corn plant. Strap shaped, 9-in.-long leaves striped with white.

DRAGON TREE. See *Dracaena draco*.

DRIMYS winteri. WINTER'S BARK. Small evergreen tree. Zones 8, 9, 14–24. Native to southern Chile and Argentina. Slender, to 25 ft. Distinguished chiefly for clean foliage and dignified presence. Stems and branches, which tend to droop gracefully, are mahogany red with aromatic bark. Bright green, leathery, fragrant leaves are elliptical, 5–10 in. long. Jasmine-scented, creamy white flowers about 1 in. wide, in small clusters. Usually multistemmed, but easily trained to single trunk. May require pruning from time to time to maintain outline of pleasing symmetry. Give plenty of water with good drainage. Will take some sun near coast; shade inland.

Drimys winteri

DROSANTHEMUM. Succulent perennials. Zones 14–24. Two ice plants described here are often confused with each other, although quite different. In both, leaves are covered with glistening dots that look like tiny ice crystals; both have typical ice plant flowers with many narrow petals. Both will endure poor soil and live with little or no irrigation once established, especially near ocean. Like sun; can be fire resistant.

Drosanthemum floribundum

D. floribundum. ROSEA ICE PLANT. Grows to 6 in. tall, but stems trail to considerable length or drape over rocks, walls. Best ice plant for controlling erosion on steep slopes. Flowers, ¾ in. wide make sheets of pale pink in late spring, early summer. Bees are fond of them.

D. hispidum. To 2 ft. tall, 3 ft. wide, less inclined to stem-root than *D. floribundum*. Showy, 1-in. purple flowers in late spring, early summer. *D. floribundum* is often sold as *D. hispidum*.

DRUMSTICKS. See *Allium sphaerocephalum*.

DRYAS. Perennials. Zones 1–6. Choice plants for rock gardens. Evergreen, or partially so; somewhat shrubby at base, forming carpet of leafy creeping stems. Shiny white or yellow strawberrylike flowers May–July; ornamental seed capsules with silvery white tails. Sun; average soil; needs less water than most perennials.

Dryas octopetala

D. drummondii. To 4 in. high. Leaves oblong, 1½ in. long, white woolly beneath. Flowers nodding, bright yellow, ¾ in. across.

D. octopetala. Leaves 1 in. long. Flowers white, 1½ in. across, erect. Mats up to 2–3 ft. high.

D. suendermannii. Hybrid between two species above. Leaves oblong, 1–1½ in. long, thick textured, similar to oak leaves. Flowers yellowish in bud, white in full bloom, nodding.

DRYOPTERIS. WOOD FERN. Native to many parts of world. Two natives of western U.S. and one exotic species are sometimes sold. Definitely drought tolerant. Grow in part shade.

D. arguta. COASTAL or CALIFORNIA WOOD FERN. Zones 4–9, 14–24. Native Washington to southern California. Dark green, finely cut, airy fronds to 2½ ft. tall. Not easy in gardens; best naturalized in woods. Avoid overwatering.

Dryopteris dilatata

D. dilatata. SPREADING WOOD FERN. Zone 4–9, 14–24. Native to much of northern hemisphere, including western U.S. Leaves even more finely cut than *D. arguta.* Fronds 1–3 ft. tall. Named varieties sometimes seen in northwestern nurseries. In southern California, best in pots. Plant in shade.

D. erythrosora. All Zones. Native to China, Japan. One of few ferns with seasonal color value: young fronds reddish, deep green in late spring and summer. Spreading habit, 1½–2 ft. tall. Shade.

DUCHESNEA indica. INDIAN MOCK STRAWBERRY. Perennial. All Zones. Grows like strawberry, with trailing stems that root firmly along ground. Bright green, long-stalked leaves with 3 leaflets. Yellow flowers ½ in. across, followed by red, ½-in., insipid-tasting fruit that stand above foliage rather than under leaves as in true strawberry. Grows readily in sun or shade without much care. Needs only moderate watering. Best used as ground cover among open shrubs or small trees. Plant 12–18 in. apart. In well-watered garden, can become rampant invader. Attracts birds.

Duchesnea indica

DUDLEYA. Rosette-forming succulents. Zones 16, 17, 21–24. Native to California, Arizona, Baja California and other parts of Mexico. About 40 species are known and some of these are common on California's coastal cliffs or inland hills. Best known in cultivation is *D. brittonii* (from Baja California), with 18-in.-wide leaf rosettes on stems that gradually lengthen into trunks 1–2 ft. tall. Leaves fleshy, covered with heavy coat of chalky powder which can be rubbed off. Striking plant when well-grown; needs bright light, shelter from rain, hail, frost. Best under glass or plastic roof. Others are also valued for use in containers, rock gardens, low borders. Very drought resistant. Full sun.

Dudleya brittonii

DUMB CANE. See *Dieffenbachia.*

DURANTA. Evergreen shrubs. Glossy green leaves arranged in pairs or whorls along stem. Attractive blue flowers in clusters attract butterflies in summer, are followed by bunches of yellow berrylike fruit. Many plants sold as *D. stenostachya* are actually *D. erecta.* Distinguishing characteristics described below.

Valued for summer flowers and fruit. Use as quick tall screen. Thrive in hot-summer areas but requires constant level of moisture. Prefer sun. Need continual thinning and pruning to keep under control.

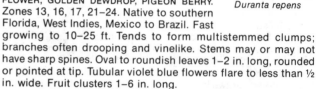
Duranta repens

D. repens (*D. erecta, D. plumieri*). SKY FLOWER, GOLDEN DEWDROP, PIGEON BERRY. Zones 13, 16, 17, 21–24. Native to southern Florida, West Indies, Mexico to Brazil. Fast growing to 10–25 ft. Tends to form multistemmed clumps; branches often drooping and vinelike. Stems may or may not have sharp spines. Oval to roundish leaves 1–2 in. long, rounded or pointed at tip. Tubular violet blue flowers flare to less than ½ in. wide. Fruit clusters 1–6 in. long.

D. stenostachya. BRAZILIAN SKY FLOWER. Not as hardy as *D. erecta,* seems to require more heat, and is not at its best in Zones 17, 24. Makes neater, more compact shrub than *D. erecta,* usually growing to about 4–6 ft. (under ideal conditions, 15 ft.). Stems are spineless. Leaves are larger (3–8 in. long) than *D. erecta* and taper to long, slender point. Lavender blue flowers are also somewhat larger, and fruit clusters grow to 1 ft. long.

DUSTY MILLER. See *Artemisia stellerana, Centaurea cineraria, C. gymnocarpa, Senecio cineraria.*

DUTCHMAN'S PIPE. See *Aristolochia durior.*

DWARF BLUE GUM. See *Eucalyptus globulus* 'Compacta'.

DWARF CHAPARRAL BROOM. See *Baccharis pilularis.*

DWARF COYOTE BRUSH. See *Baccharis pilularis.*

DWARF FLOWERING ALMOND. See *Prunus glandulosa.*

DWARF GOLDEN ARBORVITAE. See *Platycladus orientalis* 'Aureus'.

DWARF MORNING GLORY. See *Convolvulus tricolor.*

DWARF PAPYRUS. See *Cyperus isocladus.*

DWARF RED-LEAF PLUM. See *Prunus cistena.*

DWARF YAUPON. See *Ilex vomitoria* 'Nana'.

DYSSODIA tenuiloba (*Thymophylla tenuiloba*). DAHLBERG DAISY, GOLDEN FLEECE. Summer annual; may live over as perennial where winters are mild. Southwest native. To 1 ft. high. Divided, threadlike leaves make dark green background to yellow flower heads, which look much like miniature golden marguerites. Use for massed display or pockets of color. Start in flats or plant in place, in full sun and preferably in sandy soil. Needs less water than most annuals. Blooms early summer to fall, or to early winter in warm climates. Pull out plants that get ragged with age.

Dyssodia tenuiloba

EASTER CACTUS. See *Rhipsalidopsis gaertneri.*

EASTER LILY CACTUS. See *Echinopsis*.

EASTER LILY VINE. See *Beaumontia grandiflora*.

ECHEVERIA. Succulents. All make rosettes of fleshy leaves of green or gray green, often marked or overlaid with deeper colors. Flowers bell shaped, nodding, usually pink, red, or yellow, on long, slender, sometimes branched clusters. Quite drought tolerant. Good in rock gardens.

Echeveria agavoides

E. agavoides *(Urbinia agavoides)*. Zones 8, 9, 13–24. Rosettes 6–8 in. across, with stiff, fleshy, smooth, bright green, sharp-pointed leaves which may be marked deep reddish brown at tips and edges. Flower stalk to 18 in. Flowers small, red and yellow.

E. crenulata. Zones 17, 21–24. Loose rosettes on short thick stems. Leaves pale green or white-powdered, to 1 ft. long and 6 in. wide, with edges waved and crisped, purplish red. Flower clusters to 3 ft. high, with a few yellow and red flowers. Striking plant. Shelter from hottest sun; water frequently in summer.

Echeveria imbricata

E. derenbergii. Zones 17, 20–24. Small, tight rosettes spreading to form mats. The 1½-in. long leaves are grayish white with red edges and sharp tip. Flowers reddish and yellow, in 1-sided clusters to 2½ in. long.

E. elegans. HEN AND CHICKS. Zones 8, 9, 12–24. Tight, grayish white rosettes to 4 in. across, spreading freely by offsets. Flowers pink, lined yellow, in clusters to 8 in. long. Common, useful for pattern planting, edging, containers. Can burn in hot summer sun.

E. gibbiflora. Zones 17, 21-24. Striking succulent to 3 ft. tall with broad-leafed rosettes to 2½ ft. wide. Leaves gray green. Flowering stems slender, to 5 ft. tall, flowers not especially showy. Variety 'Metallica' has purplish lilac to bronzy leaves; a number of varieties and hybrids have warted, crested, and wavy-edged leaves.

E. imbricata. HEN AND CHICKS. Zones 8, 9, 12–24. Rosettes 4–6 in. across, saucer shaped, gray green. Loose clusters of small bell shaped, orange red flowers. Makes offsets very freely. Probably commonest hen and chicks in California gardens.

E. pulvinata. Zones 16, 17, 21–24. Small loose rosettes of very thick leaves covered with silvery down which later turns red or brownish. Early spring flowers are bright red.

E. secunda. HEN AND CHICKS. Zones 8, 9, 14–24. Rosettes gray green or blue green, to 4 in. across. Makes offsets freely. *E. s. glauca* (*E. glauca*) has purple-toned blue green rosettes; leaves faintly bordered purple red.

E. setosa. Zones 17, 23, 24. Dense rosettes to 4 in. across, dark green, densely covered with white, stiff hairs. Flowers red, tipped yellow. Good in rock gardens, shallow containers. Very tender.

E. 'Set-oliver'. Zones 16, 17, 21–24. Rosettes looser than in *E. setosa*. Flowers profuse, red and yellow, very showy in mass plantings.

E. hybrids. Generally have large, loose rosettes of big leaves on single or branched stems. Some have leaves crisped, waved, wattled, and heavily shaded with red, bronze, or purple. All are splendid pot plants; they do well in open ground in mild coastal gardens.

ECHINACEA purpurea *(Rudbeckia purpurea)*. PURPLE CONEFLOWER. Perennial. All Zones. Coarse, stiff plant forming large clumps of erect stems 4–5 ft. tall. Leaves oblong, 3–8 in. long. Showy flower heads with drooping purple rays and dark purple centers; blooms over long period in late summer. Coral, crimson, and white varieties exist. Use on outskirts of garden or in wide borders with other robust perennials

Echinacea purpurea

such as Shasta daisies, sunflowers, Michaelmas daisies. Plant in full sun; average soil, watering. Divide clumps in spring or fall.

ECHINOCACTUS. BARREL CACTUS. Zones 12–24. Numerous kinds of large, cylindrical cactus with prominent ribs and stout thorns. Many native to Southwest. Best known in gardens is *E. grusonii*, GOLDEN BARREL—Mexican cactus of slow growth to 4 ft. high, 2½ ft. in diameter, with showy yellow, stiff 3-in. spines and yellow, 1½–2-in. flowers at top of plant in April-May. It needs protection from hard frosts and, in hottest desert climates, some summer shade and water. Provide the first with improvised canopies of branches. Water every 2 weeks during summer.

Echinocactus grusonii

ECHINOPS exaltatus. GLOBE THISTLE. Perennial. All Zones. Rugged-looking, erect, rigidly branched plants 3–4 ft. high. Coarse, prickly, deeply cut, gray green leaves. Small steel blue flowers in round heads 2 in. across, midsummer to late fall. 'Taplow Blue' is desirable selected form. Plants often mistakenly sold under names of *E. ritro* and *E. sphaerocephalus*.

Flowers long lasting when cut; hold color when dry. Plant in full sun, ordinary soil with good drainage. Established plants tolerate dry periods; moderate watering makes plants look better. Grow from divisions in spring or fall, or sow seed in flats or in open ground in spring. Color and interesting form complement yellow and orange rudbeckias, heleniums; combine well with Michaelmas daisies and phlox.

Echinops exaltatus

ECHINOPSIS. EASTER LILY CACTUS, SEA URCHIN CACTUS. Outdoors Zones 16, 17, 21–24; grow inside sunny windows elsewhere. Small (6–10 in. high) cylindrical or globular cactus from South America, generally grown in pots. Big, long-tubed, many-petaled flowers in shades of white, yellow, pink, and red can reach 6–8 in. long. Free blooming in summer if given good light, frequent feeding, fast draining soil. Many kinds, all showy and easy. Water every 1–2 weeks spring through fall; little or no water in winter.

Echinopsis

ECHIUM. Biennials or shrubby perennials. Striking form and flower clusters. All take full sun, do well in dry, poor soil, but need good drainage. All are excellent for seacoast gardens. Very drought resistant Zones 15–17, 22–24; need weekly summer waterings in Zones 14, 18–21. Attract bees.

E. fastuosum. PRIDE OF MADEIRA. Shrubby perennial. Zones 14–24. Large picturesque plant with many coarse, heavy branches 3–6 ft. high. Hairy, gray green, narrow leaves form roundish irregular mounds at ends of stems. Great spikelike clusters of blue purple, ½-in.-long flowers stand out dramatically, well above foliage, in May-June. Branch tips and developing flower spikes may be killed by March frosts in inland areas. Use for bold effects against walls, at back of wide flower border, and on slopes. Will control erosion. Very effective with *Limonium perezii*. Prune lightly to keep plant bushy. Cut off faded flower spikes.

Echium fastuosum

(Continued on next page)

E. wildpretii. TOWER OF JEWELS. Biennial. Zones 1–17, 21–24. Striking plant from 4–10 ft. high. Its first year is spent as attractive roundish mass of long, narrow leaves covered with silvery gray hairs. In its second year it starts to grow. By mid or late spring it will form thick column of rose to rose red flowers, 6–10 ft. high and a foot or more thick. When all the countless little flowers have faded, the plant dies, leaving behind a vast amount of seed. If resulting seedlings are not hoed out, these may be grown to flower next year. An interesting oddity.

EDELWEISS. See *Leontopodium alpinum.*

EGGPLANT. For ornamental relatives see *Solanum.* Annual vegetable. All Zones in conditions noted below. Few vegetable plants are handsomer than eggplant. Bushes resemble little trees 2–3 ft. high and equally wide. Big leaves (usually lobed) are purple tinged, and drooping violet purple flowers are 1½ in. across. And, of course, big purple fruit is spectacular. Plants are effective in large containers or raised beds; a well-spaced row of them makes distinguished border between vegetable and flower garden. Most people plant large roundish or oval varieties such as

Eggplant
'Black Beauty'

'Black Beauty', 'Burpee Hybrid', or 'Early Beauty'; the Japanese, who prefer their eggplant small and very tender, prefer long, slender variety usually sold as 'Japanese'. 'White Beauty', white skinned, more nearly justifies the name "eggplant." 'Golden Yellow' has egg shaped, egg-sized yellow fruit; it's rare.

Can be grown from seed (sow indoors 8–10 weeks before date of last expected frost) but it's much easier to buy and plant nursery-grown plants. Set plants out in sun in spring when frosts are over and soil is warm. Space 3 ft. apart in loose, fertile soil. Feed once every 6 weeks with commercial fertilizer, water when soil at roots is dry, and keep weeds out. Prevent too much fruit setting by pinching out some terminal growth and some blossoms. Three to six large fruit per plant will result. If you enjoy tiny whole eggplants, allow plants to produce freely. Harvest fruit after they develop some color, but never wait until they lose their glossy shine. Dust or spray to control aphids and whiteflies.

EGLANTINE. See *Rosa eglanteria.*

EICHHORNIA crassipes. WATER HYACINTH. Aquatic plant. Zones 8, 9, 13–24. Native to tropical America. Floating leaves and feathery roots. Leaves ½–5 in. broad, nearly circular in shape; leaf stems inflated. Blooms showy, lilac blue, about 2 in. long. Upper petals with yellow spot in center, in many-flowered spikes. Attractive in small pools, ponds, but can become pest. Do not turn it loose in natural or large bodies of water. Needs warmth to flower profusely.

Eichhornia crassipes

ELAEAGNUS. Deciduous and evergreen large shrubs or small trees. Best in full sun or part shade. All are splendid screen plants. Though one kind is a tree and rest are big shrubs, and some are deciduous and some are evergreen, all grow fast as young plants to become dense, full, firm, and tough, and do it with little upkeep. All tolerate seashore conditions, heat, wind, and average to low watering. Established plants tolerate drought. Plant 10–12 ft. apart for screening.

Foliage is distinguished in evergreen forms by silvery (sometimes brown) dots that cover leaves. Reflecting sunlight, these dots give plants a special sparkle. Decidu-

Elaeagnus pungens

ous kinds have silvery gray leaves. Small, insignificant, but usually fragrant flowers are followed by decorative fruit, usually red with silvery flecks. Evergreen kinds bloom in fall. Evergreen kinds are useful as natural espaliers, clipped hedges, or high bank covers, in addition to prime role as screen plants.

E. angustifolia. RUSSIAN OLIVE. Small deciduous tree. Zones 1–3, 7–14, 18, 19. To 20 ft. high, but can be clipped as medium-height hedge. Angular trunk and branches (sometimes thorny) are covered with shredding dark brown bark that is picturesque in winter. Bark contrasts with willowlike, 2-in.-long, silvery gray leaves. Small greenish yellow flowers in early summer, very fragrant, are followed by berrylike fruit that resemble miniature olives. Can take almost any amount of punishment in interior. Does poorly and is out of character in mild-winter, cool-summer climates. Resistant to oak root fungus. Makes interesting background plant, effective barrier.

E. commutata. SILVERBERRY. Deciduous shrub. Most useful Zones 1–3. To 12 ft. with slender, open form, red brown branches, silvery leaves. Tiny fragrant flowers followed by dry, silvery berries that are good bird food. Native to Canada, northern plains, and Rocky Mountains.

E. 'Coral Silver'. Large evergreen or deciduous shrub. All Zones. Has unusually bright gray foliage, coral red berries in fall. Evergreen in Zones 19–24, deciduous or partially deciduous elsewhere.

E. ebbingei (*E. macrophylla* 'Ebbingei'). Evergreen shrub. Zones 5–24. More upright (to 10–12 ft.) than *E. pungens* (see below) and has thornless branches. Dark green leaves 2–4 in. long, silvery both sides when young, later dark green above, silvery beneath. Tiny, fragrant, silvery flowers. Red fruit; makes good jelly.

E. multiflora. Deciduous shrub. Zones 2–24. To 6 ft.; leaves silvery green above, silvery and brown below. Small fragrant flowers followed by ½-in.-long bright orange red berries on 1-in. stalks. Fruit attractive, edible but tart, much loved by birds.

E. philippinensis. Evergreen shrub. Zones 15–17, 19–24. More open and erect (to 10 ft.) than other evergreen forms with somewhat spreading and drooping branches. The 3-in.-long, olive green leaves with silvery cast are quite silvery beneath. Red fruit.

E. pungens. SILVERBERRY. Large evergreen shrub. Zones 4–24. Has rather rigid, sprawling, angular habit of growth to height of 6–15 ft.; can be kept lower and denser by pruning. Grayish green, 1–3-in.-long leaves have wavy edges and brown tinting from rusty dots. Branches are spiny, also covered with rusty dots. Overall color of shrub is olive drab. Oval fruit, ½ in. long, red with silver dust. Tough container plant in reflected heat, wind. Variegated forms listed below are more widespread than the plain olive drab variety and have a brighter, lighter look in the landscape. Both kinds make effective barrier plantings: growth is dense and twiggy, and spininess is a help, yet plant is not aggressively spiny.

E. p. 'Fruitlandii'. Zones 5–24. Leaves larger, more silvery than in other varieties.

E. p. 'Maculata'. GOLDEN ELAEAGNUS. Leaves have gold blotch in center.

E. p. 'Marginata'. SILVER-EDGE ELAEAGNUS. Leaves have silvery white margins.

E. p. 'Variegata'. YELLOW-EDGE ELAEAGNUS. Leaves have yellowish white margins.

ELDERBERRY. See *Sambucus.*

ELEPHANT'S EAR. See *Alocasia, Colocasia esculenta.*

ELEPHANT'S FOOD. See *Portulacaria afra.*

ELM. See *Ulmus.*

EMERALD RIPPLE. See *Peperomia caperata.*

EMPRESS TREE. See *Paulownia tomentosa.*

ENDIVE. All Zones in conditions noted below. Fall or late-summer annual vegetable. Botanically known as *Cichorium endivia.* This species includes curly endive and broad-leafed endive (escarole). Forms rosette of leaves. Tolerates more heat than lettuce, grows faster in cold weather. Sow in sun in late summer for maturity during rainy season (in cold-winter areas sow seed June to August). Endive matures in 90–95 days. Space plants 10–12 in. apart in rows 15–18 in. apart. When plants have reached

Endive

full size, pull outer leaves over center and tie them up; center leaves will blanch to yellow or white. 'Green Curled' is standard curly endive, 'Broad-leaved Batavian' is best broad-leafed kind. Belgian or French endives are the blanched sprouts from roots of a kind of chicory. Roots are dug after a summer's growth, then stored in the dark to sprout. See chicory.

ENDYMION *(Scilla).* ENGLISH AND SPANISH BLUEBELLS, WOOD HYACINTH. Bulbs. All Zones. They resemble hyacinths, but are taller, with looser flower clusters and fewer, broader leaves. Most dealers still sell them as *Scilla.* Full sun or part shade. Plant informal drifts among tall shrubs, under deciduous trees, among low-growing perennials. In dry-winter areas, supply water from October on. Anywhere, let dry out through summer. They thrive in pots and are good for cutting.

Endymion non-scriptus

E. hispanicus *(Scilla campanulata, S. hispanica).* SPANISH BLUEBELL. Most widely planted. Prolific, vigorous, with sturdy 20-in. stems bearing 12 or more nodding bells about ¾ in. long. Blue is most popular color, 'Excelsior' (deep blue) most popular variety. Also white, pink, rose forms. Plant in fall, 3 in. deep in mild climates, to 6 in. where winters are severe. Flowers appear in spring.

E. non-scriptus *(Scilla nonscripta).* ENGLISH BLUEBELL, WOOD HYACINTH. Flowers narrower and smaller than in Spanish bluebell, on 1 ft. spikes. Culture same as for Spanish bluebell.

ENGLISH DAISY. See *Bellis perennis.*

ENGLISH LAUREL. See *Prunus laurocerasus.*

ENKIANTHUS. Deciduous shrubs. Zones 2–9, 14–21. Native to Japan. Upright stems with tiers of nearly horizontal branches, narrow in youth, broad in age, but always good looking. Leaves, whorled or crowded at branch ends, turn orange or red in autumn. Nodding bell shaped flowers in clusters. Grow in light shade, in well-drained soil to which plenty of peat moss or ground bark has been added. Keep soil moist. Prune only to remove dead or broken branches. Plant with other acid loving

Enkianthus campanulatus

plants. Place where silhouette and fall color can be effective.

E. campanulatus. Slow growing, handsome shrub to 20 ft. in 20 years (10 ft. by 4 ft. wide in 10 years). Bluish green leaves, 1½–3 in. long, turn brilliant red in fall. In May, pendulous clusters of yellow green, red-veined, ½-in.-long bells hang below leaves. *E. c. palibinii* has deep red flowers; its variety 'Albiflorus' has white ones.

E. cernuus. Seldom over 10 ft. tall, with 1–2-in.-long leaves. White flowers. Not as well-known as its variety *rubens,* which has translucent deep red flowers in May.

E. perulatus. Grows to 6–8 ft. high. Roundish, 1–2-in.-long leaves; exceptionally good scarlet fall color. Nodding clusters of small white flowers open before leaves.

ENSETE. Big, palmlike perennials. Evergreen in Zones 17, 19–24; die back each cold winter, regrow in spring in Zones 13, 15, 16, 18; elsewhere, a container plant to grow outdoors in summer, indoors or in greenhouse over winter. Good near swimming pools.

Ensete ventricosum

E. ventricosum *(Musa ensete).* ABYSSINIAN BANANA. Lush, tropical-looking dark green leaves 10–20 ft. long, 2–4 ft. wide, with stout midrib, grow out in arching form from single vertical stem, 6–20 ft. high. Fast growing. Leaves easily shredded by winds, so plant in wind-sheltered place. Sun or part shade. Needs more water than most shrubs or trees. Flowers typically form 2–5 years after planting; plant dies to roots after flowering. Possible then to grow new plants from shoots at crown, but easier to discard, replace with new nursery plants. Flowers (inconspicuous) form within cylinder of bronze red bracts at end of stem.

E. v. 'Maurelii'. Similar to *E. ventricosum* except leaves are tinged with red on upper surface, especially along edges. Leaf stalks are dark red. Plant is slightly smaller (stems only 12–15 ft. high). 'Montbeliardii' is less squat than 'Maurelii'.

EPAULETTE TREE. See *Pterostyrax hispidus.*

EPIDENDRUM. Epiphytic or terrestrial orchids. All are easy to grow. Most species bear large clusters of blooms. On the whole they take same culture as cattleya. Those with hard round pseudobulbs and thick leathery leaves are sun and drought tolerant and need rest period. These grow in ground bark or other orchid media. Softer-textured plants with thin stemlike pseudobulbs do best with more shade and year-round moisture.

Epidendrum obrienianum

Reed-stemmed types need abundance of sun to flower, but shaded roots to provide cool root run. Mulch plants in ground beds. If sun is too hot, foliage turns bright red and burns. Grow outdoors in Zones 17, 21–24. Tip growth will burn at 28°F., plants are killed to ground at about 22°F. In cold-winter areas grow reed-stemmed plants in pots, move them indoors in winter.

Feed regularly with mild liquid fertilizer during growing season. In pure ground bark, feed at every other watering with high-nitrogen liquid feed. Feed plants grown in other media monthly. When blooms fade, cut flower stem back to within 1 or 2 joints of ground.

E. cochleatum. Native to tropical America. Pear shaped pseudobulbs 2–5 in. high with one or more leaves as long or longer. Erect flower stem bears 5–10 flowers, 2–3 in. across. Narrow, twisted yellow green sepals and petals, purplish black lip, shaped like cockleshell, with lighter veins. Blooms at various times. Hardy to about 25°F.; grows outdoors in mildest winter climates.

E. ibaguense *(E. radicans).* Native to Colombia. Erect, 2–4-ft. reedlike leafy stems. Dense, globular clusters of 1–1½-in. flowers at tips of slender stems well above foliage. Orange yellow flower, fringed lip. Bloom season varies. Numerous hybrids in shades of yellow, orange, pink, red, lavender, and white, generally sold by color rather than by name.

E. obrienianum. Best known of reed-stemmed hybrids. Dense clusters of vivid red flowers, each the shape of miniature cattleya orchid, on slender stems 1–2 ft. above foliage. Reed-stemmed hybrids need sun to bloom.

EPIGAEA repens. TRAILING ARBUTUS. Evergreen low shrublet. Zones 1–7. Native to eastern North America. Difficult to grow except under ideal conditions: acid soil well-fortified with leaf mold, pine needles, or peat moss; excellent drainage; shade from summer sun. Choice woodland ground cover. Do not fertilize. Mulch with leaf mold or peat moss when weather warms;

keep plants moist all summer. Bait for slugs. Will take any amount of cold.

Each plant can cover a patch 12–24 in. wide, stems rooting as they grow. Oval to roundish leaves 1–3 in. long. Waxy pink or white, ½-in.-wide flowers (with delightful fragrance) cluster at tips of branches, April or May.

Another species, *E. asiatica*, occasionally sold, is quite similar to the above but considered easier to grow.

Epigaea repens

EPIMEDIUM. Perennials. Zones 1–9, 14–17. Low-growing evergreen or nearly evergreen plant with creeping underground stems. Leathery, divided leaves on thin, wiry stems. Heart shaped leaflets, up to 3 in. long, unfold bronzy pink in spring, turn green in summer, bronzy in fall. Loose spikes of small, waxy-textured, pink, red, creamy yellow, or white flowers in spring. Use as ground cover under trees, among rhododendrons, azaleas, camellias; good in larger rock gardens. Need modest amount of water. Adaptable to containers. Foliage, flowers long lasting in arrangements. Divide large clumps in spring or fall by cutting through tough roots with sharp spade. Cut off old leaves in early spring.

Epimedium grandiflorum

E. grandiflorum. BISHOP'S HAT, LONGSPUR EPIMEDIUM. About 1 ft. high. Flowers 1–2 in. across, shaped like bishop's hat; outer sepals red, inner sepals pale violet, petals white with long spurs. Varieties have white, pinkish, or violet flowers. 'Rose Queen', crimson carmine flowers with white-tipped spurs, is outstanding variety.

E. pinnatum. Grows 12–15 in. high, having yellow flowers ⅔ in. across, with red petals and protruding stamens. *E. p. colchicum* (often sold as *E. p. elegans*) is larger, with more and showier flowers.

E. rubrum. To 1 ft. with showy clusters of flowers with bright crimson sepals, pale yellow or white, slipperlike petals, upcurved spurs. 'Pink Queen', rosy pink, and 'Snow Queen', white, are desirable varieties offered in specialty nurseries.

EPIPACTIS gigantea. STREAM ORCHID. Hardy terrestrial orchid. Zones 1–9, 14–24. Native from Washington to southern California, east to southern Utah and west Texas. Oval or lance shaped leaves with plaited veins. Creeping rootstocks. Stems 1–3 ft. tall. Flowers, 3–10 to stalk, greenish, purple veined, an inch wide, somewhat resemble birds in flight. Blooms June-July. Grows near brooks and is probably easiest native orchid to grow. Give it rich, moist soil in sun or partial shade.

Epipactis gigantea

EPIPHYLLUM. ORCHID CACTUS. House plants anywhere; lathhouse, shade and shelter plants in Zones 8, 9, 14–24. Growers use *Epiphyllum* to cover wide range of plants including epiphyllum itself and a number of crosses with related plants—*Heliocereus, Nopalxochia, Selenicereus, Disocactus (Chiapasia), Aporocactus*. All are similar in being jungle (not desert) cactus, and most grow on tree branches as epiphytes, like some orchids. Grow them in pots. They need rich, quick draining soil with plenty of leaf mold, peat moss, or ground bark, and sand. Overwatering and poor drainage cause bud drop. As a rule, water 1–2 times a week in summer, very little in winter.

During summer epiphyllums do best in

Epiphyllum hybrid

broken shade under trees or lath. They need protection from frost. Most have arching (to 2 ft. high), trailing stems and look best in hanging pots, tubs, or baskets. Stems are long, flat, smooth, usually notched along edges, and are quite spineless. Flowers range from medium to very large—as much as 10 in. across—and color range includes white, cream, yellow, pink, rose, lavender, scarlet, and orange. Many varieties have blends of 2 or more colors. Bloom season April-June. Feed with low-nitrogen fertilizer before and after bloom. Bait for snails and slugs. Spray to control aphids, scale, and mealybugs.

EPIPREMNUM aureum (*Pothos aureus, Raphidophora aurea, Scindapsus aureus*). POTHOS. Evergreen climbing perennial grown as house plant. Related to philodendron and similar in appearance. Takes same treatment as climbing philodendrons. Flowers are inconspicuous. Oval, leathery leaves 2–4 in. long, bright green splashed or marbled with yellow. (In greenhouse and with plenty of root room, becomes big vine with deeply cut leaves 2–2½ ft. long.) Attractive trailer for pots, window boxes, large terrariums.

Epipremnum aureum

EPISCIA. FLAME VIOLET. House plants related to African violet. Low-growing plants spread by strawberry-like runners with new plants at tips; excellent display in hanging pots. Leaves 2–5 in. long, 1–3 in. wide, are typically oval, velvety hairy, beautifully colored. Flowers somewhat resemble African violets, appear at scattered intervals through the year; plants bloom best in high humidity of greenhouse, will grow as house plants with bright light, no direct sun, lots of water.

Episcia cupreata

E. cupreata. Red flowers. *E. c. viridifolia* has green leaves with creamy veins; 'Metallica', olive green leaves with pale stripes, red edges; 'Chocolate Soldier', chocolate brown, silver-veined leaves; and 'Silver Sheen', silver leaves with darker margins.

EQUISETUM hyemale. HORSETAIL. Perennial. All Zones. Rushlike survivor of carboniferous age. Slender, hollow, 4-ft. stems are bright green with black and ash-colored ring at each joint. Spores borne in conelike spikes at end of stem. Several species, but *E. hyemale* most common. Called horsetail because many of the species have bushy look from many whorls of slender, jointed green stems that radiate out from joints of main stem.

Although effective in sunny or partly shaded garden situations, especially near water, use with caution: extremely invasive, difficult to get rid of. Best confined to containers. Useful in marshy areas, pools, roadside ditches. In open ground, root-prune rigorously, keep cutting back unwanted shoots.

Equisetum hyemale

ERANTHEMUM pulchellum (*E. nervosum*). Evergreen shrub. Outdoors. Zones 23, 24; elsewhere in greenhouses. Native to India. Grows rapidly to 2–4 ft. high. Handsome, dark green, oval, long-stalked leaves 4 in. long, in pairs, with prominent veins and somewhat scallop-toothed edges.

Deep blue (sometimes rose) tubular flowers protrude from prominent overlapping bracts in 3-in.-long solitary or branching spikes at ends of branches and among leaves, January to April.

Best grown as container plant, or in ground bed on shady, wind-sheltered patio or terrace. Give

Eranthemum pulchellum

plants loose, well-drained soil, rich in humus material. Keep plants moist at all times. Pinch back stem tips 2 or 3 times early in growing season to keep plants compact and encourage more flower production. Cut to ground to stimulate fresh new growth and overcome legginess.

ERANTHIS hyemalis. WINTER ACONITE.

Tuber. Zones 1–9, 14–17. Charming butter-cuplike plant 2–8 in. high, blooming in early spring. Each single, yellow flower, to 1½ in. across, with 5–9 petal-like sepals, sits on single, deeply lobed bright green leaf that looks like a ruff. Basal leaves round, divided into narrow lobes, appear immediately after flowers. Ideal companions for other small bulbs or bulblike plants that bloom at same time, such as snowdrop (Galanthus nivalis) and Siberian squill (Scilla sibirica). Plant tubers in August, early September before they shrivel. If tubers are dry, plump up in wet sand before planting. When dividing, separate into small clumps rather than single tubers. Plant tubers 3 in. deep, 4 in. apart, in moist, porous soil in part shade.

Eranthis hyemalis

EREMURUS. FOXTAIL LILY, DESERT CANDLE.

Perennials. Zones 1–9. Imposing lily relatives with spirelike flowering stems 6–9 ft. tall. White, pink, or yellow, bell shaped flowers, ½–1 in. wide, massed closely in graceful, pointed spikes. Blooming time: late spring, early summer. Strap shaped basal leaves in rosettes appear in early spring, fade away after bloom in summer. Magnificent in large borders against background of dark green foliage, wall, or solid fence. Fairly drought tolerant. Dramatic in arrangements; cut when lowest flowers on spike open. Plant in sun in rich, readily

Eremurus himalaicus

drained soil. Handle thick, brittle roots carefully; tend to rot when bruised or broken. When leaves die down, mark spot and avoid disturbing roots.

E. himalaicus. Leaves bright green, to 1½ ft. long. Flowers white, about 1 in. across in 2–ft. spikes on tall stems 3 ft. or more long.

E. robustus. Leaves 2 ft. or so long, in dense basal rosettes. Stems 8–9 ft. high, topped with 2–3 ft. spikes of clear pink flowers lightly veined with brown.

Shelford Hybrids. To 4–5 ft. tall; flowers in white and shades of buff, pink, yellow, and orange.

ERICA. HEATH.

Evergreen shrubs with small needlelike leaves and abundance of usually small, bell shaped, urn shaped, or tubular flowers. Hardiest kinds, native to northern and western Europe, are widely used as shrubs or ground cover plants in cool-summer, humid regions of California and Northwest. Good on slopes. South African species are tender to frost; where temperatures dip below 28°F. they are safest grown in containers and given shelter. One expert considers them about as hardy as fuchsias. A third group of heaths native to Mediterranean and southern Europe are intermediate in hardiness. All attract bees. Taller ones can be used as screens.

Erica carnea 'Springwood'

All need excellent drainage and most need acid soil (exceptions noted below). Sandy soil with peat moss and compost added is ideal; heavy clay is usually fatal. They are not heavy feeders; annual sifting of compost may be enough. If plants lose color, give light feeding of acid plant food in early spring or apply iron sulfate. Water supply should be steady, with no standing water on roots and no absolute drought. Near coast where air is moist, watering intervals are longer than inland and plants like full sun. Inland, give them light shade or afternoon shade. Prune after bloom by cutting back wood that has flowered; don't cut back into leafless wood.

Erica

NAME AND ZONES	GROWTH HABIT, SIZE	LEAVES	FLOWER COLOR, SEASON	COMMENTS
Erica arborea TREE HEATH Zones 15–17, 21–24. Southern Europe, north Africa.	Dense shrub or tree to 10–20 ft., single or many trunked, often with heavy burl at base.	Bright green, ¼ in. long. New growth lighter.	Fragrant white flowers. March-May.	Slow growing. Performs well enough in Zones 4–6 in years between big freezes. Burls are the "briar" used for making pipes.
E. a. alpina	Dense, upright, fluffy-looking shrub to 6 ft.	As above.	White. March-May.	Slow to reach blooming age, but free blooming. Slightly hardier than above.
E. australis SOUTHERN HEATH. Zones 5–9, 14–24. Spain, Portugal.	Upright, spired, 6–10 ft. high.	Dark green.	Rosy or red. Clustered at ends of shoots. March-June.	Needs protection in Northwest. There is a white form, 'Mr. Robert'.
E. blanda	See *E. doliiformis.*			
E. canaliculata (Usually sold as *E. melanthera,* and often called Scotch heather, which it is not.) Zones 15–17, 20–24.	Bushy, spreading, but with general spiry effect, to 6 ft.	Dark green above, white beneath.	Pink to rosy purple. Fall and winter.	Pink form is sold as 'Rosea', reddish purple as 'Rubra'. Excellent winter bloom in California. Sometimes called Christmas heather. One of best for Zones 20–24.
E. c. 'Boscaweniana' (Sometimes sold as *E. melanthera* 'Rosea'.)	Upright bush or small tree, to 18 ft.	As above.	Pale lilac pink to nearly white. Winter, spring.	Like *E. canaliculata,* good source of cut flowers.

(Continued on next page)

NAME AND ZONES	GROWTH HABIT, SIZE	LEAVES	FLOWER COLOR, SEASON	COMMENTS
E. carnea (E. herbacea) Zones 2–9, 14–24. European Alps.	Dwarf, 6–16 in. high. Upright branchlets rise from prostrate main branches.	Medium green.	Rosy red. Dec.-June.	Unsightly unless pruned every year. This and its varieties tolerate neutral or slightly alkaline soil. Takes part shade in hot-summer areas.
E. c. 'Ruby Glow'	To 8 in. high.	Dark green.	Deep ruby red. Jan.-June.	One of richest in color.
E. c. 'Springwood' ('Springwood White')	Spreading, to 8 in.	Light green.	White, creamy buds. Jan.-April.	Toughest, fastest growing, one of neatest heathers.
E. c. 'Springwood Pink'	Spreading mound, to 10 in.	Bright green.	Pure pink. Jan.-April.	Pinky rust new growth.
E. c. 'Vivellii'	Spreading mound, to 12 in.	Dark green, bronzy red in winter. Relatively tidy.	Carmine red. Feb.-March.	Interesting for seasonal change in foliage color as well as for bloom.
E. c. 'Winter Beauty' ('King George')	Bushy, spreading, compact, to 15 in.	Dark green.	Deep, rich pink. Dec.-April.	Often in bloom at Christmas.
E. ciliaris DORSET HEATH. Zones 4–6, 15–17. England, Ireland.	Trailing, 6–12 in.	Pale green.	Rosy red. July-Sept.	Good for massing.
E. c. 'Mrs. C. H. Gill'	Spreading, to 12 in.	Dark green.	Deep red. July-Oct.	Showy, bell-like flowers.
E. c. 'Stoborough'	As above, but taller, to 18 in.	Medium green.	White. July-Oct.	Free blooming, showy.
E. cinerea TWISTED HEATH. Zones 4–6, 15–17. British Isles, northern Europe.	Spreading mound, to 12 in.	Dark green, dainty.	Purple. June-Sept.	Forms low mat; good ground cover.
E. c. 'Atrosanguinea'	Low, spreading, bushy, to 9 in.	Dark green, dainty.	Scarlet. June-Oct.	Dwarf, slow growing.
E. c. 'C. D. Eason'	Compact, to 10 in.	Dark green.	Red. May-Aug.	Outstanding; good summer flower display.
E. c. 'P. S. Patrick'	Bushy, to 15 in.	Dark green.	Purple. June-Aug.	Sturdy long spikes, large flowers in summer.
E. darleyensis 'Darley Dale' (E. mediterranea hybrida, E. purpurascens 'Darleyensis') Zones 4–9, 14–24.	Bushy grower, to 12 in. tall.	Medium green.	Light rosy purple. Nov.-May.	Tough, hardy plant that takes both heat and cold surprisingly well. Tolerates neutral soils. In northern California, most nearly foolproof heath.
E. d. 'Furzey'	Bushy, 14–18 in. tall.	Dark green.	Deep rose pink. Dec.-April.	Spreading, vigorous plant.
E. d. 'George Rendall'	Bushy, 12 in.	Medium bluish green.	Deeper purple than 'Darley Dale'. Nov.-April.	New growth gold tinted.
E. d. 'Silberschmelze' ('Molten Silver', E. d. 'Alba', 'Mediterranea Hybrid White')	Vigorous, 18–24 in. tall.	Medium green.	White, fragrant.	Easy to maintain.
E. 'Dawn' Zones 4–9, 14–24.	Spreading mound, 12 in.	Green; new growth golden.	Deep pink. June-Oct.	Excellent ground cover. Easy to grow. Hybrid between E. ciliaris, E. tetralix.
E. doliiformis (E. blanda, E. verticillata) Zones 15–17, 20–24.	Low-growing, spiky plant to 1 ft. tall.	Rich green, needlelike.	Long, tubular, rosy red. June-Oct.	Blooms better if old blossoms are picked off as they fade.
E. 'Felix Faure' FRENCH HEATHER. Zones 15–17, 20–24.	Low, compact, to 1 ft.	Bright green.	Inch-long, tubular, lilac pink tipped white, in winter.	Often used as potted plant.
E. hyemalis (Often sold as E. hieliana or E. hyalina.) Zones 15–17, 20–24. South Africa.	Upright, spiky, to 2–3 ft.	Bright green.	Inch-long, tubular, pink and white to coral or orange, in winter.	Sometimes sold as potted plant. Orange coral color form often sold as E. hieliana or orange French heath.
E. 'John McLaren'.	See E. mammosa.			

NAME AND ZONES	GROWTH HABIT, SIZE	LEAVES	FLOWER COLOR, SEASON	COMMENTS
E. lusitanica (E. codonodes) SPANISH HEATH. Zones 5–9, 14–24. Spain, Portugal.	Upright feathery shrub, to 6–12 ft.	Light green.	Pinkish white, slightly fragrant. Jan.–March.	Remarkably profuse bloom. Needs sheltered spot in Northwest. One of best in Zones 20–24.
E. mammosa Zones 15–17, 20–24. South Africa.	Stiff, erect, to 1–3 ft. tall.	Bright green.	Variable, shades of pink. Early spring, repeating through autumn.	Many varieties. 'Jubilee', a salmon pink, is the most generally available. Usually sold as 'John McLaren'.
E. mediterranea BISCAY HEATH. Zones 4–9, 14–24. Ireland, France, Spain.	Loose, upright, 4–7 ft.	Deep green.	Lilac pink. Jan.–April.	Good background. Tolerates neutral soil. 'W. T. Rackliff' is pure white form with brown anthers.
E. mediterranea hybrida	See E. darleyensis.			
E. melanthera	See E. canaliculata.			
E. persoluta Zones 15–17, 20–24. South Africa.	Stiff, upright shrub, to 2 ft. tall.	Bright green.	Tiny, rose or white. Late winter, early spring.	Offered as pot plants or sold as cut branches.
E. regia Zones 15–17, 20–24.	To 2–3 ft.	Needlelike, dull green.	Tubular, somewhat swollen, to ¾ in. long, sticky, shiny in appearance, red. Spring.	E. r. 'Variegata', with white flowers tipped red, is showier.
E. speciosa Zones 15–17, 20–24.	To 3–4 ft. tall.	Bright green, needlelike.	Long, tubular, slightly curved, bright red with greenish tips. Sept.–June.	Nearly everblooming under ideal conditions.
E. tetralix CROSS-LEAFED HEATH. Zones 4–6, 15–17. England, northern Europe.	Upright, to 12 in.	Dark green, silvery beneath.	Rosy pink. June–Oct.	Very hardy plant. New growth yellow, orange, or red. Best in moist, peaty soil, afternoon shade.
E. t. 'Alba Mollis'	Upright, slightly spreading, to 12 in.	Silvery gray.	Clear white. June–Oct.	Foliage sheen pronounced in spring, summer.
E. t. 'Darleyensis'	Spreading, open growth, to 8 in.	Gray green.	Salmon pink. June–Sept.	Good color. Do not confuse with winter-flowering E. darleyensis (E. purpurascens darleyensis).
E. vagans CORNISH HEATH. Zones 3–6, 15–17, 20–24. Cornwall, Ireland.	Bushy, open, to 2–3 ft. tall.	Bright green.	Purplish pink. July–Sept.	Robust and hardy.
E. v. 'Lyonesse'	Bushy, rounded, to 18 in.	Bright, glossy green.	White. July–Oct.	Best white Cornish heath.
E. v. 'Mrs. D. F. Maxwell'	Bushy, rounded, to 18 in.	Dark green.	Cherry pink or red. July–Oct.	Outstanding for color and heavy bloom; widely grown.
E. v. 'St. Keverne'	Bushy, rounded, to 18 in.	Light green.	Rose pink. July–Oct.	Heavy bloom. Compact if pruned annually.
E. ventricosa Zones 15–17, 20–24.	To 6 ft., usually much less.	Medium green, needlelike.	Heavy spikes at tips of branches. Pale to medium pink, shiny, solid looking. May–July.	Occasionally sold as small pot plant in spring.

ERIGERON. FLEABANE. Perennials. Free-blooming plants with daisylike flowers; similar to closely related Michaelmas daisy (Aster), except that erigeron's flower heads have threadlike rays in 2 or more rows rather than broader rays in single row. White, pink, lavender, or violet flowers, usually with yellow centers, early summer into fall. Sun or light shade; sandy soil; moderate watering. Cut back after flowering to prolong bloom. Rock garden species need especially fast drainage.

E. glaucus. BEACH ASTER, SEASIDE DAISY. Zones 4–6, 15–17, 22–24. Native of California, Oregon coast. Burns in hot sun inland. Basal leaves in clumps. Stout, hairy stems 10–12 in. high, topped by lavender flower heads 1½–2 in. across in spring, summer. Blue green stems and foliage. Use in rock garden, border, beside path. Sun or part shade. 'Arthur Menzies' is unusually compact, mat-forming selection with lavender pink flower heads.

E. karvinskianus. (Often called Vittadinia). Zones 8, 9, 12–24. Native to Mexico. Graceful trailing plant 10–20 in. high. Leaves 1 in. long, often toothed at tips. Dainty flower heads ¾ in. across with numerous white or pinkish rays. Drought tolerant. Use as ground cover in garden beds or large containers, in rock gardens, hanging baskets, on dry walls. Naturalizes easily; stands root competition well; invasive unless controlled.

E. speciosus. All Zones. Native to coast, Pacific Northwest. Erect, leafy stemmed, 2 ft. high. Flower heads 1–1½ in. across, dark violet or lavender rays; summer bloom. E. s. macranthus,

Erigeron speciosus

ASPEN DAISY, is widespread through Rocky Mountain area. It has 3–5 flower heads to a stalk; stalks nod near top. Hybrids between *E. speciosus* and other species are available; these named sorts have larger flower heads and add white and pink to blue lavender of wild kinds.

ERIOBOTRYA. LOQUAT. Evergreen trees or big shrubs. Both kinds have large, prominently veined, sharply toothed leaves. One bears edible fruit. Attractive to birds.

  E. deflexa. BRONZE LOQUAT. Zones 8–24. Shrubby, but easily trained into small tree form. New leaves have bright coppery color which they hold for a long time before turning green. Leaves less deeply veined and not as leathery as *E. japonica,* and are more pointed and shinier. Garlands of creamy white flowers attractive in spring. No edible fruit. Good for espaliers (not on hot wall), patio planting, containers in full sun or part shade. Not drought tolerant. Fast growing.

Eriobotrya japonica

  E. japonica. LOQUAT. Zones 4–24. Grows 15–30 ft. tall, equally broad in sun, slenderer in shade. Big, leathery, crisp leaves, stoutly veined and netted, 6–12 in. long, 2–4 in. wide, sharply toothed. They are glossy deep green above and show rust-colored wool beneath. New branches woolly; small, dull white flowers in woolly 3–6 in. clusters borne in fall. These are fragrant, but not showy. Fruit 1–2 in. long, orange to yellow, sweet, aromatic, and acid with seeds (usually big) in center. Hardy to 20°F.; has survived 12°F., but fruit often injured by low temperatures.

  Plant in well-drained soil; will thrive in drought when established, but grows better with some moisture. Prune to shape; if you like the fruit, thin branches somewhat to let light into tree's interior. If tree sets fruit heavily, remove some while it's small to increase size of remaining fruit and to prevent limb breakage. Fireblight is a danger; if leaves and stems blacken from top downward, prune back 12 in. or more into healthy wood. Burn prunings and sterilize shears between cuts. Use as lawn tree for sunny or shady spots; espalier on fence or trellis, but not in reflected heat. Can be held in container for several years. Cut foliage good for indoor decorating. Plants draw bees.

  Most trees sold are seedlings, good ornamental plants with unpredictable fruit quality; if you definitely want fruit, look for a grafted variety. 'Champagne' (March-May), best in warm areas, has yellow-skinned, white-fleshed, juicy, tart fruit. 'Gold Nugget' (May-June), best near coast, has sweeter fruit with orange skin, flesh. 'MacBeth' (April-May), has exceptionally large fruit with yellow skin, cream flesh. 'Thales' is late yellow-fleshed variety.

ERIOGONUM. WILD BUCKWHEAT. Annuals, perennials, shrubs. Native to most areas of West (the few sold at nurseries are mostly native to California coast). Grow best in full sun in well-drained, loose, gravelly soil. Once established they need little water— none near coast. Useful to cover dry banks, mass among rocks, or use in rock gardens. Most available kinds withstand wind and heat well.

  Flower arrangers use flower clusters in dried bouquets. Individual blossoms are tiny but they grow in long-stemmed or branched clusters—domed, flattish, or ball-like. They turn to shades of tan or rust as seeds ripen. If you leave flower clusters

Eriogonum arborescens

on plant, seeds will drop and volunteer seedlings will appear. Transplant when they're small to extend planting or replace overgrown plants. Shrubby kinds get leggy after several years. You can do some pruning to shape if you start when plants are young, but if they've had no attention, it's better to replace them.

  E. arborescens. SANTA CRUZ ISLAND BUCKWHEAT. Shrub. Zones 14–24. Native to Santa Cruz, Santa Rosa, and Anacapa islands, southern California. Grows 3–4 (sometimes 8) ft. high, spread-

ing 4–5 ft. or more. Trunk and branches with shredding gray to reddish bark make attractive open pattern. Rather narrow, ½–1½-in.-long, gray green leaves tend to cluster at ends of branches. Long-stalked, flat clusters of pale pink to rose flowers in profusion, May-September.

  E. crocatum. SAFFRON BUCKWHEAT. Perennial. Zones 14–24. Native to Ventura County, California. Low, compact, to 18 in. high with white woolly stems. Roundish 1-in.-long leaves covered with white wool; attractive all year. Sulfur yellow flowers in broad flattish clusters, April-August.

  E. fasciculatum. CALIFORNIA BUCKWHEAT. Shrub. Zones 8, 9, 14–24. Native to foothills of California (Santa Clara to San Diego counties) and desert slopes of mountains of southern California. Forms clump of many semiupright stems 1–3 ft. high, spreading to 4 ft. Leaves usually narrow, ½–¾ in. long, vary from dark green above and white woolly beneath (typical form) to gray, hairy on both sides. White or pinkish flowers in headlike clusters, May-October. Good erosion control plant. Form 'Theodore Payne' is completely prostrate, makes attractive ground cover of lush green foliage.

  E. giganteum. ST. CATHERINE'S LACE. Shrub. Zones 14–24. Native to Santa Catalina and San Clemente islands. Differs from *E. arborescens* in its more freely branching habit, grayish white, broadly oval, 1–2½-in.-long leaves, and longer period of bloom.

  E. grande rubescens (*E. rubescens, E. latifolium rubescens*). RED BUCKWHEAT. Perennial. Zones 14–24. Native to San Miguel, Santa Rosa, and Santa Cruz islands, southern California. Woody based; branches tend to lie on ground with upright tips about 10–12 in. high, spreading to 12–18 in. Gray green oval leaves, 1–3½ in. long. Sturdy upright branches, flower stalks topped by headlike clusters of rosy red flowers.

  E. umbellatum. SULFUR FLOWER. Perennial. All Zones. Low, broad mats of woody stems set with 1-in. green leaves with white-felted undersides. Stalks, 4–12 in. tall, carry clusters of tiny yellow flowers that age to rust. They grow to timberline and above.

ERODIUM chamaedryoides. CRANE'S BILL. Perennial. Zones 7–9, 14–24. Native to Balearic Islands and Corsica. Dainty-looking but tough plant in geranium family. Forms dense foliage tuft 3–6 in. high, 12 in. across. Long-stalked, roundish, dark green leaves ⅓ in. long with scalloped edges. Profuse, cup shaped, ½-in.-wide flowers with white or rose pink, rosy-veined petals notched at tips, April to October. Good small-scale ground cover, rock plant. Plant in sun or part shade in porous soil; ample moisture. Rather slow growing.

Erodium chamaedryoides

ERYNGIUM amethystinum. SEA HOLLY, AMETHYST ERYNGIUM. Perennial. All Zones. Erect, stiff-branched thistlelike plant 2–3 ft. high, blooming July-September. Striking steel blue or amethyst, oval ½-in.-long flower heads surrounded by spiny blue bracts; upper stems also blue (flowers last long when cut, fresh or dried). Leaves sparse, dark green, deeply cut, spiny toothed. Plant in borders or fringe areas, full sun, deep sandy soil. Drought tolerant. Tap rooted; difficult to divide. Make root cuttings or sow seed in place, thin to 1 ft. Often self-sows.

Eryngium amethystinum

ERYSIMUM. BLISTER CRESS, WALLFLOWER. Perennial or annual. Closely related to wallflower (*Cheiranthus*), with similar 4-petaled flowers, mostly yellow or orange, generally quite fragrant. Most prefer full sun and can take considerable drought.

  E. hieraciifolium (usually sold as *Cheiranthus allionii* or *E. asperum*). SIBERIAN WALLFLOWER. Perennial, usually grown as annual. All Zones. Branching plants 1–1½ ft. high, smothered in spring with rich orange flowers. Leaves firm, narrow, 2–4 in.

long. Combine with yellow, orange, or bronze tulips; blue forget-me-not (*Myosotis*) or Chinese forget-me-not (*Cynoglossum*). Sow seed in fall in mild climates; elsewhere in summer for well-established plants by fall. Thin seedlings to 1 ft. apart.

E. kotschyanum. Perennial treated as annual in warm climates. Zones 1–11, 14–21. Forms attractive mats 6 in. high. Leaves pale green, finely toothed, crowded. Deep yellow flowers on 2-in. stems. Plant in sun. Use in rock gardens, rock crevices, between paving, or in small pattern plantings with mat-forming perennials such as aubrieta, dwarf candytuft (*Iberis*). If plants hump up, cut out raised portion.

*Erysimum
hieraciifolium*

ERYTHEA. See *Brahea.*

ERYTHRINA. CORAL TREE. Mostly deciduous (some nearly evergreen) trees or shrubs. Many kinds; known and used chiefly in southern California. Brilliant flowers from greenish white through yellow, light orange and light red to orange and red. Thorny plants have strong structural value, in or out of leaf. Leaves divided into 3 leaflets. Unless otherwise noted, plants do best in full sun, most soils (but best with good drainage), and with regular, deep, infrequent watering in dry season. To eliminate too-rapid, succulent growth and limb breakage in larger species (*E. caffra, E. lysistemon, E. sykesii*), give little or no summer irrigation, prune after flowering.

Erythrina caffra

E. bidwillii. Large deciduous shrub. Zones 8, 9, 12–24. To 8 ft., sometimes treelike to 20 ft. or more, wide spreading. Hybrid origin. Spectacular display—2-ft.-long clusters of pure red flowers on long willowy stalks from spring until winter; main show in summer. Cut back flowering wood when flowers are spent. Very thorny so plant away from paths and prune with long-handled shears. Best in hot sun.

E. caffra (*E. constantiana*). KAFFIRBOOM CORAL TREE. Briefly deciduous tree. Zones 21–24. Native to South Africa. Grows 24–40 ft. high, spreads to 40–60 ft. wide. Drops leaves in January; then angular bare branches produce big clusters of deep red orange, tubular flowers that drip honey. In March or earlier, flowers give way to fresh, light green foliage.

E. coralloides (sometimes sold as *E. poianthes*). NAKED CORAL TREE. Deciduous tree. Zones 12, 13, 19–24. Native to Mexico (some doubt about place of origin). To 30 ft. high and as wide or wider, but easily contained by pruning. Fiery red blossoms like fat candles or pine cones bloom at tips of naked, twisted black-thorned branches, March to May. At end of flowering season, 8–10-in. leaves develop, give shade in summer, turn yellow in late fall before dropping. Bizarre form of branch structure when tree is out of leaf is almost as valuable as spring flower display.

E. crista-galli. COCKSPUR CORAL TREE. Deciduous shrub or tree. Native to rainy sections of Brazil. Zones 7–9, 12–17, 19–24. Unusual plant with habit all its own. In frost-free areas, becomes many-stemmed, rough-barked tree to 15–20 ft. high and as wide. In colder climates, dies to ground in winter but comes back in spring like perennial (cut back dead growth). First flowers form after leaves come in spring—at each branch tip a big, loose, spikelike cluster of velvety birdlike blossoms, warm pink to wine red (plants vary). Depending on environment, there can be as many as three distinct flowering periods, spring

*Erythrina
crista-galli*

through fall. Cut back old flower stems and deadened branch ends after each wave of bloom. Leaves 6 in. long, leaflets 2–3 in. long.

E. falcata. Nearly evergreen tree. Zones 19–24. Native to Brazil and Peru. Grows to 30–40 ft. high, upright. Must be in ground several years before it flowers (may take 10–12 years). Rich deep red, or occasionally orange red, sickle shaped flowers in hanging spikelike clusters at branch ends in late winter, early spring. Some leaves fall at flowering time.

E. humeana. NATAL CORAL TREE. Normally deciduous shrub or tree (sometimes almost evergreen). Zones 12, 13, 20–24. Native to South Africa. May grow to 30 ft. but begins to wear its bright orange red flowers when only 3 ft. high. Flowers in long-stalked clusters at branch ends well above foliage (unlike many other types). Blooms continuously from late August to late November. Dark green leaves. *E. h. raja* is shrubbier and has leaflets with long pointed "tails".

Erythrina humeana

E. lysistemon (sometimes erroneously sold as *E. princeps*). Deciduous tree. Zones 13, 21–24. Native to South Africa. Similar to *E. caffra* in size; slower growing. Light orange flowers, sometimes shrimp-colored, intermittently October to May, occasionally in summer. Time of bloom varies greatly. Many handsome black thorns. A magnificent tree of great landscape value. Very sensitive to heavy, wet soil.

E. sykesii. Deciduous tree. Zones 19–24. Hybrid coral tree from Australia. Grows 24–30 ft.; spreading habit. Showy red flowers before leaves in Jan.-March. Does not form pods.

ERYTHRONIUM. Corms. Zones 1–7, 15–17. Most native to West. Dainty spring-blooming, nodding, lily shaped flowers 1–1½ in. across, on stems usually 1 ft. or less high. All have 2 (rarely 3) broad, tongue shaped, basal leaves, mottled in many species. Plant in shade or partial shade (except *E. dens-canis*) in groups under trees, in rock gardens, beside pools or streams. Plant corms in fall, 2–3 in. deep, 4–5 in. apart, in rich porous soil. Plant corms as soon as you receive them, and don't let them dry out. Growing plants need summer moisture too.

*Erythronium
tuolumnense*

E. californicum. FAWN LILY. Leaves mottled with brown. Flowers creamy white or yellow with deeper yellow band at base.

E. dens-canis. DOG-TOOTH VIOLET. European species with purple or rose flowers 1 in. long; stems 6 in. high. Leaves mottled with reddish brown. Needs more sun than others. Specialists can supply named varieties in white, pink, rose, and violet.

E. hendersonii. Flowers deeply curled back at tips, 1½ in. across, light to deep lavender, deep maroon at base surrounded by white band. Leaves mottled.

E. revolutum. Similar to *E. californicum,* with mottled leaves, large rose pink or lavender flowers, banded yellow at base. 'Rose Beauty' and 'White Beauty' are choice varieties.

E. tuolumnense. All green leaves. Flowers golden yellow, greenish yellow at base. Robust, with stems 12–15 in. tall. 'Kondo' and 'Pagoda' are extra-vigorous selections.

ESCALLONIA. Evergreen shrubs. Zones 4–9, 14–17, 20–24. Native to South America, principally Chile. Wind-hardy, clean looking, with glossy leaves. Clusters of flowers in summer and fall, nearly year round in mild climates. May freeze badly at 10°–15°F. but recover quickly. Will take direct coastal conditions and coastal winds. Grow in full sun near coast, part shade in hot interior valleys. Can take some drought once established, but look better with ample water. Tolerant of most soils but

Escallonia rubra

damaged by high alkalinity. Prune taller ones by removing ⅓ of old wood each year, cutting to the base; or shape into multi-trunked trees. Prune after flowers fade. Tip-pinch smaller kinds to keep them compact. Can be sheared as hedges, but this may sacrifice some bloom. Fast growing; good screen plants. Foliage of some exudes resinous fragrance. They attract bees.

E. 'Apple Blossom'. See *E. langleyensis.*

E. 'Balfouri'. See *E. exoniensis.*

E. bifida (*E. montevidensis*). WHITE ESCALLONIA. Tall, broad shrub (8–10 ft.) or small tree to 25 ft. Leaves dark green, glossy, 3–4 in. long. White flowers in large, rounded clusters at branch ends, late summer, fall. Big screening plant, or can be grown as multitrunked small tree. Many plants sold under this name are *E. illinita,* a smaller plant to 10 ft. tall with smaller flower clusters and pronounced resinous odor.

E. 'C. F. Ball'. See *E. rubra.*

E. 'Compakta'. To 3 ft. high with rose red flowers.

E. exoniensis. Name given to hybrids between *E. rosea* and *E. rubra.* Best selections are 'Balfouri', graceful plant to 10 ft. with drooping branchlets, narrow clusters of white, pink-tinted flowers; and 'Frades' (*E.* 'Fradesii'), compact growth to 5–6 ft. (lower with pinching). 'Frades' has glossy green leaves smaller than those of *E. laevis,* which it resembles, and prolific show of clear pink to rose flowers nearly year round. Good as espaliers.

E. 'Fradesii'. See *E. exoniensis.*

E. 'Ingramii'. See *E. rubra macrantha.*

E. 'Jubilee'. Compact 6-ft. shrub, densely leafy right to ground. Clustered pinkish to rose flowers bloom at intervals throughout year. Foliage inferior to that of *E. exoniensis.* Set 4 ft. apart for informal hedge or low screen.

E. laevis (*E. organensis*). PINK ESCALLONIA. Leafy, dense-growing shrub to 12–15 ft. Leaves bronzy green. Pink to red buds open into white to pink flowers in short, broad clusters. Early summer bloom. Use like *E. bifida.* Leaves burn in beach plantings and in high heat of interior.

E. langleyensis. Name given to hybrids between *E. rubra* and *E. virgata.* Best known selection is 'Apple Blossom', a dense-growing shrub to 5 ft., sprawling unless pinched back. Flowers pinkish white from pink buds. Blooms all summer with peaks in late spring, early fall.

E. montevidensis. See *E. bifida.*

E. organensis. See *E. laevis.*

E. rosea. Shrub to 7 ft. with shiny, oval 1½-in. leaves. Clustered flowers white to red in summer. Many closely related plants sold under this name; commonest, probably a selection of *E. franciscana,* is 10 ft. tall with tendency to throw out long uneven branches. It has chocolate-colored bark and dark green leaves ½–1 in. long. Rosy pink flowers all summer long.

E. rubra. Upright, compact shrub 6–15 ft. tall. Leaves smooth, very glossy dark green. Red or crimson flowers in 1–3-in. clusters throughout warmer months. Much used as screen or hedge, especially near coast. Compact varieties are 'C. F. Ball' (to 3 ft. with some pinching) and 'William Watson', to 4 ft., with ruddy cerise flowers, spindly habit unless pruned. *E. r. macrantha* ('Ingramii') is large-flowered variety.

E. virgata. Partially deciduous shrub to 6 ft., with ¾-in. leaves and short clusters of pale rose or white flowers. 'Gwendolyn Anley' has flesh pink flowers. These are hardiest escallonias in frostiest parts of their range of hardiness.

ESCHSCHOLZIA californica. CALIFORNIA POPPY. Perennial usually grown as annual. All Zones. Native to California, Oregon. State flower of California. Free branching from base; stems 8–24 in. long. Leaves blue green, finely divided. Single flowers vary from pale yellow to deep orange, about 2 in. wide, with satiny petals. Blooms close at night and on gray days.

Not best choice for important, close-in garden beds because unless you trim off dead flowers regularly, plants go to seed and all parts turn straw color. But can't be surpassed for naturalizing on sunny hillsides, in dry fields, vacant lots, along drives, in parking strips, in

Eschscholzia californica

country gardens. Broadcast seed in fall on cultivated, well-drained soil; if rains are late, water to keep ground moist until seeds germinate. Summer watering not necessary but forces more bloom. Full sun. For large-scale sowing, use 3–4 lbs. of seed per acre. Reseeds freely if not crowded out by weeds. Birds attracted to seeds.

There are also garden forms available in yellow, pink, rose, flame orange, red, cream, and white; Sunset strain has single flowers, Mission Bells semidouble flowers, and Ballerina semidouble flowers with frilled and fluted petals. Some seed houses sell packs of single color named varieties.

ESPOSTOA lanata. PERUVIAN OLD MAN CACTUS. Zones 12–24. Columnar cactus branching with age. Slow growing in pots, fairly fast to 8 ft. in open ground. Grow in full sun or light afternoon shade. Drought tolerant. Plant has light brown, bristly thorns ½–2 in. long, usually concealed in long, white hair that covers plant. Hair is especially long and dense near summit. Pink, 2-in.-long tubular flowers, May-June. Protect from hard frosts.

Espostoa lanata

EUCALYPTUS. Evergreen trees and shrubs. Zones 8–24. Native to Australia. Most widely planted non-native trees in California and Arizona. For several hundred miles in parts of California you never lose sight of a eucalypt. First ones were planted in California in 1856. From 1870 on, they were widely planted for windbreaks, firewood, shade, and beauty. From 1904 to 1912, thousands of acres were planted in an ill-advised hardwood timber scheme. Over the years, eucalyptus proved themselves well in these climates. They remain ever popular landscaping subjects. Reasons:

Great beauty. Some kinds are basically landscape structure trees or shrubs, with unimportant flowers. These kinds are grown for their attractive and functional form and texture. Others grow flowers as striking as roses or rhododendrons, or foliage so handsome that florists sell it. Some species serve basic landscaping functions and produce pretty flowers, too. Chart indicates noteworthy features.

Eucalyptus ficifolia

Climate tolerance. Much of Australia has either a desert, Mediterranean, or subtropical climate, as do sections of California and Arizona. Dozens of eucalypts are naturally adapted to our coast, coastal hills, valleys, deserts—with or without irrigation. Drought tolerance is common to most.

No pests. Until 1984 eucalyptus was a pest-free tree; none of its native attackers had reached here from Australia. In that year the eucalyptus longhorn beetle was observed in Southern California. Without its Australian predators to keep it in check, it is becoming a serious pest, especially on stressed trees. Symptoms are oval holes made by beetles leaving trunk, branches dying with leaves still attached.

Eucalyptus sideroxylon

Keep trees healthy. Eliminate eucalyptus firewood with underbark feeding galleries showing; burn it or bury it. Remove dead or dying trees; bury logs or cover tightly with tarps for at least 6 months. Best hope for control will come from introduced predatory insects.

Fast growth. Some tree types grow as fast as 10–15 ft. a year in early stages. Such growth rate is typically associated with short-lived trees, but not in this case; fast growing tree eucalypts can live for at least a century if planted right.

Eucalypts are influenced through their lives by their condition at planting time and the kind of planting they get. Select most vigorous looking, not biggest plants. Avoid ones with many leafless twigs or evidence of having been pruned hard. If possible, do not buy plants with canbound roots. If such plants are all that you can get, do this: wash soil off roots, spread roots out as straight and fanlike as possible in premoistened planting hole (with stem's old soil line ½–1 in. below grade level). Fill in thoroughly around fanned-out roots at once with moistened soil and irrigate heavily. If plants are topheavy, cut back and stake (chart specifically prescribes staking for certain species).

Some descriptions in the chart recommend cutting plants back to make them bushier or stouter. Do this between March and August, preferably when tree has been in ground at least a year. If possible, cut back to just above side branch or bud. If you can't find such a growth point, cut right into smooth trunk; if plant is established, new growth will break out beneath cut. Later, come back and remove all excess new branches—keep only those that are well-placed.

Best way to plant eucalyptus is directly from seed flats. Seeding is as easy as with many annuals and perennials. Sow seed on flat of prepared soil in spring or summer. Keep flat shaded and water sparingly. When seedlings are 2–3 in. high, lift gently, separate, and plant into another flat of prepared soil, spacing 3 in. apart. Or transplant into gallon cans or cleaned quart oil cans (puncture at bottom for drainage). Plant seedlings in 2–3 months when 6–12 in. high.

A eucalyptus tree in a suitable climate, properly planted and irrigated, is a vigorous, strong, and durable plant. Complete fertilizer is seldom needed, although iron often is required for eucalypts that chronically form yellow leaves.

The chart gives approximate hardiness for each eucalyptus species sold in nurseries. But it is important to remember that these temperatures are not absolute. In addition to air temperature, you must take into consideration: age of tree (generally, the older, the hardier); condition of tree or shrub; date of frost (24°F. in November is more damaging than 24°F. in January after weeks of frosts); duration of frost. As a guide: if temperatures in your area are likely to fall within frost-damage range for certain species, plant it as a risk. If they regularly fall below given range, don't plant it.

Most eucalypts have two conspicuously different kinds of foliage: soft, variously shaped juvenile leaves found on seedlings, saplings, and new branches that grow from stumps; and usually tougher adult or mature foliage. Where a species' juvenile foliage is significant, it is mentioned in the chart. Almost all eucalyptus leaves, juvenile and adult, have distinguishing pungent fragrance. Sometimes you must crush leaves to smell it. There is a common denominator to fragrance of all types, but various ones are additionally spiked with peppermint, lemon, medicinal, or other scents.

Several Australian words are used repeatedly in common names for various eucalypts. Here are their meanings as applied to eucalyptus: *gum,* a name generally applied to any eucalypt, specifically to any of various smooth-barked (often peeling) species; *ironbark,* any with hard, rough bark; *mallee,* originally native term for eucalyptus thicket, here, refers to any shrubby species with round, swollen rootstock from which grow several slender stems; *marlock,* dwarf species; *messmate,* interesting name of no particular significance, applied to several stringy-bark species; *peppermint,* any with peppermint odor in crushed leaves, usually with finely fibrous bark; *yate,* native word of western Australia, applied to certain species.

More than 500 kinds of eucalyptus have been recorded in Australia. About 150 have been grown in California and Arizona (many as solitary representatives in arboretums). A few have been grown in Oregon and Washington.

Eucalyptus

NAME	HARDI-INESS	FORM AND SIZE	LEAVES AND BARK	FLOWERS AND FRUIT	BEST FEATURES AND HOW TO ENCOURAGE THEM
Eucalyptus baueriana BLUE BOX	10°–18°F.	Fuller bodied substitute for *E. polyanthemos.*	Leaves broader and rougher than *E. polyanthemos.*	Same as *E. polyanthemos.*	Attractive round tree when young, becomes tall and straight with age.
Eucalyptus caesia (*caesia* means "bluish gray")	22°–25°F.	Graceful, weeping, open habit as mallee or small, weak-structured tree, 15–20 ft.	Gray green small leaves, contrasting with red stems. Bark white and mottled when young, curling when older.	Outstanding dusty pink to deep rose flowers in loose clusters, blooming heavily late winter to early spring. Flowering scattered rest of year. Seed capsules shaped like bells, lavender gray, ¾ in. long.	Not good in wind or in heavy soil. Use as thin screen in protected place. Or, with pruning and training, use as espalier, shrub, or multitrunked tree. Prune and stake to give it body.
E. calophylla (*calophylla* means "beautiful leaf")	25°–28°F.	Medium to large round-headed tree—90–150 ft. high in Australia, has reached 50 ft. in California.	Broad, oval leaves, 4–7 in. long. Rough, fissured bark.	Showy flowers in 1-ft. clusters—white, rose, or red, on and off all year. Bulbous seed capsules, 1½ in. wide. Light pink-flowered form often sold as *E. c.* 'Rosea'; rose pink kind is *E. c.* 'Hawkeyi'.	Sturdy, drought tolerant, easy to grow—and it produces showy flowers against nice leaves as part of the package. Similar to *E. ficifolia* in many ways (also hybridizes frequently with it).
E. camaldulensis (*E. rostrata*) RED GUM, RIVER RED GUM	12°–15°F.	Ultimately 80–120 ft. Form varies; typically has curved trunk, spreading crown, gracefully weeping branches.	Long, slender, lance shaped, medium green leaves, pendulous in varying degrees. Tan, mottled trunk.	Unimportant white to pale yellow flowers in drooping clusters, summer. Followed by many rounded, pea-sized seed capsules in long clusters. Not grown for flowers; structural tree. One of most widely planted eucalypts around world.	Mighty eucalypt for highways, broad streets, parks, skylines. Grows in lawns. Widely planted in California and Arizona valleys and deserts. Takes more heat and cold than *E. globulus.* Good in alkaline soil. Has resprouted after 11° freeze.

(Continued on next page)

NAME	HARD-INESS	FORM AND SIZE	LEAVES AND BARK	FLOWERS AND FRUIT	BEST FEATURES AND HOW TO ENCOURAGE THEM
E. cinerea (*cinerea* means "ash colored")	14°–17°F.	Medium-sized tree, 20–50 ft. high, almost as wide. Irregular outline. Can be scrawny.	Juvenile leaves gray green, roundish, 1–2 in. long, in pairs. Mature leaves long. Furrowed bark.	Small white flowers near stems in winter and spring, followed by small conical seed capsules. Flowers are incidental—decorative juvenile foliage is main reason for growing it.	Inclined to grow snakelike. Corrective pruning yields and encourages juvenile gray-foliaged branches used for indoor decorating. Fast growing. Withstands wind. Best in dry site or with fast drainage.
E. citriodora LEMON-SCENTED GUM	24°–28°F.	One of most graceful of trees, slender, tall (75–100 ft.). Trunk usually straight, sometimes curved.	Leaves long (3–7 in.), narrow, golden green, lemon scented. Trunk and branches powder white to pinkish.	Once tree gets up in the air, you'd need telescope to see flowers (lower ½ or ⅔ of tree is bare trunk). Blooms whitish, not distinctive, in clusters, mostly during winter. Seed capsules that follow are urn shaped, ⅜ in. wide.	Designer's tree. Enhances any architecture. Can grow close to walls, walks. Perfect for groves. Very fast. Weak-trunked when young. Stake stoutly. Cut back and thin often to strengthen trunk. Tolerates much or little water. Tenderness to frosts is only real drawback.
E. cladocalyx (*E. corynocalyx*) SUGAR GUM	23°–28°F.	Large, upright, graceful, round topped, very open, 75–100 ft. high. Straight trunk.	Oval or variably shaped leaves, 3–5 in. long, shiny red-dish. Tan bark peels to show cream patches.	Creamy white flowers of little significance, in dense 3-in. clusters, blooming June-August. Oval seed capsules (⅜ in. wide) in clusters. Not planted for flowers; used for structure.	Dramatic skyline tree on southern California coast. Puffy clouds of leaves separated by open spaces —a Japanese print in its mature silhouette. Tough, drought resistant. Variety 'Nana' to 20–25 ft.
E. cloeziana YELLOW MESSMATE	25°–28°F.	Medium-sized (30–50 ft.). Straight central trunk. Usually narrow.	Light green, 4-in.-long leaves, red and purple in fall, winter. Brown bark.	Small clusters of white to yellowish flowers, spring, early summer. Round seed capsules like miniature (¼ in.) half grapefruit in tight clusters.	Reddish new foliage is its best feature. Has made variable performance in California—has tendency to become chlorotic (supply iron in soil).

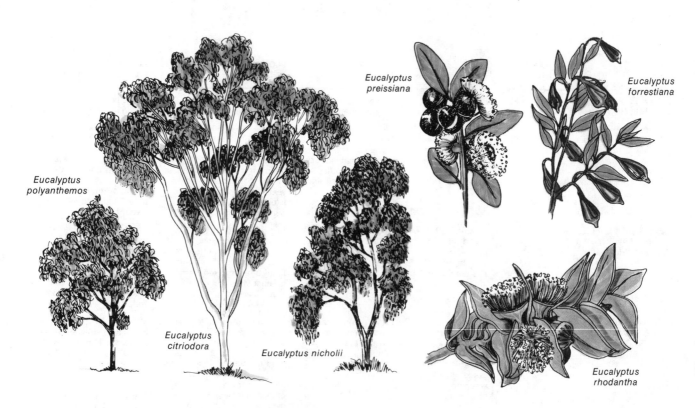

Eucalyptus polyanthemos

Eucalyptus citriodora

Eucalyptus nicholii

Eucalyptus preissiana

Eucalyptus forrestiana

Eucalyptus rhodantha

Three widely planted tree-type Eucalypts show differences in form. Eucalyptus flower size and form vary. With *E. forrestiana,* display comes from woody, red flower bases.

NAME	HARD-INESS	FORM AND SIZE	LEAVES AND BARK	FLOWERS AND FRUIT	BEST FEATURES AND HOW TO ENCOURAGE THEM
E. cornuta (*cornuta* means "horn shaped") YATE	22°–25°F.	Large-headed, spreading tree, to 35–60 ft. high. Attractive dense crown gives shade.	Lance shaped, shiny leaves, 3–6 in. long (young leaves round, gray). Bark peels in strips.	Flower buds have interesting fingerlike buff caps pushed off by opening flowers. Greenish yellow flowers make round fuzzy clusters, 3 in. wide, summer. Clusters of round seed capsules with short horns.	Appreciated for its flowers, form, and landscape uses. Grows under many kinds of soil, water, and climate conditions. Does well even when neglected. Not subject to wind breakage. Good shade tree.
E. eremophila TALL SAND MALLEE	24°–27°F.	Multitrunked, small, bushy tree, 25 ft.	Dark green, narrow, lance shaped, shiny leaves. Scaly bark.	Round, yellow, fuzzy 1–2-in. flowers in clusters, June. Opening flowers push off long pointed caps. Capsules slightly cylindrical, ¼ in. wide.	Very drought tolerant tree for banks, hillsides, beach areas. No good in lawns. Better liked in southern than in northern California.
E. erythrocorys RED-CAP GUM	23°–26°F.	Small tree, 10–30 ft., best with multiple trunk; sprawling but attractive bush.	Thick, shiny, 4–7 in., lance shaped leaves, greener than most eucalyptus leaves. White trunk.	Spectacular. Bright red caps tilt up and drop off to reveal yellow flowers; several form cluster that looks like shaving brush. Blooms any time, peaks fall to early spring. Cone shaped seed capsules.	Takes much water if drainage is good. Can be grown in lawn. To make dense multitrunked bush or tree, head back main shoots several times.
E. erythronema RED-FLOWERED MALLEE	22°–24°F.	Mallee or small, bushy, crooked or sinuous tree, 10–25 ft.	Narrow, dull green leaves 1½–3 in. long. Smooth bark in patches of pink, white, tan, pale green.	Watermelon to deep red flowers, 1 in. wide, open from conical, pointed buds, 1 in. long, pinkish green to red. Flowers often hidden by leaves. Conical, square sided seed capsules, ½ in. wide.	Trunk and flowers are its best features. You may have to thin some to make it presentable tree. Resists wind and drought. Good near ocean.
E. ficifolia RED-FLOWERING GUM	25°–30°F.	Usually single-trunked, round-headed tree to 40 ft. Compact crown. Can be multistemmed big bush.	Leaves 3–7 in. long, shape and texture of rubber plant leaves. Bark red and stringy to gray and fibrous.	Spectacular 1-ft. clusters of flowers, cream, light pink, salmon, orange, or light red (most common); all year, peaking July-August. Seed capsules 1 in. wide, like miniature dice cups with swollen bottoms.	Not like other eucalypts except *E. calophylla*. Prune off seed capsules from young trees so they won't pull branches down. Best on coast; seldom successful inland. Rarely good in lawns.
E. forrestiana FUCHSIA EUCALYPTUS	23°–27°F.	Shrub or short-trunked tree to 12 ft. (needs staking, pruning as tree).	Narrow leaves, 1½–2½ in. long. Gray brown, smooth trunk, reddish branches.	Flowers are unimportant; woody, pendant red flower bases resemble fuchsias, give decoration. Intermittent all year. Capsules 1 in. wide.	Fuchsialike flower bases last long when cut. Good performance coast or dry areas. Any soil. To strengthen, cut back when young.
E. globulus BLUE GUM	17°–22°F.	Tall, solemn trees of grandeur to 150–200 ft. Straight trunks. Heavy masses of foliage.	Sickle shaped leaves dark green, 6–10 in. long. Young leaves oval, silvery, soft. Bark sheds.	Flowers creamy white to yellow in winter and spring. Warty, ribbed, blue gray seed capsules, 1 in. wide. Fruit drop added to leaf and bark litter makes tree very messy.	Most common eucalypt in California. Very aromatic. Magnificent windbreak but too messy, greedy, and brittle for garden or city street. Needs deep soil and plenty of room. Best on coastal slopes, poor in deserts.
E. globulus 'Compacta' DWARF BLUE GUM	17°–22°F.	Multibranched, bushy, shrublike tree, as high as 60–70 ft.	Same as *E. globulus*. Foliage persists to ground for 10–15 years. More treelike shape later.	Flowers and seed capsules same as on *E. globulus*.	Lacks noble silhouette of *E. globulus*, just as greedy, almost as messy. Good low windbreak in coastal areas—can be sheared as low as 10 ft.
E. grossa COARSE-FLOWERED MALLEE	22°–26°F.	Multitrunked, spreading shrub, 9–15 ft., sometimes dense.	Thick, glistening, deep green, 3-in., broad, oval leaves. Red, green stems.	Noticeable yellow flowers in clusters open from bullet shaped buds in spring and summer. Cylindrical seed capsules, ⅜ in. wide.	Best feature is clean green foliage. Often erratic, can be made into dense hedge if pruned. Gets scraggly when old if watered heavily.
E. gunnii CIDER GUM	5°–10°F.	Medium to large, dense, vertical tree, 40–75 ft.	Mature leaves lance shaped, 3–5 in. long. Bark smooth, green, tan.	Small creamy white flowers, April-June, from shiny green, round buds. Seed capsules ¼ in. wide, bell shaped, in clusters.	Strong, vigorous, tall grower. Impressively healthy and vigorous looking. Good shade, windbreak, or privacy screening tree in cold areas (very hardy).

(Continued on next page)

NAME	HARD-INESS	FORM AND SIZE	LEAVES AND BARK	FLOWERS AND FRUIT	BEST FEATURES AND HOW TO ENCOURAGE THEM
E. kruseana KRUSE'S MALLEE	25°–28°F.	Thin, open, angular shrub, almost ground cover. Maximum: 5–8 ft. tall.	Silver blue, round, 1-in. leaves like tiny E. pulverulenta. Smooth bark.	Little (½ in.) yellow flowers along stems between round leaves. Flower bud caps cone shaped. Seed capsules size and shape of small (¼ in.) acorns.	Attractive foliage and flowers on slow-growing shrub small and dainty enough for Japanese garden. Conversation plant. Cut back frequently.
E. lehmannii BUSHY YATE	25°–28°F.	Small tree, 20–30 ft. Dense, flat-topped, wide spreading.	Light green, long-oval, 2-in. leaves, some turn red in fall. Old ones rough. Brown bark.	Apple green flowers in huge (4 in. wide) round clusters open from curved horn shaped buds in clusters. (Horns straight in form 'Max Watson.') Large fused seed capsules remain on branches.	Fast growing, densely leafed tree, very good for screening on coast, or street tree with lower branches pruned. Unpruned, branches persist to ground. Form 'Max Watson' grows low and compact.
E. leucoxylon WHITE IRONBARK	14°–18°F.	Somewhat variable, usually slender, upright, open, with pendulous branches. 20–80 ft.	Gray green, sickle shaped leaves, 3–6 in.long. Bark sheds, leaving white to mottled trunk.	White flowers intermittently, winter, spring. Goblet shaped seed capsules, ⅜ in. wide. (E. l. 'Rosea' has pink flowers, larger seed capsule, may not come true from seed.)	Free-flowering, fast growing, moderate-sized tree that tolerates many adverse conditions including heavy soil, light rocky soil, heat, wind.
E. l. macrocarpa 'Rosea' LARGE-FRUITED RED-FLOWERING GUM	14°–18°F.	Much-branched, shrublike tree, 15–25 ft., variable.	Gray green leaves. Gray to pinkish trunk.	Clear vivid crimson flowers borne profusely at early age. Seed capsules goblet shaped, ¾ in. wide.	Very ornamental tree. Good in most soils, most sites, even near beach or in desert.
E. linearis		See E. pulchella.			
E. macrandra LONG-FLOWERED MARLOCK	8°–12°F.	Round-headed, open tree to 25–35 ft. Main branches often develop curves.	Light golden green, lance shaped leaves, 2½–5 in. long. Slick bark peels in ribbons.	Cream to green flowers in clusters. Bud caps distinctive: light green fingers 1–1½ in. long, ⅛ in. wide. Seed capsules slightly elongated, too. Flowering is incidental.	Plant to hide utility pole or soften house corner. (Some nurseries mistakenly sell this as E. angulosa; real E. angulosa is a mallee with yellowish white flowers and prominently ribbed seed capsules.)
E. macrocarpa (macrocarpa means ''big-fruited'')	8°–12°F.	Erratic, sprawling shrub, 4–15 ft. Tries to be vine but stems are too stiff. Similar to E. rhodantha.	Light gray blue leaves, 2–5 in. long, round with definite point, set close to stem. Greenish white bark.	Golf ball-sized gray buds (point on top) open to show flat-topped, round, fluffy flowers 4–7 in. wide. Usually pink, also white, red, or yellowish white (seedlings vary). No stems on flowers; grow right on branch. Flat-topped, bowl shaped seed capsules, 3 in. wide.	Sprawling plant good for seasonal display in dry, sunny place. Not for irrigated areas (overwatering causes blackening of leaves). New growth begins vertical, becomes horizontal when weighted down with buds and capsules. Stems tend to die back from pruning.
E. maculata (maculata means ''spotted'')	19°–23°F.	Erect single-trunked tree, branching to make wide head. Graceful, strong. To 50–75 ft.	Dark green leaves, 3–6 in. long. Pearl gray bark patched dark red to violet.	White flowers in branch-end clusters, 1–3 in. wide. Seed capsules urn shaped, ½ in. wide, rough on outside. Not grown for flowers; landscaping tree.	Good singly or in groves. Smooth, spotted trunks are usually quite handsome; they vary in degree of spottiness. Best in sandy, well-drained soil.
E. mannifera maculosa RED-SPOTTED GUM	20°–25°F.	Tall, slender tree, 20–50 ft. Gracefully pendent branches sway prettily in wind.	Leaves ½ in. wide, 4–6 in. long, light green with gray cast. Bark brown, gray, off white.	Unimportant light-colored flowers open from pointed oval buds in clusters of 3–7, and leave ½-in. goblet shaped seed capsules.	Landscaping tree to feature in place of honor. When mature, brownish and grayish bark flakes off in summer, leaving powdery white surface. Australian aborigines paint their faces with the white dust.
E. megacornuta (megacornuta means ''big-horned'')	20°–23°F.	Big shrub or small tree, 20–30 ft. Multistemmed or single trunked. Spindly.	Shiny, bronzy green leaves. Smooth, gray to tan bark.	Clusters of St. Patrick's green flowers, 1½ in. long, each shaped like a shaving brush, open from buds that look like warty fingers. Clawlike seed capsules.	Arrangers like 2-in.-long, bronzy green buds, flowers, and seed capsules. Sometimes the form makes it acceptable for landscaping purposes.

NAME	HARD-INESS	FORM AND SIZE	LEAVES AND BARK	FLOWERS AND FRUIT	BEST FEATURES AND HOW TO ENCOURAGE THEM
E. melliodora (*melliodora* means "honey-scented")	18°–20°F.	Upright, graceful tree, 30–100 ft., with slightly weeping branches. Top fills in well.	Boat shaped to sickle shaped leaves, 2–6 in. long, grayish green. Old bark scaly, flaky, tan.	Late winter, early spring flowers are off white, in clusters about 1½ in. wide, not showy but sweet smelling (truly the smell of honey) and attractive to bees. Seed capsules goblet shaped, ¼ in. wide, in clusters.	Clean tree, well-mannered, very little litter. Good for shade tree, street tree, windbreak (takes wind very well). Form 'Rosea' has pink flowers.
E. microtheca (*microtheca* means "tiny capsules")	5°–10°F.	Bushy tree, 35–40 ft., round head. May be single or many-trunked.	Blue green, ribbon-like leaves, 8 in. long. Smooth bark.	Insignificant creamy white flowers. Seed capsules tiny (match head size) in clusters of 3–5. Seed capsules create no litter.	Strong-looking, strong-growing tree of character. Drought tolerant. No breakage from wind. One of Arizona's best eucalypts.
E. nicholii NICHOL'S WILLOW-LEAFED PEPPERMINT	12°–15°F.	Graceful, weeping tree to 40 ft. Up-right main trunk. Spreading crown.	Light green, often purple tinged, very narrow leaves, 3–5 in. long. Soft brown bark.	Small, inconspicuous whitish flowers mostly in summer. Very small, round seed capsules in roundish clusters.	Garden or street tree. Beauty is in fine-textured foliage and billowing, willowy form. Grows fast. Crushed leaves smell like peppermint.
E. niphophila SNOW GUM	0°–10°F.	Small, widespreading, open tree to 20 ft. Trunk usually crooked.	Silvery blue, lance shaped, 1½–4-in. leaves. Smooth white, peeling bark.	Creamy white flowers in tight clusters 1½ in. wide, summer. Seed capsules round, ⅜ in. wide, very gray, also in tight clusters, close to stem.	Acclaimed chiefly for its hardiness and silvery look of its leaves. Slow-growing. Drought, wind tolerant. Good on slopes. Can be picturesque.
E. orbifolia ROUND-LEAFED MALLEE	23°–25°F.	Large mallee of irregular, clambering habit. Not a tree.	Leaves nearly round (slightly pointed), 2 in. long. Thin red bark.	Little (½ in. wide) yellow flowers, in late spring. Round flower bud cap has point like Kaiser Wilhelm helmet. Seldom sets seed capsules.	Use as ground cover in difficult sunny place; native to rocky desert. Can be espaliered to show off round leaves and flowers. Slender vinelike stems.
E. orpetii ORPET HYBRID EUCALYPTUS (California hybrid)	24°–28°F.	Mallee or weak-stemmed small tree, 6–20 ft.— usually not over 10 ft.	Leaves vary in color, shape. Most are silvery green, tapered, 1½ in. long.	Many fluffy flowers, 2 in. wide, pink to red with yellow anthers, at branch ends in winter-spring. Buds and seed capsules interestingly ribbed.	Grow for attractive flowers and leaves. Cut flowers keep a week or 10 days. Believed to be hybrid between *E. macrocarpa* (or *E. orbifolia*) and *E. caesia*.
E. pauciflora GHOST GUM	10°–15°F.	Tree. Branches spread to make crown as wide as height (40 by 40 ft.). Graceful, airy, open.	All white trunk and branches and narrow, gray green leaves 3–6 in. long— hence: "ghost gum."	Insignificant flowers and little or no seed setting. Among other good points, ghost gum doesn't litter ground beneath it.	White trunk and branches and open, see-through foliage make it valuable individual display tree. Takes almost every degree of soil moisture. Good in lawns. In youth, remove erratic branches.
E. perriniana ROUND-LEAFED SNOW GUM	10°–15°F.	Small straggly tree, 15–30 ft. Best cut back as shrub.	Juvenile leaves silvery, form circle around stem, spin on stem when dry.	Many small white flowers in summer in clusters of 3. Seed capsules, also in 3s, cup shaped, ¼ in. wide.	Silvery foliage nice for arrangements. If you cut enough, silvery juvenile growth remains (mature leaves are long). Use as gray-leafed plant in border.
E. platypus ROUND-LEAFED MOORT	23°–26°F.	Large bush or small tree, 20–30 ft. Many stems; may ultimately form one trunk.	Dark, dull green leaves, round ended, 1–2 in. long, rough. Tan, smooth bark.	Many flowers, red or green (two forms), open at ends of flattened stems, make showy clusters 2 in. wide. Cluster of many ½-in., goblet shaped seed capsules.	Dense, fast, pyramidal form, good for solid screening (space 12 ft. apart). Plants give general effect of stiff birches. Hummingbirds enjoy flowers.
E. polyanthemos SILVER DOLLAR GUM	14°–18°F.	Slender, erect tree, single or multistemmed, 20–60 ft. Fairly fast.	Juvenile leaves green gray, oval or round, 2–3 in. Mature leaves lance shaped. Mottled bark.	Creamy white flowers in 1-in. clusters, spring-summer. Seed capsules are cylindrical cups, ½ in. wide, in clusters. Flowers incidental—grow it for cut foliage or landscape uses.	Popular landscaping and street tree. Excellent cut foliage. Select young trees carefully; some have leaves less round and gray than others. Grows almost anywhere. Not good in wet places.

(Continued on next page)

NAME	HARD-INESS	FORM AND SIZE	LEAVES AND BARK	FLOWERS AND FRUIT	BEST FEATURES AND HOW TO ENCOURAGE THEM
E. preissiana BELL-FRUITED MALLEE	24°–26°F.	Mallee—typically an open, many-stemmed shrub to 12 ft. Sometimes tree to 15 ft.	Oval leaves, 2–3 in. long, thick, dull bluish cast, red stems. Smooth gray bark.	Very showy. Circular, flat yellow flowers 2–3 in. wide open from brown globelike buds, 1 in. wide. Seed capsules cup shaped, ¾ in. wide. Flower color contrasts nicely with leaf, stem, trunk.	First-rate flower producer that also can hold its own as garden shrub. Cut flowers keep well. Blooms heaviest Jan.-March.
E. pulchella *(E. linearis)* WHITE PEPPERMINT	18°–22°F.	Graceful tree to 20–50 ft. with weeping branches. Can be either asymmetrical or round headed.	Long, very narrow, dark green, pendulous leaves. White to light tan bark peels in thin strips.	Clusters of tiny creamy white flowers open from pinhead-sized buds. June-Oct. Goblet shaped seed capsules, ³⁄₁₆ in. wide, in tight clusters.	Fine landscaping and street tree. Beautiful form, willowy, well-mannered. Dark, dense foliage masses contrast with light trunk. Good in light soils with little water.
E. pulverulenta *(pulverulenta means "powdered as with dust")* SILVER MOUNTAIN GUM	15°–21°F.	Irregular, sprawling small tree or large shrub, 15–30 ft. Poor form unless pruned.	Silver gray shish kebab-style juvenile foliage (stems appear to go through leaves). Ribbony bark.	Creamy white, ½-in., fuzzy flowers in 3s sandwiched between round leaves along stems. Fall to spring. Flowers are simply an extra. They are followed by ½-in.-wide, cup shaped seed capsules.	Use in garden as curiosity feature and source of branches for arrangements (use natural or gilded). Cut back often to get and encourage decorative juvenile leaf growth; mature leaves are usually long and pointed.
E. pyriformis *(pyriformis means "pear shaped")*	25°–28°F.	Shrub or treelike shrub (mallee), 10–20 ft. Long, weak, rangy stems.	Broad, oval, light green leaves 2–4 in. long. Light brown bark.	Showy, large (2–3 in. wide) flowers in clusters late winter to early summer. May be red, pink, orange, yellow, or cream. Pear shaped, 1-in. capsules.	Collector's item. Sometimes "an elegant, slender tree," sometimes "weak, rangy shrub." Flowers are best feature. Good performance in dry or sandy soil.
E. rhodantha *(rhodantha means "roselike")*	8°–12°F.	Erratic, sprawling shrub, to 4–8 ft. Branches tend to grow horizontally.	Light gray blue leaves sometimes with greenish cast, 2–4 in. long, nearly round, close to stem. Greenish white bark.	Buds same as *E. macrocarpa* but with shorter point on lid. Flowers, on 1–2-in.-long stems, same shape as *E. macrocarpa* but 3–5 in. wide and almost always carmine red. Capsules like *E. macrocarpa.* The two are similar but differ in some ways; compare them.	Sprawling plant good for almost continual flower display. For dry, sunny place and little water, same as *E. macrocarpa.* Better for spilling down slope than *E. macrocarpa* (follows terrain better). Put supports under branches to keep mud off. Makes good espalier.
E. robusta SWAMP MAHOGANY	11°–15°F.	Tall, densely foliaged, ultimately round headed, 80–90 ft.	Dark green, leathery, shiny leaves 4–7 in. long. Rough, dark red brown, stringy bark.	Attractive flowers for large tree: masses of pink-tinted creamy white flowers any time, chiefly in winter. Cylindrical ³⁄₈-in. seed capsules in clusters.	Big, strong tree performs well in moist or saline soil. Good for windy places at beach or inland. Windbreak. Attractive foliage. Darkest green eucalypt in deserts.
E. rudis DESERT GUM, SWAMP GUM	12°–18°F.	Upright, spreading, often weeping, 30–60 ft. high. Robust.	Mature leaves gray green to green, lance shaped, 4–6 in. long. Rough trunk.	White flowers in clusters, spring and summer (not showy but good for large tree). Seed capsules ¼ in. wide.	Good, large shade tree, street tree. Tolerates desert, valleys, beach, windy places, much or little water (but best with irrigation), any soil including saline.
E. saligna SYDNEY BLUE GUM	18°–20°F.	Tall, slender, shaftlike tree, dense when young, thins out later to open crown. To 60–80 ft.	Young leaves mahogany, mature ones medium green, 4–8 in. long, lance shaped. Red to pinkish bark sheds.	Flowers pinkish to cream in spring and summer, not showy. Smooth seed capsules, ¼ in. wide, in tight clusters 1 in. wide.	Probably fastest growing eucalypt ("Fastest gum in the West"); if gallon can plant not rootbound, can grow 10 ft. first year. Best near coast; not recommended inland. Can grow in lawns.
E. sideroxylon *(Often sold as E. sideroxylon 'Rosea')* RED IRONBARK, PINK IRONBARK	10°–15°F.	Varies: 20–80 ft. high, open or dense, slender or squatty, weeping or upright.	Slim blue green leaves turn bronze in winter. Furrowed, nonshedding, nearly black trunk.	Fluffy flowers, light pink to pinkish crimson, in pendulous clusters, mostly from fall to late spring. Usually, darker the foliage, darker the flowers. Seed capsules goblet shaped, ³⁄₈ in.	Use singly, as screen, or as street or highway tree. Wide variation in individuals—try to select according to characteristics you desire. Grows fast. Coast or inland. Gets chlorotic in wet adobe soils.

NAME	HARD-INESS	FORM AND SIZE	LEAVES AND BARK	FLOWERS AND FRUIT	BEST FEATURES AND HOW TO ENCOURAGE THEM
E. spathulata NARROW-LEAFED GIMLET, SWAMP MALLEE	22°–25°F.	Small, erect, multitrunked tree, 6–20 ft.	Ribbonlike leaves 2–3 in. long. Smooth red bark.	Many ½-in. cream and gold flowers open in summer from long, oval buds. Bell shaped seed capsules.	Versatile. Tolerates poor soil drainage. Bushy wind screen. Branches move nicely in breezes.
E. stellulata BLACK SALLY	12°–18°F.	Medium-sized (20–50 ft.) spreading tree, pendulous branches.	Broad elliptical leaves. Smooth gray bark changes to olive green.	White to cream flowers, Oct.-April. Not known for its flower display. Roundish seed capsules, size of small peas, in tight clusters along stem.	Unusual colored bark. Nice spreading form. Good small screening tree or shade tree.
E. tetraptera SQUARE-FRUITED MALLEE	22°–26°F.	Shrub, 4–10 ft. (occasionally to 15 ft.). Straggly but interesting.	Thick, rubbery, dark leaves, 4–5 in. long. Green to gray bark.	Big (1½ in.), smooth, salmon buds open to show big, round, red flowers. Blooms almost continuously. Seed capsules, square with 4 flanges, are 1½ in. wide.	A novelty with striking flowers, fruit, unusual form. Not for basic landscaping. Grows in sand. Wind resistant, salt tolerant. Prune to make bushy.
E. torquata CORAL GUM	27°–29°F.	Slender, upright, narrow headed, 15–20 ft. Branches often droop from weight of many flowers and seed capsules.	Light green to golden green leaves, long and narrow or blunt and round. Rough, flaky bark.	Flower buds are like little (¾ in.) Japanese lanterns. From them open beautiful coral red and yellow flowers, on and off all year. Seed capsules ½ in. long, grooved, squarish at bottom.	Grown for bloom (good cut flowers) and small size. Good as free-standing tree in narrow area or as a grove. Stake and prune or head back to make it graceful and attractive. Select individuals by plant form.
E. viminalis (viminalis means "long, flexible shoot") MANNA GUM	12°–15°F.	Tall, spreading patriarch tree to 150 ft.; drooping willowlike branches.	Light green, narrow, 4–6-in.-long leaves. Trunk whitish, bark sheds.	Little white flowers in long, thin, open clusters all year—usually too high to be seen. Small, roundish seed capsules size of peas.	Can make significant silhouette. Grows best in good soil but can take poor soil. Needs room—for ranches, parks, highways, not small gardens. Creates debris.

EUCOMIS. PINEAPPLE FLOWER. Bulbs. Zones 4–24. Unusual looking members of lily family. Thick spikes, 2–3 ft. tall, closely set with ½-in.-long flowers, are topped with cluster of leaflike bracts like a pineapple top. Bloom period July-August, but persisting purplish seed capsules carry on the show even longer. Garden or container plant, good cut flower. Sun or light shade, rich soil with plenty of humus. Some water in summer. Divide when plants become crowded. Fairly easy to grow from spring-sown seed. Interesting potted plant.

Eucomis comosa

E. bicolor. To 2 ft.; flowers green, each petal edged with purple. Attractive leaves 1 ft. long, 3–4 in. wide, with wavy edges.

E. comosa (E. punctata). Thick spikes 2–3 ft. tall set with greenish white flowers tinged pink or purple. Stems spotted purple at base. Leaves to 2 ft. long, less wavy than in E. bicolor.

EUCRYPHIA. Evergreen or semievergreen small trees or large shrubs. Zones 5–6, 15–17. Many attractive species and varieties, all quite rare. The most-sold kinds in West have shiny evergreen leaves and 2½-in.-wide pure white flowers with big tufts of yellow stamens in center. Give them neutral or slightly acid soil, ample water, and shelter from strong winds. In Zones 5 and 6, protect young plants from temperatures below 15°F.

E. lucida. Slender evergreen tree to 30 ft. Smooth-edged, glossy leaves 1½–3 in.

Eucryphia nymansensis

long. Fragrant white flowers in June, July. Native to Tasmania.

E. nymansensis. Group of hybrids between 2 species from Chile. 'Mt. Usher', best known, is small columnar evergreen tree with toothed leaves, some simple, some divided into 3–5 leaflets 2–4 in. long. Flowers often double. 'Nymansay' is somewhat faster growing. Both bloom in August, September.

EUGENIA myrtifolia. See *Syzygium paniculatum.*

E. paniculata. See *Syzygium paniculatum.*

E. smithii. See *Acmena smithii.*

E. uniflora. SURINAM CHERRY, PITANGA. Evergreen compact shrub or small tree. Zones 21–24. Very slow and open growth to 15–25 ft., usually to 6–8 ft., with equal spread. Leaves glossy coppery green deepening to purplish or red in cold weather, oval, to 2 in. long. White fragrant flowers like little brushes, ½ in. across. Fruit, size of small tomatoes, change color from green to yellow to orange to deep red, at which stage they are edible. Grow in well-drained soil and water freely. Best in moist atmosphere and sheltered spot in sun or partial shade. Can be sheared into hedge, but this will reduce flowering and fruiting. Prune to shape.

Eugenia uniflora

EUONYMUS. Evergreen or deciduous shrubs, evergreen vines. Evergreen kinds are highly valued for their foliage, texture, and form; they are almost always used as landscape structure plants, never for flower display. Some types display colorful fruit—pink, red, or yellow capsules which open to show orange red seeds in fall and attract birds. Most are best in full sun or a little shade. Need only moderate watering. Climate adaptation is quite significant because of varying degrees of hardiness and susceptibility to mildew.

E. alata. WINGED EUONYMUS. Deciduous shrub. Zones 1–9, 14–16. Slow to medium growth 7–10 ft. high to 10–15 ft. wide. Dense, twiggy, with horizontal branching and flat-topped appearance. Twigs have flat corky wings which disappear on older growth. Dark green leaves turn rich rose red in fall. Inconspicuous flowers followed by sparse crop of bright orange red fruit. Use as background, screen, or single isolated plant. Best against dark evergreens.

Euonymus japonica

Variety 'Compacta' grows 4–6 ft. tall and equally tall, has less prominent wings. Use as screen or unclipped hedge.

E. europaea. EUROPEAN SPINDLE TREE. Deciduous large shrub, small tree. Zones 1–17. Can reach 25 ft., usually much less. Easily trained into single-stem, broad-topped tree. Leaves to 3 in. long, medium green, scallop toothed; turn rose pink in fall. Flowers yellowish green, inconspicuous. Fruit showy, pink to red, capsules splitting to show bright orange seed coats. In variety 'Aldenhamensis' fruit are larger (over ¾ in.), longer stalked, more profuse, bright pink and orange.

E. fortunei. (Formerly *E. radicans acuta.*) Evergreen vine or shrub. Zones 1–17. One of best broad-leafed evergreens where temperatures drop below 0°F. Evergreen vine which trails or climbs by rootlets. Used as shrub, its branches will trail and sometimes root; allowed to climb, it will be spreading mass to 20 ft. or more. Prostrate forms can be used to control erosion. In desert climates takes full sun better than ivy *(Hedera).* Leaves dark rich green, 1–2½ in. long with scalloped-toothed edges; flowers inconspicuous. Sun or full shade. Mature growth, like that of ivy, is shrubby and bears fruit; cuttings taken from this shrubby wood produce comparatively upright plants.

E. radicans (native to Korea, Japan), once thought to be the species, was later classed as variety of *E. fortunei.* Many nurserymen have not made change in names, and still sell many varieties as forms of *E. radicans;* translate *radicans* to *fortunei* wherever you see it, except in *E. fortunei radicans.* Varieties of *E. fortunei* listed below are better known than species itself.

'Azusa'. Prostrate grower for ground cover use. Small dark green leaves with light colored veins. Undersides of leaves turn maroon in winter.

'Carrierei'. Shrubby spreading form. Plant where it can lean or sprawl against wall or fence; will not climb. Mature form bears handsome orange fruit.

'Colorata'. PURPLE-LEAF WINTER CREEPER. Same sprawling growth habit as *E. f. radicans.* Leaves turn dark purple in fall and winter. Growth is more even as ground cover than *E. f. radicans.*

'Emerald Gaiety'. Small, dense-growing, erect shrub with deep green leaves edged with white.

'Emerald 'n Gold'. Similar to above, but with gold-edged leaves.

'Golden Prince'. New growth tipped gold. Older leaves turn green. Extremely hardy; good hedge plant.

'Gracilis'. (Often sold as *E. radicans argentea variegata, E. f. variegata, E. f.* 'Silver Edge'.) Trailing, less vigorous, more restrained than the species. Leaves variegated with white or cream; lighter portions turn pinkish in cold weather. Use in hanging baskets, as ground cover in small areas, to spill over wall.

'Kewensis' ('Minima'). Delightful trailing or climbing form with very small (¼ in.) leaves. Use it to create delicate traceries against stone or wood, or as dense, fine-textured ground cover.

E. f. radicans. COMMON WINTER CREEPER. Tough, hardy, trailing or vining shrub with dark green, thick-textured, 1-in.-long leaves. Given no support, it sprawls; given masonry wall to cover, it does the job completely.

'Sarcoxie'. As hardy as *E. fortunei,* but with upright habit of *E. japonica.* To 4 ft. high. Use for hedges, as sheared tubbed plant, or as espalier.

'Silver Queen'. Seems identical to 'Carrierei' except for having white margins around leaves. (There is also an *E. japonica* 'Silver Queen'.)

'Vegeta'. BIG-LEAF WINTER CREEPER. Shrub woody enough to support itself in a mound or (with support and training) vine that will cover an area 15–20 ft. square. Irregular growth habit; sends out large branches, with side branches developing later. Attractive fruit—orange seeds in little "hat boxes"—in early fall. New spring growth an interesting chartreuse.

E. japonica. EVERGREEN EUONYMUS. Evergreen shrub. Zones 4–20. Upright, 8–10 ft. with 6-ft. spread, usually held lower by pruning or shearing. Flowers inconspicuous. Older shrubs attractive trained as trees with their curving trunks and umbrella shaped tops. Can be grouped as hedge or screen. Leaves very glossy, leathery, deep green, 1–2½ in. long, oval to roundish.

This and its varities are "cast-iron" shrubs where heat tolerance is important and soil conditions unfavorable. Notorious for mildew except in Zones 4–6, where plants grow well even in coastal wind and salt spray. To lessen risk of mildew farther south, locate plants in full sun, where air drainage is good. Since plants are also attacked by scale insects, thrips, spider **mites**, it's a good idea to include them in your regular rose spray program for mildew and insects.

Variegated forms are most popular; they are among the few shrubs that maintain variegations in full sun in such hot-summer climates as Zones 8–14, 18–20. They are labeled in many ways; there may be some overlapping in names.

'Albomarginata'. Green leaves edged white.

'Aureo-marginata'. Dark green leaves have golden yellow edge.

'Aureo-variegata'. Leaves have brilliant yellow blotches, green edges.

'Golden'. Green leaves edged yellow.

'Gold Center'. Green leaves, yellow center.

'Gold Spot'. Green edges, yellow blotches. Probably same as 'Aureo-variegata'.

'Grandifolia'. Plants sold under this name have shiny dark green leaves larger than species. Compact, well-branched, good for shearing as pyramids, globes.

'Microphylla' *(E. j. pulchella).* BOX-LEAF EUONYMUS. Compact, small-leafed, 1–2 ft. tall and half as wide. Formal looking; usually trimmed as low hedge.

'Microphylla Variegata'. Like 'Microphylla', but with leaves splashed white.

'President Gauthier'. Leaves deep green with cream-colored margins.

'Silver King'. Green leaves with silvery white edges.

'Silver Queen'. Green leaves, creamy white edges.

E. kiautschovica *(E. patens).* Evergreen shrub. Zones 1–13. Spreading shrub to 9 ft. tall; lower branches sometimes root in moist soil. Leaves partially evergreen or completely evergreen, damaged near 0°F.; light green, thinner textured than other species of evergreen euonymus. Fruit showy, pinkish with red seeds. Takes desert conditions if watered.

'Du Pont'. Compact, dense, fast growing, with dark green leaves. Hedge, screen, sheared formal plant.

'Manhattan'. Upright growth, dark green glossy leaves. Hedge, sheared formal plant, espalier.

EUPATORIUM coelestinum. MIST FLOWER. Perennial. All Zones. Upright, sparsely branched plant to 3 ft. high. Triangular, coarsely toothed leaves to 3 in. long. Light blue to violet, somewhat fragrant flowers in fluffy clusters similar to ageratum. Blooms August-September. Useful for light quality in borders with chrysanthemums, rudbeckias, Michaelmas daisies. Plant in sun or light shade; average water. Divide in spring or fall.

Eupatorium coelestinum

EUPHORBIA. SPURGE. Shrubs, subshrubs, perennials, biennials, annuals, succulents. Most have acrid, milky sap (poisonous in some species) which can irritate skin and cause pain in contact with open cuts or in eyes. What is called "flower" is really group of colored bracts. True flowers, centered in bracts, are inconspicuous. Many euphorbias are succulents; these often mimic cactus in appearance and are as diverse in form and size. Full sun. Only a few are listed below, but cactus and succulent specialists can supply scores of species and varieties.

E. characias. Shrubby evergreen perennial. Zones 4–24. Upright stems make dome shaped bush 4 ft. tall. Fairly drought resistant. Leaves crowded all along stems, narrow, blue green. Clustered flowers make round to cylindrical dense masses of chartreuse or lime green in late winter, early spring. Color holds with only slight fading until seeds ripen; then stalks yellow and should be cut out at base. New shoots have already made growth for next year's flowers. *E. c. wulfenii (E. veneta)*, commonest form, has broader clusters of yellower flowers.

Euphorbia characias wulfenii

Euphorbia pulcherrima

E. heterophylla. MEXICAN FIRE PLANT. Summer annual. To 3 ft. tall. Bright green leaves of varying shapes, larger ones resembling poinsettia; flowers unimportant. In summer, upper leaves are blotched bright red and white, giving appearance of second-rate poinsettias. Useful in hot dry borders in poor soil. Sow seed in place after frost danger is over.

E. lathyris. GOPHER PLANT, MOLE PLANT. Biennial. All Zones. Legend claims that it repels gophers and moles. Stems have milky juice which is poisonous and caustic. It could bother a gopher or mole and make him go away. Grows as tall single stem to 5 ft. by second summer, when it sets cluster of yellow flowers at top of stem. Flowers soon become seeds and plant dies. Leaves long, narrow, pointed, at right angles to stem and to each other. Flowers unimportant. Grow from seed.

E. marginata. SNOW-ON-THE-MOUNTAIN. Summer annual. To 2 ft. Leaves light green, oval, upper ones striped and margined white, uppermost sometimes all white. Flowers unimportant. Used for contrast with bright-colored bedding dahlias, scarlet sage or zinnias, or dark-colored plume celosia. To use in arrangements, dip stems in boiling water or hold in flame for a few seconds. Sow seed in place in spring—sun or part shade. Thin to only a few inches apart, as plants are somewhat rangy.

E. milii *(E. splendens)*. CROWN OF THORNS. Woody perennial or subshrub. Zones 21–24 in gardens; elsewhere as greenhouse, indoor, or summer potted plant. Shrubby, climbing stems to 3–4 ft. armed with long sharp thorns. Leaves roundish, thin, light green, 1½–2 in. long, usually found only near branch ends. Clustered pairs of bright red bracts borne nearly all year. Many varieties and hybrids vary in plant form and size, and in color of bracts—yellow, orange, pink.

Train on small frame or trellis against sheltered wall or in container. Grow in porous soil, in full sun or light shade. Tolerates drought but does better with regular watering.

E. myrsinites. Perennial. All Zones. Stems flop outward from central crown, then rise toward tip to 8–12 in. Leaves stiff, roundish, blue gray, closely set around stems. Flattish clusters of chartreuse to yellow flowers top stem ends in late winter, early spring. Cut out old stems as they turn yellow. Withstands cold, heat, drought, but is short-lived in warm-winter areas. Use in rock gardens with succulents and gray-foliaged plants.

E. obesa. BASEBALL PLANT. Succulent. House plant or indoor/outdoor pot plant. Solid, fleshy gray green sphere (or short cylinder) to 8 in., with brownish stripings, brown dots that resemble stitching on a baseball. Flowers unimportant. Good drainage, bright light, warmth, no sudden temperature change. Moderate water; keep dryish in winter.

E. pulcherrima. POINSETTIA. Evergreen or deciduous shrub. Outdoors in Zones 13, 16–24; greenhouse and indoor plant any-where. Native to Mexico. Leggy, to 10 ft. tall and more. Leaves, evergreen and coarse, grow on stiffly upright canes. Showy part of plant consists of petal-like bracts; true flowers in center are yellowish, inconspicuous. Red single form most familiar; less well-known are red doubles and forms with white, yellowish, pink, or marbled bracts. Bracts of these paler kinds often last until Easter.

Useful garden plant in well-drained soil. Prune to prevent legginess. Grow as informal hedge in frostless areas; where frosty (not severely cold) plant against sunny walls, in sheltered corners, under south-facing eaves.

Where adapted outdoors, needs no special care. Give slightly acid soil. Thin branches in summer to produce larger bracts; prune back at 2-month intervals for bushy growth (but often smaller flowers). To improve red color, feed every 2 weeks with high-nitrogen fertilizer starting when color begins to show.

To care for Christmas gift plants, keep plants in sunny window. Avoid sudden temperature changes. Keep soil moist; don't let water stand in pot saucer. When leaves fall in late winter or early spring, cut stems back to 2 buds, reduce watering to minimum. Store in cool place until late spring. When frosts are past, set pots in sun outdoors. It's difficult to bring plants into bloom again indoors. They will probably grow too tall for indoor use next winter, but may survive winter if well sheltered. Plants bloom only when they experience long nights; don't keep them where artificial light will disturb their necessary 14-hour sleep. Starting in October, put plants in dark closet for the night. Start new plants by making late summer cuttings of stems with 4 or 5 eyes (joints).

E. rigida *(E. biglandulosa)*. Evergreen perennial or subshrub. Zones 4–24. Stems angle outward, then rise up to 2 ft. Long, narrow, pointed, fleshy gray green leaves to 1½ in., their bases tightly set against stems. Flower clusters in late winter or early spring are broad, domed, chartreuse yellow in color, fading to pinkish. Stems die back after seeds ripen and should be removed. New ones take their place. Showy display plant in garden or container. Drought tolerant.

E. tirucalli. MILKBUSH, PENCILBUSH, PENCIL TREE. Zones 13, 23, 24. House plant or indoor/outdoor plant in any Zone. Tree or large shrub to possible 30 ft. tall in open ground, usually much smaller. Single or multiple trunks support tangle of light green, pencil-thick, succulent branches with no sign of a leaf. Flowers unimportant. Striking for pattern of silhouette or shadow. Thrives as house plant in driest atmosphere; needs all the light you can give it, routine soil, water, and feeding. Bleeds milky sap profusely if cut or broken.

E. veneta, E. wulfenii. See *E. characias*.

EUROPEAN BIRD CHERRY. See *Prunus padus*.

EUROPEAN CRANBERRY BUSH. See *Viburnum opulus*.

EUROPEAN MOUNTAIN ASH. See *Sorbus aucuparia*.

EUROPEAN PASQUE FLOWER. See *Anemone pulsatilla*.

EUROPEAN SPINDLE TREE. See *Euonymus europaea*.

EURYA emarginata. Evergreen shrub. Zones 4–6, 15–17, 21–24. Native to Japan. Grown for refined foliage, form. Flowers insignificant, ill scented (but only appearing on old plants). Slow-growing to 6–8 ft., but easily kept to 3–4 ft. by pruning back to bud or side branches. Branches rise at 45° angle from base of plant. Slightly teardrop shaped, dark green leathery leaves about ½ in. long, densely and symmetrically arranged along reddish brown branches. Part

Eurya emarginata

shade and same culture as rhododendrons, azaleas. *E. e. microphylla* has even smaller (¼ in.) leaves— curiosity for shaded rock garden.

EURYOPS. Shrubby evergreen perennials. Zones 14–17, 19–24. Native to South Africa. Leaves are finely divided, flower heads are daisylike. Long bloom season; cut back after flowering. They need little water once established but need excellent drainage. Fast-growing in full sun. They thrive in buffeting ocean winds but are damaged by sharp frosts. Keep old blooms picked off, and prune in June.

E. acraeus. Mounded growth to 2 ft. Leaves silvery gray, ¾ in. long. Inch-wide bright yellow daisies cover plant, May-June. Native to high South African mountains, and is hardier than others to frost.

E. pectinatus. Densely foliaged shrub to 6 ft., with 1½–2-in. yellow daisies on 6-in. stems. Leaves green to grayish green. Flowers nearly year round.

Euryops pectinatus

EUSTOMA grandiflorum *(Lisianthus russellianus).* LISIANTHUS, TULIP GENTIAN, TEXAS BLUEBELL. Biennial or short-lived perennial. All Zones. Native to high plains of the West, but garden forms introduced from Japan. Clumps of gray-green foliage send up1½-ft. stems topped by purple-blue, pink, or white tulip-shaped, 2- to 3-inch flowers all summer (if old blooms are cut off). Excellent cut flower. Can be grown with much care from dustlike seeds. Sprinkle seed on surface of potting soil; don't cover. Soak well, then cover pot with glass or plastic. At 4-leaf stage (about 2 months), place 3 or 4 plants into 6-inch pots. Buying started plants is easier. Needs sun, good garden soil, drainage, average water and fertilizing. Use in pots, border, cutting garden.

Eustoma grandiflorum

EVENING PRIMROSE. See *Oenothera.*

EVERGREEN GRAPE. See *Rhoicissus capensis.*

EVERGREEN PEAR. See *Pyrus kawakamii.*

EVERGREEN CANDYTUFT. See *Iberis sempervirens.*

EXACUM affine. GERMAN VIOLET, PERSIAN VIOLET. Summer annual grown as house or cool greenhouse plant. Small, rounded plant with egg shaped, inch-long leaves and blue, star shaped flowers with bright yellow stamen tufts in centers. Plant seeds indoors in midwinter for summer bloom, in fall for spring bloom. Five plants in 5-in. pot make attractive showing. Needs rich soil, ample water. Flowers have sweet fragrance.

Exacum affine

EXOCHORDA. PEARL BUSH. Deciduous shrubs. Perform best in Zones 3–6, satisfactory in Zones 7–9, 14–18. Loose spikelike clusters of white, 1½–2-in.-wide flowers open from profusion of pearl-like buds. Flowers bloom about same time as roundish, 1½–2-in.-long leaves expand. Give plants sunny spot, ordinary garden soil, average water. Prune after bloom to control size and form.

E. macrantha. Hybrid. The only variety available is called 'The Bride'. Compact shrub to 4 ft. tall and as broad. Flowers in late April. Plant it beneath south or west-facing windows.

E. racemosa *(E. grandiflora).* COMMON PEARL BUSH. Native to China. Loose, open, slender shrub to 10–15 ft. tall, and as wide. Blooms in April. In small gardens, trim

Exochorda racemosa

it high to make upright, airy, multistemmed small tree. In big shrub borders group three or more to give bulk, or plant against evergreens to show off flowers. Resistant to oak root fungus.

FAGUS. BEECH. Deciduous trees. Zones 1–9, 14–24. Beeches can reach 90 ft. in height, although usually much less, making broad cones with lower branches sweeping ground (unless pruned off). Smooth gray bark contrasts well with dark glossy foliage and makes handsome winter effect. Leaves turn red brown in fall and hang on tree well into winter. Later, pointed winter buds and twig structure make lacy patterns; new expanding leaves have silky sheen. Little 3-sided nuts in spiny husks are edible but inconsequential; they often fail to fill out, especially on solitary trees.

Fagus sylvatica

Grow in any good garden soil; best in full sun; moderate watering needed. Salts in soil or water stunt growth, turn leaves brown. Many feeder roots and heavy shade make lawn maintenance difficult under old or low-branched trees; good lawn trees in their early years. Woolly beech aphids cause little trouble except dripping honeydew.

Fagus sylvatica

F. grandifolia. AMERICAN BEECH. Much less widely planted than the following plants. Leaves longer (to 5 in.), narrower, turning yellow before their long-persisting red brown phase.

F. sylvatica. EUROPEAN BEECH. Leaves to 4 in. long, glossy green. Many garden varieties; here are some of the best:

'Asplenifolia'. Leaves narrow, deeply lobed or cut nearly to midrib. Delicate foliage on large, robust, spreading tree.

'Atropunicea'. COPPER BEECH, PURPLE BEECH. Leaves deep reddish or purple. Good in containers. Often sold as 'Riversii' or 'Purpurea'. Seedlings of copper beech are usually bronzy purple, turning bronzy green in summer.

'Fastigiata'. DAWYCK BEECH. Narrowly upright tree like Lombardy poplar in form. About 8 ft. wide when 35 ft. tall. In great age becomes broader, but remains narrower than species.

'Laciniata'. CUTLEAF BEECH. Narrow green leaves, deeply cut.

'Pendula'. WEEPING BEECH. Irregular, spreading form, long weeping branches reach to ground. Green leaves. Without staking to establish vertical trunk, it will grow wider than high.

'Purpurea Pendula'. WEEPING COPPER BEECH. Purple-leafed weeping form. Splendid container plant.

'Rohanii'. Purple leaves are oaklike, with rounded lobes.

'Spaethii' or 'Spaethiana'. Deepest black purple of the copper beech varieties; fades little or not at all in summer.

'Tricolor'. TRICOLOR BEECH. Green leaves marked white and edged pink. Slow to 24–40 ft., usually much less. Foliage burns in hot sun or dry winds. Choice container plant.

'Zlatia'. GOLDEN BEECH. Young leaves yellow, aging to yellow green. Subject to sunburn. Good container subject.

FAIRY DUSTER. See *Calliandra eriophylla.*

FAIRY LANTERN. See *Calochortus albus, C. amabilis.*

FAIRY LILY. See *Zephyranthes.*

FAIRY WAND. See *Dierama.*

FALLUGIA paradoxa. APACHE PLUME. Partially evergreen shrub. Zones 2–23. Native to mountains of east San Bernardino County, California, Nevada, southern Utah, Arizona, Colorado to western Texas, northern Mexico. Grows 3–8 ft. high, with straw-colored branches and flaky bark. Small, clustered, lobed leaves, deep green on top, rusty beneath. Flowers like single white roses (1½ in. wide) in April and May. Large

Fallugia paradoxa

clusters of feathery fruit follow—greenish at first, turning pink or reddish tinged—create soft-colored, changing haze through which you can see rigid branch pattern. Plant in full sun; very tolerant of heat and drought. Important erosion control plant.

FALSE ARBORVITAE. See *Thujopsis dolabrata*.

FALSE CYPRESS. See *Chamaecyparis*.

FALSE DRAGONHEAD. See *Physostegia virginiana*.

FALSE HEATHER. See *Cuphea hyssopifolia*.

FALSE INDIGO. See *Baptisia australis*.

FALSE MESQUITE. See *Calliandra eriophylla*.

FALSE SAFFRON. See *Carthamus tinctorius*.

FALSE SEA ONION. See *Ornithogalum caudatum*.

FALSE SOLOMON'S SEAL. See *Smilacina racemosa*.

FALSE SPIRAEA. See *Astilbe, Sorbaria sorbifolia*.

FAN PALM. See *Washingtonia*.

FAREWELL-TO-SPRING. See *Clarkia amoena*.

FARFUGIUM. See *Ligularia tussilaginea*.

FATSHEDERA lizei. Evergreen vine, shrub, ground cover. Zones 4–10, 12–24. Hybrid between *Fatsia japonica* and *Hedera helix,* it shows characteristics of both parents. Highly polished, 6–8-in.-wide leaves with 3–5 pointed lobes look like those of giant ivy. Shrubby like fatsia, yet sends out long trailing or climbing stems like ivy. Variety 'Variegata' has white-bordered leaves.

Leaves are injured at 15°F., tender new growth at 20°–25°F.; seems to suffer more from late frosts than from winter cold. Will take full sun only in mild, cool-summer coastal gardens. Give it partial shade and protection from hot, drying winds inland.

Fatshedera lizei

Will take heavy shade, and can even thrive indoors. Give it plenty of water. Good near swimming pools.

Fatshedera tends to go in a straight line, but it can be shaped if you work at it. Pinch tip growth to force branching. Guide and tie stems before they become brittle. Do this 2–3 times a year. If plant gets away from you, cut it back to ground; it will regrow quickly. As ground cover, cut back vertical growth every 2–3 weeks during growing season. Grown as vine or espalier, plants are heavy so give them strong supports. Even when well-grown, vine will become leafless at base. Protect leaves against pests.

FATSIA japonica *(Aralia sieboldii, A. japonica).* JAPANESE ARALIA. Evergreen shrub. Zones 4–9, 13–24. Tropical appearance with big, glossy, dark green, deeply lobed fanlike leaves to 16 in. wide on long stalks. Moderate growth to 5–8 ft. (rarely more); sparingly branched. Many roundish clusters of small whitish flowers in fall-winter, followed by clusters of small, shiny black fruit.

Takes full shade; in cool-summer climates tolerates all but hottest sun; foliage yellowish in full sun. Suffers in reflected

Fatsia japonica

heat from bright walls. Grows in nearly all soils except where too soggy. Adapted to containers. Responds quickly to ample feeding and watering. Where leaves chronically yellow, add iron to soil. Foliage damaged in coldest Portland or Seattle winters. Wash occasionally with hose to clean leaves, lessen insect attack. Bait for snails, slugs. Established plants sucker freely. Keep suckers or remove them with spade. Rejuvenate spindly plants by cutting back hard in early spring. Plants that set fruit often self-sow.

A natural landscaping choice where bold pattern is wanted. Most effective when thinned to show some branch structure. Year-round good looks for shaded entryway or patio. Useful near swimming pools. Good house plant in cool (not over 70°F.), bright room; north or east exposure good. Variety 'Moseri' grows compact and low. Variety 'Variegata' has leaves strikingly edged golden yellow to creamy white.

FAVA. See Bean, Broad.

FAWN LILY. See *Erythronium californicum*.

FEATHER BUSH. See *Lysiloma thornberi*.

FEATHERED HYACINTH. See *Muscari comosum* 'Monstrosum'.

FEIJOA sellowiana. PINEAPPLE GUAVA. Evergreen shrub or small tree. Zones 7–9, 12–24. From South America. Hardiest of so-called subtropical fruits. Normally a large plant of many stems, reaching 18–25 ft. with equal spread if not trained or killed back by frosts. Can take any amount of pruning or training to almost any shape: espalier, screen, hedge, small tree with some features of olive. Sun loving and drought tolerant but can take lawn water. Prune in late spring. Oval leaves 2–3 in. long, glossy green above, silvery white beneath. Unusual inch-wide flowers have 4

Feijoa sellowiana

fleshy white petals tinged purplish on inside and big tuft of red stamens. Petals edible; can be added to fruit salads. Blooms May or June. Attractive to bees and birds.

Fruit ripen 4–5½ months after flowering in southern California, 5–7 months in cooler areas; production is low in deserts. They are 1–4 in. long, oval, grayish green, filled with soft, sweet-to-bland, somewhat pineapple-flavored pulp. Plants grow well in valley heat, but fruit seem better flavored in cooler coastal areas.

Varieties usually available are 'Coolidge' and 'Pineapple Gem', both self-fertile. Single plants of other varieties may need pollinators.

FELICIA. South African shrubs or shrubby perennials. Daisy relatives with (generally) blue flowers.

F. amelloides *(F. aethiopica, Agathaea coelestis).* BLUE MARGUERITE. Shrubby perennial, Zones 8, 9, 13–24, grown and offered as summer annual in Zones 4–7. Called a marguerite, but not the true marguerite *(Chrysanthemum frutescens)*. About 1½ ft. tall, spreading to 4–5 ft. unless pinched or pruned back, with roughish, rather aromatic green foliage. Leaves oval, an inch long. Produces 1¼-in.-wide, sky blue, yellow-centered daisies almost continuously if dead flowers are picked off. Blooms even in mild winters.

Felicia amelloides

Grow in pots or containers, let spill over wall or raised bed, or plant in any sunny spot in garden. Needs fair amount of water for good appearance. Vigorous and likely to overgrow and look ragged; trim severely for cut flowers and prune back hard in late summer to encourage new blooming wood. One of most satis-factory perennials for warm regions.

Improved varieties include 'George Lewis', 'Midnight', and 'Rhapsody in Blue', all with very dark blue flowers; 'San Luis', 'San Gabriel', and 'Santa Anita', with extra-large (to 2½–3 in.) mid-blue flowers; 'Jolly', 1-ft.-tall dwarf with medium-blue flow-ers; and 'Astrid Thomas', compact grower with mid-blue flowers that stay open at night.

F. fruticosa (*Aster fruticosus, Diplopappus fruticosus*). SHRUB ASTER. Evergreen shrub. Zones 8, 9, 14–24. Bushy, densely branched, 2–4 ft. tall, 3 ft. wide. Leaves narrow, dark green, ½–¾ in. long. Flowers lavender, profuse, to 1 in. across. April-June bloom. Prune after flowering. Good in sunny, dry locations.

FELT PLANT. See *Kalanchoe beharensis*.

FENNEL. See *Foeniculum vulgare*.

FERN. Large group of perennial plants grown for their lovely and interesting foliage. Their leaves (fronds) are usually finely cut. They do not flower. They reproduce themselves by spores which form directly on fronds. They vary in height from a few inches to 50 ft. or more, and are found in all parts of the world. Although most live in forests, some grow in deserts, in open fields, or near timberline in high mountains.

Most spectacular are tree ferns, which display their finely cut fronds atop a treelike stem. These need moisture, rich well-drained soil, and shade (except in Zones 4–6, 17, 24, where they can stand sun). Most tree ferns are rather tender to frost, and all suffer in hot, drying winds and under extremely low humidity. Frequent watering of tops, trunks, and root area will help pull them through unusually hot or windy weather. For the various kinds of tree fern, see *Blechnum, Cibotium, Dicksonia, Sphaeropteris*.

Native ferns do not grow as high as tree ferns, but their fronds are handsome and they can perform a number of landscape jobs. Naturalize them in woodland or wild gardens, or use them to fill shady beds, as ground cover, as interplantings between shrubs, or along shady wall of house. Many endure long, dry summers in California but look lusher if given ample summer water. Some ferns native to eastern U. S. grow well in Northwest and in northern California; these take extreme cold and are usu-ally deciduous. For native ferns see *Adiantum, Asplenium, Athyrium, Blechnum, Dryopteris, Onoclea, Osmunda, Pellaea, Phyllitis, Pityrogramma, Polypodium, Polystichum, Pteridium, Woodwardia*.

Many ferns from other parts of the world grow well in the West; although some are house, greenhouse, or (in mildest climates) lathhouse subjects, many are fairly hardy. Use them as you would native ferns, unless some peculiarity of habit makes it necessary to grow them in baskets or on slabs. Some exotic ferns will be found under *Adiantum, Asplenium, Ctenitis, Cyr-tomium, Davallia, Humata, Lygodium, Microlepia, Nephrolepis, Pellaea, Pityrogramma, Platycerium, Polypodium, Polystichum, Pteris, Pyrrosia, Rumohra, Woodwardia*.

All ferns look best if groomed: remove dead or injured fronds by cutting them off near the ground or trunk—but don't cut back hardy outdoor ferns until new growth begins, since old fronds protect growing tips. Feed frequently during growing season, preferably with light applications of organic-base fertilizer—blood meal or fish emulsion are both good. Mulch with peat moss occasionally, especially if shallow fibrous roots are ex-posed by rain or irrigation.

FERNLEAF WANDERING JEW. See *Tripogandra multiflora*.

FERNLEAF YARROW. See *Achillea filipendulina*.

FERN-OF-THE-DESERT. See *Lysiloma thornberi*.

FERN PINE. See *Podocarpus gracilior*.

FEROCACTUS. BARREL CACTUS. Zones 8–24. Medium to large cactus, globular when young, cylindrical with increasing age, ribbed, spiny. Full sun; tolerates drought.

F. acanthodes. COMPASS BARREL CACTUS. Native to southern California, Nevada, Baja California. Grows slowly to 8–9 ft. Flowers yellow to orange, bell shaped, 3 in. across, bloom May-July. Grows faster on shady side of plant than on sunny side, producing curve toward the south.

F. wislizenii. FISHHOOK BARREL CACTUS. Native to Arizona, Texas, Mexico. Similar to above, with yellow or yellow-edged red flowers July-September. Hardy to near 0°F.

Ferocactus acanthodes

FESTUCA. FESCUE. Grasses, several used for lawns; one, blue fescue, used as orna-mental perennial. All Zones. Lawn fescues are classified as fine or coarse.

F. elatior. TALL FESCUE. Coarse. Tall-growing (to 30 in.), clumping pasture grass also used for erosion control and rough, drought resistant lawns. Tough blades, tol-erance of compacted soils make it good play or sports lawn. Forms no runners, so plants must be close together to make dense turf; sow 8–10 pounds of seed per 1,000 sq. ft. in fall. After grass is 2–3 in. tall, soak deeply if rains fail, soak again to 12 in. when blades begin to fold or curl. Feed lightly once a month in summer, 3 times more in fall, winter. Mow when 2 in. tall. Unmowed, makes excel-lent, deep-rooted erosion control on slopes, banks. 'Alta' is medium coarse and extremely tough against wear. 'Fawn' has narrowest leaf, finest texture. 'Goars' is fairly tolerant of saline and alkaline soils. 'Kentucky 31' is best adapted to hot-summer climates.

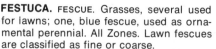

Festuca ovina glauca

F. ovina. SHEEP FESCUE. Fine. Low-growing (to 1 ft.), clumping grass with narrow, needle-fine, soft but tough leaves. *F. o. duriuscula*, HARD FESCUE, is sometimes used as lawn grass. *F. o. glauca*, BLUE FESCUE, forms blue gray tufts 4–10 in. tall. Useful ground cover for sunny or partially shaded areas, on slopes or level ground. Needs little water in Zones 1–9, 14–24; as much as lawn grass in Zones 10–13. No foot traffic. Clip back to near ground after flowering or any time plants look shabby. Does not make solid cover and needs frequent weeding. Dig overgrown clumps, pull apart, and replant as small divisions. Set 6–15 in. apart, depending on desired effect.

F. rubra. RED FESCUE. Fine blades. Principal use is as lawn grass in blends with bluegrass or other lawn grasses. Blades narrow, texture fine, color dark green. Not fussy about soil, takes some drought, some shade. Used alone, tends to grow clumpy. Mow to 1½–2 in. tall. Common red fescue is sometimes called creeping red fescue; it is one of most shade tolerant of good lawn grasses. Other creeping selections are sold as Creeping Red, 'Illahee', and 'Rainier'. *F. rubra commutata*, CHEWINGS FES-CUE, tends toward clumpiness. Unmowed, red fescues make attractive meadow on slopes too steep to mow. They are also used to overseed Bermuda lawns in winter.

FEVERFEW. See *Chrysanthemum parthenium*.

FICUS. Ornamental figs. Evergreen or deciduous trees, vines, shrubs, house plants. The average gardener would never expect to find the commercial edible fig, small-leafed climbing fig, banyan tree, and potted rubber plant under one common heading. They are classed together be-cause they all bear small or large figs.

F. auriculata (*F. roxburghii*). Briefly deciduous. Zones 20–24. Native to India. Usually takes the form of large, spreading shrub or small tree to 25 ft. high and as

Ficus elastica

wide. Full sun. Leaves are unusually large—broadly oval to round, about 15 in. across. New growth is interesting mahogany red, turning to rich green. Leaves have sandpapery texture. Large figs are borne in clusters on trunk and framework branches.

Can be shaped as small tree or espaliered. Beautiful in large container; good near swimming pools.

Grows in wind protected locations. Water young plants until established.

Ficus auriculata

F. benjamina. WEEPING CHINESE BANYAN. Evergreen tree. Outdoors in Zones 13, 23, 24; indoor plant everywhere. Native to India. To 30 ft. high and broadly spreading. Shining green, leathery, poplarlike leaves 5 in. long densely clothe drooping branches. Red figs. In frost free, wind protected locations, grow it in sun or shade, out of prevailing wind. Probably best fig for heat tolerance in Zone 13 (damaged there by any frost but recovers quickly as weather warms). Often used as small tree in entryway or patio. Good as espalier or screen.

Undoubtedly most popular indoor tree, and one of most popular house plants. Thrives on rich, steadily moist (not wet) soil, frequent light feeding, and abundant

Ficus benjamina

light. Dislikes overwatering, dark growing conditions, drafts, heat registers, and sudden changes in environment. If you get one growing happily, leave it where it is; moving it may cause it to drop leaves. (It will probably grow a new set.) Recently purchased plants often exhibit moving shock; don't rush to cure it with heavy watering.

New plants are easy to start from semihardwood cuttings taken between May and July. In mildest climates, can be used as clipped hedge.

Variety 'Exotica' has wavy-edged leaves with long, twisted tips; it is often sold simply as *F. benjamina.*

F. carica. EDIBLE FIG. See Fig, Edible.

F. deltoidea (*F. diversifolia*). MISTLETOE FIG. Evergreen shrub. Outdoors in Zones 19–24; house plant everywhere. Native to Malaya. Very slow-growing to 8–10 ft. high. Interesting open, twisted branch pattern. Thick, dark green, roundish, 2-in. leaves are sparsely stippled with tan specks on upper surface and a few black glands below. Attractive, small, greenish to yellow fruit borne continuously. Most often grown in

Ficus deltoidea

containers as patio and house plant. Grow in part shade or strong diffused light.

F. elastica. RUBBER PLANT. Evergreen shrub or tree. Outdoors in Zones 16, 17, 19–24; house plant everywhere. Native to India and Malaya. This is familiar rubber plant found in almost every florist shop. One of most foolproof indoor pot subjects. Takes less light than most big indoor plants. Leaves are thick, glossy, leathery, dark green, 8–12 in. long by 4–6 in. wide. New leaves unfold from rosy pink sheath which soon withers and drops. Let soil get fairly dry between waterings. Can become 40-ft.-high tree in Zones 23, 24. As small tree or shrub, useful in shaded "tunnel" garden entrances. Comes back in 3 months when cut to ground by frost.

F. e. 'Decora' (*F. e.* 'Belgica'). Considered superior to the species on account of broader, glossier leaves, bronzy when young.

F. e. 'Rubra'. New leaves are reddish and retain red edge as rest of leaf turns green. Grown as shrub or small tree in Zones 22–24.

F. e. 'Variegata'. Leaves are long, narrow, variegated yellow and green. Variegation is interesting when viewed close up in container, but as outdoor tree has unhealthy look.

If potted rubber plant becomes too tall and leggy, you can cut off top and select side branch to form new main shoot. Or you can get a new plant by air layering top section. When roots form,

cut branch section with attached roots and plant it in pot.

F. lyrata (*F. pandurata*). FIDDLELEAF FIG. Evergreen tree or large shrub. Outdoors in Zones 22–24. Native to tropical Africa. Dramatic structural form with huge, dark green, fiddle shaped leaves to 15 in. long and 10 in. wide, prominently veined, with glossy surface. Highly effective as indoor pot plant. In protected outdoor position, can grow to 20 ft. with trunks 6 in. wide. Good near swimming pools.

To increase branching, pinch back when young.

Ficus lyrata

F. macrophylla. MORETON BAY FIG. Huge evergreen tree. Zones 17, 19–24. Native to north New South Wales and Queensland, Australia. Grows to enormous dimensions. A tree at Santa Barbara planted in 1877 has spread of 150 ft., with massive buttressed trunk and surface roots. Blunt, oval, leathery leaves, 10 in. long and 4 in. wide, glossy green above, brownish beneath. Rose-colored leaf sheaths appear like candles at ends of branches. Purple, white-spotted, 1-in. figs.

Although tender when young, acquires hardiness with size. Shows damage at 24°–26°F. Ample water.

F. microcarpa (*F. retusa*). INDIAN LAUREL FIG. Evergreen tree. Zones 9, 15–24. Native to India, Malaya. Both this and its variety *nitida* are widely used along streets throughout southern California and in San Francisco Bay area. They differ definitely in growth habit and appearance. Both perform best with some summer water.

F. microcarpa grows moderately to 25–30 ft. It has beautiful weeping form with long drooping branches thickly clothed with 2–4-in.-long leaves with blunt tips. New leaves, light rose to chartreuse, produced almost continuously, give tree pleasing two-tone effect. Slim light gray trunk supporting massive crown may be concealed by lower trailing branches if these are not trimmed off.

F. m. nitida. Has dense foliage on upright-growing branches, and is admirably suited to formal shearing. Leaves are clear lustrous geen, similar in size to *F. microcarpa*, but more pointed at base and apex. *F. m. nitida* may be pruned at almost any time of year to size or shape desired.

Where pest free, it would be difficult to find more satisfactory tree or tub plant for warm climates.

Unfortunately, a thrips which attacks both species and its variety has become established in California. This insect is difficult to control because it quickly curls new leaves, stippling them and causing them to fall. Best control: systemic insecticides.

F. microphylla. Plants sold under this name in California are *F. rubiginosa.*

F. nekbudu (*F. utilis*). ZULU FIG. Evergreen tree. Zones 19–24. To 20 ft. tall (eventually much taller), and as wide. Leaves to 12 in. long, 6 in. wide, thick, leathery, smooth. Foliage pattern is open, revealing branching structure and smooth, pale gray bark.

F. pumila (*F. repens*). CREEPING FIG. Evergreen vine. Zones 8–24. Native to China, Japan, Australia. A most unfiglike habit; it is one of few plants which attaches itself securely to wood, masonry, or even metal in barnacle fashion.

In young stages, gives very little indication of its potential vigor. Delicate tracery of tiny, heart shaped leaves frequently seen patterned against a chimney or stucco wall is almost certain to be *F. pumila*, but in this growth phase gives no hint of its powerful character at maturity. There is almost no limit to size of vine and area it will cover. Neat little leaves of juvenile growth ultimately develop into large (2–4 in. long), leathery, oblong leaves borne on stubby branches which bear large oblong fruit. Stems in time envelop a 3 or 4-story building so completely that it becomes necessary to keep them trimmed away from windows.

It is safe to use this fig on the house if vine is cut to ground every few years. Or, control by removing fruiting stems from time to time as they form. Roots are invasive, probably more so than most other figs.

Because it is grown on walls, and thus protected, it is found in colder climates than any other evergreen fig. Will not climb on hot south or west wall, or will be unattractive yellow. Sometimes slow to begin climbing. Cut back to ground soon after planting to make new growth that will take off fast.

F. p. 'Minima'. Slender, small-leafed variety. Another tiny variety sold as *F. p.* 'Quercifolia' has lobed leaves something like tiny oak leaves. 'Variegata' has creamy white markings.

F. religiosa. PEEPUL, BO-TREE. Briefly deciduous tree. Zones 13, 19, 21, 23, 24. Native to India. Large, upright with less spread than *F. macrophylla*. Foliage is quite open and delicate, revealing structure of tree at all times. Bark is warm rich brown. Leaves roundish, 4–7 in. long, with long tail-like point, pale green, rather crisp and thin textured. They move easily even in slightest breeze, giving foliage a fluttering effect. Foliage drops completely in April or May—frightening experience to gardener who has bought an "evergreen" fig.

F. retusa. See *F. microcarpa.*

F. roxburghii. See *F. auriculata.*

F. rubiginosa. RUSTYLEAF FIG. Evergreen tree. Zones 18–24. Native to Australia. Grows to 20–50 ft., with broad crown and single or multiple trunks. Dense foliage of 5-in. oval leaves, deep green above and generally rusty, woolly beneath.

Does well in sand on beach in Santa Monica and thrives in heat of interior valleys. A few trees in coastal gardens have developed hanging aerial roots that characterize many of the evergreen figs in tropical environment. Small-leafed form is widely sold as *F. microphylla.*

F. r. australis varies from the species (if it varies at all) in having slightly less rusty leaves. Varieties 'El Toro' and 'Irvine' have exceptionally dark green leaves; 'Florida', widely distributed, has lighter green leaves. 'Variegata', with leaves mottled green and cream, is sometimes sold as house plant.

FIG, EDIBLE. For ornamental relatives see *Ficus*. Deciduous tree. Zones 4–9, 12–24. In Zones 1–3, 10, 11 as tubbed plant, protected in winter. Grows fairly fast to 15–30 ft., generally low branched and spreading; where hard freezes are common, fig wood freezes back severely and plant behaves as a big shrub.

Edible Fig

Trunks heavy, smooth, gray barked, gnarled in really old trees, picturesque in silhouette. Leaves rough, bright green, 3–5 lobed, 4–9 in. long, and nearly as wide. Winter framework, tropical-looking foliage, strong trunk and branch pattern make fig a top-notch ornamental tree, especially near patio where it can be illuminated from beneath. Fruit drop is problem immediately above deck or paving. Casts dense shade. Can be held to 10 ft. in big container, or trained as espalier along fence or wall.

Needs sun, good drainage; not particular about soil and drought resistant when established. In Zones 4–7, trees planted near or trained against south walls benefit from reflected heat. Cut back tops hard at planting. As tree grows, prune lightly each winter, cutting out dead wood, crossing branches, low-hanging branches that interfere with traffic. Pinch back runaway shoots any season. Avoid deep cultivation (may damage surface roots) and high nitrogen fertilizers (stimulate growth at expense of fruit). 'Kadota', 'Mission' are resistant to oak root fungus.

Home garden figs do not need pollenizing, and most varieties bear two crops a year: the first comes in June (July in Northwest) on last year's wood; second and more important comes in August-November from current summer's wood. Don't squeeze green or ripening figs; when ripe they come off easily. Keep picked as they ripen and protect from birds (if you can). Pick off the ripe figs and clean up fallen fruit in late fall. California pocket gophers love fig roots. To avoid, plant young figs in ample-sized wire baskets.

Varieties differ in climate adaptability, some thriving under cool coastal conditions, others needing prolonged high temperatures to bear good fruit. Familiar dried figs from the market are usually 'Calimyrna' or imported Smyrna figs. These require special pollenizers (caprifigs) and special pollenizing insect; not recommended for home gardens.

'Blue Celeste' ('Celeste', 'Celestial'). Hardy tree. Bronzy tinged

violet, pulp rosy amber; fruit resistant to spoilage, dries well on tree in California.

'Brown Turkey'. ('San Piero'. Sold in Northwest as 'Black Spanish'.) Small tree; brownish purple fruit. Adaptable to most fig climates, Arizona to Northwest. Good garden tree. Cut back hard to scaffold limbs to lessen fruit formation and subsequent fruit-drop mess.

'Conadria'. Choice white fig blushed violet; thin skinned, white to red flesh, fine flavor. Best in hot areas.

'Genoa' ('White Genoa'). Greenish yellow skin, amber to yellow flesh. Good quality, good home garden variety in California coastal and coastal valley gardens.

'Italian Everbearing'. Resembles 'Brown Turkey', but with fruit averaging somewhat larger, skin reddish brown rather than brown purple.

'Kadota' ('White Kadota'). Fruit tough skinned, greenish yellow in California's hot interior valleys where it bears best, green near coast. Commercial canning variety. Strong grower, needs little pruning. If given severe pruning, it will bear later, with fewer, larger fruit.

'Mission' ('Black Mission'). Purple black fig for desert and all California gardens. Large tree.

'Osborn Prolific'. Purplish brown fruit; good bearer in California coastal areas.

'Texas Everbearing'. Medium to large mahogany to purple fruit with strawberry-colored pulp. Bears young and gives good crop in short season areas of Southwest.

FILBERT. For ornamental relatives see *Corylus*. Deciduous nut trees. Zones 2–7. More treelike in form (15–25 ft.) than other ornamental forms of *Corylus* (this is *C. maxima*). Makes handsome, well-structured, small tree for garden or terrace. Spring to fall, roundish, ruffled-edged leaves cast pleasant spot of shade. Showy male catkins hang long and full on bare branches in winter. Crop of roundish to oblong nuts (ones sold in stores) comes as bonus in fall. A 10-year-old tree may yield up to 10 lbs. of nuts a year. Nuts form inside frilled husks.

Filbert

Set out plants in late winter or early spring, in well-drained, deep soil, full sun. Takes average water. Tree tends to sucker; clear these out 3 or 4 times a year if you wish to maintain clear trunk. Spray for aphids, bud mites, and filbert blight. Since cross-pollination is necessary, plant at least two varieties.

'Barcelona', slow or moderate growth to 18 ft. with greater spread. Roundish, large nuts.

'Du Chilly', slow to 15 ft. with equal spread. Shoots grow at right angles to limbs. Large, long nut of high quality, slow to drop and adhering to husks.

'Purpurea', ornamental variety with dark purple leaves.

'Royal', slow to 18 by 18 ft. with large nuts of excellent flavor.

'White Aveline' and 'Daviana', used as pollenizers. Light-crop varieties with medium-sized, high-quality nuts.

FINOCCHIO. See *Foeniculum vulgare azoricum.*

FIR. See *Abies.*

FIRECRACKER FLOWER. See *Dichelostemma ida-maia.*

FIRE FERN. See *Oxalis hedysaroides* 'Rubra'.

FIRETHORN. See *Pyracantha.*

FIREWHEEL TREE. See *Stenocarpus sinuatus.*

FISHTAIL PALM. *Caryota.*

FIRMIANA simplex *(F. platanifolia)*.
CHINESE PARASOL TREE. Deciduous tree.
Zones 5, 6, 8, 9, 12–24. Native to China, Japan. Small, usually slow-growing, 15–30 ft.,
with unique light gray green bark. Trunk
often has no side branches to 4–5 ft., at
which point it divides into 3 or more slender, upright and slightly spreading stems
which carry lobed, tropical-looking, 12-in.
leaves. Each stem looks as if it could be cut
off and carried away as a parasol. Large
loose, upright clusters of greenish white
flowers at ends of branches in July. Interesting fruit are like 2 opened green pea
pods with seeds on margins. Goes leafless
for long period in winter (unusual for
tropical-looking tree).

Firmiana simplex

Has been grown in mild-climate areas in all types of soil, but
best in patios and courtyards or other full-sun or morning-sun
locations protected from wind. Useful near swimming pools.
Needs irrigation when young; drought resistant when established.

FITTONIA verschaffeltii. FITTONIA. Evergreen house plant or greenhouse plant.
Native to South America. Low and creeping
with handsome foliage. Leaves dark green,
oval, 4 in. long, conspicuously veined with
red. Variety 'Argyroneura' has leaves
veined with white.

Does best when grown in north light.
High humidity, average watering, and even,
warm temperature are among its requirements. Grow from cuttings.

Fittonia verschaffeltii

FIVE-FINGER FERN. See *Adiantum pedatum*.

FLAG. See *Iris*.

FLAME PEA. See *Chorizema*.

FLAME TREE. See *Brachychiton acerifolius*.

FLAME VINE. See *Pyrostegia venusta*.

FLANNEL BUSH. See *Fremontodendron*.

FLAX. See *Linum*.

FLAX, NEW ZEALAND. See *Phormium*.

FLAXLEAF PAPERBARK. See *Melaleuca linariifolia*.

FLEABANE. See *Erigeron*.

FLOSS FLOWER. See *Ageratum houstonianum*.

FLOSS SILK TREE. See *Chorisia*.

FLOWERING ALMOND. See *Prunus triloba*.

FLOWERING CHERRY. See *Prunus*.

FLOWERING CRABAPPLE. See *Malus*.

FLOWERING MAPLE. See *Abutilon*.

FLOWERING NECTARINE. See *Prunus*.

FLOWERING PEACH. See *Prunus*.

FLOWERING PLUM. See *Prunus*.

FLOWERING QUINCE. See *Chaenomeles*.

FLOWERY SENNA. See *Cassia corymbosa*.

FOENICULUM vulgare. COMMON FENNEL.
Perennial herb, usually grown as summer
annual. To 3–5 ft. Similar to dill, but
coarser. Yellow green, finely cut leaves; flat
clusters of yellow flowers. Grow in light,
well-drained soil, full sun. Very drought tolerant. Start from seed where plants are to
be grown; thin seedlings to 1 ft. apart. Use
seeds to season bread, pudding; use leaves
as garnish for salads, fish. Young leaves
and seeds have slight licorice taste. Plants
often grow as roadside or garden weeds;
they are attractive until tops turn brown,
and even then seeds form favorite food for
wild birds.

Foeniculum vulgare

F. v. azoricum. FINOCCHIO. Lower growing; leaf bases larger
and thicker. These are edible cooked or raw in salads.

FORESTIERA neomexicana. NEW MEXICAN
PRIVET, DESERT OLIVE. Zones 1–3, 10.
Deciduous shrub. To 6–8 ft. tall, nearly as
broad. Smooth, medium green leaves 1 to
nearly 2 in. long. Flowers negligible. Fruit,
egg shaped, blue black, ¼ in. long, not always produced (some plants do not have
both male and female flowers). Fairly fast
growth makes it good screening plant in
difficult climates. Full sun. Established
plants withstand drought, but grow faster
with some water. Native to New Mexico,
Colorado, Arizona west to California.

Forestiera neomexicana

FORGET-ME-NOT. See *Myosotis*.

FORSYTHIA. Deciduous shrubs. Zones
2–11, 14–16, 18, 19. Somewhat fountain
shaped shrubs, bare branches covered with
yellow flowers February-April. Rest of the
growing season, medium green foliage
blends well with other shrubs in border
background. Rounded, pointed leaves, lush
green. Branches can be forced for indoor
bloom in winter.

Use as screen, espalier, or bank cover. Or
plant in shrub border. Tolerates most soils;
likes sun, moderate water, and feeding.
Prune established plants after bloom by
cutting to ground a third of branches that
have bloomed. Remove oldest branches,
weak or dead wood.

Forsythia intermedia

F. intermedia. Hybrids between *F. suspensa* and *F. viridissima*.
Most grow 7–10 ft. tall and have arching branches. 'Arnold
Dwarf', 20–36 in. tall and to 6 ft. wide, has few flowers which are
not especially attractive; it is useful, fast-growing ground cover
in hard climates. 'Beatrix Farrand', an upright grower to 10 ft. tall,
7 ft. broad, has branches thickly set with 2–2½-in.-wide, deep
yellow flowers marked orange.

F. i. 'Karl Sax' resembles *F.* 'Beatrix Farrand' but is lower growing, neater, more graceful. *F. i.* 'Lynwood' ('Lynwood Gold')
grows stiffly upright to 7 ft., with 4–6-ft. spread. Profuse tawny
yellow blooms survive spring storms. *F. i.* 'Spectabilis' is dense,
upright, vigorous shrub to 9 ft. with deep yellow flowers. *F. i.*
'Spring Glory' has heavy crop of pale yellow flowers.

F. suspensa. WEEPING FORSYTHIA. Dense, upright growth habit
to 8–10 ft. with 6–8-ft. spread. Drooping, vinelike branches root
where they touch damp soil. Golden yellow flowers. Useful big-
scale bank cover. Can be trained as vine; support main branches

and branchlets will cascade. *F. s.* 'Fortunei' is somewhat more upright, more available in nurseries.

F. viridissima. GREENSTEM FORSYTHIA. Stiff-looking shrub to 10 ft. with deep green foliage, olive green stems, greenish yellow flowers. 'Bronxensis' is slow growing dwarf form to 16 in. tall, for smaller shrub borders or ground cover.

FORTNIGHT LILY. See *Dietes.*

FORTUNELLA margarita. See Nagami Kumquat under *Citrus.*

FOTHERGILLA. Deciduous shrubs. Zones 3–9, 14–17. Grown principally for fall color, but small white flowers in 1–2-in. brushlike clusters are pretty. Plant in peaty soil, partial shade—especially where summers are long and hot. Average water.

Fothergilla monticola

F. major. Erect shrub to 9 ft. with roundish, 4-in.-long leaves turning orange to purplish red in autumn. Flowers appear with the leaves. Fall color early and good in San Francisco Bay area even without chilly weather.

F. monticola. Spreading plant, 3–4 ft. tall with broadly oval leaves. Flower clusters somewhat larger than in *F. major.* Fall color scarlet to crimson.

FOUNTAIN GRASS. See *Pennisetum setaceum.*

FOUQUIERIA splendens. OCOTILLO. Deciduous shrub with distinctive character. Zones 10–13, 18–20. Native to Mojave and Colorado deserts east to Texas, Mexico. Many stiff, whiplike gray stems 8–25 ft. high, heavily furrowed and covered with stout thorns. Fleshy, roundish, ½–1-in.-long leaves appear after rains, soon drop. Tubular, ¾–1-in.-long red flowers in very attractive foot-long clusters after rains in spring or summer. Can be used as screening, impenetrable hedge, or for silhouette against bare walls. Needs excellent drainage and full sun. Don't overwater. Cuttings stuck in ground will grow.

Fouquieria splendens

FOUR O'CLOCK. See *Mirabilis jalapa.*

FOXBERRY. See *Vaccinium vitis-idaea.*

FOXGLOVE. See *Digitalis.*

FOXTAIL LILY. See *Eremurus.*

FRAGARIA chiloensis. WILD STRAWBERRY, SAND STRAWBERRY. Evergreen ground cover. Grow in part shade in Zones 4–24; also in sun in Zones 4–6, 15–17, 20–24. Native of Pacific beaches and bluffs, North and South America. Forms low, compact, lush mats 6–12 in. high. Dark green glossy leaves have 3-toothed leaflets. Leaves take on red tints in winter. Large (1 in. wide) white flowers in spring. Bright red, ¾-in., seedy fruit in fall (seldom set in gardens) attract birds. Plant rooted stolons in late spring or early summer. Flat-grown plants can be planted any time. Set plants 12–18 in. apart. Needs annual mowing or cutting back (early spring) to force new growth, prevent stem buildup. Feed annually in late spring. Needs regular watering in Zones 7–16, 18–21 for good growth. In late summer, if leaves show yellowing, apply iron

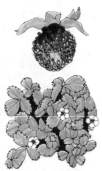

Fragaria chiloensis

sulfate. For fruiting or garden strawberry, see Strawberry.

FRAGRANT SNOWBALL. See *Viburnum carlcephalum.*

FRAGRANT SNOWBELL. See *Styrax obassia.*

FRANCESCHI PALM. See *Brahea elegans.*

FRANCOA ramosa. MAIDEN'S WREATH. Perennial. Grown as evergreen in Zones 4, 5, 8, 9, 13–24. Native to Chile. Spreading plant with basal clumps of large, wavy-margined leaves which mass up 1–2 ft. In midsummer, almost leafless, graceful flowering stems stand 2–3 ft. high; upper portions are spikes of many pure white (occasionally pinkish) tiny flowers. Ideal exposure is sun half the day or dappled sun all day. Needs just normal garden watering, very little fertilizer. Distribution seems mainly by neighborliness; more pass over back fences than through nursery channels. In just a few years, plants increase in size enough that you can divide and replant fresh new segments from outside edges of clumps.

Francoa ramosa

Good companion with foxgloves, primroses, azaleas, camellias. Good cut flowers.

FRANGIPANI. See *Plumeria rubra.*

FRANKLINIA alatamaha (*Gordonia alatamaha*). Deciduous tree. Zones 2–6, 14–17. Once native to Georgia, but apparently extinct in the wilds before 1800. Slender form, to 20–30 ft. high. Slow to moderate growth. Reddish brown bark with faint striping. Spoon shaped, bright green leaves 4–6 in. long, turn scarlet in autumn. Flowers 3 in. wide, white with center cluster of yellow stamens, open from round white buds August-September, sometimes coinciding with fall foliage color. Give it well-drained, rich, light acid soil, ample water, and partial shade in hot-summer areas (rhododendron conditions). During wet autumns in Northwest it blooms shyly. Easy to grow from seed, blooming in 6–7 years.

Franklinia alatamaha

Use for contrast in rhododendron-azalea plantings. Unusual lawn or patio tree with right soil and exposure.

FRAXINELLA. See *Dictamnus albus.*

FRAXINUS. ASH. Deciduous trees, one almost evergreen. Trees grow fairly fast, and most tolerate hot summers, cold winters, and many kinds of soil including alkaline. Chief uses as street trees, shade trees, lawn trees, patio shelter trees. Fairly pest free.

In most cases leaves are divided into leaflets. Male and female flowers (generally inconspicuous, in clusters) grow on separate trees in some species, on same tree in others. In latter case flowers are often followed by clusters of 1-seeded, winged fruit, often in such abundance they can be litter problem. When flowers are on separate trees you'll get fruit on female tree only if it grows near male tree.

Fraxinus velutina 'Modesto'

F. americana. WHITE ASH. Deciduous tree. Zones 1–11, 14–17. Native to eastern U.S. Grows to 80 ft. or more, with straight trunk and oval shaped crown. Leaves 8–15 in. long with 5–9 dark green, oval leaflets, paler beneath; turn purplish in fall. Needs some watering. Edges show burning in hot windy areas. Male and female flowers on separate trees but plants sold are generally seedlings so you don't know what you get. If both, you will get heavy crop of seed; both litter and seedlings can be problem. *F. a.* 'Rose Hill' is seedless selection that is fast growing, somewhat more pyramidal than common American ash.

F. dipetala. FOOTHILL ASH. Deciduous tree or large shrub. Zones 7–24. Native to foothills of California; also in Baja California. Treelike shrub to 6 ft. high or small tree 18–20 ft. Drought tolerant. Leaves 2–5½ in. long with 3–9 leaflets (occasionally 1) about 1 in. long. White flowers in showy, branched clusters, March-June, followed by many 1-in.-long fruit.

F. excelsior. EUROPEAN ASH. Deciduous tree. All Zones. Native to Europe, Asia Minor. Round-headed tree 60–80 ft. high, or may grow to 140 ft. Dormant buds black. Leaves 10–12 in. long, divided into 7–11 oval, toothed leaflets, dark green above, paler beneath; do not change color but drop while green.

F. e. 'Kimberly'. All Zones, but especially valued as shade tree in Zones 1–3. Is a selected male variety, so doesn't produce seed.

F. e. 'Pendula'. WEEPING EUROPEAN ASH. All Zones. Spreading, rather asymmetrical, umbrella shaped tree with weeping branches that reach ground.

F. e. 'Rancho Roundhead'. Especially adaptable to any soil, severe climate. Round form, 25–30 ft. tall.

F. holotricha. Deciduous tree. Zones 4–24. Native to eastern Balkan Peninsula. Upright, rather narrow tree to 40 ft. Leaves of 9–13 dull green, 2–3-in.-long leaflets with toothed edges. Casts light, filtered shade. Leaves turn yellow in fall, dry up, and sift down into lawn or ground cover, thus lessening litter problem.

F. h. 'Moraine'. Selected variety; more round headed than species, produces few seeds. Good lawn tree—neat, symmetrical, uniform bright yellow in fall.

F. latifolia (*F. oregona*). OREGON ASH. Deciduous tree. Zones 4–24. Native to Sierra Nevada and along coast from northern California to British Columbia. Grows to 40–80 ft. Leaves 6–12 in. long, divided into 5–7 oblong to oval, light green, hairy or smooth leaflets; end leaflet to 4 in. long, larger than side leaflets. Male and female flowers on separate trees. Will grow in standing water during winter months.

F. ornus. FLOWERING ASH. Deciduous tree. Zones 3–9, 14–17. Native to southern Europe and Asia Minor. Grows rapidly to 40–50 ft. with broad, rounded crown 20–30 ft. wide. Supplies luxuriant mass of foliage. Leaves 8–10 in. long, divided into 7–11 oval, medium green, 2 -in. -long leaflets with toothed edges. Foliage turns to soft shades of lavender and yellow in fall. In May displays quantities of fluffy, branched, 3–5-in.-long clusters of fragrant white to greenish white blossoms followed by unsightly seed clusters that hang on until late winter unless removed.

Fraxinus ornus

F. oxycarpa. Zones 3–9, 14–24. Compact, small-leafed, fine-textured ash with delicate, lacy look.

F. o. 'Flame'. Small, shiny leaves. Rich burgundy fall color. Round-headed tree to 30 ft. Seedless.

F. o. 'Golden Desert' ('Aureafolia'). Bright golden bark. Leaves open green, turn gold in July, hang on well into autumn. To 20 ft. tall, 18 ft. broad.

F. o. 'Raywood'. RAYWOOD ASH, CLARET ASH. Compact, round-headed, fast growing tree to 25–35 ft. Usually sold in California as container-grown rather than bare-root tree. Produces no seeds. Purple red fall color.

F. pennsylvanica (*F. lanceolata*). GREEN ASH. Deciduous tree. Zones 1–6. Native to eastern U.S. Moderate grower to 30–40 ft., forming compact oval crown. Gray brown bark; dense twiggy structure. Leaves 10–12 in. long, divided into 5–9 bright green, rather narrow, 4–6-in.-long leaflets. Male and female flowers on separate trees. Takes wet soil, severe cold, but foliage burns in hot, dry winds.

F. p. 'Fan West'. Seedless hybrid between green ash and Arizona ash. Light olive green leaves, good branch structure.

Takes low winter temperatures, hot desert sun and wind.

F. p. 'Marshall'. MARSHALL SEEDLESS GREEN ASH. Selected male form with large, glossy, dark green leaflets.

F. p. 'Summit'. Fast growing to 50–60 ft. Uniform, erect growth. Seedless.

F. quadrangulata. BLUE ASH. Deciduous tree. Zones 1–6. Native to central U.S. Grows rapidly to 60–80 ft. or more. Branches distinctly square, usually with flanges along edges. Oval, dark green leaflets (7–11), 2–5 in. long, with toothed edges. Foliage turns purplish in fall. Fruit may become litter problem if you have female tree with male tree to pollinate it.

F. uhdei. EVERGREEN ASH, SHAMEL ASH. Evergreen to semi-evergreen tree. Zones 9, 12–24. Native to Mexico. In mildest areas leaves stay through winter; in colder sections, trees lose most or all foliage, but often only for a short time. Sharp frosts may kill back branch tips; serious damage at about 15°F. or lower. A top favorite in southern California and low-elevation deserts.

Grows fast to 25–30 ft. in 10 years; 40 ft. in 20 years; eventually 70–80 ft. or more. Makes upright, narrow tree when young, eventually spreading. Leaves divided into 5–9 glossy, dark green leaflets about 4 in. long, edged with small teeth. Foliage may burn if subjected to hot winds. Shallow rooted; encourage deeper rooting by watering deeply. Cut back any long branches to well-placed, strong side branches when tree is young. Eliminate deep crotches by pruning out weaker branches. Texas root rot sometimes causes dieback; will kill young trees, but established trees usually survive. Resistant to oak root fungus.

F. u. 'Sexton'. SEXTON ASH. Forms very compact, rounded crown. Leaflets larger and deeper green than *F. uhdei*.

F. u. 'Tomlinson'. TOMLINSON ASH. Grows more slowly (about 18 ft. in 10 years). More upright and dense when young. Leaflets deep green, more leathery with deep wavy-toothed margins.

F. velutina. ARIZONA ASH. Deciduous tree. Native to Arizona. Zones 8, 9, 10–24. Tree withstands hot, dry conditions and cold to about −10°F. Pyramidal when young; spreading, more open when mature. Leaves divided into 3–5 narrow to oval, 3-in.-long leaflets. Male and female flowers on separate trees.

F. v. coriacea. MONTEBELLO ASH. Zones 8, 9, 13–24. Native mostly to southern California. Has broader, more leathery leaves than the species.

F. v. 'Modesto'. MODESTO ASH. Selection from tree in Westside Park, Modesto, Calif. Zones 3–24. Vigorous form of Arizona ash. Grows to about 50 ft. with 30-ft. spread. Medium green leaflets glossier than the species; turn bright yellow in fall.

In many areas following wet spring, Modesto ash leaves get scorched look. This is caused by fungus disease called anthracnose. Control by spraying with benomyl. Prune out and dispose of infected wood—it can reinfect. Verticillium wilt prevalent in agricultural areas; no control once it's started in young trees, but established trees often survive. Control aphids, psyllas, and spider mites with contact spray. Resistant to oak root fungus.

F. v. 'Rio Grande'. FAN-TEX ASH. Zones 8–24. Thrives in hot, dry climates and alkaline soils. Has very large, darker green, more succulent leaflets than Modesto ash; unfold in early spring, turn golden yellow in late fall. Foliage resistant to wind burn.

FRECKLE FACE. See *Hypoestes phyllostachya*.

FREESIA. Corms. Outdoors in Zones 8, 9, 12–24; indoors in pots anywhere. Native to South Africa. Prized for rich fragrance of flowers. Slender, branched stems to 1–1½ ft., about same height as lowest leaves; stem leaves shorter. Flowers tubular, 2 in. long, in one-sided spikes. Older variety 'Alba' has fragrant white or creamy white blooms; newer, larger-flowered varieties with 12–18-in. stems are Tecolote and Dutch Hybrids with white, pink, red, lavender, purple, blue, yellow, orange flowers, mixed or in single-color named varieties.

In mild climates plant 2 in. deep (pointed end up) in fall in sunny, well-drained soil.

Freesia hybrid

(Continued on next page)

Plants dry up after bloom, start growing again in fall with rains or watering; increase rapidly. In cold climates plant 2 in. deep, 2 in. apart in pots; grow indoors in sunny window. Keep room temperature as cool as possible at night. Easily grown from seed sown in July-August; often bloom following spring. Good in rock gardens or for cutting.

FREMONTODENDRON *(Fremontia)*. FLAN-NEL BUSH. Evergreen shrubs or small trees. Zones 7–24. Fast growing to 6–20 ft. tall. Leathery leaves dark green above with feltlike covering beneath. Yellow saucerlike flowers. Conical seed capsules, covered with bristly, rusty hairs, persist for long time; some consider them unsightly. Need excellent drainage; hillside planting best; completely drought resistant. Give plants little summer water, especially in heavy soils. Roots shallow, so stake plants while young. Pinch and prune to shape. Usually short lived. Plant with other drought tolerant shrubs—beautiful with ceanothus.

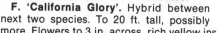

Fremontodendron 'California Glory'

F. 'California Glory'. Hybrid between next two species. To 20 ft. tall, possibly more. Flowers to 3 in. across, rich yellow inside, tinged red outside. Very prolific bloom over long period.

F. californicum. COMMON FLANNEL BUSH. Native to foothills of Sierra Nevada and California Coast Ranges, and southern California mountains. Makes eye-catching show of lemon yellow, 1–1½-in.-wide flowers in May-June; flowers bloom all at once. Roundish 1-in.-long leaves, unlobed or 3 lobed.

F. c. napense. Native to Napa, Lake, and Yolo counties in California. Somewhat shrubbier, with thinner leaves. Smaller yellow flowers sometimes tinged with rose.

F. mexicanum. SOUTHERN FLANNEL BUSH. Native to San Diego County and Baja California. To 18 ft. Leaves have 3–5 distinct lobes, 1¼–3 in. long. Flowers larger (1½–2½ in. wide), yellow often tinged orange. Flowers over longer period than *F. californicum,* but flowers form among leaves so mass effect is not as showy.

F. 'San Gabriel'. Resembles *F.* 'California Glory', but leaves are more deeply cut (maplelike).

FRENCH TARRAGON. See *Artemisia dracunculus.*

FRINGE BELLS. See *Shortia soldanelloides.*

FRINGE CUP. See *Tellima grandiflora.*

FRINGED WORMWOOD. See *Artemisia frigida.*

FRINGE HYACINTH. See *Muscari comosum.*

FRINGE TREE. See *Chionanthus.*

FRITILLARIA. FRITILLARY. Bulbs. Zones 1–7, 15–17. Native to Europe, Asia, North America; most numerous in West. Related to lilies. Give variable performance in gardens; some kinds short-lived. Unbranched stems 6 in.–4 ft. high, topped by bell-like, nodding flowers often unusually colored and mottled. Use in woodland, rock garden, or as border plants in filtered shade. Plant bulbs in fall in porous soil with ample humus. Set smaller bulbs 3–4 in. deep; largest (crown imperial) 4–5 in. deep. Most kinds should gradually dry out as foliage yellows, remain dry until late fall. Bulbs

Fritillaria imperialis

sometimes rest a year after planting or after blooming; use enough for yearly display.

F. assyriaca. Strong-growing plants 12–16 in. tall with blue green foliage, drooping maroon flowers lined with golden bronze. April-May bloom.

F. camschatcensis. Stems to 2 ft. carry 1–6 bell shaped, nearly black flowers 1–1¼ in. long. Lance shaped leaves to 4 in. long. Needs shade, leaf mold, cool soil. April-May bloom.

F. imperialis. CROWN IMPERIAL. Stout stalk 3½–4 ft., tall clothed with broad glossy leaves. Flowers large, drooping, bell shaped, red, orange, or yellow in clusters at top of stem, with tuft of leaves above. Use in borders, containers. Bulb and plant have somewhat unpleasant odor. Takes full sun near coast.

F. lanceolata. CHECKER LILY. Western native. Stems 2½ ft. high with several whorls of leaves. Flowers are bowl shaped bells, brownish purple, mottled with yellow, greenish yellow, or purple spots.

F. meleagris. CHECKERED LILY, SNAKESHEAD. Nodding 2-in. bells on 12–18 in. stems. Showy flowers, checkered and veined with reddish brown and purple, bloom in late spring. Lance shaped leaves, 3–6 in. long. There is white form. Native to damp meadows in Europe, Asia; tolerates occasional flooding. Long lived in colder regions.

F. persica 'Adiyaman'. Stems 2 to 3 ft. tall carry up to 30 deep plum-purple, 1-in. drooping flowers on the upper half. Foliage is grayish. Plant is hardy and easy, but protect emerging stems from late frosts in colder regions.

F. pudica. YELLOW FRITILLARY. Western native. To 6–12 in. tall with 1–3 nodding yellow or orange bells, April-June. Flowers turn brick red with age. Alternate lance shaped leaves, to 8 in. long.

F. recurva. SCARLET FRITILLARY. Western native. Stem 2½ ft. high; flowers are scarlet bells marked yellow inside, tinged purple outside. Blooms March-July according to climate. Lance shaped leaves in whorls, to 4 in. long.

F. verticillata thunbergii *(F. thunbergii)*. To 2 ft. tall. Flowers white or cream, checkered with green or purplish markings. Early spring bloom.

FRUITLAND ARBORVITAE. See *Platycladus orientalis* 'Fruitlandii'.

FUCHSIA. Evergreen in frost free climates, deciduous elsewhere. Shrub. Popular, showy-flowered fuchsias that come in hundreds of named varieties are forms of *F. hybrida,* and are discussed under that heading. Other species are grown almost entirely by collectors, but some are good for basic landscaping purposes. Give plenty of water and partial shade.

Fuchsia 'Swingtime'

F. arborescens. Zones 16, 17, 22–24. Big shrub to 18 ft. tall, with 8-in. leaves and large clusters of small, erect, pinkish or purplish flowers like lilacs in summer.

F. hybrida. HYBRID FUCHSIA. Here belong nearly all garden fuchsias. Zones 4–6, 15–17, 22–24 constitute finest climate in North America for growing fuchsias and region in which most varieties were developed. The next strip—Zones 2, 3, 7–9, 14, 20, 21—finds fuchsias grown, but with more difficulty. Outside of those two strips, fuchsias are little known, grown as summer annuals or in greenhouses.

Fuchsias bloom from early summer to first frost. At least 500 varieties in West, with wide variety of combinations within color range. Sepals (top parts that flare back) are always white, red, or pink. Corolla (inside part of flower) may be almost any color possible within range of white, blue violet, purple, pink, red, and shades approaching orange. Flowers have no fragrance, but hummingbirds visit them.

There is considerable difference in flower sizes and shapes. Fuchsias range from size of shelled peanuts to giants size of boy's fist. Within this range some are single, meaning that there's just one layer of closely set petals in corolla, and some are very double, with many sets of ruffled petals in corolla. Quite frequently, little-flowered types have little leaves, and big-flowered types have big leaves.

Plant forms vary extremely: from erect-growing shrubs, 3–12

ft. high to trailing types (you grow them in hanging containers), and just about every possible form between the two extremes. Specifically, you can buy or train fuchsias in these forms: hanging basket, small shrub, medium shrub, large shrub, espalier, standard (miniature tree shape).

Best environment. Fuchsias grow best in cool summer temperatures, modified sunlight, and with much moisture in atmosphere and soil. If you live where fog rolls in on summer afternoons, any place in your garden will supply these conditions. Where summers are warm, windy, dry, or sunny, seek or create favorable exposure protected from wind and in morning sun or all-day dappled shade—in short, a place where you, yourself, are comfortable on hot summer afternoons.

For containers or planting beds, soil mix should be porous (for aeration), water-retentive, and rich in organic matter.

Watering. Water as often as you can. It's almost impossible to give thriving fuchsias in well-drained containers too much water. Hanging basket fuchsias need more watering than any other form. Fuchsias in ground can go longer between watering if drainage is good. In hot-summer climates, heavy mulching (1½–3 in. deep) helps maintain soil moisture. Frequent overhead sprinkling is beneficial in several ways: keeps leaves clean, discourages pests, counteracts low humidity (especially important on windy days in inland climates). When foliage wilts in extreme heat regardless of watering, mist to cool it down.

Feeding. Apply complete fertilizer frequently. Light doses every 10 days–2 weeks, or label-recommended feedings every month, will keep plants growing and producing flowers. You can almost see fertilizer take effect. Liquid fertilizers work well.

Grow from cuttings. You can take cuttings of favorite variety and grow them into flowering plants in a few months, or—at longest—in a year. Just cut 2–3-in. stem pieces (tips preferred) and put lower halves in damp sand to root.

Summer pruning and pinching. If plant is growing leggier than you'd like, pinch out tips of branches whenever you can. Pinching forces growth into side branches, makes plant bushier. Pick off old flowers as they start to fade.

Spraying. Common pests in California are spider mites and whiteflies. If not controlled they cause leaves to yellow and drop. Frequent overhead watering will discourage red spider mites; spray undersides of leaves with miticide to control them. Spray undersides of leaves with resmethrin or orthene at 5–7 day intervals to control whiteflies. Recently in California the fuchsia gall mite has become a serious pest, causing distortion of leaves and shoots. Cut off and destroy distorted tissue. Spray plants early in season with carbaryl (sevin) or thiodan; repeat in 2 weeks. In Northwest, worst pest is aphids. Spray to control, using any good general-purpose insecticide.

Winters in cold climates. Where frosts are light, fuchsias lose their leaves; sometimes tender growth is killed. Where freezes are hard, most plants die back to hard wood, sometimes to roots. A few varieties, including 'Royal Purple', 'Checkerboard', and 'Marinka' stand outdoor exposures in winter in Zones 4–7. Generally, in Northwest, best plan is to protect outdoor fuchsias by mounding 5–6 in. of sawdust over roots (tops will be killed), and to store potted plants in greenhouse or indoors (40°–50°F. ideal) in damp sawdust. Keep soil moist (but not soggy) all winter.

Early spring pruning. Fuchsias everywhere need some pruning in early spring. In frost free areas, cut out approximately the volume of growth that formed previous summer—leave about 2 healthy leaf buds on that growth. In mild frost areas, cut out frost-damaged wood and enough more to remove most of last summer's growth. In cold-winter areas, prune lightly (remove leaves and twiggy growth) before storing. In spring, prune out broken branches and cut back into live wood.

F. magellanica. Zones 2–9, 14–24. Makes many arching, 3-ft.-long stems loaded with drooping, 1½-in.-long red and violet flowers, July to frost. Flowers frequented by hummingbirds. Leaves are oval, in groups of 2 or 3, ½–1 in. long. Where winters are mild, can reach 20 ft. trained against wall. Treat as perennial in cold-climate areas. Roots hardy with mulching; tops die back with first hard frost.

F. procumbens. Zones 16, 17, 21–24. Prostrate, spreading fuchsia to 1 ft. high for containers, shady rock gardens. Leaves ½ in. long. Tiny flowers without petals in summer. Sepals pale orange with purple tips and marked green; anthers and pollen blue. Red berries, ¾ in. long, are showy.

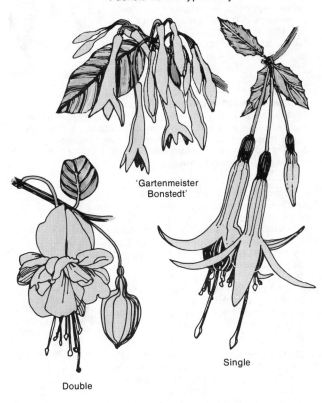

Fuchsia flower types vary.

'Gartenmeister Bonstedt'

Single

Double

FUCHSIA EUCALYPTUS. See *Eucalyptus forrestiana.*

FUNKIA. See *Hosta.*

GAILLARDIA. Perennials and annuals. All Zones. Native to central and western U.S. Low-growing, sun-loving plants with daisylike flowers in warm colors—yellow, bronze, scarlet. They thrive in sun and heat, will take some drought, need good drainage. Easy from seed and fine for cutting and borders. Often reseed.

Gaillardia grandiflora

G. grandiflora. BLANKET FLOWER. Perennial. To 2–4 ft. high. Developed from native species *G. aristata* and *G. pulchella.* Flower heads 3–4 in. across with much variation in color. They are single or double in warm shades of red and yellow with orange or maroon bands. Bloom June until frost.

They flower first year from seed. Foliage roughish, gray green. Many strains and varieties are obtainable, including dwarf and extra-large flowered kinds. 'Goblin' is especially good compact variety, 12 in. tall with large, deep red flowers bordered with bright yellow.

G. pulchella. Annual. Easy to grow. To 1½–2 ft. high. Flower heads 2 in. wide on long whiplike stems in summer. Warm shades of red, yellow, gold. Leaves soft, hairy. Plant seeds in warm soil after frost danger past.

G. p. 'Lorenziana'. Has no ray flowers (petals); instead, disk flowers are enlarged into little star-tipped bells, whole effect like balls of bright fluff. Double Gaiety strain (18 in.) has flowers that range from near-white to maroon, often with bicolors. Lollipop strain is similar, but 10–12 in. tall.

GALANTHUS. SNOWDROP. Bulbs. Zones 1–9, 14–17. Best adapted to cold climates. Closely related to, often confused with, snowflake *(Leucojum)*. White, nodding, bell shaped flowers (1 per stalk) with green tips on inner segments; larger outer segments pure white; 2–3 basal leaves. Sun or part shade. Use in rock garden, under flowering shrubs, naturalize in woodland, or grow in pots. Plant in fall, 3–4 in. deep, 2–3 in. apart, in moist soil with ample humus. Do not divide often; when needed, divide right after bloom; do not allow to dry out.

Galanthus nivalis

G. elwesii. GIANT SNOWDROP. Globular bells, 1½ in. long on 12-in. stems; 2–3 leaves, 8 in. long, ¾ in. wide. January-February bloom in mild areas (where better adapted than *G. nivalis*); March-April in cold climates.

G. nivalis. COMMON SNOWDROP. Dainty 1-in.-long bells on 6–9-in. stems in earliest spring.

GALAX urceolata *(G. aphylla).* Perennial. Zones 1–6. Often used as ground cover, although it spreads slowly. Must have medium to full shade, acid soil with much organic material, and preferably mulch of leaf mold. Regular water essential. Space plants 12 in. apart. Small white flowers on 2½-ft. stems in July. Leaves, in basal tufts, give plant its real distinction. They are shiny, heart shaped, 5 in. across; turn beautiful bronze color in fall. Leaves much used in indoor arrangements.

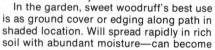
Galax urceolata

GALIUM odoratum *(Asperula odorata).* SWEET WOODRUFF. Perennial. Zones 1–6, 15–17. Attractive, low-spreading perennial that is reminiscent of deep-shaded woods. Slender, square stems 6–12 in. high, encircled every inch or so by whorls of 6–8 aromatic, bristle-tipped leaves. Clusters of tiny white flowers show above foilage in late sping and summer. Leaves and stems give off fragrant, haylike odor when dried; used to make May wine.

Galium odoratum

In the garden, sweet woodruff's best use is as ground cover or edging along path in shaded location. Will spread rapidly in rich soil with abundant moisture—can become pest if allowed to go too rampant. Self-sows freely. Can be increased by division in fall or spring.

GALTONIA candicans. SUMMER HYACINTH. Bulb. Zones 8–24. Native to South Africa. Straplike leaves, 2–3 ft. long; stout 2–4-ft. stems topped in summer with loose, spikelike clusters of drooping, funnel shaped, 1–1½-in.-long, fragrant white flowers with 3 outer segments often tipped green. Best in moderate shade with some summer irrigation. Plant behind low bushy plants. Plant 6 in. deep in rich soil in fall. Don't disturb bulbs for many years. Where ground freezes, plant in spring; mulch deeply during winter or lift bulbs after foliage dies; store at 55°–60°F. Bait for slugs and snails.

Galtonia candicans

GALVEZIA speciosa. ISLAND BUSH-SNAPDRAGON. Evergreen shrub. Zones 14–24. Native to Santa Catalina, San Clemente, Guadalupe Islands. Usually 3–5 ft. across, slightly less in height, but can climb or lean on other shrubs and reach 8

Galvezia speciosa

ft. Leaves about 1 in. long, half as wide. Flowers scarlet, tubular, 1 in. long, clustering toward tips of branches. Bloom heaviest in midspring, but intermittent throughout year. Withstands drought once established, endures light or heavy soils if drainage is adequate. Sun near coast, light shade in interior. Little summer water once well-rooted.

Galvezia speciosa

GAMOLEPIS chrysanthemoides. Evergreen shrub. Zones 8, 9, 13–24. From South Africa. Very fast growing plant to 4–6 ft. high, spreading 4–8 ft. Produces bright yellow daisylike flowers, to 1½ in. wide, almost continuously, but most heavily in spring, fall. Blooms even through frost. Quite resistant to heat and cold. Reseeds itself. Bright green leaves, 3 in. long, deeply toothed at edges. Drought tolerant but looks best when watered during dry season. Tends to untidy ranginess if not pinched or pruned regularly. Has been used as clipped hedge. Best in full sun. Not fussy about soil conditions.

Gamolepis chrysanthemoides

GARDENIA. Evergreen shrubs. White, highly fragrant flowers.

G. jasminoides. Zones 7–9, 12–16, 18–23. Native to China. Glossy bright green leaves and double, white, highly fragrant flowers. Vigorous when conditions are right: plants need ample warmth, ample water, and steady feeding. Though hardy to 20°F. or even lower, plants fail to grow and bloom well without summer heat; are hard to grow in adobe soils. Take full sun in coastal valleys; best with filtered shade in hot inland valleys; give north or east exposure in desert.

Gardenia jasminoides

Soil should drain fast but retain water, too; use plenty of peat moss or ground bark in conditioning soil. Plant high (like azaleas and rhododendrons) and avoid crowding by other plants and competing roots. Mulch plants instead of cultivating. Syringe plants in early morning except when in bloom—unless water is high in salts (residue from this water may burn leaves). Keep soil moist; where water is poor, leach salts by monthly flooding. Feed every 3–4 weeks during growing season with acid plant food, fish emulsion, or blood meal. Treat chlorosis with iron sulfate or iron chelate. Prune to remove scraggly branches, faded flowers. Use all-purpose spray or dust to control aphids, other sucking insects.

All are useful in containers, raised beds, as hedges, espaliers, low screens, or as single plants. Here are named varieties:

'August Beauty'. Grows 4–6 ft. high and blooms heavily, May-October or November. Large double flowers.

'Golden Magic'. Plants reach 3 ft. tall, 2 ft. wide in 2–3 years; eventually larger. Extra-full flowers open white, gradually age to deep golden yellow. April-September bloom, peaking in May.

'Mystery'. Best known variety, has 4–5-in. double white flowers, May-July. Tends to be rangy. Needs pruning to keep it neat. In warm southwestern gardens may bloom through November. Can reach 6–8 ft.

'Radicans'. Grows 6–12 in. high and spreads to 2–3 ft. Small dark green leaves often streaked with white. Summer flowers only 1 in. wide, but with gardenia form and fragrance. Good small-scale ground cover, container plant.

'Veitchii'. Compact 3–4½-ft. plant with many 1–1½-in. blooms May-November, sometimes even during warm winter. Prolific bloom, reliable grower.

'Veitchii Improved'. Taller (to 5 ft.) and produces larger number of slightly larger blooms.

G. thunbergia. Zones 16, 17, 21–24. Native to South Africa.

Angular-branched shrub to 10 ft. tall, 20 ft. wide. Leaves to 6 in. long, nearly black green. Winter flowers long tubed, single, 3–4 in. across. Very fragrant. Seems somewhat more tolerant of cool conditions and less than perfect soil than common gardenia, but tender to frost. With age, becomes more vigorous, flowers more profusely.

GARLAND FLOWER. See *Hedychium coronarium*.

GARLIC. For ornamental varieties see *Allium*. Perennial. Seed stores and some mail order seed houses sell mother bulbs ("sets") for planting. In mild-winter areas, plant October-December for early summer harvest. Where winters are cold, plant early in spring. Break bulbs up into cloves and plant base downward, 1–2 in. deep, 2–3 in. apart, in rows 12 in. apart. Harvest when leafy tops fall over; air-dry bulbs, remove tops and roots, and store in cool place. Giant garlic or elephant garlic has unusually large (fist-sized) bulbs and mild garlic flavor. Same culture as regular garlic.

Garlic

GARLIC CHIVES. See *Allium tuberosum*.

GARRYA. SILKTASSEL. Evergreen shrubs. Pendulous male and female catkins on separate shrubs; male catkins are exceptionally long, slender, and decorative. Both plants must be present to produce grapelike clusters of purple fruit on female plant.

Garrya elliptica

G. elliptica. COAST SILKTASSEL. Zones 5–9, 14–21. Native to Coast Ranges from southern Oregon to San Luis Obispo County, California. Shrub to 4-8 ft., or small tree, 20–30 ft. Elliptical leaves to 2½ in. long, dark green above, gray and woolly beneath, with wavy edges, densely clothe branches. Flower tassels December-February in clusters. Yellowish to greenish yellow male catkins are slender and graceful, 3–8 in. long. Pale green, rather stubby female catkins 2–3½ in. long. Female plants have clusters of purplish fruit which hang on June-September or even longer if robins don't eat it.

Excellent foliage plant for sun or part shade. Will take summer water and thrives near coast or inland as screen, informal hedge, or as display shrub.

Male variety 'James Roof' was selected for its unusually long catkins.

G. fremontii. FREMONT SILKTASSEL. Zones 4–9, 14–17. Native to Cascade Mountains, Sierra Nevada, California Coast Ranges. Differs from above in its glossy, lively yellow green leaves that are not gray and woolly beneath and have smooth edges. Catkins yellowish or purplish. Fruit purple or black. Grows 4–8 ft. high. Does best in full sun. Tolerates drought, heat, cold better than *G. elliptica*. Gets rangy in dense shade.

GAS PLANT. See *Dictamnus albus*.

GAULTHERIA. Evergreen shrubs or shrublets. Zones 4–7, 14–17 except as noted. All have urn shaped flowers and berrylike fruit. They need woodland soil and partial shade (except for native *G. shallon*). Require routine watering through dry season, tolerate wet soil. Smaller kinds are favored for rock gardens, woodland plantings in Northwest. Larger kinds are good companions for other acid-soil shrubs such as rhododendrons and azaleas.

G. cuneata. Compact shrub, 1–1½ ft. tall.

Gaultheria shallon

Leaves are ½–1 in. long, half as wide, glossy dark green, on reddish brown branches. Short clusters of white flowers in summer. White fruit, ⅜ in. wide.

G. ovatifolia. Native to mountains northern California to British Columbia, east to northern Idaho. Spreading, trailing, with upright branches to about 8 in. high. Oval, leathery dark green leaves, ¾–1½ in. long, nearly as wide. Tiny white to pinkish flowers in summer. Bright red berries ¼ in. wide in fall and winter are edible, wintergreen flavored, much liked by birds. Small-scale ground cover in woodland.

G. procumbens. WINTERGREEN, CHECKERBERRY, TEABERRY. Zones 2–7, 14–17. Native to eastern U.S. Creeping stems, upright branches to 6 in. with 2-in. oval, glossy leaves clustered toward tips. Small white summer flowers followed by scarlet berries. Leaves and fruit have flavor of wintergreen (or teaberry). Use as ground cover; plant 12 in. apart.

G. shallon. SALAL. Native Santa Barbara County, California to British Columbia. In full sun and poor, dry soil, a tufted plant 1–2 ft. tall. In shade and good soil can reach 4–10 ft. Nearly round, glossy bright green leaves 1¾–4 in. long. White or pinkish bell-like flowers on reddish stalks in loose, 6-in.-long clusters. Blooms March-June. Edible black fruit resemble large huckleberries but are bland in flavor. Birds like them.

In sun, good low bank cover. In shade and acid soil, good companion for rhododendrons, azaleas, ferns. Only neglected plantings need pruning; cut back in April, remove dead wood, and mulch with leaf mold or peat moss. Cut branches sold by florists as "lemon leaves."

GAURA lindheimeri. GAURA. Perennial. All Zones. Native to Southwest. Grows 2¼–4 ft. high. Leaves stalkless, growing directly on stem, 1½–3½ in. long. Branching flower spikes with 1-in.-long white blossoms opening from many pink buds closely set on stem. Long blooming period, with only a few blossoms opening at one time. Blossoms drop off cleanly when spent, but seed-bearing spikes should be cut to improve appearance and prevent too enthusiastic self-sowing. Plant in full sun. Can take neglect. Fairly drought tolerant. One of few long-lived perennials in southwestern gardens.

Gaura lindheimeri

GAYFEATHER. See *Liatris*.

GAZANIA. Perennials. Zones 8–24. Summer annuals anywhere. Native to South Africa. Daisy flowers give dazzling color display during peak of bloom in late spring, early summer. In mild areas they continue to bloom intermittently throughout year. Gazanias grow well in almost any soil. Once plants are established, water them about twice a month, more often in Zones 10–13. Feed once in spring with slow-acting fertilizer. Divide plants about every 3–4 years. In cold areas, carry gazanias through winter by taking cuttings in fall as you would pelargoniums.

Gazania 'Copper King'

There are basically two types—clumping and trailing.

Clumping kind (complex hybrids between a number of species) forms mounding plant of evergreen leaves. Leaves are often lobed, dark green above, gray-woolly beneath. Daily flowers, on 6–10-in.-long stems, are 3–4 in. wide. You can buy them in single colors, often marked with dark centers—yellow, orange, white, or rosy pink with reddish purple undersides. Or you can get mixture of hybrids in different colors—as plants or seeds.

Colorama strain (seeds) comes in white, yellow, gold, cream, yellow orange, red yellow, and pink. Fire Emerald strain (seeds) includes bronzy reds, lavender pinks, pure pinks, rose, orange, yellow, and cream, all usually with green center ring. Sunshine strain has 5-in. flowers that often show as many as 5 colors in each bloom.

Named hybrids of special merit are 'Aztec Queen' (multi-colored), 'Burgundy', 'Copper King', and 'Fiesta Red'; these are best used in small-scale plantings, although the last is sturdy enough for large expanses. 'Moonglow' is double-flowered bright yellow of unusual vigor; its flowers, unlike most, stay open even on dull days.

Clumping gazanias serve well as temporary fillers between young growing shrubs and as replaceable ground cover for relatively level areas that aren't subject to severe erosion. Try them in parking strips or as edgings along sunny paths. They also do well in containers or rock gardens. They can be fire retardant if reasonably well-watered.

Trailing gazania (*G. rigens leucolaena*, formerly sold as *G. uniflora* or *G. leucolaena*) grows about as tall as clumping kinds, but spreads rapidly by long trailing stems. Foliage is clean silvery gray; flowers yellow, white, orange, or bronze. New, larger flowered hybrids are 'Sunburst' (orange, black eye), and 'Sunglow' (yellow). 'Sunrise Yellow' has large, yellow, black-eyed flowers and green instead of gray foliage. New hybrids excel older kinds in length of bloom, resistance to dieback. Trailing gazania is useful on banks, level ground. Or grow it at top of wall and allow it to trail over. Attractive in hanging baskets.

GEIJERA parviflora. AUSTRALIAN WILLOW, WILGA. Evergreen tree. Zones 8, 9, 13–24. Graceful, fine-textured, to 25–30 ft. high, 20 ft. wide. Main branches sweep up and out, little branches hang down. Distant citrus relative, called Australian willow because its 3–6-in. long, narrow, medium green, drooping leaves give something of effect of weeping willow. With age, produces loose clusters of small, unimportant, creamy white flowers early spring, early fall. Well-drained soil and full sun; plant tolerates light shade but tends to be thin in foliage. Established tree resists drought but responds to ample water with faster growth. Needs pruning only to correct form (much less pruning than willow). Quite pest free.

Geijera parviflora

Has much of grace of willow, much of toughness of eucalyptus, moderate growth rate, and deep, noninvasive roots. Casts light shade. Plant singly as patio or street tree, or in colonies for attractive grove effect.

GELSEMIUM sempervirens. CAROLINA JESSAMINE. Evergreen vine. Zones 8–24. Shrubby and twining, moderate growth rate to about 20 ft. Clean pairs of shiny light green 1–4-in.-long leaves on long streamer-like branches make neat but not dense foliage pattern. Full sun. On trellis, vine will cascade and swing in wind; makes delicate green curtain of branches when trained on house. Vine can get top-heavy; if it does, cut it back severely. Fragrant, tubular yellow flowers, 1–1½ in. long, in late winter, early spring. Can be used as ground cover; keep trimmed to 3 ft. high. Moderately drought tolerant; looks best if watered regularly. All parts of plant are poisonous.

Gelsemium sempervirens

GENISTA. BROOM. Usually deciduous shrubs, but green branches give plants evergreen look. Leaves often small and short lived. Flowers yellow (rarely white or pink), sweet pea shaped. Less aggressive than other brooms *(Cytisus, Spartium)*; will not run wild. Smaller kinds attractive in rock gardens, bank plantings. Need sun, good drainage; tolerate rocky or infertile soil, drought, conditions at seashore.

Genista lydia

G. aethnensis. MT. AETNA BROOM. Zones 4–9, 12–22. Slender, nearly leafless green stems grow to 15 ft. high. Fragrant yellow flowers (⅓ in. long) scattered near ends of branches, July-August.

G. canariensis. See *Cytisus canariensis*.

G. fragrans. This white-flowered species is not in nursery trade. Plants sold under this name are *Cytisus racemosus*.

Genista lydia

G. hispanica. SPANISH BROOM. Zones 2–9, 11–22. Mass of spiny stems, with ½-in.-long leaves, to 1–2 ft. high and spreading wide. Golden yellow flowers in clusters at tips of stems, May-June.

G. lydia. (Often sold, erroneously, as *Cytisus lydia*.) Shrublet. Zones 4–6, 14–17. To 2 ft. high, spreading. Good ground cover. Bright yellow flowers in profusion at ends of shoots, June. Sets little seed.

G. monosperma. BRIDAL VEIL BROOM. Zones 16, 17, 22–24. Upright growth to 20 ft. high, 10 ft. wide, with slender, graceful, gray green, almost leafless branches. White, fragrant flowers in late winter and spring.

G. pilosa. Zones 2–9, 11–22. Fairly fast growing prostrate shrub, ultimately to 1–1½ ft. with 7-ft. spread. Intricately branched, gray green twigs. Roundish, ¼–½-in.-long leaves. Yellow flowers, May-June. 'Vancouver Gold' is best selection.

G. racemosa. See *Cytisus racemosus*.

G. sagittalis. Zones 2–9, 11–22. Plants spread along ground. Upright, winged, bright green branchlets appear jointed. Rather rapid grower to 12 in., spreading widely. Makes sheet of golden yellow bloom, late spring and early summer.

GENTIAN. See *Gentiana*.

GENTIANA. GENTIAN. Zones 1–6, 14–17. Perennials. Low, spreading, or upright plants, generally with very blue tubular flowers. Most are hard to grow, but prized by rock garden enthusiasts. Need full sun or light shade, perfect drainage, lime-free soil, ample moisture. If they thrive, they produce some of richest blues in garden.

G. acaulis. Leafy stems to 4 in. tall. Leaves 1 in. long. Rich blue flowers 2 in. long in summer. Grows well; often fails to bloom.

Gentiana acaulis

G. asclepiadea. Upright or arching stems to 1½ ft. Leaves willowlike, 3 in. long. Flowers blue, 1½ in. long, in late summer, fall. Fairly easy in cool border or rock garden.

G. clusii (*G. acaulis clusii*). Similar to *G. acaulis*. Flowers generally somewhat larger.

G. septemfida. Arching or sprawling stems 9–18 in. long. Oval leaves to 1½ in. long. Clusters of blue 2-in. flowers in late summer. Fairly easy.

G. sino-ornata. From 7-in. rosettes of bright green leaves come trailing stems which end in 2-in.-long flowers of brightest blue, early fall. Fairly easy in half shade.

GERANIUM. CRANESBILL. Perennials. Here we consider true geraniums, hardy plants. Botanically, the more common indoor/outdoor plant most people know as geranium is pelargonium. Several true geraniums have handsome, near evergreen leaves, and bloom over long period in summer and fall. Flowers attractive but not as showy as pelargonium "geranium." Borne singly or in clusters of 2 or 3, flowers have 5 overlapping petals, all alike in appearance. (Pelargonium flowers have 5 petals also, but 2 point in one direction, while other 3 point in opposite direction.) Colors include rose, blue, and purple; a few are pure pink or white. Leaves roundish or kidney shaped, lobed or deeply cut. Plants may be upright or trailing. Prefer full sun, but many tolerate light shade. Most need constant moisture for

Geranium pratense

good performance. Good in rock gardens.

G. argenteum. Zones 1–6. To 3–5 in. high. Densely covered with silky silvery hairs. Leaves basal, 5–7 lobed, 1 in. across. Flowers pink with darker veins, 1¼ in. across; notched petals, June-July.

G. dalmaticum. All Zones. Plants 3–6 in. tall, make 18-in.-wide mats in 4 years. Shell pink to white flowers. Leaves ½–¾ in. with roundish shape.

G. endressii. Zones 1–9, 14–24. Bushy, 1–1½ ft. high. Leaves deeply cut in 5 lobes, 2–3 in. across. Flowers rose pink, about 1 in. across; May-November.

G. himalayense *(G. grandiflorum).* All Zones. Wiry branching stems 1–2 ft. high. Leaves roundish, 5 lobed, long stalked, 1¾ in. across. Flowers in clusters, lilac with purple veins, red purple eye, 1½–2 in. across. Blooms all summer.

G. incanum. Zones 14–24. South African trailing ground cover plant 6–10 in. high, spreading. Least hardy of true geraniums. Spreads fast to make wide cushions of finely cut leaves; 1-in.-wide flowers of magenta pink appear spring to fall. Affected by hard frost; evergreen where frosts are light. Cut back every 2–3 years to keep neat.

G. macrorrhizum. All Zones. Plants 8–10 in. tall, spreading by underground roots. Magenta red flowers; 5–7-lobed leaves. Good ground cover plant for small areas.

G. pratense. All Zones. Common border perennial to 3 ft., branched above. Shiny green leaves, deeply 7 lobed, 3–6 in. across. Flowers about 1 in. wide, typically blue, red veined; often vary in color. Blooms June-August.

G. sanguineum. All Zones. Grows 1½ ft. high; trailing stems spread to 2 ft. Leaves roundish, 5–7 lobed, 1–2½ in. across; turn blood red in fall. Flowers deep purple to almost crimson, 1½ in. across. Other forms of limited availability. May-August bloom. White variety, 'Album', is listed. Variety 'Prostratum' *(G. lancastriense),* neater, lower, more compact, has pure pink blooms.

GERBERA jamesonii. TRANSVAAL DAISY. Perennial. Zones 8, 9, 12–24. Survives Zones 4–7 in coldframe with careful mulching, good drainage. House or greenhouse plant elsewhere. Native to South Africa. Most elegant and sophisticated of daisies. Lobed leaves to 10 in. long spring from root crowns which spread slowly to form big clumps. Slender-rayed, 4-in. daisies (one to a stem) rise directly from crowns on 18-in. erect or slightly curving stems. Colors range from cream through yellow to coral, orange, flame, and red. Flowers are first rate for arrangements; cut as soon as fully open and slit an inch at bottom of stem before placing in water. Blooms any time of year with peaks in early summer, late fall.

Gerbera jamesonii

Best in full sun; partial shade in hottest areas. Needs good soil with excellent drainage. Where drainage is poor, grow in raised beds. Plant 2 ft. apart with crowns at least ¼ in. above surface. Protect against snails and slugs. Water deeply and prevent soil from washing over crowns, then allow soil to become nearly dry before watering again. Feed frequently. Keep old leaves picked off. Let plants remain until crowded; divide February-April, leaving 2–3 buds on each division. As house or greenhouse plant, grow in bright light with night temperature of 60°F.

Wild Transvaal daisy was orange red. Plants sold as hybrids are merely seedlings or divisions in mixed colors. Specialists have bred duplex and double strains. Duplex flowers have 2 rows of rays and are often larger (to 5–6 in. across) on taller (2–2½ ft.) stems. In doubles, all flowers are rays and flowers vary widely in form—some flat, some deep, some swirled, some bicolored. Happipot strain has 4-in. flowers on 6-in. stems.

Plant as seedlings from flats, as divisions, clumps, or from cans. To grow your own from seed, sow thinly in sandy, peaty soil at 70°F. Water carefully, and allow 4–6 weeks to sprout. Takes 6–18 months to flower. Seed must be fresh to germinate well; seed specialists can supply fresh seed of single, double, or duplex strains. Doubles come about 60 percent true from seed.

GERMANDER. See *Teucrium.*

GERMAN IVY. See *Senecio mikanioides.*

GERMAN VIOLET. See *Exacum affine.*

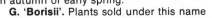

GEUM. Perennials. All Zones. Double, semidouble, or single flowers in bright orange, yellow, and red over long season (May-late summer) if dead blooms are removed. Foliage handsome; leaves divided into many leaflets. Plants evergreen except in coldest winters. Borders, cut flowers.

Grow in sun, or part shade where summers are hot. Ordinary garden soil and irrigation; need good drainage. Grow from seed sown in early spring, or divide plants in autumn or early spring.

Geum quellyon

G. 'Borisii'. Plants sold under this name make 6-in.-high mounds of foliage, foot-high leafy stems with bright orange red flowers. Use in rock garden, front of border. True *G. borisii* has yellow flowers.

G. quellyon. (Often sold as *G. chiloense, G. coccineum*). Foliage mounds to 15 in. Leafy, flowering stems to 2 ft.; flowers about 1½ in. wide. Varieties: 'Fire Opal' with semidouble orange scarlet flowers; 'Lady Stratheden', double yellow; 'Mrs. Bradshaw', double scarlet; 'Princess Juliana', double copper.

GHOST GUM. See *Eucalyptus pauciflora.*

GIANT BAMBURANTA. See *Ctenanthe oppenheimiana.*

GIANT REED. See *Arundo donax.*

GIANT SEQUOIA. See *Sequoiadendron giganteum.*

GILIA. Summer annuals. Western natives related to phlox. Useful and colorful in wild garden or in borders. Sow seed in open ground in early spring. Sun, well-drained soil. Thin plants to avoid crowding.

G. achilleifolia. YARROW GILIA. Plants to 3 ft. tall. Leaves very finely divided. Flowers (May-June) blue violet in dense clusters.

G. aggregata. See *Ipomopsis.*

G. capitata. BLUE THIMBLE FLOWER. Slender plants 8–30 in. tall. Finely cut leaves. Flowers pale blue to violet blue with blue pollen, in dense clusters like pincushions, ½–1½ in. across, June-October.

Gilia capitata

G. micrantha. See *Linanthus.*

G. rubra. See *Ipomopsis.*

G. tricolor. BIRD'S EYES. Branching plant 10–20 in. tall. Finely cut leaves. Flowers ½ in. or more wide, single or in clusters of 2–5, pale to deep violet, with yellow throat spotted purple, blue pollen. June-September.

GINGER. See *Zingiber officinale.*

GINGER LILY. See *Hedychium.*

GINKGO biloba. MAIDENHAIR TREE. Deciduous tree. Zones 1–9, 14–24. Graceful, hardy tree, attractive at any season, especially in fall when leathery, light green leaves of spring and summer suddenly turn gold. Fall leaves linger, then drop quickly and cleanly to make golden carpet where they fall. Related to conifers but differs in having leaves broad and fan shaped (1–4 in. wide) rather than needlelike. Leaf shape and veining resemble leaflets of maidenhair fern, hence

Ginkgo biloba

name. Can grow to 70–80 ft., but most mature trees are 35–50 ft. May be gawky in youth, but becomes well-proportioned with age—narrow to spreading or even umbrella shaped. Usually grows slowly, about 1 ft. a year, but under ideal conditions can grow up to 3 ft. a year.

Ginkgo biloba

Plant only male trees (grafted or grown from cuttings of male plants); female trees produce messy, fleshy, ill-smelling fruit in quantity. Named varieties listed below are reliably male. Use as street tree, lawn tree. Plant in deep, loose, well-drained soil. Be sure plant is not root bound in can. Stake young trees to keep stem straight; young growth may be brittle, but wood becomes strong with age. Water through dry seasons until 10–20 ft. high, then let it become self-sufficient. In general, ginkgos not bothered by insects or diseases. They are resistant to oak root fungus.

G. b. 'Autumn Gold'. Upright, eventually rather broad.

G. b. 'Fairmount'. Fast growing, pyramidal form. Straighter main stem than 'Autumn Gold', requires less staking and tying.

GLADIOLUS. Corms. All Zones. All have sword shaped leaves and tubular flowers, often flaring or ruffled, in simple or branching, usually one-sided spikes. Extremely wide color range. Bloom from spring to fall, depending on kind and time of planting. Superb cut flowers; also use in borders, beds behind mounding plants that cover lower parts of stems; or grow in large containers with low annuals at base. Plant in sun in rich, sandy soil.

Gladiolus hybrid

G. callianthus *(Acidanthera bicolor).* Grows 2–3 ft. tall, with 2–10 fragrant, creamy white flowers marked chocolate brown on lower segments. Flowers 2–3 in. wide, 4–5 in. long. Variety 'Murielae' is taller with purple crimson blotches. Both are excellent cut flowers. Same culture as garden gladiolus.

G. colvillei. BABY GLADIOLUS. Red and yellow hybrid, notable as ancestor of hybrid race called baby gladiolus. Latter have flaring 2½–3¼-in. flowers in short, loose spikes on 18-in. stems. Flowers white, pink, red, or lilac, solid or blotched with contrasting color. Plant 4 in. deep, October-November for May-June bloom in mild-winter areas (June-July in Northwest).

Gladiolus callianthus

G. hortulanus. GARDEN GLADIOLUS. Commonly grown garden gladiolus are complex group of hybrids derived by variation and hybridization from several species. Best-known gladiolus, with widest color range—white, cream, buff, yellow, orange, apricot, salmon, red shades, rose, lavender, purple, smoky shades and, more recently, green shades. Individual blooms are occasionally as large as 8 in. across, stems 4–6 ft. tall.

Newer varieties of garden gladiolus, up to 5 ft. tall, have sturdier spikes bearing 12–14 open flowers at one time; are better garden plants than older varieties; stand upright without staking. Another group, called miniature gladiolus, grow 3 ft. tall, have spikes of 15–20 flowers 2½–3 in. wide; are useful in gardens and for cutting. All varieties of garden gladiolus combine nicely in borders with delphiniums, Shasta daisies, gypsophila, perennial phlox.

High-crowned corms, 1½–2 in. wide, are more productive than older, larger corms (over 2 in. wide). Plant as early as possible to avoid damage by thrips. In frostless areas along southern California coast, plant nearly all year. Along most of coast, growers plant every 15 days from January-March for succession of bloom. In Zones 12, 13, plant November-February to avoid heat during bloom; plant April-June in Northwest; May-June where winters are severe. Corms bloom 65–100 days after planting.

If soil is poor, mix in complete fertilizer or superphosphate (4 lbs. per 100 sq. ft.) before planting; do not place fertilizer in direct contact with corms. Treat with bulb dust (insecticide-fungicide) before planting. Set corms about 4 times deeper than their height, somewhat less in heavy soils. Space big corms 6 in. apart, smaller ones 4 in. When plants have 5 leaves, apply complete fertilizer 6 in. from plants, water in thoroughly. Water regularly during growth. Control thrips and mites as necessary.

Cut flower spikes when lowest buds begin to open; keep at least 4 leaves on plants to build up corms. Dig corms when foliage starts to yellow; cut tops off just above corms. (In rainy areas, growers dig corms while leaves are still green to avoid botrytis infection.) Destroy tops; dry corms in shaded, ventilated area. In about 3 weeks, pull off old corms and roots, dust new corms with diazinon dust, and store at 40°–50°F. in single layers in flats or ventilated trays.

G. primulinus. This 3-ft.-tall African species with hooded primrose yellow flowers is rarely grown, but the name has been applied to its hybrids with other tall and miniature gladiolus. Strain called Butterfly gladiolus also belongs here. Flowers medium sized, frilled, with satiny sheen, vivid markings in throat. Strong, wiry 2-ft stems bear as many as 20 flowers; 6–8 open at one time. Colors include bright and pastel shades and pure white.

G. tristis. Dainty gladiolus with 2½–3-in. flowers on slender 18-in. stems. Blooms creamy to yellowish white, veined purple; fragrant at night. *G. t. concolor* has soft yellow to nearly white flowers. Blooms March and April; hardy except in severe winters. Plant corms October-November.

GLAUCIUM. HORNED POPPY, SEA POPPY. Annuals or perennials. Grow to about 2 ft. with gray green, lobed or finely cut leaves. Individual flowers short-lived, but bloom season continues June-August. Flowers followed by unusually long (to 1 ft.), slender seed capsules. Grow in full sun with other gray plants or with succulents. Fairly drought tolerant.

Glaucium flavum

G. corniculatum. Summer annual. Orange red flowers with dark spot at base.

G. flavum. YELLOW HORNED POPPY. Perennial or biennial. Zones 8–24. Grows as annual elsewhere. Orange to brilliant yellow flowers look as though they were varnished. Cutting back to new basal leaves once a year improves plant.

GLECHOMA hederacea *(Nepeta hederacea).* GROUND IVY. Perennial. All Zones, evergreen where winters seldom dip below 20°F. Trailing plant with neat pairs of round, scalloped, bright green or white-edged leaves 1½ in. across, spaced along stems. Small blue trumpet-shaped flowers in spring and summer not especially showy. Sometimes planted as small-scale ground cover or used to trail from hanging basket. To 3 in. tall with stems trailing to 18 in., rooting at joints. Can become pest in lawns.

Glechoma hederacea

GLEDITSIA triacanthos. HONEY LOCUST. Deciduous tree. Zones 1–16, 18–20. Fast growing with upright trunk, spreading, arching branches. To 35–70 ft. Leaves divided into many oval, ¾–1½-in.-long leaflets. Late to leaf out; leaves turn yellow and drop early in fall. Inconspicuous flowers followed by broad 12–18-in.-long pods filled with sweetish pulp and roundish, hard seeds.

Tolerant of acid or alkaline conditions; hardy to cold, heat, wind, some drought. Seems to do best in districts with sharply defined winters, hot summers. Good desert tree. A pod gall midge deforms leaves in some areas. No effective control.

Gleditsia triacanthos

Good lawn tree. Leafs out late and goes dormant early, giving grass added sunlight in spring and fall. Small leaflets dry up and filter into grass, decreasing raking chores. Stake until good basic branch pattern is established. Not good in narrow area between curb and sidewalk: roots on old plants will heave paving. Don't plant if you need dense shade over long season.

Trunks and branches of species are formidably thorny and pods make mess; several garden varieties of *G. t. inermis* are thornless, have few or no pods.

'Imperial'. Tall, spreading, symmetrical tree to about 35 ft. More densely foliaged than other forms; gives heavier shade.

'Moraine'. MORAINE LOCUST. Best known; fast growing, spreading tree with branches angled upward, then outward. Subject to wind breakage.

'Rubylace'. Deep red new growth. Subject to wind breakage.

'Shademaster'. More upright and faster growing than 'Moraine'—to 24 ft. tall, 16 ft. wide in 6 years.

'Skyline'. Pyramidal and symmetrical.

'Sunburst'. Golden yellow new foliage. Looks unhealthy unless combined with dark green or bronzy foliage. Defoliates easily in response to temperature changes, drought. Wind breakage. Showy against background of deep green foliage.

GLOBE AMARANTH. See *Gomphrena globosa*.

GLOBEFLOWER. See *Trollius*.

GLOBE LILY, WHITE. See *Calochortus albus*.

GLOBE THISTLE. See *Echinops exaltatus*.

GLOBE TULIP, PURPLE. See *Calochortus amoenus*.

GLORIOSA DAISY. See *Rudbeckia hirta*.

GLORIOSA rothschildiana. GLORY LILY, CLIMBING LILY. Outdoors in Zone 24; anywhere as greenhouse or summer container plant. Native to tropical Africa. Climbs to 6 ft. by tendrils on leaf tips. Lance shaped leaves 5–7 in. long. Lilylike flowers 4 in. across with 6 wavy-edged, curved, brilliant red segments banded with yellow. Grow in light shade on terrace, patio; train on trellis or frame.

Set tuberous root horizontally about 4 in. deep in light, spongy soil. Start indoors or in greenhouse in February; set out after frosts. Keep moist; feed with liquid fertilizer every 3 weeks. Dry off gradually in fall; store in pot, or lift tubers and store over winter. May survive outdoors in mild-winter areas, but likely to rot in cold wet soil.

Gloriosa rothschildiana

GLORYBOWER. See *Clerodendrum*.

GLORY LILY. See *Gloriosa rothschildiana*.

GLORY-OF-THE-SNOW. See *Chionodoxa*.

GLORY OF THE SUN. See *Leucocoryne ixioides*.

GLOXINIA. See *Sinningia speciosa*.

GOATNUT. See *Simmondsia chinensis*.

GODETIA. See *Clarkia*.

GOLDBACK FERN. See *Pityrogramma*.

GOLDEN BRODIAEA. See *Triteleia ixioides*.

GOLDEN CANDLE. See *Pachystachys lutea*.

GOLDENCHAIN TREE. See *Laburnum*.

GOLDEN CUP. See *Hunnemannia fumariifolia*.

GOLDEN DEWDROP. See *Duranta repens*.

GOLDEN DROPS. See *Onosma tauricum*.

GOLDEN EARDROPS. See *Dicentra chrysantha*.

GOLDEN FAIRY LANTERN. See *Calochortus amabilis*.

GOLDEN FLEECE. See *Dyssodia tenuiloba*.

GOLDEN FRAGRANCE. See *Pittosporum napaulense*.

GOLDEN GARLIC. See *Allium moly*.

GOLDEN GLOW. See *Rudbeckia laciniata* 'Hortensia'.

GOLDEN HINOKI CYPRESS. See *Chamaecyparis obtusa* 'Aurea'.

GOLDEN LARCH. See *Pseudolarix kaempferi*.

GOLDEN LAWSON CYPRESS. See *Chamaecyparis lawsoniana* 'Lutea'.

GOLDEN MARGUERITE. See *Anthemis tinctoria*.

GOLDEN PYRAMID ARBORVITAE. See *Platycladus orientalis* 'Beverleyensis'.

GOLDENRAIN TREE. See *Koelreuteria paniculata*.

GOLDENROD. See *Solidago*.

GOLDEN TRUMPET TREE. See *Tabebuia chrysotricha*.

GOLDEN WONDER SENNA. See *Cassia splendida*.

GOLDFISH PLANT. See *Alloplectus nummularia*.

GOLD MEDALLION TREE. See *Cassia leptophylla*.

GOMPHRENA globosa. GLOBE AMARANTH. Annual. All Zones. Stiffly branching plants, 1–3 ft. high, cover themselves in summer and fall with rounded, papery, cloverlike flower heads ¾–1 in. wide. These may be pink, purple, violet, or white. They can be dried quickly and easily, retaining color and shape for winter arrangements. Leaves are narrowly oval, 2–4 in. long, somewhat hairy. Dwarf edging varieties are only 9 in. high. 'Buddy' is purple and 'Cissy' white. Plant in full sun, late spring.

Gomphrena globosa

GOOSEBERRY. For ornamental relatives see *Ribes*. Deciduous shrub. Zones 1–6, 17. Same culture as currant. Grown for pies, canning. Lobed, somewhat maplelike leaves. Fruit often striped longitudinally, decorative. Big European dessert gooseberries do not do well in this country.

Gooseberry

(Continued on next page)

'Oregon Champion', 3–5-ft. thorny bush, is the preferred variety; green fruit. 'Pixwell', extremely hardy and with few thorns, has pink fruit. 'Poorman', favorite in Zones 1–3, has red fruit sweet enough to eat off bush. 'Welcome', as hardy as 'Poorman', has medium large, dull red fruit with tart flavor; plants are productive, nearly spineless.

GOOSE PLANT. See *Asclepias fruticosa.*

GOOSE PLUM. See *Prunus americana.*

GOPHER PLANT. See *Euphorbia lathyris.*

GORDONIA alatamaha. See *Franklinia alatamaha.*

GOURD. Summer annual vine. Many plants produce gourds; most commonly planted are the following: 1) *Cucurbita pepo ovifera,* YELLOW-FLOWERED GOURD. Produces great majority of small ornamental gourds, in many shapes and sizes. These may be all one color or striped; 2) *Luffa aegyptiaca,* DISH CLOTH GOURD, VEGETABLE SPONGE GOURD. Also has yellow flowers. Bears cylindrical gourds 1–2 ft. long, fibrous interior of which may be used in place of sponge or cloth for scrubbing and bathing; 3) *Lagenaria siceraria (L. vulgaris),* WHITE-FLOWERED GOURD. Bears gourds 3 in.–3 ft. long. May be round, bottle shaped, dumbbell shaped, crooknecked, coiled, or spoon shaped.

Gourd

All grow fast and will reach 10–15 ft. Sow seeds when ground is warm, in full sun. Start indoors if growing season is short. Gourds need all the summer heat they can get to develop fruit by frost. If planting for ornamental gourd harvest, give vines wire or trellis support to hold ripening individual fruit off ground. Plant seedlings 2 ft. apart or thin seedlings to same spacing. Give deep regular watering. Harvest when vines are dry. Cut some stem with each gourd so you can hang it up to dry slowly in cool, airy spot. When thoroughly dry, preserve with coating of paste wax, lacquer, or shellac.

GOUTWEED. See *Aegopodium podagraria.*

GRAMA GRASS. See *Bouteloua gracilis.*

GRANJENO. See *Celtis pallida.*

GRAPE. For ornamental fruit, wine, shade. Deciduous vine. All Zones (but see limitations in chart). Single grapevine can produce enough new growth every year to arch a walk, roof an arbor, form leafy wall, or put umbrella of shade over deck or terrace. Grape is one of few ornamental vines with dominant trunk and branch pattern for winter interest, bold-textured foliage, and colorful fruit.

To get quality fruit you must choose variety that fits your climate, train it carefully, and prune it regularly.

Two basic classes are: European *(Vitis vinifera)*—tight skin, winelike flavor, generally high heat requirements, cold tolerance

Grape

(Continued on page 314)

Grape

VARIETY	ZONES	SEASON	PRUNING	REMARKS
AMERICAN & AMERICAN HYBRID VARIETIES				
'Agawam'	2,3,7	Midseason to late.	Cane.	Pinkish red, aromatic, slightly foxy. Keeps well after picking. Some winter injury in coldest areas.
'Caco'	1–3,7	Midseason to late.	Cane.	Light red berries. Aromatic and vinous in flavor. Thick skinned. Good for arbors. Hardy, thrifty.
'Campbell Early' ('Island Belle')	2–7,17	Early.	Cane.	Dark purplish black with heavy bloom. High quality. Lacks foxy taste. Vine moderately vigorous. Excellent Concord type where too cool for 'Concord'.
'Catawba'	3,14–16, 19–21	Late.	Cane.	Medium-sized round, dull purplish red berries with distinctive flavor. Flavor both vinous and slightly foxy, aromatic.
'Concord'	1–3, 6–9, 14–16, 18–21	Midseason. Late in Northwest.	Cane.	Standard American slipskin. California's hot dry summer areas are not to its liking. Fruit inferior to Northwest grown.
'Concord Seedless'	1–3, 6–9	Midseason to late.	Cane.	Smaller berries than 'Concord', not so vigorous a vine.
'Delaware' (American hybrid)	3, 5–7	Early midseason.	Cane.	Small, round, light red berries with lilac bloom. Aromatic, vinous in flavor.
'Diamond' ('White Diamond')	3, 5–7, 17	Early midseason.	Cane.	Round, medium-sized, yellowish green berries of high quality. Slightly aromatic. Pleasantly tart. Vine fairly vigorous, very productive.
'Fredonia'	1–7, 17	Early.	Cane.	Large black berries with thick tough skin. Similar to 'Concord' but larger. Vigorous vine, clean foliage. Excellent for arbors.
'Golden Muscat' (American hybrid)	1–3, 6–9, 11–24	Early midseason.	Cane.	Golden green, with slipskin of American grapes but with Muscat flavor. Hybrid of 'Muscat' and green American grape, 'Diamond'. Vigorous.
'Himrod' ('Himrod Seedless') (American hybrid)	1–3, 5–7	Very early.	Cane.	Resembles 'Interlaken Seedless'.
'Interlaken Seedless' (American hybrid)	1–3, 5–7	Very early.	Cane.	Small, sweet, crisp, firm, greenish white berries. Tight skinned. Excellent flavor. Vine moderately vigorous, productive.

VARIETY	ZONES	SEASON	PRUNING	REMARKS
AMERICAN & AMERICAN HYBRID VARIETIES *(Continued from previous page)*				
'Lucile'	1–3, 6–7	Midseason.	Cane.	Small, light red berries similar to 'Caco' but thin skinned. Vine strong growing, productive.
'Moore Early'	1–3, 6–7	Early.	Cane.	Medium clusters of large berries.
'Niabell'	7–9, 14–16, 18–22	Early.	Spur or cane.	Large black berries similar to 'Concord' at its best. Excellent arbor grape. Vigorous and productive in wide range of climates. Succeeds in hot interiors where 'Concord' fails.
'Niagara'	3, 6–7	Midseason.	Cane.	Large, full clusters of medium to large green gold berries. Sweet and juicy with strong foxy flavor. Attractive vigorous vine, excellent for arbors.
'Pierce'	7–9, 14–16, 18–21	Midseason.	Cane.	Called 'California Concord'. Berries larger, vine more vigorous than 'Concord'. Stands high heat better than 'Concord'.
'Romulus' (American hybrid)	3, 6–7	Late midseason.	Cane.	Yellow seedless berries similar to 'Interlaken' but 2 weeks later. Moderate vigor but productive.
'Schuyler' (American hybrid)	3, 5–7	Early.	Spur or cane.	Medium-sized blue berries in large clusters. Very sweet and juicy. Vigorous and productive.
'Seneca'	1–7, 17	Very early.	Cane.	Sweet, aromatic, high quality white berries. Skin thin and tender, adhering to pulp. Bunches sometimes loose; not heavy yielder.
'Van Buren'	1–3, 6–7	Very early.	Cane.	Earliest of good-flavored 'Concord' type.
'Worden'	1–3, 6–7	Midseason.	Cane.	Large, round, purplish black to black berries of high Concord quality. Fairly productive; 2 weeks earlier than 'Concord'.
EUROPEAN VARIETIES				
'Black Monukka'	3, 7–9, 11–18, 18–21	Early midseason.	Cane or spur.	Medium-sized reddish black seedless berries in large loose clusters. Popular home variety. One of hardiest European grapes.
'Blackrose'	8, 9, 11–16, 18–20	Early midseason.	Cane or spur.	Beautiful black grapes, larger and more flavorful than 'Ribier'.
'Cardinal'	8, 9, 11–16, 18–21	Early.	Spur, short cane.	Large, deep red, firm, crisp. Slight Muscat flavor when fully ripe. Heavy bearer. Thin some flower clusters off when shoots are 12–18 in. long.
'Csaba' ('Pearl of Csaba')	3, 6	Very early.	Spur.	Small to medium, yellowish white, moderately firm, some Muscat flavor. One of hardiest European types. Grown in central Washington.
'Emperor'	8, 9, 18, 19	Late.	Cane or spur.	Large, reddish, very firm, crisp and crunchy. Neutral flavor.
'Exotic'	8, 9, 13–16, 18–20	Early midseason.	Spur.	Large round black berries resemble 'Ribier'.
'Italia' ('Italian Muscat')	8, 9, 11–14, 18–20	Midseason.	Spur.	Large amber yellow berries. Crisp, with sweet Muscat flavor, tender skin.
'Lady Finger'	Two grapes with long slender berries are sold under this name. See 'Olivette Blanche', 'Rish Baba'.			
'Malaga, Red'	8, 9, 11–14, 18–19	Early midseason.	Spur or cane.	Pink to reddish purple, firm, crisp, neutral flavor. Large irregular clusters. Good arbor grape.
'Malaga, White'	8, 9, 11–14, 18–19	Midseason.	Spur or cane.	Large, yellowish green; thick, tough skins. Flesh rather soft. Sweeter, more bland than 'Thompson Seedless'.
'Muscat' ('Muscat of Alexandria')	8, 9, 11–14, 18–19	Late midseason.	Spur.	Large, green to amber, round berries in loose clusters. Strongly aromatic. Renowned for its sweet, musky, aged-in-the-vat flavor.
'Olivette Blanche' ('Lady Finger')	8, 9, 11–14, 18–20	Late midseason.	Cane.	Berries long, slender, but broader, deeper green than those of 'Rish Baba'. Sometimes pink blushed. Clusters large, tight, conical. More widely grown than 'Rish Baba'.
'Perlette'	3, 7–10, 11–16, 18–21	Early.	Spur.	Earlier, larger, less sweet than 'Thompson Seedless'. Needs far less heat than most European varieties.
'Ribier'	7–9, 11–16, 18–21	Early midseason.	Spur.	Huge, black, round berries in loose clusters. Sweet and juicy but insipid. Fruit lasts well on vines. Not as flavorful as 'Blackrose'.
'Rish Baba' ('Lady Finger')	8, 9, 11–14, 18–20	Late midseason.	Cane.	Long, slender, greenish white berries sometimes slightly curved. Skins tender, brittle. Clusters slender, open.
'Ruby Seedless' ('King's Ruby')	8, 9, 13–16, 18–20	Late midseason.	Spur or cane.	Large clusters of small to medium red to reddish black seedless berries. Sweet, crisp as dessert fruit; make good raisins.
'Thompson Seedless'	8, 9, 11–14, 18, 19	Early to midseason.	Cane.	Small, sweet, mild flavored, greenish amber in big bunches. Widely planted but top quality in warm interior areas only.
'Tokay'	8, 9, 14–16, 18–20	Late midseason.	Spur.	Brilliant red to dark red. Crackling crisp with distinctive winy flavor. Reaches perfection where summer heat is high but not excessive—Zone 14.

Grape Pruning

1. December–March. Dig deep hole, plant rooted cutting from nursery, leave only top bud exposed. Set stake for training. Mound soil over bud. Object is to secure deep rooting from every bud.

2. First year: Let vine sprawl, develop as many leaves as possible to manufacture food for the developing roots. This growth made by November. Leaves have already fallen.

3. First winter: Prune vine to sturdiest cane; shorten it to 3 lowest buds. If cane is very vigorous, cut it at 2–3 ft., or at a good point for branching to begin for an arbor.

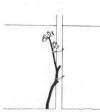

4. Second spring: When new shoots are 6–8 in. long, select 1 vigorous, upright shoot to form permanent trunk. Tie it loosely to the stake. Cut out all other shoots.

5. Second summer: When shoot reaches branching point on arbor, trellis, or fence, pinch out tip. Allow 2 strongest subsequent shoots to develop. Pinch out side shoots at 10 in.

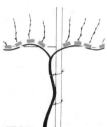

6. Third winter: Cut spindly canes on arms back to old wood. Don't prune yet for fruit production; vines are too immature. For fruit, you would leave 2 buds at the base of each cane.

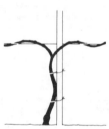

7. Third winter's finished product. On an arbor, arms would stretch out along roof level of structure. Length of arms determines size and permanent framework shape of vine.

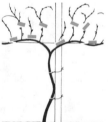

8. Fourth winter: These canes grew previous summer. To prune for fruit, cut out weak or crowding canes. Select sturdy canes 6–10 in. apart, cut each to 2 buds.

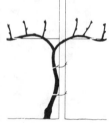

9. Fourth winter's finished product. Each bud will give 2 fruiting canes next summer. Following winter cut 1 out entirely, shorten the other to 2 buds. See Nos. 10, 11.

10. Fifth winter: These canes bore fruit the previous autumn. Cut 1 off at base. Branch at left already pruned. These short, thick branches are called spurs.

11. Fifth winter: Shorten remaining cane to 2 buds. These will give next year's fruiting canes. Pruning in subsequent years is the same. Cut out suckers on trunk and arms.

12. Well-pruned arm in its fifth year should look like this. Fruit spurs spaced approximately 6 in. apart, with 2 buds on each new cane at end of spurs.

to about 5°F.; and American (*V. labrusca*)—slipskin, "foxy" Concord-type flavor, moderate summer heat requirements, cold tolerance well below 0°F. Hybrids between classes are available; most are reasonably hardy, fall between either parent in flavor.

Choosing the right variety is important; varieties differ widely in hardiness and in heat requirements. Northwest is primarily American grape country; long warm-season areas of California, Arizona favor European varieties. Everywhere the short season, high-elevation areas must choose from American grapes.

Ideal climate for most table grapes in California is that of California's Central Valley—a long season of high heat; ideal climate in Northwest is in warmest parts of Columbia Basin. If your climate is cooler, or if growing season is shorter than ideal, look to *early ripening* varieties. Or, create warmer climate by giving vines added heat of south-facing wall.

Mildew is serious disease of European grapes (most American varieties are immune). To control, dust vines with sulfur when shoots are 6 in. long, again when they are 12–15 in., then every 2 weeks until harvest. Vines growing near lawns may need additional dustings.

To control grape leafhopper in California, add diazinon dust to sulfur at time of third sulfur dusting, just before blooming time. In Northwest, dust with diazinon in June and again in August. Grape mealybugs may infest vines in Northwest. Control with dormant oil spray in later winter and with malathion in June.

GRAPEFRUIT. See *Citrus.*

GRAPE HYACINTH. See *Muscari.*

GRAPE IVY. See *Cissus rhombifolia.*

GRAPTOPETALUM. Succulents. Zones 8–24. Native to Mexico. Leaves very thick, in loosely packed, elongated rosettes. Full sun. Needs little water. Good looking in pots or in rock gardens in mildest regions. Leaves have subtle, opalescent blending of colors. Detached leaves root easily.

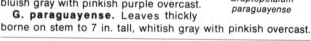

G. amethystinum. Stems to 4 in. tall, eventually leaning or sprawling. Leaves bluish gray with pinkish purple overcast.

Graptopetalum paraguayense

G. paraguayense. Leaves thickly borne on stem to 7 in. tall, whitish gray with pinkish overcast.

GRASSES. The grasses in this book are either lawn or ornamental plants—except for corn, the only cereal commonly grown in home gardens. They are described under entries headed by their botanical names; to find these, check lists below. (Two lawns are not grasses: see *Dichondra* and *Phyla*. All bamboos, which are grasses, are charted under Bamboo.)

Lawn grasses are *Agropyron*, WHEAT GRASS; *Agrostis*, BENT GRASS, RED TOP; *Bouteloua*, BLUE GRAMA; *Buchloe*, BUFFALO GRASS; *Cynodon*, BERMUDA GRASS; *Festuca*, FESCUE; *Lolium*, RYEGRASS; *Poa*, BLUEGRASS; *Stenotaphrum*, ST. AUGUSTINE GRASS; and *Zoysia*, ZOYSIA.

Ornamental grasses are *Arundo*, GIANT REED; *Briza*, RATTLESNAKE GRASS; *Coix*, JOB'S TEARS; *Cortaderia*, PAMPAS GRASS; *Festuca*, FESCUE; and *Pennisetum*, FOUNTAIN GRASS.

GRASS NUT. See *Triteleia laxa.*

GRASS TREE. See *Xanthorrhoea.*

GRECIAN LAUREL. See *Laurus nobilis.*

GREEN CARPET. See *Herniaria glabra.*

GREVILLEA. Evergreen shrubs, trees. Native to Australia. Variable in size and appearance, generally with fine textured foliage. Long, slender, curved flowers appear usually in dense clusters. Full sun.

Grevillea robusta

Once established they take poor, rocky, dry soil, but accept ordinary well-drained garden soil. Most are very drought tolerant. Rarely successful near lawns.

G. 'Aromas'. Shrub. Zones 14–24. Grows 6–8 ft. tall, 8–10 ft. wide. Long arching branches, deep green needlelike foliage. Heavy crop of deep red flowers late winter-spring, casual bloom throughout year. Endures poor soil, much drought, summer watering.

G. banksii. (Often sold as *G. banksii forsteri*.) Shrub or small tree. Zones 20–24. To 15–20 ft. Leaves 4–10 in. long, deeply cut into narrow lobes. Erect 3–6-in.-long clusters of dark red flowers bloom sporadically throughout year, heaviest in late spring. Showy used singly against high wall, near entryway, or grouped with other big-scale shrubs. Freezes at 24°F.; takes wind, drought.

G. 'Canberra'. Shrub. Zones 8–9, 12–24. Open, graceful growth to 8 ft. tall, 12 ft. wide. Bright green, needlelike, 1-in. leaves, clusters of red flowers in spring and intermittently at other times.

G. 'Constance'. Zones 8, 9, 12–24. Resembles 'Canberra' but broader in growth, orange red flowers in large clusters.

G. juniperina (*G. sulphurea*). Shrub. Zones 8, 9, 12–24. To 6 ft., with needlelike, bright green leaves, ½–1 in. long; clusters of pale yellow flowers in May and June.

G. lanigera. WOOLLY GREVILLEA. Shrub. Zones 15–24. Spreading, mounding plant 3–6 ft. tall, 6–10 ft. across. Closely set, narrow, ½-in.-long leaves; general foliage effect gray green. Clusters of narrow, curved, crimson and cream flowers profusely carried in summer; attractive to hummingbirds. Good bank cover in hot sunny areas; good transition between garden and wild areas.

G. 'Noellii'. Shrub. Zones 8, 9, 12–24. Plant sold under this name reported to be a hybrid. Grows to 4 ft. tall, 4–5 ft. wide. Densely foliaged; narrow, 1-in.-long, medium green glossy leaves. Clusters of pink and white flowers 6–8 weeks in early and midspring. Takes more water than *G. lanigera;* less drought resistant.

G. 'Pink Pearl'. Shrub. Zones 8, 9, 12–24. Resembles *G.* 'Canberra' but denser in structure, with darker green foliage, rose pink flowers.

G. robusta. SILK OAK. Tree. Zones 8, 9, 12–24. Fast growing to 50–60 (rarely 100) ft. Symmetrical, pyramidal when young. Old trees broad topped, picturesque against skyline, usually with a few heavy, horizontal limbs. Fernlike leaves are golden green to deep green above, silvery beneath. Heavy leaf fall in spring, sporadic leaf drop throughout year; frequent raking necessary. Large clusters of bright golden orange flowers in early spring; effective with jacaranda or with dark green background foliage.

Grevillea 'Noellii'

Grows in poor, compact soils if not overwatered; takes fair amount of water in fast draining soils. Brittle, easily damaged in high wind. Stake securely. To make sturdier branches, lessen wind damage, cut leading shoot back hard at planting time, shorten branches to well-balanced framework. Thrives in heat. Young trees damaged at 24°F., older plants hardy to 16°F.

Use for quick, tall screening or clip as tall hedge. One of lushest greens for low desert. Fast shade producer, showy tree for unused space far from hose bibb. Good temporary tree while you wait for slower, tougher-wooded tree to grow up.

G. rosmarinifolia. ROSEMARY GREVILLEA. Zones 8, 9, 12–24. Compact shrub to 6 ft. tall, nearly as broad. Narrow, dark green 1½-in.-long leaves (silvery beneath) somewhat like rosemary. Red and cream flower clusters (rarely pink or white) in fall, winter, with scattering at other seasons. Use as clipped or unclipped hedge in dryish places. Impervious to heat and drought.

G. sulphurea. See *G. juniperina*.

G. thelemanniana. HUMMINGBIRD BUSH, SPIDER-NET GREVILLEA. Shrub. Zones 9, 14–17, 19–24. Graceful, rounded, 5–8 ft. tall, equally wide. Dark green leaves 1–2 in. long, divided into very narrow segments. Bright red flower clusters tipped yellow. Can bloom at any season. Water plants until established, then taper off. Somewhat temperamental. Plants airier, more open, less adapted to hedge and screen use than *G. rosmarinifolia*.

G. tridentifera. Shrub. Zones 14–24. To 6 ft. tall and broader, with bright green, 3-pronged needlelike leaves; small white honey-scented flower clusters scattered all along branches. Good bank cover.

GREWIA occidentalis (usually sold as *G. caffra*). LAVENDER STARFLOWER. Evergreen shrub. Zones 8, 9, 14–24. Native to South Africa. Fast-growing, sprawling habit. Tends to branch freely in flat pattern, making natural espalier if given some support. Becomes dense with pinching and pruning. Grows 6–10 ft. tall (sometimes higher), with equal spread if unstaked.

Deep green, oblong, finely toothed leaves 3 in. long. Flowers are 1 in. wide, starlike, lavender pink with yellow centers. Blooms late spring with scattered bloom into autumn, especially if pruned after first heavy bloom.

Grewia occidentalis

Plant against warm, sunny wall or fence. Can be planted 2 ft. apart and used as tall clipped hedge or screen. If upright growth is pruned out, can be used as bank cover. Can be trained and staked to make single-trunked tree or tied in place to cover arbor or trellis. Takes wind well. Needs water, iron if chlorotic. If plants become too large or woody for their situation, cut back hard, keeping a young basal branch or two to grow on for new framework.

GRISELINIA. Evergreen shrubs. Zones 9, 15–17, 20–24. Native to New Zealand. Upright form and thick, leathery, lustrous leaves. Flowers and fruit are insignificant. Always look well groomed. Good near swimming pools.

G. littoralis. A 50-ft. tree in New Zealand, it is usually seen in California as 10-ft.-high shrub of equal spread. Leaves roundish, 4 in. long. In full sun with ample water it can reach 8 ft. in 3 years. Dense, compact screen or windbreak. Fine beach plant. Good espalier. Variety 'Variegata' has leaves marked with cream.

Griselinia littoralis

G. lucida. Slower growing, smaller, more open and slender than *G. littoralis,* with larger, 7-in.-long leaves. Excellent foliage plant for partial shade. Thrives in container. Variety 'Variegata' has white markings on leaves.

GROUND CHERRY. See *Physalis pruinosa*.

GROUND IVY. See *Glechoma hederacea*.

GROUND MORNING GLORY. See *Convolvulus mauritanicus*.

GRU-GRU PALM. See *Acrocomia*.

GUADALUPE PALM. See *Brahea edulis*.

GUATEMALAN HOLLY. See *Olmediella betschlerana*.

GUAVA. See *Psidium*.

GUERNSEY LILY. See *Nerine sarniensis*.

GUINEA GOLD VINE. See *Hibbertia scandens*.

GUM. See *Eucalyptus*.

GUM MYRTLE. See *Angophora costata*.

GUNNERA. Perennials. Zones 4–6, 14–17, 20–24. Big, bold, awesome plants to 8 ft. high with giant leaves 4–8 ft. across. Leaves, on stiff-haired stalks 4–6 ft. long, conspicuously veined, with edges lobed and cut. Given space (they need plenty) and necessary care, they can be the ultimate in summertime conversation pieces. New sets of leaves grow each spring. In mild-winter areas, old leaves remain green for more than one year. Elsewhere leaves die back completely in winter. Corncoblike 18-in. flower clusters down close to roots. Tiny fruit are red.

Gunnera chilensis

Part shade. Soil must be rich in nutrients and organic material, continually moist (but never soggy around root crown). Feed three times a year, beginning when new growth starts, to keep leaves maximum size. Give overhead sprinkling when humidity is low or drying winds occur. Use where can be focal point in summer, as beside pool or dominating bed of low, fine-textured ground cover. Makes confused scene when mixed with other plants of medium to large-sized leaves.

G. chilensis. Most common species. Lobed leaf margins are toothed and somewhat frilled. Leaves held in bowl-like way, half upright and flaring.

G. manicata. Leaves carried fairly horizontally. Spinelike hairs on leaf stalks and ribs are red. Leaf lobes are flatter, lack frills of *G. chilensis.*

GUZMANIA. Bromeliads grown as house plants or as indoor/outdoor plants in mildest coastal gardens. Pot in fast draining organic mixes, give plenty of water, frequent light feeding, and keep out of direct, hot sunlight; most come from damp jungles.

Guzmania monostachia

G. lingulata. Rosettes of glossy green leaves, 12–16 in. long, produce torchlike inflorescences of broad, brightly colored bracts and white flowers. Bracts vary from red (commonest) to orange and yellow.

G. monostachia. Rosettes produce cylindrical spike tightly shingled with short bracts. Lower ones are white striped with dark brown parallel lines; upper are orange to red with white flowers peeping out. Leaves to 16 in. long.

G. sanguinea. Rosettes, 2 ft. wide or more, gradually turn from green to scarlet as plants reach blooming size. Flowers themselves are inconspicuous.

GYMNOCALYCIUM. CHIN CACTUS. Small cactus usually grown as house plants. Plant bodies nearly globular, single or clustered, a few inches thick in most species. Flowers long tubed, showy, opening from smooth buds and lasting several days, in shades of red, pink, white, or (rarely) yellow and chartreuse. Easy to grow in good potting soil with ample water in summer, coolness and dry soil in winter. Dislike scorching sun. Best known of many is *G. mihanovichii,* PLAID CACTUS. Plants are dark green with brown markings; these markings are even stronger in *G. m. friedrichii.* The latter also has forms with pure red or pure yellow bodies known by such names as 'Ruby Ball', 'Red Head', 'Blondie', or, lumped together, as MOON CACTUS.

Gymnocalycium mihanovichii

GYMNOCLADUS dioica. KENTUCKY COFFEE TREE. Deciduous tree. Zones 1–3, 7–10, 12–16, 18–21. Native to eastern U.S. Saplings grow very fast, but slow down at 8–10 ft. Trees ultimately reach 50 ft. Narrowish habit in youth. Older trees broader, with fairly few heavy, contorted branches.

Gymnocladus dioica

These, together with stout winter twigs, make bare tree picturesque. Leaves (1½–3 ft. long, divided into many leaflets 1–3 in. long) come out late in spring; are pinkish when expanding, deep green in summer, yellow in autumn. Inconspicuous flowers followed by 6–10-in.-long flat, reddish brown pods containing hard black seeds. Average garden soil and routine watering. Established trees will take some drought, much heat and cold, poor soil. Effective for form in any cold-winter garden.

Gymnocladus dioica

GYNURA aurantiaca. PURPLE VELVET PLANT. House plant from East Indies grown for its leaves and stems which have plushlike covering of violet hairs. Leaves lance shaped, toothed, to 6 in. long, 2½ in. wide. Plant is somewhat shrubby, may reach 2–3 ft. Yellow to orange ½-in. flowers have unpleasant odor; pinch out flower buds as they form. Needs strong indirect light for best color. Give plant warmth and rich, loose, well-drained soil, average water. 'Purple Passion' or 'Sarmentosa', often sold as *G. sarmentosa,* has narrower leaves with deep lobes and climbing or trailing habit; is often called PURPLE PASSION VINE.

Gynura aurantiaca 'Sarmentosa'

GYPSOPHILA. Annuals and perennials. All Zones in conditions noted below. Much branched, upright or spreading, slender-stemmed plants, 6 in. -4 ft. tall, profusely covered in summer with small, single or double, white, pink, or rose flowers in clusters. Leaves blue green; few when plant is in bloom. Use for airy grace in borders, bouquets; fine contrast with large-flowered, coarse-textured plants. Dwarf kinds ideal in rock gardens, trailing from wall pocket, or over top of dry rock walls.

Gypsophila repens

Full sun. Routine watering. Add lime to strongly acid soils. Thick, deep roots of some perennial kinds difficult to transplant; do not disturb often. Protect roots from gophers, tender top growth from snails, slugs. For repeat bloom on perennial kinds, cut back flowering stems before seed clusters form.

G. elegans. Annual. Upright, 1–1½ ft. Leaves lance shaped, rather fleshy, to 3 in. long. Profuse single white flowers ½ in or more across. Pink and rose forms available. Plants live only 5–6 weeks; for continuous bloom, sow seed in open ground every 3–4 weeks from late spring into summer.

G. paniculata. BABY'S BREATH. Perennial. Zones 1–10, 14–16, 18–21. Much branched to 3 ft. or more. Leaves slender, sharp pointed, 2½–4 in. long. Single white flowers about $\frac{1}{16}$ in. across, hundreds in a spray, July-October. Variety 'Bristol Fairy' is improved form, more billowy, to 4 ft. high, covered with double blossoms ¼ in. wide. Grow from root grafts or stem cuttings.

G. repens. Perennial. Zones 1–11, 14–16, 18–21. Alpine native 6–9 in. high, with trailing stems 18 in. long. Leaves narrow, less than 1 in. long. Clusters of small white or pink flowers in summer. Increase by cuttings in midsummer.

HACKBERRY. See *Celtis.*

HAEMANTHUS katharinae. BLOOD LILY. Bulb. Tender South African plant closely related to amaryllis, grown in pots in greenhouse, as house plant; in mild climates move to terrace or patio for bloom in late spring. Large (4 in. diameter), white bulb stained red (hence common name). Leaves broad, wavy edged, bright green, 12–15 in. long. Sturdy succulent stem 2 ft. tall, topped by large, round clusters of sal-

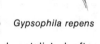

Haemanthus katharinae

mon red flowers; protruding, showy red stamens.

Put 1 bulb in 10-in. pot in rich mix in winter or early spring. Set bulb with tip at soil surface; water sparingly, keep in 70°F. temperature. When leaves appear (8–10 weeks) move outdoors (in frostless sections) to sheltered, lightly shaded spot. Water thoroughly; feed monthly with complete fertilizer; bait for snails. After bloom, gradually reduce watering; dry out plant in cool, protected place. Do not repot next season; add new mix on top, or tip out root ball, scrape off some old soil, replace with fresh.

HAKEA. Evergreen shrubs or trees. Zones 9, 12–17, 19–24. Native to Australia. Tough, drought tolerant, especially good for seacoast. Full sun. Will take poor soil.

H. laurina. SEA URCHIN, PINCUSHION TREE. Small, dense, rounded tree or large shrub, to 30 ft. Narrow, gray green, 6-in.-long leaves are often red margined. Showy flower clusters look like round crimson pincushions stuck with golden pins. Blooms in winter, sometimes in late fall. Stake young trees securely. Good small patio tree.

Hakea laurina

H. saligna. WILLOWLEAF HAKEA. Shrub to 8 ft., rarely treelike, 20 ft. Narrow, gray green leaves up to 6 in. long. Many clusters of small white flowers.

H. suaveolens. SWEET HAKEA. Dense, broad, upright shrub to 10–20 ft. tall. Stiff, dark green, 4-in. leaves, branched into stiff, needlelike, stickery segments. Fragrant small white flowers, in dense fluffy clusters, fall and winter. Useful, fast growing barrier plant, background, or screen. Good with conifers. Can be pruned into tree form.

Other hakeas are offered from time to time by experimental-minded nurserymen. Remarkably diverse in foliage and flower, all are quality shrubs or small trees for difficult sites.

HALESIA. Deciduous trees. Zones 2–9, 14–24. Both kinds give best flower display in areas of winter cold; grow best in cool, deep, humus-rich soil with ample water.

H. carolina (*H. tetraptera*). SNOWDROP TREE, SILVER BELL. Moderate growth to 20–50 ft. with 15–30 ft. spread, depending on climate. Rates high as flowering tree in May when clusters of snowflake white, ½-in., bell shaped flowers hang from graceful branches just as leaves begin to appear. Leaves 4 in. long, oval, finely toothed, turn yellow in fall. Interesting brown fruit with 4 wings hang on most of winter. Prune to single stem when young or it will grow as large shrub. Flowers show off best when you can look up into tree. Attractive as overhead planting for azaleas, rhododendrons.

Halesia carolina

H. monticola. MOUNTAIN SILVER BELL. Larger tree, 40–60 ft., with larger (3–6 in.) leaves.

HALIMIOCISTUS sahucii. Evergreen shrub. Zones 4–24. Hybrid between *Halimium umbellatum* and *Cistus salviifolius*. Combines best characteristics of both parents. Densely foliaged with 1-in., narrow, gray green leaves, it grows to 2 ft. high and spreads to 3 ft. or more. In summer, clusters of white 1–2-in.-wide flowers with center tufts of yellow stamens almost hide foliage. Good choice for sunny rock garden, dry bank, cascading over concrete retaining wall. Or, plant on sunny side of house under wide eaves where rains seldom reach. Will not live in wet soil, and can be watered with other plants only if drainage is excellent.

Halimiocistus sahucii

HALIMIUM. Evergreen shrublets. Zones 7–9, 12–24. Closely related to sunrose (*Helianthemum*) and sometimes sold under that name. Cultural requirements and uses are the same. Halimiums grow 2–3 ft. high, have gray green foliage, yellow flowers in loose clusters in spring.

H. lasianthum (*Helianthemum formosum*). Spreading plant with leaves ½–1½ in. long, ¼ in. wide. Flowers 1½ in. across, bright yellow with brownish purple blotch near base of petals.

Halimium lasianthum

H. ocymoides (*Helianthemum ocymoides*). Erect plant with leaves slightly narrower than above species. Flowers 1 in. wide, bright yellow, with black and purple blotch at base of petals.

H. umbellatum (*Helianthemum umbellatum*). Grows to 18 in. Leaves very narrow, resembling rosemary. Flowers ¾ in. across, white with yellow at base of petals. Flower clusters 4–6 in. long.

HAMAMELIS. WITCH HAZEL. Deciduous trees or large shrubs. Yellow fall foliage. Fragrant yellow flowers with very narrow crumpled-looking petals in nodding few-flowered clusters. Plants grow in sun or light shade and need moderate moisture and some peat moss, ground bark, or leaf mold in soil.

H. intermedia. Zones 4–7, 15–17. Group of hybrids between *H. mollis* and a Japanese witch hazel. Big shrubs—to 15 ft. high, with spreading habit. The following varieties are grown in Zones 4–7: 'Diane', bright red flowers, fine fall color; 'Jelena' (also known as 'Copper Beauty' and 'Orange Beauty'), spreading plant with large leaves, large flowers of yellow heavily

Hamamelis mollis

suffused with red, and orange, red, and scarlet fall foliage color; 'Magic Fire' ('Fire Charm', 'Feuerzauber'), upright plant with coppery orange flowers blended with red; and 'Ruby Glow', erect, with coppery red flowers and fine fall color. Bloom season for all these is same as for *H. mollis.*

H. mollis. CHINESE WITCH HAZEL. Zones 4–7, 15–17. Moderately slow growing shrub to 8–10 ft. or eventually small tree to 30 ft. Branches in loose zigzag pattern. Roundish leaves, 3½–6 in. long, dark green and rough above, gray felted beneath, turn good clear yellow in fall. Fragrant, rich golden yellow flowers, 1½ in. wide, with red brown calyx, bloom on bare stems. December-March. Effective against red brick or gray stone. Flowering branches excellent for flower arrangements.

H. virginiana. COMMON WITCH HAZEL. Zones 1–9, 14–16, 18–21. Native to eastern U.S. Sometimes to 25 ft. but usually 10–15 ft. high, of open, spreading, rather straggling habit. Moderately slow growing. Roundish leaves similar to *H. mollis* but not gray felted beneath; turn yellow to orange in fall. Golden yellow, ¾-in.-wide blooms appear in October, November and tend to be lost in colored foliage.

HARDENBERGIA. Evergreen shrubby vines. Native to Australia. Moderate growing to 10 ft., climbing by twining stems. Pea shaped flowers, several to many in clusters, late winter to early spring. Useful for light, delicate pattern on low walls, fences, screens, arches. Can be pegged down as a ground cover. Need light, well-drained soil in sun (partial shade in hot areas). Do not overwater. Provide support for climbing and cut back after bloom to prevent tangling. Fairly free of pests and diseases; subject to spider mites, nematodes.

H. comptoniana. LILAC VINE. Zones 15–24. Light, delicate foliage pattern; leaves divided into 3–5 dark green, narrow, 2–3-in.-long leaflets. Flowers violet blue, ½

Hardenbergia comptoniana

in. long, in long narrow clusters. Where temperatures drop below 24°F., shelter blossoms, buds, tender tops by planting under overhang.

H. violacea *(H. monophylla).* Zones 9–24. Coarser texture; leaves usually with one 2–4-in.-long leaflet. Vining or shrubby. Flowers lilac, violet to rose or white. 'Happy Wanderer' is a tough, hardy, vigorous selection that takes full sun, wind.

HAREBELL. See *Campanula rotundifolia.*

HARE'S FOOT FERN. See *Polypodium aureum.*

HARPEPHYLLUM caffrum. KAFFIR PLUM. Evergreen tree. Zones 17, 19, 21–24. Fast growth to 30–35 ft. or higher with 20–25-ft. spread. Freezes back in cold weather but makes quick recovery if temperature not below 25°F. (Usually has multiple trunks after such recovery.) Round headed, but easily trained to structurally interesting small tree. Leathery, glossy leaves of 13–15 narrow, 2½-in.-long leaflets. These unfold as rich red but turn to dark green. Clusters of very small white or greenish flowers followed by tart but edible dark red fruit resembling large olives. Fruit drop is problem near paving.

Harpephyllum caffrum

Tolerates considerable wind, heat; requires average water. Prune to shape and to remove frost-damaged wood. Well-groomed appearance and quick growth make it a good shade or decorative tree for the small garden. Striking silhouette against tall, light-colored wall.

HARRY LAUDER'S WALKING STICK. See *Corylus avellana* 'Contorta'.

HART'S TONGUE FERN. See *Phyllitis scolopendrium.*

HAWAIIAN TREE FERN. See *Cibotium glaucum.*

HAWORTHIA. Succulents of lily family. Zones 8, 9, 12–24. Extremely variable in growth habit: best-known ones resemble smaller aloes (closely related), but others make small towers of neatly stacked fleshy leaves, and there are other forms, too. Full sun; very drought tolerant. All make excellent pot plants, best in part shade. Here are 3 of dozens available from specialists.

H. attenuata. Dark green leaves heavily marked with raised white dots, grow in stemless or short-stemmed rosettes to 6 in.

Haworthia fasciata

wide. Spreads to make clumps. Flowers dull pink in 2-ft. clusters.

H. fasciata. Stemless rosettes with many 3-in.-long, narrow dark green leaves, marked strongly by crosswise bands of raised white dots. Flowers greenish white, in 6-in. clusters. Spreads freely by offsets.

H. setata. LACE HAWORTHIA. Small stemless rosettes of many leaves to 1¼ in. long, half as wide. Leaves dark green marked with whitish translucent areas and edged with long, bristly, white teeth that give lacy look.

HAWTHORN. See *Crataegus.*

HAZELNUT. See *Corylus.*

HEART OF FLAME. See *Bromelia balansae.*

HEATH. See *Erica, Daboecia.*

HEATHER. See *Calluna.*

HEAVENLY BAMBOO. See *Nandina domestica.*

HEBE. Evergreen shrubs. Zones 14–24 except as noted. Native to New Zealand. Landscaping plants grown principally for form and foliage; some give good flower display. All do better in cool coastal gardens than in interior where dry summer heat and winter frosts shorten their lives. Lower kinds are useful for edgings or ground cover; taller ones are good shrubs where sea winds and salt air are problem. Most are fast growers.

Hebe buxifolia

Will take full sun on coast; give partial shade in warm valleys. Good drainage is essential, with plenty of moisture. Prune after bloom, shortening flowering branches considerably to keep plants compact. In Southern California, fusarium wilt may cause wilting leaves, death of branches or whole plant. Shop carefully, rejecting plants that look unhealthy. If you suspect disease, avoid ammonium sulfate fertilizer. Don't replant hebes where one has died.

Closely related to *Veronica* and still often sold under that name.

H. andersonii. Hybrid between *H. speciosa* and *H. salicifolia.* Compact, to 5–6 ft. Leaves fleshy, deep green. Summer flowers in 2–4-in. spikes, white at base, violet at tip.

H. 'Autumn Glory'. Zones 5, 6, 14–24. Mounding, compact, 2 ft. high, 2 ft. wide. Oval leaves 1½ in. long. Many 2-in.-long dark lavender blue flower spikes in late summer, fall.

H. buxifolia. BOXLEAF HEBE. Rounded, symmetrical habit eventually 5 ft. tall, easily shaped into 3-ft. hedge. Deep green leaves ⅓ in. long densely crowded on branches. Small white flowers in headlike clusters in summer. One of the kinds most resistant to heat, drought, cold.

H. 'Carnea'. Grows 3–5 ft. tall. Deep green willowlike leaves 2½ in. long. Flowers rosy crimson in 2½-in.-long spikes, August–September.

H. chathamica. Ground cover shrub to 1½ ft. tall, stems trailing to 3 ft. Leaves ½ in. long, deep green. Lavender flowers in summer.

H. 'Coed'. Compact plant to 3 ft. tall, equally broad. Reddish stems densely clothed with 1½-in.-long, dark green leaves. Spikelike clusters of small, pinkish purple flowers profusely carried May–August.

H. cupressoides. Slow grower to 4–5 ft. with slender branches clothed in bright green, scalelike leaves that look like cypress. Small bluish flowers seldom produced. More widely sold is variety 'Nana', a compact, rounded, slow growing plant to 2 ft. high. Often used in containers, rock gardens, or as bonsai.

H. 'Desilor'. Dense, rounded shrub to 3 ft. tall, equally broad. Leaves somewhat smaller than in *H. elliptica.* Flowers deep purple blue in 1½-in.-long clusters May–October.

H. elliptica *(H. decussata).* Much branched shrub 5–6 ft. high. Medium-green leaves 1¼ in. long. Fragrant bluish flowers in 1½-in.-long clusters bloom in summer.

H. glaucophylla. Broad, compact, rounded shrub about 2 ft. wide. Roundish, blue green, ½-in.-long leaves. Summer flowers white, in short, dense clusters. Use as low foundation plant or divider between walk and lawn.

H. imperialis. See *H. speciosa* 'Imperialis'.

H. menziesii. Can reach 5 ft.; usually much lower. Narrow, closely spaced ¾-in.-long leaves are shiny bright green and slightly toothed. White flowers tinged lilac in short clusters; summer bloom. Spreading habit; good ground cover.

H. 'Patty's Purple'. To 3 ft. high, stems wine red. Leaves ½ in. long, dark green. Purple flowers on slender spikes in summer. Use to back flower border or mass in groups.

H. pinguifolia. Zones 5, 6, 14–24. Erect or creeping shrub 1–3 ft. tall with roundish blue green leaves ¾ in. long, often with red edges. Fat white 1-in.-long flower spikes in summer. *H. p.* 'Pagei' has leaves ½ in. across, blue gray edged rose. Grows 9 in. high, 5 ft. across. Rock garden plant.

H. 'Reevesii' *(H.* 'Evansii'*).* To 3 ft. high. Two-in.-long leaves are blend of dark green and reddish purple; flowers reddish purple, summer bloom.

H. speciosa. SHOWY HEBE. Spreading shrub 2–5 ft. high. Stout stems bear dark green, glossy leaves, 2–4 in. long. Broad, dense. Three-4-in.-long spikes of reddish purple flowers, July-September. *H. s.* 'Imperialis' shows reddish foliage, magenta flowers in summer.

HEDERA. IVY. Evergreen woody vines. Most widely planted ground cover in California. Also, often climbs on walls, fences, trellises. Sometimes planting does both—wall ivy spreads to become surrounding ground cover or vice versa. Ivy is dependable, uniform, neat. Also, it is good for holding soil—discouraging soil erosion and slippage on slopes. Roots grow deep and fill soil densely. Branches root as they grow, further knitting soil.

Ivy climbs almost any vertical surface by aerial rootlets—a factor to consider in planting against walls that need painting. Chain link fence planted with ivy soon becomes wall of foliage.

Hedera helix

Ivy grows in sun or shade in most climates; must have shade in Zones 12, 13. Its only real shortcoming is monotony. All year long you get nothing from it but green or green and white (except *H. h.* 'Baltica').

Thick, leathery leaves are usually lobed. Mature plants will eventually develop stiff branches toward top of vine which bear round clusters of small greenish flowers followed by black berries. These branches have unlobed leaves; cuttings from such branches will have same kind of leaves and will be shrubby, not vining. Such shrubs taken from variegated Algerian ivy are called "ghost ivy". *H. helix* 'Arborescens' is another variety of that type.

You can grow regular ivy from cuttings but many will die and growth will be very slow. Plants from flats grow much faster. Standard spacing: 12–18 in. Best planting time: early spring (March in California and Arizona, May in Colorado). But fall plantings, where winters are not excessively cold, require less water to get started.

Most critical needs in planting are for soil to be thoroughly pre-moistened, plant roots to be moist, and for plant tissues to be full of moisture (not wilted). Mix peat moss or ground bark into planting soil to a depth of 9–12 in., if possible. On steep slope, dig conditioner into each planting hole (6 in. deep, 6 in. wide). After spring planting, feed with high-nitrogen fertilizer. Feed again in August. For best possible growth, continue to feed in early spring and August of every year. In hot climates, the more water you give an ivy planting the better it will hold up through summer. Nevertheless, established English ivy is fairly drought tolerant.

Most ivy ground covers need trimming around edges (use hedge shears or sharp spade) 2–3 times a year. Fence and wall plantings need shearing or trimming 2–3 times a year. When ground cover builds up higher than you want, mow it with rugged power rotary mower or cut it back with hedge shears. Do this in spring so ensuing growth will quickly cover bald look.

Many trees and shrubs grow quite compatibly in ivy. But small, soft, or fragile plants will never exist for long with healthy ivy. Ivy simply smothers them out.

To kill Bermuda grass in ivy, spray with dalapon 2–3 times during Bermuda's active growing season. Chemical doesn't hurt ivy when used as directed for Bermuda. Add wetting agent to make dalapon more effective.

A bacterial leaf spot causes light green, water-soaked spots on leaves. Spots turn brown or black, edged with red or brown; ultimately stems shrivel and blacken. Physiological trouble called edema brings on same symptoms. Prevent either malady by watering early in day so foliage is dry by night. There is no chemical control for edema. To control the bacterial disease, spray infected beds with copper-bearing compounds or other locally recommended products.

If dodder, a yellow threadlike parasite, grows among ivy plants, use ammonium sulfate at 1 lb. per gal. of water. Treatment will kill ivy leaves but new leaves will replace them.

Ivy can give haven to slugs and snails. If your garden has these pests put slug-snail poison in ivy often. Ivy also harbors rodents.

H. canariensis. ALGERIAN IVY. Zones 8, 9, 12–24. Shiny, rich green leaves 5–8 in. wide with 3–5 shallow lobes, more widely spaced along stems than on English ivy. Requires more moisture than English ivy.

H. c. 'Variegata'. VARIEGATED ALGERIAN IVY. Leaves edged with yellowish white; white sometimes suffused with reddish purple in cold weather. Avoid extreme heat or desert sun.

H. colchica. PERSIAN IVY. Zones 7–9, 12–24. Evergreen leaves egg shaped to heart shaped, 3–7 in. across, up to 10 in. long. Best known for its variety 'Dentata', with faintly toothed leaves. 'Dentata Variegata' is marbled with deep green, gray green, and creamy white. Largest leaves among ivies.

H. helix. ENGLISH IVY. All Zones. Leaves dark, dull green with paler veins, 3–5 lobed, 2–4 in. wide at base and as long. Not as vigorous as Algerian ivy, better for small spaces.

H. h. 'Baltica'. Hardiest, has leaves half size of English ivy, whitish veins, turns purplish in winter. 'Bulgarica', also hardy, has larger leaves.

Many small and miniature-leafed forms are useful for small-area ground covers, hanging baskets, and training to intricate patterns on walls and in pots. Some of small-leafed forms are: 'Hahn's Self Branching', light green leaves, dense branching, part shade best; 'Conglomerata', slow-growing dwarf; 'Minima', leaves ½–1 in across with 3–5 angular lobes. Forms and colorings to be had: 'California', 'Fluffy Ruffles', 'Gold Dust', 'Gold Heart', 'Heart', 'Needlepoint', 'Ripple', 'Shamrock', and 'Star'.

HEDYCHIUM. GINGER LILY. Perennials. Outdoors in Zones 17, 22–24, greenhouse plants anywhere. Foliage handsome under ideal conditions. Leaves on two sides of stems but in one plane. Richly fragrant flowers in dense spikes open from cone of overlapping green bracts at ends of stalks. Flower in late summer or early fall. Remove old stems after flowers fade to encourage fresh new growth. Very useful in large containers but will not grow as tall as in open ground. Container plants can be moved out of sight when unattractive. Grow in light shade in soil high in organic matter. Keep it moist at all times. Frosts in mild areas can kill to ground, but new stalks appear in early spring. Useful next to swimming pools.

Hedychium gardneranum

H. coronarium. WHITE GINGER LILY, GARLAND FLOWER. Native to India, Indonesia. Grows 3–6 ft. high. Leaves 8–24 in. long, 2–5 in. broad. Foliage usually unattractive in California because, if given enough heat to bloom well, it will burn. Flowers white in 6–12-in.-long clusters, wonderfully fragrant; are good cut.

H. gardneranum. KAHILI GINGER. Native to India. Grows to 8 ft. high, the 8–18-in.-long leaves 4–6 in. wide. Clear yellow flowers with red stamens, in 18-in.-long spikes, tip branches from July to onset of cool weather.

HEDYSCEPE canterburyana. Palm. Outdoors in Zones 17, 23, 24; anywhere as house or greenhouse plant. Comes from Lord Howe Island in the South Pacific. Related to better-known Kentia palms (see *Howea*) but is smaller, broader, lower growing, with broader leaf segments and more arching, lighter green feather-type leaves. To 30 ft. Ample water.

HEIMERLIODENDRON brunonianum. See *Pisonia umbellifera*.

Hedyscepe canterburyana

HELENIUM autumnale. COMMON SNEEZE-WEED. Perennial. All Zones. Many branching, leafy stems to 1–6 ft. depending on variety. Daisylike flowers summer to early fall—rays in shades of yellow, orange, red, and copper, surrounding brown pomponlike center. Leaves 2–4 in. long, toothed. Needs full sun. Fairly drought resistant. Flowers best where summers are hot. Trim off faded blossoms to encourage more blooms. Plants can take some neglect.

Helenium autumnale

HELIANTHEMUM nummularium. SUNROSE. Evergreen shrublet. All Zones. Commonly sold under this name are a number of forms as well as hybrids between this species and others. They grow to about 6–8 in. high, and spread to 3 ft. The ½–1-in.-long leaves may be glossy green above and fuzzy gray beneath, or gray on both sides depending on the kind. They give a delightful flower display in lovely, sunny colors—flame, red, apricot, orange, yellow, pink, rose, peach, salmon, and white. Single and double-flowered forms. The 1-in.-wide flowers, in clusters, bloom April-June in California and Arizona, May-July in Northwest. Blossom lasts only a day, but new buds continue to open. Shear plants back after flowering to encourage fall bloom.

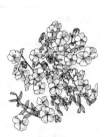

Helianthemum nummularium

Plant in full sun. Let sunroses tumble over rocks. Give them niche in dry rock wall. Set them in planter inset in sunny patio. Use them at the seashore or in rock gardens. Allow them to ramble over gentle slope. If used as ground cover, plant 2–3 ft. apart. Plant in fall or early spring—from flats, if possible. Soil drainage must be good. Do not overwater. In cold-winter areas, lightly cover them with branches from evergreens to keep foliage from dehydrating in winter.

HELIANTHUS. SUNFLOWER. Annuals and perennials. All Zones. Coarse, sturdy plants with bold flowers. All are tough, tolerant plants for full sun, any garden soil. Perennial kinds spread rapidly, may become invasive. Not for tidy gardens. All bloom in late summer, fall.

H. annuus. COMMON SUNFLOWER. Annual. From this rough, hairy plant with 2–3-in.-wide flower heads have come many ornamental and useful garden varieties. Some ornamental varieties have double yellow flower heads 5–7 in. across ('Teddy Bear', 'Sungold', 'Chrysanthemum-Flowered'); others have large orange, red brown, or mahogany heads. Best known form is

Helianthus annuus

coarse, towering (to 10 ft.) plant with small rays outside and cushiony center of disk flowers, 8–10 in. across. Usually sold as 'Mammoth Russian'. People eat the roasted seeds; birds like them raw, and visit flower heads in fall and winter. For children, annual sunflowers are big, easy to grow, and bring sense of great accomplishment. Sow seeds in spring where plants are to grow. Large-flowered kinds need rich soil, lots of water.

H. multiflorus. Perennial. To 5 ft. with thin, toothed, 3–8-in.-long leaves and numerous 3-in.-wide flower heads with yellow central disks. 'Loddon Gold' is double-flowering variety. Excellent for cutting.

H. tuberosus. JERUSALEM ARTICHOKE. Perennial. Grown to a certain extent as a commercial crop, tubers being edible. Sold in markets as "sun chokes." Plants 6–7 ft. tall, with bright yellow flower heads. Oval leaves 8 in. long. Spreads readily and can become pest. Best to

Helianthus tuberosus

harvest tubers every year and save out 2 or 3 for replanting. If controlled, a good, quick temporary screen, hedge.

HELICHRYSUM. Annual and shrubby perennial. Two quite different plants—one produces cut flowers for fresh and dried arrangements, the other is landscaping plant.

H. bracteatum. STRAWFLOWER. Summer annual. Grows 2–3 ft. high with many flower heads. Known as "everlasting" because 2½-in. pomponlike flowers are papery and last indefinitely when dried. Also good in fresh arrangements. Flowers may be yellow, orange, red, pink, or white (seeds come in mixed colors). Alternate leaves 2–5 in. long. Plant seed in place, late spring or early summer, same time as zinnias. Full sun. Dwarf forms available. Once plants well started, keep them on dry side. Inclined to have dry leaves at base. Best for hillside or dry areas.

Helichrysum bracteatum

H. petiolatum (*Gnaphalium lanatum*). Shrubby perennial. Zones 16, 17, 22–24. Woody-based plants to 2 ft. with trailing stems that spread 4 ft. or more. Grown for 1-in.-long, oval, white-woolly leaves. If flower heads form, they are ⅛ in. wide in clusters 1–2 in. wide. Full sun. Drought tolerant. Needs room; trim to keep tidy. Good in sandy soils.

HELIOPSIS helianthoides scabra (*H. scabra*). Perennial. Zones 1–16. Native to eastern U.S. Related to sunflower. Grows 3–4 ft. tall, has rough-textured foliage and yellow 3–4-in. flowers on long, wiry stems, July to fall. Flowers good for cutting. Dies back in winter; makes new growth yearly.

Plant in full sun. Drought tolerant once established. Among several named varieties are: 'Summer Sun' (seed grown) with single to double yellow flowers; and 'Incomparabilis', semidouble with gold yellow flowers 3 in. across.

Heliopsis helianthoides scabra

HELIOTROPE, GARDEN. See *Valeriana officinalis*.

HELIOTROPIUM arborescens (*H. peruvianum*). COMMON HELIOTROPE. Perennial. House or summer plant everywhere; an outdoor plant Zones 8–24. Rather tender old-fashioned plant grown for delicate, sweet fragrance of the flowers. In mild climates, grows shrubby and reaches to 4 ft. high. Flowers dark violet to white, arranged in tightly grouped, curved, one-sided spikes which form rounded, massive clusters. Veined leaves have darkish purple cast. If in pots, can be protected in winter and moved into patio or garden for spring and summer enjoyment. It takes sun or partial shade (latter best in hot-summer climates). Avoid overwatering. 'Black Beauty' and 'Iowa' are forms with deep purple flowers.

Heliotropium arborescens

HELIPTERUM roseum (*Acroclinium roseum*). Annual. Although grown for summer color in garden, valued mostly for dried cut flowers. Grows to 2 ft. tall. Daisy flower heads 1–2 in. across, carried singly; pink or white rays, thicker, brownish or greenish-colored near base. Leaves narrow, numerous near top of stems. Easily grown in full sun in warm dry soil. Sow seeds after frost where plants are to grow. Thin to 6–12 in. apart. To dry flowers, cut when fully open, after dew has dried from flowers. Tie in small bunches; hang upside down by stems in dry, cool, airy place until stems harden and leaves become brittle.

Helipterum roseum

HELLEBORUS. HELLEBORE. Perennials. Distinctive, long-lived evergreen plants for shade or half shade, blooming for several months in winter and spring. Basal clumps of substantial, long-stalked leaves, usually divided fanwise into leaflets. Flowers large, in clusters or single, centered with many stamens. Good cut flowers; sear ends of stems or dip in boiling water, then place in deep, cold water.

Plant in good soil with lots of organic material added. Ample water. Feed once or twice a year. Do not move often; plants reestablish slowly. Mass under high-branching trees on north or east side of walls, in beds bordered with ajuga, wild ginger, primroses, violets. Use them in plantings with azaleas, fatsia, pieris, rhododendrons, skimmia, and ferns.

Helleborus lividus corsicus

H. foetidus. All Zones. Grows to 1½ ft. Attractive leaves—leathery, dark green, divided into 7–11 leaflets. Flowers 1 in. wide, light green with purplish margin; bloom February-April. Drought tolerant. Good with naturalized daffodils.

H. lividus corsicus. (Sometimes sold as *H. corsicus* or *H. lividus.*) CORSICAN HELLEBORE. Zones 4–24. Leafy stems to 3 ft. Leaves divided into 3 pale blue green leaflets with sharply toothed edges. (Species *H. lividus* has leaflets with only few fine teeth on the edges or none.) Clusters of large, firm-textured light chartreuse flowers among upper leaves. In mild-winter climates blooms late fall to late spring; in Northwest blooms March-April. After shedding stamens, flowers stay attractive until summer. Best hellebore for southern California. Neutral soil. Established plants take more sun than other hellebores. Drought tolerant when established.

H. niger. CHRISTMAS ROSE. All Zones. Elegant plant to 1½ ft. tall, blooming December-April. Not adapted to mild-winter climates. Lustrous dark green leaves divided into 7–9 leaflets with few large teeth. Flowers, about 2 in. wide, white or greenish white, become purplish with age.

H. orientalis. LENTEN ROSE. All Zones. Much like *H. niger* in growth habit, but easier to transplant. Basal leaves with 5–11 sharply toothed leaflets. Blooms March-May. Flowering stems leafless, branched. Flowers greenish, purplish, or rose, often spotted or splashed with deep purple. Lenten rose often sold as Christmas rose—distinguished by different flower color, by many small teeth on leaflets (few large teeth on those of Christmas rose). Lenten rose does better in southern California than Christmas rose.

HELXINE. See *Soleirolia.*

HEMEROCALLIS. DAYLILY. Perennials with tuberous, somewhat fleshy roots; deciduous and evergreen. All Zones. Large clumps of arching, sword shaped leaves. Lilylike flowers in open or branched clusters at ends of generally leafless stems that stand well above foliage. Older yellow, orange, rust red daylilies mostly replaced by newer kinds (see below); both tall and dwarf varieties are available.

Use in borders with bearded iris, Michaelmas and Shasta daisies, poker plant *(Kniphofia),* dusty miller, agapanthus. Mass on banks under high-branching, deciduous trees, along driveways and roadsides in country gardens. Group

Hemerocallis hybrid

among evergreen shrubs, near pools, along streams. Plant dwarf daylilies in rock gardens, as edgings, as low ground covers. Good cut flowers. Cut stems with well-developed buds; buds open on successive days, though each flower slightly smaller than preceding one. Arrange individual blooms in low bowls. Snap off faded flowers daily.

Few plants tougher, more persistent, pest free. Adapt to almost any kind of soil. Sun or part shade; in hottest areas flowers fade in full sun all day—give some afternoon shade. Red-flowered daylilies need warmth to develop best color. Water thoroughly while blooming; feed with complete fertilizer in spring and midsummer. Divide crowded plants in early spring or late fall.

H. fulva. TAWNY DAYLILY, COMMON ORANGE DAYLILY. Deciduous. To 6 ft. Leaves 2 ft. or more long, 1 in. wide; flowers tawny orange red, 3–5 in. long, bloom in summer. Old variety 'Kwanso', double flowers, superseded by newer, more handsome hybrids.

H. hybrids. Deciduous or evergreen. Modern hybrids grow 1–6 ft. tall, with flowers 3–8 in. across. Color range extends far beyond basic yellow, orange, rust red; includes shell pink, vermilion, buff, apricot, creamy white, many bicolors. Early, mid-season, late varieties insure bloom from May to September or October (in mild climates). Some varieties bloom twice a year (or even more often); some bloom in evening. Flowers single, semidouble, double; vary in shape from broad-petaled to narrow and twisted. Especially noteworthy are tetraploids ("tetras"), which have unusually heavy-textured flowers.

H. lilioasphodelus (*H. flava*). LEMON DAYLILY. Deciduous. To 3 ft. Leaves 2 ft. long. Fragrant, clear yellow, 4-in. flowers in June. Old-timer, worthwhile for fragrance and moderate size.

HEMIGRAPHIS. House plants. Acanthus relatives with arching or trailing stems and opposite pairs of toothed or scalloped leaves. Give them rich house plant mix, subdued light, ample water, moderate feeding. Foliage plants generally grown in hanging pots or baskets. Flowers not showy.

H. alternata (*H. colorata*). Heart shaped, 3-in. leaves are grayish above, wine red underneath.

Hemigraphis 'Exotica'

H. 'Exotica'. WAFFLE PLANT. Leaves longish oval, heavily puckered between veins in waffle or seersucker effect, purplish green above, purple red underneath. Exact name uncertain.

HEMLOCK. See *Tsuga.*

HEN AND CHICKENS. See *Sempervivum tectorum.*

HEN AND CHICKS. See *Echeveria.*

HEPATICA. LIVERLEAF. Perennials. Zones 1–11, 14–16. Attractive woodland plants for damp, shady places. Related to anemones. In really cold areas may bloom before snow melts. Flower stems are 4–6 in. high and carry several white, brilliant blue violet, or rose pink flowers about ¾ in. across. Flowers followed by silky fruits. Just the beautiful foliage is reason enough for planting—it's soft and furry when new, bronzed and thick when mature. Requires normal summer watering.

H. acutiloba. Leaves have 3 pointed lobes; flowering stems are usually taller than leaf stems.

H. americana. Leaves have 3 very blunt lobes.

Hepatica americana

HERALD'S TRUMPET. See *Beaumontia grandiflora.*

HERB-OF-GRACE. See *Ruta graveolens.*

HERBS. This category includes all plants that at some time in history have been considered valuable for seasoning, medicine, fragrance, or general household use. As you look through lists of plants you can recognize certain herbs because they bear the species name *officinalis* (meaning: sold in shops, edible, medicinal, recognized in the pharmacopoeia).

Today's herb harvest is used almost entirely for seasoning of foods. Herbs are versatile as garden plants. Some creep along ground making fragrant carpets. Others are shrublike and can be clipped to make formal hedges or grown informally in shrub or perennial borders. Many make attractive container plants. Those with gray foliage are striking contrast to green-leafed plants. However, many herbs do have distinctly weedy look, especially when planted beside regular ornamental plants.

Many are hardy and adaptable. Although hot, dry, sunny conditions with poor but well-drained soil are usually considered best for most herbs, some thrive in shady, moist locations with light soil rich in humus.

Following are lists of herbs for specific landscape situations:

Kitchen garden. This can be sunny raised bed near kitchen door, planter box near the barbecue, or a portion of vegetable garden. Plant basic cooking herbs: basil *(Ocimum)*, chives, dill *(Anethum graveolens)*, sweet marjoram *(Origanum majorana)*, mint *(Mentha)*, oregano *(Origanum vulgare)*, parsley, rosemary *(Rosmarinus)*, sage *(Salvia officinalis)*, savory *(Satureja)*, tarragon *(Artemisia dracunculus)*, thyme *(Thymus)*. The connoisseur may wish to plant: angelica, anise *(Pimpinella anisum)*, caraway *(Carum carvi)*, chervil *(Anthriscus cerefolium)*, coriander *(Coriandrum sativum)*, common fennel *(Foeniculum vulgare)*.

Ground cover for sun. Prostrate rosemary, mother-of-thyme *(Thymus praecox arcticus, T. serpyllum)*, lemon thyme *(T. citriodorus)*, woolly thyme *(T. pseudolanuginosus)*, caraway-scented thyme *(T. herba-barona)*.

Ground cover for shade or part shade. Chamomile *(Chamaemelum nobile)*.

Ground cover for shade. Sweet woodruff *(Galium odoratum)*.

Perennial or shrub border. Common wormwood *(Artemisia absinthium)*, Roman wormwood *(A. pontica)*, small burnet *(Poterium sanguisorba)*, lavenders *(Lavandula)*, monarda, rosemary, rue *(Ruta graveolens)*, scented geraniums *(Pelargonium)*, tansy *(Tanacetum vulgare)*.

Hedges. Formal clipped hedge—hyssop *(Hyssopus officinalis)*, santolina, germander *(Teucrium)*. Informal hedge—lavenders, winter savory *(Satureja montana)*.

Gray garden. Common wormwood, Roman wormwood, English lavender *(Lavandula angustifolia)*, germander, horehound *(Marrubium vulgare)*, sage, woolly thyme.

Rock garden. French lavender *(Lavandula dentata)*, sage, woolly thyme, mother-of-thyme, winter savory.

Herbs for moist areas. Angelica, mints, parsley, sweet woodruff.

Herbs for part shade. Chervil, costmary *(Chrysanthemum balsamita)*, lemon balm *(Melissa officinalis)*, parsley, sweet woodruff.

Herbs for containers. Crete dittany *(Origanum dictamnus)*, chives, costmary, lemon verbena *(Aloysia triphylla)*, sage, pineapple sage *(Salvia elegans)*, summer savory *(Satureja hortensis)*, sweet marjoram, mints, small burnet.

Potpourris and sachets. Costmary, English lavender flowers, lemon balm, sweet woodruff, lemon verbena, lemon-scented geranium *(Pelargonium crispum)*, rose geranium *(P. graveolens)*, monarda.

Drying leafy herbs for cooking. Cut leafy herbs for drying early in day before sun gets too hot, but after dew has dried on foliage. Oil content highest then. Leafy herbs ready from time flower buds begin to form until flowers are half open. (Exceptions: parsley can be cut any time; sage and tarragon may take on strong taste unless cut early in summer.) Don't cut perennial herbs back more than one third; annual herbs may be sheared back to about 4 in. from ground. Generally you can cut 2 or 3 crops for drying during summer. Don't cut perennial herbs after September or new growth won't have chance to mature before cold weather.

Before drying, sort weeds and grass from herbs, remove dead or insect-damaged leaves. Wash off loose dirt in cool water; shake or blot off excess moisture. Tie woody-stemmed herbs such as sweet marjoram or thyme in small bundles and hang upside down from line hung across room. Room for drying

herbs should be dark to preserve color, have good air circulation and warm temperature (about 70°F.) for rapid drying to retain aromatic oils. If drying area is fairly bright, surround herb bundles with loose cylinders of paper.

For large-leafed herbs such as basil, or short tips that don't bundle easily, dry in tray made by knocking bottom from nursery flat and replacing it with screen. On top of screen place double thickness of cheesecloth. Spread leaves out over surface. Stir leaves daily.

With good air circulation and low humidity, leafy herbs should be crumbly dry in few days to a week. Strip leaves from stems and store whole in airtight containers—glass is best—until ready to use. Label each container with name of herb and date dried. Check jars first few days after filling to make sure moisture doesn't form inside. If it does, pour out contents and dry few days longer.

Seed herbs. Gather seed clusters such as dill, anise, fennel, caraway when they turn brown. Seeds should begin to fall out of them when gently tapped. Leave little of stem attached when you cut each cluster. Collect in box. Flail seeds from clusters and spread them out in sun to dry for several days. Then separate chaff from seed and continue to dry in sun for another 1½–2 weeks. Store seed herbs same way as leafy ones.

HERCULES' CLUB. See *Aralia spinosa*.

HERMANNIA verticillata *(Mahernia verticillata)*. HONEYBELLS. Evergreen perennial or subshrub. Zones 14–24. Straggly plant to 1 ft. tall, 3 ft. wide. Leaves 1 in. long, finely divided. Yellow, bell shaped, fragrant flowers in spring, then blooms sporadically all year. Needs good drainage. For longer plant life, keep dead flowers cut. Good in hanging basket or above wall. Needs full sun.

Hermannia verticillata

HERNIARIA glabra. GREEN CARPET, RUPTURE WORT. Evergreen perennial. All Zones. Trailing plant under 2 or 3 inches with crowded, tiny, bright green leaves less than ¼ in. long. Bloom negligible.

Grows vigorously in full sun in hottest places, but does well in moist shade too. Foliage turns bronzy red in cold winters.

Spreads well, but won't grow out of control; use it between stepping stones, on mounds, with rocks, or in parking strips. Endures occasional footsteps, but not constant traffic.

Herniaria glabra

HESPERALOE parviflora. Evergreen perennial. Zones 10–16, 18–21. Native to Texas, northern Mexico. Makes dense, yuccalike clump of very narrow, swordlike leaves 4 ft. long, about 1 in. wide. Pink to rose red, 1¼-in.-long, nodding flowers in slim 3–4-ft.-high clusters in early summer, with repeat bloom frequent in milder climates. On older plants spikes can reach 8–9 ft. Effective combined with other desert plants. Good large container plant with loose, relaxed look. Full sun; drought tolerant.

H. p. engelmannii, similar to species but 1-in.-long flowers are more bell shaped.

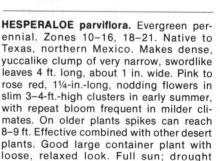

Hesperaloe parviflora

HESPERIS matronalis. DAME'S ROCKET, SWEET ROCKET. Perennial, sometimes short lived. All Zones. Stems to 3 ft. Leaves rather coarse, dark green. Clusters of fragrant lavender purple to white flowers look something like stock, something like phlox, something like mustard bloom (except for color). Easy from seed in sun or light shade, ordinary soil, moderate water. Self-sows in many gardens.

HETEROCENTRON elegans (*Schizocentron elegans.*) SPANISH SHAWL.
Perennial. Zones 17, 21–24; with protection from frost, lives over in Zones 15, 16, 18–20. Creeping, vinelike habit. Oval leaves ½ in. or less wide with 3 well-marked veins. Leaves and stems often acquire a red color as the season advances. In summer, 1-in.-wide magenta flowers appear among the leaves; calyx remains after blossom has withered. Grow in shade. When used as ground cover, plants in bloom give appearance of a carpet covered with bougainvillealike blossoms. Good subject for hanging baskets.

Hesperis matronalis

HETEROMELES arbutifolia (*Photinia arbutifolia*). TOYON, CHRISTMAS BERRY, CALIFORNIA HOLLY.
Evergreen shrub or small tree. Zones 5–24. Native to Sierra Nevada foothills, southern California to Baja California, California Coast Ranges. Dense shrub 6–10 ft. tall or multitrunked small tree 15–25 ft. tall. Thick, leathery, glossy dark green leaves 2–4 in. long with bristly, pointed teeth. Small white flowers in flattish clusters, June-July. Bright red (rarely yellow) clustered berries, November-January. Birds relish them; bees also attracted to plant. *H. a. macrocarpa*, from Channel Islands, has larger berries.

Heterocentron elegans

Improves under cultivation. Drought tolerant, but thrives with summer water in well-drained soil. Needs some summer water in desert. Full sun or part shade. If trimmed to give abundance of year-old wood, it produces even more berries than in the wilds. Can be pruned to form small single-trunked tree. Valuable as screen, bank planting, erosion control. Fire retardant if kept moist.

Heteromeles arbutifolia

HEUCHERA. ALUM ROOT, CORAL BELLS.
Perennials. Compact, evergreen clumps of roundish leaves with scalloped edges. Slender, wiry stems 15–30 in. high bear open clusters of nodding, bell shaped flowers ¼ in. or more across, in carmine, reddish pink, coral crimson, red, rose, greenish, or white. Bloom April-August. Use as edgings, mass in borders, in front of shrubs, in rock gardens, as ground cover. Flowers attract hummingbirds. Dainty, long-lasting in cut arrangements.

Heuchera sanguinea

Sun, light shade in hot inland areas. Best with plenty of water. Divide clumps every 3 or 4 years in fall or spring (in colder sections). Use young, vigorous, rooted divisions; discard older woody rootstocks. Sow seed in spring.

H. maxima. ISLAND ALUM ROOT. Zones 15–24. Native to Channel Islands, southern California. Foliage clumps 12–24 in. across. Leaves roundish, heart shaped, lobed, shining dark green. Flowers whitish or pinkish; hundreds in each narrow, 18–30-in.-long cluster. Blooms February-April. Partial shade; moisture. Good ground cover in untamed parts of garden.

H. micrantha. All Zones. Native to California, Washington, Oregon, Idaho. Adapts easily to garden conditions. Plant in protected spots in cold areas. Long-stalked, roundish leaves 1–3 in. long, hairy on both sides, toothed and lobed. Flowers whitish or greenish, about ⅛ in. long, in loose clusters on leafy stems 2–3 ft. high.

H. sanguinea. CORAL BELLS. All Zones. Native to Mexico and Arizona. Universal favorite. Makes neat foliage tufts of round 1–2-in.-long leaves with scalloped edges. Slender, wiry stems 14–24 in. tall bear open clusters of nodding, bell shaped, bright red or coral pink flowers. White, pink, crimson varieties available. Good edging for beds of delphinium, iris, lilies, peonies, roses.

H. 'Santa Ana Cardinal'. Zones 14–24. Outstanding hybrid between garden forms of *H. sanguinea* and *H. maxima*. Unusually vigorous, free flowering. Clumps 3–4 ft. wide. Vibrant rose red flowers, 50–100 in a spike, on 24-in. stems. Blooms 3–5 months, almost all year in mild areas.

HIBA CEDAR. See *Thujopsis dolabrata*.

HIBBERTIA.
Evergreen shrubs and vines with yellow flowers, most natives of Australia.

H. cuneiformis (*Candollea cuneiformis*). Evergreen shrub. Zones 13, 15–24. Native to Australia. Pleasing appearance and substance, to 4 ft. and somewhat broader. Small, 1-in.-long, polished green leaves tapered at base and toothed at tip. Flowers, like clear yellow wild roses, are carried all along new growth, March-June. Prune after flowering to control outline. Needs food and water in average amounts but exceptionally fast drainage. Takes sun or light shade. Resists wind well. Associate with rockroses (*Cistus*), sunroses (*Helianthemum*), and *Aster frikartii*.

Hibbertia cuneiformis

H. scandens (*H. volubilis*). GUINEA GOLD VINE. Evergreen vine. Zones 16, 17, 21–24. Native to Australia. Fast growing, shrubby, climbing by twining stems to 8–10 ft. Luxuriant foliage handsome all year in ideal climate. Waxy, dark green leaves, 3 in. long by 1 in. wide. Clear bright yellow flowers, like single roses, start to appear in May and will continue to bloom into October. Thrives in part shade, but will also grow in hot sun. Requires ample water. Recovers quickly from burning by light frosts. Use it to cover stone or tile walls, or as ground cover. Good for small garden areas trained on trellis or against low fence. Can also use in containers.

Hibbertia scandens

HIBISCUS.
Five species are grown in West—an annual, a perennial, two deciduous shrubs, and one evergreen shrub. In Hawaii and warmest areas of coastal southern California several more species are grown.

H. huegelii. See *Alyogyne*.

H. moscheutos. PERENNIAL HIBISCUS, ROSE-MALLOW. Perennial. Zones 1–21. Hardy. To 6–8 ft. high. Stems rise each year and bloom starts in late June, continuing to frost. Plants die down in winter. Oval, toothed leaves deep green above, whitish beneath. Flowers largest of all hibiscus; some reach 12 in. across. Plants need regular deep watering and protection from winds that may burn flowers. A 2-in.-deep mulch will help conserve moisture. Feed at 6–8-week intervals during growing season. Sun.

Hibiscus rosa-sinensis

Varieties available as plants are 'New Blood Red', 7-in., deep blood red flowers with reflexed petals; 'Giant Raspberry Rose', 10–12-in., rich, deep rose flowers; 'Ruffled Cerise', 8-in. flowers; 'Strawberry Rose', 8-in. flowers; 'Super Clown', 9-in. flowers of ivory white suffused with pink, tips of petals shaded deep rose, deep red eye; and 'Super White', 8–12-in. white flowers with rose red centers.

Can be grown from seed, often flowering first year if planted early. Mallow Marvels strain grows to 3 ft., has big flowers in white to crimson shades. Southern Belle strain (4–5 ft.) has 8–10-in. blooms, is available as mix or in pink, white, red, rose, and bicolor pink and white.

H. mutabilis. CONFEDERATE ROSE. Deciduous shrub. Zones 4–24. Shrubby or treelike in warmest climates, it behaves more like perennial in colder areas, growing flowering branches from woody base or short trunk. Three-5-lobed broad, oval leaves. Summer flowers 4–6 in. wide, opening white or pink and changing to deep red by evening. Variety 'Rubra' has red flowers. Requires sun; average water.

H. rosa-sinensis. CHINESE HIBISCUS, TROPICAL HIBISCUS. Evergreen shrub. Zones 9, 12, 13, 15, 16, 19–24. House plant or indoor/outdoor plant in cold-winter areas. One of showiest flowering shrubs. Reaches 30 ft. in tropics, but seldom over 15 ft. tall even in mildest parts of California. Glossy foliage varies somewhat in size and texture depending on variety. Growth habit may be dense and dwarfish or loose and open. Summer flowers 4–8 in. wide, may be single or double. Colors range from white through pink to red, from yellow and apricot to orange.

Plants require good drainage; to check, dig hole 18 in. across and as deep. Fill with water; if water hasn't drained in hour or so find another planting area, improve drainage, or plant in raised bed or container. Plants also need sun, heat, and protection from frost and wind (especially ocean wind). In warm inland areas they generally grow best if partially shaded from very hot afternoon sun. In cool coastal climates such as San Francisco's, they never get heat enough to thrive or bloom. Where winter temperatures frequently drop below 30°F., even hardier varieties will need overhead protection of roof overhang or evergreen tree. Where temperatures drop much lower, grow plants in containers and shelter them indoors over winter. Or grow them as annuals, setting out fresh plants each spring.

Feed plants monthly (container plants twice monthly) from April to early September. Let growth harden after that. Water deeply and frequently. All varieties are quite susceptible to aphids.

Can be used as screen planting, in containers, as espaliers, or as free-standing shrubs or small trees. To keep mature plants growing vigorously, prune out about ⅓ of old wood in early spring. Pinching out tips of stems in spring and summer increases flower production. Prune poorly shaped young plants when set out in spring to develop good branch structure. Here are a few of many varieties sold in the West:

'Agnes Galt'. Big single pink flowers. Vigorous, hardy plant to 15 ft. Prune to prevent legginess.

'American Beauty'. Broad, deep rose flowers. Slow growth to 8 ft. tall. Irregular form.

'Bride'. Very large, palest blush to white flowers. Slow or moderate growth to open 6 ft.

'Brilliant' ('San Diego Red'). Bright red single flowers in profusion. Tall, vigorous, compact, to 15 ft. Hardy.

'Butterball'. Fully double pure yellow flowers on compact bush, 4–6 ft. tall.

'Butterfly'. Small, single bright yellow flowers. Slow, upright growth to 6 ft.

'California Gold'. Heavy yield of yellow, red-centered, single flowers. Slow or medium growth to a compact 7 ft.

'Crown of Bohemia'. Double gold flowers; petals shade to carmine orange toward base. Moderate or fast growth to 10 ft. Bushy, upright. Hardy.

'Diamond Head'. Large, double, deep red flowers—nearly black red. Compact growth to 5 ft.

'Ecstasy'. Large (5–6 in.) single bright red flowers with striking white variegation. Upright growth to 6 ft.

'Fiesta'. Single bright orange flowers 6–7 in. wide; white eye zone at flower center edged red. Petal edges ruffled. Strong, erect growth to 6–7 ft.

'Fullmoon'. Double pure yellow flowers. Moderately vigorous growth to a compact 8 ft.

'Golden Dust'. Bright orange single flowers with yellow orange centers. Compact, thick-foliaged plant 4–6 ft. tall.

'Hula Girl'. Large, single, canary yellow flowers have deep red eye. Compact growth to 7 ft. Flowers stay open several days.

'Kate Sessions'. Flowers large, single, broad petaled, red

tinged gold beneath. Moderate growth to 10 ft. Upright, open habit.

'Kona'. Double ruffled pink flowers. Vigorous, upright, bushy, to 15–20 ft. Prune regularly. 'Kona Improved' has fuller flowers of richer pink color.

'President'. Flowers single, 6–7 in. wide, intense red shading to deep pink in throat. Upright, compact, 8 ft. tall.

'Red Dragon' ('Celia'). Flowers small to medium, double, dark red. Upright, compact, 6–8 ft. tall.

'Rosea'. Heavy producer of double rose red flowers.

'Ross Estey'. Flowers very large, single, with broad, overlapping petals of pink shading coral orange toward tips. Flowers heavy textured, lasting 2–3 days on bush. Vigorous grower to 8 ft. Leaves unusually large, ruffled, polished dark green.

'Sundown' ('Jigora'). Flowers double salmon orange. Plant bushy, to 7 ft.

'Vulcan'. Large single red flowers with yellow on back of petals open from yellow buds. Flowers often last more than day. Compact grower, 4–6 ft. tall.

'White Wings'. Single, white, narrow-petaled flowers with small red eye. Profuse. Vigorous, open, upright growth to 20 ft.; prune to control legginess. Compact form with somewhat smaller flowers is available; it is generally sold under the name of 'White Wings Compacta'.

H. sabdariffa. ROSELLE, JAMAICA SORREL, JAMAICA FLOWER. Annual. Tall (4–5 ft.), narrowish plant with 3–5-lobed oval leaves, grown for fleshy calyces which surround bases of yellow flowers. These red calyces are used for making sauce, jelly, cool drinks, or teas; dried, they are known as Jamaica flowers. Their flavor is reminiscent of cranberry or currant. Plants need long, hot summer to ripen flowers; they do well in all interior valleys where frosts come late. Bloom begins as days shorten; early frosts prevent harvest. Give tomato culture; space plants 1½–2 ft. apart in rows. Can be used as narrow temporary hedge.

H. syriacus. ROSE OF SHARON, SHRUB ALTHAEA. Deciduous shrub. Zones 1–21. To 10–12 ft. tall, upright and compact when young, spreading and open with age. Easily trained to single trunk with treelike top. Leaves medium sized, often 3 lobed, coarsely toothed. Summer flowers single or double, 2½–3 in. across. Single flowers slightly more effective, opening somewhat larger; but singles produce many unattractive capsule-type fruit.

Grows easily in sun or part shade. Water requirements moderate; established plants take some drought. Prune to shape; for bigger flowers, cut back (in winter) previous season's growth to 2 buds. Resistant to oak root fungus.

Best varieties, some hard to find, are these: 'Albus', single, pure white, 4-in. flowers; 'Anemoniflora' ('Paeoniflora'), semidouble, red with deeper crimson eye; 'Ardens', double, purple; 'Boule de Feu', double, deep violet-pink; 'Coelestis', single, violet blue with reddish purple throat; 'Collie Mullens', double, magenta rose with crimson eye; 'Diana', large pure white that drops clean and forms few seed pods; 'Lucy', double, magenta rose with red eye; 'Purpurea', semidouble, purple, red at base of petals; 'Red Heart', pure white with deep red center; 'Woodbridge', single, magenta rose with red eye.

HILLS OF SNOW. See *Hydrangea arborescens* 'Grandiflora'.

HIMALAYAN POPPY. See *Meconopsis betonicifolia.*

HINDU-ROPE PLANT. See *Hoya carnosa* 'Compacta'.

HIPPEASTRUM. AMARYLLIS. Bulbs. Zones 12, 13, 19, 21–24; elsewhere as pot plant in greenhouse, indoors, or in frostproof outdoor area. Native to tropics and subtropics. Many species useful in hybridizing, but only hybrids generally available; usually sold as giant amaryllis or Royal Dutch amaryllis. Named varieties or color selections in reds, pinks, white, salmon, near

Hippeastrum hybrid

orange, some variously marked and striped. From 2 to several flowers, often 8–9 in. across, form on stout, 2-ft. stems. Where grown outdoors, flowers bloom in spring. Where grown indoors, they bloom just a few weeks after planting. Leaves broad, strap shaped, usually appearing after bloom, growing through summer, disappearing in fall.

Usually grown in pots. Pot in rich, sandy mix with added bonemeal or superphosphate. Plant in November-February. Allow 2-in. space between bulb and edge of pot. Set upper half of bulb above soil surface. Firm soil, water well, then keep barely moist until growth begins. Wet, airless soil causes root rot.

To force early bloom indoors, keep in warm dark place until rooted. Growers maintain bottom heat and air temperatures of 70°–85°F. until flower stalk 6 in. tall, then put in warm, light shade. In homes, keep in warm but not-too-dry atmosphere. Can grow in sunny indoor window boxes. Increase watering as leaves form. Feed lightly every 2 weeks through flowering period.

When flowers fade, cut off stem, keep up watering; feed to encourage leaf growth. When leaves yellow, withhold water, let plants dry out. Repot in late fall or early winter.

HIPPOCREPIS comosa. Perennial ground cover. Zones 8–24. Forms mat 3 in. high; spreads to 3 ft. Leaves divided into 7–15 medium green, oval, ¼–½-in.-long leaflets. Flowers golden yellow, sweet pea shaped, ½ in. long, in loose clusters of 5–12. Blooms in spring; some repeat bloom in summer. Drought resistant and takes poor soils, but lusher looking with good soil, adequate water. Sun. Roots bind soil on steep banks. Bank cover, rock garden, small-scale lawn substitute (mow once just after flowers fade). Set 1 ft. apart. Takes light foot traffic.

Hippocrepis comosa

HIPPOPHAE rhamnoides. SEA BUCKTHORN. Deciduous shrub. Zones 1–6. Fountain shaped shrub to 10–15 ft., rarely a small tree. Willowlike leaves to 3 in. long, ¼ in. wide, dark gray green above, silvery white beneath. Flowers inconspicuous. Female plants bear masses of bright yellow orange fruit ¼ in. long, if pollinated by nearby male plant. Fruit colors by September, lasts far into winter; birds won't eat it. Tolerates wide range of soils and treatments—drought resistant. Likes sun, good drainage.

Hippophae rhamnoides

HOGAN CEDAR. See *Thuja plicata* 'Fastigiata'.

HOHERIA. Evergreen trees and deciduous trees or shrubs. Native to New Zealand. Leaves are bright green, leathery, toothed, 3–5 in. long, 1½–2 in. wide. Flowers form in clusters among leaves, are pure white, about 1 in. wide. Keep moist.

H. glabrata. MOUNTAIN RIBBONWOOD. Deciduous tree or large shrub. Zones 5–6. To 40 ft. high, usually much less. Attractive with azaleas or rhododendrons. Summer bloom.

H. populnea. NEW ZEALAND LACEBARK. Evergreen tree. Zones 4–6, 15–17, 21–24. In growth habit as graceful as birch; in addition it puts on good show of flowers late summer into fall. Grows fast to eventual 50–60 ft., but enjoyable for many years as 20–30-ft., slender tree. Like birch, it's ideal for multiple planting and groves. Has deep, well-behaved root system. Inner bark is interestingly perforated and used in New Zealand for ornamental purposes.

Hoheria glabrata

HOLLY. See *Ilex.*

HOLLYFERN. See *Cyrtomium falcatum.*

HOLLYHOCK. See *Alcea rosea.*

HOLLYLEAF CHERRY. See *Prunus ilicifolia.*

HOLLYLEAF REDBERRY. See *Rhamnus crocea ilicifolia.*

HOLLYLEAF SWEETSPIRE. See *Itea ilicifolia.*

HOLODISCUS. Deciduous shrubs related to *Spiraea* and similar in appearance. All are western natives.

H. discolor. CREAM BUSH, OCEAN SPRAY. Deciduous shrub. Zones 1–7, 14–17. Native to California Coast Ranges, Sierra Nevada; north to British Columbia east to Rocky Mountains. May grow to 20 ft. in moist, rich soil and partial shade. Fairly drought tolerant. In dry, sunny situations, such as east of Cascades in Oregon and Washington, may get to only 3 ft. Triangular leaves, deep green above, white-hairy beneath, to 3 in. long, edges coarsely toothed. Nodding, branched clusters (sometimes to 12 in.

Holodiscus discolor

long) of small, creamy white flowers tip branches May-July, make quite a show, attract birds. Flowers fade to tannish gold and brown, remain attractive for long time. Prune back after flowering.

H. dumosus. MOUNTAIN SPRAY, ROCK SPIRAEA. Zones 1–3, 10. Native to shady canyons in Rockies from Wyoming south. Generally smaller than *H. discolor* and with narrower flower clusters, but can reach 15 ft. Coarsely toothed leaves, less than 1 in. long.

HOMALOCLADIUM platycladum. RIBBON BUSH, CENTIPEDE PLANT. Strange shrubby plant. Zones 8, 9, 12–24. Novelty or collector's plant, sometimes grown in raised beds or containers. Grows in sun or shade. Usually leafless, with long, narrow, flat, bright green, jointed stems reaching 2–4 ft. tall, usually less in pots. Small, narrow leaves sometimes show on stem edges. Flowers inconspicuous. Red berrylike fruit.

HONESTY. See *Lunaria annua.*

HONEY BELLS. See *Hermannia verticillata.*

HONEY BUSH. See *Melianthus major.*

HONEY LOCUST. See *Gleditsia triacanthos.*

HONEYSUCKLE. See *Lonicera.*

HONG KONG ORCHID TREE. See *Bauhinia blakeana.*

HOOP PINE. See *Araucaria cunninghamii.*

HOP. See *Humulus.*

HOP BUSH, HOPSEED BUSH. See *Dodonaea viscosa.*

HOP TREE. See *Ptelea trifoliata.*

HOREHOUND. See *Marrubium vulgare.*

Homalocladium platycladum

HORNBEAM. See *Carpinus.*

HORNED POPPY. See *Glaucium.*

HORSE BEAN. See Bean, Broad.

HORSECHESTNUT. See *Aesculus.*

HORSEMINT. See *Monarda.*

HORSERADISH. All Zones. A large, coarse, weedy-looking perennial plant grown for its large, coarse, white roots, which are peeled, grated, and mixed with vinegar or cream to make a condiment. Does best in rich, moist soils in cool regions. Grow it in some sunny out-of-the-way corner. Start with roots planted 1 ft. apart in late winter or early spring. Dig full grown roots in fall, winter, or spring. It's best to dig just a few outside roots at a time; then you'll have your horseradish fresh and hot.

Horseradish

HORSETAIL. See *Equisetum hyemale.*

HORSETAIL TREE. See *Casuarina equisetifolia.*

HOSTA *(Funkia).* PLANTAIN LILY. Perennials. Zones 1–10, 12–21. Their real glory is in their leaves—typically heart shaped, shiny, distinctly veined. Flowers come as a dividend: thin spikes topped by several trumpet shaped flowers grow up from foliage mounds in summer, last for several weeks. Sun, light shade, or heavy shade (north side of house). Need regular summer watering. Feeding once a year will bring on extra leafy splendor. Blanket of peat moss around plants will prevent mud from splattering plants. Slugs and snails love the leaves; bait 3–4 times a year. All forms go dormant (collapse almost to nothing) in winter; new fresh leaves grow from roots in early spring. Good in containers. In ground, plants last for years, clumps expand in size, shade out weed growth. Few plants have undergone so many name changes; to be quite sure you are getting the one you want, buy it in full leaf.

Hosta decorata

H. decorata (H. 'Thomas Hogg'). Plants to 2 ft. high. Oval leaves, 6 in. long, bluntly pointed tips, green with silvery white margins. Lavender 2-in.-long flowers.

H. 'Honeybells'. Large grass green leaves. Fragrant lavender lilac flowers on 3-ft. stems.

H. lancifolia (H. japonica). NARROW LEAFED PLANTAIN LILY. Leaves dark green, 6 in. long not heart shaped, but tapering into the long stalk. Pale lavender flowers, 2 in. long, on 2-ft. stems.

H. plantaginea (H. grandiflora, H. subcordata). FRAGRANT PLANTAIN LILY. Scented white flowers, 4–5 in. long, on 2-ft. stems. Leaves bright green, to 10 in. long.

H. sieboldiana (H. glauca). Blue green leaves, 10–15 in. long, heavily veined. Many slender, pale lilac flowers nestle close to leaves. A showpiece plant near shaded pool or woodland path.

H. undulata (H. media picta, H. variegata). WAVY-LEAFED PLANTAIN LILY. Leaves 6–8 in. long, have wavy margins, variegated white on green. Foliage used in arrangements. Pale lavender flowers on 3-ft. stalks.

H. ventricosa (H. caerulea). BLUE PLANTAIN LILY. Deep green broad leaves, prominently ribbed. Blue flowers on 3-ft. stems.

HOTTENTOT FIG. See *Carpobrotus.*

HOUSELEEK. See *Sempervivum.*

HOWEA. Palms. Outdoors in Zones 17, 21–24; anywhere as house or greenhouse plant. Native to Lord Howe Island. These feather palms are the kentia palms of florists. Slow growing; with age, leaves drop to show clean, green trunk ringed with leaf scars. Ideal pot plants.

H. belmoreana. SENTRY PALM. Less common than *H. forsterana,* smaller and more compact, with over-arching leaves 6–7 ft. long. As a pot plant stands some watering neglect, drafts, dust.

H. forsterana. PARADISE PALM. Larger than *H. belmoreana,* with leaves to 9 ft. long and long, drooping leaflets. Average water.

Howea forsterana

Howeas (usually under the name of kentias) are the classic parlor palms. Keep fronds clean and dust-free to minimize spider mite problem.

HOYA. WAX FLOWER, WAX PLANT. Shrubby or climbing house plants, one used outdoors in mild climates. Thick, waxy, evergreen leaves and tight clusters of small waxy flowers. Commonly grown in sunny windows. Do best in rich, loose, well-drained soil. Bloom best when potbound; usually grown in containers even outdoors. Do not prune out flowering wood; new blossom clusters appear from stumps of old ones.

H. bella. House or greenhouse plant. Shrubby, to 3 ft., with slender, upright branches which droop as they grow older; small leaves. Tight clusters of white, purple-centered ½-in. flowers in summer. Best in hanging basket. Average water.

Hoya carnosa

H. carnosa. WAX FLOWER, WAX PLANT. Indoor plant or outdoors in Zones 15–24 with overhead protection—but even there it is quickly damaged by temperatures much below freezing. Vining to 10 ft. Has 2–4-in.-long oval leaves; big, round, tight clusters of creamy white flowers ½ in. across, each flower with a perfect 5-pointed pink star in center. Fragrant, summer blooming. Red young leaves give additional touch of color. Water deeply in summer, then allow soil to go partially dry before watering again. In cool climates let plant go dormant in winter, giving only enough water to keep it from shriveling. Outdoors, train on pillar or trellis in shade; indoors, train on wire in sunny window.

'Variegata' has leaves edged with white suffused with pink. Color is variable and may change with age of plant, amount of available light. It is not as vigorous or hardy as the green form. 'Exotica' shows yellow and pink variegation. 'Krinkle Kurl' has crinkly leaves very closely spaced on short stems; it looks like a severe case of aphid damage. It is often sold as *H. c.* 'Compacta' or as the HINDU-ROPE PLANT.

HUCKLEBERRY. See *Vaccinium ovatum, V. parvifolium.*

HUMATA tyermannii. BEAR'S FOOT FERN. Outdoors in Zones 17, 23, 24; elsewhere an indoor or greenhouse plant. Native to China. This small fern has furry, creeping rhizomes that look something like bear's feet. Fronds 8–10 in. long, very finely cut, rising at intervals from the rhizome. Like *Davallia* in appearance and uses, but slower growing. Average water, partial shade.

Humata tyermannii

HUMMINGBIRD BUSH. See *Grevillea thelemanniana.*

HUMMINGBIRD FLOWER. See *Zauschneria.*

HUMULUS. HOP. Annual and perennial vines. Extremely fast growth. Need much water. Full sun. Large, deeply lobed leaves. Useful for summer screening on trellises or arbors.

H. japonicus. JAPANESE HOP. Summer annual vine. To 20–30 ft. Flowers do not make true hops. Variety 'Variegatus' has foliage marked with white. Flowers in greenish clusters like pine cones. Sow seeds in spring where plants are to grow.

H. lupulus. COMMON HOP. Perennial vine. All Zones. The plant that grows hops used to flavor beer. Grow from roots (not easy to find in nurseries) planted in rich soil, early spring. Place thick end up, just below soil surface. Furnish supports for vertical climbing. Shoots come forth in May and grow quickly to 15–25 ft. by midsummer. Give roots copious water once rapid growth starts. Leaves 3–5 lobed, toothed. Squarish, hairy stems twine vertically; to get horizontal growth, twine stem tips by hand. Light green hops (soft, flaky, 1–2-in. cones of bracts and flowers) form in August-September. They're attractive and have fresh piny fragrance. Cut back stems to ground after frost turns them brown. Regrowth comes the following spring. Tender hop shoots can be cooked as a vegetable.

Humulus lupulus

H. l. neomexicanus (H. americanus), native to central and southern Rockies, scarcely differs from the cultivated hop noted above.

HUNNEMANNIA fumariifolia. MEXICAN TULIP POPPY, GOLDEN CUP. Perennial, usually treated as annual. Bushy, open, 2–3 ft. high, with very finely divided blue green leaves. Its flowers are clear soft yellow, cup shaped, 3 in. across, with crinkled petals; bloom July-October. Related to California poppy. Showy plant in masses; striking with scarlet *Zauschneria californica,* or with blues of ceratostigma, echium, or penstemon. Blooms last for a week in water if cut in bud. Plant from nursery flats or sow seed in place in warm, dry, sunny position and later thin seedlings to 12 in. apart. Reseeds. Plants need excellent drainage, will die out if overwatered.

Hunnemannia fumariifolia

HYACINTH BEAN. See *Dolichos lablab.*

HYACINTHUS. HYACINTH. Bulbs. All Zones. As garden plants, best adapted in cold-winter climates. Bell shaped, fragrant flowers in loose or tight spikes rise from basal bundle of narrow bright green leaves. All spring blooming. Plant in fall. Where winters are cold, plant in September-October. In mild areas plant October-December.

H. amethystinus. See *Brimeura.*
H. azureus. See *Muscari azureum.*
H. orientalis. COMMON HYACINTH. Grows to 1 ft., with fragrant, bell shaped, white, pale blue, or purple blue flowers. Two basic forms are the Dutch and the Roman or French Roman.

Hyacinthus orientalis

DUTCH HYACINTH, derived from *H. orientalis* by breeding and selection, has large dense spikes of waxy, bell-like, fragrant flowers in white, shades of blue, purple, pink, red, cream, buff, and salmon. Size of spike directly related to bulb size.

Biggest bulbs are desirable for exhibition plants or for potting; second size is most satisfactory for bedding outside. Small bulbs give smaller, looser clusters with flowers more widely spaced. These are sometimes called miniature hyacinths. Set the larger bulbs 6 in. deep, smaller bulbs 4 in.

Hyacinths look best when massed or grouped; rows look stiff, formal. Mass bulbs of a single color beneath flowering tree or in border. Leave bulbs in ground after bloom, continue to feed and water until foliage yellows. Flowers tend to be smaller in succeeding years, but maintain same color and fragrance.

Choice container plants. Pot in porous mix with tip of bulb near surface. After potting, cover containers with thick mulch of sawdust, wood shavings, or peat moss to keep bulbs cool, moist, shaded until roots well formed; remove mulch, place in full light when tops show. Also grow hyacinths in water in special hyacinth glass, the bottom filled with pebbles and water. Keep in dark, cool place until rooted, give light when top growth appears; place in sunny window when leaves have turned uniformly green.

ROMAN or FRENCH ROMAN HYACINTH (*H. o. albulus*), has white, pink, or light blue flowers loosely carried on slender stems; usually several stems to a bulb. Earlier bloom than Dutch hyacinths, well-adapted to mild-winter areas, where they naturalize under favorable conditions. Where winters are cold, grow in pots for winter bloom.

HYBOPHRYNIUM braunianum (*Bamburanta arnoldiana*). BAMBURANTA. Perennial. Zones 22–24; elsewhere indoor plant. Grown for foliage only and not for flowers. Tall-growing canes suggest bamboo in habit; spreading leaves all along stems are oval and very short stalked. Shade or semishade. Best in containers. Needs light soil, good drainage, abundant water. Give light feedings frequently (every 2–4 weeks).

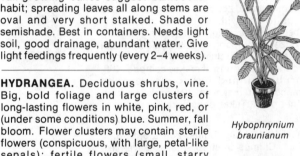

Hybophrynium braunianum

HYDRANGEA. Deciduous shrubs, vine. Big, bold foliage and large clusters of long-lasting flowers in white, pink, red, or (under some conditions) blue. Summer, fall bloom. Flower clusters may contain sterile flowers (conspicuous, with large, petal-like sepals); fertile flowers (small, starry petaled); or cluster of small fertile flowers surrounded by ring of big sterile ones. The last named are called the lace cap hydrangeas. Sterile flowers last long, often holding up for months, gradually fading in color. Effective when massed in partial shade or planted in tubs on paved terrace.

Easy to grow in rich, porous soil; dependent on heavy watering. Protect against overhead sun inland; in cool coastal gardens they can take full sun. Fast growing—prune to control size and form; cut out stems that have flowered, leaving those which have not. To get biggest flower clusters, reduce number of stems; for numerous middle-sized clusters nicely spaced, keep more stems.

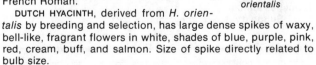

Hydrangea macrophylla

H. anomala. CLIMBING HYDRANGEA. Deciduous vine. Zones 1–21. Climbs high by clinging aerial rootlets. Shrubby and sprawling without support. Roundish, 2–4-in.-long green, heart shaped leaves. Mature plants develop short, stiff, flowering branches with flat white flower clusters, 6–10 in. wide, in lace cap effect. *H. anomala petiolaris* (*H. petiolaris*), commoner form in cultivation, is scarcely different.

H. arborescens. SMOOTH HYDRANGEA. Deciduous shrub. Zones 1–21. Upright, dense to 10 ft. with oval, grayish green 4–8-in. leaves. White flowers in 6-in. roundish clusters, June to frost; a few large sterile flowers. Much better is variety 'Grandiflora', HILLS OF SNOW, with very large clusters made up of large sterile flowers.

H. macrophylla (*H. hortensia, H. opuloides, H. otaksa*). BIG-LEAF HYDRANGEA, GARDEN HYDRANGEA. Deciduous shrub. Zones 2–24. Symmetrical, rounded habit, to 4–8, even 12 ft. with thick, shining, coarsely toothed leaves to 8 in. long. Flowers white, pink, red, or blue in big clusters.

Pink and red forms often turn blue or purple in acid soils.

(Continued on next page)

Florists grow French hybrids as pot plants, controlling flower color by controlling soil mix. Blue-flowering plants from the florist may show pink flowers when planted out in neutral or alkaline soil. Plants can be made (or kept) blue by soil application of aluminum sulfate; plants can be kept red or made redder by liming or applying superphosphate in quantity to soil; treatment is not effective unless started well ahead of bloom.

Great performer in areas where winters are fairly mild, disappointing where plants freeze to ground every year. May never bloom under these conditions. Protect in Zones 2, 3 by hilling soil or leaves over bases of plants.

There are hundreds of named varieties, and plants may be sold under many names. Florists' plants are usually French hybrids, dwarfer (1–3 ft. tall) and with larger flowers than old garden varieties. Two varieties are unmistakable: 'Domotoi' has clusters of pink or blue double sterile flowers; 'Tricolor' (usually sold as 'Variegata'), a lace cap, has dark green leaves strongly marked with cream and light green.

H. paniculata 'Grandiflora'. PEEGEE HYDRANGEA. Deciduous shrub. Zones 1–21. Upright, of coarse texture, can be trained as a 25-ft. tree. Best as a 10–15-ft. shrub. Leaves 5 in. long, turn bronzy in fall. White flowers in upright 10–15-in.-long clusters slowly fade to pinky bronze.

H. quercifolia. OAKLEAF HYDRANGEA. Deciduous shrub. Zones 1–22. Broad rounded shrub to 6 ft. with very handsome, deeply lobed, oaklike, 8-in.-long leaves that turn bronze or crimson in fall. Creamy white flowers in open clusters, June. Pruned to ground each spring, it makes compact, 3-ft. shrub. Thinned out to well-spaced branches, it makes a distinguished container plant. Takes considerable sun.

*Hydrangea
quercifolia*

HYMENOCALLIS. Bulbs. Zones 5, 6, 8, 9, 14-24. Clumps of strap shaped leaves like amaryllis. In June and July, 2-ft. stems bear several very fragrant flowers that resemble daffodils except that center cup has 6 slender, spiderlike, free segments. Unusual summer-blooming plant for borders or containers. Plant in rich, well-drained soil in late fall or early winter in frostless areas; after frosts in colder climates. Likes sun or light shade. Set bulbs with tips 1 in. below surface. Water well during growth and bloom; dry off when foliage begins to yellow. Dig and wash bulbs, dry in inverted position; do not cut off fleshy roots. Store in open trays at 60°–75°F.

*Hymenocallis
narcissiflora*

H. festalis. Free flowering, with 4 or more pure white flowers, the cup with very narrow curved segments. Leaves resemble those of *H. narcissiflora*.

H. narcissiflora (*Ismene calathina*). BASKET FLOWER, PERUVIAN DAFFODIL. Leaves 1½–2 ft. long, 1–2 in. wide. White, green-striped flowers grow 2–5 in cluster. Variety 'Advance' has pure white flowers, faintly lined with green in throat.

H. 'Sulfur Queen'. Primrose yellow flowers with light yellow, green-striped throat. Leaves like those of *H. narcissiflora*.

HYMENOCYCLUS. See *Malephora*.

HYMENOSPORUM flavum. SWEETSHADE. Evergreen small tree or large shrub. Zones 8, 9, 14–23. Native to Australia. Offers slow to moderate growth to 20–40 ft. with 15–20-ft. spread. Graceful, upright, slender, open habit in first 10 years. Leaves shiny dark green, 2–6 in. long, 1–2 in. wide, with tendency to cluster near ends of twigs and branches. Clusters of yellow flowers bloom in early summer with pronounced orange

*Hymenosporum
flavum*

blossom honey fragrance.

Best away from coastal winds. Should have fast soil drainage, routine feeding, and well-spaced deep watering rather than lawn watering. Full sun or light shade. Early training necessary as branches spread out in almost equal threes, creating weak crotches that are likely to split. Strengthen branches by frequent pinching and shortening. As single tree, needs staking for several years. Attractive planted in small groves, in which case trees can grow without staking, training, or pruning.

Hymenosporum flavum

HYPERICUM. ST. JOHNSWORT. Shrubs and perennials, evergreen or semievergreen. Zones 4–24, except as noted below. Best in mild, moist coastal areas. Open, cup shaped, 5-petaled flowers range in color from creamy yellow to gold, and have prominent sunburst of stamens in center. Leaves neat, vary in form and color. Plants useful for fresh green of foliage and summer flower color. Mass planting, ground cover, informal hedges, borders. Sun near coast, part shade in hot-summer areas. Any soil. Most kinds stand some drought, but are better with water.

Hypericum calycinum

H. beanii (*H. patulum henryi*). To 4 ft., with light green, oblong leaves on graceful, willowy branches. Evergreen. Flowers brilliant golden yellow, 2 in. across, July-October. Shabby winter appearance in cold-winter areas. Good for low, untrimmed hedge, mass planting.

H. calycinum. AARON'S BEARD, CREEPING ST. JOHNSWORT. Evergreen shrub; semideciduous where winters are cold. Zones 2–24. Grows to 1 ft. tall; spreads by vigorous underground stems. Leaves short stalked, to 4 in. long, medium green in sun, yellow green in shade. Flowers bright yellow, 3 in. across. Tough, dense ground cover for sun or shade; competes successfully with tree roots, takes poor soil, some drought. Fast growing, will control erosion on hillsides. Can invade other plantings unless confined. Plant from flats or as rooted stems; set 18 in. apart. Clip or mow off tops every 2–3 years during dormant season.

H. coris. Evergreen subshrub. To 6–12 in. or more high. Leaves narrow, ½–1 in. long, in whorls of 4–6. Flowers yellow, ¾ in. across, in loose clusters. Bloom April-June. Good ground cover or rock garden plant.

H. 'Hidcote'. (*H. patulum* 'Hidcote'). Rounded shrub to 4 ft., semievergreen in colder climates, where freezing keeps height closer to 2 ft. Leaves 2–3 in. long. Flowers yellow, 3 in. wide; blooms all summer.

H. kouytchense. Semievergreen. Twiggy, rounded shrub 1½–2 ft. tall, 2–3 ft. wide, with 2-in. pointed oval leaves. Flowers golden yellow, 2-3 in. across, heavily produced July-August.

H. moseranum. GOLD FLOWER. Evergreen shrub or perennial. To 3 ft. tall where winters are mild; grows as hardy perennial in cold-winter areas. Moundlike habit with arching, reddish stems. Leaves 2 in. long, blue green beneath. Flowers golden yellow, 2½ in. across, in clusters of 1–5, bloom June-August. Cut back in early spring.

H. patulum henryi. See *H. beanii*.

H. patulum 'Hidcote'. See *H.* 'Hidcote'.

H. 'Rowallane'. Evergreen shrub. Upright to 3–6 ft., rather straggly growth. Flowers bright yellow, 2½–3 in. across, profuse in late summer and fall. Leaves 2½–3½ in. long. Remove older branches annually.

H. 'Sungold'. See *H. kouytchense*.

HYPOCYRTA nummularia. See *Alloplectus nummularia*.

HYPOESTES phyllostachya (*H. sanguinolenta*). FRECKLE FACE, PINK POLKA-DOT PLANT. Indoor foliage plant. Can reach 1-2 ft. tall. Slender stems. Leaves 2-3 in. long, oval, spotted irregularly with pink. A selected form known as 'Splash' has larger spots. Blooms very seldom. Plant in loose, peaty mixture in pots or planters. Feed with liquid fertilizer. Pinch tips to make bushy.

HYSSOPUS officinalis. HYSSOP. Perennial herb. All Zones. Compact growth to 1½–2 ft. Narrow, dark green, pungent leaves; profusion of dark blue flower spikes from July to November. There are also white and pink-flowered forms. Fairly drought resistant. Full sun or light shade.

Hypoestes phyllostachya

IBERIS. CANDYTUFT. Annuals, perennials. All Zones. These are free-blooming plants with clusters of white, lavender, lilac, pink, rose, purple, carmine, or crimson flowers, early spring to summer. Use annuals for borders, cutting; perennials for edging, rock gardens, small scale ground covers, containers.

Sow seed of annual kinds in place or in flats in fall (in mild areas) or in early spring. Set transplants 6–9 in. apart. Plant perennials in sun or partial shade in fall or spring; water deeply—moderately drought tolerant; shear lightly after bloom to stimulate new growth.

Hyssopus officinalis

I. amara. HYACINTH-FLOWERED CANDYTUFT, ROCKET CANDYTUFT. Annual. Fragrant white flowers in tight, round clusters that elongate into hyacinthlike spikes on 15-in. stems. Narrow, slightly fuzzy leaves.

I. sempervirens. EVERGREEN CANDYTUFT. Perennial. Grows 8–12 or even 18 in. high, spreading about as wide. Leaves narrow, shiny dark green, good looking all year. Flower clusters pure white, on stems long enough to cut for bouquets; bloom early spring to June; first flowers as early as November in mild areas. Lower, more compact varieties are 'Little Gem', 4–6 in. tall; 'Purity', 6–12 in. tall, wide spreading; 'Snowflake', 4–12 in. tall, 1½–3 ft. wide, broader, more leathery leaves, larger flowers in larger clusters on shorter stems, extremely showy in spring and with sporadic bloom all year in milder areas.

Iberis sempervirens

I. umbellata. GLOBE CANDYTUFT. Annual. Bushy plants 12–15 in. high. Lance shaped leaves to 3½ in. long. Flowers in pink, rose, carmine, crimson, salmon, lilac, and white. Dwarf strains 'Dwarf Fairy' and 'Magic Carpet' grow to 6 in. tall, in the same colors.

ICE PLANT. Succulent perennials, subshrubs, or annuals. Once conveniently lumped together as *Mesembryanthemum,* now classified under several different names. A brief summary of plants under new names:

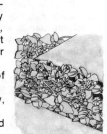

Delosperma 'Alba'

Carpobrotus. Coarse, sturdy ice plants of beach and highway plantings.

Cephalophyllum. Slow spreading, hardy, showy flowers.

Delosperma. Good ground cover and bank cover.

Dorotheanthus. Annuals for summer bloom.

Drosanthemum. Profuse pink or purple flowers, useful on steep banks.

Lampranthus. Large flowering, brilliantly colorful as ground cover, in rock gardens.

Malephora. Ground covers with good-looking foliage, long bloom season.

Mesembryanthemum. Annuals of little ornamental value are the only plants left here. One is sometimes seen as naturalized roadside planting in California.

Oscularia. Dainty form, fragrance.

Descriptions of each of above are given under the listed names. All tolerate drought when established, but look best with some summer water; amount depends on heat, humidity. Plants require little summer water in coastal areas, more inland. Too much water can lead to dieback. Give just enough to keep plants looking lively. Feed lightly when fall rains begin, and again after bloom. All need full sun, take most soils; won't take walking on.

IDESIA polycarpa. Deciduous tree. Zones 4–9, 14–17, 19–24. Native to Japan, China. To 50 ft. tall, usually much less, with strongly horizontal branch structure and broad crown. The leaves are thick, heart shaped, 6–10 in. long, nearly as wide, on 5–7-in. stalks. Yellow green flowers (June and July) in 10-in.-long, drooping clusters, fragrant but not showy; male and female flowers usually on separate trees. Fruit in clusters on female trees; individual berries the size of peas, turning from green to brown to red, ornamental. Needs some summer water. Unusual lawn or shade tree. Large leaves and broad crown give idesia an exotic look; berries are handsome in fall

Idesia polycarpa

and early winter, but you must have both male and female plants for fruiting.

ILEX. HOLLY. Evergreen shrubs or trees (deciduous types rarely grown in the West). English holly is most familiar, but other species are becoming popular, especially in warmer, drier parts of the West. Hollies range from foot-high dwarfs to 50-ft. trees. Leaves may be tiny or large, toothed or smooth, green or variegated. Plants sold as Dutch holly are simply hollies without marginal spines. Berries may be red, orange, yellow, or black.

Most holly plants are either male or female, and generally both plants must be present for female to bear fruit. There are exceptions: some female holly plants will set fruit without pollination, and hormone sprays may induce berry set on female flowers. Safest way to get berries is to have plants of both sexes, or to graft male branch onto female plant. Male plants will have no berries.

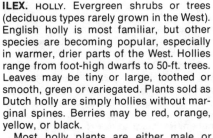

Ilex aquifolium

Holly prefers rich, slightly acid, good garden soil; it tolerates sun or shade, is most compact and fruitful in sun. (See descriptions for exceptions.) It needs ample water with good drainage. Add thick mulch rather than cultivating around plant. Attractive background plant, useful as barrier.

Scale and mealybug can attack in all holly-growing areas. Holly bud moth and leaf miner need attention on English holly in Northwest. Two sprays a year generally give good control. Use an oil late in March for scale and bud moth. Spray with systemics or malathion during May for leaf miner. Birds will eat fruit.

I. altaclarensis 'Wilsonii' (*I. wilsonii*). WILSON HOLLY. Shrub or tree. Zones 3–24. Hybrid between English holly and a Canary Island species. One of best hollies, especially in warmer regions. Takes sun, shade, wind, almost any soil. Moderately drought tolerant. Usually a 6–8-ft. shrub, but easily grown as 15–20-ft. single-stemmed tree. Leaves to 5 in. long, 3 in. wide, thick, leathery, rich green, evenly spine toothed. Heavy producer of bright red berries. Use as standard tree, espalier, shrub, screen, clipped hedge.

I. aquifolium. ENGLISH HOLLY, CHRISTMAS HOLLY. Shrub or tree. Zones 4–9, 14–24; at its best in Zones 4–6, 15–17. Native to southern and central Europe, British Isles. Slow growth to 40 ft., usually much less. Highly variable in leaf shape, color, and degree of spininess. Note that male plants will not have berries; females may or may not. Some varieties produce infertile berries without a pollinator but these berries are usually small, slow to develop, and quick to drop. English holly needs protection from sun in hot dry areas and soil conditioning where soils are alkaline. Resistant to oak root fungus. Best-known include:

I. a. 'Angustifolia'. Grows as compact, narrow pyramid. Very narrow (½ in. wide, 1½ in. long) spiny leaves. Small brilliant red berries.

'Balkans'. Hardiest English holly. Seed collected in Yugoslavia. Smooth, upright, dark green leaves. Red berries.

'Big Bull'. Very ornamental male with large, nearly smooth-edged leaves.

'Boulder Creek'. Typical English holly with large leaves. Brilliant red berries.

'Ciliata Major'. Vigorous, erect holly with purple bark on young shoots. Large leaves are flat, long spined, with high gloss, olive-tinged dark green. Good berry producer.

'Ferox'. HEDGEHOG, PORCUPINE HOLLY. Male with sterile pollen. Twisted, fiercely spined leaves give it its common names.

'Fertilis'. Sets light crop of seedless berries without pollination.

'Little Bull'. Very ornamental compact male with small leaves.

'San Gabriel'. Bears seedless berries without pollination.

'Sparkler'. Strong, upright grower. Heavy crop of glistening red berries at an early age.

'Teufel's Deluxe'. Exceptionally dark green leaves. Large, early-ripening red berries.

'Teufel's Zero'. Upright with long slender branches, weeping. Dark red berries ripen early. Unusually hardy.

'Van Tol'. Smooth, glossy green leaves. Early to mature. Large dark red berries.

Varieties with variegated leaves. Leaves edged with silver: 'Argenteo Marginata', 'Silvery', 'Silver Queen' (male), 'Silver King'. Leaves with silver centers: 'Argentea Mediopicta', 'Silver Star', 'Silver Milkmaid'. Leaves with golden margins: 'Aureomarginata', 'Golden Queen' (male), 'Lily Gold'. Leaves with golden centers: 'Golden Milkmaid', 'Pinto'.

I. aquipernyi. Shrub. Zones 4–9, 14–24. Hybrid between *I. aquifolium* and *I. pernyi.* The variety 'Brilliant' grows 8–10 ft. (possibly to 20 ft.), with cone shaped habit and dense foliage. Leaves short stalked, densely set on branches, twice as large as *I. pernyi,* with few but very pronounced teeth. Heavy crop of red berries without pollination. Resistant to oak root fungus.

I. cornuta. CHINESE HOLLY. Shrub or small tree. Zones 4–24; best in Zones 8, 9, 14–16, 18–21. Needs long warm season to set fruit. Give it east or north exposure in desert climates. Dense or open growth to 10 ft. Typical leaves glossy, leathery, nearly rectangular, with spines at the 4 corners and at tip. Berries exceptionally large, bright red, long lasting. Great variation among varieties in fruit set, leaf form, spininess. In following list, all bear fruit without pollinator except those noted:

'Berries Jubilee'. Dwarf, dome shaped plant with large leaves and very heavy crop of large bright red berries. Leaves larger, spinier than 'Burfordii' on much smaller plant.

'Burfordii'. BURFORD HOLLY. Widely planted throughout California. Leaves nearly spineless, cupped downward. Useful as espalier.

'Carissa'. Extremely dwarf, dense grower with small leaves; smaller than 'Rotunda'. Use for small containers, low hedge. No berries.

'Dazzler'. Compact, upright growth. Glossy leaves have a few stout spines along wavy margins. Loaded with berries.

'Dwarf Burford' ('Burfordii Nana'). Resembles 'Burfordii' but much smaller; plants 5 years old not likely to exceed 1½ ft. in height, spread. Small (1½ in.) light green spineless leaves, densely set.

'Femina'. Very spiny leaves. Good berry producer.

'Rotunda'. DWARF CHINESE HOLLY. Compact low grower. A 6-year-old may be 18 in. high and as wide. Does not produce berries. A few stout spines and rolled leaf margins between them make medium light green leaves nearly rectangular.

'Willowleaf'. Large shrub or small tree with dense spreading growth pattern. Long, narrow, dark green leaves. Good crop of dark red berries.

I. crenata. JAPANESE HOLLY. Shrub. Zones 2–9, 14–24. Looks more like a boxwood than a holly. Dense, erect, usually to 3-4 ft., sometimes 20 ft. Narrow, finely toothed leaves, ½–¾ in. long. Berries are black. Extremely hardy and useful where winter cold limits choice of polished evergreens for hedges, edgings. All grow best in slightly acid soil. Sun or shade. Varieties sold:

'Convexa'. (Often sold as *I. c. bullata.*) Compact, rounded shrub to 4–6 ft. and broader than tall. Leaves, ½ in. long, roundish with edges cupped downward. Handsome clipped or unclipped.

'Glory'. Small, dense grower; round bush with tiny leaves. Male plant (no fruit).

'Green Island'. Low and spreading, to 24 in. high.

'Green Thumb'. Compact, upright to 20 in. Deep green leaves.

'Helleri'. Dwarf to 12 in. high, 2 ft. wide.

'Hetzii'. Similar to 'Convexa' with larger leaves, more vigorous growth.

'Mariesii'. Smallest and slowest growing of Japanese hollies. Only 8 in. high in 10 years.

I. latifolia. Tree. Zones 4–7, 15–17, 20–24. Native to China and Japan. Largest leaves of hollies, 6–8 in. long, dull dark green, thick and leathery, finely toothed. Slow-growing tree with stout branches to 50–60 ft. Berries in large clusters, large, dull red.

I. meserveae. Zones 3–24. Hybrids between *I. aquifolium* and species from far northern Japan. Apparently the hardiest of hollies that have true holly look. Dense, bushy plants 6–7 ft. tall with purple stems and spiny, blue green, glossy leaves. Varieties include: 'Blue Angel', crinkly foliage, large berries; 'Blue Prince', male plant for pollination; and 'Blue Princess', deep green Christmas holly foliage, many clusters of berries along stems.

I. 'Nellie Stevens'. Shrub. Zones 4–9, 14–24. Hybrid between *I. cornuta* and *I. aquifolium.* Leaves suggest both parents. Showy berries. Fast growing, large, can be trained as tree.

I. opaca. AMERICAN HOLLY. Tree. Zones 2–9, 15, 16, 19–23. Native to eastern U.S. Slow growing, pyramidal or round headed, to 50 ft. Leaves 2–4 in. long, dull or glossy green with spiny margins. Berries red, not as numerous as on *I. aquifolium.* Plant is resistant to oak root fungus. Some of the many varieties are occasionally available in the West. They include 'Brilliantissima', 'East Palatka', 'Howard', 'Manig', 'Mrs. Sarver', 'Old Heavy Berry', 'Rosalind Sarver'.

I. pernyi. Shrub or small tree. Zones 4–9, 14–24. Slow growth to 20–30 ft. Glossy, square-based leaves closely packed against branchlets, 1–2 in. long, with 1–3 spines on each side. Berries red, set tightly against stem.

I. 'San Jose Hybrid'. Shrub or small tree. Zones 4–9, 14–24. Hybrid with *I. altaclarensis* 'Wilsonii' as one parent. To 15–20 ft. Resembles *I. altaclarensis* but with leaves somewhat longer and narrower. Growth upright, berry production heavy.

I. vomitoria. YAUPON. Shrub or small tree. Zones 3–9, 11–24. Native to southeastern U.S. Stands extremely alkaline soils better than other hollies. Large shrub or small tree to 15–20 ft. Often sheared into columnar form. Narrow, inch-long, dark green leaves. Tiny scarlet berries in profusion, without pollinator. The following varieties are available:

'Nana'. DWARF YAUPON. Low shrub. Compact to 18 in. high and twice as wide. Refined, attractive. Formal when sheared.

'Pride of Houston'. Large shrub or small tree, upright, freely branching. Use as screen or hedge.

'Stokes'. Dark green leaves, close set, compact. Smaller growing than 'Nana'.

IMMORTELLE. See *Xeranthemum annuum.*

IMPATIENS. BALSAM, TOUCH-ME-NOT, SNAPWEED. Summer annuals, perennials. Annual kinds grow best in sun, perennials in partial shade in all but coastal areas. Flowers attract birds. Ripe seed capsules burst open when touched lightly and scatter seeds explosively.

I. balsamina. BALSAM. Summer annual. Erect, branching, 8–30 in. tall. Leaves 1½–6 in. long, sharply pointed, deeply toothed. Flowers large, spurred, borne among leaves along main stem and branches. Colors plain or variegated, in white, pink, rose, lilac, red. Double camellia-flowered forms most used, compact, bushy. Sow seeds in early spring, set out plants after frost in full sun (light shade in hot areas). Needs lots of water.

Impatiens wallerana

I. glandulifera *(I. roylei)*. Summer annual. Coarse, much branched, to 3–4 ft. Leaves 2–6 in. long, sharply toothed. Flowers large, pale lavender to purple, in clusters of 3 or more on long stalks. Grows easily, naturalizes where water is available.

I. holstii. See *I. wallerana*.

New Guinea hybrids. Summer annuals. A varied group of striking plants developed from number of species native to New Guinea. Plants can be upright or spreading; they usually have very large leaves, these often variegated with cream or red. Flowers are usually large (though not profuse); colors include lavender, purple, pink, red, orange. Best used as pot plants; give ample water and fertilizer; need somewhat more light than conventional bedding impatiens. Many named kinds, ranging from spreading 8 in. to erect 24 in.

I. oliveri. OLIVER'S SNAPWEED, POOR MAN'S RHODODENDRON. Perennial. Zones 15–17, 21–24; elsewhere as greenhouse or indoor/outdoor container plant. Shrubby to 4–8 ft. tall, as much as 10 ft. wide. Bears many lilac, pale lavender, or pinkish slender-spurred flowers 2¼ in. across. Glossy dark green leaves to 8 in. long in whorls along stems. Blooms in partial or deep shade. Along coast grows in full sun, takes sea breezes, salt spray. Needs some summer water. Inland, frosts kill it to ground; regrows in spring.

I. repens. House plant. Trailer, with juicy red stems, tiny (fingernail-sized) bright green leaves, bright yellow 1½-in. flowers appearing from time to time, with heaviest bloom in summer, early fall. Best in hanging pot with rich soil, summer feeding, regular watering, strong indirect light.

I. sultanii. See *I. wallerana*.

I. wallerana. BUSY LIZZIE. Perennial, usually grown as summer annual. Includes plants formerly known as *I. holstii* and *I. sultanii*. Rapid, vigorous growth: tall varieties (usually called *I. holstii*) to 2 ft.; dwarf, 4–8 in.; semidwarf, 8–12 in. Dark green, glossy, narrow 1–3-in.-long leaves on pale green, juicy stems. Flowers 1–2 in., scarlet, pink, rose, violet, orange, or white.

Useful for bright flowers for many months in partial shade with begonias, fatsia, ferns, fuchsias, hydrangeas. Grow from seed, cuttings, or buy plants from flats. Rich, moist soil. Perhaps *the* most useful summer annual for shady gardens—especially in warm-summer climates. Improved strains of dwarf 6–12-in. plants are Cinderella, Elfin, and Minette. In 12–15 in. range are Imp, Shade Glow, and Shady Lady. For big flowers, get Futura and Shade King (6–12 in.) or Grande (12–15 in.); all have 2½-in. flowers. Fancifrills strain has fully double flowers that look like miniature camellias; they perform best as pot plants or house plants. Singles with white markings are Crazy Quilt, Ripple, and Zig Zag.

INCARVILLEA delavayi. Perennial. All Zones. Fleshy roots. Basal leaves 1 ft. long, divided into toothed leaflets. Stems to 3 ft., topped with clusters of 2–12 trumpet shaped flowers 3 in. long and wide; rosy purple outside, yellow and purple inside. Blooms May-July. Sun or light shade. Deep, porous soil. Roots rot in winter in water-logged soils. Sow seeds in spring for bloom following year. In extremely cold climates lift and store roots like dahlias. Cover with soil; do not let them dry out.

Incarvillea delavayi

INCENSE CEDAR. See *Calocedrus decurrens*.

INDIA HAWTHORN. See *Raphiolepis indica*.

INDIAN BEAN. See *Catalpa bignonioides*.

INDIAN CURRANT. See *Symphoricarpos orbiculatus*.

INDIAN FIG CACTUS. See *Opuntia ficus-indica*.

INDIAN MOCK STRAWBERRY. See *Duchesnea indica*.

INSIDE-OUT FLOWER. See *Vancouveria planipetala*.

IOCHROMA cyaneum *(I. lanceolatum, I. purpureum, I. tubulosum)*. Evergreen shrub. Zones 16, 17, 19–24. To 8 ft. or more with oval to lance shaped leaves, 5–6 in. long, of dark, dull green. Clusters of purplish blue, tubular, drooping, 2-in.-long flowers in summer. Seedlings sometimes vary to purplish rose or pink. Buy in bloom to get color you want. Fast-growing, soft-wooded shrub that looks best espaliered or tied up against wall. Best in full sun. Prune it hard after bloom, and give it plenty of water, protection from hard frosts. Subject to infestation by measuring worms; spray with any broad-scope insecticide.

Iochroma cyaneum

IPHEION uniflorum *(Brodiaea uniflora, Triteleia uniflora)*. SPRING STAR FLOWER. Bulb. Zones 4–24. Native to Argentina. Flattish, bluish green leaves which smell like onions when bruised. Spring-blooming flowers 1½ in. across, broadly star shaped, white tinged blue, on 6–8-in. stems. Edging, ground cover in semiwild areas, under trees, large shrubs. Plant in fall in any soil; sun or part shade. Not fussy about water. Easy, persisting and multiplying for years.

Ipheion uniflorum

IPOMOEA. MORNING GLORY. Perennial or annual vines. Includes many ornamental vines and the sweet potato; does not include wild morning glory or bindweed *(Convolvulus arvensis)*. Ipomoeas may self-sow, but they don't spread by underground runners. Full sun. Don't need much water once established.

I. acuminata *(I. leari)*. BLUE DAWN FLOWER. Perennial. Zones 8, 9, 12–24. Vigorous, vines rapidly to 15–30 ft. Leaves dark green; flowers bright blue, fading pink, 3–5 in. across, clustered. Use to cover large banks, walls. Blooms in 1 year from seed; grows from cuttings, divisions, and layering of established plants.

Ipomoea tricolor

I. alba *(Calonyction aculeatum)*. MOON-FLOWER. Perennial vine grown as summer annual, as greenhouse plant in coldest climates. Fast-growing (20–30 ft. in one season) shade for arbor, trellis, or fence in summer. Effective combined with annual morning glory 'Heavenly Blue'. Luxuriant leaves 3–8 in. long, heart shaped, closely spaced on stems. Flowers fragrant, white (rarely lavender pink), often banded green, 6 in. long and across. Theoretically flowers open only after sundown, but will stay open on dark, dull days. Seed hard; abrade or soak 1–2 days for faster sprouting.

I. batatas. See SWEET POTATO.

I. nil. MORNING GLORY. Summer annual. Includes rare large-flowered Imperial Japanese morning glories and a few varieties of common morning glory, including rosy red 'Scarlett O'Hara'. For culture, see *I. tricolor* below.

I. quamoclit *(Quamoclit pennata)*. CYPRESS VINE, CARDINAL CLIMBER. Summer annual twining to 20 ft. Leaves 2½–4 in. long, finely divided into slender threads. Flowers are scarlet tubes 1½ in. long, flaring at mouth into 5-pointed star. Usually scarlet, rarely white.

I. tricolor. MORNING GLORY. Summer annual. Flowers showy, funnel shaped to bell-like, single or double, in solid colors of blue, lavender, pink, red, white, usually with throats in contrasting colors; some bicolored, striped. Most morning glories open only in morning, fade in afternoon; bloom until frost. Large heart shaped leaves.

Use on fence, trellis, as ground cover; or in containers trained on stakes or wire cylinder, or allow to cascade. For cut flowers, pick stems with buds in various stages of development, place in deep vase. Buds open on consecutive days.

Sow seeds in place in full sun after frost. To speed sprouting, notch seed coat with knife or file, or soak in warm water for 2 hours. Some growers sell scarified seed. For earlier start, sow seeds indoors in small pots or plant bands. Set out plants 6–8 in. apart. Ordinary soil; water moderately; do not feed.

'Heavenly Blue' morning glory twines to 15 ft. Flowers 4–5 in. across, pure sky blue, yellow throat. 'Pearly Gates' has large pure white flowers. Other color forms available.

IPOMOPSIS. Biennials or short-lived perennials. Erect single stems, finely divided leaves, and tubular red, or yellow and red flowers. Startling in appearance, best massed; individual plants are very narrow. Sow seed spring or early summer for bloom following year. Sun, good drainage; quite drought tolerant.

I. aggregata *(Gilia aggregata)*. Biennial. Native California to British Columbia, east to Rocky Mountains. To 2½ ft. tall. Flowers in long, narrow cluster, red marked yellow, sometimes yellow, an inch or so long. June-September.

I. rubra *(Gilia rubra)*. Biennial or perennial. Native to southern U.S. To 6 ft. tall. Flowers red outside, yellow marked red inside. Summer bloom.

Ipomopsis aggregata

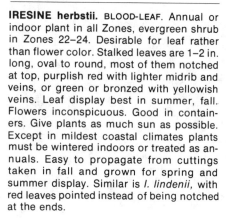

Iresine herbstii

IRESINE herbstii. BLOOD-LEAF. Annual or indoor plant in all Zones, evergreen shrub in Zones 22–24. Desirable for leaf rather than flower color. Stalked leaves are 1–2 in. long, oval to round, most of them notched at top, purplish red with lighter midrib and veins, or green or bronzed with yellowish veins. Leaf display best in summer, fall. Flowers inconspicuous. Good in containers. Give plants as much sun as possible. Except in mildest coastal climates plants must be wintered indoors or treated as annuals. Easy to propagate from cuttings taken in fall and grown for spring and summer display. Similar is *I. lindenii*, with red leaves pointed instead of being notched at the ends.

IRIS. Bulbs, rhizomes. All Zones, exceptions noted below. Large and remarkably diverse group of about 200 species, varying in flower color and form, cultural needs, and blooming season, although majority flower in spring or early summer. Leaves swordlike or grasslike. Flowers showy, complex in structure. The 3 inner segments (petals or standards) are usually erect, arching or flaring; 3 outer ones (sepals or falls) hang or curve back. The following

Tall Bearded Iris

best known and most widely adapted species and varieties are listed in four main groups: bulbous irises, crested, beardless, and bearded. The last three have rhizomes. The "beard" is a tuft of hair on falls.

Listings below are necessarily incomplete. Iris specialists devote whole catalogues to varieties of irises (the most widely grown of which are tall bearded), and many new varieties appear every year. Other specialists can furnish lesser-known species. Few irises (except bulbous) appear in retail nurseries.

BULBOUS IRISES

All have bulbs that become dormant in summer, can be lifted, stored until time to plant in fall. Flowers dainty, sometimes orchidlike.

I. reticulata. VIOLET-SCENTED IRIS. Bulb has netted outer covering. Long-tubed, 2–3-in., delicately fragrant, violet purple flowers edged gold. Stems 6–8 in. tall. Blooms March-April, or late January-early February in mild areas. Thin, 4-sided, blue green leaves appear after bloom. Well-adapted to pot culture. Cut flowers keep well. Named varieties are sometimes obtainable: 'Cantab' has pale blue flowers with orange markings, 'Harmony' is sky blue marked yellow, and 'J. S. Dijt' is reddish purple. These are sometimes sold in mixture. Similar in appearance but bright yellow in color is *I. danfordiae*. Plant bulb 3–4 in. deep in well-drained soil. Full sun. Good in rock gardens.

I. xiphioides. ENGLISH IRIS. Zones 1–6, 15–17, 21–24. Plant to 18 in.; flowers larger than Dutch irises, have velvety texture of Japanese irises. Early summer blooms (after Dutch iris) are bluish purple, wine red, maroon, blue, mauve, white; no yellows. Needs partial shade in warm-summer areas; moist, cool, acid soil; full sun where cool. In Zones 1–3, some gardeners find it easier than Dutch irises; no top growth in autumn that is liable to freeze. Set bulbs 3–4 in. deep, 4 in. apart in fall.

Spanish iris. Derived from species native to Spain, its surrounding areas, and north Africa. The species are not grown commercially, but from them have been developed many varieties and color strains. Related to the two following kinds, Spanish irises have smaller flowers and bloom about two weeks later than Dutch irises. Culture is the same as for Dutch irises.

Dutch iris. Some growers lump Spanish and Dutch irises together; others consider them separate. Dutch irises acquired their name because the process of selecting and hybridizing them was first carried out by Dutch growers. The result was a group of lovely irises with long straight stems and flowers in many clear colors—white, blue, orange, purple, mauve, yellow brown, and bicolors. They flower in March-April in warm climates, May-June in colder areas. Flowers are 3–4 in. across on stems 1½–2 ft. tall. They make excellent cut flowers.

Plant in sun 4 in. deep, 3–4 in. apart in October-November. Bulbs hardy, but in coldest climates, mulch in winter. Ample water during growth. After bloom let foliage ripen before digging, store bulbs in cool, dry place; do not let bulbs stay out of ground more than 2 months. Dutch irises are good in containers; plant 5 bulbs in 5–6-in. pot.

Dutch Iris

Wedgwood iris. Zones 4–24. These are often sold as Dutch irises, but actually they are the result of a series of crosses between Dutch iris antecedents and Moroccan native *I. tingitana*. Flowers are large, in shades of lavender blue with yellow markings. Bulbs are larger than those of Dutch irises. They are also more tender and plants bloom several weeks earlier. Outstanding for cutting, containers, early color in borders (plant behind bushy annuals or perennials to hide floppy leaves). The light blue 'Wedgwood' is best known, blooms at same time as 'King Alfred' daffodils.

CRESTED IRISES

Dainty, closely related to bearded irises, generally shade tolerant. Flowers distinguished by small narrow crest at base of falls (outer petals). All are subject to slug, snail damage.

I. cristata. Leaves 4–6 in. long, ½ in. wide, from slender, greenish, free-running rhizomes. Lavender or light blue or white flowers with golden crests in April-May. Hardy to −10°F. Cool, damp soil, light shade, summer water. Divide crowded plantings right after bloom or in fall after leaves die down. Good in rock gardens.

I. japonica. Sometimes called orchid iris; considered most beautiful of crested irises. Widely branched, 2-ft. stems bear pale lavender, fringed flowers with orange crests, late spring. Outside only in milder climates; grow in containers in coldest areas.

I. tectorum. ROOF IRIS. Broad, ribbed leaves 1 ft. tall. Flowers purple blue with white crests, or pure white, late spring. Rich, somewhat acid soil, half shade, ample water. Best in mild, moist areas; short-lived in very cold or dry climates. Planted on thatched roofs in Japan, good in rock gardens.

BEARDLESS IRISES

This group varies in size, appearance, and garden use. Distinguished by lack of beard (tufts of hairs on falls), rhizomes with many fibrous roots, need for moisture—some need much more than others.

I. ensata (formerly *Iris kaempferi*). JAPANESE IRIS. Graceful, upright sword shaped leaves with distinct raised midrib. Stems to 4 ft. bear 1, 2, or more large (4–12 in.), flat, velvety, single or double flowers in late June-July. Colors are purple, violet, pink, rose, red, or white, often edged in contrasting shade.

Iris ensata

Use in moist borders, at edge of pools or streams, grow in boxes or pots plunged halfway to rim in pond or pool during growing season. Plant in fall or spring. Set rhizomes 2 in. deep, 18 in. apart in rich, moist, acid soil. Provide sun in cool-summer areas, light shade in warm sections; shelter from wind; lots of water while growing and blooming. Not adapted to hot, dry climates. If soil or water is alkaline, apply aluminum sulfate or iron sulfate (1 oz. to 2 gal. water) several times during growing season. Divide crowded clumps in late summer or fall. Use rhizomes from outer edge of clump, cut back foliage halfway, replant quickly.

I. foetidissima. GLADWIN IRIS. Hardy iris with evergreen leaves to 2 ft., ill smelling if bruised. Stems 1–1½ ft. tall; spring flowers unshowy, subtly attractive in shades of blue gray and chartreuse (a rare form is pale yellow). Real attraction is large seed capsules which open in autumn to show numerous round, scarlet seeds, admired by flower arrangers. There are also orange and yellow selected forms. Plant will grow in sun or quite deep shade; needs little care; extremely drought resistant.

I. missouriensis. WESTERN BLUE FLAG. Native to meadows and streambeds throughout the West, including Rocky Mountains. Grows 1–2 ft. tall. Spring flowers nearly 3 in. wide, pale blue lavender or white, veined bluish purple. Full sun to light shade. Established clumps tolerate drought after blooming season.

I. pseudacorus. YELLOW FLAG, YELLOW WATER IRIS. Tall (leaves to 5 ft., flower stems to 6–7 ft.) iris with 2–3-in. bright yellow flowers (there are forms with ivory-colored flowers). Needs acid, damp to wet soil. Thrives in shallow water. Decorative in pools or at edges of ponds. Full to light shade. Can seed itself prolifically, become a pest in favored locations, unless seed capsules are removed.

I. sibirica. SIBERIAN IRIS. Graceful iris for perennial borders, cut flowers. Leaves somewhat grassy, narrow, erect, 1–2½ ft. high. Flower stems 2–3½ ft. Flowers shaped like those of Dutch irises appear as midseason bearded irises fade; range from pale to deep blue, purple, purple red, or white; excellent named varieties. Full sun; acid to neutral soil; plenty of water during growing season. Need dividing infrequently; best performance from well-established clumps. When old clumps begin to get hollow in center, divide in September-October.

I. unguicularis (*I. stylosa*). WINTER IRIS. Zones 5–24. Dense clumps of narrow, dark green 1–2-ft. leaves. Lavender blue flowers, with 6–9-in. tubes that look like stems, appear in November (where winters are mildest) to January-March. Use along paths, in borders. In Zones 5–7, grow next to sunny wall or house foundation. Good cut flowers; cut in bud, let flowers open indoors. Slugs attracted to flowers. Sun or shade; any soil; much or little water. To reveal flowers partly concealed by foliage, cut back tallest leaves in September; also divide overgrown clumps at this time, or in March-April after flowering.

Louisiana Irises

A group consisting of 3 or more species, mostly native to Mississippi delta, have given rise to hybrids of great beauty and grace. Among the species are: *I. fulva,* with unusual coppery red color; *I. giganticaerulea,* great size, height, good blue color; *I. brevicaulis,* also blue, with hardiness and flower substance. Hybrids somewhat like Japanese irises, but more graceful in form, with colors including red, white, yellow, pink, purple, blue. Height ranges from 2-5 ft. Mulch where ground freezes. Need rich, neutral or acid soil, ample water during growing season, partial shade in hot regions.

Pacific Coast Irises

Following 4 species native to Pacific coast are used in western gardens. Selections and hybrids of these irises also available from specialists. Where summer temperatures are high and soils heavy, these irises are difficult to grow; give them light shade and lighten soil with organic material. Under these conditions selections and hybrids of *I. douglasiana* are tougher than the others. Good in rock gardens.

I. douglasiana. Zones 4–24. Native to California coast from Santa Barbara north to Oregon. Large clump of evergreen 1–1½-ft. leaves. Stems 1–2 ft., often branched, with 2 to 3 or more flowers in white, cream, yellow, or lavender blue to deep reddish purple. Naturalize on banks, in fringe areas of garden. Full sun or light shade; tolerates many soils. Once established, withstands summer drought but will also accept some summer water.

I. innominata. Zones 4–24. From mountains of northern California, southwestern Oregon. Clumps of evergreen, 15-in. leaves. Flowers on 6–10-in. stems, clear yellow to orange, lavender, purple, brick red. Best forms are golden yellow with brown stripes. Woodland or rock garden plant.

I. munzii. Zones 5–9, 14–24. Native to Sierra Nevada foothills in Tulare County, California. Gray green leaves to 2 ft. Large lavender blue to deep blue flowers on 2½-ft. stems in spring. Best forms nearly true sapphire.

I. tenax. Zones 4–17. From Washington and Oregon. Dense clumps of 6–12-in. leaves that are deciduous. Dainty flowers, dark purple blotched white, blue, lavender, pink, apricot, cream, and white on 6–12-in. stems. Rock garden. Porous soil, sun or light shade.

Spuria Irises

This name was originally given to a group of species with similar habits, flower form, and culture. Of these only *I. orientalis,* usually sold as *I. ochroleuca,* is much grown today. It grows 3–5 ft. tall, and its white flowers have deep yellow blotches on the falls. Improved hybrids are replacing the species. They vary in height from 2–6 ft. They have somewhat larger flowers than the species and come in many shades—yellow, buff, bronze, lavender, blue, chartreuse, white.

All form clumps of stiff, erect, narrow, deep green leaves. Flowers, similar to Dutch irises, form on one side of tall rigid stems, bloom in spring, early summer. Stately plants in borders, for cutting. Full sun or light shade, rich soil, ample moisture while growing, little or no summer water needed. Best dividing time is early fall. Difficult to dig after firmly established. Best performance on established clumps. Plants often fail to bloom first year after dividing.

BEARDED IRISES

Probably most irises grown fall into this group. Many species, varieties, and many years of hybridizing by growers and iris fanciers have contributed to this great array of beautiful irises. All are characterized by having a beard (tuft of hairs) on the falls. Bearded irises can be separated into seven groups described below. (Note that the Aril group needs slightly different cultural requirements.)

Bearded irises need good drainage, full sun in cool climates, light shade in hottest areas. Adapt to most soils; feeding in early spring and after bloom will suffice.

Plant between July 1 and October 31; in cold-winter climates the earlier part of this season is safer. Near coast, plant any time during this period. Set rhizomes 1–2 ft. apart, with top just below surface; spread roots well. Rhizomes grow from end with leaves; point that end in direction you want growth to take. For quick show, plant 3 rhizomes 12 in. apart, two with growing ends pointed outward, the third aimed to grow into the space between them. On slopes, set rhizomes with growing end facing upward. Water to settle soil, start growth. Take care not to overwater later—once in 2 weeks sufficient in most sections; established clumps need only occasional watering in cool areas. In warm climates, soak deeply 2 or 3 times during hot season. After 3 or 4 years clumps are likely to be overcrowded. Lift and divide at best season for planting in your growing area. Divide rhizomes with sharp knife; discard older woody center; plant healthy sections with good fan of leaves. Trim leaves, roots to 6 in. for convenient handling. Let cut ends heal for several hours to a day before planting.

In late autumn remove old or dry leaves. Where winters are severe, mulch plantings to prevent alternate freezing, thawing.

Dwarf and Median Irises

These are smaller in plant size, stature, and flower size than taller beardeds but have flowers of generally tall bearded iris form. Median iris is collective term for Standard Dwarfs, Intermediates, Border Beardeds, and Miniature Tall Beardeds.

Miniature Dwarf Bearded Iris. To 10 in. tall. Flowers large for size of plant, earliest to bloom of bearded irises (about 6 weeks before main show of tall beardeds). Hardy, fast to multiply. Fine in rock gardens, front of borders. Wide range of colors.

Standard Dwarf Bearded Iris. Larger than miniature dwarfs, these range from 10–15 in. tall; flowers are larger (2–3 in. across) and bloom is very profuse.

Intermediate Bearded Iris. These bloom later than dwarfs but 1–3 weeks before tall bearded irises. Height is 15–28 in., flowers 3–5 in. across. Most are hybrids between standard dwarfs and tall bearded varieties, resemble larger standard dwarfs (as compared to border bearded irises in same height range, which are slightly smaller replicas of tall beardeds). Some give second bloom in fall.

Border Bearded Iris. Blooming at the same time as tall bearded irises, these are useful in smaller gardens. They grow 15–28 in. tall—proportionately smaller versions of tall beardeds in the same range of colors.

Miniature Tall Bearded Iris. Ranging from 15–28 in. high, these resemble tall bearded irises reduced in every proportion—slim stems, small flowers (2–3 in. wide), narrower, finer foliage. Blooming same time as tall beardeds, they are especially favored for cutting and arrangements—hence their original name Table Irises.

Tall Bearded Iris

Among very choicest perennials for borders, massing, cutting. Adapted in all climates, easy to grow. From 2½–4 ft. high. All colors but pure red and green; patterns of two or more colors, blendings of colors produce infinite variety of flowers. Many named varieties available. Modern hybrids free-branching, some with flowers ruffled, fringed. Some give second bloom in late summer, fall, or winter. Climate, growing conditions, and varieties must be right; consult specialists' catalogues for most suitable reblooming varieties.

Aril Iris

Little-known group with strange and often remarkably beautiful flowers. Mostly from semidesert areas of the Near East and central Asia, they need perfect drainage, limy soil, and no summer water. Two main groups are Oncocyclus, in which a number of species have huge, domed flowers in lavender, gray, silver, maroon, and gold, often subtly veined and stippled with deeper hues; and Regelias, with smaller, narrower blooms. Oncocyclus are difficult; Regelias and Oncogelias (hybrids between the two) are only relatively easy. For the average gardener, Arilbred (or Oncobred) irises—crosses between Arils and tall bearded irises—are more satisfactory, being nearly as easy as the latter to grow and having some of the exotic beauty of the former.

IRISH MOSS. See *Sagina subulata.*

IRONBARK. See *Eucalyptus.*

ISLAND BUSH SNAPDRAGON. See *Galvezia.*

ISMENE calathina. See *Hymenocallis narcissiflora.*

ISOTOMA fluviatilis. See *Laurentia.*

ITEA ilicifolia. HOLLYLEAF SWEETSPIRE. Evergreen shrub or small tree. Zones 4–24. Usually graceful, open, arching shrub, 6–10 ft. tall, rarely to 18 ft. Leaves glossy, dark green, oval, 4 in. long, spiny toothed. Small, greenish white, lightly fragrant flowers in nodding or drooping narrow clusters to 12 in. long. Fall bloom. Blooms sparsely where winters are very mild. Not a striking plant, but extremely graceful. Needs ample moisture and good soil; stands sun or partial shade near coast, should have part shade inland. Good near pools or waterfalls, as espalier against dark wood or stone backgrounds. Good informal screen.

Itea ilicifolia

IXIA. AFRICAN CORN LILY. Corm. Zones 5–24. Garden kinds are hybrids of several South African species. Swordlike leaves, wiry stems 18–20 in. long, topped in May-June with spikelike clusters of 1–2-in. cup shaped flowers in cream, yellow, red, orange, pink, all with dark centers. Long-lasting when cut. In mild areas, plant corms 3 in. deep in early fall; in Zones 5, 6, delay planting until after November 1. Set corms 4 in. deep in sheltered spot, full sun. Apply protective mulch. Can be left in ground several seasons; when crowded, lift in summer, replant in fall. In mild climates, plants reseed freely and are quite drought tolerant. In coldest areas, grow in pots like freesias; plant 6–8 corms 1 in. deep in 5-in. pot. Keep cool after bringing indoors—not over 55°F. night temperature.

Ixia maculata

ITHURIEL'S SPEAR. See *Triteleia laxa.*

IVY. See *Hedera.*

IXIOLIRION tataricum *(I. montanum).* Bulb. Zones 5–24. Native to central Asia. Narrow, greenish gray leaves; wiry stems, 12–16 in. high, bear loose clusters of violet blue, trumpet shaped, 1½-in. flowers in late May-June. Plant in sun in fall; set bulbs 3 in. deep, 6 in. apart. In cold areas, plant in warm, sheltered location and mulch to protect leaves from severe frost in spring. Average water.

Ixiolirion tataricum

JACARANDA mimosifolia (often sold as *J. acutifolia*). JACARANDA. Deciduous to semievergreen tree. Zones 13, 15–24. Native to Brazil. Grows 25–40 ft. high, 15–30 ft. wide. Open, irregular, oval head, sometimes multitrunked or even shrubby. Finely cut, fernlike leaves, usually dropping in February-March. New leaves may grow quickly or branches may remain bare until flowering time. Many 8-in.-long clusters of lavender blue, 2-in. tubular flowers, usually in June but can bloom any time April-September. 'Alba', with white flowers, is sometimes seen. White form has lusher foliage, longer blooming period, and sparser flowers. All forms have roundish flat seed capsules, quite decorative in arrangements.

Fairly hardy after it attains some mature, hard wood; young plants are tender below 25°F. but often come back from freeze to make multistemmed, shrubby plants. Takes wide variety of soils but best in sandy soil. Needs regular but not frequent irrigation. Too little water stunts it; too much encourages lush, loose, tender growth. Often fails to flower in path of ocean winds or where there isn't adequate heat. Resistant to oak root fungus.

Stake to produce single, sturdy trunk. Prune to shape. Usually branches profusely at 6–10 ft. In hillside gardens, a nice tree to look down on from above (downslope from deck or terrace), or to view against sky (planted on top of knoll). But it's also widely used in flat valley floor gardens.

Jacaranda mimosifolia

JACOBEAN LILY. See *Sprekelia formosissima.*

JACOBINIA carnea. See *Justicia carnea.*

JACOB'S LADDER. See *Polemonium caeruleum.*

JADE PLANT. See *Crassula argentea.*

JAMAICA FLOWER, JAMAICA SORREL. See *Hibiscus sabdariffa.*

JAPANESE ANGELICA TREE. See *Aralia elata.*

JAPANESE ARALIA. See *Fatsia.*

JAPANESE FELT FERN. See *Pyrrosia lingua.*

JAPANESE FLOWERING APRICOT. See *Prunus mume.*

JAPANESE FLOWERING PLUM. See *Prunus mume.*

JAPANESE LACE FERN. See *Polystichum polyblepharum.*

JAPANESE PAGODA TREE. See *Sophora japonica.*

JAPANESE SNOWBALL. See *Viburnum plicatum.*

JAPANESE SNOWBELL, JAPANESE SNOWDROP TREE. See *Styrax japonicus.*

JAPANESE SPURGE. See *Pachysandra terminalis.*

JAPAN PEPPER. See *Zanthoxylum piperitum.*

JASMINUM. JASMINE. Evergreen or deciduous shrubs or vines. This is one of the first plants that comes to mind when one thinks of fragrance. Yet not all jasmines are fragrant. Also, one of best known and most fragrant plants commonly called jasmine—the star jasmine—is not a true jasmine at all but a *Trachelospermum.* All jasmines thrive in regular garden soil, sun or partial shade, and need frequent pinching and shaping to control growth. All need some watering; the larger-leafed kinds suffer from drought the most. Low-growing, shrubby kinds make good hedges.

Jasminum mesnyi

J. floridum. Evergreen or partially evergreen, shrubby, sprawling, or half-climbing shrub. Zones 4–9, 12–24. To 3–4 ft. Leaves divided into 3 (rarely 5) small leaflets ½–1½ in. long. Clusters of golden yellow, scentless, ½–¾-in. flowers over a long season in spring, summer, fall.

J. grandiflorum. *(J. officinale grandiflorum).* SPANISH JASMINE. Semievergreen to deciduous vine. Zones 5–9, 12–24. Rapid growth to 10–15 ft. Glossy green leaves with 5–7 leaflets 2 in. long. Flowers fragrant, white, 1½ in. across, in loose clusters. Blooms all summer. Dry flowers stay on plant. Gives open, airy effect along fence tops or rails.

J. humile. ITALIAN JASMINE. Evergreen shrub or vine. Zones 5–9, 12–24. Erect willowy shoots reach to 20 ft. and arch to make 10-ft. mound. Can be trained as shrub or, planted in a row, clipped as hedge. Light green leaves with 3–7 leaflets 2 in. long. Fragrant clusters of bright yellow ½-in. flowers July–September. *J.h.* 'Revolutum' has larger, dull dark green leaves; flowers 1 in. across, up to 12 in cluster. Side clusters make even larger show.

J. magnificum. See *J. nitidum.*

J. mesnyi *(J. primulinum).* PRIMROSE JASMINE. Evergreen shrub. Zones 4–24; protected spots in Zone 3. Long, arching branches 6–10 ft. long. Leaves dark green with 3 lance shaped 2–3-in. leaflets; square stems. Flowers bright lemon yellow, to 2 in. across, semidouble or double, unscented. They are scattered singly through plant, November-April in mild-winter areas, February-April in colder climates. Needs space. Best tied up at desired height and permitted to spill down in waterfall fashion. Use to cover pergola, banks, large walls. Will control erosion. Can be clipped as 3-ft.-high hedge. Whatever form, plants may need occasional severe pruning to avoid brushpile look. Sun or part shade.

J. nitidum. (Often sold as *J. magnificum.*) ANGELWING JASMINE. Evergreen vine. Zone 13; semideciduous Zones 12, 16, 19–21. Needs long warm growing season to bloom satisfactorily. Not reliably hardy below 25°F. Moderate growth to 10–20 ft. Leathery, uncut, medium glossy green leaves to 2 in. long. Flowers shaped like 1-in.-wide pinwheels; very fragrant, white above, purplish beneath, purplish in bud, in 3-flowered clusters, late spring and summer. Responds well to drastic pruning. Shrubby ground cover. Good container plant.

Jasminum nitidum

J. nudiflorum. WINTER JASMINE. Deciduous viny shrub. Zones 3–21; best adapted in cooler climates. To 10–15 ft. with slender, willowy branches. Glossy green leaves with 3 leaflets. Yellow 1-in. flowers in January-March before leaves unfold. Not fragrant. Train like *J. mesnyi.* Will control erosion.

J. officinale. COMMON WHITE JASMINE, POET'S JASMINE. Semievergreen to deciduous twining vine. Zones 5–9, 12–24. Resembles *J. grandiflorum* but is taller (to 30 ft.), with smaller flowers (to 1 in. across). Somewhat tenderer than *J. grandiflorum.*

J. parkeri. DWARF JASMINE. Evergreen shrub. Zones 5–9, 12–24. Dwarf, twiggy, tufted habit. To 1 ft. tall, 1½–2 ft. across. Leaves bright green, ½–1 in. long, made up of 3–5 tiny leaflets. Small yellow flowers profusely borne in May, June. Not fragrant. Good rock garden shrub; containers. Drought tolerant.

J. polyanthum. Evergreen vine. Zones 5–9, 12–24. Fast climbing, strong growing to 20 ft. Finely divided leaflets. Flowers fragrant, white inside, rose colored outside; in dense clusters, February-July in Zones 22–24, April in colder areas. Needs sun to bloom well; regular summer watering; prune annually to keep it from tangling. Use as climber, ground cover, in containers.

J. sambac. ARABIAN JASMINE. Evergreen shrub. Zones 13, 21, 23. In Hawaii also called pikake, favorite flower for leis, used in making perfume; in Orient added to tea to make jasmine tea. Tender. To 5 ft. tall. Leaves undivided, glossy green, to 3 in. long. Flowers white, ¾–1 in. across, powerfully fragrant, in clusters. Grow as small compact shrub on trellis, or in container.

JERUSALEM ARTICHOKE. See *Helianthus tuberosus.*

JERUSALEM CHERRY. See *Solanum pseudocapsicum.*

JERUSALEM SAGE. See *Phlomis fruticosa.*

JERUSALEM THORN. See *Parkinsonia aculeata.*

JEWEL MINT OF CORSICA. See *Mentha requienii.*

JICAMA. See *Pachyrhizus erosus.*

JOB'S TEARS. See *Coix lacryma-jobi.*

JOHNNY-JUMP-UP. See *Viola tricolor.*

JOJOBA. See *Simmondsia chinensis.*

JONQUIL. See *Narcissus jonquilla.*

Junipers

NAME	SYNONYMS OR NURSERYMEN'S NAMES	SIZE, HABIT	CHARACTERISTICS
GROUND COVERS			
Juniperus chinensis 'Alba' VARIEGATED PROSTRATA JUNIPER	*J. prostrata variegata.* *J. squamata variegata.* *J. davurica variegata.*	To 18 in. by 4–5 ft.	See *J. c.* 'Parsonii'. Patches of creamy yellow variegation. Not as rugged grower as green forms. Variegations burn in hot sun.
J. c. 'Parsonii' PROSTRATA JUNIPER	*J. squamata* 'Parsonii'. *J. davurica* 'Parsonii'. *J. prostrata.*	To 18 in. by 8 ft. or more.	Selected form. Slow growing. Dense short twigs on flat, rather heavy branches.
J. c. procumbens JAPANESE GARDEN JUNIPER	*J. procumbens.*	To 3 ft. by 12–20 ft.	Feathery yet substantial blue green foliage on strong, spreading branches.
J. c. procumbens 'Nana'	*J. procumbens* 'Nana'. *J. procumbens* 'Compacta Nana'.	To 12 in. by 4–5 ft. Curved branches radiating in all directions.	Shorter needles and slower growing than *J. procumbens*. Often sold as *J. compacta* 'Nana'. Blue green foliage spreads rapidly. Give it some protection in hot climates.
J. c. procumbens 'Variegata'	*J. procumbens* 'Variegata'.	To 3 ft. by 8–10 ft.	*J. procumbens* with creamy white patches of foliage.
J. c. 'San Jose'	*J. procumbens* 'San Jose'. *J. japonica* 'San Jose'. *J. chinensis procumbens* 'San Jose'.	Two ft. by 6 ft. or more. Prostrate, dense.	Dark sage green with both needle and scale foliage. Heavy trunked, slow growing. One of the best.
J. c. sargentii SARGENT JUNIPER, SHIMPAKU	*J. sargentii, J. sargentii viridis.*	To 1 ft. by 10 ft. Ground hugging.	Gray green or green. Feathery. Classic bonsai plant. *J. c. sargentii* 'Glauca' has blue green foliage. *J. c. sargentii* 'Viridis' has bright green foliage.
J. c. 'Seaspray'		To 8 in. tall.	Gray green foliage stays very dense, covering center limbs even in hot climates.
J. communis saxatilis	*J. c. montana.* *J. c. sibirica.*	To 1 ft. by 6–8 ft. Prostrate, trailing.	Variable gray, gray green. Upturned branchlets like tiny candles. Native alpine.
J. communis 'Hornibrookii'		To 1 ft. by 4 ft.	Attractive, rugged branching pattern.
J. conferta SHORE JUNIPER	*J. littoralis, J. conferta litoralis.* Plants so named may be a grower's selected form.	To 1 ft. by 6–8 ft. Prostrate, trailing.	Bright green, soft needled. Excellent for seashore and will stand valley heat if given moist, well-drained soil. 'Blue Pacific' is denser, bluer, more heat tolerant form.
J. horizontalis 'Bar Harbor' BAR HARBOR JUNIPER		To 1 ft. by 10 ft. Hugs ground.	Fast growing. Feathery, blue gray foliage turns plum color in winter. Foliage dies back in center to expose limbs as plant ages, especially in hot climates.
J. h. 'Blue Chip'		To 12 in. tall.	Silvery blue foliage.
J. h. 'Douglasii' WAUKEGAN JUNIPER		To 1 ft. by 10 ft. Trailing.	Steel blue foliage turns purplish in fall. New growth rich green.
J. h. 'Emerald Spreader'		To 6 in. tall.	Dense feathery bright green foliage.
J. h. 'Emerson's Creeper'	*J. h.* 'Marshall's Creeper'.	To 6 in. tall.	Extremely hardy; bluish green.
J. h. 'Hughes'		To 6 in. tall.	Showy silvery blue.
J. h. 'Plumosa' ANDORRA JUNIPER	*J. depressa plumosa.*	To 18 in. by 10 ft. Wide spreading.	Gray green in summer, plum color in winter. Flat branches, upright branchlets. Plumy. Smaller more compact form is *J. h.* 'Youngstown'.
J. h. 'Prince of Wales'		To 8 in. tall.	Medium-green foliage turns purplish in fall.
J. h. 'Turquoise Spreader'		To 6 in. tall.	Dense turquoise green foliage.
J. h. 'Venusta'		To 12 in. by 10 ft.	Similar to 'Bar Harbor'.
J. h. 'Webberi'		To 12 in. by 6–8 ft. Spreading, matlike.	Bluish green. Heavy texture. Turns purplish in fall.
J. h. 'Wiltonii' BLUE CARPET JUNIPER	*J. horizontalis* 'Blue Rug'.	To 4 in. by 8–10 ft. Flattest juniper.	Intense silver blue. Dense, short branchlets on long, trailing branches. Similar to 'Bar Harbor' but tighter; it rarely exposes limbs.
J. h. 'Yukon Belle'		To 6 in. tall.	Silvery blue foliage. Hardy in coldest climates.
J. sabina 'Arcadia'		To 12 in. by 10 ft.	Bright green, lacy foliage.
J. s. 'Blue Danube'		To 18 in. by 5 ft.	Blue green foliage.
J. s. 'Broadmoor'		To 14 in. by 10 ft. Dense, mounding.	Soft, bright green foliage.

NAME	SYNONYMS OR NURSERYMEN'S NAMES	SIZE, HABIT	CHARACTERISTICS
J. s. 'Buffalo'		To 8–12 in. tall by 8 ft. Lower than tamarix juniper.	Soft, feathery, bright green foliage. Very wide spreading.
J. s. 'Scandia'		To 12 in. by 8 ft.	Low, dense, bright green.
J. s. 'Tamariscifolia' TAMARIX JUNIPER, TAM	J. tamariscifolia.	To 18 in. by 10–20 ft. Symmetrically spreading.	Dense, blue green. Widely used. Recently introduced is 'New Blue'.
J. scopulorum 'White's Silver King'		To 10 in. by 6–8 ft. Dense, spreading.	Pale silver blue foliage.
J. virginiana 'Silver Spreader'	J. v. prostrata.	To 18 in. by 6–8 ft.	Silvery green, feathery, fine textured. Older branches become dark green.
SHRUBS			
J. chinensis 'Ames'		To 6 ft. Broad-based pyramid.	Blue green foliage. Slow growing. Massive.
J. c. 'Armstrongii' ARMSTRONG JUNIPER		Four ft. by 4 ft. Upright.	Medium green. More compact than Pfitzer juniper.
J. c. 'Blaauw' BLAAUW'S JUNIPER, BLUE SHIMPAKU		Four ft. by 3 ft. Vase shaped.	Blue foliage. Dense. Compact.
J. c. 'Blue Point'		To 8 ft. Dense pyramid.	Blue foliage. Needs no shearing.
J. c. 'Blue Vase' TEXAS STAR JUNIPER		3 ft. by 3 ft. Dense, blocky.	Blue prickly foliage. Good traffic stopper.
J. c. 'Corymbosa'	Probably a J. chinensis form.	To 10–15 ft. Irregular cone.	Much like Hollywood juniper but without twisted branches. Dark green.
J. c. 'Corymbosa Variegata' VARIEGATED HOLLYWOOD JUNIPER	J. chinensis 'Torulosa Variegata'.	To 8–10 ft. Irregular cone.	Variegation of creamy yellow. Growth more regular than Hollywood juniper.
J. c. 'Fruitland'		Three ft. by 6 ft. Compact, dense.	Like a Pfitzer—but more compact.
J. c. 'Golden Armstrong'		Four ft. by 4 ft. Full, blocky.	Between golden Pfitzer and Armstrong juniper in appearance.
J. c. 'Gold Coast'	J. 'Coasti Aurea'.		Similar to, or identical with, J. c. 'Golden Armstrong'.
J. c. 'Hetzii' HETZ BLUE JUNIPER	J. chinensis hetzi glauca. J. glauca hetzi.	To 15 ft. Fountainlike.	Blue gray. Branches spread outward and upward at 45° angle.
J. c. 'Maneyi'		To 15 ft. Semierect, massive.	Blue gray. Steeply inclined, spreading branches.
J. c. 'Mint Julep'		Four to 6 ft. by 6 ft. Vase shaped.	Mint green foliage, arching branches.
J. c. 'Mordigan'		To 7 ft. by 5 ft. Irregular, upright.	Dark green foliage. Taller, narrower, more blocky than Pfitzer.
J. c. 'Pfitzerana' PFITZER JUNIPER		To 5–6 ft. by 15–20 ft. Arching.	Feathery, gray green. Sharp needled foliage. 'Pfitzerana Aurea' is golden form.
J. c. 'Pfitzerana Blue-Gold' GOLDEN PFITZER JUNIPER		To 3–4 ft. by 8–10 ft.	Blue gray foliage with creamy yellow variegations.
J. c. 'Pfitzerana Compacta' NICK'S COMPACT PFITZER JUNIPER	J. pfitzeriana nicksi, J. nicksi compacta.	To 2 ft. by 4–6 ft. Densely branched.	Compact. Gray green foliage.
J. c. 'Pfitzerana Glauca'		To 5–6 ft. by 10–15 ft. Arching branches.	Silvery blue foliage.
J. c. 'Pfitzerana Mordigan Aurea'		Three ft. by 5 ft.	A denser, smaller golden Pfitzer.
J. c. 'Pfitzerana Nana'		Four ft. by 2 ft.	Dense, nearly globular green juniper.
J. c. 'Pfitzerana Old Gold'	May be same as J. c. 'Golden Armstrong'.		See J. c. 'Golden Armstrong'.
J. c. 'Pfitzerana Plumosa'		Two ft. by 5 ft.	Horizontal branching, table topped Pfitzer.
J. c. 'Plumosa Aurea'	J. japonica aurea, J. bandai-sugi aurea, J. procumbens aurea.	Three ft. by 3 ft. Vase shaped.	Semiupright, spreading, with bright gold new growth.
J. c. 'Torulosa' HOLLYWOOD JUNIPER	J. c. 'Kaizuka'.	To 15 ft. Irregular, upright.	Rich green. Branches with irregular, twisted appearance. Give it enough room.

(Continued on next page)

NAME	SYNONYMS OR NURSERYMEN'S NAMES	SIZE, HABIT	CHARACTERISTICS
J. communis depressa PASTURE or OLDFIELD JUNIPER		To 4 ft. Wide spreading.	Gray green. Too large for average garden use.
J. communis depressa 'Aurea'			As *J. c.* 'Torulosa'; golden new foliage.
J. sabina 'Arcadia'		To 1½ ft. by 4–5 ft.	Rich green, lacy. Like a very low, flat-topped Pfitzer.
J. sabina 'Blue Danube'		To 3–4 ft. by 5 ft. Semierect.	Blue green, upright habit with flat branching.
J. sabina 'Scandia'		One ft. by 4 ft.	More yellow green than 'Arcadia'.
J. sabina 'Variegata' HOARFROST JUNIPER		To 3–4 ft. by 6 ft.	Upright, spreading, lacy branch pattern. Every twig bears small white tip.
J. squamata 'Blue Star'		To 2 ft. by 5 ft.	Regularly branching, silver blue.
J. squamata 'Meyeri' MEYER or FISHBACK JUNIPER		To 6–8 ft. by 2–3 ft. Upright.	Oddly angled stiff branches. Broad needled. Blend of green, gray, and reddish foliage.
J. squamata 'Prostrata'		To 1 ft. by 6 ft.	Slow, very flat, gray green.
J. scopulorum 'Lakewood Globe'		To 4–6 ft. Globe.	Blue green foliage.
J. scopulorum 'Silver Star'		Three ft. by 6–8 ft.	Silvery gray. Wide spreading.
J. scopulorum 'Table Top Blue'		Six by 8 ft.	Gray. Massive. Flat topped.
J. virginiana 'Tripartita'	*J. tripartita.*	To 4–5 ft. Upright, arching.	Green. Branches ascend from base, then spread out. Fast growing.
COLUMNAR TYPES			
J. chinensis 'Columnaris' CHINESE BLUE COLUMN JUNIPER	*J. chinensis* 'Columnaris Glauca'.	To 12–15 ft.	Blue green, narrow pyramid.
J. c. 'Foemina'	*J. foemina, J. sylvestris, J. chinensis* 'Reeves'.	To 12–15 ft.	Dark green. Broad column with outward-spraying branchlets.
J. c. 'Hetz's Columnaris'		To 12–15 ft.	Rich green. Dense column. Scale foliage predominant, branchlets threadlike.
J. c. 'Keteleeri' KETELEER JUNIPER		To 20 ft.	Bright green, broad pyramid with loose, ascending branches.
J. c. 'Mountbatten'		To 12 ft.	Gray green narrow column with needlelike juvenile foliage.
J. c. 'Obelisk'		To 20 ft.	Dense stiff column. Steel blue foliage.
J. c. 'Pyramidalis'	*J. excelsa* 'Stricta'.	To 15–30 ft.	Blue gray needlelike foliage. Narrow pyramid broadening with age.
J. c. 'Robusta Green'		To 20 ft.	Brilliant green, dense-tufted column.
J. c. 'Spartan'	*J. c. densaerecta* 'Spartan'.	To 20 ft.	Rich, green, dense column.
J. c. 'Wintergreen'		To 20 ft.	Deep green, dense-branching pyramid.
J. communis 'Compressa'		To 2 ft.	Dwarf, for rock gardens.
J. communis 'Stricta' IRISH JUNIPER	*J. c. hibernica, J. c. fastigiata.*	To 12–20 ft.	Dark green. Very narrow column with closely compact branch tips.
J. excelsa 'Stricta'.	See *J. chinensis* 'Columnaris'.		
J. excelsa 'Variegata' VARIEGATED SPINY GREEK JUNIPER	*J. e. stricta variegata.*	Probably to 20 ft.	Thick, full, blue green pyramid with creamy white or yellowish branch tips.
J. scopulorum 'Blue Haven'	*J. s.* 'Blue Heaven'.	To 20 ft.	Neat, compact, narrow gray blue pyramid.
J. s. 'Cologreen'			Narrow, bright green column.
J. s. 'Emerald Green'			Compact, bright green pyramid.
J. s. 'Erecta Glauca'			Gray blue, upright pyramid. Very similar to 'Pathfinder'.
J. s. 'Gray Gleam'			Gray blue, symmetrical column. Slow grower.
J. s. 'Moffetii'			Silvery green column.
J. s. 'Pathfinder'			Gray blue, upright pyramid.
J. s. 'Welchii'			Silvery green. Very narrow spire.
J. s. 'Wichita Blue'			Broad, silver blue pyramid.

NAME	SYNONYMS OR NURSERYMEN'S NAMES	SIZE, HABIT	CHARACTERISTICS
J. virginiana 'Burkii' BURK RED CEDAR		15–20 ft. or more.	Steel blue. Dense pyramid. Turns plum color in winter.
J. v. 'Cupressifolia' HILLSPIRE JUNIPER		15–20 ft.	Dark green compact pyramid with same color in winter.
J. v. 'Manhattan Blue'	*J. scopulorum* 'Manhattan Blue'.	10–15 ft.	Blue green, compact pyramid.
J. v. 'Skyrocket'		10–15 ft.	Narrowest blue gray spire.
TREES			
J. californica CALIFORNIA JUNIPER		Shrubby or to 40 ft.	Yellowish to rich green. Useful in desert areas.
J. deppeana pachyphlaea ALLIGATOR JUNIPER	*J. pachyphlaea.*	Shrubby or to 60 ft.	Blue gray foliage, strikingly checked bark like alligator hide.
J. monosperma		To 40 ft.	Similar to *J. osteosperma;* bluish green.
J. osteosperma UTAH JUNIPER	*J. utahensis.*	Shrubby or to 20–30 ft.	Yellowish green foliage. Adapted to high desert.
J. occidentalis WESTERN JUNIPER		To 50–60 ft.	Massive, long-lived mountain native.
J. scopulorum			Seldom grown; see varieties above.
J. virginiana EASTERN RED CEDAR		Forty–50 ft. or more.	Conical dark green tree becoming reddish in cold weather.

JOSEPH'S COAT. See *Amaranthus tricolor.*

JOSHUA TREE. See *Yucca brevifolia.*

JUBAEA chilensis *(J. spectabilis).* CHILEAN WINE PALM. Palm with fat trunk patterned with scars of leaf bases. Zones 15–24. Slow grower to 50–60 ft. Feather-type leaves 6–12 ft. long. Flowers insignificant. Needs regular watering during dry seasons until well established. Very hardy for a palm (20°F.).

Jubaea chilensis

JUDAS TREE. See *Cercis siliquastrum.*

JUGLANS. See *Walnut.*

JUJUBE. See *Ziziphus.*

JUNIPER. See *Juniperus.*

JUNIPER MYRTLE. See *Agonis juniperina.*

JUNIPERUS. JUNIPER. Evergreen shrubs and trees. Most are hardy. All Zones; ones that do not tolerate extreme desert heat or mountain cold are not sold in these critical areas. Coniferous plants with fleshy, berrylike cones. Foliage is needlelike, scalelike, or both. Junipers are most widely used woody plants in West. There's a form for almost every landscape use. Western nurserymen offer more than a hundred junipers under many more than a hundred names. In the chart these offerings are grouped by common use and listed by botanical names with accompanying synonyms, nurserymen's names, and common names. If you can't locate a juniper in the first column, look for one of its alternate names in next column to the right.

Juniperus chinensis 'Torulosa'

The ground cover group includes types ranging from a few inches to 2 or 3 ft. If you are planning large scale plantings, some of the taller junipers (such as the Pfitzer) could be included in this group. Prostrate and creeping junipers are almost indispensable to rock gardens. As ground cover, space plants 5–6 ft. apart; or for faster coverage, 3–4 ft., removing every other plant when they begin to crowd. In early years, mulch will help keep soil cool and weeds down. Or interplant with annuals until junipers cover.

Juniperus conferta

Shrub types range from low to quite tall, from spreading to stiffly upright and columnar. You can find a juniper in almost any height, width, shape, or foliage color. Use columnar forms with care; they become quite large with age. Many serve well as screens or windbreaks in cold areas.

Juniperus horizontalis

Tree types are not widely used. They are interesting for picturesque habit of trunk and branch; are tough, drought resistant.

Junipers succeed in every soil type the West offers, acid or alkaline, heavy or light. However, you can expect root rot (yellowing and collapse) if soil is waterlogged. Avoid planting junipers so close to lawn sprinkling systems that their roots stay wet. Well-established junipers in reasonably retentive soil can thrive on little or no summer water—except in hottest interior or desert areas. In summer-cool climates they are best grown in full sun but will accept light shade. In hot areas they do well with partial shade.

Pests to watch for: spider mites (gray or yellow, dry-looking plants, fine webbing on twigs); aphids (sticky deposits, falling needles, sooty mildew); twig borers (browning and dying branch tips). Control first two with malathion or other contact spray. Sevin or diazinon sprays in mid-June and early July (one month earlier in southern California) will control the latter. One important disease is juniper blight; twigs and branches die back. Control with copper sprays in July and August.

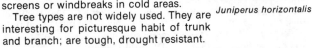

JUPITER'S BEARD. See *Centranthus ruber.*

JUSTICIA. Subtropical shrubs, a few growing in deserts of California and Arizona. Name includes plants formerly known as *Beloperone* and *Jacobinia*.

J. brandegeana *(Beloperone guttata).* SHRIMP PLANT. Evergreen. Zones 12, 13, 15–17, 21–24, and anywhere as indoor/outdoor plant, or annual. Native to Mexico. Will grow to 3 by 4-ft. mound but can be kept much lower. Leaves egg shaped, to 2½ in. long, apple green, often dropping in cold weather or in soil too wet or too dry. Tubular flowers, white spotted purple, enclosed in coppery bronze, overlapping bracts forming compact, drooping spikes 3 in. long (lengthening to 6–7 in. if allowed to remain on plant). In total, spike formation somewhat resembles large shrimp. Flowers attract birds.

*Justicia
brandegeana*

Will take sun but bracts and foliage fade unless grown in partial shade. Variety called 'Chartreuse' has spikes of chartreuse yellow which sunburn more easily than those of the coppery kind. To shape plant, pinch continuously in early growth until compact mound of foliage is obtained, then let bloom. To encourage continued bushiness, cut back stems when flower bracts turn black. Good for pot or tub, for close-up planting near terraces, patios, entryways.

Justicia carnea

J. californica. CHUPAROSA, CALIFORNIA BELOPERONE. Deciduous. Zones 10–13. Native to edges of Colorado Desert to Arizona and northern Mexico. A low, gray green shrub 2–5 ft. high, spreading to 4 ft. Arching branches appear almost leafless. Small, roundish, ¼-in. leaves. Tubular bright red flowers, 1½ in. long in clusters, give good show of color in April-May. Full sun. Often freezes to ground in winter but comes back quickly in spring. Very drought tolerant.

J. carnea *(Jacobinia carnea).* BRAZILIAN PLUME FLOWER. Evergreen shrub. Zones 8, 9, 13–24; house or greenhouse plant anywhere. Erect, soft-wooded plant with heavily veined leaves to 10 in. Dense clusters of pink to crimson tubular flowers bloom on 4–5 ft. stems, midsummer to fall. Shade, rich soil, ample water. Cut back in early spring to encourage strong new growth. Tops freeze back at 29° F. in any case.

J. ghiesbreghtiana. See *J. spicigera.*

J. leonardii. Zones 12–24. Shrub to 3 ft. with velvety leaves to 6 in. long. Small clusters of 1½-in. scarlet flowers appear off and on through warmer weather. Often sold in California as *Anisacanthus thurberi,* a related plant. Full sun. Drought tolerant.

J. spicigera (often sold as *J. ghiesbreghtiana* or, in Arizona, as *Anisacanthus thurberi*). To 6 ft., with leaves that may be smooth or velvety and with few-flowered clusters of 1½-in. orange or orange red flowers. Full sun. Drought tolerant.

KADSURA japonica. SCARLET KADSURA. Twining evergreen vine. Zones 7–9, 14–22. Grown for its foliage and berries. On support, grows fast to 15–20 ft. Needs some summer watering. Leaves highly polished, leathery, dark green, oval, 2–4 in. long, toothed. Leaves turn reddish beneath with cold weather. Flowers yellowish white, ¾ in. across, inconspicuous. Bright scarlet fruit in roundish, headlike 1-in.-wide clusters, fall and winter. Need male and female plants to secure fruit on female. Without pollination, an attractive all-foliage vine. Train around pillar or on fence or pergola. Takes full sun near coast; best in partial shade inland.

Kadsura japonica

KAFFIRBOOM CORAL TREE. See *Erythrina caffra.*

KAFFIR LILY. See *Clivia miniata, Schizostylis coccinea.*

KAFFIR PLUM. See *Harpephyllum caffrum.*

KAHILI GINGER. See *Hedychium gardneranum.*

KALANCHOE. Succulents grown principally as house plants. Some hardy outdoors in mildest coastal regions, but safest even there with protection of lath, eaves, or other overhead structure. Shapes and sizes varied. Flowers fairly large, bell shaped, erect or drooping, brightly colored in a few species. Sun or light shade. Need very little water.

*Kalanchoe
blossfeldiana*

K. beharensis. (Often sold as *Kitchingia mandrakensis.*) FELT PLANT. Outdoors Zones 21–24, house plant anywhere. Stems usually unbranched, to 4–5 ft., possibly 10 ft. Leaves at tips of stems, usually 6–8 pairs, each leaf 4–8 in. or more long, half as wide, triangular to lance shaped, thick, and thickly covered with dense, white to brown feltlike hairs. Flowers not showy; foliage strikingly waved and crimped at edges. Hybrids between this and other species differ in leaf size, color, and degree of felting and scalloping. Striking in big rock garden, raised bed, in sun or considerable shade.

K. blossfeldiana. House plant; some hybrids hardy Zones 17, 21–24. Leaves fleshy, dark green edged red, shiny, smooth edged or slightly lobed, 2½ in. long, 1–1½ in. wide. Small bright red flowers in big clusters held above leaves. Hybrids and named varieties come in dwarf (6 in.) and extra-sturdy (18 in.) sizes and in different colors, including yellow, orange, salmon. 'Pumila' and 'Tetra Vulcan' are choice dwarf seed-grown selections. Blooms winter, early spring. Popular house plant at Christmas time.

K. daigremontiana. MATERNITY PLANT. House plant. Upright, single-stemmed plant 18–36 in. tall. Leaves fleshy, 6–8 in. long, 1¼ in. or more wide, gray green spotted red. Leaf edges are notched; young plants sprout in notches—these root even on the plant. Flowers clustered, small, grayish purple.

K. fedtschenkoi. Zones 17, 21–24. Flowering stems upright, to 2 ft. Sterile stems spreading, rooting. Grown chiefly for leaves—fleshy, scallop toothed, lavender gray in color, ½–2 in. long. Brownish pink flowers attractive, not showy. Used as pot plant or for foliage color in mixed plantings of succulents.

K. flammea. House plant; some hybrids hardy Zones 17, 21–24. Lightly branched, 12–16 in. tall, with fleshy, gray green, 2½-in. leaves and many-flowered clusters of orange red or yellow flowers in winter and spring.

K. laciniata *(K. coccinea).* Zones 17, 21–24. To 4 ft. Leaves greenish bronze to red, to 5 in. long, fleshy, smooth edged, scalloped, or cut. Clusters of ¼-in. yellow, orange, or red flowers late winter and spring.

K. manginii. Zones 17, 21–24. Stems spreading or trailing, to 12 in. long. Inch-long green leaves thick and fleshy. Drooping bell shaped, inch-long flowers are bright red. Hanging basket plant.

K. pinnata *(Bryophyllum pinnatum).* AIR PLANT. Zones 17, 21–24. Fleshy stems eventually 2–3 ft. tall. Leaves fleshy; early ones undivided, scalloped; later ones divided into 3–5 leaflets, these also scalloped. Produces many plantlets in notches of scallops. Leaves can be removed and pinned to curtain, where they will produce plantlets until they dry up. Flower color ranges from greenish white to reddish. Takes sun or considerable shade. Likes moisture.

K. tomentosa. PANDA PLANT. House plant. Eventually 18 in. tall, branched. Leaves very fleshy, 2 in. long, coated with dense, white, felty hairs. Leaf tips and shallow notches in leaves strongly marked dark brown.

K. uniflora. Zones 17, 21–24. Trailing plant; inch-long, thick, fleshy leaves have a few scallops near rounded tips. Inch-long flowers are pinkish or purplish red. Hanging basket plant.

KALE AND COLLARDS. Vegetable crops that live 1–2 years. The type of kale known as collards is a large smooth-leafed plant like a cabbage that does not form a head. Planted in early spring or late summer, collards will yield edible leaves in fall, winter, and spring. 'Georgia' and 'Vates' are typical varieties. Collards not widely grown in the West.

Kale

Slightly more popular are curly kales like 'Dwarf Blue Curled' and 'Dwarf Siberian'; these are compact clusters of tightly curled leaves. They make decorative garden or container plants as well as supplying edible leaves. One kind, flowering kale, has brightly colored foliage, especially toward centers of rosettes. Grow just like late cabbage. Harvest leaves for cooking by removing from outside of cluster; or harvest entire plant.

KALMIA. Evergreen shrubs. Zones 1–7, 16, 17. Related to rhododendron. All have clusters of showy flowers and grow in part shade. All need regular watering.

K. latifolia. MOUNTAIN LAUREL, CALICO BUSH. Native to eastern U.S. Slow growing to 6–8 ft. or more, with equal spread. Glossy, leathery, oval leaves, 3–5 in. long, dark green on top, yellowish green beneath. Clusters of pink buds open to pale pink flowers in apple blossom effect, May-June. Varieties range from white or near red. Flowers 1 in. across, clusters to 5 in. across. Hardy well below 0°F. Shares rhododendron's cultural needs—moist atmosphere, partial shade, acid soil rich in humus. Has proved difficult to grow in Zones 16, 17 even under these conditions; seems to do better in containers there.

Kalmia latifolia

K. microphylla (*K. polifolia microphylla*). WESTERN LAUREL, ALPINE LAUREL. Low plant has spreading branches with erect branchlets, small dark green leaves whitish underneath, and rounded clusters of extremely showy, ½-in., rose to purple flowers in summer. Full sun. Will grow in very moist, acid soils.

Typical high mountain form is 8–11 in. tall with leaves up to ¾ in. long. A taller variety, *K. m. occidentalis*, to 2 ft. tall and with slightly larger leaves, grows in coastal lowlands north to Alaska.

KALMIOPSIS leachiana. Evergreen shrub. Zones 4–6, 14–17. Native to mountains of southwest Oregon. Rhododendron relative, slow growing to 1 ft. tall, with 2-ft. spread. Many branches densely clothed with thick dark green leaves. Flowers abundantly in early spring with leafy clusters of ½-in. rose pink flowers. Does best in light shade. Takes same culture as rhododendron or azalea. Sometimes reblooms.

Kalmiopsis leachiana

KANGAROO PAW. See *Anigozanthos*.

KANGAROO THORN. See *Acacia armata*.

KANGAROO TREEBINE. See *Cissus antarctica*.

KATSURA TREE. See *Cercidiphyllum japonicum*.

KENILWORTH IVY. See *Cymbalaria muralis*.

KENTIA PALM. See *Howea*.

KENTUCKY COFFEE TREE. See *Gymnocladus dioica*.

KENYA IVY. See *Senecio macroglossus*.

KERRIA japonica. Deciduous shrub. Zones 1–21. Green branches give welcome winter green in cold areas. Open, graceful, rounded shrub to 8 ft., with a 5–6-ft. spread. Leaves bright green, heavily veined, somewhat triangular, 2–4 in. long with toothed edges, turning yellow in fall. Flowers (March-May) like small, single, yellow roses. Variety 'Pleniflora' has double, yellow, inch-wide flowers and is the more commonly planted form.

Kerria japonica
'Pleniflora'

Give kerria part shade (will take sun in cooler areas) and room to arch and display its form. Water until established and growing. Drought tolerant after that. Remove suckers and prune heavily after bloom, cutting out branches that have flowered and all dead or weak wood. Cut green branches are a favorite subject in Japanese arrangements.

KHAT. See *Catha edulis*.

KING PALM. See *Archontophoenix cunninghamiana*.

KINNIKINNICK. See *Arctostaphylos uva-ursi*.

KIWI, HARDY KIWI. See *Actinidia*.

KLEINIA. See *Senecio*.

KNIPHOFIA uvaria (*Tritoma uvaria*). RED-HOT POKER, TORCH-LILY, POKER PLANT. Perennial. Zones 1–9, 14–24. Native to South Africa. Likes full sun or a little shade. Quite heat and drought tolerant. Has been in cultivation long enough to give rise to garden varieties with some range in size, color. Typical plant is coarse with large, rather dense clumps of long grasslike leaves. Flower stalks (always taller than leaves) are about 2 ft. in dwarf kinds and 3–6 ft. tall in larger kinds. The many drooping, orange red or yellow, tubular flowers of the typical plant overlap, forming pokerlike clusters 12 in. long. Named varieties, in both dwarf and taller forms, come in soft or saffron yellow, cream white, or coral. Flowers attract hummingbirds, are good in flower arrangements.

Kniphofia uvaria

Flowering time varies—spring through summer. Cut out flower spikes after bloom. Cut old leaves at base in fall; new leaves will replace them by spring. Increase by root divisions. Poker plant is useful in large borders with other robust perennials such as hemerocallis, *Echinops exaltatus*.

KNOTWEED. See *Polygonum*.

KOCHIA scoparia. SUMMER CYPRESS. Summer annual. Grow these foliage plants close together as low, temporary hedge or individually for their gently rounded form—like fine-textured coniferous shrubs. To 3 ft. Branches densely clothed with very narrow, soft, light green leaves, making plants too dense to see through. Insignificant flowers. Sow in full sun. Tolerates high heat and will perform well in short summer areas. Shear to shape if necessary.

Kochia scoparia

K. s. trichophylla. MEXICAN FIRE BUSH, BURNING BUSH. Same as above, but foliage turns red at first frost. Can reseed profusely enough to become pest; hoe out unwanted seedlings when small.

KOELREUTERIA. Deciduous trees. Small yellow flowers in large loose clusters in summer. Colorful fruit are fat, papery capsules which seem to resemble clusters of little Japanese lanterns; used in arrangements.

K. bipinnata (*K. integrifoliola*). CHINESE FLAME TREE. Zones 8–24. Slow to moderate growth to 20–40 ft. or taller, spreading, eventually flat topped. Leaves 1–2 ft. long, divided into many oval leaflets, holding onto tree until December, then turning yellow briefly before dropping. Capsules 2 in. long, orange, red, or salmon-colored, showy in late summer and fall, in large clus-

*Koelreuteria
paniculata*

ters. Fruit formation not always dependable. Takes to most well-drained soils and moderate watering. Stake and prune to develop high branching. Good patio shade tree, lawn, or street tree. Roots deep, not invasive. Good tree to plant under. A similar species, *K. elegans* (*K. formosana*, *K. henryi*), is occasionally seen. It is less hardy and less widely sold.

K. paniculata. GOLDENRAIN TREE. Zones 2–21. Slow to moderate growth to 20–35 ft. with 10–40-ft. spread. Open branching, giving slight shade. Leaves to 15 in. long, with 7–15 toothed or lobed leaflets, 1–3 in. long. Flower clusters in summer, 8–14 in. long. Fruit buff to brown in fall, hanging late. Takes cold, heat, drought, wind, alkaline soil; needs regular watering when young. Prune to shape; can be gawky without pruning. Valuable as street, lawn, or terrace tree in difficult soils and climates. The variety 'Kew' or 'Fastigiata' is erect and narrow—3 ft. wide by 25 ft. tall.

KOHLRABI. All Zones in conditions noted below. Cool-season, annual vegetable related to cabbage. The edible portion is bulblike enlarged portion of the stem, formed just above soil surface. Ordinary leaves grow above. Varieties: 'Early White Vienna' and 'Early Purple Vienna'. Similar in size and flavor, they differ only in skin color. Sow seed ½ in. deep in full sun and in rich soil about 2 weeks after average date of last frost. Follow first planting with successive plantings 2 weeks apart. In warm-winter areas plant again in late fall

Kohlrabi

and early winter. Space rows 18 in. apart; thin seedlings to 4 in. apart. To control aphids, dust or spray with rotenone. Harvest when round portions are 2–3 in. wide. Slice them and eat raw like cucumbers or cook them like turnips.

KOLKWITZIA amabilis. BEAUTY BUSH. Deciduous shrub. Zones 1–11, 14–20. Growth upright, graceful to 10–12 ft., arching in part shade, denser and lower in full sun. Leaves gray green. Clusters of small pink, yellow-throated flowers bloom heavily in May in California, June in Northwest and mountain states. Flowers followed by conspicuous pinkish brown, bristly fruit that prolong color. Thin out after bloom; to enjoy the fruit, prune lightly in early spring, removing wood which has bloomed year

Kolkwitzia amabilis

before. Brown, flaky bark gradually peels from stems during winter. Sun. Average water needs.

KOREAN GRASS. See *Zoysia tenuifolia*.

KOWHAI. See *Sophora tetraptera*.

KRUSE'S MALLEE. See *Eucalyptus kruseana*.

KUMQUAT. See *Citrus*.

LABURNUM. GOLDENCHAIN TREE. Deciduous trees or large shrubs. Zones 1–10, 14–17. Upright growth; usually pruned into single-stemmed tree; can be shrubby if permitted to keep basal suckers and low branches. Bark green, leaves bright green, divided into 3 leaflets (like clover). Flowers yellow, sweet pea shaped, in hanging clusters like wisteria.

Protect from afternoon sun in hot regions. Well-drained soil, adequate water. Subject to chlorosis in alkaline soils; use iron. Prune and trim regularly to keep plants tidy. Remove seed pods if possible. Not only are they poisonous, but too heavy a crop is drain on plant's strength. Hand-

Laburnum watereri

some in bloom. Use as a single tree in lawn or border, group in front of neutral background, or space regularly in long borders of perennials, rhododendrons, or lilacs. In Wales, a tunnel of laburnums trained over a series of arches is one of the world's most startling horticultural sights when plants are in bloom. Pests seldom a problem, but beware of mites.

L. alpinum. SCOTCH LABURNUM. To 30–35 ft. Flower clusters 10–15. in. long. Blooms late spring. The variety 'Pendulum' has weeping branches.

L. anagyroides. COMMON GOLDENCHAIN. To 20–30 ft. high, often wide-spreading and bushy. Flower clusters 6–10 in. long in late spring. Like Scotch laburnum, it has a weeping variety, 'Pendulum'.

L. watereri. Hybrid between the two preceding species; has flower clusters 10–20 in. long. Most widely grown variety is 'Vossii', most graceful of the lot. Can be espaliered.

LACEBARK. See *Hoheria*.

LACE FERN. See *Microlepia strigosa*.

LACHENALIA. CAPE COWSLIP. Bulbs. Hardy outdoors only in Zones 16, 17, 24; usually grown in pots indoors or in greenhouses. Native to South Africa. Strap shaped, succulent leaves, often brown spotted. Tubular, pendulous flowers in spikes on thick, fleshy stems; bloom in winter, early spring. Plant in August-September; put 6 bulbs in 5–6-in. pot; set 1–1½ in. deep to prevent flowering stems from falling over. Water, keep cool and dark until roots form and leaves appear. When growth becomes active, water thoroughly, bring plants into light. Keep cool (50°F. night temperature). Feed when flower spikes show. When leaves start to yellow, gradually dry out plants. Keep dry during summer.

*Lachenalia
bulbiferum*

L. aloides (*L. tricolor*). Flowers yellow, inner segments tipped red, outer tipped green, on stems 1 ft. tall or less. Leaves usually 2 to a plant, 1 in. wide, about as tall as or taller than flower stems. Variety 'Aurea' is bright orange yellow; 'Nelsonii', bright yellow tinged green; 'Pearsonii' slightly taller, yellow orange with reddish orange buds and flower bases.

L. bulbiferum (*L. pendula*). Basal leaves to 2 in. wide. Flowers 1½ in. long, coral red and yellow, purple tipped, in spikes 12–15 in. tall. 'Superba', improved form, has orange red flowers.

LADY FERN. See *Athyrium filix-femina*.

LADY-OF-THE-NIGHT. See *Brassavola nodosa*.

LADY PALM. See *Rhapis*.

LADY'S SLIPPER. See *Cypripedium*, *Paphiopedilum*.

LAELIA. Epiphytic orchids. Greenhouse or indoor/outdoor plants—the three which are hardy in sheltered locations outdoors in Zones 16, 17, 21–24. Foliage and flowers resemble cattleyas. Color range includes red, orange, and yellow, but most are in the white-pink-lavender-purple range. Plants perform best in filtered shade. Grow on slab of tree bark or tree fern (hapuu) or in media used for cattleyas. Tack slabs on wall in patio, hang from tree trunk, or grow in pots on patio. During summer feed several times with fish emulsion or fertilizer packaged especially for orchids. Let potting medium dry out between waterings.

Laelia anceps

L. albida. Transparent white, 2-in. flowers with yellow rib in throat, lavender flush in lip. Bloom 2–8 on stem in winter and early spring. Fragrant. Oval 1–2-in.-high pseudobulbs topped by pair of narrow leaves.

L. anceps. Rose violet flowers to 4 in. across with yellow throat lined purple. Blooms 2–6 on stem in autumn and winter. Four-sided pseudobulb, 3–5 in. high, bearing one, sometimes two, 5–9-in.-long leaves. Repot these plants as infrequently as possible.

L. autumnalis. Rose purple, 4-in. flowers with white at base of lip. Fragrant blooms, 3–9 on erect stem, in fall and winter. Pseudobulbs 2–4 in. high bear 2–3 leathery, 4–8-in.-long leaves.

LAGENARIA. See Gourd.

LAGERSTROEMIA indica. CRAPE MYRTLE. Deciduous shrub or tree. Root hardy and sometimes treated as perennial in Zones 1–3; hardy in Zones 4–6 but doesn't flower freely except in hottest summers; excellent in Zones 7–9, 12–14, 18–21; generally a shrub in Zones 10, 11; mildew is serious problem in Zones 15–17, 22–24. Native to China. Dwarf shrubby forms and shrub-tree forms, 6–30 ft. tall, are available. Slow-growing as shrub, spreads as wide as high; trained as tree, becomes vase shaped with most attractive trunk and branch pattern. Smooth gray or light brown bark flakes off to reveal smooth pinkish inner bark.

Lagerstroemia indica

Spring foliage light green tinged bronze red; mature leaves 1–2 in. long, oval, deep glossy green. Fall foliage yellow, more rarely orange to red. Crinkled, crepelike, 1½-in. flowers in rounded, slightly conical clusters, 6–12 in. long, at ends of branches; smaller clusters form lower down on branches. Colors in shades of red, rose, pink, rosy orchid, purple, soft pink, white. Long flowering period, July-September.

Plant in full sun; feed moderately; water infrequently but deeply—drought resistant. Where soil is alkaline or water high in salts, treat chlorosis or marginal leaf burn by occasional leaching and applications of iron. Check mildew with sprays just before plants bloom. Prune in dormant season to increase flowering wood the next summer. With dwarf shrub forms, remove spent flower clusters and prune out small twiggy growth. With large shrubs and trees cut back branches 12–18 in.

Many color selections are available in bush form and trained as trees. In whites: 'White', 'Glendora White'; pinks: 'Shell Pink' ('Near East'), 'Pink'; reds: 'Durant Red', 'Gray's Red', 'Rubra', 'Watermelon Red', 'Watermelon Red Improved'; other colors: 'Lavender', 'Purple', 'Select Purple', 'Majestic Orchid'. 'Peppermint Lace' has rose pink flowers edged with white. These are the dwarfer, shrubby forms (to 5–7 ft.): 'Petite Embers' (rose red), 'Petite Orchid', 'Petite Pinkie', 'Petite Red Imp' (dark red), 'Petite Snow', 'Snow White'.

Selections called Indian Tribes have heavy foliage with considerable resistance to mildew. 'Catawba' has dark purple flowers, 'Cherokee' has bright red. 'Potomac' and 'Seminole' have pink bloom. 'Powhatan' has light lavender flowers and is a dense, globular shrub.

Strain called Crape Myrtlettes grows from seed, flowering in late summer from March sowing. They have full range of crape myrtle colors, grow to 12–14 in. during first year, eventually to 3–4 ft. Can be grown in pots or hanging baskets. Can be espaliered.

LAGUNARIA patersonii. PRIMROSE TREE, COW ITCH TREE. Evergreen tree. Zones 13, 15–24. Native to South Pacific and Australia. Rather fast growth to 20–40 ft. Young trees narrow and erect; old trees sometimes spreading, flat topped. Densely foliaged. Leaves thick, oval, olive green, gray beneath, 2–4 in. long. Flowers hibiscuslike, 2 in. wide, pink to rose, fading nearly white in summer. Brown seed capsules hang on long time. Flower arrangers like them because capsules split into 5 sections, revealing bright brown seeds. Handle carefully; pods also contain short, stiff fibers which can cause skin irritation.

Lagunaria patersonii

Foliage burns at 25°F. but recovers quickly. Tolerates wide variety of soils and growing conditions. Resists ocean wind, salt spray; tolerates soils and heat of low deserts. Best flowering under coastal conditions. Plant individually as garden tree or in groups as showy windbreak or screen. Needs little water once established.

LAMB'S EARS. See *Stachys byzantina*.

LAMIUM maculatum. DEAD NETTLE. Perennial. All Zones. Trailing stems sprawl along ground or hang from wall or container to length of 6 ft. or more. Heart shaped leaves in neat pairs, 1½–2 in. long, bluntly toothed at edges, green with silvery white markings along the midrib. Flowers pink to white. 'Variegatum' has green and silver leaves; 'Beacon Silver' is silver with narrow green edge. Usually seen as hanging basket plant; can be used as ground cover in shade. Needs rich soil, plenty of water. Deciduous in cold winters. Partially evergreen where winters are mild, but old, shabby stems should be cut off to make room for fresh new growth.

Lamium maculatum

LAMPRANTHUS. ICE PLANT. Succulent subshrub. Zones 14–24. Most of the blindingly brilliant ice plants with large flowers belong here. Plants erect or trailing, woody at base; leaves fleshy, cylindrical or 3-sided. Select in bloom for the color you like. Plant in full sun. Need little or no summer water. Cut back lightly after bloom to eliminate fruit capsules, encourage new leafy growth. Good at seashore. Attract bees.

L. aurantiacus. To 10–15 in. tall. Foliage gray green; leaves an inch long, 3 sided. Flowers (February-May) 1½–2 in. across, bright orange. Variety 'Glaucus' has bright yellow flowers; 'Sunman' has golden yellow flowers. Plant 15–18 in. apart for bedding, borders, low bank cover.

Lampranthus spectabilis

L. filicaulis. REDONDO CREEPER. Thin creeping stems, fine-textured foliage. Spreads slowly to form mats 3 in. deep. Flowers small, pink. Early spring bloom. Use for small-scale ground cover, mound or low bank cover.

L. productus. To 15 in. tall, spreading to 1½–2 ft. Gray green, fleshy leaves tipped bronze. Flowers an inch wide, purple. Blooms heavily January-April. Scattered bloom at other times. Plant 1–1½ ft. apart.

L. spectabilis. TRAILING ICE PLANT. Sprawling or trailing, to 12 in. tall, 1½–2 ft. wide. Gray green foliage. Makes carpets of gleaming color, March-May. Flowers 2–2½ in. across, very heavily borne. Available in pink, rose pink, red, purple. Set plants 1–1½ ft. apart.

LANTANA. Evergreen and deciduous vining shrubs—deciduous only in very cold winters. Seldom freeze in Zones 17, 23, 24. May freeze but recover quickly in Zones 12, 13, 15, 16, 18–22. In Zones 8–10, 14 often persist, but may need replacement after hard winter. Elsewhere, an annual. Fast-growing, valued for profuse show of color over long season—every month in the year in frost-free areas.

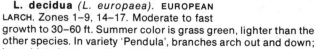

Lantana montevidensis

Not particular as to soil. Plant in full sun. Subject to mildew in shade or continued overcast. Prune hard in spring to remove dead wood and prevent woodiness. Water deeply but infrequently; feed lightly. Too much water and fertilizer cuts down on bloom. Shrubby kinds used as substitutes for annuals in planting beds or containers, as low hedges, foundation shrubs. Spreading kinds excellent bank covers, will control erosion. Effective spilling from raised beds, planter boxes, hanging baskets. Crushed foliage has strong, pungent odor that is objectionable to some people. Birds attracted to plants.

L. camara. One species used in development of kinds sold at nurseries. Coarse, upright to 6 ft. Rough dark green leaves. Flowers in 1–2-in. clusters, yellow, orange, or red.

L. montevidensis (*L. sellowiana*). The other species used in cross breeding. This one is sold at nurseries. A little hardier than *L. camara*, it's a well-known ground cover whose branches may trail to as much as 3 or even 6 ft. Dark green leaves, 1 in. long, with coarsely toothed edges; sometimes tinged red or purplish, especially in cold weather. Rosy lilac flowers in 1–1½-in.-wide clusters. A white-flowered variety is sold as 'Velutina White'.

The following list gives some of the named kinds of lantana that are available. Some are merely forms of *L. camara*, or hybrids between the forms. Others are hybrids between *L. camara* and *L. montevidensis*.

'Carnival' ('Dwarf Carnival'). 1½–2 ft. by 4 ft. Pink, yellow, crimson, lavender.

'Christine'. To 6 ft. tall, 5 ft. wide, cerise pink. Can be trained into small patio tree.

'Confetti'. To 2–3 ft. by 6–8 ft. Yellow, pink, purple.

'Cream Carpet'. To 2–3 ft. by 6–8 ft. Cream with bright yellow throat.

'Dwarf Pink'. To 2–4 ft. by 3–4 ft. Light pink. Rather tender.

'Dwarf White'. To 2–4 ft. by 3–4 ft.

'Dwarf Yellow'. To 2–4 ft. and as wide as high.

'Gold Mound'. To 1½–2 ft. by 6 ft. Yellowish orange.

'Irene'. To 3 ft. by 4 ft. Compact. Magenta with lemon yellow.

'Kathleen'. To 2 ft. by 5–6 ft. Blend of soft rose and gold.

'Orange'. To 4 ft. by 3 ft.

'Pink Frolic'. To 2–3 ft. by 6–8 ft. Pink and yellow.

'Radiation'. To 3–5 ft. by 3–5 ft. Rich orange red. Try it as staked small patio tree.

'Spreading Sunset'. To 2–3 ft. by 6–8 ft. Vivid orange red.

'Spreading Sunshine'. To 2–3 ft. by 6–8 ft. Bright yellow.

'Sunburst'. To 2–3 ft. by 6–8 ft. Bright golden yellow.

'Tangerine'. To 2–3 ft. by 6–8 ft. Burnt orange.

LAPAGERIA rosea. CHILEAN BELLFLOWER. Evergreen vine. Zones 5, 6, 15–17, 23, 24. The national flower of Chile. Likes high humidity, moderate summer temperatures. Slender stems twine to 10–20 ft. Leaves glossy, leathery, oval, to 4 in. long. Blooms scattered through late spring, summer, and

Lapageria rosea

fall. Beautiful, 3-in.-long, rosy red, pendant, bell shaped flowers (frequently spotted with white) have unusually heavy, waxy sub-

stance; hold up as long as 2 weeks after cutting. Give it partial shade, wind protection, loose soil with plenty of peat moss, ground bark, or sawdust, and ample water. Protect from snails and slugs.

LARCH. See *Larix*.

LARIX. LARCH. Deciduous conifers. Slender pyramids with horizontal branches and drooping branchlets. Needles (½–1½ in. long) soft to touch, in fluffy tufts. Woody roundish cones, ½–1½ in. long, are scattered all along branchlets. Notable for spring and fall color, and winter pattern. In spring, new needle tufts are pale green and new cones bright purple red. In fall, needles turn brilliant yellow and orange before dropping. Winter interest is enhanced by many cones which create a delightful polka dot pattern against sky. Not particular as to soils; accept lawn watering. Not for warm winter climate or dry soils. Plant with dark evergreen conifers as background or near water for reflection. They attract birds.

Larix decidua

L. decidua (*L. europaea*). EUROPEAN LARCH. Zones 1–9, 14–17. Moderate to fast growth to 30–60 ft. Summer color is grass green, lighter than the other species. In variety 'Pendula', branches arch out and down; branchlets hang nearly straight down.

L. kaempferi. JAPANESE LARCH. Zones 1–9, 14–19. Fast growing to 60 ft. or more. Summer foliage color a soft bluish green. Most frequently planted larch in West. Can be dwarfed in containers.

L. occidentalis. WESTERN LARCH, TAMARACK. Zones 1–7. Native to Cascades of Washington and Oregon, eastern Oregon, northern Rocky Mountains. Needles sharp and stiff. Grows to 150–200 ft. as timber tree, 30–50 ft. in gardens.

LARKSPUR. See *Consolida ambigua*.

LARREA tridentata (sometimes sold as *L. divaricata*). CREOSOTE BUSH. Evergreen shrub. Zones 10–13, 19. One of commonest native shrubs in deserts of southeastern California, Arizona, southern Utah, Texas, northern Mexico. Grows with many upright branches 4–8 ft. high. Straggly and open in shallow, dry soil. Attractive, dense, rounded but spreading where water accumulates. Leathery, yellow green to dark green leaves divided into 2 tiny crescents ⅜ in. long. Gummy secretion makes leaves look varnished and yields distinctive creosote odor, especially after rain. Small yellow flowers off and on all year, followed by small roundish fruit covered with shiny white or rusty hairs. Full sun. With water and fertilizer, grows taller, more dense, with larger shiny dark green leaves. Use as wind or privacy screens, or trim into more formal hedge.

Larrea tridentata

LATHYRUS. Annual vines or bushlike perennial vine. In this group is one of the best known garden flower producers—the delightfully fragrant and colorful sweet pea.

You will find through this book flower descriptions that say "sweet pea shaped" or "sweet pealike." The flower of the sweet pea is typical of the many members of the pea family (*Leguminosae*). This means that each flower has 1 large, upright, roundish petal (banner or standard), 2 narrow side petals (wings), and 2 lower petals that are somewhat united, forming a boat shaped structure (keel). Leaves are alternate.

Lathyrus odoratus

L. latifolius. PERENNIAL SWEET PEA. All Zones. Strong-growing vine up to 9 ft., with blue green foliage. Flowers usually reddish purple, often white or rose. Single colors—white and rose—sometimes sold. Long bloom season: June to September, if not allowed to go to seed. Plants grow with little care. May escape and become naturalized. Use as bank cover, trailing over rocks, on trellis, fence. Sun.

L. odoratus. SWEET PEA. Spring or summer annual. Bears many spikelike clusters of crisp-looking flowers with a clean sweet fragrance, in single colors and mixtures. Color mixtures include deep rose, blue, purple, scarlet, white, cream, amethyst on white ground, salmon, salmon pink on cream. Sweet peas make magnificent cut flowers in quantity. Bush types offer cut flowers the same as vine types, and require no training; both need sun.

To hasten germination, soak seeds for a few hours before planting. Treat seeds with fungicide. Sow seeds 1 in. deep and 1–2 in. apart. When seedlings are 4–5 in. high, thin to not less than 6 in. apart. Pinch out tops to encourage strong side branches. Where climate prevents early planting or soil is too wet to work, start 3–4 seeds in 2¼–3-in. peat pots, indoors or in protected place, and set out when weather has settled. Plant 1 ft. apart, thinning to 1 strong plant. This method is ideal for bush types. Protect young seedlings from birds with wire screen. Set out bait for slugs and snails. Never let vines lack for water. Soak heavily when you water. Cut flowers at least every other day and remove all seed pods.

For vining sweet peas, provide trellis, strings, or wire before planting. Seedlings need support as soon as tendrils form. Free-standing trellis running north and south is best. When planting against fence or wall keep supports away from wall to give air circulation.

Here is a special method of soil preparation—not essential, but producing most perfect flowers on extra long stems: dig trench 12–18 in. deep. Mix 1 part peat moss, ground bark, or sawdust to 2 parts soil. Add complete commercial fertilizer according to label directions as you mix. Backfill trench with mix. This extra deep digging is not necessary in good garden soils. Regular monthly feeding with commercial fertilizer will keep vines vigorous and productive.

The many varieties of vine-type sweet peas are best understood if grouped by time of bloom.

Early flowering. (Early Flowering Multiflora, Early Multiflora, formerly Early Spencers.) The name "Spencer" once described a type of frilled flowers (wavy petals) that is now characteristic of almost all varieties. The "Multiflora" indicates that the plants carry more flowers per stem than the old "Spencers." The value of Early Flowering varieties is that they will bloom in midwinter when days are short. (Spring and summer-flowering types will not bloom until days have lengthened to 15 hours or more.) Where winter temperatures are mild (Zones 12, 13, 17, 21–24), sow seeds in August or early September for late December or January bloom. Use these varieties for forcing in greenhouse. They are not heat resistant. Generally sold in mixed colors.

Spring flowering. (Spring Flowering Heat Resistant Cuthbertson Type, Cuthbertson's Floribunda, Floribunda—Zvolanek strain.) Seeds are packed in both mixtures and single-color named varieties. Wide color range: pink, lavender, purple, white, cream, rose, salmon, cerise, carmine, red, blue. Royal or Royal Family are somewhat larger flowered, more heat resistant.

In Zones 7–9, 12–24, plant between October and early January. Elsewhere, February to April, or just as soon as soil can be worked.

Summer flowering. (Galaxy, Plenti-flora.) Available in named varieties and mixtures in wide color range. Heat resistant, they bloom from early summer on. Large flowers, 5–7 on long stems. Heat resistance is relative; not enough for Zones 7–15, 18–21.

Bush type. The so-called bush type sweet peas are strong vines with predetermined growth, heights. Unlike vining types that reach 5 ft. and more, these stop their upward growth at 12–30 in.

Bijou. To 12 in. Full color range in mixtures and single varieties. Flowers 4–5 on 5–7-in. stems. Useful and spectacular in borders, beds, window boxes, containers. Not as heat resistant or as long stemmed as Knee-Hi, performs better in containers.

Jet Set. Bushy, self-supporting plants 2–3 ft. tall. All colors.
Knee-Hi. To 30 in. Large, long-stemmed flowers 5–6 to the stem. Has all the virtues and color range of Cuthbertson Floribundas in self-supporting, bush-type vines. Provides cutting-type flowers in mass display in beds and borders. Growth will exceed 30 in. where planting bed joins fence or wall. Keep in open area for uniform height. Follow same planting dates as spring flowering sweet peas.

Little Sweethearts. Rounded bushes, 8 in. tall, bloom over a long season. Full range of colors.

L. splendens. PRIDE OF CALIFORNIA. Perennial vine to 8–10 ft. Zones 14–24. Clusters of 3 to 10 deep red sweet peas in March-April. Native to chaparral in San Diego County and adjacent Baja California. Start from seed in pots in fall or spring, plant out in fall or winter. Needs little water first years, none once established. Long-lived in dry, well drained soil.

LAURENTIA fluviatilis (*Isotoma fluviatilis*). BLUE STAR CREEPER. Perennial ground cover plant. Zones 4, 5, 8, 9, 14–24. Creeping, spreading plant that grows only 2–3 in. tall. Pointed, oval leaves ¼ in. long give plant look of baby's tears (*Soleirolia*). Pale blue starlike flowers, slightly broader than the leaves, spangle plantings in late spring, summer, with a scattering at other times. Will grow in part shade or full sun and can take foot traffic. Plant pieces 6–12 in. apart for cover within a year. Feed lightly once a month, spring to fall. Looks good around stepping stones.

Laurentia fluviatilis

LAUREL. See *Laurus, Prunus, Umbellularia californica.*

LAURUS nobilis. SWEET BAY, GRECIAN LAUREL. Evergreen tree or shrub. Zones 5–9, 12–24. Slow growth to 12–40 ft. Natural habit is compact, broad-based, often multistemmed, gradually tapering cone. Leaves leathery, aromatic, oval, 2–4 in. long, dark green; traditional bay leaf of cookery. Clusters of small yellow flowers followed by ½–1-in.-long black or dark purple berries.

Not fussy about soil, but needs good drainage; requires little water when established. In hot-summer climates, best in filtered shade or afternoon shade. Spray for black scale and laurel psyllid. Tends to sucker heavily. Dense habit makes it a good large background shrub, screen, or small tree. Takes well to clipping into formal shapes—globes, cones, topiary shapes, standards, or hedges. A classic formal container plant. 'Saratoga' has broader leaves, a more treelike habit, and is resistant to psyllid.

Laurus nobilis

LAURUSTINUS. See *Viburnum tinus.*

LAVANDULA. LAVENDER. Evergreen shrubs or subshrubs. Native to Mediterranean region. Prized for fragrant lavender or purple flowers used for perfume, sachets. Grayish or gray green aromatic foliage. Plant as hedge, edging, or in herb gardens; in borders with plants needing similar conditions—cistus, helianthemum, nepeta, rosemary, santolina, verbena.

All need full sun; loose, fast draining soil. Little water or fertilizer. Prune immediately after bloom to keep plants compact, neat. For sachets, cut flower clusters or strip flowers from stems just as color shows; dry in cool shady place.

L. angustifolia (*L. officinalis, L. spica, L. vera*). ENGLISH LAVENDER. Zones 4–24. Most

Lavandula angustifolia

widely planted. Classic lavender used for perfume and sachets. To 3–4 ft. high and across. Leaves gray, smooth on margins, narrow, to 2 in. long. Flowers lavender, ½ in. long, on 18–24-in.-long spikes in July-August. Dwarf varieties: 'Compacta' ('Compacta Nana'), to 8 in. tall, 12–15 in. wide; 'Hidcote', slow growing to 1 ft. tall, with very gray foliage and deep purple flowers; 'Munstead', most popular dwarf, 18 in. tall, with deep lavender blue flowers a month earlier than the species. 'Twickel Purple', 2–3 ft. high, with purple flowers in fanlike clusters on extra-long spikes. Attractive to bees.

L. dentata. FRENCH LAVENDER. Zones 8, 9, 12–24. To 3 ft. tall. Gray green, narrow leaves, 1–1½ in. long, with square-toothed edges. Lavender purple flowers in short spikelike clusters topped with tuft of petal-like bracts. In mild-winter areas, blooms almost continually.

L. latifolia. SPIKE LAVENDER. Zones 4–24. Much like English lavender in appearance, but with broader leaves and flower stalks frequently branched.

L. stoechas. SPANISH LAVENDER. Zones 4–24. Stocky plant 1½–3 ft. tall with narrow gray leaves ½–1 in. long. Flowers dark purple, about ⅛ in. long, in dense, short spikes topped with tuft of large purple petal-like bracts. Bloom in early summer.

LAVATERA. TREE MALLOW. Annuals, shrubs. Flowers resemble single hollyhocks. Needs sun, accepts routine watering or drought, good soil or poor.

L. arborea. Zones 14–24. Southern European plant naturalized along northern California coast. Evergreen shrub to 15 ft. tall. Maplelike leaves have 5–9 lobes and scalloped edges. Flowers purplish red with darker veins, 2 in. across, June-July. There is variety with white-variegated leaves.

L. assurgentiflora. Zones 14–24. Native to Channel Islands, but naturalized on California coastal mainland. Erect shrub to 12 ft., or treelike. Maplelike leaves 3–5 in. long, lobed and toothed. Rosy lavender white-striped flowers 2–3 in. wide, almost throughout the year, heaviest April-August. Resists drought, wind, salt spray. Use as fast-growing windbreak hedge. Will reach 5–10 ft. and bloom first year from seed. Shear to keep dense.

Lavatera assurgentiflora

L. trimestris. ANNUAL MALLOW. Annual. To height of 3–6 ft. from spring-sown seed. Leaves roundish, angled on upper part of plant, toothed. Flowers satiny, to 4 in. across; named varieties in white, pink, rosy carmine. July-September bloom if spent flowers are removed to halt seed production. Thin seedlings to allow ample room to spread. Colorful, fast-growing summer hedge or background planting.

LAVENDER. See *Lavandula.*

LAVENDER COTTON. See *Santolina chamaecyparissus.*

LAVENDER MIST. See *Thalictrum rochebrunianum.*

LAVENDER STARFLOWER. See *Grewia occidentalis.*

LAYIA platyglossa. TIDYTIPS. Spring and summer annual. California native. Member of sunflower family. Often obtained in mixed wildflower packets, or from dealers in seeds of native plants. Rapid growth to 5–16 in. high. Flower heads about 2 in. across; the rays are light yellow with neatly marked white tips. Can grow in rather heavy soil but won't take standing water. Will naturalize on banks or other well-drained sites with poor soil and little competition from grasses. Give seedlings a good start by preparing soil as for any garden bed. Sow seeds in sunny place in autumn, and water occa-

Layia platyglossa

sionally if winter rains fail to materialize.

LEATHERLEAF FERN. See *Rumohra adiantiformis.*

LEDEBOURIA socialis (*Scilla violacea*). Bulb. Indoor/outdoor or house plant. Clustered purple bulbs an inch long rest on surface of earth. Each has 1–5 fleshy oval leaves 2–8 in. long and tapered at either end. Leaf color is big attraction: gray green leaves are heavily spotted dark green on upper surface, unspotted purple underneath. Bulbs spread by offsets to make big clumps. Spikelike clusters of small green and white flowers are graceful, but not showy. Thrives in bright light or partial shade (not hot sunlight) with routine house plant care and little watering. Easy to propagate by division of bulb clusters. Sometimes sold by dealers in cactus and succulents.

Ledebouria socialis

LEEA coccinea. Large house plant; outdoors in sheltered gardens Zones 23, 24. Vigorous, upright grower to 6 ft. or more. Leaves large, divided and subdivided into leaflets 4–6 in. long. General effect is fernlike and lacy. Grows well in bright light (not hot sunlight); survives fairly heavy shade, but grows very little. Feed regularly; let soil surface dry between waterings. Best with room to spread up and out. Flowers red, not especially showy.

Leea coccinea

LEEK. For ornamental relatives see *Allium.* An annual vegetable—an onion relative that doesn't form distinct bulb. Edible bottoms resemble long fat green onions and have mild flavor. Leeks need a very rich soil that should never completely dry out. Best in cool weather. Sow in early spring in sunny spot. (In cold-winter areas, sow indoors and set out plants in June or July.) When plants have made considerable top growth, draw soil up around fat, round stems to make bottoms white and mild. Plants grow 2–3 ft. high. Do not let soil into bases of leaves. Begin to harvest in late autumn. Where winters are cold, dig plants with roots and plant them closely in boxes of soil in cool but frost free location. Where winters are mild, dig as needed from late fall until spring.

Leek

LEMAIREOCEREUS thurberi. ORGANPIPE CACTUS. Zones 12–24. Native to Arizona, Mexico. Columnar, treelike cactus branching from base (also from top, if injured). Dark green or gray green stems, with 12–17 ribs, grow slowly to 15 ft. Spines black, ½–1 in. long. Purplish, white-edged, 3-in. flowers May-June. Full sun. Needs excellent drainage and very little watering. Night blooming. Fruit 1½ in. long, red tinged olive green, filled with sweet red pulp that is edible.

Lemaireocereus thurberi

LEMON. See *Citrus.*

LEMON BALM. See *Melissa.*

LEMONADE BERRY. See *Rhus integrifolia.*

LEMON BOTTLEBRUSH. See *Callistemon citrinus.*

LEMON-SCENTED GUM. See *Eucalyptus citriodora.*

LEMON VERBENA. See *Aloysia triphylla.*

LENTEN ROSE. See *Helleborus orientalis.*

LEONOTIS leonurus. LION'S TAIL. Perennial. Zones 8–24. Shrubby, branching, 3–6 ft. with hairy stems. Leaves 2–5 in. long, with coarsely toothed edges. Tubular, 2-in.-long flowers, in dense whorls, deep orange, covered with fine furlike hairs. Blooms summer into fall. Plant in full sun. Drought resistant. Striking if kept well-groomed.

Leonotis leonurus

LEONTOPODIUM alpinum. EDELWEISS. Perennial. Zones 1–9, 14–24. Short-lived, white, woolly plants 4–12 in. high, with small flower heads closely crowded on tips of stems and surrounded by collar of slender white, woolly leaves radiating out from below flower heads like arms of starfish. The tiny bracts of flower heads, also white and woolly, are tipped with black. Blooms June-July. Sun, plenty of water, and excellent drainage. Seeds germinate easily. Good in rock gardens.

Leontopodium alpinum

LEOPARD PLANT. See *Ligularia tussilaginea* 'Aureo-maculata'.

LEOPARDS BANE. See *Doronicum.*

LEPTOSPERMUM. TEA TREE. Evergreen shrubs or small trees. Zones 14–24. Native to Australia, New Zealand. Soft and casual looking (never rigid or formal)—partly because of branching habit. Substantial, useful landscape structure plants the year around. All make springtime display of flowers along stem among small leaves. The flowers (white, pink, or red) are basically alike; about ½ in. wide with petals arranged around hard central cone or cup. Single flowers look like tiny single roses. Petals fall to leave woody, long-lasting seed capsules about ¼ in. wide.

Leptospermum laevigatum

Need good soil drainage and full sun. Need moisture when first planted; established plants are drought tolerant. Subject to chlorosis in alkaline soils. Apparently pest free above ground; sometimes succumb quickly to root troubles where drainage is poor. All take some surface shearing but in real pruning cut back only to side branches, never into bare wood. Called "tea tree" because Captain Cook brewed leaves of *L. scoparium* into tea to prevent scurvy among his crew. Good near ocean.

L. citratum. See *L. petersonii.*

L. laevigatum. AUSTRALIAN TEA TREE. Large shrub or small tree. To 30 ft. high, often as wide. Lives long and well with little care if soil conditions right (well-drained, slightly acid). Oval or teardrop shaped leaves to ⅜ in. wide, 1 in. long, dull green to gray green. The plant has two basic uses and the uses determine its appearance:

(1) Solitary plants allowed to grow full size develop picturesque character with muscular-looking, twisted and gracefully curved, shaggy, gray brown trunks, up to 24 in. diameter at the base. Equally handsome branches range out from trunk and carry canopies of fine-textured foliage. Some pendulous branches weep down from foliage canopies. Single white flowers appear in great numbers along branches in spring.

(2) Planted close together (1½–6 ft.) to make windbreak, thick natural screen, or clipped hedge, plants do not develop any visible branching character but do make solid bank of fine-textured green foliage, highlighted in spring by white flowers.

L. l. 'Compactum'. Similar to above but smaller—to 8 ft. high, 6 ft. wide—and slightly more open and loose. Does not flower as heavily as *L. laevigatum.*

L. l. 'Reevesii'. Leaves are rounder, slightly bigger and more densely set than on *L. laevigatum,* and plant grows only to 4–5 ft. high and wide. Heavier looking than either of the preceding two kinds.

L. lanigerum (*L. pubescens*). Erect growth to 8–15 ft. high. Noted for silky or downy surfaces on young shoots and on undersides of dark gray green, tiny, narrow leaves (⅛ in. wide, ½ in. long). Flowers white, single, ¾ in. wide, appear singly on short leafy twigs in late spring.

L. nitidum 'Macrocarpum'. Shrub 6 ft. tall with reddish new growth, purplish bronze older foliage. Leaves like *L. lanigerum* (plant is also called *L. lanigerum* 'Macrocarpum'). Spring flowers nearly 1 in. wide, chartreuse yellow with dark green disk.

L. petersonii (*L. citratum*). Big shrub or small tree 15–20 ft. tall with open-branching, see-through quality and graceful weeping branches. Pale green leaves, 1–2 in. long, less than ¼ in. wide, have strong, pleasant lemon scent when crushed. White flowers with green centers in summer. Attractive multistemmed small tree.

L. scoparium. NEW ZEALAND TEA TREE, MANUKA. Ground cover to large shrub. True species *L. scoparium* is of no interest in western U.S. but its many varieties are valuable. These are not as bold of form or quite as serviceable in hedges and screens as the kinds listed above, but they have showier flowers. Hardier than other species. Leaves are tiny (from almost needlelike and ¼ in. long to ⅛ in. wide and ½ in. long), pointed, densely set. Many white to pink flowers to ½ in. across in spring or summer.

L. s. 'Florepleno'. Double pale pink flowers on compact bush. Blooms late winter to early spring, often with repeat bloom in late summer, fall.

L. s. 'Gaiety Girl'. Slow growing to 5 ft. Midspring flowers double, pink with lilac tint. Foliage reddish.

L. s. 'Helene Strybing'. Seedling of *L. s.* 'Keatleyi'; resembles parent except that flowers are somewhat smaller, much deeper pink.

L. s. 'Horizontalis'. Ground cover or hanging basket shrub 1 ft. high, 3 ft. wide. Single pink flowers, spring.

L. s. 'Keatleyi'. Tallest (6–10 ft.) most open and rangy of *L. scoparium* varieties—most inclined to develop picturesque habit. Single pink flowers, paler at edges, are extra large, sometimes as big as a quarter. Spring bloom, may repeat in summer.

L. s. 'Nanum'. Low, rounded shrub to 2 ft. high. Single flowers light pink, darker at center.

L. s. 'Pompon'. Compact to 6–8 ft. high. Many double pink flowers in late spring or summer. Dark green foliage.

L. s. 'Red Damask'. To 6–8 ft., dense in habit, double ruby red flowers, red-tinged leaves. Heavy bloom midwinter to spring.

L. s. 'Ruby Glow'. Compact, upright 6–8-ft. shrub with dark foliage, double, oxblood red flowers (¾ in. wide) in great profusion (entire shrub looks red) in winter, spring.

L. s. 'Snow White'. Spreading, compact plant 2–4 ft. high. Medium-sized double white flowers with green centers, December-spring.

L. s. 'Waerengi'. Low, spreading ground cover shrub to 8–12 in. high, 18–24 in. wide. Many soft, pliant, arching twigs, reddish tinged. Soft, densely set leaves. Scattering of single pale pink flowers in spring.

LETTUCE. Summer annual in Zones 1–7, 10, 11. Cool-season annual in Zones 8, 9, 12–24. Indispensable salad plant and easy to grow. There are four principal types.

Lettuce

Crisphead lettuce is most familiar kind in markets, most exasperating for home gardener to produce. Heads best when monthly average temperatures are around 55°–60°F. In cool coastal areas it does well over long season; inland, timing becomes critical. Best varieties: various strains of

'Great Lakes', 'Imperial', and 'Iceberg'.

Butterhead or Boston types have loose heads with green, smooth outer leaves and yellow inner leaves. Good varieties: 'Bibb' ('Limestone') and 'Buttercrunch'. 'Mignonette' ('Manoa') stands heat without bolting (going to seed) quickly.

Lettuce

Loose-leaf lettuce makes rosettes rather than heads, stands heat better than the others, is summer mainstay in warm climates. Choice selections: 'Black-seeded Simpson', 'Oak Leaf', 'Slobolt', 'Prizehead' or 'Ruby' (red-tinged varieties), and 'Salad Bowl', with deeply cut leaves.

Romaine lettuce has erect, cylindrical heads of smooth leaves, the outer green, the inner whitish. Stands heat moderately well. Try 'White Paris', 'Parris Island', 'Dark Green Cos', or 'Valmaine'.

Loose, well-drained soil; in hot-summer areas light shading in midday helps. Water regularly, feed lightly and frequently. Sow in open ground at 10-day intervals, starting after frost as soon as soil is workable. Barely cover seeds; space rows 8–12 in. apart. Thin head lettuce or romaine to 12 in. apart, moving seedlings with care to extend the plantings. Leaf lettuce can be grown 4 in. apart; harvest some whole plants as they begin to crowd.

In milder climates, make later sowings in late summer, fall. Where summers are very short, sow indoors, move seedlings outdoors after last frost. Control snails, slugs, earwigs with bait *on the ground*—not on the plants. Harvest when heads or leaves are of good size; lettuce doesn't stand long before going to seed, becoming quite bitter in the process. Loose-leaf lettuce can be harvested over a long period, removing a few leaves from each plant in the row until bloom stalks start to grow.

LETTUCE FERN. See *Polypodium aureum* 'Mandaianum'.

LEUCOCORYNE ixioides (*L. odorata*). GLORY OF THE SUN. Bulb. Zones 13, 16, 19, 21–24. Native to Chile. Closely related to *Brodiaea*. Narrow grasslike leaves to 1 ft. Slender, wiry stems, 12–18 in. high, bear 4–6 lavender blue, white-centered, beautifully scented flowers, 2 in. across. Blooms in March-April. In mild-winter climates use in rock gardens or naturalize in sections that get little summer watering. Use with ixia, sparaxis, freesia, tritonia, or grow in pots like freesias. Excellent, long-lasting cut flowers.

Leucocoryne ixioides

Outdoors, plant bulbs in fall, 6 in. deep, 3–4 in. apart in sun, in light, perfectly drained soil. Give ample water until after bloom, then let bulbs dry out. Bulbs tend to move downward in soil; confine them by planting in containers or laying wire screen across bottom of planting area.

LEUCODENDRON argenteum. SILVER TREE. Evergreen tree or large shrub. Zones 17, 20–24. Native to South Africa. Young trees (the most spectacular in effect) narrow and stiffly upright; mature trees spreading, with tortuous, gray-barked trunk, irregular silhouette. Can reach 40 ft. Silky, silvery white leaves 3–6 in. long densely cover the branches—it's a foliage plant; flowers and fruit are inconsequential. Foliage good for arrangements.

Leucodendron argenteum

Needs fast draining soil, some water during summer. Will not thrive in clay, alkaline soil, or soil with animal manure. Needs sunlight and humid air; takes ocean winds but not dry winds. Striking appearance and cultural problems make it hard to use. Small plants are picturesque container subjects for 3–4 years. Larger plants effective on slopes with boulders, succulents, and pines in sheltered seaside gardens. Use singly or in groups.

LEUCOJUM. SNOWFLAKE. Bulbs. Strap shaped leaves and nodding, bell shaped white flowers with segments tipped green. Easy and permanent. Naturalize under deciduous trees, in shrub borders, orchards, or cool slopes. Plant 4 in. deep in fall. Do not disturb until really crowded; then dig, divide, and replant after foliage dies down.

Leucojum aestivum

L. aestivum. SUMMER SNOWFLAKE. All Zones. Most commonly grown. Leaves 12–18 in. long. Stems 18 in. long carry 3–5 flowers; variety 'Gravetye Giant' has as many as 9 flowers to a stem. In mild-winter areas blooms November through winter; flowers with narcissus in colder areas.

L. vernum. SPRING SNOWFLAKE. Zones 1–6; not successful in hot, dry climates. Leaves 9 in. long. Stems 1 ft. tall bear single large, nodding, white flowers in very early spring (late winter in warmer areas). Needs rich moist soil.

LEUCOPHYLLUM frutescens (*L. texanum*). TEXAS RANGER. Evergreen shrub. Zones 7–24. Native to Texas, Mexico. Compact, slow-growing, silvery-foliaged shrub to 5–12 ft. tall, 4–6 ft. wide. Does well in desert areas, taking any degree of heat and wind. Tolerates some alkali if drainage is good. Thrives with little water near sea, but needs heat to produce its rose purple, 1-in.-long, bell shaped summer flowers. Leaves small, silvery white beneath. Useful either as round-headed gray mass, as clipped hedge, or in mixed dry plantings. *L. f. alba* has white flowers; purple-flowered variety 'Compactum' is smaller and denser than the type.

Leucophyllum frutescens

LEUCOSPERMUM. PINCUSHION. Evergreen shrubs. Zones 15–17, 21–24. South African shrubs related to *Protea;* see that entry for culture. Like proteas, difficult to grow but spectacular flowers reward extra effort. Flowers are actually clusters of long, slender tubular flowers that make up large thistlelike head. These make spectacular cut flowers, lasting a month in water. Leaves are narrow ovals, stalkless and crowded along stems. Bloom peaks in late winter, early spring, but can start earlier, last up to 6 months in mild winters. Well-established plants can take several degrees of frost, and side buds will produce flowers even if main flower buds freeze.

Leucospermum reflexum

L. nutans. NODDING PINCUSHION. Compact plants 4 ft. tall and as wide. Flower clusters 4 in. across, individual tube flowers curving gracefully outward, then inward again, coral with yellow tips. Best of kind for cut flowers.

L. reflexum. ROCKET PINCUSHION. Sprawling plant to 12 ft. tall with attractive gray foliage. Orange rose, 4-in. heads; as flowers age, "pins" curl downward, giving shaggy look.

LEUCOTHOE. Evergreen shrubs. Related to *Pieris*. All have leathery leaves and clusters of urn shaped white flowers. Need acid, woodsy, deep soil and some shade; do best in woodland gardens or as facing for taller broad-leafed evergreens. Best used in masses; not especially attractive individually. Bronze-tinted winter foliage is a bonus.

Leucothoe davisiae

L. axillaris. Zones 4–7, 15–17. Native to southeastern U.S. Very like *L. fontanesiana*, but with shorter-stalked, sharply pointed leaves.

L. davisiae. SIERRA LAUREL. Zones 1–7, 15–17. Upright shrub to 3½ ft. Leaves oblong or egg shaped, to 3 in. long, glossy rich green. Flowers white, in erect clusters 2–4 in. long. Blooms in summer. Grows in bogs and wet places in Sierra Nevada, Trinity, and Siskiyou mountains.

L. fontanesiana *(L. catesbaei).* DROOPING LEUCOTHOE. Zones 4–7, 15–17. Borderline hardiness in Zones 1–3. Native to eastern U.S. Slow grower to 2–6 ft.; branches arch gracefully. Leathery, 3–6-in.-long leaves turn bronzy purple in fall (bronzy green in deep shade). Spreads from underground stems. Drooping clusters of creamy white, lily-of-the-valleylike flowers in spring. Variety 'Rainbow', with leaves marked yellow, green, and pink, grows 3–4 ft. tall.

*Leucothoe
fontanesiana*

Requires summer water in first 2–3 summers but later can take fair amount of drought. Can be controlled in height to make 18-in. ground cover in shade; just cut older, taller stems to ground. Branches cut in bloom are decorative.

LEVISTICUM officinale. LOVAGE. Perennial. All Zones. This herb is sometimes grown for its celery-flavored seeds, leaves, and stems. Reaches 2–3, even 6 ft., with cut and divided, glossy deep green leaves. Flattish clusters of greenish yellow small flowers. Full sun. Ordinary garden care suits it. Grow from seeds or divisions.

*Levisticum
officinale*

LEWISIA. Perennials. Zones 1–7. Beautiful, often difficult plants for rock gardens, collections of alpine plants. All need excellent drainage; plant with fine gravel around crowns. Of many offered by specialists these are outstanding:

L. cotyledon. Native to northern California and southern Oregon. Rosettes of narrow, fleshy, evergreen leaves bear 10-in. stems topped by large clusters of 1-in. flowers of white or pink striped with rose or red. Spring to early summer bloom is extremely showy. *L. c. howellii* is similar, but leaves are wavy edged and flowers somewhat larger. Same culture as *L. tweedyi* (below). Can be grown in pots in fast draining sterilized soil or growing mixes.

Lewisia tweedyi

L. rediviva. BITTERROOT. Native to mountains of the West. State flower of Montana. Fleshy roots; short stems with short, succulent, strap shaped leaves to 2 in. long that usually die back before flowers appear (seemingly from the bare earth) in spring. Flowers look like 2-in.-wide rose or white waterlilies—borne singly on short stems. Full sun. Water sparingly. Not difficult if drainage is excellent.

L. tweedyi. Native to mountains, south central Washington. Stunning with big, satiny, salmon pink flowers, 1–3 to a stem, above fleshy, evergreen, 4-in. leaves. Grow in full sun or light shade. Water sparingly. Must have perfect drainage around root crown to prevent rot. Prune out side growths to keep root crown open to air.

LIATRIS. GAYFEATHER. Perennials. Zones 1–3, 7–10, 14–24. Native to eastern and central United States. Showy plants. Basal tufts of narrow grassy leaves grow from thick, often tuberous rootstock. Tufts lengthen in summer to tall, narrow stems densely set with narrow leaves and topped by narrow plume of small rosy purple (sometimes white) fluffy flower heads.

They need full sun, endure heat, cold, drought, and poor soil; are best used in mixed perennial borders. The rosy purple

Liatris spicata

color calls for careful placing to avoid color clashes.

L. callilepis. Plants grown and sold under this name by Dutch bulb growers are *L. spicata.*

L. scariosa. Grows 1–3 ft. high. Each flower head in the cluster is ½–1 in. wide.

L. spicata. To 6 ft., usually only 2–3 ft., with 15-in.-long flower plumes; each individual flower head to ⅓ in. wide.

LIBOCEDRUS. See *Calocedrus.*

LICORICE FERN. See *Polypodium glycyrrhiza.*

LIGULARIA tussilaginea *(L. kaempferi, Farfugium japonicum).* Perennial. Zones 4–10, 14–24. House plant or indoor/outdoor plant in all Zones. Speckled variety 'Aureo-maculata', LEOPARD PLANT, has leaves 6–10 in. broad, evergreen, thick and rather leathery, speckled and blotched with cream or yellow, all rising directly on 1–2 ft. stems from rootstock. Nearly kidney shaped but shallowly angled and toothed. Flower stalks 1–2 ft. tall bear a few flower heads, yellow rayed, 1½–2 in. broad.

*Ligularia
tussilaginea
'Aureo-maculata'*

Choice foliage plant for shady beds or entryways. Good container plant. Tops hardy in 20°F. temperatures; plants die back to roots at 0°F., put on new growth again in spring. Needs routine summer watering. Bait for snails and slugs. *L. t.* 'Argentea' has deep green leaves irregularly mottled, particularly on edges, with gray green and ivory white. 'Crispata' has curled and crested leaf edges.

LIGUSTRUM. PRIVET. Deciduous or evergreen shrubs or small trees. Most widely used in hedges. Can also be clipped into formal shapes and featured in tubs or large pots. One type is a common street tree. All have abundant, showy clusters of white to creamy white flowers in late spring or early summer. Fragrance is described as "pleasant" to "unpleasant" (never "wonderful" or "terrible"). Flowers draw bees. On clipped hedges, fewer flowers grow because most of the flower bearing branches get trimmed off. Small, blue black, berrylike fruit follow blossoms. Birds eat fruit, thus distributing seeds which make privet plants come up like weeds.

Ligustrum lucidum

Most grown easily in sun or in some shade, and in any soil. Give them lots of water. In some areas they are subject to lilac leaf miner which disfigures leaves.

Confusion exists in identity of certain privets in nurseries. The one sold as *L. japonicum* usually turns out to be the small tree—*L. lucidum.* The true *L. japonicum* is usually sold as *L. texanum.* Actually two (or more) forms of *L. japonicum* are available and one is sold as *L. texanum.* The tall shrubby kind is the true species; the lower-growing, more densely foliaged form probably should be called *L. japonicum* 'Texanum'. In a similar fashion the smaller-leafed hardy privets used for hedging are often confused: *L. amurense, L. ovalifolium,* and *L. vulgare* look much alike, and any is likely to be sold as common privet—a name that belongs to *L. vulgare.*

L. amurense. AMUR PRIVET, AMUR RIVER NORTH PRIVET. All Zones. Deciduous in coldest areas, where it is much used for hedge and screen planting. Partially evergreen in milder climates, but seldom planted there. In appearance much like *L. ovalifolium;* foliage less glossy.

L. ibolium 'Variegata'. Zones 3–24. Semideciduous. Variegated form of a hybrid between *L. ovalifolium* and another Japanese privet. Resembles *L. ovalifolium,* but bright green leaves have creamy yellow edges.

L. japonicum. (Often sold as *L. texanum.*) JAPANESE PRIVET, WAXLEAF PRIVET. Evergreen shrub. Zones 4–24. Dense, compact growth habit to 10–12 ft., but can be kept lower by trimming.

(Continued on next page)

Roundish oval leaves 2–4 in. long, dark to medium green and glossy above, distinctly paler to almost whitish beneath; have thick, slightly spongy feeling. Excellent plants for hedges, screens, or for shaping into globes, pyramids, other shapes, or small standard trees. Sunburns in hot spells. In areas of caliche soil, or where Texas root rot prevails, grow it in containers.

L. j. 'Rotundifolium' (*L. j.* 'Coriaceum'). Grows to 4–5 ft. and has nearly round leaves to 2½ in. long. Part shade in inland valleys.

L. j. 'Silver Star'. Leaves are deep green, with gray green mottling and startlingly creamy white edges. Good contrast with deep green foliage.

L. j. 'Texanum'. Very similar to species but lower growing to 6–9 ft. and has somewhat denser, lusher foliage. Useful as windbreak.

L. lucidum. GLOSSY PRIVET. Evergreen tree. Zones 5, 6, 8–24. Makes a round-headed tree that eventually reaches 35–40 ft. Can be kept lower as a big shrub, or may form multiple-trunked tree. Leaves 4–6 in. long, tapered, pointed, glossy, dark to medium green on both sides; feel leathery but not slightly spongy like *L. japonicum*. Flowers in especially large feathery clusters followed by profusion of fruit. Fine street or lawn tree. Fast growing, somewhat drought resistant but looks better with water. Can grow in narrow areas. Performs well in large containers. Or plant 10 ft. apart for tall privacy screen. Useful as windbreak.

L. ovalifolium. CALIFORNIA PRIVET. Semideciduous shrub; evergreen only in mildest areas. Zones 4–24. Inexpensive hedge plant, once more widely used in California. Grows rapidly to 15 ft,, but can be kept sheared to any height. Dark green, oval, 2½-in.-long leaves. Set plants 9–12 in. apart for hedges. Clip early and frequently to encourage low, dense branching. Greedy roots. Well-fed, well-watered plants hold leaves longest. Tolerates heat.

L. o. 'Aureum' (sold as *L. o.* 'Variegatum'). GOLDEN PRIVET. Leaves have broad yellow edge.

L. 'Suwannee River'. Evergreen shrub. All Zones. Reported to be hybrid between *L. japonicum* 'Rotundifolium' and *L. lucidum*. Slow growing to 18 in. tall in 3 years, eventually 3–4 ft.; compact habit. Dark green leaves leathery, somewhat twisted. No fruit produced. Low hedge, foundation planting, containers.

L. 'Vicaryi'. VICARY GOLDEN PRIVET. Deciduous shrub. All Zones. This one has yellow leaves—color strongest on plants in full sun. To 3–4 ft. high. Best planted alone; color does not develop well under hedge shearing.

L. vulgare. COMMON PRIVET. Deciduous shrub. All Zones. To 15 ft., unsheared. Light green leaves less glossy than those of California privet. Clusters of black fruit conspicuous on unpruned or lightly pruned plants. Root system less greedy than California privet. Variety 'Lodense' ('Nanum') is dense, dwarf form which reaches only 4 ft., with equal spread.

LILAC. See *Syringa*.

LILAC MARIPOSA. See *Calochortus splendens*.

LILAC VINE. See *Hardenbergia comptoniana*.

LILIUM. LILY. Bulbs. All Zones. Most stately and varied of bulbous plants. For many years only species—same as plants growing wild in parts of Asia, Europe, and North America—were available; many of these were difficult and unpredictable.

Around 1925 lily growers entered upon a significant breeding program. Using species with desirable qualities, they bred new hybrids and also developed strains and varieties that were healthier, hardier, and easier to grow than the original species. They were able to produce new

Lilium auratum

forms and new colors and, what is more important, they evolved the methods for growing healthy lilies in large quantities. Now the new forms and new colors are the best garden lilies, but it is

still possible to get some desirable species lilies.

Lilies have three basic cultural requirements: (1) a deep, loose, well-drained soil; (2) ample moisture year-round—they never stop growing completely; (3) coolness and shade at roots, and sun or filtered shade at tops where the flowers form.

Plant bulbs as soon as possible after you get them. If you must wait, keep them in cool place until you plant. If bulbs are dry, place them in moist sand or peat moss until scales get plump and new roots begin to sprout.

In coastal fog belts, plant lilies in open sunny position, but protect them from strong winds. In warmer, drier climates, light or filtered shade is desirable.

If soil is deep, well-drained, and contains ample organic material, it will grow good lilies. If it is heavy clay, or very sandy and deficient in organic matter, add peat moss, ground bark, or sawdust. Spread 3–4-in. layer of such material over surface; on top of it, broadcast complete fertilizer (follow label directions for pre-planting application), and thoroughly blend both into soil as you dig to a depth of at least 12 in.

Before planting bulbs, remove any injured portions, and dust cuts with sulfur or a special anti-fungus seed and bulb disinfectant.

For each bulb, dig a generous planting hole (6–12 in. deeper than depth of bulb). Place enough soil at bottom of hole to bring it up to proper level for bulb (see below). Set bulb with its roots spread; fill in hole with soil, firming it in around bulb to eliminate air pockets. If your area is infested with gophers, you may have to plant each bulb in a 6-in. square wire basket made of ½-in. hardware cloth. The depth of the basket will depend on the planting depth—see next paragraph.

Planting depths vary according to size and rooting habit of bulb. General rule is to cover smaller bulbs with 2–3 in. of soil; medium-sized bulbs with 3–4 in.; and larger bulbs with 4–6 in. Never cover Madonna lilies with more than 1 in. of soil. Planting depth can be quite flexible. It's better to err by planting shallowly than too deeply. Lily bulbs have contractile roots that draw them down to proper depth. Ideal spacing for lily bulbs in 12 in. apart; you can plant as close as 6 in. apart for densely massed effect.

After planting, water well, and mulch area with 2–3 in. of organic material to conserve moisture, keep soil cool, and reduce weed growth.

Lilies need constant moisture to about 6 in. deep. You can reduce watering somewhat after tops turn yellow in fall, but never allow roots to dry out completely. Flooding is preferable to overhead watering, which may help to spread disease spores. Pull weeds by hand if possible; hoeing may injure roots.

Virus or mosaic infection is a problem. No cure exists. To avoid it, buy healthy bulbs from reliable sources. Dig and destroy any lilies that show mottling in leaves or seriously stunted growth. Control aphids, which spread the infection. Control botrytis blight, a fungus disease, with appropriate fungicide. Control gophers; they relish lily bulbs.

Remove faded flowers. Wait until stems and leaves turn yellow before you cut them back.

If clumps become too large and crowded, dig, divide, and transplant them in spring or fall. With care, lily clumps can be lifted at any time, even in bloom.

Lilies are fine container plants. Place one bulb in deep 5–7-in. pot or five in a 14–16-in. pot. First, fill pot ⅓ full of potting mix. Then place bulb with roots spread and pointing downward; cover with about an inch of soil. Water thoroughly and place in deep coldframe or greenhouse that is heated (in colder climates) just enough to keep out frost. During root forming period, keep soil moderately moist. When top growth appears, add more soil mixture and gradually fill pot as stems elongate. Leave 1 in. space between surface of soil and rim of pot for watering. Move pots onto partially shaded terrace or patio during blooming period.

When foliage turns yellow, withhold water somewhat but do not let soil become bone dry, since lilies never go completely dormant. You can repot bulbs in late fall or early spring.

The official classification of lilies lists eight divisions of hybrids (not all of them available in nurseries) and a ninth division of species. Following are the lilies ordinarily available to western gardeners.

DIVISION 1. ASIATIC HYBRIDS
Subdivision a. Upright flowering. Compact growth.

Golden Chalice Hybrids. Stems 1½–3 ft. tall. Colors range from lemon yellow to apricot orange. 'Golden Wonder', 2½–4½ ft. tall, is soft golden yellow variety. Blooms in May.

Mid-Century Hybrids. Strong growing, hardy, tolerant of most soils. Plants are 2–4 ft. tall. July bloom in most climates, June in Zones 18–24. Colors range from yellow through orange to red; most dotted with black. Upward facing, wide open flowers spread like branches of candelabra. Many excellent named varieties; notable ones are: 'Enchantment' (nasturtium red) especially adapted to warm climates and pot culture, 'Chinook' (salmon), 'Cinnabar' (orange red), 'Connecticut King' (yellow), and 'Sterling Star' (white to cream).

Rainbow Hybrids. Tulip shaped flowers golden yellow through orange to dark red, usually with dark spots, in upward facing clusters; bloom in June. Stems 3–4 ft. tall.

Subdivision b. Outward facing flowers, but otherwise similar to group 1a. Varieties include 'Connecticut Lemonglow', 'Corsage', 'Paprika', 'Prosperity', and 'Sunrise'.

Subdivision c. Drooping flowers on long stalks, but otherwise similar to groups 1a and 1b.

Fiesta Hybrids. Hardy, vigorous, sun loving, bloom in July. Nodding flowers with strongly recurved segments in pale yellow through gold to deep maroon. Selections from Fiesta Hybrids are: Bronzino strain, sand, mahogany, and amber; Burgundy strain, cherry red, claret, and burgundy; Citronella strain, golden and lemon yellow flowers with small black dots; Golden Wedding strain, large golden yellow flowers.

Harlequin Hybrids. Largely derived from *L. cernuum.* June-July bloom. To 5 ft. tall. Flowers open with recurved segments; ivory white through pale lilac and old rose to violet and purple, with intermediate shades of salmon, terra cotta, and amber pink. Most are pink and tangerine. Selected varieties are 'Bittersweet', 'Connecticut Yankee', 'Discovery', Hallmark Strain, 'Hornback's Gold', and 'Sonata'.

DIVISION 2. Mostly hybrids between *L. martagon* and *L. hansonii.* All bloom in June. 'Achievement' is pale yellow, almost ivory white, 3 ft. tall. 'Gay Lights', 5 ft. tall, has pinkish bronze flowers, often as many as 30 on a stem. Paisley strain, 3½–5 ft. tall, has many flowers to a stem. Segments recurved (curved sharply backward); colors range through yellow, orange, lilac, purple, tangerine, and mahogany.

DIVISION 3. CANDIDUM HYBRIDS. As with *L. candidum* (see Division 9), plant bulbs in fall, only 1–2 in. deep.

L. testaceum. Six-12 handsome apricot yellow flowers on a stem. Same waxlike appearance and perfume as *L. candidum,* a parent. (*L. chalcedonicum* is other parent.) Lime loving.

DIVISION 4. AMERICAN HYBRIDS. Derived from *L. parryi, L. pardalinum,* and other North American species. High growers. Plant 4 in. deep in well-drained, enriched soil.

Bellingham Hybrids. The result of crosses between number of West Coast native lilies. Recurved flowers, 20 or more on 6-ft. stems in late June-July. Yellow through orange to bright orange red, spotted brown or reddish brown. Named varieties are 'Afterglow' and 'Sunset'.

DIVISION 6. AURELIAN HYBRIDS. Derived from Asiatic species excluding *L. auratum* and *L. speciosum.* All grow 3–6 ft. high, bloom July-August.

Subdivision a. Trumpet-type flowers in clusters of 12–20, tipping 5–6 ft. stems. Includes golden and lemon yellow strains such as Golden Clarion, Golden Splendor and Royal Gold; other strains, Copper King, Moonlight, and Regale; and the Olympic hybrids.

Olympic Hybrids. Trumpet shaped lilies bloom July-August on plants to 6 ft. high. Flowers range from pure white through cream, yellow, soft pink, or icy green, shaded on outside with greenish brown or wine. Many choice named varieties available such as 'Green Dragon', 'Quicksilver', 'Carrara'. Also available in strains such as Black Dragon, Green Magic, and pure white Sentinel.

Subdivision b. Shallow, bowl shaped flowers that face out. Flower colors include white, yellow, cream; many with orange throats shading into cream at segment tips. Includes Heart's Desire strain and 'Thunderbolt'.

Subdivision c. Pendant flower type. Includes 'Pendant'.

Subdivision d. Sunburst type with flared flowers that open flat and have narrow segments. Includes Golden Sunburst and Sunburst hybrids.

DIVISION 7. ORIENTAL HYBRIDS. Lilies derived from Far Eastern species *L. japonicum, L. rubellum, L. speciosum* and *L. auratum* (the latter two being the most important species of Japan) and any crosses of these with *L. henryi.*

Subdivision b. Hybrids bearing bowl shaped flowers. Derived from *L. auratum* and *L. speciosum.* Exquisitely beautiful flowers in August—"Queens" of all lilies. Includes *L. auratum* Melridge strain, 'Cover Girl', 'Empress of India', Little Rascal, Magic Pink, Red Band hybrids, and 'Red Baron'.

Subdivision c. Flat-faced flowers with recurving blooms. Includes Imperial Crimson, Imperial Gold, Imperial Pink, Imperial Silver, and Oriental hybrids.

Subdivision d. Hybrids with flat flowers. Includes 'Black Beauty', Celebrity, Jamboree, and 'Journey's End'.

DIVISION 9. SPECIES AND VARIANTS.

L. auratum. GOLD-BAND LILY. August or early September bloom on 4–6-ft. plants. Flowers fragrant, waxy white spotted crimson, with golden band on each segment. 'Platyphyllum' is most robust selection, with flowers nearly a foot wide.

L. candidum. MADONNA LILY. Pure white, fragrant blooms on 3–4-ft. stems in June. Unlike most lilies, dies down soon after bloom, makes new growth in fall. Plant while dormant in August. Does not have stem roots; set top of bulb only 1–2 in. deep in sunny location. Bulb quickly makes foliage rosette which lives over winter, lengthens to blooming stem in spring. Subject to diseases that shorten its life. The lily of medieval romance, a sentimental choice for many gardeners.

Lilium candidum

L. cernuum. Only 12–20 in. tall, with lilac flowers often dotted dark purple. Summer blooming; perfectly hardy. Sun.

L. chalcedonicum. The famous scarlet Turk's cap lily from the Near East. Now rare. Sweetly scented blooms, 6–10 per stem (each stem to 4½ ft. high), in July.

L. columbianum. COLUMBIA LILY. Dainty species bearing about 20–30 golden orange lilies on 2 ft. stems in July and August. Native from British Columbia to northern California.

L. concolor. To 2 ft., with 5–7 scarlet, unspotted, star shaped flowers on wiry stems. Needs full sun and perfect drainage. 'Coridion' is a citron yellow variety.

L. formosanum. Long white Easter lily flowers appear very late. Plant bulbs 5–6 in. deep to allow for heavy stem roots. Easy, quick from seed, but tender and virus prone. Stems to 5 ft. tall.

L. hansonii. Sturdy lily to 4 ft. or more, with many thick-textured orange flowers spotted brown. June-July. Needs light shade. Highly resistant or immune to virus.

L. henryi. Slender stems to 8–9 ft. topped by 10–20 bright orange flowers with sharply recurved segments. Summer bloom. Best in light shade.

L. humboldtii. HUMBOLDT LILY. Native of open woodlands in Sierra Nevada. Grows 3–6 ft. tall. Nodding recurved flowers of bright orange with large maroon dots. Early summer bloom. *L. h. ocellatum* (*L. h. magnificum*) is larger, finer, easier to grow.

L. japonicum. Deep pink to purple, fragrant, trumpet shaped blooms on 2–3-ft. stems in July.

L. kelloggii. Elegant honey-scented lily from the Pacific Northwest. Reflexed petals open waxy white in May-June and mature to mauve pink with heavy maroon spots. Pyramid form 3–4 ft. tall. No stem roots.

L. lancifolium (*L. tigrinum*). TIGER LILY. To 4 ft. or more with pendulous orange flowers spotted black. Summer bloom. An old favorite.

(Continued on next page)

L. lankongense. Long-lived lily in garden. Heavily scented rosy mauve and crimson-spotted Turk's cap blooms, 20–30 on a stem. Grows to 3 ft. tall; blooms in August.

L. longiflorum. EASTER LILY. Very fragrant, long white trumpet shaped flowers on short stems. Usually purchased in bloom at Easter as forced plant. Set out in garden after flowers fade. Sun or part shade, good drainage. Stem will ripen and die down. Plant may rebloom in fall; in 1–2 years may flower in midsummer, its normal bloom season. Varieties include 'Tetraploid', 1–1½ ft. tall; 'Croft', 1 ft. tall; 'Estate', to 3 ft. Not for severe winter climates. Don't plant forced Easter lilies near other lilies; may transmit virus.

L. martagon. TURK'S CAP LILY. Purplish pink, recurved, pendant flowers in June-July on 3–5-ft. stems. Slow to establish, but is long-lived and makes big clumps. *L. m. album*, pure white, is one of the most appealing lilies. There also is deep wine purple variety that blooms July-August; may be sold as *L. m. dalmaticum.* It is properly *L. m. cattaniae.*

L. monadelphum. Bright yellow Turk's cap lily folds back its petals like stars—20–30 blooms on 4 ft. stem. Needs moisture. Slow to establish, but will be hardy and long lived.

L. nepalense. Large, pendulous, trumpet shaped flowers, soft green with purple centers in July-August. Stems 1½–4 ft. tall. Needs long, warm growing season, humidity.

L. pardalinum. LEOPARD LILY. California native. Recurved flowers orange or red shading to yellow, with brown spotting in center. Spring-summer bloom on stems 4–8 ft. high.

L. pumilum. A coral red lily that loves sun, but needs shade for its roots. One–20 scented flowers on wiry 18-in. stems. Blooms in May and June.

L. regale. REGAL LILY. Superseded in quality by modern hybrid trumpet lilies, but still popular and easy. To 6 ft., with white, fragrant flowers in July.

L. rubellum. Fragrant, pink, satiny flowers show well against its dark green foliage. To 30 in. high. Leafs out early and blooms in May and June.

L. rubescens. Native to Pacific Northwest and northern California. Fragrant, waxy white, purple-speckled flowers later turn pink. Plant in fall. Keep on dry side after bloom. Let dry out as foliage yellows. Grows to 3 ft. Blooms midsummer.

L. speciosum. Grows 2½–5 ft. tall. Large, wide, fragrant flowers with broad, deeply recurved segments in August-September; white, heavily suffused rose pink, sprinkled with raised crimson dots. 'Rubrum', red; 'Album', pure white; also other named forms. Best in light and afternoon shade; needs rich soil with plenty of leaf mold. New varieties are 'Crimson Glory', 'Grand Commander', and 'White Glory'.

L. superbum. TURK'S CAP LILY. Eastern North American native. Grows to 6 ft. and more. Blooms July and August. Brilliant orange flowers like *L. pardalinum*, but larger. Flushed with yellow at center and brown spotted. Effective red anthers. Likes to be wet while growing.

L. tigrinum. See *L. lancifolium.*

L. wardii. From high mountains of Tibet. Purple pink Turk's cap blooms have purple anthers and orange pollen. Scented. Thirty or more flowers on a 4-ft. stem. Blooms July, August.

L. washingtonianum. West Coast native. Lilies in large open clusters change from white to deep rose, with waxy texture and translucence. Carnation scented. Grows to 4–6 ft. Plant bulbs 10 in. deep in partial shade. Blooms June, July. Keep on dry side after bloom.

LILLY-PILLY TREE. See *Acmena smithii.*

LILY. See *Lilium.*

LILY-OF-THE-NILE. See *Agapanthus.*

LILY-OF-THE-VALLEY. See *Convallaria majalis.*

LILY-OF-THE-VALLEY ORCHID. See *Odontoglossum pulchellum.*

LILY-OF-THE-VALLEY SHRUB. See *Pieris japonica.*

LILY-OF-THE-VALLEY TREE. See *Clethra arborea, Crinodendron patagua.*

LILY TURF. See *Liriope* and *Ophiopogon.*

LIME. See *Citrus.*

LIMEQUAT. See *Citrus.*

LIMONIUM *(Statice).* SEA LAVENDER. Annuals, perennials. Large, leathery basal leaves contrast with airy clusters of small, delicate flowers on nearly leafless, many-branched stems. Tiny flowers consist of two parts: an outer, papery envelope which is the calyx; and an inner part called the corolla which is often of a different color. Flowers good for cutting; keep color even when dried.

Limonium perezii

Tolerate heat, strong sun, some drought when established. Need good drainage; otherwise tolerant of many soils. Often self-sow.

Sow annual kinds indoors, move to garden when weather warms up for spring-summer bloom. Or sow outdoors in early spring for later bloom.

L. bonduellii. Summer annual or biennial. All Zones. Grows 2 ft. tall, with 6-in. basal leaves lobed nearly to midrib. Flower stems are distinctly winged; calyx is yellow, tiny corolla deeper yellow.

L. latifolium. Perennial. Zones 1–10, 14–24. To 2½ ft. tall. Leaves to 10 in. long with smooth edges. Calyx is white and corolla bluish; white and pink kinds exist. Summer bloom. Vigorous plants may show a yard-wide haze of flowers.

L. perezii. Perennial. Zones 13, 16, 17, 20–24. Often freezes Zones 14, 15, 18, 19. Leaves up to 12 in. long, including stalks, rich green. Summer bloom over long season. In the flowers, calyx is rich purple and the tiny corolla white. Flower clusters may be 3 ft. tall, nearly as wide. First-rate beach plant. Damaged by 25°F. temperatures; can be fire retardant. Often naturalizes along southern California coast. Useful even where it freezes out occasionally; nursery-grown seedlings develop fast.

L. sinuatum. Summer annual. Growth habit like *L. bonduellii*, with lobed leaves and winged stems but calyx blue, lavender, or rose, corolla white. Widely grown as a fresh or dried cut flower.

L. suworowii. See *Psylliostachys.*

LINARIA. TOADFLAX. Annuals or perennials. They have brightly colored flowers that resemble small, spurred snapdragons. Very narrow, medium green leaves. Easy to grow. Full sun or light shade. Best in masses; individual plants rather wispy.

L. cymbalaria. See *Cymbalaria muralis.*

L. maroccana. BABY SNAPDRAGON, TOADFLAX. Summer annual—winter annual Zones 10–13. To 1½ ft. Flowers in red and gold, rose, pink, mauve, chamois, blue, violet, and purple, blotched with different shade on the lip. Spur is longer than flower. Fairy Bouquet strain is only 9 in. tall and has larger flowers in pastel shades. Northern Lights strain has reds, oranges, and yellows as well as two-color forms. Flowers June-September. Sow in quantity for a show.

Linaria maroccana

L. purpurea. Perennial. All Zones. Narrow, bushy, erect growth to 2½–3 ft. Blue green foliage and violet blue flowers. 'Canon Went' is a pink form. Summer blooming. Fairly drought tolerant.

LINDEN. See *Tilia.*

LINDERNIA grandiflora *(Ilysanthes grandiflora)*. BLUE ANGEL TEARS. Perennial used as house plant. Native to Florida. Makes compact mat which eventually sprawls or trails (if in a hanging pot). Pairs of roundish, bright green, ½-in. leaves resemble those of pimpernel (*Anagallis*). Tiny (less than ½ in.) flowers look pale blue but are actually white with purple stripes. Bloom season April-November, sometimes longer. Rich soil, ample water, occasional feeding, dim light or (better) strong filtered light.

Lindernia grandiflora

LINGONBERRY. See *Vaccinium vitis-idaea minus.*

LINNAEA borealis. TWINFLOWER. Low, delicate perennial. Zones 1–7, 14–17. Native of northern California to Alaska, Idaho, and much of northern hemisphere. Dainty, flat evergreen mats with 1-in.-long, glossy leaves. Spreads by runners. Pale pink, paired, fragrant trumpet shaped flowers, ⅓ in. long on 3–4-in. stems. Collector's item or small-scale ground cover for woodland garden. Keep area around plants mulched with leaf mold to induce spreading. In Zones 4–6 will grow in full sun if well watered. Must have shade in Zones 14–16.

Linnaea borealis

LINUM. FLAX. Annuals, perennials. All Zones. Flaxes are drought resistant, sun loving plants with erect, branching stems, narrow leaves, and abundant, shallow-cupped, 5-petaled flowers blooming from late spring into summer or fall. Each bloom lasts but a day, but others keep coming on. (The flax of commerce—*L. usitatissimum*—is grown for its fiber and seeds, which yield linseed oil.)

Use in borders; some naturalize freely in waste places. Full sun. Light, well-drained soil. Most perennial kinds live only 3–4 years. Easy from seed; perennials also from cuttings; difficult to divide.

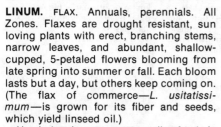
Linum perenne

L. flavum. GOLDEN FLAX. Perennial. (Often called yellow flax, a name correctly applied to closely related *Reinwardtia indica*.) Erect, compact, 12–15 in. tall, somewhat woody at base; grooved branches, green leaves. Flowers golden yellow, about 1 in. wide, in branched clusters, April-June.

L. grandiflorum 'Rubrum'. SCARLET FLAX. Annual. Bright scarlet flowers, 1–1½ in. wide, on slender, leafy stems 1–1½ ft. tall. Narrow grayish green leaves. Also comes in rose-colored form. Sow seed thickly in place in fall (in mild areas) or early spring. Quick easy color in borders, over bulbs left in ground. Good with gray foliage or white-flowered plants. Reseeds, but doesn't become a nuisance. Seed often incorporated into wild flower seed mixtures.

L. narbonense. Perennial. Wiry stems to 2 ft. high. Leaves blue green, narrow. Flowers large, 1¾ in. across, azure blue with white eye, in open clusters. Best variety, 'Six Hills', rich sky blue flowers.

L. perenne. PERENNIAL BLUE FLAX. Most vigorous blue-flowered flax with stems to 2 ft., usually leafless below. Branching clusters of light blue flowers, profuse from May-September. Flowers close in shade or late in the day. Self-sows freely.

LION'S TAIL. See *Leonotis leonurus.*

LIPPIA citriodora. See *Aloysia triphylla.*

LIPPIA repens. See *Phyla nodiflora.*

LIPSTICK PLANT. See *Aeschynanthus radicans.*

LIQUIDAMBAR. SWEET GUM. Deciduous trees. Valuable for form, foliage, and fall color, easy culture. Moderate growth rate; young and middle-aged trees generally upright, somewhat cone shaped, spreading in age. Lobed, maplelike leaves. Flowers inconspicuous; fruit are spiny balls which ornament trees in winter, need raking in spring.

Liquidambar styraciflua

Neutral or slightly acid good garden soil; chlorosis in strongly alkaline soils hard to correct. Plant from containers or from ball and burlap; be sure roots are not canbound. Stake well. Prune only to shape. Trees branch from ground up, look most natural that way, but can be pruned high for easier foot traffic.

Good street trees. Form surface roots which can be nuisance in lawns or parking strips. Effective in tall screens or groves, planted 6-10 ft. apart. Brilliant fall foliage. Leaves color best when trees are in full sun and in well-drained soil; fall color less effective in mildest climates or in mild, late autumns.

For best appearance, should be watered deeply once a month in heavy soils, twice a month in sandy soils through dry season.

L. formosana. CHINESE SWEET GUM. Zones 4–9, 14–24. To 40–60 ft. tall, 25 ft. wide. Free-form outline; sometimes pyramidal, especially when young. Leaves 3–5 lobed, 3–4½ in. across, violet red when expanding, then deep green. In southern California leaves turn yellow beige in late December-January before falling. Farther north leaves turn red. Variety 'Afterglow' has lavender purple new growth, rose red fall color.

L. orientalis. ORIENTAL SWEET GUM. Zones 5–9, 14–24. Native to Turkey. To 20–30 ft., spreading or round headed. Leaves 2–3 in. wide, deeply 5 lobed, each lobe again lobed in lacy effect. Leafs out early after short dormant period. Fall color varies from deep gold and bright red in cooler areas to dull brown purple in coastal southern California. Resistant to oak root fungus.

L. styraciflua. AMERICAN SWEET GUM. Zones 1–9, 14-24. Grows to 60 ft. (much taller in its native eastern U.S.). Narrow and erect in youth, with lower limbs eventually spreading to 20–25 ft. Tolerates damp soil; resistant to oak root fungus. Good all-year tree: in winter, branching pattern, furrowed bark, corky wings on twigs, and hanging fruit give interest; in spring and summer, leaves (5–7 lobed, 3–7 in. wide) are deep green turning purple, yellow, or red in fall. Even seedling trees give good color (which may vary somewhat from year to year), but for uniformity, match trees while they are in fall color or buy budded trees of a named variety, such as the following:

'Burgundy'. Leaves turn deep purple red, hang late into winter or even early spring if storms are not heavy.

'Festival'. Narrow, columnar. Light green foliage turns to yellow, peach, pink, orange, and red.

'Palo Alto'. Turns orange red to bright red in fall.

LIRIODENDRON tulipifera. TULIP TREE. Deciduous tree. Zones 1–10, 14–23. Native to eastern U.S. Fast growth to 60–80 ft., with eventual spread to 40 ft. Straight columnar trunk, with spreading, rising branches that form tall pyramidal crown. Bright yellow green, lyre shaped leaves 5–6 in. long and wide; these turn bright yellow (or yellow and brown) in fall. Tulip shaped flowers in late spring are 2 in. wide, greenish yellow, orange at base. Handsome at close range, they are not showy on the tree, being high up and well-concealed by leaves. They are not usually produced until tree is 10–12 years old.

Liriodendron tulipifera

Give this tree room; deep, rich, well-drained neutral or slightly acid soil; and plenty of summer water. Best where constant wind from one direction won't strike it. Control scale insects and aphids as necessary. Not bothered by oak root fungus.

Good large shade, lawn, or roadside tree. One of the best deciduous trees for southern California; it turns yellow there most autumns. Spreading root system makes it hard to garden under. Columnar variety 'Arnold' is useful in narrow planting areas; it will bloom 2–3 years after planting.

LIRIOPE and OPHIOPOGON. LILY TURF. Evergreen grasslike perennials. Zones 5–10, 12–24 (*L. spicata* in all Zones). The two plants are similar in appearance and both belong to the lily family. They form clumps or tufts of grasslike leaves. White or lavender flowers grow in spikelike or branched clusters and in some kinds make quite a show. Last well in flower arrangements.

Use as casual ground cover in small areas. Also attractive as borders along

Liriope muscari

paths, or between flower bed and lawn, among rock groupings, or in rock gardens. Grow well along streams and around garden pools. Try under bamboo or to cover bare soil at base of trees or shrubs in large containers. None satisfactory as mowed lawn. Tolerate indoor conditions in pots or planter beds.

Plant in shade in inland areas or foliage may turn yellow; along coast plant in sunny location. Well-drained soil. Ample moisture needed but fleshy roots enable plants to withstand brief lapses in watering. Become ragged and brown with neglect. Cut back shaggy old foliage after new leaves appear. Plants don't need heavy feeding. Bait or spray for snails and slugs. Increase plants by dividing in early spring before new growth starts.

Plants look best from spring until cold weather of winter. Extended frosts may cause plants to turn yellow; it takes quite a while for them to recover. Can show tip burn on leaves if excess salts in soil, or if kept too wet where drainage is poor.

The chart compares the kinds you can buy, describes leaves and flowers, mentions uses and cultural needs.

Liriope and Ophiopogon

NAME	GROWTH FORM	LEAVES	FLOWERS	COMMENTS
LIRIOPE muscari BIG BLUE LILY TURF	Forms large clumps but does not spread by underground stems. Rather loose growth habit 12–18 in. high.	Dark green. To 2 ft. long, ½ in. wide.	Dark violet buds and flowers in rather dense 6–8-in.-long spikelike clusters on 5–12-in.-long stems (resemble grape hyacinths), followed by a few round, shiny black fruit.	Profuse flowers July-August. Flowers held above leaves in young plants, partly hidden in older plants. Many garden varieties.
L. m. 'Majestic'	Resembles *L. muscari* but more open clumps and somewhat taller growing.	Similar to above.	Dark violet flowers and buds in clusters that look somewhat like cockscombs on stems 8–10 in. long.	Heavy flowering. Clusters show up well above leaves on young plants.
L. m. 'Silvery Sunproof'	Open growth, strongly vertical, partly arching, 15–18 in. high.	Leaves with gold stripes that turn white as they mature.	Lilac flowers in spikelike clusters rise well above foliage in early summer.	One of the best for open areas and flowers. Best in full sun along coast; inland partial or full shade.
L. m. 'Variegata' (May be sold as *Ophiopogon jaburan* 'Variegata')	Resembles *L. muscari*, but somewhat looser, softer.	New leaves green, 12–18 in. long, edged with yellow, becoming dark green second season.	Violet buds and flowers in spikelike clusters well above foliage. Flower stalk 12 in. high.	Does best in part shade.
L. spicata CREEPING LILY TURF	Dense ground cover that spreads widely by underground stems. Grows 8–9 in. high.	Narrow (¼ in. wide) deep green grasslike leaves, soft and not as upright as *L. muscari*.	Pale lilac to white flowers in spikelike clusters barely taller than leaves.	Hardy in All Zones. Inland, it looks rather shabby in winter. Should be mowed every year in spring prior to new growth development to get best effect. Good ground cover for cold areas where *Ophiopogon japonicus* won't grow.
OPHIOPOGON jaburan (Often sold as *Liriope gigantea*)	Eventually forms large clump growing from fibrous roots.	Dark green, somewhat curved, firm leaves 18–36 in. long, about ½ in. wide.	Small, chalk white flowers in nodding clusters, somewhat hidden by leaves in summer. Metallic violet blue fruit.	Does best in shade. Fruit is very attractive feature; good for cutting O. j. "Vittatus" has leaves striped lengthwise with white, aging to plain green. Similar, perhaps identical, is *Liriope muscari* 'Variegata', sometimes sold as *L. exiliflora* 'Vittata'.
O. japonicus MONDO GRASS	Forms dense clumps that spread by underground stems, many of which are tuberlike. Slow to establish as ground cover.	Dark green leaves ⅛ in. wide, 8–12 in. long.	Flowers light lilac in short spikes usually hidden by the leaves. Summer blooming. Fruit blue.	In hot dry areas grow in some shade. Can be cut back. Easy to divide. Set divisions 6–8 in. apart. Roots will kill at 10°F. Looks best in partial shade but will take full sun along coast.
O. planiscapus 'Arabicus' (O. arabicum)	Makes tuft 8 in. high and about 1 ft. wide.	Leaves to 10 in. long. New leaves green but soon turn black.	White sometimes flushed pink in loose spikelike clusters in summer.	Probably best grown in container; valuable as a novelty, as black-leafed plants are rather rare.

LISIANTHUS. See *Eustoma.*

LITCHI chinensis. LITCHI, LITCHI NUT. Evergreen tree. Zones 21–24. Slow-growing, round-topped, spreading, 20–40 ft. tall. Leaves have 3–9 leathery, 3–6-in.-long leaflets that are coppery red when young, dark green later. Inconspicuous flowers. Fruit, red and juicy when ripe, is enclosed in brittle, warty covering. Dried fruit have raisin-like texture, sweet flavor.

Needs frost free site, acid soil, ample water, moist air, feeding with nitrogen. Has fruited in a few warm areas near San Diego. Look for named varieties if you're interested in food production.

Litchi chinensis

LITHOCARPUS densiflorus. TANBARK OAK. Evergreen tree. Zones 4–7, 14–24. Native to Coast Ranges from southern Oregon to Santa Barbara County, California. Reaches 60–90 ft. under forest conditions; in the open, tree is lower, broader, its lower branches sometimes touching the ground. Leathery, 1½–4-in. sharply toothed leaves covered with whitish or yellowish wool upon expanding; later smooth green above, gray green beneath. Tiny whitish male flowers in large branched clusters have odd odor which some find offensive. Acorns in burlike cups.

Lithocarpus densiflorus

Stands some drought when established. As street or lawn tree resembles holly oak, but has lusher foliage. One of the few broad-leafed evergreen trees for Zone 6. Tends to be shrubby in Zones 4, 5.

LITHODORA diffusa *(Lithospermum diffusum, L. prostratum).* Perennial. Zones 5–7, 14–17. Prostrate, somewhat shrubby, slightly mounded, broad mass 6–12 in. tall. The evergreen leaves are narrow, ¾–1 in. long; foliage and stems are hairy. In May-June (and often later) plants become sprinkled with tubular flowers ½ in. long and brilliantly blue. Full sun or light shade in hot exposures. Loose, well-drained, lime free soil. Needs some summer watering. Rock gardens, walls.

Lithodora diffusa

'Heavenly Blue' and 'Grace Ward' are selected varieties of good form and color.

LITHOPS. STONEFACE. Succulents. Best grown indoors. Among the best-known "living rocks" or "pebble plants" of South Africa. Shaped like inverted cones 2–4 in. high; tops are shaped like stones with a fissure across the middle. From this fissure emerges the large flower (it looks like an ice plant flower) and new leaves. Many species, all interesting. Grow in pots of fast draining soil. Water sparingly in summer; must be kept dry during cool winter weather. Fairly hardy in mild winters but subject to rot outdoors in damp winter air and cold wet soil.

Lithops

LITHOSPERMUM. See *Lithodora.*

LIVINGSTONE DAISY. See *Dorotheanthus bellidiformis.*

LIVISTONA. Palms. Zones 13–17, 19–24. Native from China to Australia. These fan palms somewhat resemble Washingtonia, but generally have shorter, darker, shinier leaves. All hardy to about 22°F. Irrigate regularly for luxuriant appearance.

L. australis. In ground grows slowly to 40–50 ft. Has clean, slender trunk with interesting-looking leaf scars. Dark green leaves 3–5 ft. wide. Good potted plant when young.

L. chinensis. CHINESE FOUNTAIN PALM. Slow-growing; 40-year-old plants are only 15 ft. tall. Self-cleaning (no pruning of old leaves needed) with leaf-scarred trunk. Outer edges of 3–6-ft., roundish, bright green leaves droop strongly.

L. decipiens. To 30–40 ft. in 20 years. Stiff, open head of leaves 2–5 ft. across, green on top, bluish beneath, on long spiny stems. Good in pots, gardens.

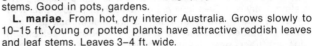
Livistona australis

L. mariae. From hot, dry interior Australia. Grows slowly to 10–15 ft. Young or potted plants have attractive reddish leaves and leaf stems. Leaves 3–4 ft. wide.

LOBELIA. Perennials or annuals. Tubular, lipped flowers look like those of honeysuckle or salvia.

L. cardinalis. CARDINAL FLOWER. Perennial. Zones 1–7, 13–17. Native to eastern U.S. Erect, single-stemmed, 2–4 ft. high with saw-edged leaves set directly on the stems. Spikes of flame red, inch-long flowers. Summer bloom. Needs constant moisture through growing season, rich soil (bog plant in nature). Sun or part shade.

L. erinus. Summer annual. Popular and dependable edging plant. Compact or trailing growth habit with leafy, branching stems. Flowers ¾ in. across, light blue to violet (sometimes pink, reddish purple, or white) with white or yellowish throat. Blooms early summer to frost; lives over winter in mild areas.

Lobelia erinus

Takes about 2 months for the seed in flats to grow to planting-out size. Moist rich soil. Part shade in hot areas, full sun where summers are cool, foggy. Self-sows where adapted.

Trailing kinds are graceful as ground cover in large planters or in smaller pots, where stems, loaded with flowers, spill over the edges. Compact varieties make good edging, masses.

'Cambridge Blue' has clear, soft blue flowers, light green leaves on compact 4–6-in. plant. 'Crystal Palace' has rich, dark blue flowers on a compact plant with bronze green leaves. Takes morning or late afternoon sun inland. 'Rosamond' has carmine red flowers with a white eye. 'White Lady' is pure white. Three trailing varieties for hanging baskets or wall plantings are 'Hamburgia', 'Blue Cascade', and 'Sapphire'.

LOBIVIA. Cactus. Grow outdoors in part shade in Zones 16, 17, 21–24; as house plant, or indoor/outdoor plant anywhere. Small globular or cylindrical shapes with big showy flowers in shades of red, yellow, pink, orange, purplish, lilac. Flowers sometimes nearly as big as plants, like flowers of *Echinopsis* but shorter, broader. Many species offered. Usually grown in pots by collectors. Need full sun or light shade, porous soil, ample water during summer bloom and growth, occasional feeding.

Lobivia hybrid

LOBIVOPSIS. Cactus. Hybrids between *Lobivia* and *Echinopsis.* Extremely free flowering with big, long-tubed flowers on small plants. Culture, hardiness same as for *Echinopsis;* grow in fairly good-sized pots (5-in. pot for a 3-in. plant), feed monthly in summer and water freely during bloom season. Paramount Hybrids come in red, pink, orange, rose, and white. Some may show a dozen or more 6-in.-long flowers on

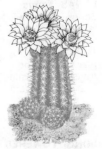
Lobivopsis hybrid

a 3–4-in. plant. Will take part shade, but bloom most heavily in full sun. Keep cool, dry in winter.

LOBULARIA maritima. SWEET ALYSSUM. Summer or winter annual Zones 10–24; summer annual anywhere. Low, branching, trailing plant to 1 ft. tall. Leaves narrow or lance shaped, ½–2 in. long. Tiny, white, four-petaled flowers crowded in clusters; honeylike fragrance. Spring and summer bloom in cold regions; where winters are mild, blooms year-round from self-sown seedlings. Has run wild in parts of the West.

Lobularia maritima

Easy, quick, dependable. Blooms from seed in 6 weeks, grows in almost any soil. Best in sun, but takes light shade. Useful for carpeting, edging, bulb cover, temporary filler in rock garden or perennial border, between flagstones, in window boxes or containers. Attracts bees. If you shear plants halfway back 4 weeks after they come into bloom, new growth will make another crop of flowers, and plants won't become rangy.

Garden varieties better known than the species; these varieties self-sow too, but seedlings tend to revert to taller, looser growth, less intense color, smaller flowers.

'Carpet of Snow' (2–4 in. tall), 'Little Gem' (4–6 in.), and 'Tiny Tim' (3 in.) are good compact whites. 'Tetra Snowdrift' (12 in.) has long stems, large white flowers. 'Rosie O'Day' (2–4 in.) and 'Pink Heather' (6 in.) are lavender pinks. 'Oriental Night' (4 in.) and 'Violet Queen' (5 in.) are rich violet purples.

LOCUST. See *Robinia.*

LOGANBERRY. See Blackberry.

LOLIUM. RYEGRASS. Annual or perennial lawn grasses used for lawns, pasture, and soil reclamation. Not considered choicest lawn grass, but useful in special conditions and for special uses. Plants clump instead of running, and do not make tight turf; heavy sowing helps overcome this. Often mixed with other lawn grass species for low-cost, large-area coverage in cool-summer climates. In Bermuda grass country, often sowed in fall on reconditioned Bermuda lawns to give winter green.

L. multiflorum. ITALIAN RYEGRASS. Larger, coarser than perennial ryegrass. Basically an annual; some plants live for several seasons in mild climates. Fast, deep rooted.

Lolium perenne

Hybrid between the two is COMMON or DOMESTIC RYEGRASS, often used as winter cover on soil or on winter-dormant lawns.

L. perenne. PERENNIAL RYEGRASS. Finer texture than above, deep green with high gloss. Disadvantages are clumping tendency and tough flower and seed stems that lie down under mower blades. Advantages are fast sprouting and growth. Best in cool-summer climates. 'Manhattan' is finer, more uniform. Other varieties are 'Pennfine', 'Derby', 'Yorktown', 'Loretta'.

LOMARIA. See *Blechnum.*

LONAS annua (*L. inodora*). Annual. All Zones. Stems to 1 ft. tall, finely divided leaves, 2-in.-wide, flat-topped clusters of yellow flower heads that suggest yarrow. Takes coastal fog and wind. Sow where plants will bloom, or grow in flats, then transplant. Summer bloom in most areas, year-round bloom in Zone 17.

Lonas annua

LONDON PRIDE. See *Saxifraga umbrosa.*

LONG-FLOWERED MARLOCK. See *Eucalyptus macrandra.*

LONG-LEAFED YELLOW-WOOD. See *Podocarpus henkelii.*

LONICERA. HONEYSUCKLE. Evergreen or deciduous shrubs or vines. Most kinds valued for tubular, often fragrant flowers. Easily grown in sun, or light shade inland. Vining kinds need support when starting out. Flowers of most kinds yield abundant nectar for hummingbirds; fruit of shrubby kinds attract many seed and fruit-eating birds. Most need average summer water once established.

Lonicera hildebrandiana

L. ciliosa. Deciduous vine. Zones 1–9, 14–24. Native to mountains, British Columbia and Montana south to northern California and Arizona. To 15 ft. Leafs out early. Leaves oval, 1–3 in. long, green above, pale beneath. Flowers reddish orange, 1½ in. long in terminal whorl, May-July; followed by small red fruit.

L. 'Clavey's Dwarf'. Deciduous shrub. Zones 1–9, 14–24. Dense, to 3 ft., rarely to 6 ft. tall, with equal spread. Flowers white, small, not showy. Blue green leaves. Useful foundation plant or low unclipped hedge in colder regions.

L. fragrantissima. WINTER HONEYSUCKLE. Deciduous shrub, partially evergreen in mild-winter areas. Zones 1–9, 14–24. Arching, rather stiff growth to 8 ft. Leaves oval, dull dark green above, blue green beneath, 1–3 in. long. Creamy white flowers ⅝ in. long on previous year's wood, in early spring to fall depending on climate. Flowers not showy, but have rich fragrance, like *Daphne odora*. Red berrylike fruit. Can be used as clipped hedge or background.

L. heckrottii. GOLD FLAME HONEYSUCKLE, CORAL HONEYSUCKLE. Deciduous or semideciduous vine, or small shrub. Zones 2–24. Vigorous, to 12–15 ft. with oval, 2-in., blue green leaves. Free blooming spring to frost. Clustered flowers, 1½ in. long, bright coral pink outside, rich yellow within, open from coral pink buds. Train as espalier, or on wire along eaves. Subject to aphids. Varieties sold as 'Gold Flame' and 'Pink Gold Flame' are similar, if not identical.

L. hildebrandiana. GIANT BURMESE HONEYSUCKLE. Evergreen vine. Zones 9, 14–17, 19–24. Big, fast-growing, with 4–6-in., glossy, dark green, oval leaves on supple, ropelike stems. Tubular, fragrant flowers to 6–7 in. long, open white, then turn yellow to dull orange; slow to drop. Summer bloom. Plants occasionally have dark green, inch-wide, berrylike fruit. Most widely planted kind in southern California. Any good soil, occasional feeding, plenty of water. Thin out older stems occasionally and remove some growth that has bloomed. Striking along eaves, on arbor or wall.

L. involucrata. TWINBERRY. Deciduous shrub. Zones 1–9, 14–17, 21–24. Native to moist areas, California to Alaska and eastward. Densely foliaged plants 5–10 ft. high. Dark green, oval leaves 2–5 in. long. Small (½ in. long), tubular, paired flowers, yellowish tinged red, each surrounded by 2 united bracts that enlarge as fruit forms, becoming bright red and finally black. The twin berries are black. Plants bloom March-July.

L. japonica. JAPANESE HONEYSUCKLE. Evergreen vine, partly or wholly deciduous in coldest regions. Zones 2–24. Rampant. Leaves deep green, oval. Flowers white, tinged purplish, with sweet fragrance. Late spring, summer bloom. Several varieties are grown, all better known than the species itself: *L. j.* 'Aureoreticulata', GOLDNET HONEYSUCKLE, leaves veined yellow, especially in full sun. *L. j.* 'Halliana', HALL'S HONEYSUCKLE, most vigorous and most widely grown, climbs to 15 ft., covers 150 sq. ft.; flowers pure white, changing to yellow, attractive to bees. *L. j.* 'Purpurea', probably same as *L. j. chinensis,* leaves tinged purple underneath, flowers purplish red, white inside.

Of the above, Hall's honeysuckle most commonly used as bank and ground cover, for erosion control in large areas; unless curbed can become a weed, smothering less vigorous plants. Needs severe pruning once a year to prevent undergrowth from building up and becoming fire hazard. Cut back almost to framework with shears. Train as privacy or wind screen on chain link or wire fence. Fairly drought resistant when established, tolerates poor drainage. As ground cover set 2–3 ft. apart.

L. korolkowii. Deciduous shrub. Zones 1–9, 14–24. Arching form to 12 ft. Leaves oval, 2 in. long, bluish green. A profusion of small rose-colored flowers in May-June are followed by bright red fruit in early fall. Use in cold areas as big background shrub. Takes desert heat. *L. k.* 'Zabelii' has broader leaves, deeper rose flowers.

L. nitida. BOX HONEYSUCKLE. Evergreen shrub. Zones 4–9, 14–24. To 6 ft. with erect, densely leafy branches. Tiny (½ in.), oval, dark green, shiny leaves. Attractive bronze to plum-colored winter foliage. Flowers (in June) fragrant, creamy white, ½ in. long. Berries translucent, blue purple. Rapid growth, tending toward untidiness, but easily pruned as hedge or single plant. Takes salt spray, resistant to oak root fungus.

L. pileata. PRIVET HONEYSUCKLE. Semievergreen shrub. Zones 2–9, 14–24. Low, spreading, with stiff horizontal branches, to 3 ft. Dark green, 1½-in., privetlike leaves; small, white, fragrant flowers in May; translucent violet purple berries. Sun, or light shade inland. Good bank cover with low-growing euonymus or barberries. Does well at seashore.

L. sempervirens. TRUMPET HONEYSUCKLE. Evergreen or semievergreen twining vine, shrubby if not given support. Zones 3–24. Showy, unscented orange yellow to scarlet trumpet flowers 1½–2 in. long, in whorl at end of branches in summer. Fruit scarlet. Oval leaves, 1½–3 in. long, bluish green beneath.

L. tatarica. TATARIAN HONEYSUCKLE. Deciduous shrub. Zones 1–9, 14–21. Forms big, upright, dense mass of twiggy branches; looser and more attractive in partial shade. Oval, 2-in.-long, dark green or bluish green leaves. Small pink or rose flowers in late spring, early summer. Bright red fruit. Neat-appearing plants for backgrounds, screens, windbreaks.

LOQUAT. See *Eriobotrya japonica.*

LOROPETALUM chinense. Evergreen shrub. Zones 6–9, 14–24. Borderline Zones 4, 5. Generally 3–5 ft. tall, possibly up to 12 ft. in great age. Neat, compact habit, with tiered, arching or drooping branches. Leaves roundish, light green, soft, 1–2 in. long. Occasional leaf turns yellow or red throughout the year for nice touch of color. Flowers white to greenish white, in clusters of 4–8 at ends of branches. Each flower has 4 narrow, inch-long, twisted petals. Bloom heaviest March-April, but some bloom likely to appear any time.

Loropetalum chinense

Full sun in fog belt; sun or partial shade inland. Needs rich, well-drained soil and lots of water. Subtle beauty, good in foregrounds, raised beds, hanging baskets, woodland gardens, as ground cover. In Northwest needs protection against hard freezes.

LOTUS. Subshrubs or perennials, often with completely prostrate trailing stems. (For plants with common name LOTUS, see *Nelumbo.*) Leaves divided into leaflets. Flowers sweet pea shaped, pink through shades of red to yellow. Full sun to part shade. Need some summer water.

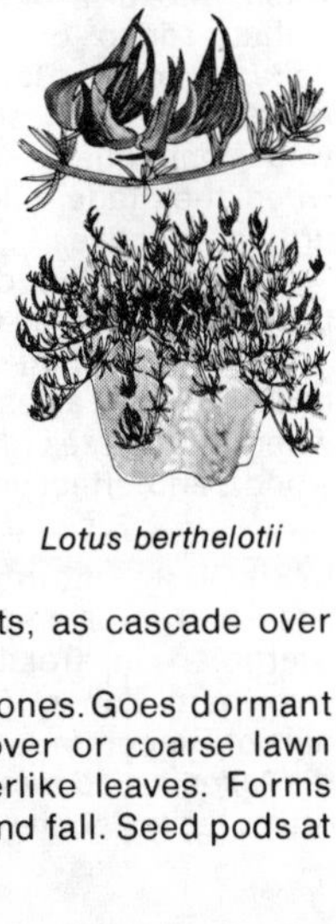

Lotus berthelotii

L. berthelotii. PARROT'S BEAK. Zones 9, 15–24. Trailing perennial with stems 2-3 ft. long, thickly covered with silvery gray foliage and very narrow, 1-in.-long, scarlet blossoms. Blooms June-July. Dies back in cold weather, suffers root rot in poor drainage. Space 24 in. apart as ground cover, and cut back occasionally to induce bushiness. Also very effective in hanging baskets, as cascade over wall or rocks.

L. corniculatus. BIRDSFOOT TREFOIL. All Zones. Goes dormant where winters are cold. Use as ground cover or coarse lawn substitute. Makes mat of dark green cloverlike leaves. Forms clusters of small yellow flowers in summer and fall. Seed pods at top of flower stem spread like bird's foot, hence common name. Sow seeds or set out plants. Takes much water in hot, dry months. Should be mowed occasionally.

L. mascaensis. Perennial. Zones 16, 17, 20–24. Partially erect and bushy; will cascade in hanging containers, above walls. Narrow, silky gray leaflets. Bright yellow flowers, ½–¾ in. long in small clusters. Trim to induce flat growth. Short-lived; freezes back at 30°F.

LOVAGE. See *Levisticum officinale.*

LOVE-IN-A-MIST. See *Nigella damascena.*

LOVE-LIES-BLEEDING. See *Amaranthus caudatus.*

LOW BULRUSH. See *Scirpus cernuus.*

LUFFA. See Gourd.

LUMA apiculata *(Myrceugenella apiculata, Myrtus luma).* Evergreen shrub or small tree. Zones 14–24. Slow growth to 6–8 (possibly 20) ft. tall, equally wide. Old plants develop beautiful, smooth, cinnamon-colored bark. Dense foliage; leaves close together, ½–1 in. long, oval to roundish, dark green. Flowers white to pinkish, a little more than ½ in. across, with 4 petals and a large brush of stamens in the center. Fruit blue black, less than ½ in. wide, is edible but not especially tasty. Resembles common myrtle (*Myrtus*) but is denser and darker green. Fairly drought tolerant.

Luma apiculata

LUNARIA annua *(L. biennis).* MONEY PLANT, HONESTY. Biennial. Zones 1–10, 14–24. Old-fashioned garden plant grown for the translucent silvery circles (about 1¼ in. across) that stay on flower stalks and are all that remain of ripened seed pods after outer coverings drop with seeds. Plants 1½–3 ft. high, with coarse, heart shaped, toothed leaves. Flowers resemble wild mustard blooms, but are purple or white, not yellow. Plant in an out-of-the-way spot in poor soil, or in a mixed flower bed where shining pods can be admired before they are picked for dry bouquets. Tough, persistent, can reseed and become weedy.

Lunaria annua

LUNGWORT. See *Pulmonaria.*

LUPINUS. LUPINE. Annuals, perennials, shrubs. Leaves are divided like fingers into many leaflets. Flowers sweet pea shaped, in dense spikes at ends of stems. Many species native to western U.S., ranging from beach sand to alpine rocks. Only best and easiest kinds covered here; native plant seed specialists can supply many others.

All need good drainage; are not otherwise fussy about soil. Start from seed sown winter-early spring. Hard-coated seeds often slow to sprout, germinate quicker after soaking in hot water or after having coats scratched or cut.

Lupinus
Russell Hybrids

L. arboreus. Shrub. Zones 14–17, 22–24. Native to California coastal areas. Grows to 5–8 ft. tall. Flower clusters in March-June, 4–16 in. long, usually yellow but sometimes lilac, bluish, white, or some mixture of those colors. Drought resistant. Striking beach plant.

(Continued on next page)

L. hartwegii. Summer annual. Native to Mexico. Grows 1½–3 ft. tall and comes in shades of blue, white, and pink. Easy from seed sown April-May where plants are to bloom. Flowers in July-September.

L. nanus. SKY LUPINE. Spring annual; Zones 8, 9, 14–24. California native, 8–24 in. high; flowers rich blue marked white. Sow seeds in fall or winter for spring bloom. Sow California poppies with it for contrast. April-May flowers. Self-sows readily where it gets little competition. Excellent for barren banks.

L. polyphyllus. Perennial. All Zones. Native to moist places, northern California to British Columbia. Grows 1½–4 ft. tall, with dense flower clusters, 6–24 in. long, in summer. Flowers blue, purple, or reddish. One important ancestor of the Russell Hybrids. Needs fair amount of water. Control aphids.

L. Russell Hybrids. RUSSELL LUPINES. Perennials. Zones 1–7, 14–17. Large, spreading plants to 4–5 ft., with long, dense spikes of flowers in May-June. Little Lulu and Minarette strains are smaller growing (to 18 in.). Colors white, cream, yellow, pink, blue, red, orange, purple. Many bicolors. Grow from seed or buy started plants from flats, pots. Striking border plant where summers aren't too hot and dry. Keep soil moist, give plants good air circulation to help avoid mildew. Often short-lived.

LYCASTE. Epiphytic and terrestrial orchids. Greenhouse plants—do fine outdoors during frost free months. Native to Central America. Plants have large oval pseudobulbs bearing 1–5 plaited leaves. Long-lasting fragrant flowers produced in profusion are predominantly green; some are pink, white, yellow, or brown.

Lycaste virginalis

Thrive in cool (50°–55°F. night, 10°F. higher day) location in bright light, good ventilation, and moist but very well-drained soil. Plant in pots of U.C.-type mix or commercial house plant mix. Reduce watering to minimum as growth matures and bulbs swell to encourage bloom set. Increase watering when new growth appears, but keep water off leaves until mature to prevent rot. Many species and hybrids are available from specialists; this is the best known:

L. virginalis *(L. skinneri).* Native to Guatemala. Old plants produce large numbers of 5–7 in. flowers, each on single stem, in winter. Color varies from white with yellow lip to rose pink with pink, crimson-spotted lip. Plant grows 15–24 in. tall.

LYCHNIS. Annuals, perennials. Hardy, old-fashioned garden flowers, all very tolerant of adverse soils.

L. chalcedonica. MALTESE CROSS. Perennial. Zones 1–9, 11–24. Loose, open, growing 2–3 ft. high, with hairy leaves and stems. Grow in full sun to light shade; keep moist. Flowers in dense terminal clusters, scarlet, the petals deeply cut. June-July bloom. Plants effective in large borders with white flowers, gray foliage. There is a white variety, 'Alba'.

Lychnis coronaria

L. coeli-rosa *(Silene coeli-rosa, Agrostemma coeli-rosa, Viscaria coeli-rosa).* Summer annual. Single, saucer shaped, 1-in. flowers cover foot-tall plants in summer. Blue and lavender are favorite colors; white and pink are also available, most with contrasting lighter or darker eye spot. Leaves long, narrow, and pointed. Good cut flowers with long bloom season. Sow seed March-April in moist, rich soil. In Zones 8, 9, 12–24 sow in fall for winter, spring bloom.

L. coronaria. CROWN-PINK, MULLEIN-PINK. Annual or perennial. All Zones. Plants 1½–2½ ft., with attractive, silky, white foliage and, in spring and early summer, magenta to crimson flowers a little less than an inch across. Effective massed. Reseeds copiously, but any surplus is easily weeded out.

L. viscaria 'Splendens'. Perennial. Zones 1–9, 11–24. Compact, low evergreen clumps of grasslike leaves to 5 in. long. Flower stalks to 1 ft. with clusters of pink to rose ½-in. flowers in

summer. A double-flowered variety, 'Splendens Flore Pleno', is a good rock garden plant and lasts well when cut.

LYCORIS. SPIDER LILY. Bulbs. Narrow, strap shaped leaves appear in spring, ripen, and die down before bloom starts. Clusters of red, pink, or yellow flowers on bare stems up to 2 ft. in late summer, fall. Flowers spidery looking with narrow, wavy-edged segments curved backward, and long stamens. Grow in garden beds, depending on hardiness, or as pot plants. Some kinds are tender, some half hardy. Bulbs available July-August. Set 3–4 in. deep (note exception below) in good soil and in full sun to

Lycoris radiata

light shade; give ample water during growth, but let plants dry out during dormant period in late summer. Don't disturb plantings for several years. When potting, set with tops exposed; don't use too large pots; best growth with crowded roots.

L. africana *(L. aurea).* GOLDEN SPIDER LILY. Outdoors in Zones 16, 17, 19–24; indoor/outdoor container plants elsewhere. Bright yellow 3-in. flowers in September-October.

L. radiata. Zones 4–9, 12–24. Best known and easiest. Coral red flowers with gold sheen; stems 18 in. 'Alba' has white flowers. Will take light shade. Give protection in cold-winter climates. August-September bloom.

L. squamigera *(Amaryllis hallii).* All Zones. Funnel shaped, fragrant, pink or rosy lilac 3-in. flowers in clusters on 2-ft. stems. August bloom. Hardiest lycoris; winters in colder regions if bulbs are planted 6 in. deep in protected location, as against a south wall.

LYGODIUM japonicum. CLIMBING FERN. Perennial. Zones 8, 9, 14–24. Native to Southeast Asia. Delicate, lacy-textured, tightly twining climber to 8 ft., with light green leaflets. Fertile (spore-bearing) leaflets much narrower than the sterile ones. Grow on post or trellis, or in hanging basket. Grow in light to heavy shade and keep roots moist. Hardy to 30°F.

LYONOTHAMNUS floribundus. CATALINA IRONWOOD. Evergreen tree. Zones 15–17, 19–24. Native to Channel Islands off coast of southern California. The species, with merely lobed or scallop-toothed leaves, is seldom seen in cultivation; *L. f. asplenifolius,* FERNLEAF CATALINA IRONWOOD, is well-known. Moderate growth to 30–60 ft. with a 20–40 ft. spread. Redwood-colored bark peels off in long, thin strips. Young twigs often reddish. The 4–6-in. leaves are divided into 3–7 deeply notched or lobed leaflets, deep glossy green above, gray hairy beneath. Small white blossoms in large, flat 8–18-in. clusters. These stand out well from foliage, but should be cut off when they fade. Old clusters turn brown, are unattractive.

Lygodium japonicum

Needs excellent drainage and should be pruned in winter to shape and control growth. Sometimes shows chlorosis in heavy soils. Easiest to grow near coast where it tolerates much drought. Handsome in groves (like redwood), and effective with redwood, Torrey pines.

Lyonothamnus floribundus

LYSILOMA thornberi. FEATHER BUSH, FERN-OF-THE-DESERT. Shrub or small tree, evergreen in frostless areas, deciduous elsewhere. Zones 10, 12–24. Native to foothills of Rincon Mountains of Arizona. To 12 ft. Makes broad canopy of finely cut bright green leaves somewhat like acacia. Some-

Lysiloma thornberi

times killed by heavy frosts, but usually comes back. Flowers tiny, white, in ½-in. heads. May-June bloom. Seed pods flat, ridged, 4–8 in. long, 1 in. wide. Takes desert heat and drought when established. Good informal background shrub, patio tree, transitional planting between garden and desert.

Lysiloma thornberi

LYSIMACHIA nummularia. MONEYWORT, CREEPING JENNIE. Perennial. Zones 1–9, 14–24. Evergreen creeping plant with long runners (to 2 ft.) that root at joints. Forms pretty light green mat of roundish leaves. Flowers about 1 in. across, yellow, form singly in leaf joints. Summer blooming. Requires moisture and shade (full sun near coast). Best use is in corners where it need not be restrained. Will spill from wall, hanging basket. Good ground cover (plant 12–18 in. apart) near streams. 'Aurea' has yellow leaves, needs shade.

Lysimachia nummularia

LYTHRUM salicaria. Perennial. All Zones. Showy magenta-flowered plants for pond margins or moist sunny areas. Grows in clumps 2 ft. wide with 2½–5-ft. stems; ¾-in. flowers densely set on the top 8–18 in. Narrow leaves clothe lower stem. Hybrids known as 'Roseum Superbum', 'Morden's Pink' or 'Morden's Gleam' grown in the West. Valued for cut flowers in late summer and fall. In borders, tone down magenta by planting with white flowers.

Lythrum salicaria

MACADAMIA. MACADAMIA NUT, QUEENS- LAND NUT. Evergreen trees. Zones 9, 16, 17, 19–24. Clean, handsome ornamental tree where frosts are light. Where best adapted (Zones 23, 24), produces clusters of hard-shelled, delicious nuts; pick when they fall.

Best in deep, rich soil. Takes some drought when established but grows slowly if kept dry. Stake young trees. Prune to shape.

Most trees are sold under the name *M. ternifolia.* They are nearly always one of the species described below. Look for grafted, named varieties of proven nut bearing ability. All are resistant to oak root fungus.

Both species reach 25–30 ft. tall and more, 15–20 ft. wide (larger when very old). Long (5–12 in.), glossy, leathery leaves. Mature foliage is durable and attractive for cutting. Small flowers in winter and spring are white to pink in dense, hanging, 1-ft. clusters.

M. integrifolia. SMOOTH-SHELL MACADAMIA. Best near coast. Leaves are smooth edged. Nuts ripen in late fall to May.

M. tetraphylla. ROUGH-SHELL MACADAMIA. Best inland. Spiny leaves. Shell thinner, tree more open than *M. integrifolia.* Nuts appear fall through February.

Macadamia tetraphylla

MACFADYENA unguis-cati (*Doxantha unguis-cati, Bignonia tweediana*). CAT'S CLAW, YELLOW TRUMPET VINE. Zones 8–24. Partly deciduous vine that loses all its leaves when winters are cold. Climbs high and fast by hooked, clawlike, forked tendrils. To 25–40 ft. Leaves divided into 2 oval, glossy green, 2-in. leaflets. Yellow trumpets to 2 in. long, 1¼ in. across, early spring.

Grows near coast, but faster and stronger where summer heat is high—even

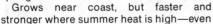

Macfadyena unguis-cati

on south walls in Zones 12 and 13. Will cling to any support— stone, wood, fence, tree trunk. Some even are seen clinging to undersides of freeway overpasses. Tends to produce leaves and flowers at ends of stems; cut back some stems nearly to ground to stimulate new growth lower down, and prune whole plant hard after bloom. Needs little dry season water once established.

MACLURA pomifera. OSAGE ORANGE. Deciduous tree. All Zones; little planted outside Zones 1, 3, 10–13. Fast growth to 60 ft. with spreading, open habit. Thorny branches. Leaves to 5 in. long, medium green. If there's a male plant present, female plants may bear 4-in. inedible fruit (hedge-apples) which somewhat resemble bumpy, yellow green oranges. Can stand heat, cold, wind, drought, poor soil, moderate alkalinity. Easily propagated by seed, cuttings, root cuttings; easily transplanted. Useful as big, tough, rough-looking hedge or background. Prune to any size from 6 ft. up. Pruned high, becomes desert shade tree, but needs some water until established. Not bothered by oak root fungus.

Maclura pomifera

MADAGASCAR JASMINE. See *Stephanotis floribunda.*

MADAGASCAR PERIWINKLE. See *Catharanthus roseus.*

MADEIRA VINE. See *Anredera cordifolia.*

MADRONE, MADROÑO. See *Arbutus menziesii.*

MAGIC FLOWER. See *Cantua buxifolia.*

MAGNOLIA. Deciduous or evergreen trees and shrubs. A great number of magnificent flowering plants with a remarkable variety of colors, leaf shapes, and plant forms. The following classification by general appearance may help you find the magnolias that interest you (the chart lists all the kinds alphabetically).

EVERGREEN MAGNOLIAS

To gardeners in California and Arizona, magnolia usually means *M. grandiflora,* the big evergreen with glossy leaves and big, white, fragrant flowers. This one stands pretty much by itself. Generally considered a street or lawn tree, it can also be used as an espalier or grown in a large container for a few years. Foliage is good in arrangements. Known for heat resistance and tolerance of damp soil, it has many named forms for different uses.

Other evergreen magnolias are *M. delavayi, M. virginiana,* and *M. 'Freeman',* a hybrid between *M. grandiflora* and *M. virginiana.*

Magnolia grandiflora

DECIDUOUS MAGNOLIAS WITH SAUCER FLOWERS

This group includes the saucer magnolia (*M. soulangiana*) and its many varieties, often miscalled "tulip trees" because of shape and bright colors of their flowers. Included here are the yulan magnolia (*M. heptapeta*) and lily magnolia (*M. quinquepeta*). All are hardy to cold, thriving in various climates throughout the West; but early flowers of all forms are subject to frost damage, and all do poorly in hot, dry, windy areas. Related to

Magnolia soulangiana

(Continued on page 365)

Magnolia

NAME	ZONES	DECIDUOUS OR EVERGREEN	HEIGHT	SPREAD	BLOOMS AT AGE:	FLOWERS	USES	REMARKS
Magnolia acuminata CUCUMBER TREE	1–9, 14–21	Dec.	60–80 ft.	25 ft.	12 yrs.	Small, greenish yellow, appear after leaves. Late spring, summer. Not showy. Handsome reddish seed capsules, red seeds.	Shade or lawn tree.	Dense shade from glossy 5–9-in. leaves. Hardy to cold; dislikes hot, dry winds.
M. a. cordata (*M. cordata*) YELLOW CUCUMBER TREE, YELLOW MAGNOLIA	4–9, 14–21	Dec.	To 35 ft.	To 35 ft.	12 yrs.	Larger (to 4 in.), chartreuse yellow outside, pure yellow within, appear as leaves start to expand. Mild lemon scent.	Lawn or border tree for large properties. Slow-growing.	Lower, shrubbier than *M. acuminata*. Showier, but not ordinarily a tree you can walk or sit under. 'Miss Honeybee' is good selection with pale yellow flowers.
M. campbellii	6–9, 14–21	Dec.	60–80 ft.	40 ft.	20 yrs. Grafts bloom younger.	Magnificent 6–10-in. bowls, deep rose outside, paler within. Central petals cupped over rose stamens. Very early flowering.	Plant in lee of evergreens to protect flowers from storm winds. Make it focus of garden and give it room.	Best in Zones 15–17. 'Alba', 'Strybing White' are white forms; 'Hendricks Park', 'Late Pink', good pinks.
M. c. mollicomata	4–9, 14–21	Dec.	50–80 ft.	40 ft.	10 yrs. Grafts less— perhaps 5 yrs.	Pale to rose pink. 'Lanarth' variety pinkish purple. Early flowering.	Shrubbier than above, blooms at earlier age. Leaves (as in *M. campbellii*) purplish when 8–12 in. long, heavily veined.	A little hardier than *M. campbellii*. 'Maharaja' has white and purple flowers to 15 in., 'Maharanee' white flowers to 10 in.
M. dawsoniana DAWSON MAGNOLIA	4–9, 14–21	Dec.	40–50 ft.	25–30 ft.	10 yrs. from grafts.	Large (8–10 in.), white with rose shading. Narrow petals, slightly pendulous. Profuse bloom. Early flowering. Slight perfume.	Big plant for big garden. Makes magnificent show—a little untidy close up.	Very dark green leaves. Quite cold hardy when established, needs hardening off in fall. 'Chyverton' is selected salmon, fading pink.
M. delavayi	7–9, 14–21	Ev.	20–30 ft.	20 ft.	4–5 yrs.	Dull creamy white, 6–8 in. wide. Fragrant, short-lived; flowers shatter day they open. Long summer bloom period.	Use as single tree or giant shrub in lawn or large corner. Hard to train as single-stemmed tree.	Foliage is the feature; leaves 8–14 in. long, 5–8 in. wide, stiff, leathery, gray green, tropical looking.
M. denudata. See *M. heptapeta.*								
M. fraseri (*M. auriculata*)	2–9, 14–21	Dec.	To 50 ft.	20–30 ft.	10–12 yrs.	Creamy to yellowish white, 8–10 in. wide. Blooms May-June when leaves are full grown.	Single lawn tree or wood-land tree. Rose red 5-in. seed capsules showy in summer.	Leaves 16–18 in. long, parchmentlike, in whorls at ends of branches. Effect is that of parasols. Handsome dark brown fall color.
M. 'Freeman'	4–12 14–24	Ev.	10–15 ft.	5 ft.	8 yrs. from seed.	White, 5 in. across, very fragrant. Summer bloom.	Narrow, dense, columnar ever-green tree for small gardens. Foliage like *M. grandiflora* but smaller.	Hybrid between *M. virginiana* and *M. grandiflora*. A very old tree has been known to reach 50 ft.

NAME	ZONES	DECIDUOUS OR EVERGREEN	HEIGHT	SPREAD	BLOOMS AT AGE:	FLOWERS	USES	REMARKS
M. globosa	5–9 14–21	Dec.	To 20 ft.	20 ft.	10 yrs.	White, fragrant, cupped or globe shaped, nodding or drooping. June.	Use as big shrub in lawn, woodland edge, above a wall (to look up into flowers).	Leaves 5–8 in. long, half as wide, rusty furry beneath. Tree tender when young.
The southern magnolia in all its forms is something of a "sacred cow" in western gardens: on the one hand it is loved for its pretty foliage (while it's on the tree) and its glorious flower display; on the other hand, it is cursed or tolerated for the big, hard (almost like plastic) fallen leaves, fallen flower parts, and fallen seedheads that need to be picked or raked up daily or weekly from May through September.								
M. grandiflora SOUTHERN MAGNOLIA, BULL BAY	4–12 14–24	Ev.	To 80 ft.	40 ft.	15 yrs., sometimes much less. From grafts or cuttings, 2–3 yrs.	Pure white, aging buff; large (8–10 in. across), powerfully fragrant. Carried throughout summer and fall.	Street or lawn tree, big containers, wall or espalier plant. In cool-summer areas it appreciates warm wall or pocket. Glossy leathery leaves 4–8 in. long.	Unpredictable in form and age of bloom. Grafted plants more predictable. Does well in desert heat if out of wind. Needs warm wall in Zones 4–5. Expect breakage, yearly pruning in Zones 6–7.
M. g. 'Edith Bogue'	Same.	Same.	To 35 ft.	20 ft.	2–3 yrs. from grafts.	As in *M. grandiflora*. Young plants slower to come into heavy bloom than some other varieties.	One of hardiest selections of *M. grandiflora*. Original tree from New Jersey. Shapely vigorous tree.	Has withstood −24°F. The one to try in coldest regions. Keep it out of strong winds.
M. g. 'Majestic Beauty'	Same.	Same.	35–50 ft.	20 ft.	2 yrs. from grafts.	Very large, to 12 in. across, with 9 petals.	Vigorous, dense-branching street or shade tree of broadly pyramidal form.	Leaves exceptionally long, broad and heavy. Most luxuriant of southern magnolias; however, not the densest or most symmetrical.
M. g. 'Samuel Sommer'	Same.	Same.	30–40 ft.	30 ft.	Same.	Very large and full; to 10–14 in. across, with 12 petals.	Like the other grafted magnolias that bloom young, this will need pruning to become single-trunked tree. Can grow as multistemmed tree.	Leaves large, leathery, glossy, with heavy rusty red felting on underside; very dark green above. Fairly fast growing.
M. g. 'St. Mary'	Same.	Same.	Usually 20 ft.	20 ft.	Same.	Heavy production of full-sized flowers on small tree.	Fine where standard-sized magnolia would be too tall. Good espalier and pot subject.	Left alone it will form a big, dense bush. Pruned and staked, it makes a small tree.
M. g. 'Victoria'	Same.	Same.	To 20 ft.	15 ft.	2–3 yrs. from grafts.	Same as *M. grandiflora*.	Withstands −10°F. with little damage, but plant out of wind.	Parent plant grew in Victoria, B.C. Foliage exceptionally broad, heavy, dark green. 'Pioneer' is as hardy but leaves are not as dark green.
M. heptapeta (*M. conspicua, M. denudata*) YULAN MAGNOLIA	2–9 14-24	Dec.	To 35 ft.	30 ft.	6–7 yrs.	White, fragrant, sometimes tinged purple at base. Held erect, somewhat tulip shaped, 3–4 in. long spreading to 6–7 in. Early; often a few in summer.	Place it where it can show off against dark background or sky. Cut flowers striking in Oriental arrangements.	Tends toward irregular form—no handicap in informal garden or at woodland edge. Leaves 4–7 in. long.

(Continued on next page)

NAME	ZONES	DECIDUOUS OR EVERGREEN	HEIGHT	SPREAD	BLOOMS AT AGE:	FLOWERS	USES	REMARKS
M. hypoleuca (M. obovata)	4–9 14–21	Dec.	To 50 ft.	25 ft.	15 yrs.	To 8 in. across, creamy, fragrant. Appear in summer after leaves expand.	Only for big lawn or garden. Flowers are high up in tree.	Leaves impressive—up to 18 in. long; they tend to obscure flowers.
M. kobus KOBUS MAGNOLIA	2–9 14–24	Dec.	To 30 ft.	20 ft.	15 yrs.	White, to 4 in. across; early.	Hardy, sturdy tree for planting singly on lawn or in informal shrub and tree groupings.	Variety 'Wada's Memory' (M. kewensis 'Wada's Memory') is a better garden plant; blooms young, grows faster, has bigger flowers, copper red new growth.
M. kobus stellata.	See M. stellata.							
M. liliiflora.	See M. quinquepeta.							
M. loebneri	2–9 14–24	Dec.	Slow to 12–15 ft.	12–15 ft.	3 yrs.	Narrow, strap shaped petals like star magnolia, but fewer, larger. Plants bloom early and young.	Use in lawn, shrub border or woodland edge.	Group of hybrids between M. kobus and M. stellata. 'Ballerina' is white with faint pink blush on opening; 'Leonard Messel' has pink flowers, deeper in bud; 'Merrill' ('Dr. Merrill') is a very hardy, free flowering white.
M. macrophylla BIGLEAF MAGNOLIA	2–9 14–21	Dec.	To 50 ft. Slow.	30 ft.	12–15 yrs.	White, fragrant to 12 in. across, appearing after leaves are out May-July.	Show-off tree with leaves 12–30 in. long, 9–12 in. wide. Needs to stand alone. Striking foliage but hard to blend with other textures.	Plant where it is out of the wind; huge leaves easily tattered, branches brittle.
M. officinalis	4–9 14–21	Dec.	To 50 ft.	25 ft.	15 yrs.	To 8 in. wide, fragrant, creamy white. Appear after leaves in May.	Much like M. hypoleuca. Use for big, exotic-looking tree.	M. o. biloba has 18 in. long leaves notched at tips.
M. quinquepeta (M. liliiflora) LILY MAGNOLIA	2–9 14–24	Dec.	To 12 ft.	15 ft.	4–5 yrs.	White inside, purplish outside. Selections sold as 'Gracilis', 'Nigra' and 'O'Neill' darker purple red outside, pink inside.	Shrub border; strong vertical effect in big flower border. Blooms over long spring, summer season.	Good cut flower if buds taken before fully open. Spreads slowly by suckering. Leaves 4–6 in. long. 'Royal Crown', hybrid with M. veitchii, has pink candle shaped buds which open to 10-in. flowers.
M. salicifolia ANISE MAGNOLIA	2–9 14–21	Dec.	18–30 ft. Slow.	12 ft.	2–10 yrs.	White, narrow petaled, to 4 in. across. Early.	Usually upright with slender branches, graceful appearance. In front of trees, use as shrub border. Leaves (3–6 in. long) bronze red in fall.	An upright, large-flowered selection named 'Else Frye' is sold. Variety 'W. B. Clarke' blooms young, heavily.
M. sargentiana robusta	5–9 14–24	Dec.	To 35 ft.	35 ft.	10–12 yrs.; 8–10 yrs. from grafts.	Huge (8–12 in.) mauve pink bowls which open erect, then nod to horizontal. Early to midseason.	Must have ample room and protection from stormy winds which would tear early blooms.	One of most spectacular of flowering plants. Leaves 6–8 in. long. Not for hot, dry areas.

NAME	ZONES	DECIDUOUS OR EVERGREEN	HEIGHT	SPREAD	BLOOMS AT AGE:	FLOWERS	USES	REMARKS
M. sieboldii (Sometimes sold as *M. parviflora*) OYAMA MAGNOLIA	4–9 14–24	Dec.	6–15 ft.	6–15 ft.	5 yrs.	White, cup shaped, centered with crimson stamens; fragrant. Begins in May and flowers open continuously over long period.	Nice planted upslope or at the top of wall so people can look into flowers. Good for small gardens.	Popular in Zones 4–6 for fragrance, long bloom, restrained growth. Buds like white Japanese lanterns. Leaves 3–6 in. long.
M. sinensis CHINESE MAGNOLIA	4–9 14–24	Dec.	15–20 ft.	20–30 ft.	8–10 yrs. Less from grafts.	White, hanging, cup shaped, fragrant, 3–5 in. wide. May and well into summer. Red stamens.	Usually a big shrub. Foliage glossy, thick, and leathery.	Long bloom, fragrance and crimson stamens make it a charming plant. Can be staked and pruned into a small tree.
M. soulangiana SAUCER MAGNOLIA (Often erroneously called TULIP TREE)	1–10 12–24	Dec.	To 25 ft.	25 or more ft.	3–5 yrs.	White to pink or purplish red, variable in size and form, blooming before leaves expand. Generally about 6 in. across.	Lawn ornament, anchor plant in big corner plantings. Foliage good green, rather coarse, leaves 4–6 in. (or more) long.	Seedlings highly variable; shop for named varieties. Hybrid of *M. heptapeta* (*M. denudata*) and *M. quinquepeta* (*M. liliiflora*).
M. s. 'Alba' (*M. s.* 'Amabilis', *M. s.* 'Alba Superba')	Same.	Same.	To 30 ft.	Same.	Same.	Flowers suffused purple, opening nearly pure white, large. Early.	As above. Rather more upright in growth than most.	
M. s. 'Alexandrina'	Same.	Same.	To 25 ft.	Same.	Same.	Deep purplish pink, white inside, large. Midseason.	As above. Large, rather heavy foliage.	Late bloom helps it escape frosts in colder sections.
M. s. 'Brozzonii'	Same.	Same.	Same.	Same.	Same.	Huge, to 8 in. across. White, very slightly flushed at base. Early.	Large, vigorous plant.	One of handsomest whites.
M. s. 'Burgundy'	Same.	Same.	Same.	Same.	Same.	Large, well-rounded, deep purple halfway up to petal tips, then lightening to pink. Early.	San Francisco's Japanese Tea Garden has many of these artfully pruned and thinned to picturesque shapes.	
M. s. 'Coates Soulangiana'	Same.	Same.	Same.	Same.	Same.	Large, attractive flowers resemble those of 'Royal Crown'. (See under *M. quinquepeta*).	Large, shrubby.	
M. s. 'Grace McDade'	Same.	Same.	Same.	Same.	Same.	Flowers very large, perhaps to 10 in. across, white with pink tinting at base of petals. Early.	Striking with background of evergreens.	
M. s. 'Lennei' (*M. lennei*)	Same.	Same.	Same.	Same.	Same.	Very large, rather globe shaped, deep purple on outside, white on inside. Late.	Plant spreading, vigorous.	Very late bloom helps it escape frosts in cold areas.

(Continued on next page)

NAME	ZONES	DECIDUOUS OR EVERGREEN	HEIGHT	SPREAD	BLOOMS AT AGE:	FLOWERS	USES	REMARKS
M. s. 'Lennei Alba' (*M. lennei* 'Alba')	1–10 12–24	Dec.	To 25 ft.	25 or more ft.	3–5 yrs.	As *M. s.*'Lennei', except white in color, slightly smaller, earlier. Midseason.	Plant spreading, vigorous.	Two plants sold under this name. One form common in California is smaller in flower, creamy white, and earlier.
M. s. 'Lilliputian'	Same.	Same.	Smaller grower than others.	Same.	Same.	Pink and white, somewhat smaller than other *M. soulangiana* varieties. Late flowering.	Good where a smaller magnolia is called for.	Late blooming.
M. s. 'Norbertii'	Same.	Same.	To 25 ft.	Same.	Same.	White, stained purple on outside. Late.	Upright dense habit.	
M. s. 'Pink Superba'	Same.	Same.	Same.	Same.	Same.	Large, deep pink, white inside. Early.	Best where late frosts are not a problem.	Identical to *M. s.* 'Alba' except for flower color.
M. s. 'Purpliana'	Same.	Same.	Same.	Same.	Same.	Reddish purple, blooms early.	Same.	
M. s. 'Rustica Rubra'	Same.	Same.	Same.	Same.	Same.	Large, cup shaped, deep reddish purple flowers. Midseason.	Tall, vigorous grower for large areas. More treelike than many varieties.	Blooms somewhat past midseason. Big 6-in. seed pods of dark rose.
M. sprengeri 'Diva'	5–9 14–24	Dec.	To 40 ft.	30 ft.	7 yrs. from grafts.	To 8 in. wide, rose pink outside, white suffused pink with deeper lines inside. Scented; early to midseason.	One of the brightest in color; young plants broad, twiggy.	Highly colored, erect, spectacular flowers. Buds seem more frost resistant than those of *M. sargentiana robusta*.
M. stellata STAR MAGNOLIA	1–9 14–24	Dec.	To 10 ft.	20 ft.	3 yrs.	Very early white flowers with 19–21 narrow, strap shaped petals. Profuse bloom in late winter, early spring.	Slow growing, shrubby, fine for borders, entryway gardens, edge of woods.	Quite hardy but flowers often nipped by frost in Zones 1–7. Fine texture to twig and leaf. Fair yellow and brown fall color.
M. s. 'Centennial'	Same.	Same.	Same.	Same.	Same.	Large (5 in.) flowers, white, faintly marked pink.	Same.	
M. s. 'Dawn'	Same.	Same.	Same.	Same.	Same.	To 40–50 pink petals.	Same.	
M. s. 'Rosea' PINK STAR MAGNOLIA	Same.	Same.	Same.	Same.	Same.	Pink buds, flowers flushed pink, fading white.	As above. Place where you can see flowers from living or family room; they often bloom so early that you won't want to walk out to see them.	In cold regions plant these early flowering sorts in a north exposure to delay bloom as long as possible, lessen frost damage.
M. s. 'Royal Star'	Same.	Same.	Same.	Same.	Same.	White, 25–30 petals, blooms 2 weeks later than *M. stellata*.	Same uses as above. Faster growing.	
M. s. 'Rubra'	Same.	Same.	Same.	Same.	Same.	Rosy pink flowers.	More treelike in form than other *M. stellata* varieties.	

NAME	ZONES	DECIDUOUS OR EVERGREEN	HEIGHT	SPREAD	BLOOMS AT AGE:	FLOWERS	USES	REMARKS
M. s. 'Waterlily'	1–9 14–24	Dec.	To 10 ft.	20 ft.	3 yrs.	White. Larger flowers than *M. stellata*; broader, more numerous petals.	Leaves, like those of tall star magnolias, are modest in size (2–4 in. long); give finer foliage texture than other magnolias.	Faster growing than most star magnolias.
M. thompsoniana THOMPSON MAGNOLIA	4–9 14–24	Dec.	10–20 ft.	10 ft.	4 yrs.	July flowering. Creamy white, fragrant, 4–5 in. across.	Big shrub for semishaded location, fragrant bloom at a dull season.	Long (4–10 in.) narrow leaves nearly white underneath. Hybrid of *M. tripetala* and *M. virginiana*. Variety 'Urbana' is hardier.
M. tripetala UMBRELLA TREE, UMBRELLA MAGNOLIA	2–9 14–24	Dec.	To 40 ft.	25 ft.	10–12 yrs.	Large (to 10 in.) white flowers appear in summer after leaves expand. Flower odor considered unpleasant by many.	Shade or lawn tree. Plant out of strong wind.	Leaves in whorls at branch ends, to 2 ft. long. Resembles *M. macrophylla*.
M. veitchii VEITCH MAGNOLIA	4–9 14–24	Dec.	30–40 ft.	30 ft.	4–5 yrs.	Blooms early, before leaves. Rose red at base, shading to white at tips, to 10 in. across.	Needs plenty of room and protection from wind. Fast-growing branches are brittle. Spectacular tree.	This hybrid between *M. campbellii* and *M. heptapeta* is exceptionally fast growing and vigorous. 'Rubra' has smaller purple red flowers.
M. virginiana (*M. glauca*) SWEET BAY	4–9 14–24	Dec. or semi-ever-green.	To 50 ft. Usually less.	20 ft.	8–10 yrs.	Nearly globular, 2–3 in. wide, creamy white, fragrant, June to September.	Prefers moist, acid soil. Grows in swamps in eastern U.S. Usually a massive, semi-evergreen shrub.	Variable in leaf drop. Some plants quite evergreen. Leaves grayish green, nearly white beneath, 2–5 in. long.
M. watsonii WATSON MAGNOLIA	4–9 14–24	Dec.	To 20 ft.	20 ft.	12 yrs.	Creamy white, with crimson anthers, June-July after leaves expand. Often 5–6 in. across, fragrant.	Big shrub or stiff-looking small tree. At its best standing alone. Many think it a difficult plant to grow.	Hybrid between *M. sieboldii* and *M. hypoleuca*, a big-leafed Japanese species. Leaves 4–8 in. long, dark green, nearly white underneath.
M. wilsonii WILSON MAGNOLIA	4–9 14–24	Dec.	To 25 ft.	25 ft.	10 yrs.	White, with red stamens, pendulous, 3–4 in. across, fragrant. May and June.	Blooms at 4 ft., and tends to remain shrubby. Plant high on bank where flowers can be looked up to. Better in light shade.	Rich purple brown twigs and narrow, tapered leaves, 3–6 in. long with silvery undersides.

these, but more tender to cold (and heat), are the big Oriental magnolias from western China and the Himalayas—*M. campbellii, M. dawsoniana, M. sargentiana robusta, M. sprengeri* 'Diva'. Most spectacular of all, these are borderline hardy in Zones 4 and 5, and subject to frost and storm damage to early flowers.

DECIDUOUS MAGNOLIAS WITH STAR FLOWERS

This garden group includes *M. kobus, M. stellata* and its varieties (the star magnolias), and *M. salicifolia*. All are hardy, slow-growing, early-blooming plants with wide climatic adaptability.

LATE-FLOWERING MAGNOLIAS

These show fragrant, rather globular flowers during late spring and early summer and include *M. sieboldii, M. sinensis, M. watsonii*, and *M. wilsonii*. Blooming after leaves appear, they make less splash than saucer magnolias, but they have quiet beauty, rich fragrance, and a fairly long bloom season.

OTHER MAGNOLIAS

Less widely planted are a group of magnolias which bloom with or after the appearance of the leaves but are generally considered foliage plants or shade trees: *M. acuminata,* a big shade tree with inconspicuous flowers; *M. hypoleuca* and *M. officinalis,* big trees with big leaves and large, but not noticeable flowers; and the eastern American *M. fraseri, M. macrophylla,* and *M. tripetala,* middle-sized trees with huge leaves, flowers.

A few specialists list even more varieties than are shown in the chart on pages 360–365.

Balled and burlapped plants are available in late winter and early spring, container plants any time. Do not set plants lower than their original soil level. Stake single-trunked or very heavy plants against rocking by wind, which will tear the thick, fleshy, sensitive roots. Set stakes in planting hole before placing tree (to avoid damaging fleshy roots). If you plant your magnolia in a lawn, try to provide a good-sized area free of grass for a watering basin. Water deeply and thoroughly, but do not drown the plants. Thick mulch will help hold moisture and reduce soil temperature. It will also make hand weeding easier. Surrounding grass cuts reflected heat.

Prevent soil compaction around root zone; this means reducing foot traffic to a minimum. Prune only when absolutely necessary. Best time is right after flowering, and best way is to remove entire twig or limb right to the base. Paint wound with tree seal.

Damaging creatures and diseases are few. Watch for scale and aphids at any time and for spider mites in hot weather. Snails and slugs eat lower leaves of shrubby magnolias. Bait or spray will control them. Magnolias are not immune to oak root fungus (*Armillaria*), but they seem somewhat resistant.

Carefully pick planting site for any magnolia. Except for *M. grandiflora* magnolias are hard to move once established, and many grow quite large. They never look their best when crowded, and may be severely damaged by digging around their roots, as might be necessary if you add other plants. They need moist, well-drained, rich soil, neutral or slightly acid. Add plenty of organic matter at planting time—leaf mold, peat moss, or ground bark. Full sun (light shade in desert regions).

More bothersome are deficiency problems: chlorosis from lack of iron in alkaline soils, and nitrogen starvation. Iron chelates will remedy the first condition, fertilizer will fix the second. Burning of leaf edges usually means salt damage from either overfertilizing, mineral salts in the soil, or salts in the irrigation water. This last is a problem in southern California and is usually the factor limiting success of magnolias in the deserts. Regular, frequent, deep, heavy waterings will help leach out the salts and carry them to lower soil levels—*if* drainage is good. In the Northwest, late frosts sometimes burn leaf edges.

Uses are discussed in more detail in the chart. Generally speaking, larger deciduous magnolias are at their best standing alone against some background that will display their flowers and, in winter, their strongly patterned, usually gray limbs, and big, fuzzy flower buds. Smaller deciduous magnolias show up well in large flower or shrub borders, and make choice ornaments in the Oriental garden, where they are good companions for pine, bamboo, nandina, and azaleas. And all magnolias are excellent trees to grow in lawns.

MAHERNIA verticillata. See *Hermannia.*

MAHOBERBERIS miethkeana. Evergreen shrub. All Zones. Resembles *Mahonia aquifolium,* one of its parents; also has some traits of its barberry parent. Some leaves divided into leaflets. Leaves (or leaflets) oval, leathery, spiny or merely toothed, dark green showing bronzy purple in fall, winter. Dense, upright growth to 6–8 ft.; gets leggy, but can be pruned back. Clustered yellow flowers in early spring. Plant under some protection from wind and full sun. Drought tolerant. *M. aquisargentii* is a similar plant.

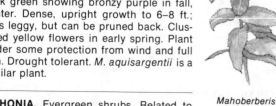
Mahoberberis miethkeana

MAHONIA. Evergreen shrubs. Related to barberry (*Berberis*) and described under

that name by some botanists. Easily grown; good looking all year. Leaves divided into leaflets that usually have spiny teeth on edges. Yellow flowers in dense rounded to spikelike clusters, followed by blue black (sometimes red) berrylike fruit. Generally disease resistant; sometimes foliage is disfigured by small looper caterpillar. All are drought tolerant, attract birds.

Mahonia aquifolium

M. aquifolium. OREGON GRAPE. Zones 1–21. Native British Columbia to northern California. State flower of Oregon. To 6 ft. or more with tall, erect habit; spreads by underground stems. Leaves 4–10 in.-long, with 5–9, very spiny-toothed, oval, 1–2½-in.-long leaflets that are glossy green in some forms, dull green in others. Young growth ruddy or bronzy; scattered mature red leaves through year (more pronounced in fall); purplish or bronzy leaves in winter, especially in cold-winter areas or where grown in full sun. Flowers in 2–3-in.-long clusters, March-May; fruit blue black with gray bloom, edible (make good jelly).

Takes any exposure in most areas; north exposure best in Zones 12, 13 (where chlorosis is also a problem); in Zones 9–14, 18–21 it looks best growing in shade. Control height and form by pruning; cut to ground any woody stems that extend too far above mass; new growth quickly fills in.

For uniformity, plant one of the varieties grown from cuttings or divisions. 'Compacta' averages about 2 ft. tall and spreads freely to make broad colonies. New foliage is glossy and light to coppery green; mature foliage is matte medium green. 'Orange Flame', 5 ft. tall, has bronzy orange new growth, glossy green mature leaves that turn wine red in winter.

Plant in masses as foundation planting, in woodland, in tubs, as low screen or garden barrier. Resistant to oak root fungus (*Armillaria*) and especially valuable where gardens are heavily infested by it.

M. bealei. LEATHERLEAF MAHONIA. All Zones. To 10–12 ft., with strong pattern of vertical stems, horizontal leaves over a foot long divided into 7–15 thick, leathery, broad leaflets as much as 5 in. long, yellowish green above, gray green below, edges spiny toothed. Flowers in erect, 3–6-in.-long, spikelike clusters at ends of branches in earliest spring. Berries powdery blue. Takes sun in fog belt; best in partial shade elsewhere. Plant in rich soil with ample organic material incorporated. Water generously. Truly distinguished plant against stone, brick, wood, glass.

M. fortunei. Zones 8–24. Stiffly upright with unbranched 5–6-ft. stems and 6–8-in. leaves divided into 7–13 rather narrow, 2–4-in.-long, dark dull green, toothed leaflets. Flowers (October-November) in short, narrow clusters. More tender than other mahonias, not so showy; pretty in quiet way where vertical effect is desired. Needs shade. Rare.

M. fremontii. DESERT MAHONIA. Zones 8–24. Native to deserts of Southwest. Erect habit, many stems, 3–12 ft. tall. Leaves with 3–5 thick, 1-in.-long leaflets are gray green to yellowish green; edges have very sharp, tough spines. Flowers in 1–1½-in.-long clusters, May-June; fruit dark blue to brown. Grow in full sun or light shade.

M. 'Golden Abundance'. Zones 1–21. Dense, heavily foliaged shrub, 5–6 ft. tall. Glossy green leaves with red midribs; heavy bloom and fruit set.

M. lomariifolia. Zones 6–9, 14–24. Showy plant with erect, little-branched stems to 6–10 ft. Young plants often have single, vertical unbranched stem; with age, plants produce more almost vertical branches from near base. Clustered near ends of these branches are the leaves, to 24 in. long, which are held horizontally. Leaves have outline of stiff, crinkly, barbed ferns. They are made of as many as 47 thick, spiny, glossy green leaflets arranged symmetrically along both sides of central stem. Yellow flowers in winter or earliest spring grow in long, erect clusters at branch tips,

Mahonia lomariifolia

just above topmost cluster of leaves. They are followed by powdery blue berries which birds eat.

Needs shade at least in afternoon to keep its deep green. Prune stems at varying heights to induce branching. Dramatic in entryways, on shaded patios, against shaded wall, in containers. Vertical habit, high leaf masses make it dramatic plant for silhouette lighting effect. Good choice for narrow areas. Just don't place it so close to walk that sharp needles on its leaflets scratch passers-by.

M. nervosa. LONGLEAF MAHONIA. Zones 2–9, 14–17. Native British Columbia to northern California. Low shrub, 2 ft. (rarely 6 ft.) tall. Spreads by underground stems to make good cover. Leaves clustered at stem tips, 10–18 in. long, with 7–21 glossy, bristle-toothed, green, 1–3¾-in.-long leaflets. Yellow flowers in upright clusters 3–6 in. long, April-June. Blue berries. Best in shade; will take sun in cooler areas, becoming very compact. Woodland ground cover, facing for taller mahonias, low barrier planting.

M. nevinii. NEVIN MAHONIA. Zones 8–24. Native to scattered localities, southern California. Many-branched shrub, 3–10 ft. tall, with gray foliage. Leaves with 3–5 leaflets, about 1 in. long, bristly or spiny. Flowers in loose, 1–2-in.-long clusters, March-May, followed by red berries. Sun or light shade, any soil, much or little water. Resistant to oak root fungus. Use individually or as screen, hedge, barrier.

M. pinnata. CALIFORNIA HOLLY GRAPE. Zones 8, 9, 14–24. Native southern Oregon to southern California. Similar to Oregon grape, but leaves are more crinkly, spiny; often lots of red and orange in new growth; plants may grow taller in ideal coastal conditions. Takes drought better than Oregon grape. In Zones 8, 9, 14, 18–21 it's best in light shade. For uniformity, plant selection 'Ken Hartman'.

M. repens. CREEPING MAHONIA. Zones 1–21. Native northern California, eastward to Rocky Mountains. Creeps by underground stems. To 3 ft. tall, spreading habit. Dull bluish green leaves have 3–7 spine-toothed leaflets, turn bronzy in winter. Yellow flowers, April-June, followed by blue berries in short clusters. Good ground cover in sun, partial shade. Will control erosion.

MAIDENHAIR FERN. See *Adiantum*.

MAIDENHAIR TREE. See *Ginkgo biloba*.

MAIDEN'S WREATH. See *Francoa ramosa*.

MAJORANA hortensis. See *Origanum majorana*.

MALCOLMIA maritima. VIRGINIAN STOCK. Summer annual. To 8–15 in., single-stemmed or branching from base, covered with nearly scentless 4-petaled flowers. Colors include white, yellow, pinks, and lilacs to magenta. Leaves are oblong. Sow in place any time except in hot or very cold weather. As with sweet alyssum (*Lobularia maritima*), seed-sowing to bloom takes only 6 weeks. Does not readily reseed. Demands moderately rich soil and full sun for best performance. Good bulb cover.

Malcolmia maritima

MALEPHORA (*Hymenocyclus*). ICE PLANT. For comparison with other ice plants, see Ice Plant. Dense, smooth, gray green to blue green foliage highly resistant to heat, wind, exhaust fumes, fire. Widely used in streetside and freeway plantings. Drought tolerant. Full sun. Flowers over long season, but blooms are scattered rather than in sheets. Attractive to bees.

Malephora luteola

M. crocea. Zones 11–24. Trailing plant to 6 in. high with smooth, gray green foliage, sparse production of reddish yellow flowers nearly throughout year, heaviest in spring. *M. c. purpureo-crocea* has salmon flowers, bluish green foliage. Both are good for erosion control on moderately steep slopes. Hardiest of trailing ice plants. Plant 1–1½ ft. apart.

M. luteola. Zones 15–24. To 1 ft. Light gray green foliage, yellow flowers, May-June and throughout year. Bloom sparse. Not for erosion control.

MALLEE. See *Eucalyptus*.

MALTESE CROSS. See *Lychnis chalcedonica*.

MALUS. CRABAPPLE. Deciduous trees, rarely shrubs. Zones 1–11, 14–21. Handsome pink, white, or red flowers and fruit which is edible, or showy, or sometimes both. For crabapples we use in jellies, see CRABAPPLE. Ornamental crabapples include at least two hundred named kinds, and new ones appear with each year's new catalogues. Chart describes most-used kinds.

Most kinds grow 6–30 ft. high. Leaves are

Malus floribunda

(*Continued on page 369*)

Malus-Crabapple

NAME	GROWTH RATE, HEIGHT & SPREAD	STRUCTURE	FOLIAGE	FLOWERS	FRUIT
MALUS 'Almey'	Moderate to 15 by 15 ft.	Upright growth.	Young leaves purplish, mature ones bronze green. Susceptible to rust and apple scab.	Single scarlet, white at base. April bloom.	Scarlet, hangs on well.
M. 'American Beauty'	Moderate to 30 by 18 ft.	Upright growth.	Bronzy green.	Large, double red.	Sparse, red.
M. arnoldiana ARNOLD CRABAPPLE	Fairly rapid, 20 by 30 ft.	Broad, spreading, with long arching branches.	Medium texture, fairly large leaf.	Buds red. Flowers pink, fading white, fragrant, to 2 in. across.	Yellow and red. Sept. through Nov.
M. atrosanguinea CARMINE CRABAPPLE	Moderate to 18 by 18 ft.	Upright branches, drooping tips. Open, irregular, rather sparse.	Purplish green, with more sheen than average crabapple.	Fragrant, crimson to rose pink; profuse; late April-May.	Yellow, aging brown and hanging on through winter in withered state.

(*Continued on next page*)

NAME	GROWTH RATE, HEIGHT & SPREAD	STRUCTURE	FOLIAGE	FLOWERS	FRUIT
M. baccata 'Columnaris'	Moderate to 30 by 5–8 ft.	Narrow, upright, columnar, spreading somewhat in old plants.	Dense. Resistant to rust in Northwest.	White, fragrant 1-in. flowers in April.	Yellow and scarlet.
M. coronaria 'Charlotte'	Moderate to 30 by 30 ft.	Rounded, broad at base of crown.	Dense.	Pink, double, 2 in. across. Late May; fragrant.	Large, green, sparsely produced.
M. 'Dolgo'	Moderate to 40 by 40 ft.	Willowy, spreading; prune for good framework.	Reddish green, dense.	Early spring blooming. Flowers profuse, white, single.	Cherrylike clusters of red, 1¼-in. fruit, Aug.-Oct. Flavor good.
M. 'Dorothea'	Moderate to 25 by 25 ft.	Dense, rounded.	Dense, fine textured.	May blooming, double, 2-in. pink flowers. Blooms young.	Marble sized, bright yellow; effective fall and early winter.
M. floribunda JAPANESE FLOWERING CRABAPPLE	Moderate to 20 by 30 ft.	One form is rounded, dense, with irregular, angular branches. The other is more upright.	Dense, fine textured. Resistant to rust in Northwest.	Red to pink in bud, opening white. Extremely profuse.	Small, yellow and red, Aug.-Oct.
M. 'Hopa'	Fast to 25 by 20 ft.	Upright branches spreading with weight of fruit.	Dense, dark green with brownish cast. Subject to rust in Northwest. Very susceptible to scab and fireblight.	Fragrant, single, rose red, 1½ in. April flowering. One of best in southern California.	Orange red, coloring early. Profuse. Good for jelly.
M. hupehensis (M. theifera) TEA CRABAPPLE	Moderate to 15 by 20 ft.	Rigid branches grow in 45° angles from short trunk. Side branches short, spurlike. General effect Y shaped.	Dense on side branches, but these are spaced well apart from each other.	Deep pink buds, pink flowers fading white, fragrant. Early May. Very profuse.	Not ornamental.
M. ioensis 'Plena' BECHTEL CRABAPPLE	Moderate to 25 by 20 ft. 'Klehm's Improved Bechtel' is a better grower.	Coarse branches, rather angular, eventually vase shaped.	Sparse, coarse, soft green.	Large, very double, pink, fragrant. Resemble rambler rose flowers. M. ioensis 'Nova' has deeper flower color.	Rarely borne, green, not ornamental.
M. 'Katherine'	Slow to 20 by 20 ft.	Loose and open.	Dark green, not dense.	Double, light pink fading white, very large—to 2¼ in. Alternate bloom; heavy one year, light the next.	Dull red, not especially showy.
M. micromalus (M. kaido) MIDGET CRABAPPLE (Kaido is Japanese for crabapple)	Slow to 20 by 15 ft.	One strain is upright and dense. The other is smaller with irregular branches.	Dark green.	Single, unfading pink, very profuse in April. Fragrant.	Red or greenish red, not showy.
M. 'Oekonomierat Echtermeyer' ('Pink Weeper') WEEPING CRABAPPLE	Moderate to 15 ft. Spread depends on pruning.	Weeping branches. Usually grafted high on a standard crabapple. Cut out branches that grow stiffly upright.	Opening purplish, later bronzy green.	Purplish red, 1½ in. wide, all along drooping branchlets.	Purple red, 1 in., effective in fall.
M. 'Pink Perfection'	Moderate to 20 by 20 ft.	Full, rounded crown.	Thick, heavy, green; holds color to fall.	Red buds open to large double pink flowers.	Yellow and insignificant.
M. 'Pink Spire'	Moderate to 15 by 10 ft.	Narrow, upright grower.	Red purple in spring, turning bronzy green.	Rose pink.	Small, purplish red.
M. 'Purple Wave'	Moderate to 10–15 by 10 ft.	Spreading, broad headed.	Dark purplish green.	Large, single to semidouble, rose red fading to purplish pink.	Dark purple red, 1 in.
M. purpurea 'Aldenhamensis' ALDENHAM CRABAPPLE	Fast to 20 by 20 ft.	Somewhat irregular round head, dense.	Purplish leaves and purplish bark on twigs.	Semidouble, purplish red, large. May, sometimes reblooming in fall.	Purplish red, 1 in.

NAME	GROWTH RATE, HEIGHT & SPREAD	STRUCTURE	FOLIAGE	FLOWERS	FRUIT
M. p. 'Eleyi' ELEY CRABAPPLE	Fast to 20 by 20 ft.	Irregular, open, graceful.	Dark green, with reddish veins and stalks. Subject to apple scab.	Wine red, 1¼ in., April.	Heavy bearer of ¾-in. purple red fruit.
M. 'Radiant'	Fast to 20 by 20 ft.	Broad, rounded crown.	New foliage purple red, aging green.	Deep red buds open to deep pink single blooms.	Bright red, ½ in. wide. Color in midsummer.
M. 'Red Jade'	Moderate to 15 by 15 ft.	Long, slender, weeping branches. Charming, irregular habit.	Dark green.	Small, white, profuse in April-May.	Heavy crop of bright red fruit hold late into fall, are showy on weeping branches.
M. 'Red Silver'	Fast to 15 by 15 ft.	Irregular, branches angular with tips drooping slightly.	Reddish or purplish bronze silvered with silky hairs.	Deep wine red, April.	Dark purplish red, ¾ in., good for jelly.
M. 'Royalty'	Moderate to 15 by 15 ft.	Dense, moundlike crown. Extremely cold hardy.	Same dark purple as purple-leaf plum. Resists scab.	Single, purplish crimson.	Dark red, nearly ¾ in. across.
M. sargentii SARGENT CRABAPPLE	Slow to 10 by 20 ft.	Dense, broad shrub with zigzag branching.	Dark green, often lobed at base.	White, small but profuse, fragrant. Pink in *M. s.* 'Rosea'. Mid-May.	Red, tiny, profuse, lasting late.
M. scheideckeri SCHEIDECKER CRABAPPLE	Moderate to 20 by 15 ft.	Dense, upright.	Dense, dark green.	Semidouble, rose pink. April to May.	Small, yellow, holding into November.
M. 'Snowcloud'	Moderate to 25 by 12 ft.	Upright, narrow.	Dark green, glossy, heavy textured.	Pink buds open to double white flowers.	Yellow, sparse and insignificant.
M. 'Snowdrift'	Moderate to 20–25 by 20 ft.	Rounded, dense crown.	Good green; scab resistant.	Red buds open into single white flowers. Long bloom period.	Orange red fruit, less than ½ in. across, hang on long time.
M. 'Strathmore'	Moderate to fast to 20 by 10 ft.	Narrow, upright, pyramidal.	Reddish purple leaves hold color all summer; deepen to scarlet in fall. Subject to apple scab.	Deep pink to reddish pink.	Small red fruit.
M. tschonoskii	Fast to 40 by 30 ft.	Symmetrical broad cone.	Dark green, white beneath, turning to orange, purple, and scarlet in fall.	Single white 1-in. flowers, not showy.	One-in.-wide green apples with red cheeks are not showy.
M. zumi calocarpa	Moderate to 25 by 15 ft.	Pyramidal, dense, branching, branchlets weeping.	Densely foliaged; larger leaves lobed.	Opening soft pink, fading white; fragrant; late April-early May.	Small, ½ in., glossy, bright red, holding well into winter.

pointed ovals, often fuzzy, from deep green to nearly purple. Longer-lived than flowering peaches, hardier and more tolerant of wet soil than flowering cherries or other flowering stone fruit, flowering crabapples are among the most useful and least troublesome of flowering trees, even if spring color is less striking than that of flowering peach or cherry. Plant bare-root in winter or early spring; set out container plants any time. Good well-drained garden soil is best, but crabapples will take mildly acid or alkaline soil, or rocky soil. They take heat. Prune only to build good framework or to correct shape; annual pruning is neither necessary nor desirable.

Malus floribunda

Malus sargentii

Diseases and pests are few; fireblight can be a problem, but usually is not. The same pests that affect apple also prey on crabapple; controls are simple. If you or your neighbors grow apples, or if you wish to use crabapples from your tree, spray to control codling moth. Scale, aphids, spider mites, and tent caterpillars may require spraying. Scab, powdery mildew, and crabapple rust are serious problems in the Northwest. Ask your nurseryman about rust-resistant varieties. Fungicide sprays will control them. Some are rust resistant; see chart. Most are resistant to oak root fungus. Birds are attracted to fruit.

Make fine lawn trees, or use in rows along driveways or walks. Planted near fences they will heighten screening effect, provide blossoms and fruit, and still give planting room for primroses, spring bulbs, or shade loving summer bedding plants. Good espaliers.

MAMMILLARIA. Cactus. Zones 8–24. Small, cylindrical or globe shaped, either single-stemmed or clustered. Plants mostly grow 2–6 in. high. Flowers generally small, arranged in circle near top of plant, red, pink, yellow, or white. Easy to grow in sun; give ample water during summer. Chiefly grown in pots by collectors. Specialists offer as many as 100 species.

For the plant sold as *M. vivipara,* see *Coryphantha.*

MANDARIN ORANGE. See *Citrus.*

Mammillaria candida

MANDEVILLA. Evergreen or deciduous vines. Known for showy flowers. Includes plants formerly known as *Dipladenia.*

M. 'Alice du Pont' (*Mandevilla splendens, M. amabilis, Dipladenia splendens, D. amoena*). House or greenhouse plant; outdoors Zones 21–24. Evergreen vine to 20–30 ft., much less as usually grown in pots or tubs. Twining stems produce dark green, glossy, oval leaves 3–8 in. long. Clusters of flowers appear among leaves from April-November. Flowers 2–4 in. across, pure pink. Even very small plant in 4-in. pot will bloom. Give plant frame, trellis, or stake for support. Pinch young plant to induce bushiness. Rich soil, ample water while it's putting on growth; full sun coastal areas, part shade inland. Spray for spider mites.

Mandevilla 'Alice du Pont'

M. laxa (*M. suaveolens*). CHILEAN JASMINE. Deciduous vine. Zones 4–9, 14–21. Twines to 15 ft. or more. Leaves are long ovals, heart shaped at base, 2–6 in. long. Summer flowers white, clustered, 2 in. across, trumpet shaped, powerfully fragrant (like gardenia). Sun, rich soil, ample water. If plant becomes badly tangled, cut it to ground in winter; it will bloom on new growth. Root hardy to about 5°F.

MANGIFERA indica. MANGO. Evergreen tree. Zones 23, 24. Grows to large size in tropics. In mildest parts of southern California often survives for years, but may remain shrubby and is likely to fruit only in most favored, frost free locations. Yellow to reddish flowers in long clusters at branch ends. Fruit that follow are oval, to 6 in. long, green to reddish or yellowish; contain large seeds and flesh that's peach flavored with varnish or turpentine overtones. Leaves are large and handsome, often coppery red or purple at time of expanding, later dark green and 8–16 in. long. Needs steady moisture, but tolerates fairly poor, shallow soils.

Mangifera indica

MANGO. See *Mangifera indica.*

MANNA GUM. See *Eucalyptus viminalis.*

MANUKA. See *Leptospermum scoparium.*

MANZANITA. See *Arctostaphylos.*

MANZANOTE. See *Olmediella betschlerana.*

MAPLE. See *Acer.*

MARANTA leuconeura. PRAYER PLANT, RABBIT TRACKS. Perennial. House or greenhouse plant with leafy stems, usually less than 1 ft. high. Leaves 7–8 in. long and half as wide, short stalked, becoming whitish along midrib and veins; brown

Maranta leuconeura

spots toward margin account for name "rabbit tracks." Leaves fold upward at night; hence other common name, "prayer plant." In variety *kerchoviana,* undersurface of leaves is grayish and spotted with red. Small flowers are white with purple spots.

Grow out of direct sunlight. Must have warmth, occasional trimming, lots of water, and regular feeding (fish emulsion is good) to be at its best. Excellent in dish gardens, terrariums, or shallow pots.

MARGUERITE. See *Chrysanthemum frutescens.*

MARIGOLD. See *Tagetes.*

MARIPOSA LILY. See *Calochortus venustus.*

MARJORAM. See *Origanum majorana.*

MARLOCK. See *Eucalyptus.*

MARMALADE BUSH. See *Streptosolen jamesonii.*

MARRUBIUM vulgare. HOREHOUND. Perennial herb. All Zones. To 1–3 ft. Wrinkled, woolly, aromatic, gray green leaves; white mintlike flowers in whorls on foot-long, branching stems. Grows in poor, sandy, dry soil, full sun. Sow seeds in spring in flats; later transplant to 12 in. apart. As garden plant, it's rather weedy looking but can serve as edging in gray garden. Used for medicinal purposes and in candy. Foliage lasts well in bouquets.

Marrubium vulgare

MARSH MARIGOLD. See *Caltha palustris.*

MATERNITY PLANT. See *Kalanchoe daigremontiana.*

MATILIJA POPPY. See *Romneya coulteri.*

MATRICARIA recutita (*M. chamomilla*). CHAMOMILE. Summer annual. This is the chamomile which yields a fragrant tea with overtones of pineapple. Plants grow 2–2½ ft. tall, with finely cut, almost fernlike foliage and daisylike white and yellow flower heads an inch (or less) wide. Grows easily in full sun, ordinary soil from seed sown in late winter or spring. Needs little or no irrigation once started. Has become naturalized in some areas. Dried flowers are the parts used in making tea.

Plants or seeds sold as *Matricaria* 'White Stars', 'Golden Ball', and 'Snowball' are varieties of *Chrysanthemum parthenium.* Chamomile sold as walk-on ground cover is *Chamaemelum nobile* (*Anthemis nobilis*). Its flowers also yield medicinal-tasting, rather bitter tea.

Matricaria recutita

MATTHIOLA. STOCK. Annuals (technically, biennials or perennials grown as annuals). All have gray green, long, narrow leaves and flowers in erect clusters.

M. incana. STOCK. Valued for fragrance, cut flowers, garden decoration. Leaves oblong to 4 in. long. Flowers single or double, an inch wide, in spikes. Colors include white, pink, red, purple, lavender, cream. Blues and reds are purple toned, yellows tend toward cream. Spicy-sweet fragrance.

Matthiola incana

Stock needs light, fertile soil, good drainage, cool weather. Valuable winter flowers in Zones 8, 9, 12–24—there, set out plants in early fall for winter or early spring bloom. Plants take moderate frost, but will not set flower buds if nights are too chilly; late planting will mean late flowers. Where rainfall is heavy, plant in raised beds to insure good drainage, prevent root rot. In Zones 1–7, 10, 11, plant in earliest spring to get bloom before hot weather.

Many strains available. Column stock and Double Giant Flowering are unbranched, 2–3 ft. tall, and can be planted 6–8 in. apart in rows; ideal for cutting. Giant Imperial strain is branched, 2–2½ ft. tall, comes in straight colors or mixed. Trysomic or Ten Weeks stock is branched, 15–18 in tall. Trysomic Seven Weeks strain is 12–15 in. tall.

M. longipetala bicornis. EVENING SCENTED STOCK. Summer annual. Foot-tall plant with lance shaped leaves to 3½ in. long. Small purplish flowers are closed and inconspicuous by day, wonderfully fragrant at night. Full sun. Routine watering.

MATTRESS VINE. See *Muehlenbeckia complexa.*

MAYBUSH, MAYDAY TREE. See *Prunus padus.*

MAYPOP. See *Passiflora incarnata.*

MAYTENUS boaria. MAYTEN TREE. Evergreen tree. Zones 8, 9, 14–21. Slow to moderate growth to an eventual 30–50 ft.; 20 ft. by 15 ft. in spread at 12 years is typical. Long, pendulous branchlets hang down from branches, giving tree daintiness and grace. Habit and leaves (1–2 in. long) somewhat like small-scale weeping willow. Better tree for patio than weeping willow—neater and without invasive roots. Flowers and fruit inconspicuous.

Maytenus boaria

Good drainage a necessity. Stake securely when planting. There will be much side growth; remove unwanted growth along trunk, or, if you wish, preserve some side branches for multiple trunk effect. Will take some drought when established, but is lusher and greener with adequate water. Sometimes may show partial defoliation after cold snaps or at blooming time; recovery is rapid. Resistant to oak root fungus. For uniformity, plant cutting-grown variety 'Green Showers'; the weeping branchlets of this variety are densely clad with deep green leaves that are a little broader than most seedling trees.

Choice lawn tree. Locate to display its pattern effectively—against walls in entryway or patio, in featured raised planting beds, near outdoor living areas.

MAZUS reptans. Perennial. Zones 1–7 (freezes to ground in winter), 14–24 (evergreen). Slender stems creep and root along ground, send up leafy branches 1–2 in. tall. Leaves an inch long, narrowish, bright green, with a few teeth on edges. Flowers (spring, early summer) in clusters of 2–5, purplish blue with white and yellow markings, about ¾ in. across. In shape, the flowers resemble those of mimulus. Sun or very light shade; rich, moist soil. Rock gardens or small-scale ground cover. Takes very light foot traffic.

Mazus reptans

MEADOW RUE. See *Thalictrum.*

MEADOW SAFFRON. See *Colchicum autumnale.*

MEADOW SWEET. See *Astilbe.*

MECONOPSIS. Perennials. Rare plants related to poppy. Ardent collectors and shade garden enthusiasts sometimes attempt the many species offered by specialist seed firms. Most are difficult; two listed here are not too hard in right climate.

Meconopsis betonicifolia

M. betonicifolia *(M. baileyi)*. HIMALAYAN POPPY. Zones 1–7, 17. Tall, leafy, short-lived perennial 2–4 ft. tall with hairy leaves and 3–4-in.-wide silky poppies of sky blue or rosy lavender, centered with yellow stamens. Needs shade, humid air, coolness, loose, acid soil, summer watering. Try it with rhododendrons.

M. cambrica. WELSH POPPY. Zones 1–9, 14–17. Short-lived perennial with 3-in. yellow or orange flowers on 1-ft. stems. Fairly easy, self-sows. Gray green divided leaves. Full sun or light shade near coast, part shade inland. Can take a little or a lot of summer water.

MEDAKE. See *Arundinaria simonii* under Bamboo.

MEDITERRANEAN FAN PALM. See *Chamaerops humilis.*

MELALEUCA. Evergreen trees and shrubs. Narrow, sometimes needlelike leaves, and clustered flowers with prominent stamens. Each cluster resembles a bottlebrush, and some melaleucas are called bottlebrushes, although that name is more generally applied to *Callistemon*. Clusters of woody seed capsules hang on for several years, forming odd, decorative cylinders around twigs and branches. Flowers attract birds.

Melaleuca linariifolia

Most melaleucas stand heat, wind, poor soil, drought, and salt air; exceptions, noted below, are important. Most are vigorous and fast growing; control by cutting back selected branches to a well-placed side branch. Shearing makes plants dense and lumpish. Smaller melaleucas are good screening materials; some of the larger ones are useful as flowering or shade trees. Many have interestingly contorted branches and bark that peels in thick paperlike layers.

M. armillaris. DROOPING MELALEUCA. Shrub or small tree. Zones 9, 12–24. To 15–30 ft. Furrowed gray bark peels in strips near base of trunk. Drooping branches. Light green, needlelike leaves to 1 in. long. Fluffy white flowers in 1–3½-in.-long spikes, spring to fall. Tough and adaptable, especially useful in sea winds. Clipped hedge or unclipped informal screen (prickly leaves a real deterrent), or, with training, a sprawling shrub or small tree. Becomes picturesque with age.

M. decussata. LILAC MELALEUCA. Large shrub or small tree. Zones 9, 12–24. Grows 8–20 ft. tall with equal spread. Brown, shreddy bark. Tiny (½ in. long) leaves close-set on arching, pendulous branches. Lilac to purple flowers in 1-in. spikes, late spring-summer. Will stand some neglect. Use it to supply big masses of fine-textured, bluish foliage. Thinning will improve its appearance by showing off trunk, branch character.

M. elliptica. Shrub or small tree. Zones 9, 12–24. To 8–15 ft. high. Brown, shreddy bark. Roundish, ½-in.-long leaves mostly at ends of fanlike branches. Large, showy, red to crimson bottlebrushes to 3½ in. long, on side branches, early spring to fall.

M. ericifolia. HEATH MELALEUCA. Shrub or small tree. Zones 9, 12–24. To 10–25 ft. Bark tan or gray, soft, fibrous. Dark green, needlelike, 1-in. leaves like those of heather. Yellowish white flowers in 1-in. spikes; blooms early spring. Fast-growing and tolerant of alkaline soil and poor drainage; good near beach. Attractive multitrunked tree.

M. hypericifolia. DOTTED MELALEUCA. Shrub. Zones 9, 12–24. Grows 6–10 ft. tall, with thin, peeling bark, drooping branches. Coppery green to dull green 1¼-in. leaves, bright orange red flowers in dense 2-in. clusters, late spring through winter—often hidden by foliage. Can be clipped into hedge, but will bloom more profusely as informal, unclipped screen. Not suited right at beach, but takes ocean wind, drought.

M. linariifolia. FLAXLEAF PAPERBARK. Tree. Zones 9, 13–23. To 30 ft., with umbrellalike crown. White bark sheds in papery flakes. Slender branchlets. Bright green or bluish green, 1¼-in.-long leaves are stiff, needlelike. Numerous fluffy spikes of small white flowers in summer give effect of snow on branches. Young plants willowy, need staking until trunk firms up; prune out lower branches to shape.

M. nesophila. PINK MELALEUCA. Tree or large shrub. Zones 9, 13, 16–24. Fast growth to 15–20, possibly 30 ft. Grows naturally as small tree; unpruned, produces gnarled, heavy branches that sprawl or ascend in picturesque patterns. Thick, spongy bark. Gray green, thick, roundish, 1-in. leaves. Roundish (to inch-wide) mauve flower brushes at branch ends, produced most of year, fade to white with yellow tips. Takes beach winds and spray; poor, rocky soil; desert heat; much water or practically no water. Use as big informal screen, tree, or shear as hedge.

M. quinquenervia (usually sold as *M. leucadendra*). CAJEPUT TREE. Tree. Zones 9, 13, 16, 17, 20–24. Upright, open growth to 20–40 ft. Young branches pendulous. Trunk has thick, spongy, light brown to whitish bark that peels off in sheets. Leaves stiff, narrowly oval, pale green, shiny, 2–4 in. long. Young leaves have silky hairs. Foliage turns purple with light frost. Flowers yellowish white (sometimes pink or purple), in 2–3-in. spikes, summer and fall. Can take much or little water. Good street tree.

M. styphelioides. Tree. Zones 9, 13–24. Grows 20–40 ft. Pendulous branchlets; lacy, open growth habit. Thick, pale, spongy, light tan bark becomes charcoal with age, peels off in papery layers. Leaves to ¾ in. long, ¼ in. wide, sometimes twisted, prickly to touch, light green. Creamy white flowers in 1–2-in. brushes, summer through fall. Thrives in any soil; resistant to oak root fungus. Good lawn tree. Best trained with multiple trunks.

MELAMPODIUM leucanthum. Short-lived perennial. Zones 1–3, 10–13. Native to Arizona, New Mexico, Mexico, Texas. Foot-tall, foot-wide clumps of narrow gray foliage are topped by clouds of inch-wide daisies, white with yellow centers. Rays are broad and full, and plant is showy when in bloom. In mild-winter climates it blooms off and on during winter months and more heavily from April to October—if given water. Where freezing temperatures are routine, expect spring and summer bloom only. Plants need full sun and fast draining soil; in nature they grow principally in decomposed granite. If plants become too straggly for good looks, cut them back in autumn.

Melampodium leucanthum

MELIA azedarach. CHINA-BERRY. Deciduous tree. Zones 6, 8–24. Spreading tree to 30–50 ft. high. Leaves 1–3 ft. long, cut into many 1–2-in.-long, narrow or oval, toothed leaflets. Loose clusters of lilac flowers in spring or early summer, fragrant in evening, followed by ½-in. yellow, hard, berrylike fruit. Fruit poisonous if eaten in quantity, but birds enjoy them.

M. a.'Umbraculiformis'. TEXAS UMBRELLA TREE. Less picturesque but far more common. It has dense, spreading, dome shaped crown and drooping leaves. Grows to 30 ft. Gives rich green color, dense shade in hottest, driest climates, even in poor alkaline soil. Leaves turn gold in autumn. Stands all except strongest ocean winds. Sometimes suckers, and wood is brittle, but is valuable in areas where trees are hard to grow.

Melia azedarach 'Umbraculiformis'

MELIANTHUS major. HONEY BUSH. Evergreen shrub. Zones 8, 9, 12–24. Soft-wooded plant of very fast growth to 12–14 ft., easily kept much lower. Stems upright or sprawling and spreading, slightly branched. Striking foliage. Leaves a foot long, grayish green, divided into 9–11 strongly toothed leaflets—have disagreeable odor when brushed or bruised. Flowers reddish brown, 1 in. long, in foot-long spikes, late winter, early spring.

Melianthus major

Adaptable in most soils, most locations, but best in some shade in desert and other hot gardens. To get tall plants, stake a few stems; for sprawling, bulky effect, shorten some stems in early spring before new growth begins. Needs grooming. Spray to control whitefly. Excellent when used as silhouette in raised beds, sprawling over wall, in containers, with succulents or foliage plants.

M. minor. Rare plant occasionally seen at plant sales or collectors' gardens. Leaves are much smaller (6–7 in.), on shorter (3 ft.) plants.

MELISSA officinalis. LEMON BALM, SWEET BALM. Perennial herb. All Zones. To 2 ft. Light green, heavily veined leaves with lemon scent. White flowers unimportant. Shear occasionally to keep compact. Spreads rapidly. Grow in rich moist soil in sun or part shade. Very hardy. Propagate from seed or root divisions. Self-sows. Leaves used in drinks, fruit cups, salads, with fish. Dried leaves help give lemon tang to sachets, potpourris. Cut branches keep well in arrangements.

Melissa officinalis

MELON, MUSKMELON, CANTALOUPE. Annual. (The true cantaloupe, a hard-shelled melon, is rarely grown in this country.) To ripen to full sweetness, a melon needs 2½–4 months of heat. Foggy summer days or cool days don't help. Gardeners in cool-summer climates should plant melons in warmest southern exposures. Both in cool-summer climates and interior short-summer climates, start plants indoors in peat pots a few weeks before last frost date. Truly tropical plants, melons perish in even light frost.

Melon

Melons need considerable space (dimensions described below) in full sun. You can grow melons on sun-bathed trellises, but heavy fruit have to be supported in individual cloth slings.

Principal types are muskmelons ("cantaloupes") and late melons. The former are ribbed and have a netted skin and (usually) salmon-colored flesh; these are most widely adapted to various western climates. Good muskmelons (best types for cooler climates) are 'Hale's Best', 'Honey Rock', and the hybrids 'Ambrosia', 'Mainerock' (early), 'Samson', and 'Saticoy'. Hybrids excel others in disease resistance and uniformity of size and quality. Recent introductions among small, tasty, highly perfumed melons from Mediterranean (and hybrids of these), are white-fleshed 'Ha-Ogen' and orange-fleshed 'Chaca' and 'Charentais'. Late melons will ripen only where there is a long, hot, rather dry summer (Zones 8, 9, 12–14, 18, 19). 'Persian', 'Honey Dew', 'Honey Ball', 'Golden Beauty Casaba', and 'Crenshaw' are typical late melons.

Except as noted above, sow seeds 2 weeks after average date of last frost. Soil should be light and well drained. Best planted on gently rounded mounds 6 ft. wide, a few inches high at center, and as long as your garden will permit. On south side of mounds make furrows 10 in. wide and 6 in. deep for irrigation. Water well until furrows are filled. Plant 6 or 7 seeds about 1 in. deep, spaced within an 8–10-in. circle, 6 in. or so away from furrow. Space these circles (hills) 3 ft. apart. This system permits watering plants from below without wetting foliage.

When plants are well established, thin each hill to the best two, and begin to train them away from furrow. Fill furrow with water from time to time, but do not keep soil soaked. Feed (again in furrow) every six weeks. Harvest muskmelon and 'Persian' melon when stems begin to crack away from melon end. 'Honey Dew' and 'Casaba' fruit are ready when rinds turn yellow; 'Crenshaw' melons turn mostly yellow, but show some green even when ripe. Most reliable way to determine degree of ripeness of these melons is to smell blossom end. Ripe ones have pleasant, fruity perfume.

MENTHA. MINT. Perennial herbs and ground cover. Spread rapidly by underground stems. Once established, surprisingly drought tolerant. Can be quite invasive. Grow almost anywhere but perform best in light, medium-rich, moist soil, partial shade. Contain in pot or box to keep in bounds. Propagate from runners. Keep flowers cut off. Replant every 3 years.

M. gentilis. GOLDEN APPLE MINT. All Zones. To 2 ft. Smooth, deep green leaves, variegated yellow. Flowers inconspicuous. Use in flavoring foods. Foliage excellent in mixed bouquets.

M. piperita. PEPPERMINT. All Zones. To 3 ft. Strong-scented, toothed, 3-in.-long leaves. Small purple flowers in 1–3-in.

Mentha spicata

spikes. Leaves good for flavoring tea. *M. p. citrata,* ORANGE MINT, BERGAMOT MINT grows to 2 ft. and has broad, 2-in.-long leaves, small lavender flowers. Used in potpourris, or like other mints in flavoring foods. Crushed leaves have slight orange flavor.

M. pulegium. PENNYROYAL. Zones 4–24. Creeping plant grows a few inches tall with nearly round 1-in. leaves. Small lavender flowers in tight, short whorls. Strong mint fragrance and flavor; reputed to be poisonous in large quantities, but such quantities not needed to flavor sauces. Needs cool, moist site, with shade in hottest areas.

M. requienii. JEWEL MINT OF CORSICA. Creeping, mat forming perennial. Zones 5–9, 12–24. Spreads at moderate to rapid rate, grows only ½ in. high. Tiny, round, bright green leaves give mossy effect. Tiny light purple flowers in summer. Set divisions 6 in. apart for ground cover in sun or part shade. Needs moisture, and disappears during winter in colder areas. Delightful minty or sagelike fragrance when leaves are bruised or crushed under foot.

M. spicata. SPEARMINT. All Zones. To 1½–2 ft. Dark green leaves, slightly smaller than peppermint; leafy spikes of purplish flowers. Use leaves fresh from garden or dried for lamb, in cold drinks, as garnish, in apple jelly.

M. suaveolens (usually sold as *M. rotundifolia*). APPLE MINT. All Zones. Stiff stems grow 20–30 in. tall. Rounded leaves are slightly hairy, gray green, 1–4 in. long. Purplish white flowers in 2–3 in. spikes. Leaves have apple-mint fragrance. *M. s.* 'Variegata', PINEAPPLE MINT, has leaves with white markings, faint fragrance of pineapple.

MENTZELIA. BLAZING STAR. Annuals, biennials, or perennials. All Zones. Native to desert or semidesert areas of western U.S. They tolerate heat, wind, poor soil but require good drainage and full sun. Star shaped yellow blossoms are large and showy.

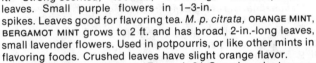

M. laevicaulis. Biennial or short-lived perennial to 3–3½ ft. tall, rough and ungainly with 3–7-in.-long, narrow leaves.

Mentzelia lindleyi

Spectacular pale yellow, 4-in.-wide stars open in evening; plant often called evening star. It requires summer drought and excellent drainage. Best use is on bare banks, where it's perfectly at home.

M. lindleyi. Summer annual 1–4 ft. tall, usually narrow, sometimes spreading to 1½ ft. Leaves light green, rough with short hairs. Flowers bright yellow with orange or reddish center ring

and big brush of yellow stamens. Blooms April to June. Sow seed in fall, winter, or earliest spring where plants are to bloom; give ample water until plants come into bloom, then reduce or stop watering. Use alone or in wildflower mixtures.

MERATIA. See *Chimonanthus.*

MERTENSIA. Perennials. Zones 1–21. Resemble giant forget-me-nots, and are related to them. Plants appear and flower early, go dormant soon after seeding, usually before midsummer. Foliage usually smooth gray green or blue green. Flowers nodding, in loose, gradually uncoiling clusters, pink or lavender in bud opening to blue bells, sometimes with pinkish cast. Hardy and attractive in shade with ample moisture during growth and bloom. Good with ferns, trilliums in woodland gardens or with naturalized daffodils.

Mertensia virginica

M. ciliata. CHIMING BELLS, MOUNTAIN BLUEBELL. Native to damp places in Rocky Mountains. Grows 1–3 ft. tall, with ½–¾-in. flowers. Several other species grow in mountainous areas of West; most are lower growing.

M. virginica. VIRGINIA BLUEBELLS. From eastern U.S., and most widely planted species. Grows 1–2 ft. tall; flowers are 1 in. long.

MERYTA sinclairi. PUKA. Shrub or small tree. Zones 17, 23, 24. House plant anywhere. Young plants have single, upright stems several feet tall with huge (8–20 in.),

Meryta sinclairi

leathery, oval, dark green leaves. Older plants eventually branch and become broad, rounded trees 15–18 ft. tall. Flowers, fruit inconspicuous, not often seen outside its native New Zealand. Rich soil, ample water and feeding, light shade.

MESCAL BEAN. See *Sophora secundiflora.*

MESEMBRYANTHEMUM crystallinum. ICE PLANT. Summer annual. Least ornamental of many plants commonly called *Mesembryanthemum* or ice plant, but now considered the only true *Mesembryanthemum.* Grow in full sun. Needs little or no water once established. For other, showier kinds used as ground covers or ornamentals, see entry under ICE PLANT.

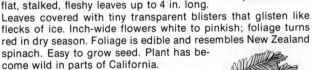

M. crystallinum is a sprawling plant a few inches tall and several feet wide with oval, flat, stalked, fleshy leaves up to 4 in. long.

Mesembryanthemum crystallinum

Leaves covered with tiny transparent blisters that glisten like flecks of ice. Inch-wide flowers white to pinkish; foliage turns red in dry season. Foliage is edible and resembles New Zealand spinach. Easy to grow seed. Plant has become wild in parts of California.

METASEQUOIA glyptostroboides. DAWN REDWOOD. Deciduous conifer. Zones 3–9, 14–24. To 80–90 ft. high. Looks somewhat like coast redwood *(Sequoia sempervirens)* but differs in several ways. Cones are much smaller than those of coast redwood. Leaves are soft to the touch and light, bright green; those of coast redwood are dark green and somewhat stiff. Dawn redwood's light brown branchlets turn upward; those of coast redwood usually stand out horizontally. Most important, foliage of dawn redwood turns light bronze in the

Metasequoia glyptostroboides

autumn and then it falls; coast redwood is evergreen.

Stands temperatures from −15° to 105°F., but suffers winter wind damage in cold, dry areas. Salt winds cause foliage burn, as does hot sunlight in enclosed areas. Grows best in moist, well-drained soil containing peat moss or leaf mold; takes lawn watering well. Resistant to oak root fungus.

Best use is in groves, where it brings something of the beauty of a redwood grove to cold-winter areas. However, also good for single planting—swelling buds and bright, silky new needles are real treat in spring. Structurally interesting even when bare. Trunks of older trees show rugged, fluted bases. Grows very fast when young, sometimes 4–6 ft. a year in California, less in colder areas. Young tree will grow satisfactorily in large tub or box.

MESQUITE. See *Prosopis glandulosa torreyana.*

MESSMATE. See *Eucalyptus.*

METAKE. See *Pseudosasa japonica* under Bamboo.

METROSIDEROS. Evergreen trees or large shrubs. Native to New Zealand. Plants generally branch heavily from ground up, require careful staking and pruning to bring into tree form. Leaves firm, leathery, densely spaced on branches. Flowers, clustered at ends of branches, are red (rarely yellow or white). Dense, clustered stamens make the show; along coast, trees rival *Eucalyptus ficifolia* in flower color.

Best near coast; frost, dry air limit success inland. Most dependable first-line trees near beach, tolerating wind and salt spray. Water through the first two dry seasons; then they should be drought resistant. Useful lawn trees; good street trees, but can break sidewalk growing in narrow parking strip.

Metrosideros excelsus

M. excelsus (*M. tomentosus*). NEW ZEALAND CHRISTMAS TREE, POHUTUKAWA. Zones 17, 23, 24. Grows to 30 ft. or more; foliage on young plants smooth glossy green; older plants develop leaves which are dark green above, white, woolly underneath. Dark scarlet flowers in big clusters cover ends of branches in May-July (December in New Zealand, hence common name "Christmas Tree"). "Pohutukawa" means "drenched with spray," and describes very well seashore conditions where wild plants grow. There is a yellow-flowered variety, 'Aurea'.

M. kermadecensis (*M. villosus*). Zones 17, 20–24. Shrubby, fairly upright plant. Smaller than *M. excelsus,* with smaller grayish leaves, red flowers produced sporadically through year. Showier than *M. excelsus* when in bloom. Has withstood 22° F. *M. v.* 'Variegata' has leaves with creamy markings.

M. robustus. NORTH ISLAND RATA. Zones 17, 23, 24. To 45 ft. or more. Leaves 1–1½ in. long, dark green, roundish. New shoots and foliage coppery red. Flowers (in midsummer) scarlet. Blooms young.

M. umbellatus (*M. lucidus*). SOUTHERN RATA. Zones 16, 17, 20–24. Slow growth to large bush, eventually may become tree 45–60 ft. tall. New leaves flushed red; mature leaves 1–3½ in. long, silky when young, later glossy. Midsummer flowers are scarlet. This bush is slow-growing, as well as very slow to come into bloom (15–20 years). Tolerant of frosts and constant wind. Needs plenty of water.

MEXICAN BLUE PALM. See *Brahea armata.*

MEXICAN FAN PALM. See *Washingtonia robusta.*

MEXICAN FIRE BUSH. See *Kochia scoparia trichophylla.*

MEXICAN FIRE PLANT. See *Euphorbia heterophylla.*

MEXICAN FLAME VINE. See *Senecio confusus.*

MEXICAN GRASSTREE. See *Nolina longifolia.*

MEXICAN ORANGE. See *Choisya ternata.*

MEXICAN PALO VERDE. See *Parkinsonia aculeata.*

MEXICAN SHELL FLOWER. See *Tigridia pavonia.*

MEXICAN STAR. See *Milla biflora.*

MEXICAN SUNFLOWER. See *Tithonia rotundifolia.*

MEXICAN TREE FERN. See *Cibotium schiedei.*

MEXICAN TULIP POPPY. See *Hunnemannia fumariifolia.*

MICHAELMAS DAISY. See *Aster.*

MICHELIA. Evergreen trees or shrubs. Related to magnolias, but with numerous flowers borne among leaves rather than singly at ends of branches.

Michelia doltsopa

M. doltsopa. Big evergreen shrub or tree. Zones 14–24. Ultimate size in this country not known, but tall tree in its native Himalayas. Has grown to 25 ft. in as many years in San Francisco. Varies from bushy to narrow and upright; choose plants for desired form and prune to shape. Leaves thin, leathery, dark green, 3–8 in. long, 1–3 in. wide. Flowers open from brown furry buds that form in profusion among leaves near branch ends; blooms open January-March. Flowers creamy or white, slightly tinged green at base of petals, 5–7 in. wide, fragrant, with 12–16 1-in.-wide petals. They somewhat resemble flowers of saucer magnolia (*M. soulangiana*). Needs rich soil, ample water.

M. figo (*M. fuscata*). BANANA SHRUB. Evergreen shrub. Zones 9, 14–24. Slow growth to 6–8 ft., possibly to 15 ft. Dense habit, with glossy, 3-in.-long, medium green leaves. Heavy bloom season March-May, but plants often show scattered bloom throughout the summer. Flowers 1–1½ in. wide, creamy yellow shaded brownish purple, resembling small magnolias. Notable feature is powerful, fruity fragrance; most people think it resembles smell of ripe bananas. Rich, well-drained soil in sun; partial shade best in hottest climates. Ample water. Fragrance best in warm, wind free spot. Choice plant for entryway, patio, or near bedroom window. Good espalier subject, container plant.

MICROLEPIA. Ferns. Sturdy, useful for landscaping shaded areas in mild climates. All can take fairly dry soil.

M. firma. Zones 17, 23, 24. Native to India. Fronds dull green, delicately cut, triangular, to 3 ft. long. Surfaces densely hairy. Hardy to 28° F.

M. platyphylla. Zones 15–17, 19–24. Large coarse fern, to 10 ft. or higher. Leaflets broad, coarsely toothed, bluish green to yellow green.

M. strigosa. (sometimes sold as *M. speluncae*). LACE FERN. Zones 17, 23, 24. Native to tropical Asia. Robust fern with delicate fronds. Grows 2–3 ft. tall. Hardy to 28°F.

Microlepia strigosa

MICROMERIA chamissonis. See *Satureja douglasii.*

MIGNONETTE. See *Reseda odorata.*

MILFOIL. See *Achillea millefolium.*

MILKBUSH. See *Euphorbia tirucalli.*

MILLA biflora. MEXICAN STAR. Bulb. Zones 13, 16–24. Native to Arizona, New Mexico, northern Mexico. Grasslike basal leaves. Clusters of white, green-striped buds open to flat, starlike, fragrant flowers that are white inside, green outside. Spring bloom. Stems to 18 in. high. Hardy (with mulch) in fairly cold winters. Average water. Plant in October in sunny border, rock garden, or as edging. Or plant in pots for late winter, early spring bloom indoors. Plants sold under this name are often *Zephyranthes candida,* a plant with rushlike leaves and white, long-tubed flowers in late summer, fall.

Milla biflora

MILTONIA. PANSY ORCHID. Epiphytic orchids. Greenhouse or indoors. Native to tropical or subtropical Americas. Many lovely large-flowered hybrids listed in catalogs. Flower colors: yellow, white, red, or blends of these colors. Blooms, single or in clusters on arching stems, are flat, resemble pansies in appearance, and last a month or more on plant (not good cut flower). Plants have short pseudobulbs, long, graceful light green leaves that produce clump of foliage a foot or more in diameter. Thrive in shade in cool tempera-

Miltonia hybrid

ture. Keep moist and medium warm when flower spikes are forming; water less frequently in winter. Grow in finely cut but firmly packed osmunda fiber or in fine-sized ground bark or prepared, bark-based mix.

MIMOSA. Gardeners from East and South often use this word for silk tree *(Albizia julibrissin).* Also, *Acacia baileyana* and other fine-leafed acacias are sometimes called "mimosa."

MIMOSA pudica. SENSITIVE PLANT. Tender perennial usually grown as houseplant curiosity. To 18 in. high or less. Leaves finely cut into tiny leaflets. These leaves and branchlets, when touched or otherwise disturbed, droop and fold up with astonishing speed. They quickly expand again. Small pink "silk tree" blossoms. Grow from seed indoors or in bright light in a warm greenhouse. They will grow outdoors, but are not sufficiently attractive for garden. Transplant carefully to 4-in. pots. Avoid overwatering. Their only use is to dem-

Mimosa pudica

onstrate movement in plants; children find them fascinating.

MIMULUS. MONKEY FLOWER. Perennials, some grown as annuals, or shrubby evergreen perennials. The latter, often known as *Diplacus,* are showy, drought tolerant plants for Zones 7–9, 14–24. They grow 1–4 ft. tall and branch from base. Narrow, glossy dark green leaves are often sticky. Tubular, lipped flowers, 1–3 in. long, bloom over long period in late spring, summer. Pruned after first flowering, they often

Mimulus hybridus

bloom again in fall or, with some water, flower repeatedly throughout most of the year. Prune in spring before growth starts. Sow seed or set out plants in fall for bloom next summer. Make cuttings of most desirable plants to preserve best colors (easy to root in moist sand). Need sun, well-drained soil. Flowers attract birds.

M. cardinalis, M. hybridus, M. lewisii need partial shade except in fog belt, damp soil. Good in pots.

M. aurantiacus *(Diplacus aurantiacus).* STICKY MONKEY FLOWER. California native to 4 ft. tall, with sticky foliage and 1½-in., buff orange, funnel shaped flowers. Drought tolerant.

M. bifidus *(Diplacus grandiflorus).* PLUMAS MONKEY FLOWER. Large, pale yellow to peach pink flowers resemble those of deciduous azaleas.

M. cardinalis. Perennial. Zones 4–24. Native to Oregon, California, Nevada, and Arizona. To 1–2 ft. with rather floppy stems. Leaves light green, 1–4½ in. long, sharply toothed, sticky. Flowers 1½–2 in. long, scarlet, 2 lipped, bloom July-October. Takes lots of heat if given partial shade and plenty of water.

M. hybridus *(M. tigrinus).* All Zones. Short lived, usually grown as annual. Leaves smooth, succulent, toothed. Flowers 2–2½ in. across, yellow, splotched and spotted with brown and maroon; blooms spring and summer. Plant in shade with ferns, primroses, polemonium, tradescantia. Good in pots and hanging baskets. Sow seed in spring for summer bloom. Set out plants in rich, moist soil. Queen's Prize and Monarch are choice strains.

M. lewisii. Perennial, often grown as annual. All Zones. Native to streams and wet places in western mountains. Plants erect to 2½ ft. high, slightly sticky. Leaves 1–3 in. long, irregularly toothed. Flowers rose red or pink, about 2 in. long, sometimes blotched or streaked maroon, with yellow lines in throat. Adapted to wet but well-drained places in rock gardens.

M. longiflorus *(Diplacus longiflorus).* Much-branched, 3-ft. shrub. Native to coastal southern California. Flowers vary from cream to orange yellow; *M. l. rutilus* has velvety red flowers. Many hybrids have been raised in shades of cream, yellow, orange, copper, rose, salmon, red, and mahogany. These are not quite so tough as wild species; they appreciate water every week or two in summer.

Mimulus longiflorus

MINA lobata *(Quamoclit lobata).* SPANISH FLAG. Perennial vine Zones 20–24, summer annual elsewhere. Fast-twining morning glory relative that grows quickly from hard-coated seeds. Grows to 20 ft. in first year. Heart shaped leaves 3 in. across. Flowers in long, slender garlands open orange red, fade to yellow and white. Good for covering posts, stumps, fences, outbuildings, or for quick summer shading for west or south facing terrace. Notch seeds with knife or soak in warm water until they swell, then plant in average garden soil. Routine watering and feeding.

Mina lobata

MING ARALIA. See *Polyscias fruticosa.*

MINT. See *Mentha.*

MIRABILIS jalapa. FOUR O'CLOCK. Perennial in Zones 4–24; summer annual in Zones 1–3. Tuberous roots can be dug and stored like dahlia roots. Erect, many-branched stems grow quickly to form mounded clumps, 3–4 ft. high and wide. Trumpet shaped flowers open in midafternoon—red, yellow, or white with variations of shades between. Deep green, oval, 2–6-in.-long leaves and strong, bushy habit give substance and character of

Mirabilis jalapa

shrubs (even though only temporary or seasonal). Jingles strain is lower growing than old-fashioned kinds, has elaborately splashed and stained flowers in two or three colors all at once. Sow seed in sunny, open location in early spring for blooms from midsummer through fall. Reseeds readily. Drought tolerant.

MIRROR PLANT. See *Coprosma repens.*

MIST FLOWER. See *Eupatorium coelestinum.*

MOCCASIN FLOWER. See *Cypripedium.*

MOCK ORANGE. See *Philadelphus.*

MOLE PLANT. See *Euphorbia lathyris.*

MOLUCCELLA laevis. BELLS-OF-IRELAND, SHELL FLOWER. Summer annual. Single-stemmed or branched, about 2 ft. high. Flowers are carried almost from base in whorls of 6. Showy part of flower is large shell-like or bell-like calyx—apple green, very veiny and crisp textured; small white tube of united petals in center is inconspicuous. As cut flowers, spikes of little bells are attractive fresh (long lasting) or dried (be sure to remove unattractive leaves).

Moluccella laevis

Needs sunny location and loose, well-drained soil. Sow seed in early spring or late fall; if weather is warm, refrigerate seed for a week before planting. For long spikes, water and fertilize regularly.

MONARDA. BEE BALM, OSWEGO TEA, HORSEMINT. Perennials. All Zones, but not long-lived where winters are warm, summers long and hot. Bushy, leafy clumps, 2–4 ft. tall, spread rapidly at edges but are not really invasive. Six-in.-long, oval dark green leaves have strong, pleasant odor between those of mint and basil. In summer, stems are topped by tight clusters of long-tubed flowers much visited by humming-birds. Sun (light afternoon shade in hottest summer climates). Need lots of water. Plant 10 in. apart. Divide every 3 or 4 years.

Monarda didyma

M. didyma. Scarlet flowers. Heavily aromatic leaves to 4 in. long. Native to eastern U.S.

Garden selections and hybrids include scarlet 'Adam', pink 'Croftway Pink' and 'Granite Pink', lavender 'Violet Queen', and 'Snow White'. A very old variety, 'Cambridge Scarlet', is still widely grown. Pale colors may be best in some color schemes, but scarlets are showiest and most typical.

M. fistulosa. Rosy lavender flowers. Takes moist or average soils. Native from eastern U.S. to Rocky Mountains.

MONDO GRASS. See *Ophiopogon japonicus* under *Liriope* and *Ophiopogon.*

MONEY PLANT. See *Lunaria annua.*

MONEYWORT. See *Lysimachia nummularia.*

MONKEY FLOWER. See *Mimulus.*

MONKEY HAND TREE. See *Chiranthodendron pentadactylon.*

MONKEY PUZZLE TREE. See *Araucaria araucana.*

MONKSHOOD. See *Aconitum.*

MONSTERA. Evergreen vines. Related to philodendron and resembling them in leaf gloss and texture. Most have cut and perforated foliage.

M. deliciosa (often sold as *Philodendron pertusum*). SPLIT-LEAF PHILODENDRON. Zones 21–24; house plant anywhere. Even-tually of great size if planted in open ground bed in greenhouse or (in mildest areas) outdoors. Long, cordlike roots hanging from stems root into soil, help support plant on trees or on moss "totem poles." Leaves on youngest plants uncut; mature leaves heavy, leathery, dark green, deeply cut and perforated. Flowers may form on big plants; they are something like callas, with thick, 10-in. spike surrounded by white, boatlike bract. If heat, light, and humidity are high, spike may ripen into edible fruit—delicious only when fully ripe.

Monstera deliciosa

Best in filtered shade with rich soil, ample water, stout support. For best results indoors, grow in container with good drainage, feed occasionally, and keep leaves clean. In poor light or low humidity new leaves will be smaller. If tall plants get bare at base, replant in larger container and add younger, lower plant to fill in; or cut plant back and let new shoots start.

M. friedrichsthalii. SWISS CHEESE PLANT. House or greenhouse plant. Leaves smaller, thinner in texture than *M. deliciosa;* edges are wavy, not deeply cut. Leaves are perforated by series of oval holes on either side of midrib.

MONTANOA. DAISY TREE. Evergreen shrubs or small trees. Zones 16, 17, 20–24. Give them good soil, ample water, full sun, and groom by cutting off dead flower heads. Useful for winter flowers, tropical effects, background.

Montanoa bipinnatifida

M. arborescens. To 12 ft. or more, usually seen as multitrunked tree branching from base. The 6-in. oval leaves are medium green, slightly toothed and rough textured. Covered with small white daisylike flower heads in winter. Needs little pruning.

M. bipinnatifida. To 7–8 ft. Bold-textured shrub with large, deeply lobed leaves. Flower heads to 3 in. across, mostly composed of white ray flowers to give double effect; some yellow in center of heads. Blooms all fall, early winter. Prune hard after bloom; new stems grow quickly.

M. grandiflora. To 12 ft., with large deeply cut leaves, 3-in. daisies in fall, winter. Flowers have sweet scent of freshly baked cookies. Prune like *M. bipinnatifida.*

MONTBRETIA. See *Crocosmia crocosmiiflora, Tritonia.*

MONTEZUMA CYPRESS. See *Taxodium mucronatum.*

MOON CACTUS. See *Gymnocalycium mihanovichii friedrichii.*

MOONFLOWER. See *Ipomoea alba.*

MORAEA IRIDIOIDES. See *Dietes.*

MORAINE LOCUST. See *Gleditsia triacanthos* 'Moraine'.

MORETON BAY CHESTNUT. See *Castanospermum australe.*

MORNING GLORY. See *Ipomoea.*

MORUS. MULBERRY. Deciduous trees. Leaves of variable form, size, and shape—often on same tree. Fruit look like miniature blackberries and are favored by birds. Most important kinds to home gardeners, however, are fruitless forms of *M. alba.*

Morus alba

M. alba. WHITE MULBERRY, SILKWORM MULBERRY. All Zones. Fruit-bearing form grows to 20–60 ft., has inconspicuous flowers followed by rather insipid, sweet fruit which stains patios, clothing. 'Pendula' or 'Tea's Weeping' is low growing, strongly weeping variety. 'Chaparral' is a nonfruiting weeping mulberry with deeply cut, dark green leaves.

Morus alba

Fruitless forms are better for home gardens. Excellent desert shade trees—bright green foliage, rapid growth in hot climates and alkaline soils. Resistant to Texas root rot. Take some drought once established, but grow faster with water and feeding. Beach plantings in southern California very successful. Difficult to garden under because of heavy surface roots. To 35 ft. tall, somewhat wider spread; often 20 ft. by 20 ft. in 3 years (slower in cool climates). 'Fan-San', 'Fruitless', 'Kingan', and 'Stribling' ('Mapleleaf') are good varieties.

Stake new plants carefully; they develop large crowns rather fast, and these may snap from slender young trunks in high winds. For first few years branches may grow so long that they droop from own weight; shorten such branches to a well-placed upward growing bud. Do not prune heavy branches to stubs; these are likely to rot.

M. nigra. BLACK or PERSIAN MULBERRY. Zones 4, 5, 7–24. To 30 ft. with short trunk, dense, spreading head. Takes some drought once established. Heart shaped leaves to 8 in. long. Fruit large, juicy, dark red to black.

M. papyrifera. See *Broussonetia*.

MOSES-IN-THE-BOAT, MOSES-IN-THE-CRADLE. See *Rhoeo spathacea*.

MOSS CAMPION. See *Silene acaulis, S. schafta*.

MOSS PINK. See *Phlox subulata*.

MOTHER FERN. See *Asplenium bulbiferum*.

MOTHER-IN-LAW'S TONGUE. See *Sansevieria*.

MOTH ORCHID. See *Phalaenopsis*.

MOUNTAIN ASH. See *Sorbus*.

MOUNTAIN BLUEBELL. See *Mertensia ciliata*.

MOUNTAIN CRANBERRY. See *Vaccinium vitis-idaea minus*.

MOUNTAIN GARLAND. See *Clarkia unguiculata*.

MOUNTAIN IRONWOOD. See *Cercocarpus betuloides*.

MOUNTAIN LAUREL. See *Kalmia latifolia*.

MOUNTAIN MAHOGANY. See *Cercocarpus*.

MOUNTAIN PAPAYA. See *Carica pubescens*.

MOUNTAIN PRIDE. See *Penstemon newberryi*.

MOUNTAIN RIBBONWOOD. See *Hoheria glabrata*.

MOUNTAIN SILVER BELL. See *Halesia monticola*.

MOUNTAIN SPRAY. See *Holodiscus dumosus*.

MOUNTAIN WHITETHORN. See *Ceanothus cordulatus*.

MOURNING BRIDE. See *Scabiosa atropurpurea*.

MT. AETNA BROOM. See *Genista aethnensis*.

MUEHLENBECKIA. WIRE VINE. Evergreen vines. Unusual plants with thin wiry stems, tiny leaves, insignificant flowers. Routine summer watering. Sun to medium shade.

M. axillaris (*M. nana*). CREEPING WIRE VINE. Zones 3–9, 14–24. Small, dense, creeping plant to a few inches or mounding up to 1 ft. high, spreading by underground stems. Leaves ⅛ in. long, dark glossy green, closely spaced. Rock garden plant or small-scale ground cover. Deciduous where winter chill is pronounced.

Muehlenbeckia axillaris

M. complexa. MATTRESS VINE, WIRE VINE. Zones 8, 9, 14–24. Climbs to 20–30 ft. or more, or sprawls with no support. Dense tangle of thin black or brown stems. Leaves vary in shape, ⅛–¾ in. long. Tough vine for beach planting; good screen for old stump or rock pile.

MULBERRY. See *Morus*.

MULLEIN. See *Verbascum*.

MULLEIN PINK. See *Lychnis coronaria*.

MURRAYA paniculata (*M. exotica*). ORANGE JESSAMINE. Evergreen shrub. Zones 21–24. To 6–15 ft. tall and wide, sometimes grown as small single or multitrunked tree. Open habit; graceful, pendulous branches with dark green, glossy leaves divided into 3–9 oval, 1–2-in. leaflets. White, ¾-in., bell shaped flowers have jasmine fragrance. Blooms late summer and fall, sometimes spring as well. Mature plants have small red fruit.

Best in high shade or a half-day's sun without reflected heat. Needs rich soil, ample water, frequent feeding. Recovers beauty slowly after cold wet winters. Good as hedge or filler; also for shaping. Fast growing; attracts bees.

Murraya paniculata

Dwarf variety usually sold as *M. exotica* is slower growing, more upright and compact, to 6 ft. tall, 4 ft. wide. Leaves lighter green; leaflets smaller, stiffer. Bloom usually less profuse.

MUSA. BANANA. Perennials, some treelike in size. For commonest bananas, see *Ensete*. Kinds described here include tall, medium, and dwarf (2–5 ft.) plants. All have soft, thickish stems and spread by suckers or underground roots to form clumps. Leaves are long, broad, spectacular, easily tattered by strong winds (a banana plant outdoors should be in wind-sheltered spot). Most kinds are tender and should be grown in tubs, either beside a sunny window, in a greenhouse, or in such a location in winter and outdoors in warm season.

Musa paradisiaca seminifera

Attractive near swimming pools. Give all types rich soil, plenty of water, heavy feeding. Fast-growing.

M. acuminata 'Dwarf Cavendish' (*M. cavendishii, M. nana*). Zones 21–24. Plants 6–8 ft. tall have leaves 5 ft. long, 2 ft. wide. Large, heavy flower clusters with reddish to dark purple bracts, yellow flowers. In warmest southern California coastal gardens can bear sweet, edible 6-in. bananas. Plant out of wind near south wall.

M. coccinea. Zones 21 (warmest parts), 23, 24. Grows 6–8 ft. tall; leaves 2–3 ft. long. Flower bracts are fiery red tipped yellow. Striking cut flower.

M. ensete. See *Ensete ventricosum*.

M. mannii. Zones 23, 24. To 6–8 ft., with 4 ft. leaves; stems and midribs black. Rose-colored bracts, seedy 3-in. bananas.

M. maurelii. See *Ensete ventricosum* 'Maurelii'.

M. ornata *(M. rosacea, M. rosea)*. Zones 23, 24. Grows 8–12 ft. tall, with 5-ft. leaves. Short, erect flower stalk has pinkish bracts, yellow orange flowers.

M. paradisiaca *(M. sapientum)*. Zones 16, 19–24; root hardy but damaged by frost in Zones 9, 14, 15. Many ornamental and edible forms. Commonest often called *M. p. seminifera.* Grows to 20 ft., with leaves to 9 ft. Makes large clumps. Drooping flower stalk with powdery purple bracts; fruit (usually seedy and inedible) sometimes follow.

M. velutina. Zones 23, 24. Grows to 3–4 ft., with 3-ft. leaves green above, bronzy beneath. Pink upright bracts, orange flowers, velvety pink fruit.

MUSCARI. GRAPE HYACINTH. Bulbs. All Zones. Clumps of narrow, grassy, fleshy leaves appear in autumn and live through cold and snow. Small, urn shaped, blue or white flowers in tight spikes in early spring. Plant 2 in. deep in fall, setting bulbs in masses or drifts under flowering fruit trees or shrubs, in edgings and rock gardens, or in containers. Grow in sun or light shade. Need little or no water in summer. Very long lived. Lift and divide when bulbs become crowded.

Muscari armeniacum

M. armeniacum. Bright blue flowers on 4–8-in. stems above heavy cluster of floppy foliage. 'Cantab' has clear light blue flowers, blooms later, is lower growing, has neater foliage.

M. azureum *(Hyacinthus azureus)*. Something between hyacinth and grape hyacinth in appearance. The 4–8-in. stalks have tight clusters of bell shaped (not urn shaped) flowers. Fragrant flowers are sky blue.

M. botryoides. Medium blue flowers on 6–12-in. stems. 'Album' is white variety.

M. comosum. FRINGE OR TASSEL HYACINTH. Unusual, rather loose cluster of shredded-looking flowers—greenish brown fertile ones, bluish purple sterile ones. Stems 12–18 in. high. Leaves about same length and ⅜–1 in. wide.

M. c. 'Monstrosum' *(M. c. 'Plumosum')*. FEATHERED OR PLUME HYACINTH. Sterile violet blue to reddish purple flowers with finely divided and twisted segments. Also 12–18 in. high.

M. tubergenianum. Stems to 8 in. tall; flowers at top of spike dark blue; lower flowers light blue. Leaves neater.

MUSTARD. Summer annual. Curly-leaf mustards somewhat resemble curly-leaf kales in appearance; they are cooked like spinach or cabbage, or young leaves are sometimes eaten raw in salads or used as garnishes. Fast and easy grower, ready for the table in 35–60 days. Sow in early spring and make successive sowings when young plants are established. Plants thrive in cool weather but quickly go to seed in heat of summer. Sow in late summer for fall use. In mild-winter areas, plant again in fall and winter. Thin seedlings to stand 6 in. apart in rows. Water well. Harvest leaves from outside as needed. Mustard spinach or tendergreen mustard has smooth, dark green leaves. It ripens earlier than curly mustard and is more tolerant of hot, dry weather.

Mustard

MYOPORUM. Evergreen shrubs or small trees. Bell shaped flowers attractive at close range but not showy; fruit small but colorful. Features are dark green, shining leaves with translucent dots, fast growth, toughness. All take full sun, are fire retardant.

M. debile. Shrub. Zones 15–17, 19–24. Low growing, with trailing branches. To 1

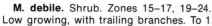

Myoporum laetum

---

ft. tall. 2–4 ft. wide. Narrow dark green leaves. Flowers in spring, ½ in. across, pink; fruit ½ in. wide, rose colored. Drought resistant. Rock garden, banks.

M. insulare. Shrub or tree. Zones 8, 9, 15–17, 19–24. Generally shrubby near coast, taller and more treelike inland. Grows to 20–30 ft. Leaves and flowers much like those of *M. laetum* but somewhat smaller. Fruit are bluish purple. Culture and uses same as *M. laetum;* plants more drought resistant.

M. laetum. Shrub or tree. Zones 8, 9, 14–17, 19–24. Temperatures in low 20s can inflict severe damage. Exceptionally fast growth to 30 ft., 20-ft. spread. Dense foliage of rather narrow, 3–4-in.-long leaves. Natural habit a broad-based, billowing mass of dark green. Attractive multitrunked tree if staked and pruned; thin to prevent top heaviness and wind damage. Flowers in clusters of 2–6 in summer, about ½ in. wide, white with purple markings. Small reddish purple fruit.

Superb for seaside use—effectively blocks sound, wind, sun, blown sand (won't take drought, however). Can also make good ground cover; keep branches pegged down so they'll root and spread. Not for tailored garden areas or near pools; some leaf drop at all times, invasive roots.

M. l. 'Carsonii'. Cutting-grown selection; has darker, larger, broader leaves with fewer translucent dots; keeps its foliage right down to base of plant. Grows even faster than species.

M. parvifolium. *(M. p. 'Prostratum')*. Ground cover. Zones 14–16, 18–24. Bright green, ½–1-in. leaves densely cover plant. Summer flowers are ½ in. wide, white, followed by purple berries. Grows to 3 in. high, 9 ft. wide. Plant 5 ft. apart. Plants will fill in within 6 months, branches rooting where stems touch moist ground. No traffic. Moderately drought resistant but better with some summer water.

MYOSOTIS. FORGET-ME-NOT. Annual or biennial, perennial. Exquisite blue flowers, tiny but profuse. Best in partial shade; grows easily and thickly as ground cover. Give ample water.

Myosotis sylvatica

M. scorpioides. Perennial. All Zones. Similar in most respects to *M. sylvatica,* but grows lower, blooms even longer, and roots live over from year to year. Flowers, ¼ in. wide, are blue with yellow centers, pink, or white. Bright green, shining, oblong leaves. Spreads by creeping roots.

M. sylvatica (often sold as *M. alpestris*). Annual or biennial. All Zones. To 6–12 in. Soft, hairy leaves, ½–2 in. long, set closely along stem. Tiny, clear blue, white-eyed flowers, to ⅓ in. wide, loosely cover upper stems. Long bloom season, beginning in late winter or early spring. Flowers and seeds profusely for a long season. With habit of reseeding, will persist in garden for years unless weeded out. Improved strains available, best of which are 'Blue Ball', 'Blue Bird', and 'Ultramarine'.

MYRICA. Evergreen and deciduous shrubs. The first one is from the Pacific Coast, the other from the Atlantic.

Myrica californica

M. californica. PACIFIC WAX MYRTLE. Evergreen shrub or tree. Zones 4–6, 14–17, 20–24. Native to coast and coastal valleys, southern California to Washington. At the beach a low, flattened mass; out of wind, big shrub or tree to 30 ft., usually with many upright trunks. In garden, one of best-looking of native plants. Great virtue is clean-looking foliage throughout year. Branches densely clad with glossy, dark green leaves, 2–4½ in. long, about ½ in. wide, toothed on edges, paler beneath. Spring flowers inconspicuous; fall fruit are purplish nutlets coated with wax, attractive to birds. Useful screen or informal hedge, 6–25 ft. tall. Can be used as clipped hedge. Drought tolerant.

M. pensylvanica *(M. caroliniensis)*. BAYBERRY. Deciduous or partly evergreen shrub. Zones 4–7. Native to eastern U.S. Dense, compact growth to 9 ft. Leaves to 4 in. long, narrowish, glossy green, dotted with resin glands, fragrant in odor. Flowers inconspicuous. Fruit tiny, roundish, covered with white wax—the bayberry wax used for candles. Tolerates poor, sandy soil; takes sun. Resistant to oak root fungus. Usually needs some summer water.

MYROBALAN. See *Prunus cerasifera*.

MYRRHIS odorata. SWEET CICELY. Perennial. All Zones. Thin, branching stems grow upright to 2–3 ft. Lacy, delicate green leaf consists of several finely cut pairs of leaflets so that mature plants resemble fern. In early summer, small white flowers appear in terminal clusters about 2 in. wide. Seeds and leaves have slight anise flavor—spicy green seeds flavor salads. Roots can be eaten raw or cooked. Shade or semishade.

Myrrhis odorata

Moderately rich, moist, well-drained soil. Seeds planted in fall make seedlings in spring. Increase stock by dividing roots.

(Another plant called sweet cicely, native to woods in western states, is entirely different. It is *Osmorhiza*).

MYRSINE africana. AFRICAN BOXWOOD. Evergreen shrub. Zones 8, 9, 14–24. To 3–8 ft.; slightly floppy when young, but stiffens up into dense, rounded bush easily kept at 3–4 ft. with moderate pinching, clipping. Stems vertical, dark red, closely set with very dark green, glossy, roundish, ½-in. leaves (excellent cut foliage). Insignificant flowers.

Grows well in full sun or part shade with reasonable drainage. Smog resistant; relatively pest free, although susceptible to red spider mites and, occasionally, brown scale. Drought tolerant. Good for low hedges, clipping into formal shapes, low green backgrounds, foundations, narrow beds, containers.

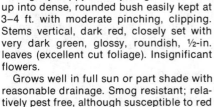
Myrsine africana

MYRTLE. See *Myrtus, Vinca*.

MYRTUS. MYRTLE. Evergreen shrubs. Included here are several of most useful, basic evergreen shrubs for California and Arizona gardens. Drought resistant.

M. communis. TRUE MYRTLE. Zones 8–24. Rounded form to 5–6 ft. high and 4–5 ft. wide; old plants can reach treelike proportions—15 ft. tall, 20 ft. across. Glossy bright green, pointed 2-in. leaves, pleasantly aromatic when brushed or bruised. White, sweet scented, ¾-in.-wide flowers with many stamens in summer, followed by bluish black, ½-in. berries. Grows well in part shade but also will take hot bright sun.

Myrtus communis

Any soil, but good drainage is essential—tip chlorosis occurs if drainage is poor. Good formal or informal hedge or screen. Can also be trained to reveal attractive branches.

M. c. 'Boetica'. Heavy, stiff, gnarled branches rise 4–6 ft. from base. Leaves large, leathery, very dark green, upward pointing, very fragrant. Popular in desert.

M. c. 'Buxifolia'. BOXLEAF MYRTLE. Small elliptical leaves.

M. c. 'Compacta'. DWARF MYRTLE. Slow-growing, small, compact, with densely set small leaves. Very popular for low edgings, foundation plantings. Excellent low, compact, formal hedge.

M. c. 'Compacta Variegata'. VARIEGATED DWARF MYRTLE. Similar to 'Compacta', but leaves are edged in white.

M. c. 'Microphylla'. Dwarf myrtle with tiny, close-set, overlapping leaves.

M. c. 'Variegata'. VARIEGATED MYRTLE. Leaves white edged.
M. luma. See *Luma apiculata*.
M. ugni. See *Ugni molinae*.

NADEN CHERRY. See *Prunus serrulata* 'Takasago'.

NAKED CORAL TREE. See *Erythrina coralloides*.

NAKED LADY. See *Amaryllis belladonna*.

NANDINA domestica. HEAVENLY BAMBOO, SACRED BAMBOO. Evergreen or semideciduous shrub. Zones 5–24. Loses leaves at 10° F.; killed to ground at 5° F., but usually recovers fast. Not a bamboo but a member of barberry family; reminiscent of bamboo in its lightly branched, canelike stems and delicate, fine-textured foliage.

Nandina domestica

Slow to moderate growth to 6–8 ft. (can be held at 3 ft. indefinitely by pruning oldest canes to ground). Leaves intricately divided into many 1–2 in., pointed, oval leaflets, creating lacy pattern. New foliage pinkish and bronzy red on expanding, later soft, light green. Picks up purple and bronze tints in fall; often turns fiery crimson in winter, especially in some sun and with some frost. Flowers pinkish white or creamy white in loose, erect, 6–12-in. clusters at branch ends, late spring or summer. Shiny red berries follow if plants are grouped; single plants seldom fruit heavily.

Sun or shade; colors better in sun, but needs some shade in low desert and hot valley regions. Best in rich soil with ample water, but plants tolerate drought when established, even competing with tree roots in dry shade. Apply iron sulfate or chelates to correct chlorosis in alkaline soils. Resistant to oak root fungus. Most useful for light, airy vertical effects; narrow, restricted areas. Good hedge, screen, tub plant, bonsai. Dramatic with night lighting. Makes highly satisfactory indoor plant if given plenty of light and placed away from warm, dry air currents.

Varieties include:

'Alba'. White berries, little fall color.

'Compacta'. Lower growing than species (4–5 ft.) with narrower, more numerous leaflets giving it lacy look.

'Harbour Dwarf'. Lower growing (1½–2 ft.) than 'Compacta', much more freely spreading. Underground rhizomes send up stems several inches from parent plants. Orange red to bronzy red winter color. Good ground cover.

'Moyers Red'. Standard-sized plant with broad foliage. Brilliant red winter color in Zones 5–7.

'Nana' ('Nana Compacta', 'Nana Purpurea'). At least two plants grown under these names. One has coarse foliage with broad, somewhat cupped leaflets. It is purplish green in summer, reddish purple in winter. Very slow to spread, it is best as container plant or as single plant among rocks or in prominent corner where its domelike growth is emphasized. The other has finely cut leaves with narrow leaflets and is green in summer, bright red in winter. It spreads fairly fast, making good small-scale ground cover. Both grow about 1 ft. tall. The two are often mixed in nurseries, so select plants carefully to get kind you want.

'Pygmaea'. Dwarf nandina with extremely dense clumping habit. Stems mostly 8–10 in. tall, with occasional stems to 3 ft. Turns bright red in fall, winter. (Other varieties may be sold under this name.)

'Royal Princess' ('Chinensis', 'Chinese Princess'). Clumps are open rather than tight, making for broad shrubs with see-through quality. Foliage fine textured; colors well in winter.

'Stribling Little Princess'. Dense, tight clumps 3–4 ft. tall; very slow-growing, slow to spread.

'Umpqua Chief'. Shorter than species (5–6 ft.), fast-growing, vigorous. Red spots appear on foliage early in fall, deepening and blending to overall bright red in winter.

'Umpqua Princess'. Clumps grow 3–4 ft. tall. Leaves narrow, giving fine texture, see-through look. Winter color not especially bright.

(Continued on next page)

'Umpqua Warrior'. Tallest and fastest grower, inclined to floppiness in its tallest stems. Large leaflets, good winter color.

NANKING CHERRY. See *Prunus tomentosa.*

NARCISSUS. DAFFODIL. Bulbs. All Zones. Most valuable spring-flowering bulbous plants for most regions of West: they are permanent, increasing from year to year; they are hardy in cold and heat; they are useful in many garden situations; they provide fascinating variety in flower form and color; and gophers won't eat them.

Narcissus-daffodil

Leaves straight and flat (strap shaped) or narrow and rushlike. Flowers composed of ring of segments ("petals") at right angles to trumpet or crown (also called cup) in center. Flowers may be single or clustered. Colors are basically yellow and white, but have many variations—orange, red, apricot, pink, cream.

Use under trees and flowering shrubs, among ground cover plantings, near water, in rock gardens and patios, or in borders. Naturalize in sweeping drifts where space is available. Good in containers, fine cut flowers.

Flowers usually face sun; keep that in mind when selecting planting place.

Plant bulbs as early in fall as obtainable. In southern California and the deserts of Arizona, wait until November so soil can cool. Look for solid, heavy bulbs. Number one double-nose bulbs are best; number one round, single-nose bulbs are second choice.

Trumpet

Short-cupped

Large-cupped

Double

Cyclamineus hybrid

Jonquilla hybrid

Poeticus

Triandrus hybrid

N. bulbocodium

Miscellaneous split-cup

Tazetta

Narcissus come in groups called "divisions." Flowers (except doubles) have 6 segments (perianth) and a cup.

Plant with 5–6 in. of soil over top of bulbs, smaller bulbs covered by 4–5 in. Set bulbs 8 in. apart and you won't have to divide for at least 2–3 years. Full sun is best, but flowers of late-blooming kinds last better in light shade.

Water well after planting; if fall rains are on schedule, further watering is usually unnecessary. Continued watering may be necessary where winters are dry. Water while growing and blooming. Control snails and slugs; they relish leaves and flowers of all kinds of narcissus and are particularly abundant during their flowering season.

Let foliage ripen naturally after bloom. Lift and divide clumps of daffodils when flowers get smaller and fewer in number; wait until foliage has died down. Don't break away forcibly any bulbs that are tightly joined to mother bulb; remove only those that come away easily. Replant at once, or store for only a short time—preferably not over 3 weeks.

To grow in containers, set bulbs close together, with tips level with soil surface. Place pots in well-drained trench or coldframe and cover with 6–8 in. of moist peat moss, wood shavings, sawdust, or sand. Look for roots in 8–10 weeks (tip soil mass from pot carefully). Remove pots with well-started bulbs to greenhouse, cool room, or sheltered garden spot to bloom. Keep well-watered until foliage yellows; then plant in garden. Can sink pots or cans of bulbs in borders when flowers almost ready to bloom, lift containers when flowers fade.

Following are the 11 generally recognized divisions of daffodils, and representative varieties in each division:

Trumpet daffodils. Trumpet is as long as or longer than surrounding flower segments. Yellows are most popular: old variety 'King Alfred' best known, top seller, although newer 'Unsurpassable' and 'William the Silent' are superior. White varieties include 'Mount Hood', 'Cantatrice', 'Empress of Ireland'. Bicolors, with white segments, yellow cup are 'Spring Glory', 'Trousseau'. Reverse bicolors like 'Spellbinder' have white cup and yellow segments.

Large-cupped daffodils. Cups are more than ⅓, but less than equal to, length of flower segments. Yellows are 'Carlton', 'Carbineer', 'Galway'; white, 'Ice Follies'; bicolors 'Binkie' and 'Mrs. R. O. Backhouse'.

Small-cupped daffodils. Cups not more than ⅓ length of segments. Less widely available, for specialists. Varieties include 'Aircastle', 'Chinese White'.

Double daffodils. 'Yellow Cheerfulness'; 'Mary Copeland', white and bright red; 'White Lion', creamy white and yellow; 'Texas', yellow and orange scarlet; 'Windblown', white and pale lemon.

Narcissus-double

Triandrus Hybrids. Cups not less than ⅔ length of flower segments. Clusters of medium-sized, slender-cupped flowers. 'Thalia' is a favorite white with 2–3 beautifully proportioned flowers per stem. 'Silver Chimes' has 6 or more white flowers with yellow cups.

Cyclamineus Hybrids. Early medium-sized flowers with recurved segments. Gold, yellow, primrose, and white with yellow cup. Examples are 'February Gold', 'February Silver', 'Peeping Tom'.

Jonquilla Hybrids. Clusters of 2–4 rather small, very fragrant flowers. Yellow, orange, ivory white like 'Trevithian' and 'Suzy'.

Tazetta and *Tazetta Hybrids.* These are Polyanthus or bunch-flowered daffodils with small-cupped white and yellow flowers in clusters. Good varieties are 'Golden Dawn' and 'Matador'. Also includes Poetaz narcissus, such as 'Geranium', paper white narcissus, and *N. tazetta* 'Orientalis' (Chinese sacred lilies). These last, along with 'Cragford' (white, scarlet cup) and 'Grand Soleil d'Or' (golden yellow) can be grown indoors in bowls of pebbles and water. Keep dark and cool until growth is well along, then bring slowly into light.

Poeticus narcissus. POET'S NARCISSUS. White flowers with shallow, broad cups of

Narcissus tazetta 'Orientalis'

yellow, edged red. 'Actaea' is largest; white flower segments, yellow, red-rimmed cup.

Species, varieties, and *hybrids.* Many species and their varieties and hybrids delight the collector. Most are small, and some are true miniatures for rock gardens or very small containers. *N. bulbocodium,* HOOP PETTICOAT DAFFODIL. To 6 in. tall, has little upward-facing flowers that are mostly trumpet, with very narrow pointed segments. Deep and pale yellow varieties. *N. cyclamineus,* 6 in. high, backward-curved lemon yellow segments and narrow, tubular golden cup. *N. jonquilla,* JONQUIL. Round rushlike leaves. Clusters of early, very fragrant, golden yellow flowers with short cups. *N. asturiensis* (usually sold as *N.* 'Minimus'), very early miniature trumpet flowers on 3-in. stems. *N. triandrus,* ANGEL'S TEARS. Clusters of small white flowers.

Narcissus bulbocodium

Miscellaneous. This group serves as a catch-all for a variety of new flower forms. Typical are 'Baccarat', light yellow with deeper yellow trumpet cut into 6 equal lobes; and 'Cassata', white with ivory split trumpet; segments lie flat along petals.

NARROW-LEAFED GIMLET. See *Eucalyptus spathulata.*

NASTURTIUM. See *Tropaeolum.*

NATAL CORAL TREE. See *Erythrina humeana.*

NATAL IVY. See *Senecio macroglossus.*

NATAL PLUM. See *Carissa grandiflora.*

NEANTHE bella. See *Chamaedorea elegans.*

NECTARINE. See Peach and Nectarine.

NEEDLE PALM. See *Rhapidophyllum hystrix.*

NELUMBO (*Nelumbium*). LOTUS. Perennials. All Zones. These are water plants. If you acquire started plants in containers, put them in pond with 8–12 in. of water over soil surface. If you get roots, plant in spring, horizontally, 4 in deep, in container (12–18 in. deep) of fairly rich soil. Place soil surface 8–12 in. under water. Huge round leaves attached at center to leaf stalks grow above water level. Large fragrant flowers form in summer, may grow above leaves or lower than leaves. Ornamental woody fruit perforated with holes in salt shaker effect.

Nelumbo nucifera

Good for dried arrangements. Roots should not freeze; where freezing is possible, cover pond or fill it deeper with water.

N. lutea. (*Nelumbium luteum*). AMERICAN LOTUS. Similar to following but somewhat smaller in leaf and flower. Flowers are pale yellow.

N. nucifera (*Nelumbium nelumbo*). INDIAN or CHINESE LOTUS. Round leaves, 2 ft. or more wide, carried 3–6 ft. above water surface. Pink flowers, one to each stem, 4–10 in. wide. White, rose, and double varieties available.

NEMESIA strumosa. Winter/spring annual in Zones 15–17, 21–24; summer annual elsewhere. To 10–18 in., with irregularly shaped flowers. Full sun. Every color of spectrum (except green) appears in these ¾-in. blossoms on their 3–4-in.-long spikes. Sometimes flowers are bicolored. Sutton's strain is larger flowered. There is also dwarf form, 'Nana Compacta'. Lance shaped, toothed leaves.

Nemesia strumosa

Sow outdoors in spring in cold climates, spring or fall where winters are mild, or buy in flats. Time plantings of this rapid grower to avoid frost but to bloom during cool weather. Does best in rich soil, moist but not wet. Pinch back to induce bushiness. Excellent bulb cover and container subject (handsome hanging basket plant). Small bed of nemesia edged with blue lobelias or violas makes dazzling patio planting.

NEMOPHILA. Annuals. Often used as low cover for bulb bed. Broadcast seed in fall (mild winter regions) or early spring, in sun or part shade. Will reseed if growth conditions are ideal. Need constant moisture. Both listed here are native to western U.S.

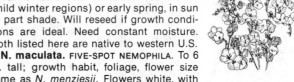

N. maculata. FIVE-SPOT NEMOPHILA. To 6 in. tall; growth habit, foliage, flower size same as *N. menziesii.* Flowers white, with fine purple lines; small dots and one large dot on each of the 5 lobes.

Nemophila menziesii

N. menziesii (*N. insignis*). BABY BLUE EYES. To 6–10 in. tall, branching from base. Blooms as freely in gardens as it does in the wilds. Cup shaped flowers about 1 in. across are sky blue with whitish center. Leaves have rounded lobes. Spring blooming period short. Nice bulb cover.

NEOPANAX arboreus (*Nothopanax arboreum*). Evergreen tree. Zones 16–24. Moderately fast to 15–25 ft. Outline dense, vase shaped. Large, glossy deep green leaves divided fanwise into 3–7 leaflets 3–8 in. long, 1–3 in. wide. Flowers greenish brown, in large clusters, not showy. Rich soil, ample water. Takes part sun or considerable shade. Useful for rich, dark, dense foliage mass. Can be trained as multitrunked small tree 6–8 ft. high; good tub subject for shady terrace or even indoors.

Neopanax arboreus

NEOREGELIA. House plants. Sometimes grown in sheltered gardens in Zones 21–24. Bromeliads with rosettes of leathery leaves, often strikingly colored or marked, and with short spikes of usually inconspicuous flowers buried in hearts of rosettes. Need light, open, fast draining planting mix that holds moisture but does not exclude air. Feed lightly. Keep water in cup at the base of rosette. Can also be grown on tree branch with sphagnum moss around roots. Filtered shade or strong indirect light.

Neoregelia carolinae

N. carolinae. Many narrow, shiny leaves 1 ft. long, 1½ in. wide. Medium green leaves turn rich red at base as plant approaches bloom. *N. c.* 'Tricolor' has leaves striped lengthwise with white. Center turns bright red.

N. spectabilis. PAINTED FINGERNAIL PLANT. Leaves 1 ft. long, 2 in. wide are olive green with bright red tips. In strong light plant takes on bronzy color.

NEPAL CAMPHOR TREE. See *Cinnamomum glanduliferum.*

NEPETA. Perennials, ground covers. All Zones. Vigorous spreading plants of mint family. Plant in full sun. Normal watering.

N. cataria. CATNIP. Perennial plant 2–3 ft. high with downy, gray green leaves and clustered lavender or white flowers at branch tips in June. Easy grower in light soil in full sun; reseeds readily. Plant attractive to cats. Sprinkle its dried leaves over their food, or sew some into toy cloth mouse. Some people use it to flavor tea.

Nepeta cataria

(Continued on next page)

N. faassenii (usually sold as *N. mussinii*). CATMINT. Makes soft, gray green, undulating mounds to 2 ft. high. Leaves aromatic and (like catnip) attractive to cats, who enjoy rolling in plantings of it. Lavender blue, ½-in. flowers in loose spikes make display in early summer. If dead spikes prove unsightly, shear them back; this may bring on another bloom cycle. Set 12–18 in. apart for ground cover.

N. hederacea. See *Glechoma*.

NEPHROLEPIS. SWORD FERN. (For native western sword fern, see *Polystichum munitum*.) Tough, easy-to-grow ferns for garden or house.

Nephrolepis exaltata 'Bostoniensis'

N. cordifolia. (Often sold as *N. exaltata*.) SOUTHERN SWORD FERN. Zones 8, 9, 14–24. Bright green, narrow, upright fronds in tufts to 2–3 ft. tall. Fronds have closely spaced, finely toothed leaflets. Roots often have small roundish tubers. Plant spreads by thin, fuzzy runners and can be invasive if not watched. Will not take hard frosts but otherwise adaptable—easily moved, tolerant of poor soil, light or heavy shade, erratic watering. Can be used in narrow, shaded beds.

N. exaltata. SWORD FERN. Outdoors in Zones 23, 24; house plant anywhere. Taller (to 5 ft.) than *N. cordifolia*, and with fronds to 6 in. wide.

N. e. 'Bostoniensis'. BOSTON FERN. House plant. Spreading and arching in habit, with graceful, eventually drooping fronds. Classic parlor fern of grandmother's day. Many more finely cut and feathery forms exist; 'Fluffy Ruffles', 'Rooseveltii', and 'Whitmanii' are among best known. North light in cool room suits it. Plant in well-drained fibrous soil. Feed every month with dilute liquid fertilizer; water whenever soil surface dries out.

NEPHTHYTIS. See *Syngonium*.

NERINE. Bulbs. Zones 5, 8, 9, 13–24. Native to South Africa. Usually grown in pots, but can grow outdoors year around in mildest regions. Wide-leafed kinds need shade in warmer climates. Strap shaped basal leaves appear during or after bloom. Flowers funnel shaped with 6 spreading segments bent back at tips; in rounded clusters on 12–24-in. stems. Bloom August through January, depending on kind.

Nerine curvifolia 'Fothergillii Major'

Plant August-December. Put 1 bulb in 4-in. pot, 3 in 5–6-in. pot. Cover only lower half of bulb. Wait for signs of flower stalk before watering. Water through winter and spring. In May, move pots outdoors to lightly shaded spot. Gradually dry off. Withhold water from July until growth resumes. Do not repot until quite crowded. To grow outdoors, plant in sun in perfectly drained soil; set bulb 3 in. deep. Do not disturb or divide for several years.

N. bowdenii. The hardiest; grows outdoors in milder parts of Northwest. Glossy green leaves 1 in. wide, 6–12 in. long. Flowers to 3 in. long, soft pink, marked deeper pink, in clusters of 8–12 on 2-ft. stems. Forms with taller stems, larger flower clusters come in deeper pink, crimson, and red. Blooms in fall; as late as December in southern California.

N. curvifolia. Best known is variety 'Fothergillii Major', with clusters of 2-in.-wide, scarlet flowers overlaid with shimmering gold. Long stamens topped by greenish yellow anthers. Bloom stalks to 18 in. Leaves 1 ft. long.

N. filifolia. Leaves narrow, grassy, evergreen, 6–8 in. long. Flowers 1 in. wide, rose red with narrow, crinkled petals, in clusters of 8–12 on stems 1 ft. tall. Fast multiplier.

N. masonorum. Resembles *N. filifolia*, but smaller, with 4–12 1-in.-wide flowers on 9-in. stems.

N. sarniensis. GUERNSEY LILY. Large clusters of iridescent crimson 1½-in.-long flowers on 2-ft. stalks. Pink, orange scarlet, and pure white varieties. Leaves green, 1 ft. long, ¾ in. wide.

NERIUM oleander. OLEANDER. Evergreen shrub. Zones 8–16, 18–23. One of the basic shrubs for desert and hot interior valleys. Moderate to fast growth; most varieties reach maximum height of 8–12 ft. and as wide. Ordinarily broad and bulky, but easily trained into handsome single or many-trunked tree resembling (when out of bloom) an olive tree. Narrow leaves, dark green, leathery, and glossy, 4–12 in. long, attractive all seasons; form with golden

Nerium oleander

variegations in leaves is sometimes available. Flowers 2–3 in. across, clustered at twig or branch ends, May or June to October. Number of varieties have fragrant flowers. Varieties include double and single flower forms, with color range from white to shades of yellow, pink, salmon, and red. 'Sister Agnes', single white, is most vigorous grower, often reaching 20 ft. tall; 'Mrs. Roeding', double salmon pink, grows only 6 ft. tall and has proportionally smaller leaves, finer foliage texture than big oleanders.

'Petite Pink' and 'Petite Salmon' are small growers easily kept to 3–4 ft. 'Algiers' (single dark red) and 'Casablanca' (single pure white) are intermediate between dwarfs and tall plant varieties in size.

Not at all particular about soil; it withstands considerable drought, poor drainage, soil with relatively high salt content. Thrives in heat and strong light, even reflected light from paving. Weak or leggy growth and few flowers in shade or ocean fog.

Prune in early spring to control size and form. Cut out old wood that has flowered. Cut some branches nearly to ground. To restrict height, pinch remaining tips or prune them back lightly. To prevent bushiness at base, pull (don't cut) unwanted suckers.

Chief insect pests are yellow oleander aphid (one spring spraying usually controls), and scale insects (spray in midsummer crawler stage with cygon, diazinon, malathion, or sevin). One disease is bacterial gall which causes warty growth and splitting on branches, also blackened, deformed flowers (control by pruning out infected parts, making cuts well below visible damage—or completely remove infected plants).

All parts of plant are poisonous if eaten. Caution children against eating leaves or flowers; keep prunings, dead leaves away from hay or other animal feed; don't use wood for barbecue fires or skewers. Smoke can cause severe irritation. However, dwarf kinds are fire retardant.

Use as screens, windbreaks, borders for road or driveway, tubs, background plantings, small single or multitrunked trees. Use freely where deer are a problem—they don't touch it. Single white oleanders give cool look to hot-climate garden.

For another plant called yellow oleander, see *Thevetia*.

NERTERA granadensis (*N. depressa*). BEAD PLANT. Perennial. Extremely tender, generally grown as house plant. Sometimes used as rock garden subject or small-scale ground cover in Zones 17, 22–24. Prostrate habit. Tiny, smooth, rounded leaves make dense green mat an inch or so high; berrylike, ¼-in., bright orange fruit may last from midsummer into winter. Small green flowers are a lesser attraction. Plant in sandy loam with some leaf mold. Must have shade, constant moisture. Fine terrarium or dish-garden plant.

Nertera granadensis

NET BUSH. See *Calothamnus*.

NEW MEXICAN PRIVET. See *Forestiera neomexicana*.

NEW ZEALAND BRASS BUTTONS. See *Cotula squalida*.

NEW ZEALAND BUR. See *Acaena microphylla*.

NEW ZEALAND CHRISTMAS TREE. See *Metrosideros excelsus*.

NEW ZEALAND FLAX. See *Phormium.*

NEW ZEALAND LACEBARK. See *Hoheria populnea.*

NEW ZEALAND LAUREL. See *Corynocarpus laevigata.*

NEW ZEALAND SPINACH. Perennial vegetable, Zones 15–17, 21–24, a summer annual elsewhere. Cook and serve it like spinach. Differs chiefly in that it can be harvested through warm season; real spinach comes in cool season. You harvest greens from plants by plucking off top 3 in. of tender stems and attached leaves. A month later new shoots grow up for another harvest. Plants are spreading, 6–8 in. high, evergreen in mild-winter areas but going dormant in heavy frosts. Sow seed in full sun in early spring after frosts. Water deeply and often. Feed 1–2 times a year with complete fertilizer. Though heat tolerant, also thrives in cool, damp conditions at shore and is often seen growing wild.

New Zealand Spinach

NEW ZEALAND TEA TREE. See *Leptospermum scoparium.*

NICHOL'S WILLOW-LEAFED PEPPERMINT. See *Eucalyptus nicholii.*

NICOTIANA. Tender perennials grown as summer annuals. May live over in mild-winter areas. Upright-growing plants with slightly sticky leaves and stems. Flowers tubular, usually broadly flaring at ends into 5 pointed lobes; grow near top of branched stems in summer. Usually grown for fragrance of flowers which often open at night or on cloudy days; some kinds open during day time. Large, soft, oval leaves. Plant in full sun or part shade. Require normal summer watering. Some kinds reseed readily.

Nicotiana alata

N. alata (*N. affinis*). To 2–3 ft. high. Very fragrant large white flowers open towards evening. There are 3 good varieties: 'Dwarf White Bedder' ('White Bedder') grows only 1 ft. high. Flowers stay open during day. 'Lime Green' and 'Lime Sherbet' grow 2½ ft. high. Greenish yellow flowers not very fragrant but excellent in flower arrangements.

N. sanderae. Flowers of most kinds stay open all day. Represented in gardens by 2 varieties: 'Crimson Bedder', to 1 ft. high; flowers rich deep crimson, slightly fragrant. 'Crimson King', to 2½ ft.; dark velvety, crimson flowers, slightly fragrant.

Sensation strain (Sensation Mixed, Daylight Sensation). Compact plants to 2½ ft. high. Flower colors—white, mauve, red, chocolate, chartreuse, lime green. Blooms open in daytime. Amount of fragrance varies according to environment.

N. sylvestris. To 5 ft. Rather coarse foliage, but sweetly fragrant, large white flowers in candelabralike clusters.

NIDULARIUM innocentii. Perennial. Outdoors in Zones 23, 24; greenhouse plant anywhere. Stemless bromeliad, best adapted to pot culture and shady, moist, warm atmosphere. Leaves straplike, 8 in. long or more, spiny toothed along margin to pointed tip, reddish purple on underside. Smaller, bractlike, brilliant red leaves make flattened, nestlike rosette at center of leaves, from which rises dense bunch of white flowers with erect petals. Appropriately named, *Nidularium* means "bird's nest."

Nidularium innocentii

NIEREMBERGIA. CUP FLOWER. Perennials. Flowers tubular but flaring into saucerlike or bell-like cup. Need sun, good soil, average water.

N. frutescens. See *N. scoparia.*

N. hippomanica violacea (*N. h. caerulea*). DWARF CUP FLOWER. Zones 8–24. To 6–12 in. high. Much-branched mounded plant. Stiff, very narrow, ½–⅔-in.-long leaves. Covered all summer with blue to violet, widely spreading, bell-like flowers almost an inch across. Trimming back to induce new growth seems to lengthen life. Good edging plant for semishade in desert regions. 'Purple Robe' is readily available variety.

Nierembergia repens

N. repens (*N. rivularis*). WHITE CUP. Zones 5–9, 14–17. Prostrate 4–6-in. mat of bright green leaves covered in summer with white flowers as large or larger than the preceding and of same shape. For best performance, don't crowd it with more aggressive plants and water it occasionally during the dry season.

N. scoparia (*N. frutescens*). TALL CUP FLOWER. Zones 8–24. To 3 ft.; shrubby with somewhat woody stems. Leaves ¾ in. long, narrow. Saucer shaped flowers 1 in. wide, white tinged blue. Can be trimmed to low rounded shape.

NIGELLA damascena. LOVE-IN-A-MIST. Spring annual. Branching, to 1–2½ ft. high. All leaves, even those that form collar under each flower, are finely cut into threadlike divisions. Blue, white, or rose flowers, 1–1½ in. across, are solitary on ends of branches. Curious papery-textured, horned seed capsules very decorative in dried bouquets; fresh material gives airiness in bouquet or in mixed border. Sow seeds on open ground in full sun or part shade. Plants come quickly into bloom in spring and dry up in summer. Will reseed. "Miss Jekyll', semidouble cornflower blue blossoms, is superior variety; 'Persian Jewels' is superior mixed strain.

Nigella damascena

NIGHT JESSAMINE. See *Cestrum nocturnum.*

NIKAU PALM. See *Rhopalostylis sapida.*

NINEBARK. See *Physocarpus.*

NOLINA. Evergreen shrubs. Yucca and century plant relatives with narrow, tough, grassy leaves on thick trunk. Desert or dry landscape plants. Sun, any soil, good drainage. Take much drought when established. Flowers not important.

N. longifolia. MEXICAN GRASSTREE. Zones 16, 19–24. Native to central Mexico. In youth forms fountain of 3-ft.-long, 1-in.-wide grasslike leaves. In time, fountains top thick trunks (6–10 ft. tall, sometimes with a few branches). Grows fast with plenty of water and feeding, but needs neither when established.

Nolina longifolia

N. parryi. Native to southern California deserts. Zones 13–24. Smaller than above: 3-ft. trunk, leaves to 3 ft. long, ¾ in. wide.

NORFOLK ISLAND PINE. See *Araucaria heterophylla.*

NORSE FIRE PLANT. See *Columnea* 'Stavanger'.

NORTH ISLAND RATA. See *Metrosideros robustus.*

NOTHOPANAX. See *Neopanax.*

NYMPHAEA. WATER LILY. Water plants. All Zones. Leaves float and are rounded, with deep notch at one side where leaf stalk is attached. Showy flowers either float on surface or stand above it on stiff stalks. Cultivated water lilies are largely hybrids that cannot be traced back to exact parentage. There are hardy and tropical types. Both kinds need full sun in order to bloom. Hardy kinds come in white, yellow, copper, pink, and red. Tropical types add blue and purple; recent introductions in tropicals include yellows and an unusual greenish blue. Some tropicals in the white—pink—red color range are night bloomers; all others close at night.

Nymphaea

Hardy kinds are easiest for beginners. Plant them from February through October in mild-winter areas, April through July where freezes prevail. Set 6-in.-long pieces of rhizome in nearly horizontal position with bud end up, on soil at pool bottom or in boxes of at least 8-in. depth. Top of soil should be 8–12 in. below water surface. Do not use redwood containers; they can discolor water. Enrich soil with 1 lb. of complete fertilizer (3–5 percent nitrogen) for each lily you plant.

Groom plants by removing spent leaves and blooms. They usually bloom throughout warm weather and go dormant in fall, reappearing in spring. If you live in very cold area, protect as you would *Nelumbo*. Tropical kinds begin to grow and bloom later in summer, but they last longer in fall, too, often up to first frost. Buy started tropical plants and set at same depth as hardy rhizomes. Tropical types go dormant but do not survive really low winter temperatures. They usually live longer where orange trees grow. Where winters are colder, store dormant tubers in damp sand over winter or buy new plants each year.

NYSSA sylvatica. SOUR GUM, TUPELO, PEPPERIDGE. Deciduous tree. Zones 3–10, 14–21. One of best lawn trees for fall color; dependable color even in mild-winter areas. Slow to moderate growth to 30–50 ft., spreading to 15–25 ft. Pyramidal when young; spreading, irregular, and rugged in age. Crooked branches, twigs, and dark, red-tinged bark make dramatic picture against winter sky. Leaves dark green, glossy, 2–5 in. long, turning hot, coppery red in fall before dropping; come out rather late in spring. Flowers are inconspicuous; fruit bluish black, shaped like small olives—attractive to birds. Grows well in any soil, takes much or little water, withstands occasional drought, tolerates poor drainage.

Nyssa sylvatica

OAK. See *Quercus.*

OCEAN SPRAY. See *Holodiscus discolor.*

OCHNA serrulata *(O. multiflora).* BIRD'S-EYE BUSH. Evergreen shrub. Zones 14–24. Slow, spreading growth to 4–8 ft. high and as wide. Oblong leaves, 2–5 in. long, are leathery, finely toothed, bronzy in spring, deep green later. Early summer flowers are size of buttercups; when yellow petals fall, sepals turn vivid red. Next, 5 or more green seedlike fruit protrude from red center. They later turn glossy jet black, in strong contrast with red sepals; at this stage children see the configuration as bright eyes and big ears of a mouse.

Ochna serrulata

Partial shade, slightly acid soil; fairly drought tolerant once established. Good tub or box subject; makes good small espalier. Sometimes grown indoors.

OCIMUM. BASIL. Summer annual herbs. One of the basic cooking herbs. Leaves in varying shades of green and purple. One type—'Dark Opal'—is attractive enough to be sold for borders and mass plantings. Sow seed of any basil in early spring; plant outdoors after frost. Requires warm soil, full sun. Space plants 10–12 in. apart. Fertilize once during growing season with complete fertilizer. Water regularly to keep growth succulent. Occasional overhead watering keeps foliage clean and bright. Keep flower spikes pinched out to prevent seeding, subsequent death of plant.

Ocimum basilicum

O. basilicum. SWEET BASIL. To 2 ft. Shiny green, 1–2-in.-long leaves; spikes of white flowers. Forms with purple or variegated leaves have purple flowers. Most popular basil for cooking. Use fresh or dry; gives a pleasant, sweet, mild flavor to tomatoes, cheese, eggs, fish, shellfish, poultry stuffing, salads. There is a dwarf, small-leafed kind that thrives in pots.

O. 'Dark Opal'. Large-leafed basil, known for its ornamental qualities. Dark purple bronze foliage; spikes of small lavender pink flowers. Grows 12–18 in. tall with spread of about 1 ft. Attractive in mass planting with dusty miller or 'Carpet of Snow' sweet alyssum.

OCONEE BELLS. See *Shortia galacifolia.*

O'CONNOR'S LEGUME. See *Trifolium fragiferum.*

OCOTILLO. See *Fouquieria splendens.*

OCTOPUS TREE. See *Schefflera actinophylla.*

ODONTOGLOSSUM. Epiphytic orchids. Outdoors in Zones 23, 24; greenhouse or indoors in winter everywhere. Few other orchids have as many natural crosses or as much variation between species. In general, pseudobulbs are flat and oval in shape with 2 or 3 pairs of leaves sheathing base and two more at top. In most cases flower stalks reach well above foliage.

Odontoglossum pulchellum

Plant in medium or fine ground bark. Transplant after flowering in fall or in early spring, never in hot summer weather. Don't plant in oversize pot; plants thrive under crowded conditions. Plants need abundant moisture year around, good ventilation but no drying winds; 45°–55° F. temperature preferable (not above 65°F. in winter and as low as possible in summer). Thrive in well-lighted location, but burn in hot summer sun. Species listed here can be grown in garden beds, Zones 23, 24. Elsewhere, grow in pots or on slabs, suspended from trees, in protected patio or lathhouse in summer, indoors or in cool greenhouse in winter.

O. crispum. Large, 2–3-in. white flowers, often tinged rose, blotched with red, crowded on 15–30-in.-long stem. Usually blooms late spring, early summer, but may bloom any time. Oval 2–4-in.-high pseudobulbs; narrow, 9–15-in.-long leaves.

O. grande. TIGER ORCHID. Bright yellow flowers with mahogany brown stripes. Blooms 5–7 in. across, arranged 3–7 per stalk to 12 in. long. Blooms in fall, lasting 3–4 weeks. Pseudobulbs 2–4 in. high with 2 dull green, broad, lance shaped leaves 8–10 in. long. After bulbs mature, keep plant on dry side until growth shows again. Good cut flower.

O. pulchellum. LILY-OF-THE-VALLEY ORCHID. Six or more 1-in. flowers, white with touch of yellow in lip, borne on 10-in. stems in spring. Flowers have fragrance of lily-of-the-valley. Pseudobulbs, 2–3 in. high, have stiff, narrow, 8–12-in.-long leaves. Keep on dry side from time growth matures until signs of new growth appear.

OENOTHERA. EVENING PRIMROSE. Biennials, perennials. All Zones. Valued for showy, early summertime flowers in tough, rough places.

O. berlandieri (*O. speciosa childsii*). MEXICAN EVENING PRIMROSE. Perennial. During summer bloom period, stems with their profusion of rose pink, 1½-in. flowers are 10–12 in. high; stems then die back. Blooms in daytime. Once established, thrives with little or no care. Invasive if not controlled. Good ground cover for dry slopes, parking strips.

Oenothera berlandieri

O. biennis. Biennial. From very large fleshy roots grow much-branched plants 3–4 ft. high. Basal leaves lance shaped, to 6 in. long. Yellow flowers open in evening. Stems green to red.

O. erythrosepala (*O. lamarckiana*). Biennial or short-lived perennial. Escaped from gardens along coast, northern California to British Columbia. Tall unbranched plant to 2–6 ft. high. Bright yellow flowers an inch or more across are open from late afternoon until morning, turn orange red as they fade. Crinkled leaves. Reseeds readily; can become something of a pest but is easily weeded out.

O. hookeri. Biennial. Western native. To 2–6 ft. high. Bright yellow, 3½-in. flowers open late afternoon to sunrise. Hairy elliptical leaves.

O. missourensis. Perennial. Prostrate, sprawling stems to 10 in. long. Soft, velvety 5-in. leaves. In late spring or summer, clear yellow flowers 3–5 in. across. One of most beautiful of evening primroses. Good rock garden subject.

O. tetragona. SUNDROPS. Perennial. To 2 ft.; reddish stems, good green foliage. Daytime display of 1½-in.-wide, yellow blossoms throughout summer. Needs very little attention. Several varieties.

OKRA. Warm-season annual vegetable crop that grows well under same conditions as sweet corn. Plant when ground begins to warm up. Soak seed 24 hours before planting to speed germination. Water regularly and fertilize at least once. Pods grow on large, erect, bushy plants with tropical-looking leaves. Harvest pods every 2 or 3 days. Best size is 1–3 in. long; over-ripened pods are tough and they shorten plant's bearing life. In containers, variety 'Red River' has tropical look. In large tub in warm spot, one plant can yield enough to make it worth growing.

Okra

OLD MAN. See *Artemisia abrotanum.*

OLD MAN CACTUS. See *Cephalocereus senilis.*

OLD WOMAN. See *Artemisia stellerana.*

OLEA europaea. OLIVE. Evergreen tree. Zones 8, 9, 11–24. Along with palms, citrus, and eucalyptus, olives stand out like regional trademarks along avenues and in gardens of California and southern Arizona. The trees' beauty has been appreciated in those areas since they were introduced to mission gardens for oil.

Willowlike foliage is a soft gray green that combines well with most colors. Smooth gray trunks and branches become gnarled and picturesque in maturity. Trees grow slowly, eventually reaching 25–30 ft. high and as wide; however, young trees put on height (if not substance) fairly fast. Begin training early. For single trunk, prune

Olea europaea

out or shorten side branches below point where you want branching to begin, stake tree firmly, cut off basal suckers. For several trunks, stake lower branches or basal suckers to continue growth at desired angles.

Large old olive trees can (with reasonable care) be boxed and transplanted with near certainty of survival.

Olive trees need full sun. They're most lush when growing in deep, rich soil, but will also grow in shallow, alkaline, or stony soil and with little fertilizer. If planted in lawn areas, mound soil up to base of trunks. They thrive in areas of hot, dry summers, but also perform adequately in coastal areas. Take temperatures down to 15° F. Withstand heavy pruning—thinning each year shows off branch pattern to best advantage, and removing flowering-fruiting branches reduces or eliminates fruit crop, which is usually a nuisance.

Olives blacken and drop from tree late in the year. Without leaching and processing, olives off the tree are inedible. Fruit can stain paving and harm a lawn if not removed. In addition to pruning, spray with fruit-control hormones when tiny white flowers appear, to reduce crop. Or spread tarpaulin at dropping time, knock off all fruit, and dispose of it. So-called fruitless varieties are not always reliably barren; see list.

Watch for scale insects and spray as needed. Olive knot occasionally forms galls on twigs and branches, eventually killing them; prune out infected wood, sterilizing instruments after each cut. Verticillium wilt is serious in some areas; it is sometimes possible to get olives that have been grown on resistant understocks.

These varieties are sold:

'Fruitless'. Landscaping variety. Advertised as nonfruiting, but some have borne fruit.

'Manzanillo'. Landscaping and commercial variety with lower, more spreading growth habit than most. Large fruit.

'Mission'. Landscaping and commercial variety. Taller, more compact, and hardier than 'Manzanillo'. Smaller fruit than most, but has fine flavor and high oil content.

'Sevillano'. Commercial variety. Very large fruit, low oil content.

'Skylark Dwarf'. Neat, compact, large, dense shrub. Sets fruit very lightly. Leaves smallish (1–1½ in. long), deep blue green above, gray beneath.

'Swan Hill'. Landscaping variety. Fruitless because of flower deformity.

OLEANDER. See *Nerium oleander.*

OLIVE. See *Olea europaea.*

OLIVER'S SNAPWEED. See *Impatiens oliveri.*

OLMEDIELLA betschlerana. GUATEMALAN HOLLY, COSTA RICAN HOLLY, MANZANOTE. Evergreen shrub or small tree. Zones 9, 14–24. Fairly fast to 20–25 ft., 10–15-ft. spread. Dense, dark green foliage, new growth bronzy. Leaves resemble English holly, but have less prominent spines. Inconspicuous flowers. Female trees are capable of producing a few inedible fruit, size of small orange. Young plants tender (plant after spring frosts); established plants hardy to 19° F. Sun or shade on coast; partial shade and ample water in inland valleys. Train as single or multitrunked tree, or as big bush densely foliaged to base. Use as background plant, street or lawn tree, tall screen, barrier, trimmed hedge, container plant. Dry leaves very stickery; don't use near pool.

Olmediella betschlerana

OLNEYA tesota. DESERT IRONWOOD. Evergreen tree. Zones 12, 13. Grows slowly to 25–30 ft. with equal spread. Branches erect in youth, later spreading. Gray green leaves divided into many ¾-in. leaflets; each leaf has 2 spines at its base. In early summer clusters of pinkish lavender ½-in.-long sweet pealike flowers put on good show. Old leaves fall after bloom, with new ones replacing them quickly. Pods, 2 in. long, follow.

Name comes from extremely hard, heavy heartwood. Plant grows near washes where some deep water is usually available. Tree is deciduous in hard frosts and cannot endure prolonged freezes, but tolerates any amount of summer heat.

Olneya tesota

ONCIDIUM. Epiphytic orchids. Greenhouse or indoors. Native from Florida to Brazil, and from sea level to high, cool mountains. In general, growth habit similar to odontoglossums. Hundreds of species and hybrids available. Most species have yellow flowers spotted or striped with brown; a few have white or rose-colored blooms.

Water generously during growing season, sparingly during dormant period—just enough to keep pseudobulbs from shriveling. Give more light than odontoglossums. Give definite rest period to Mexican and Central American species. Potting medium same as for odontoglossums. Most species grow well under conditions recommended for cattleyas. Excellent cut flower.

Oncidium splendidum

O. cheirophorum. Colombia. Miniature species with fragrant, bright yellow ½-in. flowers with green sepals. Dense, branched clusters in fall. Plant is seldom over 6 in. high, with bright green grasslike leaves.

O. crispum. Brazil. Shiny brown, 1½–3-in. flowers with yellow and red at base of segments. Borne in profusion on 1–1½-ft., arching stems any time throughout year. Rough, flat, usually dark brown pseudobulbs 3–4 in. high; leathery 6–9-in. lance shaped leaves. Never let plants dry out completely.

O. flexuosum. Brazil. Many 1-in. flowers on branched stems 2–3 ft. long. Sepals and petals very small, barred green and brown, lip quite large and bright yellow. Flattened, egg shaped pseudobulbs to 2 in., with two strap shaped, thin leaves below and two above. Tolerates and blooms well in great range of temperatures and light conditions. Excellent kind for beginners.

O. papilio. BUTTERFLY ORCHID. West Indies. Flowers 4–5 in. long, 2½ in. across. Top sepals and petals stand erect, are brown with bands of yellow; lower sepals and petals curve downward and are yellow with bands of brown. Lip yellow, edged brown. Flowers open one at a time on 2–3-ft.-long stalk which continues to produce buds on old flower stems for several years. Blooms any time of year. Rounded, dark purple pseudobulbs. Olive green leaves, mottled with brownish purple.

O. splendidum. Guatemala and Mexico. Branched, 2–3-ft., erect flower stems produce 3-in. flowers in profusion in winter. Sepals and petals yellow green, barred and blotched with reddish brown, recurved at tips; large flat, clear yellow lip. Two-inch pseudobulbs bear one stiff leathery leaf 9–15 in. high.

O. varicosum. DANCING LADY. Brazil. Golden yellow, 2-in. flowers barred with reddish brown appear in great profusion in 3-ft.-long, branched, arching sprays in fall and winter. Oblong, 3–4.-in.-high pseudobulbs bear pair of 6–9-in.-long leaves.

ONION. For ornamental relatives see *Allium.* Onions are biennials grown as annuals. Grow them from seed or sets (small bulbs). Sets are easiest for beginners, but seed gives larger crop for smaller investment. In mild climates, sets can go in 1–1½ in. deep and 1–2 in. apart all winter long and through April. Where winters are cold, plant sets in earliest spring. Start pulling green onions in 3 weeks or so; any not needed as green onions can grow on for

Onion

later harvest as dry onions when tops wither. Plant seed in early spring in rows 15–18 in. apart. Soil should be loose, rich, and well drained. When seedlings are pencil sized, thin to 3–4 in. apart, transplanting thinnings to extend plantings. Trim back tops of transplants about half way. In some areas onion plants (field-grown transplants of near pencil size or seedlings growing in pots) are available.

Do not let onions go dry; they are shallow rooted and need moisture fairly near the surface. Also feed plants, especially early in season: the larger and stronger the plants grow, the larger bulbs they form. For same reason, carefully eliminate weeds that compete for light, food, and water. When most of the tops have begun to yellow and fall over, dig bulbs and let them cure and dry on top of ground for several days. Then pull off tops, clean, and store in dark, cool, airy place.

Of the more familiar varieties, look for 'Crystal Wax Bermuda', 'Southport White Globe', and 'White Sweet Spanish' if you like white onions. Good yellow varieties are 'Early Yellow Globe', 'Yellow Globe Danvers', and 'Utah Sweet Spanish'. Fine red variety is 'Southport Red Globe'. An unusual onion is the long, red, very mild 'Italian Red' or 'Red Torpedo'.

ONOCLEA sensibilis. SENSITIVE FERN. Zones 1–9, 14–24. Native to eastern U.S. Coarse-textured fern with 2–4-ft. sterile fronds divided nearly to midrib; fertile fronds smaller, with clusters of almost beadlike leaflets. Fronds come from underground creeping rhizome which can be invasive in wet, rich soil. Dies down in winter. Takes sun if moisture is adequate. Fronds seem coarse to many gardeners.

Onoclea sensibilis

ONOSMA tauricum. GOLDEN DROPS. Perennial. Zones 1–9, 14–17. Low-growing irregular clumps to 8 in. high, spreading to 18 in. wide, with rough, dull green, narrow, 1–2-in.-long leaves. One main vertical stem with smaller, drooping side branches. Fragrant, long, tubular, yellow, 1½-in. flowers in fiddleneck clusters at tips of main stalk and side branches. Sun or part shade. Plant in well-drained soil and avoid overwatering. Use in rock gardens, or include in low planting scheme of grays and yellows.

Onosma tauricum

OPHIOPOGON. See *Liriope* and *Ophiopogon.*

OPUNTIA. Cactus. Many kinds of varied appearance. Most species fall into one of two sorts: those having flat, broad joints; or those having cylindrical joints. First are often called prickly pears, the second chollas, but terms are rather loose. Hardiness is variable. Flowers are generally large and showy. The fruit is a berry, often edible. Need little or no water once established.

O. bigelovii. TEDDYBEAR CACTUS. Zones 11–24. Native to Arizona, Nevada, California, northern Mexico. Treelike plant of slow growth to 2–8 ft. Woody trunk covered with

Opuntia microdasys

black spines. Branches cylindrical, easily detached, covered with vicious, silvery yellow spines. Flowers pale green, yellow, or white marked with lavender, 1–1½ in. wide. April bloom. Grows freely in hottest, driest deserts.

O. ficus-indica. Zones 8, 9, 12–24. Big shrubby or treelike cactus to 15 ft., with woody trunks and smooth, flat green joints 15–20 in. long. Few or no spines, but has clusters of bristles. Yellow flowers 4 in. across, spring or early summer. Large fruit, red or yellow, edible, often sold in markets. Handle it carefully—bristles break off easily and are irritating.

O. microdasys. BUNNY EARS. Zones 13–24. Mexico. Fast growth to 2 ft. high, 4–5 ft. wide (much smaller in pots). Pads flat, thin, nearly round, to 6 in. across, velvety soft green with neatly spaced tufts of short golden bristles in polka dot effect. *O. m.* 'Albispina' has white bristles. Small round new pads atop larger old ones give plant silhouette of animal's head. Favorite with children.

ORANGE. See *Citrus*.

ORANGE CLOCK VINE. See *Thunbergia gregorii*.

ORANGE JESSAMINE. See *Murraya paniculata*.

ORCHID. Each of the kinds of orchids available to westerners is described fully in this book under its name (i.e. *Cattleya, Cypripedium, Laelia*, etc.). Here we explain orchid growers' terms that are used in those descriptions.

EPIPHYTIC
Some orchids are epiphytic, growing high in branches of trees in tropical or subtropical jungles, clinging to bark, but obtaining their nourishment from air, rain, and whatever decaying vegetable matter they can trap in their root systems.

POTTING AND GROWING
Potting materials for cattleyas (most commonly grown kind) will work for most epiphytic orchids: osmunda fiber, hapuu (tree fern stem), or ground bark. Most popular now is bark, which is readily available, easy to handle, and fairly inexpensive. Use fine grade for small pots 3 in. or less, medium grade for 4-in. pots and larger. It's sensible to use ready-made mixes sold by orchid growers; these are generally blended for proper texture and acidity.

Water plants about once a week—when mix dries out and becomes lightweight. Feed plants with a commercial water soluble orchid fertilizer about once every two weeks during the growing season. To provide humidity for plants in house, fill a waterproof metal or plastic tray with gravel and add enough water so top of gravel is dry. Stretch hardware cloth over top of pan, leaving about an inch between gravel and wire for air circulation. Set pots on top. Maintain water level.

PSEUDOBULB
Epiphytic orchids have thickened stems called pseudobulbs which serve as storage for food and water, making it possible for the plants to survive seasons of drought. These may be short and fat like bulbs, or erect and slender. They vary from green to brown in color. Leaves may grow along pseudobulbs or from their tips.

TERRESTRIAL
Some orchids are terrestrial, with their roots growing in loose, moist soil rich in humus—often in wooded areas, but sometimes in open meadows as well. These orchids require constant source of moisture and food. Most native orchids fall under this classification.

SEPALS, PETALS, LIP, AND POUCH
Segments of an orchid flower include 3 sepals and 3 petals; one of the petals, usually the lowest one, is referred to in descriptions as a lip. This lip is usually larger and more brightly colored than other segments. Sometimes it is fantastically shaped, with various appendages and markings. It may be folded into a slipperlike "pouch."

RAFTS, BARK
Nearly all orchids, terrestrial or epiphytic, are grown in pots. A few are grown on "rafts" or slabs of bark or wood, or in baskets of wood slats; a few natives are grown in open ground.

TEMPERATURE REQUIREMENTS
Below, we list orchids according to their temperature requirements.

Many of the cool-growing orchids are hardy enough to grow outdoors in mild-winter climate areas; some are native to our western states.

Temperate-climate orchids can be grown in pots on a window sill along with other house plants, but will perform best if provided with additional humidity. An excellent method of supplying humidity is described above. Most temperate-climate orchids can be moved outdoors in summer in the shade of high-branching trees, on the patio, or in a lathhouse.

Warm-climate orchids need greenhouse conditions to provide uniform warmer temperatures and high humidity they require.

Cool-climate orchids: *Bletilla, Calypso, Cymbidium, Cypripedium, Epidendrum, Epipactis, Laelia, Odontoglossum, Paphiopedilum* (green-leafed forms), *Pleione*. Some of these are hardy out of doors in mildest parts of California. Some are thoroughly hardy.

Temperate-climate orchids: *Brassavola, Cattleya, Coelogyne, Dendrobium, Epidendrum, Laelia, Lycaste, Miltonia, Oncidium, Paphiopedilum* (mottled-leafed forms).

Warm-climate orchids: *Phalaenopsis, Vanda*.

ORCHID CACTUS. See *Epiphyllum*.

ORCHID TREE. See *Bauhinia*.

ORCHID VINE. See *Stigmaphyllon ciliatum*.

OREGANO. See *Origanum vulgare*.

OREGON BOXWOOD. See *Paxistima myrsinites*.

OREGON GRAPE. See *Mahonia aquifolium*.

OREGON MYRTLE. See *Umbellularia californica*.

ORGANPIPE CACTUS. See *Lemaireocereus thurberi*.

ORIENTAL ARBORVITAE. See *Platycladus orientalis*.

ORIENTAL GARLIC. See *Allium tuberosum*.

ORIGANUM. Subshrubs or perennials, some short-lived. Mint relatives with strongly and pleasantly scented foliage and tight clusters of small flowers. Bracts in flower clusters overlap, giving effect of small pine cones. Sun; little water; good drainage but are not fussy about soil.

Origanum majorana

O. dictamnus (*Amaracus dictamnus*). CRETE DITTANY. Perennial. Zones 8–24. Native to Mediterranean area. Aromatic herb with slender, arching stems to 1 ft. long. Thick, roundish leaves to ¾ in. long, white-woolly and somewhat mottled. Flowers pink to purplish, ½ in. long; rose purple fruit in conelike heads. Blooms summer to fall. Shows up best when planted individually in rock garden, in container, in hanging basket.

O. majorana (*Majorana hortensis*). SWEET MARJORAM. Perennial herb in Zones 4–24; summer annual elsewhere. To 1–2 ft. Tiny, oval, gray green leaves; spikes of white flowers in loose clusters at top of plant. Grow in fairly moist soil, full sun. Keep blossoms cut off and plant trimmed to prevent woody growth. Propagate from seeds, cuttings, or root divisions. It's a favorite herb for seasoning meats, salads, vinegars, casserole dishes. Use leaves fresh or dried. Often grown in container indoors on window sill in cold-winter areas.

O. vulgare. OREGANO, WILD MARJORAM. Perennial herb. All Zones. Upright growth to 2½ ft. Spreads by underground stems. Medium-sized oval leaves; purplish pink blooms. Grow in sun, medium-rich soil; needs good drainage, average watering. Keep trimmed to prevent flowering. Replant every 3 years. Leaves, fresh or dried, are used in many dishes and sauces, especially Italian and Spanish ones.

ORNAMENTAL PEAR. See *Pyrus.*

ORNITHOGALUM. Bulbs. Zones 5–24. Leaves vary from narrow to broad and tend to be floppy. Flowers mostly star shaped, in tall or rounded clusters. Most bloom in April-May. Grow in sun. Use in borders or grow in pots.

Ornithogalum caudatum

O. arabicum. STAR OF BETHLEHEM. Handsome clusters of 2-in., white, waxy flowers with beady black pistils in centers. Stems 2 ft. tall. Floppy leaves to 2 ft. long, 1 in. wide, bluish green. Bulbs hardy except in coldest winters; in cool-summer climates, bulbs may not bloom second year after planting because of lack of sufficient heat. Wet-winter, dry-summer plant. Can be grown in pots. Excellent cut flower.

O. caudatum. PREGNANT ONION, FALSE SEA ONION. House plant. Grown for bulb and foliage rather than for tall wands of small green and white flowers. Leaves are strap shaped, hang downward, and grow to 5 ft. long. Big, gray green, smooth-skinned bulb (3–4 in. thick) grows on, not in, the ground. Bulblets form under skin and grow quite large before they drop out and root. Hardy to 25°F.; will lose leaves in extended drought. Does best with 4 hours of sun daily.

O. thyrsoides. CHINCHERINCHEE. Tapering, compact clusters of white 2-in. flowers with brownish green centers. Leaves bright green, upright, 2 in. wide, 10–12 in. long. Flower stems 2 ft. high. Usually considered tender, but has survived cold winters in sheltered south or southwest location when well mulched. Average water. Long-lasting cut flower.

O. umbellatum. STAR OF BETHLEHEM. Probably hardiest of group. May naturalize widely once it's established—can become pest. Clusters of 1-in.-wide flowers, striped green on outside, top 1-ft. stems. Grasslike leaves about as long as flower stems. Cut flowers last well but close at night. Give adequate water for good performance.

OSAGE ORANGE. See *Maclura pomifera.*

OSCULARIA. Subshrubs. Zones 15–24. Low plants with erect or trailing branches. To 1 ft. tall. Leaves very thick and fleshy, triangular, blue green with pink flush. Flowers to ½ in. across, fragrant in late spring, early summer. Full sun. Need little water. Best in pots, hanging baskets, rock gardens, borders. Can be used for small-scale ground cover.

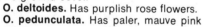

Oscularia deltoides

O. deltoides. Has purplish rose flowers.

O. pedunculata. Has paler, mauve pink flowers.

OSMANTHUS. Evergreen shrubs or trees. All have clean, leathery, attractive foliage and inconspicuous but fragrant flowers. Take considerable drought once established. Good in full sun but perform well in light to medium shade. Tolerate broad range of soils, including heavy clays.

O. decorus. See *Phillyrea decora.*

O. delavayi (*Siphonosmanthus delavayi*). DELAVAY OSMANTHUS. Shrub. Zones 4–9, 14–21. Slow-growing, graceful, to 4–6 ft., with arching branches spreading wider. Leaves dark green, oval, to 1 in. long, with toothed edges. White, fragrant flowers in profusion (largest of any osmanthus) in clusters of 4–8, March-May. Partial shade in hot-summer areas. Attractive all year. Easily controlled by pruning. Good choice for foundations, massing. Handsome on retaining wall where branches hang down.

Osmanthus fragrans

O. fortunei. Shrub. Zones 5–10, 14–24. Hybrid between O.

heterophyllus and *O. fragrans.* Slow, dense growth to 20 ft. Usually seen about 6 ft. high. Leaves oval, hollylike, to 4 in. long. Small, fragrant white flowers in spring, summer.

O. f. 'San Jose'. Similar in appearance but has cream to orange flowers in October.

O. fragrans. SWEET OLIVE. Shrub. Zones 8, 9, 12–24. Moderate growth to 10 ft. and more with age. Broad, dense, compact. Can be pruned to upright growth where space is limited. Can train as small tree, hedge, screen, background, espalier, container plant. Pinch out growing tips of young plants to induce bushiness. Leaves glossy, medium green, oval, to 4 in. long, toothed or smooth edged. Flowers tiny, white, inconspicuous except in their powerful, sweet, apricotlike fragrance. Bloom heaviest in spring and early summer, but is scattered throughout year in mild-winter areas. Young plants grow best in some shade, but tolerate sun as they mature. In Zones 12, 13, grow in east or north exposure.

O. f. aurantiacus. Leaves less glossy and more narrow than those of *O. fragrans.* Concentrates its crop of wonderfully fragrant orange flowers in October.

O. heterophyllus (*O. aquifolium, O. ilicifolius*). HOLLY-LEAF OSMANTHUS. Shrub. Zones 3–10, 14–24. Useful as hedge. A number of varieties are available:

O. h. 'Gulftide'. Similar to 'Ilicifolius' but more compact.

O. h. 'Ilicifolius'. Dense, symmetrical upright growth to 6–8 ft., eventually to 20 ft. Leaves dark green, strongly toothed, hollylike, to 2½ in. long. Fragrant white flowers in fall, winter, early spring. Excellent for screening, background.

O. h. 'Purpureus' (*'Purpurascens'*). Dark purple new growth, with purple tints through summer.

O. h. 'Rotundifolius'. Slow-growing to 5 ft., with roundish small leaves and few spines along edges.

O. h. 'Variegatus'. Slow-growing to 4–5 ft., with densely set leaves edged creamy white. Useful to light up shady areas.

OSMAREA burkwoodii. Evergreen shrub. Zones 4–9, 14–17. Slow-growing to 6 ft. and as wide. Bushy, compact, well-foliaged with dark green, glossy, toothed leaves 1–2 in. long. Small, fragrant white flowers in clusters, in April-May. Hybrid between *Osmanthus delavayi* and *Phillyrea decora.* Similar to *Osmanthus delavayi* but does not flower as freely. Sun or part shade. Drought tolerant. Makes good hedge.

Osmarea burkwoodii

OSMUNDA regalis. ROYAL FERN. All Zones, best in Zones 4–6. Big fern with twice-cut fronds and large leaflets, with texture coarser than that of most ferns but extremely handsome. Fertile leaflets small, clustered at tips of fronds. Can reach 6 ft. in moist, shady places. Leaves die back in winter.

Osmunda regalis

OSTEOSPERMUM. AFRICAN DAISY. (For other African daisies see *Arctotis, Dimorphotheca.*) Evergreen subshrubs or perennials. Zones 8, 9, 14–24. South African plants closely related to *Dimorphotheca* (Cape marigold) and often sold as such. Except for trailing perennial *O. fruticosum,* all are spreading, mounded shrubby plants with medium-green foliage and profusion of daisylike flowers over long season (best spring, summer). Leaves variable in size and shape, larger on young plants and vigorous young shoots, 2–4 in. long, narrowish oval, smooth edged or with a few large teeth. Flowers, on long stems, open only in sunlight.

Grow in full sun. Plants look best with

Osteospermum fruticosum

moderate watering and good garden soil, but will stand drought and neglect when established. Tip-pinch young plants to induce bushiness; cutting back old, sprawling branches to young side branches will keep plants neat, often induce repeat bloom. Use in borders or mass plants along driveways, paths, on slopes, in front of screening shrubs. Grow from seeds or cuttings (named varieties from cuttings only).

O. barberae (*Dimorphotheca barberae*). To 2–3 ft. tall, a little wider. Flower heads 2–3 in. across; rays pinkish lilac inside, with deep purplish blue stripes on reverse; dark purple blue centers. Blooms from fall through spring, frequently through summer.

O. 'Buttersweet'. Plant form resembles that of *O. barberae*. Flower heads have primrose yellow rays fading to cream near center, lavender to brownish zone at base, lavender blue to brownish center. Backs of rays yellow with pronounced brown stripe. Spring to frost.

O. ecklonis (*Dimorphotheca ecklonis*). Grows 2–4 ft. tall, equally broad. Long stems bear 3-in. flower heads with white rays (tinged lavender blue on backs), dark blue center. Blooms early summer to frost.

O. fruticosum (*Dimorphotheca fruticosa*). TRAILING AFRICAN DAISY, FREEWAY DAISY. Spreads rapidly by trailing, rooting branches. Rooted cuttings will cover circle 2–4 ft. across in year; plants grow to 6–12 in. tall. Leaves shorter, thicker than in other species. Flowers intermittently during year, most heavily November-March. Heads to 2 in. across; rays lilac above, fading nearly white by second day, deeper lilac beneath and in bud; dark purple center. Excellent ground cover for sunny areas; good bank cover. Needs well-drained soil. Does well at seashore. Fire retardant when well watered. Will spill over wall or grow in hanging basket (tip-pinch to induce bushiness). Used as annual (fall planting) in Zones 12, 13. White form (sold as 'Hybrid White', 'White Cloud', 'Snow White') grows more upright, blooms in sheets in late winter and early spring. Deep purple varieties are 'African Queen' and 'Burgundy Mound'.

O. 'Golden Charm'. Resembles *O.* 'Buttersweet', but rays, centers are bright yellow.

OSWEGO TEA. See *Monarda*.

OUR LORD'S CANDLE. See *Yucca whipplei*.

OXALIS. Perennials; some grow from bulbs or rhizomes. Leaves divided into leaflets (most commonly in manner of clover leaves—3 leaflets). Flowers pink, white, shades of rose, or yellow. Can go completely dry in summer. One yellow-flowered kind (*O. corniculata* and its purple-leafed form) is considered an aggressive weed everywhere in West. Some cultivated kinds can spread aggressively, may become weeds. All except *O. oregana* can be grown as house plants anywhere—keep them in sunny window.

Oxalis oregana

O. acetosella. WOOD SORREL, SHAMROCK. One of several plants known as shamrock. See Shamrock.

O. adenophylla. Zones 4–9, 14–24. Low (4 in. high), dense, compact tuft of leaves, each leaf with 12–22 crinkly, gray green leaflets. Flowers are 1 in. wide, on 4–6-in. stalks, bell shaped, lilac pink with deeper veins, in late spring. Plant roots in fall. Needs good drainage, full sun. Good rock garden plant.

O. bowiei. Zones 4–9, 14–24. Cloverlike leaves of 3 leaflets topped by 12-in.-high stems with pink or rose purple summer flowers 1½–2 in. across. Has survived 0°F. with only light mulching, but better known as house plant.

O. crassipes. Zones 8, 9, 14–24. Compact evergreen plant seems to bloom at all seasons. At top of 6–18-in.-high stalks are small pink flowers. Enough open at one time to be effective. There is a white-flowered form, *O. c.* 'Alba', and a blush pink one, *O.c.* 'Pinkie'.

O. hedysaroides 'Rubra'. FIRE FERN. House plant. Shrubby,

with erect stems to 3 ft. Flowers yellow, not especially showy. Leaves of 3-in. leaflets, maroon red in color. Bright light. Let soil dry out between waterings.

O. hirta. Zones 8, 9, 14–24. Makes many upright, branching stems to 1 ft. high that gradually fall over with weight of leaves and flowers. Leaves cloverlike, small, set directly against stems or on very short stalks. General effect is feathery. Flowers (late fall or winter) bright rose pink, 1 in. wide. Plant bulbs in fall. Quite drought tolerant. Good in rock gardens, hanging baskets.

O. oregana. REDWOOD SORREL, OREGON OXALIS. Zones 4–9, 14–24. Native to coastal forests from Washington to California. Creeping white roots send up velvety, medium green, cloverlike leaves 1½–4 in. wide on stems 2–10 in. high. Flowers to 1 in. across, pink or white veined with lavender, borne in spring, sometimes again in fall. Interesting ground cover for part shade to deep shade in mild-winter, cool-summer areas. Good with ferns. Looks most lush when watered frequently.

O. pes-caprae (*O. cernua*). BERMUDA BUTTERCUP. Zones 8, 9, 14–24. Clusters of bright green cloverlike leaves (often spotted with dark brown) spring directly from soil in fall. Above them in winter and spring rise stems up to 12 in. long topped with clusters of inch-wide, bright yellow flowers. This handsome plant is best grown in pots or baskets; it spreads rapidly by rhizomes and bulbs, and it can become a troublesome pest in an open garden.

O. purpurea (*O. variabilis*). Zones 8, 9, 14–24. Low growing (4–5 in. tall), with large cloverlike leaves and rose red flowers an inch across, November-March. Spreads by bulbs and rhizomelike roots, but is not aggressive or weedy. Plant bulbs in fall. Improved kinds with larger flowers sold under the name Grand Duchess; flowers are rose pink, white, or lavender.

O. regnellii. House plant. Erect stem to nearly 1 ft. tall has many long-stemmed drooping leaves, each with 3-in.-long leaflets shaped like triangles attached by their points—three-quarters of an iron cross. Flowers white, dainty. Same culture as *O. hedysaroides* 'Rubra'.

OXERA pulchella. Zones 22–24. Evergreen vine or vining shrub. As a shrub, mounding to 6 ft. tall; with support, can be trained to 10 ft. Leaves leathery, glossy, very dark green, oblong, to 5 in. long. Clusters of white, waxy 2-in. trumpets give winter or spring display of unusual quality at varying times of year. Refined appearance. Best in high shade or cool, sunny spot. Average water.

Oxera pulchella

OXYDENDRUM arboreum. SOURWOOD, SORREL TREE. Deciduous tree. Zones 3–9, 14–17. Native to eastern U.S. Slow growth to 15–25 ft., eventually to 50 ft. Slender trunk, slightly spreading head. Leaves 5–8 in. long, narrow, somewhat resemble peach leaves; bronze tinted in early spring, rich green in summer, orange and scarlet in autumn. Creamy white, bell shaped flowers in 10-in.-long, drooping clusters at branch tips in late July-August. In autumn, when foliage is brilliant scarlet, branching clusters of greenish seed capsules extend outward and downward like fingers; capsules turn light silver gray and hang on late into winter.

Oxydendrum arboreum

Best known in areas with cool summers, well-defined winters. Requires acid soil, ample water. Not competitive plant—doesn't do well in lawns or under larger trees. Avoid underplanting with anything needing cultivation. Good shade tree for patio or terrace. Distinguished branch and leaf pattern, spring leaf color, summer flowers, fall color. Young plants are good container subjects.

PACHISTIMA. See *Paxistima*.

PACHYRHIZUS erosus. JICAMA. Annual vine. Zones 7–16, 18–24. Grown for its edible root, which looks like large turnip and tastes something like water chestnut. Twining or scrambling vines are attractive, with luxuriant deep green foliage and pretty purple or violet flower clusters. Leaves have 3 leaflets, each the size of hand; upright spikes of sweet pealike flowers appear in late summer. They should be pinched out for maximum root production, but you can allow seed for next year's crop to form on a plant or two. Needs long warm growing season and good garden soil. Sow seeds in full sun after danger of frost, 1–1½ in. deep, 6–12 in. apart in rows. Do not let plants go dry, and feed once or twice in early and midsummer. Tubers form as days begin to grow shorter and should be harvested before first frost.

Pachyrhizus erosus

Although roots are delicious, seeds are poisonous and should not be eaten.

PACHYSANDRA terminalis. JAPANESE SPURGE. Evergreen subshrub. Zones 1–10, 14–21. Use it as ground cover in shade. Spreads by underground runners. In deep shade, stems reach 10 in.; in dappled shade, 6 in. Leaves are rich dark green, 2–4 in. long, in clusters atop stems; yellowish in full sun. Small fluffy spikes of fragrant white flowers in summer; white fruit follow.

Pachysandra terminalis

Set 6–12 in. apart in rich, preferably acid soil. Give plenty of water, especially while getting established. Feed during growing season for best color. May spread moderately, but is not aggressive or weedy. Good transition between walks or lawns and shade-loving shrubs.

'Variegata' has leaves edged with white.

PACHYSTACHYS lutea. GOLDEN CANDLE. Evergreen shrub. Zones 21–24. House plant anywhere. Soft-wooded shrub related to shrimp plant *(Justicia brandegeana)* and resembling it, but broader, more erect and open, with brighter green foliage. Leaves to 6 in. long, 2 in. wide. Branches tipped with 3–6-in. spikes of neatly overlapping golden yellow bracts. True flowers, slender white tubes, appear from between bracts. Flowers last only a few days, but spike is attractive for many weeks. Blooms throughout warm weather—nearly all year in greenhouse, with peak production in summer. Needs rich soil, partial shade, ample water. Occasional thorough leaching will prevent salt burn in areas where water is salt laden.

Pachystachys lutea

Pinch tips to encourage bushy growth; plant can grow to 5–6 ft. high and as wide under most favorable conditions, but usually tops out at 3 ft. Where grown outdoors may need protection from frost.

PACIFIC WAX MYRTLE. See *Myrica californica.*

PAEONIA. PEONY. Practically all garden peonies are hybrids. These fall into two principal classes, herbaceous and tree peonies.

Herbaceous Peonies. Perennials. Zones 1–11, 14–16. Well-grown clumps reach 2–4 ft. tall and spread wider from thickened, tuberous roots. Large, deep green, attractively divided leaves make effective background for spectacular mid to late

Paeonia

spring flowers. These may be: single (uncommon but very effective); single filled with mass of narrow, yellow, petal-like structures (Japanese type); semidouble; or fully double. Colors range from pure white through pale creams and pinks to red. Flowers may reach 10 in. across. Newer kinds have deeper reds and chocolate tones. There is even a pure yellow. Many have fragrance of old-fashioned roses.

Paeonia

Herbaceous peonies bloom really well only when they experience pronounced winter chilling period. Winter cold and summer heat not a problem, but flowers do not last well where spring days are hot and dry—in such areas choose early-blooming varieties and give plants some afternoon shade and ample water. Where they grow best—in Zones 1–7—they thrive in full sun.

Can grow in most soils, but because they live long, prepare soil well, at least 18 in. deep. Keep manure from direct contact with roots. Plant in early fall, being careful that eyes on tubers are no deeper than 2 in.; deeper planting may prevent blooming. Feed established clumps like other plants. Provide support for heavy flowers. Cut off stems carefully just below soil surface in fall after leaves turn brown. Fairly pest free; to control botrytis, which browns buds and spots leaves, spray with copper fungicide or benomyl before buds open; cut out and destroy all withered buds, stems, or brown-spotted leaves.

To divide in early fall, dig, cut off foliage, hose dirt from root cluster, and divide carefully into sections with at least 3 eyes (pink growth buds). But don't divide clump unless absolutely necessary.

They are choice cut flowers, and are a mainstay of big perennial borders. Can be planted in bays of big shrub borders.

Tree Peonies. Deciduous shrubs. Zones 2–12, 14–21. Descendants of *P. suffruticosa*, Chinese shrub to 6 ft. tall; yellow and salmon varieties are hybrids of this and *P. lutea*, Tibetan plant with yellow flowers. Irregular, picturesque branching habit from 3–6 ft. tall, eventually as wide. Leaves large, divided, blue green to bronzy green.

Flowers very large, up to 1 ft. across, single to fully double. Japanese types have single to double flowers held erect above foliage; silky petals range from white through pink and red to lavender and purple. European types have very heavy double flowers that tend to droop and hide their heads; colors range chiefly through pinks and rosy shades. Hybrids with *P. lutea* have fully double to single flowers in yellow, salmon, or sunset shades; singles and semidoubles hold up their flowers best.

Very hardy to cold, and less dependent on winter chill than herbaceous peonies; can get botrytis in humid climates. Fragile blooms come in early to midspring and should be sheltered from strong winds. Give plants afternoon shade in hot-summer climates. Plant in fall or earliest spring (from containers any time) in rich, deep, well-prepared soil away from competing tree roots. Plants are long-lived, so take special pains to improve soil with peat moss or ground bark. Plant deep, setting plant several inches deeper than it grew in nursery can or growing field. Water regularly in summer. To prune, remove spent flowers and cut back to live wood in spring when buds begin to swell.

Varieties available are many, and some nurseries sell unnamed seedlings; select the latter in bloom to get desired form and color.

PAINTED DAISY. See *Chrysanthemum coccineum.*

PAINTED FINGERNAIL PLANT. See *Neoregelia spectabilis.*

PAINTED-TONGUE. See *Salpiglossis sinuata.*

PALM. It's difficult to generalize about any plant family as large and widespread as palms. Generally speaking, they have single, unbranched trunks of considerable height; some grow in clusters, though, and some are dwarf or stemless. Again generally speaking, the leaves are divided into many leaflets, either like ribs of a fan (fan palms) or like a feather, with many parallel leaflets growing outward from a long central stem. But some palms have undivided leaves.

Most palms are tropical or subtropical; a few are surprisingly hardy (to be seen in Edinburgh, London, and southern Russia, as well as Portland and Seattle).

Palms offer great opportunity for imaginative planting. In nature they grow not only in solid stands but also in company with other plants, notably broad-leafed evergreen trees and shrubs. They are effective near swimming pools. Most young palms prefer shade and all tolerate it; this fact makes them good house or patio plants when they are small. As they grow, they can be moved into sun or part shade, depending on species.

Growth rates vary but keeping plants in pots usually slows growth of faster-growing kinds. If temperatures are in the 60s or higher, fertilize potted palms often and wash them off frequently to provide some humidity, clean the foliage, and dislodge some of the insects which (indoors, at any rate) are protected from their natural enemies and can increase at an unnatural rate.

To pot a palm, supply good potting soil, adequate drainage, and not too big a container. As with all potted plants, pot or repot a palm in a container just slightly larger than the one it's in.

Some shade-tolerant palms such as *Rhapis, Chamaedorea,* and *Howea* may spend decades in pots indoors. Others that later may reach great size—*Phoenix, Washingtonia, Chamaerops*—make charming temporary indoor plants but must eventually be moved.

To plant palm of 5-gallon size in ground, dig hole 3 ft. wide and 8 in. deeper than root ball. At bottom place 1 or 2 cubic ft. of manure, fortified sawdust, or other organic amendment, with a handful or two of blood meal added. Put 6-in. layer of soil over this, set palm, and fill around it with mixture of half native soil, half fortified sawdust, ground bark, or peat moss. Water well, and continue watering throughout summer and fall. Give gallon-sized palms the same treatment scaled down.

Palms, even big ones, transplant easily in late spring or early summer. Since new roots form from base of trunk, root ball need not be large. New root system will form and produce lush new growth. During transplant of large palms, tie leaves together over center "bud" or heart, and stiffen or secure the latter by tying leaf mass to a length of 2-by-4 tied to trunk.

Palms need little maintenance; reasonably fertile soil and adequate water will produce thriving plants. All palms with a tropical background do their growing during warm portions of year. Winter rains wash them down and leach accumulated salts from soil. Washing with a hose is beneficial, especially for palms exposed to dust and beyond reach of rain or dew. Washing helps keep down spider mites and sucking insects which find refuge in long leaf stems.

Feather palms and many fan palms look neater when old leaves are removed after they have turned brown. Make neat cuts close to trunk, leaving leaf bases. Some palms shed old leaf bases on their own. Others, including arecastrums and chamaedoreas, may hold old bases. You can remove them by slicing them off at the very bottom of base (be careful not to cut into trunk).

Many palm admirers say that dead leaves of *Washingtonia* should remain on tree, the thatch being part of the palm's character. If you also feel this way, you can cut lower fronds in a uniform way close to trunk, but leave leaf bases which present a rather pleasant lattice surface.

Here are 10 roles that the right kinds of palms can fill (palms named in each listing are described under their own names elsewhere in this book):

Sturdy palms for park and avenue plantings, and for vertical effects in large gardens: *Archontophoenix, Arecastrum, Brahea, Jubaea, Livistona, Phoenix canariensis, P. dactylifera, P. loureiri , P. rupicola, Rhopalostylis, Sabal, Washingtonia.*

Small to medium-sized palms for sheltered areas in frost free gardens: *Archontophoenix, Caryota, Chamaedorea, Chamaerops, Chrysalidocarpus, Hedyscepe, Howea.*

Small to medium-sized palms for gardens in areas of occasional frosts: *Acoelorrhaphe, Acrocomia totai, Brahea, Butia, Chamaedorea cataractarum, C. elegans, C. klotzschiana, C. seifrizii, Chamaerops, Livistona, Phoenix roebelenii, Rhapidophyllum, Trachycarpus, Trithrinax.*

Hardy palms for cold areas: (Those marked with asterisk have withstood very cold winters in various parts of the world.) *Chamaerops, Brahea armata, B. edulis, *Jubaea, Livistona, *Phoenix canariensis, P. dactylifera, P. loureiri, *Rhapidophyllum, Rhapis, Sabal mexicana, S. minor, S. palmetto, *Trachycarpus, Washingtonia filifera.*

Frost becomes more damaging to palms as it extends its stay and is repeated. Light frosts for half an hour may leave no damage, but the same degree during a period of four hours may damage some palms, kill others. Simplest damage is burned leaf edges, but frost may affect whole leaves, parts of trunks, or crown. Damage in crown is usually fatal (some have recovered). Hardiness is also a matter of size; larger plants may pass through severe frosts unharmed while smaller ones perish.

Garden palms for seaside planting: Palms in southern California beach plantings should be washed off occasionally to keep them free from salt accumulations. The following palms are listed in order of their salt tolerance, most tolerant first: *Washingtonia robusta, Phoenix dactylifera, P. canariensis, P. reclinata, Chamaerops, Brahea edulis, Butia, Sabal domingensis, S. palmetto.*

Palms for inland and desert: *Butia, Chamaerops, Brahea armata, Livistona chinensis, L. mariae, Phoenix canariensis, P. dactylifera, P. loureiri, P. sylvestris, Sabal mexicana, S. minor, Washingtonia.*

Palms to grow under trees, lath, overhangs, or indoors (indoor palms should occasionally be brought outdoors into mild light): *Acoelorrhaphe, Archontophoenix, Caryota mitis, C. ochlandra, C. urens, Chamaedorea, Hedyscepe, Howea,* young *Livistona, Phoenix reclinata* (when young), *P. roebelenii, Rhapis, Rhopalostylis, Trachycarpus* (when young).

Palms near swimming pools: Palms have great value near swimming pools because they do not drop leaves. Mature plants of *Phoenix reclinata* or *Chamaerops humilis,* with their curved trunks arching near the pool, give feeling of tropical island. But whether palm trunks are curved or upright, or topped with either fan or feather leaves, they can create beautiful mirror effects in the water.

Palms as ground covers: Young palms, especially those that grow slowly such as *Livistona chinensis* or *Chamaerops humilis,* can be used effectively as ground covers. They'll stay low from 5–10 years, especially if they're in gardens that need little care. When they get too tall, move them to another location in garden where you need height.

Palms to light at night: Because of their stateliness and their spectacular leaves, palms are good subjects for night lighting. You can back light them, light them from below, or direct lights to silhouette palms against light-colored building wall.

PALMETTO. See *Sabal.*

PALO VERDE. See *Cercidium.*

PAMPAS GRASS. See *Cortaderia selloana.*

PANAMIGA, PANAMIGO. See *Pilea involucrata.*

PANDA PLANT. See *Kalanchoe tomentosa.*

PANDOREA. Evergreen vines. Zones 16–24. Leaves divided into glossy oval leaflets; flowers trumpet shaped, clustered. Climb by twining.

P. jasminoides (*Bignonia jasminoides, Tecoma jasminoides*). BOWER VINE. Fast to 20–30 ft. Slender stems, distinguished glossy foliage, medium to dark green. Leaves have 5–9 egg shaped leaflets 1–2 in. long. Flowers (June-October) 1½–2 in. long, white with pink throats, dropping cleanly after bloom. 'Alba' has pure white flowers; 'Rosea' has pink flowers with rose pink throats. Plant in lee of prevailing wind.

Pandorea jasminoides

(Continued on next page)

Ample moisture, sun near coast, part shade inland. Prolonged freezes will kill it.

P. pandorana *(Bignonia australis, Tecoma australis).* WONGA-WONGA VINE. Glossy foliage handsome all seasons. Flowers smaller (to ¾ in. long), yellow or pinkish white, throat usually spotted brown purple. Grows in sun or shade. Needs room to grow. Requires little water once established. Prune ends of branches heavily after spring bloom.

PANSY. See *Viola.*

PANSY ORCHID. See *Miltonia.*

PAPAVER. POPPY. Annuals, perennials. Provide gay color in spring and summer for borders and cutting. All kinds need full sun, ordinary soil, good drainage, not too much water, light feeding until established.

P. burseri *(P. alpinum).* ALPINE POPPY. Perennial. All Zones; best adapted in colder climates. Will bloom first spring from fall or early spring sowing. Short-lived rock garden poppy with leaves in a basal rosette and flower stalk 5–8 in. high. Blue green, nearly hairless divided leaves. Spring flowers 1–1½ in. across, white, orange, yellow, salmon.

Papaver orientale

P. nudicaule. ICELAND POPPY. Perennial, grown as annual in warm-winter areas. All Zones. Divided leaves with coarse hairs. Slender, hairy stems 1–2 ft. high. Flowers cup shaped, to 3 in. across, slightly fragrant, yellow, orange, salmon, rose, pink, cream, or white. In mild climates blooms winter and early spring from plants set out in fall. Where winters are cold, sow seed in earliest spring for summer bloom. To prolong bloom, pick flowers frequently. Several good strains available; Champagne Bubbles is showiest. Cover young plants with screen to protect from birds. Both this and Alpine poppy make excellent cut flowers; sear cut ends in flame before placing in water.

P. orientale. ORIENTAL POPPY. Perennial. Zones 1–17. Short-lived in warm-winter climates. Strong, bold plants to 4 ft. Coarse, hairy, divided leaves. Flowers single or double, 3–6 in. across, in brilliant and pastel shades. Many named varieties. Plants die back in midsummer; new leafy growth appears in early fall, lasts over winter, develops rapidly in warm weather. Combine with bearded iris, lupine, nepeta, violas. Baby's breath *(Gypsophila)* makes good summer filler when poppies go dormant.

P. rhoeas. FLANDERS FIELD POPPY, SHIRLEY POPPY. Summer annual. Slender, branching, hairy, 2–5 ft. high. Leaves short, irregularly divided. Flowers 2 in. or more across, single and double, in red, pink, white, orange, scarlet, salmon, bicolor. Selections with single scarlet flowers, black bases sold as 'American Legion' or 'Flanders Field'. Broadcast seed mixed with fine sand. Sow successively for bloom from spring through summer. Take cut flowers when buds first show color. Remove seed capsules (old flower bases) weekly to prolong the bloom season.

PAPAYA. See *Carica papaya.*

PAPER MULBERRY. See *Broussonetia papyrifera.*

PAPHIOPEDILUM. LADY'S SLIPPER. Terrestrial orchids. Cool greenhouse or indoor plants. This name applies to lady's slipper orchids (sometimes sold as *Cypripedium*) native to tropical regions of Asia. Under this name fall large-flowered hybrids grown commercially for cut flowers. Blooms are perky, usually one, occasionally two or more to stem. Many of them shine as if they'd been lacquered. Flowers may be white, yellow, green with white stripes,

Paphiopedilum insigne

pure green, or combination of background colors and markings in tan, mahogany brown, maroon, green, and white.

Graceful arching foliage (no pseudobulbs) either plain green or mottled. Usually plain-leafed forms flower in winter, mottled-leafed forms flower in summer. Most plants at orchid dealers' establishments are hybrids.

In general, mottled-leafed forms do best with about 60°–65° F. night temperatures, 70°–85° F. day temperature. Plain-leafed forms require 55°–65° F. night temperatures, and 65°–75° F. day temperatures. They have no rest period, so should be kept moist at all times. A good potting medium: equal parts ground bark and sandy loam. Don't plant in oversize pot; plants thrive when crowded. Hardiest kinds can be grown in pots indoors, treated as house plants. They thrive in less light than most orchids require.

P. insigne. Polished lady slipper-type flowers on stiff, brown, hairy stems any time October-March. Sepals and petals green and white spotted and striped brown; pouch reddish brown. Hardy to brief exposures of 28°F.

PAPYRUS. See *Cyperus papyrus.*

PARADISE PALM. See *Howea forsterana.*

PARIS DAISY. See *Chrysanthemum frutescens.*

PARKINSONIA aculeata. JERUSALEM THORN, MEXICAN PALO VERDE. Deciduous tree. Zones 11–24; especially valuable in Zones 12 and 13. Rapid growth at first, slowing to eventual 15–30 ft. high and wide. Yellow green bark, spiny twigs; picturesque form. Sparse foliage; leaves 6–9 in. long, with many tiny leaflets which quickly fall in drought or cold. Numerous yellow flowers in loose 3–7-in.-long clusters. Long bloom season in spring, intermittent bloom throughout year.

Tolerates alkaline soil. Very drought tolerant. Stake young trees, train for high or low branching. Requires minimum attention once established. Does not do well with lawn watering. As shade tree, it filters sun rather than blocking it. Thorns, sparse foliage rule it out of tailored gardens. Flowering branches attractive in arrangements. Litter drop a problem on hard surfaces.

Parkinsonia aculeata

PARROT BEAK. See *Clianthus puniceus.*

PARROTIA persica. PERSIAN PARROTIA. Deciduous tree or large shrub. Zones 4–6, 15–17. Native to Persia. Choice and colorful; attractive all seasons of year. Most dramatic display comes in fall. Usually leaves turn from golden yellow to orange to rosy pink and finally scarlet. Slow-growing to 30 ft. or more, but tends to be shrub or multitrunked tree to 15 ft. Bark attractive in winter: smooth, gray, flakes off to leave white patches. Thick foliage is made up of lustrous, dark green, oval 3–4-in.-long leaves. It is drought tolerant once it becomes established.

Its flowers with red stamens are in dense heads surrounded by woolly brown bracts. They appear in spring before leaves open to give tree hazy red effect.

Parrotia persica

To train as tree, stake and shorten lower side branches. Allow upper branches to take their wide-spreading habit. When tree reaches desired height, remove lower shortened side branches cleanly.

PARROT'S BEAK. See *Lotus berthelotii.*

PARSLEY. Biennial herb treated as annual. All Zones. The 6–12-in.-high plants with their tufted, finely cut, dark green leaves make attractive edging for herb, vegetable, or flower garden. Attractive in boxes and pots. You can use the leaves fresh or dried as seasoning, fresh as garnishes. Parsley is most satisfactorily grown anew every year. Grow in partial shade if possible, or in sun. Buy plants at nursery or sow seed in place (April in Zones 1–7; December-May in Zones 8–11, 14–24; September-October in Zones 12, 13). Soak seed in warm water 24 hours before planting. Even then, it may not sprout for several weeks—an old story says that parsley seeds must go to the devil and come back before sprouting. Thin seedlings to 6–8 in. apart. Water regularly.

Parsley

Most attractive and most widely used are curled leaf kinds. For quantity production, ease of culture (and possibly superior flavor), try Italian or flat-leafed parsley (grows 2–3 ft. tall). Turnip-rooted or Hamburg parsley is grown for its fleshy, turnip shaped root, which is used as a cooked vegetable; leaves also make acceptable garnish.

PARSLEY PANAX. See *Polyscias fruticosa*.

PARSNIP. Biennial vegetable. All Zones. Needs deep, well-prepared, loose soil for long roots; some varieties are 15 in. long. Grow in full sun. In cold-winter areas plant seeds in late spring, harvest in fall and leave surplus in ground to be dug as needed in winter. In mild-climate areas sow in fall and harvest in spring; in such areas parsnips can't stay in ground even in winter, as they will become tough and woody. Soak seeds in water 24 hours before planting to improve germination. Sow seeds ½ in. deep in rows 2 ft. apart; thin seedlings to 3 in. apart.

Parsnip

PARTHENOCISSUS (*Ampelopsis*). Deciduous vines. Cling to walls by sucker discs at ends of tendrils. Superb and dependable fall leaf color, orange to scarlet. Flowers are insignificant. Ample water, moderate feeding. Grow in most exposures, sun or quite a bit of shade. Attractive to birds. Think twice before planting them against wood or shingle siding; they can creep under, and their clinging tendrils are hard to remove at repainting time.

Parthenocissus quinquefolia

P. henryana. SILVERVEIN CREEPER. Zones 4–9, 14–17. Resembles smaller (to 20 ft.), less aggressive Virginia creeper. Leaves formed by 5 leaflets, 1–2½ in. each, which open purplish, turn dark bronzy green with pronounced silver veining and purple undersides. Color is best in shade; colors fade to plain green in strong light. Rich red autumn foliage. Clings to walls, but needs some support to get started. Also good wall spiller, small scale ground cover. Rare.

P. inserta. VIRGINIA CREEPER, WOODBINE. All Zones. Western form of *P. quinquefolia*. Native to Rocky Mountains and eastward. Tendrils have few or no sucker discs; plants tend to scramble rather than cling.

P. quinquefolia. VIRGINIA CREEPER. All Zones. Big, vigorous vine that clings or runs over ground, fence, trellis. Looser growth than Boston ivy, and can be used to drape its trailing branches over trellis. Leaves divided into 5 separate 6-in. leaflets with saw-toothed edges. Good ground cover on slopes; can control erosion. Sun or shade. *P. q.* 'Engelmannii' has smaller leaves, denser growth.

P. tricuspidata. BOSTON IVY. All Zones. Semievergreen in mild-winter areas. Glossy leaves variable in shape, usually 3 lobed or divided into 3 leaflets, up to 8 in. wide. Clings tightly to make fast, dense, even wall cover. This is ivy of the "Ivy League;" covers brick or stone in areas where English ivy freezes. North or east walls only in Zones 12, 13. Variety 'Beverly Brooks' has large leaves, good fall color, is fast-growing. Most leaves are divided into 3 leaflets. 'Lowii' has smaller (1½ in.), deeply lobed leaves. 'Veitchii' has small leaves, the younger ones purplish. Vine with leaves strongly resembling those of *P. tricuspidata* is *Ampelopsis brevipedunculata*.

Parthenocissus tricuspidata

PARTRIDGE BREAST. See *Aloe variegata*.

PASQUE FLOWER. See *Anemone pulsatilla*.

PASSIFLORA. PASSION VINE. Evergreen, semievergreen, or deciduous vines. Climb by tendrils to 20–30 ft. Name comes from manner in which flower parts symbolize elements of passion of the Lord; the lacy crown could be a halo or crown of thorns; the five stamens the five wounds; the ten petal-like parts the ten faithful apostles.

Passiflora alatocaerulea

Vigorous, likely to overgrow and tangle themselves; to keep plant open and prevent buildup of dead inner tangle, prune excess branches back to base or juncture with another branch. Do this annually after second year. Tolerant of many soils; average water and feeding. Favorite food plant of caterpillars of gulf fritillary butterfly.

Use on trellises or walls for their vigor and bright showy flowers, or use as soil-holding bank cover. Full sun. In cold-winter climates use as greenhouse or house plants.

P. alatocaerulea (*P. pfordtii*). Evergreen or semievergreen vine. Zones 12–24; root hardy perennial in Zones 5–9. Hybrid between *P. alata, P. caerulea*. Best known, most widely planted, probably least subject to caterpillars. Leaves 3 in. long, 3 lobed. Fragrant 3½–4-in. flowers, white shaded pink and lavender. Crown deep blue or purple. Blooms all summer. In colder areas give it warm place out of wind; plant against wall or under overhang. Mulch roots in winter. Forms no fruit.

P. caerulea. BLUE CROWN PASSION FLOWER. Evergreen or semievergreen vine. Zones 12–24; root hardy perennial in Zones 5–9. Leaves smaller than *P. alatocaerulea,* 5 lobed. Flowers smaller, greenish white, crown white and purple. Fruit small, orange-colored, oval.

P. edulis. PASSION FRUIT. Semievergreen vine. Zones 15–17, 21–24. Leaves 3 lobed, deeply toothed, light yellow green. Flowers white with white and purple crown, 2 in. across. Fruit deep purple, fragrant, 3 in. long, delicious in beverages, fruit salads, sherbets. Fruit produced in spring and fall. There is a yellow-fruited variety.

P. incarnata. MAYPOP. All Zones. Perennial vine. Only if you live in really cold area and want very hardy passion flower. Native to eastern U.S. Spreads prodigiously by root runners, dies back at first frost. Flowers 2 in. across, white with purple and white crown. Fruit 2 in. long, yellowish green, edible. Grow from seed.

P. 'Incense'. Zones 5–24. Hybrid between the preceding and an Argentinian species. Hardy to 0°F., even holding its foliage through short cold spells—deciduous otherwise. Flowers are 5 in. wide, violet with lighter crown, scented like sweet peas. Egg shaped 2-in. fruit drop when ripe, turn olive to yellow green. Fragrant, tasty pulp.

P. jamesonii. Evergreen vine. Zones 14–24. Especially good in Zones 17, 24. Glossy leaves 3 lobed. Flowers long tubed (to 4 in.), salmon to coral, profuse all summer. Fast-growing bank, fence cover.

P. manicata. Evergreen vine. Zones 17, 23, 24. Leaves 3 lobed. Flowers to 4 in. across, scarlet with narrow blue crown.

(Continued on next page)

P. mollissima. Evergreen vine. Zones 12–24. Soft green foliage; leaves 3 lobed, deeply toothed. Long-tubed pink to rose flowers 3 in. across. Yellow 2-in. fruit. Rampant growth makes it good bank cover, but problem planted with trees, shrubs.

P. racemosa *(P. princeps)*. Evergreen vine. Zones 23, 24. Tall, slender. Leathery leaves fairly pest free. Showy deep rose maroon to coral flowers with purple and white crown hang from main stems in long wiry clusters.

PASSION FRUIT. See *Passiflora edulis*.

PASSION VINE. See *Passiflora*.

PAULOWNIA tomentosa *(P. imperialis)*. EMPRESS TREE. Deciduous tree. All Zones; young trees may need protection in Zones 1–3; flowers to be expected only in Zones 4–9, 11–24. Somewhat similar to catalpa in growth habit, leaves. Fast to 40-50 ft. with nearly equal spread. Heavy trunk and heavy, nearly horizontal branches. Foliage gives tropical effect; leaves are light green, heart shaped, 5–12 in. long, 4–7 in. wide. Best with some summer irrigation. If tree is cut back annually or every other year, it will grow as billowy foliage mass with giant-sized leaves up to 2 ft. However, this pruning will reduce flower production.

Paulownia tomentosa

Flower buds form in autumn and persist over winter; they are brown and size of small olives. Buds open before leaves in early spring to form upright clusters (6–12 in. long) of trumpet shaped 2-in.-long, fragrant flowers of lilac blue with darker spotting and yellow stripes inside. Flowers are followed by top shaped seed capsules 1½-2 in. long. They hang on tree so that both seed capsules and flower buds are present at same time. Does not flower well where winters are very cold (buds freeze) or very mild (buds may drop off). In areas of strong winds, leaves will be damaged. Bark is apt to sunburn in Zones 7–14, 18–21. Give it a place where falling flowers and leaves are not objectionable. Not tree to garden under because of dense shade and surface roots.

PAUROTIS wrightii. See *Acoelorrhaphe wrightii*.

PAXISTIMA *(Pachystima, Pachistima)*. Evergreen shrubs. Zones 1–10, 14–21. Low growing with small, shiny, leathery leaves, insignificant flowers. Hardiness and compact habit make them useful as low hedges, edgings, ground cover. Full sun near coast; partial shade, ample water in hot interiors. Best in well-drained soil.

Paxistima canbyi

P. canbyi. Native to mountains, eastern U. S. Makes mat 9–12 in. tall, with narrow leaves ¼–1 in. long, ¼ in. wide. Foliage dark green, turning bronze in fall and winter.

P. myrsinites. OREGON BOXWOOD. Native to mountains in West. Dense growth to 2–4 ft. (usually much less), easily kept lower by pruning. More compact in sun. Leaves larger than *P. canbyi.*

PEA. Cool-season vegetable. Easy crop to grow when conditions are right, and delicious when freshly picked. They need coolness and humidity and must be planted at just the right time. If you have space and don't mind the bother, grow tall (vining) peas on trellises, strings, or screen; tall peas reach 6 ft. or more and bear heavily. Bush types are more commonly grown in home gardens; they require no support. Grow either type in full sun. A good tall variety is 'Alderman'. Fine bush varieties are 'Green Arrow', 'Little Marvel', 'Morse's Progress No. 9', 'Freezonian', and 'Blue

Pea

Bantam'. An unusually good vegetable (and one indispensable to Oriental cooking) is edible-podded snow or sugar pea— 'Mammoth Melting Sugar' is tall-vining variety; 'Dwarf Gray Sugar' is a bushy one. 'Sugar Snap' is an edible-podded pea with full complement of full-sized peas inside; instead of shelling, you merely string and snap, just like green beans.

Soil should be nonacid, water retentive but fast draining. Peas are hardy and should be planted just as early in spring as ground can be worked. Where winters are mild and spring days quickly become too warm for peas, plant from October through February, later dates applying where winters are coldest. Sow 2 in. deep in light soil, shallower (½–1 in.) in heavy soil or in winter. Moisten ground thoroughly before planting; do not water again until seedlings have broken through surface. Leave 24 in. between rows and thin seedlings to stand 2 in. apart. Successive plantings several days apart will lengthen bearing season, but don't plant so late that summer heat will overtake ripening peas; most are ready to bear in 60–70 days.

Plants need little fertilizer, but if soil is very light give them one application of complete fertilizer. If weather becomes warm and atmosphere dry, supply water in furrows; overhead water encourages mildew. Provide support for climbing peas as soon as tendrils form. When peas begin to mature, pick *all* pods that are ready; if seeds ripen, plant will stop producing. Vines are brittle; steady them with one hand while picking with the other. Above all—shell and cook (or freeze) peas right after picking.

PEACH AND NECTARINE. Peach *(Prunus persica)* and nectarine *(Prunus persica nucipersica)* trees look alike and have same general cultural needs. Nectarine fruit differ from peaches only in having smooth skins and (in some varieties) a slightly different flavor. Climate adaptation of nectarine is more limited.

Peach

In terms of landscaping and fruit growing, there are four kinds of peaches: flowering peaches, fruiting peaches, flowering-fruiting (dual-purpose) peaches, and dwarf fruiting peaches that form large bushes. Here we consider the three groups of fruiting peaches. For strictly flowering peaches, see *Prunus*.

A regular fruiting peach tree grows fast to 25 ft. high and spreads as wide; well-pruned trees are usually less than 15 ft. tall and 15–18 ft. wide. The peach starts bearing large crops when 3–4 years old and reaches its peak at 8–12 years.

Peaches do best if they get some chilling in winter and clear hot weather during growing season. Peaches generally set few flowers and pollinate poorly where spring is cool and rainy. Only specially selected varieties do well in extremely mild-winter areas. Lack of winter chilling results in delayed foliation, few fruit, and eventual death of tree. The high desert satisfies chilling requirements but late frosts make early-blooming varieties risky. Few are satisfactory in mild-winter areas of low desert.

To save space, you can graft different varieties on one tree or plant 3 or 4 varieties in one hole.

Peaches require well-drained soil and regular fertilizing program. Prune these trees more heavily than any other fruit trees. When planting bare-root tree, cut back to 2 ft. above ground. New branches will form below cut. After first year's growth, select three well-placed branches for scaffold limbs. Remove all other branches. On mature trees, each dormant season cut off 2/3 of previous year's growth by removing 2 of every 3 branches formed last year; or head back each branch to 1/3 its length. Or, head back some branches and cut out others. Can be trained as espaliers.

Peaches and nectarines tend to form too much fruit even with good pruning. Remove (thin) some excess fruit when they are about 1 in. wide. If growth becomes weak and leaves yellowish, feed with nitrogen fertilizer. In hot, dry summers, irrigate several times while fruit is on tree.

Protect all kinds of peaches and nectarines from peach leaf curl and peach tree borer. Two dormant sprayings, one in November and again in January before the buds swell, will control leaf curl. Use Bordeaux mixture or lime sulfur. Sprays combining oil and lime sulfur or fixed copper will control both scale insects and peach leaf curl. Borers attack at or just below ground level. Pull away soil to expose 2–3 in. of roots. Spray with sevin or diazinon in early June and every 3 weeks until mid-August.

FLOWERING-FRUITING PEACHES

These dual purpose peaches were developed in southern California for southern California conditions, but are widely adapted. Zones 7–9, 12–22. Most likely to succeed in Zone 13 is 'Daily News Four Star'.

'Daily News Three Star'. Deep pink double flowers. Highly colored red freestone with white flesh, in midsummer.

'Daily News Four Star'. Salmon pink double flowers. Highly colored red fruit with white flesh. Freestone. Midseason.

'Saturn'. Large, deep pink double flowers. High quality. Yellow-fleshed freestone. Midseason.

NATURAL DWARF PEACHES AND NECTARINES

Most fruit trees are dwarfed by grafting standard varieties on dwarfing root stocks. In case of peaches and nectarines, best dwarfs are genetic (natural) dwarf varieties. These are sold:

'Bonanza'. Peach. Blooms and bears fruit at 2 ft. high, 2 years old. Will eventually reach 6 ft. Semidouble rose pink flowers. Blushed red, yellow-fleshed freestone of good size and flavor. Early.

'Empress'. Peach. Semidwarf, reaching 4–5 ft. Pink to red skin, yellow-fleshed cling of large size and fine flavor. Early August.

'Flory'. Peach. Grows slowly to 5 ft., with equal spread. White-fleshed freestone. Bland flavor. Ripens July.

'Garden Delight'. Nectarine. Slow to 5–6 ft. Medium-sized, yellow-fleshed freestone. Midseason.

'Garden Gold'. Peach. To 5–6 ft. Medium-sized, yellow-fleshed freestone. Midseason.

'Garden Sun'. Peach. To 5–6 ft. Medium-sized, yellow-fleshed freestone. Early summer.

'Golden Gem'. Peach. To 5–6 ft. Double pink bloom. Large, yellow, red-blushed skin, yellow freestone. Midseason.

'Golden Glory'. Peach. To 5 ft. Large yellow-fleshed freestone. Skin golden with red blush. Heavy bearer. Ripens mid to late August.

'Golden Prolific'. Nectarine. Slow growing to 5 ft. Large yellow-fleshed freestone. Skin yellow, mottled with orange red. Ripens midseason.

'Golden Treasure'. Peach. To 5–6 ft. Golden, red-blushed, large yellow-fleshed freestone. Early August.

'Nectarina'. Nectarine. To 5–6 ft. Skin deep red and yellow. Orange-fleshed freestone ripening in late July.

'Silver Prolific'. Nectarine. Slow growing to 5–7 ft. Large yellow-fleshed freestone. Skin light yellow, blushed red. Rich flavor. Midseason.

'Southern Belle'. Nectarine. To 5 ft. Large yellow-fleshed freestone. Midseason. Low winter chilling requirement.

'Southern Flame'. Peach. To 5 ft. Large, yellow with red blush, yellow flesh. Freestone. Moderately low chilling requirement. Early midseason.

'Southern Rose'. Peach. To 5 ft. Large, yellow blushed red. Freestone. Needs little chilling. Ripens midseason.

'Southern Sweet'. Peach. To 5 ft. Medium-sized yellow fruit of good flavor. Freestone. Heavy bearer. Fairly low chilling requirement. Early ripening.

'Sunbonnet'. Nectarine. To 5 ft. Red skin, yellow flesh. Clingstone. Fairly low chilling requirement. Early midseason.

Peach and Nectarine

NAME	ZONES	FRUIT	COMMENTS
PEACHES			
'Australian Saucer'	13, 18–24	White fleshed, flattened end to end. Sweet, faint bitterish overtone. Very little acid. Freestone. Early.	Requires very little chilling and is nearly evergreen in mild regions.
'Autumn Gold'	3, 6–9, 14–16	Medium to large yellow freestone. Yellow skin striped red. Good quality. Ripens late in September.	Keeps well if picked when firm-ripe.
'Babcock'	15–16, 19–24	White freestone, small to medium, sweet flavor with some tang. Early.	Needs little winter chilling. Old-timer.
'Belle' ('Belle of Georgia')	10–12, 18–19	Large white freestone of fine flavor, attractive appearance. Early midseason.	Old favorite for table use.
'Blazing Gold'	3, 6, 8, 9, 14–16	Yellow freestone, small to medium, firm fleshed, good flavor. Early.	Not as high quality in Zones 3, 6 as in 8, 9, 14–16.
'Bonita'	15–24	Large yellow freestone with medium blush, firm flesh, fine flavor. Ripens in midseason.	Bred for mild-winter areas.
'Cardinal'	4–9, 14–16, 18	Medium to large clingstone. Bright red, yellow fleshed. One of the best early varieties.	Has ability to set fruit in cool, rainy spring weather.
'Dixired'	2, 3, 6–9, 14	Attractive red cling with yellow flesh. Very good flavor. Early.	Has tendency to split pits.
'Desertgold'	8, 9, 12, 13, 23	Medium-sized yellow semicling of good quality. Ripens late April-early May in low desert, early June in San Joaquin Valley.	Very early bloom rules it out wherever spring frosts are likely.
'Early Amber'	18–23	Medium yellow semicling. Yellow skin with dark red blush. Ripens late April.	Low chilling requirement; good producer in warm-winter areas.
'Early Crawford'	1–3, 6–12, 14, 18	Medium-sized yellow freestone, blushed red. Firm flesh, excellent flavor. A week earlier than 'Elberta'.	Fruit irregular in shape and in ripening, but an old favorite.

(Continued on next page)

NAME	ZONES	FRUIT	COMMENTS
'Early Elberta' ('Improved Elberta', 'Gleason Elberta', 'Lemon Elberta')	2–11, 14, 15	Superior in color and flavor to 'Elberta'. Freestone. Ripens week earlier than 'Elberta'.	Needs somewhat less heat than 'Elberta' and less winter chill; less subject to fruit drop. Thin well for good-sized fruit.
'Elberta'	1–3, 6–11, 14	Medium to large yellow freestone, skin blushed red, high quality. Midseason (later in Zone 6).	Needs good amount of winter chilling, high summer heat to ripen to full flavor.
'Fay Elberta' ('Gold Medal' in Northwest)	2, 3, 6–11, 14, 15, 18, 19	More colorful than 'Elberta', keeps a little better. Yellow-fleshed freestone. Ripens with 'Elberta'.	Has large, handsome single flowers. Thin it well.
'Flordasun'	18–23	Small yellow semicling. Faint blush over yellow skin. Fair to good flavor. Mid to late April.	Fruit becomes freestone when fully ripe.
'Fortyniner'	5–9, 14–16, 18	Large yellow freestone. Bright red blush over yellow. Good to excellent flavor. Early midseason.	Resembles 'J. H. Hale', the parent; about 1 week earlier.
'Giant Elberta'	1–3, 6	Large yellow-fleshed freestone of good quality. Early midseason.	Similar to 'July Elberta' in season, appearance, quality.
'Gold Dust'	6–9, 11, 14–16	Small to medium yellow freestone, high blush, good quality. Early.	Like 'Blazing Gold', but ripens 1 week later.
'Golden Blush'	18, 19	Medium large yellow-fleshed freestone of good flavor. Midseason.	Fast-growing, vigorous tree.
'Golden Jubilee'	2, 3, 5, 6	Medium yellow freestone of fair flavor. Tender. Ripens 3 weeks before 'Elberta'.	Good early peach in Zones 2, 3.
'Halberta' ('Hal-Berta Giant')	1–3, 6–11, 14, 18	Very large yellow freestone, very smooth skinned. Ripens with 'Elberta'.	Needs pollenizing; any other peach except 'J. H. Hale' or 'Indian Free' will do.
'Halehaven'	1–3, 6–11, 14–16	Medium to large, highly colored yellow freestone. Ripens 2 weeks ahead of 'Elberta'.	Fine large yellow freestone to use fresh or canned. Fruit and leaf buds very winter hardy.
'Halford'	1–3, 7–12, 14–16, 18	Large yellow cling. Heavy bearer. Mid to late August.	Basically a commercial canning peach.
'Halloween'	3, 7–9, 14, 15	Large yellow freestone. Yellow skin, red blush. Early October.	Tree productive. Fruits very late.
'Indian Blood Cling' ('Indian Cling')	1–3, 6–11, 14–16	Medium red-skinned clingstone. Flesh firm, yellow streaked red. Late.	Old variety with small but devoted band of enthusiasts. Good for preserves.
'Indian Free'	7–11, 14–16	Large, round, yellow freestone, deep red at pit. Tart until fully ripe. Late midseason.	Needs pollenizing by any other peach.
'J. H. Hale'	1–3, 7–11, 14–16	Very large, highly colored yellow freestone of high quality. Fine keeper. Ripens with 'Elberta'.	Needs pollenizing by any other peach except 'Halberta', 'Indian Blood'.
'Jim Bowie'	2, 3, 7–10, 18	Large yellow freestone. Yellow with slight blush. Sweet, very juicy. September.	Hardy, vigorous, spreading tree.
'July Elberta'	2, 3, 6–12, 14–16, 18, 19	Medium large, yellow-fleshed freestone of high quality. Ripens a month ahead of 'Elberta'.	Prolific bearer. May need extra thinning to get size.
'Loring'	2, 3, 6–9, 14, 15	Large, attractive yellow freestone. Skin with red blush, little fuzz. Good quality. Midseason.	Bears well where spring brings unpredictable weather.
'Mayflower'	2, 3, 10, 11	Medium white freestone. Greenish white skin blushed red. Tender, juicy. May-June.	Needs considerable winter chill to bear well.
'Meadowlark'	11, 12, 18, 20	Yellow-fleshed freestone much resembling 'Elberta'. Early.	Developed for these climate zones.
'Melba'	2, 3, 10, 11	Large white freestone. Pale yellow skin. Sweet, juicy. Long ripening season.	Sets fruit well in cold unsettled spring weather.
'Miller's Late'	7–11, 14, 18	Medium-sized yellow freestone peach of fair flavor. Very late ripening.	If you have to have peaches in mid-October. In cool-autumn areas, ripen off tree.
'Nectar'	7–11, 14–16	Medium to large white freestone peach of excellent flavor. Early midseason.	White peach fanciers consider it the best.
'Orange Cling' ('Miller Cling')	1–3, 7–12, 14–16, 18	Large, late clingstone peach with firm, deep yellow flesh. Late.	A favorite for home canning.
'Pacific Gold' ('Rochester')	3–6	Small yellow freestone with medium blush, yellow flesh. Early midseason.	Long ripening season. One of best in western Washington and Oregon for fresh use. Dependable producer.

NAME	ZONES	FRUIT	COMMENTS
'Polly'	1–3, 10	Medium white freestone. White skin blushed red. Juicy, excellent flavor. Late midseason.	Tree and buds very hardy to cold.
'Ranger'	3, 5–9, 14–16, 18	Medium large, highly colored freestone, yellow fleshed, good flavor. Early midseason, a month before 'Elberta'.	Heavy fruit bud set. High yielder. Excellent early canner.
'Redglobe'	3, 6–11, 14–16	Highly colored, firm-fleshed yellow freestone of good flavor. Three weeks before 'Elberta'.	Good for canning or freezing. Sometimes sets light crop in Zone 6.
'Redhaven'	3, 5, 12, 14–16	Brightly blushed yellow freestone. Long ripening season permits numerous pickings. Ripens 3–4 weeks ahead of 'Elberta'.	Colors up early so taste-test for ripeness. Thin early and well. One of best for planting. 'Early Redhaven' ripens 2 weeks earlier.
'Redskin'	1–3, 6–12, 14–16	Medium to large yellow freestone. Heavy red blush. Excellent quality fresh, canned, or frozen. Midseason.	Tree productive, needs less winter chill than 'Elberta'.
'Redwing'	18–24	Small, highly colored white freestone. Soft fleshed. Early.	Low winter chilling requirement.
'Rio Grande'	8–10, 15, 18–20	Medium to large yellow freestone. Red blush. Good quality. Early June.	Medium-sized productive tree with showy flowers.
'Rio Oso Gem'	3, 7–9, 14, 15	Medium large, yellow-fleshed freestone of excellent flavor. Ripens week later than 'Elberta'.	Small tree. Not vigorous. One of best.
'Robin'	18, 20	Small white clingstone. Bright color, soft flesh. Very early.	Mild flavor, low acid.
'Rochester' ('Pacific Gold')	3–6	Small yellow freestone with medium blush, yellow flesh. Early midseason.	Long ripening season. One of best for western Washington and Oregon for fresh use. Dependable producer.
'Rubidoux'	18, 20	Medium large yellow freestone, firm flesh, good keeper. Late midseason.	Developed specifically for these climate zones.
'Sam Houston'	2, 3, 6–11, 14–16, 18–20	Medium to large yellow freestone of 'Elberta' type. Ripens late June.	Needs less winter chill than 'Elberta'. Sets heavy crop, needs thinning.
'Shanghai'	14–16, 18–24	Medium white freestone. Red blush. Soft, juicy, very sweet flesh. Late midseason.	Vigorous tree. Fruit too soft for canning, freezing. Very fine flavor.
"Southland"	3, 6–9, 14–16	Attractive medium to large yellow-fleshed freestone. Midseason.	Not consistently productive in Zone 6.
'Springtime'	18–23	White semicling of high color, good flavor. Ripens late May–early June.	One of earliest.
'Strawberry Cling'	7–9, 14–16, 18–20	Large, creamy white marbled red. Clingstone. Flesh white, juicy, richly flavored. Early midseason.	Favorite with home canners.
'Strawberry Free'	7–9, 14–16, 18–20	Medium-sized white freestone. Medium blush, firm flesh, excellent flavor. Early midseason.	Old favorite of those who like white peaches.
'Summerset'	7–9, 14–16, 18, 19	Large yellow freestone with attractive red blush. Firm flesh is good for canning, freezing. Late.	Vigorous, productive tree.
'Sundar'	8, 9, 14, 18, 19	Large white freestone. Skin blushed red, rather tough. Juicy, sweet. Late.	Needs little winter chill.
'Tejon'	18–22	Small to medium semifreestone, very juicy, yellow flesh. Very early.	Very low chilling requirement.
'Tropi-berta'	8, 9, 14–16, 18–24	Large yellow freestone with red blush. Juicy with good flavor. Late midseason.	Very low chilling requirement.
'Ventura'	18–24	Medium-sized attractive yellow freestone. Very smooth skin. Midseason.	Developed especially for these climate zones.
'Veteran'	4–6	Medium-sized yellow freestone of good flavor. Ripens 10 days earlier than 'Elberta'.	Resembles 'Elberta' but rounder, less fuzzy. Sets fruit under adverse conditions.
'White Heath Cling' ('Heath')	7–11, 14–16	Medium to large, firm-fleshed, white clingstone, excellent flavor. Late.	Distinctive flavor, and a favorite for home canning.
NECTARINES			
'Fantasia'	3, 7–9, 14–16, 18–22	Large, bright yellow and red, freestone. Firm flesh. Ripens mid-July.	Short chilling requirement.

(Continued on next page)

NAME	ZONES	FRUIT	COMMENTS
'Flame Kist'	7–9, 14–16, 18–22	Large, yellow blushed red clingstone. Late.	Resistant to cracking; thin out tree to bring sunshine in on fruit and improve color.
'Flaming Gold'	7–9, 14, 15	Large yellow freestone. Skin blushed red. Early midseason.	Showy fruit.
'Flavortop'	3, 7–9, 14–16, 18, 19	Large, red with yellow undertone, freestone. Good quality.	Vigorous, productive tree.
'Freedom'	7–9, 11	Large, highly colored, yellow-fleshed freestone of high quality. Early midseason.	Beautiful fruit.
'Gold Mine'	7–9, 14–16, 18–24	Red blush, white-fleshed freestone. Late midseason.	Low winter chilling requirement.
'Gower'	7–9, 11, 14, 15	White freestone. Late midseason.	Good nectarine flavor.
'Independence'	7–9, 14–16, 18, 19	Large red freestone with yellow flesh of good flavor. Early.	Moderately vigorous, productive tree.
'John Rivers'	7–9, 14, 15	White freestone or semifreestone. Early.	Earliest good variety.
'Le Grand'	7–9, 14, 15	Very large, bright red and yellow nectarine. Firm yellow flesh. Clingstone. Ripens midseason.	Attractive and holds well. Many variants of this are entering trade—earlier and later, more colorful forms: 'Early Le Grand', 'Late Le Grand', 'Red Grand,' 'Ruby Grand', 'Sun Grand'.
'Panamint'	7–9, 14–16, 18–24	Bright red skin, yellow flesh, freestone. Midseason.	Very low chilling requirement.
'Pioneer'	7–9, 14–16, 18–23	Yellow overlaid with red. Flesh yellow touched with red. Freestone. Rich, distinctive flavor. Midseason.	Large pink flowers.
'Silver Lode'	7–9, 14–16, 18–20	White flesh, freestone, scarlet and white skin. Early.	Low chilling requirement.
'Stanwick'	7–9, 14, 15	Greenish white shaded purple red. White-fleshed freestone. Late.	Excellent flavor. Good for freezing.
'Stribling Giant Free'	7–9, 11	Resembles 'Freedom'.	More uniform production than 'Freedom'.
'Stribling White Free'	7–9, 11, 14–16	Large white nectarine blushed red. Sweet white flesh. Early.	Good home orchard tree.
'Sunred'	18–23	Medium, bright red. Semifreestone. Yellow flesh, good flavor. Very early.	Best in warm-winter areas.

PEACH LEAFED BLUEBELL. See *Campanula persicifolia.*

PEANUT. Summer annual. Best where summers are long and warm and soil is not acid. Plants resemble small sweet pea bushes 10–20 in. high. After bright yellow flower fades, "peg" (shootlike structure) develops at flower's base, grows down into soil and develops peanuts underground. Soil must be light-textured to admit penetration by the pegs. Sandy soil in full sun is ideal. Tender to frost but worth growing as novelty even in cool regions.

Buy seeds (unroasted peanuts) from mail order seed firms. Plant when soil warms up, setting nuts 2 in. deep in rows 3 ft. apart. Space shelled 'Jumbo Virginia' seeds 10 in. apart, 'Spanish' 4 in. apart (unshelled seeds 20 in. apart). Fertilize at planting time. Water regularly, especially at blossom time, up to 2 weeks before harvest. In 110–120 days after planting, foliage begins to yellow and plants are ready to dig. Loosen soil around plants and pull them up. Cure peanuts on vines in warm, airy place out of sunlight for 2–3 weeks, then strip from plants.

Peanut

PEANUT CACTUS. See *Chamaecereus sylvestri.*

PEAR *(Pyrus communis).* Deciduous fruit tree. Zones 1–11, 14–18. Pyramidal tree with strongly vertical branching; grows 30–40 ft. tall, sometimes more. Long-lived. Leaves are leathery, glossy, bright green. Clustered white flowers are handsome in early spring.

Takes damp, heavy soil better than most fruit trees; resistant to oak root fungus in soil. Good looking enough for garden use, and mature trees need little pruning, but trees need spraying for codling moth, aphids, and other pests. Fireblight can be serious problem. It makes entire branches die back quickly. Cut out blighted branches well below dead part; wash pruning tools with disinfectant between each cut.

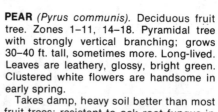

Pear

Train trees early to good framework of main branches, then prune lightly to keep good form, eliminate crowding branches. Pears on dwarfing understock are good small garden trees, excellent espaliers.

See chart on page 399 for description of pear varieties.

PEAR, ORIENTAL OR ASIATIC. Deciduous trees. All Zones. Descendants of *Pyrus pyrifolia (P. serotina)* and *P. ussuriensis*, two Asiatic species. Fruit differs from European pears in being generally round, firm to hard in texture, crisp and usually gritty to the bite. Often called apple pears because of roundness and crispness. Shouldn't be compared to European varieties for eating fresh; true value lies in firmness when cooked or when mixed with other fruit and vegetables in salads. Culture is same as for other pears. Trees often sold as apple pears, but are not hybrids of these fruits. Varieties available include 'Chojuro',

'Hosui', 'Ishiiwase', 'Kikusui', 'Niitaka', 'Nijisseiki' ('Twentieth Century'), 'Okusankichi' ('Late Korean'), 'Shinko', 'Shinseiki', 'Tsu Li', 'Ya Li', and 'Yakumo'.

PEARL BUSH. See *Exochorda*.

Pear

NAME	CLIMATE ADAPTABILITY	FRUIT CHARACTERISTICS	COMMENTS
'Anjou', 'd' Anjou' ('Beurre d'Anjou')	A favorite late variety in Northwest, northern California mountains.	Medium to large, round or short necked, yellow to russeted yellow. Fine flavor, late ripening.	Tree upright and vigorous. Not always consistent in bearing. Moderately susceptible to fireblight. There is a red-skinned selection, 'Red d'Anjou'.
'Bartlett'	Widely adaptable, but not at its best in mild winters. In southern California will succeed at high elevations or in cold canyon or valley floors.	Medium to large, with short but definite neck. Thin skinned, yellow or slightly blushed, very sweet and tender. Standard summer pear of fruit markets.	Generally sets fruit without pollination, but may require pollinator in cool California coastal areas and Northwest. Any variety except 'Seckel' will do. Tree form not the best, and somewhat subject to fireblight. Nevertheless a good home variety.
'Bosc' ('Beurre Bosc', 'Golden Russet')	Best in Northwest or at high altitudes farther south.	Medium to large, quite long necked, interesting and attractive in form. Heavy russeting on green or yellow ground color. Fine flavor. Midseason.	Large, upright, vigorous tree. Needs attention to pruning in youth. Highly susceptible to fireblight. Does not ripen well in cold storage; ripen it at room temperature.
'Clapp Favorite'	Very hardy to cold; good garden tree in Northwest, intermountain areas.	Resembles 'Bartlett'. Early, soft, and sweet.	Tree productive and shapely. Good foliage; highly susceptible to fireblight.
'Comice' ('Doyenne du Comice', 'Royal Riviera')	At its best in Hood River and Medford regions of Oregon, Santa Clara County in California.	Large to very large, roundish to pear shaped, thick skinned, russeted greenish yellow, sometimes blushed. Superb flavor and texture. Late.	Big, vigorous tree but slow to reach bearing age. Moderately susceptible to fireblight. Bears well only when soil, climate, and exposure are right. Bears better in Northwest with pollinator.
'Douglas'	Has short chilling requirement, but is also quite hardy.	Small to medium, oval in shape, greenish yellow. Flavor sweet to acid. Texture tender, with some grittiness.	Like other hybrids with Oriental pear, this one is highly resistant to fireblight.
'Fan Stil'	Low winter chilling requirements, high tolerance to heat and cold. Grown in high desert.	Medium sized, yellow with slight red blush. Crisp, juicy. August.	Vigorous, upright growth. Highly resistant to fireblight. Consistent bearer.
'Flemish Beauty'	Grown in Northwest.	Medium to large roundish pear, yellow, with pronounced red blush. Fine flavor. Early midseason.	Large, productive, very hardy tree. Fruit best ripened off tree.
'Garber'	Same as 'Fan Stil'.	Resembles 'Kieffer' but more rounded in form, lighter in color. Quality similar.	Tree moderately vigorous, somewhat resistant to fireblight.
'Kieffer'	Same as 'Fan Stil'.	Medium to large, oval, greenish yellow blushed dark red. Gritty in texture, fair in flavor. Best picked from tree and ripened at 65°F. Late.	Oriental pear hybrid, and quite resistant to fireblight. Good pear for extreme climates.
'Le Conte'	Same as 'Fan Stil'.	Resembles 'Kieffer'. Roundish, gritty, late.	Most tolerant to summer heat; somewhat resistant to fireblight.
'Max-Red Bartlett'	See 'Bartlett'.	Like 'Bartlett' except bright red in skin color and somewhat sweeter.	Red color extends to twigs and tints leaves. Needs pollinator in Northwest.
'Monterrey'	Same as 'Fan Stil'. Originated in Monterrey, Mexico.	Large, apple shaped fruit with yellow skin. Flavor good with little grit cell content. August-September.	Probably cross between an Oriental and a European pear. Fireblight resistance not evaluated.
'Moonglow'	Wide climate tolerance.	Somewhat like 'Bartlett' in looks. Flesh juicy, soft. Flavor good. Ripens 2 weeks before 'Bartlett'.	Tree upright, vigorous, very heavy bearer. Very resistant to fireblight.
'Seckel' ('Sugar')	Widely adaptable.	Very small, very sweet and aromatic. Roundish to pear shaped, yellow brown. Flesh granular. Early midseason.	Tree fairly resistant to fireblight, highly productive.
'Sure Crop'	Prolonged bloom period makes it safe bearer where spring frosts come late.	Resembles 'Bartlett' in looks and flavor. Bears August-September.	Consistent annual bearer. Fairly resistant to fireblight.
'Winter Bartlett'	See 'Bartlett'.	Smaller than 'Bartlett', firmer, later in ripening.	Tree spreading, loose, somewhat susceptible to fireblight.
'Winter Nelis'	Northwest. Mountains, cold valley floors in Southern California.	Small to medium, roundish, dull green or yellowish, rough. Very fine flavor. Late.	Very fine keeper, fine for baking but not attractive pear. Tree moderately susceptible to fireblight. Needs pollinator.

PECAN. See *Carya illinoensis.*

PEDILANTHUS tithymaloides. DEVIL'S BACKBONE. House plant. Cultivated varieties seldom exceed 1½ ft., are usually much less. Erect, fleshy, cylindrical stems have milky juice. Leaves in 2 rows, like ribs attached to backbone. Flowers small, in dense clusters atop stems; red bracts are showy parts. Commonest is 'Variegatus', with 4-in.-long oval leaves of light green variegated with white and pink. 'Nana Compacta' has dark green leaves crowded together on short, erect stems. Plants need warmth, good light, house plant soil, and regular water.

Pedilanthus tithymaloides 'Variegatus'

PEEPUL. See *Ficus religiosa.*

PELARGONIUM. GERANIUM. Shrubby perennials. Zones 17, 24 are ideal climates; next best are Zones 15, 16, 22, 23; possible but less easy are Zones 8, 9, 12–14, 18–21; elsewhere a pelargonium or geranium is house plant or summer bedding plant.

Geranium here is used as a common name; it's hard to be both botanically correct and conversationally clear. Pelargoniums, *to the botanist,* are all evergreen perennials or shrubby perennials that endure light frosts but not hard freezes and have slightly asymmetrical flowers in clusters. Most come from South Africa. In gardeners' conversation, a pelargonium is a Martha (or Lady) Washington geranium (or pelargonium). To the botanist, a geranium is one of many annual or perennial plants, mostly from the northern hemisphere, that have symmetrical flowers borne singly or in clusters; some are weeds, some valued perennial border or rock garden plants. To the gardener, a geranium is an ivy geranium, a fancy-leafed geranium, a common geranium, or a scented geranium; all are species or varieties of *Pelargonium.* Gardeners also use the word to speak of the whole works—all true geraniums and all true pelargoniums.

Most garden geraniums can be divided among 3 species of *Pelargonium:* Martha Washington geranium *(P. domesticum);* common geranium *(P. hortorum)*—this group also includes variegated forms usually referred to as fancy-leafed or colored-leafed geraniums—and ivy geranium *(P. peltatum).* In addition, many other species have scented leaves.

All geraniums do well in pots. Common geraniums grow well in garden beds; Martha Washington geraniums are also planted in beds, but tend to get rangy. Some varieties of Martha Washington are used in hanging baskets. Ivy geraniums are good in hanging containers, raised beds, as ground cover, bank cover. Use scented geraniums in close-up situations—in pots or in ground (in mild areas). For good bloom on potted geranium indoors, place it in a sunny window or in the brightest light possible.

In the garden, plant geraniums in full sun in coastal areas, light shade in hot-summer climates; never in dense shade. Plant in any good, fast draining soil. If soil is alkaline, add peat moss, or nitrogen-fortified ground

Pelargonium crispum

Pelargonium domesticum

Pelargonium graveolens

Pelargonium hortorum

Pelargonium peltatum

bark or sawdust, to planting bed. Water common geraniums growing in ground when soil dries to about 1 in. below surface—best slightly on dry side. In warm weather, water Martha Washington geraniums deeply once a week. Water ivy geraniums every 10 days–2 weeks. Geraniums of any kind in good garden soil need little feeding; if in light sandy soil feed 2–3 times during active growing season.

Pelargonium tomentosum

Remove faded geranium flowers regularly to encourage new bloom. Pinch growing tips in early growth stages to force side branches. Prune after last frost, using tip cuttings to start new plants. With proper pinching and support it is possible to raise standard ("tree") or espalier geraniums.

Geraniums in pots bloom best when somewhat potbound. When needed, repot only in next larger pot. In warm weather, water common geraniums in pots every other day; Martha Washington geraniums may need daily watering.

To control tobacco budworm on common geraniums, use sevin or diazinon or orthene as soon as worms appear in summer, fall; see page 58. Control aphids and whiteflies on Martha Washington geraniums with all-purpose spray. Use a miticide to control red spider mites on ivy geraniums.

P. domesticum. LADY WASHINGTON PELARGONIUM, MARTHA WASHINGTON GERANIUM, REGAL GERANIUM. Erect or somewhat spreading, to 3 ft. More rangy than common geranium. Leaves heart shaped to kidney shaped, dark green, 2–4 in. broad, with crinkled margins, unequal sharp teeth. Large showy flowers 2 in. or more across in loose rounded clusters, in white and many shades of pink, red, lavender, purple, with brilliant blotches and markings of darker colors. Blooms in spring and summer.

P. hortorum. COMMON GERANIUM, GARDEN GERANIUM. Most popular, widely grown. Shrubby, succulent stemmed, to 3 ft. or more; older plants grown in open (in mild areas) become woody. Leaves round or kidney shaped, velvety and hairy, soft to the touch, edges indistinctly lobed and scallop toothed; most varieties show zone of deeper color just inside leaf margin. Some are plain green; others, colored-leafed or fancy-leafed varieties, have zones, borders, or splashes of brown, gold, red, white, or green in various combinations. Some also have highly attractive flowers. Flowers single or double, not as large as Lady Washington, flatter, usually in solid colors, many more flowers to a cluster. Many varieties in white and shades of pink, rose, red, orange, and violet. Flowers appear spring through fall.

There are also dwarf-growing, cactus-flowered, and other novelty kinds. Tough, attractive geraniums for outdoor bedding can be grown from seed, flowering the first summer. Sprinter series is earliest to bloom; plants of both it and the Carefree series need no pinching. Double Dip selections have double flowers. All are available in single colors or in mixture.

P. peltatum. IVY GERANIUM. Trailing plants to 2–3 ft. or longer. Leaves rather succulent, glossy, bright green, 2–3 in. across, ivylike, with pointed lobes. Few to several 1-in., single or double flowers in rounded clusters are white, pink, rose, red, and lavender, 2 upper petals blotched or striped. Many named varieties. Flat-grown plants for ground cover usually labeled only by color. 'L'Elegante' has foliage strongly edged with white, and other varieties have white or yellow veins in leaves.

Scented geraniums. Many species and varieties are grown for fragrance of their leaves, which may resemble various fruit, flowers, herbs, or spices. They are fun to collect and have a few limited uses—in sachets, for flavoring sauces or jellies, for scenting fingerbowls. Mostly, people just like to brush the foliage and enjoy the pleasant perfume. Common names describe the fragrances. Fairly common are lemon-scented geranium, *P. crispum; P. graveolens,* rose geranium (there are other rose geraniums); lime-scented geranium, *P. nervosum;* and apple-scented geranium, *P. odoratissimum.*

P. tomentosum. PEPPERMINT-SCENTED GERANIUM. Large, 3–5-in.-wide, lobed leaves, velvety to the touch. Spreads to about 2–4 ft. Small white flowers in fluffy clusters. Use as ground cover in partial shade in frost free gardens. Leafy branches are striking draped over wall or hanging from basket.

PELLAEA. CLIFF-BRAKE. Ferns. Small plants, not striking in appearance, but with charmingly detailed foliage. The first two tolerate summer drought, but look dry. Second two are good house plants.

P. andromedifolia. COFFEE FERN. Zones 6-9, 14-24. Native to California, southern Oregon. Finely cut fronds of gray green to bluish green on thin wiry stalks. To 18 in. high. With shade and ample water will remain green.

P. mucronata. BIRD'S-FOOT FERN. Zones 2-11, 14-24. Larger than the preceding, with gray green, airy fronds and narrow leaflets arranged in threes.

P. rotundifolia. ROUNDLEAF FERN. Zones 14-17, 19-24. Small fern with spreading fronds to 1 ft. long. Nearly round leaflets are evenly spaced about ¾ in. across. Pretty fern to contrast with finer-textured ferns or to show off in pots, baskets, or raised beds. Filtered shade. Hardy to 24°F.

P. viridis (*P. adiantoides*). Zones 14-17, 19-24. Fronds to 2 ft. long, fresh green leaflets oval to lance shaped. Ground cover, rock garden, containers. Filtered shade. Hardy to 24°F.

*Pellaea
rotundifolia*

PENCILBUSH, PENCIL TREE. See *Euphorbia tirucalli.*

PENNISETUM setaceum (*P. ruppelii*). FOUNTAIN GRASS. Perennial grass. All Zones. Dense rounded clump to 4 ft. Narrow arching leaves 2 ft. long. Hollow 3-4-ft. stems in summer tipped with fuzzy, showy, coppery pink or purplish flower spikes. Use in dry locations, as in gravel beds; as focal point in low ground covers. Any soil; full sun; drought resistant; goes dormant in winter. Cut stems for arrangements before flowers go to seed; a pest if not controlled. Variety 'Cupreum', reddish brown leaves, dark plumes, does not set seed; grow from divisions or cuttings.

*Pennisetum
setaceum*

PENNYROYAL. See *Mentha pulegium.*

PENSTEMON. BEARD TONGUE. Perennials, evergreen shrubs and shrublets. A few are widely grown; most others are sold only by specialists. All have tubular flowers in bright reds and blues (commonest) but also soft pinks through salmon and peach to deep rose, lilac, deep purple, white, and rarely yellow. Hummingbirds are attracted to flowers. Of some 250 species, most are native to western U.S.—some on highest mountains, some in the desert, others in forest glades, foothills, or plains, from Canada into Mexico. Many are showy in bloom, and possibilities for hybridization are rich.

*Penstemon
heterophyllus
purdyi*

All penstemons best in full sun (light shade in hot-summer climates). Need fast drainage; many kinds best in loose, gravelly soil, with infrequent watering. Usually short-lived (3-4 years). In dry years or with little water, plants of wild species may thrive; in too rich soil and with too much water they may die quickly. Hybrids and selections tend to be easier to grow alongside regular garden plants.

P. antirrhinoides. Evergreen shrub. Zones 8-24. Native to southern California and northern Baja California. Stiffly spreading, much branched, 3-6 ft. tall. Leaves are narrow, to ½ in. long. Flowers bright yellow, ½-¾ in. long, very broad, in leafy clusters; buds brownish red. Blooms April-June. Dormant in summer, loses lower leaves; use in fringe areas of garden. Water little in summer.

P. barbatus. Perennial. All Zones. Native to mountains from Colorado and Utah to Mexico. Open, somewhat sprawling habit,

to 3 ft. Bright green leaves, 2-6 in. long. Long, loose spikes of red flowers about 1 in. long; early summer bloom. Selections include 'Prairie Dusk', deep purple flowers on 2-ft. spikes; 'Prairie Fire', scarlet flowers on 30-in. spikes; and 'Rose Elf', deep rose on 30-in. spikes. All are short-lived in warm-winter areas, tolerate extreme cold.

P. barrettiae. Perennial. Zones 1-7. Native to Columbia River gorge in Oregon and Washington. Shrubby, branching, to 1 ft. high. Leaves leathery, blue green, to 3 in. long, toothed. Flowers abundant in short spikes, rose purple, 1-1½ in. long. Blooms April-June.

P. cordifolius. Evergreen shrub. Zones 8, 9, 14-24. Native to coast of southern California. Loose branching, half climbing, with flexible, arching branches to 10 ft.; fuchsialike leaves ½-1½ in. long. Red tubular flowers 1-1½ in. long, in dense clusters at tips of stems; April-June. Yellow-flowered forms exist. Little water in summer if soil is heavy.

P. davidsonii (*P. menziesii davidsonii*). Perennial. Zones 1-7. Native to high mountains of Sierra Nevada and western Nevada north to Washington. Mat-forming alpine to 3 in. high. Leaves oval, to ½-¾ in. long. Flowers violet blue, 1-1½ in. long; July-August. Ideal for gravelly slope in rock garden.

P. gloxinioides. BORDER PENSTEMON, GARDEN PENSTEMON. Perennial treated as annual in cold-winter climates. Plants so named are selections of *P. hartwegii* or hybrids between it and *P. cobaea*. All Zones. Compact, bushy, upright stems to 2-4 ft. tall. Tubular flowers in loose spikes at ends of stems, in almost all colors but blue and yellow. Mass in borders, or group with other summer-flowering plants.

*Penstemon
gloxinioides*

Plant in full sun; partial shade in hot-summer areas. Subject to root rot in heavy, wet soil. In mild climates, set out flat-grown plants in fall for bloom in April. Older plants, if cut back after main bloom, flower again later in summer on side branches. Easy to grow from seed; several good mixed-color strains available. For plants in separate colors, make softwood cuttings from desirable plants. Some nurseries sell cutting-grown plants in separate colors.

P. heterophyllus purdyi. Perennial. Zones 6-24. Native to Sierra Nevada foothills and Coast Ranges of California. Stems upright or spreading, 12-24 in. high. Narrow, pointed leaves 1-3 in. long. Spikelike clusters of flowers varying from rosy lavender to intense gentian blue. Blooms April-July. Most nurseries that stock this plant sell it as 'Blue Bedder' penstemon.

P. newberryi. MOUNTAIN PRIDE. Perennial. Zones 1-9. Native to higher elevations of Sierra Nevada. Matted plant to 20 in. high, woody at base. Leaves thick, roundish, toothed, ½-1½ in. long. Flowers rose red, about 1 in. long; June-August.

P. pinifolius. Small shrublet. All Zones. Spreading 4-6 in. tall (rarely to 2 ft.) with crowded needlelike leaves ¾ in. long. Coral to scarlet flowers 1½ in. long. Rock garden or low border plant.

P. rupicola. Evergreen subshrub. Zones 1-7. Native to Cascade and Siskiyou Mountains. Trailing, much branched, to 4 in. high. Leaves roundish, blue green, fine toothed, ⅓-¾ in. long. Flowers bright rose crimson, ½-1½ in. long; June-August. Gravel or perfectly drained soil a must. Beautiful in rock gardens, in dry wall near miniature campanulas. Lesser known, white-flowered form is available; it needs half shade, is somewhat more difficult than species.

PEONY. See *Paeonia.*

PEPEROMIA. Perennials. House or greenhouse plants grown for foliage. Evergreen, often succulent; usually prostrate or trailing. Tiny flowers in dense, small, slender spikes. Use in planters, dish gardens, or other containers. Can be used as ground cover in large indoor planting. Grow in north light, or in diffused light protected from direct sun (as by wide overhang). Cool

Peperomia caperata

or warm temperature. Light, well-drained soil; not too much water. Propagate by stem, crown, or leaf cuttings (insert lower ½ of leaf in 2-in. pot of ½ sand, ½ leaf mold).

Following are a few of many sold by house plant specialists.

P. argyreia *(P. sandersii)*. WATERMELON PEPEROMIA. Compact, nearly stemless, with rosette of round, 3–5-in.-long, gray striped leaves on long red stems.

P. caperata. EMERALD RIPPLE. Plants 3–4 in. tall. Leaves rich green, heart shaped, deeply veined, borne densely on very short, reddish stalks. Tiny greenish white flowers in spikes. 'Little Fantasy' is miniature variety.

P. metallica. Erect, dark red stems. Narrow, waxy leaves of copper with a metallic luster and silver green band down leaf center.

P. obtusifolia. Old favorite with thick, upright or trailing stems to 6 in.; dark green, fleshy, round, 4-in. leaves. 'Minima', miniature form, has dense stems; oval, stalked leaves 1½–2 in. long, dark green above, paler beneath. Several variegated forms are available.

P. rotundifolia *(P. nummariifolia, P. prostrata)*. Tiny, dark green, round, ¼-in. leaves often reddish underneath, along slender, trailing stems.

PEPPER. The two basic kinds of peppers are sweet and hot. First kind always remains mild, even when flesh ripens to red. These include big stuffing and salad peppers commonly known as bell peppers; best known of these are 'California Wonder' and 'Yolo Wonder'. Hybrid varieties have been bred for earliness, high yield, or disease resistance. Other sweet types are thick walled, very sweet pimientos used in salads, cooking, or for canning; sweet cherry peppers for pickling; and long slender peppers used for cooking—Italian frying peppers and Hungarian sweet yellow peppers.

Pepper (Bell)

Hot peppers range from pea sized to long, narrow 6–7 in., but all are pungent, their flavor varying from mild heat of Italian peperoncini to almost incandescent chilipiquin. 'Anaheim' is mild but spicy pepper used for making canned green chiles. 'Long Red Cayenne' is used for drying, 'Hungarian Yellow Wax (Hot)', 'Jalapeno' and 'Fresno Chile Grande' for pickling. Mexican cooking utilizes an entire palette of peppers—'Ancho', 'Mulato', and 'Pasilla' are a few.

All grow on handsome, bushy plants. 1½–2 ft. tall. Use plants as temporary low informal hedge, or grow and display them in containers. Certain kinds have been bred for house plant use: 'Ball Christmas' and 'Red Boy' are typical ornamental forms with small erect fruit that change from green through whitish and purple to bright red.

Buy started plants at nursery, or sow seed indoors 8–10 weeks before average date of last frost. Set out when weather becomes warm, spacing plants 18–24 in. apart. Grow in full sun. Water thoroughly but not frequently as plants grow, and feed once or twice with commercial fertilizer after plants become established, before blossoms set. Sweet peppers are ready when they have reached good size, but keep their flavor until red-ripe. Pimientos should only be picked when red-ripe. Pick hot peppers when they are fully ripe. Control cutworms with baits. Control aphids, whiteflies with all-purpose vegetable garden dust or spray.

PEPPER GRASS. See Cress, Garden.

PEPPERIDGE. See *Nyssa sylvatica*.

PEPPERMINT. See *Eucalyptus, Mentha piperita*.

PEPPERMINT TREE. See *Agonis flexuosa*.

PEPPER TREE. See *Schinus*.

PEPPERWOOD. See *Umbellularia californica*.

PERILLA frutescens. SHISO. Summer annual. Sturdy, leafy plant to 2–3 ft. tall. Deeply toothed leaves egg shaped, to 5 in. long. Kind most commonly seen has bronzy or purple leaves that look much like coleus. Fancy Fringe strain has leaves deeply cut and fringed, deep bronzy purple in color. Use leaves as vegetable or flavoring (taste is something like mint, something like cinnamon) and use long, thin clusters of flower buds as a vegetable to fry in tempura batter. Extremely fast and easy to grow in sun or light shade with average water. In the Orient, seeds are pressed for edible oil.

Perilla frutescens

PERIWINKLE. See *Vinca*.

PERNETTYA mucronata. Evergreen shrub. Zones 4–7, 15–17. Compact growth to 2–3 ft. tall, spreading by underground runners to make clumps. Glossy, dark green, oval or narrow, ⅓–¾-in.-long leaves give fine-textured look. Some leaves turn red or bronzy in winter. Tiny white to pink, bell shaped flowers in late spring, followed by very colorful berries.

Berries are ½ in. across, fleshy, with metallic sheen, purple, white, red, rose, pink, or near black. They hold until knocked off by hard rain or frost, possibly until early spring. Plants set more fruit if you grow several for cross-pollination.

Pernettya mucronata

Acid, peaty soil; ample water. Full sun in cold-winter regions, partial shade where summers are long and hot. Can be invasive; control by root-pruning with spade. Tops often need regular pruning to stay attractive. Use as informal low hedge or border, in tubs or window boxes.

PERSIAN VIOLET. See *Exacum affine*.

PERSIMMON *(Diospyros)*. Deciduous trees. Two species are grown in West; one is well-known fruit tree with outstanding ornamental qualities. Both are resistant to oak root fungus in soil.

Oriental or Japanese Persimmon *(Diospyros kaki)*. Zones 7–9, 14–16, 18–23; borderline in Zones 4–6; grows in Zones 10–13, but rarely fruits. To 30 ft. or more with wide-spreading branches. New leaves soft, light green in spring, becoming dark green, leathery broad ovals to 6–7 in. long, 2–3½ in. wide. In late autumn leaves turn yellow, orange, or scarlet even in warm-winter climates. Then, after leaves drop, orange scarlet fruit light tree for weeks; when these drop, handsome branch structure justifies featured spot in garden.

Persimmon

Easy to grow. Prune only to remove dead wood, shape tree, or open up too dense interior. Only problem is fruit drop, common in young trees. To avoid it, be consistent in feeding and watering. Space deep irrigations so that root zone is neither too wet nor too dry. Feed plants in late winter or early spring; overfeeding with nitrogen causes excessive growth, excessive fruit drop. Mature plants usually bear consistently.

Persimmon fruit can be dried; pick when hard-ripe with some stem remaining. Peel and hang up by string in sun. Dried fruit has flavor something like litchi or very high quality prune.

One of best fruit trees for ornamental use; good garden or small shade tree. Can be espaliered. Available varieties:

'Chocolate'. Brown-flecked, very sweet flesh.

'Fuyu'. Nonastringent, even when underripe, firm fleshed (like an apple), reddish yellow, about size of baseball but flattened like tomato. Similar but larger is 'Giant Fuyu'.

'Hachiya'. Shapeliest tree for ornamental use. This variety yields big (4 in. long, 2½–3 in. broad), slightly pointed persimmons usually found in produce stores. Pick before fully ripe to outwit birds, but allow to become soft-ripe before eating; astringent unless mushy.

'Tamopan'. Astringent until fully ripe; very large, turban shaped.

American Persimmon *(Diospyros virginiana)*. Zones 3–9, 14–16, 18–23. Moderate-growing small tree to 20–30 ft. with broad oval crown, attractive gray brown bark fissured into deep checkered pattern. Glossy, broad, oval leaves to 6 in. long. New foliage bronzy or reddish; leaves turn yellow, pink, and red in fall. Fruit round, yellow to orange (often blushed red), 1½–2 in. wide, very puckery until soft-ripe, then very sweet.

PERUVIAN DAFFODIL. See *Hymenocallis narcissiflora*.

PERUVIAN LILY. See *Alstroemeria*.

PERUVIAN OLD MAN CACTUS. See *Espostoa lanata*.

PETUNIA hybrida. COMMON GARDEN PETUNIA. Tender perennial grown as summer annual. (In mild-winter desert areas, planted in fall for color from spring to early summer.) Fragrant flowers single and funnel shaped to very double, in many colors from soft pink to deepest red, light blue to deepest purple, cream, yellow, and pure white. Leaves thick, broad, and slightly sticky to touch.

Petunia hybrida

Plant in full sun in good garden soil; water regularly. Single-flowered kinds will grow in poor soil if it's well drained; tolerate alkalinity. Plant 8–18 in. apart depending on size of variety. After plants established, pinch back about half for compact growth. Feed monthly with complete fertilizer. Near end of summer, cut back rangy plants about half to force new growth. In some areas, smog causes spots on leaves of seedlings—plants outgrow damage in clear periods. White-flowered kinds are most susceptible. Tobacco budworm may be a problem in some areas. See 'Corn earworms,'' page 58, for control.

To most gardeners, petunias are of two main types: doubles or singles. Doubles are heavily ruffled, many petaled flowers resembling carnations; singles are funnel shaped (either ruffled or smooth edged) with open throats. Both doubles and singles come as Grandifloras (very large flowers) or Multifloras (smaller flowers but more of them).

Most newer varieties of petunias (F_1 hybrids, produced by crossing two different varieties) are more vigorous, more uniform in color, height, and growth habit than ordinary petunias. Most are hand pollinated to produce seed, thus are somewhat more expensive than petunias grown from open-pollinated seed.

F_1 Hybrid Grandiflora: Sturdy plants, 15–27 in. high, 24–36 in. across. Flowers usually single, ruffled or fringed, to 4½ in. across, in pink, rose, salmon, red, scarlet, blue, white, pale yellow, or striped. Cascade series of petunias belongs here. Cascading growth habit makes them especially good for hanging containers. Large, single flowers are 4–5 in. across in white, pink, red, and blue. Double Hybrid Grandifloras with heavily ruffled flowers come in all the above colors except yellow.

F_1 Hybrid Multiflora: Plants about same size as F_1 Hybrid Grandiflora, but flowers generally smooth edged and smaller (to 2 in. across), single or double. Neat compact growth, ideal for bedding, massed planting. Many named varieties in pink, rose, salmon, yellow, white, blue. Multifloras resistant to botrytis disease which disfigures blossoms and later foliage of other kinds in humid weather. Satin and Joy series of petunias belong in F_1 Hybrid Multiflora strain. Flowers single, to 2½ in. wide, with satiny texture in white, cream, pink, coral, red, and blue. 'Summer Sun' is genuinely bright yellow petunia.

F_2 Hybrid Grandiflora and Multiflora petunias look like their F_1 seed parents, but are variable in color and somewhat so in growth pattern.

Particularly large flowers (4–6 in. wide) mark Giants of California petunias. Heavy frilling and showy throat markings make them good subjects for close-up viewing in pots or window boxes. Hybrid Frolic series has flowers to 8 in. wide.

PHAEDRANTHUS buccinatorius. See *Distictis buccinatoria*.

PHALAENOPSIS. MOTH ORCHID. Epiphytic orchids. Greenhouse and house plants. Thick, broad, leathery leaves, no pseudobulbs. Long sprays of 3–6-in.-wide, white, cream, pale yellow, or light lavender pink flowers in spring-fall; some are spotted, barred, or have contrasting lip color. Leaves are rather flat, spreading, to 12 in. long. Flower sprays may be from 3–5 ft. long.

Phalaenopsis

Although very popular commercially, they are more for the advanced amateur than beginner. They require warmer growing conditions than most orchids (minimum 60°–70° F. at night and 70°–85° F. during the day), fairly high humidity, and moist potting medium at all times. Good location is near bathroom or kitchen window with light coming through a gauzelike curtain (foliage burns easily in direct sun). Give them same potting medium as for cattleyas. When cutting flowers, leave part of main stem so another set of flowers can develop from dormant buds. Many lovely, large-flowered hybrids. Some smaller-flowered new hybrids give promise of being easier to grow, taking somewhat lower nighttime temperatures.

PHASEOLUS caracalla. See *Vigna caracalla*.

PHILADELPHUS. MOCK ORANGE. Deciduous shrubs. White, usually fragrant flowers bloom in late spring (some species early summer). Most are large vigorous plants of fountain form with medium green foliage. Full sun (part shade in hottest-summer areas), ordinary garden soil and watering. Prune every year just after bloom, cutting out oldest wood and surplus shoots at base. Taller ones are striking in lawns or as background and corner plantings. Smaller kinds can be planted near foundations or used as low screens or informal hedges.

Philadelphus lemoinei

P. coronarius. SWEET MOCK ORANGE. Zones 1–17. Strong growing, 8–10 ft. tall. Oval leaves 1–4 in. long. Clusters of very fragrant, 1½-in.-wide flowers in June. Old favorite. 'Aureus' has bright golden leaves which turn yellow green in summer, does not grow as tall.

P. gordonianus. See *P. lewisii*.

P. lemoinei. Zones 1–17. This hybrid includes many garden varieties, most to 5–6 ft. tall and all with very fragrant flowers in clusters. Leaves oval, to 2 in. long. Double-flowered 'Enchantment' is best-known variety.

P. lewisii. WILD MOCK ORANGE. Zones 1–17. Native to western North America. Erect and arching habit (tall race from west of the Cascades is often called *P. gordonianus*). Satiny, fragrant blooms nearly 2 in. across; oval leaves 2–4 in. long. Blooms June-July. Somewhat drought tolerant, especially the form native to California. State flower of Idaho.

P. mexicanus. EVERGREEN MOCK ORANGE. Zones 8, 9, 14–24. Best used as vine or bank cover; long supple stems with 3-in. evergreen leaves will reach 15–20 ft. if given support. Fragrant creamy flowers in small clusters bloom in spring and early summer, or intermittently.

P. purpureomaculatus. Zones 2–17. Group of hybrids including moderate-sized shrubs with flowers showing purple centers. 'Belle Etoile' has upright growth, to 5 ft. tall; fragrant, fringed, single flowers to 2½ in. Leaves oval to 2 in. long.

P. virginalis. Zones 1–17. Another hybrid which has produced several garden varieties, the flowers of which tend to be double.

(Continued on next page)

Tall (6-8 ft.) varieties include 'Minnesota Snowflake' and 'Virginal', both double, and 'Natchez', with 2-in. single flowers. Lower growing are double 'Glacier' (3–4 ft.), and 'Dwarf Minnesota Snowflake' (2–3 ft.).

PHILLYREA decora (*Osmanthus decorus*). Evergreen shrub. Rare. Zones 4–9, 14–21. Slow growth to 6–8 ft. Neat, glossy leaves 3–5 in long, dark green above, yellowish green beneath. Small pure white flowers April-May. Male and female flowers on different plants; if both sexes are present, small red fruit follow bloom, turn purplish black in late fall.

Phillyrea decora

Has foliage quality of camellia or skimmia but grows well in ordinary garden soils and exposures. Needs little water once established.

PHILODENDRON. Evergreen vines and shrubs. Philodendrons are tough, durable, fast-growing plants grown for their attractive, leathery, usually glossy leaves. They fall into two main classes; each species and variety in list that follows is designated in one of these categories:

Arborescent and relatively hardy. These become big plants 6–8 ft high (sometimes higher) and as wide. They develop large leaves and sturdy, self-supporting trunks. They will grow indoors, but need much

Philodendron bipennifolium

more space than most house plants. They grow outdoors in certain milder climate zones—see individual descriptions. As outdoor plants they do best in sun with shade at midday but can survive considerable shade. Use them for tropical jungle effects, or as massive silhouettes against walls or glass. Excellent in large containers; effective near swimming pools.

Vining or self-heading and tender. These forms can only be house plants. There are many kinds, with many different leaf shapes and sizes. Vining types do not really climb and must be tied to or leaned against support until they eventually shape themselves to it. The support can be almost anything, but certain water absorbent columns (sections of tree fern stems, wire and sphagnum "totem poles," slabs of redwood bark) serve especially well because they can be kept moist, and moist columns help plants grow better. Self-heading types form short, broad plants with sets of leaves radiating out from central point.

Whether in containers or open ground, a philodendron should grow in rich, loose, well-drained soil. House plant philodendrons grow best in good light but not direct sun that comes through a window. All prefer soil to be kept moist but will not take soggy soil. Feed lightly and frequently for good growth and color. Dust leaves of indoor plants once a month (commercial leaf polishes are available).

It's the nature of most philodendrons—especially when grown in containers—to drop lower leaves, leaving bare stem. To fix leggy philodendron you can air-layer leafy top and, when it develops roots, sever it and replant it. Or cut plant back to short stub and let it start over again. Often the best answer is to throw out overgrown, leggy plant and replace it with new one. Aerial roots form on stems of some kinds; push them into soil or cut them off—it won't hurt plant.

Flowers may appear on old plants if heat, light, and humidity are high; they somewhat resemble callas, with boat shaped bract surrounding club shaped spikelike structure. Flower bracts are usually greenish, white, or reddish.

Here are the kinds. Note that the great favorite—the so-called "split-leaf philodendron"—is not a philodendron at all, but a *Monstera*.

P. bipennifolium (usually sold as *P. panduriforme*). FIDDLE-LEAF PHILODENDRON. Vining. Fairly fast climber with rich green 10-in. leaves oddly lobed to resemble violin (or horse's head; no two leaves are exactly alike). Excellent house plant but sparse foliage on older plants suggests planting in multiples for dense effect.

P. bipinnatifidum. Arborescent. Zones 15–24. Similar to *P. selloum*, but carries more leaves at a time and has more deeply and evenly cut leaves with reddish veins. Next to *P. selloum*, hardiest for outdoor use.

P. cordatum. See *P. scandens oxycardium*.

P. domesticum (usually sold as *P.* 'Hastatum'). Vining. Fairly fast, open growth. Leaves 1 ft. long, arrow shaped, deep green. Subject to leaf spot if kept too warm and moist. A number of selections and hybrids have become available; these are more resistant to leaf spot and tend to be more compact and upright. Some, possibly hybrids with *P. erubescens*, have much red in new foliage and in leaf stalks. 'Emerald Queen' is a choice deep green, 'Royal Queen' a good deep red.

Philodendron domesticum

P. erubescens. Vining. Leaves 9 in. long, arrow shaped, reddish beneath, dark green above, on reddish leaf stalks.

P. 'Evansii'. Arborescent. Zones 20–24. Hybrid of *P. speciosum* and *P. selloum*. Elephant-ear lobes are scalloped and ruffled, but not deeply cut. Leaves on mature plants may reach 4–5 ft. long.

P. 'Florida'. Vining. Hybrid of *P. pedatum* and *P. squamiferum*. Leaves heavy textured, split into 5 broad, sharp-pointed lobes, with pronounced veins and reddish undersurface.

P. 'Florida Compacta'. Vining. Compact, slow to climb with deep green leaves similar to 'Florida' in shape. Leaf stalks red.

P. guttiferum. Vining. Slow, dense growth with narrow, pointed, very stiff, deep green leaves on short, broad, flattened leaf stalks. Close-held leaves give shingled effect to foliage.

P. 'Hastatum'. See *P. domesticum*.

P. imbe. Vining. Foot-long, narrow, arrow shaped leaves held well out from plant horizontally. Rich green above, red beneath.

P. laciniatum. See *P. pedatum*.

P. 'Lynette'. Self-heading. Makes close cluster of foot-long, broadish, bright green leaves with strong patterning formed by deeply sunken veins. Good table top plant.

P. 'Mandaianum'. Vining. Leaves arrow shaped, 12–15 in. long, dark green above, maroon underneath, on maroon stalks. Deeper in color than *P. erubescens*.

P. oxycardium. See *P. scandens oxycardium*.

P. panduriforme. See *P. bipennifolium*.

P. pedatum (usually sold as *P. laciniatum*). Vining. Dark green 8-in. leaves deeply slashed into unequal broad, sharp-pointed lobes. Holds lower leaves well.

P. pertusum. See *Monstera deliciosa*. This is commonly sold as SPLIT-LEAF PHILODENDRON.

P. scandens oxycardium (usually sold as *P. oxycardium* or *P. cordatum*). Vining. Commonest philodendron. Leaves heart shaped, deep green, usually 5 in. or less in length in juvenile plants, up to foot long on mature plants in greenhouses. Easily grown (cut stems will live and grow for some time in vases of water). Thin stems will climb fast and high, or trail gracefully. Grow on moisture retentive columns or train on strings or wires to frame a window or hang from a rafter.

Philodendron scandens oxycardium

P. selloum. Arborescent. Zones 8, 9, 12–24. Hardiest of big-leafed philodendrons used outdoors. Leaves to 3 ft. long, deeply cut. Variety 'Lundii' is more compact.

P. squamiferum. Vining. Much like *P. pedatum* in appearance, but with red, bristly leaf stalks and deeply sunken leaf veins.

P. verrucosum. Vining. Heart shaped, 8-in. leaves are dark bronzy green with paler veins, deep green edges, purplish undersides. Leaf stalks are red with green bristles. Showy; not as tough and undemanding as most philodendrons.

Philodendron squamiferum

P. wendlandii. Self-heading. Compact clusters of a dozen or more foot-long, broadly lance shaped leaves of deep green on short, broad stalks. Useful where tough, compact foliage plant is needed for table top or low, broad planting area.

PHLOMIS fruticosa. JERUSALEM SAGE. Shrubby perennial. All Zones. Deserving old-time garden plant, rugged and woody. Coarse, woolly, gray green wrinkled leaves. Yellow flowers 1 in. long in tight, ball shaped whorls around upper part of 4-ft. stems; bloom in early summer. Combine with echinops, eryngium, helenium, helianthus, kniphofia, rudbeckia. Full sun; adapted to poor soil, dry slopes. Resistant to oak root fungus. Stays evergreen in mild winters. Cut back ⅓ in fall to keep in shape. With summer water it will produce several waves of bloom; cut back after each flowering for repeat performance.

Phlomis fruticosa

PHLOX. Annuals, perennials. Most are natives of North America. Wide variation in growth form. All of them have showy flower clusters that are attractive to birds. Give them sun, average garden soil, and water unless otherwise noted.

Phlox paniculata

P. carolina (*P. suffruticosa*). THICK-LEAF PHLOX. Perennial. Zones 1–14, 18–21. To 3–4 ft. tall. Early flowers about ¾ in. wide, white with pale pink eye to magenta, in clusters 15 in. long. Shiny foliage, free from mildew and red spider mites which often attack summer phlox. 'Miss Lingard' is excellent white-flowered variety to 3 ft. tall.

P. divaricata. SWEET WILLIAM PHLOX. Perennial. Zones 1–17. To 12 in., with slender leafy stems and creeping underground shoots. Leaves oval, 1–2 in. long, ¾ in. wide. Flowers bluish or pinkish blue varying to white, ¾–1½ in. across, somewhat fragrant, in open clusters; bloom in spring. Use in rock gardens, as bulb cover (see *Tulipa*). Light shade, good, deep soil, average water. *P. d. laphamii* has best blue color.

P. drummondii. ANNUAL PHLOX. Summer annual. Grows 6–18 in. tall, with leafy, erect stems more or less covered with rather sticky hairs. Flowers numerous, showy, in close clusters at top of stems. Bright and pastel colors (no blue or orange); some with contrasting eye. Tall strains in mixed colors are Finest and Fordhook Finest. Dwarfs (6 in. tall) include Beauty (smooth-edged flowers) and Twinkle (fringed, starry-pointed flowers), in many colors, excellent for low bedding, edgings. Bloom from early summer until frost if faded flowers are removed. Plant in spring in colder climates—in fall in mild areas of southern California and desert. Give full sun and light, rich loam.

P. nivalis. TRAILING PHLOX. Perennial. Zones 4–7. Trailing plants form loose mats of narrow evergreen foliage 4–6 in. tall. Big pink or white flowers in fairly large clusters in late spring or early summer. Excellent in rock garden. 'Camla' is fine salmon pink variety.

P. paniculata. SUMMER PHLOX. Perennial. Zones 1–14, 18–21. Long-lived. Thrives in full sun, but in hottest areas colors may bleach. Leaves 2–5 in. long, narrow and tapering to slender point. Flowers in summer, 1 in. wide, in large, dome shaped clusters on 3–5-ft. stems, fragrant. White, shades of lavender, pink, rose or red; some with eyes of contrasting color. Many named varieties. Mulch around plant to keep roots cool. Plants subject to mildew at end of blooming season. Divide plants every few years, replanting young shoots from outside of clump. Plants do not come true from seed, but Beltsville Beauty strain will give good colors. Plant seed in fall or freeze in ice cubes for month before sowing.

P. subulata. MOSS PINK. Perennial. Zones 1–17. Mat forming, to 6 in. with ½-in., stiffish, needlelike, evergreen leaves on creeping stems. The ¾-in. flowers range in color from white through pinks to rose and lavender blue. Late spring or early summer

bloom, according to climate. Makes sheets of brilliant color in rock gardens. Ground cover. Grow in loose, not too rich soil. After flowering, cut back halfway. Moderately drought tolerant.

P. suffruticosa. See *P. carolina.*

PHOENIX. DATE PALM. Mostly large feather palms, but one a dwarf. Trunks patterned with bases of old leaf stalks. Small yellowish flowers in large hanging sprays followed by clusters of often edible fruit (one species bears dates of commerce). Phoenix palms hybridize freely; buy from reliable nurseryman who knows his seed or plant source.

Phoenix canariensis

P. canariensis. CANARY ISLAND DATE PALM. Zones 9, 12–24. Big, heavy-trunked plant to 60 ft. tall, with 50-ft. spread composed of a great many gracefully arching fronds. Slow-growing until it forms trunk, then speeds up a little. Young plants do well in pots for many years, looking something like pineapples. Grow on slopes, in parks, big spaces, along wide streets; not for small city lots. Hardy to 20° F. Slow to develop new head of foliage after hard-frost damage.

Phoenix dactylifera

P. dactylifera. DATE PALM. Zones 9, warmer parts of 11, 12–24. The date palm of Indio, California, and of Palm Springs golf courses and classic palm of movie desert oases. Native of Middle East. Very tall palm (as much as 80 ft.) with slender trunk and gray green waxy leaves; leaflets stiff and sharp pointed. Suckers from base; natural habit is clump of several trunks. Principal commercial variety in California is 'Deglet Noor'. Too stiff and large for most home gardens, but adaptable and does well in seaside, desert gardens. Leaves killed at 20° F. but plants have survived 4°–10° F.

Phoenix roebelenii

P. loureiri (*P. humilis*) Zones 9, 12–24. Resembles smaller, more slender and refined Canary Island date palm. Slow grower to 10–18 ft. tall. Leaves dark green, flexible, 10 ft. long. Good in containers or in the garden. Hardy to 20° F. Rare.

P. reclinata. SENEGAL DATE PALM. Zones 23, 24. Native to tropical Africa. Makes picturesque clumps from offshoots, with several curving trunks 20–30 ft. high. Offshoots can be removed to make single-trunk trees. Fertilize for fast growth. Below 28° F. expect trouble.

P. roebelenii. PIGMY DATE PALM. Outdoors in Zones 23, 24; house plant anywhere. Native to Laos. Fine-leafed, small-scale palm. One stem grows slowly to 6 ft. or so. Curved leaves from dense crown. Good pot plant. Requires moisture. Does best in shade or part shade, but not successful in dark indoor corners.

P. rupicola. CLIFF DATE PALM. Zones 17, 19–24. From India. Stately as Canary Island date palm, but much smaller, reaching only 25 ft. in height. Slender stem; lower leaves droop gracefully. Hardy to 26° F.

P. sylvestris. SILVER DATE PALM. Zones 14–17, 19–24. Native to India. Hardy and beautiful date palm with single trunk to 30 ft. covered with old leaf bases. Trunk tapers from wide base to narrow top. Crown of gray green leaves is thick and round. Hardy to 22° F.

PHORMIUM. NEW ZEALAND FLAX. Evergreen perennials. Zones 7–24; may freeze to ground but regrow in Zones 5, 6. Big dramatic plants composed of many swordlike, stiffly vertical leaves in fan pattern. Flowers dull red or yellow, 1–2 in. long, in clusters on stems that reach high above leaves. Use as point-of-interest display plant or near

Phormium tenax 'Variegatum'

swimming pools. Grow in full sun to light shade. Sturdy, fast-growing in almost any soil or exposure—heat or cold, salt air or ocean spray; will take much or little water, even poor drainage to a point (in very poorly drained soil, crown rot can be problem). Subject to summer rot in low desert; replacement plants set out in fall will grow quickly. Use as windbreak along coast; grow in containers anywhere. Increase by dividing large clumps.

P. colensoi *(P. cookianum).* Leaves to 5 ft. long 2½ in. wide; less rigid than *P. tenax.* Flowers yellow or amber yellow, on 7-ft. spikes. Not common, but useful for its moderate size.

P. tenax. NEW ZEALAND FLAX. Large, bold plant tending to spread. Leaves to 9 ft. long and as wide as 5 in. Nursery plants in containers are deceptively small. Allow plenty of garden room for size of mature plant. Reddish brown flower stalks bear many dark red to yellowish flowers. Variants in leaf color are available; 'Atropurpureum' is purple red; 'Bronze' brownish red; 'Rubrum' has deepest coloring, dark purplish red; 'Variegatum' has green leaves striped with creamy white. 'Tiny Tim' grows 3–4 ft. tall, has bronzy leaves striped yellow.

PHOTINIA. Evergreen or deciduous shrubs or small trees. Attractive foliage and fruit color. Related to hawthorn, pyracantha. Sun, good garden soil. In Northwest, with-hold water in late summer to ripen growth, lessen frost damage. Prune to shape; never allow new growth to get away and make long, bare switches. Use as screens, background.

Photinia fraseri

P. arbutifolia. See *Heteromeles arbutifolia.*

P. fraseri. Evergreen shrub. Zones 4–24. Moderate growth to 10 ft. tall, spreading wider. Leaves glossy dark green above, lighter beneath, 2–5 in. long. New growth bright bronzy red, showy. White flower clusters in early spring resemble those of *P. glabra.* Attractive to birds. Good espalier or small single-stemmed tree. Cut branches excellent in arrangements. Control aphids. Resists mildew where other kinds susceptible. Sometimes chlorotic in Zones 12, 13. Heat resistant.

P. glabra. JAPANESE PHOTINIA. Evergreen shrub. Zones 4–24. Broad, dense growth to 6–10 ft or more. Leaves oval, broadest toward tip, to 3 in. long. New growth coppery; scattered leaves of bright red give touch of color through fall and winter. Summer pruning will restrict size of plant to neat 5 ft. and give continuing show of new foliage. White flowers with hawthorn fragrance in 4-in.-wide clusters. Berries red, turning black. May take setback with prolonged freeze, but usually recovers. Mildew is a problem in many areas.

P. serrulata. CHINESE PHOTINIA. Evergreen shrub or small tree. Zones 4–16, 18–22. Broad, dense growth to 35 ft., but easily held to 10 by 10 ft. Leaves stiff, crisp, deep green, to 8 in. long, prickly along edges. New growth bright copper; scattered crimson leaves in fall, winter. Flowers white, in flat clusters 6 in. across, March-May. Bright red berries often last until December. May freeze badly in continued 0°–10° F. cold but usually recovers. Mildew can be expected almost anywhere. Fairly drought resistant when established. *P. s.* 'Aculeata' (often sold as *P. s.* 'Nova' or *P. s.* 'Nova Lineata') is more compact, has midrib and main leaf veins of ivory yellow.

P. villosa. Deciduous shrub or small tree. Zones 1–6. To 15 ft. tall, with spread of 10 ft. Leaves 1½–3 in. long, dark green. New foliage pale gold with rosy tints when expanding, bright red in fall. White flowers in 1–2-in.-wide clusters in midspring. Bright red fruit nearly ½ in. long decorate plant in fall, early winter.

PHYGELIUS capensis. CAPE FUCHSIA. Perennial in Northwest, tending to be shrubby in milder climates. Zones 4–9, 14–24.

Phygelius capensis

Perhaps it's called fuchsia because flowers are pendant, but it is really related to penstemons and snapdragons. Stems 3–4 ft. high. Leaves 1–5 in. long, scalloped on margins, large at plant base, smaller toward top. Flowers red, tubular, slightly curved, 2 in. long, in loosely branched clusters July-September. Looks a bit weedy; use in outskirts of garden. Plant in sun in good garden soil. Water requirement average. Spreads by underground roots. Prune for neat appearance. In colder areas, mulch to protect roots. Rare, but easy from seed.

PHYLA nodiflora *(Lippia repens).* LIPPIA. Perennial. Zones 8–24. Creeps and spreads to form flat, ground hugging mat sturdy enough to serve as lawn. Leaves to ¾ in. long, gray green. Small lilac to rose flowers in tight round heads ½ in. across, spring-fall. Flowers attract bees; if objectionable, mow off tops. Full sun, average soil. Goes dormant, unattractive in winter. Feed regularly, especially in early spring to bring it out of dormancy fast. Drought tolerant once established, but looks best with regular water. Particularly useful in desert areas, but subject to nematodes.

Phyla nodiflora

PHYLLITIS scolopendrium. HART'S TONGUE FERN. Zones 2–24 but difficult in desert areas or areas with poor quality water. Needs humus, some limestone chips if soil is poor in calcium. Native to Europe, eastern United States. Odd fern with undivided, strap shaped leaves 9–18 in. long. Fanciers collect various dwarf, crested, or forked varieties. In Pacific Northwest it is quite hardy and easy in full sun to full shade; seems fussy where summers are long and dry. Striking in woodland gardens, rock gardens, with rhododendrons and azaleas. Durable container plant; grows from tight crown so may occupy same pot for many years.

Phyllitis scolopendrium

PHYLLOSTACHYS. See Bamboo.

PHYSALIS. Perennials or annuals. Fruit are surrounded by loose, papery husk (enlarged calyx of flower). One is ornamental, others edible.

P. alkekengi *(P. franchetii).* CHINESE LANTERN PLANT. Perennial often grown as annual. All Zones. Plant angularly branched, 1–2 ft. high. Long, creeping, whitish, underground stems; may become invasive without control. Leaves long stalked, light green, 2–3 in. long. Flowers white, rather inconspicuous, appearing in leaf joints. Ornamental part of plant is calyx which forms around ripened berry as loose, papery, bright orange red, 2-in.-long, inflated envelope shaped like lantern. Dry leafless stalks hung with these gay lanterns make choice winter arrangements. Sow seed in spring in light soil. Sun or light shade. Will grow with minimal water but plants will be smaller than those receiving regular watering. Increase by root division in fall or winter. Dwarf variety, 'Pygmy,' grows to 8 in., makes good pot plant.

Physalis alkekengi

P. ixocarpa. TOMATILLO. Annual of bushy, sprawling growth to 4 ft. Fruit about 2 in. wide, swelling to fill—sometimes to split open—the baggy calyx. Fruit yellow to purple, but most often picked green and used (cooked) in Mexican cuisine. Ripe fruit very sweet.

P. pruinosa. GROUND CHERRY, STRAWBERRY TOMATO. Tender perennial grown as annual. Bushy, 1½ ft. high. Leaves 2–4 in. long. Flowers bell shaped, ⅜ in. long, whitish yellow marked with 5 brown spots. Seedy yellow fruit are sweet, rather insipid, can be used for pies or preserves (after removing papery husks). Grow in same way as tomatoes. Plants sprawl quite a bit and are slow to start bearing, but eventually productive where summers are long and warm. Several species resemble this, one of them *P. peruviana,* the *poha* of Hawaii.

PHYSOCARPUS. NINEBARK. Deciduous shrubs. Grown Zones 1–3, 10, undoubtedly hardy in any climate with pronounced winters. Name comes from peeling bark, which often shows several layers. Plants resemble spiraeas and are closely related, with round clusters of tiny white flowers in spring or early summer. Sun or shade, average soil. Average water requirement.

Physocarpus capitatus

P. capitatus. Native to mountains in the Northwest, northern California, and northern Rocky Mountain states. To 8 ft. tall, with toothed and lobed 2-in. leaves and dense clusters of white flowers.

P. monogynus. MOUNTAIN NINEBARK. Rocky Mountain native 3–4 ft. tall with 1½-in. leaves and few-flowered clusters of pinkish to white flowers. Brilliant fall colors, mostly orange and red.

P. opulifolius intermedius. DWARF NINEBARK. Grows 4–5 ft. tall. Many white to pinkish flowers in each cluster. Fall color reddish brown. *P. o.* 'Luteus' has leaves that are yellow in sunlight, yellow green in shade.

PHYSOSTEGIA virginiana. FALSE DRAGONHEAD. Perennial. All Zones. (Sometimes called obedience plant because flowers, if twisted on stem, remain in position.) Slender, upright, leafy stems to 4 ft. Leaves oblong, 3–5 in. long, toothed, pointed at tip. Flowers funnel shaped, 1 in. long, glistening white, rose pink, or lavender rose, in dense, 10-in.-long spikes. Summer bloom. Spiky form useful in borders, cut arrangements. Combine with taller erigerons, *Scabiosa caucasica,* Michaelmas daisies. Sun or part shade. Any good garden soil, regular watering. Stake taller stems to keep upright. Cut to ground after bloom. Vigorous; divide every 2 years to keep in bounds. 'Vivid', 2 ft. tall, has rose pink flowers. 'Summer Snow', white, especially good, is least invasive.

Physostegia virginiana

PICEA. SPRUCE. Evergreen trees and shrubs. Zones 1–6, 14–17, except as noted. The large cone-bearing trees take on pyramidal or cone shape. Many kinds have dwarf varieties that are useful where adapted, in foundation plantings, rock gardens, and in containers. Spruces have no special soil requirements. Dwarf forms need reasonably cool location and ample water. Birds are attracted to spruce. Most trees are attacked by small, dull green aphids in late winter. Unless you check plants at that time to see if aphids are on foliage, their attack may not be noticed until weather warms and needles start dropping. Start spraying in February and repeat monthly until May. Pine needle scale

Picea pungens 'Glauca'

(flat and white) may cause sooty mold. Spray when scale insects are in crawler stage in May. In Rocky Mountain states, spruces may be bothered by spider mites (see page 59 for control) and tussock moths.

Prune to shape only. If a branch grows too long, cut back to a well-placed side branch. To slow growth and make more dense, remove part of each year's growth to force side growth. When planting larger spruces, don't place them too near buildings, fences, or walks. They need space to grow in. Except in Zones 1–3, they can be grown in containers for years as living Christmas trees.

P. abies *(P. excelsa).* NORWAY SPRUCE. Native to northern Europe. Not as good in Rocky Mountain states as North American native spruces. Fast growth to 100–150 ft. Stiff, deep green, attractive pyramid in youth; in age branches tend to grow horizontally, with branches drooping strongly, and branches at base dying back. Extremely hardy and wind resistant, it is valued for windbreaks in cold areas. Norway spruce has produced a number of varieties. Some of the best are:

Picea abies 'Nidiformis'

P. a. 'Clanbrasiliana'. Very dwarf. Forms tight, compressed ball, 2 ft. across in 20 years.

P. a. 'Maxwellii'. Picturesque, rounded dwarf with heavy short twigs, 2 ft. high and 3 ft. wide in 20 years.

P. a. 'Mucronata'. Dense dwarf, rounded in youth, growing into broad pyramid with age. Reaches 3 ft. in 20 years and has appearance of larger spruces in miniature.

P. a. 'Nidiformis'. BIRD'S NEST OR NEST SPRUCE. Very compact, dark green foliage; grows as flattened globe, eventually to 3 ft. high and 4–6 ft. across.

P. a. 'Pendula'. Growing naturally, it spreads over ground with height of about 1½ ft. and spread of 10 ft. It will cascade downward from rocks or walls. When staked it becomes dense irregular column with branches trailing downward to 8 ft. or more with outward sweeping, recurved tips.

P. a. 'Procumbens'. Close-branched, irregular growth with upturned branch ends. Slow to 2 ft. high, 5 ft. across.

P. a. 'Pygmaea'. Broad rounded cone, very dense, 2 ft. high and 3 ft. across in 20 years.

P. a. 'Remontii'. Irregular, wide, cone shaped dwarf, 3 ft. high, 4 ft. wide at base in 20 years, eventually to 20 ft.

P. a. 'Repens'. Low, irregular, rounded to 1½ ft. high and 3 ft. wide in 20 years. Fanlike branches held in layers.

P. a. 'Sherwood Gem'. Dense, heavily foliaged, regular, flattened globe to 2 ft. high, 4 ft. wide.

P. a. 'Sherwoodii'. Rugged, picturesque, compact but irregular in growth habit. Parent tree, 60 years old, is 5 ft. tall and 10 ft. across.

P. brewerana. BREWER'S WEEPING SPRUCE. Zones 4–7, 14–17. To 100 –120 ft. in its native Siskiyou Mountains in California and Oregon. Branchlets are pendulous, hanging vertically to 7–8 ft. or more. Rare in the wilds and in gardens. Tenderer than most spruces and requires much moisture and cool temperatures.

P. engelmannii. ENGELMANN SPRUCE. Densely pyramidal tree to 150 ft., native from southwest Canada to Oregon and northern California, east to the Rockies. Resembles blue green forms of Colorado spruce, but needles are softer and tree is not so spreading at base. Even 25-ft. specimens will be densely branched to ground. Popular lawn tree in Rocky Mountain area.

P. glauca. WHITE SPRUCE. Native to Canada and northern U.S. Conical tree to 60–70 ft., dense when young, with pendulous twigs and silver green foliage. Best in very cold-winter climates.

P. g. 'Conica'. (Often sold as *P. albertiana.*) DWARF ALBERTA OR DWARF WHITE SPRUCE. Compact pyramidal tree of slow growth to 7 ft. in 35 years. Short, fine needles are soft to the touch, bright grass green when new, gray green when mature. Handsome tub plant—a miniature Christmas tree for many years. Or, fine small formal pyramid for garden. Thoroughly hardy to cold, but needs shelter from hot or cold drying winds and from strong reflected sunlight.

P. g. densata. BLACK HILLS SPRUCE. Slow-growing, dense pyramid, it can reach 20 ft. in height in 35 years. Use it in containers, or plant it out in groves for screening or for alpine meadow effects.

P. pungens. COLORADO SPRUCE. Zones 1–10, 14–17. To 80–100 ft. Very stiff, regular, horizontal branches forming broad pyramid. Foliage varies in seedlings from dark green through all shades of blue green to steely blue. Often grown outside zones where it thrives; it survives there but seldom looks its best.

P. p. 'Glauca'. COLORADO BLUE SPRUCE. Positive gray blue color.

P. p. 'Koster'. KOSTER BLUE SPRUCE. Even bluer than 'Glauca' but growth habit sometimes irregular.

(Continued on next page)

P. p. 'Moerheimii'. Same blue as 'Koster' but tree has more compact and symmetrical shape.

P. p. 'Pendens'. KOSTER WEEPING BLUE SPRUCE. Gray blue with weeping branchlets.

P. p. 'Thomsen'. Palest blue white of all spruces. Vigorous, symmetrical habit.

P. sitchensis. Zones 4–6, 14–17. SITKA SPRUCE. Native Alaska to California. Tall pyramidal tree to 100–150 ft. with wide-spreading, horizontal branches. Thin, quite narrow needles are prickly to the touch, bright green and silvery white in color. Requires moisture in soil and moist atmosphere to look its best. Very subject to Cooley spruce gall, a conelike growth on new shoots caused by aphids. Treat as for scale.

PICKEREL WEED. See *Pontederia cordata.*

PIERIS. Evergreen shrubs. Leathery leaves and clusters of small, white, urn shaped flowers. Foliage and form excellent year through; flower buds in early winter look like strings of tiny greenish pink beads. These begin to open February to April. At (or just after) bloom season, tinted new growth begins to appear. Related to rhododendron and azalea, they have same

Pieris japonica

cultural needs and make good companion plants. Fairly easy in coastal valleys of Northwest, they become increasingly fussy and often less satisfactory south and inland. Require some shade, particularly in afternoon. Where water is high in salts, they need careful leaching. Protect from wind for maximum beauty. Prune by removing spent flowers. Splendid in containers, in Oriental and woodland gardens, in entryways where year-round quality is essential.

P. 'Forest Flame' (*P.* 'Flame of the Forest'). Hybrid between *P. japonica* and form of *P. forrestii* with especially bright red spring foliage. It combines new foliage brilliance of latter with some of hardiness of former. Growing satisfactorily in Zones 2 and 3 where sheltered from drying winds and hot sun. Flowering is profuse, and flower clusters are broader and heavier than those of *P. japonica.* Grows 6–7 ft. tall and ultimately as wide.

P. floribunda (*Andromeda floribunda*). MOUNTAIN PIERIS. Zones 2–9, 14–17; but needs protection in Zones 2, 3. Compact, rounded shrub 3–6 ft. tall with elliptical, dull green 1½–3-in. leaves. New growth pale green. Blossoms in upright clusters. Very hardy to cold, and takes hotter, dryer air than the others. Takes sun west of Cascades in Northwest. Somewhat rare.

P. forrestii (*P. formosa forrestii*). CHINESE PIERIS. Zones 5–9, 14–17. Dense, broad grower to 10 ft. tall with greater spread. Leaves shiny, leathery, dark green, to 6 in. long. New growth ranges from brilliant scarlet (in best forms) to pale salmon pink. Large, heavy clusters of tiny white flowers on branch tips in April, May. Buy when plants are making new growth; cutting-grown plants from best selections show their quality then. These may be offered as variety 'Bright Red'. Makes good espalier in shaded locations.

P. japonica (*Andromeda japonica*). LILY-OF-THE-VALLEY SHRUB. Zones 1–9, 14–17; in Zones 1–3 it requires protection from sun and wind, generous watering. Upright, dense, tiered growth to 9–10 ft. Mature leaves glossy dark green, 3 in. long; new growth bronzy pink to red. Drooping clusters of flower buds form in autumn and are attractive even before opening to white, pink, or nearly red flowers in February-May. Buds themselves are often dark red. Responds well to frequent feeding—a must in heavy rainfall areas where leaching of nutrients would cause yellowing of foliage. Takes full sun in cool, humid climates, part shade elsewhere. Many horticultural varieties, some rare. For unusual habit or foliage: 'Bert Chandler'; new foliage turns from salmon pink through cream to white, then pale green; 'Compacta', smaller grower than parent; 'Crispa', smaller grower with wavy-edged leaves of great distinction; 'Mountain Fire', with fiery red new growth; 'Pygmaea', tiny dwarf less than 1 ft. tall, with narrow leaves 1 in. long or less, and very few flowers; and 'Variegata', medium-sized, slow-growing compact plant with leaves prettily marked with creamy white, tinged pink in spring.

Varieties grown principally for flower characteristics include: 'Christmas Cheer', bicolor white and deep rose red, with rose red flower stalks, early bloom; 'Coleman', pink flowers opening from red flower buds; 'Daisen', similar to 'Christmas Cheer', but with broader foliage; 'Dorothy Wyckoff', white flowers from deep red flower buds; 'Flamingo', heavy blooming, with rose pink flowers; 'Pink', shell pink fading to white; 'Valley Rose', low growing, compact, light pink; and 'White Cascade', an extremely heavy flower producer.

P. taiwanensis. Not completely tested; probably Zones 5–7, 14–17. Similar to *P. japonica,* but with somewhat larger, more erect flower clusters. Hybrid with *P. japonica,* 'Snowdrift', has unusually heavy bloom of pure white.

PIGEON BERRY. See *Duranta repens.*

PIGGY-BACK PLANT. See *Tolmiea menziesii.*

PILEA. Perennials. Grown in house or greenhouse. Juicy-stemmed foliage plants with inconspicuous flowers. Plant in porous soil mix (1 part sand, 1 part leaf mold, 1 part peat moss). Water thoroughly; don't water again until soil surface is dry. Feed monthly with house plant food. Grow at 65°–70° F. temperature. Light shade or bright light best; plant gets leggy in heavy shade.

Pilea microphylla

P. cadierei. ALUMINUM PLANT. Grows 1–1½ ft. tall. Erect, fast-growing with succulent stems. Leaves fleshy, toothed, 3–4 in. long; vivid green to bluish green with conspicuous silvery blotches. Flowers tiny.

P. depressa. Low, spreading or trailing, rooting where stems touch ground. Leaves roundish, broader toward tips. Used in terrariums, as ground cover in larger mixed plantings.

P. involucrata. PANAMIGA, PANAMIGO. Freely branching plant 6–8 in. tall. Leaves roundish oval, to 2 in. long, brownish green above, purplish beneath, heavily veined in seersucker effect.

P. microphylla. ARTILLERY PLANT. Grows ½–1½ ft. tall, with many spreading branches and fine twigs. Leaves very tiny, thickly set, bright green. Total effect somewhat fernlike. Called artillery plant because flowers forcibly discharge pollen.

P. nummulariifolia. CREEPING CHARLIE (one of several plants so named). Resembles *P. depressa,* but leaves more rounded, more evenly scalloped along edges. Good small hanging basket plant.

PIMELEA prostrata (usually sold as *P. coarctata*). Zones 4–7, 14–17. Evergreen shrublet. Makes gray, fine-leafed, compact mat 3–6 in. high and a foot or more wide. Clusters of tiny white 4-petaled flowers appear over long spring and summer bloom period; they look like tiny daphne flowers (plants are related). Flowers have faint sweet fragrance. White berries follow. Full sun, except in very hot locations where light shade helps. Needs good drainage,

Pimelea prostrata

nonalkaline soil, average water, light feeding. Use in rock gardens or as small-scale ground cover.

PIMPERNEL. See *Anagallis.*

PIMPINELLA anisum. ANISE. Annual herb. All Zones. Bright green, toothed, basal leaves. Tiny white flowers in umbrellalike clusters on 2-ft. stems in June. Start from seed in place when ground warms up in spring. Does not transplant easily. Grow in light soil, full sun; regular water. Use fresh leaves in salads, seeds for flavoring cookies, confections.

Pimpinella anisum

PINCUSHION FLOWER. See *Scabiosa*.

PINCUSHION TREE. See *Hakea laurina*.

PINDO PALM. See *Butia capitata*.

PINE. See *Pinus*.

PINEAPPLE. Bold, distinctive house plant that may bear fruit. Plant is rosette of long, narrow leaves with sawtooth edges. Cut leafy top from market pineapple. Root base of top in water or damp sand-peat moss. When roots have formed, move to 7 or 8-in. pot of rich soil. Keep plants in greenhouse or in sunny room where temperatures stay above 68° F. Water overhead when soil gets dry. Feed every 3–4 weeks with liquid fertilizer. Fruit forms, if you're lucky, in 2 years, on top of sturdy stalk at center of clump. Home-grown pineapple fruit is much smaller than commercial fruit. Sometimes available as house plant is variety with foliage variegated in pink, white, and olive green.

Pineapple

PINEAPPLE FLOWER. See *Eucomis*.

PINEAPPLE GUAVA. See *Feijoa sellowiana*.

PINK. See *Dianthus*.

PINK CEDAR. See *Acrocarpus fraxinifolius*.

PINK DIOSMA. See *Coleonema pulchrum*.

PINK IRONBARK. See *Eucalyptus sideroxylon*.

PINK POLKA-DOT PLANT. See *Hypoestes phyllostachya*.

PINK POWDER PUFF. See *Calliandra haematocephala*.

PINON. See *Pinus edulis*.

PINUS. PINE. Evergreen trees, rarely shrubs. See chart for climate adaptability. Pines are great individualists of garden, differ-

ing not only among species but also in ways they respond to sun, wind, and soil type. The number of long, slender needles in a bundle and size and shape of cones are two chief characteristics by which pines are classified.

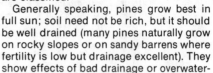
Pinus pinea

Generally speaking, pines grow best in full sun; soil need not be rich, but it should be well drained (many pines naturally grow on rocky slopes or on sandy barrens where fertility is low but drainage excellent). They show effects of bad drainage or overwatering by general poor appearance and unusual number of yellowing needles, especially on older growth. Most pines fairly to very drought tolerant; general exceptions are the 5-needled species. Polluted air causes abnormal needle drop, poor growth, and can kill trees. Pines require little if any fertilizing; heavy feeding encourages too-rapid, rank growth. Never use fertilizer high in nitrogen.

Pines are subject to a number of pests, but healthy, well-grown plants will stay that way with comparatively little attention. Most pines with 5 needles to a bundle are subject to disease called white pine blister rust. Pines with 2 or 3 needles in a bundle are sometimes attacked by European pine shoot moth in Northwest (symptoms are distorted or dead new shoots). Aphids usually show their presence by sticky secretions, sooty mildew, yellowing needles. Engraver beetles sometimes bore into bark of Monterey, and Ponderosa, Bishop, Coulter, Shore, Aleppo, and Torrey pines in California. Healthy trees usually survive with little damage, but trees weakened by drought, smog, or mites and other pests often die. Consult knowledgeable local nurseryman about pines likely to be bothered by pests, disease, or environmental stress in your area. Also, birds like to feast on seeds contained in pinecones.

All pines can be shaped, and usually improved, by some pruning. To slow a pine's growth or to fatten up a rangy one cut back candles of new growth when new needles begin to emerge. Cut them back halfway or even more. Leave a few clusters of needles if you want growth to continue along branch. To shape a pine in Oriental manner is trickier, but not really difficult; it's just a matter of cutting out any branches that interfere with the effect, shortening other branches, and creating an upswept look by removing all twigs that grow downward. Cutting vertical main trunk back to well-placed side branch will induce side growth, and wiring or weighting branches will produce cascade effects.

It is unlikely that any one nursery will have *all* pines described in chart; in fact, any nursery which has even as many as half of them is remarkably well stocked. Ask your nurseryman for help in locating any of the rarer ones you may wish to try. Specialists in bonsai plants often stock a wide variety of pines.

Pine

NAME	GROWTH RATE, SIZE	GROWTH HABIT	NEEDLES AND CONES	CLIMATE ADAPTABILITY	REMARKS
Pinus albicaulis WHITEBARK PINE Native to high mountains of Canada, Washington, Oregon, northern California, western Nevada, and east into Idaho, western Wyoming, central Montana.	Very slow to 20–40 ft., usually much less.	Prostrate, spreading, or semiupright. Often multitrunked. In youth, slender and symmetrical.	Needles: in 5s, 1½–3 in., dark green, dense. Cones: 3 in., roundish, purple.	Hardy timberline tree. Does well east of Cascades in Northwest. Dislikes warm, low elevation climates.	Usually dug in mountains and sold by collectors as "alpine" conifer. Good for rock gardens, bonsai.

(Continued on next page)

NAME	GROWTH RATE, SIZE	GROWTH HABIT	NEEDLES AND CONES	CLIMATE ADAPTABILITY	REMARKS
P. aristata BRISTLECONE PINE Native to high mountains of West; very local and widely scattered.	Very slow to 45 ft., usually not above 20 ft.	Dense, bushy, heavy trunked, with ground-sweeping branches. In youth a symmetrical, narrow-crowned tree with mature look.	Needles: in 5s, 1–1½ in., dark green, whitish below flecked with white dots of resin. Cones: 3½ in., dark purplish brown.	Hardy. Does well at sea level in cool-summer areas of coastal California. Somewhat variable in Northwest. Does well along front range of Rocky Mountains. Best as pot plant in southern California.	So slow-growing it is good for years as container plant. Needles persist many years, making crown extremely dense. Very old trees in California's White Mountains are now considered new species, *P. longaeva*.
P. attenuata KNOBCONE PINE Native to northern and central Cascades in Oregon, Siskiyous, Sierra Nevada foothills in California, south to Baja.	Rapid to 20–80 ft.	Open, irregular, and rough. In youth, rounded and regular. Some populations are far more dense, symmetrical. Habit depends, to some extent, on seed source.	Needles: in 3s, 3–5 in., yellow green. Cones: narrowly oval and asymmetrical, light brown, to 6 in.	Quite hardy; adaptable to most areas from Puget Sound south to Baja California.	Very drought tolerant when established. Grows well in poor soils. Holds its cones for many years.
P. balfouriana FOXTAIL PINE Native to California mountains: northern Coast Range and southern Sierras.	Very slow to 20–50 ft.	In youth a symmetrical, narrow cone. As it matures it becomes spreading with stout lower branches and irregular upper branches.	Needles: in 5s, to 1½ in., glossy green in dense tufts at branch tips, lasting many years. Cones: narrow, cylindrical, drooping, to 5 in. long.	Hardy, often timberline tree.	Best planted as shrub that in much time can outgrow shrub status. Candidate for container, bonsai, rock garden.
P. banksiana JACK PINE Native from Nova Scotia, New York, Minnesota, west to Alberta.	Slow to moderate to 70 ft.; usually lower, shrubby.	Crooked, open, picturesque, with slender, spreading branches.	Needles: in 2s, 1 in. long, bright green, twisted. Cones: 2 in., conic-oblong, light brown.	Northernmost pine of North America. Very hardy. Well-adapted to areas with long summer days.	Rare tree in nurseries. Cones persist 12–15 years. Needles yellowish in winter.
P. brutia (*P. halepensis brutia*) CALABRIAN PINE Native to eastern Mediterranean, Southern Russia, southern Italy.	Rapid growth, especially in youth, to 30–80 ft.	Denser, more erect than related *P. halepensis*, closer to classic pine tree shape.	Needles: in pairs, 5–6½ in. long, dark green. Cones: like those of Aleppo pine but not stalked and not bent backward toward trunk.	Thrives in heat, drought, wind, indifferent soil. Cannot take temperatures much below 0°F.	Faster, shapelier tree than *P. halepensis*; form is less interesting in maturity. Good possibilities as commercial Christmas tree.
P. bungeana LACEBARK PINE Native to northern and central China.	Slow to 75 ft.	Often with several trunks, spreading. Sometimes shrubby. Picturesque.	Needles: in 3s, 3 in. long, bright green. Cones: 2–2½ in. long, roundish, light yellowish brown.	Hardy to sub-zero cold, tolerates heat of California's Central Valley.	Smooth, dull gray bark flakes off like sycamore bark to show smooth, creamy white branches and trunk.
P. canariensis CANARY ISLAND PINE Native to Canary Islands.	Fast, to 60–80 ft., sometimes less.	In youth a slender, graceful pyramid. Later a tiered structure; finally a round-crowned tree.	Needles: in 3s, 9–12 in., blue green in youth, dark green when older. Cones: 4–9 in., oval, glossy brown.	Tender in Northwest but excellent in northern coastal and southern California. Has been severely damaged (even killed) at 10°F. Needles freeze at about 20°F., hang on tree.	Resistant to oak root fungus. Very young plants are gawky, but soon outgrow it. Drought tolerant, but needs water in southern California.
P. cembra SWISS STONE PINE Native to northern Asia, northern Europe.	Extremely slow to 70 ft or higher.	Spreading, short branches form narrow, dense pyramid, becoming broad, open, and round topped with age. In youth, handsome.	Needles: in 5s, 3–5 in., dark green. Cones: 3½ in., oval, light brown.	Very hardy (to –35°F.) Good in Northwest and Rocky Mountain region.	Resistant to white pine blister rust. Rare tree. Extremely slow growth and dense, regular foliage make a good plant for small gardens.
P. cembroides MEXICAN PINON PINE Native from Arizona to Baja California and northern Mexico.	Slow to 10–25 ft.	Stout, spreading branches form round-topped head. In youth rather rangy.	Needles: in 3s, sometimes 2s, 1–2 in., slender, dark green. Cones: 1–2 in., roundish, yellowish or reddish brown.	Has succeeded in Northwest west of Cascades and in California coastal and valley gardens. Excellent in Rocky Mountain Zone 2.	Most treelike of pinons. Drought resistant, good in desert soils.

NAME	GROWTH RATE, SIZE	GROWTH HABIT	NEEDLES AND CONES	CLIMATE ADAPTABILITY	REMARKS
P. contorta BEACH PINE, SHORE PINE Native along coast from Mendocino County, California to Alaska.	Fairly fast to 20–35 ft.	Nursery-grown trees compact, pyramidal, somewhat irregular. Trees collected along coast dwarfed, contorted by winds.	Needles: in 2s, 1¼–2 in., dark green, dense. Cones: 1–2 in., light yellow brown.	Hardy anywhere, but not at its best in hot, dry areas.	Good-looking in youth. Dense foliage, takes training well. One of best small pines for small gardens. Does well in containers.
P. c. latifolia (*P. c. murrayana*) LODGEPOLE PINE Native to Blue Mountains of eastern Oregon; Cascade Mountains of Washington; throughout Rocky Mountains. Plants from California and Oregon mountains have been called *P. c. murrayana*.	Rather slow to 80 ft., sometimes 150 ft., usually low, bushy tree in cultivation.	In cultivation rather irregular, open branched, attractive. Planted close, they grow tall, slim trunked. Solitary trees in mountains heavy trunked, narrow, dense.	Needles: in 2s, 1½–3 in., yellow green. Cones: 1½ in., shiny brown, persist many years.	Hardy. Widely adaptable except in areas of drought and low humidity.	All forms of *P. contorta* excellent in small garden, wild garden, or large rock garden.
P. coulteri COULTER PINE Native to dry, rocky California mountain slopes: Mt. Diablo, Mt. Hamilton, Santa Lucia ranges and mountains of southern California, south to Baja California.	Moderate to fast, 30–80 ft.	Shapely open growth, lower branches spread widely, persist. Sometimes develops several divergent leaders, producing "oak tree' shape.	Needles: in 3s, 5–10, even 14 in., deep green, stiff. Cones: 10–13 in., buff-colored, heavy, persist many years.	Hardy. Adaptable to area west of Cascades. Resistant to heat, drought, wind. Good in high desert.	Excellent in gardens where not crowded. Too spreading for small gardens. Huge cones attractive but potentially dangerous around play areas, patios, parked cars.
P. densiflora JAPANESE RED PINE Native to Japan.	Rapid when young. May reach 100 ft., usually much less.	Broad, irregular head. Often develops two or more trunks at ground level.	Needles: in 2s, 2½–5 in., bright blue green or yellow green, slender. Cones: 2 in., oval or oblong, tawny brown.	Hardy to −20°F., but not tree for desert areas. Will not tolerate hot, dry, or cold winds.	Handsome pine for informal effects, especially multitrunked trees. Makes moderate shade for woodland gardens. Variety 'Oculus-draconis', DRAGON EYE PINE, has 2 yellow bands on each needle; seen endwise, branch has concentric green and yellow bands. 'Pendula' is dwarf with sprawling branches.
P. d. 'Umbraculifera' TANYOSHO PINE Native to Japan.	Slow to moderate. 12–20 ft.	Broad, flat topped, with numerous trunks from base. Spread greater than height.	Same as above.	Same as above. Has performed well in Denver.	Gallon and 5-gallon-sized trees frequently bear cones. Good for containers, rock and Oriental gardens.
P. edulis (*P. cembroides edulis*) PINON, NUT PINE Native to California's Little San Bernardino and New York Mountains, east to Arizona, New Mexico, and Texas, north to Wyoming.	Slow to 10–20 ft.	Horizontal branching tree; low, round or flat-crowned in age; bushy and symmetrical in youth.	Needles: usually in 2s, dark green, ¾–1½ in., dense, stiff. Cones: 2 in., roundish, light brown.	Hardy. Thrives in coastal California, Northwest, Denver, higher desert areas. Drought resistant.	Beautiful small pine for containers, rock gardens. Collected plants bring look of age into new gardens. Cones contain edible seeds (pine nuts).

(Continued on next page)

NAME	GROWTH RATE, SIZE	GROWTH HABIT	NEEDLES AND CONES	CLIMATE ADAPTABILITY	REMARKS
P. eldarica Native to Caucasus Mountains of southern Russia, Afghanistan, Pakistan.	See *P. brutia.*	See *P. brutia.*	See *P. brutia.*	One of best desert pines, it also thrives near coast.	Something of a mystery pine; may be *P. brutia* from Afghanistan and Pakistan. Widely sold selection from Pakistan seed is sold as MONDELL PINE.
P. flexilis LIMBER PINE Mountains of northern Arizona, Utah, Nevada, southeastern California, and eastern slope of Rocky Mountains from Alberta to Texas.	Slow, to 20–30 ft. in gardens.	Thick trunk, open round top, many limber branches that may droop at decided angle to trunk.	Needles: in 5s, to 3 in., slightly curved or twisted, dark green. Cones: to 5 in. long, ovoid-conic, buff to buff-orange.	Hardy. Grows well on hot, dry, rocky slopes. Drought tolerant.	Smaller and more irregular at higher elevations. Young plants rather straggly appearing. Shapes well with shearing, can be used for bonsai. Susceptible to white pine blister rust.
P. halepensis ALEPPO PINE Native to Mediterranean region.	Moderate to rapid growth to 30–60 ft.	Attractive as 2 year old; rugged character at 5 years; in age, open irregular crown of many short, ascending branches.	Needles: usually in 2s, 2½–4 in., light green. Cones: 3 in., oval to oblong, reddish to yellow brown.	Semihardy. Thrives in desert heat, drought, and wind, good at seashore. Tender when young; established trees can take near-zero temperatures.	Most useful in poor soils and difficult, arid climates. Handsomer trees can be found for cooler, moister gardens. Standard desert pine. Sometimes bothered by mites in southern California, temporary dieback in Tucson area.
P. halepensis brutia See *P. brutia.*					
P. jeffreyi JEFFREY PINE Native to mountains of California, southern Oregon, western Nevada, Baja California.	Moderate to 60–120 ft.	Symmetrical in youth; straight trunked with short, spreading, often pendulous branches. Upper branches ascending, form open, pyramidal.	Needles: in 3s, 5–8 in., blue green. Cones: 6–12 in., reddish brown, oval. Cone doesn't feel prickly when you hold it in hand (*P. ponderosa* cone does).	Hardy. High altitude tree not at best in low areas. Drought resistant. Slow growing in Seattle.	Attractive in youth with silver gray bark and bluish foliage. One of best natural bonsai trees. Furrows of bark have vanilla odor.
P. lambertiana SUGAR PINE Native to Sierra Nevada and California's higher Coast Ranges; high mountains of southern California, Baja California; north to Cascades of central Oregon.	Slow in youth, then faster, to 200 ft. or higher.	Young trees narrow, open pyramids with spreading, rather pendulous branches. Old trees usually flat topped with wide-spreading open head.	Needles: in 5s, 3–4 in., dark bluish green. Cones: 10–20 in., cylindrical, light brown.	Hardy but temperamental. Grows well in Seattle.	World's tallest pine. Susceptible to white pine blister rust, but usually safe if no currants or gooseberry bushes (alternate hosts of blister rust) nearby.
P. monophylla SINGLELEAF PINON PINE Native to southeastern California south to Baja California, east to Utah, Arizona.	Very slow to 10–25 ft.	Young trees slender, symmetrical, narrow crowned. In maturity a small round-headed tree, with crooked trunk, open and broad topped in great age.	Needles: usually carried singly, ¾–1½ in., gray green, stiff. Cones: 2 in., wide, roundish, brown.	Hardy and drought resistant. Only pinon common in southern California.	Good bonsai or rock garden plant—or shrub of great character in dry, rocky places. Cones contain edible seeds (pine nuts). Rare in nurseries.
P. montezumae MONTEZUMA PINE Native from Mexico to Guatemala.	Moderately fast. To 70 ft. or more in the wilds, usually much less in cultivation.	Broad, fairly dense, with horizontal, somewhat drooping branches.	Needles: usually in 5s, to 12 in., drooping gracefully; deep, often bluish green. Cones: to 12 in., conical, yellow, reddish, or dark brown.	Unlikely to survive in low temperatures.	Rare, striking pine with unusually long needles. Does well in San Francisco Bay Area. Substitute *P. wallichiana* in colder areas.

NAME	GROWTH RATE, SIZE	GROWTH HABIT	NEEDLES AND CONES	CLIMATE ADAPTABILITY	REMARKS
P. monticola WESTERN WHITE PINE Native to northern California, north to British Columbia, east to Montana.	Fast first years, then slow to moderate to 60 ft.	Attractive, narrow, open crown in youth; spreading, somewhat drooping branches in age form pyramid.	Needles: in 5s, 1½–4 in., blue green, white banded beneath, fine and soft. Cones: 5–11 in., light brown, slender.	Very hardy.	Susceptible to white pine blister rust throughout Northwest and northern California.
P. mugo (*P. montana*) SWISS MOUNTAIN PINE Native to mountains of Spain, central Europe to Balkans.	Slow to variable heights.	Variable. Prostrate shrub, low shrub, or pyramidal tree of moderate size.	Needles: in 2s, 2 in., dark green, stout, crowded. Cones: 1–2 in., oval, tawny to dark brown.	Hardy but suffers in desert heat.	In nurseries, generally a bushy, twisted, somewhat open pine. *P. m. pumilio* is eastern European form, shrubby and varying from prostate to 5 or 10 ft.
P. mugo mugo MUGHO PINE Native to eastern Alps and Balkan states.	Slow to 4 ft.	From infancy on a shrubby, symmetrical little pine. May become spreading in age.	Needles: darker green than *P. mugo*. Cones: a little shorter than those of *P. mugo*.	Very hardy; as above.	One of most widely used pines because of low growth habit. Excellent container plant. Pick plants with dense pleasing form. Good in rock gardens.
P. muricata BISHOP PINE Native to northern coast of California, Santa Cruz Island, northwestern Baja California.	Rapid to 40–50 ft.	Open, pyramidal when young; dense, rounded in middle life; irregular in age.	Needles: in 2s, 4–6 in., dark green, crowded. Cones: 2–3 in., borne in whorls of 3, 4, or 5; broadly oval, brown.	Takes wind and salt air. Not reliably hardy in Northwest or interior.	Many people prefer *P. muricata* to Monterey pine because of its slower growth rate, greater denseness in youth.

(Continued on next page)

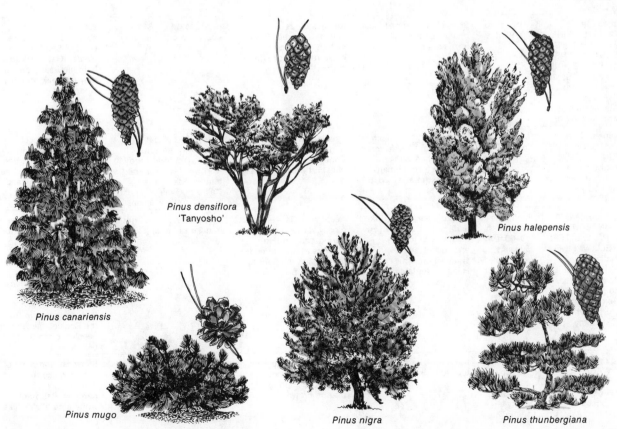

Pinus canariensis

Pinus densiflora 'Tanyosho'

Pinus halepensis

Pinus mugo

Pinus nigra

Pinus thunbergiana

These widely planted pines show great range of outlines and textures.

NAME	GROWTH RATE, SIZE	GROWTH HABIT	NEEDLES AND CONES	CLIMATE ADAPTABILITY	REMARKS
P. nigra (Formerly *P. austriaca*) AUSTRIAN BLACK PINE Native to Europe, western Asia.	Slow to moderate, usually not above 40 ft. in gardens.	Dense, stout pyramid with rather uniform crown. Branches in regular whorls; in age, broad and flat topped.	Needles: in 2s, 3–6½ in., stiff, very dark green. Cones: 2–3½ in., oval, brown.	Very hardy. Adaptable to winter cold and wind.	Tree of strong character which will serve either as landscape decoration or as windbreak in cold regions. Oak root fungus resistant.
P. palustris LONGLEAF PINE Native to Virginia and Florida to Mississippi; along coast of southeastern United States.	Slow for 5–10 years, then fast to 55–80 ft.	Gaunt, sparse branches ascend to form open, oblong head.	Needles: in 3s, to 18 in. on young trees, to 9 in. on mature. Dark green. Cones: 6–10 in., dull brown.	Grows in northern and southern California. In native habitat it occasionally takes frosts down to 5°F. but is used to generally warm winters.	Gallon-sized plants look like fountains of grass. Take several years to outgrow this stage. Larger young plants resemble green mops. Good tree for experimenters. Control chlorosis with iron chelates.
P. parviflora JAPANESE WHITE PINE Native to Japan and Formosa.	Slow to moderate to 20–50 ft. or higher.	In open ground a broad pyramid nearly as wide as high.	Needles: in 5s, 1½–2½ in., bluish gray to green. Cones: 2–3 in., oval, reddish brown.	Hardy. Grows well in Seattle and in northern California. Will survive −20°F.	Widely used for bonsai or container plant.
P. patula JELECOTE PINE Native to Mexico.	Very fast to 40–80 ft.	Symmetrical pyramid with widely spaced tiers of branches.	Needles: in 3s, to 12 in., grass green, slender, hanging straight down. Cones: to 4½ in., conic-ovoid, lustrous pale brown.	Hardy to 15°; a borderline case in Seattle or inland, thriving in coastal California.	Graceful tree casts a light shade, provides handsome silhouette. One of fastest-growing pines in the world. Treat for chlorosis. Oak root fungus resistant.
P. peuce MACEDONIAN PINE Native to Yugoslavia, Bulgaria, and Albania.	Slow to moderate growth to 80 ft.	Shapely, dense, erect, narrow cone shape.	Needles: in 5s, slender, 3–4½ in. long, blue green. Cones: slender, curved, 4–6 in. long.	Not widely tested. Hardy to 0°F. and somewhat below. Successful near Denver. Drought tolerant.	Very attractive tree. Similar to *P. wallichiana* but more compact with shorter needles. Rare in nurseries.
P. pinaster CLUSTER PINE, FRENCH TURPENTINE PINE, MARITIME PINE Native to Atlantic coast of France, western Mediterranean, northern Africa.	Very fast to 80–90 ft.	Spreading or sometimes pendulous branches form pyramidal head.	Needles: in 2s, 5–9 in., stiff, glossy green. Cones: 4–7 in., conic-oblong, clustered, glossy light brown.	Hardy to 0°F. Best near coasts, in coastal valleys.	Well-adapted to sandy soil, ocean exposure. Used in San Francisco's Golden Gate Park to help bind sand dunes. May be weak rooted when young.
P. pinea ITALIAN STONE PINE Native to southern Europe and Turkey.	Moderate to 40–80 ft.	In youth, a stout, bushy globe; in middle life, thick trunk topped with umbrella form of many branches. In age, broad and flat topped.	Needles: in 2s, 5–8 in., bright to gray green, stiff. Cones: 4–6 in., glossy, chestnut brown, broadly oval.	Hardy. Takes heat and drought when established. Old trees hardy in Northwest, young ones tender. Good in California valleys, coast; successful in Tucson.	Excellent in beach gardens. Eventually too large for small gardens. Splendid roadside tree. Young trees are handsome, old trees striking.
P. ponderosa PONDEROSA PINE, WESTERN YELLOW PINE Native from British Columbia to Mexico, east to Nebraska, Texas, and northeast Oklahoma.	Moderate to rapid to 50–60 ft. in 50 years, eventually to 150 ft. or more.	In youth, straight trunked and well-branched. In age stately, with loosely arranged branches in spirelike crown. Handsome plated bark.	Needles: in 3s, 4–11 in., glossy yellow green to dark green, firm, in clusters at branch ends. Cones: 3–5 in., light to red brown, prickly to touch.	Very hardy, but not good in desert heat and wind.	Bushy, attractive tree at all ages. Eventually for large gardens only. Oddly enough, small ones make fine bonsai or large container plants. *P. p. arizonica* has needles in 5s, sometimes 3s and 4s. *P. p. scopulorum* from the Rockies has shorter needles, often drooping branches.
P. pumila DWARF SIBERIAN PINE Native to exposed sites in eastern Asia mainland and nearby islands.	Very slow, shrubby, perhaps to 10 ft. after many years.	Naturally dwarf, tending toward prostrate habit.	Needles: in 5s, to 2 in., blue green. Cones: ovoid to 2 in. long, orange brown.	Very hardy, in nature growing on exposed, windswept sites.	Slowness and habit of growth make this a natural for rock gardens. Resistant to white pine blister rust.

NAME	GROWTH RATE, SIZE	GROWTH HABIT	NEEDLES AND CONES	CLIMATE ADAPTABILITY	REMARKS
P. pungens TABLE MOUNTAIN PINE Native from New Jersey to Georgia.	Fairly slow to 20–60 ft.	Stout, spreading branches form broad, open, often flat topped or irregular picturesque crown.	Needles: in 2s or 3s, 2–3 in., stiff, prickly, dark green. Cones: 3½ in., bright brown, persist many years.	Hardy. Thriving in Seattle and in northern California.	Somewhat resembles Japanese red pine. Useful where informal, rather open pine is desirable. Large, abundant, deep purple catkins are decorative.
P. radiata MONTEREY PINE Native to California central coast.	Very fast to 80–100 ft.	Shapely broad cone in youth, then drops lower branches to develop rounded or flattish crown.	Needles: in 3s or 2s, 3–7 in., bright green. Cones: 3–6 in., lopsided, clustered; persist many years.	Most widely planted pine in California even in areas where it is poorly adapted. Not reliably hardy when temperatures drop below 15°F. Best where summers are cool. Not for high or low desert areas nor for California's central valley. Good in sea wind, but not on shallow soils.	Very fast-growing, 6 ft. a year when young; 50 ft. in 12 years. Often shallow rooted, subject to blowdown. Prune to maintain denseness (see introduction to Pines). In coastal California gets many pests, suffers smog damage, water molds. Oak root fungus resistant.
P. resinosa NORWAY PINE, RED PINE Native to eastern United States.	Medium to 70 ft.	Dense crown, slightly drooping branches.	Needles: in 2s, 4–6 in. long, dark shiny green. Cones: 2 in. long, shiny brown.	Very hardy to cold. Popular in Northwest.	Bark reddish brown on older trees.
P. roxburghii (*P. longifolia*) CHIR PINE, INDIAN LONGLEAF PINE Native to Himalayan foothills.	Medium fast to 60–80 ft. or more.	Slender pyramid in youth with long, drooping foliage; later broad, spreading, with round-topped, symmetrical head.	Needles: in 3s, 8–13 in., slender, light green. Cones: 4–7 in., conic-oval.	Adapted to California coastal areas, lower Oregon coast. Oddly, successful in Tucson.	Rare pine. Similar in many ways to Canary Island pine.
P. sabiniana DIGGER PINE Native to California foothills.	Fast to 40–50 ft.	Wild trees in dry areas are sparse, open. Main trunk divides into secondary trunks.	Needles: in 3s, 8–12 in., gray green, lacy. Cones: 6–10 in., oblong-oval, contain edible seeds.	Though native to dry foothills, and very drought resistant, thrives in Seattle and is quite hardy there.	Unusual tree for large gardens. Bulky yet lacy, almost transparent crown. Little shade under Digger pine. Very ornamental.
P. strobus WHITE PINE, EASTERN WHITE PINE Native Newfoundland to Manitoba, south to Georgia, west to Illinois and Iowa.	Slow in seedling stage, then fast to 100 ft. or more.	Symmetrical cone with horizontal branches in regular whorls. In age, broad, open, irregular.	Needles: in 5s, 2–4 in., blue green, soft. Cones: 3–8 in., slender, often curved.	Hardy in any cold but burns in windy areas. Needs regular water supply.	Fine textured and handsome in form and color. Subject to blister rust. 'Pendula' has weeping, trailing branches. 'Prostrata' is low, spreading shrub with trailing branches.
P. s. 'Nana' DWARF WHITE PINE	Very slow to 3–7 ft.	Broad bush usually twice as wide as tall.	As above but needles shorter.	Hardy wherever *P. strobus* grows successfully.	Useful in containers or rock gardens.
P. sylvestris SCOTCH PINE Native to northern Europe, Asia.	Moderate to 70–100 ft.	Straight, well-branched pyramid in youth; irregular and picturesque in age, with drooping branches.	Needles: in 2s, 1½–3 in., blue green, stiff. Cones: 2 in., gray to reddish brown.	Very hardy. Not for desert areas; often turns red brown in cold winters, but recovers. Wind resistant.	Popular as Christmas tree and in landscaping. Reddish bark, sparse foliage have own charm. Select young trees with good green winter color; some turn yellowish, even when winter is mild. Excellent in flower arrangements. Many other garden forms: 'Nana' and 'Watereri' are dwarfs, 'Pendula', a weeping tree. All are rare.
P. s. 'Fastigiata'	As above.	Dense, narrow column.	As above.	As above.	Handsome, very densely foliaged plant.

(Continued on next page)

NAME	GROWTH RATE, SIZE	GROWTH HABIT	NEEDLES AND CONES	CLIMATE ADAPTABILITY	REMARKS
P. thunbergiana (*P. thunbergii*) JAPANESE BLACK PINE Native to Japan.	Fast to 100 ft. in Northwest. Slow to moderate to 20 ft. in southern California and desert.	Spreading branches form broad, conical tree, irregular and spreading in age.	Needles: in 2s, 3–4½ in., bright green, stiff. Cones: 3 in., brown, oval.	Hardy. Widely planted throughout California, in western Washington and Oregon, with watering in intermediate and high desert.	Handsome tree in youth. Takes to pruning like cloth to scissors; shear it into Christmas tree form or make it into cascade. Excellent in planters or as bonsai.
P. torreyana TORREY PINE Native to California's San Diego coast and Santa Rosa Island.	Fast to 40–60 ft., sometimes higher.	Broad, open, irregular, picturesque habit when exposed to sea winds.	Needles: in 5s, 8–13 in., light gray green to dark green. Cones: 4–6 in., chocolate brown.	Although native to the coast, it accepts inland, even high desert, conditions, with temperatures as low as 12°F. Stands drought.	Less open growth when grown in heavy soil. Don't prune: cut branches die back to trunk. Oak root fungus resistant.
P. wallichiana (*P. griffithii, P. excelsa*) HIMALAYAN WHITE PINE Native to Himalayas.	Slow to moderate to 40 ft. in gardens, 150 ft. in wilds.	Broad, conical.	Needles: in 5s, 6–8 in., blue green, slender, drooping. Cones: 6–10 in., light brown.	Hardy to about –10°F. Performance in dry, hot areas not good.	Resistant to blister rust. Eventually large, but good form and color make it good choice for featured pine in big lawn or garden.

PISONIA umbellifera (*P. brunoniana, Heimerliodendron brunonianum*). Zones 23, 24 or house plant anywhere. Evergreen shrub. Green-leafed wild plant from New Zealand. Can grow from 12–20 ft. tall and spread nearly as wide in frost free locations. Rare in West. Commoner is *P. u.* 'Variegata', MAP PLANT, with 4–6 in.-long oval leaves strongly variegated pale green and creamy white on medium green background. It is not likely to exceed 4–6 ft. in height. Flowers are not showy; fruit are ribbed, 1 in. long, extremely sticky. Fruit are seldom seen here. Plants, indoors or out, need regular watering and feeding, warm, even temperature with freedom from wind or warm drafts, and good light (but not strong, hot sun). Usually seen as a pot plant 2–3 ft. tall and as wide.

Pisonia umbellifera

PISTACHE. See *Pistacia*.

PISTACHIO, PISTACHIO NUT. See *Pistacia vera*.

PISTACIA. PISTACHE. Deciduous or semievergreen trees. Divided leaves on all species. Flowers not showy. Female trees bear fruit after several years if male trees are nearby. Of species described, only one bears edible fruit (nuts): *P. vera*. Others are ornamental trees.

Verticillium wilt (see page 65) may strike established trees. Minimize susceptibility by planting in well-drained soils, watering deeply and infrequently.

P. atlantica. MT. ATLAS PISTACHE. Semievergreen or deciduous. Zones 8–24. Slow to moderate growth to 60 ft. More regular and pyramidal than other pistaches, especially as young tree. Leaflets 7–11, narrow, rounded at tip, glossy medium green. Fruit dark blue or purple. Needs sun, good drainage. Takes desert heat and winds; tolerates drought when established. Holds its foliage very late—all winter in mild climate. Not widely grown as ornamental, but is much used as understock for pistachio (*P. vera*).

P. chinensis. CHINESE PISTACHE. Deciduous. Zones 8–16, 18–23. Moderate growth to 60 ft. tall, 50 feet. wide. Young trees

Pistacia chinensis

often gawky and lopsided, but with reasonable care older trees become dense and shapely. Leaves with 10–16 paired leaflets 2–4 in. long by ¾ in. wide. Foliage colors beautifully in fall —scarlet, crimson, orange, sometimes yellow tones. Only tree to color scarlet in desert. Fruit on female trees bright red, turning dark blue. Not fussy as to soil or water; accepts moderately alkaline conditions, lawn watering (though verticillium wilt is a danger), or no summer watering at all (this only in deep soils). Resistant to oak root fungus. Stake young trees and prune for first few years to develop head high enough to walk under. Reliable tree for street or lawn, patio or garden corner planting. 'Keith Davey', selected male variety, has scant fruit production and is neater, easier to shape.

P. vera. PISTACHIO, PISTACHIO NUT. Deciduous. Zones 7–12, 14, 15, 18–21. Broad, bushy tree to 30 ft. high, with one or several trunks. Leaves have 3–5 roundish, 2–4-in.-long leaflets. Fruit reddish, wrinkled, borne in heavy clusters. Inside husks are hard-shelled pistachio nuts. Be sure to include male tree in your planting. 'Peters' is the male variety most planted, 'Kerman' is principal fruiting (female) variety. When planting, avoid rough handling; budded tops are easily broken away from understock. Pistachios are inclined to spread and droop; stake them and train branches to good framework of 4 or 5 limbs beginning at 4 ft. or so above ground. Established trees will take considerable drought.

PITANGA. See *Eugenia uniflora*.

PITCHER PLANT. See *Sarracenia*.

PITTOSPORUM. Evergreen shrubs and trees. Some forms have attractive fragrant flowers and some have pretty fruit, but pittosporums as a group are valued most by Californians for their foliage and form. All make basic, dependable shrubs or trees— the kind of plants that can be a garden's all-year backbone. Some make good clipped hedges; all have pleasing outlines when left unclipped. Good as windbreaks.

Pittosporum tobira

Although they are fairly drought resistant, all respond with greener, lusher growth when watered regularly and when fed at least once each spring or summer with nitrogenous or complete fertilizer. All are susceptible to aphids and scale insects. Black sooty covering on leaves (mold growing on insects' honeydew secretions) is sure sign. All grow best in full sun to half shade.

P. crassifolium. Zones 9, 14–17, 19–24. Will grow to 25 ft. high in 8–10 years, but can easily be kept 6–10 ft. high and 6–8 ft. wide by yearly pruning. Gray green leaves, 1–2 in. long with rounded ends, densely set on branches. Clusters of little (¼ in. wide) maroon flowers in late spring. Conspicuous fruit. Notably wind resistant, and tolerates even salt-laden ocean winds. Good seaside plant. 'Nana' is dense dwarf form 3 ft. tall or a little more and equally wide.

P. eugenioides. Zones 9, 14–17, 19–22. Excellent hedge plant or freestanding shade tree. Good as screen or background plant. Leaves 2–4 in. long have distinctly wavy edges and medium glossy finish. Depending on environment, leaf color may be yellow green to medium green. On unpruned plants, clusters of fragrant, yellow, ½-in. flowers form in spring. To grow as hedge, plant gallon-can plants 18 in. apart in row. Force bushiness by shearing off 2–6 in. of plant tops several times each year between February and October. Begin clipping sides when necessary. As freestanding tree (to 40 ft. high, 20 ft. wide), develops handsome curving gray trunk and lush foliage canopy.

P. napaulense (P. floribundum). GOLDEN FRAGRANCE. Zones 15–17, 20–24. This shrub, to 12 ft. high, 8 ft. wide, is not like the others. Main differences: Leaves are thin, leathery texture, 4–8 in. long, 1–2 in. wide, shiny, pointed at tips; flowers are golden yellow, intensely fragrant, and in 3-in. clusters protruding beyond branch tips in spring. Use as display plant or fragrance maker, not as hedge or screen plant.

P. phillyraeoides. WILLOW PITTOSPORUM. Zones 9, 12–24. Also different from typical pittosporums. This one's a weeping plant with trailing branches and deep, dusty green leaves, very narrow, 3 in. long. Grows slowly to 15–20 ft. high, 10–15 ft. wide. Always best standing alone; strong structure shouldn't be smothered by other foliage. Good by pool or patio. Small, yellow, bell shaped, fragrant flowers borne along drooping branches in late winter, early spring, followed by deep yellow fruit. If drainage is poor, water very infrequently but deeply. Tolerates heat and drought better than most other pittosporums. Has even naturalized in some desert areas.

P. rhombifolium. QUEENSLAND PITTOSPORUM. Zones 12–24. Slow-growing shrub or tree, to 15–35 ft. Glossy rich green leaves are nearly diamond shaped, to 4 in. long. Small white flowers in late spring. Very showy, yellow to orange, ½-in., round fruit in clusters from fall through winter. Fruit contrast nicely with foliage. Growth is open enough that you can see fruit. As small tree, well suited for patio (if litter of sticky fruit won't pose a problem) or lawn. Or use several as not-too-dense screen that needs little pruning. Resistant to oak root fungus.

P. tenuifolium (P. nigricans). Zones 9, 14–17, 19–24. This is quite similar in most ways (size, growth habit, uses, culture) to P. eugenioides. Main difference is in leaves and twigs, and therefore in total texture effect. This one has shorter (1–1½ in.), more oval leaves than P. eugenioides; leaf edges are less wavy, and color is deeper green. Small twigs and leaf stems are darker. Altogether, then, this one is finer textured, darker, and a little denser. If pruning allows flower formation, they will be dark purple, ½ in. wide in clusters. Plants more tolerant of beach conditions than P. eugenioides. There are varieties with bronzy purple foliage and variegated leaves.

P. tobira. TOBIRA. Zones 8–24; borderline hardiness in Zones 4–7. Broad, dense shrub or small tree, 6–15 ft. tall, rarely to 30 ft. Can be held to 6 ft. by careful heading back and thinning (tobira does not respond as well to shearing as do some other pittosporums). Foliage clean looking, dense; leaves leathery, shiny dark green, 2–5 in. long, rounded at ends. Clusters of creamy white flowers at branch tips in early spring have fragrance of orange blossoms. Flowers become round, green fruit that turn brownish in fall and split to show orange seeds. Best for screens, massing, or individually as crooked-stemmed, freestanding small tree. Effective in containers. Variety 'Variegata' is smaller, usually growing to about 5 ft. high and as broad. Foliage is gray green edged white. Sometimes loses many leaves in winter. 'Wheeler's Dwarf' has same handsome leaves as P. tobira but on extremely dense-growing 1–2-ft. shrub. Choice for foreground or low boundary plantings, even small-scale ground cover. Good near swimming pools.

P. undulatum. VICTORIAN BOX. Zones 14 and 15 (in frost-sheltered locations) 16, 17, 21–24. Moderately fast growth to 15 ft., then slow to 30–40 ft. high, equal width. Planted 5–8 ft. apart, can be kept to 10–15-ft. dense screen by pruning (not shearing). Good background plant. Makes dense single or multitrunked, dome shaped tree of great beauty. Leaves medium to dark green, glossy, wavy edged, 4–6 in. long. Fragrant creamy white flowers in early spring. Yellowish orange fruit open in fall to show sticky, golden orange seeds which are messy on lawn or paving. Lawn or street tree, screen, in big container. Strong roots become invasive with age.

P. viridiflorum. CAPE PITTOSPORUM. Zones 15–17, 20–24. Shrub or tree to 25 ft. Leaves to 3 in. long, sharp pointed or blunt, often inrolled at edges. Flowers fragrant, yellowish green, in dense clusters. Orange yellow fruit. Resembles large P. tobira; serves similar uses, also has great value as street or garden tree. Good as screen.

PITYROGRAMMA. GOLDBACK FERN. Finely cut fronds, dark green above, heavily coated beneath with bright golden or silvery white powder. Grow in light shade.

P. hybrida. Zones 23, 24. Large fern of hybrid origin. Brilliantly gold-backed fronds to 2–3 ft. long, broad, finely cut. Hardy to 32° F.

P. triangularis. Zones 4–9, 14–24. Native California to Alaska. Small fern with fronds 7 in. long, 6 in. wide, often much less in dry woods. Reverse of fronds strikingly golden (silver in some varieties). Dormant in summer, therefore drought tolerant.

*Pityrogramma
triangularis*

PLAID CACTUS. See *Gymnocalycium mihanovichii.*

PLANE TREE. See *Platanus.*

PLANTAIN LILY. See *Hosta.*

PLATANUS. PLANE TREE, SYCAMORE. Deciduous trees. All grow large, have lobed, maplelike leaves. Older bark sheds in patches to reveal pale, smooth, new bark beneath. Brown, ball-like seed clusters hang from branches on long stalks through winter; prized for winter arrangements. Somewhat drought tolerant but are better with some deep watering in summer. Subject to blight (anthracnose) which causes early, continued leaf fall; P. racemosa especially susceptible. See pages 64 and 65 for controls. Also rake up and dispose of dead leaves; fungus spores can overwinter on them. Chlorosis may be a problem in desert.

Platanus acerifolia

P. acerifolia. (Often sold as P. orientalis.) LONDON PLANE TREE. Zones 2–24. Fast growth to 40–80 ft., 30–40-ft. spread. Upper trunk and limbs cream-colored, smooth. Leaves are 3–5 lobed, 4–10 in. wide. Tolerates most soils, stands up beautifully under city smog, soot, dust, reflected heat. Can be pollarded to create dense, low canopy.

Watch for spider mites and scale. Good street, park, or lawn tree. Used in lines and blocks for formal plantings—avenues, screens, masses.

P. occidentalis. AMERICAN SYCAMORE, BUTTONWOOD. All Zones. Similar to London plane tree; new bark is whiter, tree is out of leaf longer. Very hardy. Occasionally grows with multiple or leaning trunks. Old trees near streams sometimes reach huge size and have heavy trunks.

P. racemosa. CALIFORNIA SYCAMORE. Zones 4–24. Native along streams in California foothills and Coast Ranges. Fast growth to robust 50–100 ft. Main trunk often divides into spreading or leaning secondary trunk. Attractive patchy, buff-colored bark.

(Continued on next page)

Smooth branches often gracefully twisted and contorted. Deeply lobed, yellowish green leaves 4–9 in. long. Susceptible to leaf miner, red spider mites. Leaves naturally turn dusty brown too early in autumn to be considered as fall color. In mild coastal areas brown leaves hang on until new leaf growth starts. In winter the ball-like seed clusters hang 3–7 together along single stalk. For native or wild gardens, or for big informal gardens generally. Tolerant of much heat, wind. With care in pruning can be trained into picturesque multitrunked clump.

P. wrightii (*P. racemosa wrightii*). ARIZONA SYCAMORE. Zones 10–12. Native along streams and canyons in mountains of south and east Arizona, needs regular watering during dry season. To 80 ft. Resembles *P. racemosa;* leaves more deeply lobed, seed clusters have individual stalks branching from common stalk.

PLATYCERIUM. STAGHORN FERN. Odd epiphytic ferns from tropical regions. In nature, they grow on trees; gardeners grow them on slabs of bark or tree fern stem, occasionally in hanging baskets or on trees. Most should be kept on the dry side, watering only when slab or moss to which plant is attached is actually dry to the touch. Two kinds of fronds: sterile ones are flat, pale green aging tan and brown—they support plant and accumulate organic matter to help feed it; fertile fronds are forked, resembling deer antlers. Striking decoration for lanai, shaded patio.

Platycerium bifurcatum

P. bifurcatum (often sold as *P. alcicorne*). Zones 15–17, 19–24. From Australia and New Guinea. Surprisingly hardy; survives 20°–22° F. with only lath structures for shelter. Fertile fronds clustered, gray green, to 3 ft. long. Makes numerous offsets which can be used in propagation.

P. grande. Zones 23, 24. From Australia. Fertile and sterile fronds both forked, the former broad but divided somewhat like moose antlers to 6 ft. long. Protect from frosts. Don't overwater.

PLATYCLADUS orientalis (*Thuja orientalis, Biota orientalis*). ORIENTAL ARBORVITAE. Evergreen shrubs, trees. All Zones; damaged by severe winters in Zone 1. Shrubby forms common, but tree from which they originate, a 25–50-ft. plant, is very rarely seen. Leaves scalelike, on twigs that are arranged in flat, vertical planes. Juvenile foliage needlelike; some varieties keep juvenile foliage throughout life. Cones small, fleshy, woody when ripe. Less hardy to cold than American arborvitae (*Thuja occidentalis),* but tolerates heat and low humidity better. In Rocky Mountains grows best when in part shade; shade during winter is especially helpful. Has survived well in nematode infested soils. Give good drainage, ample water, and protect from the reflected heat of light-colored walls or pavement. Blight of leaves and twigs in Northwest is easily controlled by copper sprays in early fall and by pruning out and destroying diseased growth. Spray for spider mites.

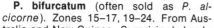

Platycladus orientalis

Widely used around foundations, as pairs or groups by doorways or gates, singly in lawns or borders, or in formal rows. Most stay small, but some forms often end up bigger than space they're meant for. Varieties are:

'Aureus' ('Aureus Nana', 'Berckmanii'). DWARF GOLDEN ARBORVITAE, BERCKMAN DWARF ARBORVITAE. Dwarf, compact, golden, globe shaped, usually 3 ft. tall, 2 ft. wide. Can reach 5 ft.

'Bakeri'. Compact, cone shaped, with bright green foliage.

'Beverleyensis'. BEVERLY HILLS ARBORVITAE, GOLDEN PYRAMID ARBORVITAE. Upright globe to cone shaped, somewhat open habit. Branchlet tips golden yellow. Can grow to 10 ft. tall, 10 ft. wide in time. Give it room.

'Blue Cone'. Dense, upright, conical; good blue green color.

'Bonita' ('Bonita Upright', 'Bonita Erecta'). Rounded, full, dense cone to 3 ft. tall. Dark green with slight golden tinting at branch tips.

'Fruitlandii'. FRUITLAND ARBORVITAE. Compact, upright, cone shaped shrub with deep green foliage.

'Raffles'. Resembles 'Aurea' but denser in growth, smaller, brighter in color.

PLATYCODON grandiflorus. BALLOON FLOWER. Perennial. All Zones. Upright branched stems to 3½ ft. Leaves light olive green, 1–3 in. long. Balloonlike buds open into 2-in.-wide, star shaped flowers in blue violet, white, or soft pink. Bloom June-August if spent flowers (not entire stems) are removed.

Platycodon grandiflorus

Use in borders with astilbe, campanula, francoa, hosta, rehmannia. Plant in sun near coast; light shade in warmer areas. Protect roots from gophers. Good soil, moderate watering. Completely dormant in winter; mark position to avoid digging up fleshy roots. Takes 2–3 years to get well established. Easy to grow from seed. Variety *mariesii* is dwarf form 12–18 in. high. 'Apoyama', 2–3-in. dwarf in pots, grows to size of *mariesii* in open ground.

PLECTRANTHUS. SWEDISH IVY. Perennials. Outdoors in Zones 22–24; elsewhere lathhouse or greenhouse foliage plants. Leaves somewhat thickish, with scalloped edges and prominent veins. Small white or bluish flowers in spikes. Grow as ground cover in small semishady to shady areas, southern California coast. Especially good trailing over wall or edge of planter or raised bed. As indoor or lathhouse plant, grow in hanging pot or wall container. Among easiest plants to grow. Will root in water or soil, take moderate or deep shade (though it prefers good light without direct sun), require fairly little water once established. Most people remove flower buds before bloom for more compact plants; alternative method is to allow plant to bloom, then cut it back afterward. Following are the best known of many species and varieties:

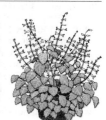

Plectranthus oertendahlii

P. australis. Shining dark green leaves. There are white-variegated forms.

P. coleoides 'Marginatus'. Somewhat less trailing in habit, leaves green and gray green with cream edge.

P. oertendahlii. Leaf veins silvery, margins purplish, scalloped, veins purplish beneath.

PLEIONE. Terrestrial orchids. Outdoors in Zones 5–9, 14–24. Native to southeast Asia. Many species. All are deciduous. Plant is a pseudobulb bearing 1 or 2 leaves. Leaves to 8 in. long in largest species, narrowly oval and pleated. Flowers resemble a cattleya, appear before foliage in early spring. Grow them in pots with leaf mold or in peaty soil. Keep on dry side in winter. Shade.

Pleione bulbocodioides

P. bulbocodioides. (*P. formosana*). One or two 2½–3-in. flowers on 3–5-in. stem in spring. Lavender purple sepals and petals, paler lavender lip marked with brown and yellow.

PLEIOSPILOS. SPLIT ROCK. Succulents. Grow in pots; let them summer outside anywhere; bring indoors where winters are cold; leave outdoors in winter with overhead protection in Zones 16, 17, 21–24. Plants have 1–3 pairs of leaves that very much resemble gray or gray green rounded pebbles; size varies according to species, from 1 in. long to slightly more than 3 in. Flowers large in relation to leaf size,

Pleiospilos nelii

resembling those of ice plants, yellow or white. For culture see *Lithops.* Of many kinds offered, *P. nelii* and *P. bolusii* are best known.

PLEROMA splendens. See *Tibouchina urvilleana.*

PLOVER EGGS. See *Adromischus festivus.*

PLUM and PRUNE. Varieties of edible plums and prunes commonly grown in West are described in accompanying chart. Noted there beneath each variety is group to which it belongs—Japanese (*Prunus salicina*), European (*P. domestica*). A third category, important only where climate is unusually severe, is a complex group of hybrids involving Japanese plum, several species of native American wild plums, and the native sand cherry (*P. besseyi*). Originating in Canada, the Dakotas, and Minnesota, they are exceptionally tolerant of cold and wind. Typical varieties are 'Compass', 'Pipestone', 'Sapa', 'Sapalta', and 'Waneta'. They are eaten fresh, cooked, or made into preserves. Pollination is often difficult with these hybrids; inquire of local nurserymen about effective and available pollinators. Damson plum (*P. insititia*) is often considered a type of European plum; it intercrosses with European plums freely.

Plum

As orchard trees, both Japanese and European plums reach a height of 15–20 ft. with a spread somewhat wider than high. Differences in growth habit are discussed below under pruning and thinning. All have white flowers. Leaves are broadly oval with serrated edges to about 3 in. long, turn tawny yellow in fall. Fruit of Japanese plums range in color from green through yellow and brilliant red to deep purple black. With few exceptions fruit is larger than that of European plum, juicier, with pleasant blend of acid and sugar. Most Japanese plums are used for fresh fruit only. European plums range in color from green and yellow to almost black. Prunes are European plums that have high sugar content which enables them to be sun dried

without fermenting at the pit. As fresh fruit they are sweeter than other plums.

European plums and prunes bloom late and are better adapted than early blooming Japanese plums to areas with late frosts or cool, rainy spring weather. Most European varieties have moderately high chilling requirement that rules them out of extremely mild winter areas. Pollination requirements are listed in the chart; pollenizers recommended are not the only combinations possible, but those listed have worked.

You can grow plums in many soil types but, of course, they do best in well-drained fertile soil. Best growth, fruit development come with periodic deep watering in summer even though established trees are fairly drought tolerant.

For larger fruit and vigorous growth, fertilize heavily. Orchardists give Japanese plums 1–3 lbs. of actual nitrogen a year; European plums, 1–2 lbs.

Train young trees to vase shape. After selecting framework branches, cut back to lateral branches. If tree tends to grow upright, cut to outside branches; if it is spreading, cut to inside branches.

Japanese plums make tremendous shoot growth and rather severe pruning is necessary at all ages.

European plums do not branch as freely and selection of framework branches is limited. Prune to avoid formation of V-crotches. Mature trees require little pruning—mainly thinning out annual shoot growth.

European plums and prunes do not require as heavy fruit thinning as the Japanese. Heavy bearing of Japanese varieties results in much small fruit and possibly damage to tree. Thin drastically as soon as fruit are big enough to be seen. Space fruit 4–6 in. apart.

Control insects and diseases like this: dormant spray for scale, mite eggs, aphids. Or use recommended control (page 60) in early spring to kill scale in crawler stage. Spray when buds show white for twig borer and aphids; use insecticide containing sevin or diazinon. Brown rot and fruit and leaf spot may be severe in humid areas. To control, spray with wettable sulfur weekly as fruit matures. If borers attack, control as with peaches. To control mites and insects after leaves form, use an all-purpose fruit tree insecticide, following carefully the instructions on spray label.

Plum and Prune

NAME	ZONES	POLLINATION	FRUIT	REMARKS
'Beauty' JAPANESE (*Prunus salicina*)	7–10, 12, 14–20	Self-fertile; yield improved by pollination with 'Santa Rosa'.	Medium sized, bright red skin, amber flesh streaked with scarlet, good flavor. Very early.	Fruit softens quickly.
'Bluefre' EUROPEAN (*P. domestica*)	2–12, 14–22	Self-fertile.	Large, blue skin. Firm yellow green flesh, small pit, freestone. Early midseason. Productive.	Good canning variety. Fruit lasts on tree 30 days after ripening.
'Burbank' JAPANESE	2–12, 14–20	'Beauty', 'Santa Rosa'.	Large, red. Amber yellow flesh of excellent flavor. Midseason.	Good choice in regions where hardiness to cold is important.
'Burmosa' JAPANESE	5–10	'Santa Rosa', 'Mariposa'.	Large, pinkish red. Light amber flesh. Early.	Handsome, delicious plum but softens quickly.
'Casselman' JAPANESE	2, 3, 7–12, 14–22	See 'Santa Rosa'.	Resembles 'Late Santa Rosa' but lighter in color, ripening later.	Not subject to cracking of skin.
'Damson' ('Blue Damson') EUROPEAN (*P. insititia*)	2–23	Self-fertile.	Small, purple or blue black, green fleshed, very tart.	Makes fine jam and jelly. Strains of this variety sold as 'French Damson', 'Shropshire'.
'Duarte' JAPANESE	2–12, 14–20	'Beauty', 'Santa Rosa', 'Satsuma', 'Howard Miracle'.	Medium to large, dull red, silvery markings. Deep red flesh. Midseason.	Firm and keeps well. Sweet flesh, fine flavor, tart skin.
'Eldorado' JAPANESE	7–10, 12, 14–20	'Santa Rosa', 'Wickson'.	Medium large, flattened, black red. Firm, somewhat dry, amber flesh. Midseason.	Good keeper. Holds shape well for canning, slicing.

(Continued on next page)

NAME	ZONES	POLLINATION	FRUIT	REMARKS
'Elephant Heart' JAPANESE	2, 3, 7–12, 14–22	'Santa Rosa'.	Very large dark red plum with rich red flesh. Freestone, highly flavored. Midseason to late.	Skin tart; some prefer it peeled. Long harvest season.
'French Prune' ('Agen') EUROPEAN (*P. domestica*)	2, 3, 7–12, 14–22	Self-fertile.	Small, red to purplish black. Very sweet and mild. Late.	Standard drying prune of California. Suitable for drying or canning.
'Green Gage' (*P. d. italica*) EUROPEAN	2–12, 14–22	Self-fertile.	Small to medium, greenish yellow, amber fleshed. Good flavor. Midseason.	Very old variety; still a favorite for eating fresh, for cooking, canning, or jam. Selected strain sold as 'Jefferson'.
'Hollywood'	See FLOWERING PLUM under Prunus.			
'Howard Miracle' JAPANESE	7–10, 14–20	'Santa Rosa', 'Laroda', 'Wickson'	Medium-sized, yellow with red blush. Yellow flesh with spicy, pineapplelike flavor. Midseason.	More acid than most Japanese plums, but truly distinctive in flavor.
'Imperial' ('Imperial Epineuse') EUROPEAN	7–12, 14–18	'French Prune' or other European plums.	Large, reddish purple to black purple, greenish yellow flesh, sweet, highly flavored, fine quality. Late midseason.	Excellent fresh. Makes a premium dried prune, canned product.
'Inca' JAPANESE	7–9, 12–24	'Beauty', 'Wickson', 'Kelsey', 'Santa Rosa', 'Satsuma'.	Medium-sized, yellow-skinned, yellow-fleshed fruit. Firm fleshed. Late.	Good home variety. Fruit holds well. Discarded commercially. Very low chilling requirement.
'Italian Prune' ('Fellenburg') EUROPEAN	2–12, 14–18	Self-fertile.	Medium-sized, purplish black, sweet prune. Late midseason.	Standard for prunes in the Northwest. Excellent fresh and for canning. Can be dried. 'Early Italian' ripens 2 weeks earlier.
'Kelsey' JAPANESE	7–12, 14–18	'Beauty', 'Formosa', 'Wickson', 'Inca'.	Large, green to greenish yellow splashed red. Yellow, firm, sweet flesh. Nonjuicy. Late midseason.	Holds for several weeks off tree.
'Laroda' JAPANESE	7–12, 14–18	'Santa Rosa', 'Late Santa Rosa'.	Large, medium red. Light amber flesh. Thin, tender skin. Firm. Midseason.	Very sweet. Firm fleshed, but cooks apart easily.
'Late Santa Rosa' JAPANESE	7–12, 14–22	Self-fertile.	Medium to large, purplish crimson. Amber flesh red near skin, tart-sweet sprightly flavor. Late.	Follows 'Santa Rosa' by a month.
'Mariposa' ('Improved Satsuma') JAPANESE	7–12, 14–22	'Beauty', 'Santa Rosa', 'Wickson', 'Late Santa Rosa', 'Inca'.	Large, purple red, deep red flesh. Nearly freestone. Sweet flavor. Midseason.	Good for cooking and eating.

PLUM, FLOWERING. See *Prunus.*

PLUM YEW. See *Cephalotaxus.*

PLUMBAGO. See *Ceratostigma.*

PLUMBAGO auriculata (*P. capensis*). CAPE PLUMBAGO. Semievergreen shrub or vine. Zones 8, 9, 12–24. Unsupported, a sprawling, mounding bush to 6 ft. tall, 8–10 ft. wide; with support can reach 12 ft. or more. In Zone 12 usually a 2-ft. shrub. Leaves light to medium green, 1–2 in. long, fresh looking. Flowers, an inch wide, in phloxlike clusters, varying (in seedling plants) from white to clear light blue. Select plants in bloom. Blooms mostly in March-December, throughout year in warm, frost free areas. Hot desert sun bleaches flowers. Takes poor soil and (once established) very little water, but good drainage is important.

Plumbago auriculata

Young growth blackens, leaves drop in heavy frosts, but recovery is good. Prune out damaged growth after frost danger is past. In coldest climates, plant in spring so plants have greatest chance to become established before frosts. Propagate from cuttings. Slow to start, but tough. Good cover for bank, fence, hot wall; good background and filler plant. 'Alba' is white-flowered variety.

For other plants called plumbago, see *Ceratostigma.*

PLUME CEDAR, PLUME CRYPTOMERIA. See *Cryptomeria japonica* 'Elegans'.

PLUME HYACINTH. See *Muscari comosum* 'Monstrosum .

PLUMERIA. Evergreen and deciduous shrubs or small trees. Have open, gaunt character with thick branches, leathery pointed leaves clustered near branch tips. Clustered flowers are large, showy, waxy, very fragrant. Tender to frost; won't take cold wet soil. Sun near coast, part shade inland. Keep dryish in winter. Grow in containers, shelter from frosts. When frosts can be expected, move container indoors to bright window for continued bloom; or move to frost free garage or shed, give little water throughout winter. Feeding late in year will result in soft growth that will be nipped by lightest frosts. All are easy to grow from cuttings.

Plumeria rubra acutifolia

P. obtusa. SINGAPORE PLUMERIA. Evergreen shrub or small

NAME	ZONES	POLLINATION	FRUIT	REMARKS
'Nubiana' JAPANESE	2–12, 14–20	Self-fertile.	Large, deep black purple, amber-fleshed plum. Sweet and firm. Midseason.	Good for cooking and eating. Turns red when cooked. Good keeper.
'Peach Plum' JAPANESE	2–12, 14–20	Self-fertile.	Large, brownish red. Yellow fleshed, nearly freestone. Good flavor. Early midseason.	Matures rapidly.
'President' EUROPEAN	2–12, 14–20	'Imperial'.	Large, purplish blue, amber fleshed, attractive. Flavor not outstanding. Late.	Used for cooking, eating fresh. Not for drying.
'Queen Ann' JAPANESE	7–12, 14–18	'Laroda'.	Large, dark purple, heart shaped fruit with amber flesh. Rich flavor when fully ripe. Late.	Holds shape well when cooked.
'Santa Rosa' JAPANESE	2, 3, 7–12, 14–23	Self-fertile.	Medium to large, purplish red with heavy blue bloom. Flesh yellow to dark red near skin and of rich, pleasing, tart flavor. Early.	Most important commercial and home variety. Good canned if skin is removed.
'Satsuma' JAPANESE	2–12, 14–22	'Beauty', 'Santa Rosa', 'Wickson', 'Duarte'.	Small to medium, deep, dull red. Dark red, solid, meaty flesh, mild, sweet. Small pit. Early midseason.	Preferred for jams and jellies. Sometimes called blood plum because of its red juice.
'Shiro' JAPANESE	2–12, 14–22	'Beauty', 'Santa Rosa'.	Large, golden yellow plum with yellow flesh of good quality. Early midseason.	Tree productive and hardy.
'Stanley' EUROPEAN	2–12, 14–22	Self-fertile.	Large, purplish black with yellow flesh. Sweet and juicy. Midseason.	Good canning variety; resembles larger 'Italian Prune'.
'Sugar' EUROPEAN	2–12, 14–22	Self-fertile.	Medium, somewhat larger than 'French Prune'. Very sweet, highly flavored. Early midseason.	Good fresh, for home drying and canning. Trees tend to bear heavily in alternate years.
'Tragedy' EUROPEAN	2–12, 14–20	'President'.	Small to medium, deep blue with heavy bloom. Green amber flesh. Early.	Too tart for drying; good for eating fresh or cooking.
'Yellow Egg' EUROPEAN	2–12, 14–20	Self-fertile.	Large, oval, bright yellow, yellow fleshed, soft, sweet. Midseason.	Handsome, good-flavored plum for eating fresh, canning.
'Wickson' JAPANESE	2–12, 14–22	'Santa Rosa', 'Beauty'.	Large, showy yellow turning yellow red when ripe. Firm yellow flesh of fine flavor. Early midseason.	Good keeper. Makes a fine-textured pink sauce.

tree. Zone 24. Leaves dark green, 6 in. long, 2 in. wide, very glossy. White, fragrant flowers 2 in. across bloom during warm weather. Very tender.

P. rubra. PLUMERIA, FRANGIPANI. Deciduous shrub or small tree. Zones 12, 13, 19, 21–24. In cold-winter climates, grown in greenhouse or as indoor-outdoor plant. Thick, pointed, 8–16-in.-long leaves drop in winter or early spring. Flowers in clusters, 2–2½ in. wide, red, purplish, pink, yellow, or white, blooming June–November. Many varieties available in Southern California. Blooms best in full sun (afternoon shade best in desert). Where frosts occur, best grown in containers, moved to shelter when needed.

POA. BLUEGRASS. Perennial or annual grasses. One is the most important cool-season lawn grass, one a sometimes attractive weed, others are occasionally cultivated meadow grasses. Leaves of all have characteristic boat-prow tip. Must have regular water. They all perform best in maximum available sunlight.

P. annua. ANNUAL BLUEGRASS. Usually considered cool-season weed of lawns, it often furnishes much of the green in winter lawns. Bright green, soft in texture, it would be attractive except for seed heads and propensity to die off just when you need it—when rain lessens in late spring. Dis-

Poa pratensis

courage it by maintaining thick turf of good grasses.

P. pratensis. KENTUCKY BLUEGRASS. Rich blue green lawn grass, excellent in Zones 1–7. Okay but troublesome in Zones 8–11, 14–17. Difficult in Zones 12, 13, 18–24. Many selections are available as seed or sod.

P. trivialis. ROUGH-STALKED BLUEGRASS. Fine-textured bright green grass occasionally used in shady lawn mixtures for its tolerance of shade, damp soil.

PODOCARPUS. Evergreen trees, shrubs. Versatile plants grown for good-looking foliage, interesting form; adaptable to many climates, many garden uses, such as screen or background plantings. Foliage generally resembles that of related yews *(Taxus)*, but leaves of better-known species are longer, broader, lighter in color.

Grow easily (if slowly) in ordinary garden soil, in sun or partial shade. Some shade best in hot valleys. Will grow many years in containers. Not especially drought tolerant. Best with year-round regular water. Practically pest free; sometimes troubled by chlorosis, especially in cold, wet, heavy soil.

Podocarpus gracilior

P. elongatus. See *P. gracilior*.

P. falcatus. Tree. Zones 8, 9, 14–24. Native to South Africa.

(Continued on next page)

Slow growth. Differs from *P. gracilior* in technical details. For culture and uses, see *P. gracilior*.

P. gracilior. (Often sold as *P. elongatus*.) FERN PINE. Tree, often grown as espaliered vine, even as hanging basket plant. Zones 8, 9, 12 (warmest areas), 13–24. Native to east Africa, where it grows to 70 ft. Old trees in California reach 60 ft. tall.

Habit and foliage variable with age of plant and method of propagation. Leaves on mature wood closely spaced, soft grayish or bluish green, 1–2 in. long, narrow. Plants grown from cuttings or grafts taken from such wood will be limber branched, slow to make vertical growth, and will have grayish or bluish short leaves. Such plants are usually sold as *P. elongatus*.

Leaves on seedlings, vigorous young plants, and unusually vigorous shoots of mature plants are twice as long, more sparsely set on branches, and dark glossy green. Seedlings are more upright in growth than plants grown from cuttings or grafts, and branches are less pendulous, more evenly spaced. Such plants are usually sold as *P. gracilior*. Stake these plants until strong trunk develops. With age, foliage will become more dense, leaves shorter and bluish or grayish green in color.

Cutting-grown and grafted plants are slow to begin upright growth; branches are supple and limber, and dominant, upright trunk is slow to form. Such plants are excellent for espaliering or for growing as vines along fences or eaves. With age they will become trees, either with single or multiple stems. Stake well to support heavy foliage masses.

Sun or light shade; needs shade in Zone 13. Among cleanest and most pest free choices for street or lawn tree, patio or flower bed tree, espalier, hedge, big shrub, or container plant. Choice entryway plant or indoor/outdoor plant. Young plants sometimes used in dish gardens.

P. henkelii. LONG-LEAFED YELLOW-WOOD. Tree. Zones 8, 9, 14–24. Handsome, erect, slow-growing tree with masses of drooping foliage. Leaves 5–7 in. long, ⅓ in. wide; on old trees in its native South Africa, leaves are smaller. Young trees to 10 ft. are strikingly handsome; older, larger ones not yet seen here.

P. macrophyllus. YEW PINE. Shrub or tree. Zones 4–9, 12–24. Has been grown in Zones 3, 11 with shelter from wind, hot sun, deep snow. More tolerant of heat, drought than other *Podocarpus*. Ultimately grows to 50 ft. high. Bright green leaves are 4 in. long and are broader than those of *P. gracilior*. Grows indoors or out, in tubs or open ground. Generally narrow and upright, but limber enough to espalier. Easily pruned to shape. Tub plant, large shrub, street or lawn tree (with staking and thinning), screen planting, topiary, clipped hedge.

P. m. maki. SHRUBBY YEW PINE. Smaller, slower growing than yew pine (to 6–8 ft. in 10 years). Dense, upright form. Leaves to 3 in. long, ¼ in. wide. One of the very best container plants for outdoor or indoor use, and fine shrub generally.

P. nagi. Tree. Zones 8, 9, 14–24. Slow growth to 15–20 ft. (80–90 ft. in its native Japan). Branchlets drooping, sometimes to a considerable length. Leaves 1–3 in. long, ½–1½ in. wide, leathery, smooth, sharp pointed. Takes considerable shade or sun, indoors or out. More treelike in youth than other podocarpus species. Makes decorative foliage pattern against natural wood or masonry. Plant in groves for slender sapling effect. Excellent container plant.

P. nivalis. ALPINE TOTARA. Shrub. Zones 4–9, 14–17. Broad, low, spreading plant eventually 2–3 ft. tall and 6–10 ft. wide. The dark olive green needles are ¼–¾ in. long, densely clothe branches. Resembles yew *(Taxus)*. Attractive ground cover or large rock garden shrub.

P. totara. TOTARA. Tree. Zones 8, 9, 14–24. Reaches 100 ft. in New Zealand; likely to reach 25–30 ft. in gardens. Dense, rather narrow, with leathery, stiff, pointed, gray green leaves to 1 in. long. General appearance like that of yew.

POHUTUKAWA. See *Metrosideros excelsus*.

POINCIANA. See *Caesalpinia*.

POINSETTIA. See *Euphorbia pulcherrima*.

POISON OAK. See *Rhus diversiloba*.

POKER PLANT. See *Kniphofia uvaria*.

POLEMONIUM. Perennials. Zones 1–11, 14–17. Plants for shaded or half-shaded borders or under trees. Lush rosettes of finely divided, fernlike foliage; clusters of bell shaped flowers in summer. Combine with bleeding heart, campanulas, ferns, hellebores, hosta, and lilies. Cool, moist conditions; good drainage. Grow from seed, or divide after flowering or in spring. Many species are choice wildflowers from western mountains. Following are the ones generally available in nurseries.

Polemonium caeruleum

P. caeruleum. JACOB'S LADDER. Clusters of lavender blue pendulous flowers 1 in. long on leafy, 1½–2-ft.-high stems.

P. reptans. Best known is its variety 'Blue Pearl', a dwarf, spreading plant 9 in. tall. Profuse display of blue flowers in April and May. Good in shaded, dampish rock garden.

POLIANTHES tuberosa. TUBEROSE. Tuber. Garden plant in Zone 24; elsewhere planted in containers, moved outdoors after frosts. Native to Mexico. Noted for powerful, heady fragrance. Flowers white, tubular, loosely arranged in spikelike clusters on stems to 3 ft., summer-fall. Basal leaves long, narrow, grasslike. Single forms are graceful, but double variety 'The Pearl' is best known and most widely available.

Long, slender bulblike tubers always show a point of green if alive and healthy. *Polianthes tuberosa* Start indoors like tuberous begonias or plant outside after soil is warm. Plant 2 in. deep, 4–6 in. apart. Needs steady heat, sun or part shade. Water after leaves appear and heavily through growth season. Feed with acid-type fertilizer if soil or water is alkaline. Dry out when leaves yellow in fall, dig, and store in a warm place. Or plant 3 tubers in 6-in. pot and treat as above. Tubers will bloom year after year; divide clumps every 4 years.

POLYANTHUS. See *Primula polyantha*.

POLYGALA. Evergreen shrub, shrublets. Flowers irregular, with slight resemblance to sweet peas. Average water.

Polygala dalmaisiana

P. chamaebuxus. Shrublet. Zones 4–6. To 6–8 in. tall, spreading slowly by underground stems. Leaves dark green, 1–1½ in. long, shaped like those of boxwood. Flowers (April-May, and sporadically throughout year) creamy white or yellow and white, sometimes marked with red. *P. c. grandiflora* has flowers of rosy purple and yellow. Sun or filtered shade. Rock gardens.

P. dalmaisiana. SWEET-PEA SHRUB. Evergreen shrub. Zones 8, 9, 12–24. To 5 ft. tall, spreading habit, usually bare at base of plant. Leaves to 1 in. long. Useful for continuous production of purplish pink, oddly shaped flowers. Sun or light shade. Color hard to handle; use it with whites or blues, preferably with low, bushy plants which conceal its legginess. May be sheared frequently to promote more compact bushy growth. Good temporary filler.

POLYGONATUM. SOLOMON'S SEAL. Perennials. Zones 1–7, 15–17. Arching, leafy stems grow from slowly spreading underground rhizomes. Greenish white, bell shaped blossoms hang down beneath bright green leaves in spring. Plants disappear over winter. Attractive for form and flowers in woodland garden with ferns, hosta, wild ginger. Need shade, loose, woodsy soil, ample water. Attractive in containers. (For the western native false Solomon's seal, see *Smilacina*.)

P. biflorum. Stems to 3 ft.; 1–3¾-in. flowers in clusters beneath 4-in. leaves.

P. commutatum. Stems possibly to 6 ft. From 2–10 flowers to a cluster, leaves to 7 in. long.

P. odoratum (*P. japonicum*). To 3½ ft. tall, with 2-flowered clusters beneath 4–6-in. leaves. 'Variegatum' has leaves edged white.

Polygonatum biflorum

POLYGONUM. KNOTWEED. Evergreen and deciduous perennials and vines. Sturdy, sun-loving plants with jointed stems and small white or pink flowers in open sprays. Some kinds tend to get out of hand and need control.

P. affine. Evergreen perennial. Zones 4–9, 14–17. Tufted plant 1–1½ ft. tall. Leaves mostly basal, 2–4½ in. long, finely toothed, deep green, turn bronze in winter. Flowers bright rose red, in dense, erect spikes 2–3 in. long August-October. Informal border or ground cover. Sun or shade, average soil, ample water.

P. aubertii. SILVER LACE VINE. Deciduous in Zones 1–7, 10–12; evergreen in Zones 8, 9, 13–24. Rapid growing; can cover 100 square feet in a season. Leaves heart shaped, glossy, wavy edged, 1½–2½ in. long. Flowers creamy white, small, in frothy mass from late spring to fall. Use as fast-growing screen on fences, arbors, on hillsides, at seashore. Water deeply once a month. Can prune severely (to ground) each year; bloom will be delayed until August. Sun, average soil.

P. baldschuanicum. BOKHARA FLEECEFLOWER. Deciduous vine. All Zones. Much like *P. aubertii* in appearance, growth, vigor, and uses. Flowers are pink, fragrant, somewhat larger, and grow in large drooping clusters.

P. capitatum. Evergreen perennial. Zones 8, 9, 12–24. Rugged, tough, trailing ground cover to 6 in. high, spreads to 20 in. Leaves 1½ in. long; new leaves dark green, old leaves tinged pink. Stems and flowers (in small round heads) also pink. Blooms most of year. Leaves discolor and die in temperatures below 28° F. Good ground cover for waste places or in confined areas where invasive roots can be held in check. Sun or shade—will even grow under pines. Best with regular water but will endure drought. Seeds freely and can be grown as an annual where winters are cold.

P. cuspidatum. JAPANESE KNOTWEED. Perennial. All Zones. Tough, vigorous plant forming large clumps of red brown wiry stems 4–8 ft. high. Leaves nearly heart shaped, to 5 in. long. Greenish white blooms in late summer-fall. Extremely invasive; keep away from choice plants; useful in untamed parts of garden. Prefers ample water but may survive without irrigation in heavy soils. Cut to ground in late fall or winter. Often called bamboo or Mexican bamboo because of jointed stalks.

P. c. compactum (*P. reynoutria*). Fast-growing ground cover 10–24 in. high with creeping roots, can become a nuisance near choice plants. Stiff, wiry red stems. Pale green leaves, 3–6 in. long, heart shaped and red veined, turn red in fall. Plants die to ground in winter. Dense, showy clusters of small flowers, red in bud and pale pink when open, late summer. Ground cover for sunny, dry banks, fringe areas of garden. Controls erosion on hillsides.

P. vacciniifolium. Evergreen perennial. Zones 4–7. Prostrate, with slender, leafy branching stems radiating 2–4 ft. Leaves ½ in. long, oval and shining, turning red in fall. Flowers rose pink in dense, upright, 2–3-in. spikes on 6–9-in. flower stalks, late summer. Excellent bank cover or drapery for boulder in large rock garden. Needs ample summer water. Increase by cuttings.

Polygonum cuspidatum compactum

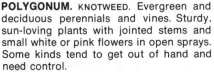

POLYPODIUM. Ferns. Widespread and variable group, some native to West.

P. aureum. HARE'S FOOT FERN. Zones 15–17, 19–24; house plant anywhere. From tropical America. Needs shade and regular voluminous watering. Big fern for hanging basket culture. Heavy brown creeping rhizomes, coarse fronds 3–5 ft. long, blue green in color. Fronds drop after frost, but plants recover fast. *P. a.* 'Mandaianum', sometimes called LETTUCE FERN, has frilled and wavy frond edges. Both make showy display plants.

P. coronans. See *Aglaomorpha coronans*.

P. glycyrrhiza (*P. vulgare occidentale*). LICORICE FERN. Zones 4–6, 14–24. Native to coastal strip from Alaska to California.

Polypodium aureum 'Mandaianum'

Forms mats with creeping rhizomes. Once-cut fronds resemble smaller (to 18 in.) sword ferns. *P. hesperium (P. vulgare columbianum),* which grows from Pacific Coast into Rocky Mountains, is smaller (to 10 in.). In the wilds they tend to grow on rocks or dead logs; in the garden give them leaf mold or other organic material and shade (except right on the coast). Grows best with summer water but can survive without it.

P. heracleum. See *Aglaomorpha heracleum*.

P. scouleri. LEATHERY POLYPODY. Zones 4–6, 15–17. Native along seacoast from British Columbia to California. Thick, glossy fronds are once-cut, may reach 18 in. long and 6 in. across at base. Often grows on trees, rocks, spreading slightly by short rhizomes. In the ground it tends to be clump forming. Good for woodland gardens, naturalizing. Culture as for *P. glycyrrhiza*.

P. subauriculatum 'Knightiae'. KNIGHT'S POLYPODY. Zone 24, greenhouse and house plant everywhere. Long (to 3 ft. or more and 1 ft. wide) gracefully drooping fronds are once-cut with fringed edges.

Makes spectacular hanging container specimen when well grown—like a magnified Boston fern. Grown outdoors, old fronds are shed in spring, quickly replaced by new ones. Needs shade, routine house plant watering.

POLYSCIAS. Evergreen shrubs (small trees in tropics) used as house plants. Like many other aralia relatives, grown for their handsomely divided leaves. Flowers are unimportant; seldom produced outside tropics. As house plants they grow slowly, maintain their shapeliness for many years. They are considered fussy as house plants, needing fresh air but no drafts, good light but not direct, strong sunlight, and just enough water. Plants that fail usually do so because of overwatering or mite damage. Misting is useful, along with light feeding; if plant is doing well, don't move it. They appreciate warmth and humidity.

Polyscias fruticosa 'Elegans'

P. balfouriana. To 25 ft. tall. Leaves have three 2–4-in. toothed leaflets. Plain green form can grow out of doors in mildest southern California gardens. 'Marginata', commoner than species, has white-edged leaflets. 'Pennockii' has white to pale green leaflets with irregular green spots.

P. fruticosa. MING ARALIA, PARSLEY PANAX. Grows 6–8 ft. tall. Leaves finely divided and redivided into multitude of narrow, toothed segments. 'Elegans' is small-growing, extremely densely foliaged variety.

P. guilfoylei 'Victoriae'. Compact grower with deeply slashed and cut leaflets with white edges.

POLYSTICHUM. Ferns. Medium-sized, evergreen fronds on hardy symmetrical plants. Among most useful and widely planted ferns in West; they blend well with other plants and are easy to grow.

P. dudleyi. Zones 4–9, 14–24. Native to Coast Ranges of northern California. Re-

Polystichum munitum

sembles *P. munitum* but has broader, shorter, more finely cut fronds. Not always easy to find, but choice. Prefers summer moisture.

P. munitum. SWORD FERN. All Zones. Native from California to Alaska and Montana. Most-seen fern of redwood forests. Leathery, shiny dark green fronds 2–4 ft. long, depending on soil and available moisture. Fronds once-cut, texture medium coarse, long-lasting when cut. Old plants may have 75–100 fronds. Good plant for shady beds, along house walls, big scale ground cover, in mixed woodland plantings. Grows best in rich soil with organic matter and ample water.

P. polyblepharum (usually sold as *P. setosum*). JAPANESE LACE FERN, TASSEL FERN. Zones 4–9, 14–24. Handsome, dense, lacy. Resembles *P. setiferum* but is taller, darker green, somewhat coarser, fronds somewhat more upright (to 2 ft.). Same culture, uses as *P. setiferum*.

P. setiferum. Zones 4–9, 14–24. Low-growing fern with spreading, finely cut fronds, giving effect of dark green lace. Many cultivated varieties: 'Proliferum' makes plantlets on midribs of older fronds; these make for a dense, lacy plant and can be used for propagation. Northwestern specialists offer many fancy varieties as "English ferns." All are splendid in shaded rock gardens or for bedding with tuberous begonias and other shade plants. Regular summer water.

POMEGRANATE. See *Punica granatum*.

POMPON TREE. See *Dais cotinifolia*.

PONTEDERIA cordata. PICKEREL WEED. Perennial. All Zones. Water plant grown as companion to waterlilies. Roots grow in soil beneath water. Long-stalked leaves stand well above water; these are heart shaped, to 10 in. long and 6 in. wide. Short spikes of bright blue flowers top 4 ft. (or less) stems. Best planted in pots of rich soil and sunk in not more than 12 in. of water where leaves will ultimately grow in sun to light shade. Gives wild-pond look to informal garden pool. Dormant in winter.

PONYTAIL. See *Beaucarnea recurvata*.

Pontederia cordata

POOR MAN'S ORCHID. See *Schizanthus pinnatus*.

POOR MAN'S RHODODENDRON. See *Impatiens oliveri*.

POPCORN. See Corn.

POPLAR. See *Populus*.

POPPY. See *Papaver*.

POPULUS. POPLAR, COTTONWOOD, ASPEN. Deciduous trees. All known for rapid growth. Eminently suitable for country places where fast growth, toughness, and low maintenance are considerations. Although most kinds can grow anywhere in the West, they are grown and appreciated far more in the cold-winter, hot-summer interior regions. Appearance, performance poorer in mild winter zones and near coast where temperature extremes are minimal. Best with regular deep watering. Some appear to be drought tolerant if roots grow deep enough to tap water table or other underground water. *Do not plant near water or sewer lines, septic tanks or their leach lines.* Roots are invasive—not for city streets, lawns, or small gardens.

Populus nigra 'Italica'

P. acuminata. LANCELEAF COTTONWOOD. All Zones. Thrives at elevations to 7,500 ft. in Rocky Mountains. To 60 ft. tall, with egg shaped, sharply pointed leaves to 4 in. long, glossy green above, pale beneath.

P. alba. WHITE POPLAR. All Zones. Fast growth to 40–60 ft., broad and wide spreading. The 5-in.-long leaves, usually with 3–5 lobes, are white-woolly underneath. A "lively" tree, even in light breezes, with flickering white and green highlights. Good tree for desert. Tolerates wide range of soils. Suckers profusely—an advantage if planted as windbreak, otherwise a problem.

P. a. 'Pyramidalis'. (Usually sold as *P. bolleana*.) BOLLEANA POPLAR. Narrow columnar form. Good for country windbreaks or sun screens. Suckers freely; may send up new shoots from roots many feet from main trunk.

P. angustifolia. NARROWLEAF COTTONWOOD. All Zones. Grows at elevations to 8,000 ft. To 60 ft. tall, with narrow leaves 5 in. long, 1½ in. wide.

P. balsamifera (*P. candicans*) BALM-OF-GILEAD. All Zones. Fast to 30–60 ft., broad topped. Suckers profusely. Triangular leaves 4½–6 in. long, 3–4 in. wide. Two cottonless selections are 'Idahoensis' or 'Idaho Hybrid' and 'Mojave Hybrid', similar fast-growing, large selections. The latter has nearly white bark. All thrive in Zones 11, 12, 13.

P. brandegeei (*P. monticola*). Zones 12, 13. Desert native tree to 40–60 ft. Resembles *P. fremontii* but has smooth white bark like quaking aspen. Good to line a long driveway.

P. canadensis. CAROLINA POPLAR. All Zones. Fast growth to 40–150 ft. Triangular leaves are 4 in. long with toothed edges. Has deservedly bad reputation for invading and breaking sewer lines. *P. c.* 'Eugenei' is somewhat narrower grower. 'Siouxland' is disease resistant selection.

P. canescens 'Macrophylla'. All Zones. Fast-growing, large tree with exceptionally large leaves (to 9 in. long on vigorous young shoots). Leaves white underneath, bark pale gray on older trees.

P. fremontii. WESTERN OR FREMONT COTTONWOOD. Zones 7–24. Fast to 40–60 ft. or more. Leaves are thick, glossy yellow green, 2–4 in. broad, triangular, coarsely toothed; turn bright lemon yellow in fall, remain on tree practically all winter in Zones 12, 13. Small greenish yellow flowers in long, slender catkins appear before leaves. Female trees later bear masses of cottony seeds that blow about and become a nuisance; be sure to plant male trees (easily grown from cuttings). Requires little water except in desert where weekly watering is needed during hot weather if roots haven't tapped underground source.

P. nigra 'Italica'. LOMBARDY POPLAR. All Zones. Fast to 40–100 ft. Beautiful columnar tree with upward reaching branches. Suckers profusely; invasive roots are a problem. Indispensable to country driveways, valuable both as windbreak and skyline decoration. Bright green, triangular 4-in.-long leaves turn beautiful golden yellow in fall. Subject to blight of branchlets in many areas. Healthy and attractive in cold, dry, interior climates. *P. n. thevestina* has white bark.

P. tremuloides. QUAKING ASPEN. Zones 1–7. Native throughout western mountains. Fast growing to 20–60 ft. Trunk and limbs smooth, pale gray green to whitish. Dainty, light green, round leaves that flutter and quake in slightest air movement. Brilliant golden yellow fall color. Generally performs poorly or grows slowly at low elevations. Needs moist soil. Plants are occasionally offered in nurseries: some are collected, but many are raised from seed or cuttings and are more easily transplanted into gardens. Good background tree for native shrubs and wildflowers. Apt to suffer from sudden dieback or from borers.

P. trichocarpa. BLACK COTTONWOOD. Zones 1–7. Native along mountain streams and wet lowlands west of Cascades, California to Alaska. Tall, spreading tree to 40 ft. in 15 years, 150–180 ft. in age. Heavy limbed, with dark gray, furrowed bark; wood very brittle. Leaves 3–5 in. across, triangular, deep green above and distinctly silver below; attractive when ruffled by breeze. Male trees shed quantities of catkins; female trees release myriad cottony seeds if male trees present.

PORK AND BEANS. See *Sedum rubrotinctum*.

PORT ORFORD CEDAR. See *Chamaecyparis lawsoniana.*

PORTUGAL LAUREL. See *Prunus lusitanica.*

PORTULACA grandiflora. PORTULACA, ROSE MOSS. Summer annual. Useful warm-weather plants for brilliant color, early summer until frost. Plants 6 in. high, 18 in. across. Leaves fleshy, succulent, cylindrical, pointed, 1 in. long. Trailing, branched reddish stems, also succulent. Flowers roselike, lustrous, in red, cerise, rose pink, orange, yellow, white, pastel shades; single and double strains sold.

Portulaca grandiflora

Flowers open fully only in sun, close in late afternoon. Available as single colors or mixes in either single flowered or double (Prize Strain, Magic Carpet, Sunglo, Sunkiss) strains.

Use on hot dry banks, in parking strips, rock gardens, gravel beds, patio insets, shallow containers, hanging baskets, among succulents, as edgings. Plant in full sun. Any soil; best in sandy loam. Sow seed in place after weather is warm or plant flat-grown plants in late spring. Although drought tolerant, better with occasional watering. Plants self-sow.

PORTULACARIA afra. ELEPHANT'S FOOD, PURSLANE TREE, SPEKBOOM. Succulent. Outdoors Zones 13, 16, 17, 22–24; outdoors with overhead protection Zones 8, 9, 12–15, 18–21; house plant anywhere. Native to South Africa. Thick juicy-stemmed shrub to 12 ft. tall and nearly equal width, usually much smaller in pots. Looks a bit like jade plant *(Crassula argentea)* and is sometimes sold as "miniature jade plant." Elephant's food is faster growing, more loosely branched, has more limber, tapering branches, and smaller (½ in. long) leaves. In South Africa, bears tiny pink flowers in clusters; seldom blooms in western U.S.

Portulacaria afra

Small plants are good, easy pot plants; where hardy can be used as fast-growing informal screen, un-clipped hedge, or cut back as high-growing ground cover. Forms with variegated leaves ('Foliis Variegatis' and 'Variegata') are slower growing, smaller than species. Another form has larger, inch-long leaves. All are tolerant of drought and are fire resistant as well. Same culture as jade plant; will endure desert sun and heat, which jade plant will not.

POTATO. For ornamental relatives, see *Solanum.* Tuberous-rooted perennial grown as annual. Though not most widely grown of home garden vegetables, potatoes can be most satisfying. Two lbs. of certified seed potatoes (potatoes raised under disease free conditions) can give you 50 lbs. of potatoes for eating. The many diseases and pests that plague commercial growers are not likely to plague home gardeners. Potatoes need sandy, fast draining soil; tubers become deformed in heavy, poorly drained soil. Locate in full sun. For early crops, plant in spring as soon as soil can be worked, or in midwinter where frosts are not severe; for fall and winter use, plant from mid-May to mid-June.

Potato

The aboveground potato plant is a sprawling, bushy, dark green plant with much-divided leaves somewhat like a tomato plant's. Clustered inch-wide flowers are pale blue. Round yellow or greenish fruit very rarely seen.

Buy certified (inspected, disease free) seed potatoes from seed or feed store. Cut potatoes into chunky pieces about 1½ in. square with at least 2 eyes. Place chunks 4 in. deep and 18 in. apart. Do not plant if soil is very wet. After top growth appears, give plants an occasional soaking.

Dig early (or new) potatoes when tops begin to flower; dig mature potatoes when tops die down. Dig potatoes carefully to avoid bruises and cuts. Well-matured potatoes free of defects keep best in storage. Store in cool dark place at 40°F. Where ground doesn't freeze, late potatoes can remain in ground until needed. Dig before spring (or mild winter) temperatures start them into growth again.

Another method of planting is to prepare soil so surface is loose, plant potato eyes ½–1 in. deep, water well, and cover with 12–18 in. of straw, hay, or dead leaves; surround with fence of chicken wire to keep loose material from blowing away. Potatoes will develop on surface of soil or just beneath, will require little digging.

POTATO VINE. See *Solanum jasminoides.*

POTENTILLA. CINQUEFOIL. Evergreen and deciduous perennials and shrubs. Hardy plants useful for ground covers and borders. Leaves are bright green or gray green, divided into small leaflets. Small, mostly single, roselike flowers cream to bright yellow, white or pink to red. Give them full sun (they tolerate part shade in hot summer areas) and moderate water.

Potentilla fruticosa

EVERGREEN PERENNIALS
P. cinerea. Zones 1–17. Matted stems 2–4 in. high. Leaves divided fanwise into 5 wedge shaped, gray-hairy leaflets toothed at tip, white-woolly underneath. Flowers are pale yellow, ½ in. wide. Ground cover or rock plants for sun, part shade.

P. nepalensis 'Willmottiae' (*P. n.* 'Miss Willmott'). All Zones. Good performance near coast. Grows to 10 in. high, spreads to 18 in. Leaves divided fanwise into 5 roundish, 2–3-in.-long, green leaflets. Branching clusters of salmon pink flowers ½–1 in. wide. Borders, cut flowers.

P. tabernaemontanii (*P. verna, P. verna* 'Nana'). SPRING CINQUEFOIL. All Zones. Dainty bright green, tufted creeper 2–6 in. high. Leaves divided into 5 leaflets. Butter yellow flowers ¼ in. wide, 3–5 in clusters in spring and summer. Stands more moisture than other potentillas. Needs some shade where summers are hot and dry. May turn brown in cold winters. Fast-growing ground cover, bulb cover. Makes good lawn substitute for no-traffic situations. Smothers weeds effectively when well established.

DECIDUOUS SHRUBBY POTENTILLAS
There's a group of shrubby potentillas (Zones 1–21) that are most often sold as named forms of *P. fruticosa,* which is native to northern latitudes everywhere, including Cascade, Olympic, and Rocky mountains. These potentillas all have leaves divided into 3–7 leaflets; some are distinctly green on top, gray beneath; others look more gray green. In full sun, all bloom cheerfully from June-October in spite of poor soil, heat, and little water. Best in well-drained soil with moderate water.

'Gold Drop' (variety 'Farreri') grows to 2 ft. high, 3 ft. wide. Deep yellow, ¾-in.-wide flowers.

'Hollandia Gold'. Deep yellow flowers to 2 in. wide on gray green 2–3-ft. shrubs.

'Jackman's Variety'. Flowers bright yellow, to 1½ in. wide. Blooms profusely. Shrub to 4 ft. tall, somewhat wider.

'Katherine Dykes' can reach 5 feet but usually stays much lower, spreading at least as wide as high. Pale yellow, inch-wide flowers.

'Klondike'. Deep yellow flowers 1½–2 in. wide on dense-growing 2-ft. shrubs.

'Longacre'. Yellow inch-wide flowers on bright green, cushiony plants 3 ft. wide, 1 ft. tall.

'Moonlight' ('Maanely's'). Pale yellow to white 1-in. flowers on 1½-ft. shrubs. Foliage dark blue green, furry.

'Mount Everest'. Pure white, yellow-centered flowers 1½ in. wide on upright, bushy plant to 4½ ft.

(Continued on next page)

'Primrose Beauty'. Consider it a 'Klondike' with pale yellow flowers.

'Red Ace'. Bright red flowers with yellow reverse, 1½ in. wide. Shrub reaches 2 ft. tall by 3–4 ft. wide. Flowers fade to yellow as they age (very quickly in hot-summer climates or under poor growing conditions).

'Snowflake' grows 2–4 ft. high. Semidouble, white blossoms.

'Sutter's Gold' grows 1 ft. high, spreading to 3 ft. Clear yellow flowers an inch wide.

'Tangerine'. Bright yellow orange flowers 1½ in. wide on 2½-ft. shrub.

POTERIUM sanguisorba *(Sanguisorba minor).* SMALL BURNET, SALAD BURNET. Perennial herb. All Zones. To 8–12 in. high. Leaves with deeply toothed leaflets grow in rosette close to ground. Unusual, thimble shaped pinkish white flowers borne on long stems.

Grow in sun, poor soil, with adequate moisture, good drainage. Keep blossoms cut. Don't cut plant back more than half. Self-seeds almost too freely if flowers not cut. Also propagated from division of roots (divide each year). Bushy ornamental. Good in containers. Leaves give cucumber aroma to salads, vinegar, cream cheese.

*Poterium
sanguisorba*

POTHOS aureus. See *Epipremnum aureum.*

POT MARIGOLD. See *Calendula officinalis.*

PRATIA angulata. Perennial. Zones 4–9, 12–24. May be killed or badly damaged in coldest Zone 4 winters. New Zealand plant with creeping stems; used as ground cover (no traffic) or rock garden plant. Stems root at joints to form dense, shiny dark green mats. Leaves roundish, ½ in. long, with a few teeth. Flowers white or bluish white, nearly ¾ in. wide, on 2-in. stalks. Flowers oddly shaped, with 2-lobed upper lip and 3-lobed lower lip. Likes rich soil and abundant water. Takes full sun in cool climates;

Pratia angulata

needs shade where summer temperatures are high. Thrives even in low desert if growing conditions are right. Plant 6–8 in. apart for fairly fast cover.

PRAYER PLANT. See *Maranta leuconeura.*

PREGNANT ONION. See *Ornithogalum caudatum.*

PRICKLY PEAR. See *Opuntia.*

PRICKLY POPPY. See *Argemone.*

PRIDE OF CALIFORNIA. See *Lathyrus splendens.*

PRIDE OF MADEIRA. See *Echium fastuosum.*

PRIMROSE. See *Primula.*

PRIMROSE TREE. See *Lagunaria patersonii.*

PRIMULA. PRIMROSE. Perennials; a few short-lived perennials treated as annuals. Fanciers reserve the name "primrose" for *Primula vulgaris,* but gardeners generally call both this plant and polyanthus *(P. polyantha),* "English primrose."

Out of some 600 species of primroses, only a few are widely adapted and distributed over the West. Long hot summers and low humidity are limiting factors. But almost any primrose can be grown to perfection in cool, moist climates of western Oregon and Washington, and north coastal California. Most primroses are quite hardy; many thrive east of the Cascades and in the intermountain region.

Primula malacoides

Specialty nurseries, mainly in the Northwest, offer seeds and plants of many kinds of primroses. Fanciers exchange seeds and plants through primrose societies.

To systematize this large group of plants, specialists have set up sections—or groups of species—that strongly resemble each other, often hybridize with each other, and usually respond to the same kind of care.

(Continued on page 428)

Primula

NAME	SECTION	ZONES	LEAVES	FLOWERS	REMARKS
PRIMULA acaulis See *P. vulgaris.*					
P. alpicola MOONLIGHT PRIMROSE	Sikkimensis	1–6, 17	Long-stalked, wrinkled, forming dense clumps in time.	Sulfur yellow, spreading, bell shaped, in clusters on 20-in. stalk. Summer.	Powerfully fragrant. Flowers sometimes white or purple. Somewhat tender in coldest areas.
P. auricula AURICULA	Auricula	1–6, 17, 22–24 (in shade, preferably in pots).	Evergreen rosettes of broad, leathery leaves, toothed or plain edged, gray green, sometimes with mealy coating.	Clusters of yellow, cream, rose, purple, or brownish; fragrant; white or yellow eye. Early spring.	Three classes: Show Auriculas, usually grown in pots under glass to protect flowers against weather; garden Auriculas, sturdier; and alpine Auriculas. Flowers in shades of white, yellow, orange, pink, red, purple, blue, brownish. Double forms available.
P. beesiana	Candelabra	1–6, 17	Long leaves taper gradually into leaf stalk. Leaves (including stalks) reach 14 in.	Reddish purple, in 5–7 dense whorls on a 2-ft. flower stem. Mid or late spring.	Somewhat variable in color, but usually reddish purple with yellow eye. Very deep rooted; needs deep watering.

NAME	SECTION	ZONES	LEAVES	FLOWERS	REMARKS
P. bulleyana	Candelabra	1–6, 15–17	Like *P. beesiana*, but with reddish midribs.	Bright yellow, opening from orange buds. Whorls open in succession over long season in mid and late spring.	Plants disappear in late fall; mark the spot. Older plants can be divided after bloom or in fall. Showy at woodland edge.
P. burmanica	Candelabra	1–6, 17	Like *P. beesiana*, but broader, longer stalked.	Like *P. beesiana*, but with more densely clustered flowers of deeper purple with yellow eye.	One of best and easiest of Candelabra section.
P. cockburniana	Candelabra	1–6, 17	Leaves 4–6 in. long, rather few in clump.	Flowers orange scarlet, in 3–5 whorls on 10–14-in. stalks.	Smaller and less vigorous than other Candelabra types. Striking color, most effective when massed.
P. denticulata (Often sold as *P. d. cachemiriana* or *P. cachemiriana*.)	Denticulata	1–6	Leaves 6–12 in. long, only half grown at flowering time.	Dense, ball shaped clusters on foot-high, stout stems. Color ranges from blue violet to purple. Very early spring bloom.	Pinkish, lavender, and white varieties are available. Not adapted to warm-winter areas.
P. florindae	Sikkimensis	1–6, 17	Leaves broad, heart shaped, on long stems.	As many as 60 fragrant, yellow, bell shaped, nodding flowers top 3-ft. stems in summer.	Will grow in a few inches of running water, or in damp, low spot. Plants late to appear in spring. Hybrids have red, orange, or yellow flowers.
P. helodoxa	Candelabra	1–6, 17	Leaves smooth, large, nearly or quite evergreen in mild climates, unlike those of most Candelabra primroses.	5–7 whorls of large, golden yellow flowers in early to midspring. Stalks to 4 ft. tall.	Needs shade, much water. One of the most spectacular and stately for bog, damp woodland, waterside.
P. Inshriach hybrids	Candelabra	1–6, 17	Typical, lush Candelabra foliage.	Tiered flower clusters in bright and pastel shades of yellow, red, orange, peach, salmon, pink, purple. Midspring to summer.	Easily grown from seed, blooming second year.
P. japonica	Candelabra	1–6, 17	Leaves 6–9 in. long, to 3 in. wide.	Stout stems to 30 in. with up to 5 whorls of purple flowers with yellow eyes. May-July. 'Miller's Crimson' is excellent variety.	White and pink varieties are obtainable. One of toughest and hardiest of Candelabras. Needs semishade; lots of water.
P. juliae	Vernales	1–6, 17	Smooth, roundish leaves ½–1 in. long rise directly from creeping rootstock.	Flowers ¾–1 in. across, purplish red with yellow eyes, borne singly on 1-in. stems. Bloom in early spring, appearing before or with new leaves.	Makes little flower-covered mats of great beauty.
P. juliae hybrids JULIANA PRIMROSE	Vernales	1–6, 17	Tuftlike rosettes of bright green leaves.	Flowers borne singly (cushion type) or in clusters. Very early.	Many named forms in white, blue, yellow, orange red, pink, or purple. Excellent for edging, borders, woodland, rock garden.
P. kewensis	Verticillata	17. Greenhouse or house plant elsewhere.	Leaves 4–8 in. long, coarsely toothed, either deep green or powdered with white.	Borne in whorls on 18-in. stems, golden yellow, profuse. Long bloom season in winter, spring; scattered bloom possible any time.	Best as house plant, lathhouse Zones 15–16, 18–24. Long-lived with reasonable care. Hybrid between *P. floribunda*, *P. verticillata*.
P. malacoides FAIRY PRIMROSE BABY PRIMROSE	Malacoides	12–24	Rosettes of soft, pale green, oval, long-stalked leaves 1½–3 in. long. Edges lobed and cut.	Borne in loose, lacy whorls along numerous upright stems, 12–15 in. high. White, pink, rose, red, lavender, in February-May.	Splendid for winter-spring color in mild-winter areas of California and Arizona. Set out plants in October-November. Use under high-branching trees, spring bulbs, in containers. Grown as annual; stands light frost. Indoor or cool greenhouse pot plant in cold climates.
P. obconica	Obconica	15–24	Large, roundish, soft-hairy leaves on long, hairy stems; hairs cause skin irritation to some people.	Flowers 1½–2 in. wide in large, broad clusters on stems to 1 ft. tall. Shades of white, pink, lavender, and reddish purple. Tends to be nearly everblooming in mild regions.	Perennial, best treated as annual. Use for bedding in shade where winters are mild, as house plant in cold regions.
P. Pagoda hybrids	Candelabra	1–6, 17	Typical, lush Candelabra foliage.	Tiered clusters of orange, red, yellow, pink, tangerine flowers on 2–3-ft. stems. Late spring through summer.	These are very fine Candelabra hybrids developed near Portland, Oregon.

(Continued on next page)

NAME	SECTION	ZONES	LEAVES	FLOWERS	REMARKS
P. polyantha POLYANTHUS PRIMROSES (Often called English primroses.) A group of hybrids.	Vernales	1–10, 12–24	Fresh green leaves in tight clumps.	Flowers 1–2 in. across in large full clusters on stems to 12 in. high. Almost any color. Blooms from winter to early and midspring. Most adaptable and brilliant of primroses. Usually treated as annuals in desert and other hot-summer areas.	Fine, large-flowered strains are Clarke's, Barnhaven, Pacific, and Santa Barbara. Novelties include Gold Laced, mahogany petals edged with gold. Miniature Polyanthus have smaller flowers on shorter stalks. All excellent for massing in shade, for planting with bulbs, or as container plants.
P. polyneura	Cortusoides	1–6, 17	Leaves long stalked, broad, lobed and toothed, green above, to 4 in. long.	Flower stems 9–18 in. high, with 1, 2, or more whorls of erect rose, purplish, or red flowers with orange yellow eyes. Spring bloom.	Handsome, spreading plant for shade; needs fast drainage, somewhat less water than Candelabra types.
P. pulverulenta	Candelabra	1–6, 17	Leaves a foot or more long, deep green, wrinkled.	Flowers red to red purple, purple eyed, in whorls on 3-ft. stems thickly dusted with white meal.	Bartley strain has flowers in pink and salmon range. Also a fine white with orange eye.
P. sieboldii	Cortusoides	1–6, 14–17	Leaves scalloped, toothed, on long, hairy stalks.	Flowers pink, rose, or white, clustered 1–1½ in. across. Stalk 4–8 in. high. Blooms in late spring.	Tolerates more heat and drought than most primroses. Spreads from creeping rootstocks. Often goes dormant in late summer. Easily propagated by cuttings of the rootstock.
P. sikkimensis	Sikkimensis	1–6, 17	Leaves scanty, 3–5 in. long, with short stalks.	Up to 2 dozen yellow, bell shaped, nodding flowers on slender, 20-in.-high stalk. Summer bloom.	Largely supplanted by *P. florindae*, which is taller and somewhat easier to grow.
P. sinensis CHINESE PRIMROSE	Sinenses	Green-house or house plant.	Leaves on long stalks, roundish, lobed, toothed, soft, hairy, 2–4 in. long.	Flowers white, pink, lavender, reddish, coral; 1½ in. or more wide, many in a cluster on 4–8-in. stems. Stellata varieties have star shaped flowers in whorls.	Tender, scarce. Favorite European pot plant; imported seed available from specialists.
P. veris COWSLIP	Vernales	1–6, 17	Leaves similar to those of Polyanthus primroses.	Bright yellow, fragrant flowers ½–1 in. wide in early spring. Stem 4–8 in. high.	Naturalize in wild garden or rock garden. Charming, but not as sturdy as Polyanthus primroses.
P. vialii (*P. littoniana*)	Muscarioides	1–6, 17	Leaves to 8 in. long, 1½–2½ in. wide, hairy, irregularly toothed.	Flowers violet blue, fragrant, ¼–½ in. across, opening from bright red calyces. Stems erect, 1–2 ft. high. Dense, narrow spikes 3–5 in. long.	Not long-lived, but quite easy from seed in cool-winter areas. For collectors. Use in rock gardens.
P. vulgaris (*P. acaulis*) PRIMROSE, ENGLISH PRIMROSE	Vernales	1–6, 17	Tufted; leaves much like those of Polyanthus primroses.	Flowers one to a stalk; vigorous garden strains often have 2 or 3 to a stalk. Early spring bloom. White, yellow, red, blue, and shades of bronze, brownish, and wine.	Generally found only in cool moist climate. Double varieties available. Blues and reds especially desirable. Use in woodland, rock garden, as edging. Nosegay and Biedermeier strains exceptionally heavy blooming.

Primulas most commonly grown in the West fall into 11 of the 34 primula sections. Following are basic characteristics and requirements of these sections. To learn how to grow particular species, note which section it belongs to in accompanying chart.

Section Auricula. More than 20 species native to European Alps. Rosettes of thick leaves, often with mealy coating or white

Primula polyantha

margin. Strong fleshy stems to 8 in. high bear clusters of yellow, cream, purple, rose, or brownish flowers; often fragrant. They grow in full sun in their native habitat but in most of western U.S. do best in light shade—full sun in coastal areas. Tolerate more sun than Polyanthus primroses.

Section Candelabra. Native to and most abundant in meadows, bogs, or open woodland, principally in Himalayan region. Vigorous growing; larger species have semierect leaves.

Flowers in whorls, one above another on 2–3-ft. stems. Best in massed plantings. Need rich soil, partial shade, and much water; will take bog conditions.

Section Cortusoides. Called woodland primulas. Spread by underground creeping roots. Leaves long-stalked, oblong and somewhat lobed. Bell shaped flowers in whorls. After setting seed, plants become dormant and lose their leaves. Extremely hardy; can take somewhat drier conditions than other primroses, but thrive in rich moist soil with ample humus. Need shade.

Section Denticulata. Native to Himalayan meadows and moist slopes 6,000–14,000 ft. high. Winter over as large scale-covered buds, from which emerge in spring a cluster of leaves and stout stalk topped with ball-like cluster of flowers. Grow best where winters are cold; mild days in fall and winter may force blossoms too early.

Section Malacoides. Semihardy primroses from western

China, usually treated as annuals. Planted in mild-winter areas in early fall for bloom in winter and early spring. In cold climates grow in greenhouse. Leaves long-stalked, usually lobed. Flowers in whorls.

Section Muscarioides. Short-lived, rather difficult, usually treated as biennials. Flowers in this Chinese and Tibetan group are tightly crowded into long clusters resembling those of miniature red-hot pokers or grape hyacinths. For collectors.

Section Obconica. Semitropical, short-lived primroses from western China. Thick rhizomes; long-stalked, hairy leaves. Large, showy flower clusters over long period in winter and spring. Good in pots. Hairy leaves irritate skin of some people.

Section Sikkimensis. Similar to Candelabra primroses, except that bell shaped, drooping flowers on long stems are carried in single large cluster, rarely with second, lower whorl. Leaves have distinct stalks. Need abundant water, will take bog conditions.

Section Sinenses. Like Obconica section includes semitropical, short-lived plants. Best grown indoors in pots, either in greenhouse or cool, bright window.

Section Vernales. Includes familiar species sometimes called English primroses—*P. vulgaris* and *P. polyantha.* Tuftlike rosettes of leaves, with flowers borne singly or in clusters on stiff stems. Grow best in rich soil with lots of humus. Partial shade inland, full sun in coastal fog belt.

Section Verticillata. Densely leafy tufts produce many stems bearing long-tubed yellow flowers. Long-lived, with long bloom season. Rather tender plants grown in pots.

Accompanying chart does little more than introduce the great primrose group. Enthusiasts will be able to find and grow dozens of other species, some a real challenge to grow to flowering. But primroses in chart are not difficult if you live in the cool, moist primula belt and give plants rich soil, ample water, and shade.

PRINCE'S FEATHER. See *Amaranthus hybridus erythrostachys.*

PRINCESS FLOWER. See *Tibouchina urvilleana.*

PRIVET. See *Ligustrum.*

PROSOPIS glandulosa torreyana (Often sold as *P. chilensis.*) MESQUITE. Deciduous tree or large shrub. Zones 8–14. Native to deserts in the Southwest. One of the wide-spreading shade trees that helps make outdoor living more comfortable in the desert. To 30 ft. high and over 40 ft. wide, with many tiny bright green leaflets all through thicketlike tops. Leaflets and their stems make airy kind of shade. Mesquite also serves well as screen or windbreak. Usually several trunks branch out at ground level. Small greenish yellow flowers in 1½–2½-in.-long spikes. Flat seed pods 2–6 in. long.

Prosopis glandulosa torreyana

Best in deep soil where taproot will go down great distances for water. Tolerates drought, alkaline conditions, or irrigated lawn. Survives in shallow, rocky soil, but will be shrubby. Plant known as *P. alba,* Argentine mesquite, is evergreen except in coldest winters or cold locations. Makes a better shade tree because canopy of blue green foliage is more luxurious. Young plants very thorny.

"Reese hybrid" is evergreen tree of uncertain origin. Fast, may reach 30 ft. high, 60 ft. wide in 10 years.

PROSTANTHERA rotundifolia. ROUND-LEAFED MINT BUSH. Evergreen shrub. Zones 8, 9, 14–24. Dense, rounded growth to 4–10 ft. Tiny roundish leaves to ⅓ in. long, dark

Prostanthera rotundifolia

green above, paler beneath. Flowers (April-May) blue purple, trumpet shaped, to ½ in. long, profusely carried in short clusters. Takes sun or light shade, tolerates some drought.

PROTEA. Evergreen shrubs. Zones 16, 17, 21–24. Beautiful flowering plants from South Africa. Tubular flowers in large, tight clusters are surrounded by brightly colored bracts; effect is that of large, very colorful artichoke or thistle. Superb cut flowers, they hold their color for weeks, and even after fading they retain their shape.

Protea cynaroides

Difficult to grow; definitely not for beginners. They need perfect drainage (preferably on slopes), moderate summer water, protection from dry winds, good air circulation, full sun. Most need acid soil; some accept alkaline soil. Smaller species will grow in containers. Young plants tender to cold; older plants of most species hardy to 25°–27°F. They bloom in 3–4 years from seed, but are not long-lived plants.

Some 150 species grow in South Africa. These few seem to do best here:

P. cynaroides. KING PROTEA. To 3–5 ft. tall with open, spreading habit. Leaves oval, leathery. Flower heads to 11–12 in. across. Bracts pale pink to crimson, flowers white (midsummer to winter, early spring). Needs regular watering throughout year. Can be grown in tubs.

P. neriifolia. To 10 ft., 6–8 ft. wide. Leaves narrow, shaped like oleander leaves. Flower heads (autumn, winter) 5 in. long, 3 in. wide. Bracts pink to salmon, with black, furry tips. Will take 17°F. and grow in alkaline soil.

P. susannae. To 6 ft. tall, fairly compact. Lance shaped leaves; foliage heavy scented. Flower heads to 4 in. long, pink shading to brown at base. Has proven among the easiest to grow in California, withstanding alkaline soil and dry air.

PROVENCE BROOM. See *Cytisus purgans.*

PRUNE. See *Plum.*

PRUNUS. Deciduous and evergreen trees and shrubs. Fruit trees that belong to *Prunus* are better known as "stone fruits" and are described individually elsewhere in this encyclopedia under their common names. See Almond, Apricot, Cherry (sweet, sour, and Duke), Peach and Nectarine, Plum and Prune.

Prunus cerasifera

Take away the fruit trees and you have left the ornamentals, of which there are two classes: (1) evergreens, used chiefly as structure plants (hedges, screens, shade trees, street trees); and (2) deciduous flowering fruit trees (and shrubs) closely related to fruit trees mentioned above and valued for their springtime flower display as well as for attractive form and texture of foliage, shape. Following, in alphabetical order, are descriptions of evergreen forms. After that comes alphabetical listing of the flowering kinds, with certain ones charted.

EVERGREEN FORMS

P. caroliniana. CAROLINA LAUREL CHERRY. Evergreen shrub or tree. Zones 7–24. Native North Carolina to Texas. As upright shrub, it can be well-branched from ground up and useful as formal, clipped hedge or tall screen to 20 ft. Can be sheared into formal shapes. Trained as tree, will become broad topped and reach 35–40 ft. Attractive trained as multistemmed tree. Densely foliaged with glossy green smooth-edged leaves 2–4 in. long. Small creamy white flowers in 1-in. spikes, February-April. Fruit black, ½ in. or less in diameter. Varieties with greater denseness and less height are 'Bright 'n Tight' and 'Compacta'.

Litter from flowers and fruit is problem when planted over paved areas. Appearance best in coastal areas. Often shows salt burn and chlorosis in alkaline soils but does withstand desert heat and wind. Give it average soil, full sun, pruning to shape. Once established it's quite drought tolerant.

P. ilicifolia. HOLLYLEAF CHERRY. Evergreen shrub or small tree. Zones 7–9, 12–24. Native to California Coast Ranges and Baja California. Grows at moderate rate to 20–30 ft., usually broader than high. Mature leaves deep, rich green, 1–2 in. long, resemble those of holly. New leaves, from March to May, are light green, contrasting pleasantly with dark older foliage. Often, variations in leaf color and size occur from plant to plant. Creamy white flowers, ½ in. across, in spikes 3–6 in. long, appear with new leaves in March. Round fruit, ½–¾ in. wide, turn from green to red, then reddish purple (never as dark or black as those of Catalina cherry). Hybrids between hollyleaf and Catalina cherry appear frequently when plants are grown from seeds collected where both grow.

Hollyleaf cherry can be grown in almost any soil but thrives best in coarse, well-drained types. May be attacked by whiteflies in moist, shady situations. For control, see page 61. Does best in sun but will take light shade. Once established it will require no irrigation in normal rainfall years. Growth rate and appearance are improved by deep but infrequent watering. When buying plants avoid rootbound, large plants. A gallon can size, properly grown (no coiled roots) will generally outgrow larger plant in 5 gallon can. Use as small tree, tall screen, or formal clipped hedge of any height from 3–10 ft. (space plants 1 or 1½ ft. apart, train as described under *Pittosporum eugenioides*). It has unusually high resistance to oak root fungus (*Armillaria*), like *P. lyonii*. Very large, old trees resemble California live oak (*Quercus agrifolia*).

P. laurocerasus. ENGLISH LAUREL. Evergreen large shrub or small tree. Zones 4–9, 14–24; best performance in Zones 4–6, 15–17. Hardy to 5°F.; varieties listed below hardier. Native from southeastern Europe to Iran. Generally seen as clipped hedge. As tree, fast-growing to 30 ft. tall and as wide. Leaves leathery, glossy dark green, 3–7 in. long, 1½–2 in. wide. Flowers creamy white in 3–5-in.-long spikes in summer, often hidden by leaves. Small black fruit in late summer and fall. No special soil requirements. Where adapted, it's a fast-growing, greedy plant that's difficult to garden under or around. Generous watering and fertilizing will speed growth and keep treetop dense. Grows best in part shade in hot-summer areas. Full sun elsewhere. Few pests. May be troubled occasionally by scale (see page 60 for control). Fungus may cause reddish brown spots on leaves. Use combination fungicide-insecticide-miticide to prevent further damage.

Prunus laurocerasus 'Zabeliana'

Stands heavy shearing, but at expense of considerable mutilation of leaves; best pruned not by shearing but one cut at a time, cutting overlong twigs just above a leaf. Maintenance of hedge is problem because of fast growth. Best used as tree or tall unclipped screen. Three dwarf forms of *P. laurocerasus* are sold, 'Mt. Vernon', 'Nana', and 'Otto Luyken'. All have leaf size reduced to match their 4–6 ft. (or less) height and spread.

P. l. 'Schipkaensis'. SCHIPKA LAUREL. Zones 2–9, 14–17. Smaller plant than species, with narrow leaves 2–4½ in. long.

P. l. 'Zabeliana'. ZABEL LAUREL. Zones 3–9, 14–21. This narrow-leafed variety has branches which angle upward and outward from base. To 6 ft. high in time, with equal or greater spread. More tolerant of full sun than English laurel. Use as low screen, divider, or big foundation plant. With branches pegged down it makes an effective bank cover. Can be espaliered. Planted in narrow strip between house and walk, half the branches will lie on ground and rest will fan up the wall.

P. lusitanica. PORTUGAL LAUREL. Evergreen shrub or tree. Zones 4–9, 14–24. Native to Portugal and Spain. Slower growing than English laurel. Becomes densely branched large shrub 10–20 ft. high or multitrunked spreading tree to 30 ft. or more; trained to single trunk, it is used as formal street tree. Dense-branching habit and attractive dark green foliage make it useful background plant. Leaves glossy dark green, to 5 in. long. Small creamy white flowers in 5–10-in. spikes extend beyond leaves in spring and early summer, followed by long clusters of bright red to dark purple, ⅓-in. fruit. Takes heat, sun, and wind better than English laurel. Reasonably drought tolerant.

P. l. azorica. Native to Azores and Canary Islands where it grows 60–70 ft. high. Here, it grows into gigantic columnar bush 20 ft. high and half as wide. Exceptionally dark green and glossy foliage.

P. lyonii (*P. integrifolia, P. ilicifolia integrifolia*). CATALINA CHERRY. Evergreen shrub or tree. Zones 7–9, 12–24. Native to Channel Islands off southern California. Seen as broad, dense shrub in hedges and screens, clipped and informal. Trained as tree it will reach 45 ft. in height with spread of over 30 ft. and trunk 6–8 in. in diameter. Leaves 3–5 in. long, dark green, smooth margined or faintly toothed. (Leaves of young plants are more definitely toothed and usually are similar to hollyleaf cherry.) Creamy white flowers in clusters 4–6 in. long are borne in profusion in April and May. Fruit, ¾–1-in. black cherries, ripen August-September. Fruit is sweet but insipid, large stoned.

When used as patio tree or street tree over sidewalks, fruit litter is objectionable. Best planted in full sun. Quite drought tolerant; may be short-lived in heavy soil with regular garden watering. Seldom troubled with diseases or pests. May be attacked by whitefly. For control, see page 61. Valuable as tall screen or hedge. Can be held to any height desired by pruning. Rates high in resistance to oak root fungus (*Armillaria*).

Flowering Cherry

NAME	ZONES	FORM	HEIGHT & SPREAD	FLOWERS & SEASON
Prunus 'Accolade'	2–9, 14–17	Small tree with spreading branches, twiggy growth pattern. Very vigorous.	To 20 ft. or more, equally wide.	Semidouble, pink, 1½ in. wide, in large drooping clusters. Midseason. Hybrid between *P. sargentii* and *P. subhirtella*.
P. campanulata TAIWAN FLOWERING CHERRY	7–9, 14–23	Graceful, densely branched, bushy, upright, slender small tree. Performs well in California climates where other flowering cherries fail.	To 20–25 ft.; not as wide as high.	Single, bell shaped, drooping, in clusters of 2–5. Strong positive color—electric rose, almost neon purple pink. Blooms early, along with flowering peach.
P. sargentii SARGENT CHERRY	1–7, 14–17	Upright spreading branches form rounded crown. Orange red fall foliage.	To 40–50 ft. and more, not as wide as high.	Single blush pink flowers in clusters of 2–4. Midseason. 'Columnaris' is more narrow and erect than typical *P. sargentii*.
P. serrula BIRCH BARK CHERRY	1–7, 14–16	Valued for beauty of its bark—glossy mahogany red color.	To 30 ft. and as wide.	Small white flowers are almost hidden by new leaves. Midseason.

NAME	ZONES	FORM	HEIGHT & SPREAD	FLOWERS & SEASON
P. serrulata JAPANESE FLOWERING CHERRY	2–7, 14–20	The species is known through its many cultivated varieties. Best of these are listed below.		
'Amanogawa'		Columnar tree. Use as small Lombardy poplar.	To 20–25 ft. tall, 8 ft. wide.	Semidouble, light pink with deep pink margins. Early midseason.
'Beni Hoshi' ('Pink Star')		Fast grower with arching, spreading branches; umbrella shaped in outline.	To 20–25 ft. high and as wide.	Vivid pink single flowers with long, slightly twisted petals hang below branches. Midseason.
'Kwanzan' ('Kanzan', 'Sekiyama')		Branches stiffly upright, form inverted cone.	To 30 ft. high, 20 ft. wide.	Large, double. Deep rosy pink in pendant clusters displayed before or with red young leaves. Midseason.
'Ojochin'		Upward sweeping, rather stiff branches, compact growth.	To 25–30 ft. and as wide.	Single pink buds open white or white flushed pink. Midseason.
'Shirofugen'		Wide horizontal branching.	To 25 ft. and as wide.	Double, long stalked, pink, fading to white. Latest to bloom.
'Shirotae' ('Mt. Fuji')		Strong horizontal branching.	To 20 ft., wider than high.	Semidouble, pink in bud, white when fully open, purplish pink as flower ages. Early.
'Shogetsu'		Spreading growth, arching branches.	To 15 ft., wider than high.	Semidouble and very double, pale pink, often with white centers. Late.
'Takasago' ('Sieboldii') NADEN CHERRY		Low, rounded head. Slow growth.	To 12–15 ft.	Large, semidouble, pale pink. Midseason.
'Ukon'		Open sparse growth. Pinch branch tips in young plants to induce denser branching. Orange red autumn color.	To 30 ft. and as wide.	Large, semidouble, greenish yellow. Midseason.
P. subhirtella 'Autumnalis'	2–7, 14–20	Loose branching, bushy with flattened crown.	To 25–30 ft. and as wide.	Double, white or pinkish white in autumn as well as early spring. Often blooms in warm spells in January and February.
P. s. 'Hally Jolivette'		Small, bushy, upright.	To 8 ft., 6 ft. wide.	Double white flowers; pink buds. Early. This (and occasionally other cherries) is grafted on *P. serrula* trunks, which give four-season interest because of showy bark.
P. s. 'Pendula' SINGLE WEEPING CHERRY		Usually sold grafted at 5–6 ft. high on upright-growing understock. Graceful branches hang down, often to ground.	Slow to 10–12 ft. and as wide.	Single small pale pink blossoms in profusion. Midseason.
P. s. 'Rosea' (Usually sold as *P. s.* 'Whitcombii'.)		Wide-spreading, horizontal branching.	To 20–25 ft., spreading to 30 ft.	Buds almost red, opening to pink single flowers. Profuse, very early bloom. Northwest favorite.
P. s. 'Yae-shidare-higan' DOUBLE WEEPING CHERRY		Same as *P. s.* 'Pendula'.	Same as *P. s.* 'Pendula'.	Double rose pink. Midseason.
P. yedoensis YOSHINO FLOWERING CHERRY	2–7, 14–20	Curving branches; graceful, open pattern.	Fast to 40 ft., with 30 ft. width.	Single, light pink to nearly white, fragrant. Early.
P. y. 'Akebono' (Sometimes called 'Daybreak'.)		Variety is smaller than species.	To 25 ft. and as wide.	Flowers pinker than *P. yedoensis*.

FLOWERING FRUIT

Flowering Cherry. The several species and many varieties commonly called flowering cherries are described in accompanying chart. They perform best in Zones 4–6, 15–17. Cold-hardy enough for Zones 2–3, they suffer severe damage where winters are dry, sunny, and windy. Their cultural requirements are identical. They require fast draining, well-aerated soil. If your soil is heavy clay, plant in raised beds. Give them full sun. Somewhat drought tolerant but best with moderate watering during summer. Do as little pruning as possible. Cut while tree is in bloom and use branches in arrangements. Remove awkward or crossing branches. Pinch back occasional overly ambitious shoot to force branching.

Pests and diseases are not usually a problem. Infestations of tadpole shaped slugs and yellowish to greenish caterpillars may skeletonize leaves unless sprayed with insecticide. If branch or two dies back, treat tree for cherry dead-bud as explained on page 63. Plants in heavy soil sometimes subject to root rot, for which there is no cure, during winter. Affected tree usually will bloom, then send out new leaves which will suddenly collapse.

Use flowering cherries as their growth habit indicates. All are good trees to garden under. Large spreading kinds make good shade trees. Smaller cherries are almost a necessity in Oriental gardens.

Flowering Nectarine. There is one important flowering nectarine: 'Alma Stultz'. Fast growing to 20 ft. and as wide as high, in early spring it covers itself with large, 2–2½-in.-wide, waxy-petaled fowers that look somewhat like azalea blossoms. They are rosy white shaded pink, and the color deepens with age. Deliciously fragrant. White-fleshed fruit is sparsely produced. Plant appearance, cultural needs same as peach.

Flowering Peach. Flowering peach is identical to fruiting peach in growth habit and height. But it's more widely adapted than fruiting peaches—flowering peaches can be grown in

Zones 2–24. However, they may be caught by late frosts in Zones 2, 10, 11, and suffer from delayed foliation in 13, 23, 24. Heavy pruning necessary for good show of flowers. Cut branches back to 6-in. stubs at flowering time. Multibranched new growth will be luxuriant by summer's end and it will flower profusely the following spring. Cultural requirements, insect and disease control are same as for fruiting peaches. Use flowering peaches as giant seasonal bouquets. Place them where they will give maximum effect when in bloom and where they will be fairly unobtrusive out of bloom—behind evergreen shrubs, fence or wall.

Some peach varieties produce showy blossoms and good fruit. These are described in this encyclopedia under Peaches and Nectarines. The following varieties are strictly "flowering" in the sense that their blooms are showy and their fruit is either absent or worthless. Early-flowering varieties are best choices for regions where spring comes early and is hot.

'Burbank'. Double pink. Late.

'Double White'. Midseason.

'Early Double Pink'. Very early.

'Early Double Red'. Deep purplish red or rose red. Very early and brilliant, but color likely to clash with other pinks or red.

'Early Double White' blooms with 'Early Double Pink'.

'Helen Borchers'. Clear pink, 2½-in.-wide flowers. Late.

'Icicle'. Double white flowers. Late.

'Late Double Red'. Later by 3–4 weeks than 'Early Double Red'.

'Peppermint Stick'. Flowers striped red and white; may also bear all-white and all-red flowers on same branch. Midseason.

'Royal Red Leaf'. Foliage red, deepening to maroon. Deep pink flowers. This might be classed as flowering-fruiting as it bears red, white-fleshed, edible fruit. Late.

'Weeping Double Pink'. Smaller than other flowering peaches, with weeping branches. Requires careful staking and tying to develop main stem of suitable height. Midseason.

'Weeping Double Red'. Similar to above, but with deep rose red flowers. Midseason.

'Weeping Double White'. White version of weeping forms listed above.

Flowering Plum. The many species and varieties of flowering plums are grouped in chart form.

Flowering plums will grow in almost any soil. If soil is wet for long periods, plant 6–12 in. above grade level in raised bed. Expect attacks from aphids, slugs, caterpillars, spider mites. Spray with all-purpose fruit tree spray. Check trunk at and just below ground level for peach tree borers. Spray with sevin or diazinon (see Peach).

One of the most adaptable and choicest medium-sized flowering trees for lawn, patio, terrace, or small street tree is *P. blireiana*. It also does well in planters and large tubs. In choosing plum to be planted in paved area check its fruiting habits. When a flowering plum is planted in a patio, prune to establish head at height to walk under. As tree develops, prune out crossing and inward-growing branches.

P. besseyi. WESTERN SAND CHERRY. Zones 1–3, 10. Deciduous shrub 3–6 ft. tall. White flowers in spring followed by sweet black cherries nearly ¾ in. in diameter. Used for pies, jams, jellies. Shrubs withstand heat, cold, wind, drought.

P. fruticosa. Like *P. besseyi*, but 2–3 ft. tall, with smaller red purple fruit.

P. glandulosa. DWARF FLOWERING ALMOND. Deciduous shrub. Zones 1–10, 12, 14–19. Native to Japan, China. Much branched, upright, spreading growth to 6 ft. tall. Leaves light green, narrow and pointed, to 4 in. long. Flowers, set close to slender branches, appear early, before leaves, and turn branches into long wands of blossoms. In species, seldom seen in gardens, flowers are single, pink, or white, and only ½ in. wide. Flowers of commonly available varieties are double, 1–1¼ in. across, resembling light fluffy pompon chrysanthemums. Variety 'Alboplena' has double white flowers; 'Sinensis' has double pink

Flowering Plum

NAME	ZONE	GROWTH HABIT	LEAF, FLOWER, FRUIT
Prunus americana WILD PLUM, GOOSE PLUM	1–3, 10	Thicket-forming shrub or small tree to 15–20 ft. Extremely tough and hardy.	Dark green foliage follows profusion of 1-in. clustered white flowers. Fruit yellow to red, to 1 in., sour but good for jelly.
P. blireiana Hybrid between *P. cerasifera* 'Atropurpurea' and *P. mume*.	2–12, 14–22	Graceful, to 25 ft. high, 20 ft. wide branches long and slender.	Leaves reddish purple, turning greenish bronze in summer. Flowers semidouble, fragrant, pink to rose. February-April. Fruit none or very few.
P. cerasifera CHERRY PLUM, MYROBALAN	2–22	Used as rootstock for various stone fruits. Will grow to 30 ft. and as wide.	Leaves dark green. Flowers pure white, ¾–1 in. wide. Small red plums, 1–1¼ in. thick, are sweet but bland. Self-sows freely.
P. c. 'Allred'	2–22	Upright, slightly spreading, 20 ft. tall, 12–15 ft. wide.	Leaves red, flowers white. Fruit red, 1¼-in. wide, tart. Good for preserves, jelly.
P. c. 'Atropurpurea' (*P.* 'Pissardii') PURPLE-LEAF PLUM	2–22	Fast-growing to 25–30 ft. high, rounded in form.	New leaves copper red, deepening to dark purple, gradually becoming greenish bronze in late summer. White flowers. Sets heavy crop of small red plums.
'Hollywood' Hybrid between *P. c.* 'Atropurpurea' and Japanese plum 'Duarte'.	2–22	Upright grower to 30–40 ft., 25 ft. wide.	Leaves dark green above, red beneath. Flowers are light pink to white. February-March. Good quality red plums 2–2½ in. wide.
'Krauter Vesuvius'	2–22	Smaller growing than *P. c.* 'Atropurpurea', to 18 ft. high, 12 ft. wide; upright, branching habit.	Darkest of flowering plums. Leaves purple black. Flowers light pink. February-March. Fruit none or few.
'Newport'	2–22	To 25 ft. high, 20 ft. wide.	Purplish red leaves. Single pink flowers. Will bear a few fruit.
'Thundercloud'	2–22,	More rounded form than *P. c.* 'Atropurpurea' to 20 ft. high, 20 ft. wide.	Dark coppery leaves. Flowers light pink to white. Sometimes sets good crop of red fruit.
P. cistena DWARF RED-LEAF PLUM	2–12, 14–22	Dainty, multibranched shrub to 6–10 ft. Can be trained as single-stemmed tree, good for planting in small patios.	Purple leafed; white to pinkish flowers in early spring. Fruit blackish purple in July.

flowers. Prune back hard, either just after blooming or when in bloom, using cut wands for arrangements. Can be used as flowering hedge.

P. maackii. AMUR CHOKECHERRY. Zones 1–3, 10. Deciduous tree 25–30 ft. tall. Bark of trunk is yellowish and peeling, like birch bark. Leaves strongly veined, rather narrow and pointed, to 4 in. long. Small white flowers in narrow clusters 2–3 in. long. Fruit is black, ¼ in. thick. Native to Manchuria and Siberia, it is extremely hardy to cold and wind.

P. mume. JAPANESE FLOWERING APRICOT, JAPANESE FLOWERING PLUM. Deciduous tree. Zones 2–9, 12–22. (Blooms may be frosted in Zones 2, 3.) Neither true apricot nor plum. Considered longest lived of flowering fruit trees, it eventually develops into gnarled, picturesque 20-ft. tree. Leaves to 4½ in. long, broadly oval. Flowers are small, profuse, with clean, spicy fragrance. January-February in mild areas, February-March in cold-winter areas. Fruit is small, inedible. Prune heavily. Let tree grow for a year, then prune back all shoots to 6-in. stubs. Next year cut back half the young growth to 6-in. stubs; cut back other half following year, and continue routine in succeeding years.

Varieties are:

'Dawn'. Large ruffled double pink.

'Matsubara Red'. Double dark red.

'Peggy Clarke'. Double deep rose flowers with extremely long stamens and red calyx.

'Rosemary Clarke'. Double white flowers with red calyx. Very early.

'Viridicalyx'. Double white with green calyx.

'W. B. Clarke'. Double pink flowers on weeping plant. Effective large bonsai or container plant, focus of attention in winter garden scene.

P. padus. EUROPEAN BIRD CHERRY, MAYDAY TREE, MAYBUSH. Tree. Zones 1–3, 10. Moderate growth rate to 15–20 ft., occasionally taller, rather thin and open in habit while young. Dark, dull green oval leaves 3–5 in. long are among the first to unfold in spring.

Small white flowers in drooping 3–6-in. slender clusters make big show in May, nearly hiding foliage. Small black fruit that follow are bitter, but much loved by birds. Any soil, average water. Tolerates much cold.

P. tomentosa. NANKING CHERRY. Like *P. besseyi*, extremely tough, hardy fruiting shrub; grows 6–8 ft. tall. Fruit scarlet, up to ½ in. wide.

P. triloba. FLOWERING ALMOND. Small tree or treelike large shrub. Zones 1–11, 14–20. One of several plants known as "flowering almond." Slow growth to 15 ft., usually 8–10 ft. with equal spread. Rather broad 1–2½-in.-long leaves and double pink flowers about 1 in. wide in very early spring. A white-flowered form is sometimes available. Useful where quite hardy small flowering plant of definite tree form is needed. Also is sold as multitrunked shrub.

P. virginiana. CHOKECHERRY. Shrub or small tree. Grown Zones 1–3, 10. Leaves 2–4 in. long. Flowers appear after leaves have unfolded; they are tiny, white, in 3–6-in. slender clusters. Astringent fruit is ½–⅓ in. thick, dark red to black. Gives good display of autumn foliage color. *P. v. demissa*, western chokecherry, is native to Pacific Coast, Sierra Nevada, Great Basin area and northern Rockies. It is drought and heat tolerant. *P. v. melanocarpa*, BLACK CHOKECHERRY, has smoother leaves and blacker, sweeter fruit. With average garden watering it grows into 20–25-ft. tree. Its variety 'Shubert' has leaves that open green, then turn red as they mature. Tends to sucker freely.

PSEUDOLARIX kaempferi (*Chrysolarix kaempferi, C. amabilis*). GOLDEN LARCH. Deciduous conifer. Zones 2–7, 14–17. Slow-growing to 40–70 ft. high, often nearly as broad at base. Wide-spreading branches, pendulous at tips, grow in whorls to form symmetrical, pyramidal tree. Needles 1½–2 in. long, about ⅛ in. wide, clustered in tufts except near branch ends where they are single. Foliage effect feathery, bluish green, turning golden yellow in fall. Cones and bare branches make interesting winter

Pseudolarix kaempferi

patterns. Give it sunny, open spot sheltered from cold winds. Best in deep, rich, well-drained, acid or neutral soil. Needs regular supply of moisture. Fine for spacious lawns.

Pseudolarix kaempferi

PSEUDOPANAX. Evergreen shrubs or trees. Slow-growing. Leaves of *P. crassifolius*, *P. ferox* highly variable; young plants have long, narrow spiny-toothed leaves; mature plants have divided or undivided leaves of no very remarkable shape. Young plants odd and decorative. Flowers inconspicuous. Take sun or deep shade; respond to average garden water.

P. crassifolius. LANCEWOOD. Zones 16, 17, 21–24. In time, a 50-ft. tree. Usually seen as single-stem plant 3–5 ft. tall with rigid, drooping leaves to 3 ft. long, less than 1 in. wide, strongly toothed, reddish bronzy in color. Upright growth habit—good choice for narrow areas.

P. ferox. Zones 16, 17, 21–24. Eventually a 20-ft. tree. Young plants with leaves 12–18 in. long, 1 in. wide, strongly toothed.

P. lessonii. Zones 17, 20–24. Moderate growth to 12–20 ft. tall. In open ground an effective multistemmed tree. Leaves dark green, leathery, divided into 3–5 leaflets 1–3 in. long. July-August flowers inconspicuous. Withstands wind. Excellent container plant—confining roots keeps plant shrubby.

Pseudopanax lessonii

PSEUDOSASA. See Bamboo.

PSEUDOTSUGA. Conifers. The two species are quite similar but there's a great difference in status—the first is little known and the second is most prominent tree in Pacific Northwest.

P. macrocarpa. BIGCONE SPRUCE. Zones 1–3, 10, 11, 18, 19. Native to southern California. Stout-trunked; grows to about 60 ft. tall. Needles similar to *P. menziesii*. Has much larger cones—4–7½ in. long, 2–3 in. wide; 3-pronged bracts on cones barely protrude from each scale. Drought tolerant.

P. menziesii (*P. taxifolia*). DOUGLAS FIR. Zones 1–10, 14–17. Since pioneer days, Northwesterners have been gardening under and near this magnificent native tree.

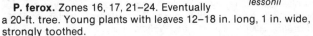

Pseudotsuga menziesii

Its entire range includes not only western Oregon and Washington but also extends east to the Rocky Mountains, north to Alaska, and south into many forested parts of northern California.

Sharply pyramidal form when young; widely grown and cherished as Christmas tree. Grows 70–250 ft. in forests. Densely set, soft needles, dark green or blue green, 1–1½ in. long, radiate out in all directions from branches and twigs. Sweet fragrance when crushed. Ends of branches swing up. Pointed wine red buds form at branch tips in winter. These open in spring to apple green tassels of new growth that add considerably to tree's beauty. Reddish brown cones are oval, about 3 in. long, and have obvious 3-pronged bracts. Unlike upright cone of true firs (*Abies*), these hang down.

Best suited to its native areas or to areas with similar summer-winter climates. Will grow in any except undrained, swampy soils. Does well in sun or considerable shade, and can take wind. Environment influences its appearance: where summers are dry, it is dense with shorter spaces between branches; where there is much moisture or too much shade, it tends to look awkward, thin, and gawky, especially as young tree. As garden tree, its height is difficult to control; you can't keep it down without butchering it. Yet it serves well as 10–12 ft. clipped hedge—plant young trees 2 ft. apart and keep them topped and trimmed. Resistant to oak root fungus (*Armillaria*).

(Continued on next page)

P. m. glauca. The common form in Rocky Mountains. Usually has more bluish green needles. It is much hardier to winter cold than Pacific Coast trees. Compact, weeping, and other forms exist, but are grown mostly in arboretums and botanic gardens.

PSIDIUM. GUAVA. Evergreen shrubs or small trees. White flowers (composed principally of brush of stamens). Berrylike fruit, good in jellies, pastes. Best in rich soils, but adaptable, taking some drought when established.

P. guajava. GUAVA. Zones 23, 24. Taller than strawberry guava, with strongly veined leaves to 6 in. long. Semideciduous briefly in spring; new leaves attractive salmon color. Fruit 1–3 in. across; white, pink, or yellow flesh; musky and mildly acid.

P. littorale *(P. cattleianum).* LEMON and STRAWBERRY GUAVAS. Zones 9, 15–24 (14 in sheltered locations). Moderate, open growth to 8–10 ft. as shrub; can be trained as multitrunked, 10–15-ft. tree. Especially beautiful bark and trunk—greenish gray to golden brown. Leaves glossy green, to 3 in. long; new growth bronze. Two principal varieties: *P. l. littorale,* LEMON GUAVA, has yellow fruit 1½ in. thick with white, sweet-tart, somewhat resinous flesh, fairly dense growth. *P. l. longipes,* STRAWBERRY GUAVA, has dark red fruit. Both make good informal hedges or screens, container plants.

Psidium littorale longipes

PSYLLIOSTACHYS suworowii *(Limonium* or *Statice suworowii).* Summer annual. Rosettes of 8-in.-long narrow leaves produce 18-in.-tall spikes of lavender pink tiny flowers. Spikes are very slender, single or branched, and cylindrical, reminiscent of slender, furry, highly refined rats' tails. They are excellent in flower arrangements, fresh or dry. Sow seed in pots or open ground seed bed when danger of frost is over; transplant to 1 ft. apart. Needs sun, average soil with good drainage, average water.

Psylliostachys suworowii

PTELEA trifoliata. WAFER ASH, HOP TREE. Deciduous shrub, small tree. Zones 1–3, 10. Slow to moderate growth to 15 ft., but often shrubby. Leaves divided into 3 leaflets. Summer flowers small, inconspicuous. Seeds are disks up to 1 in. wide—seed surrounded by thin, flat, nearly circular wing. Not related either to ash or hop, but rather to the orange; leaves have tiny oil glands like citrus, and strong scent that most people find pleasant. Once established, it can get along with very little water, even in poor rocky soil. Yellow fall color.

Ptelea trifoliata

PTERIDIUM aquilinum. BRACKEN. Fern. All Zones. Worldwide native. Variety *pubescens* is native to West. Fronds coarse, much divided, rising directly from deep, running rootstocks. Grows from 2 ft. to as much as 7 ft. under good conditions. Takes full sun to medium shade; reasonably drought tolerant—goes dormant if not enough water to sustain foliage. Occurs wild in many places and can be tolerated in untamed gardens, but beware of planting it: deep rootstocks can make it tough, invasive weed.

Pteridium aquilinum pubescens

PTERIS. BRAKE. Ferns. Mostly small ferns of subtropical or tropical origin, and mostly used in dish gardens or small pots; some are big enough for landscape use. For best garden performance,

keep soil moist but not saturated for any length of time.

P. cretica. Zones 17, 23, 24. To 1½ ft. tall with comparatively few, long narrow leaflets. Numerous varieties exist: some have forked or crested fronds, some are variegated. Variety 'Wimsettii', light green form with forked tips on mature plants, is so dense and frilly that it doesn't look like a fern.

P. 'Ouvrardii'. Zones 17, 22–24. Dark green 12–30-in.-tall fronds have extremely long, narrow ribbonlike divisions. Splendid massed or grouped with azaleas, camellias.

P. quadriaurita 'Argyraea'. SILVER FERN. Zone 24. From India. Fronds 2–4 ft. tall, rather coarsely divided, heavily marked white. Showy, but white markings seem out of place on ferns. Protect from frost and snails.

P. tremula. AUSTRALIAN BRAKE. Zones 16, 17, 22–24. Extremely graceful 2–4-ft. fronds on slender, upright stalks. Good landscape fern, with excellent silhouette. Fast-growing, but tends to be short lived.

Pteris cretica

PTEROCARYA stenoptera. CHINESE WINGNUT. Deciduous tree. Zones 5–24. Fast to 40–90 ft., with heavy, wide-spreading limbs. Shows its kinship to walnuts clearly in its leaves, 8–16 in. long and divided into 11–23 finely toothed, oval leaflets. Foot-long clusters of small, one-seeded, winged nuts hang from branches. Good-looking tree, but with only one real virtue: it succeeds well in compacted, poorly aerated soil in play yards and other high-traffic areas. Aggressive roots make it unsuitable in lawn and garden.

P. fraxinifolia, CAUCASIAN WINGNUT, is similar, has slightly larger leaflets, longer nut clusters.

Pterocarya stenoptera

PTEROSTYRAX hispidus. EPAULETTE TREE. Deciduous tree. Zones 5–10, 14–21. Possibly to 40 ft., but more usually held to 15–20 ft. with 10-ft. spread. Trunk single or branched, branches open, spreading at the top.

Light green leaves, gray green beneath, 3–8 in. long, rather coarse. Creamy white, fringy, lightly fragrant flowers in drooping clusters 4–9 in. long, 2–3 in. wide. Blooms in early summer. Gray, furry, small fruit in pendant clusters hang on well into winter, are attractive on bare branches.

Plant in sunny location in well-drained soil, give average garden watering. Prune to control shape, density. Best planted where you can look up into it—on bank beside path, above a bench, or in raised planting bed. It is a choice selection when planted at edge of a woodland area or as focal point in large shrub border.

Pterostyrax hispidus

PTYCHOSPERMA macarthuri *(Actinophloeus macarthuri).* Zones 23, 24. Native to New Guinea. Feather palm with several clustered, smooth green stems 10–15 ft. high. Soft green leaflets with jagged ends. Requires part shade in frost free coastal locations. Requires abundant water to look its best.

Ptychosperma macarthuri

PUKA. See *Meryta sinclairi.*

PULMONARIA. LUNGWORT. Perennials. Zones 1–9, 14–17. Long-stalked leaves mostly in basal clumps, with few on flower bearing stalks. Flowers funnel shaped, blue or purplish, in drooping clusters from April-June. Will grow in shade that discourages most flowering plants. Use with ferns, azaleas, rhododendrons; good under early spring-flowering trees, with blue scillas, pink tulips. Creeping roots. Need moist, porous soil.

Pulmonaria saccharata

P. angustifolia. COWSLIP LUNGWORT. Tufts of narrowish, dark green leaves. Flowers dark blue, in clusters on 6–12-in. stems. Blooms in spring at same time as primroses. Divide in fall after leaves die down.

P. saccharata. BETHLEHEM SAGE. Grows to 1½ ft., spreads to 2 ft. White-spotted, roundish, evergreen leaves. Flowers reddish violet or white.

PUMPKIN. Annual vine related to gourds, melons, squash. Here's how to grow jumbo-sized pumpkins for Halloween. Varieties that grow to 30–40 in. across are 'Big Tom' (or 'Connecticut Field'), 'Jack O'Lantern', and 'Big Max'. Plant seeds in mid-May or early June. Choose sunny location. Allow vine area of 8–12 ft. in diameter. After soil is cultivated, scoop hole 4 in. deep right under where you will plant seeds. Put shovelful of manure in hole and cover it with enough soil to make ground level again.

Pumpkin

Plant 6–8 seeds, 1 in. deep, within a circle 6 in. wide. If you want more than one set of vines, plant such circles 8 ft. apart. Water seeds after planting. When plants are 4–6 in. high, cut off tops of all but two best plants in circle. Water when you see signs of slightest wilting. Try not to wet foliage. When small pumpkins are tennis ball sized, remove all but 3 or 4 on each vine (for extra-large pumpkins, remove all but one). Remove fruit toward ends of vines; save those near main stem. Continue removing later flowers. In late summer, slide wooden shingle under pumpkins to protect from wet soil (not necessary if soil is sandy).

Smaller pumpkins with finer grained, sweeter flesh are 'Small Sugar' or 'Sugar'. Grow 'Lady Godiva' for its seeds; they have no hulls and can be roasted, salted, and eaten as nuts.

PUNICA granatum. POMEGRANATE. Deciduous tree or shrub. Zones 7–24; also Zones 5 and 6 if used against south or west wall. Showy flowers. Some varieties yield pomegranates. Narrow, glossy bright green to golden green leaves, bronzy new growth, brilliant yellow fall color except in Zone 24. All varieties tolerate great heat and will live and grow well in alkaline soil that would kill most plants. Need sun for best bloom and fruit. When established, nonfruiting varieties need little water, but will take a lot if drainage is good. In desert areas, the leaf-footed plant bug (seriously) may drill holes in fruit, causing it to spoil. Control with spray of diazinon, malathion, or sevin in late spring.

Punica granatum

'Alba Plena'. Shrubby, 6–10 ft. tall. Flowers double, creamy white or yellowish from yellow, waxy calyx. June-August. New growth bright green. Fruit (pale yellow) seldom forms.

'Chico'. DWARF CARNATION-FLOWERED POMEGRANATE. Compact bush can be kept to 18 in. tall if pruned occasionally. Double orange red flowers over long season. No fruit. Excellent under lower windows, in containers, as edging.

'Double Red'. Arching shrub to 12 ft. high with double orange red flowers, no fruit.

'Legrellei' ('Mme. Legrelle'). Dense 6–8-ft. shrub with double creamy flowers heavily striped coral red. No fruit.

'Nana'. DWARF POMEGRANATE. Dense shrub to 3 ft., nearly evergreen in mild winters. Blooms when a foot tall or less.

Orange red single flowers followed by small, dry, red fruit. Excellent garden or container plant; effective bonsai.

'Wonderful'. Best-known fruiting pomegranate. Grow it as 10-ft. fountain shaped shrub, tree, or espalier. Burnished red fruit in autumn follow orange red, single flowers up to 4 in. across. Will not fruit in cool coastal areas. Drought followed by flooding will cause fruit to split. Water deeply and regularly if fruit is important.

PURPLE CONEFLOWER. See *Echinacea purpurea*.

PURPLE GLOBE TULIP. See *Calochortus amoenus*.

PURPLE HEART. See *Setcreasea pallida* 'Purple Heart'.

PURPLE-LEAF PLUM. See *Prunus cerasifera* 'Atropurpurea'.

PURPLE ORCHID TREE. See *Bauhinia variegata*.

PURPLE OSIER. See *Salix purpurea*.

PURPLE VELVET PLANT. See *Gynura aurantiaca*.

PURSLANE TREE. See *Portulacaria afra*.

PUSCHKINIA scilloides. Bulb. All Zones. Closely related to *Scilla* and *Chionodoxa*. Flowers bell-like, pale blue or whitish with darker, greenish blue stripe on each segment, in spikelike clusters on 3–6-in. stems. Leaves broad, strap shaped, upright, bright green, a little shorter than flower stems. Plant bulbs 3 in. deep, 3 in. apart in fall; locate in sun to slight shade. Will grow for years without disturbance. Best in cold climates, will withstand some summer drought. *P. s. libanotica*, a more vigorous plant, is variety usually sold. *P. s.* 'Alba' has white flowers.

Puschkinia scilloides

PUSSY EARS. See *Calochortus tolmiei, Cyanotis somaliensis*.

PUYA berteroniana (usually sold as *P. alpestris*). Evergreen perennial. Zones 9, 13–17, 19–24. Native to Chile. Big, spectacular flowering plant. Massive flower clusters, resembling giant asparagus stalks as they develop, grow from crowded clump of 2-ft.-long, 1-in.-wide swordlike leaves, gray green, with sharp spines on edges and sharp tips. Flower cluster, including stalk, gets 4–6 ft. high. Blooms late April to early June. Cluster contains 2-in. bell shaped flowers, metallic blue green and steely turquoise, accented with vivid orange anthers. Stiff, spiky branchlet ends protrude from cluster.

Puya berteroniana

Use in rock gardens, on banks, or in large containers. Good with cactus, succulents, aloes. Full sun. Soil can be poor. Fairly drought tolerant once established.

PYRACANTHA. FIRETHORN. Evergreen shrubs. Grown widely for bright fruit, evergreen foliage, variety of landscape uses, and easy culture. All grow fast and vigorously with habit from upright to sprawling; nearly all have thorns. All have glossy green leaves, generally oval or rounded at ends, ½–1 in. wide and 1–4 in. long. All bear flowers and fruit on spurs along wood of

Pyracantha coccinea

last year's growth. Clustered flowers are small, fragrant, dull creamy white, effective because numerous.

Pyracantha coccinea

Fruit vary in color, size, season, and duration. Some color in late summer; others color late and hang on until birds, storms, or decay clear them out in late winter. Plants need full sun and do best where soil is not constantly wet; keep them away from lawn sprinklers. Control size and form by pinching young growth or by shortening long branches just before growth starts. Cut out branches that have berried back to well-placed side shoot. Subject to fireblight, scale, and woolly aphids, red spider mites. In coastal areas, apple scab sometimes a problem in early spring: can nearly defoliate plants.

Use as espaliers on wall or fence, as barrier plantings, screens, rough hedgerows or barriers along roads. Can be trained as standards; often clipped into hedges or topiary shapes (which spoils their rugged informality and often their fruit crop). Low-growing kinds are good ground covers.

P. angustifolia 'Gnome'. All Zones except coldest parts of Zone 1. Dwarf, spreading, densely branched shrub with orange fruit. One of the hardiest.

P. coccinea. All Zones except coldest parts of Zone 1. Rounded bush to 8–10 ft. (20 ft. trained against wall). Flowers March-April; red orange berries in October, November. Best known for its varieties 'Government Red' (red berries), 'Kasan' (red orange, long-lasting berries), 'Lalandei' and 'Lalandei Monrovia' (orange berries), 'Lowboy' (low, spreading, orange fruit) and 'Wyattii' (orange red berries coloring early). Best species for cold-winter areas. 'Lalandei' is hardiest of all.

P. 'Duvalii'. Zones 4–24. Large, bright red berries in very dense clusters. Shrub 12–25 ft. tall; good espalier. Tightly clustered fruit sometimes mold in wet autumns.

P. fortuneana (*P. crenatoserrata, P. yunnanensis*). Zones 4–24. Spreading growth to 15 ft. tall, 10 ft. wide. Limber branches make it good espalier plant. Berries orange to coral, lasting through winter. Variety 'Graberi' has huge clusters of dark red fruit that color in midfall, last through winter; growth more upright than species.

P. koidzumii (*P. formosana*). Zones 4–24. Big upright shrub to 10 ft. tall, 8 ft. wide. Large scarlet fruit in big clusters. Many pyracanthas of mixed parentage are sold as *P. koidzumii* varieties.

P. 'Lodense'. Zones 4–24. Low, dense, compact (usually under 3 ft.) pyracantha with small, closely set leaves, sparse crops of orange red fruit hidden by leaves. Edgings, low barriers.

P. 'Mohave'. Zones 3–24. Shrub to 12 ft. tall and wide. Heavy producer of big orange red fruit that colors in late summer and lasts into winter. One of reddest of the very hardy pyracanthas. Reported to be resistant to fireblight by National Arboretum, its originator.

P. 'Red Elf'. Zones 4–9, 12–24. Low growing, compact, densely branched, with bright red fruit. Small enough for container culture. Less susceptible to fireblight than most pyracanthas. Apparently the same as plant sold as 'Leprechaun'.

P. 'Rosedale'. Zones 4–24. Upright, tall growth with supple branches well adapted to espalier work. Bright red fruit is earliest to color, hangs late, is well distributed along branches.

P. 'Ruby Mound'. Zones 4–9, 12–24. Long, arching, drooping branches make broad mounds. Fruit bright red.

P. 'Santa Cruz' (*P. 'Santa Cruz Prostrata'*). Zones 4–24. Low growing, branching from base, spreading. Easily kept below 3 ft. by pinching out occasional upright branch. Red fruit. Plant 4–5 ft. apart for ground, bank cover.

P. 'Stribling'. Zones 4–24. Tall, upright to 15 ft., with pendulous branches. Red berries.

P. 'Tiny Tim'. Zones 4–24. Compact plant to 3 ft. tall. Small leaves, few or no thorns. Berries red. Prune once a year when fruit begins to color, shortening any runaway vertical shoots. Informal low hedge, barrier, tub plant.

P. 'Victory'. Zones 4–24. To 10 ft. tall, 8 ft. wide. Dark red fruit color late and hold on well.

P. 'Walderi' (*P. 'Walderi Prostrata'*). Zones 4–24. Low-growing (to 18 in., with a few upright shoots that should be cut out),

wide-spreading ground cover plant with red berries. Plant 4–5 ft. apart for fast cover.

P. 'Watereri'. Zones 3–24. To 8 ft. tall, equally wide. Very heavy producer of bright red, long-lasting fruit. Northwest favorite.

PYRETHRUM roseum. See *Chrysanthemum coccineum*.

PYROSTEGIA venusta (*P. ignea, Bignonia venusta*). FLAME VINE. Evergreen vine. Zones 13, 16, 21–24. Fast to 20 ft. or more, climbing by tendrils. Leaves with oval, 2–3-in. leaflets. Orange tubular flowers 3 in. long in clusters of 15–20 are impressive sight during fall, early winter. Any soil. Will take some shade, but best in full sun. Thrives in low desert and other hot climates; outstanding against west wall.

Pyrostegia venusta

PYRROSIA lingua. (Often sold as *Cyclophorus lingua.*) JAPANESE FELT FERN. Zones 14–17, 19–24. Dark green, broad, undivided, lance shaped fronds with feltlike texture from creeping rootstocks. Fronds to 15 in. tall, densely clustered. Most often used in baskets, but makes choice ground cover for small areas. Can take full sun along coast, part shade in other areas. Foliage color better with some shade. Requires only moderate watering. Slow grower.

Pyrrosia lingua

PYRUS. ORNAMENTAL PEAR. Deciduous or evergreen trees. Commercial fruiting pear is described under Pear. Following are ornamental species. Most are subject to fireblight (see under Pear). All are best in full sun, will get along with no more than moderate summer watering once established.

P. calleryana. Deciduous tree. Zones 2–9, 14–21. Grows to 25–50 ft. Strong horizontal branching pattern. Leaves 1½–3 in. long, broadly oval, scalloped, dark green, very glossy and leathery. Flowers clustered, pure white, ¾–1 in. wide; very early bloom; in coldest zones, flower crop may be destroyed by late freezes in some years. Fruit very small, round, inedible. Fairly resistant to fireblight; rich purplish red fall color.

Pyrus kawakamii

'Bradford', original introduction, has strongly horizontal limbs, has reached 50 ft. in height, 30 ft. width. 'Aristocrat' is more pyramidal, with upcurving branches. 'Redspire' is similar, with yellow to red fall color. 'Capital' and 'Whitehouse' are narrowly columnar.

P. communis. See Pear.

P. kawakamii. EVERGREEN PEAR. Evergreen shrub or tree. Zones 8, 9, 12–24. Partially deciduous in coldest winters in coldest zones. Branchlets drooping; leaves glossy, oval, pointed. Clustered white flowers appear in sheets and masses in winter-early spring. Small fruit seldom seen, inedible.

Without support evergreen pear becomes broad, sprawling shrub or in time a multitrunked small tree. With willowy young branches fastened to fence or frame, it makes a good-looking espalier. To make tree of it, stake one or several branches, shorten side growth, and keep staked until trunk is self supporting. Beef up framework branches by shortening (when young) to upward-facing buds or branchlets. Established, well-shaped plants need little pruning or shaping. Heavily pruned evergreen pears, such as those espaliered on small frames, seldom flower.

Tolerant of many soils, easy to grow wherever it doesn't freeze. Spray for aphids and watch for fireblight, which can disfigure or destroy plants.

P. pyrifolia. SAND PEAR, JAPANESE SAND PEAR. Deciduous tree. Zones 1–9, 14–21. Like common pear in appearance, but has glossier, more leathery leaves which turn brilliant reddish purple in fall. Fruit small, woody, gritty. Improved forms of this tree, *P. p. culta,* are grown for their fruit by Japanese.

P. ussuriensis. Deciduous tree. Planted Zones 1–3, 10; hardy to any cold but flowers may be damaged by late freezes. Grows 20–30 ft. tall. Leaves roundish, glossy green turning bright red in fall. Flowers white, 1½ in. across. Fruit 1–1½ in. wide, yellow green, hard, inedible.

QUAIL BUSH. See *Atriplex lentiformis.*

QUAKING GRASS. See *Briza maxima.*

QUAMOCLIT lobata. See *Mina lobata.*

QUAMOCLIT pennata. See *Ipomoea quamoclit.*

QUEEN PALM. See *Arecastrum romanzoffianum.*

QUEENSLAND KAURI. See *Agathis robusta.*

QUEENSLAND NUT. See *Macadamia.*

QUEENSLAND UMBRELLA TREE. See *Schefflera actinophylla.*

QUEEN'S TEARS. See *Billbergia nutans.*

QUEEN'S WREATH. See *Antigonon leptopus.*

QUERCUS. OAK. Deciduous or evergreen trees. Western home owners acquire oak trees in either of two ways: they either set out a nursery plant or plant an acorn (or a jay or squirrel plants an acorn for them). Or, they move where a native oak tree remains from the days when the land was wild.

Quercus coccinea

The method of acquisition is quite significant. An oak tree planted in a garden will grow vigorously and fast (1½–4 ft. a year). It will very likely not experience any unusual pest attacks or poor health—whether it's a western native or not. Old wild trees, on the other hand, quite frequently cannot handle the surfeit of water and nutrients that they get in a garden and must be given special treatment.

Special treatment for existing native oaks. If possible, do not raise or lower grade level between trunk and drip line. If you must alter grade, put a well around base of trunk so that grade level there is not changed. Never water within 4 ft. of trunk or allow water to stand within that area. Any of a number of sucking and chewing insects and mites feed upon existing native oaks. Most of the time these creatures are kept in check by birds, other insects and mites, and by insect-and-mite troubles that we don't even know about. But once in a while an outbreak of some organism—usually oak moth larvae—gets bad enough to need artificial control. When that happens, call a commercial arborist or pest control firm to diagnose and treat it, because an oak tree is too big for a homeowner to reach with his limited spray equipment.

Oak root fungus *(Armillaria)* is a way of life in many California neighborhoods that once were oak forests. Get advice of arborist on how to sustain infected trees. All old oaks, infected with the disease or not, can benefit from feeding and deep watering—fertilize and irrigate only out near drip line.

Old, existing, native oaks also benefit from periodic grooming to remove dead wood. Arborists should not cut thick branches unless they have good reasons for doing so. Excessive pruning may stimulate succulent new growth that will be subject to mildew.

How to plant an acorn. Select shiny, plump, fallen acorns, free of worm holes. Remove caps. Plant acorns on or just beneath soil surface and put up screen to protect from jays and squirrels. Surer way is to gather newly sprouted acorns or to sprout fresh ones between layers of damp peat moss (takes 2 weeks). Plant those with strong root sprouts. Make crater deep so acorn can be just covered with soil. At bottom of crater poke vertical hole to take sprouted tap root. Insert root and press soil around it. Water. Expect first leaves in 6–8 weeks. If you plant several acorns in one area you can thin later to best seedling. After planting, water weekly (when there is no rain) the first 2 months, then monthly.

How to transplant an oak. It seems not to hurt oak seedling of any size up to 5–8 ft. to have its vertical root cut in transplanting if root ball is otherwise big and firm enough. Tree may wilt or lose leaves after roots are cut but if watered well it should show new growth in 4–6 weeks. Oak seedlings from nursery containers usually will not show spiralling of tap roots at bottom of containers. The better growers will cut a seedling's tap root when planting into nursery container so young oak will develop branching root system.

How to train a young oak. By nature, many young oaks grow twiggy. Growth is divided among so many twigs that none elongate fast. To promote fast vertical growth, pinch off tips of unwanted small branches, meanwhile retaining all leaf surface possible in order to sustain maximum growth.

Most are drought tolerant. In the following list, oaks native to the western U.S. or to the Mediterranean region need no watering after they are established (but water them through the first one or two dry seasons).

Q. agrifolia. COAST LIVE OAK. Evergreen tree. Zones 7–10, 12, 14–24. Native to California Coast Ranges. Round-headed, wide-spreading tree to 20–70 ft. high, often with greater spread. Smooth dark gray bark. Dense foliage of rounded, hollylike, 1–3-in.-long leaves, slightly glossy on upper surface. As planted tree from nursery or acorn, it can grow as high as 25 ft. in 10 years, 50 feet in 25 years. Attractive green all year unless hit by oak moth larvae. Has greedy roots and drops almost all its old leaves in early spring just when gardening time is most valuable. Regardless of these faults, it's a handsome and quite worthwhile shade tree or street tree. Can be sheared into handsome 10–12-ft. hedge.

Quercus agrifolia

Q. bicolor. SWAMP WHITE OAK. Deciduous tree. Zones 1–3, 10. Medium to slow growth to 60 ft., rarely more. Leaves dark shiny green, up to 7 in. long, with shallow lobes or scallops, silvery white underneath. Bark of trunk and branches flakes off in scales. Tolerates wet soil; also thrives where soil is well drained.

Q. chrysolepis. CANYON LIVE OAK. Evergreen. Zones 5–9, 14–24. Native to mountain slopes and canyons of California, southern Oregon. Handsome round-headed or somewhat spreading tree to 20–60 ft., with smooth whitish bark. Oval, 1–2-in.-long leaves are shiny medium green above, grayish or whitish beneath. Leaf edges are smooth or toothed. Acorn cups, covered with golden fuzz, look like turbans.

Q. coccinea. SCARLET OAK. Deciduous. All Zones. Native to eastern U.S. Moderate to rapid growth in deep rich soil. Can reach 60–80 ft. High, light, open-branching habit. Leaves bright green, to 6 in. long, with deeply cut, pointed lobes. Leaves turn bright scarlet in sharp autumn nights (Zones 1–11, 14, 15, 18–20); color less well where autumn is warm. Roots grow deep. Good street or lawn tree. Fine to garden under.

Q. douglasii. BLUE OAK. Deciduous. All Zones. Native to foothills around California's Central Valley. Low branching, wide spreading, to 50 ft. high. Finely textured light gray bark and decidedly bluish green leaves, shallowly lobed, oval, almost squarish. Good in dry hot situations. Fall colors attractive—pastel pink, orange, yellow.

Q. dumosa. CALIFORNIA SCRUB OAK. Evergreen shrub 3–10 ft. tall, rarely small tree. Zones 4–9, 14–24. Evergreen leaves ½–1 in. long, shiny green, lightly spine edged or smooth. Sometimes grown for landscaping wild gardens, erosion control. Very drought tolerant; thrives in poor, rocky soil. *Q. durata* is similar but with leaves dull green and covered with fine hair.

Q. emoryi. EMORY OAK. Evergreen. Zones 10–13. Handsome

tree to 60 ft. (usually smaller in gardens), native to lower mountain slopes in Arizona, New Mexico, Texas, and northern Mexico. Leathery oval leaves, 2–3 in. long, sometimes turn golden just before new growth starts in late spring. Grows well in low desert, tolerates variety of soils. Needs periodic deep watering during summer.

Q. engelmannii. MESA OAK. Evergreen. Zones 18–24. Native to southern California. Wide-spreading tree of character, to 60 ft. high. Leaves oval or oblong, 2 in. long, usually smooth edged. In its area, it has the same cherished native status as the coast live oak.

Q. gambelii *(Q. utahensis).* ROCKY MOUNTAIN WHITE OAK. Deciduous. Zones 1–3, 10. Grows slowly to 20–30 (rarely 50) ft., often in colonies from underground creeping root system. Leaves 3–7 in. long, half as wide, dark green turning yellow, orange, or red in fall. Is characteristic oak of Arizona's Oak Creek Canyon and Colorado foothills south of Denver.

Q. garryana. OREGON WHITE OAK, GARRY OAK. Deciduous. Zones 4–6, 15–17. Native from British Columbia south to Santa Cruz Mountains of California. Slow to moderate growth to 40–90 ft., with wide, rounded crown, branches often twisted. Bark grayish, scaly, checked. Leaves 3–6 in. long with rounded lobes, leathery, dark glossy green above, rusty or downy on lower surface. Casts moderate shade and has deep nonaggressive root system—good shelter for rhododendrons (but don't plant them within 4 ft. of tree's trunk).

Q. ilex. HOLLY OAK, HOLM OAK. Evergreen. Zones 4–24. Native to Mediterranean region. Moderate growth rate reaching 40–70 ft. high, equal spread. Leaves variable in shape and size, usually 1½–3 in. long, ½–1 in. wide, either toothed or smooth edged, dark, rich green on upper surface, yellowish or silvery below.

Tolerates wind and salt air; will grow in constant sea wind, but tends to be shrubby there. Inland, growth rate can be moderately fast but this varies with soil and water conditions. Good evergreen street or lawn tree where coast live oak is difficult to maintain, but it lacks open grace of coast live oak. Can take hard clipping into formal shapes or hedges.

Q. kelloggii. CALIFORNIA BLACK OAK. Deciduous. Zones 5 (inland portions), 6, 7, 15, 16, 18–21. Native to mountains from southern Oregon to southern California. Moderate growth rate to 30–80 ft. Dark, furrowed and checked bark. Handsome foliage; unfolding leaves are soft pink or dusty rose, becoming bright glossy green and turning yellow or yellow orange in fall. Leaves 4–10 in.

Quercus kelloggii

long and 2½–6 in. wide, deeply lobed, with lobes ending in bristly points. Good moderate-sized tree for spring and fall color, winter trunk and branch pattern.

Q. lobata. VALLEY OAK, CALIFORNIA WHITE OAK. Deciduous. Zones 1–3, 6–16, 18–21. Native to interior valleys, Sierra foothills, and Coast Ranges away from direct coastal influence. California's mightiest oak, often reaching 70 ft. or more with equal or greater spread. Trunk and limbs massive, with thick, ashy gray, distinctly checkered bark. Limbs often picturesquely twisted; outer branches long and drooping, sometimes sweeping ground. Deeply lobed

Quercus lobata

leaves, lobes rounded; 3–4 in. long, deep green above, paler beneath.

Tolerates high heat and moderate alkalinity in its native range. Best in deep soils where it can tap ground water—and in such situations it can grow fast (2½–3 ft. a year). Magnificent tree for shading really big outdoor living area (debris makes it difficult for beds of small plants or heavily used paved areas). This is tree that gives much of California's Central Valley its parklike look.

"Oak balls" are lightweight, corky spheres about size of tennis balls, black and tan when they fall. They result from insect activity, do not harm tree.

Q. macrocarpa. BUR OAK, MOSSY CUP OAK. Deciduous. Zones 1–11, 14–24. Native to eastern U.S. Rugged looking, to 60–75 ft.

Quercus macrocarpa

high, 30 ft. wide. Leaves are glossy green above and whitish beneath, 8–10 in. long, broad at tip, tapered at base, deeply lobed. Large acorns form in mossy cup. Similar to *Q. bicolor* but faster growing, more tolerant of adverse conditions.

Q. myrsinifolia. JAPANESE LIVE OAK. Evergreen. Zones 4–7, 14–24. A 30–50-ft. tree in its native China and Japan. Leaves 2½–4 in. long, narrow, toothed toward tips, glossy dark green. New foliage purplish. Graceful rather than sturdy (like most oaks), not easily recognized as an oak unless seen with its acorns.

Q. palustris. PIN OAK. Deciduous. All Zones. Native to eastern U.S. Moderate to fairly rapid growth to 50–80 ft. Slender and pyramidal form when young, open and round-headed at maturity. Brownish gray bark. Lower branches tend to droop almost to ground; if lowest whorl is cut away, branches above will adopt same habit. Only when fairly tall will it have good clearance

Quercus palustris

beneath its lowest branches. Glossy dark green leaves, deeply cut into bristle-pointed lobes; in brisk fall weather leaves turn yellow, red, and finally russet brown. Many hang on in winter.

Less drought tolerant than most other oaks. Develops chlorosis in alkaline soils; treat with iron chelate. Needs ample water and good drainage. Stake young trees and give only corrective pruning. Plant where its spread will not interfere with walks, drives, or street traffic, or trim it often. Unlike western oaks, it is a fine tree for lawns.

Q. phellos. WILLOW OAK. Deciduous. Zones 1–4, 6–16, 18–21. Native to eastern U.S. To 50–90 ft., somewhat like pin oak in growth habit and spreading nature. Bark smooth, gray. Leaves unlike those of other common oaks, somewhat resemble willow leaves; 2½–5 in. long, ⅓–1 in. wide, smooth edged, turning yellowish before falling. In warmer zones, may hold dead foliage

Quercus phellos

through winter. Of all oaks is most delicate in foliage pattern. Grown and used same way as pin oak.

Q. robur. ENGLISH OAK. Deciduous. Zones 2–12, 14–21. To 90 ft. with rather short trunk and very wide, open head in maturity. Fairly fast growth. Leaves 3–4½ in. long, with 3–7 pairs of rounded lobes. Leaves hold until late in fall and drop without much color change. Variety 'Fastigiata', UPRIGHT ENGLISH OAK, is narrow and upright, like Lombardy poplar when young, branches out to broad, pyramidal shape when mature.

Q. rubra *(Q. rubra maxima, Q. borealis).* RED OAK, NORTHERN RED OAK. Deciduous. Zones 1–12, 14–24. Fast growth to 90 ft. Broad, spreading branches and round-topped crown. Leaves 5–8 in. long by 3–5 in. wide, with 3–7 pairs of sharp-pointed lobes. New leaves and leaf stalks are red in spring and turn to dark red, ruddy brown, or orange in fall. Needs fertile soil and plenty of water. Stake young plants. High-branching habit and reasonably open head make it good tree for big lawns, parks, broad avenues. Its deep roots make it good tree to garden under.

Q. shumardii. SHUMARD RED OAK. Deciduous. Zones 4–9, 14–17. Very similar to scarlet oak *(Q. coccinea),* slightly less hardy. Fall color yellow to red.

Q. suber. CORK OAK. Evergreen. Zones 5–7 (with occasional winter damage), 8–16, 18–23. Native to Mediterranean region. Moderate growth rate to 70–100 ft. high with equal spread. Trunk and principal limbs covered with thick corky bark (cork of commerce). The 3-in. toothed leaves are shining dark green above, gray beneath. General effect is fine textured. Needs good

Quercus suber

drainage; is fairly tolerant of different soil types, but is likely to yellow in alkaline soils. Established trees can take considerable drought. One of best oaks for desert.

Good garden shade tree with interesting contrast between fairly light-textured foliage and massive, fissured trunk. Value as street or park tree diminishes when children find out how easy it is to carve bark.

Q. vacciniifolia. HUCKLEBERRY OAK. Evergreen shrub. Zones

4–7, 14–17. Native to mountains of California. Low (to 2 ft.), with sprawling stems and smooth-edged gray green leaves ¾–1¼ in. long. Sometimes planted in wild gardens, large rock gardens, mountain summer home gardens.

Q. virginiana. SOUTHERN LIVE OAK. Evergreen, partly or wholly deciduous in cold-winter regions. Zones 4–24. Native to eastern U.S. Moderate to fast growth to eventual 60 ft., with broad, spreading, heavy-limbed crown twice as wide. Leaves 1½–5 in. long, smooth edged, shining dark green above and whitish beneath. Thrives on ample water and does best in deep rich soil. In hot interior climates, is most attractive of all evergreen oaks. Best oak for lawn planting in low desert.

Q. wislizenii. INTERIOR LIVE OAK. Evergreen. Zones 7–9, 14–16, 18–21. Native to Sierra foothills and east side of California's Central Valley. To 30–75 ft. high, often broader than high. Wide-spreading branches form dense crown. Oblong leaves to 4 in. long, glossy green, smooth or spiny edges. Handsome tree for parks and big lawns. Sparse, angular young plants fail to hint at tree's ultimate beauty.

QUILLAJA saponaria. SOAPBARK TREE. Evergreen tree. Zones 8, 9, 14–24. Usually to 25–30 ft.; occasionally to 60 ft. Young plants are dense columns foliaged right down to ground; old trees develop broad, flattened crown. Branchlets are pendulous, especially on younger plants, and general effect of young tree is that of narrow, bushy, weeping live oak. Leaves are 2 in. long, oval to nearly round, rather leathery, shiny green. White flowers are ½ in. across; handsome brown 1-in. fruit open into star form. Tends toward multiple trunks and excessive bushiness but responds quickly to pruning. Younger trees may blow down in strong winds without firm staking and occasional thinning. Fairly tolerant of different soils, and even of drought, once well rooted. Good narrow screening tree. Can be pruned as tall hedge.

Quillaja saponaria

QUINCE, FLOWERING. See *Chaenomeles.*

QUINCE, FRUITING. Deciduous shrub or small tree. All Zones. Slow to 10–25 ft. Unlike flowering quince *(Chaenomeles)* its branches are thornless.

Generally overlooked by planters of flowering fruit trees and home orchard trees, yet the following virtues make common quince worth considering as ornamental. In spring it wears white or pale pink 2-in.-wide flowers at tips of leafed-out branches. Attractive, oval, 2–4-in. leaves, dark green above, whitish beneath, turn

Quince, Fruiting

yellow in fall. Fruit are yellow, fragrant. Its winter form can be dramatic in pattern of gnarled and twisted branches.

Best in heavy well-drained soil but tolerates wet soil. Avoid deep cultivation, which damages shallow roots and causes suckers. Prune only to form trunk and shape frame; thin out and cut back only enough to stimulate new growth. Do not use high-nitrogen fertilizer, as this results in succulent growth which is susceptible to fireblight.

Large, fragrant fruit are inedible when raw but useful in making jams and jellies. Here are some popular varieties (fruit ripen from late September to October);

'Apple' ('Orange'). Old favorite. Round, golden-skinned fruit. Tender orange yellow flesh.

'Cooke's Jumbo'. Very large yellowish green fruit with white flesh. Can be nearly twice size of other quinces.

'Pineapple'. Roundish, light golden fruit. Tender white flesh; pineapplelike flavor.

'Smyrna'. Round to oblong fruit, lemon yellow skin. Strong quince fragrance.

RABBIT TRACKS. See *Maranta leuconeura.*

RADICCHIO. See *Chicory.*

RADISH. You can pull radishes for the table 3 weeks after you sow seed (slowest kinds take 2 months). They need continual moisture and some added nutrients to grow well. Supply nutrients by blending rotted manure into soil before planting, or—about 10 days after planting—feed beside row as for carrots, or feed with liquid fertilizer. Sow seeds in full sun early in spring, as soon as ground can be worked, and at weekly intervals until warm weather approaches. Can be grown in light shade as weather warms. In mild areas, radishes also make fall and winter crop.

Radish

Sow seeds ½ in. deep and thin to 1 in. apart when tops are up. Space rows 12 in. apart. Most familiar kinds are short, round, red or red and white ones like 'Cherry Belle', 'Crimson Giant', and 'Scarlet White-Tipped'. These should be used just as soon as they reach full size. Slightly slower to reach edible size are long white radishes, of which 'Icicle' is best known. Late radishes 'Long Black Spanish' and 'White Chinese' grow 6–10 in. long and can be stored in moist sand in frost free place for winter use.

RANGPUR LIME. See *Citrus.*

RANUNCULUS. Tubers, perennials. A very large group (up to 250 species); the two listed are only ones grown to any extent.

R. asiaticus. PERSIAN RANUNCULUS, TURBAN RANUNCULUS. Tuber. All Zones (tubers lifted and stored after foliage dies down). Flowers are semidouble to fully double, 3–5 in. wide, 1–4 on stalks up to 18 in. or more tall. Blooms in many shades of yellow, orange, red, pink, cream, and white. Large tubers produce many stalks, 50–75 blooms. The most popular strain is Tecolote; it includes colors listed above straight or in mixture, as well as picotee (edged) blends. Bloomingdale is a dwarf (8 to 10 inch) strain. Use in borders with Ice-

Ranunculus asiaticus

land poppies, snapdragons, nemesias. Plant for follow-up color in daffodil beds. Superb cut flowers. Leaves bright fresh green, almost fernlike.

In mild-winter areas, plant tubers in November; in the desert, October. In western Washington, Oregon, plant November or mid-February. Later planting gives later bloom. Need perfect drainage, full sun. Set tubers (prongs downward) 2 in. deep, 6–8 in. apart; plant ½–1 in. deep in heavy soil. Tubers come dry and hard; plump up after absorbing moisture. Water thoroughly after planting; unless weather is very hot and dry, do not water again until sprouts show above ground (10 days–2 weeks). Tubers rot if overwatered before roots form. In warm dry regions, some soak tubers 3–4 hours before planting. Can start tubers in flats of moist sand, plant when sprouted and rooted. To protect young sprouts from birds, cover with netting. After blooms fade, let plants dry out, lift, cut off tops, and store tubers in dry, cool place. Flat-grown seedlings sold in some areas in fall. In coldest climates grow ranunculus in greenhouse, plant after frosts. Early hot spell may shorten bloom period in such areas.

R. repens 'Pleniflorus'. CREEPING BUTTERCUP. Perennial. All Zones. Vigorous plant with thick fibrous roots and runners growing several feet in a season, rooting at joints. Leaves glossy, roundish, deeply cut, toothed. Flowers are fully double, button shaped, bright yellow, about 1 in. across, on stems 1–2 ft. high. Spring bloom. Ground cover in moist soil, filtered or deep shade. Can be invasive in flower beds and lawns.

Single form, *R. repens,* is as aggressive, or more so; under favorable conditions is a major weed.

RAOULIA australis. Perennial. Zones 7–9, 13–24. Carpeting plant. Stems up to 6 in. long form very close mats. Stems are hidden by small gray leaves that overlap them completely. Inconspicuous pale yellow flowers in spring. Useful in dry rockery: needs sandy soil, full sun, moderate water, perfect drainage.

Raoulia australis

RAPHIOLEPIS. Evergreen shrubs. Zones 8–10, 12–24; grown as worthwhile risk in Zones 4–7. These shrubs, with their glossy, leathery leaves, make attractive dense background plantings, large-scale ground covers, low dividers, or informal hedges. And they offer more than constant greenery of most basic landscaping shrubs. From late fall or midwinter to late spring they carry profusion of flowers ranging from white to near red. Dark blue berrylike fruit (not especially showy) follow flowers. New leaves often add to color range with tones of bronze and red.

Raphiolepis indica

Most stay low. With few exceptions the taller kinds rarely get higher than 5–6 ft.; with pruning they can be kept at 3 ft. almost indefinitely. Prune from beginning if you want sturdy, bushy, compact plants; pinch back tips of branches at least once each year, after flowering. For more open structure, let it grow naturally and occasionally thin out branches. Encourage spreading by shortening vertical branches. Pinch side branches to encourage upright growth.

Most kinds are easy to grow in full sun; in light shade they are less compact, bloom less. Raphiolepis stand fairly dry conditions but also tolerate frequent waterings they get when planted near lawn or flower bed. Aphids occasionally attack. Fungus sometimes causes leaf spotting, especially during cold wet weather—to control, destroy infected leaves, spray with fungicide, avoid overhead watering. In desert, plants will burn in reflected heat; need some sheltering shade in Zone 13. Fireblight a problem in some areas.

R. delacouri. Pink-flowered hybrid of *R. indica* and *R. umbellata.* To 6 ft. tall. Small pink flowers in upright clusters, October-May. Leaves smaller than most. Name is often used incorrectly for many different plants.

R. indica. INDIA HAWTHORN. White flowers tinged with pink are about ½ in. across. Leaves pointed, 1½–3 in. long. Plants grow 4–5 ft. high. Grown infrequently but its varieties (below) are widely grown and sold. Varieties differ mainly in color of bloom and size and form of plant. Even plants of same variety may vary. Flower color is especially inconsistent. Flowers in warmer climates and exposures are usually lighter. Bloom is paler in fall than in spring.

R. i. 'Ballerina'. Deep rosy pink flowers. Stays low (not much taller than 2 ft.) and compact (no wider than 4 ft.). Leaves take on reddish tinge in winter.

R. i. 'Bill Evans'. Light pink flowers, larger than most. Plants grow fast and vigorously. Usually to 5–7 ft. high. Upright, open, irregular. Thick, glossy, roundish leaves resemble those of *R. umbellata* more than *R. indica.*

R. i. 'Clara'. White flowers on compact plants 3–5 ft. high, about as wide. Red new growth.

R. i. 'Coates Crimson'. Crimson pink flowers. Compact, spreading plants grow slowly, stay small—2–4 ft. high and as wide. Best in part shade and with regular watering.

R. i. 'Enchantress'. Pink flowers. Faster, more vigorous, and taller than 'Coates Crimson', color not as deep.

R. i. 'Fascination'. Deep rosy pink flowers with white centers. Taller than 'Ballerina' but more compact than most raphiolepis.

R. i. 'Jack Evans'. Bright pink flowers. To about 4 ft. with wider spread. Compact and spreading. Leaves sometimes have purplish tinge.

R. i. 'Pink Cloud'. Pink flowers. Compact growth to 3 ft. high, 3–4 ft. wide. Very similar to *R. i.* 'Springtime'.

R. i. 'Pink Lady'. Deep pink flowers. Vigorous grower 4–5 ft. tall, 4–6 ft. wide. Resembles 'Enchantress'.

R. i. 'Rosea'. PINK INDIA HAWTHORN. This was the first of selected, named seedlings. Very light to medium pink flowers. Slow growth to 3–5 ft. high, 5–6 ft. wide. Growth looser and more graceful than that of most of the stiffer, more compact newer varieties. New growth bronzy.

R. i. 'Rosea Dwarf'. Denser, more compact grower than 'Rosea'; flowers pale pink. Foliage purplish in winter.

R. i. 'Snow White'. White flowers. Growth habit about like 'Jack Evans'. Leaves paler than on most varieties.

R. i. 'Springtime'. Deep pink flowers. Vigorous, upright to 4–6 ft. high.

R. 'Majestic Beauty'. Fragrant light pink flowers in clusters to 10 in. wide. Leaves 4 in. long. Larger in every detail than other raphiolepis; can reach 15 ft. Thought by some to be hybrid between *Raphiolepis* and *Eriobotrya.* Use as background shrub or small tree with single or multiple trunk.

R. umbellata *(R. u. ovata, R. ovata).* Easily distinguished from *R. indica* by its roundish, leathery, dark green leaves, 1–3 in. long. White flowers about ¾ in. wide. Vigorous plants 4–6 ft. tall, sometimes to 10 ft. In full sun, thick and bushy.

RASPBERRY. Shrubs with biennial stems. For ornamental relatives, see *Rubus.* These need slowly warming, lingering springtime to reach perfection. Best in Zones 4–6, 15–17, but can be grown (perhaps with some setbacks or difficulties) anywhere else in West. Loose clusters of white flowers; berries ripen either in summer or in fall.

Raspberry

Most popular and heaviest bearers are red raspberries. These can be grown as free-standing shrubs and staked, but in Northwest (where they grow tall) they are easiest handled tied to wires fastened between two stout posts. Upper wire should be 4 or 5 ft. above the ground, the lower 2½ ft.

Set plants 2½–3 ft. apart in rows 7–9 ft. apart. Well-drained soil is essential. Best production is in full sun; in warmer zones outside of best raspberry climates, satisfactory production may come from plants grown in light shade. Set plants about an inch deeper than they grew originally, and cut back cane that rises from roots, leaving only enough to serve as marker. Plant should produce 3–5 sturdy canes first year; these will bear the next year and should be cut out at ground level after fruiting.

Second year canes will come up all around parent plant and even between hills and rows. Remove all except 8–12 closely spaced, vigorous canes that come up near crown—be sure to pull up all suckers away from crown. Tie selected canes to top wire. In spring before growth begins cut them back to 4½–5½ ft. Fruit-bearing laterals will appear from these canes.

Fall-bearing raspberries differ slightly in pruning needs; these ripen canes earlier in summer and fruit laterals form and bear fruit near top of cane. Cut off upper portion that has borne fruit; lower parts of cane will fruit next spring; cut out cane after it has fruited along its whole length. In mild California climates some growers have had success with handling fall-bearing raspberry canes as annuals. After canes finish fruiting, cut all of them off as close to the ground as possible; use powerful rotary mower in large berry patch. In spring new canes appear to bear new crop. Ease of maintenance helps make up for loss of earliest berries.

Plants need plenty of water, especially during blossoming and fruiting. Feed at blossoming time.

'Bababerry'. Everbearer. Needs little winter chill, stands heat.

'Canby'. Large, bright red berries. Thornless, hardy.

'Cuthbert'. Medium berries of good quality.

'Durham'. Medium-sized, firm berries of good quality. Fall bearing; starts to ripen 2 weeks before 'Indian Summer'

'Fairview'. Variety for coastal Northwest. Bears young and heavily. Early variety of good quality.

'Heritage'. Small red berries are tasty, a bit dry. Bears June and again in September.

'Indian Summer'. Small crops of large, red, tasty berries in late spring and again in fall; fall crop often larger.

'Latham'. Older, very hardy variety for intermountain areas. Late. Berries often crumbly. Mildews in summer-humid regions.

'Meeker'. Large, bright red, firm fruit on long willowy laterals.

'Newberg'. Hardy, late-ripening variety. Large light red berries. Takes heavy soil fairly well.

'Puyallup'. For west of the Cascades. Large soft berries with very good flavor. Midseason.

'Ranere' ('St Regis'). Everbearing. Long bearing season, from midspring to frost in California. Berries small, bright red. Needs steady irrigation for long bearing.

'September'. Medium to small berries of good flavor. A few fruit in June, good crop in fall.

'Sumner'. Hardy, with some resistance to root rot in heavy soils. Fine fruit. Early.

'New Washington'. Smallish fruit of high quality. Hardy, but needs well-drained soil.

'Willamette'. Large, firm dark red berries which hold color and shape well.

Tasty novelty is 'Golden West', with yellow berries of excellent quality.

RASPBERRY, BLACK or BLACKCAP. Shrub with biennial stems. For ornamental relatives, see *Rubus*. Best Zones 4–6; fails to thrive in California. Resembles regular red raspberry in many ways (see illustration for Raspberry), but blue black fruit is firmer, seedier, and has more distinct flavor. Plants differ from red raspberries in not suckering from roots; new plants form when arching cane tips root in soil. Plant in good garden soil in sun to light shade, give regular summer water for best crop. You need no trellis. Head back new canes at 18–24 in. to force laterals. At end of growing season, cut out all weak canes (under ½ in.; if all are small leave best two), and remove canes that fruited during current season. In late winter or early spring, cut back laterals to 10–15 in. on strong canes, 3–4 in. on weak ones. Fruit is produced on sideshoots from these laterals. If you prefer trellising, head new canes at 2–3 ft.

Varieties usually sold are 'Cumberland', an old variety; 'Morrison', large berry on productive vine; and 'Munger', most popular commercial variety. 'Sodus', purple raspberry, is hybrid between red and black raspberry. Vigorous variety; head new canes at 30–36 in.

RATTAN PALM. See *Rhapis humilis*.

RATTLESNAKE GRASS. See *Briza maxima*.

REDBERRY. See *Rhamnus crocea*.

REDBUD. See *Cercis*.

RED-CAP GUM. See *Eucalyptus erythrocorys*.

RED CHOKEBERRY. See *Aronia arbutifolia*.

RED CLUSTERBERRY. See *Cotoneaster lacteus*.

RED-FLOWERED MALLEE. See *Eucalyptus erythronema*.

RED FLOWERING GUM. See *Eucalyptus ficifolia*.

RED GUM, RIVER RED GUM. See *Eucalyptus camaldulensis*.

RED-HOT POKER. See *Kniphofia uvaria*.

RED HUCKLEBERRY. See *Vaccinium parvifolium*.

RED IRONBARK. See *Eucalyptus sideroxylon*.

REDONDO CREEPER. See *Lampranthus filicaulis*.

RED RIBBONS. See *Clarkia concinna*.

RED SPIKE ICE PLANT. See *Cephalophyllum* 'Red Spike'.

RED-SPOTTED GUM. See *Eucalyptus maculosa*.

REDTOP. See *Agrostis gigantea*.

RED VALERIAN. See *Centranthus ruber*.

REDWOOD, COAST REDWOOD. See *Sequoia sempervirens*.

REDWOOD SORREL. See *Oxalis oregana*.

REHMANNIA elata *(R. angulata)*. Perennial. Zones 7–10, 12–24. Impressive thing about this plant is that it blooms in sun or shade from mid-April to November. Flower stalks rise to 2–3 ft., loosely set with 3-in.-long, tubular flowers that look something like big gaping foxgloves. Common form is rose purple with yellow, red-dotted throat; there is fine white and cream form that must be grown from cuttings or division. Coarse, deeply toothed leaves. Spreads by underground roots and forms big evergreen clumps where winters are mild. Deciduous where winters are colder. Easy to grow; main requirements are rich soil, ample water, some shade. Handsome, long-lasting cut flowers.

Rehmannia elata

REINWARDTIA indica *(R. trigyna)*. YELLOW FLAX. Perennial. Zones 8–10, 12–24. Grows shrublike to 3–4 ft., has alternate leaves. Brilliant yellow, 2-in. flowers form in great profusion at an unusual season: in late fall and early winter. Blooms do not last long, but for weeks new ones open daily.

Sun or part shade. Pinch to make more compact. Spreads by underground roots. Increase by rooted stems; divide in spring. Good choice for winter color in flower garden or with shrubs.

Reinwardtia indica

RESEDA odorata. MIGNONETTE. Summer annual. To 12–18 in. tall; rather sprawling habit. Light green leaves. Not particularly beautiful plant, but well worth growing because of remarkable flower fragrance. Dense spikes of bloom become loose and open as blossoms mature. Small greenish flowers tinged with copper or yellow. Flowers dry up quickly in hot weather.

Sow seed in early spring—or late fall or winter in Zones 15–24. Successive sowings give long bloom period. Best in rich soil with regular watering. Sun in cool sections, part shade inland. Plant in masses to get full effect of fragrance, or spot a few in flower bed. Suitable for pots. There are other forms with longer flower spikes and brighter colors, but they are less fragrant.

Reseda odorata

RETINISPORA pisifera. See *Chamaecyparis pisifera*.

RHAMNUS. Evergreen or deciduous shrubs or trees. Small flowers in clusters are rather inconspicuous; plants are grown for form and foliage, occasionally for show of berrylike fruit.

R. alaternus. ITALIAN BUCKTHORN. Evergreen shrub. Zones 4–24. Fast, dense growth to 12–20 ft. or more, spreading as

Rhamnus californica

wide. Close planting or pruning will keep it narrow. Easily trained as multistemmed or single-stemmed small tree. Leaves oval to oblong, bright shiny green, ¾–2 in. long. April flowers tiny, greenish yellow. Fruit black, ¼ in. long.

Rhamnus californica

Easily sheared or shaped. Takes drought, heat, wind, as well as regular watering. Grows in full sun or part shade. Valuable as fast screen or tall clipped hedge. Trained to single stem, makes good plant for tall screen above 6-ft. fence. *R. a.* 'John Edwards' is cutting-grown and thus uniform in size, shape. *R. a.* 'Variegata' (*R. a.* 'Argenteo-variegata') has leaves edged with creamy white; striking against dark background. Cut out plain green branches that occasionally appear.

R. californica. COFFEEBERRY. Evergreen shrub. Zones 4–24. Native to southwest Oregon, California, Arizona, New Mexico. Low and spreading or upright, 3–15 ft. tall. Leaves 1–3 in. long, shining dark green above to dull green above (depending on variety), paler beneath (in some forms gray hairy beneath). Large berries green, then red, then black when ripe. Near ocean, plants tend to be broad, spreading; taller in woodland or in hills. 'Eve Case', a dense, compact form propagated from cuttings, grows 4–8 ft. tall, with equal spread. Selected coastal form, *R. c.* 'Seaview', can be kept to 18 in. high, 6–8 ft. wide if upright growth is pinched out. Both 'Eve Case' and 'Seaview' have foliage that is distinctly broader, flatter, brighter green than the species. Coffeeberries grow in full sun to half shade; not particular as to soil. Drought tolerant, but the two broader-leafed varieties look better with some summer water.

R. cathartica. COMMON BUCKTHORN. Deciduous. Zones 1–3. Big shrub or tree to 15–20 ft. Leaves bright glossy green, 1–2½ in. long by half as wide, turning yellow before falling off in autumn. Short twigs often spine tipped. Fruit are black, ¼ in. thick. Useful hedge or small tree in coldest, driest areas. Tolerates drought, poor soil, wind.

R. crocea. REDBERRY. Evergreen shrub. Zones 14–21. Native to Coast Ranges, Lake County to San Diego County, California. To 2–3 ft. high and spreading, with many stiff or spiny branches. Leaves roundish, ½ in. long, glossy dark to pale green above, golden or brownish beneath, often finely toothed. Small bright red fruit August-October. Full sun to part shade; best with some shade inland from its native territory. Less drought tolerant than its holly-leaf form (following).

R. c. ilicifolia. HOLLY-LEAF REDBERRY. Evergreen shrub. Zones 7–16, 18–21. Native to Coast Ranges and Sierra Nevada foothills, mountains of southern California, Arizona, Baja California. Multistemmed, or often treelike, 3–15 ft. Leaves roundish, ½–1¼ in. long, spiny toothed. Good ornamental plant for dry banks or informal screen in hot-sun areas. Drought resistant.

R. frangula. ALDER BUCKTHORN. Deciduous shrub or small tree. Zones 1–7, 10–13. To 15–18 ft. tall. Leaves roundish, 1–3 in. long, half as wide. Fruit turns from red to black on ripening. Sun to part shade; established plants need only moderate summer watering. *R. f.* 'Columnaris', TALLHEDGE BUCKTHORN, grows 12–15 ft. tall, 4 ft. wide. Set 2½ ft. apart for tight, narrow hedge that needs minimum of trimming and can be kept as low as 4 ft.

R. purshiana. CASCARA SAGRADA. Deciduous shrub or small tree. Zones 1–9, 14–17. Native from northern California to British Columbia and Montana. To 20–40 ft., with smooth gray or brownish bark. Leaves elliptical, prominently veined, dark green, 1½–8 in. long, to 2 in. wide, usually somewhat tufted at ends of branches. Foliage turns good yellow in fall. Round black fruit attract birds. Will grow in dense shade or full sun with ample water. Picturesque branching pattern. Bark has medicinal value.

RHAPHIDOPHORA aurea. See *Epipremnum aureum.*

RHAPIDOPHYLLUM hystrix. NEEDLE PALM. Zones 7–9, 12–24. Hardy, slow-growing fan palm from southeastern U. S. Upright or creeping stems 5 ft. high. Rounded leaves, 3–4 ft. across, dark green above, silvery

Rhapidophyllum hystrix

beneath. Well provided with strong black spines. Makes impenetrable hedge. Hardy to 10°F. Tolerates damp soil.

RHAPIS. LADY PALM. Fan palms which form bamboolike clumps with deep green foliage. Trunks covered with net of dark, fibrous leaf sheaths. Slow-growing, choice, expensive.

R. excelsa. LADY PALM. Zones 12–17, 19–24. Small, slow, 5–12 ft. tall, often much lower. Best in shade, but will take considerable sun near the beach. Must have shade, shelter from heat and cold, in Zones 12–14. Well-drained soil. One of the finest container palms; resists poor light, dust, and drought, but responds quickly to better light and fertilizer. Hardy to 20°F.

Rhapis excelsa

R. humilis. RATTAN PALM, SLENDER LADY PALM. Zones 16, 17, 20–24. Tall, bamboolike stems (to 18 ft.) give charming, graceful, tropical air. Larger, longer leafed than *R. excelsa,* less tolerant of sun and wind. Hardy to 22°F.

RHIPSALIDOPSIS gaertneri (*Schlumbergera gaertneri*). EASTER CACTUS. House plant; lathhouse or covered terrace plant in Zones 16, 17, 21–24. For culture and general description, see *Schlumbergera.* Much like *S. bridgesii* but plant more upright (has same drooping branches), joints of stems are not as flat. Flowers to 3 in. long, bright red, upright or horizontal rather than drooping. Blooms April, May, often again in September. There are many varieties in shades of pink and red.

Rhipsalidopsis gaertneri

RHODODENDRON (including azalea). Evergreen or deciduous shrubs, rarely trees. Very large group, of approximately 800 species. There are over 10,000 named varieties in the International Register, of which perhaps 2,000 are currently available. Botanists have arranged species into series and subseries: one of these series includes plants called azaleas.

The climate adaptation pattern of azaleas is very different from that of rhododendrons. For example, evergreen azaleas are planted by the hundreds of thousands in southern California, where rhododendrons are far less frequent and require more special attention.

Rhododendron 'Pink Pearl'

The West's finest rhododendron climates are found in Zones 4–6, 15–17. However, gardeners in every climate of the West—except deserts and areas of coldest winters—can find ways to grow certain varieties. Even some adventuresome desert gardeners have succeeded with container-grown plants.

Basic soil and water requirements of rhododendrons and azaleas are much the same. They require acid soil. They need more air in root zone than any other garden plants but at the same time, they need constant moisture supply. In other words, they need soil that drains rapidly and at the same time retains moisture. Soils rich in organic matter have those qualities. If your soil lacks those qualities, add liberal quantities of organic matter such as peat moss, ground bark, sawdust, or leaf mold.

If your garden soil is clay or alkaline, planting in raised beds is simplest way to give these plants conditions they need. Make beds 12–24 in. above soil level. Liberally mix organic materials into top 12 in. of soil beneath raised bed, then fill bed with mixture of 50% organic material (at least half peat moss), 30% soil, 20% sand. This mixture will be well aerated but moisture retentive and will permit alkaline salts to leach through.

Plant azaleas and rhododendrons with top of root ball slightly above soil level. Never allow soil to wash in and bury stems.

Plants are surface rooters and benefit from mulch. Good mulch materials are pine needles, oak leaves, and wood byproducts such as redwood and fir bark or chips. Never cultivate soil around these plants.

Sun tolerance of azaleas and rhododendrons differs by species and varieties. Most can take full sun in cool-summer areas. Ideal location is filtered shade of tall trees. East and north side of house and fence are next best. Too dense shade makes lanky, sparse-blooming plants.

Fertilize when growth starts in spring, at bloom time or immediately afterward, and repeat monthly until August. Use commercial acid fertilizer and follow directions carefully; to be extra safe, cut portions in half and feed twice as often.

Both azaleas and rhododendrons need special attention where soil or water is high in dissolved salts—as in many areas in California. To avoid damage, plant in containers or raised beds and periodically leach the mix by heavy watering—enough to drain through mix 2 or 3 times. If leaves turn yellow while veins remain green, plants have iron deficiency called chlorosis; apply iron chelate to soil or spray with iron solution.

Insects and diseases are seldom much of a problem. Root weevil larvae feed on roots. Adult weevils notch leaves but damage usually is minor. You can prevent larvae from developing in soil by applying diazinon, orthene, or sevin to soil and working it in to depth of 6 in. at planting time. Or you can kill adults as they emerge from soil in April through May. Use poison bait or spray plant and soil with orthene and repeat every 2 weeks until there is no sign of leaf feeding. In western Oregon the obscure root weevil (gray in color) is part of the root weevil group; control with malathion.

Poor drainage can result in root rot, which shows in yellowing, wilting, and collapse of plants. Too much sun causes bleaching or burning in leaf centers. Wind and soil salts burn leaf edges; windburn shows up most often on new foliage, saltburn on older leaves. Late frosts often cause deformed leaves.

Prune evergreen azaleas by frequent pinching of tip growth from after flowering to August if you wish a compact plant with maximum flower production.

Prune large-flowered rhododendrons early in spring at bloom time if needed. Early spring pruning will sacrifice some flower buds but is the best time for extensive pruning. Plant's energies will be diverted to dormant growth buds, which will then be ready to push out early in the growing season. Tip-pinch young plants to make them bushy; prune older, leggy plants to restore shape by cutting back to side branch, leaf whorl, or to cluster of dormant buds. (Some varieties will not push new growth from dormant buds.) Prune off faded flower heads or break off spent flower trusses; take care not to injure new growth buds just beneath truss.

KINDS OF RHODODENDRONS

Most people know rhododendrons as big, leathery-leafed shrubs with stunning, rounded clusters of white, pink, red, or purple blossoms. But there are other rhododendrons—dwarfs a few inches high; giants to 40, even 80 ft. in their native southeast Asia; and a host of species and hybrids in every size between, in a color range that includes scarlet, yellow, near-blue, and a constellation of blends in the orange-apricot-salmon range.

Listed here are a number of the most generally available kinds.

Heights given are for plants 10 years old; older plants may be taller, and crowded or heavily shaded plants may reach up faster. Bloom seasons are approximate and vary with weather and location.

Ratings for plant quality should be regarded as judgments that may change as a plant is tested more thoroughly by rhododendron specialists who establish the ratings. Furthermore, one rating cannot blanket performance of plant in a dozen different climates.

The list includes only a portion of the best species and hybrids grown in the West.

To give some idea of the great variety of experiences to be had with rhododendrons, we have brought together a few classifications from the alphabetical list of species and hybrids that follows.

There are a number of "ironclad" hardy hybrids that surprisingly do well in southern California: 'Cunningham's White', 'Fastuosum Flore Pleno', 'Gomer Waterer', 'Madame Mason', 'Mars', and 'Scarlet King'.

California specials—rhododendrons too tender for Northwest gardens. Many of them fragrant: R. burmanicum, 'Countess of Haddington', 'Countess of Sefton', 'Forsterianum', 'Fragrantissimum', 'Saffron Queen'.

Good performers in California, rated low in Northwest: 'Anah Kruschke', 'Antoon Van Welie', 'Rainbow', 'Sappho', 'Unknown Warrior', 'Van Nes Sensation'.

For outdoor planting in California's frost free and nearly frostless zones (17, 23, 24) are the Malesian rhododendrons from tropics of southeast Asia. These also are fine container plants (even indoors) so they can be grown in colder zones if brought inside for duration of winter. Typically, plants flower on and off throughout the year rather than in one blooming season. Waxy-textured flowers in loose clusters are in exciting shades of yellow, gold, orange, vermilion, salmon, pink. Species, named hybrids, and unnamed seedlings are offered by some specialty growers. Among the most widely available are: R. brookeanum, R. javanicum, R. konori, R. laetum, R. lochae, R. macgregorae, 'Golden Gate', 'George Budgen', 'Pink Delight', 'Valentine'.

Highly regarded, dependable, popular, easy to grow, widely adapted: 'Anna Rose Whitney', 'Betty Wormald', 'Britannia', 'Countess of Derby' ('Eureka Maid'), 'Crest', 'David', 'Jan Dekens', 'Loder's White', 'Mrs. E. C. Stirling', 'Mrs. G. W. Leak' ('Cottage Gardens Pride'), 'Pink Pearl', 'Purple Splendour', 'The Hon. Jean Marie de Montague'.

From their general appearance you could call them azaleas. Low-growing rhododendron species, hybrids of great charm: R. chryseum, R. impeditum, R. intricatum, R. keiskei, R. moupinense, R. pemakoense, 'Blue Bird', 'Blue Tit', 'Blue Diamond', 'Ocean Lake', and 'Sapphire'.

Dwarfs and low growers with distinctive foliage and bell shaped or funnel shaped flowers, not in typical trusses: 'Bow Bells', 'Bric-a-Brac', 'Cilpinense', 'Racil', 'Snow Lady'.

RHODODENDRON RATINGS & HARDINESS

We have followed the American Rhododendron Society's system for rating plants for quality and hardiness.

Quality is expressed this way: 3/3. Flower quality is listed first, shrub quality second; 5 is superior, 4 above average, 3 average, 2 below average, 1 poor. A 5/5 rating is near perfection.

Hardiness rating indicates minimum temperatures a well-matured plant can take without serious injury.

'A. Bedford'. 4/3. –5°F. Lavender blue, darker flare, large trusses. To 6 ft. Late May.

'Alice'. 3/4. –5°F. Deep pink, fading to pale rose. Reliable, easy to grow. Flowers good for cutting. To about 6 ft. April and May.

'Anah Kruschke'. 2/3. –10°F. Lavender purple. Color not the best, but plant has good foliage, tolerates heat, not fussy about soil. To 5 ft. May.

'Anna Rose Whitney'. 4/3. +5°F. Big, rich, deep pink trusses on compact, 5-ft. plant with excellent foliage. May.

'Antoon Van Welie'. 3/3. –5°F. Carmine pink. Big trusses of 'Pink Pearl' type on 6-ft. plant. Late May.

R. augustinii. 4/3. +5°F. Open, moderate growth to 6 ft. Leaves to 3 in. long. Flowers 2–2½ in. wide in clusters of 3–4, blue or purple in best named forms. May.

'Beauty of Littleworth'. 4/3. –5°F. Tall, vigorous plant. Bears light pink buds, white flowers in conical trusses. Young plants are slow to reach blooming age.

'Betty Wormald'. 4/3. –5°F. Carmine pink, darker markings on upper petals. Tall trusses. Informal growth to 6 ft. April, May.

'Blue Diamond'. 5/4. 0°F. Compact, erect growth to 3 ft. Small leaves; lavender blue flowers cover plant in April. Takes considerable sun in Northwest.

(Continued on next page)

'Blue Peter'. 4/3. −10°F. Broad, sprawling growth to 4 ft.; needs pruning. Large trusses of lavender blue flowers blotched purple. May.

'Blue Tit'. 4/4. 0°F. To 2–3 ft. Small leaves on dense twiggy plant. Flowers lighter than 'Blue Diamond', near true blue.

'Bow Bells'. 3/4. 0°F. Compact, rounded growth to 4 ft. Leaves rounded. Flowers bright pink, bell shaped, in loose clusters. May. New growth bronzy.

'Bric-a-Brac'. 4/4. +5°F. Low, compact grower to 3 ft. with greater spread. New growth dark red; leaves small. Flowers in pairs, pure white with chocolate anthers. Splendid for massing, containers. Protect March flowers from late frost.

'Britannia'. 4/4. −5°F. Bright red, ruffled flowers in large, rounded truss. May. Slow-growing, rounded shrub to 4 ft. Beautiful foliage yellows in too much sun.

'Broughtonii Aureum'. 3/2. 0°F. Azalea-rhododendron hybrid of loose, willowy growth to 4 ft. Foliage dull green. Soft yellow flowers blotched orange in rounded trusses. Has shown good heat, sun resistance in California. Late May.

'Burgundy'. 4/3. −5°F. Name describes color. Medium height, compact plant.

R. calophytum. 4/4. −5°F. Small stocky tree, to 4 ft. Noted for big leaves—4 in. wide, 10–14 in. long. Trusses of white or pink flowers with deep blotch. Protect from wind. March and April.

'Carita'. 4/4. +5°F. Large, pale primrose yellow, 12–13 flowers in truss. Late April. Outstanding flowers and foliage, but latter yellows badly in sun.

'Christmas Cheer'. 2/4. −5°F. Pink to white in tight truss. Can take full sun. To 3 ft. Early bloom (February-March) compensates for any lack in flower quality.

R. chryseum. 2/2. −15°F. Dwarf (1 ft.) densely branched plant with 1-in. leaves. Flowers are small, bright yellow bells, 4–5 in cluster. April to May.

'Cilpinense'. 4/4. +5°F. Funnel shaped flowers of apple blossom pink fading white; loose clusters nearly cover plants in March. Low, spreading growth to 2½ ft.; small leaves. Easy to grow. Effective massed. Protect blossoms from late frosts.

'CIS'. 4/2. +10°F. Flowers (in large trusses) are red in throat to cream yellow at edges of flower. To 3 ft. May.

'Conemaugh'. 4/3. −15°F. Dainty, lavender pink flowers in miniature trusses. Light, airy, open. To 3 ft. March.

'Cornubia'. 4/3. +15°F. Strong, upright growth to 7 ft. Blood red flowers in large clusters February-March.

'Cotton Candy'. 4/4. 0°F. Large flowers in soft pink shades carried in tall trusses. Dark green foliage on medium height plant.

'Countess of Derby' ('Eureka Maid'). 4/3. −5°F. Rose pink, with deeper blotch. Easy, vigorous grower to 5 ft. Resembles 'Pink Pearl'. May.

'Countess of Haddington'. 4/4. +20°F. Light pink to white, waxy, tubular, fragrant flowers in compact trusses. To 5 ft. May.

'Countess of Sefton'. 3/3. +20°F. Large, tubular, fragrant, white flowers in loose truss. Not as rangy as 'Fragrantissimum'. To 4 ft. Late April.

'Crest'. 5/3. −5°F. Primrose yellow. Outstanding. To 5 ft. April, May.

'Cunningham's White'. 2/3. −15°F. White with greenish yellow blotch. Hardy old-timer. Late May.

'Cynthia'. 3/3. −10°F. Rosy crimson trusses in May. Dependable, strong grower to 6 ft.

'David'. 4/3. +5°F. Blood red trusses in May. Compact growth to 5 ft.

'Dora Amateis'. 4/4. −15°F. Semidwarf, rather small-foliaged plant; compact, spreading, good for foreground. Profuse bloomer with green-spotted white flowers.

'Elizabeth'. 4/4. 0°F. Several forms available. Broad grower to 3 ft. tall with middle-sized leaves. Blooms very young. Bright red, waxy, trumpet shaped flowers in clusters of 3–6 at branch ends and in upper leaf joints. Main show in April; often reflowers in October. Very susceptible to fertilizer burn, salts in water.

'Elizabeth H. Hobbie'. 4/4. −10°F. Spreading dwarf plants have especially attractive shiny leaves; small trusses contain brilliant red, bell shaped blossoms. Fine foreground, rock garden plant.

'Else Frye'. 5/3. +15°F. Long, limber growth makes this a natural for informal espalier. Considerable pinching needed for compact plant. Early season flowers are white with pink flush and gold throats.

'Evening Glow'. 4/3. 0°F. One of the relatively small group of good yellow-flowered rhododendrons. Loose trusses carry bright yellow blossoms in May. Foliage is light green. Best in light shade.

Fabia. 3/3. +10°F. Group of hybrids with 6–8 nodding flowers to a truss. Early May. Low, spreading growth; 4 ft. 'Tangerine' has vermilion orange flowers; 'Roman Pottery' terra cotta; 'Exbury' pale apricot tinted pink (not to be confused with Exbury hybrid azaleas).

R. falconeri. 3/3. +5°F. One of the unusual tree rhododendrons (others not listed here). To 25 ft. high and wide. Leathery leaves 6–12 in. long, reddish felted beneath. Creamy white to pale yellow flowers, 2 in. wide in clusters. Blooms when 15–20 years old.

'Fastuosum Flore Pleno'. 3/3. −10°F. Double mauve flowers in May. Dependable, hardy old-timer. To 5 ft.

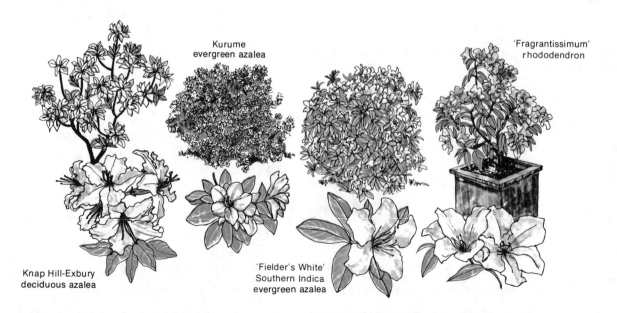

Kurume
evergreen azalea

'Fragrantissimum'
rhododendron

Knap Hill-Exbury
deciduous azalea

'Fielder's White'
Southern Indica
evergreen azalea

All are rhododendrons, though the three at left are usually called azaleas; deciduous or evergreen, all require acid soil.

R. forrestii repens. 3/3. +5°F. Low, spreading dwarf. To 6 in. Tubular, bright red flowers in small clusters. April-May. Not easy to grow. Needs perfect drainage.

'Forsterianum'. 5/4. +20°F. Tubular, frilled, fragrant white flowers tinted pink. March bloom; buds often damaged by frost in colder areas without overhead protection. Open, rangy growth to 5 ft. Attractive glossy, red brown, peeling bark and medium-scale, glossy foliage.

'Fragrantissimum'. 4/3. +20°F. Large, funnel shaped white flowers touched with pink, April-May. Powerfully fragrant. Loose, open, rangy growth with medium-sized, bright green, bristly leaves. With hard pinching in youth, a 5-ft. shrub. Easily trained as espalier or vine, reaching to 10 ft. or more. Can spill over wall. Grow as container plant in Northwest; overwinter indoors in bright but cool room.

'Gomer Waterer'. 3/4. −15°F. White flushed lilac. Hardy old-timer. To 5 ft. Late May.

R. impeditum. 2/3. −10°F. Twiggy, dwarf, dense shrub to 1 ft. with closely packed, tiny, gray green leaves. Small flowers mauve to dark blue, April or May. Takes full sun in cooler areas. Needs *excellent* drainage to avoid root rot.

R. intricatum. 2/3. −15°F. Compact, upright to 3 ft. Mauve to lilac blue. April, May.

'Jan Dekens'. 2/3. 0°F. Big, high trusses of rich pink, frilled flowers in May. Excellent habit and foliage. To 6 ft.

'Janet Blair'. 4/3. −15°F. Ruffled pastel flowers blend pink, cream, white and gold; large blossoms come in rounded trusses. Vigorous, tall and spreading.

'Jean Marie de Montague'. See 'The Hon. Jean Marie de Montague'.

R. keiskei. 2/1. −5°F. At least two forms are available. The very dwarf, very compact form makes 6-in.-high shrublet. Taller form will reach 3 ft., and is more open in growth. Both forms produce lovely lemon yellow bells in great profusion, 3–5 in a cluster. March-May.

'Leo'. 5/3. −5°F. Rounded to dome shaped trusses are packed with rich cranberry red blooms. Medium height plant is well clothed in large dark green leaves.

'Letty Edwards'. 3/3. 0°F. Pale yellow with greenish tinge. One of older yellows. Several forms—one with pinkish tinge, another sulfur yellow. Sets buds as youngster. Foliage does not yellow in sun. To 5 ft. Mid-May.

Loderi. 5/4. 0°F. Spectacular group of hybrids with tall trusses of 6–7-in.-wide flowers in shades of pink or white. Fragrant; early May bloom. Informal, open growth to 8 ft. Too large for small garden. Slow to reach blooming age and not easy to grow. Difficult to maintain good foliage color. Best known are 'King George', with white flowers opening from blush buds; 'Pink Diamond', with blush flowers; and 'Venus', with shell pink flowers.

'Loder's White'. 5/5. 0°F. Big trusses of flowers open white tinged pink and mature pure white. May. Shapely growth to 5 ft. Blooms freely even when young. Best white for most regions.

'Lord Roberts'. 3/3. −10°F. Handsome dark green foliage and rounded trusses of black-spotted red flowers. Growth is more compact, flowers more profuse in sun.

R. macrophyllum (*R. californicum*). COAST RHODODENDRON, WESTERN RHODODENDRON. Unrated. +5°F. Native near coast northern California to British Columbia. Rangy growth 4–10 ft. or to 20 ft. in some locations. Leaves dark green, leathery, 2½–6 in. long; flower trusses rosy, rose purple, rarely white. May-June. Rarely sold; in Northwest, collect only with a permit.

'Madame Mason' ('Madame Masson'). 3/3. −5°F. White with light yellow flare on upper petal. Needs pruning to keep it compact. To 5 ft. Late May.

'Mars'. 4/3. −10°F. Dark red. Outstanding in form, foliage, flowers. To 4 ft. Late May.

'Moonstone'. 4/4. −5°F. Flaring bells age from pale pink to creamy yellow in April. Attractive dense, dwarf growth to 2 ft. Leaves neat, small, rounded. Fine facing taller rhododendrons, as low foundation planting with 'Bow Bells'.

R. moupinense. 4/2. 0°F. Open, spreading. To 1½ ft. Small (1½ in. long), oval leaves. White or pink flowers, spotted red. New spring foliage deep red. February to March.

'Mrs. Betty Robertson'. 3/3. +5°F. Pale yellow, large truss.

May. Low, compact grower to 3 ft. Good foliage, does not burn in sun.

'Mrs. Charles E. Pearson'. 4/4. −5°F. Bluish mauve blotched orange brown; fades to light pink. Big trusses. May.

'Mrs. E. C. Stirling'. 4/4. −5°F. Opens blush pink, becomes light pink. May. Easy to grow. Vigorous growth to 5 ft.

'Mrs. Furnival'. 5/5. −10°F. Clear pink flowers with light brown blotch in upper petals, in tight, round trusses. Late May. Compact growth to 4 ft.

'Mrs. G. W. Leak' ('Cottage Gardens Pride'). 4/4. +5°F. Deep pink, deep brown flare on upper petals. Strong growth to 5 ft. May.

R. mucronulatum. 4/3. −25°F. Deciduous rhododendron with open growth to 5 ft. Makes up for bare branches by flowering in January-February. Flowers generally bright purple; there is pink form, 'Cornell Pink'.

Naomi. 4/4. −10°F. Group of top-notch hybrids with trusses of fragrant 4–5-in. flowers in May. Bloom younger than Loderi hybrids; lower, more compact, hardier. To 4–5 ft., and leggy unless carefully pruned while young. 'Exbury' (rosy pink blended with yellow); 'Nautilus' (pale pink, frilled, centered with creamy yellow and veined rose); and 'Stella Maris' (pink and yellow) are three best known in this outstanding group. Take it easy with fertilizers.

'Ocean Lake'. 3/3. −5°F. Low azalealike plant with flowers of deep violet.

R. pemakoense. 2/3. 0°F. Compact, spreading. To 1½ ft. Tiny (1½ in. long) leaves. Flowers pinkish purple, very free blooming. Useful in rock gardens. March-April.

'Pink Pearl'. 3/3. −5°F. Rose pink, tall trusses in May. To 6 ft. and more. Open, rangy growth without pruning. Dependable grower and bloomer in all except coldest climates.

'Praecox'. 3/3. −5°F. Small, rounded leaves cover compact and upright plant up to 4 ft. tall. Trusses of lavender pink flowers early in season.

'Purple Splendour'. 4/3. −10°F. Ruffled, rich deep purple blotched black purple. Informal growth to 4 ft. Hardy and easy to grow. May.

R. racemosum. 3/3. −10°F. Several forms include 6-in. dwarf, 2½-ft. compact upright shrub, and tall 7-footer. Pink inch-wide flowers in clusters of 3–6 all along stems in March-April. Easy; sun tolerant in cooler areas.

'Racil'. 3/2. −5°F. Shell pink, funnel shaped flowers in open clusters. Most useful. To 2 ft. April.

'Radium'. 4/3. +5°F. Medium height plant produces loose trusses of brilliant red flowers in late May.

'Rainbow'. 1/2. 0°F. Light pink center, carmine edges. Very showy. Heavy foliage. Strong growth to 5 ft. April bloom.

'Rosamundi'. 2/3. −5°F. Ball-like trusses of pink flowers appear in early season. Plant is slow, compact, to 4 ft. high and wide.

'Rose Elf'. 4/5. 0°F. Dwarf, spreading plant for foreground, rock garden. Very heavy production of blush pink, nodding flowers. Small dark leaves turn bronzy in full sun.

'Saffron Queen'. 4/3. +20°F. Sulfur yellow, darker spots on upper petals. April bloom. Flowers, trusses, foliage smaller than 'Pink Pearl' type. To 3 ft.

'Sapphire'. 4/4. 0°F. Bright blue, small azalealike flowers in March, April. Twiggy, rounded, dense shrublet to 1½ ft. Foliage gray green, leaves tiny.

'Sappho'. 3/2. −5°F. White, dark purple spot in throat. May. Easy to grow, gangly without pruning. Use it back of border.

Scarlet King. Group of hybrids. Too recent for rating. +20°F. These New Zealand hybrids thrive in warm-winter conditions, yet perform well in average rhododendron situations. Habit of growth varies. Free flowering. Rich red flowers late April-May.

'Scarlet Wonder'. 5/5. −10°F. Outstanding dwarf (to 2 ft.) of compact growth. Shiny, quilted foliage forms backdrop for many bright red blossoms.

'Scintillation'. 4/5. −10°F. Medium height, compact plant covered in lustrous, dark green leaves. Rounded trusses carry gold-throated pink flowers.

'Snow Lady'. 4/4. 0°F. White, black stamens. Wide, fragrant, flat flowers in clusters. To 3 ft. April.

'Susan'. 3/4. −5°F. Silvery lavender flowers in large trusses.

(Continued on next page)

May. Handsome foliage. To 4 ft.

'The Hon. Jean Marie de Montague'. 3/4. 0°F. Brightest scarlet red in May. Good foliage. To 5 ft.

'Trilby'. 3/4. –10°F. Dark red flowers are accented by nearly black center spots and are complemented by olive to gray green leaves. Compact, upright plant of medium height.

'Unique'. 3/5. +5°F. Apricot buds open to deep cream, fade to light yellow; trusses tight, rounded. April, early May. Outstanding neat, rounded, compact habit. To 4 ft.

'Unknown Warrior'. 3/2. +5°F. Light soft red, fades quickly when exposed to bright sun. Easy to grow. To 4 ft. April.

'Van Nes Sensation'. 3/4. 0°F. Pale lilac flowers in large trusses. Strong grower. To 5 ft. May.

'Vulcan'. 3/4. –5°F. Bright brick red flowers in late May, early June. New leaves often grow past flower buds, partially hiding flowers. To 4 ft.

R. yakusimanum. 4/4. –20°F. Clear pink bells changing to white, about 12 in truss. Late May. Dense, spreading growth to 3 ft. New foliage gray felted; older leaves with heavy tan or white felt beneath. Hybrids of this plant perform well in Rocky Mountain gardens.

KINDS OF EVERGREEN AZALEAS

The evergreen azaleas sold in the West fall into 12 groups and one species. In many cases the group to which a variety belongs indicates kind of growth and flowering that you can expect, hardiness, and amount of sun plants can take. But group characteristics are rather elastic. Here are the groups, zones in which they perform best, and descriptions of groups' characteristics.

Belgian Indica. Zones 14–24. This is a group of hybrids originally developed for greenhouse forcing. Where lowest temperatures are 20°–30°F, many of them serve very well as landscape plants. Their foliage is lush and full. Large flowers open in profusion during their flowering season. Among most widely sold are 'Albert and Elizabeth' (white and pink), 'California Sunset' (white and pink), 'Chimes' (dark red), 'Fred Sanders' (salmon pink), 'Mme. Alfred Sanders' (cherry red), 'Orange Sanders' (salmon orange), 'Orchidiflora' (orchid pink), 'Paul Schame' (salmon), and 'Red Poppy'. 'Violetta' (deep purple) and 'William Van Orange' (orange red) have pendant growth suitable for hanging baskets.

Brooks hybrids. Zones 8, 9, 14–24. Bred in Modesto, California, for heat resistance, compactness, and large flowers. Best-known are 'Flamingo' (red), 'Madonna' (white), 'Red Cap', and 'Red Wing'.

Gable hybrids. Zones 4–9, 14–24. Developed to produce azaleas of Kurume type that would take 0°F. temperatures. In Zones 4–6, they may lose some leaves but they bloom heavily from late April through May. Frequently sold are 'Caroline Gable' (bright pink), 'Herbert' (purple), 'Louise Gable' (pink), 'Pioneer' (pink), 'Purple Splendor', 'Purple Splendor Compacta' (less rangy growth), 'Rosebud' (pink), and 'Rose Greeley' (white).

Glenn Dale hybrids. Zones 4–9, 14–24. Developed primarily for hardiness. But they do drop some leaves in cold winters. Some grow tall and rangy, others low and compact. They vary from rapid to slow-growing. Some have small leaves like Kurumes; others have large leaves. Familiar varieties are 'Anchorite' (orange), 'Aphrodite' (pale pink), 'Buccaneer' (orange red), 'Everest' (white), 'Geisha' (white, striped red), and 'Glacier' (white).

Gold Cup hybrids. Zones 14–24. Originally called Mossholder-Bristow hybrids. Plants combine large flowers of Belgian Indicas with vigor of Rutherfordianas. Good landscape plants where temperatures don't go below 20°F. Some popular varieties are 'Easter Parade' (pink and white), 'Sun Valley' (white), and 'White Orchid' (white with red throat).

Kaempferi hybrids. Zones 2–7. Based on *R. kaempferi,* the torch azalea, a hardy group with orange red flowers. Somewhat hardier than Kurumes, taller and more open in growth. Nearly leafless in coldest winters. Hardy to –15°F. Flowers cover plants in early spring. Similar in every way to Vuykiana hybrids. Among those sold are 'Fedora' (salmon rose), 'John Cairns' (orange red), and 'Palestrina' (white).

Kurume. Zones 4–9, 14–24. Compact, twiggy plants, densely foliaged with small leaves. Small flowers borne in incredible profusion. Plants mounded or tiered, handsome even out of bloom. Hardy to 5°–10°F. Grow well outdoors in half sun. Many varieties available, most widespread of which are 'Bridesmaid' (salmon), 'Coral Bells' (pink), 'Hexe' (crimson), 'Hino-crimson' (bright red), 'Hinodegiri' (cerise red), 'Sherwood Orchid' (red violet), 'Sherwood Red' (orange red), 'Snow', 'Vivid' (scarlet), and 'Ward's Ruby' (dark red).

Macrantha. Zones 4–9, 14–24. Includes azaleas sometimes referred to as Gumpo, Chugai, and Satsuki hybrids. Hardy to 5°F. Plants low growing; some true dwarfs—many are pendant enough for hanging baskets. Large flowers late, often in June. Popular varieties are 'Bunkwa' (blush pink), 'Flame Creeper' (orange red), 'Gumpo' (white), 'Gumpo Pink' (rose pink), 'Hi Gasa' (bright pink), 'Rosaeflora' (rose pink), 'Shinnyo-No-Tsuki' (violet red, white center).

Pericat. Zones 4–9, 14–24. Hybrids originally developed for greenhouse forcing, but as hardy as Kurumes. Similar to Kurumes but flowers tend to be somewhat larger. Varieties sold are 'Mme. Pericat' (light pink), 'Sweetheart Supreme' (blush pink), and 'Twenty Grand' (rose pink).

Rutherfordiana. Zones 15–24. Greenhouse plants, good in garden where temperatures don't go below 20°F. Bushy 2-4-ft. plants with handsome foliage. Flowers intermediate between Kurume and Belgian Indica. Available varieties include 'Alaska' (white), 'Constance' (light orchid pink), 'Dorothy Gish' (brick red), 'Firelight' (rose red), 'L. J. Bobbink' (orchid pink), 'Purity' (white), 'Rose Queen' (deep pink), and 'White Gish' (pure white).

Southern Indica. Zones 8, 9, 14–24. Varieties selected from Belgian Indicas for sun tolerance and vigor. Most take temperatures of 10°–20°F., but some are damaged at 20°F. Generally speaking, they grow faster, more vigorously, and taller than the other kinds. Many varieties are sold, among which are these popular ones: 'Brilliant' (carmine red), 'Duc de Rohan' (salmon pink), 'Elegans Superba' (watermelon pink, sometimes sold as 'Pride of Mobile'), 'Fielder's White', 'Formosa' (brilliant rose purple, also sold as 'Coccinea', 'Phoenicia', 'Vanessa'), 'George Lindley Taber' (light pink), 'Glory of Sunninghill' (orange red), 'Imperial Countess' (deep salmon pink), 'Imperial Princess' (rich pink), 'Imperial Queen' (pink), 'Iveryana' (white with orchid streaks), 'Orange Pride' (bright orange), 'Pride of Dorking' (brilliant red), 'Prince of Wales' (rose red), 'Southern Charm' (watermelon pink, sometimes sold as 'Judge Solomon'), and 'White April'.

Vuykiana hybrids. See description of Kaempferi hybrids above. Varieties sold are 'Blue Danube' (violet blue), 'Vuyk's Rosy Red', and 'Vuyk's Scarlet'.

R. mucronatum ('Indica Alba', 'Ledifolia Alba'). Zones 4–9, 14–24. Spreading growth to 6 ft. (but usually 3 ft.); large, hairy leaves. White or greenish flowers 2½–3 in. across March-April. Variety 'Sekidera' ('Indica Rosea', 'Ledifolia Rosea') has white flowers flushed and blotched rose, February, March.

KINDS OF DECIDUOUS AZALEAS

Very few deciduous shrubs can equal deciduous azaleas in show and range of color. Their evergreen relatives can't match them in yellow, orange, and flame red range or in bicolor contrasts. They are at their best in Zones 4–7, 15–17. Also perform well in coastal valley Zone 14 (even in full sun) if well watered. Deciduous types tend to be less particular about soil, watering than most evergreen sorts. Fall foliage color an added bonus: often brilliant orange red to maroon.

Ghent hybrids. Extremely hardy. Many will take –25°F. temperatures. Upright growth variable in height. Flowers generally smaller than those of Mollis hybrids. Color ranges in shades of yellow, orange, umber, pink, and red. May flowering.

Knap Hill-Exbury hybrids. Plants vary from spreading to upright, from 4–6 ft. tall. Flowers are large (3–5 in. across), in clusters of 7–18, sometimes ruffled or fragrant, white through pink and yellow to orange and red, often with contrasting blotches. Wide petals give squarish look to flowers.

Both Knap Hill and Exbury azaleas come from same original crosses; first crosses were made at Knap Hill, and subsequent improvements were made at both Exbury and Knap Hill. The ''Rothschild'' azaleas are Exbury plants. Ilam hybrids are from same original stock, further improved in New Zealand.

A hundred or more named varieties are available in Northwest and northern California. If you want to be sure of color and size of flower of plant you buy, choose from named varieties. But don't consider all seedlings as inferior plants. Generally it's best to select seedlings in bloom.

Mollis hybrids. Hybrids of *R. molle* and *R. japonicum*. Upright growth 4–5 ft. Similar to *R. molle* but with larger (2½–4 in.) flowers in clusters of 7–13. Colors range from chrome yellow through poppy red. Good fall foliage color. Bloom in May.

Occidentale hybrids. Hybrids between *R. occidentale* and Mollis hybrids. Flowers same size as Mollis hybrids; plants taller, to 8 ft. Colors range from white flushed rose and blotched yellow to red with orange blotch.

Viscosum hybrids. Hybrids between Mollis azaleas and *R. viscosum*. Deciduous shrubs with color range of Mollis but with added fragrance from *R. viscosum*.

R. calendulaceum. FLAME AZALEA. Hardy to −10°F. Native to mountains of eastern U.S. Variable growth 4–10 ft. tall. Tubular, flaring flowers in clusters of 5–25. Colors range from gold and orange to scarlet. May-June bloom.

R. japonicum. JAPANESE AZALEA. Hardy to −10°F. Upright, fast growth to 6 ft. Flowers, 2–3 in., in clusters of 6–12, in salmon red, orange, and orange red. Variety *aureum* has rich yellow flowers. Blooms in May.

R. luteum (*R. flavum*). PONTIC AZALEA. Tall growing to 8 ft. Flowers are single yellow with darker blotch; fragrant. Blooms in May.

R. molle. CHINESE AZALEA. Hardy to −10°F. Erect grower to 6 ft. April flowers 2½ in. wide in clusters of 6–10, yellow to golden orange. Foliage turns yellow to orange in late fall.

R. occidentale. WESTERN AZALEA. Hardy to −5°F. Zones 4–24. Native to mountains and foothills of California and Oregon. Erect growth to 6–10 ft. Funnel shaped flowers in clusters May-June. Color varies from white to pinkish white with yellow blotch; some are heavily marked carmine rose. Fragrant.

R. prinophyllum (*R. roseum, R. nudiflorum*). Hardy to −25°F. Up to 12 ft. Clove-scented flowers are clear deep pink to violet red, sometimes paler, usually blotched with darker brown red; tubular, funnel shaped, in trusses of 5–9, about 1¾ in. across. Blooms in May.

R. quinquefolium. Hardy to 0°F. Shrub or small tree up to 25 ft., usually smaller. Flowers, in trusses of 1–3, up to 2 in. wide, pure white with green spots. Blooms April-May. Very attractive foliage, especially in fall color.

R. schlippenbachii. ROYAL AZALEA. Hardy to −20°F. Native to Korea. Densely branched shrub to 6–8 ft. Leaves in whorls of 5 at tips of branches. Large (2–4 in.), pure light pink flowers in clusters of 3–6. April-May. There's no pink to compare with it. Good fall color—yellow, orange, scarlet, crimson. Protect from full sun to avoid leaf burn.

R. vaseyi. PINKSHELL AZALEA. Hardy to −20°F. Upright, irregular, spreading to 15 ft. Pink, almost white flowers in clusters of 5–8 in May.

R. viscosum. Hardy to −25°F. Up to 15 ft. Fragrant, sticky, white flowers, occasionally with some pink in them; in clusters of 4–12, about 1½ in. across. June-July.

RHOEO spathacea (*R. discolor*). MOSES-IN-THE-CRADLE, MOSES-IN-THE-BOAT. Perennial. Outdoor plant in Zones 16, 17, 20–24; sheltered spots in Zones 12–15, 18, 19. House plant everywhere. Stems to 8 in. high. Leaf tufts grow to 6–12 in. wide, with dozen or so broad, sword shaped, rather erect leaves which are dark green above and deep purple underneath. Flowers are interesting rather than beautiful. Small, white, 3-petaled, they are crowded into boat shaped bracts borne down among leaves. Best used as pot plant or in hanging

Rhoeo spathacea

basket. Tough plant which will take high or low light intensity and casual watering, low humidity and heat on a desert patio. Avoid overwatering, keep water out of leaf axils. Variety 'Variegata' has leaves striped red and yellowish green.

RHOICISSUS capensis (*Cissus capensis*). EVERGREEN GRAPE. Evergreen vine with tuberous roots. Outdoors in Zones 16, 17, 21–24; house plant anywhere. Leaves roundish to kidney shaped, scallop toothed, something like true grape in size and appearance. New growth (stem and leaf) rosy rusty with red hairs, mature leaves strong light green tinged coppery, rusty hairy beneath. Flowers insignificant. Takes full sun outdoors but roots need shade, moisture. Will take heavy shade as house plant. Good overhead screen or ground cover in milder regions. Slow-growing.

Rhoicissus capensis

RHOPALOSTYLIS. Zones 17, 23, 24. Feather palms with clean, long trunks. Moderate growth rate. Need shade and ample water; do best in frost free gardens. Rare.

R. baueri. From Norfolk Island. Grows to 50 ft.; beautiful curving, arching leaves 6–9 ft. long.

R. sapida. NIKAU PALM. From New Zealand. Grows to 30 ft. Good pot plant where small space dictates upright palm. On outdoor plants, feathers 4–8 ft. long stand upright from prominent bulge at top of clean, long trunk. (Often called shaving brush palm.)

Rhopalostylis sapida

RHUBARB. Grows best in Zones 1–11, grown also in 14–24. Unconventional vegetable. It is used, as fruit is, in sauces and pies. And, its delicious leaf stalks bear poisonous leaves; always discard leaves when preparing rhubarb. A perennial, it grows from large fleshy rhizomes. Treated as annual in Zones 10, 11; set out in fall for winter, spring harvest—plant rots in heat of late spring, early summer. Big, elongated, heart shaped, crinkled leaves and red-tinted leaf stalks are showy enough to qualify for display spot in garden. Flowers are insignificant, in spikelike clusters. Preferred varieties are 'Victoria' (greenish stalks), 'Cherry' ('Crimson Cherry'), 'MacDonald', and 'Strawberry' (red stalks).

Rhubarb

Plant in late winter or early spring. Divisions should contain at least one bud. Soil should be deep, rich, and well drained. Place tops of divisions at soil line. Space divisions 3–4 ft. apart. Give plants some shade in hot inland gardens. Irrigate freely when active top growth indicates that roots are growing. Permit plants to grow two full seasons before harvesting. During next spring you can pull off leaf stalks (to cook) for 4 or 5 weeks; older, huskier plants will take up to 8 weeks of pulling. Harvest stalks by grasping near base and pulling sideways and outward; cutting with knife will leave stub that will decay. Never remove all leaves from a single plant. Stop harvesting when slender leaf stalks appear. After harvest, feed and water freely. Cut out any blossom stalks that appear.

RHUS. SUMAC. Evergreen or deciduous shrubs or trees. Of the ornamental sumacs, deciduous kinds are hardy anywhere and thrive in poor soils. They tend to produce suckers, expecially if their roots are disturbed by soil cultivation. They need some water. Evergreen sumacs will grow in almost any soil, but they need good drainage; soggy soils may kill them. Evergreen types are fire resistant if fairly well watered. They are not as hardy as deciduous kinds.

Rhus typhina

Rhus includes poison oak and poison ivy, both of which may cause severe dermatitis on contact; even breathing smoke from burning plants is harmful. If you have either on your property, it's best to destroy plants with chemical brush killer.

Poison oak (*R. diversiloba*) is most common in California, western Oregon, and western Washington. In the open or in filtered sun, it grows as dense leafy shrub. Where shaded, as in coast redwood country, it becomes tall-climbing vine. Its leaves are divided into 3 leaflets, edges of which are scalloped, toothed, or lobed. Very similar is poison ivy (*R. radicans*) which grows in eastern Oregon, eastern Washington (and eastward), but it's more sprawling in growth habit and rarely climbs. Foliage of both turns bright orange or scarlet in the fall—beautiful but to be avoided. It's hardest to identify bare branches in winter and early spring; even brushing against these can cause typical rash.

R. aromatica. FRAGRANT SUMAC. Deciduous shrub. Zones 1–3, 10. Fast growing, 3–5 ft. tall, spreading much wider. Leaves divided into 3 leaflets, fragrant when brushed against or crushed. Tiny yellowish flowers in spring. Chief use: coarse bank cover, ground cover for poor, dry soils. Red fall color. Two available varieties are 'Low Grow' (to about 2 ft.) and 'Green Mound' (to 4 ft. tall).

R. choriophylla. Evergreen shrub. Zones 10–13. Native to New Mexico, Arizona, northern Mexico. To 6 ft. Leaves divided into 5–9 leaflets 2 in. long. Well adapted to cultivated desert gardens; less touchy about summer water than *R. ovata* and a good substitute for *R. integrifolia*. *R. virens* is similar but with smaller leaflets (to 1½ in. long).

R. cotinus. See *Cotinus coggygria*.

R. glabra. SMOOTH SUMAC. Deciduous large shrub or small tree. Zones 1–10, 14–17. Native to eastern Oregon, eastern Washington, British Columbia, and eastward in North America. Upright to 10 ft., or sometimes treelike to 20 ft. In the wilds spreads by underground roots to form large patches. Very similar in appearance to staghorn sumac (*R. typhina*), but it usually grows lower and its branches are not velvety.

Leaves are divided into 11–23 rather narrow, 2–5-in.-long toothed leaflets, deep green above, whitish beneath; turn brilliant scarlet in fall. Inconspicuous greenish flowers followed by showy autumn display of scarlet fruit in conical clusters which last on bare branches well into winter. Very drought and heat tolerant. Garden use same as staghorn sumac. *R. g. cismontana*, dwarf variety that grows in Rocky Mountains, is 3–4 ft. tall, has smaller leaves with fewer leaflets. *R. g.* 'Laciniata' has deeply cut and slashed leaflets giving fernlike appearance.

R. integrifolia. LEMONADE BERRY. Evergreen shrub. Zones 15–17, 20–24. Native to coastal southern California, Channel Islands, and Baja California. Generally 3–10 ft. high and as wide, rarely treelike to 30 ft. Oval to nearly round, leathery dark green leaves, 1–2½ in. long, with smooth or shallowly toothed edges. White or pinkish flowers in dense clusters February-March, sometimes January-July. Small flat, clustered fruit, reddish, gummy, with acid pulp which can be used to flavor drinks—hence common name.

Set plants out in fall or winter. Although drought resistant, they thrive best if watered deeply once a month during summer months. Will also take normal garden watering if drainage is good. Grows best near coast. Very susceptible to verticillium wilt wherever it is present. Makes wonderful ground cover on rocky slopes exposed to salt laden winds; one plant eventually sprawls over wide area, even down cliffs. In less windy places, use it as tall screen or background. Makes excellent espalier against fences and walls. Can be trimmed to dense formal hedge and kept only 10 in. wide. Useful in erosion control.

R. lancea. AFRICAN SUMAC. Evergreen tree. Zones 8, 9, 12–24. Slow-growing to 25 ft. with open spreading habit, graceful weeping outer branchlets. Leaves divided into 3 willowlike, dark green leaflets 4–5 in. long. Pea-sized, yellow or red berrylike fruit grow in clusters on female tree, can be messy on pavement.

Popular tree in desert areas because it can take high summer heat. Established plants are drought resistant, but will also thrive in lawns. Hardy to 12°F. Stake and prune to establish form you want. Makes attractive airy tree with interesting branch pattern and effective dark red, rough bark. You can train it to single trunk or let it grow as multitrunked tree looking somewhat like olive. Also useful for screens, clipped hedges, or background

plantings. Old plants easy to transplant if grown under dry conditions. Susceptible to Texas root rot in Zones 12 (especially) and 13.

R. laurina. LAUREL SUMAC. Evergreen shrub. Zones 20–24. Native mostly to coastal foothills of southern California and Baja California. Grows rapidly to 6–15 ft.; sometimes almost treelike, with rounded crown. Gets rangy unless pruned and trimmed. Attractive reddish branchlets. Laurel-like leaves, 2–4 in. long, light green, often with pink margins and pink leaf stalks; foliage pleasantly aromatic. Small whitish flowers in dense, branched clusters 2–6 in. long; bloom May-July, sometimes to December. White berrylike fruit attracts birds. More tender to frost than native sugar bush or lemonade berry. Sometimes freezes in its native range but comes back quickly from stump. Very drought tolerant. Useful as espalier plant or as clipped hedge. Good bank cover where frost is rare. Aids in erosion control.

R. ovata. SUGAR BUSH. Evergreen shrub. Zones 7–24. Native to dry slopes away from coast in southern California, Baja California, Arizona. Upright or spreading shrub 2½–10 ft. high. Glossy leathery leaves, 1½–3 in. long, differ from *R. integrifolia* in being somewhat trough shaped and with pointed tip instead of rounded. White or pinkish flowers in dense clusters, March-May; followed by small, reddish, hairy fruit coated with sugary secretion. Culture and use same as lemonade berry and can substitute for same in inland areas. Can be used along coast but not where exposed to salt spray and sea winds. In desert, plant in fall or winter; hard to establish in hot weather. Very heat and drought tolerant.

R. trilobata. SQUAWBUSH, SKUNKBUSH. Deciduous shrub. Zones 1–3, 10. Similar in most details to *R. aromatica*, but scent of bruised leaves considered unpleasant by most people. Clumping habit makes it a natural low hedge. Brilliant yellow to red fall color. Very tolerant of heat and drought.

R. typhina. STAGHORN SUMAC. Deciduous shrub or small tree. Zones 1–10, 14–17. Upright growing from 15 to sometimes 30 ft., spreading wider. Very similar to *R. glabra*, except branches are covered with velvety short brown hairs, like deer's antler "in velvet." Leaves divided into 11–31, 5-in.-long, toothed leaflets deep green above, grayish beneath; they turn rich red in fall. Tiny greenish flowers in 4–8-in.-long clusters in June-July are followed by clusters of fuzzy crimson fruit which last all winter, gradually turn brown. *R. t.* 'Laciniata' is variety with deeply cut leaflets. It doesn't grow quite as big as species, and is said to have richer color in fall.

Both staghorn sumac and smooth sumac take extreme heat and cold and will grow in any except most alkaline soils. Big divided leaves give tropical effect; when they turn color, show is brilliant. Bare branches make fine winter silhouette, fruit are decorative. Good among evergreens that show off bright fall foliage color. You can also grow them in large containers.

R. virens. See *R. choriophylla*.

RHYNCHOSPERMUM. See *Trachelospermum*.

RIBBON BUSH. See *Homalocladium platycladum*.

RIBES. CURRANT, GOOSEBERRY. (See these entries for fruiting currants and gooseberries.) Deciduous and evergreen shrubs. Those without spines are called currants; those with, gooseberries. Number of native species are ornamental; four are sold in nurseries. Flowers, fruit attract birds.

Ribes sanguineum

R. alpinum. ALPINE CURRANT. Deciduous shrub. Zones 1–3, 10. Spineless shrub 4–5 ft. tall (rarely taller) of dense twiggy growth. Roundish toothed and lobed leaves ½–1½ in. across appear very early in spring. Flowers and fruit inconspicuous. Good hedge plant. Sun or shade, average water.

R. aureum. GOLDEN CURRANT. Deciduous shrub. All Zones. Native to inland regions of West. Erect growth, 3–6 ft. tall with light green, lobed, toothed leaves. Clusters of small, bright yellow, spicily fragrant (usually) flowers are 1–2½ in. long. Spring bloom. Summer berries are yellow to red to black. Plant in full sun to part shade. Prefers moderate summer watering.

R. laurifolium. Evergreen shrub. Zones 4–6, 14–17. To 4–6 ft. tall, spreading. Leaves leathery, toothed, to 5 in. long, 2½ in. wide. Flowers, in earliest spring, are unshowy greenish yellow but form in elegant drooping clusters to 2½ in. long. Grows in part shade, needs some summer water.

R. sanguineum. PINK WINTER CURRANT, RED FLOWERING CURRANT. Deciduous shrub. Zones 4–9, 14–24. Native California to British Columbia in Coast Ranges. To 4–12 ft. tall. Leaves are 2½ in. wide, maplelike. Flowers, March-June, are deep pink to red, small, 10–30 in 2–4-in. drooping clusters. Berries blue black, with whitish bloom. Variety *glutinosum* (more southerly in origin) is commonest in nurseries; it has 15–40 flowers to cluster, generally deep or pale pink. 'Elk River Red', occasionally sold in Northwest, has rich red flowers. 'King Edward VII' is lower-growing variety with red flowers. Plant in sun to light shade. Fairly drought tolerant, but best with moderate water, some shade where summer is hot and dry.

R. speciosum. FUCHSIA-FLOWERING GOOSEBERRY. Nearly evergreen shrub. Zones 8, 9, 14–24. Native near coast from Santa Clara County south to Baja California. Erect, 3–6 ft. tall with spiny, often bristly stems. Thick green 1-in. leaves resemble those of fruiting gooseberry. Deep crimson to cherry red drooping flowers are fuchsialike, with long protruding stamens. January-May bloom. Berries gummy, bristly. Excellent barrier planting. Sun near coast, light shade inland. With a little summer water is nearly evergreen, otherwise is deciduous summer through fall. Tolerates much drought and heat when established, but loses leaves in summer.

Ribes speciosum

R. viburnifolium. CATALINA PERFUME, EVERGREEN CURRANT. Spreading evergreen shrub. Zones 8, 9, 14–24. Native to Catalina Island, Baja California. Low-growing plant. To 3 ft. tall and much wider (to 12 ft.). Low-arching or half-trailing wine red stems may root in moist soil. Leaves leathery, roundish, dark green, inch across, fragrant (some say like pine, others like apples) after rain or when crushed. Flowers light pink to purplish, February-April. Berries red. Ground or bank cover for sun or half shade on coast, part shade inland. Useful in erosion control. Foliage yellows in hot sun. Spider mites sometimes a problem in coastal areas. Drought tolerant when established. Excellent ground cover under native oaks where heavy watering is undesirable. Cut out upright-growing stems to keep low.

RICE PAPER PLANT. See *Tetrapanax papyriferus*.

RICINUS communis. CASTOR BEAN. Summer annual. Bold and striking shrublike plant. Can provide tall screen or leafy background in a hurry; grows to 6–15 ft. in a season with full sun, plenty of heat and moisture. Where winters are mild, will live over and become quite woody and treelike. Has naturalized in small areas in many climates.

Should not be planted in area where small children play—large, mottled, attractive, shiny seeds are poisonous. Also, foliage or seeds occasionally cause severe contact allergies.

Ricinus communis

Large lobed leaves are 1–3 ft. across on vigorous young plants, smaller on older plants. Small white unimpressive flowers are borne in clusters on foot-high stalks, followed by attractive prickly husks which contain seeds. Grown commercially for castor oil extracted from seeds. Many horticultural varieties: 'Zanzibarensis' has very large green leaves; 'Dwarf Red Spire' is lower-growing (to 6 ft.) plant with red leaves and seed pods.

RIVER RED GUM. See *Eucalyptus camaldulensis*.

ROBINIA. LOCUST. Deciduous trees or shrubs. All Zones. Leaves divided like feathers into many roundish leaflets; clusters of white or pink sweet pea shaped flowers midspring to early summer. They are hardy everywhere, fairly fast growing, and well adapted to dry hot regions. Will take poor soil, much drought when established. Drawbacks: wood is brittle, roots aggressive, plants often spread by suckers.

R. ambigua. Name given to hybrids between black locust and *R. viscosa*—seldom-grown pink flowering locust. Best known varieties are:

R. a. 'Decaisneana'. To 40–50 ft. tall, 20 ft. wide. Flowers like black locust, but pale pink.

Robinia pseudoacacia

R. a. 'Idahoensis'. IDAHO LOCUST. Deciduous tree of moderately fast growth to shapely 40 ft. Flowers bright magenta rose in 8-in. clusters; one of showiest of locusts in bloom. Good flowering tree for Rocky Mountain gardens.

R. hispida. ROSE ACACIA. Deciduous shrub. Spreading, suckering habit, usually 6–8 ft. high. Branches and leaf stalks with bright red bristles. Leaves 6–10 in. long, with 7–13, oval to round, dark green leaflets 1½–2½ in. long and half as wide. Flowers are deep rose, 1¼ in. long, in clusters 2–3 in. long and as wide with 5–10 flowers. Pods very rarely produced.

R. h. macrophylla. Better known than species. Nearly free of bristles; large, more brightly colored flowers; rounder leaflets. Often grafted on 6 or 8-ft. black locust trunks to produce small round-headed standard tree 12–15 ft. tall, equally broad. Such trees need stout stakes until well-established.

R. pseudoacacia. BLACK LOCUST. Deciduous tree. Fast growth to 75 ft., with rather open, sparse-branching habit. Deeply furrowed brown bark. Thorny branchlets. Leaves divided into 7–19 leaflets 1–2 in. long. Flowers white, fragrant, ½-¾ in. long, in dense hanging clusters 4–8 in. long. Beanlike, 4-in.-long pods turn brown and hang on tree all winter.

Emigrants brought seeds with them from eastern U. S. and black locust is now common everywhere in West. In California's Gold Country it has gone native. Very drought tolerant. With pruning and training in its early years, is truly handsome flowering tree, but so common, and so commonly neglected, that it's often overlooked.

Has been used as street tree, but not good in narrow parking strips or under power lines. Wood is extremely hard, tough; trees difficult to prune out where not wanted.

R. p. 'Frisia'. Leaves yellow; new growth nearly orange. Thorns, new wood red.

R. p. 'Pyramidalis' ('Fastigiata'). Very narrow, columnar tree.

R. p. 'Tortuosa'. Slow growing, with twisted branches. Clusters few flowered.

R. p. 'Umbraculifera'. Dense, round headed. Usually grafted 6–8 ft. high on another locust. Very few flowers.

R. 'Purple Robe'. Resembles Idaho locust but has darker, purple pink flowers, reddish bronze new growth, blooms 2 weeks earlier and over a longer period.

ROCHEA coccinea (*Crassula coccinea*). Succulent. Outdoors in Zones 17, 23, 24; greenhouse plant anywhere. From South Africa. Shrubby well-branched plant 1–2 ft. Leaves closely set on stems, 1–1½ in. long by half as wide. Flowers once a year in late spring or summer. Bright scarlet blooms are 2 in. long, fragrant, in flat clusters at tops of stems.

In greenhouse, give plants rich, porous soil. Keep cool, in bright light, and on dryish side until January; then increase warmth, water. In mild-winter-area gardens, root cuttings in late spring or very early summer; grow rooted plants in porous, peaty soil with feeding. Plants will flower following summer.

Rochea coccinea

ROCKCRESS. See *Arabis.*

ROCK JASMINE. See *Androsace.*

ROCK SPIRAEA. See *Holodiscus dumosus.*

ROCKROSE. See *Cistus.*

ROCKY MOUNTAIN THIMBLEBERRY. See *Rubus deliciosus.*

ROHDEA japonica. Perennial. Zones 4–9, 14–24. Grown for its dense clumps of evergreen foliage. Leaves broadly strap shaped, usually arched and recurving, dark green, to 2 ft. long and 3 in. wide. Cream-colored flowers in thick short spike among leaves followed by short dense cluster of red berries. Spreads slowly by thick rhizomes; old plants have many foliage clumps.

Rohdea japonica

Grow it in shade outdoors; or pot it up as house plant. Tough and sturdy. Needs average water. Many varieties with crested and variegated leaves are collector's items in Japan. Some are available from specialists here.

ROMAN WORMWOOD. See *Artemisia pontica.*

ROMNEYA coulteri. MATILIJA POPPY. Perennial. Zones 5–10, 12–24. Native to southern California and Mexico. Spectacular plant growing to 8 ft. or more. Stems and deeply cut 3–4-in. leaves are gray green. Flowers up to 9 in. wide, with 5 or 6 white, crepe paperlike petals surrounding round cluster of golden stamens. Fragrant. Bloom June-July. Flowers handsome in arrangements; if cut in bud, will open in water, last for a few days.

Romneya coulteri

Use on hillsides as soil binder, along roadsides and in marginal areas, in wide borders. Invasive, spreading by underground roots; don't place near less vigorous plants. Needs full sun. Tolerates varying amounts of water, varying soil types—including loose gravelly soil, little water. Withhold summer irrigation to keep growth in check. Cut nearly to ground in early fall. New shoots emerge after first rains. May be propagated from root cuttings in fall. In Zones 12, 13 set out new plants in fall; spring plantings often rot in high summer temperatures.

RONDELETIA. Evergreen shrubs. Borderline in Zones 8, 9, 18; reasonably safe in Zones 14–17, 19–24. Tubular flowers in clusters are brightly colored, sometimes fragrant. Best in slightly acid soil in part shade (sun along coast). Feed and water generously. Prune when young to make compact. Remove old spent flowers. Shelter from hard frosts. Rare.

Rondeletia cordata

R. amoena. Medium to fast growth to 6–8 (possibly 15) ft. Glossy golden green to dark red green, 5-in., oval leaves. New growth bronzy. Clustered flowers light salmon pink, yellow in throat. Late winter, spring, and intermittently later on.

R. cordata. Similar to *R. amoena,* but with shining green smooth leaves. Flowers near red in bud, open to become salmon pink in February-March, often into June.

ROSA. ROSE. Deciduous, bushy or climbing shrubs (a few are evergreen in mildest zones). Undoubtedly the best-loved and most widely planted of shrubs in the West, and in all other temperate parts of world. Even though the most popular kinds are not completely hardy in colder zones, they will survive cold winters with some protection and perform year after year.

To grow roses well is not difficult, but to be successful you must follow certain guidelines.

1. Select varieties suited to your climate.
2. Buy best plants available (No. 1 grade is tops).
3. Locate and plant them properly.
4. Attend to their basic needs: water, nutrients, any necessary pest and disease control, and pruning.
5. In Zones 1–3 provide some sort of winter protection.

Hybrid Tea rose 'Seashell'

Climate

The American Rose Society rates modern roses by a scale of 1–10. The higher the rating, the better is the rose based on national average of scores. Highest-rated roses generally will perform well in most climates and would be good choices for novice grower. Lower-rated roses, however, may do especially well in certain regions and fail in others. Rating, therefore, does not always tell the entire story. The following general tips will guide your selection based on rose's description.

In cool-summer areas, you should, if possible, avoid varieties having unusually great number of petals; many of these tend to "ball" (open poorly or not at all). Many varieties with deep color tones tend to appear "muddy" in cool summers; pastel colors seldom appear off-color or unattractive. Choose varieties noted as being disease resistant and plant them in open areas where air circulation is good. Watch for foliage diseases—primarily mildew, rust, and black spot—and use appropriate fungicide sprays if any appear.

In hot-summer areas, rose plants grow vigorously, but hot sun causes flowers to open quickly, fade, and sometimes sunburn. There, best flowering is in spring and fall (sometimes winter, too) with plants going nearly dormant in summer. Varieties with few petals (under 30) are usually disappointing in hottest weather, when they can go from bud to flat-open bloom in several hours; fuller-petalled flowers open more slowly and last longer. In such areas any rose flowers will last longer if plants are located to receive midday or afternoon shade in summer. Also avoid planting roses where they will receive reflected heat from light-colored walls—especially in south or west exposures.

In cold-winter areas (for roses this is Zones 1–3), most modern roses will not survive winter low temperatures. You will need to give plants some sort of winter protection. Certain old roses, species, and modern shrub roses will endure winter freezing in coldest zones without sustaining much damage.

In any region, most certain guide to best roses is nearby municipal or private rose garden. Whatever varieties you see performing well in your area are safest choices for planting in your garden.

Buying Plants

All roses are available as bare-root plants from late fall through early spring. In Zones 4–24, they may be planted throughout winter, but in coldest regions (Zones 1–3) you plant in fall or spring—before ground freezes or after it has thawed. Bare-root plants are always the best buy, and they are graded according to strict standards: No. 1, 1½, and 2. Grades 1 and 1½ are most satisfactory, in that order; Number 2 plants, if they live, may develop into decent bushes, but it will take them several years longer than huskier Number 1 and 1½ plants. Reputable retail nurseries and specialist rose growers who sell by mail through catalogues offer Number 1 plants and often will replace plants that fail to grow. Frequently you will find packaged bare-root roses sold at attractive prices in supermarkets and department stores. These can be good buys if you purchase as soon as plants appear for sale, but the longer you wait the more the plants are enticed into premature growth or are dried out under high storage temperatures in market or store. Be prepared, too, for a number of these bargain roses to be mislabeled.

If you wish to plant roses during their growing season, you can buy (at greater cost than bare-root) roses growing in containers.

That way you get a chance to see bloom on an unfamiliar rose variety before you decide to buy. And, you are assured that the plant has put on healthy root and top growth following its bare-root transplanting. Look for plants growing in large containers (5 gallon is best), as that is a guarantee that minimum amount of root system was cut off to fit in container. Also try to buy only roses that were planted in containers toward the end of most recent dormant season; they will be in generally better condition than will plants that have been container grown for a year or more. Avoid plants that show considerable dead or twiggy growth. Container-grown roses may be planted in a garden any time after rooting is sufficiently advanced to hold soil ball together—usually 3 months after having been planted in containers.

The advent of molded paper containers has added a new wrinkle to planting of container-grown roses: you can plant the pot without having to disturb the rose. Cut or tear holes in the sides and bottom of paper pot so roots can easily grow into garden soil. Then dig a hole and plant the container with rose, making sure plant is at proper depth as described under bare-root planting. Within a year, planted pot will have decomposed.

The presence of a plant patent number on a variety's tag is no assurance of quality. It simply means that for variety's first seventeen years, patent holder receives a royalty on each sale. Many are excellent roses, and many without patents are also excellent. Quite a number of the latter at one time had patents that have now expired.

Location and Planting

For best results, plant roses where they will receive full sun all day (exceptions noted under "Climate"). Avoid planting where roots of trees or shrubs will steal water and nutrients intended for roses. To lessen any problem with foliage diseases, plant roses where air circulates freely (but not in path of regular, heavy winds). Generous spacing between plants will also aid air circulation. How far apart to plant varies according to growth habit of roses and according to climate. The colder the winter and shorter the growing season, the smaller will be bushes; where growing season is long and winters are mild, there is hardly a time when roses will not be able to grow—so bushes can attain greater size. But some varieties naturally make small plants while others will become tall and massive, and those relative size differences will hold in any climate. In coldest zones you might plant most vigorous sorts 3 ft. apart, whereas in milder zones same roses might require 6-ft. spacing.

Soil for roses should drain reasonably well; if it does not, best alternative is to plant in raised beds. Dig soil deeply, incorporating organic matter such as ground bark, peat moss, compost; this preparation will help aerate dense clay soils and will improve moisture retention of sandy soils. Add complete fertilizer to soil at same time, and dig supplemental phosphorus and potash into planting holes: this gets nutrients down to where roots can use them.

Healthy, ready-to-plant bare-root roses should have plump, fresh-looking canes (branches) and roots. Plants that have dried out slightly in shipping or in nursery can be revived by burying them, tops and all, for a few days in moist soil, sand, or sawdust. Just before planting any bare-root rose, it is a good idea to immerse entire plant in water for several hours to be certain all canes and roots are plumped up. Plant according to directions for bare-root planting on page 44, being sure to make holes large enough to spread out roots without bending or cutting back. Just before planting, cut broken canes and broken roots back to below breaks. Set plant in hole so that bud union ("knob" from which canes grow) is just above soil level. Even growers in coldest zones find this successful, and plants produce more canes when planted this way, as long as plants are well protected during winter. After you have planted a rose and watered it well, mound soil, damp peat moss, or sawdust over bud union and around canes to conserve moisture. Gradually (and carefully) remove it when leaves begin to expand.

Basic Needs

All roses require water, nutrients, some pruning, and, at some point in their lifetime, some pest and disease control.

Water is needed at all times during growing season for best performance of most popular garden roses. Inadequate water slows or halts growth and bloom. Water deeply so that entire root system is moistened. How often to water depends on soil type and weather; refer to watering chapter, pages 48–52, for guidelines. Big well-established plants will need more water than will newly set plants, but you will need to pay closer attention to watering frequency of new plants in order to get them well established.

Basin flooding is a simple way to water individual rose plants, and with a modified drip irrigation system (see page 52) many plants can be watered this way at one time. Overhead sprinkling is often practiced in hot, dry regions; sprinkling removes dust, freshens foliage, and is partial control for aphids and spider mites. Disadvantages are that it will wash off spray residues, may leave mineral deposits on foliage if water is hard, and in some areas may encourage foliage diseases by keeping foliage and atmosphere damp. If you sprinkle, do it early in the day to be sure foliage dries off by nightfall. Even if you irrigate in basins, give plants an occasional sprinkling to clean dust off foliage.

Mulch, spread 2–3 inches deep, will help save water, keep soil surface from baking hard, keep soil cool in summer, deter weed growth, and build healthy soil structure (well aerated, permeable by water and roots). See pages 51–52 for mulch suggestions.

Nutrients, applied fairly regularly, will produce the most gratifying results. In mild-winter climates, begin feeding established plants with complete commercial fertilizer in February. Elsewhere, give first feeding just as growth begins. Fertilizer application should be timed in relation to bloom period. Ideal time to make subsequent feedings is when a blooming period has come to an end and new growth is just beginning for next cycle of bloom. Depending on expected arrival of freezing temperatures, you stop feeding in late summer or fall—generally about 6 weeks before earliest normal hard frost. In Zones 1–3, last application may be around August 1; in Zones 4–7 and 10, last feeding may be from early to late September. Milder zones may go as late as mid-October for crop of late fall flowers.

Dry commercial fertilizer, applied to soil, is most frequently used. A variation on that type is slow-release fertilizer that provides nutrients over prolonged period; follow directions on package for amount and frequency. Liquid fertilizers are useful in smaller gardens in which roses are basin watered; most liquids can also be used as foliage fertilizers—sprayed on rose leaves, which absorb nutrients immediately for quick tonic.

Pest and disease control may not constitute a regular part of your rose growing activities, but the need for certain controls usually arises during growing season. Descriptions of pests and diseases, along with recommended controls, appear on pages 55–66.

Principal rose pests are aphids, spider mites, and (in some areas) thrips. If you don't want to rely on natural predators, begin aphid control when aphids first appear and repeat as needed until they are gone or their numbers are severely reduced. Spring is prime aphid time. Spider mites are hot-weather pests, capable of inflicting severe damage—especially to underwatered plants and weak bushes. They work on leaf undersides, stippling leaves and giving them silvery cast; in severe infestations leaves fall off. Spider mites also can sap growth to the point that flower production stops. Thrips do their damage inside rose buds, making brown streaks on petals, browning petals completely, or turning entire buds brown or so misshapen that flowers may not open. Control is difficult because tiny thrips are hidden in rose petals, difficult to reach by contact insecticides; systemic insecticides are usually most successful for thrips control.

Mildew, rust, and black spot are "big 3" of rose foliage diseases. First line of defense for all three is thorough dormant season cleanup of all dead leaves and other debris from previous season; this is simplest right after you have pruned plants. Then, before new growth begins, spray plants and soil with dormant season spray of oil or lime sulfur (calcium polysulfide). This will destroy many disease organisms that otherwise might live over winter to reinfect plants in spring; overwintering insect eggs also are dispatched with these sprays.

Mildew, a gray to white furry coating on leaves, thrives under conditions of high humidity but no rain; it needs dry leaves on which to grow. Poor air circulation, as in crowded plantings or plants grown against a wall, encourages mildew development in regions where it is likely to occur. Rose varieties differ in their susceptibility to mildew; degree of mildew resistance is noted in detailed descriptions in Sunset's book *How to Grow Roses.* Rust usually appears first in late spring as small bright orange spots beneath leaves. In severe infestations, entire leaf undersurface will be covered with orange powder and leaves may drop off. Rust is easily spread by air currents and by rain or sprinkling; it needs damp leaves on which to grow. Black spot is most devastating of the three foliage diseases and may be found in parts of the Northwest and Rocky Mountain states, rarely in California and the Southwest. Summer rainfall areas are its home, as the disease spreads in water. Symptoms are black spots with irregular, fringed margins on leaves and sometimes on stems; leaves turn yellow around the spots, and if infection is unchecked entire plants will defoliate. Replacement of all foliage is a strain on plant, and roses weakened by the effort are likely to suffer more winter damage in the coldest zones (which are zones where black spot is most prevalent).

Chlorosis is not a disease but usually a symptom of iron deficiency: leaves turn light green to yellow but veins remain dark green. This can be a major problem in Zones 12 and 13. Iron chelate gives fastest relief to problem. Iron sulfate is also effective but slower to take effect.

Pruning, done properly each year, will contribute to health and longevity of your rose plants. Sensible pruning is based on these facts about growth of roses:

A. Blooms are produced on new growth. Unless pruning promotes strong new growth, flowers will come on spindly outer twigs and be of poor quality.

B. The more healthy wood you retain, the bigger plant will be. And the bigger the plant, the more flowers it can produce. Also, nutrients are stored in woody canes (branches), so the larger plant will be the stronger plant. Therefore, prune conservatively; *never* chop down vigorous 6-ft. bush to 18-in. stubs unless you want only a few huge blooms for exhibition. (Exception: in coldest zones, where plant freezes back to its winter protection, you will remove dead wood in spring and be left with equivalent of severely pruned plant.)

C. Best pruning time for most roses (certain climbers and shrub types excepted) is at the end of dormant season when growth buds begin to swell. Exact time will vary according to locality.

General pruning guidelines. The following five pruning practices apply to all roses except certain shrub and species roses, for which special instructions are indicated in their descriptions.

1. Use sharp pruning shears; make all cuts as shown on page 69.

2. Remove wood that is obviously dead, and wood that has no healthy growth coming from it; branches that cross through plant's center and any that rub against larger canes; branches that make bush appear lopsided; any old and unproductive canes that have been replaced by strong new ones during past season.

3. Cut back growth produced during previous year, usually making cuts above outward-facing buds (except for very spreading varieties where some cuts to inside buds will promote more height without producing many crossing branches). As a general rule, remove ⅓ to no more than ½ the length of previous season's growth (exception for coldest zones is noted in point B above). The ideal result is a "V" shaped bush with relatively open center.

4. If any suckers have grown (growth produced from rootstock instead of from rose variety growing on it), completely remove them. Dig down to where suckers grow from rootstock and pull them off with downward motion; that removes growth buds that would produce additional suckers in subsequent years. Let wound air dry before you replace soil around it. *Be certain you are removing a sucker rather than a new cane growing from the bud union of the budded variety.* Usually you can note a distinct difference in foliage size and shape, and size of thorns, on sucker growth. If in doubt, let the presumed sucker grow until you can establish its difference from budded rose. (A sucker's flowers will be different; a flowerless, climbing cane from a shrub rose is almost certainly a sucker.)

5. Consider cutting for flowers as form of pruning. Cut off enough stem to support flower in vase, but don't deprive plant of too much foliage. Leave on plant a stem with at least two sets of 5-leaflet leaves.

The most widely planted modern roses, Hybrid Teas and Grandifloras, can be pruned successfully according to guidelines above. A few additional tips apply to four other popular types:

Floribunda and Polyantha roses are grown for quantities of flowers they produce in clusters, so amount of bloom rather than quality of individual flower is the objective. Cut back previous season's growth only by ¼, and leave as many strong new canes and stems as plant produced. Most produce more canes per bush than do Hybrid Teas and Grandifloras. If you grow Floribundas or Polyanthas as hedge or border of one variety, cut back all plants to uniform height.

Climbing roses divide into two general types: those that bloom in spring only (which includes a large category known as natural climbers, discussed on page 454), and those that bloom off and on in other seasons as well as in spring (which includes the very popular climbing sports of Hybrid Tea roses). All climbers should be left unpruned for first 2–3 years after planting; remove only dead and weak, twiggy wood, but allow plants to get established and produce their long, flexible canes. Most bloom comes from lateral branches that grow from long canes, and greatest number of those flowering branches develop when long canes are spread out horizontally as along a fence. Types that bloom only in spring produce strong new growth after they flower, and that new growth bears flowers the following spring. Prune these climbers just *after* they bloom, removing oldest canes that show no signs of producing strong new growth. Repeat-flowering climbers (many are climbing sports of bush varieties) are pruned at same time as you would prune bush roses in your locality. Remove oldest, unproductive canes and any weak, twiggy growth; then cut back lateral branches on remaining canes to within 2–3 buds from canes.

Pillar roses are not quite bush or climber. They produce tall, somewhat flexible canes that bloom profusely without having to be trained horizontally as are climbers. Prune pillar roses according to general guidelines for bush roses.

Tree roses, more properly called "standards," are an artificial creation: a bush rose budded onto a 2–3-ft.-high understock stem. Most important is to securely stake trunk to prevent its breaking from weight of bush it supports. A ½-in. metal pipe makes good permanent stake; use cross "X" tie between stake and trunk to hold secure. General pruning guidelines apply, with particular attention to maintaining symmetrical plant.

Winter Protection

Where winter low temperatures regularly reach 10°F. and lower, some amount of winter protection is needed for all modern roses—bushes, climbers, and standards. Healthy, well-ripened plant will withstand winter better than weak, actively growing one; your first step to protection is preparation. Time your last fertilizer application so that bushes will have ceased putting on new growth by expected date of first sharp frosts; leave last crop of blooms on plants to form hips which will help ripening process by stopping growth. Keep plants well watered until soil freezes.

After a couple of hard freezes have occurred and night temperatures seem to remain consistently below freezing, mound soil over base of each bush to height of 12 in. Get soil from another part of garden; do *not* scoop soil from around roses, exposing surface roots. With soft twine, tie canes together to prevent whipping around in wind, and cut excessively long canes back to about 4 ft. When mound has frozen, cover it with evergreen boughs, straw, or other fairly lightweight material that will act as insulation to keep mounds frozen. Your objective is to prevent alternate freezing and thawing of mound (and canes it covers), maintaining plant at constant temperature of 15°–20°F. A cylinder of wire mesh around soil mound will help keep it and insulating material in place.

Remove protection in early spring when you are reasonably certain hard frosts will not recur. Gradually remove soil mounds as they thaw; do it carefully to avoid breaking new growth that may have begun under the soil.

Use of manufactured styrofoam rose cones eliminates the labor of mounding and unmounding; just a bit of soil over the cone's base plus a rock or brick on top will hold it in place over the bush. Disadvantages are: cost and availability; need to cut rose down to fit cone over it, perhaps pruning more severely than if plant were mounded to endure winter cold; moisture condensation inside cone as days begin warming. To avoid condensation problem, get cones with removable tops that can be opened for air circulation on warm late-winter days.

Climbing roses should be mounded in same manner, but in addition you will have to protect all of their canes. Where winter lows are in −10° to +5°F. range, wrap canes in burlap stuffed with straw for insulation. Where temperatures normally go below −10°F., remove canes from their support, gently bend them to ground, secure them in that position and cover with soil. A wiser plan in such climates is to plant only climbers known to be successful in your area or reputed to be hardy in similar climates.

Standards, or tree roses, may be insulated as described for climbers but it still is a gamble: the part you want—the head of the tree—is the most exposed. Some rosarians wrap with straw and burlap, then construct a plywood box to cover insulated plant. Others dig their standards each year and heel them in a cool garage, basement, or shed, then replant in spring. Simpler is to grow standards in large containers, then in fall move to cool shed or garage where temperature won't drop below 10°F.

MODERN ROSES

Types described below constitute majority of roses offered for sale and planted by hundreds of thousands each year. Those that have been All-America Rose Selections, recognized on basis of performance in nationwide test gardens, are indicated by AARS; those with an asterisk (*) are rated 8.0 or higher by the American Rose Society.

Hybrid Teas

This, the most popular class of rose, outsells all other types combined. Flowers are large and shapely, generally produced one to a stem on plants that range from 2–6 ft. or more, depending on variety. Many thousands of varieties have been produced since the class first appeared in 1867; hundreds are catalogued and new ones appear each year. In color groups that follow are listed most popular Hybrid Teas.

Red. 'Christian Dior' (AARS), *'Chrysler Imperial' (AARS), 'Crimson Glory', 'Jamaica', 'Kentucky Derby', *'Mister Lincoln' (AARS), 'Oklahoma', 'Red Devil', 'Red Masterpiece'.

Pink. 'Bewitched' (AARS), *'Century Two', 'Charlotte Armstrong' (AARS), *'Dainty Bess' (single), *'Duet' (AARS), 'Electron' (AARS), 'First Love', 'First Prize' (AARS), 'Friendship' (AARS), 'Jadis', 'Miss All-American Beauty' (AARS), 'Perfume Delight' (AARS), 'Portrait' (AARS), *'Royal Highness' (AARS), 'South Seas', *'Swarthmore', 'Taj Mahal', 'Texas Centennial', *'Tiffany' (AARS).

Multicolors, Blends. *'Chicago Peace', *'Double Delight', *'Granada' (AARS), 'Helen Traubel' (AARS), 'Medallion' (AARS), 'Seashell' (AARS), 'Snowfire', 'Sunrise-Sunset', 'Sunset Jubilee', 'Talisman', 'Yankee Doodle' (AARS), *'Wini Edmunds'.

Orange, Orange Tones. 'Command Performance', 'Firelight', *'Fragrant Cloud', 'Futura', 'Gypsy' (AARS), 'Mojave' (AARS), 'Oldtimer', *'Tropicana' (AARS).

Yellow. 'Apollo' (AARS), 'Autumn Gold', 'Eclipse', 'Golden Gate', 'Irish Gold', 'King's Ransom' (AARS), 'Lowell Thomas' (AARS), 'McGredy's Yellow', 'Oregold' (AARS), *'Peace' (AARS), 'Summer Sunshine', 'Sutter's Gold' (AARS).

White. *'Garden Party' (AARS), 'John F. Kennedy', 'Kaiserin Auguste Viktoria', 'Matterhorn' (AARS), *'Pascali' (AARS), 'Virgo', 'White Masterpiece'.

Lavender. 'Heirloom', *'Lady X', 'Paradise' (AARS), 'Sterling Silver'.

Grandifloras

Vigorous plants sometimes 8–10 ft. high with Hybrid Tea-type flowers borne singly or in long-stemmed clusters. This class is very close to Hybrid Teas, and some varieties have been switched from one class to the other. Valuable for its large number of cuttable flowers per plant and its mass color effect in garden. Good barrier plants.

Red. 'Candy Apple', 'Carrousel', 'John S. Armstrong' (AARS), 'Scarlet Knight' (AARS).

Pink, Pink Blend. 'Aquarius' (AARS), 'Camelot' (AARS), 'Cherry-Vanilla', *'Pink Parfait' (AARS), *'Queen Elizabeth' (AARS), 'Sonia'.

Orange, Blend. 'Arizona' (AARS), 'Comanche' (AARS), 'Montezuma', 'Prominent', 'Sundowner' (AARS).

Yellow. 'Buccaneer', 'Golden Girl'.

White. 'Mount Shasta'.

Floribundas

Originally developed from Hybrid Teas and Polyanthas, these are noted for producing quantities of flowers in clusters on vigorous and bushy plants. Flowers and plants generally are smaller than most Hybrid Teas. Excellent for providing masses of color in landscape: informal hedges, borders, barriers, massing, containers. Some varieties have climbing forms.

Red. *'Europeana' (AARS), 'Frensham', 'Garnette', 'Happy Talk', 'Merci', 'Red Pinocchio', *'Sarabande' (AARS).

Pink. *'Betty Prior' (single), 'Bon Bon' (AARS), 'Faberge', *'Gene Boerner' (AARS), 'Rosenelfe', 'Rose Parade' (AARS).

Orange, Blend. 'Apricot Nectar' (AARS), 'Bahia' (AARS), 'Cathedral', 'Circus' (AARS), 'Fashion' (AARS), 'First Edition', *'Little Darling', *'Matador', 'Redgold' (AARS), 'Spartan', 'Woburn Abbey'.

Yellow. 'Goldilocks', 'Spanish Sun', 'Sunsprite'.

White. *'Iceberg', 'Ivory Fashion' (AARS), 'Saratoga' (AARS).

Lavender. *'Angel Face' (AARS).

| Grandiflora rose 'Camelot' | Floribunda rose 'Cathedral' | Polyantha rose 'Margo Koster' |

Polyanthas

Small flowers (less than 2 in. wide) are carried in large sprays. Plants are vigorous, many-caned, nearly everblooming, and quite disease resistant. Uses are same as for Floribundas but color range is more limited. Four varieties are most often sold: 'Cecile Brunner' (often called the "Sweetheart Rose") has light pink flowers that are of best hybrid tea form; 'Perle d'Or' is similar but color is apricot orange; 'Margo Koster' has coral orange, very double flowers that resemble ranunculus; 'The Fairy' produces huge clusters of small light pink flowers.

Miniature roses

True roses 6–12 in. tall or a little taller, with miniature canes, foliage, and flowers. They are derived in part from *R. chinensis minima (R. roulettii)* and come in white, pink, red, or yellow. Everblooming. Can be grown indoors in cool, bright window; use 6-in. pots and rich potting soil. Use outdoors in rock gardens, window boxes, or containers. Plants are hardier than Hybrid Teas, but shallow roots demand constant water, careful feeding, and mulching. Nearly all miniatures are grown from cuttings (therefore no suckers from rootstock).

Many new varieties are put on market each year. Among the best are these, all rated 8.0 or higher.

Red. 'Beauty Secret', 'Dwarfking', 'Kathy', 'Robin', 'Royal Ruby', 'Scarlet Gem', 'Sheri Anne', 'Starina', 'Top Secret'.

Pink. 'Baby Betsy McCall', 'Chipper', 'Gypsy Jewel', 'Judy Fischer', 'Opal Jewel', 'Pixie Rose', 'Willie Winkie'.

Orange, Blend. 'Anytime', 'Baby Darling', 'Hula Girl', 'Janna',

'Jeanie Williams', 'Kathy Robinson', 'Magic Carousel', 'Mary Adair', 'Mary Marshall', 'Over the Rainbow', 'Peachy', 'Rosmarin', 'Toy Clown'.

Yellow. 'Yellow Doll'.

White. 'Cinderella', 'Easter Morning', 'Popcorn', 'Simplex', 'Starglo', 'White Angel'.

Miniature rose

Climbing rose
'Climbing
Mrs. Sam McGredy'

Climbing Roses

Two general categories comprise climbing roses: large-flowered natural climbers and climbing sports of bush roses (Hybrid Teas, Floribundas, Grandifloras, Polyanthas, Miniatures). See "Pruning" for description of major differences in pruning procedure. Here are the most popular varieties in the two categories.

Large-flowered Climbers

Red. 'Blaze', *'Don Juan', *'Dortmund' (single), 'Paul's Scarlet Climber', 'Red Fountain', 'Tempo'.

Pink. 'Blossomtime', 'Coral Dawn', *'Galway Bay', 'New Dawn', 'Rhonda'.

Orange, Blend. 'America' (AARS), 'Coralita', *'Handel', 'Joseph's Coat', *'Royal Sunset'.

Yellow. 'Golden Showers' (AARS), 'High Noon' (AARS), 'Royal Gold'.

White. 'White Dawn'.

Climbing Sports

Red. 'Cl. Crimson Glory' (HT), 'Cl. Chrysler Imperial' (HT), 'Cl. Etoile de Hollande' (HT).

Pink. 'Cl. Cecile Brunner' (Poly.), 'Cl. Charlotte Armstrong' (HT), 'Cl. Dainty Bess' (HT, single), *'Cl. First Prize' (HT), 'Cl. Queen Elizabeth' (Gr.), 'Cl. Tiffany' (HT).

Orange, Blend. 'Cl. Margo Koster' (Poly.), 'Cl. Mrs. Sam McGredy' (HT), 'Cl. Talisman' (HT), 'Cl. Tropicana' (HT).

Yellow. 'Cl. Goldilocks' (Fl) 'Cl. Peace' (HT).

White. 'Cl. Snowbird' (HT).

OLD ROSES

Some of the wild or species roses and their immediate hybrid offspring are still grown by fanciers and sold by specialists. Many are valuable landscape or flowering shrubs. All are as hardy as modern Hybrid Teas, except where noted. Three old rose garden types (Hybrid Perpetual, Tea, China) are an important source of vigor, delicate form, and everblooming quality in modern roses. Refer to "Climate" on page 450.

Hybrid Perpetuals

Before Hybrid Teas became popular, these were *the* garden roses. Plants are big, vigorous, and hardy to −30°F. if cut back to 18 in. when ground freezes and mounded with soil until new growth pushes out in spring. Often very susceptible to rust. They need more frequent feeding and watering than Hybrid Teas to produce repeated bursts of bloom. Prune high and thin out oldest canes. Flowers are big (to 7 in. wide), opulent, full-petaled, and have strong old-rose fragrance. Buds often are shorter and plumper than average Hybrid Tea bud. Colors range from white through many shades of pink to deep red. Examples are 'Paul Neyron', 'Ulrich Brunner', 'American Beauty'. Though now officially classed as a Hybrid Tea, the old favorite white 'Frau Karl Druschki' typifies Hybrid Perpetual growth and flower.

Tea Roses

One of the parents of Hybrid Teas. Primarily adapted to climates of little seasonal change, with short rest periods (best in Zones 8, 9, 12–24). All resent heavy pruning; thin out weak growth and let plants develop into large shrubs. Flowers are refined, well formed, in tones of soft cream, light yellow, apricot, buff, pink, and rosy red, produced throughout warm weather. 'Maman Cochet', 'Duchesse de Brabant', 'Catherine Mermet', are among those still available commercially. Hybrids with *Rosa moschata* were responsible for famous Tea-Noisettes 'Lamarque' and 'Marechal Niel'. Variant of the tea rose, *R. odorata*, is *R. o. gigantea*. Its celebrated hybrid is rampant pale pink climber 'Belle Portugaise' ('Belle of Portugal').

China Roses

Original China rose, *R. chinensis,* has smooth stems, glossy foliage, and single, pink to red, usually clustered flowers over long period. One source of dependable recurrent bloom habit of modern roses, hybrid Chinas have diverse parentage. A hybrid China, 'Gloire de Rosomanes' (better known as 'Ragged Robin') was once widely used as understock and is still widely planted as hedge. Vigorous grower to 6–10 ft., it has semidouble, cherry red, fragrant flowers over a long season. *R. chinensis* 'Minima' is an important parent of modern miniature rose. In its own right it is good pot plant or rock garden plant 9–10 in. high, with tiny red single or double flowers in spring and scattered repeat bloom. Closely allied to China roses are hybrids of *R. borboniana,* Bourbon rose. Pinks 'La Reine Victoria', 'Madame Pierre Oger', 'Souvenir de la Malmaison' are best known.

Other old garden rose types available from nursery rose specialists are:

R. alba. WHITE OR YORK ROSE. Associated with England's War of the Roses. Semidouble, flat, ivory white flowers. Garden hybrids grow vigorously, make erect shrubs. Wood is green, smooth; leaves gray green, cool looking. Garden varieties are pink 'Celestial', 'Königin von Dänemark', 'Maiden's Blush'.

R. banksiae. LADY BANKS' ROSE. Evergreen climber (deciduous in cold winters). Zones 4–24. Vigorous grower to 20 ft. or more. Aphid resistant, almost immune to disease. Stems have almost no prickles; leaves with 3–5 leaflets to 2½ in. long, glossy and leathery. Flowers small, yellow or white, in large clusters late spring to midsummer depending on zone and season. Good for covering banks, ground, fence, or arbor in mild climates. The two varieties sold are 'Alba Plena', whose white, double flowers smell like violets; and 'Lutea', which has scentless double yellow flowers.

R. bracteata. Climbing shrub with large, single, creamy white blossoms. Naturalized in southeastern U. S. Its celebrated offspring is 'Mermaid', evergreen or semievergreen climber (Zones 4–24). Vigorous (to 30 ft.), thorny, with glossy, leathery, dark green leaves and many single, creamy yellow, lightly fragrant flowers, 5 in. across, in summer, fall, and intermittently through winter in mildest zones. Tough, disease resistant, thrives in sun or part shade, beach or inland. Plant 8 ft. apart for quick ground cover, or use to climb wall (will need tying), run along fence, or climb tree.

R. centifolia. CABBAGE ROSE. Deciduous shrub. Rose of Dutch painters. Open growing, to 6 ft. tall, with prickly stems. Flowers pink, double, nodding, very fragrant; blooming in late spring, early summer. Selections range from pale pink to purplish. *R. c. muscosa,* MOSS ROSE, is grown in many named kinds. Moss roses have flower stalks and bases covered with hairy, green "moss" and were a Victorian favorite. Flowers are mostly double, pink, white, or red, intensely fragrant with old-rose fragrance; some varieties bloom only one season each year; others, such as 'Salet', bloom repeatedly.

R. damascena. DAMASK ROSE. Deciduous shrub to 6 ft., with pale green, downy foliage, long arching canes, and loosely double, very fragrant pink blooms in clusters. "Rose of Castile" of Spanish missions. Source of attar of roses. Garden hybrids include blush pink 'Celsiana'; 'Mme. Hardy', white; and celebrated "York and Lancaster" with blooms sometimes pink, sometimes white, or two colors mixed.

R. eglanteria *(R. rubiginosa).* SWEET BRIAR, EGLANTINE. Deciduous shrub or climber. All Zones. Vigorous growth to 8–12 ft. Stems prickly; leaves dark green, fragrant (like apples), especially after rain. Flowers single, pink, 1½ in. across, appearing singly or in clusters in late spring. Fruit red orange. Can be used as hedge, barrier, screen; plant 3–4 ft. apart and prune once a year in early spring. Can be held to 3–4 ft. Naturalized in some parts of West. Good hybrid forms: 'Lady Penzance', 'Lord Penzance'.

R. foetida (R. lutea). AUSTRIAN BRIER. Deciduous shrub. All Zones. Slender, prickly stems 5–10 ft. long, erect or arching. Leaves dark green, smooth, or slightly hairy. May drop early in fall. Flowers (May-June) single, bright yellow, 2–3 in. across, with odd scent. Best known by its variety 'Bicolor', AUSTRIAN COPPER ROSE, 4–5-ft.-tall shrub with brilliant coppery red flowers, petals of which are yellow on backs. This species and its variety are source of orange and yellow in modern roses.

Austrian brier does best in warm, fairly dry, well-drained soil and in full sun. Needs reflected heat in Zones 4–6. Prune only to remove dead or worn-out wood.

R. gallica. FRENCH ROSE. Deciduous shrub. Prickly, often bristly stems to 3–4 ft. tall from creeping rootstocks. Leaves smooth, dark green. Flowers red, fragrant, 2–2½ in. across. All have old-rose fragrance, and some, like 'Rosa Mundi', are strikingly striped red on white. Flowers pink through slate blue and purple, often mottled with these colors.

R. harisonii. HARISON'S YELLOW ROSE. Deciduous shrub. All Zones. Thickets of thorny stems to 6–8 ft.; fine-scale foliage; flowers (in late spring) profuse, semidouble, bright yellow, fragrant. Occasionally reblooms in fall in warmer climates. Showy fruit. Hybrid between Austrian brier and Scotch rose. Very old rose that came west with pioneers and still persists in gold country and around old farm houses. Vigorous growth, disease free, hardy to cold and (once established) resistant to drought. Useful deciduous landscaping shrub.

R. hugonis. FATHER HUGO'S ROSE, GOLDEN ROSE OF CHINA. Deciduous shrub. All Zones. Dense growth to 8 ft. Stems arching or straight, with bristles near base. Handsome foliage; leaves deep green, 1–4 in. long with 5–11 tiny leaflets. Flowers profusely in May-June; branches become garlands of 2-in.-wide, bright yellow, faintly scented flowers. Useful in borders, as screen or barrier plantings, against fence, trained as fan on trellis. Will take high filtered afternoon shade. Prune out oldest wood to ground each year to shape plant, get maximum bloom.

R. moschata. MUSK ROSE. Vigorous, arching,deciduous shrub with clustered ivory white flowers of musky odor. Parent of Tea-Noisettes. Available are many HYBRID MUSKS, large 6–8-ft. shrubs or semiclimbers. Flowers, in clusters or large trusses, are almost everblooming, in red, pinks, buff, yellow, and white; heavily fragrant. Some produce decorative orange or red hips in fall. Musks grow and bloom in afternoon shade or broken shade as well as in sun. Popular varieties are 'Belinda', 'Cornelia' (pink); 'Nymphenburg', 'Penelope' (salmon); 'Buff Beauty' (buff apricot); 'Will Scarlet' (single red); and 'Kathleen' (single pink, like apple blossoms).

R. multiflora. Deciduous shrub. All Zones. Arching growth on dense, vigorous plant 8–10 ft. tall and as wide. Susceptible to mildew, spider mites. Many clustered, small white flowers (like blackberry blossoms) in June; profusion of ¼-in. red fruit in fall. Promoted as hedge but truly useful for this purpose only on largest acreage—far too large and vigorous for most gardens. Spiny and smooth forms available; spiny form best for barrier hedge. Set plants a foot apart for fast fill-in. Can help control erosion. Birds love fruit.

R. roxburghii. CHESTNUT ROSE. Deciduous. Zones 2–24. Spreading plant with prickly stems 8–10 ft. long. Bark gray, peeling. Light green, very fine-textured, ferny foliage; immune to mildew; new growth bronze and gold tipped. Buds and fruit are spiny like chestnut burs. Flowers generally double, soft rose pink, very fragrant; appear in June. If stems are pegged down, makes good bank cover, useful in preventing erosion; normally a big shrub for screen or border.

R. rugosa. RAMANAS ROSE, SEA TOMATO. Deciduous shrub. All Zones. Vigorous, very hardy shrub with prickly stems, 3–8 ft. tall. Leaves bright glossy green, with distinctive heavy veining which gives them crinkled appearance. Flowers are 3–4 in. across and, in the many varieties, range from single to double and from pure white and creamy yellow through pink to deep purplish red, all wonderfully fragrant. Bright red fruit, an inch or more across,

are shaped like tomatoes, edible but seedy; sometimes used for preserves.

All Rugosas are extremely tough, hardy, and make fine hedges; help prevent erosion. They take hard freezes, wind, drought, salt spray at ocean. Foliage remains quite free of diseases and insects except possibly aphids. Among most widely sold are 'Blanc Double de Coubert' (double white), 'Frau Dagmar Hastrup' (single pink), 'Hansa' (double purplish red), 'Will Alderman' (double pink). Two unusual Rugosa hybrids are 'F. J. Grootendorst' and 'Grootendorst Supreme' — their double flowers with deeply fringed petals resemble carnations more than roses.

R. sericea pteracantha. Deciduous shrub. Single, 1½–2-in., white, mostly 4-petalled flowers. A rose to grow for its decorative thorns. New shoots have inch-long winged, bright red prickles that are actually translucent.

R. spinosissima (R. pimpinellifolia). SCOTCH ROSE, BURNET ROSE. Deciduous shrub. All Zones. Suckering, spreading shrub 3–4 ft. tall. Stems upright, spiny and bristly, closely set with small, ferny leaves. Handsome bank cover on good soil; helps prevent erosion. Spring flowers white to pink, 1½–2 in. across. Fruit dark brown or blackish. Many varieties range to deep rose of yellow. 'Frühlingsgold', 'Frühlingsmorgen', 'Stanwell Perpetual' are among most widely sold. Best-known variety is R. p. altaica, sometimes 6 ft. tall with larger leaves and 3-in. white flowers garlanding branches.

R. wichuraiana. MEMORIAL ROSE. Vine. All Zones; evergreen or partially evergreen in Zones 4–24. Trailing plant,making stems 10–12 ft. long in one season. Stems root in contact with moist soil. Leaves 2–4 in. long, with 5–9 smooth, shining leaflets ¼–1 in. long. Flowers white, to 2 in. across, in clusters of 6–10. Blooms midsummer. Good ground cover in relatively poor soil.

ROSA DE MONTANA. See Antigonon leptopus.

ROSARY VINE. See Ceropegia woodii.

ROSE. See Rosa.

ROSEA ICE PLANT. See Drosanthemum floribundum.

ROSE ACACIA. See Robinia hispida.

ROSE APPLE. See Syzygium jambos.

ROSE CRESS. See Arabis blepharophylla.

ROSELLE. See Hibiscus sabdariffa.

ROSE-MALLOW. See Hibiscus moscheutos.

ROSEMARY. See Rosmarinus officinalis.

ROSE MOSS. See Portulaca grandiflora.

ROSE OF SHARON. See Hibiscus syriacus.

ROSMARINUS officinalis. ROSEMARY. Evergreen shrub, herb. Zones 4–24. Rugged, picturesque, to 2–6 ft. high. Narrow, aromatic leaves glossy dark green above, grayish white beneath. Small clusters of light lavender blue, ½-in. flowers in winter, spring; occasionally repeat in fall. Flowers attract birds, bees. Leaves widely used as seasoning.

Endures hot sun and poor soil, but good drainage is a must. Once established needs some watering in desert, little or no watering elsewhere. Feeding and excess water result in rank growth, subsequent woodi-

Rosmarinus officinalis

ness. Control growth by frequent tip-pinching when plants are small. Prune older plants lightly; cut to side branch or shear.

Some taller varieties are useful as clipped hedges or in dry borders with native and gray-leafed plants. Greatest use for lower growing varieties is as ground or bank covers. Set container-grown plants or rooted cuttings 2 ft. apart for moderately quick cover. Feed lightly, thin occasionally, and head back gently to encourage new growth. Useful in erosion control.

R. o. 'Collingwood Ingram' *(R. ingramii).* To 2–2½ ft. tall, spreads 4 ft. or more. Branches curve gracefully. Flowers rich, bright blue violet. Tallish bank or ground cover with high color value. Variety 'Benenden Blue' may be same.

R. o. 'Lockwood de Forest' *(R. lockwoodii, R. forrestii).* Resembles *R. o.* 'Prostratus', but has lighter, bright foliage, bluer flowers.

R. o. 'Prostratus'. DWARF ROSEMARY. To 2 ft. tall with 4–8 ft. spread. Will trail over wall or edge of raised bed to make curtain of green. Pale lavender blue flowers. Fire resistant if reasonably well watered.

R. o. 'Tuscan Blue'. Rigid upright branches to 6 ft. tall grow directly from base of plant. Leaves are rich green, flowers blue violet.

ROUND-LEAFED MALLEE. See *Eucalyptus orbifolia.*

ROUND-LEAFED MINT BUSH. See *Prostanthera rotundifolia.*

ROUND-LEAFED MOORT. See *Eucalyptus platypus.*

ROUND-LEAFED SNOW GUM. See *Eucalyptus perriniana.*

ROUNDLEAF FERN. See *Pellaea rotundifolia.*

ROUNDLEAF LAURUSTINUS. See *Viburnum tinus* 'Robustum'.

ROUND-HEADED GARLIC. See *Allium sphaerocephalum.*

ROYAL FERN. See *Osmunda regalis.*

ROYAL TRUMPET VINE. See *Distictis* 'Rivers'.

RUBBER PLANT. See *Ficus elastica.*

RUBUS. BRAMBLE. Best known for edible members blackberry and raspberry (see separate entries), the brambles include many ornamental plants, generally little known and not much resembling their thornier relations.

Rubus deliciosus

R. calycinoides. Evergreen shrub. Zones 4–6, 14–17, little tested elsewhere. Creeping stems make mat that spreads 1 ft. a year. Densely packed leaves are shiny green with crinkled look above, felted underneath, 1½ in. across, nearly round, ruffled. Small white flowers resemble strawberry flowers; salmon-colored berries rarely seen. Needs good drainage, average soil, sun or light shade. Attractive ground cover, rock garden plant. Some drought tolerance.

R. deliciosus. ROCKY MOUNTAIN THIMBLEBERRY, BOULDER RASPBERRY. Deciduous shrub. Grown Zones 1–5, 10, not widely tested elsewhere. Graceful shrub with arching, thornless branches; reaches 3–5 ft. Leaves bright green, nearly round, lobed. Flowers, 2–3 in. across, look like single white roses. May-June bloom. Fruit attracts birds. Good drainage, dryish soil, sun or light shade.

RUDBECKIA. Annuals, biennials, perennials. All Zones. Garden rudbeckias are descendants of wild plants from eastern United States. All are tough, easy plants which thrive in any except soggy soils; full sun. Showy flowers are good for cutting and brighten summer and autumn borders.

R. hirta. GLORIOSA DAISY, BLACK-EYED SUSAN. Biennial or short-lived perennial; can be grown as annual, blooming first summer from seed sown in early spring. To 3–4 ft., with upright branching habit, rough, hairy stems and leaves. Wild black-eyed Susan has single daisylike flowers 2–4 in. across, with orange yellow rays and black purple center.

Rudbeckia hirta

Gloriosa Daisy strain has single daisies 5–7 in. wide in shades of yellow, orange, russet, or mahogany, often zoned or banded. 'Irish Eyes' has golden yellow flowers with light green centers that turn brown as they mature. 'Pinwheel' has mahogany and gold flowers. Gloriosa Double Daisy strain has somewhat smaller (to 4½ in.) double flower heads, nearly all in lighter yellow and orange shades. 'Marmalade' is lower growing, good bedding plant.

R. laciniata 'Hortensia'. GOLDEN GLOW. Perennial to 6–7 ft. tall, spreading by underground stems, sometimes aggressively. Leaves deeply lobed, light green. Flowers (summer and fall) double, bright yellow. Tolerates heat remarkably well. Good summer screen or tall border plant. Does not seed, but spreads rapidly, is easily divided. Spray to control aphids. Variety 'Goldquelle' grows to 2½ ft., is less aggressive.

R. purpurea. See *Echinacea.*

RUE. See *Ruta graveolens.*

RUMOHRA adiantiformis. (Usually sold as *Aspidium capense.*) LEATHERLEAF FERN. Zones 14–17, 19–24. Fronds are deep glossy green, triangular, finely cut, to 3 ft. tall. They are firm textured and last well when cut for arrangements. Although it does best in partial shade, this fern will grow in full sun. Hardy to 24°F. Needs moderate water.

Rumohra adiantiformis

RUPTURE WORT. See *Herniaria glabra.*

RUSCUS. BUTCHER'S BROOM. Evergreen shrublets. Zones 4–24. Unusual plants with some value as small-scale ground cover, curiosity, or source of dry arrangement material and Christmas greens. Flattened leaf-like branches do work of leaves. They bear tiny greenish white flowers in centers of upper surfaces. If male and female plants are present, or if you have plant with male and female flowers, bright red (sometimes yellow) marble-sized fruit follow flowers. Spread by underground stems. Best in shade but will take sun, except in hot desert areas. They tolerate water, drought, competition from tree roots. Subject to iron chlorosis in desert. Will grow indoors.

Ruscus hypoglossum

R. aculeatus. To 1–4 ft. tall with branched stems. Leaves are 1–3 in. long, a third as wide, spine tipped, leathery, dull dark green. Fruit ½ in. across, red or yellow.

R. hypoglossum. To 1½ ft., unbranched stems. "Leaves" to 4 in. long, 1½ in. wide, glossy green, not spine tipped. Fruit ¼–½ in. across. Faster spreading than *R. aculeatus.* Superior as small-scale ground cover. Shade tolerant.

RUSSIAN OLIVE. See *Elaeagnus angustifolia.*

RUTABAGA. See Turnip and Rutabaga.

RUTA graveolens. RUE, HERB-OF-GRACE. Perennial herb. All Zones. To 2–3 ft. Aromatic, fernlike blue green leaves; small, greenish yellow flowers; decorative brown

Ruta graveolens

seed capsules. Sow seeds in flats, transplant to 12 in. apart. Good garden soil with additions of lime to strongly acid soil. Full sun; average to minimal water. Plant at back of border. Dry seed clusters for use in wreaths or swags. 'Jackman's Blue' is dense, compact, and fine gray blue in color.

RYEGRASS. See *Lolium.*

SABAL. PALMETTO. Zones 12–17, 19–24. Native from North Carolina to South America. Large, slow-growing fan palms, some with trunks, some without. Large clusters of inconspicuous flowers appear among leaves when plants are mature. Hardy, all withstanding 20°–22°F., some even lower temperatures. Take sun in youth. Average garden water except *S. uresana.*

Sabal palmetto

S. domingensis. (Often sold as *S. blackburniana* or *S. umbraculifera.*) HISPANIOLAN PALMETTO. Largest palmetto, ultimately 80 ft. or more, with immense green fans 9 ft. across.

S. mexicana *(S. texana).* OAXACA PALMETTO. Leaf stems hang on trunk in early life, then fall to show attractive, slender trunk. Grows 30–50 ft. high.

S. minor. Leafy green palm, usually trunkless, but sometimes with trunk to 6 ft. Old leaves fold at base, hang down like inverted umbrella.

S. palmetto. CABBAGE PALM. Zones 10, 12–17, 19–24. Trunk grows slowly to 20 ft., much taller in its native southeastern states. Big 5–8-ft. green leaves grow in dense globular head.

S. uresana. SONORAN PALMETTO. Native to northwestern Mexico. To 30 ft., faster growing than most palmettos. Drought tolerant. Silver gray to blue gray leaves, 6 ft. wide.

SACRED FLOWER OF THE INCAS. See *Cantua buxifolia.*

SAFFLOWER. See *Carthamus tinctorius.*

SAGE. See *Salvia.*

SAGINA subulata. IRISH MOSS, SCOTCH MOSS. Perennial. Zones 1–11, 14–24. Commoner of two different plants of similar appearance, each sold in green (Irish) and golden green (Scotch) form. Both make dense, compact, mosslike masses of very slender leaves on slender stems. Both are grown primarily as ground covers for limited areas in full sun, semishade. Useful to fill in between paving blocks. In cool coastal gardens they can seed themselves, become pests.

Sagina subulata

Although they look like moss, these plants won't grow well under conditions that suit true mosses. They need good soil, good drainage, ample water, and occasional feeding of slow-acting, nonburning fertilizer. In hot places, give partial shade; they don't do well in deep shade. They take some foot traffic and tend to hump up in time; control humping by occasionally cutting out narrow strips. Control snails, slugs, cutworms. Cut squares from flats and set 6 in. apart for fast cover. Plant so that soil line of squares is at or slightly below planted soil surface to avoid lumpiness.

The two plants involved are: *Arenaria verna* (usually called *Arenaria verna caespitosa*), and *Sagina subulata.* Former has tiny white flowers in few-flowered clusters. Latter (far more common) bears flowers singly and differs in other technical details. In common usage, however, green-colored forms of two species are called Irish moss, and golden green forms (*Arenaria verna* 'Aurea' and *Sagina subulata* 'Aurea') are called Scotch moss.

SAGO PALM. See *Cycas revoluta.*

SAGUARO. See *Carnegiea gigantea.*

ST. AUGUSTINE GRASS. See *Stenotaphrum secundatum.*

ST. CATHERINE'S LACE. See *Eriogonum giganteum.*

ST. JAMES LILY. See *Sprekelia formosissima.*

ST. JOHN'S BREAD. See *Ceratonia.*

ST. JOHNSWORT. See *Hypericum.*

SAINTPAULIA ionantha. AFRICAN VIOLET. Evergreen perennial. Probably most popular house plant in the United States. Fuzzy heart shaped leaves with smooth edges, grow in rosettes up to 1 ft. wide. Pale lavender flowers grow in clusters of 3 or more. On hybrids and named varieties leaves are plain or scalloped, green or variegated; flowers are purple, violet, pink, white, or variegated. Best in east window with roof

Saintpaulia ionantha

overhang or suffused morning sun. Keep where temperatures average 60°–70°F. Preferably humidity should be high; if house air is quite dry, increase humidity around plants by setting each plant on a saucer filled with wet gravel.

African violets won't take just any potting mix. They need: acid conditions (use plenty of leaf mold); suitable soil conditioner such as builder's sand or vermiculite; good loam (preferably sterilized if you use garden soil); and small amount of slow acting fertilizer such as bone meal or manure. One good mix is 3 parts leaf mold, 1 part loam, ½ part builder's sand, and small amount of bone meal. (For a number of other good mixes, see *Sunset* book *How to Grow African Violets.*) Don't use too large a pot—African violets bloom best when roots are crowded.

Water plants from top or below, but avoid watering crown or leaves. Wick-irrigated pots work well. Use water at room temperature or slightly warmer, wet soil thoroughly, let potting mixture become dry to the touch before watering again. Don't let water stand in pot saucers for more than 2 hours after watering plants. If plant is well established, feed—only when soil is moist—with slightly acid fertilizer once every 2–4 weeks. Propagate from seeds, leaf cuttings, or divisions. Most common pests are aphids, cyclamen mites, thrips, and mealybugs.

SALAD BURNET. See *Poterium sanguisorba.*

SALAL. See *Gaultheria shallon.*

SALIX. WILLOW. Deciduous trees or shrubs. Most kinds best where there are pronounced winters. Very fast growing. Will take any soil, and most kinds will even tolerate poor drainage. One important need is plenty of water. All have invasive roots, are hard to garden under. Most are subject to tent caterpillars, aphids, borers, spider mites.

Salix babylonica

Weeping willows find their best use as single trees near stream or lake. With training they can become satisfactory shade trees for patio or terrace. All leaf out very early in spring, hold leaves late (until Christmas in milder climates).

Shrubby willows are grown principally for their catkins ("pussy willows"), their colored twigs, as screen plants, or for erosion control on stream or river banks.

S. alba tristis (*S. babylonica aurea, S.* 'Niobe'). GOLDEN WEEPING WILLOW. Tree. All Zones. To 80 ft. or more, with greater

---

spread. One-year-old twigs are bright yellow, quite pendulous. Leaves are bright green or yellow green, paler beneath.

Left to its own way, this (and other weeping willows) will head too low to furnish usable shade. Stake up main stem and keep it staked—right up to 15–18 ft. Shorten side branches and remove them as they lose their vigor; keep early growth directed into a tall main stem and high-branching scaffold limbs. This treatment will make a tree you can walk under. Subject to twig blight in Northwest; use copper spray on new foliage. Texas root rot a problem in desert.

S. babylonica. WEEPING WILLOW. Tree. All Zones. To 30–50 ft. with equal or greater spread. Smaller than golden weeping willow, with longer (3–6 in.) leaves, and even more pronounced weeping habit. Greenish or brown branchlets. Train to be full-fledged weeper as described under *S. alba tristis.*

Variety 'Crispa' ('Annularis'), RINGLEAF or CORKSCREW WILLOW, interesting oddity, has leaves twisted and curled into rings or circles and is somewhat narrower in spread.

S. blanda. WISCONSIN WEEPING WILLOW. Tree. All Zones. To 40–50 ft. or more, spreading wider. Less strongly weeping habit than *S. babylonica*; leaves broader, more bluish green. 'Fan', FAN GIANT BLUE WEEPING WILLOW, is resistant to borers and blight.

S. caprea. FRENCH PUSSY WILLOW, PINK PUSSY WILLOW. Shrub or small tree. All Zones. To 25 ft. Broad leaves 3–6 in. long, dark green above, gray hairy beneath. Fat, inch-long, pinkish gray woolly catkins before leaves in very early spring. Forces easily indoors, and can be cut for winter arrangements. For large gardens that can spare room for unusual shrubs, or for naturalizing. Can be kept to shrub size by cutting to ground every few years.

S. discolor. PUSSY WILLOW. Shrub or small tree. All Zones. To 20 ft., with slender, red brown stems and bright green 2–4-in.-long, oval leaves, bluish beneath. Catkins of male plants (usually only kind sold) are feature attraction—soft, silky, pearl gray, and up to 1½ in. long. Branches can be cut in winter for early bouquets.

S. gracilistyla. ROSE-GOLD PUSSY WILLOW. Shrub. All Zones. Upright, spreading to 6–10 ft. tall, with 2–4-in.-long, ½–1¼-in.-wide leaves, gray green above, bluish green beneath. Plump, 1½-in.-long, furry gray catkins show numerous stamens with rose and gold anthers. Good-looking in garden or in arrangements. Cutting branches for indoor use will help curb its size; every 3 or 4 years cut back whole plant to short stubs. You'll be rewarded by especially vigorous shoots with large catkins.

S. matsudana. HANKOW WILLOW. Tree. All Zones. Upright, pyramidal growth to 40–50 ft. Leaves narrow, bright green, 2–4 in. long, ½ in. wide. Can thrive on less water than most willows. This plant and its varieties are popular in high desert and plateau areas.

S. m. 'Navajo'. GLOBE NAVAJO WILLOW. Large, very tough and hardy, spreading round-topped tree to 70 ft. tall, equally wide.

S. m. 'Tortuosa'. TWISTED HANKOW WILLOW, CORKSCREW WILLOW. To 30 ft. high, with 20-ft. spread. Branches and branchlets fantastically twisted into upright, spiralling patterns. Use for silhouette value; cut branches good in arrangements.

S. m. 'Umbraculifera'. GLOBE WILLOW. To 35 ft. with equal spread. Round, umbrella shaped head with upright branches, drooping branchlets.

S. purpurea. PURPLE OSIER, ALASKA BLUE WILLOW. Shrub. All Zones. To 10–18 ft. high with purple branches, 1–3-in.-long dark green leaves markedly bluish underneath. Variety 'Gracilis' ('Nana'), DWARF PURPLE OSIER, often seen in cold-winter regions, has slimmer branches and narrower leaves; it is usually grown as clipped hedge and kept 1–3 ft. high and equally wide. General effect is fine textured; color effect blue gray. Grows easily from cuttings. Good background plant.

S. sachalinensis 'Sekka' (*S. s.* 'Setsuka'). Shrub or small tree. All Zones. Leaves 2–4 in. long, ½ in. wide, green above, silvery beneath. Catkins silvery, up to 2 in. long. Big feature: flattened branches often 1–2 in. wide, twisted and curled, picturesque in arrangements.

SALPIGLOSSIS sinuata. PAINTED-TONGUE. Summer annual. Upright open habit, to 2–3 ft. tall. Sticky leaves and stems. Leaves to 4 in. long, narrowly oblong. Flowers much like petunias in

Salpiglossus sinuata

shape and size (2–2½ in. wide), but more unusual in coloring—shades of mahogany red, reddish orange, yellow, purple and pink tones, marbled and penciled with contrasting color.

Seeds are rather difficult to start, especially when sown directly in garden bed. Good method: In late winter or early spring, plant in potting mixture in peat pots, several seeds to pot. Keep in warm, protected location; seeds should sprout in 7–10 days. Thin to one seedling per pot. Later, when young plants are well established and all danger of frost is past, plant in sunny location. Best in rich soil; don't overwater. Pinch out tips of growing plants to induce branching. Best bloom in late spring and early summer, but plants will endure until frost. Good background plant for border; handsome cut flowers.

SALSIFY, OYSTER PLANT. Hardy biennial grown in all Zones for edible root. Root looks something like parsnip and has creamy white flesh that tastes a little like oysters. Plant grows to 4 ft. tall; leaves are narrow, grasslike. Plant in rich, deep, sandy soil, spaded deep. Culture is same as for parsnips. It takes 150 days to grow to maturity. Cooked, mashed salsify, mixed with butter and beaten egg, can be made into patties and sauteed until brown to make mock oysters. If plant is allowed to overwinter it will produce flower stalk topped by large head of lavender purple, dandelion flowers followed by white, cottony, dandelionlike seeds.

Salsify

SALTBUSH. See *Atriplex.*

SALT CEDAR. See *Tamarix chinensis.*

SALVIA. SAGE. Annuals, perennials, shrubs. Flowers in whorls, sometimes distinctly spaced, sometimes pushed close together so they appear as one dense spike. Tubular flowers vary in color from deep blue through purple to bright red. Shrubby kinds need little summer water; perennials need moderate water.

S. azurea grandiflora (*S. pitcheri*). Perennial. Zones 1–11, 14–24. To 5 ft. tall with hairy, 2–4-in.-long leaves. Gentian blue flowers, ½ in. long, provide mass of color from early July to frost. Full sun.

S. clevelandii. Shrub. Zones 10–24. Native to chaparral slopes of San Diego County. Rounded form to 4 ft. tall. Foliage and flowers have delightful fragrance. Smooth gray green leaves about an inch long. Blue ¾-in. flowers May-August. Sun, well-drained soil, practically no water in summer. For best appearance, prune after frosts have passed. Use with plants that have similar cultural requirements.

Salvia officinalis

S. elegans (*S. gracilistyla, S. rutilans*). PINEAPPLE SAGE. Perennial herb. Zones 8–24. To 2–3 ft. Use woolly light green leaves fresh or dried as seasoning; milder, more fruity scent and taste than garden sage. Scarlet flowers in fall. Tender to frost, otherwise same care as garden sage.

S. farinacea. MEALY-CUP SAGE. Perennial; annual where winters are cold. All Zones. Fast growth to 3-ft. mound. Gray green, 4-in.-long leaves. Spikes of violet blue, ½-in.-long flowers rise well above mound. Use with other annuals and perennials or by itself as foundation plant. Favorite of flower arrangers. 'Blue Bedder', 'Catima', and 'Victoria' are best varieties; last named is 18-in. dwarf.

S. greggii. Evergreen shrub. Zones 8–24. Upright branching, bushy plant to 3–4 ft. tall. Leaves ½–1 in. long, medium green. Flowers an inch long, rosy red, in loose spikelike clusters late spring and summer. Ordinary garden soil and watering, full sun or light shade. Drought tolerant near coast. Can be sheared into a hedge.

S. leucantha. MEXICAN BUSH SAGE. Shrub. Zones 10–24. To 3–4 ft. tall and as wide; graceful habit. Long, slender, velvety purple or deep rose spikes with small white flowers; blooms summer and fall. Tolerates drought. Cut old stems to the ground; new ones bloom continuously. Grow from clump or pieces of old clumps with roots attached. Sun or light shade.

S. leucophylla. PURPLE SAGE. Shrub. Zones 10–24. Native to southern Coast Ranges and mountains of southern California. To 2–6 ft. tall with white stems and gray, crinkly 1–3-in. leaves which drop in dry seasons. Flowers light purple, ½ in. long, in 3–5 whorled clusters May-June. Heat and drought tolerant.

S. officinalis. GARDEN SAGE. Perennial herb. All Zones. To 18–24 in. high. Narrow, gray green, 1–2-in.-long leaves. Tall spikes of violet blue (rarely red or white) flowers attractive to bees in early summer. Variety 'Tricolor' has leaves variegated with white and purple red. Poor but well-drained soil, full sun. Fairly drought resistant. Cut back after bloom; fertilize if you cut continually. Divide every 3–4 years. Propagate from cuttings, layers, or seeds. Excellent for rock gardens and containers. Fragrant, colorful cut flower. Use leaves (fresh or dried) for seasoning meat, sausage, cheese, poultry.

S. patens. GENTIAN SAGE. Perennial, evergreen in mild climates; use as annual where winters are cold. All Zones. To 2½ ft. stems with arrow shaped, hairy, 2–5-in.-long, green leaves. Deep dark blue flowers 2 in. long. Sun or part shade.

S. sclarea. CLARY SAGE. Biennial. Coarse-foliaged plant to 3–4 ft. Summer flower fountains of bluish white and rose. Easy from seed. Said to have medicinal value as eyewash.

S. splendens. SCARLET SAGE. Annual. Sturdy plant 1–3 ft. high (depends on variety) with dark green leaves topped by tall dense clusters of magnificent scarlet flowers. Also rose, lavender, white varieties. Blooms early summer to frost. 'Scarlet Pygmy' and 'St. John's Fire' are extremely dwarf varieties. Start from seed (slow) or buy young plants from nursery. Thrives in full sun, but will also flower in part shade. Any soil; water generously. Cut flowers don't last. Strong color is best with gray foliage or white flowers.

SAMBUCUS. ELDERBERRY. Deciduous shrubs or trees. In their natural state, these western natives are rampant, fast growing, wild looking. But they can be tamed to a degree. Use them in same way as spiraea or other large deciduous shrubs. In large gardens, they can be effective as screen or windbreak. To keep them dense and shrubby, prune hard every dormant season. New growth sprouts readily from stumps. Sun or light shade, average water. Will take

Sambucus caerulea neomexicana

wet conditions with good drainage. Elders are a confusing lot, and botanists in different regions tend to assign different names to same plant. Generally speaking there are black and blue-fruited kinds (edible by humans) and red-fruited kind with poisonous fruit. But birds eat fruit of all elders.

S. caerulea (*S. glauca*). BLUE ELDERBERRY. Zones 1–17. Native California north to British Columbia, east to Rockies. Shrub 4–10 ft. tall or spreading tree to 50 ft. Leaves 5–8 in. long, divided into 5–9 rather firm, toothed, 1–6-in.-long leaflets. Small white or creamy white flowers in flat-topped clusters 2–8 in. wide, April-August. Clusters of blue to nearly black ¼-in. berries usually covered with whitish powder. Berries edible, often used in jams, jellies, pies, and wine—if birds don't get them first. Forms from southern California and desert states (*S. c. mexicana* and *S. c. neomexicana*) have fewer leaflets of grayer green, and berries are fewer, smaller, drier.

S. callicarpa (*S. racemosa callicarpa*). COAST RED ELDERBERRY, RED ELDERBERRY. Zones 4–7, 14–17. Native to coastal regions, northern California to British Columbia. Shrub to 8 ft. or small tree to 20 ft. Leaves 3–6 in. long, divided into 5–7 smooth,

sharply toothed leaflets. Flowers creamy white, in dome shaped clusters 2–5 in. across. Small berries are bright red, reputed to be poisonous. Requires ample water.

S. canadensis. AMERICAN ELDERBERRY. Zones 1–7, 14–17. Spreading, suckering shrub to 6–8 ft., seldom grown except in cold-winter climates. Almost tropical looking in foliage, each leaf having 7 leaflets up to 6 in. long. Flat, creamy white flower clusters to 10 in. wide in summer are followed by purple black fruit of good flavor. Fruit used for pies, both flowers and fruit for wine. Needs sun, good soil, ample water, hard pruning each year. In March cut back all last year's growth to a few inches. Named fruiting varieties include 'Adams', 'Johns', and many more. Plant any two varieties for pollination.

Ornamental varieties include 'Aurea', with golden green foliage, golden in full sun; and 'Laciniata', CUTLEAF or FERNLEAF ELDER, with finely cut foliage.

S. pubens. Zones 1–3. Shrubby, usually 2–4 ft. tall, possibly to 15 ft. Loose, tall flower clusters followed by bright red fruit later in season.

S. racemosa. RED ELDERBERRY, EUROPEAN RED ELDERBERRY. Zones 1–3. Native northern latitudes in North America, Europe, Asia. Bushy shrub 8–10 ft.; leaves 3–6 in. long, divided into 5 or 7 smooth, sharply toothed leaflets. Small creamy white flowers in dome shaped clusters to 2½ in. wide, May-July, followed by bright red berries. Golden cutleaf variety is called 'Plumosa Aurea'.

SAND CHERRY. See Plum and Prune.

SANDHILL SAGE. See *Artemisia pycnocephala*.

SAN JOSE HESPER PALM. See *Brahea brandegeei*.

SAND PEAR. See *Pyrus pyrifolia*.

SAND STRAWBERRY. See *Fragaria chiloensis*.

SAND VERBENA. See *Abronia*.

SANDWORT. See *Arenaria*.

SANGUINARIA canadensis. BLOODROOT. Perennial. Zones 1–6. This member of poppy family gets its common name because of the orange red juice that seeps from cut roots and stems. Big, deeply lobed grayish leaves. In early spring, 1½-in. white or pink tinged flowers are borne singly on 8-in. stalks. For damp, shaded rock garden where it can spread, or for leafy soil beneath trees or open shrubs. 'Multiplex' has double flowers.

Sanguinaria canadensis

SANGUISORBA minor. See *Poterium sanguisorba*.

SANSEVIERIA trifasciata (often sold as *S. zeylanica*). BOWSTRING HEMP, SNAKE PLANT, MOTHER-IN-LAW'S TONGUE. Evergreen perennials. Outdoors Zones 13–24, protected locations Zone 12. House plants everywhere. Appreciated for thick, patterned leaves that grow in rosettes from thick rhizomes. Leaves 1–4 ft. tall, 2 in. wide, rigidly upright or spreading slightly at top, dark green banded gray green. *S. t.* 'Laurentii' is identical, but adds broad creamy yellow stripes on leaf edges. Dwarf variety 'Hahnii' has rosettes of broad triangular leaves 6 in. long, dark green with silvery banding. Plant piles up to make mass

Sansevieria trifasciata 'Laurentii'

1 ft. tall, equally wide. Serves as good small pot plant or focus for dish garden.

First common name comes from use of tough fibers in leaves as bowstrings; second comes from banding or mottling on leaves, which resembles some snakeskins; third probably comes from toughness of leaves and plants' persistence under neglect. Erect, narrow clusters of greenish white, fragrant flowers seldom appear.

No special soil requirements; water seldom but thoroughly. If grown outdoors, shelter from midday sun, which makes leaves pale and unsightly. Indoors they will grow in much or little light, seldom need repotting, and withstand considerable neglect—dry air, uneven temperatures, and light, capricious watering.

SANTOLINA. Herbs, evergreen subshrubs. All Zones. These have attractive foliage, a profusion of little round flower heads, and stout constitutions. Good as ground covers, bank covers, or low clipped hedges. Grow in any soil in full sun. Both species are aromatic if bruised, and both look best if kept low by pruning. Clip off spent flowers. Cut back in early spring. May die to ground in coldest areas, but roots will live and resume growth. Needs little or no water where summers are cool.

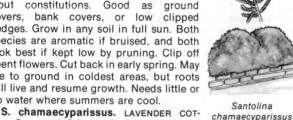

Santolina chamaecyparissus

S. chamaecyparissus. LAVENDER COTTON. Can reach 2 ft., but looks best clipped to 1 ft. or less. Brittle, woody stems densely clothed with rough, finely divided, whitish gray leaves. Bright yellow buttonlike heads in summer on unclipped plants. Plant 3 ft. apart as ground cover, closer as edging for walks, borders, foreground plantings. Replace after a few years if woodiness takes over.

S. virens. Similar to lavender cotton, but narrower, deep green leaves of striking texture; plants look something like puffs of green smoke. Creamy chartreuse flowers. Faster than *S. chamaecyparissus,* tolerates more water. Fire retardant.

SANVITALIA procumbens. CREEPING ZINNIA. Summer annual. Not really a zinnia, but looks enough like it to fool most people. Plants grow only 4–6 in. high, but spread or trail 1 ft. or more. Leaves are like miniature (to 2 in. long) zinnia leaves. Flower heads nearly 1 in. wide, with dark purple brown centers and bright yellow rays. Bloom lasts from midsummer until frost. Plants take much drought and heat once established;

Sanvitalia procumbens

need sun and good drainage. Sow seeds from mid-March (low desert) to May or even June (where soil is slow to warm up). Good hanging basket or pot plants, temporary fillers in borders, slope and bank covers, edgings. Avoid overhead watering.

SAPIUM sebiferum. CHINESE TALLOW TREE. Deciduous tree. Zones 8, 9, 12, 14–16, 18–21. To 35 ft. with dense round or conical crown of equal width. Outstanding fall color. Tends toward shrubbiness, multiple trunks, suckering, but easily trained to single trunk. In colder areas unripened branch tips freeze back each winter; new growth quickly covers damage, but may require thinning. Leaves are poplarlike, roundish, tapering to slender point, light green. Foliage is dense, but general effect is airy; leaves flutter in lightest breeze. If tree is in full sun and has moderate autumn chill its foliage turns brilliant, translucent, neon red. Some trees color plum purple,

Sapium sebiferum

yellow, orange, or mixture of colors. If possible, select your tree while it is in fall color; a few specimens have shown nondescript yellow instead of flaming red. Tiny yellowish flowers in spikes at branch tips; fruit small, clustered, grayish white, waxy coating.

Hardy to 10°–15°F. Grows in most soils, but does somewhat better in mildly acid conditions. Give it ample water for fast growth and prune only to correct shape. Stake young plants securely. Good lawn or street tree, patio or terrace shade. Resistant to oak root fungus. Good screening against low summer sun or objectionable view. Gives light to moderate shade.

SAPONARIA ocymoides. Perennial. All Zones. Trailing habit, to 1 ft. high and 3 ft. across. Leaves oval, dark green; in spring plants are covered with small pink flowers in loose bunches shaped much like phlox. Any soil; easy to grow. Useful for covering walls and as ground cover in little-used areas.

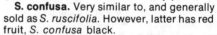

Saponaria ocymoides

SAPOTE, WHITE. See *Casimiroa.*

SARCOCOCCA. Evergreen shrubs. Zones 4–9, 14–24 (see *S. saligna* for exception). Native to Himalayas, China. Of great value in landscaping shaded areas—under overhangs, in entryways, beneath low-branching, evergreen trees. They maintain slow, orderly growth and polished appearance in deepest shade. Will take sun in cool-summer areas. Grow best in soil rich in organic matter. Add peat moss, ground bark, or the like to planting bed. Average garden water. Scale insects only pests.

S. confusa. Very similar to, and generally sold as *S. ruscifolia.* However, latter has red fruit, *S. confusa* black.

Sarcococca ruscifolia

S. hookerana humilis (*H. humilis*). Low growing, seldom more than 1½ ft. high, it spreads by underground runners to 8 ft. and more. Dark green, glossy, narrow oval, pointed leaves (1–3 in. long, ½–¾ in. wide) closely set on branches. Fragrant, tiny white flowers, hidden in foliage in early spring, are followed by glossy blue black fruit. Good ground cover in shade.

S. ruscifolia. Slow growth (6 in. a year) to 4–6 ft., with 3–7-ft. spread. Glossy, waxy, deep green, wavy-edged leaves, 2 in. long, densely set on branches. Flowers (in early spring) small, white, nearly hidden in foliage, but fragrant enough to be noticed many feet away, are followed by red fruit. Will form natural espalier against wall, branches fanning out to form dark patterns.

S. saligna. Least hardy of species. Killed to ground in Zones 4–6 at lows of 8°F. Grows to 3–4 ft. high with weeping branches. Dark green willowlike leaves, 3–5 in. long, 1–1½ in. wide. Fragrant light yellow flowers. Purple fruit.

SARGENT CHERRY. See *Prunus sargentii.*

SARRACENIA. PITCHER PLANT. Perennials. Zones 4–7, house plants (or terrarium plants) nearly anywhere. Leaves rise from creeping rhizome, look like hollow tubes or "pitchers." These leaves trap and digest insects in same manner as our western native pitcher plant—see Darlingtonia. Not easy to grow, requiring boggy, acid soil and high humidity. Will not tolerate hot dry air, strong fertilizers, or extended irrigation with hard water. Grow in bogs, in pots of

Sarracenia flava

wet sand-sphagnum mix, or try them in terrariums or enclosed, humid, glass frames. Give rainwater or distilled water.

S. flava. Leaves 1–2 ft. tall, erect, yellowish green veined red. Flowers solitary on 1–2-ft. stalks, yellow, 4–5 in. across.

S. purpurea. Green to purple red leaves 6–10 in. tall, rather plump. Flowers purple red or greenish, to 2 in. across.

SASA. See *Bamboo.*

SASSAFRAS albidum. SASSAFRAS. Deciduous tree. Zones 4–6, 10, 12, 14–17. Fast to 20–25 ft., then slower to eventual 50–60 ft. Dense and pyramidal, with heavy trunk and rather short branches. Sometimes shrubby. Pleasantly aromatic tree; bark of roots sometimes used for making tea. Leaves 3–7 in. long, 2–4 in. wide; shape may be oval, lobed on one side (mitten shaped), or lobed on both sides. They turn to orange and scarlet in fall, better some years than others. Flowers inconspicuous. Best in sandy, well-drained soil; won't take long summer drought or alkaline soil. Hard to transplant. Suckers badly if roots cut during cultivation.

Sassafras albidum

SATUREJA. Annual and perennial herbs, sometimes shrublike. Aromatic foliage.

S. douglasii *(Micromeria chamissonis).* YERBA BUENA. Creeping perennial. Zones 4–9, 14–24. Native from Los Angeles County to British Columbia (plant for which San Francisco was given its original name of Yerba Buena). Slender stems root as they grow, spreading to 3 ft. Roundish, 1-in.-long leaves with scalloped edges have strong minty scent. Small white or lavender-tinted flowers April-September. Needs rich, moist soil for best appearance, sun along coast, part shade inland. Dried leaves make pleasant tea.

Satureja montana

S. hortensis. SUMMER SAVORY. Summer annual. Upright to 18 in. with loose, open habit. Rather narrow, ½–1½-in.-long aromatic leaves. Delicate, ⅛-in.-long pinkish white to rose flowers in whorls. Grow in light soil rich in humus. Full sun; average water. Excellent container plant. Sow seed where plants are to be grown; thin to 18 in. apart. Use fresh or dried leaves as mild seasoning for meats, fish, eggs, soups, vegetables; favorite with beans. German name *Bohnenkraut* means "bean herb." And some believe that planting it among beans will keep whiteflies away.

S. montana. WINTER SAVORY. Perennial or subshrub. All Zones. Low, spreading, 6–15 in. high. Stiff, narrow to roundish ½–1-in.-long leaves. Profusion of white to lilac ⅜-in.-long blooms in whorls, attractive to bees. Grow in sandy, well-drained soil; give little to moderate water. Sun. Fire resistant if fairly well watered. Keep clipped. Clip at start of flowering season for drying. Propagate from seed (germinates slowly), cuttings, divisions. Space plants 18 in. apart in rows. Use as edging in herb border, or in rock garden. Use leaves fresh or dried. Not as delicate in flavor as summer savory.

SAUROMATUM guttatum *(Arum cornutum).* VOODOO LILY. Tuber. Zones 5, 6, 8, 9, 14–24; also grown as house plant. Flower is composed of 12-in.-long, greenish yellow flower bract marked deep purple, surrounding long blackish purple central spike. Bloom has extremely strong, unpleasant odor. Large, deeply lobed, fanlike, tropical-looking leaves on 3-ft stalks appear after flowers. Big tuber will bloom without planting if large enough; just place it on window sill or table. After bloom, plant in big pot or in garden. Loose, slightly acid soil. Light shade or sun, average water.

S. g. venosum, commonly called SNAKE LILY, has leaves 10–12 in. long, spotted stalk.

Sauromatum guttatum

SAVIN. See *Juniperus sabina.*

SAVORY. See *Satureja.*

SAXIFRAGA. SAXIFRAGE. Perennials. Some native to western mountains and foothills, most from Europe. They thrive best in rock gardens of Northwest, where specialists grow dozens of kinds. Most saxifrages grow in full sun or light shade in cooler regions. They require good drainage, light soil; easily rotted by soggy soil, but can't take drought. Bergenias, once classified as saxifrages, are still often sold as such.

Saxifraga umbrosa

S. rosacea *(S. decipiens, S. sternbergii).* Zones 1–7, 14–17. Cushion-forming, spreading plant—typical "mossy saxifrage." Spreads fairly rapidly; narrow, fleshy leaves are divided into 3–5 narrow lobes. In Northwest, foliage turns crimson in late fall. Flower stalks rise in spring to 8–9 in. tall and display wide-open flowers of white. Afternoon shade best in cool-summer areas; shade essential where summers are hot. Many named varieties and hybrids exist, with flowers of pink, rose, and red.

S. stolonifera *(S. sarmentosa).* STRAWBERRY GERANIUM. Zones 1–9, 14–24; house plant everywhere. Creeping plant that makes runners like strawberry. Nearly round, white-veined leaves to 4 in. across, pink underneath, blend well with pink azaleas. Flowers white, to 1 in. across, in loose, open clusters to 2 ft. tall. Used as house plant in hanging baskets or pots. Ground cover where hard freezes are infrequent. Shade or part shade, considerable moisture.

S. umbrosa. LONDON PRIDE. Zones 1–7, 14–17. Rosettes of shiny green, tongue-shaped leaves 1½ in. long. Open cluster of pink flowers on wine red flower stalk, blooms in May. Does best in shade. Good ground cover for small areas; effective near rocks, stream beds. Needs ample water.

Saxifraga stolonifera

SCABIOSA. PINCUSHION FLOWER. Annual, perennials. Stamens protrude beyond curved surface of flower cluster, giving illusion of pins stuck into a cushion. Easy to grow; need sun. Bloom begins in midsummer, continues until winter if flowers are cut. Good in mixed or mass plantings. Excellent for arrangements.

S. atropurpurea (usually sold as *S. grandiflora).* PINCUSHION FLOWER, MOURNING BRIDE. Annual; may persist as perennial where winters are mild. Grows to 2½–3 ft. tall. Oblong, coarsely toothed leaves. Many long, wiry-stemmed flower clusters 2 in. or more across, in colors from blackish purple to salmon pink, rose, white.

S. caucasica. PERENNIAL PINCUSHION FLOWER. Perennial. All Zones. To 2½ ft. high. Leaves vary from finely cut to uncut. Flowers blue to bluish lavender or white depending on variety. Flower clusters 2½–3 in. across appear from June to frost.

S. columbaria. Perennial. Zones 4–24. To 2½ ft. tall. Leaves gray green, finely cut. Flowers to 3 in. across; lavender blue, pink, white varieties. Does particularly well in Zones 22–24.

Scabiosa columbaria

SCAEVOLA 'Mauve Clusters'. Shrubby perennial. Zones 8–9, 14–24. Evergreen, nearly ever-blooming (in mild climates) ground cover or rock garden plant from Australia. Forms mats 4–6 in. tall, eventually 3 to 5 ft. across. Lilac-mauve flowers in clusters are ½ inch wide, fan-shaped (all petals on one side). Has no special pests, takes moderate drought once established; 2 soakings a month are adequate. Set plants 3 ft. apart for ground cover, or try in hanging basket. Needs little fertilizer, but iron sulfate deepens flower color.

Scaevola

SCARLET LARKSPUR. See *Delphinium cardinale, D. nudicaule.*

SCARLET WISTERIA TREE. See *Sesbania tripetii.*

SCHEFFLERA. Evergreen large shrubs, small trees. Fast-growing, tropical-looking plants; long-stalked leaves divided into leaflets which spread like fingers of hand. House plants everywhere, they can also be grown outdoors in mildest California climates. Grow well near swimming pools. All need rich soil, routine watering, full sun or light shade near coast, light shade inland.

Schefflera actinophylla

S. actinophylla (*Brassaia actinophylla*). QUEENSLAND UMBRELLA TREE, OCTOPUS TREE, SCHEFFLERA. Outdoors Zones 21–24; precariously hardy Zones 16–20 with protection of overhang. As garden plant, grows fast to 20 ft. or more. "Umbrella" name comes from way giant leaves are held. Horizontal tiers of long-stalked leaves are divided into 7–16 large (to 12 in.) leaflets that radiate outward like ribs of umbrella. "Octopus" comes from curious arrangement of flowers in narrow clusters to 3 ft. long that spread horizontally. Color changes from greenish yellow to pink to dark red. Tiny dark purple fruit. Use for striking tropical effects, for silhouette, and for foliage contrast with ferns and other foliage plants. Cut out tips occasionally to keep it from becoming leggy. Overgrown plants can be cut nearly to ground; they will branch and take better form.

As house plant give standard rich potting mix, occasional feeding, bright light. Let mix become dry between waterings. Wash leaves occasionally and mist to discourage mites.

S. arboricola (*Heptapleurum arboricolum*). HAWAIIAN ELF SCHEFFLERA. Outdoors Zones 23, 24. As outdoor plant can reach 20 ft. or more, with equal or greater spread, but easily pruned to smaller dimensions. Leaves very dark green, much smaller than those of *S. actinophylla,* with 3-in. leaflets which broaden toward rounded tips. If stems are planted at angle, they continue to grow at that angle, which can give attractive multistemmed effects. Flowers clustered in flattened spheres 1 ft. wide, yellowish aging to bronze. General plant effect denser, darker, less treelike than *S. actinophylla.* Same care as latter plant. Loves humidity.

Schefflera arboricola

S. digitata. NEW ZEALAND SCHEFFLERA. Zones 17, 23, 24. Grows 10–20 ft. tall, generally with grouped leaning stems. Leaves with 5–10 leaflets, each 3–7 in. long, sometimes deeply lobed, dark, dull green; new leaves light green with brown tinge. Clusters of greenish flowers followed by clustered purplish black fruit.

SCHINUS. PEPPER TREE. Evergreen trees. Commonly planted in lowland parts of California and Arizona. Pepper trees are praised by some gardeners, heartily disliked by others. Fruit attracts birds. Actually, the two species discussed here are quite different from one another, and each should be judged on its own merits.

Schinus molle

S. molle. CALIFORNIA PEPPER TREE. Evergreen tree. Zones 8, 9, 12–24. Fast to 25–40-ft. height and spread. Trunks of old trees are heavy and fantastically gnarled, with knots and burls that frequently sprout leaves or small branches. Bark is light brown, rough. Limbs heavy, branchlets light and gracefully drooping. Bright green leaves are divided into many narrow 1½–2-in.-long leaflets. Numerous tiny, yellowish white summer flowers in drooping 4–6-in. clusters give way to pendant clusters of rose-colored berries in fall, winter. (Some trees have nearly all male flowers; these will not fruit.)

Grows in any soil, tolerates drought when established, and will even get along with poor drainage.

Stake young plants; prune for high branching if you wish to walk under them. To avoid heart rot, keep large pruning cuts sealed until well healed over. Spray for scale. Subject to root rot diseases in infected soils—especially Texas root rot in the desert.

There's room for argument when it comes to usefulness. Some gardeners object to their messy litter, scale infestation, and greedy surface roots; and yet many newcomers to California consider them to be one of our most strikingly handsome trees. Probably the brightest green of desert-tolerant trees. Fire resistant if reasonably well watered. Properly used, they are splendid. Don't plant them between sidewalk and curb, near house foundations, patio paving or entrances, in lawns, or near sewers or drains. Do plant them along roads or rustic streets without curbs—if you can give them room to spread. They are fine trees for shading play area or rustic, gravel surfaced, informal lounging area. One different use: plant young pepper trees 2 ft. apart and prune into a graceful, billowy hedge.

S. terebinthifolius. BRAZILIAN PEPPER. Evergreen tree. Zones 13, 14 (sheltered), 15–17, 19–24. Moderate growth rate to 30 ft., with equal spread. Differs from California pepper in its nonpendulous growth; in its darker green, coarser, glossy leaves with only 5–13 leaflets instead of many; and in bright red berries that are very showy in winter. With very little training it makes broad, umbrella shaped crown. Stake young trees well and prune to make fairly high crown. Also popular as multitrunked tree. Variations in foliage and growth habit are often pronounced. When selecting tree, try to choose one that has rich foliage and that has already set berries.

Feed and water infrequently and deeply to discourage surface roots. To reduce possibility of storm breakage, shorten overlong limbs and do some late-summer thinning so wind can pass through. Subject to verticillium wilt. Good shade tree for patio or small garden.

SCHIPKA LAUREL. See *Prunus laurocerasus* 'Schipkaensis'.

SCHIZANTHUS pinnatus. POOR MAN'S ORCHID, BUTTERFLY FLOWER. Winter-spring annual in Zones 15–17, 21–24; summer annual in Zones 1–6. To 1½ ft. high. Great quantities of small orchidlike flowers. Flowers have varicolored markings on pink, rose, lilac, purple, or white background and are quite showy against their ferny foliage. Sensitive to frost and to heat; best in cool coastal regions. Buy plants in pots, or start seeds indoors about 4 weeks ahead of planting time (germination is slow). Plant in filtered shade.

Schizanthus pinnatus

Combines well with *Primula malacoides* and cineraria, and shares same cultural requirements. Good pot subject. Often grown in greenhouses and conservatories.

SCHIZOCENTRON elegans. See *Heterocentron elegans.*

SCHIZOSTYLIS coccinea. CRIMSON FLAG, KAFFIR LILY. Rhizome. Zones 5–9, 14–24; best in mild-winter climates. Narrow, evergreen leaves, 18 in. tall, resemble those of gladiolus. Spikes of showy, crimson, starlike, 2½-in. flowers bloom on slender 18–24-in. stems in October–November. Variety 'Mrs. Hegarty' has rose pink flowers. Excellent cut flower spikes—each flower lasts 4 days, others follow.

Plant in sun. Provide light shade in hot areas. Add peat moss or leaf mold to soil; water freely during growth. Divide overgrown clumps.

Schizostylis coccinea

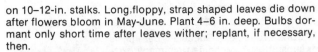

SCHLUMBERGERA. CACTUS. House plants; lathhouse or covered terrace plants in Zones 16, 17, 21–24. These cactus, in nature, live on trees like certain orchids. Plants often confused in nursery trade; many hybrids, selections differ principally in color. Remember, they come from jungle—give them rich porous soil with plenty of leaf mold and sand. Water frequently (but avoid soggy soil) and feed often with liquid fertilizer. Feed as often as every 7–10 days. If grown outdoors in summer, give half shade.

Schlumbergera bridgesii

S. bridgesii. (Often sold as *Zygocactus truncatus.*) CHRISTMAS CACTUS. Old favorite. Grown right, plants may be 3 ft. across, with arching, drooping branches made up of flattened, scalloped, smooth, bright green, spineless, 1½-in. joints; and may have hundreds of many-petaled, long-tubular, 3-in.-long, rosy purplish red flowers at Christmas time.

S. gaertneri. See *Rhipsalidopsis gaertneri.*

S. truncata (*Zygocactus truncatus*). CRAB CACTUS. Joints 1–2 in. long, sharply toothed, with 2 large teeth at end of last joint. Flowers short tubed, with spreading, pointed petals, scarlet. November-March. Many varieties in white, pink, salmon, orange.

Schlumbergera truncata

SCIADOPITYS verticillata. UMBRELLA PINE. Evergreen tree. Zones 4–9, 14–24; borderline Zones 1–3. To 100–120 ft. in its native Japan, but not likely to exceed 25–40 ft. in western gardens. Very slow grower. Young plants are symmetrical, dense, rather narrow; older plants open up and branches tend to droop. Small scalelike leaves grow scattered along branches, bunched at branch ends. At branch and twig ends grow whorls of 20–30 long (3–6 in.), narrow, flattened, firm, fleshy needles of glossy dark green (they radiate out like spokes in umbrella). In time, 3–5-in.-long woody cones may appear.

Plant in rich, well-drained, neutral or slightly acid soil. Full sun in cool-summer areas or near coast; afternoon shade in interior valleys. Give ample water. Watch for mites in hot, dry weather. Can be left unpruned or can be thinned to create Oriental effect. Choice decorative tree for open ground or container use. Good bonsai subject. Boughs are beautiful and long lasting in arrangements.

Sciadopitys verticillata

SCILLA. SQUILL, BLUEBELL. Bulbs. All Zones; exceptions noted below. All have basal, strap shaped leaves and bell shaped or starlike flowers in clusters on leafless stalks. Best planted in informal drifts among shrubs, under deciduous trees, among low-growing spring perennials. Good in pots, for cutting. Dormant in summer.

S. bifolia. First to bloom. Carries up to 8 turquoise blue, inch-wide, starlike flowers on 8-in. stems. White, pale purplish pink, or violet blue varieties. Plant 2 in. deep, 3–5 in. apart.

S. hispanica. See *Endymion hispanicus.*

S. nonscripta. See *Endymion nonscriptus.*

S. peruviana. PERUVIAN SCILLA. Outdoors all year in Zones 14–17, 19–24; in colder climates grow in pots (1 to a 6-in. pot, 3 to a 9–10-in. pot). Actually native to Mediterranean. Bluish purple, starlike flowers—50 or more in large dome shaped cluster,

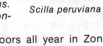

Scilla peruviana

on 10–12-in. stalks. Long, floppy, strap shaped leaves die down after flowers bloom in May-June. Plant 4–6 in. deep. Bulbs dormant only short time after leaves wither; replant, if necessary, then.

S. siberica. SIBERIAN SQUILL. Satisfactory only in cold-winter areas. Very early blooming, with loose spikes of intense blue flowers on 3–6-in. stems. 'Spring Beauty', with darker blue stripes, is choice. Also comes in white, purplish pink, and violet blue varieties.

S. tubergeniana. Blooms in January, at same time as snowdrops (*Galanthus*). Pale blue flowers, 4 or more on 4-in. stalks; 3 or more stalks to each bulb. Plant 2–3 in. deep.

S. violacea. See *Ledebouria socialis.*

SCIMITAR SHRUB. See *Brachysema lanceolatum.*

SCINDAPSUS pictus. Perennial vine grown as house or greenhouse plant. Resembles more familiar green and yellow pothos (*Epipremnum aureum*) in appearance, but the egg shaped leaves are dark green mottled with gray green. Leaves are also thinner in texture, and average somewhat larger (to 6 in., compared with 2–4-in. leaves of pot grown pothos). Flowers insignificant. Variety 'Argyraeus' is most often grown; its markings are more prominent, larger, nearly silver, and leaves have a silky sheen. Needs same care as pothos and other philodendron relatives, but is fussier about drainage, good atmospheric humidity, careful watering and feeding, and bright (but not strong) light.

Scindapsus pictus

SCIRPUS cernuus (*Isolepis gracilis*). LOW BULRUSH. Grasslike perennial. Zones 7–24. To 6–10 in. high, usually less. Drooping, green, threadlike stems topped by small brown flower spikelet. Ample moisture is all it needs to grow; occasional division and resetting will keep it small. Ideal for edge of shallow pond; highly attractive for streamside effect in Japanese gardens. Good pot subject.

Scirpus cernuus

SCOTCH BROOM. See *Cytisus scoparius.*

SCOTCH HEATHER. See *Calluna vulgaris.*

SCOTCH MOSS. See *Sagina subulata.*

SEA BUCKTHORN. See *Hippophae.*

SEA FIG. See *Carpobrotus.*

SEAFORTHIA elegans. See *Archontophoenix cunninghamiana.*

SEA HOLLY. See *Eryngium amethystinum.*

SEA LAVENDER. See *Limonium.*

SEA PINK. See *Armeria.*

SEA POPPY. See *Glaucium.*

SEASIDE DAISY. See *Erigeron glaucus.*

SEA TOMATO. See *Rosa rugosa.*

SEA URCHIN. See *Hakea laurina.*

SEA URCHIN CACTUS. See *Echinopsis*.

SEDUM. STONECROP. Succulent perennials or subshrubs. They come from many parts of world and vary in hardiness, cultural needs; some are among hardiest succulent plants. Some are tiny and trailing, others upright. Leaves fleshy, highly variable in size, shape, and color; evergreen unless otherwise noted. Flowers usually small, starlike, in fairly large clusters, sometimes brightly colored.

Sedum rubrotinctum

Smaller sedums are useful in rock gardens, as ground or bank cover, in small areas where unusual texture, color are needed. Some smaller sedums are prized by collectors of succulents, who grow them as pot or dish garden plants. Larger kinds good in borders or containers, as shrubs. Most kinds propagate very easily by stem cuttings—even detached leaves will root and form new plants. Soft and easily crushed, they will not take foot traffic; otherwise they are tough, low-maintenance plants. Set ground cover kinds 10–12 in. apart. Sedums take full sun or considerable shade, need little water in summer. Grow well near swimming pools.

S. acre. GOLDMOSS SEDUM. All Zones. Evergreen plant 2–5 in. tall, with upright branchlets from trailing rooting stems. Tiny light green leaves; clustered yellow flowers in mid or late spring. Extremely hardy but can get out of bounds, become weed. Good plant to use as a ground cover, between stepping stones, or on dry walls.

S. album (often sold as *S. brevifolium*). All Zones. Creeping evergreen plant 2–6 in. tall. Fleshy leaves ¼–½ in. long, light to medium green, sometimes red tinted. Flowers white or pinkish white. Ground cover.

S. altissimum. See *S. sediforme, S. reflexum*.

S. amecamecanum. See *S. confusum* for plant sold under this name. True *S. amecamecanum (Sedadia amecamecana)* resembles *S. confusum*, but is rare in gardens.

S. anglicum. All Zones. Low, spreading plants 2–4 in. tall. Dark green fleshy leaves to ⅛ in. long. Flowers (spring) pinkish white. Ground cover.

S. brevifolium. Zones 8, 9, 14–24. Europe, north Africa. Tiny, slowly spreading plants, 2–3 in. high with tightly packed, fleshy leaves less than ⅛ in. long. Leaves gray white, flushed with red. Flowers pinkish or white. Sunburns in hot dry places. Needs good drainage. Best in rock garden, with larger succulents in pots, containers, miniature gardens.

S. confusum. Zones 8, 9, 14–24. Native to Mexico. Plants spreading, branching, 6–12 in. tall. Leaves, ¾–1½ in. long, fleshy, shining light green, tend to cluster in rosettes toward branch ends. Dense clusters of yellow flowers in spring. Good ground cover, but sometimes plagued by dieback in wet soils, hot weather; looks best during cooler weather. Use in borders, pots, containers, as edging, in miniature gardens.

S. dasyphyllum. Zones 8, 9, 12, 14–24. Mediterranean, north Africa. To 2 in. tall; tiny leaves closely packed on stems, soft blue green. Spring flowers small, white. Good color for small areas. Ground cover.

S. dendroideum. Zones 8, 9, 12, 14–24. Native to Mexico. To 2 ft. Branching, spreading plant with rounded, fleshy leaves 2 in. long, yellow green, often bronze tinted. Flowers deep yellow, in spring and early summer.

S. d. praealtum (*S. praealtum*). Like the one above but taller (to 3–5 ft.), with lighter yellow flowers and less bronze tinting on leaves. Both plants good for low-maintenance informal hedge or space divider; especially useful along semirural streets or lanes where watering is difficult.

S. guatemalense. See *S. rubrotinctum*.

S. lineare (often sold as *S. sarmentosum*). All Zones. Spreading, trailing, rooting stems to 1 ft. long, closely set with very narrow, fleshy light green leaves 1 in. long. Flowers yellow, star shaped, profuse in late spring, early summer. Ground cover. Vigorous spreader. 'Variegatum', with white-edged leaves, is favorite pot or herbarium plant.

S. moranense. Zones 8–24. Native to Mexico. Small, spreading, much branched plants to 3 in. tall. Leaves small, fleshy,

cylindrical, bright green turning reddish in sun or in cool weather. Flowers sparse, small, white. Rock garden subject or ground cover for small areas.

S. morganianum. DONKEY TAIL, BURRO TAIL. Safely outdoors in Zones 17, 22–24; house plant everywhere; much used under protection of lath or eaves in Zones 13–16, 18–21. Makes long, trailing stems that grow to 3–4 ft. in 6–8 years. Thick, fleshy, light gray green leaves overlap each other along stems to give braided or ropelike effect. Flowers (rarely seen) pink to deep red. Choice plant if well grown. Because it grows such long, pendulous stems, most practical place to grow it is in hanging pot or wall pot. In mildest areas near coast try it at top of walls or high up in rock garden. Rich, fast draining soil. Protect from wind and give half shade; water freely and feed

Sedum morganianum

2–3 times during summer with liquid fertilizer. Relatives that have same culture and same uses: *S.* 'Burrito', with fat tails 1 in. thick composed of densely packed ½-in. leaves; GIANT DONKEY TAIL (often sold as *S. orpetii*), with somewhat shorter, thicker tails; and *Sedeveria* 'Super Giant Donkey Tail', with still thicker, shorter tails.

S. oxypetalum. Zones 16, 17, 21–24. Native of Mexico. Grows to 3 ft. high, usually much less. Even tiny plants have look of a gnarled tree. Leaves 1–1½ in. long; flowers dull red, fragrant. Evergreen or semievergreen in mildest areas, deciduous elsewhere. Handsome pot plant.

S. reflexum (often sold as *S. altissimum*). Zones 8–24. Much like *S. sediforme*, but with shorter leaves, yellow flowers. Ground cover.

S. rubrotinctum (*S. guatemalense*). PORK AND BEANS. Zones 8, 9, 12 (with a little shade and water), 14–24. Sprawling, leaning stems 6–8 in. tall. Leaves like jelly beans, ¾ in. long, green with reddish brown tips, often entirely bronze red in sun. Flowers reddish yellow. Easily detached leaves root readily. Rock garden or pot subject, small-scale ground cover.

S. sediforme (*S. altissimum*). Zones 8–24. Native to Mediterranean region. Spreading, creeping plants to 16 in. tall. Leaves light blue gray, fleshy, to 1½ in. long, narrow, closely set on stems. Flowers small, greenish white. Use in rock garden, for blue green effects in carpet or pattern planting, as small-scale ground cover.

S. sieboldii. All Zones. Native to Japan. Spreading, trailing, unbranched stems to 8–9 in. long. Fleshy leaves in 3s, nearly round, stalkless, toothed in upper half, blue gray edged red. Plant turns coppery red in fall, dies to ground in winter. Each stem shows a broad, dense, flat cluster of dusty pink flowers in autumn. *S. s.* 'Variegatum' has leaves marked yellowish white. Beautiful rock garden or hanging basket plant. Light shade, occasional water in hot interior gardens.

Sedum sieboldii

S. spathulifolium. All Zones. Native from California's Coast Ranges and Sierra Nevada north to British Columbia. Leaves blue green tinged reddish purple, spoon shaped, fleshy, packed into rosettes on short, trailing stems. Flowers light yellow, spring-summer. Ground cover. 'Cape Blanco' is a selected form with good leaf color. 'Purpureum' has deep purple leaves. Good in sunny or partially shaded rock gardens. Needs no water, after it's rooted, in cool-summer climates.

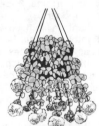

Sedum spathulifolium

S. spectabile. All Zones. China, Japan. Upright or slightly spreading stems to 18 in. tall, well set with blue green, roundish, fleshy, 3-in. leaves. Flowers pink, in broad, dense clusters atop stems in late summer, autumn. Dies down in winter. 'Brilliant' has deep rose red flowers, 'Carmen' is soft rose, and 'Meteor', brightest, has carmine red flowers. Sun, average garden water.

S. spurium. All Zones. Evergreen perennial plant with trailing stems. Leaves thick, inch or so long, nearly as wide, dark green or bronzy tinted. Flowers pink, in dense clusters at ends of 4–5-in. stems in summer. Garden variety called 'Dragon's Blood' has bronzy leaves and rosy red flowers. Rock garden, pattern planting subject, ground cover.

S. stahlii. Zones 8, 9, 14–24. Native to Mexico. Twiggy, trailing, 4–8 in. tall. Leaves like tiny (¼–½ in.) beans closely packed toward ends of stems. Leaves dark green, usually brown tinted or quite brown. Yellow flowers summer or autumn. Use in rock garden, miniature garden, pots, or as limited area ground cover.

S. telephium. All Zones. To 2 ft. Resembles *S. spectabile,* leaves somewhat narrower. If stalks are not cut after bloom, 6-in. dome shaped flower clusters turn to purple clusters of seeds on top of bare stalks. Garden varieties: 'Autumn Joy', to 30 in., with coppery rose bloom; 'Indian Chief', coppery red flowers.

SEGO LILY. See *Calochortus nuttallii.*

SEMIARUNDINARIA. See Bamboo.

SEMPERVIVUM. HOUSELEEK. Succulents. All Zones (shade in Zones 12, 13). Evergreen perennial plants with tightly packed rosettes of leaves. Little offsets cluster around parent rosette. Flowers star shaped, in tight or loose clusters, white, yellowish, pink, red, or greenish, pretty in detail but not showy. Summer bloom. Blooming rosettes die after setting seed, but easily planted offsets carry on. Good in

Sempervivum tectorum

rock gardens, containers, even in pockets on boulders or pieces of porous rock. All need sun in most climates; shade in Zones 12, 13, good drainage, and generous summer watering (except on coast). Many species, all good; these are fairly common:

S. arachnoideum. COBWEB HOUSELEEK. Europe. Tiny gray green rosettes, ¾ in. across, of many leaves joined by fine hairs which give a cobweb-covered look to plant. Spreads slowly to make dense mats. Flowers bright red on 4-in. stems; seldom blooms.

S. tectorum. HEN AND CHICKENS. Rosettes gray green, 4–6 in. across, spreading quickly by offsets. Leaves tipped red brown, bristle pointed. Flowers red or reddish in clusters on stems to 2 ft. tall. Easy in rock gardens, borders, pattern planting.

SENECIO. Perennials, shrubs, vines. Daisy relatives which range from garden cineraria and dusty miller to vines, shrubs, perennials, succulents, even a few weeds. Succulents are often sold as *Kleinia,* an earlier name.

S. cineraria. DUSTY MILLER. Shrubby perennial. All Zones (needs protection Zones 1–3). Spreading plant to 2–2½ ft.; woolly-

Senecio cineraria

white leaves cut into many blunt-tipped lobes. Clustered heads of yellow or creamy yellow flowers at almost any season. Plant gets leggy unless sheared occasionally. Easy to grow, needs only light watering. Fire resistant if fairly well watered. Use in combination with bright-flowered, sun-loving annuals and perennials. Striking in night garden.

S. confusus. MEXICAN FLAME VINE. Evergreen or deciduous vine. Zones 12 (possibly), 13, 16–24. Sometimes grown as annual or perennial in colder climates. Twines to 8–10 ft. in frost free areas; dies back to ground in mild frost, comes back fast from roots. Leaves light green, rather fleshy, 1–4 in. long, ½–1 in. wide, coarsely toothed. Daisylike flowers in large clusters at ends of branches, ¾–1 in. wide, startling orange red with golden centers. Blooms all year where winters are mild. Sun or light shade; moist, light soil. Use on trellis, column, to cascade over bank or wall, or in hanging basket.

S. greyi. Evergreen shrub. Zones 5–9, 14–24. Spreading plant that grows 4–5 ft. high. Stiff, slightly curving stems bear 3½-in.-long, leathery leaves of gray green outlined by silvery white.

Profusion of 1-in.-wide, yellow daisies in 5-in.-wide, flattish clusters comes in summer—effective contrast with gray foliage. Plants usually sold as *S. greyi* are similar but somewhat smaller *S. compactus* and hybrids between the two.

Senecio greyi

Full sun, not-too-rich soil, good drainage, little or moderate water. Prune yearly to remove oldest or damaged growth, stimulate new wood. Attractive with geraniums, zauschneria, cistus, rosemary, purple or red-leafed shrubs. Cut branches effective in arrangements, especially with scarlet and orange flowers; long lasting.

S. hybridus (*S. cruentus*). CINERARIA. Perennial in Zones 16, 17, 22–24; grown as summer annual elsewhere. Valuable for bright colors in cool, shady places; not for hot, dry climates. Most commonly grown are the large-flowered, dwarf kinds generally sold as Multiflora Nana or Hybrida Grandiflora. These are compact 12–15-in.-tall plants with lush, broad green leaves and broad clusters of 3–5-in.-wide daisies that cover top of plant. Will self-sow when adapted. Colors range from white through

Senecio hybridus

pink and purplish red to sensational blues and purples, often with contrasting eyes or bands. Bloom late winter and early spring in mild regions, spring and early summer elsewhere. Plants sold as *Cineraria stellata* are taller (to 2½–3 ft.) with looser clusters of smaller, starlike daisies; these often self-sow.

Frost is hazard to fall-planted cinerarias; plant in spring, or protect by planting under shrubs, trees, overhang, or lath. Plant in shade in cool, moist, loose, rich soil. Water generously and often, but avoid soggy soil, which brings on stem rot. Principal pests are leaf miners, spider mites, slugs, snails.

To grow in large pots for patio display, begin by setting transplants in 3 or 4-in. pots in mixture of rich soil, leaf mold, sand. After several weeks (or before they become potbound) shift into 5–6-in. pots. Feed every 2 weeks with liquid fertilizer. Never let plants dry out.

Effective in mass plantings or combined with ferns, tuberous or other begonias, foliage plants. Use to decorate lanais, shaded terraces, sitting areas. Usually discarded after bloom.

S. jacobsenii. Succulent perennial. Zones 15–17, 21–24. Stems creeping or trailing, to 2 ft. long, slightly branching; leaves neatly disposed all along stems, 2–3 in. long, ½–1 in. wide, thick, fleshy, dark green, broadest toward tips. Small heads of orange flowers. Good hanging basket plant. Sun or light shade, moderate to light watering.

S. leucostachys. See *S. vira-vira.*

S. macroglossus. KENYA IVY, NATAL IVY, WAX VINE. Evergreen vine. House plant. Twining or trailing vine with thin, succulent stems and thick, waxy or rubbery leaves 2–3 in. across. Leaves are shaped like ivy leaves with 3, 5, or 7 shallow lobes. Flowers are tiny yellow daisies. Grow in sunny window and water only when soil becomes dry. Can grow out of doors in low desert if given north or east exposure. 'Variegatum' has leaves sharply splashed with creamy white.

S. mandraliscae (*Kleinia mandraliscae*). Zones 12 (protected spots), 13, 16, 17, 21–24. Somewhat shrubby, with spreading branches to 12–18 in. tall, spreading wider. Leaves cylindrical, 3–3½ in. long, slightly curved, strikingly blue gray.

S. mikanioides. GERMAN IVY. Perennial vine. Zones 14–24. Evergreen in mildest areas, deciduous elsewhere. Twines to 18–20 ft. Leaves roundish, with 5–7 sharply pointed lobes, ivylike, ½–3 in. long. Winter flowers are small yellow daisies without rays. Trailer in window boxes, or screening

Senecio mandraliscae

vine. Plant in sun to semishade. Water sparingly. Can become a weed in coastal California.

(Continued on next page)

S. petasitis. VELVET GROUNDSEL, CALIFORNIA GERANIUM. Perennial or shrubby perennial. Zones 15–17, 21–24, greenhouse plant anywhere. Bulky plant 6–8 (or more) ft. tall, equally wide. Leaves evergreen, tropical looking, large, lobed, fanlike, velvety to touch, to 8 in. across. Blooms in midwinter, with large clusters of small, bright yellow daisylike flowers standing well above mass of plant. Best in sheltered locations in full sun. Needs ample water, some feeding. Prune hard after bloom to limit height and sprawl. Can be kept 2–4 ft. tall in big pots or tubs. Good filler in tropical garden.

S. rowleyanus. STRING OF BEADS. Succulent. Trailing or hanging stems to 6–8 ft. set with ½-in. spherical green leaves. Small white carnation-scented flowers. Hanging basket. Sun or shade near coast, shade inland. Moderate water. Hardy to 25°F.

S. serpens (*Kleinia repens*). Zones 16, 17, 21–24. Like *S. mandraliscae*, but grows 1 ft. tall, has 1½-in.-long light gray or bluish leaves.

Senecio rowleyanus

S. stapeliiformis. Succulent. House plant or indoor/outdoor plant. Stems look like candles 6–8 in. tall and ¾ in. thick, gray green marked with dark green lines. Tiny leaves, lined up in vertical rows along stems, eventually harden into blunt spines. Red flowers. Grow in shallow pots to accommodate creeping rhizome, and give little water in spring, less in summer. Sun or partial shade, excellent drainage.

S. vira-vira (*S. leucostachys*, *S. cineraria* 'Candissimus'). Subshrub. All Zones. To 4 ft. tall; broad, sprawling habit. Leaves like *S. cineraria* but more finely cut into much narrower, pointed segments, whiter. Flowers (summer) not showy, creamy white. In full sun brilliantly white, densely leafy; in part shade looser, more sparsely foliaged with larger, greener leaves. Tip-pinch young plants to keep them compact. Needs light watering.

Senecio serpens

SENNA. See *Cassia*.

SENSITIVE FERN. See *Onoclea sensibilis*.

SENSITIVE PLANT. See *Mimosa pudica*.

SENTRY PALM. See *Howea belmoreana*.

SEQUOIA sempervirens. COAST REDWOOD. Evergreen tree. Zones 4–9, 14–24. Native to parts of Coast Ranges from Curry County, Oregon, to Monterey County, California. Tallest of the world's trees, and one of West's most famous native trees (equally famous is its close relative *Sequoiadendron*, giant sequoia or big tree). Fine landscaping tree—fast growing (3–5 ft. a year), substantial, pest free, and almost always fresh looking and woodsy smelling.

Its red brown, fibrous-barked trunk goes straight up (unless injured). Nearly parallel sides on redwood's trunk indicate tree has fared well (if redwoods struggle they develop trunks with noticeable taper).

Sequoia sempervirens

Branches grow straight out from trunk and cup up a little at outer end. Branchlets hang down slightly from branches. Flat, pointed, narrow leaves (½–1 in. long) grow in one plane on both sides of stem like feather. Leaves are medium green on top, grayish underneath. Small round cones are 1 in. long.

Plant in full sun to half shade. One of best growing places is in or directly next to a lawn. Redwood thrives on luxurious supply of water (in 10–20 years, however, tree may defeat lawn). Away from lawns it needs occasional feeding and regular summer watering (at least for first 5 years). Resistant to oak root fungus.

Here's a planting mix recipe for a 1 or 5-gallon-size redwood. It makes a redwood grow well in just about any soil—it's especially useful in Zones 7–9, 14–16, 18–24. Dig a hole 18 in. wide and 3 ft. deep. Pile the excavated soil and thoroughly mix into it 1 lb. of iron sulfate and 2 cubic ft. of cattle manure. Throw the blended mix back into the hole and saturate it (to leach out salts and ammonia). After mix dries enough to be workable, remove enough from the center to make room for the root ball. Use removed mix to make a watering dike about 10 in. out from the tree trunk.

Troubles the tree encounters are mostly physiological: (1) Not enough water or hot, dry sites make it sulk and grow slowly; (2) Too much competition from bigger trees and structures makes it grow lanky, thin, and open; (3) Lack of available iron makes needles turn yellow every summer, especially on new growth—apply iron sulfate or chelated iron; (4) It's normal for oldest leaves to turn yellow, then brown, and then drop in late summer and early fall.

Count on branch spread at base (tip to tip) of 14–30 ft. Although mature, centuries-old natives surpass 350 ft. in height, 70–90 ft. seems to be most to expect in garden in one owner's lifetime; trees can reach this height in 25 years. Use redwood singly as shade tree, tree to look up into or to hang a swing from, or tree to be seen from 2 blocks away. Or, plant several in a grove or in a 40-ft.-diameter circle—inside it's cool, fragrant, and a fine spot for fuchsias, begonias, and people on hot summer days. For grove or circle planting, space trees 7 ft. apart. Trees can be planted 3–4 ft. apart and topped at least once a year to make beautiful hedge.

Redwoods vary greatly in form, texture, and color. Some are dense and some are open; some are pendulous, others bristly; foliage colors may be any shade from light green to deep blue green; branch angles vary from a slight up-tilt to almost straight down. These characteristics are determined mostly by heredity—a tree will have them all its life.

Until the 1970s, all redwoods at nurseries were grown from seed, with each seedling inheriting a slightly different set of characteristics. But now there are named varieties available, vegetatively propagated, with certain definite growth and color characteristics. 'Aptos Blue' has dense blue green foliage on nearly horizontal branches with branchlets hanging down. 'Santa Cruz' has light green foliage, soft texture, branches pointing slightly down. 'Soquel' has fine texture, somewhat bluish green foliage, horizontal branches that turn up at tips, and a sturdy, stout trunk with little suckering. 'Los Altos' has deep green foliage of heavy texture on horizontal, arching branches.

Variety 'Adpressa' ('Albo spica') is a dwarf for rock garden use—up to 3 ft. high and 6 ft. wide; its new growth is tipped white, which deepens to green as summer advances.

SEQUOIADENDRON giganteum (*Sequoia gigantea*). BIG TREE, GIANT SEQUOIA. Evergreen tree. All Zones. Native to west slope of the Sierra Nevada from Placer County to Tulare County. Most massive trunk in the world and one of tallest trees, reaching 325 ft. in height with 30-ft. trunk diameter. It has always shared fame and comparisons with its close relative, the coast redwood (*Sequoia*). But, horticulturally, similarities are rather few.

Dense foliage of giant sequoia (more bushy than coast redwood) is gray green; branchlets are clothed with short, overlapping, scalelike leaves with sharp points. It's a somewhat prickly tree to reach into. Dark reddish brown cones, 2–3½ in. long. Bark is

Sequoiadendron giganteum

reddish brown and generally similar to that of coast redwood.

Giant sequoia is hardier to cold than coast redwood. It grows a little slower—2–3 ft. a year. It also needs less water. Plant in deep soil, preferably in full sun, and water deeply but infrequently once trees are established.

Primary use is as featured tree in large lawn (roots may surface there in due time) or other open space. Trees hold lower branches throughout their long youth, and are likely to get too broad for the small garden. In essence, then, giant sequoia is easier to grow than coast redwood and more widely adaptable to cold, dry climates but it doesn't have as many landscape uses. Variety 'Pendulum' has drooping branches—and must be staked to coax it into vertical habit.

SERVICE BERRY. See *Amelanchier.*

SESBANIA tripetii *(Daubentonia tripetii).* SCARLET WISTERIA TREE. Deciduous shrub or small tree. Zones 7–9, 12–16, 18–23. Native to Argentina. Neither a wisteria nor a tree, and flower color is more burnt orange than scarlet. Fast growing to 8–10 ft. high and 6–8 ft. wide, with fernlike leaves. Showy, drooping clusters of yellow and orange red, sweet pea shaped flowers from May through summer. Pods that follow are 4-angled and winged. Remove pods as they form to prolong flowering.

Sesbania tripetii

Give full sun and warmest spot in garden. Prune severely in early spring to thin and shorten side branches to stubs. Average water.

Not long-lived plant and appears a little out of place with glossy-leafed, refined plants, but valued for exciting color and quick effects. Most often seen trained into flat-topped standard tree on 6-ft. trunk. Can be grown in containers, blooming quite heavily in 12-in. pots.

SETCREASEA pallida 'Purple Heart'. PURPLE HEART. Perennial. Zones 12–24. Freezes, recovers from roots Zones 12–18; house plant anywhere. Stems a foot or more high, inclined to lop over. Leaves rather narrowly oval and pointed, very strongly shaded with purple, particularly underneath. Use discretion in planting, or the vivid foliage may create harsh effect (pale or deep purple flowers are inconspicuous). Pinch back after bloom. Plants are generally unattractive in winter. Will take light shade; color best in sun. Frosts may kill tops, but growth resumes in warm weather and recovery is fast.

Setcreasea pallida 'Purple Heart'

SHADBLOW, SHADBUSH. See *Amelanchier.*

SHALLOT. Small onionlike plant that produces cluster of edible bulbs from single bulb. Prized in cooking for its distinctive flavor. Plant either sets (small dry bulbs) or nursery plants in fall in mild climates, early spring in cold-winter areas. Leaves 12–18 in. high develop from each bulb. Tiny lavender or white flowers sometimes appear. Ultimately 2–8 bulbs will grow from each original set. At maturity (early summer if fall planted, late summer if spring planted), bulbs are formed and tops yellow and die. Harvest by pulling clumps and dividing bulbs. Let outer skin dry for about a month so that shallots can be stored for 4–6 months. Some seed firms sell sets; nurseries with large stocks of herbs may sell growing plants. If you plant sets, place in ground so that tips are just covered.

Shallot

SHAMROCK. Around St. Patrick's Day nurseries and florists sell "shamrocks." These are small potted plants of *Medicago lupulina* (hop clover, yellow trefoil, black medick), an annual plant; *Oxalis acetosella* (wood sorrel), or *Trifolium repens* (white clover). The last is most common.

All have in common leaves divided into 3 leaflets (symbolic of the Trinity). They can be kept on a sunny window sill or planted out, but have little ornamental value and are likely to become weeds.

SHASTA DAISY. See *Chrysanthemum maximum.*

SHEEP BUR. See *Acaena.*

SHELL FLOWER. See *Alpinia zerumbet, Moluccella laevis.*

SHELL GINGER. See *Alpinia zerumbet.*

SHE-OAK. See *Casuarina.*

SHEPHERDIA argentea. SILVER BUFFALOBERRY. Deciduous shrub. Grown Zones 1–3, 10. Native to many western habitats, from the plains of Canada and the Midwest to California. Spreading, suckering shrub 5–6 ft. tall (rarely to 12 ft.) with spine-tipped branchlets. Leaves 1 in., longish ovals, silvery on both upper and lower surfaces. Plants either male or female; if both are present, latter bear ¼-in. berries of bright red or orange, sour but edible and used for jams and jellies. Flowers not showy. Good plant for attracting birds. Withstands any amount of cold and wind, most soils (including considerable alkali), and puts up with drought once established.

Shepherdia argentea

SHIBATAEA. See Bamboo.

SHIMPAKU. See *Juniperus chinensis sargentii.*

SHISO. See *Perilla frutescens.*

SHORTIA. Perennials. Zones 1–7. Beautiful small evergreen plants. Spread slowly by underground stems. Need shade, moisture. Acid, leafy or peaty soil. Grow with azaleas or rhododendrons.

S. galacifolia. OCONEE BELLS. Forms clump of round or oval glossy green leaves 1–3 in. long, with scalloped-toothed edges. Single, nodding white bell, 1 in. wide, with toothed edges, tops each of the many 4–6-in.-high stems in March-April.

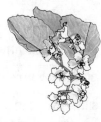
Shortia galacifolia

S. soldanelloides. FRINGE BELLS. Coarsely toothed-round leaves form clumps similar to above. Flowers differ in being pink to rose in color, with deeply fringed edges.

S. uniflora 'Grandiflora'. Like *S. galacifolia* but with indented and wavy-edged leaves and flowers that are large fringed bells of clear soft pink.

SHOOTING STAR. See *Dodecatheon.*

SHRIMP PLANT. See *Justicia brandegeana.*

SHRUB ALTHAEA. See *Hibiscus syriacus.*

SHRUB ASTER. See *Felicia fruticosa.*

SIBERIAN PEASHRUB. See *Caragana arborescens.*

SIBERIAN WALLFLOWER. See *Erysimum hieraciifolium.*

SIERRA LAUREL. See *Leucothoe davisiae.*

SIERRA STAR TULIP. See *Calochortus nudus.*

SILENE. Perennials. Many species, some with erect growth habit, others cushionlike. Sun, part shade.

S. acaulis. CUSHION PINK, MOSS CAMPION. Perennial. Zones 1–11, 14–16, 18–21. Mosslike mat of bright green, narrow leaves about ⅝ in. long. Reddish purple flowers, ½ in. across, borne singly, March-April. For gravelly, damp but well-drained spot in rock garden.

S. californica. CALIFORNIA INDIAN PINK. Perennial. Zones 7–11, 14–24. Native to California and southern Oregon foothills. Loosely branching to 6–16 in. tall. Foliage somewhat sticky. Flaming red, 1¼-in.-wide flowers, with petals cleft and fringed. Spring blooming. Occasionally sold in seed packets. Needs well-drained soil; let it dry off in summer.

Silene californica

S. coeli-rosa. See *Lychnis coeli-rosa.*

S. schafta. MOSS CAMPION. Perennial. Zones 1–9, 14–16, 18–21. Forms tuft of upright, rather wiry stems to 6–12 in. high. Leaves small, tongue shaped. Stalks with 1–2 rose purple flowers bloom late summer, autumn. Average water.

SILK OAK. See *Grevillea robusta.*

SILKTASSEL. See *Garrya.*

SILK TREE. See *Albizia julibrissin.*

SILVER BELL. See *Halesia carolina.*

SILVERBERRY. See *Elaeagnus commutata, E. pungens.*

SILVER BUFFALOBERRY. See *Shepherdia argentea.*

SILVER DOLLAR GUM. See *Eucalyptus polyanthemos.*

SILVER FERN. See *Pteris quadriaurita* 'Argyraea'.

SILVER LACE VINE. See *Polygonum aubertii.*

SILVER MOUNTAIN GUM. See *Eucalyptus pulverulenta.*

SILVER SPREADER. See *Artemisia caucasica.*

SILVER TREE. See *Leucodendron argenteum.*

SILVERVEIN CREEPER. See *Parthenocissus henryana.*

SIMMONDSIA chinensis. JOJOBA, GOATNUT. Evergreen shrub. Zones 10–13, 19–24. Native to deserts of southern California, Arizona, Mexico. Dense, rigid-branching, spreading shrub 3–6 (rarely to 16) ft. tall. Foliage dull gray green; leaves leathery, 1–2 in. long, to ½ in. wide. Flowers inconspicuous; male and female on different plants. If both are present, female plants bear edible, nutlike fruit about ¾ in. long. Flavor like filbert, slightly bitter until cured. High oil content of fruit gives plant possible commercial use as crop for marginal land.

Simmondsia chinensis

Young plants rather tender; when established will take 15°F. Needs little water. Likes full sun, heat. Of particular value as clipped hedge, foundation planting in desert garden.

SINARUNDINARIA. See Bamboo.

SINGLE WEEPING CHERRY. See *Prunus subhirtella* 'Pendula'.

SINNINGIA speciosa *(Gloxinia speciosa).* GLOXINIA. Tuber. House plant, or pot plant for shaded terrace or patio. Leaves oblong, dark green, toothed, fuzzy, 6 in. or longer. Flowers are spectacular—large, velvety, bell shaped, ruffled on edges. Come in blue, purple, violet, pink, red, or white. Variable; some flowers have dark dots or blotches, others contrasting bands at the flower rims. Leaves occasionally white veined. Tubers usually available December-March. Plant 1 in. deep in rich, loose mix. Water sparingly until first leaves appear; increase watering after roots form. Apply water around base of plant, or from below; don't water on top of leaves. When roots fill pot, shift to larger pot. Feed regularly during growth. After bloom has finished, gradually dry off plants and store tubers in cool dark place with just enough moisture to keep them from shriveling. Repot in January-February.

Sinningia speciosa

SIPHONOSMANTHUS delavayi. See *Osmanthus delavayi.*

SISYRINCHIUM. Perennials. Zones 4–24. Related to iris. Narrow, rather grasslike leaves. Small flowers, made up of 6 segments, open in sunshine. Pretty but not showy, best suited for informal gardens or naturalizing. Sun or light shade, average water. Will endure some drought.

S. bellum. BLUE-EYED GRASS. Native to coastal California. To 4–16 in. tall. Narrow green or bluish green leaves. Flowers purple to bluish purple, ½ in. across, bloom early to midspring.

S. californicum. YELLOW-EYED GRASS. Native to coast of California and Oregon. Dull green leaves, broader, slightly taller than those of blue-eyed grass. Yellow flowers open May-June. Can grow in wet, low, or poorly drained places.

Sisyrinchium bellum

S. macounii. Native to Northwest. Dwarf plant with broad leaves, large flowers. Best-known form is *S. m.* 'Album', 4–6 in. tall with 1-in.-wide white flowers on 6-in. stems. Long bloom season in spring. Good container or rock garden plant.

S. striatum. Larger than other sisyrinchiums; leaves are iris-like, 1 ft. long, up to 1 in. wide, attractive gray green. Spikelike flower clusters grow to 2½ ft., with many pale yellow, brown-streaked ½-in. flowers in spring. Attractive for foliage clumps of gray, with old leaves fading to black. Can self-sow and become attractive nuisances.

SKIMMIA. Evergreen shrubs. Zones 4–9, 14–22 (grows best in Zones 4–6, 17; needs special handling elsewhere). Slow growing, compact with glossy rich green leaves neatly arranged. Clusters of tiny white flowers open from clusters of pinkish buds held well above foliage. Blooms April-May. Red hollylike fruit in fall and through December if pollination requirements are met.

When massed, forms level surface of leaves; individual plants are dense mounds. Light to moderate shade preferable; full sun yellows leaves, heavy shade makes plants lanky, inhibits bloom.

Skimmia japonica

No special soil requirement in Northwest. In California's alkaline soils add at least 50 percent peat moss or the like to planting soil. In Northwest, skimmia is attacked by special skimmia mite that gives leaves sunburned look. Also expect attacks by thrips and red spider mites. Plants need ample water, but water mold is a problem in hot regions. Good shrub under low windows. Use to flank entryways. Plant beside shaded walks. Blends well with all shade plants. Good in containers.

S. foremanii. Hybrid between following two species. Resembles *S. japonica* but more compact, with broader, heavier, darker green leaves. Seems to take northern California conditions better than either parent. Plants may be male, female, or self-fertile.

S. japonica. Variable in size. Slow growth to 2–5 ft. tall, 3–6 ft. wide. Leaves 3–4 in. long, an inch wide, oval, short pointed, mostly clustered near twig ends. Flowers fragrant, in 2–3-in. clusters. Bright red berries on female plants if male plant present, and worth effort of planting both. Form with ivory white berries is available. *S. j.* 'Macrophylla' is a male form with large leaves and flowers. Rounded, spreading shrub to 5–6 ft. high.

S. reevesiana *(S. fortunei).* Dwarf, dense-growing shrub 2 ft. tall. Self-fertile, with dull crimson fruit. Fragrant flowers.

SKY FLOWER. See *Duranta repens, Thunbergia grandiflora.*

SKUNKBUSH. See *Rhus trilobata.*

SMALL BURNET. See *Poterium sanguisorba.*

SMALL SOAPWEED. See *Yucca glauca.*

SMILACINA racemosa. FALSE SOLOMON'S SEAL. Perennial. Zones 1–7, 15–17. Grows 1–3 ft. tall. Each single arching stalk has several 3–10-in.-long leaves, hairy beneath. Stalk topped by fluffy, conical cluster of fragrant, small, creamy white flowers in March-May, followed by red, purple-spotted berries. Most common form in West is variety *amplexicaulis,* whose leaves sheath stem at base. You see it commonly in shaded woods—California to British Columbia, east to Rockies. Sun or shade, water during spring growth. Can go dry in summer if in shade.

Smilacina racemosa

SMOKE TREE. See *Cotinus coggygria, Dalea spinosa.*

SNAIL VINE. See *Vigna caracalla.*

SNAKE LILY. See *Sauromatum guttatum* 'Venosum'.

SNAKE PLANT. See *Sansevieria.*

SNAKESHEAD. See *Fritillaria meleagris.*

SNAPDRAGON. See *Antirrhinum majus.*

SNAPWEED. See *Impatiens.*

SNEEZEWEED. See *Helenium.*

SNOWBALL. See *Viburnum.*

SNOWBELL. See *Styrax.*

SNOWBERRY. See *Symphoricarpos.*

SNOW BUSH. See *Ceanothus cordulatus.*

SNOWDROP. See *Galanthus.*

SNOWDROP TREE. See *Halesia carolina.*

SNOWFLAKE. See *Leucojum.*

SNOWFLAKE TREE. See *Trevesia.*

SNOW GUM. See *Eucalyptus niphophila.*

SNOW-IN-SUMMER. See *Cerastium tomentosum.*

SNOW-ON-THE-MOUNTAIN. See *Euphorbia marginata.*

SOAPBARK TREE. See *Quillaja saponaria.*

SOCIETY GARLIC. See *Tulbaghia violacea.*

SOLANDRA maxima (usually sold as *S. guttata*). CUP-OF-GOLD-VINE. Evergreen vine. Zones 17, 21–24; with overhead protection in Zones 15, 16, 18–20. Fast, sprawling, rampant growth to 40 ft. Fasten to support. Large, broad, glossy leaves 4–6 in. long. Blooms February-April and intermittently at other times. Flowers golden yellow striped brownish purple, bowl shaped, 6–8 in. across.

Solandra maxima

Full sun near coast; needs cool, shaded roots in hot inland valleys. Prune to induce laterals and more flowers. Can be cut back to make rough hedge. Takes salt spray directly above tide line; stands wind, fog. Use on big walls, pergolas, along eaves, or as bank cover.

SOLANUM. Evergreen and deciduous shrubs and vines. Includes, in addition to potato and eggplant (described under their own names), a number of ornamental plants. Ordinary garden care suits most of them.

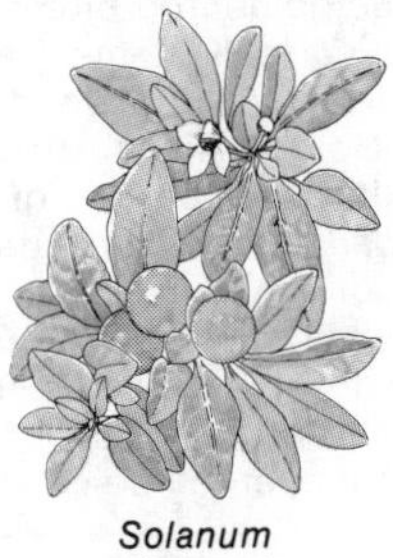
Solanum pseudocapsicum

S. jasminoides. POTATO VINE. Evergreen or deciduous vine. Zones 8, 9, 12–24. Fast growth to 30 ft.; twining habit. Leaves 1½–3 in. long, evergreen in milder winters, medium to purplish green. Flowers pure white, or white tinged blue, an inch across, in clusters of 8–12. Nearly perpetual bloom; heaviest in spring. Sun or part shade. Grown for flowers or for light overhead shade. Cut back severely at any time to prevent tangling, promote vigorous new growth; control rampant runners that grow along ground.

S. pseudocapsicum. JERUSALEM CHERRY. Evergreen shrub. Zones 23, 24; anywhere pot or container plant for indoor use, outdoor summer decoration. Grows 3–4 ft. high. Foliage deep green; leaves 4 in. long, smooth, shiny. Flowers ½ in. wide, white. Fine show of scarlet (rarely yellow) ½-in. fruit like miniature tomatoes, October-December. Fruit may be poisonous; caution children against eating them. Usually grown as annual. In Zones 23, 24, blooms, fruits, and seeds itself through year. The many dwarf strains (to 12 in. high) are more popular than taller kinds, have larger (to 1 in.) fruit.

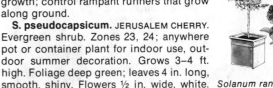

Solanum rantonnetii

S. rantonnetii. Evergreen or deciduous shrub or vine. Zones 12, 13 in protected patios, 15–24. As free-standing plant makes 6–8-ft. shrub. Can be staked into tree form. With support can grow to vine 12–15 ft. or more. Informal, fast growing, not easy to use in tailored landscape. Evergreen in mild winters; leaves drop in severe cold, branch tips may die back. Oval leaves to 4 in. long, bright green. Flowers violet blue, yellow centered, 1 in. wide, blooming throughout warm weather, often nearly throughout year. Apparently all plants in cultivation are variety 'Grandiflorum'. Wild species has flowers only half as large.

Prune severely to keep it a neat shrub. Give it support when used as vine; or let it sprawl as ground cover.

S. wendlandii. COSTA RICAN NIGHTSHADE. Deciduous vine.

(Continued on next page)

Zones 16, 21–24. Tall, twining vine with prickly stems. Leaves larger than those of other species (4–10 in. long), lower ones divided into leaflets. Leaves drop in low temperatures even without frost. Slow to leaf out in spring. Big clusters of 2½-in. lilac blue flowers. Use to clamber into tall trees, to cover pergola, to decorate eaves of large house.

SOLEIROLIA soleirolii (Helxine soleirolii). BABY'S TEARS, ANGEL'S TEARS. Perennial. Zones 8–24; in Zones 4–7 a summer cover that renews itself from root fragments and seeds. Creeping plants with tiny round leaves make lush medium green mats 1–4 in. high. Flowers inconspicuous. Tender, juicy leaves and stems easily injured, but aggressive growth habit quickly repairs damage. Roots easily from pieces of stem and can become invasive pest.

Soleirolia soleirolii

Grows best in shade, but takes full sun near coast if water supply is ample. Freezes to black mush in hard frosts, but comes back fast. Cool-looking, neat cover for ferns or other shade loving plants. Can be used to carpet terrariums or space under greenhouse benches. There is golden green variety.

SOLIDAGO. GOLDENROD. Perennial. All Zones. Not as widely known and grown in far West as Rockies and eastward. A few can be grown here. Varieties of garden origin are sometimes sold. They grow 1–3 ft. high (sometimes to 5 ft.), with characteristic goldenrod plume of yellow flowers topping leafy stems. Varieties differ chiefly in size and in depth of yellow shading. 'Golden Mosa', to 3 ft., has light yellow flowers color of "mimosa" (Acacia baileyana). Plants grow best in not-too-rich soil, in full sun or light shade. Average water requirement. Good meadow planting with black-eyed Susan and Michaelmas daisies, or can be used in border for summer-fall color.

Solidago

SOLLYA heterophylla (S. fusiformis). AUSTRALIAN BLUEBELL CREEPER. Evergreen shrub or vine. Zones 8, 9, 14–24. Grows 2–3 ft. tall as loose, spreading shrub; given support and training, climbs to 6–8 ft. Foliage light and delicate; leaves narrow, glossy green, 1–2 in. long. Clusters of ½-in.-long, brilliant blue, bell shaped flowers appear through most of summer.

Full or part sun in coastal areas, part shade inland. Drought tolerant when established, but looks better with regular watering and frequent pruning to fatten it up. Dies if drainage is poor. Spray to control scale insects. Will grow under eucalyptus trees. Use as ground cover, border planting, along steps, on half-shaded banks. Plant over low wall, where its branches can spill downward. Good container plant.

Sollya heterophylla

SOLOMON'S SEAL. See Polygonatum.

SOPHORA. Deciduous or evergreen trees or shrubs. Leaves divided into numerous leaflets. Drooping clusters of sweet pea shaped flowers are followed by pods bearing seeds.

S. arizonica. Evergreen shrub. Zones 10, 12, 13, possibly 11. To 6–10 ft. with gray green foliage, clusters of 1-in. lavender flowers. Takes heat and drought, prefers occasional deep irrigation. Slow growing, rare.

Sophora japonica

S. japonica. JAPANESE PAGODA TREE, CHINESE SCHOLAR TREE. Deciduous tree. All Zones. Moderate growth to 20 ft.; from this point it grows slowly to 40 ft., with equal or greater spread. Young wood smooth, dark gray green. Old branches and trunk gradually take on rugged look of oak. Dark green, 6–10-in. leaves divided into 7–17 oval, 1–2-in.-long leaflets. Long, open, 8–12-in. clusters of yellowish white, ½-in.-long flowers, July-September. Pods are 2–3½ in. long, narrowed between big seeds in bead necklace effect. Unreliable bloom where summers are cold and damp. Not fussy as to soil, water; no special pests or diseases. Resistant to oak root fungus. 'Regent' is exceptionally vigorous, uniform grower. One of best spreading trees for giving shade to lawn or patio. Good tree for Rocky Mountain area, but subject there to damage from ice storms.

Sophora japonica

S. secundiflora. MESCAL BEAN, TEXAS MOUNTAIN LAUREL. Evergreen shrub or tree. Zones 8–16, 18–24. Can be trained into 25-ft. tree with short, slender trunk or multiple trunks, narrow crown, and upright branches. Very slow growth, especially in cool-summer regions. Leaves 4–6 in. long, divided into 7–9 glossy, dark green, oval leaflets, 1–2 in. long. Blooms February-April; inch-wide, violet blue, wisterialike flowers are carried in drooping 4–8-in. clusters. Rarely a white-flowered form appears. Flowers have sweet fragrance. Silvery gray, woody, 1–8-in.-long seed pods open on ripening to show bright red ½-in. seeds which are decorative but poisonous—remove pods before they mature. Thrives in hot sun and alkaline soil, but needs good drainage and some water. Choice small tree for street, lawn, or patio. Untrained, it is good large screen, bank cover, or espalier.

S. tetraptera. KOWHAI, YELLOW KOWHAI. Evergreen or deciduous shrub or small tree. Zones 15–17. Slow growing to 15–20 ft. Is slender, open, rather narrow tree which drops its leaves in spring just before blooming. Leaves 3–6 in. long, divided into tiny leaflets, their number ranging from 20–40. Flowers bright golden yellow, 2 in. long, in hanging clusters of 4–8. Seed pods with 4 wings, narrowed between seeds, grow 2–8 in. long. Rather tender; doesn't take drought and low humidity. Well-drained soil, ample water, full sun or partial shade.

SORBARIA sorbifolia (Spiraea sorbifolia). FALSE SPIRAEA. Deciduous shrub. Zones 1–10, 14–21. Spreads by suckering to cover large areas if not curbed. Grows 3–8 ft. tall, less in poor, dry soil. Leaves are fernlike, 6–12 in. long, with up to 23 toothed, deep green leaflets. Stems topped in summer by branching clusters (to 1 ft. long) of tiny white flowers. These should be cut off after they have faded.

General effect is lush, almost tropical, especially in rich, moist soil. Sun or light shade. Tolerates some drought when established. Thin clumps drastically or cut back near ground in earliest spring; plants bloom on new wood.

Sorbaria sorbifolia

SORBUS. MOUNTAIN ASH. Deciduous trees, rarely shrubs. Zones 1–10, 14–17. Grown for finely cut, somewhat fernlike foliage, clustered white flowers, and bright fruit. All stand winter cold, can endure strong winds, low humidity, extreme heat. Average garden soil, sun or light shade, good drainage, average garden watering. Where adapted they are good small garden or street trees, though fruit can be messy over paving. Fruit is generally red, but rarely available white, pink, or golden varieties and species show up; all are attractive to birds. Some may be difficult to transplant. Cankers a problem when trees are under stress. Watch for fireblight.

Sorbus aucuparia

S. aucuparia. EUROPEAN MOUNTAIN ASH. Moderate to rapid growth to 20–30 ft. with 15–20 ft. spread; may grow much larger. Sharply rising branches make dense oval to round crown. Leaves have 9–15, 1–2-in. leaflets, dull green above, gray green below. They turn yellow, orange, or red in fall. Flat clusters, 3–5 in. wide, of tiny white flowers bloom in late spring followed by clusters of orange red, berrylike, ¼-in. fruit which color in midsummer, may hang until spring unless birds eat them. Fruit especially attractive against background of conifers. 'Cardinal Royal' has especially large bright red berries that color early.

S. tianshanica. TURKESTAN MOUNTAIN ASH. Large shrub or small tree to 16 ft. Leaves 5–6 in. long, with 9–15 leaflets to 2 in. long, ½ in. wide. Loose clusters of ¾-in. flowers 3–5 in. across, followed by bright red fruit. Neat form, slow growth; excellent plant for small garden.

SORREL, WOOD OR REDWOOD. See *Oxalis.*

SORREL TREE. See *Oxydendrum arboreum.*

SOUR GUM. See *Nyssa sylvatica.*

SOURWOOD. See *Oxydendrum arboreum.*

SOUTHERN RATA. See *Metrosideros umbellatus.*

SOUTHERN SWORD FERN. See *Nephrolepis cordifolia.*

SOUTHERNWOOD. See *Artemisia abrotanum.*

SPANISH BAYONET. See *Yucca aloifolia.*

SPANISH BLUEBELL. See *Endymion hispanicus.*

SPANISH BROOM. See *Genista hispanica, Spartium junceum.*

SPANISH DAGGER. See *Yucca gloriosa.*

SPANISH FLAG. See *Mina lobata.*

SPANISH SHAWL. See *Heterocentron elegans.*

SPARAXIS tricolor. HARLEQUIN FLOWER. Corm. Zones 9, 13–24. Native to South Africa. Closely related to and similar to ixia in uses and culture. Small funnel shaped flowers in spikelike clusters on 12-in. stems. Flowers come in yellows, pinks, purples, reds, and white. Usually blotched and splashed with contrasting colors. Blooms over long period in late spring. Leaves are sword shaped. Use in borders, rock gardens, containers, for cutting. Naturalize like freesias in mild climates. Plant in full sun in fall; set corms 2 in. deep, 2–3 in. apart.

Sparaxis tricolor

SPARMANNIA africana. AFRICAN LINDEN. Evergreen shrub, tree. Zones 17, 21–24; with special protection 15, 16, 18–20; house plant anywhere. Fast to 10–20 ft., usually as thicket, multitrunked from base, especially if frosted back or pruned to control size; slower, smaller in container or as house plant. Dense, coarse foliage. Leaves broad, angled, to 9 in. across, light green, heavily veined, velvety with coarse hairs. Flowers white with brush of yellow stamens, 1–1½ in. across, clustered, borne in midwinter to early spring.

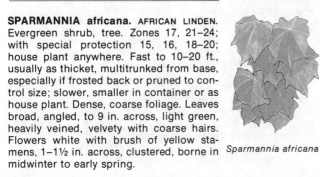

Sparmannia africana

Ample water and feeding, sun or shade. Susceptible to spider mites. Prune heavily every few years to give desired height and control legginess. Best used for furnishing bulk and mass near entryways, screening, combining with tropical foliage plants. Grows well near pools. Easily propagated by cuttings.

SPARTIUM junceum. SPANISH BROOM. Evergreen shrub. Zones 5–9, 11–24. Grows 6–10 ft. to make dense, bushy shrub of many green, erect, almost leafless stems. Bright yellow, fragrant, 1-in.-long flowers in clusters at branch ends bloom continuously from July to frost in north, March to August south. Flowers followed by hairy seed pods. All parts of plant are poisonous if eaten.

Gaunt-looking woody shrub, but pruning will fatten it up. Does best with little water, in full sun. Takes poor, rocky soil. Has naturalized many places in West. Good rough bank cover with native shrubs, but where best adapted is capable of crowding out desirable native plants. Easily controlled in garden.

Spartium junceum

In southern California, especially Zone 24, extremely subject to caterpillars in summer. By fall, they often leave plants without flowers or stems—may resprout at base in winter. Aphids are a problem at blooming time.

SPATHIPHYLLUM. Evergreen perennial. House plant. Dark green leaves are large, oval or elliptical and narrowed to a point, erect on slender leaf stalks that rise directly from soil. Flowers resemble calla lilies or anthuriums—central column of closely set tiny flowers surrounded by leaflike white flower bract.

Loose, fibrous potting mixture; weekly feedings of dilute liquid fertilizer. Grow in good light, but avoid hot sunny windows; they can endure low light. They like ample water. One of the few flowering plants that grows and blooms readily indoors. Most common are 'Clevelandii', 2 ft., and 'Mauna Loa', to 3 ft.

Spathiphyllum 'Clevelandii'

SPEAR LILY. See *Doryanthes palmeri.*

SPEARMINT. See *Mentha spicata.*

SPEEDWELL. See *Veronica.*

SPEKBOOM. See *Portulacaria afra.*

SPHAEROPTERIS cooperi *(Cyathea, Alsophila cooperi,* often sold as *A. australis).* AUSTRALIAN TREE FERN. Zones 15–24. Fastest growing of the fairly hardy tree ferns; can go from 1 ft. to 6 ft. spread in a year. Eventually 20 ft. tall. Broad fronds are finely cut, bright green, to 12 ft. long.

Chaffy scales on trunk. Is hardy to possibly 20°F., but with damage to fronds. Reasonably safe in sheltered places along the coast and in warm coastal valleys. Established plants will take full sun in the coastal fog belt and part shade elsewhere.

Sphaeropteris cooperi

SPICE BUSH. See *Calycanthus occidentalis.*

SPIDER FLOWER. See *Cleome spinosa.*

SPIDER LILY. See *Lycoris.*

SPIDER PLANT. See *Chlorophytum comosum.*

SPIDERWORT. See *Tradescantia andersoniana.*

SPIKED CABBAGE TREE. See *Cussonia spicata.*

SPINACH. All Zones. Sow according to schedules on pages 83–84 to mature during fall, winter, and spring. Long daylight of late spring and heat of summer make it go to seed too fast. It requires rich soil that drains well. Make small sowings at weekly intervals to get succession. Grow in sun. Space rows 18 in. apart.

After seedlings start growing, thin plants to 6 in. apart. Give plants plenty of water; one feeding will encourage lush foliage. When plants have reached full size, harvest by cutting off entire clump at ground level.

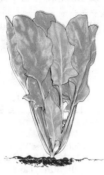

Spinach

SPIRAEA. Deciduous shrubs. Zones 1–11, 14–21. Easy to grow in all kinds of soils, in sun or light shade, average water. Varying in form, height, and flowering season. They provide generous quantities of white, pink, or red flowers.

Prune according to form and time of bloom. Those with loose graceful look need annual renewal of new growth. Remove old wood that has produced flowers—cutting back to ground. Most shrubby types require less severe pruning.

Spiraea bumalda 'Anthony Waterer'

Prune spring-flowering kinds when they finish blooming. Or, even better, cut flowering branches for arrangements; they have graceful lines, good keeping qualities. Prune summer-flowering species in late winter or very early spring. See chart for descriptions of kinds available.

SPLIT-LEAF PHILODENDRON. See *Monstera deliciosa.*

SPLIT ROCK. See *Pleiospilos.*

Spiraea

NAME	GROWTH HABIT	FLOWERS	SEASON
S. billiardi Hybrid—*S. douglasii* and *S. salicifolia.*	To 4–6 ft. high with arching branches. Foliage green above, gray green beneath.	Tiny pale pink flowers in fluffy, 8-in.-long clusters at ends of branches. *S. b.* 'Macrothyrsa' and *S. b.* 'Rosea' have flowers of brighter pink.	July-August.
S. bullata Native to Japan.	To 1–1½ ft., dense growing, with roundish, puckered leaves that hang on all winter in mild climates.	Pink flowers in small dense clusters. Used in edgings, rock gardens.	July-August.
S. bumalda Hybrid between *S. japonica* and *S. albiflora.*	Rounded, dense, to 2–3 ft. tall. Narrow oval leaves 1–4 in. long.	Flowers deep pink to nearly white in flat-topped clusters.	June to fall.
S. b. 'Anthony Waterer' DWARF RED SPIRAEA Most commonly available form of *S. bumalda.*	Same as above but with a maroon tinge.	Flowers bright carmine in flat-topped clusters.	June to fall.
S. b. 'Froebelii'	Same growth habit but taller, to 3–4 ft. Good fall coloring.	Flowers rosy red, in flat-topped clusters 3 in. across.	June to fall.
S. b. 'Goldflame'	Grows 3–4 ft. tall. New leaves bronze, turning yellow as they expand.	Flowers rosy red.	June to fall.
S. cantoniensis (*S. reevesiana, S. reevesii*) REEVES SPIRAEA	Upright with arching branches to 5–6 ft. Small dark green leaves turn red in fall. Pinch back occasionally.	White flowers in dense clusters along branches.	June-July.
S. densiflora Native California to British Columbia, east to Wyoming.	Mounding to 2 ft. Leaves oval or elliptic, to 1½ in. long, green above, paler beneath. Best in cool-summer climates.	Flowers rose-colored, in dense clusters to 1½ in. across.	June.
S. douglasii WESTERN SPIRAEA Native California to British Columbia, east to Rocky Mountains.	Suckering shrub to 4–8 ft. tall, with 1½–3-in. leaves of dark green, velvety white beneath. Useful in large-scale native plantings near creeks.	Flowers pale pink to deep rose in dense, steepled 8-in.-long clusters at ends of branches.	July-August.
S. nipponica tosaensis 'Snowmound' Native to Japan.	Compact spreading growth to 2–3 ft. Dense foliage of small blue green leaves.	White flowers in round clusters all along stems make wands of white.	June.
S. prunifolia BRIDAL WREATH SPIRAEA, SHOE BUTTON SPIRAEA Native to Korea, China, Formosa.	Graceful, to 6 ft. high with equal spread. Small dark green leaves turn rich red in fall.	Small double white flowers like little rosettes all along branches.	April-May.
S. thunbergii Native to Japan, China.	Showy, billowy to 5 ft., with many arching branches. Turns soft reddish brown in fall.	Round clusters of small white flowers all along branches.	April.
S. vanhouttei Hybrid between *S. cantoniensis* and *S. trilobata.* Probably most commonly planted.	Fountain shaped growth to 6 ft. Blue green leaves on arching branches.	Showy snow white flowers in rounded clusters wreathe branches.	June-July.

SPREKELIA formosissima (often sold as *Amaryllis formosissima*). JACOBEAN LILY, ST. JAMES LILY, AZTEC LILY. Bulb. Zones 9, 12–24 as all-year garden plants; everywhere in pots or as spring-fall garden plants. Native to Mexico. Foliage resembles daffodils. Dark crimson blooms resemble orchids, with 3 erect segments, 3 lower ones rolled together into tube at base, then separating again into drooping segments. Stems 12 in. tall. Plant in fall, setting bulbs 3–4 in. deep and 8 in. apart in full sun. Blooms 6–8 weeks after planting. Most effective in groups. In mild climates may flower several times a year, with alternating moisture and drying out. Where winters are cold, plant outdoors in spring, lift plants in fall when foliage yellows and store over winter (leave dry tops on). Or grow in pots like amaryllis *(Hippeastrum),* only slightly cooler. Repot every 3–4 years.

Sprekelia formosissima

SPRING STAR FLOWER. See *Ipheion uniflorum.*

SPRUCE. See *Picea.*

SPURGE. See *Euphorbia.*

SPURGE LAUREL. See *Daphne laureola.*

SQUARE-FRUITED MALLEE. See *Eucalyptus tetraptera.*

SQUASH. This edible annual comes in two forms. Those that are harvested and cooked in the immature state are called summer squash; this group includes scalloped white squash, yellow crookneck and straightneck varieties, and cylindrical, green or gray zucchini or Italian squash. Winter squash varieties have hard rinds and firm, close-grained, fine-flavored flesh. They store well and are used for baking and for pies. They come in variety of shapes—turban, warted, and banana are a few—and variety of sizes and colors.

Crookneck squash

Many summer squashes grow on broad, squat bushes rather than on vines; these help economize on space. 'Early Summer Crookneck' and 'Early Prolific Straightneck' are good yellow summer squash. 'Early White Bush' (white) and 'Scallopini Hybrid' (green) are fine scalloped varieties. 'Ambassador Hybrid', 'Aristocrat Hybrid', and 'Burpee Hybrid' are productive zucchini varieties.

Fall and winter squash for storing are the small 'Bush Table Queen', 'Acorn', 'Butternut', and 'Buttercup'; and the large 'Hubbard', 'Blue Hubbard', and 'Jumbo Pink Banana.' Spaghetti squash looks like any other winter squash but when you cook it (bake or boil) and open it, you find flesh is made up of long, spaghetti-sized strands. It has nutty flavor.

Bush varieties of summer squash can be planted 2 ft. apart in rows; planted in circles ("hills") they need more room, so space "hills" 4 by 4 feet. Runner-type winter squash needs 5-ft. spacing in rows, 8 by 8 ft. in "hills." Roots will need ample water, but keep leaves and stems as dry as possible; irrigate in basins or furrows. Plant summer squash in full sun; winter squash tolerates light shade but does better in full sun. Harvest summer squash when they are still small and tender; seeds should still be soft and you should be able to pierce rind easily with your thumbnail. Late squash should stay on vines until thoroughly hardened; harvest these with an inch of stem and store in cool (55°F.), frost free place.

SQUAWBUSH, SKUNKBUSH. See *Rhus trilobata.*

SQUILL. See *Scilla.*

SQUIRREL'S FOOT FERN. See *Davallia trichomanoides.*

STACHYS byzantina *(S. lanata, S. olympica).* LAMB'S EARS. Perennial. All Zones. Soft, thick, white-woolly, rather tongue shaped leaves grow densely on spreading 12–18-in. stems. Flower stalks, with many whorls of small purplish flowers, form in June-July but plant is most useful for foliage effect. Rain smashes it down, makes it mushy. Frost damages leaves. Cut back in spring. Use to contrast with dark green and differently shaped leaves such as strawberry or some sedums. Good edging plant for paths, flower border; highly effective edging for bearded iris. Excellent ground cover under high-branching oaks. Average soil, sun or light shade, light water but not absolute drought, good drainage.

Stachys byzantina

STACHYURUS praecox. Deciduous shrub. Zones 4–6 best; also 14–17. Slow to 10 ft., with spreading, slender, polished chestnut brown branches. Pendulous flower stalks 3–4 in. long, each with 12–20 unopened buds, hang from branches in fall-winter. These open (February-March) into pale yellow or greenish yellow bell shaped flowers ⅓ in. wide. Berrylike fruit in August-September. Bright green leaves, 3–7 in. long, are toothed, taper to sharp tip. Leaves often somewhat sparse. Fall color pleasant (but not bright) rosy red and yellowish.

Stachyurus praecox

Grow under deciduous trees to shelter winter buds from heavy freezes. With ample water will take full sunshine, give brighter fall color. Appropriate in woodland garden.

STAGHORN FERN. See *Platycerium.*

STAPELIA. STARFISH FLOWER, CARRION FLOWER. Succulents. House plants; outdoors Zones 24; 12, 13, 16–23 with lath or some other shelter. Plants resemble cactus, with clumps of 4-sided, spineless stems. Flowers (summer) are large, fleshy, shaped like 5-pointed stars; they usually have elaborate circular fleshy disk in center. Most smell like carrion; odor is not usually offensive on plants blooming outside in summer. They need cool, dry rest period in winter, sun and moderate water in summer. Best managed in pots. Good desert succulent, tolerating extreme heat.

Stapelia variegata

S. gigantea. Remarkable novelty, with 9-in.-tall stems and flowers 10–16 in. across, brown purple marked yellow, with fringed edges.

S. variegata. Commonest. Stems to 6 in. Flowers to 3 in. across, yellow heavily spotted and barred dark purple brown. There are many hybrids and color variants. Flowers not strongly scented; plant takes light frost.

STAR BUSH. See *Turraea obtusifolia.*

STARFISH FLOWER. See *Stapelia.*

STAR JASMINE. See *Trachelospermum.*

STAR OF BETHLEHEM. See *Campanula isophylla, Ornithogalum arabicum, O. umbellatum.*

STAR OF PERSIA. See *Allium christophii.*

STAR TULIP. See *Calochortus uniflorus, C. nudus.*

STATICE. See *Limonium.*

STENOCARPUS sinuatus. FIREWHEEL TREE. Evergreen tree. Zones 16, 17, 20–24. Slow to 30 ft., with a spread of 15 ft. Foliage dense, shiny. Leaves on young plants to 12 in. long, lobed like oak leaves; on older plants leaves are smaller and usually unlobed. Tubular, 2–3-in. scarlet and yellow flowers arranged in clusters like spokes of wheel. Has been adopted by Rotary Clubs as mascot. Plants will not bloom until established for several years. Bloom season varies; plants may flower at any time, but early fall is usually peak season. Blooms will sometimes come out of the trunk's bark, making most unusual effect.

Stenocarpus sinuatus

Rather tender, especially when young. Best in deep, rich, well-drained, acid soil. Needs occasional deep watering even when well established. Prune to shape in early years. Where climate, soil, and water are right, it can be showy flowering tree for use near patio or terrace. Good lawn tree. Good near swimming pools; has little leaf drop. Popular as indoor pot plant with beautiful juvenile leaves.

STENOLOBIUM stans. See *Tecoma stans.*

STENOTAPHRUM secundatum. ST. AUGUSTINE GRASS. Perennial lawn grass. Zones 12, 13, 18–24. Tropical or subtropical coarse-textured grass that spreads fast by surface runners that root at joints. Leaves very dark green, up to ⅜ in. wide, on coarse, wiry, flattened stems. Turns brown during short winter dormancy, can creep into flower beds or other plantings, requires power mower to deal with heavy blades, produces thick thatch. On the other hand it is easily removed from flower beds because of shallow roots, tolerates much wear, has few pests, is fairly salt tolerant, and endures shade better than other subtropical grasses. Water requirement moderate to high. Plant from sod, plugs, or stolons. Mow 1 in. high once a week during growing season.

Stenotaphrum secundatum

STEPHANOTIS floribunda. MADAGASCAR JASMINE. Evergreen vine. Zones 23, 24; house or indoor/outdoor plant everywhere. Moderate growth to 10–15 ft. (more if grown in open ground). Can be kept small in pots. Leaves glossy green, waxy, to 4 in. long. Flowers funnel shaped, white, waxy, very fragrant, 1–2 in. long in open clusters. Blooms June through summer as outdoor plant; grown indoors and properly rested by some drying out, will bloom 6 weeks after resuming growth. Favorite flower in bridal bouquets.

Stephanotis floribunda

Grown outdoors, does best with roots in shade, tops in filtered sun. Needs warmth, support of frame or trellis. As indoor/outdoor plant, feed and water liberally, but dry out somewhat before bringing indoors. Grow in bright light out of direct sun. Watch for scale, mealybug.

STERNBERGIA lutea. Bulb. All Zones. Narrow 6–12-in. leaves appear in fall same time as flowers, and remain green for several months after blooms have gone. Flowers 1½ in. long, resemble large golden crocuses on 6–9-in. stems. Flowers give pleas-

Sternbergia lutea

ant autumn surprise in borders, rock gardens, and near pools. Good cut flowers. Plant bulbs as soon as available—August or September. Set 4 in. deep, 6 in. apart, in sun. In coldest climates give sheltered location. Lift, divide, replant in August, but only when bulbs become crowded.

STERCULIA. See *Brachychiton.*

STEWARTIA. Deciduous shrubs or trees. Zones 4–6, 14–17, 20, 21. These are all-season performers: bare and exhibiting distinctive branch pattern in winter; leafing out in spring; displaying white flowers like single camellias in summer; and in autumn offering colored foliage. Slow growing. Best in moist, acid soil with high content of organic matter. Need ample moisture when young, otherwise leaves burn. Take sun, but prefer partial shade in warm climates.

Stewartia koreana

S. koreana. KOREAN STEWARTIA. Tree. To 20–25 ft.; may reach eventual 50 ft. Rather narrow pyramidal habit. Leaves dark green, to 4 in. long, somewhat silky underneath, turning orange or orange red in fall. Flowers June-July, white with yellow orange stamens, to 3 in. across, on short stalks among leaves. Possibly only a variety of Japanese stewartia.

S. monadelpha. TALL STEWARTIA. Tree. To 25 ft., with upward-angled slender branches, 1½–2½-in.-long leaves. Summer flowers 1½ in. across, the stamens with violet anthers. Outstanding red fall leaf color.

S. ovata. MOUNTAIN STEWARTIA. Shrub or small tree. To 15 ft. Slender habit. The 2½–5-in. grayish green leaves turn brilliant orange in fall. Three-inch flowers with frilled petals bloom in summer.

S. pseudocamellia. JAPANESE STEWARTIA. Tree. To 60 ft. Leaves 1–3 in. long, turning bronze to dark purple in fall. July-August flowers to 2½ in. across with orange anthers.

STIGMAPHYLLON. ORCHID VINE. Vines, evergreen or partially deciduous. Tall twiners of fairly fast growth to 20–30 ft. Leaves borne in pairs; upper leaves have long-stalked clusters of bright yellow flowers of irregular shape, somewhat resembling oncidium orchids. Heaviest bloom July-September, but may carry some bloom all year in mildest climates. Do best in rich soil, with shade at roots and ample water. Furnish support and prune out dead or straggling growth.

Stigmaphyllon ciliatum

S. ciliatum. Zones 19–24. Foliage open and delicate, and plants easily kept small. Leaves heart shaped, 1–3 in. long, with a few long bristly teeth on edges. Clusters of 3–7 flowers 1½ in. across.

S. littorale. Zones 15–24. Larger, coarser vine with larger (to 5 in. long) oval leaves and larger clusters (10–20) of smaller flowers (1 in. across). Extremely vigorous; can climb to tops of tall trees if allowed to.

STOCK. See *Matthiola.*

STOKES ASTER. See *Stokesia laevis.*

STOKESIA laevis. STOKES ASTER. Perennial. Zones 1–9, 12–24. Rugged and most adaptable plant. Much branched, with stiff erect stems 1½–2 ft. high. Smooth, firm-textured, medium green leaves, 2–8 in. long, spiny, toothed at bottom. Flower heads asterlike, blue, purplish blue, or white, 3–4 in. across. Composed of button of small flowers in center, surrounded by ring of larger flowers. Blooms summer,

Stokesia laevis

early autumn. Leafy, curved, finely toothed bracts surround tight unopened flower buds. Several varieties; 'Blue Danube' is selected form. Sun, average water, good drainage. Good in pots. Long-lasting cut flower.

STONECRESS. See *Aethionema.*

STONECROP. See *Sedum.*

STONEFACE. See *Lithops.*

STORAX, CALIFORNIA. See *Styrax officinalis californicus.*

STRANVAESIA davidiana. Evergreen shrub or small tree. Zones 4–11, 14–17. Informal, wide-spreading, 6–20 ft. high; moderate growth rate. Leaves oblong, smooth edged, to 4 in. long; new foliage reddish. Some leaves turn bronze or purple in late fall and winter—good foil for clusters of showy red berries that form at same time. White flowers in 4-in. clusters, June.

Best if given plenty of room, sun, not-too-rich soil. In hot interior gardens, protect from hot winds and supply adequate water. Subject to fireblight. Looks good with strong-growing native plants, or as screen or background. Berried branches are handsome as holiday cut foliage.

Stranvaesia davidiana

S. d. undulata *(S. undulata).* Lower growing, to irregularly shaped 5-ft. shrub. New foliage and branch tips are colorful bronzy red. Leaves are wavy along edges.

STRAWBERRY. All Zones. Plants are 6–8 in. tall, spreading about 12 in across with long runners. Toothed, roundish, medium green leaves, white flowers. Plant strawberries in sunny location and in soil that is well drained, fairly rich. To harvest just a few berries, you can simply plant a dozen or so plants, spaced 14–18 in. apart in sunny patch within flower or vegetable garden, or even in boxes or tubs on patio.

Strawberry

To bring in big crop of berries, plant in rows. If soil is heavy or poorly drained, set plants in rows along raised mounds 5–6 in. high and 28 in. from center to center. Use furrows between mounds for irrigation and feeding. Set plants 14–16 in. apart.

If your soil drains well or if furrow irrigation would be difficult, plant on flat ground, 14–18 in. apart, in rows 18 in. apart, and irrigate by overhead sprinkler. Flat ground method best where salinity is a problem. Strawberries are difficult to grow in desert or other regions where soil and water salinity are very high.

In Northwest most gardeners set plants 2–3 ft. apart in rows 4–5 ft. apart, let runners fill in until plants are 7–10 in. apart, then keep additional runners pinched off. Keep the rows 20–30 in. wide.

Planting season is usually determined by when your nursery can offer plants. In mild-winter areas plants set out in late summer or fall produce crop following spring. Other than that, rule is to plant in early spring. Everbearers will give summer and fall crop from spring plantings; pinch off earliest blossoms to increase plant strength.

Set plants carefully; crown should be above soil level, topmost roots ¼ in. beneath soil level (buried crowns rot; exposed roots dry out). Mulch to keep down weeds, conserve moisture, keep berries clean.

(Continued on next page)

Strawberry

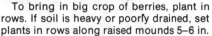

NAME	DESCRIPTION	ADAPTABILITY	RESISTANCE
'Chief Bemidji'	Everbearer. Bright red fruit of fine flavor.	Hardy to −40°. Not thoroughly tested in milder areas.	
'Fort Laramie'	Everbearer. Good yield of large, bright red berries over long season. Excellent flavor.	Tolerates −30°F. without mulch. Hardy in mountain states, high plains.	
'Fresno'	Good-sized fruit is less firm than 'Tioga'. Bears same times as 'Lassen'. Heavy cropper.	Tolerates some salinity. Suggested variety San Joaquin Valley, southern California, California coastal valleys.	Highly subject to verticillium wilt.
'Hood'	Berry is large, cone shaped, bright red. Bears same times as 'Northwest'. Fine for jam, fresh use. Not best freezer.	Similar to 'Northwest'.	Resists mildew.
'Lassen'	Medium large berry with spring and fall crops. Use fresh or for freezing.	Good in southern California, inland valleys. Takes warm winters.	Moderate resistance to alkalinity. Highly subject to yellows.
'Marshall' ('Banner', 'Oregon Plum', 'Oregon', 'Pacific', 'Dewey')	Large, deep crimson fruit in late June. Excellent flavor.	Good in Northwest where yellows not prevalent.	Susceptible to yellows and red stele.
'Nisqually'	Everbearer. Medium large, medium red fruit.	Developed for Northwest.	Tolerant of mildew.
'Northwest'	Big, good-looking berry for use fresh, frozen, in preserves. June-July in Northwest.	Very popular in Washington, Oregon.	Resistant to yellows. Susceptible to red stele; give good drainage.
'Ogallala'	Everbearer. Hybrid with wild Rocky Mountain berry.	Very cold tolerant. Blossoms fairly frost resistant.	
'Olympus'	Average-sized light red fruit in midseason. No runners; vigorous plants bear on branching crowns.	Good in southwestern Washington and northwestern Oregon.	Some botrytis resistance. Resists red stele where best adapted; susceptible in northwestern Washington.
'Ozark Beauty'	Everbearer. Large, long-necked berries. Mild, sweet flavor. Produces many runners.	Wide climate adaptability. Tolerates much cold.	

(Continued on next page)

NAME	DESCRIPTION	ADAPTABILITY	RESISTANCE
'Paris Spectacular'	Everbearer. Large, showy fruit of fine flavor. Good variety for hanging baskets, barrels. Hanging, unrooted runners will fruit.	Wide climate adaptability. Good performance in California as hanging basket plant.	
'Puget Beauty'	Sweet, glossy red. Good fresh, frozen, and for jam. Main crop June; light crop in August.	Good variety for heavy soils in Northwest.	Some resistance to red stele and mildew.
'Quinault'	Everbearer. Fruit is large, attractive, tasty, rather soft. Good producer of runners.	Developed for Northwest.	
'Rainier'	Good-sized red berries that hold size throughout long main crop season. Fine flavor; fine home garden variety. Vigorous plant producer.	Best in Northwest, west of Cascades.	Fair tolerance to root rot.
'Red Rich'	Medium large everbearer. Red clear through. June-October.	Good in all strawberry climates.	Moderate resistance to salinity. Susceptible to yellows, wilt.
'Sequoia'	Medium to large, red fruit. Tastiest of modern strawberries. Prolific. Bears for many months.	Developed in and for coastal California, but with wide climate adaptability, even in coldest winters.	Resistant to alkalinity, yellows, and most leaf diseases.
'Shasta'	Large, firm berries of good flavor midseason and throughout summer in California.	Excellent in California's central coastal counties.	Resistant to mildews, some viruses.
'Shuksan'	Medium-sized dark red, soft, mealy berries in midseason.	Very cold hardy, tolerant of alkalinity. Good east of Cascades.	Resistant to botrytis fruit rot.
'Tioga'	Yield, size, and appearance better than 'Lassen'.	Grows well in all strawberry areas of California.	Resistant to yellows. Susceptible to wilt.
'20th Century' ('Utah Centennial')	Medium to large fruit of high quality. Spring and fall crop.	Good in cold-winter areas, northern California inland valleys.	

Strawberries need frequent deep soaking, especially in bearing season. In summer-arid areas they may need water every 2–3 days if soil is sandy, every week to 10 days if soil is heavy. In humid Northwest early berries may ripen without irrigation, but everbearers will need summer water.

Feed plants twice a year—once when growth begins, again after first crop. In California and Southwest, nitrogen is especially necessary. Northwest growers usually apply superphosphate at planting time and use complete fertilizers high in phosphorus.

Most varieties are reproduced by offset plants at ends of runners. You can (a) pinch off all runners, which will give large plants and small yields of big berries; or (b) permit offset plants to grow either 7–10 in. apart or even closer, which will give heavy yields of somewhat smaller berries. When your plants have made enough offsets, pinch off further runners. (Some varieties make few or no offsets.)

Strawberries are subject to red stele (root rot), yellows (virus) and verticillium wilt (soil-borne fungus). Spray or dust to control aphids and spider mites; do not use chemicals if fruit has set. Control snails and slugs. Replace plants every 3 years (everbearers every other year). Use your own runner-grown plants only if disease free.

See variety chart for choices in regular strawberries.

Novelty strawberries. So-called climbing strawberries do not climb. Instead they produce, at ends of runners, plantlets that bear fruit without rooting into soil. These plantlets must be tied to trellis. In cold winters they freeze; to keep plants going, bring down and root occasional plantlet to replace parent. Better still, grow strawberries in more conventional way.

Alpine strawberries, wild strawberries, or *fraises de bois* are worthwhile novelty. Plants produce no runners, but bear numbers of tiny, long, slender berries from spring to fall. Fruit is fragrant and tasty. Raise from seed sown in early spring to fruit first summer. Extend plantings by dividing older plants. Often naturalizes in partially shaded, well-watered gardens. Attractive informal low edging plant. Varieties are 'Alexandria', 'Baron Solemacher', and 'Harzland'. Occasionally seed of white or yellow forms is offered.

STRAWBERRY GERANIUM. See *Saxifraga stolonifera.*

STRAWBERRY TOMATO. See *Physalis pruinosa.*

STRAWBERRY TREE. See *Arbutus unedo.*

STRAWFLOWER. See *Helichrysum bracteatum.*

STREAM ORCHID. See *Epipactis gigantea.*

STRELITZIA. BIRD OF PARADISE. Evergreen perennials. Tropical plants of extremely individual character. Need full sun in coastal areas, light shade inland. Both kinds are good to use by pools—make no litter and seem to withstand some splashing.

S. nicolai. GIANT BIRD OF PARADISE. Zones 22–24. This one is grown for its dramatic display of bananalike leaves; flowers are incidental. Treelike, clumping, many stalks to 30 ft. Gray green, leathery, 5–10-ft. leaves are arranged fanlike on erect or curving trunks. Floral envelope is purplish gray, flower is white with dark blue tongue.

Strelitzia reginae

Feed young plants frequently to push to full dramatic size, then give little or no feeding. Goal is to acquire and maintain size without lush growth and need for dividing. Keep dead leaves cut off and thin out surplus growths. Endures temperatures to 28°F.

S. reginae. BIRD OF PARADISE. Outdoors in Zones 22–24; under overhangs where heat can be trapped, Zones 9, 12–21. Damaged at 28°–29°F., and recovers slowly; do not attempt where frost is likely. This one is grown for its spectacular flowers, startlingly like tropical birds. Orange, blue, and white flowers on long stiff stems bloom intermittently throughout year, but best in cool season. Last extremely long. Official city flower of Los Angeles. Trunkless plants grow 5 ft. high with leathery, long-stalked, blue green, 1½-ft.-long leaves, 4–6 in. wide. Benefits greatly from frequent and heavy feedings. Divide infrequently since large crowded clumps bloom best. Good in containers.

STREPTOCARPUS. CAPE PRIMROSE. Evergreen perennials. Outdoors in Zones 17, 22–24; house plants everywhere. Related to African violets and gloxinias (*Sinningia*), and are something between them in appearance. Leaves are fleshy, sometimes velvety. Flowers are trumpet shaped, with long tube and spreading mouth. Long bloom season; some flower intermittently all year. Indoors, handle like African violets. Outdoors, give shady, cool, moist situation. Many species and hybrids of interest to fanciers. Most generally available are hybrids.

Streptocarpus hybridus

Large Flowered Hybrids (Giant Hybrids). Clumps of long narrow leaves and 1-ft.-tall stems with long-tubed 1½–2-in.-wide flowers in white, blue, pink, rose, red, often with contrasting blotches. Usually bloom after 1 year from seed.

Nymph series. Long-blooming plants grown from leaf cuttings. 'Constant Nymph', midblue, is best known; other named sorts available in purple, rose, red, white, pink. Flowers resemble the above.

Wiesmoor Hybrids. Flowers fringed and crested, up to 4–5 in. wide, on 2-ft. stems. Grow from seed.

S. saxorum. Unlike others; shrubby, much branched perennial making spreading mound of furry, gray green, 1½-in.-long, fleshy leaves. Long-stemmed flowers appear in waves over much of year, pale blue and white, 1½ in. wide. Makes splendid hanging pot plant. Give African violet conditions, perhaps a bit more light. Hybrids are beginning to appear: 'Concord Blue', with large flowers, blooms continuously.

STREPTOSOLEN jamesonii. MARMALADE BUSH. Evergreen viny shrub. Outdoors in Zones 17, 23, 24; indoor/outdoor plant or with careful protection, Zones 13, 15, 16, 18–24. To 4–6 ft. tall and as wide (to 10–15 ft. trained against wall, bank, trellis). Leaves ribbed, oval, 1½ in. long. Flowers are 1 in. across in large, loose clusters at branch ends. Color ranges from yellow to brilliant orange, mostly the latter.

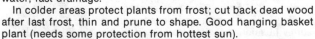
Streptosolen jamesonii

Big bloom season April-October (in most frost free parts of Zones 23, 24 occasionally everblooming, with good display in midwinter). Grow it in warm spot with ample water, fast drainage.

In colder areas protect plants from frost; cut back dead wood after last frost, thin and prune to shape. Good hanging basket plant (needs some protection from hottest sun).

STRING OF BEADS. See *Senecio rowleyanus*.

STYRAX. Deciduous trees. Pretty white bell-like flowers in hanging clusters.

S. japonicus. JAPANESE SNOWDROP TREE, JAPANESE SNOWBELL. Deciduous tree. Zones 3–10, 14–21. Slow to moderate growth to 30 ft. Trunk slender, graceful; branches often strongly horizontal, giving the tree a broad, flat top. Leaves oval, dark green, to 3 in. long with scalloped edges; turn red or yellow in fall. White, faintly fragrant flowers ¾ in. long, hang on short side branches in June. Leaves angle upward from branches while flowers hang down, giving parallel green and white tiers.

Styrax japonicus

Needs reasonably good, well-drained garden soil. Full sun or part shade. Plenty of water. Prune to control shape; tends to be shrubby unless lower side branches suppressed. Splendid tree to look up into; plant it in raised beds near outdoor entertaining areas, or on high bank above path. Roots are not aggressive.

S. obassia. FRAGRANT SNOWBELL. Deciduous tree. Zones 3–10, 14–21. To 20–30 ft. tall, rather narrow in spread. Roundish leaves 3–8 in. long, deep green. June flowers fragrant, ¾–1 in. long, carried in 6–8-in. drooping clusters at ends of branches. Culture same as *S. japonica*. Good against background of evergreens, or for height and contrast above border of rhododendrons and azaleas.

S. officinalis californicus *(S. californica).* CALIFORNIA STORAX. Zones 8, 9, 14–24. Shrub to 4–12 ft. Trunks gray, leaves 1–2 in. long, green above, gray underneath. Flowers (April-June) fragrant, white, drooping in clusters of 2 or 3, about an inch long. Native to foothills of Sierra Nevada, inner Coast Range. *S. o. fulvescens*, very similar, is native to mountains of southern California. Endures drought, heat, rocky soil.

SUCCULENT. Strictly speaking, a succulent is any plant that stores water in juicy leaves, stems, or roots to withstand periodic drought. Practically speaking, fanciers of succulents exclude such fleshy plants as epiphytic orchids and include in their collections many desert plants (yuccas, puyas) which are not fleshy. Although cactus are succulents, common consent sets them up as separate category (see Cactus).

Most succulents come from desert or semidesert areas in warmer parts of the world. Mexico and South Africa are two very important sources. Some (notably sedums and sempervivums) come from colder climates, where they grow on sunny, rocky slopes and ledges.

Succulents are grown everywhere as house plants; in milder western climates many are useful and decorative as landscaping plants, either in open ground or in containers. When well grown and well groomed, they look good throughout year, in bloom or out. Although considered low-maintenance plants, they look shabby if neglected. They may live through extended drought but will drop leaves, shrivel, or lose color. Amount of irrigation needed depends on summer heat, humidity of atmosphere. Plants in interior valleys may need water every week or two; near coast water less. Give plants just enough water to keep them healthy, plump of leaf, and attractive.

One light feeding at start of growing season should be enough for plants in open ground. Larger-growing and later-blooming kinds may require additional feeding.

Some succulents make good ground covers. Some are sturdy and quick growing enough for erosion control on large banks. Other smaller kinds are useful among stepping stones or for creating patterns in small gardens. Most of these come easily from stem or leaf cuttings, and a stock can quickly be grown from a few plants. See: *Echeveria,* Ice plant, *Portulacaria, Sedum, Senecio.*

Large-growing succulents have decorative value in themselves. See: *Aeonium, Agave, Aloe, Cotyledon, Crassula, Doryanthes, Dudleya, Echeveria, Kalanchoe, Portulacaria, Yucca.*

Many succulents have showy flowers. For some of the best see *Aloe,* some species of *Crassula, Hoya,* Ice plant, *Kalanchoe, Rochea.*

Some smaller succulents are primarily collectors' items, grown for odd form or flowers. See smaller species of *Aloe, Ceropegia, Crassula, Echeveria, Euphorbia, Graptopetalum, Haworthia, Lithops, Pleiospilos, Stapelia.*

A few words of caution to growers of succulents:

1. Not all succulents like hot sun; read species descriptions carefully. Some do not thrive in interior valley or desert summer heat, even if given some shade.

2. Variety of forms, colors, textures offers many possibilities for handsome combinations, but the line between successful grouping and jumbled medley is thin. Beware of using too many kinds in one planting. Mass a few species instead of putting in one of each.

3. You can combine succulents with other types of plants, but plan combinations carefully. Not all plants look right with them.

SUGAR BUSH. See *Rhus ovata.*

SUGAR GUM. See *Eucalyptus cladocalyx.*

SULFUR FLOWER. See *Eriogonum umbellatum.*

SUMAC. See *Rhus.*

SUMMER CYPRESS. See *Kochia scoparia.*

SUMMER FORGET-ME-NOT. See *Anchusa capensis.*

SUMMER HOLLY. See *Comarostaphylis diversifolia.*

SUMMER HYACINTH. See *Galtonia candicans.*

SUMMER LILAC. See *Buddleia davidii.*

SUMMERSWEET. See *Clethra alnifolia.*

SUNDROPS. See *Oenothera tetragona.*

SUNFLOWER. See *Helianthus.*

SUNROSE. See *Helianthemum nummularium, Halimium.*

SURINAM CHERRY. See *Eugenia uniflora.*

SWAMP GUM. See *Eucalyptus rudis.*

SWAMP MAHOGANY. See *Eucalyptus robusta.*

SWAMP MALLEE. See *Eucalyptus spathulata.*

SWAN PLANT. See *Asclepias fruticosa.*

SWAN RIVER DAISY. See *Brachycome iberidifolia.*

SWAN RIVER PEA SHRUB. See *Brachysema lanceolatum.*

SWEDISH IVY. See *Plectranthus.*

SWEET ALYSSUM. See *Lobularia maritima.*

SWEET BALM. See *Melissa.*

SWEET BAY. See *Laurus nobilis, Magnolia virginiana.*

SWEET BRIAR. See *Rosa eglanteria.*

SWEET BRUSH. See *Cercocarpus betuloides.*

SWEET CICELY. See *Myrrhis odorata.*

SWEET GUM. See *Liquidambar.*

SWEET OLIVE. See *Osmanthus fragrans.*

SWEET PEA. See *Lathyrus odoratus.*

SWEET-PEA SHRUB. See *Polygala dalmaisiana.*

SWEET PEPPERBUSH. See *Clethra alnifolia.*

SWEET POTATO. This vegetable is the thickened root of trailing tropical vine closely related to morning glory (*Ipomoea*). Zones 8, 9, 14, 18–21. Requires long frost free season; much space; warm, well-drained, preferably sandy loam soils; and considerable work in getting started. Vegetables are, moreover, tricky to store. All in all, only devoted gardeners will take trouble to order plants from specialist growers. Mark off rows 3 ft. apart, and ditch between them to form planting ridges 6–9-in. high. Set shoots with roots 5–6 in.

Sweet Potato

deep so that only stem tips and leaves are exposed. Plants should be 14–16 in. apart. They tolerate dry soil once established. Harvest before first frost; dig carefully to avoid cutting or bruising roots. Dry in sun, then cure by storing 10–14 days in dry place at temperatures between 85°–95°F. Then store in cool (not below 55°F.) place to await use. Sometimes grown for its attractive foliage; handsome vine in hanging basket.

To grow sweet potato vine as house plant, push 3 toothpicks firmly into sweet potato at equal distances around tuber; these will support potato within rim of glass or jar of water. Adjust water level so it just touches tip end of tuber; it doesn't matter which end. Keep water touching base. Sprouts will grow from tuber and in 6 weeks you'll have lush vine with very attractive foliage. Vine will continue to grow until tuber shrivels. If nothing happens for several weeks, your sweet potato probably has been kiln dried or treated to prevent sprouting. Occasionally planted to cascade from high raised beds; tolerates desert heat if well watered.

SWEET ROCKET. See *Hesperis matronalis.*

SWEETSHADE. See *Hymenosporum flavum.*

SWEET SULTAN. See *Centaurea moschata.*

SWEET WILLIAM. See *Dianthus barbatus.*

SWEET WOODRUFF. See *Galium odoratum.*

SWISS CHARD. One of the easiest and most practical of vegetables for home gardens in all Zones. Sow big, crinkly, tan seeds ½–¾ in. deep in spaded soil, in sunny position, any time from early spring to early summer. Thin seedlings to 12 in. apart. Water enough to keep them growing. About 2 months after sowing (plants are generally 1–1½ ft. tall) you can begin to cut outside leaves from plants as needed for meals. New leaves grow up in center of plants. Yield all summer and seldom bolt to seed (if one does, pull it up and throw it away). In desert, plant in fall; doesn't stand up to summer heat there.

Swiss Chard

Regular green and white chard looks presentable in flower garden. Rhubarb chard has red stems, reddish green leaves, and makes attractive plant in garden beds or containers. Its leaves are valuable in floral arranging and tasty when cooked, too—sweeter and stronger flavored than green chard.

SWISS CHEESE PLANT. See *Monstera friedrichsthalii.*

SWORD FERN. See *Nephrolepis* and *Polystichum munitum.*

SYCAMORE. See *Platanus.*

SYDNEY BLUE GUM. See *Eucalyptus saligna.*

SYMPHORICARPOS. Deciduous shrubs. North American natives. Low growing, often spreading by root suckers. Flowers are small, pink-tinged or white, in clusters or spikes. Attractive round, berrylike fruit remain on stems after leaves fall; nice in winter arrangements, attract birds. Best used as wild thicket in sun or shade, erosion control on steep banks.

Symphoricarpos albus

S. albus (*S. racemosus*). COMMON SNOWBERRY. All Zones. Upright or spreading shrub 2–6 ft. tall. Leaves roundish, dull green, ¾–2 in. long (to 4 in. and often lobed on sucker shoots). Pink flowers in May-June, white fruit ½ in. wide from late summer to winter. Drought tolerant. Fruits best in sun.

S. chenaultii. All Zones. Hybrid of garden origin. Resembles *S. orbiculatus,* but red fruit is lightly spotted white and leaves are larger. *S. c.* 'Hancock' is 1-ft. dwarf of special value as woodland ground or bank cover.

S. mollis. CREEPING SNOWBERRY, SPREADING SNOWBERRY. Zones 4–24. Like common snowberry, but usually less than 18 in. high, earlier flowering, fewer flowers, smaller fruit. Spreads like ground cover. Best in part shade; tolerates drought.

S. orbiculatus (*S. vulgaris*). CORAL BERRY, INDIAN CURRANT. All Zones. Resembles common snowberry, but with profusion of small purplish red fruit in clusters.

SYMPHYTUM officinale. COMFREY. Perennial. All Zones. Deep-rooted, clumping perennial to 3 ft. Basal leaves 8 in. or more in length, upper leaves smaller, all furry with stiff hairs. Flowers not showy, ½ in. long, usually dull rose, sometimes white, creamy, or purple. Leaves have been used as food for people or stock, or dried as medicinal tea. They contain a poison, pyrrolizidine, and should not be used internally. Plants

Symphytum officinale

take full sun or partial shade, average garden water. Leaves grow all year in coastal southern California. Plants go dormant elsewhere. To keep leaf production high, cut out flowering stalks and mulch each spring with compost. Grow from root cuttings.

SYNGONIUM podophyllum (often sold as *Nephthytis afzelii*). Evergreen climbing perennial grown as house plant. Succeeds outdoors in sheltered patios in Zones 13, 23, 24. Dwarf, slow growing. Related to philodendron. It has long-stalked, arrow-shaped, dull green leaves, sometimes lobed. Flowers insignificant. Easy to grow in pots of rich house plant mix. Useful in terrarium, dish garden, as a trailer, or trained against support in manner of vining philodendron. Can grow to 10–15 feet with support. Many varieties include 'Ruth Fraser', silvery leaves bordered green; 'Trileaf Wonder', green leaves covered with whitish powder; 'California Silver Wonder', narrow silvery leaves.

Syngonium podophyllum

SYRINGA. LILAC. Deciduous shrubs, rarely small trees. Best known is common lilac (*S. vulgaris*) and its many named varieties, but there are other species of great usefulness. Best where winter brings pronounced chill, but some bloom well with light chilling. Sun; light shade in hottest areas. All like alkaline soil; in areas where soils are strongly acid, add lime and cultivate into

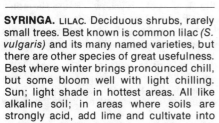
Syringa vulgaris

soil beneath drip line of plants. Average watering best, but can take some drought when established. Do not, however, limit water when plants are coming into bloom and making new growth. Control growth during early years by pinching and shaping. Flower buds for next year form in pairs where leaves join stems. After bloom, remove spent flower clusters just above points where buds are forming. Heavy pruning results in loss of much of next year's bloom. Thin out dead and weak wood at same time.

Renovate old, overgrown plants by cutting a few of oldest stems to the ground each year. Leaf miner scale and stem borer are only important pests; bacterial blight, leaf spot, downy mildew are occasional problems.

S. chinensis (*S. rothomagensis*). CHINESE LILAC. Zones 1–11, 14–16, 18–21. Hybrid between common and Persian lilacs. Moderate growth rate to 15 ft., usually much less. More graceful than common lilac, and with finer-textured foliage. Airy, open clusters of fragrant rose purple flowers in May, April in warmer Zones. Profuse bloom. Does well in mild-winter, hot-summer climates. Variety 'Alba' has white flowers.

S. hyacinthiflora. Zones 1–12, 14–16, 18–22. Hybrids between common lilac and *S. oblata,* a Chinese species which confers earliness and fragrance on the cross. 'Excel' and 'Grace McKenzie' (both single, lilac) can bloom as early as March 1. Other varieties are 'Alice Eastwood' (double, magenta), 'Blue Hyacinth' (single, lavender blue), Clarke's Giant (single, lavender blue, large flowers), 'Esther Staley' (single, magenta), 'Gertrude Leslie' (double, white), 'Pocahontas' (single, purple), 'Purple Heart' (single, purple), and 'White Hyacinth' (single, white).

S. josikaea. HUNGARIAN LILAC. Zones 1–11, 14–16, 18–21. Dense, upright growth to 12 ft. Dark green foliage. Flowers lilac purple, slightly fragrant, in narrow clusters 4–7 in. long. Blooms in May, April in warmer Zones.

S. laciniata (*S. persica laciniata*). Zones 1–12, 14–16, 18–21. Moderate growth to 8 ft. tall, open habit, good rich green foliage color. Leaves to 2½ in. long, divided nearly to midrib into 3–9 segments. Many small clusters of fragrant flowers in April, May.

S. patula (*S. palibiniana, S. velutina*). KOREAN LILAC. Zones 1–9, 14–16. Dense, twiggy growth to eventual 8–9 ft., but stays at 3 ft. many years. Flowers pink to lavender, in clusters to 5 in. long. Blooms April to May. Sometimes grafted high to make 3-ft. standard tree. 'Miss Kim' is dwarf (to 3 ft.) lavender blue variety.

S. persica. PERSIAN LILAC. Zones 1–12, 14–16, 18–21. Graceful, loose form to 6 ft., with arching branches and 2½-in.-long leaves. Many clusters of pale violet, fragrant flowers appear all along branches in May, April in warmer areas.

S. prestoniae. Zones 1–12, 14–16. To 10–15 ft. tall. Group of extra-hardy hybrids developed in Canada. Medium to large shrubs that bloom after other lilacs have finished on new spring growth. 'Isabella' (single, lilac), 'Jessica' (single, violet), 'Nocturne' (blue), and 'Royalty' (purple to violet) are good selections. For 'James MacFarlane' (sometimes sold as member of this group) see *S. swegiflexa.*

S. reticulata (*S. japonica, S. amurensis japonica*). JAPANESE TREE LILAC. Large shrub easily trained as single-stemmed 30-ft. tree. Zones 1–12, 14–16. Bark smooth, something like cherry in its gloss. Leaves large (to 5 in. long). White flower clusters to 12 in. appear in late spring, early summer. Flowers showy, but not fragrant; they have smell of privet flowers. Useful small shade or street tree in difficult climates.

S. swegiflexa. Zones 1–9, 14–16. To 12 ft. Single pink flowers open from deep reddish buds. Clusters to 8 in. long. Blooms 3 weeks after common lilac. Sometimes sold as pink pearl lilac. Hybrid between two hardy Chinese species, *S. reflexa* and *S. sweginzowii.* 'James MacFarlane' is best-known variety.

S. vulgaris. COMMON LILAC. Zones 1–11, cooler locations of 12. In Zones 14–16, 18–22 plants often bloom irregularly because of failure to break dormancy after mild winters. It was once recommended that plants be gradually but completely dried off beginning in August. It is now felt that such treatment can harm the plant, possibly kill it. Water may be restricted at this time, but should always be available. The Descanso Hybrids were developed in southern California to accept mild winters.

Best known is 'Lavender Lady' (lavender); other varieties are 'Blue Boy' (blue), 'Chiffon' (lavender), 'Forrest K. Smith' (light lavender), 'Sylvan Beauty' (rose lavender), and 'White Angel'. These do exceptionally well in Zones 18–22.

These bulky shrubs can eventually reach 20 ft. tall, with nearly equal spread. Leaves roundish oval, pointed, dark green, to 5 in. long. Flowers pinkish or bluish lavender ('Alba' has pure white flowers) in clusters to 10 in. long or more. Flowers in May; fragrance is legendary. Excellent cut flowers. Lilac fanciers swear these are more fragrant than newer varieties.

Varieties, often called French hybrids, number in the hundreds. They generally flower a little later than species and have larger clusters of single or double flowers in wide range of colors. Singles are often as showy as doubles, sometimes more so. All lilacs require 2–3 years to settle down and produce flowers of full size and true color. Here are just a few of the many choice varieties:

'Charles Joly' (double, dark purplish red), 'Miss Ellen Willmott' (double, pure white), 'Ludwig Spaeth' (single, reddish purple to dark purple), 'President Lincoln' (single, Wedgwood blue), 'President Poincare' (double, two-tone purple), 'Sensation' (single, wine red with white picotee edge), 'William Robinson' (double, pink).

SYZYGIUM. Evergreen shrubs or trees. Closely related to *Eugenia,* and usually sold as such in nurseries. Foliage rich green, often tinted coppery; new foliage brightly tinted. Flowers conspicuous for tufts of stamens that look like little brushes. Fruit are soft, edible, handsomely colored. Grow best in sun with ample water. Tolerate shade.

S. jambos (*Eugenia jambos*). ROSE APPLE. Zones 18–24. Slow growth to 25–30 ft., usually much smaller and shrubby. Leaves 5–8 in. long, narrow, thick, shiny, coppery green; new growth pinkish. Greenish white flower brushes 2–3 in. across in clusters at branch ends. Spring bloom. Fruit greenish or yellow sometimes blushed pink, 1–2 in. wide, is sweetish, with mild flavor, fragrance of rosewater. Slow growth means little or no pruning.

Syzygium paniculatum

S. paniculatum (*Eugenia myrtifolia, E. paniculata*). BRUSH CHERRY, AUSTRALIAN BRUSH CHERRY. Zones 16, 17, 19–24. Unclipped, a handsome, narrowish tree, single or multitrunked, dense foliage crown, 30–60 ft. tall. Usually clipped into formal shapes and hedges, and a most popular hedging, background, and screening plant in mild, nearly frost free areas. Young foliage reddish bronze; mature leaves oblong, 1½–3 in. long, rich glossy green, often bronze tinged. Flowers white or creamy, ½ in. wide, with feathery tufts of stamens. Fruit is rose purple, showy, ¾ in. long, edible but insipid.

Will not stand heavy frost; foliage burns at 25°–26°F. and even old plants may die if temperature drops much lower. Thrives in well-drained garden soil. Hedges need frequent clipping to stay neat, and heavy root systems make it hard to grow other plants nearby; new red foliage, showy fruit make it worth the effort. Don't plant where dropping fruit will squish on pavement.

Variety 'Compacta' is smaller, denser in growth. Very popular hedging plant. 'Brea' and 'Globulus' are also dwarf and compact, with bronzy amber foliage color. 'Red Flame' has new growth of exceptionally bright red.

TABEBUIA. Briefly deciduous, sometimes evergreen trees. Zones 15, 16, 20–24. Worth a try in Zone 13. Fast growth to 25–30 ft. Very showy trumpet shaped flowers grow 2–4 in. long in rounded clusters which become larger, more profuse as trees mature, and may contain as many as 23 flowers. Leaves dark olive green, usually divided into 3–7 leaflets arranged like fingers of hand.

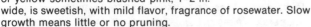

Tabebuia chrysotricha

Useful as patio trees or as free-standing flowering trees for display. Tolerate many soils and degrees of maintenance, but respond well to feeding and frequent watering. Once established, can also take much drought. Good drainage essential. Stake while young and keep plants to single leading shoot until 6–8 ft. tall, then allow to develop freely. Hardy to about 24°F.

T. avellanedae (*T. ipe*). More erect, larger growing than *T. chrysotricha.* Leaves dark green, smooth. Tree usually evergreen. Flowers 2–3 in. long, lavender with white throat banded yellow. Blooms late winter, sometimes again late summer to fall. Does not bloom as young tree.

T. chrysotricha (sometimes sold as *T. pulcherrima*). GOLDEN TRUMPET TREE. Rounded, spreading growth to 25 ft. Leaves with 5 leaflets (2–4 in. long, 1–2 in. wide); young twigs, undersides of leaves covered with tawny fuzz. Flowers are 3–4 in. long, golden yellow, often with maroon stripes in throat. Bloom heaviest April-May, when trees lose leaves for brief period. May give lighter bloom at other times with leaves present. Blooms young.

TAGETES. MARIGOLD. Summer annuals. Robust, free-branching, nearly trouble-free plants ranging from 6 in.–4 ft. tall and with flowers from pale yellow through gold to orange and brown maroon. Leaves finely divided, ferny, usually strongly scented. Bloom period early summer to frost if old flowers are picked off. In desert, bloom best in fall, until frost. Handsome, long-lasting cut flowers; strong scent permeates a room, but some odorless varieties are available. Easy from seed, which sprouts in a few days in warm soil; to get earlier bloom, start seeds in flats or buy flat-grown plants. Full sun, ample water. Smog will damage tender young plants, but they toughen up.

Tagetes erecta

T. erecta. AMERICAN MARIGOLD, AFRICAN MARIGOLD (often sold simply as tall marigold). Original strains were plants 3–4 ft. tall with single flowers. Modern strains are more varied, and most have fully double flowers. They range from dwarf (14 in.) Space Age series with 3-in. flowers and even shorter (12 in.) Guys and Dolls with 4-in. flowers through semidwarf Lady and Galore series (18–20 in.) with 3½-in. flowers to tall (to 3 ft.) Climax and Gold Coin marigolds with 5-in. flowers. Novelty tall strains are the odorless Hawaii and the near-white First Whites (28–30 in.), both with 4-in. flowers.

Triploid Hybrids, crosses between African and French marigolds, have exceptional vigor and a long bloom season. Most are 12–15 in. tall and have enormous profusion of 2-in. flowers. Series to look for are Nugget and Triple, both obtainable as yellow, gold, orange, red, or a mixture.

Avoid overhead watering on taller kinds, or stems will sag and perhaps break. To make tall-variety plants stand as stout as possible (and perhaps not need staking), dig planting holes extra deep, strip any leaves off lower 1–3 in. of stem and plant with stripped portion below soil line.

T. filifolia. IRISH LACE. Mounds of bright green, finely divided foliage, 6 in. high and as wide, resemble unusually fluffy round ferns. Used primarily as edging plant for foliage effect, but tiny white flowers in late summer, fall are attractive. Resembles heather more than marigold.

T. patula. FRENCH MARIGOLD. Varieties from 6–18 in. tall, in flower colors from yellow to rich maroon brown; flowers may be fully double or single, and many are strongly bicolored. Among best for edging are Extra Dwarf Doubles, 6 in. tall, 10 in. wide, very floriferous: 'Petite Gold' (golden yellow), 'Petite Harmony' (mahogany and gold), 'Petite Orange', 'Petite Yellow', and 'Brownie Scout' (golden splashed red). Slightly taller are double red and gold 'Bolero' (12 in.) and bright orange 'Tangerine' (15 in. tall).

T. tenuifolia (*T. signata*). SIGNET MARIGOLD. Relatively little-planted species. Fewer ray flowers on smaller flower heads, but incredibly profuse in bloom. Foliage finely cut. 'Golden Gem' ('Ursula'), golden orange; and 'Lemon Gem', bright yellow, grow 8 in. tall.

TALLHEDGE BUCKTHORN. See *Rhamnus frangula* 'Columnaris'.

TALL SAND MALLEE. See *Eucalyptus eremophila*.

TAM. See *Juniperus sabina* 'Tamariscifolia'.

TAMARACK. See *Larix occidentalis*.

TAMARIX. TAMARISK. Deciduous and evergreen-appearing shrubs and trees. In deserts of California and Arizona they have no equal in resistance to wind, drought, and they will grow in saline soils that are toxic to other plants. Fire retardant if reasonably well watered. Nurseries can't keep them in containers long because they form deep tap roots. But they are easy to grow from ½–1-in.-thick cuttings set in place and kept watered.

Tamarix aphylla

There is much confusion in labeling of tamarisks in the nurseries. For the gardener there are three kinds—evergreen-appearing tree, spring flowering, and spring through summer flowering.

Evergreen-appearing tree

    T. aphylla (*T. articulata*). ATHEL TREE. Widely used in Zones 10–13; useful in some difficult situations in Zones 7–9, 14–24. Heavily damaged at 0°F. temperature but comes back rapidly. Excellent windbreak tree. Fast growth from planted cuttings to 10 ft. or more in 3 years; eventually 30–50 ft. and more in 15 years with deep soil and water.

    Greenish jointed branchlets give tree its evergreen appearance. Takes on grayish look in late summer where soils are saline, due to secretions of salt. True leaves are minute. White to pinkish, very small flowers grow in clusters at ends of branches in late summer, but flowering is not as spectacular as other tamarisks. Not good selection for highly cultivated garden because its roots are too competitive.

Spring-flowering tamarisks

    These are hardy and adapted in all Zones. Fast growth to 6–15 ft., depending on culture. Graceful, airy, arching branches with reddish bark. Pink flowers in clusters on branches of previous year. Prune after bloom in spring to maintain graceful effect, limit height, and produce new flowering wood.

    T. africana. Bears its flowers in 1–2-in.-long upright clusters of white or very pale pink. Rare. For plants sold and widely used under this name in California, see *T. parviflora*.

    T. parviflora (often sold as *T. tetrandra*). Profuse display of pink, 4-petaled flowers. This plant is sometimes sold as *T. africana* in California.

Spring through summer-flowering tamarisks

    T. chinensis (*T. pentandra, T. juniperina, T. ramosissima, T. japonica*). SALT CEDAR. The many names result from the variability in flower color, bloom season, and plant habit. Blooms may come from March to October and vary from white through cream and various pinks to deep purple; they may bloom on last year's wood before growth begins or later in summer on new wood. Looks best if pruned to ground in early spring; if so treated will stay 6–12-ft. shrub and bloom heavily July to fall, giving masses of large plumes. Unpruned it can become 20–30-ft. rank-growing shrub with highly competitive root system. Tiny leaves are pale blue green.

TANACETUM vulgare. COMMON TANSY. Perennial herb. All Zones. Coarse garden plant with history of medicinal use. To 3 ft. Finely cut, bright green, aromatic leaves; small buttonlike flowers. Any soil, full sun. Fairly drought tolerant. Good in Rocky Mountain area. Start from seed or division

Tanacetum vulgare

of roots. Thin clumps yearly to keep in bounds. Foliage and flowers keep well in bouquets.

    T. v. crispum. FERN-LEAF TANSY. To 2½ ft.; more decorative.

TANBARK OAK. See *Lithocarpus densiflorus*.

TANGELO. See *Citrus*.

TANGERINE. See *Citrus*.

TANGOR. See *Citrus*.

TANSY. See *Tanacetum vulgare*.

TARO. See *Colocasia esculenta*.

TARRAGON, FRENCH or TRUE. See *Artemisia dracunculus*.

TASMANIAN TREE FERN. See *Dicksonia antarctica*.

TASSEL FERN. See *Polystichum polyblepharum*.

TASSEL FLOWER. See *Amaranthus caudatus*.

TASSEL HYACINTH. See *Muscari comosum*.

TAXODIUM. Deciduous or evergreen trees. Conifers of considerable size bearing short, narrow, flat, needlelike leaves in graceful sprays. Cones are scented. One is native to the southeastern U.S., the other to Mexico, but both show remarkably wide adaptation to colder and dryer climates.

Taxodium distichum

    T. distichum. BALD CYPRESS. Deciduous tree. Zones 1–9, 14–24. Also thrives in wet places in Zones 10, 12, 13. In nature can grow into 100-ft.-tall, broad-topped tree, but young and middle-aged garden trees are pyramidal. Foliage sprays very delicate and feathery; leaves about ½ in. long, very narrow, and of delicate, pale, yellow-toned green. Foliage turns bright orange brown in fall before dropping. Any soil except alkaline. Takes extremely wet conditions (even thrives in swamps), but also will tolerate rather dry soil. Hardy in all except coldest mountain areas. No particular pests or diseases. Requires only corrective pruning—removal of dead wood and unwanted branches. Outstanding tree to plant on the banks of a stream, lake, or pond. Will tolerate wet lawn conditions.

    T. mucronatum. MONTEZUMA CYPRESS. Evergreen tree in mild climates; partially or wholly deciduous in cold regions. Zones 5, 6, 8–10, 12–14. Has strongly weeping branches. Fast grower in its youth; with ample water will reach 40 ft. in 14 years; it's likely to reach eventual 75 ft. in gardens. Established plants are fairly drought tolerant, but growth is slow under drought conditions. Extremely graceful, fine-textured evergreen for large lawns.

TAXUS. YEW. Evergreen shrubs or trees. Zones 3–9, 14–24. Conifers, but instead of cones they bear fleshy, scarlet (rarely yellow), cup shaped, single-seeded fruit. Fruit (seeds) and foliage poisonous if eaten. In general, yews are more formal, darker green, and more shade and moisture tolerant than most cultivated conifers. Slow growing, long-lived, tolerant of much shearing and pruning. Excellent basic landscape plants for hedges, screens.

Taxus baccata 'Stricta'

    Easily moved even when large, but slow growth makes big plants a luxury item. Tolerate many soil conditions, but will not

thrive in strongly alkaline or strongly acid soils. Once established, fairly drought tolerant. Grow well in shade or sun, but
reflected light and heat from hot south or west wall will burn
foliage. Even cold-tolerant kinds show needle damage when exposed to bright winter sun, dry winds, very low temperatures.

Only female plants produce berries, but many do so without
male plants nearby. Considered disease free; the few pests include vine weevils, scale, and spider mites. All yews benefit from
being washed off with water from hose every 2 weeks during hot,
dry weather.

T. baccata. ENGLISH YEW. Slow growth to 25–40 ft., with wide-
spreading branches forming broad, low crown. Needles ½–1½
in. long, dark green and glossy above, paler underneath. Red
fruit have poisonous seeds. Garden varieties are far more common than the species.

T. b. 'Adpressa' (usually sold as *T. brevifolia,* which is really
the native western yew). Wide-spreading, dense shrub, 4–5 ft.
high, with leaves about ½ in. long.

T. b. 'Aurea'. More compact than species, with new foliage
golden yellow spring to autumn, then turning green.

T. b. 'Erecta'. Erect and formal. Less compact than Irish yew,
and with smaller leaves.

T. b. 'Repandens'. SPREADING ENGLISH YEW. Long, horizontal,
spreading branches make 2-ft.-high ground cover. Useful low
foundation plant. Will arch over wall.

T. b. 'Repandens Aurea'. Golden new growth; otherwise like
spreading English yew.

T. b. 'Stricta' ('Fastigiata'). IRISH YEW. Makes column of very
dark green. Slow growing to 20 ft. or higher. Leaves larger than
on English yew. Many crowded upright branches tend to spread
near top, especially in snowy regions or where water is ample,
growth lush. Branches can be tied together with wire. Plants that
outgrow their space can be reduced by heading back and thinning; old wood sprouts freely. Striking against big wall, in corner
plantings, or as background planting. Very drought tolerant
once established.

T. b. 'Stricta Aurea'. New foliage has golden color.

T. b. 'Stricta Variegata'. Like Irish yew, except that the leaves
show yellowish white variegations.

T. brevifolia. WESTERN OR OREGON YEW.   Zones 1–6, 14–17.
Native of moist places, California north to Alaska, inland to Montana. Tree of loose, open growth to 50–60 ft. with needles of dark
yellowish green 1 in. or less in length. Very difficult to grow.
Most plants sold under this name are *T. baccata* 'Adpressa' or *T.
cuspidata* 'Nana'.

T. cuspidata. JAPANESE YEW. Tree to 50 ft. in Japan. Most useful yew in cold-winter areas east of the Cascade mountains. Varieties will grow in shaded areas of Rocky Mountain gardens.
Usually grown as compact, spreading shrub. Leaves ½–1 in.
long, usually in two rows along twigs, making flat or V-shaped
spray. Foliage dark green above, tinged yellowish underneath.

T. c. 'Capitata'. Plants sold under this name are probably ordinary *T. cuspidata* in its upright, pyramidal form. Dense, slow
growth to 10–25 ft. Can be held lower by pinching new growth.
Fruits heavily.

T. c. 'Densiformis'. Much branched, very low, dense, spreading plant with dark green foliage.

T. c. 'Nana' (often sold as *T. brevifolia*). Grows slowly (1–4 in. a
year) to 3 ft. tall and spreads to 6 ft. (in 20 years). Good low
barrier or foundation plant.

T. media. Group of hybrids between Japanese and English
yew. Intermediate between the two in color of green and texture.

T. m. 'Brownii'. Slow-growing, compact, rounded yew eventually 4–8 ft. tall. Good for low, dense hedge.

T. m. 'Hatfieldii'. Broad columnar or pyramidal yew of good
dark green color. Grows 10 ft. or taller.

T. m. 'Hicksii'. Narrow, upright yew, slightly broader at center
than at top and bottom; to 10–12 ft.

TEA. See *Camellia sinensis.*

TEABERRY. See *Gaultheria procumbens.*

TEA TREE. See *Leptospermum.*

TECOMA. Various trumpet vines once
lumped together here now have different
names. What remains is showy large shrub
or small tree.

T. australis. See *Pandorea pandorana.*

T. capensis. See *Tecomaria.*

T. jasminoides. See *Pandorea jasminoides.*

T. stans (*Stenolobium stans*). YELLOW
BELLS, YELLOW TRUMPET FLOWER, YELLOW
ELDER. Evergreen shrub or small tree.
Zones 12, 13, 21–24. In mildest-winter areas
can be trained as tree. Usually large shrub
where frosts are common, much of wood
dying back; quick recovery in warm

Tecoma stans

weather, and very rapid, bushy growth to 20 ft. Leaves divided
into 5–13, toothed, 1½–4-in.-long leaflets. Flowers bright yellow,
bell shaped, 2 in. across in large clusters. Blooms June to
January. Needs heat, water, deep soil, fairly heavy feeding. Cut
faded flowers to prolong bloom, prune to remove dead and
brushy growth. Very showy mass in large garden. Boundary
plantings, big shrub borders, screening. *T. s. angustata,* with
narrow leaflets, is kind best adapted to Arizona desert climates.

TECOMARIA capensis (*Tecoma capensis*).
CAPE HONEYSUCKLE. Evergreen vine or
shrub. Zones 12, 13, 16, 18–24; Zones 14,
15 with protection. Native to South Africa.
Can scramble to 15–25 ft. if tied to support.
With hard pruning a 6–8-ft. upright shrub.
Leaves divided into many dark, glistening
green leaflets. Total foliage effect is of informality and fine texture. Brilliant orange
red, tubular, 2-in. blossoms grow in compact clusters, October through winter.

Tecomaria capensis

Needs good soil drainage. Takes sun, heat, wind, salt air,
some drought when established. Tolerates light shade. Use as
espalier, bank cover (especially good on hot, steep slopes),
coarse barrier hedge.

Variety 'Aurea' has yellow flowers and lighter green foliage;
it's smaller-growing and less showy. Requires more heat to perform well.

TEDDY BEAR. See *Cyanotis kewensis.*

TEDDYBEAR CACTUS. See *Opuntia bigelovii.*

TELLIMA grandiflora. FRINGECUPS. Perennial. Zones 4–9, 14–17. Creeping rootstocks send up roundish, lobed leaves to 4
in. across on leafstalks up to 8 in. long.
Leaves are light green, softly hairy, somewhat like those of piggyback plant (*Tolmiea*). Small urn shaped flowers with tiny
fringed petals open green, age to deep red;
these are not showy, but are attractively
disposed along tall (to 30 in.), slender
stems. Evergreen where winters are mild,
deciduous in colder parts of its native
range—central California north to southern Alaska. Choice with ferns in woodland
garden. Needs water when growing. Takes
summer drought if shaded.

Tellima grandiflora

TERNSTROEMIA gymnanthera (*T. japonica*). Evergreen shrub.
Zones 4–9, 12–24. It takes a long time to reach 6–8 ft., and is
usually seen as rounded plant 3–4 ft. tall and 4–6 ft. wide.
Glossy, leathery foliage is the feature; rounded oval to narrow
oval leaves are 1½–3 in. long, with red stalks. New growth
bronzy red; mature foliage deep green to bronzy green to
purplish red, depending on season, exposure, and plant itself.
Plants in deep shade tend to be dark green; with some sun,
leaves may be bronzy green to nearly purple red. Red tints are
deeper in cold weather.

Summer flowers not showy but fragrant, ½ in. wide, creamy yellow. Fruit (uncommon on small plants) resemble little holly berries or cherries, yellow to red orange; they split open to reveal shiny black seeds.

Full sun to partial shade (full shade in desert). Ample moisture—and more sun plants get, greater the water need. Leaves turn yellow if soil isn't acid enough—feed with acid plant food. Pinch out tip growth to encourage compact growth. Use as basic landscaping shrub, informal hedge, tub plant. Good near pools. Grows well and blends well with camellias (to which it is related), azaleas, nandina, pieris, ferns. Cut foliage keeps well.

Ternstroemia gymnanthera

TETRAPANAX papyriferus *(Aralia papyrifera).* RICE PAPER PLANT. Evergreen shrub. Zones 15–24. This is an often multi-stemmed plant of fast growth (to 10–15 ft.). Big, bold leaves 1–2 ft. wide, deeply lobed, on long stalks, in clusters at ends of stems, gray green above, white-felted beneath. Fuzz on new growth irritating if it gets in eyes or down the neck. Tan trunks often curve or lean. Big branched clusters of creamy white flowers on tan furry stems show in December.

Sun or shade (midday shade in hottest summer areas). Young plants sunburn easily, older ones adapt. Nearly any soil. Needs

Tetrapanax papyriferus

only average garden watering, but for best appearance, should never be drought stressed. Few pests; seems to suffer only from high winds (which break or tatter leaves) or frost (foliage severely damaged at 22°F. though plant will survive). Plants recover fast from freezes, often put up suckers to form thickets. Digging around roots stimulates suckering.

Use as silhouette against walls, in patios; combine with other sturdy, bold-leafed plants for tropical effect.

TETRASTIGMA voinieranum *(Cissus voinierana).* Evergreen vine. Zones 13 (shade only), 17, 20–24. Climbs by tendrils or covers ground rapidly. Stems thick, fleshy. Fast growth to 50–60 ft. New growth covered with silvery fuzz. Leaves glossy, dark green, up to 1 ft. across, divided fanwise into 3–5 oval, leathery leaflets with toothed edges. Flowers, fruit rarely seen. Needs ample water; feed until well established. Plant so roots are shaded while top can run out or up to sun. Good eave-line decoration. Large-scale bank or ground cover in Zones 17, 23, 24. Good near swimming pools.

Tetrastigma voinieranum

TEUCRIUM. GERMANDER. Evergreen shrubs or subshrubs. Tough plants for sun and heat, enduring poor, rocky soils; established plants are quite drought tolerant. They can't stand wet or poorly drained soils, will take ordinary garden watering where drainage is good.

T. chamaedrys. All Zones. Low growing (to 1 ft. tall), spreading to 2 ft., with many upright stems woody at base. Toothed dark green leaves, ¾ in. long, densely set on stems. In summer red purple or white ¾-in. flowers form in loose spikes. White flowered form is looser. Attractive to bees. Use as edging, foreground, low clipped hedge, or small-scale ground cover. To keep neat, shear back once or twice a year to force side branching. As ground cover, set

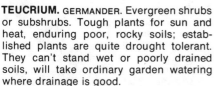

Teucrium chamaedrys

2 ft. apart. Fire-retardant plant if reasonably well watered.

T. c. 'Prostratum'. Foliage and flowers similar to *T. chamaedrys,* but growth habit is very prostrate (4–6 in. high and spreading to 3 ft. or more).

T. fruticans. BUSH GERMANDER. Zones 4–24. Loose, silvery-stemmed shrub to 4–8 ft. tall and as wide or wider. Leaves 1¼ in. long, gray green above, silvery white beneath, giving overall silvery gray effect. Lavender blue, ¾-in.-long flowers in spikes at branch ends through most of year. Thin and cut back in late winter, early spring.

Use plant as an informal hedge, against a fence or screen, in mass at end of lawn area, but far enough from sprinklers to avoid overwatering. Attractive with reddish or purplish-leafed plants.

TEXAS MOUNTAIN LAUREL. See *Sophora secundiflora.*

TEXAS RANGER. See *Leucophyllum frutescens.*

TEXAS UMBRELLA TREE. See *Melia azedarach* 'Umbraculiformis'.

THALICTRUM. MEADOW RUE. Perennials. All Zones; most species short lived in Zones 18–24. Leaves resemble those of columbines; openly leafy stems on most species are 3–6 ft. in height, topped by airy clusters of small flowers. Summer bloom. Give wind-protected location with plenty of moisture and light shade. Superb for airy effect; delicate tracery of leaves and flowers is particularly effective against dark green background. Pleasing contrast to sturdier perennials. Foliage good in flower arrangements.

Thalictrum aquilegifolium

T. aquilegifolium. Grows 2–3 ft. tall. Foliage bluish green. Flowers white, lilac, or purple.

T. dipterocarpum. CHINESE MEADOW RUE. Plants 3–6 ft. Lavender to violet flowers, yellow stamens. Long lived everywhere.

T. minus. A somewhat variable species. The form most often sold reaches to 3 ft. when in flower. Foliage bluish green; flowers, consisting mostly of stamens, yellow.

T. rochebrunianum. Flowers white with pale yellow stamens. Clumps 4–6 ft. tall. 'Lavender Mist' has lavender flowers.

THEA sinensis. See *Camellia sinensis.*

THEVETIA. Evergreen shrubs, small trees. Fast-growing plants with narrow leaves; showy funnel shaped, yellow or apricot flowers in clusters. They thrive in heat, take full sun, very little frost. Like their relatives the oleanders, they are poisonous.

T. peruviana *(T. neriifolia).* YELLOW OLEANDER. Zones 12 (with careful protection), 13, 14 (sheltered locations), 21–24. Fast growth typically to 6–8 ft. or more. Can be trained into 20-ft. small tree. Leaves 3–6 in. long, very narrow, with edges rolled under. Leaves are deep green, glossy, with inconspicuous veins. Flowers bloom any time (mostly June-November); are fragrant,

Thevetia peruviana

yellow to apricot, 2–3 in. long, in clusters at branch ends.

Takes any amount of heat and sun. Best with ample water, good drainage. Shallow rooted. Protect from wind or prune to lessen wind resistance. Can be grown as tree or pruned into 6–8-ft. hedge, background planting, or screen. In cold-winter areas, mound dry sand 6–12 in. deep around base of stem. If top is frozen, new growth will bloom same year.

T. thevetioides. GIANT THEVETIA. Zones 12 and 13 (with winter protection), 22–24. Fast, open growth to 12 ft. tall, 12 ft. wide. Leaves darker green than *T. peruviana,* resemble those of oleander but corrugated, heavily veined beneath. Flowers brilliant yellow, to 4 in. across, in large clusters, June-July and into winter Desert heat wilts summer flowers.

THREADLEAF FALSE ARALIA. See *Dizygotheca.*

THRIFT. See *Armeria.*

THUJA (sometimes spelled Thuya, and always so pronounced). ARBORVITAE. Evergreen shrubs or trees. Neat, symmetrical, even, geometrical plants which run to globes, cones, or cylinders. Scalelike leaves in flat sprays; juvenile foliage feathery, with small needlelike leaves. Small cones with few scales. Foliage in better-known varieties is often yellow green, or bright golden yellow.

Thuja plicata

T. occidentalis. AMERICAN ARBORVITAE. Tree. Zones 2–9, 15–17, 21–24. Native to eastern U.S. Upright, open growth to 40–60 ft. with branches that tend to turn up at ends. Leaf sprays bright green to yellowish green. Foliage turns brown in severe cold, will scorch badly in winter in coldest, windiest, Rocky Mountain gardens unless plants are shaded, watered. Needs moist soil, moist air to look its best. Spray for red spider mites.

Typical plant is seldom seen but certain garden varieties are fairly common. Among them, taller kinds make good unclipped or clipped screens. Lower-growing kinds often planted around foundations, along walks or walls, as hedges. Some good varieties are:

'Douglasii Pyramidalis'. Tall, vigorous green pyramid of fairly fast growth.

'Fastigiata' ('Pyramidalis', 'Columnaris'). Is a narrow, tall, dense, columnar plant which can grow to 25 ft. high, 5 ft. wide. Can be kept lower by pruning. Good plant for tall (6 ft. or more) hedges and screens, especially in cold regions and damp soils. Set 4 ft. apart for neat, low-maintenance screen.

'Globosa' ('Nana' and 'Pumila' are very similar, if not identical). GLOBE ARBORVITAE, TOM THUMB ARBORVITAE. Small, dense, rounded, with bright green foliage. Usually 2–3 ft. tall, with equal spread, but eventually larger.

'Little Gem' ('Pumila'). Dense, dark green; slow growth to 2 ft. tall, 4 ft. across. Larger in great old age.

'Nana'. Small, round, dense, to 1½–2 ft. in height.

'Rheingold' ('Improved Ellwangeriana Aurea'). Cone shaped, slow-growing, bright golden plant which has mixture of scalelike and needlelike leaves. Even very old plants seldom exceed 6 ft.

'Umbraculifera'. Globe shaped in youth, gradually becoming flat topped. At 10 years it should be 4 by 4 ft.

'Woodwardii'. Widely grown dense, globular shrub of rich green color. May attain considerable size with age, but is small plant over reasonably long period. If you can wait 72 years, it may be 8 ft. high by 18 ft. wide.

T. orientalis. See *Platycladus.*

T. plicata. WESTERN RED CEDAR. Tree. Zones 1–9, 14–24. In those zones with hot summers, must have summer shade to avoid foliage burn. Grows from coastal northern California north to Alaska and inland to Montana. Plants from inland seed are hardy anywhere in West; those from coastal seed less hardy to cold. Can reach over 200 ft. in coastal belt of Washington, but usually much less in gardens. Slender, drooping branchlets set closely with dark green scalelike leaves, form flat, graceful, lacy sprays. Cones are ½ in. across, cinnamon brown. Prefers cool, moist (but not soggy) soil. In areas where native, established plants may get along with little or no summer water.

Single trees are magnificent on large lawns, but lower branches spread quite broadly and trees lose their characteristic beauty when these are cut off.

Here are a few of its varieties:

'Aurea'. Younger branch tips golden green.

'Fastigiata'. HOGAN CEDAR. Very dense, narrow, erect; fine for tall screen.

'Striblingii'. Dense, thick column 10–12 ft. tall, 2–3 ft. wide. For moderate-height screen planting or can be used as an upright sentinel.

THUJOPSIS dolabrata. FALSE ARBORVITAE, DEERHORN CEDAR, HIBA CEDAR. Evergreen tree. Zones 1–7, 14–17. Needs part shade in Zone 14, warmest parts of 15. Pyramidal, coniferous, of very slow growth to 50 ft. high, often shrubby. Foliage resembles *Thuja*, but twigs are coarser, very glossy, branching in deerhorn effect. Will grow in part shade. Best where summers are cool, humid; may get by with little summer water there. Where summers are hotter and drier, requires more shade and moisture. Plant as single tree where foliage details can be appreciated. Slow growth makes it good container plant. 'Nana' is dwarf variety. 'Variegata' has white branch tips.

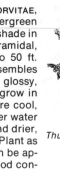

Thujopsis dolabrata

THUNBERGIA. Perennial vines. Noted for showy flowers. Tropical in origin, but some are hardy in milder parts of California and Zone 13, and others grow fast enough to bloom the first season and, hence, be treated as annuals. Best with regular garden watering.

Thunbergia alata

T. alata. BLACK-EYED SUSAN VINE. Perennial, grown as summer annual in cold-winter areas. May live over in mild climates. Trailing or twining, small plant with triangular, 3-in. leaves. Flowers are flaring tubes to 1 in. wide, orange, yellow, or white, all with purple black throat. Start seed indoors, set plants out in good soil in sunny spot as soon as weather warms. Use in hanging baskets, window boxes, as ground cover in small, sunny spots, or train on strings or low trellis.

T. grandiflora. SKY FLOWER. Zones 16, 21–24. Vigorous twiner to 20 ft. or more, with lush, green, 8-in., heart shaped leaves. Slightly drooping clusters of tubular, flaring, 2½–3-in., delicate, pure blue flowers. Blooms fall, winter, spring. Takes year to get started, then grows rapidly. Will come back to bloom in a year if frozen back. Full sun near coast, part shade inland. Use to cover arbor, lathhouse, or fence; makes dense shade. There is a white variety.

T. gregorii (T. *gibsonii*). ORANGE CLOCK VINE. Zones 21–24; warm lathhouse or greenhouse in Zones 13, 16, 17; or grow as summer annual. Twines to 6 ft. tall, or sprawls over ground to cover 6-ft. circle. Leaves 3 in. long, toothed, evergreen. Flowers tubular, flaring, bright orange, borne singly on 4-in. stems. Blooms nearly all year in mildest areas, in summer where winters are cool. Plant 3–4 ft. apart to cover wire fence, 6 ft. apart as ground cover. Plant above wall, over which vine will cascade, or grow in hanging basket. Easy and showy; watch color conflicts with pink and red flowers.

THYME. See *Thymus.*

THYMOPHYLLA tenuiloba. See *Dyssodia.*

THYMUS. THYME. Ground covers, erect shrubby perennial herbs. All Zones. Foliage usually heavily scented. Plants attract bees. Grow in warm, light, well-drained soil that is fairly dry. Full sun to light shade. Stands some neglect but will need periodic summer watering in hottest zones. Restrain plants as needed by clipping back growing tips. Propagate from cuttings taken early in summer, or sow seed. Plant ground cover kinds 6–12 in. apart in fall or spring.

Thymus vulgaris

T. citriodorus. LEMON THYME. Small shrub, erect or spreading, 4–12 in. tall. Tiny (to ⅜ in.) leaves have lemon scent. Flowers palest purple. Variegated forms are 'Argenteus' (silver) and 'Aureus' (gold).

T. herba-barona. CARAWAY-SCENTED THYME. Ground cover. Fast-growing, forms thick, flat mat of dark green, ¼-in.-long leaves with caraway fragrance. Rose pink flowers in headlike clusters. Can use leaves to flavor vegetable dishes.

T. lanuginosus. See *T. pseudolanuginosus.*

T. praecox arcticus (*T. serpyllum, T. drucei*). MOTHER-OF-THYME, CREEPING THYME. Ground cover. Forms flat mat, the upright branches 2–6 in. high. Roundish, ¼-in.-long, dark green, aromatic leaves. Small purplish white flowers (white in one form) in headlike clusters, June-September. Good for small areas or filler between stepping stones where foot traffic is light. Soft and fragrant underfoot. Leaves can be used in seasoning and in potpourris. Rose red variety is sold as 'Reiter's'.

T. pseudolanuginosus (*T. lanuginosus*). WOOLLY THYME. Ground cover. Forms flat to undulating mat 2–3 in. high. Stems densely clothed with small gray-woolly leaves. Seldom shows its pinkish flowers. Plants become slightly rangy in winter. Use in rock crevices, between stepping stones, to spill over bank or raised bed, to cover small patches of ground.

T. vulgaris. COMMON THYME. Shrubby perennial herb. To 6–12 in. high. Narrow to oval, ¼-in.-long, fragrant, gray green leaves. Tiny lilac flowers in dense whorls, June and July. Low edging for flower, vegetable, or herb garden. Good container plant. Use leaves fresh or dried for seasoning vegetable juices, fish, shellfish, poultry stuffing, soups, vegetables.

T.v. 'Argenteus'. SILVER THYME. Has leaves variegated with silver.

TI. See *Cordyline terminalis.*

TIBOUCHINA urvilleana (*T. semidecandra, Pleroma splendens*). PRINCESS FLOWER. Evergreen shrub or small tree. Zones 14 and 15 (sheltered locations), 16, 17, 21–24; excellent greenhouse plant anywhere. Native to Brazil. Fast, rather open growth to 5–18 ft. Large, oval, velvety, 3–6-in.-long leaves are strongly ribbed, velvety green, often edged red. Branch tips, buds, new growth shaded with orange and bronze red velvety hairs. Older leaves add spots of red, orange, or yellow, especially in winter. Brilliant royal purple, 3-in.-wide flowers in clusters at ends of branches appear intermittently May-January.

Tibouchina urvilleana

Best in somewhat acid, well-drained soil with roots in shade, top in sun; give average water. Protect from strong wind. Minimize legginess by light pruning after each bloom cycle, heavier pruning in early spring. Resprouts quickly after heavy pruning. Pinch tips of young plants to encourage bushiness. Feed after spring pruning and lightly after each bloom cycle. If buds fail to open, look for tobacco budworm.

TIDYTIPS. See *Layia platyglossa.*

TIGER FLOWER. See *Tigridia.*

TIGER ORCHID. See *Odontoglossum grande.*

TIGRIDIA pavonia. TIGER FLOWER, MEXICAN SHELL FLOWER. Bulb. All Zones if treated like gladiolus; leave bulbs in ground only in mild-winter areas. Leaves narrow, ribbed, swordlike, 12–18 in. long; shorter leaves on 18–30-in. flower stalks. Showy bright flowers, 3–6 in. across, with 3 large segments forming triangle, joined with 3 smaller segments to form center cup. Larger segments usually vivid solid color—orange, pink, red, yellow—or white. Smaller segments usually spotted or blotched with darker colors. Immaculata strain in solid colors, unspotted. Bloom July-August;

Tigridia pavonia

each flower lasts one day, but others follow for several weeks.

Plant after weather warms in rich, porous soil in groups of 10–12. Set bulbs 2–4 in. deep, 4–8 in. apart. Full sun near coast,

afternoon shade in warmer areas. Or, plant 6–8 bulbs in 9-in. pot. During active growth water regularly, and feed every 2 weeks with mild solution of liquid fertilizer. In colder areas dig and store after foliage ripens. Do not break bulbs apart until just before planting in spring. Plants in open ground require division every 3–4 years. Easily grown from seed; may bloom first year. Control red spider mites, starting when leaves are few inches tall. Protect from gophers.

TILIA. LINDEN. Deciduous trees. Dense, compact crowns. Much used for street and park planting in Europe. All have small, quite fragrant, yellowish white flowers in drooping clusters. All respond well to deep, rich soil and plenty of water. All grow at slow to moderate rate (not fast trees). Young trees need staking and shaping. Older trees need only corrective pruning. Under certain circumstances, aphids cause disagreeable drip of honeydew and accompanying sooty mildew.

Tilia cordata

T. americana. AMERICAN LINDEN, BASSWOOD. Zones 1–17. To 40–60 ft. with 20–25-ft. spread. Straight trunk; dense, compact, narrow crown. Dull dark green leaves 4–6 in. long, 3–4 in. wide, sometimes larger, heart shaped. Loose clusters of fragrant yellowish white flowers in June-July. 'Fastigiata' and 'Pyramidalis' are upright-branching, narrow forms.

T. cordata. LITTLE-LEAF LINDEN. Zones 1–17. To 30–50 ft. with 15–30-ft. spread. Form densely pyramidal. Leaves 1½–3 in. long, equally broad or broader, dark green above, silvery beneath. Flowers in July. Attracts bees. Excellent medium-sized lawn or street tree. Given space to develop its symmetrical crown, it can be fine patio shade tree (but expect bees in flowering season). It is hardiest linden. 'Greenspire' and 'Rancho' are forms with especially upright or conical shapes.

T. euchlora. CRIMEAN LINDEN. Zones 1–17. To 25–35 ft., perhaps eventually to 50 ft., almost as wide. Branches slightly pendulous. Leaves oval or roundish, 2–4 in. long, rich glossy green above, paler beneath. Yellowish white flowers in July. Use in same way as little-leaf linden—form is broader, shade and foliage less dense. 'Redmond' is pyramidal in habit.

T. tomentosa. SILVER LINDEN. Zones 1–21. To 40–50 ft. high, 20–30 ft. wide. Light green, 3–5-in.-long leaves, silvery beneath, turn in slight breeze. Drought resistant once established.

TILLANDSIA. Perennials. Outdoors Zones 22–24; house plants anywhere. Bromeliads (pineapple relatives) grown in pots of loose, fast draining soil mix or as epiphytes on tree branches or slabs of bark. Best known is *T. usneoides*, the "Spanish moss" of the South. Similar is Arizona native *T. recurvata*.

Tillandsia cyanea

Leaf rosettes of some are bright green, of others gray and scaly or scurfy; the latter require bright light and are drought resistant. They are often mounted on plaques of wood or bark and used as wall ornaments indoors or outside (where hardy). Let potting mix dry out between waterings.

T. cyanea. Rosette of bright green, arching, 12-in. leaves produces showy flower cluster—flattened plume of deep pink or red bracts from which violet blue flowers emerge 1 or 2 at a time for long period.

T. ionantha. Miniature rosettes of short-furred, silvery gray leaves to 2 in. long. Small tubular flowers are violet; at bloom time center of rosette turns red. Tough and undemanding plant.

T. lindenii (*Vriesea lindenii*). Like *T. cyanea*, but plume is green or green marked rose.

TIPU TREE. See *Tipuana tipu.*

TIPUANA tipu. TIPU TREE. Deciduous or semievergreen tree. Zones 12 (warmest locations), 13–16, 18–24. Fast to 25 ft.; can reach eventual 35–50 ft. Broad silhouette with flattened crown usually wider than high; can be pruned to umbrella shape to make narrower, denser crown. Leaves divided into 11–21, 1½-in.-long, oblong, light green leaflets. Blooms June-July with clusters of sweet pea shaped flowers, apricot to yellow. Blooms followed by 2½-in. pods. Hardy to 25°F.; well-ripened wood will take 18°F. with minor damage. Any soil except strongly alkaline. Established trees need occasional deep soaking, young plants more frequent irrigation. Flowers best in warm-summer areas out of immediate ocean influence. Good street or lawn tree. Useful shade canopy for patio or terrace, although flower litter can be slight problem. Brittle branches problem in windy areas.

Tipuana tipu

TITHONIA rotundifolia (*T. speciosa*). MEXICAN SUNFLOWER. Perennial grown as summer annual. Husky, rather coarse, gaudy plant; rapid growth to 6 ft. tall. Spectacular flower heads 3–4 in. across with orange scarlet rays and tufted yellow centers. Blooms July to frost. Inflated hollow stems; cut with care for bouquets so as not to bend stalks. Leaves velvety green. Sow seed in place in spring, in not-too-rich soil. Full sun. Drought resistant and heat resistant, good choice for desert gardens. Belongs in background where flowers can be seen above other plants. 'Torch', lower growing variety to 4 ft., makes bushy summer hedge, is useful filler in new shrub borders.

Tithonia rotundifolia

TOADFLAX. See *Linaria.*

TOBIRA. See *Pittosporum tobira.*

TOLMIEA menziesii. PIGGY-BACK PLANT. Zones 5–9, 12–24; house plant everywhere. Native to Coastal Ranges from northern California northward to Alaska. Chief asset is abundant production of attractive 5-in.-wide basal leaves—shallowly lobed and toothed, rather hairy. Leaves can produce new plantlets at junction of leaf stalk and blade. Tiny reddish brown flowers top 1–2-ft.-high stems, are rather inconspicuous. Tolerates wet soil. Good ground cover for shade. As house plant, needs filtered light, cool temperatures, frequent watering. Mealybugs, spider mites are occasional

Tolmiea menziesii

pests. Makes handsome hanging basket plant. Start new plants any time of year. Take leaf with plantlet and insert in moist potting mix so base of plantlet contacts soil. Or float leaf with plantlet in bowl of water—roots will form.

TOMATILLO. See *Physalis ixocarpa.*

TOMATO. The vines are easy to grow and they yield delicious fruit abundantly—that must be why tomatoes are just about the most widely grown of all garden plants, edible or otherwise. There is a sea of opinion among amateur and commercial growers about how the plants can best be grown. If you have developed your own particular scheme for growing them, continue to follow it. But, if you're a novice or dissatisfied with your previous attempts,

Tomato

you may find useful the following information about growing tomatoes (word "vine" is used to denote tomato plant—it's really a sprawling plant incapable of climbing, but by common usage it's a vine).

First, choose varieties suited to your climate that will yield kind of tomatoes you like on kind of vines that you can handle. Plant a few of early, midseason, and late varieties for production over long period; some are described at the end of this section.

To grow your own tomato plants from seed, sow in early March in pot of light soil mix or in a ready-made seed starter, sold at stores. In pots, cover seed with ½ in. of fine soil. Firm soil over seeds. Keep soil surface damp. Place seed container in coldframe or sunny window (sun and ideally a 65°–70°F. temperature, though range of 50°F. at night to 85°F. daytime will give acceptable results). Transplant seedlings when 2 in. high into 3 or 4-in. pots. Keep these pots in sunny area, and grow them to transplant size.

Time to plant tomato seedlings—ones that you grew from seed (above) or ones that you buy from a nursery or garden store—depends on where you live: February or early March in Zones 12, 13; April, May, or early June in Zones 7–9, 14–24; May or early June in Zones 1–6, 10, 11. Typically, 6 plants can supply a family.

Plant in sunny position in well-drained soil. Space plants 18 in.–3 ft. apart (staked or trained) to 3–4 ft. apart (untrained). Make planting hole extra deep. Set seedlings in hole so lowest leaves are just above soil level. Additional roots will form on buried stem and provide stronger root system.

When selecting tomato varieties you may find some noted as *determinate,* others as *indeterminate.* Determinate types are bushier and not as suitable for staking or trellising. Indeterminate ones are more vinelike, need more training, and generally have longer bearing period.

Tomato management and harvest will be most satisfying if you train plants to keep them mostly off the ground (left alone, they will sprawl and some fruit will lie on soil, often causing rot, pest damage, and discoloration). Commonest training method for indeterminate varieties is to drive 6-ft.-long stake (at least 1-by-1-in. size) into ground a foot from each plant. Tie plants to these stakes as they grow.

Slightly easier in the long run, but more work at planting time, is to grow each plant in wire cylinder made of concrete reinforcing screen (6-in. mesh). Form cylinder with 1½-ft. diameter. Screen is manufactured 84 in. wide, which is just right for cylinder height. Most indeterminate vines can grow to top of such a cylinder. Put stakes at opposite sides of cylinder and tie it firmly to them. As vine grows, poke protruding branches back inside cylinder every week. Reach through screen to pick fruit.

Or for a novelty, plant in large suspended container and let vine cascade down (quite useful and practical with small-fruited tomatoes).

Irrigate tomato plants frequently during early part of the season, less frequently after fruit begins to ripen. Tomato plant sends its roots deep, so water heavily when you do water.

If soil is fairly rich, you won't need to fertilize at all. But in ordinary soils, give light application of fertilizer every 2 weeks or at alternate waterings from the time first blossoms set until end of harvest.

If diseases or insects trouble or threaten plants, protect them with all-purpose vegetable dust or spray—a mixture that contains both an insecticide and a fungicide.

If your plants grow, set fruit, and then shrivel, wilt, and die, they may have been sabotaged by gophers. If no gopher evidence is found, plants probably are suffering from verticillium or fusarium wilt or both. Pull and dispose of such plants. Diseases live over in soil, so the next year plant in different location and try one of the wilt-resistant varieties suited to your climate. Some tomato problems—leaf roll, blossom-end rot, cracked fruit—are physiological, usually corrected (or prevented) by maintaining uniform soil moisture. A mulch will help.

If you have done everything right and your tomatoes have failed to set fruit in the spring, use hormone to spray on blossoms. Tomatoes often fail to set fruit when night temperatures drop below 55°F. In chilly-night areas, select cold-tolerant varieties (especially small-fruited strains). Fruit-setting hormone often speeds up bearing in the earlier part of the season. Tomatoes can also fail to set fruit when temperatures rise above 100°F., but hormones are not effective under those conditions.

Harvest fruit when they have turned full red and juicy; keep ripe fruit picked to extend season. When frost is predicted, harvest all fruit, green and partly ripe. Store these at 58°F. and bring into 70°F. to ripen as needed.

TOMATO VARIETIES

Following are kinds of tomatoes you can buy as seeds or started plants—listings are arranged according to fruit and vine types.

Wilt-resistant tomatoes. Several varieties are valued especially for their resistance to verticillium or fusarium wilt. Varieties with the letters "VF" after their names tolerate verticillium and fusarium; those marked VFN also tolerate nematodes.

Main crop or standard tomatoes. 'Ace' and 'Ace' types are large tomatoes of very fine flavor that bear well in California's interior and inner coastal valleys. 'Pearson' and 'Pearson Improved' will set fruit under wide range of temperatures and produce well in California's coastal and interior valleys. 'Stone' is late-maturing variety with scarlet red globular fruit on large vines; it is southern California favorite. 'Manalucie' is another good main crop variety for warm areas. 'Pritchard' produces fairly early main crop and is useful in northwestern gardens.

Early tomatoes. "Early" means more than early harvest. Early varieties set fruit at lower night temperatures than midseason or late varieties; most will ripen fruit in cool-summer climates. Name 'Earliana' covers several varieties such as 'Early Market', 'First Early', 'Morse's 498', and 'Pennheart'. 'Early Girl' gives high yield of medium-small tomatoes beginning early and lasting through season. Early types grown in Oregon and Washington include 'Bonny Best', 'John Baer', and 'Valiant', all large-vine types; and 'Willamette', a small-vine type.

Cool-summer tomatoes. Where summers are unusually cool, nurseries offer locally adapted varieties: in Seattle you'll find 'Seattle Best of All'; in San Francisco look for 'Frisco Fogger'.

Hybrid tomatoes. Hybrid vigor makes these tomatoes grow more strongly and rapidly, produce larger and more uniform fruit than other varieties. And they produce fruit in climate extremes. Of many hybrids, 'Beefmaster' (VFN); 'Burpee Hybrid', a medium to large main crop variety; 'Big Boy', a very large, thick, round red tomato; 'Better Boy' (VFN); 'Wonder Boy'; and 'Spring Giant' are well known.

Yellow orange tomatoes. 'Jubilee' and 'Sunray' are strikingly handsome golden orange tomatoes. They taste just like good red tomatoes and look good too, especially sliced and mixed with sliced red tomatoes. There are even white tomatoes: 'New Snowball' and 'White Beauty' are interesting novelties with very low acid content.

Large-fruited tomatoes. These are home gardener's specials. They are poor shippers. Unless they are grown locally, you won't find them at your produce market. Among the best are 'Ponderosa', 'Beefsteak' ('Crimson Cushion'), 'Big Boy', 'Big Girl' (VF), 'Beefmaster' (VFN), 'Bragger', 'Spring Giant' (VF). Fruit is very large, broad, rather shallow, very meaty, and mild in flavor. All varieties need moderate heat and are not recommended where nights are cool or in coastal areas. Vines are large.

Small-fruited tomatoes. Ripe fruits are size of large marbles or small plums, but there's nothing small about vines of small-fruited tomatoes. Trained against wall they will reach 8 ft. and spread almost as wide. These varieties set fruit well under greater climate extremes than do larger-fruited varieties. Many shapes and colors are available as indicated by their names: 'Red Cherry', 'Red Plum', 'Red Pear', 'Yellow Cherry', 'Yellow Pear', 'Yellow Peach'. Extra-heavy producer of small, sweet cherry tomatoes is 'Sweet 100'. 'Basket Pak' produces tomatoes to 1½ in. wide. Dwarf varieties that will grow in small pots or containers are 'Tiny Tim', 'Small Fry' (VFN), 'Pixie', 'Toy Boy', 'Patio', 'Salad Top', 'Tumbling Tom', 'Early Salad', 'Atom'. A special type of extra-meaty tomato is often grown for making tomato paste and puree. These smallish, long, slim varieties with little seed pulp include 'San Marzano' and 'Roma'.

TORCH-LILY. See *Kniphofia uvaria.*

TORENIA fournieri. WISHBONE FLOWER. Summer annual. Compact, bushy, to 1 ft. high. Flowers look like miniature gloxinias, light blue marked deeper blue, bright yellow throat; white also available. Blooms summer and fall. Stamens arranged in shape of wishbone. Full sun where summers are cool and short, part shade elsewhere. Needs much water. Sow seed in flats, transplant to garden when frosts are over. Good for borders, pots, window boxes.

Torenia fournieri

TORREYA californica. CALIFORNIA NUTMEG. Evergreen tree. Zones 7–9, 14–24. Conifer native to cool shaded canyons in scattered California mountain regions below 4,500 ft. elevation. Wide, open pyramidal crown, becoming domelike with age; slow growing to 15–50 ft. high with trunk 1–3 ft. in diameter. Branches are horizontal, slender, somewhat drooping at tips. Leaves dark green with two whitish bands underneath, flat, rigid, sharp pointed, 1¼–2½ in. long, ⅛ in. wide, in flat sprays. Fruit plumlike, pale green with purplish markings. Easy to grow; needs occasional watering in summer months.

TOTARA. See *Podocarpus totara.*

TOUCH-ME-NOT. See *Impatiens.*

Torreya californica

TOWER OF JEWELS. See *Echium wildpretii.*

TOYON. See *Heteromeles arbutifolia.*

TRACHELOSPERMUM (*Rhynchospermum*). STAR JASMINE. Evergreen vines or sprawling shrubs. Used as ground covers, spillers, or climbers.

T. asiaticum. Zones 6–24. Twines to 15 ft. or sprawls on the ground with branchlets rising erect. Leaves smaller, darker, duller green than *T. jasminoides.* Flowers smaller, creamy yellow or yellowish white, fragrant, blooming April-June. Regular watering, sun (best with part shade in desert to avoid foliage burn).

T. jasminoides. STAR JASMINE. Zones 8–24. One of most widely used plants in California and Arizona. Given support, is twining vine to 20 ft., slow to start but eventually moderately fast growing. Without

Trachelospermum jasminoides

support and with some tip-pinching, a spreading shrub or ground cover 1½–2 ft. tall, 4–5 ft. wide. New foliage glossy light green; mature leaves lustrous dark green, to 3 in. long. Flowers white, to 1 in. across, profuse in small clusters on short side branches, sweetly fragrant. Blooms June-July; May-June in desert. Attractive to bees. *T. j. 'Variegatum'* has leaves variegated with white; it is rare.

To grow as vine, start with plant that has been staked, or that at least has not been tip-pinched to make it shrubby. Provide support immediately. Use heavy cord to lead vine in direction you wish it to take. Train on posts, baffles, walls, fences, trellises, wherever its fragrance can be enjoyed, or where night lighting can pick out white blossoms. Give some shade in hottest areas. Cut back older plants about ⅓ each year to prevent inner growth becoming too woody and bare.

To grow as bank or ground cover, set plants 1½–3 ft. apart (depending on how fast you want cover). Cut back upright shoots. Feed in spring, late summer. Spray for scale, mealybug, red spider mites. Keep well watered and weeded. In 3–4 years growth is thick enough to discourage most annual weeds.

Use in raised beds, entry gardens, for edging along walks or drives, to extend lawn, or to cover ground under trees and shrubs that need summer water.

TRACHYCARPUS. Palms. Fan leafed. Plants of moderate size and great hardiness. Characteristic blackish fiber grows at least at tops of all but oldest trunks. Need regular watering.

T. fortunei (sometimes sold as *Chamaerops excelsa*). WINDMILL PALM. Indoor potted palm anywhere; outdoors Zones 4–24. Native to China. Moderate to fast growth to 30 ft. in warm-winter areas. Trunk is dark, usually thicker at top than at bottom, covered with dense, hairy-looking fiber. Leaves 3 ft. across on 1½-ft. toothed stalks. Responds to water and feeding, but isn't demanding. Sometimes becomes untidy and ruffled in high winds. Hardy to 10°F. or lower.

Trachycarpus fortunei

T. martianus. Zones 15–17, 19–24. Native to Himalayas. Slower, taller, more slender than *T. fortunei*. Trunk without fiber except at top, ringed with leaf scars. Hardy to 22°F. Rare.

T. takil. Zones 15–17, 19–24. Native to western Himalayas. Very slow grower with heavy, inclined trunk. Can reach 20 ft., but is dwarf for many years. Rare.

TRACHYMENE coerulea (*Didiscus coeruleus*). BLUE LACE FLOWER. Late spring annual; blooms in summer where weather is cool. To 2 ft. tall. Flowers small, lavender blue, numerous, in flat-topped clusters 2–3 in. across and quite lacy in appearance, as are divided leaves. Sow seeds in place in spring for summer bloom. Needs regular watering, sunny location, but won't take too much heat.

Trachymene coerulea

TRADESCANTIA. Perennials. Long-trailing, indestructible plants often grown indoors, or outdoors as ground cover for shaded areas. Most are used as pot plants or hanging basket plants; these can also be used as ground covers, but are likely to prove invasive. The long-stemmed, rambling kind is often called inch plant or wandering Jew—a name also often applied to related *Callisia, Tripogandra,* and especially *Zebrina.*

Tradescantia fluminensis

T. albiflora. WANDERING JEW, GIANT INCH PLANT. Zones 12–24. Trailing, or sprawling and rooting at joints. Leaves 2–3 in. long. Flowers small, white. 'Albovittata' has leaves that are finely and evenly streaked with white. 'Aurea' ('Gold Leaf') has chartreuse yellow foliage. 'Laekenensis' ('Rainbow') has bandings of white and pale lavender purple. Variegated forms are unstable and tend to revert to green; keep solid green growths pinched out. Easiest care in well-drained soil with average water and strong light but not hot, direct sunlight. Can take considerable shade. Trailing stems will live long time in water, rooting quickly and easily. Renovate overgrown plants by cutting back severely or by starting new pots with fresh tip growth.

T. andersoniana (usually sold as *T. virginiana*). SPIDERWORT. All Zones. Grows in clumps 1½–3 ft. tall, with long, deep green, erect or arching grasslike foliage. Three-petaled flowers open for only a day, but buds come in large clusters and plants are seldom out of bloom during summer. Named garden varieties come in white and shades of blue, lavender, purple, pink, and purplish rose to near red. Needs ample water and tolerates boggy conditions. Any soil. Sun or shade. Propagate by division.

T. blossfeldiana. Zones 12–24. Fleshy, furry stems spread and lean, but do not really hang. Leaves to 4 in. long are dark, shiny green above, purple and furry underneath. Flowers showier than those of most trailing or semitrailing tradescantias: clusters of furry purplish buds open into ½-in. pink, white-centered flowers. Grow in full sun in coastal valleys, full sun or partial shade inland. Average water requirement.

T. fluminensis. WANDERING JEW. Zones 12–24; house plant everywhere. Prostrate or trailing habit. Fast growing. Succulent stems have swollen joints where 2½-in.-long, dark green, oval or oblong leaves are attached ('Variegata' has leaves striped yellow or white). Tiny white flowers are not showy. Very easy to grow. In warmer areas can be grown in shade as ground cover. Excellent for window boxes and dish gardens, or for under greenhouse bench. A few stems placed in glass of water will live long time, and will even make some growth.

T. multiflora. See *Tripogandra multiflora*.

T. navicularis. CHAIN PLANT. House plant. Compact plant with short, barely trailing branches packed with fleshy, folded brownish purple leaves. Miniature plants form along stems, detach for propagation. Tiny purple red flowers. Grow as succulent.

T. sillamontana. House plant. Short trailing or ascending branches with 2–2½-in. leaves densely coated with soft white fur. Tiny rose purple flowers. Avoid overwatering.

TRAILING AFRICAN DAISY. See *Osteospermum fruticosum*.

TRAILING ARBUTUS. See *Epigaea repens*.

TRANSVAAL DAISY. See *Gerbera*.

TREE FERN. See *Blechnum, Cibotium, Dicksonia, Sphaeropteris*.

TREE MALLOW. See *Lavatera*.

TREE-OF-HEAVEN. See *Ailanthus altissima*.

TREE TOMATO. See *Cyphomandra betacea*.

TREVESIA. SNOWFLAKE TREE. Evergreen shrubs or small trees. Zones 21–24; house plants everywhere. Resemble *Fatsia japonica* in growth habit, but taller (10–20 ft.), more treelike. Leaves on long stalks, are 1–2 ft. across, deeply lobed like fatsia, but each lobe is deeply cut. Leaves have lacy look resembling outline of enormous snowflake. Flowers unimportant. Several have been cultivated; best known is *T. palmata* 'Micholitzii'.

Trevesia palmata 'Micholitzii'

Take filtered sun or afternoon shade; loose, leafy, fast draining soil with liberal water and feeding. Watch for mealybug, spider mites. Indoors, give good light but not hot sun from west or south window. Young plants are good tub subjects, indoors or outdoors. Grow well near pools.

TRICHOSPORUM. See *Aeschynanthus*.

TRICHOSTEMA lanatum. WOOLLY BLUE CURLS. Evergreen shrub. Zones 14–24. Native to dry, sunny slopes of Coast Ranges, California. Much branched, neat plant, 3–5 ft. high. Leaves pungently aromatic when bruised, narrow, 1¼–2 in. long, upper surface shining dark green, under surface white, woolly; leaf edges rolled under. Flowers, in separated clusters along the long stalk, are blue with conspicuous arching stamens. Stalks and parts of flowers are covered with blue, pink, or whitish wool. Blooms April-June; throughout summer and early fall if old flower stems are cut back. Needs excellent drainage. Do not water in summer. Good choice for sunny hillsides.

Trichostema lanatum

TRICUSPIDARIA dependens. See *Crinodendron patagua*.

TRIFOLIUM. CLOVER. Scores of species, most of them field crops. Two are perennials of garden importance.

T. repens. WHITE CLOVER, WHITE DUTCH CLOVER. All Zones. Sometimes used to mix with lawn grass or dichondra seed. Useful for deep rooting (with some drought resistance) and ability to take nitrogen

Trifolium repens

from air and put it into the soil through root bacteria action. Can stain clothing of small children who play on it, and heads of white blossoms attract bees. Prostrate stems root freely and send up lush cover of 3-part leaves with ¾-in. leaflets. Thrives in full sun to half shade. *T. r. minus* is one of the shamrocks.

T. fragiferum. STRAWBERRY CLOVER. Zones 4–24. An Australian strain of this forage crop known as O'Connor's Legume is used as a ground or bank cover for its deep rooting (6–7 ft.) and tolerance of heat, drought, and moderate salinity. Sow seed at 2–8 oz. per 1000 sq. ft. and water well until established. With average water makes 6–7-in. mat of green clover leaves.

TRILLIUM. WAKE ROBIN. Perennials. Early spring-blooming plants of the lily family. Whorl of three leaves tops each stem, and from center of these springs single flower with three maroon or white petals. Plant thick, deep-growing, fleshy rhizomes in shady, woodsy location. Never let plants completely dry out. Let them alone; they will gradually increase.

Trillium ovatum

T. chloropetalum (*T. sessile californicum*). Zones 4–9, 14–17. Western native. To 1–1½ ft. high. Flower, with greenish white to yellowish petals about 2½ in. long, sits without a stalk on the three large (6 in. long) mottled leaves. *T. c. giganteum* has deep maroon petals.

T. grandiflorum. Zones 1–6. Stout stems 8–18 in. Leaves 2½–6 in. long. Flower is stalked, nodding, white aging to rose.

T. ovatum (*T. californicum*). Zones 1–6, 14–17. Western native similar to *T. grandiflorum* but with narrower petals, and flowers are usually upright on stalks. Effective in shady part of wildflower garden or among ferns, azaleas, or Polyanthus primroses.

TRINIDAD FLAME BUSH. See *Calliandra tweedii*.

TRIPOGANDRA multiflora (*Tradescantia multiflora*). BRIDAL VEIL, FERNLEAF WANDERING JEW. Perennial used as house plant, usually in hanging pot or basket. Resembles common wandering Jews (*Tradescantia* and *Zebrina*) in most details and in culture, but is finer in texture, with smaller (1–2 in. long), narrower leaves, thinner stems. Leaves dark green above, purple underneath. Tiny white flowers are freely produced on slender, almost hairlike stalks. Stems can trail to considerable length—a yard or even more. Plants need

Tripogandra multiflora

same culture and conditions as *Tradescantia albiflora* and *T. fluminensis* but are less hardy to cold and low humidity.

TRISTANIA. Evergreen trees. Zones 19–24; also grown in Zones 15–18, but hardiness is questionable where temperatures drop below 26°F. Related to eucalyptus. The two species grown in California are of manageable size, and both have brightly colored shedding bark in addition to handsome evergreen foliage.

T. conferta. BRISBANE BOX. Moderate to fast growth rate to 30–60 ft. Trunk and limbs resemble those of madrone, with reddish brown bark peeling away to show smooth, light-colored new bark under-

Tristania conferta

neath. Growth habit is rather upright, crown eventually broad and rounded. Leaves are 4–6 in. long, oval, leathery, bright green; they tend to cluster toward tips of branchlets. Flowers in clusters of 3–7 in summer, ¾ in. across, white to creamy. Fruit is woody capsule something like that of eucalyptus.

Tristania conferta

Takes almost any soil, but young plants get better start with good soil and liberal watering; established plants are quite drought resistant. Pinch and prune to get more twiggy growth. Not bothered by insects or diseases, but chlorosis sometimes a problem in Los Angeles area. Good street or lawn tree.

T. laurina. Slow-growing, rather formal-looking small tree or shrub. Trees 8 years old are 10 ft. tall and 5 ft. across, with remarkably dense and rounded crown. Trunk is covered with mahogany colored bark which peels to show satiny white new bark. Leaves to 4 in. long, usually narrow, but varying to somewhat broader, heavy textured, glossy medium green. Flowers small, yellow, clustered, are borne with sufficient profusion to put on good show in late spring or early summer. Fruit similar to *T. conferta* but only ¼ in. across. Young plants are densely shrubby, and can be kept that way with a little pinching. May be trained, like olives, as multistemmed trees. To make a single-stemmed tree, stake plant and shorten side branches. Remove shortened side branches when treelike growth pattern is established; then only light shaping will be necessary. Good tub subject. Variety 'Elegant' has broad leaves that open red and hold color until shaded by newer growth; they then turn green.

TRITELEIA. Corms. Plants under this name were formerly know as *Brodiaea*. General descriptions and culture are same as for *Brodiaea*, which differs only in technicalities. Species below quite heat and drought tolerant.

T. grandiflora (*Brodiaea douglasii, B. grandiflora*). Flowering stalk to 2 ft. tall, many blue to white 1¼-in.-long trumpets.

T. ixioides (*B. ixioides*). PRETTY FACE, GOLDEN BRODIAEA. Flower stalk to 2 ft.; flowers 1 in. across, golden yellow with purple black midrib and veins.

T. laxa (*B. laxa*). ITHURIEL'S SPEAR. Flower stalk to 2½ ft.; purple blue 1½ in. trumpets.

Triteleia laxa

T. 'Queen Fabiola'. Flower stem to 30 in. tall; flowers deep violet. Good cut flower.

T. tubergenii. Flower stem to 2½ ft. tall; flowers light blue.

T. uniflora. See *Ipheion*.

TRITOMA uvaria. See *Kniphofia uvaria*.

TRITONIA (*Montbretia*). Corms. Zones 9, 13–24. Native of South Africa. Related to freesia, ixia, and sparaxis. Leaves are narrow, sword shaped. Branched flower stems carry short, spikelike clusters of brilliant flowers. Grow in sun. Give regular watering through blooming period, after which foliage dies down and plants will withstand drought. Good in rock gardens, borders, pots. Long-lasting cut flowers.

T. crocata. Often called flame freesia. Flower stems to 12–18 in. Flowers orange red, funnel shaped, 2 in. long. Variety *miniata* has bright red blooms. 'Princess Beatrix' has deep orange flowers. Others come in white and shades of pink, salmon, yellow, and apricot.

Tritonia crocata

T. hyalina. Flowers bright orange; narrower segments than *T. crocata*, with transparent area near base. More dwarf than *T. crocata*.

TROLLIUS. GLOBEFLOWER. Perennials. All Zones. Shiny, finely cut, dark green leaves. Yellow to orange flowers resemble those of ranunculus. Bloom season late spring to late summer. Need shade or part shade, rich soil, plenty of moisture. Subject to aphids. Valuable for bringing bright color to shady area; particularly happy choice near pool. Excellent cut flowers.

T. europaeus. To 1–2 ft. tall. Flowers yellow, 1½ in. across. Some varieties have orange flowers.

T. ledebouri. Plant so called by nurseries grows to 2 ft. tall. Flowers gold orange, 2 in. across. Variety 'Golden Queen' reaches 4 ft., has 4-in.-wide flowers.

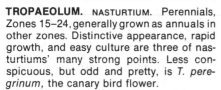

Trollius ledebouri

TROPAEOLUM. NASTURTIUM. Perennials, Zones 15–24, generally grown as annuals in other zones. Distinctive appearance, rapid growth, and easy culture are three of nasturtiums' many strong points. Less conspicuous, but odd and pretty, is *T. peregrinum,* the canary bird flower.

T. majus. GARDEN NASTURTIUM. Two main kinds: climbing ones trail over the ground or climb to 6 ft. by coiling leaf stalks; dwarf kinds are compact, up to 15 in. tall. Both have round, shield shaped, bright green leaves on long stalks. Flower colors range through maroon, red brown, orange, yellow, and red to creamy white. Flowers are broad and have a long spur, refreshing fragrance. Young leaves, flowers, and unripe seed pods have peppery flavor like watercress, may be used in salads.

Tropaeolum majus

Easy in most well-drained soils in sun; best in sandy soil. Should have regular summer watering. Sow early spring. Grows and blooms quickly, often reseeds itself. In Zones 12 and 13, plant seeds in fall against sunny wall; plants will bloom from winter until heat of late spring. If hard frosts kill seedlings just plant more seeds. Has become naturalized in some California beach areas. Needs no feeding in average soils.

Climbing or trailing kinds will cover fences, banks, stumps, rocks. Use dwarf kinds for bedding, to cover fading bulb foliage, quick flower color in ground or in pots. Good cut flowers.

In dwarf forms (most sold) you can get seeds of mixed colors in several strains, or a few separate colors including cherry rose, mahogany, gold. Also both single and double-flowered forms.

T. peregrinum. CANARY BIRD FLOWER. Climbs to 10–15 ft. Leaves are deeply 5-lobed. Flowers ¾–1 in. across, canary yellow, frilled and fringed, with green curved spur. Best in light shade, moist soil.

TRUMPET CREEPER. See *Campsis.*

TRUMPET VINE. See *Bignonia, Campsis.*

TSUGA. HEMLOCK. Coniferous evergreen trees and shrubs. Zones 1–7, 14 (part shade only) to 17, except *T. canadensis.* These are mostly gigantic trees with unusually graceful foliage. Branches horizontal to drooping; needlelike leaves flattened and narrowed at the base to form distinct, short stalks. Small, medium brown cones hang down from branches. Best in acid soil, with ample moisture, high summer humidity, protection from hot sun and wind.

T. canadensis. CANADA HEMLOCK. Zones 3–7, 17. Dense, pyramidal tree to 90 ft. tall in its native eastern states, much smaller here. Has tendency to grow 2 or more trunks. Outer branchlets droop gracefully. Dark green needles, white banded beneath, about ½ in. long, are mostly arranged in opposite rows on branchlets. Oval cones about ¾ in. long grow on short stalks. Fine lawn tree or background planting. Can be clipped into outstandingly beautiful hedge, screen. One variety, 'Pendula', SARGENT WEEPING

Tsuga canadensis

HEMLOCK, is low, broad plant 2–3 ft. high and twice as wide, with pendulous branches; it is good plant for large rock gardens. Many other dwarf or pendulous varieties exist.

T. heterophylla. WESTERN HEMLOCK. Native along coast from Alaska to northern California, inland to northern Idaho and Montana. Handsome tree with narrow, pyramidal crown. Grows fairly fast to 125–200 ft. high. Somewhat drooping branchlets and fine-textured, dark green to yellowish green foliage give fernlike quality. Short needles ¼–¾ in. long grow in two rows; whitish bands beneath. A profusion of small 1-in. cones droop gracefully from branch tips. Needs water in dry seasons. Picturesque large conifer for background use, hedges, or screens.

T. mertensiana. MOUNTAIN HEMLOCK. Native to high mountains from Alaska south through the higher Sierra Nevada in California and to northern Idaho and Montana. Grows to 50–90 ft. high in the wilds, but much less and more slowly in home gardens. Foliage blue green with a silvery cast; has ½–1-in.-long needles growing all around stems to give branchlets plump, tufty appearance. Cones 1½–3 in. long. Trees at timberline frequently grow in horizontal or twisted fashion. Slow-growing under lowland conditions. Thrives on cool slope with plenty of organic matter in soil. Least adapted to lowland, hot summer areas. Decorative in large rock garden. Good for containers, bonsai.

TUBEROSE. See *Polianthes tuberosa.*

TUCKEROO. See *Cupaniopsis.*

TULBAGHIA. Perennials. Zones 13–24. Many narrow leaves grow from central point to make broad clumps. Clusters of star shaped flowers rise above clumps on long stems. Full sun, average watering. Evergreen in mild climates. Frost damage at 20°–25°F. with quick recovery.

T. fragrans. Leaves to 12–14 in. long or more, an inch wide, gray green. Flowers are fragrant, lavender pink, 20–30 on 1½–2-ft. stalk. Blooms in winter. Good cut flower.

T. violacea. SOCIETY GARLIC. Leaves bluish green, narrow, to 12 in. long. Flowers rosy lavender, 8–20 in cluster on 1–2-ft. stems. Some bloom most of year, with peak in spring and summer. Leaves, flower stems have onion or garlic odor if cut or crushed. Unsatisfactory cut flower for this reason (but can be used as seasoning). One form has creamy stripe down the center of each leaf. Variety 'Silver Lace' has white-margined leaves.

Tulbaghia violacea

TULIP. See *Tulipa.*

TULIPA. TULIP. Bulbs. All Zones. Best adapted to cold-winter climates. Tulips vary considerably in color, form, height, and general character. Some look stately and formal; others dainty and whimsical; a few are bizarre. Together, the species (the same as those growing in the wilds) and hybrids provide color March-May in the garden, in containers, and for cutting.

Use larger tulips in colonies or masses with low, spring-blooming perennials such as alyssum, arabis, aubrieta, iberis, *Phlox divaricata*; or annuals such as forget-me-not, sweet alyssum, pansies, or violas. Plant smaller, lower-growing species in rock gardens, near paths, in raised beds, or

Darwin hybrid tulip

in patio or terrace insets for close-up viewing. Tulips are superb container plants; see page 75 for container culture. More unusual kinds, such as Double Early, Rembrandt, and Parrot strains, seem more appropriate in containers than in garden.

Need sun most of the day while in bloom; can be planted under deciduous trees that leaf out after tulips fade (good practice in hot-summer areas). Light shade helps prolong bloom of late-blooming kinds. Good light should come from overhead; otherwise, stems will lean toward light source. Rich sandy soil is ideal, although tulips will grow in any good soil with fast drainage. Plant bulbs 2½ times as deep as they are wide, and 4–8 in. apart depending on ultimate size of plant. Plant bulbs in October except where weather is still warm. In Southwest store tulip bulbs at 40°–45°F. for 6–8 weeks before planting in November or December (or even as late as end of January). Plant bulbs at least 6–8 in. deep in warmer areas to provide necessary cool root run. Give plants ample water during growing and flowering period. Need is much less after flowering, particularly if bulbs deeply planted or shaded in summer.

Gophers, field mice, and aphids consider tulips a great delicacy. To protect from rodents, plant bulbs in baskets of ¼-in. wire mesh. To control aphids, spray twice a month in growing season or use systemic insecticide.

Tulips have been classified into many divisions. Following are the most important of these divisions, listed in approximate order of bloom:

Single Early tulips. Large single flowers of red, yellow, or white grow on 10–16-in. stems. Much used for growing or forcing indoors in pots. Also grown outdoors, blooming in March to mid-April, except in warm-winter climates.

Double Early tulips. Double peonylike flowers to 4 in. across bloom on 6–12-in. stems. Same colors, same bloom season as Single Early tulips. In rainy areas mulch around plants or surround with ground cover to keep mud from splashing short-stemmed flowers. In colder climates effective massed in borders for early bloom.

Mendel tulips. Single flowers grow on stems to 20 in. tall. Bloom after Single and Double Early kinds, before Darwin tulips. Shades of white, rose, red, orange, yellow.

Triumph tulips. Single flowers on medium-height (20 in.), very sturdy stems. Bloom earlier than Darwin tulips and (like Mendel tulips) are valuable in providing continuity of bloom.

Darwin tulips. Most popular of late April-May-flowering tulips. Graceful, stately plants with large oval or egg shaped flowers, square at base, usually with stems to 30 in. tall. Clear, beautiful colors of white, cream, yellow, pink, red, mauve, lilac, purple, maroon, and near black.

Darwin Hybrids. Spectacular group bred from Darwin tulips and huge, brilliant species *T. fosterana.* Bloom before Darwins; have enormous, brightly colored flowers on 24–28-in. stems. Most are in scarlet orange to red range; some have contrasting eyes or penciling; some measure 7 in. across. Most popular tulips in southern California.

Breeder tulips. Large oval to globular flowers on stems to 35 in. tall. May blooming. Unusual colors include orange, bronze, purplish, mahogany—often overlaid with flush of contrasting shade. Called Breeders because Dutch growers once grew them primarily to breed the much admired "broken" (variegated) tulips.

Lily-flowered tulips. Once included in Cottage division; now separate group. Flowers are long and narrow, with long pointed segments. Graceful, slender stemmed, fine in garden (where they blend well with other flowers) or for cutting. Stems 20–26 in. tall. May blooming. Full range of tulip colors.

Cottage tulips (often called May-flowering tulips). About same size and height as Darwins. Flower form variable, long oval to egg shaped to vase shaped, often with pointed segments. May blooming.

Rembrandt tulips. "Broken" (variegated) Darwin tulips. Scarlet striped white, white flamed lilac purple, white edged red are characteristic patterns. Color variegation due to transmittable virus disease; don't plant near valued solid-color tulips.

Bizarre tulips. "Broken" Breeder or Cottage tulips. Flowers have yellow background marked bronze, brown, maroon, or purple. See planting caution under Rembrandt tulips.

Bybloems (Bijbloemens). "Broken" Breeder or Cottage tulips with white background marked rose, lilac, or purple. See planting caution under Rembrandt tulips.

Parrot tulips. May-flowering tulips with large, long, deeply fringed and ruffled blooms striped and feathered in various colors. Many have descriptive names like 'Blue Parrot', 'Red Par-

rot'. Good in containers, unusual cut flowers. See planting caution under Rembrandt tulips.

Double Late tulips (often called Peony Flowered). Large, heavy blooms like peonies. They range from 18–22 in. tall; flowers may be damaged by rain or wind in exposed locations.

Seven divisions include varieties and hybrids of *T. batalinii, T. eichleri, T. fosterana, T. greigii, T. kaufmanniana,* and *T. marjolettii,* and another division that includes all other species. Most important:

Hybrids and varieties of *T. fosterana,* including huge, fiery red variety 'Red Emperor' ('Mme. Lefeber'), 16 in. tall.

Varieties and hybrids of *T. kaufmanniana,* 5–10 in. tall, very early blooming, in white, pink, orange, and red, often with markings, some with leaves patterned brown.

Three fairly new novelty groups include:Fringed tulips, variations from Single Early, Double Early, and Darwin tulips, finely fringed on edges of segments; Viridiflora tulips, 10–20 in. tall, flowers edged or blended green with other colors—white, yellow, rose, red, or buff; and Multiflowered, 3–6 flowers on each 20–27-in. stem, flowers white, yellow, pink and red, May bloom.

Most species tulips—wild tulips—are low growing and early blooming with shorter, narrower foliage than garden hybrids, but there are exceptions. Generally best in rock gardens or wild gardens where plantings can remain undisturbed for many years. Those noted as being "easy" are also good container subjects.

Following are outstanding species:

T. acuminata. Flowers have long, twisted spidery segments of red and yellow on 18-in. stems. May. Easy.

T. batalinii. Single, soft yellow flowers on 6–10-in. stems. Very narrow leaves. April.

T. biflora. Small flowers, off-white inside, greenish gray purple outside, yellow at base; several blooms on each 8-in. stem. March.

T. clusiana. LADY or CANDY TULIP. Slender, medium-sized flowers on 9-in. stems. Rosy red on outside, white inside. Easy, grows well in mild-winter areas. Give sheltered position in colder areas. April-May.

T. c. chrysantha (*T. stellata chrysantha*). To 6 in. tall, blooms April. Outer segments rose carmine shading to buff at base; inner segments bright yellow.

T. eichleri. Big scarlet flowers with black bases margined buff on 12-in. stems. Blooms late March.

T. greigii. Scarlet flowers 6 in. across, on 10-in. stems. Foliage mottled or striped with brown. Early flowering.

T. kaufmanniana. WATERLILY TULIP. Medium-large creamy yellow flowers marked red on outside and yellow at center. Stems 6 in. tall. Very early bloom. Easy, permanent in gardens. Many choice named varieties.

T. linifolia. Scarlet, black-based, yellow-centered flowers on 6-in. stems in late April. Handsome with *T. batalinii.*

Tulipa kaufmanniana

T. praestans. Cup shaped, orange scarlet flowers, 2–4 to 10–12-in. stem, in early April. Variety 'Fusilier' is shorter, has 4–6 flowers to a stem.

T. saxatilis. Fragrant, yellow-based pale lilac flowers open nearly flat, 1–3 to each 1-ft. stem. Early bloom. Dependable in warm-winter areas.

T. stellata chrysantha. See *T. clusiana chrysantha.*

T. sylvestris. Yellow 2-in. flowers, 1 or 2 on 1-ft. stem. Late flowering. Good in warm-winter areas.

T. tarda (*T. dasystemon*). Each 3-in. stem has 3–6 upward facing, star shaped flowers with golden yellow centers, white-tipped segments.

T. turkestanica. Vigorous tulip with up to 8 flowers on each slender 1-ft. stem. Flowers slender in bud, star shaped when open, gray green on the outside, off-white with yellow base inside. Early March bloom. Easy.

TULIP TREE. See *Liriodendron tulipifera, Magnolia soulangiana.*

TUPELO. See *Nyssa sylvatica.*

TUPIDANTHUS calyptratus. Evergreen shrub or small tree. Zones 19–24. Grows to 20 ft. Single or multiple trunk. Leaves to 20 in. wide, divided fanwise into 7–9 leathery, glossy, bright green, stalked leaflets about 7 in. long by 2½ in. wide. Resembles the better known schefflera, but branches from base and makes broader, denser shrub.

*Tupidanthus
calyptratus*

Needs rich, well-drained soil, plenty of food, moderate water, and sheltered location. Best in partial shade but will take full sun in cooler coastal gardens. Can be pruned into almost any form. Is good small tree for sheltered lanai, entryway, or patio. Grows well near pools. Splendid plant for large tubs and containers. As container plant indoors give same care as *Schefflera actinophylla.* Effective when grown against fence or wall as triple-trunked small tree.

TURNIP AND RUTABAGA. Biennial vegetables grown as cool-season annuals for their colorful, flavorful roots. Foliage of turnips is also a useful green vegetable. Different varieties give a nice choice of colors and shapes. Colors: white, white topped with purple, creamy yellow. Shapes: globe, flattened globe. Rutabaga is tasty kind of turnip with large yellowish roots. It's a late-maturing crop that stores well in the ground; turnips are quick growing and should be harvested and used as soon as they are big enough. Plant in full sun. Roots are milder flavored if soil is kept moist, become more pungent under drier conditions.

Turnip

In cold-winter areas, plant turnips or rutabagas in April for early summer harvest, or in July or August for fall harvest. In mild-winter areas, grow as winter crop by planting September through March.

TURRAEA obtusifolia. STAR BUSH. Evergreen shrub. Outdoors in Zones 22–24; protect from frosts in Zones 15, 16, 19–21. Native to South Africa. Slow growth to 4–5 ft. tall, 4 ft. wide, with many drooping branchlets, some lower branches nearly prostrate. Leaves 2 in. long, dark green, glossy, polished. Many pure white flowers in loose clusters, star shaped, with narrow petals, 1½ in. across. Long bloom season reaches peak in September, October. Temperamental: needs good drainage and either light shade of high-branched trees or eastern exposure without strong reflected heat. Hardy to 26°F. Water deeply.

Turraea obtusifolia

TWINBERRY. See *Lonicera involucrata.*

TWINFLOWER. See *Linnaea borealis.*

TWINSPUR. See *Diascia barberae.*

UGNI molinae (*Myrtus ugni*). CHILEAN GUAVA. Evergreen shrub. Zones 14–24. Slow to moderate growth to 3–6 ft. tall. Scraggly and open in youth, it matures into compact, rounded plant. Foliage is dark green with bronze tints; leaves are oval, leathery, ½ in. long, whitish beneath, with edges slightly rolled under. White, rose-

Ugni molinae

tinted flowers in late spring, early summer; they are principally little brushes of stamens. Purplish or reddish ½-in. fruit follow. These have fragrance of baking apples, and pleasant flavor. Can be used fresh or in jams and jellies.

Takes sun near coast, part shade in hot areas; neutral to acid soil; ample water. Tidy, restrained plant for patios, terraces, near walks and paths where passers-by can pick and sample fruit, enjoy its fragrance.

ULMUS. ELM. Deciduous or partially evergreen trees. Easy to grow in any fairly good soil; will survive in most poor ones. Best with normal watering, but will tolerate low moisture conditions at expense of good growth, plant health. Root systems are aggressive, close to surface, and you'll have trouble growing other plants under them. Branch crotches often narrow, easily split. Many of the larger ones are tasty to leaf beetles, bark beetles, leafhoppers, aphids, and scale, making them either time-consuming or messy or both. Dutch elm disease, formerly a problem in the East and Midwest, has reached western states. For description, measures to take, see page 64.

Ulmus americana

U. americana. AMERICAN ELM. Zones 1–11, 14–21. Fast-growing tree which can reach 100 ft. or more with nearly equal—sometimes even greater—spread. Form is stately, with stout trunk dividing into many upright main branches at same height; outer branches are pendulous, silhouette vase shaped. Rough-surfaced, toothed leaves are 3–6 in. long. Leafs out very late where winters are mild. Fall color yellow. Pale green papery seeds in spring blow about, are messy.

Grows best in deep soil, with 70–75-ft. circle to spread in. Roots send up suckers, can make thickets; will lift pavement if crowded. Leaf and bark beetles weaken and disfigure trees; scale causes drip and sooty mildew. The only really recommendable use for such a tree has been for very large gardens, out-of-the-way places, on broad boulevards unencumbered by utility lines, or in parks. Now its attack by Dutch elm disease in the West rules out recommendation for planting under any circumstances.

U. carpinifolia. SMOOTH-LEAFED ELM. Zones 1–11, 14–21. To 100 ft. Wide-spreading branches, weeping branchlets. Leaves 2–3½ in. long, shiny deep green above. Culture, uses, precautions same as for American elm.

U. glabra. SCOTCH ELM. Zones 1–11, 14–21. To 120 ft. tall. Nonsuckering. Leaves 3–6 in. long, oval, sharply toothed, rough surfaced, on very short stalks. Old trees sometimes seen, but scarcely grown nowadays. Variety 'Camperdownii', CAMPERDOWN ELM, has weeping branches that reach to ground, making tent of shade. Generally 10–20 ft. tall.

U. hollandica. DUTCH ELM. Zones 1–11, 14–21. To 100 ft. or more. Suckers freely. Name covers a number of hybrids between Scotch and smooth-leafed elm.

U. parvifolia (often sold as *U.p.* 'Sempervirens'). CHINESE ELM, CHINESE EVERGREEN ELM. Zones 8, 9, 12–24. Evergreen or deciduous according to winter temperatures and tree's individual heredity. So-called evergreen elm usually sold as 'Sempervirens'; this may be evergreen most winters, lose its leaves in unusual cold snap (new leaves come on fast). Very fast growth to 40–60 ft., with 50–70-ft. spread. Often reaches 30 ft. in 5 years. Extremely variable in form, but generally spreading, with long, arching, eventually weeping branchlets. Trunks of older trees have bark which sheds in patches somewhat like sycamore. Leaves leathery, ¾–2½ in. long, ⅓–1⅓ in. wide, oval, evenly toothed. Round fruit form in fall while leaves are still on tree.

Stake young trees until trunks can carry weight of branches. Stake and head leading shoot higher than other shade trees to compensate for weeping. Rub or cut out small branches along trunk for first few years. Shorten overlong branches or strongly weeping branches to strengthen tree scaffolding. Older trees may need thinning to lessen chance of storm damage. Very little bothered by pests or diseases except Texas root rot in desert.

Good for patio shade in milder portions of West. Useful for sun screening. With careful pruning, useful as a street tree.

Varieties are 'Brea', with larger leaves, more upright habit; and 'Drake', with small leaves, weeping habit. Both are more or less evergreen. 'True Green' has small deep green leaves, is round headed, more evergreen than others.

Word of caution: Siberian elm is sometimes sold as Chinese elm. Siberian elm flowers in spring, has stiffer habit and thinner, less glossy leaves.

U. procera. ENGLISH ELM. Zones 1–11, 14–21. To 120 ft. Suckers profusely. Tall trunk with broad or tall dense crown of branches. Foliage holds dark green color later in fall than American elm. Same precautions apply to this tree as to American elm.

U. pumila. SIBERIAN ELM. All Zones. Most useful in Zones 1–3, 10, 11. To 50 ft. Leaves ¾–2 in. long, ⅓–1 in. wide, dark green, smooth. Extremely hardy and tough, enduring cold, heat, drought, and poor soil. Under worst conditions grows slowly, may even be shrub. As fast-growing tree, is suitable for windbreaks or shelterbelts. Has brittle wood, weak crotches, and is not desirable as single garden tree. Root system troublesome in gardens, but possibly useful in holding soil in problem areas against wind or water erosion. Papery, winged seeds disperse seedlings over wide area.

UMBELLULARIA californica. CALIFORNIA LAUREL, CALIFORNIA BAY, OREGON MYRTLE, PEPPERWOOD. Evergreen tree. Zones 4–10, 12–24. Native to southwestern Oregon, California Coast Ranges, lower elevations of Sierra Nevada. In the wilds it varies from huge gumdrop shaped shrub (on windy hillsides near coast) to tall and free-ranging tree 75 ft. high and over 100 ft. wide (in forests). Leaves are 3–5 in. long, 1 in. wide, pointed at tip, medium to deep yellow green and glossy on top, dull light green beneath.

Umbellularia californica

As sure identification, crush a leaf—if it's this plant it will be powerfully aromatic. A little of the crushed fragrance is pleasant, but too much can cause a headache.

Leaves are sometimes used as more potent substitute for true bay leaves (*Laurus nobilis*) in soups and stews. Tiny yellowish flowers in clusters give plant yellowish cast in spring. They are followed by olivelike, green, inedible fruit that turn purple.

In gardens, plants tend to grow slowly (about 1 ft. a year) to 20–25 ft. high and as wide. Grows best and fastest in deep soil with ample water, but tolerates many other conditions, including drought. Will grow in deep shade and ultimately get big enough to become shade maker itself—casts very dense shade unless thinned. Always neat. Good for screening, background plantings, or tall hedges. Often multitrunked. Good patio or street tree when thinned to one or a few trunks.

UMBRELLA PINE. See *Sciadopitys verticillata*.

UMBRELLA PLANT. See *Cyperus alternifolius*.

UMBRELLA TREE. See *Magnolia tripetala, Schefflera actinophylla*.

URBINIA agavoides. See *Echeveria agavoides*.

VACCINIUM. Evergreen and deciduous shrubs. Excellent ornamental shrubs with clusters of bell shaped flowers and colorful, edible fruit, which attract birds. All require acid soil and ample leaf mold, peat moss, or ground bark. Good woodland garden subjects.

Vaccinium ovatum

V. corymbosum. See Blueberry.

V. ovatum. EVERGREEN HUCKLEBERRY. Zones 4–7, 14–17. Evergreen shrub. Native Santa Barbara County north to British Columbia. Erect shrub 2–3 ft. in sun, to 8–10 ft. in shade. Young plants spreading, older plants taller than wide, compact. Leathery, lustrous dark green leaves, ½–1¼ in. long; new growth bronzy. Flowers (March-May) are white or pinkish. Berries black with whitish bloom, good in pies, jams, jellies, syrups.

Best in partial shade; will take full sun in cool-summer areas. Can be trimmed into hedge or grown in container. Cut branches popular for arrangements.

V. parvifolium. RED HUCKLEBERRY. Zones 2–7, 14–17. Deciduous shrub. Native Sierra Nevada and northern California Coast Ranges to Alaska. Slow growth to 4–12, rarely 18 ft. Branches are green, thin, on spreading or cascading plant with intricate, filmy winter silhouette. Leaves thin, oval, ½–¾ in. long, light green. Flowers greenish or whitish, April-May, fine for arrangements. Berries clear, bright red, showy, and delicious in jams, jellies, and pies. Needs highly acid humus soil, moisture, partial shade.

V. vitis-idaea. COWBERRY, FOXBERRY. Zones 2–7, 14–17. Evergreen shrub. Slow growth to 1 ft. tall, spreading by underground runners to 3 ft. Leaves glossy, dark green, ⅓–1 in. long; new growth often brightly tinged red, orange. Flowers, clustered, white or pinkish, bloom in May. Edible sour, red berries are something like tiny cranberries, are esteemed for preserves, syrups. Handsome little plants for small-scale ground cover, informal edging around larger acid-soil plantings. Good in wet areas. With ample water, will take full sun in cool-summer areas. *V. v. minus,* MOUNTAIN CRANBERRY, LINGONBERRY, is smaller, with leaves ⅛–½ in. long. Attractive container plant.

VALERIANA officinalis. VALERIAN, GARDEN HELIOTROPE. Perennial herb. All Zones.

Valeriana officinalis

True heliotrope is *Heliotropum. Centranthus ruber* is called red valerian. Both of these plants are more common than *Valeriana officinalis*. Tall straight stems grow to about 4 ft. high. Bulk of leaves remain fairly close to ground. They are light green, in pairs that are further divided into 8–10 pairs of narrow leaflets. Tiny fragrant flowers are white, pink, red, or lavender blue, in rounded clusters at ends of stems. Plant spreads and can become invasive. Roots are strong smelling.

Plant in sun or part shade. Start new plants from seeds or divisions. Grow in mixed herb or flower borders but don't allow it to crowd other plants. Use cut flowers in arrangements.

V. rubra. See *Centranthus*.

VALLOTA speciosa. SCARBOROUGH LILY. Bulb. Zones 16, 17, 23, 24 outdoors; anywhere in containers. Native to South Africa. Strap shaped evergreen leaves are 1–2 ft. long. Clusters of bright orange vermilion, funnel shaped, 2½–3-in.-wide flowers grow on 2-ft. stalks. Blooms summer and early fall. White-flowered form rarely available. Survives out of doors where frosts are very light and infrequent; succeeds even in competition with tree roots. Excellent container plant. Plant June-July or just after flowering. Set bulbs with tips just below surface. Use smallest pots possible; repot or divide only when absolutely necessary; blooms best when roots are crowded. Prefers light shade, tolerates full sun along coast. Fertilize monthly during active growth. Water regularly except during semidormant period in winter and spring, but never let plant dry out completely.

Vallota speciosa

VANCOUVERIA. Deciduous and evergreen perennials. These close relatives of *Epimedium* have the same uses in garden. Leaves are divided into numerous leaflets. Flowers in late spring, early summer. In cool-summer areas will grow with little summer water; elsewhere prefers regular watering. Attractive

ground cover for tree-shaded beds. Cut foliage is attractive in bouquets.

V. chrysantha. Evergreen. Zones 5, 6, 14–17. Native to Siskiyou Mountains. To 8–16 in. tall. Bronzed, gray green leaves, 1½ in. long and wide. Small yellow flowers 4–15 to the stalk, each flower ½ in. wide.

V. hexandra. Deciduous. Zones 4–6, 14–17. Native to coastal forests from northern California to Washington. To 4–16 in. tall. Leaflets 1–2½ in. long, light green; fresh appearance all summer. Flower stalks usually 3-flowered, white flowers to ½ in. across, drooping, petals and sepals sharply bent backward.

Vancouveria planipetala

V. planipetala (V. parviflora). INSIDE-OUT FLOWER. Evergreen, sometimes deciduous in cold-winter areas. Zones 4–6, 14–17. To 2 ft. in height. Light to medium green leaflets, shallowly lobed, 1½ in. long and wide. Flowers are white, even smaller than on V. hexandra, but with 25–50 flowers in cluster.

VANDA. Epiphytic orchids. Greenhouse or indoors. Beautiful orchids, but difficult to flower in coastal fog belts where light is limited. Plants grow erect, with leaves arranged opposite each other up the stem. Flowers grow on stalk formed in leaf joints.

Plant in osmunda fiber, tree fern fiber, or ground bark. Support stem against stake of tree fern stem about ⅔ height of plant to provide anchor for aerial roots. Vandas fall into two general groups according to leaf type. Those with pencil-like leaves (terete)

Vanda coerulea

require much light, high humidity, night temperatures above 50°F. Only tropical greenhouse conditions are suitable. Kinds with strap shaped leaves require less light, lower temperatures, will grow and flower under more usual cool greenhouse atmosphere. Water very lightly during winter. They need plenty of light all year, but especially from November to February in order to set flower buds. Many species, hybrids may be grown.

V. coerulea. India. Large 3–4-in. flowers vary in color from pale to dark blue on 1–2-ft.-long stems in late summer, early fall. Plants grow 1–2 ft. high with rigid, dark green, 6–10-in.-long strap shaped leaves.

V. teres. Burma. The flower so frequently used in making leis; often flown in from Hawaii. Sepals white tinged rose, petals deep rose, side lobes of lip yellow, lower lobe rose lined and spotted with yellow. Flowers, 3–4 in. across, grow 2–5 on stalk from May to September. Cylindrical, slightly tapered leaves (terete) clothe slender 2–7-ft. climbing stems. Needs winter rest, much light.

VANILLA TRUMPET VINE. See Distictis laxiflora.

VARIEGATED GINGER. See Alpinia sanderae.

VARIEGATED SPINY GREEK JUNIPER. See Juniperus excelsa 'Variegata'.

VAUQUELINIA californica. ARIZONA ROSEWOOD. Evergreen shrub or small tree. Zones 9–13. Upright, sometimes rather contorted growth to as much as 20 feet, with dark gray to reddish brown bark. Leaves lance shaped, edges lightly toothed, to 3 in. long and ½ in. wide, leathery bright green with lightly woolly undersides. White flowers grow in loose, flattened clusters at branch tips, each flower ¼ in. across with 5 petals; late spring. Woody seed capsules, about ¼ in. long, develop in summer, persist through fall, winter.

Vauquelinia californica

Rather open-growing shrub or small tree for desert landscapes, dry margins of cultivated desert gardens.

VELTHEIMIA viridifolia. Bulb. Zones 23, 24 outdoors; Zones 13, 16–22 outdoors with winter shelter; anywhere in containers as house plant or summer patio plant. Native to South Africa. Some name confusion in the nursery trade. It is probable that all sold are V. viridifolia or a variety of it. Unique and beautiful plant with clump of broad, shining deep green, wavy-margined leaves 1 ft. long, 3 in. wide. Beautiful even without bloom. Heavy clusters of pale rose, green-tipped, tubular, drooping flowers on 12-in., stout, brown-marked stem, resemble red-hot poker (Kniphofia). Blooms in winter or early spring. Set bulbs with upper ⅓ above surface. Grow cool and keep barely moist until roots start to form. Increase watering,

Veltheimia viridifolia

light, and warmth as growth begins. Fertilize every 2 weeks through growing season. Dry off as foliage ripens in summer; resume watering in September when new growth begins. Outdoors, protect from hot sun and wind.

VELVET GROUNDSEL. See Senecio petasitis.

VELVET PLANT. See Gynura aurantiaca.

VERBASCUM. MULLEIN. Biennials, perennials. All Zones. Stately, sun loving, summer blooming plants. Broad leaves closely set on stem. Shallow-dished flowers in straight spikes. A large group, some of them weedy. They self-sow freely. Start biennial sorts from seed in spring; sow in place or in containers (but transplant to ground when 2 in. high). Drought tolerant when established, but best flower show with some water, fertilizer.

V. blattaria. MOTH MULLEIN. Biennial. Low clumps of smooth, dark green, cut or toothed leaves. Flower spikes 1½–2½ ft. high with pale yellow or white blooms, purple stamens. Flowers open with morning light.

Verbascum bombyciferum

V. bombyciferum 'Arctic Summer'. Biennial. Foot-high rosettes of furry gray green oval leaves. Stems, to 6 ft. or more, are powdery white with 1½-in. yellow flowers.

V. olympicum. Stems to 5 ft. high. Large leaves, 2 ft. or more long, white, with soft, downy hairs. Bright yellow 1-in. flowers clustered in many long spikes.

V. phoeniceum. PURPLE MULLEIN. Stems 2–4 ft. high. Leaves smooth, only hairy on underside. Purple flowers in slender spikes half the height of plant or more.

VERBENA. Perennials, some grown as annuals. They need sun and heat in order to thrive, and are drought resistant. Set 2 ft. apart for ground cover; growth is fast. Species listed below adjust effectively to planting in parking strips, along sides of driveways, and on dry banks, walls, and rock crevices where they display their colors all summer. All like good air circulation, dislike wet foliage.

V. gooddingii. Short-lived perennial native to Southwest. To 1½ ft. high, spreading. Oval leaves deeply cut. Flowers in heads top short spikes, are usually pinkish lavender. Sow in early spring for summer bloom. Can reseed itself where moisture is adequate. Good performer in desert heat.

Verbena peruviana

V. hybrida (V. hortensis). GARDEN VERBENA. Short-lived perennial in Zones 8–24; usually grown as annual. Many-branched plants 6–12 in. high and spreading 1½–3 ft. Oblong, 2–4-in.-long leaves are bright green or gray green, with toothed margins. Flowers in flat compact clusters, 2–3 in. wide. Colors include white, pink, bright red, purple, blue, and combinations. Variety 'Amethyst' is good sky blue; 'Blaze' has bright red flowers with practically no white in centers; 'Sparkle' is red with prominent "eye" in flower center; 'Miss Susie' is good double salmon pink. Subject to mildew—there will be less chance of it if you water deeply and not too often. If used as perennial, prune severely in winter or early spring. Good ground cover in Zones 12, 13 if Bermuda grass can be kept out of it.

V. peruviana (*V. chamaedryfolia*). Perennial, often grown as annual. Zones 8–12. Spreads rapidly, forms very flat mat. (Planted 2 ft. apart, can make solid cover in a season.) Leaves are neat, small, closely set. Flat-topped flower clusters on slender stems lavishly cover foliage. In original form, corolla tube is white, spreading lobes rich scarlet. Hybrids spread somewhat more slowly, have slightly larger leaves and stouter stems, and are available in several colors: 'Starfire', red; 'Appleblossom', 'Cherry Pink', 'Princess Gloria', 'Little Pinkie', 'Raspberry Rose' in pink and rose tones; many purplish varieties; and a very fine pure white. Especially popular in southern California and in desert areas.

V. rigida (*V. venosa*). Perennial. All Zones. Spreading plants, 10–20 in. tall. Leaves rough, dark green, 2–4 in. long, strongly toothed. Lilac to purple blue flowers in cylindrical clusters on tall, stiff stems summer and fall. Takes considerable drought; useful in low-maintenance gardens. Can be grown as annual; blooms in 4 months from seed.

V. tenera maonettii. Creeping perennial. Zones 8–24. Leaves cut to midrib and lobes cut again. Flat clusters of pink flowers with distinct white margins.

VERONICA. SPEEDWELL. Perennials (for shrubby plants sold as *Veronica*, see *Hebe*). All Zones. Handsome plants ranging from 4 in.–2½ ft. in height. Small flowers (¼–½ in. across) are massed to display effectively the white, rose, pink, pale or deep blue color. Use in sunny borders and rock gardens. Most need regular watering; prostrate, mat-forming kinds will tolerate less frequent attention.

V. grandis holophylla. Many stems to 24 in. high are densely clothed with dark green, very glossy leaves. Long stalks of rich deep blue flowers show above foliage.

Veronica hybrid

V. hybrids. These include a number of midsummer-blooming, upright bushy perennials ranging from 10–18 in. high. Choice varieties: 'Barcarole', to 10 in. tall, rose pink flowers; 'Crater Lake Blue', prostrate with flower stems to 10 in. tall, bright blue flower spikes; 'Icicle', 15–18 in. tall, white flower spikes.

V. incana. Leaves to 3 in. long, grayish, on gray to white, woolly stems. Bright blue flowers in dense, narrow, 6-in. spikes on stems 1–2 ft. high. Striking contrast between foliage, stem, and flower colors.

V. longifolia subsessilis. Clumps of upright stems to 2 ft. tall topped by close-flowered spikes of deep blue flowers about ½ in. across in midsummer. Stems are leafy and rather closely set with narrow, pointed leaves.

V. pectinata. Forms prostrate mats that spread by creeping stems which root at joints. Roundish, ½-in.-long leaves with scallop-toothed or deeply cut edges. Flowers are profuse, deep blue with white center, in 5–6-in. spikes among the leaves. Good as a rock plant or in wall crevices.

V. prostrata (*V. rupestris*). Has tufted, hairy stems, some of which are prostrate. Leaves ½–¾ in. long. Flower stems to 8 in. high are topped by short cluster of pale blue flowers. 'Heavenly Blue' is almost entirely prostrate, with flower stems reaching up to 6 in. high. Bright blue flowers.

V. repens. Shining green, ½-in.-long leaves clothe prostrate stems, give mosslike effect. Flowers ¼ in. wide, lavender to white in few-flowered clusters in spring. Takes sun or some shade; fast growing with regular watering. Good cover

Veronica prostrata

for small bulbs, small-scale ground cover, or paving plant.

V. saturejoides. Many tufted stems spread by creeping roots. Roundish, ½-in.-long leaves closely overlap on stems. Dark blue flowers in short, compact spikes appear in May. Fine rock plant.

V. spicata. Much like *V. longifolia subsessilis* but less robust and with shorter flower spikes. Miniature variety, 'Nana', grows 6 in. high, with violet blue flowers June-July.

VIBURNUM. Deciduous or evergreen shrubs, rarely small trees. Large and diverse group of plants with clustered, often fragrant flowers and clusters of 1-seeded, often brilliantly colored fruit much liked by birds. Some are valuable for winter flowers. They tend to fall into groups determined by landscape use.

Evergreen viburnums used principally as foliage plants are *V. cinnamomifolium, V. davidii, V. japonicum, V. propinquum,* and *V. rhytidophyllum.*

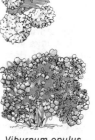

Viburnum opulus 'Roseum'

Evergreen viburnums used as foliage and flowering plants are *V. odoratissimum, V. suspensum, V. rigidum,* and *V. tinus.*

Partially deciduous viburnums grown for flowers are *V. burkwoodii* and *V. macrocephalum.* They are nearly evergreen in mild climates and have showy flowers.

Deciduous viburnums grown for fragrant flowers are *V. bitchiuense, V. bodnantense, V. carlcephalum, V. carlesii, V.* 'Carlotta', *V. burkwoodii* 'Chenault', *V. farreri,* and *V. juddii.*

Deciduous viburnums for showy flowers, fall leaf color include *V. dentatum, V. lentago, V. opulus* (also has showy fruit), *V. o.* 'Roseum', *V. plicatum, V. p. tomentosum, V. prunifolium,* and *V. trilobum.*

Deciduous viburnums valued for fruit color are *V. dilatatum, V. ichangense,* and *V. wrightii.*

Viburnums, with few exceptions noted in descriptions, tolerate alkaline and acid soils. They do well in heavy, rich soils with ample moisture, though many are somewhat tolerant of drought. Useful near swimming pools. Many have unusually wide range in climate adaptability; note *V. burkwoodii* and *V. tinus* 'Robustum' for examples. They grow in sun or shade. Most evergreen kinds look better with some protection from sun where summers are hot and long. Prune to shape to prevent legginess; some evergreen kinds can be sheared. Aphids, thrips, spider mites, and scale are likely to be problems. Use an all-purpose insecticide-miticide spray in early spring at 2-week intervals. Keep sulfur sprays off viburnum foliage.

V. bitchiuense. Deciduous shrub. Zones 4–9, 14–24. To 10 ft. Leaves oval, 1½–3½ in. long, downy. Flowers (May) pink aging white, very fragrant. Fruit black, not showy. Somewhat more open habit than *V. carlesii.*

V. bodnantense. Deciduous shrub. Zones 4–9, 14–24. To 10 ft. or more. Oval leaves 1½–4 in. long are deeply veined, turn dark scarlet in fall. Flowers deep pink fading paler, very fragrant, in loose clusters October-April. Fruit are red, not showy. This plant is a hybrid; there are several varieties. Best known is 'Dawn' ('Pink Dawn'). Flower buds freeze in coldest Northwest winters.

V. burkwoodii. Deciduous shrub in coldest areas, nearly evergreen elsewhere. Zones 1–10, 14–24. To 6–12 ft. tall, 4–5 ft. wide. Leaves dark green, glossy above, white hairy beneath, to 3½ in. long. Purplish in cold weather. Flowers, in dense 4-in. clusters, pink in bud, open white, very fragrant, February-March. Fruit blue black, not showy. Early growth is straggly, mature plants dense. Can be trained as espalier.

V. b. 'Chenault' (*V. chenaultii*). Deciduous shrub. Zones 1–9, 14–24. To 4–6 ft. tall, 3–4 ft. wide. Leaves and flowers are much like those of *V. burkwoodii,* though plant is more compact, more deciduous than the latter.

V. carlcephalum. FRAGRANT SNOWBALL. Deciduous shrub. Zones 1–11, 14–24. To 8–10 ft. tall, 4–5 ft. wide. Leaves dull grayish green, downy beneath, 2–3½ in. long. Flowers long-lasting, waxy white, fragrant; bloom in dense 4–5-in. clusters in spring, early summer. No fruit. Showy as common snowball, but has added fragrance.

(Continued on next page)

V. carlesii. KOREAN SPICE VIBURNUM. Deciduous shrub. Zones 1–11, 14–24. To 4–8 ft. tall, 4–5 ft. broad. Leaves are like those of *V. carlcephalum.* Flowers pink in bud, opening white, in 2–3-in.-wide clusters, sweetly fragrant, March-May. Fruit blue black, in summer. Loose, open habit. Best in part shade summer, sun in spring, winter.

V. 'Carlotta'. Deciduous shrub. Zones 3–9, 14–24. Like a bigger-flowered *V. carlesii,* with different fragrance. Dense clusters of waxy flowers.

V. chenaultii. See *V. burkwoodii* 'Chenault'.

V. cinnamomifolium. Evergreen shrub. Zones 5–9, 14–24. To 10–20 ft. tall, equally wide. Leaves 3–6 in. long, 1–3 in. wide, leathery, glossy dark green, strongly 3-veined. Flowers pink in bud opening white, individually tiny, in flattish clusters 6 in. across, April. Faintly honey scented. Fruit is shiny blue black, small. Looks like a much-magnified *V. davidii.* Use in screens, background. Best in acid soil with plenty of water.

V. davidii. Evergreen shrub. Zones 4–9, 14–24. To 1–3 ft. tall, 3–4 ft. wide. Leaves are glossy dark green, deeply veined, to 6 in. long. Flower clusters to 3 in. wide, white, bloom from dull pinkish red buds, not showy. Fruit metallic turquoise blue. For abundant berry production set out more than one plant.

Use as foundation shrub, in foreground plantings, with ferns, azaleas, other acid soil plants in part shade. Extremely valuable in Zones 4–6, 17.

V. dentatum. ARROWWOOD. Deciduous shrub. Zones 1–9, 14–21. To 15 ft. with many stems from base tending to form clumps or thickets. Oval, coarsely toothed leaves to 3 in. long, turn glossy red in autumn. Flowers white, in flattish 4-in. clusters, spring; blue black fruit in late spring to summer, is relished by birds. Use in woodland plantings, as background or screen shrub. Grows well in sun or shade, moist or dry soil.

V. dilatatum. LINDEN VIBURNUM. Deciduous shrub. Zones 3–9, 14–16. To 10 ft. tall, broad, compact. Leaves nearly round, 2–5 in. long, gray green. Flowers are tiny, creamy white, in 5-in.-wide clusters in early summer. Showy bright red fruits are produced best where summers are warm; they ripen in September, hang on into winter.

V. farreri (*V. fragrans*). Deciduous shrub. Zones 4–9, 14–24. To 10–15 ft. tall, and as wide. Leaves are oval, heavily veined, smooth green, 1½–3 in. long. Turn soft russet red in fall. Flowers white to pink, in 2-in. clusters, fragrant. Bloom November-March. Blossoms will stand to 20°–22°F., freeze in colder temperatures. Fruit bright red. Prune to prevent leggy growth. *V. f.* 'Album' (*V. f.* 'Candidissimum') has pure white flowers. *V. f.* 'Nanum' is lower growing (to 2 ft.), with pink flowers.

V. ichangense. Deciduous shrub. Zones 4–9, 12–20. To 6 ft. tall, with oval, long (1½–2½ in.), pointed leaves. Profuse clusters of white fragrant flowers in late spring. Heavy crop of bright red fruit in fall, early winter. Leggy open shrub best grown in borders for fruit display.

V. japonicum. Evergreen shrub or small tree. Zones 5–10, 12, 14–24. To 10–20 ft. tall. Leaves are leathery, glossy dark green, to 6 in. long. Sparse bloom; flowers in spring bloom in 4-in. white, fragrant clusters. Red fruit is sparse but very attractive. Big bulky shrub or small tree for background plantings. Best with some shade in warmer areas. Control aphids.

V. juddii. Deciduous shrub. Zones 3–9, 14–24. To 4–8 ft. tall. Hybrid between *V. carlesii, V. bitchiuense.* More spreading and bushy than *V. carlesii,* otherwise similar to it.

V. lantana. WAYFARING TREE. Deciduous shrub or small tree. Zones 1–12, 14–20. To 8–15 ft. tall. Leaves are broadly oval, to 5 in. long, downy on both sides; turn red in fall. Flowers tiny, white, in 2–4-in. clusters, May or June. Fruit bright scarlet turning black, showy. Variety 'Mohican' is smaller, to 6 ft. high and 8 ft. wide. Fruit remain orange red. Use in woodland or background plantings. Will take dryish conditions.

V. lentago. NANNYBERRY. Deciduous shrub or small tree. Zones 1–9, 14–21. Will grow as single-trunked tree up to 30 ft. or as massive shrub to lesser height. Creamy white flowers in flat clusters grow to 4–5 in. across in spring. Edible fruit red at first, change to blue black, remaining on plant into winter. Glossy foliage turns purplish red in fall.

Grows in shade as well as sun. Use as large background shrub, small tree. Good in shade of taller trees, at woodland edge.

V. macrocephalum macrocephalum (V. m. 'Sterile'). CHINESE SNOWBALL. Deciduous shrub in coldest areas, nearly evergreen elsewhere. Zones 1–9, 14–24. To 12–20 ft. tall, with broad, rounded habit. Leaves oval to oblong, dull green, 2–4 in. long. Big rounded flower clusters to 6–8 in. are composed of sterile flowers. Blooms April-May. No fruit. Spectacular bloom clusters; plant good for espaliers, display.

V. odoratissimum. SWEET VIBURNUM. Evergreen shrub (briefly deciduous in colder-winter areas). Risky in coldest winters in Zones 8, 9, 14; reliable in 15–24. To 10–20 ft. tall, broader than tall. Leaves bright green, 3–8 in. long, have glossy, varnished-looking surface. Conical 3–6-in. clusters of white, lightly fragrant flowers, May. Fruit red, ripening black. Variety 'Emerald Lustre' has larger leaves. Use as big screen or single plant.

V. opulus. EUROPEAN CRANBERRY BUSH. Deciduous shrub. Zones 1–9, 14–24. To 10–20 ft. Lobed, maple shaped leaves 2–4 in. long and wider are dark green, turn red in fall. Flower clusters 2–4 in. across, white, rimmed with ¾-in.-wide sterile white flowers in lace cap effect, May. Large red, showy fruit. Needs careful spraying to control aphids.

V. o. 'Compactum'. Same as *V. opulus* except for smaller plant size: 4–5 ft. high and wide.

V. o. 'Nanum'. Dwarf form of *V. opulus.* To 2 ft. tall, 2 ft. wide. Needs no trimming as low hedge. Can take poor, wet soils. No flowers, fruit.

V. o. 'Roseum' (V. o. 'Sterile'). COMMON SNOWBALL. To 10–15 ft. Resembles *V. opulus* except that flower clusters resemble snowballs, 2–2½ in. through and composed entirely of sterile flowers (so no fruit).

V. plicatum plicatum (V. tomentosum 'Sterile'). JAPANESE SNOWBALL. Deciduous shrub. Zones 1–9, 14–24. To 15 ft. tall and as wide. Oval, dull dark green, strongly veined leaves 3–6 in. long. Leaves turn purplish red in fall. Snowball clusters of white sterile flowers 2–3 in. across, borne in opposite rows along horizontal branches; May. Less subject to aphids than *V. opulus.* Horizontal branching pattern, fall color, flowers all attractive.

V. p. tomentosum. DOUBLEFILE VIBURNUM. Resembles plant above, but flat flower clusters are 2–4 in. wide, edged with sterile 1–1½-in.-wide flowers in lace cap effect. Fruit red, showy, not always profuse. *V. p. t.* 'Mariesii' has larger sterile flowers.

V. propinquum. Evergreen shrub. Zones 5–9, 14–24. To 4 ft. tall. Leaves narrowish oval, 3 veined, 2–3½ in. long, dark glossy green. New growth bronzy. Greenish white flowers bloom in clusters 1½–3 in. wide. Fruit blue black, small. Resembles bushier *V. davidii* with twiggier outline, smaller leaves.

V. prunifolium. BLACK HAW. Deciduous shrub. Zones 1–9, 14–21. Upright to 15 ft. and spreading as wide. Can be trained as small tree. Common name comes from dark fruit and plant's resemblance to hawthorn (*Crataegus*). Oval leaves, to 3 in. long and finely toothed, color red in autumn. Abundant clusters of creamy white flowers in spring are followed by edible blue black fruit to ½ in. long in fall, winter. Use as dense screen or barrier, attractive specimen shrub, or small tree. Best in sun.

V. rhytidocarpum. See *V. rhytidophyllum.*

V. rhytidophylloides. See *V. rhytidophyllum.*

V. rhytidophyllum. LEATHERLEAF VIBURNUM. Evergreen shrub. Zones 2–9, 14–24. Narrow, upright shrub to 6–15 ft. tall, is fast-growing in colder areas, slow in Zones 18–24. Leaves narrowish, to 4–10 in. long, deep green and wrinkled above, densely fuzzy underneath. Flowers off-white, in clusters 4–8 in. across, in spring. Fruit scarlet, turning black. Cold-hardy, but tattered looking where cold winds blow. Some think it striking, others merely coarse. Two hybrids (neither significantly different from species): *V. rhytidocarpum* and *V. rhytidophylloides* 'Willowwood'.

V. rigidum. CANARY ISLAND VIBURNUM. Evergreen shrub. Zones 15–24. Resembles *V. tinus* but has larger flower clusters, larger leaves to 6 in. long. Grows upright to 6–10 ft. with equal or greater spread. Flowers in late winter, early spring are followed by blue fruit that later turn black. Uses same as for *V. tinus.*

Viburnum rhytidophyllum

V. suspensum. SANDANKWA VIBURNUM. Evergreen shrub. Risky in coldest winters Zones 8–10, 13–24; reliable in Zones 15–24. To 8–10 ft. tall and as broad. Leaves oval, 2–4 in. long, leathery, glossy deep green above, paler beneath. Flowers white, in 2–4-in. loose clusters in early spring. Fragrance objectionable to some people. Fruit red turning black, not long lasting. Takes sun or considerable shade. Serviceable screen, hedge, with dense foliage. Watch for thrips, spider mites, aphids.

V. tinus. LAURUSTINUS. Evergreen shrub or small narrow tree. Zones 4–10, 12, 13 (in coolest locations), 14–23. To 6–12 ft. tall, half as wide. Leaves dark green, oval, leathery, slightly rolled under at edges, 2–3 in. long. New stems wine red. Tight clusters of pink buds open to white flowers November-spring. Lightly fragrant. Fruit, bright metallic blue, last through summer. Dense foliage right to ground makes it good plant for screens, hedges, clipped topiary shapes. Mildews near ocean. May be bothered by spider mites.

V. t. 'Dwarf'. Similar to above, but grows only 3–5 ft. tall, equally wide. Low screens, hedges, foundation plantings.

V. t. 'Lucidum'. SHINING LAURUSTINUS. Leaves larger than *V. tinus*; plant less hardy, but more resistant to mildew near coast.

V. t. 'Robustum'. ROUNDLEAF LAURUSTINUS. Leaves coarser, rougher than in *V. tinus*, less pink in flowers. More resistant to mildew. Makes excellent, small narrow tree.

V. t. 'Spring Bouquet'. Foliage is slightly smaller, darker green than *V. tinus*. Plant is fairly compact, upright to about 6 ft.; good for hedges.

V. t. 'Variegatum'. Zones 4–9, 14–23. Like *V. tinus,* except that leaves are variegated with white and pale yellow.

V. trilobum. CRANBERRY BUSH. Deciduous shrub. Zones 1–11, 14–20. To 10–15 ft. tall. Leaves are much like those of *V. opulus*; turn red in fall. Lace cap flowers and fruit similar to those of *V. opulus.* Less susceptible to aphid damage than *V. opulus.*

V. wrightii. Deciduous shrub. Zones 4–9, 14–17. To 6–10 ft. tall, with narrow, erect habit. Leaves smooth, bright green, oval, 2–5 in. long, 1–2½ in. wide. Flowers small, white, in 2–4-in.-wide clusters, May. Fruit (most valuable feature) is showy, bright red, lasts many months.

VICTORIAN BOX. See *Pittosporum undulatum.*

VIGNA caracalla (*Phaseolus caracalla*. Often sold as *P. gigantea*.) SNAIL VINE. Perennial vine. Zones 12–24. Looks much like pole bean in foliage and general appearance. Climbs to 10–20 ft. Flowers (spring and summer) are fragrant, cream marked purple or pale purple. Common name comes from twisted keel petals which are coiled like snail shell. Odd and pretty. Cut to ground when frost kills tops. Plant in full sun. Will accept overwatering. Summer screen or bank cover.

Vigna caracalla

VINCA. PERIWINKLE, MYRTLE. Evergreen perennials. Trailing habit; extensively used as ground covers, for pattern plantings, and for rough slopes and otherwise unused areas. Both species can be extremely invasive in sheltered and forested areas, outcompeting many native and cultivated plants.

Vinca minor

V. major. Zones 5–24. Long trailing stems root as they spread, carry many 1–3-in., somewhat broad-based, oval, dark green, glossy leaves (white-variegated form also common). Short flowering branches with lavender blue flowers 1–2 in. across. Will mound up 6–12 in., possibly to 2 ft. high. Tough plant, quite easy to grow. Needs shade and some moisture to look its best, but will take sun if watered generously. If used as ground cover, shear close to ground occasionally to bring on fresh new growth.

V. minor. DWARF PERIWINKLE. Perfect miniature of *V. major,* except leaves are more often oblong, have shorter stalks, are more closely spaced. Also requires more care—2 or 3 good

soakings per month and feeding several times a year. In Zones 1–3, 7, 10–13, grow only in shade. Lavender blue flowers an inch across; also forms with white, double blue, and deeper blue flowers; variegated foliage. 'Bowles' Variety' has larger blue flowers.

V. rosea. See *Catharanthus roseus.*

VIOLA. VIOLET, PANSY. Perennials; some treated as annuals. Botanically speaking, violas, pansies, and violets are all perennials belonging to genus *Viola.* Pansies and violas, however, are generally treated as annuals, especially in mild-winter areas.

Viola wittrockiana

All three grow best in rich, moist soil. Plant violas and pansies in full sun in coastal areas, in partial shade in warmer sections. Violets need shade from hot afternoon sun; in desert and other hot-summer climates, plant in full shade.

Violas and pansies are invaluable for winter and spring color in mild regions, from spring through summer in cooler areas. They provide mass color in borders and edgings, as ground covers for spring-flowering bulbs, and in containers outdoors. Pansies also give colorful displays in pots and boxes. Sweet violets are notorious hosts to spider mites.

V. alba. PARMA VIOLET. Zones 4–9, 14–24. Small, sweetly fragrant, double blue purple flowers. Plant and growth habit similar to *V. odorata.* Give it rich soil, cool location, regular water. Individual plants send out runners that form new crowns. Use as small-scale ground cover in woodland gardens.

V. cornuta. VIOLA, TUFTED PANSY. All Zones. Tufted plants 6–8 in. high. Smooth, wavy-toothed, ovalish leaves. Purple, pansylike flowers, about 1½ in. across, have slender spur. Newer strains and varieties have larger flowers with shorter spurs, in solid colors of purple, blue, yellow, apricot, ruby red, and white. Crystal strain has especially large flowers in clear colors.

In mild-winter climates, sow seed of violas in late summer, set out plants in fall for color from late winter or early spring to summer. In cold regions, sow seed in September or early spring; transplant September-sown seedlings to coldframe, keep there over winter, set plants outside in spring. Named varieties of violas such as 'Maggie Mott' and 'Pride of Victoria' also increased by division or cuttings.

V. hederacea. AUSTRALIAN VIOLET. Zones 8, 9, 14–24. Tufted plant 1–4 in. high, spreads by stolons at slow to moderate rate to several feet in time. Leaves kidney shaped. Flowers, ¼–¾ in. across, nearly spurless, are white or blue fading to white at petal tips. Summer bloom; plant goes dormant at about 30°F. Use as ground cover in shade or in sun with abundant water.

V. odorata. SWEET VIOLET. All Zones. The violet of song and story. Tufted, long runners root at joints. Leaves dark green, heart shaped, toothed on margins. Flowers are fragrant, short spurred, deep violet, bluish rose, or white. Large, long-stemmed (to 6 in.) deep purple 'Royal Robe' is widely used. 'Royal Elk' has single, fragrant, long-stemmed violet-colored flowers; 'Charm' grows in clumps, has small white flowers; 'Rosina' is pink flowered. Plant size varies from 2 in. for smallest varieties, to 8–10 in. for largest. Plants spread by runners at moderate rate. Take full sun near coast and in cool-summer areas.

Remove runners and shear rank growth in late fall for better spring flower display. For heavy bloom, feed in very early spring, before flowering, with complete fertilizer.

V. priceana. See *V. sororia.*

V. sororia (*V. priceana*). CONFEDERATE VIOLET. All Zones. Stemless, with sturdy rootstock. Leaves are somewhat heart shaped, to 5 in. wide. Flowers ½–¾ in. across, white, heavily veined with violet blue, flat-faced like pansies. Self-sows readily; best in woodland garden. Good ground cover among rhododendrons.

V. tricolor. JOHNNY-JUMP-UP. Annual or short-lived perennial. To 6–12 in. tall with oval, deeply lobed leaves. Tufted habit. Purple and yellow flowers resemble miniature pansies. Color forms available in blue or in mix including yellow, lavender, mauve, apricot, red. Spring bloom. Self-sows profusely.

V. tricolor hortensis. See *V. wittrockiana.*

V. wittrockiana (*V. tricolor hortensis*). PANSY. Excellent strains with flowers 2–4 in. across, in white, blue, mahogany red, rose, yellow, apricot, purple; also bicolors. Petals striped or blotched. Plants grow to about 8 in. high. F_1 and F_2 hybrids more free flowering, heat tolerant.

Sow pansy seed from mid-July to mid-August. In mild-winter areas, set out plants in fall for bloom from late winter or early spring to summer. In cold sections, transplant seedlings into coldframe, set out plants in spring; or sow seed indoors in January or February, plant outdoors in spring. Or, plant nursery plants in spring. Pansies need rich, cool, moist soil with protection from hottest sun. To prolong bloom, pick flowers (with some foliage) regularly, remove faded blooms before they set seed. In warmer climates, plants get ragged by midsummer, should be removed.

VIOLET. See *Viola.*

VIOLET TRUMPET VINE. See *Clytostoma callistegioides.*

VIRGINIA BLUEBELLS. See *Mertensia virginica.*

VIRGINIA CREEPER. See *Parthenocissus inserta, P. quinquefolia.*

VIRGINIAN STOCK. See *Malcolmia maritima.*

VISCARIA coeli-rosa. See *Lychnis coeli-rosa.*

VITEX. CHASTE TREE. Deciduous and evergreen shrubs or trees. Two species sold in the West. Both have divided leaves and clustered flowers.

V. agnus-castus. CHASTE TREE. Deciduous shrub or small tree. Zones 4–24. Growth is slow in cold climates, fast in warmer areas. Size varies from 6 ft. in Northwest to 25 ft. in low desert. Habit broad and spreading, usually multitrunked. Leaves are divided fanwise into 5–7 narrow, 2–6-in.-long leaflets that are dark green above, gray beneath. Conspicuous 7-in. spikes of lavender blue flowers appear in summer and fall.

Vitex agnus-castus

Tolerates many types of soils, but requires plenty of summer heat for richly colored, profuse bloom. In rich, moist soils it grows luxuriantly, but has paler flowers. Good for summer flower color in shrub border. Trained high, makes good small shade tree. Resistant to oak root fungus. Varieties are: 'Alba', white flowers; 'Latifolia' (often sold as *V. macrophylla*), sturdy, with large leaflets; and 'Rosea', with pinkish flowers.

V. lucens. NEW ZEALAND CHASTE TREE. Evergreen tree. Zones 16, 17, 22–24. Slow to moderate growth to 40–60 ft. Leaves with 3–5 shining, glossy, corrugated-looking, roundish, 5-in.-long leaflets. Pink winter buds open to lavender pink 1-in. flowers in loose clusters. Fruit bright red, resembling small cherry. Needs deep, rich soil, ample water, and protection from frost while young. Luxuriant near coast; tolerates sea breezes.

VITIS. See *Grape.*

VOODOO LILY. See *Sauromatum guttatum.*

VRIESEA. Perennial. Outdoors in most frost free parts of Zones 22–24. House plant anywhere. Bromeliads (pineapple relatives) with rosettes of long, leathery leaves and oddly shaped flower clusters. Grow as epiphytes in pockets of sphagnum moss on branches or in pots of loose, highly organic mix. Keep leaf bases filled with water, and water mix occasionally. Mist if grown

Vriesea hieroglyphica

in hot, dry rooms. Feed lightly and often. Give strong light, but not direct, hot sun.

V. hieroglyphica. Rosettes of 30–40 leaves each 3 ft. long, 3 in. wide, dark green with pronounced cross-banding of blackish purple. Flower spike greenish, with dull yellow flowers.

V. lindenii. See *Tillandsia lindenii.*

V. splendens. FLAMING SWORD. Rosettes of up to 20, 1½-ft. leaves of dark green barred transversely with blackish purple. Flower stalk like a 1½–2-ft.-wide feather of bright red bracts from which small yellow flowers emerge. 'Chantrierei' is brightly colored selection.

WAFER ASH. See *Ptelea trifoliata.*

WAKE ROBIN. See *Trillium.*

WALDSTEINIA fragarioides. BARREN STRAWBERRY. Zones 2–9, 14–17. Evergreen strawberrylike ground cover 2–3 in. high, spreading 6–8 in. Leaves consist of 3 wedge shaped leaflets to 2 in. long, glossy green turning bronze in autumn. Yellow 5-petaled flowers grow to ¾ in. across, spring. Full sun to light shade, ordinary garden watering.

Waldsteinia fragarioides

WALLFLOWER. See *Cheiranthus cheiri, Erysimum.*

WALNUT (*Juglans*). Deciduous trees. Usually large and spreading, with leaves divided into leaflets. Oval or round nuts in fleshy husks. English walnut (*J. regia*) is a well-known orchard tree in many parts of the West; American native species are sometimes planted as shade trees with incidental bonus of edible nuts or are used as understock for grafting English walnut. English and California black walnut trees are notorious as hosts to aphids. The pests and their honeydew exudation are so inevitable that you should not plant either tree where branches will arch over patio or automobile parking place.

J. californica. SOUTHERN CALIFORNIA BLACK WALNUT. Zones 18–24. Native to southern California. Treelike shrub or small tree 15–30 ft., usually with several stems from ground. Leaves 6–12 in., with 9-19 leaflets to 2¼ in. long. Roundish, ¾-in. nuts have good flavor but extremely hard, thick shells. Not commercially grown, but worth saving if it grows as native. Takes drought and poor soil. Resistant to oak root fungus.

Walnut

J. cinerea. BUTTERNUT. Zones 1–9, 14–17. Native to eastern U. S. To 50–60 ft., with broad, spreading head. Resembles black walnut (*J. nigra*), but is smaller; leaves have fewer leaflets; nuts are oval or elongated rather than round. Flavor is good, but shells are thick and hard. Needs only moderate amount of summer water.

J. hindsii. CALIFORNIA BLACK WALNUT. Zones 5–9, 14–20. Native to scattered localities in northern California. Tree 30–60 ft. tall, with single trunk and broad crown. Leaves have 15–19, 3–5-in. leaflets. Widely used as rootstock for English walnut in California. Tree is resistant to oak root fungus (*Armillaria*) and drought tolerant.

J. major (*J. rupestris major*). NOGAL, ARIZONA WALNUT. Zones 10, 12–13. Native to Arizona, New Mexico, northern Mexico. Broad tree to 50 ft. Leaves have 9–13 leaflets. Round, small, thick-shelled nuts in husks that dry on tree. Takes desert heat and wind, needs deep soil, some water.

J. nigra. BLACK WALNUT. Zones 1–9, 14–21. Native to eastern U.S. High-branched tree grows to 150 ft. (usually not over 100 ft. in the West) with round crown, furrowed blackish brown bark. Leaves have 15–23 leaflets, each 2½–5 in. long. Nuts 1–1½ in. across, thick-shelled and very hard, but with rich flavor. Improved varieties (scarce) with thinner shells are 'Thomas', 'Stabler', and 'Ohio'. Big, hardy shade tree for big places. Fairly drought tolerant. Don't plant near vegetable or flower gardens, rhododendrons or azaleas. Black walnut inhibits their growth, either through root competition or by a substance that inhibits growth of other plants. Long dormant season.

J. regia. ENGLISH WALNUT. Zones 4–9, 14–23; some varieties in zones 1–3. Native to southwest Asia, southeast Europe. To 60 ft. high, with equal spread, fast growing, especially when young. Smooth gray bark on trunk and heavy horizontal or upward-angled branches. Leaves with 5–7 leaflets, rarely more, 3–6 in. long. The tree is hardy to −5°F., but certain varieties are injured by late and early frosts in colder regions. Strains from the Carpathian mountains of eastern Europe are hardy in all but the coldest mountain areas.

English walnut should not be planted as landscape tree except on very large lots. It's out of leaf a long time, messy when in leaf (drip and sooty mildew from aphid exudations), and messy in fruit (husks can stain). It needs deep soil and deep watering. Many people are allergic to the wind-borne pollen.

To thrive, these need deep soil moisture and they need to have bases of trunks kept dry to prevent fungus attack and rot. Deep, slow irrigation in basins is ideal; where tree must grow with lawn sprinkling, keep base of trunk dry by digging away earth down to level of first roots, replacing it with coarse gravel or rock. Or pave area near trunk with brick or stone on sand. Keep other plants out under drip line where feeder roots grow.

Established plants take some drought, but in dry-summer areas need deep, regular watering for top-quality nuts. Old plants need pruning only to remove dead wood or correct shape. Young plants grow fast, should be trained to make central leading shoot and branch high enough for comfortable foot traffic. Shorten overlong side branches.

Spray for aphids, scale insects, codling moths, spider mites. Walnut husk fly attacks husks, making them adhere to and disfigure nuts. Control with repeated malathion sprays.

Walnut husks open in fall, dropping nuts to ground. Hasten drop by knocking nuts from tree. Pick up nuts immediately. Remove any adhering husks. Dry in single layer spread out in airy shade until kernels become brittle, then store.

In Zone 3 grow Carpathian or Hardy Persian walnuts. In Zones 4–7, 'Adams', 'Franquette', 'Idaho', and 'Mayette' bloom late enough to escape spring frosts, yield high-quality nuts. Gardeners in Zones 8, 9 can grow 'Carmelo' (bears huge nuts), 'Drummond', 'Eureka', 'Hartley', 'Payne', 'Idaho', or 'Serr' (bears at early age). Best varieties for Zones 14–16 are 'Carmelo', 'Concord', 'Franquette', 'Hartley', 'Mayette', 'Payne', 'Serr', or 'Wasson'. In Zones 18–20 grow 'Drummond', 'Payne', or 'Placentia'. In Zones 21–23, best choice is 'Placentia'. Variety 'Laciniata' with deeply cut leaflets is occasionally sold.

WANDERING JEW. See *Callisia, Tradescantia, Tripogandra, Zebrina.*

WARMINSTER BROOM. See *Cytisus praecox.*

WASHINGTON THORN. See *Crataegus phaenopyrum.*

WASHINGTONIA. Palms. Zones 8, 9, 11–24. Native to California, Arizona, northern Mexico. Fan shaped leaves. These two are the most widely planted palms in California.

W. filifera. CALIFORNIA FAN PALM. Fast grower to 60 ft. In native stands in Southwest deserts, it always grows near springs or other moist spots. Takes desert heat and some drought, but thrives on moisture in well-drained soil. Long-stalked leaves stand well apart in open crown. As leaves mature, they bend down to form a petticoat of thatch which develops in straight lines, tapering inward toward trunk at lowest edge of petticoat. Trunk is much more robust than that of its Mexican cousin, even

Washingtonia robusta

though cousin's name is "robusta." Hardy to around 18°F.

Use young trees in containers. In landscape can serve as street or parkway planting, in groves, or in large gardens as single trees or in groups.

W. robusta. MEXICAN FAN PALM. Taller (to 100 ft.), more slender, more widely sold than California fan palm. Leaf stalks are shorter, with distinguishing reddish streak on undersides. More compact crown, less smooth thatch. Very fast growing. Old plants take on natural curvature; young ones started at an angle will grow upright to produce a bend. Hardy to 20°F. Takes poor soil or drought, but grows faster with good conditions.

WATERCRESS. All Zones. This small perennial plant grows naturally in running streams. You can plant seed in flats or pots and transplant seedlings to moist banks, where they will grow rapidly. Or insert cuttings of watercress from the market into wet soil in or near the stream; these root readily. Be quite certain the stream is free from pollution before planting out in such a location. It can also be grown in wet place in garden, but requires some shade in warm inland gardens. Or, grow it in pots of soil placed in tub of water; water should be changed at least weekly by running hose slowly into tub. Plant grows to 10–15 in. with small roundish leaflets. Flowers are insignificant.

Watercress

WATER HAWTHORN. See *Aponogeton distachyus.*

WATER HYACINTH. See *Eichhornia crassipes.*

WATER LILY. See *Nymphaea.*

WATERMELON. Annuals. These need a long growing season, more heat than most other melons, and more space than other vine crops—space "hills" (circles of seed) 8 ft. by 8 ft. Other than that, culture is as described under Melon. If you garden in a commercial watermelon growing area—Zones 8, 9, 12–14, 18–21—choose any variety that suits your fancy. If your summers are short or cool (Zones 1–6, 15–17, 22–24) choose one of the fast-maturing ("early") varieties. Those listed in catalogs and on seed packets at 70–75 days to harvest are best.

Watermelon

WATSONIA. Deciduous and evergreen perennials growing from corms. Zones 4–9, 12–24. Gardeners in Zones 1–3 can experiment growing them like gladiolus, lifting and storing corms over winter. Native to South Africa. Flowers are smaller, generally more tubular than gladiolus, on taller, branched stems. They grow in fall and winter and hence are of limited use where winters are severe. All are good cut flowers. Plant late summer or early fall; plants produce foliage in autumn. Full sun, little to moderate summer water needs except for newly planted corms. Stake tall stems if grown in pots. In mild climates they can remain undisturbed for many years. Lift and divide overcrowded clumps in summer after bloom, divide, and replant as quickly as possible.

Watsonia pyramidata

Of about 70 species the following are best known:

W. beatricis. Evergreen. Leaves 30 in. long; July-August flowers 3 in. long, bright apricot red, on somewhat branched, 3½-ft.

stems. Selected hybrids in colors from peach to nearly scarlet.

W. pyramidata. Deciduous. Blooms late spring, early summer. Rose pink to rose red 2½-in. flowers in spikelike clusters on 4–6-ft. branched stems. Leaves are 2½ ft. long, 1 in. wide. Many excellent large-flowered hybrids in pink, white, lavender, red. *W. p. ardernei* (often listed as *W. ardernei*), pure white.

WATTLE. See *Acacia.*

WAXFLOWER, GERALDTON. See *Chamelaucium uncinatum.*

WAX FLOWER, WAX PLANT. See *Hoya.*

WAX VINE. See *Senecio macroglossus.*

WAYFARING TREE. See *Viburnum lantana.*

WEDELIA trilobata. WEDELIA. Perennial. Zones 12, 13, 21–24. Trailing plant that roots wherever stems touch damp earth. Foliage evergreen; leaves somewhat fleshy, dark glossy green, to 4 in. long and half as wide, with a few coarse teeth or shallow lobes toward tips. Inch-wide flower heads resemble tiny yellow zinnias or marigolds. Blooms nearly throughout the year in sun; blooms sparsely in shade. Spreads fast by creeping, rooting stems; easily propagated by lifting rooted stems or by placing tip cuttings in moist soil. Best in sandy, fast

Wedelia trilobata

draining soils but will take others if drainage is acceptable. Reasonably salt tolerant. Killed to ground by frost, it makes fast comeback. Tolerates high heat of desert. Plant 18 in. apart, water regularly, feed lightly. Cut back hard if plantings mound up or become stemmy.

WEEPING BOTTLEBRUSH. See *Callistemon viminalis.*

WEEPING CHERRY. See *Prunus.*

WEEPING CHINESE BANYAN. See *Ficus benjamina.*

WEEPING MYALL. See *Acacia pendula.*

WEEPING WILLOW. See *Salix babylonica.*

WEIGELA. Deciduous shrubs. Zones 1–11, 14–17. Valuable for voluminous flower display late in spring season (May-June in Northwest, earlier in California). Funnel shaped flowers grow singly or in short clusters all along previous season's shoots. When weigelas finish blooming their charm fades—they aren't outstandingly attractive out of bloom. Most are rather coarse leafed and stiff, becoming rangy unless pruned

After flowering, cut back branches that have bloomed to unflowered side branches. Leave only 1 or 2 of these to each

Weigela florida

stem. Cut some of the oldest stems to ground. Thin new suckers to a few of the most vigorous. A simpler method you can employ every other year is to cut back entire plant about halfway just after blooms fade. Resulting new growth will be dense and will provide plenty of flowers the next spring.

Use as backgrounds for flower borders, as summer screens, in mixed shrub borders. Can grow in full sun to part shade. Need at least moderate summer watering.

Many garden varieties are complex hybrids of four species; names are often mixed in nursery trade.

W. 'Bristol Ruby'. To 6–7 ft. tall, nearly as wide. Ruby red flowers in late spring, some repeat bloom midsummer and fall.

W. 'Bristol Snowflake'. Resembles 'Bristol Ruby', but has white flowers.

W. florida (*W. rosea*). Fast growth to 8–10 ft. tall. Flowers pink to rose red, 1 in. long, in May and June.

W. f. 'Variegata'. Bright green foliage variegated with cream. Popular and showy.

W. 'Java Red'. Compact, mounding plant to 6 ft. or wider. Flowers deep pink opening from red buds. Foliage deep green tinted purple.

W. middendorffiana. Dense, broad shrub to 3–4 ft. tall. Leaves 2–3 in. long, 1–1½ in. wide, wrinkled, dark green. Flowers (April, May) are sulfur yellow marked orange, an inch long and as wide, clustered at ends of branches. Best in cool, moist place; less rugged than other weigelas.

W. 'Newport Red' (also sold as *W.* 'Vanicekii', 'Cardinal', 'Rhode Island Red'). To 6 ft. tall, with brilliant red flowers 1–1½ in. across in May-June.

W. praecox. Similar to *W. florida* but blooms several weeks earlier and grows to about 6 ft. tall. Flowers pink to rose with yellow throats.

WELSH POPPY. See *Meconopsis cambrica.*

WESTERN HOUND'S TONGUE. See *Cynoglossum grande.*

WESTERN LAUREL. See *Kalmia microphylla.*

WESTERN MAIDENHAIR. See *Adiantum pedatum.*

WESTERN RED CEDAR. See *Thuja plicata.*

WESTERN SAND CHERRY. See *Prunus besseyi.*

WESTRINGIA rosmariniformis. Evergreen shrub. Zones 14 (damaged in coldest winters), 15–17, 19–24. Native to Australia. Spreading, rather loose growth to 3–6 ft. tall, half again as wide. Leaves medium green to gray green above, white below, slightly finer, filmier in texture than rosemary. Small white flowers February through spring in colder areas, all year in milder climates.

Westringia rosmariniformis

Needs light, well-drained soil in sun. Little to average water. Good near coast; very wind tolerant. Effective on sunny banks and in borders with lavender; charming with *Podocarpus gracilior.*

WHEATGRASS. See *Agropyron.*

WHITE BLADDER FLOWER. See *Araujia sericifera.*

WHITE CEDAR. See *Chamaecyparis thyoides.*

WHITE CLOVER, WHITE DUTCH CLOVER. See *Trifolium repens.*

WHITE CUP. See *Nierembergia repens.*

WHITE FLOSS SILK TREE. See *Chorisia insignis.*

WHITE FORSYTHIA. See *Abeliophyllum distichum.*

WHITE GLOBE LILY. See *Calochortus albus.*

WHITE IRONBARK. See *Eucalyptus leucoxylon.*

WHITE MARIPOSA LILY. See *Calochortus venustus.*

WHITE MUGWORT. See *Artemisia lactiflora.*

WHITE ORCHID TREE. See *Bauhinia variegata* 'Candida'.

WHITE PEPPERMINT. See *Eucalyptus pulchella*.

WHITE SAPOTE. See *Casimiroa edulis*.

WHITE TRAILING ICE PLANT. See *Delosperma* 'Alba'.

WILD GINGER. See *Asarum caudatum*.

WILD HYACINTH. See *Dichelostemma pulchellum*.

WILD INDIGO. See *Baptisia australis*.

WILD LILAC. See *Ceanothus*.

WILD MARJORAM. See *Origanum vulgare*.

WILD PLUM. See *Prunus americana*.

WILD STRAWBERRY. See *Fragaria chiloensis*.

WILGA. See *Geijera parviflora*.

WILLOW. See *Salix*.

WILLOW-LEAFED JESSAMINE. See *Cestrum parqui*.

WINDFLOWER. See *Anemone*.

WINDMILL PALM. See *Trachycarpus fortunei*.

WINTER ACONITE. See *Eranthis hyemalis*.

WINTER CREEPER. See *Euonymus fortunei*.

WINTERGREEN. See *Gaultheria procumbens*.

WINTER HAZEL. See *Corylopsis*.

WINTER'S BARK. See *Drimys winteri*.

WINTERSWEET. See *Chimonanthus praecox*.

WIRE VINE. See *Muehlenbeckia*.

WISHBONE FLOWER. See *Torenia*.

WISTERIA. Deciduous vines. All Zones (but some flower buds damaged in cold winters in coldest parts of Zone 1). Twining, woody vines of great size, long life, and exceptional beauty in flower. So adaptable they can be grown as trees, shrubs, or vines.

To get off to a good start, buy cutting-grown or grafted wisteria; seedlings may not bloom for many years. With grafted plants, keep suckers removed or they may take over. Wisterias are not fussy about soil, but they need good drainage, ample water during bloom or growth. In alkaline soil, watch for chlorosis and treat with iron chelates or iron sulfate.

Pruning and training are important for bloom production and control of plant's size, shape. Let newly set plants grow to establish framework you desire, either single or multitrunked. Remove stems that interfere with desired framework, pinch back side stems and

Wisteria sinensis

long streamers, rub off buds that develop on trunk for single-trunked specimens. For multiple trunks, select as many vigorous stems as you wish and let them develop. If plant has only one stem, pinch it back to encourage others to develop. Remember that main stem will become good-sized trunk, and that weight of mature vine is considerable. Give firm support, and tie developing stems where you want them.

Tree wisterias can be bought ready-trained; or you can train your own. Remove all but one main stem, and stake this one securely. Tie stem to stake at frequent intervals; plastic tape best to prevent girdling. When plant has reached height at which you wish head to form, pinch or prune out tip to force branching. Shorten branches to beef them up. Pinch back long streamers, rub off all buds that form below head. Replace stakes and ties as needed.

Wisterias can be trained as big shrubs or multistemmed,small, semiweeping trees; permit well-spaced branches to form the framework, shorten side branches, and nip long streamers. Unsupported plants make vigorous bank cover.

Young plants should be well fed and watered; blooming-size, established plants flower better with less food and water. Prune blooming plants every winter, cutting back or thinning out side shoots from main or structural stems and shortening back to 2–3 buds the flower-producing spurs that grow from these shoots. You'll have no trouble recognizing fat flower buds on these spurs.

In summer cut back long streamers before they tangle up in main body of vine; save those you want to use to extend height or length of vine and tie them to support—eaves, wall, trellis, arbor. If old plants grow rampantly but fail to bloom, withhold all nitrogen fertilizers for an entire growing season (buds for the next season's bloom are started in early summer). If that fails to produce bloom the next year, you can try pruning roots in spring—after you're sure no flowers will be produced—by cutting vertically with spade into plant's root zone.

W. floribunda (often sold as *W. multijuga*). JAPANESE WISTERIA. Leaves are 12–16 in. long, divided into 15–19 leaflets. Violet or violet blue, fragrant flowers in 18-in. clusters appear with leaves in April-May. Flowers begin to open at base of cluster, gradually open toward tip, prolonging bloom season but making less spectacular burst of color than Chinese wisteria. Long clusters give extreme beauty of line. Many varieties obtainable in white, pink, and shades of blue, purple, lavender, usually marked with yellow and white. 'Longissima' ('Macrobotrys'), very long (1½–3 ft.) clusters of violet flowers; 'Longissima Alba', white flowers in 2-ft. clusters.

Japanese wisteria blooms best in full sun.

W. sinensis. CHINESE WISTERIA. Most widely planted throughout West. Leaves divided into 7–13 leaflets. Plants bloom before leaves expand in April-May. Flower clusters are shorter (to 12 in.) than those of Japanese wisteria, but make quite a show by opening nearly full length of cluster at one time. Violet blue, slightly fragrant. Will bloom in considerable shade. *W. s.* 'Alba' is white-flowering form.

W. venusta (often sold as *W. v.* 'Alba'). SILKY WISTERIA. Broad leaves and leaflets have silky hairs. Individual flowers are white, very large, long-stalked, in short, heavy clusters that open all at once. Very profuse bloom when leaves begin to open in April. Plant in full sun for best bloom. *W. v.* 'Violacea' has fragrant, purple blue flowers. Older plants (especially in tree form) remarkably profuse in bloom.

WITCH HAZEL. See *Hamamelis*.

WONGA-WONGA VINE. See *Pandorea pandorana*.

WOODBINE. See *Parthenocissus*.

WOOD FERN. See *Dryopteris*.

WOOD HYACINTH. See *Endymion non-scriptus*.

WOODRUFF. See *Galium odoratum.*

WOOD SORREL. See *Oxalis acetosella.*

WOODWARDIA. CHAIN FERN. Large, strong-growing ferns. The only common species in cultivation is native giant chain fern.

Woodwardia fimbriata

W. fimbriata (often sold as *W. chamissoi* or *W. radicans*). GIANT CHAIN FERN. Zones 4–9, 14–24. Native British Columbia to Mexico, always in moist places. The largest native fern, it can reach 9 ft. tall in wet coastal forests. Fronds twice cut, rather coarse in texture, with strong upright or spreading silhouette. Excellent near pool or brook, against shaded wall, in woodland gardens. Slow to establish if dug from clumps; nursery plants grown from spores or tissue culture are vigorous and rapid. Ultimately withstands neglect.

W. orientalis. Zones 17, 22–24. Native to Japan, Formosa. Broad, arching, drooping fronds to 8 ft. long, of leathery texture and quite red when immature, deep green later. Produces many plantlets on fronds. Stunning in shaded, moist raised beds, where its fronds will cascade; or massed at woodland edge. Needs partial shade. Hardy to 26°F.

W. radicans. EUROPEAN CHAIN FERN. Zones 15–17, 19–24. Southern Europe to China. Resembles *W. fimbriata* but more arching and drooping, the fronds broader at the base. Forms bulblets at tips of fronds; these root while attached to plant. To 3 ft. tall, fronds 4–6 ft. long, 1½–2 ft. wide. Uses, culture as for *W. orientalis.*

WOOLLY BLUE CURLS. See *Trichostema lanatum.*

WOOLLY SENNA. See *Cassia tomentosa.*

WORMWOOD. See *Artemisia.*

XANTHORRHOEA. GRASSTREE. Perennials. Zones 16, 17, 20–24. Native to Australia. Dense tufts of narrow, long, grasslike leaves radiate out from top of thick, woody, nearly black, very slow-growing stem. White flowers grow in dense, narrow spike on tall stem. Drought resistant. Best used with yuccas, century plants, succulents in full sun and dry, loose, sandy soil.

Xanthorrhoea preissii

X. preissii. BLACKBOY. Stem is slow growing, but in age may reach 15 ft. Leaves 2–4 ft. long, about ⅛ in. wide. Flower spike 1–3 ft. long, on stem of equal length.

X. quadrangulata. Trunk reaches several feet high. Leaves 1½ ft. long. Spike and its stem may reach 12–15 ft.

XANTHOSOMA. Cormlike tubers. Best adapted Zones 23, 24; in protected gardens Zones 12, 13, 16, 17, 21, 22; or anywhere as indoor or greenhouse plant in winter, outdoors in summer. Tropical foliage plants related to *Alocasia.* All have big arrow shaped leaves on long stalks. Flowers clustered on spike surrounded by callalike bract (spathe), usually greenish or yellowish and more curious than attractive. Rich soil, ample water. Use with ferns, begonias, schefflera in warm filtered shade, humus soil. Protect from hard frosts.

X. sagittifolium. Trunklike stem to 3 ft. Dark green leaves 3 ft. long on 3-ft. stems. Spathes greenish white, 7–9 in. long.

Xanthosoma violaceum

X. violaceum. Stemless, forming clumps by offsets. Leaves to 2 ft. long, 18 in. wide, dark green above, lighter beneath, purplish veins and margin, powdery appearance. Leaf stalks 2½ ft., purple, with heavy, waxy, bluish or grayish cast. Spathes yellowish white, large.

XERANTHEMUM annuum. COMMON IMMORTELLE. Summer annual. To 2½ ft. tall. Everlasting flower; fluffy heads of papery bracts up to 1½ in. across in pink, lavender, white, shades of violet purple. Scant foliage is silvery green. Sow seed in spring in place in full sun. Accepts almost any soil, regular watering. Cut flowers dried for winter bouquets.

Xeranthemum annuum

XYLOSMA congestum (*X. senticosum*). Evergreen or deciduous shrub or small tree. Zones 8–24. Usually loose, graceful, spreading shrub 8–10 ft. tall and as wide or wider. Height is easily controlled. Leaves are shiny, yellowish green, long-pointed oval in shape, clean and attractive. New growth bronzy. Flowers insignificant, rarely seen. Some plants are spiny.

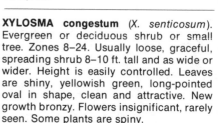

Xylosma congestum

Left alone, plants develop angular main stem that takes its time zigzagging upward. Meanwhile side branches grow long and graceful, arching or drooping, sometimes lying on the ground. Easily trained as espalier. If shrub is staked and side growth pruned, can be made into 15–30-ft. spreading tree. Variety 'Compacta' grows more slowly, reaches half the size of species.

Adaptable to most soils; heat tolerant; established plants survive with little water but look better with adequate water, moderate feeding. Best growth in full sun or filtered shade. Spray as necessary to control occasional scale or red spider mites. Apply iron chelates or iron sulfate for chlorosis.

One of the handsomest, easiest, and most versatile of the all-foliage, landscape structure plants. Unattractive appearance in nursery cans (especially in winter, when plants may be nearly bare of leaves) and slow start in ground may discourage the gardener. Plants actually are hardy to 10°F., but may lose many (or all) leaves in sharp frosts. Plant normally sheds many old leaves in April when new growth begins. Frost at that time will kill new growth. Well-established plants usually evergreen except in coldest seasons, and new leaves come fast.

Use as single or multitrunked tree, arching shrub, ground or bank cover (prune out erect growth), espalier on wall or fence, clipped or unclipped hedge (twine long branches together to fill in gaps faster), container shrub in large (18 in. or more) container.

YANGTAO. See *Actinidia chinensis.*

YARROW. See *Achillea.*

YATE. See *Eucalyptus cornuta.*

YAUPON. See *Ilex vomitoria.*

YELLOW BELLS. See *Tecoma stans.*

YELLOW CUCUMBER TREE. See *Magnolia acuminata cordata.*

YELLOW ELDER. See *Tecoma stans.*

YELLOW-EYED GRASS. See *Sisyrinchium californicum.*

YELLOW FLAX. See *Reinwardtia indica*.

YELLOW FRITILLARY. See *Fritillaria*.

YELLOW LADY SLIPPER. See *Cypripedium calceolus pubescens*.

YELLOW MESSMATE. See *Eucalyptus cloeziana*.

YELLOW OLEANDER. See *Thevetia peruviana*.

YELLOW TRUMPET FLOWER. See *Tecoma stans*.

YELLOW TRUMPET VINE. See *Anemopaegma chamberlaynii, Macfadyena unguis-cati*.

YELLOW WOOD. See *Cladrastis lutea*.

YERBA BUENA. See *Satureja douglasii*.

YESTERDAY-TODAY-AND-TOMORROW. See *Brunfelsia pauciflora* 'Floribunda'.

YEW. See *Taxus*.

YEW PINE. See *Podocarpus macrophyllus*.

YOUNGBERRY. See Blackberry.

YUCCA. Evergreen perennials, shrubs, trees. Yuccas grow over much of North America, and hardiness depends on species. All have clusters of tough, sword shaped leaves and large clusters of white or whitish flowers. Some are stemless while others reach tree size. Best in full sun in well-drained soil. Most take considerable drought when established—many are true desert plants. Most will accept garden watering. Useful near swimming pools. Fire retardant if reasonably well watered.

Yucca whipplei

Group with agaves, cactus, succulents in desert gardens or grow with various softer leafed tropical foliage plants. Taller kinds make striking silhouettes, and even stemless species make important and vertical effects when in bloom. Some have stiff, sharp-pointed leaves; keep these away from walks, terraces, other well-traveled areas.

Young plants of some species can be used as indoor plants. They withstand dry indoor atmosphere and will grow well in hot, sunny windows. Buy gallon-can size or smaller; plant out in garden when they become too large for house. Successful indoors are *Y. aloifolia* (but beware of sharp-pointed leaves), *Y. elephantipes, Y. filamentosa, Y. gloriosa, Y. recurvifolia*.

Y. aloifolia. SPANISH BAYONET. Zones 7–24. Native southern U.S. Slow growth to 10 ft. or more, trunk either single or branched, or sprawling in picturesque effect. Sharp-pointed leaves to 2½ ft. long and 2 in. wide densely clothe stems. Leaves are dark green; in *Y. a.* 'Variegata' they are marked yellow or white. Flowers white sometimes tinged purple, to 4 in. across in dense, erect clusters to 2 ft. tall. Summer bloom. Sharp-spined leaf tips a hazard if plant is near walkway.

Y. baccata. DATIL YUCCA. All Zones. Native to deserts of southern California, Nevada, to Colorado and Texas. Grow as single stemless rosettes or sometimes in clumps with short, leaning trunks to 3 ft. Leaves 2 ft. long, 2 in. wide. Flowers (May-June) fleshy, red brown outside, white inside, in dense clusters 2 ft. long. Fleshy fruit was eaten by Indians.

Y. brevifolia. JOSHUA TREE. Zones 8–24. Native to deserts of southern California, Nevada, Utah, Arizona. Tree of slow growth to 15–30 ft. with heavy trunk and few, heavy branches. Leaves clustered near ends of branches, short, broad, sword shaped. Old, dead leaves hang on a long time. Flowers (February-April) greenish white, in dense, heavy, foot-long clusters.

Collected plants sometimes available; nursery plants are very slow to make trunks. Best in dry, well-drained soil in desert gardens. Difficult under average garden conditions.

Y. elata. SOAPTREE YUCCA. Zones 7–24. Native to Arizona, New Mexico, west Texas, and northern Mexico. Slow growth to 6–20 ft. with single or branched trunk. Leaves to 4 ft. long, ½ in. wide. White summer flowers bloom in very tall spikes.

Y. elephantipes (*Y. gigantea*). GIANT YUCCA. Zones 12 and 13 (protected from sun, hard frosts), 16, 17, 19–24. Native to Mexico. Fast growing (to 2 ft. a year), eventually 15–30 ft. tall, usually with several trunks. Leaves 4 ft. long, 3 in. wide, dark rich green, not spine tipped. Striking silhouette alone or combined with other big-scale foliage plants; out of scale in smaller gardens. Large spikes of creamy white flowers in spring. Does best in good, well-drained soil with ample water.

Y. filamentosa. All Zones. Native to southeastern U.S. Much like *Y. flaccida,* but with stiffer, narrower leaves, narrower flower clusters. Variety 'Bright Eagle' has leaves margined in creamy white.

Y. flaccida. Zones 1–9, 14–24. Native of southeastern U.S. Stemless. Leaves to 2½ ft. long, 1 in. wide, with long, loose fibers at edges of leaves. Flowers white, in tall branching clusters to 4–7 ft. or more in height. Lightly fragrant in the evening. One of hardiest, most widely planted in colder regions.

Y. glauca. SMALL SOAPWEED. All Zones. Native Texas, New Mexico to Montana, South Dakota. Stemless or short stemmed. Leaves 1–2½ ft. long. Summer flowers greenish white in tall narrow clusters.

Y. gloriosa. SPANISH DAGGER, SOFT-TIP YUCCA. Zones 7–9, 12 and 13 (protected from frost, reflected heat), 14–24. Much like *Y. aloifolia,* generally multitrunked to 10 ft. tall. Blooms late summer. Leaf points soft, will not penetrate skin. Good green color blends well with lush, tropical-looking plants. Easy garden plant, but overwatering may produce black areas on leaf margins. There is a variegated form.

Y. harrimaniae. All Zones. Native to Colorado and Southwest. Short stemmed or stemless; clumps single or clustered. Leaves yellowish or bluish green, 4–18 in. long, ½–1½ in. wide. Summer flowers greenish white, 2–2½ in. across, in erect, unbranched clusters 1–3 ft. tall. May be slow to bloom in coldest climates.

Y. recurvifolia (*Y. pendula*). Zones 7–10, 12–24. Native southeastern U.S. Single, unbranching trunk to 6–10 ft. tall, or lightly branched in age. Can be cut back to keep single trunked. Spreads by offsets to make large groups. Leaves, 2–3 ft. long, 2 in. wide, beautiful blue gray green, are spine tipped, sharply bent downward. Leaf tips bend to touch, are not dangerous. Less stiff and metallic looking than most yuccas. Flowers (in June) are large, white, in loose, open cluster 3–5 ft. tall. Easy to grow under all garden conditions.

Y. schidigera (*Y. mohavensis*). Zones 10–24. Native to deserts of California, Nevada, Arizona, Baja California. Trunk 3–12 ft. tall, single or branched. Tough, sharp-tipped leaves 2–3 ft. long, 1–2½ in. wide, yellowish green. Flowers (April-May) in 2-ft. clusters, creamy or purple tinted.

Y. schottii (*Y. macrocarpa*). Zones 7–9, 11–24. Native to Arizona, New Mexico, northern Mexico. Treelike with unbranched or branched trunk 6–20 ft. tall. Leaves gray green to yellow green, 1½–3 ft. long, 1½ in. wide, tipped with sharp spines. Summer flowers are white, 1–2 in. long, in branched clusters 1–3 ft. long

Y. torreyi. TORREY YUCCA. Zones 7–24. Native to west Texas. Trunk to 10–15 ft., usually not branched. Leaves to 3 ft. long, stiff, sharp pointed. White summer flowers in dense, heavy, fat-looking clusters partially hidden by leaves.

Y. whipplei. OUR LORD'S CANDLE. Zones 2–24. Native to southern California mountains, California coast, Baja California. Stemless, with dense cluster of rigid, gray green leaves 1–1¾ ft. long. These are needle tipped; don't plant where people can walk into them.

(Continued on next page)

Flowering stems to 6–14 ft. long. Drooping, bell shaped, 1–2-in. creamy white blossoms in large branched spikes 3–6 ft. long. Plants die after blooming and producing seed. New plants come from seeds or offsets.

YUSHANIA. See *Bamboo.*

ZABEL LAUREL. See *Prunus laurocerasus* 'Zabeliana'.

ZANTEDESCHIA. CALLA. Rhizomes. Zones 5, 6, 8, 9, 14–24. Native to South Africa. Basal clumps of long-stalked, shining, rich green, arrow or lance shaped leaves, sometimes spotted white. Flower bract surrounds central spike that is tightly covered with tiny true flowers.

Common calla tolerates many soils. Full sun near coast, partial shade in hot-summer areas. Thrives on heavy watering, even grows in bogs. Nearly evergreen in mild areas, deciduous where winters are cold. Set rhizomes 4–6 in. deep, 1–2 ft. apart.

Zantedeschia aethiopica

Golden, pink, and spotted callas need slightly acid soil, moderate water with drainage, and a resting season. Plant 2 in. deep, 12 in. apart. In mild climates they survive in well-drained, open ground beds. If drainage is poor or frosts heavy, dry off gradually in late summer, dig, and store at 40°–50°F. in dry soil, sawdust, or peat moss. To grow in pots, set 2 in. deep (1 rhizome to 6-in. pot), water sparingly until leaves appear. Then water freely, feed weekly with mild solution of complete fertilizer. Reduce watering after bloom to dry off plants, then withhold entirely until new growth begins.

Z. aethiopica. COMMON CALLA. Forms large clump of leaves 18 in. long, 10 in. wide. Pure white or creamy white 8-in.-long bracts on 3-ft. stems appear mostly spring and early summer. Variety 'Godefreyana' smaller than species, flowers very heavily. 'Hercules' larger than species, has big bracts that open flat, curve backward. 'Childsiana' is 12 in. tall. 'Minor' 18 in., bracts 4 in. long.

Z. albomaculata. SPOTTED CALLA. Grows to 2 ft. Leaves spotted white. Bracts 4–5 in. long, creamy yellow or white with purplish crimson blotch at base. Spring-summer bloom.

Z. elliottiana. GOLDEN CALLA. To 18–24 in., with bright green, white-spotted leaves 10 in. long by 6 in. wide. Flower bracts 4–5 in. long, changing from greenish yellow to rich golden yellow. June-July. Tolerates full sun, even in hot-summer areas.

Z. rehmannii. RED OR PINK CALLA. To 12–18 in., with narrow, lance shaped, unspotted green leaves 1 ft. long. Pink or rosy pink bracts to 4 in. long. Blooms May. 'Superba' deeper pink, improved variety, generally sold rather than species. Hybrids of this and other callas available; flowers range through pinks and yellows to orange and buff tones, with some purplish and lavender tones on yellow grounds.

ZANTHOXYLUM piperitum. JAPAN PEPPER. Deciduous shrub or small tree. Zones 6–9, 14–17. Dense, to 20 ft. Leaves, to 8 in. long divided into 7–11, 2-in.-long, oval leaflets. Main leaf stalk prickly. Form sometimes seen in California nurseries has yellow main leaf stalk, yellow blotches at base of each leaflet. Flowers are inconspicuous, green. Small, black, aromatic fruit ground and used as seasoning in Japan.

Ordinary garden soil, full sun, moderate water.

Zanthoxylum piperitum

ZAUSCHNERIA. CALIFORNIA FUCHSIA, HUMMINGBIRD FLOWER. Perennials or subshrubs. Zones 4–10, 12–24. These California natives can take dry, hot summers and give many pretty red flowers against gray foliage from summer to fall but they never will become completely domesticated. Most grow a bit rangy,

spread into other garden beds with invasive roots, go to seed and reseed themselves, and become twiggy and ungroomed through the winter. Use them in full sun in informal gardens, at summer cabins, on banks or hillsides. All have small, gray or gray green, narrow leaves, ½–1½ in. long, and bright scarlet, trumpet shaped flowers, 1½–2 in. long. The flowers attract birds.

Z. californica. Stems upright or somewhat arching, 1–2 ft. tall. Plants sometimes shrubby at base. Evergreen in mild-winter climates.

Zauschneria californica

Z. c. latifolia (*Z. septentrionalis,* often sold as *Z. latifolia* 'Etteri') is a perennial that makes mats of closely set stems about 6 in. high. Dies to ground in winter.

Z. cana. Stems woody at base, sprawling. Foliage dense; leaves very narrow, silvery. Evergreen in mild-winter climates.

ZEBRA BASKET VINE. See *Aeschynanthus marmoratus.*

ZEBRA PLANT. See *Calathea zebrina.*

ZEBRINA pendula. WANDERING JEW. Evergreen perennial. This house plant has much the same growth habit and leaf shape as *Tradescantia fluminensis,* but is not as hardy. Small clusters of flowers are purplish rose and white. Known mostly in its variegated forms. *Z. pendula* 'Quadricolor' has purplish green leaves with longitudinal bands of white, pink, and carmine red. *Z. p.* 'Purpusii' has leaves of dark red or greenish red. Other varieties add white, pink, and cream to prevailing colors. When selecting a location indoors, remember that variegated plants need more light than all-green ones.

Zebrina pendula

ZELKOVA serrata. SAWLEAF ZELKOVA. Deciduous tree. Zones 3–21. A good shade tree, it grows at moderate to fast rate, eventually to 60 ft. or higher, and equally wide. Smooth gray bark like that of beech. Leaves similar to those of elm (2–3½ in. long by 1½ in. wide) but rougher textured with sawtooth margins. Carefully train young trees to develop strong framework—head back excessively long pendulous branches to force side growth, thin competing branches to permit full development of the strongest. Water deeply to encourage deep rooting. Very pest resistant; sometimes gets red spider mites.

Zelkova serrata

Fall foliage color varies from yellow to dark red to dull reddish brown. Variety 'Village Green' is somewhat hardier, faster growing than species, with arching branches; silhouette reminiscent of American elm (*Ulmus americana*).

ZENOBIA pulverulenta (*Andromeda speciosa*). Deciduous shrub. Zones 4–7, 14–17. Native southeastern U.S. Slow growth to 2–4, possibly 6 ft. Open, loose growth. Leaves pale green, 1–2 in. long, half as wide; new growth heavily dusted with bluish white powder in pearly gray effect. Flowers white, bell shaped, ½ in. across, grow in loose clusters at ends of branches. Blooms June-July in Northwest. Sometimes spreads by underground stems.

Related to heaths and heathers; needs acid, uniformly moist soil, partial shade in warm exposures.

Zenobia pulverulenta

ZEPHYR FLOWER. See *Zephyranthes.*

ZEPHYRANTHES. ZEPHYR FLOWER, FAIRY LILY. Bulbs. Zones 1–9, 14–24. Bright green, rushlike leaves. Funnel shaped flowers with six similarly shaped segments appear singly on hollow stems, usually in late summer or early fall, often throughout the year if kept alternately wet and dry. In the wilds, flowers appear a few days after a rain (hence, often called rain lilies).

Zephyranthes candida

Use in rock garden or foreground of border. Good in pots. Plant late summer or early fall; set bulbs 1–2 in. deep, 3 in. apart. Full sun, although *Z. candida* takes light shade. In cold climates, plant in spring and lift in fall; or mulch heavily over winter months.

Z. ajax. Hybrid between *Z. candida* and *Z. citrina.* Free flowering, light yellow. Evergreen. Leaves to 8 in. long.

Z. candida. Rushlike, glossy evergreen leaves to 1 ft. in large clumps. Crocuslike flowers 2 in. long, glossy textured, pure white outside, tinged rose inside, borne singly on stems as long as leaves; blooms in late summer, autumn.

Z. citrina. Fragrant, lemon yellow, 2-in. flowers; narrow, ridged leaves. Stems 10 in. tall.

Z. grandiflora. Flowers 4 in. across, rose pink, look like small amaryllis; 8-in. stems. Leaves 12 in. long, appearing with flowers in late spring, early summer.

Z. hybrids. 'Alamo' has deep rose pink flowers flushed yellow. 'Apricot Queen', low growing, has yellow flowers stained pink. 'Prairie Sunset', large, light yellow flowers suffused with pink, appearing after rain or a watering. 'Ruth Page' is rich pink.

ZINGIBER officinale. TRUE GINGER. Perennial with thick rhizomes. Zones 9, 14–24. Rhizomes are the source of ginger used in cooking. Stems 2–4 ft. tall. Narrow, bright green glossy leaves to 1 ft. long. Flowers (rarely seen) are yellowish green, with purple lip marked yellow, not especially showy, in summer. Tropical in origin, ginger needs heat and humidity, shade from hottest sun. Buy roots (fresh, not dried) at grocery store in early spring; cut into 1–2-in.-long sections with well-developed growth buds. Let cut ends dry, then plant just underground in rich, moist soil. Water cautiously until top and root growth are active, then heavily. Feed once a month.

Zingiber officinale

Plants are dormant in winter; rhizomes may rot in cold, wet soil. Plant with tree ferns, camellias, fuchsias, begonias. Harvest roots at any time—but allow several months for them to reach some size.

ZINNIA. Summer annuals. Long-time garden favorites for colorful, round flower heads in summer and early fall. Distinctly hot-weather plants, they do not gain from being planted early; merely stand still until weather warms up. Subject to mildew in foggy places, or when given overhead water, and when autumn brings longer nights, more dew, and more shade. Sow seeds where plants are to grow (or set out nursery plants) in May–July. Give plants good garden soil in sunny place. Feed and water generously but always water by soaking soil, not by overhead sprinkling.

Zinnia elegans

Most garden zinnias belong to *Z. elegans,* but the other two species are grown.

Z. angustifolia. Compact plants to 8 in. tall. Leaves very narrow. Inch-wide flower heads orange, each ray with a paler stripe. Blooms in six weeks from seed, continues late into fall. 'Classic'

grows 8–12 in. tall, spreads to 2 ft. Can be perennial where winters are mild. Good in hanging baskets.

Z. elegans. Plant height ranges from 1–3 ft., leaves to 5 in., flower head size from less than 1 in. to as much as 5–7 in. across; forms include full doubles, cactus flowered (with quilled rays), crested (cushion center surrounded by rows of broad rays); colors include white, pink, salmon, rose, red, yellow, orange, lavender, purple, and green.

Many strains are available, from dwarf plants with small flowers to 3-ft. sorts with 5-in. blooms. Extra dwarf (to 6 in. tall) are the Mini series and Thumbelina strain. Other small-flowered kinds on larger (12 in.) but still compact plants are Cupid and Buttons; still taller (to 2 ft.) but small flowered are the Lilliputs. Peter Pan strain has 3-in. blooms on bushy dwarf plants to 12 in.; Whirligig has large bicolored flowers on 18-in. plants. Large-flowered strains with 2–3-ft. plants include California Giants, Dahlia Flowered, Giant Cactus Flowered, Ruffles, State Fair, and Zenith.

Z. haageana. Plants compact, 1–1½ ft. tall, 3-in. leaves narrower than on common zinnias. Double strains Persian Carpet (1 ft. tall) and Old Mexico (16 in. tall) have flowers in strong shades of mahogany red, yellow, and orange, usually mixed in the same flower head. Colorful, long blooming.

ZIZIPHUS jujuba. CHINESE JUJUBE. Deciduous tree. Zones 7–16, 18–24; hardy in Zones 4–6 but fruit ripens only in warmest summers. Slow to moderate growth rate to 20–30 ft. Branches spiny, gnarled, somewhat pendulous. Leaves glossy, bright green, 1–2 in. long, with 3 prominent veins. Clusters of small yellowish flowers in May-June. Shiny reddish brown datelike fruit in fall have sweet applelike flavor; candied and dried, they resemble dates.

Ziziphus jujuba

Deep rooted, it takes well to desert conditions, tolerating drought, saline and alkaline soils. Grows better in good garden soil with regular, deep watering. Thrives in lawns. No serious pests, but subject to Texas root rot in deserts. Prune in winter to shape, encourage weeping habit, or reduce size. Attractive silhouette, foliage, fruit, and toughness make it a good decorative tree, especially for high desert. Foliage turns a good yellow in fall.

Fruit of seedlings are ½–1 in. long. Two cultivated varieties are 'Lang' (1½–2-in.-long fruit, bears young) and 'Li', with 2-in.-long fruit.

ZOYSIA. Perennial grasses used for lawns and ground covers. They tend to spread slowly, are fairly deep rooted and drought tolerant. Thrive in sun but tolerate some shade. Dormant and straw-colored during the winter; turn green in spring. Plant using sod, sprigs, stolons, or plugs. Cut lawns ¾ in. high.

Zoysia tenuifolia

Z. japonica 'Meyer'. MEYER ZOYSIA. Zones 12, 13. Resembles bluegrass in appearance and texture. Turns brown earliest in winter, turns greens latest in spring.

Z. matrella. MANILA GRASS. Zones 8, 9, 12–14, 18–24. Also similar to bluegrass in appearance. Holds color into winter a little better than Meyer.

Z. tenuifolia. KOREAN GRASS. Hardy in Zones 8, 9, 12–24; best in Zones 18–24. Creeping, fine-textured, bumpy. Makes a beautiful grassy meadow or gives mossy Oriental effect in areas impossible to mow or water often. The farther inland, the longer the dormant season.

Z. tenuifolia 'Emerald'. EMERALD ZOYSIA. Zones 8, 9, 12–14, 18–24. Wiry, dark green, prickly looking turf. Dense, wiry blades hard to cut. More frost tolerant than other zoysias.

ZUCCHINI. See Squash.

Glossary

To prepare a comprehensive gardening book, it is necessary to use a number of special words that derive from the art of horticulture and the science of botany. These gardening terms serve as a sort of shorthand in explanations and descriptions. Grouped in this glossary are the special words and phrases used in this book: some are particular to the world of plants, others are familiar words that take on new meanings when applied to gardening.

In addition to these gardening terms, certain other words describe specific large groups of plants—bamboo, bromeliad, cycad, cactus, fern, herb, orchid, palm, succulent. These words are fully explained in their alphabetical places in the Western Plant Encyclopedia.

Acid soil, Alkaline soil. Acidity and alkalinity describe one aspect of the soil's chemical reaction: the concentration of hydrogen ions (an ion is an electrically charged atom or molecule). The relative concentration of hydrogen ions is represented by the symbol pH followed by a number. A pH of 7 means that the soil is neutral, neither acid nor alkaline. A pH below 7 indicates acidity, above 7 indicates alkalinity.

Many plants will grow well over a range of pH from slightly acid to slightly alkaline; some garden favorites are more particular. Usually they need an acid soil (most rhododendrons, azaleas, heathers, for example). Soils in areas with high rainfall tend to be acid. Areas where rainfall is light tend to have alkaline soils. For more information, see page 34.

Actual (as in actual nitrogen). Sometimes we recommend a certain amount of actual nitrogen; to calculate it, multiply the total weight of fertilizer by the percentage of the particular nutrient. A 25-pound bag of fertilizer that contains 5 percent nitrogen will yield 1¼ pounds actual nitrogen (25 pounds × .05 = 1.25 pounds). The same formula will allow you to calculate actual phosphorus or potash. It will also allow you to calculate the real nutritive value of a given fertilizer.

Alkaline soil. See **Acid soil.**

Annual. A plant that completes its life cycle in a year or less is called an annual. Seed germinates and the plant grows, blooms, sets seed, and dies—all in one growing season. Examples are marigolds *(Tagetes)* and zinnias. The phrase "grow as an annual" or "treat as an annual" means to set out a plant in spring after the last frost, enjoy it from spring through fall, and pull it out or let the frosts kill it at the end of the year. (Some plants that desert gardeners treat as annuals are planted in fall, grow and bloom during winter and spring, and then are killed by summer heat.)

Backfill. Backfill soil is returned to a planting hole after a plant's roots have been positioned. Sometimes backfill is simply the soil dug out to create the planting hole; more often it is mixed with some organic soil amendments to improve its texture.

Balled and burlapped (sometimes abbreviated B and B). From late fall to early spring, some nurseries sell shrubs and trees with a large *ball* of soil around the roots, wrapped in *burlap* to hold the soil together. Usually these are plants that cannot be offered BARE ROOT.

Bare root. In winter and early spring, nurseries offer many deciduous shrubs and trees, and some perennials, with all soil removed from their roots. These are dormant plants dug from growing fields, trimmed and freed of soil, and then protected against drying out until planting.

Biennial. This type of plant completes its life cycle in two years. Two familiar biennials are foxglove *(Digitalis)* and Canterbury bells *(Campanula medium)*. Typically you plant seeds in spring and set out the seedling plants in summer or fall. The plants bloom the following spring, then set seed and die.

Bolt. Annual flowers and vegetables that grow too quickly to flowering stage at the expense of developing well otherwise are said to *bolt*. This happens most often when plants are set out too late in the year or when unseasonably hot weather rushes the growth.

Bonsai. A Japanese term, bonsai is one of the fine arts of gardening: growing carefully trained, dwarfed plants in containers selected to har-monize with the plants. The objective is to create in miniature scale a tree or landscape; often the dwarfed trees take on the appearance of very old, gnarled specimens. To get the desired effect the bonsai craftsman meticulously wires and prunes branches, and trims roots.

Bracts. These modified leaves may grow just below a flower or flower cluster (not all flowers have bracts). Usually bracts are green, but in some cases they are conspicuous and colorful, constituting what people regard as "flowers" (examples are bougainvillea, dogwood, and poinsettia).

Broadcast. To broadcast means to scatter seed by hand over the soil surface; the ground may be a prepared surface, as for a lawn, or uncultivated, as in scattering wildflower seed.

Broad-leafed. The phrase "broad-leafed evergreen" refers to a plant that has green foliage all year but is not an evergreen CONIFER such as a juniper, with needlelike or scalelike foliage. A broad-leafed weed is any weed that is not a grass.

Bud. This word has several definitions. A flower bud is one that develops into a blossom. A growth bud may be at the tip of a stem *(terminal)* or along the sides of a stem *(lateral);* these buds will produce new leafy growth (see page 30). Finally, *to bud* a plant is to propagate by a process similar to grafting (see page 41).

Bulb. In everyday conversation, any plant that grows from a thickened underground structure is referred to as a "bulb." But a true bulb is one particular type of underground stem. (Others, defined in this glossary and on pages 75–77, are Corms, Rhizomes, Tubers, and Tuberous roots). The true bulb is more or less rounded and composed of fleshy scales (actually modified leaves) that store food and protect the developing plant inside. The outer scales dry to form a papery covering. Slice an onion in half from top to bottom to see a typical example.

Caliche. A soil condition found in some areas of the arid Southwest, caliche is a deposit of calcium carbonate (lime) beneath the soil surface. For help in dealing with it, see "Shallow soil" (page 34).

Calyx. See *Sepals* under **Flower parts.**

Cambium layer. See **Grafting.**

Catkin. A catkin is a slender, spikelike, and often drooping flower cluster. Catkins are either male or female: in some plants the male catkins are borne on one individual plant, the female on another (cottonwoods, willows); or both male and female catkins may be produced on each individual plant (alders, birches).

Chilling requirement. Many deciduous shrubs and trees (fruit trees in particular) and perennials need certain amounts of cold weather in winter in order to grow and bloom well during the following year. Where winters are mild and these plants fail to get the necessary winter chill, their performance will be disappointing: plants fail to flower or fruit well, and often the plant declines in health and vigor even to the point of dying. With some of these plants (apples and lilacs, for example) varieties have been developed that require less winter cold than is normal for the type. Gardeners in milder winter areas should choose varieties with low chilling requirements.

Chlorosis. When a leaf looks yellower than it should (especially between the leaf veins), it often is chlorotic or suffering from *chlorosis.* Frequently chlorosis is caused by a plant's inability to obtain the iron it needs to produce green coloring. For one way to correct this condition, see IRON CHELATE.

Complete fertilizer. Any plant food that contains all three of the primary nutrient elements—nitrogen, phosphorus, potassium—is a complete fertilizer.

Composite family (Compositae). This enormous family of plants includes all the flowers known as daisies—and many more. What appears to be an individual flower actually is many small flowers tightly grouped into a head and surrounded by BRACTS that form a cup (involucre). A typical daisy is composed of two kinds of flowers: *disk flowers* are the small tubular flowers that usually are tightly packed together to form the round, cushionlike center of a daisy; *ray flowers* are those that appear to be petals (each "petal" is an individual ray flower) surrounding the central disk flowers. Some composites have disk flowers only (chamomile and santolina, for example); others, such as most dahlias, marigolds, and zinnias, have blossoms that consist only of ray flowers.

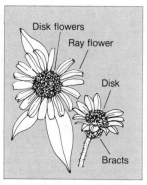

Conifer. Conifer is a more precise word for the plants many people call "evergreens," such as cedars, cypresses, junipers, and pines. Leaves on most are narrow and needlelike or tiny and scalelike. Not all conifers are evergreen, but all bear their seeds in cones or in modified conelike structures.

Conservatory. Originally a conservatory was a greenhouse for displaying rather than growing plants; now it is simply a fancy greenhouse.

Corm. Technically, a corm is a thickened underground stem capable of producing roots, leaves, and flowers during the growing season. Gladiolus and crocus are two familiar plants that grow from corms. A corm differs from a bulb in that food is stored in the solid center tissue, whereas in bulbs food is stored in scales. See also BULB and pages 75–77.

Corolla. See *Petals* under **Flower parts.**

Cuttings. These are portions of stem or root, sometimes called "slips," that can be induced to form roots and develop into new plants. A more complete description is on pages 38–39.

Daisy flower. See **Composite family.**

Damping off. This plant disease, caused by fungi in the soil, makes small seedlings rot, wilt, or fall over and die, just before or soon after they break through the soil.

Deciduous. Any plant that sheds all of its leaves at one time each year (usually in fall) is deciduous.

Defoliation. This refers to the unnatural loss of a plant's leaves, usually to the detriment of the plant's health. Defoliation may result from high winds that strip foliage away, intense heat (especially if accompanied by wind) that critically shrivels or wilts leaves, drought, unusually early or late frosts that strike a plant still in active growth, or severe attacks by insects or diseases.

Dieback. In dieback, a plant's stems die, beginning at the tips, for a part of their length. Causes are various: not enough water, nutrient deficiency, plant not adapted to climate in which it is growing, severe insect, mite, or disease injury.

Disk flower. See **Composite family.**

Dividing. This is the easiest way to increase perennials, bulbs, and shrubs that form clumps of stems with rooted bases. Procedural information is on pages 37–38.

Double flower. A double flower has an indefinite number (usually large) of petals that give it an unusually full appearance.

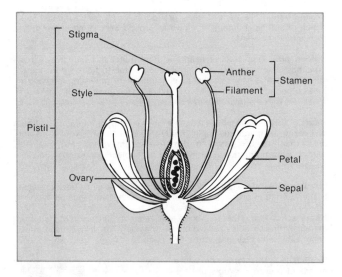 ...

Dividing

Drainage. Drainage refers to the movement of water through the soil in a plant's root area. When this happens quickly, the drainage is "good," "fast," or the soil is "well drained"; when it happens slowly the drainage is said to be "slow," "bad," or soil is "poorly drained." For plants to grow, water must pass through soil. Plant roots need oxygen as well as water, and soil that remains saturated deprives roots of necessary oxygen. Fast drainage (water disappears from a shrub planting hole in 10 minutes or less) is typical of sandy soils; slow drainage (water still remains in planting hole after an hour) is found in clay soils and where hardpan exists. Refer to pages 33–35 for more information on soils and drainage.

Drip line. The circle that you would draw on the soil around a tree directly under its outermost branch tips is called a drip line. Rainwater tends to drip from the tree at this point. The term is used in connection with feeding, watering, and grading around existing trees and shrubs.

Dust. This word defines a type of insecticide or fungicide and its method of application. Several insecticides and fungicides are manufactured as powders so finely ground that they are *dust.* You put the product into a special applicator (sometimes the container is the applicator) and *dust* it onto the plants. If you do this in early morning when air is still, the dust makes a large cloud, the particles of which slowly settle as a thin, even coating over everything. The advantage of dusting over spraying is convenience: no mixing, fast application, and easy clean-up.

Epiphyte. These plants grow on another plant for support but receive no nourishment from the host plant. Familiar examples are cattleya orchids and staghorn ferns. These are often mistakenly called *parasites;* true parasites steal nourishment from the host.

Espalier. This is a tree or shrub trained so its branches grow in a flat pattern—against a wall or fence, on a trellis, along horizontal wires. Espaliers may be formal and geometric, or informal.

Evergreen. This kind of plant never loses all leaves at one time. For plants many people call "evergreens," see CONIFER. Also refer to BROAD-LEAFED.

Everlastings. Flowers that hold their shape and color when dried are called everlastings. See list on page 115.

Eye. This undeveloped growth bud ultimately will produce a new plant or new growth. The "eyes" on a potato will, when planted, produce new potato plants. Eye is synonymous with one definition of BUD.

Family. See **Plant classification.**

Fertilize. In popular usage, this word has two definitions: to fertilize a flower is to apply pollen (the male element) to a flower's pistil (the female element) for the purpose of setting seed. See POLLINATION. To fertilize a plant is to apply nutrients (plant food, usually referred to as fertilizer).

Flower parts. The flower parts illustrated above are described on this page and the next, starting from the outside and moving toward the center:

Sepals make up the outer circle. Usually these are green, but in some flowers (fuchsias and irises, for example) they are brightly colored and petal-like. Collectively they are called a *calyx.*

Petals form the next circle of flower parts, inward from the sepals. In showy flowers, it is usually the petals that make the show. Collectively a flower's petals are called the *corolla.* Petals may be separate, as in camellias and roses, or united into tubular, cupped, or bell-like shapes as in petunias.

Stamens are the flower parts containing the male reproductive elements. Typically a stamen consists of a slender stalk (the *filament*) topped by an *anther* (most often a yellow color) which contains the grains of pollen—the male element needed to fertilize the flower in order to produce seed. Some plants produce flowers having only stamens (male) or only pistils (female). These can be either on the same or separate plants. Many flowers contain both male and female elements.

Pistils, in the very center part of the flower, bear the female reproductive parts. Typically, each pistil consists of an ovary at the base, in which seeds will form following POLLINATION, and a stalklike tube called the *style* that rises from the ovary. The style is topped by the *stigma,* the part that receives the pollen.

Forcing.   Forcing is a process of hastening a plant along to maturity or a marketable state, or of growing a plant to the flowering or fruiting stage out of its normal season, usually by growing it under shelter, as in a greenhouse, where temperature, humidity, and light can be controlled.

Formal.   The term formal means regular, rigid, and geometric. In gardening, it is variously applied to flowers, methods of training, and styles of garden design. A formal double flower, as in some camellias, consists of layers of regularly overlapping petals. Examples of formal plant training are rigidly and geometrically structured espaliers and evenly clipped hedges. Formal gardens are those laid out in precise geometric patterns, often containing formal hedges and espaliers.

Foundation plant.   This outmoded but persistent term originally described a plant used to hide the foundation of a house. Since many of today's homes lack high or even visible foundations, the term has come to mean any shrub you plant near the house walls.

Frond.   In the strictest sense, fronds are the foliage of ferns. Often, however, the word is also applied to the leaves of palms and is even used to designate any foliage that looks fernlike.

Genus.   See **Plant classification.**

Girdling.   This refers to the choking of a branch by a wire, rope, or other inflexible material. It occurs most often in woody plants that have been tightly tied to a stake or support. As the tied limb increases in girth, the tie fails to expand in diameter and cuts off supplies of nutrients and water to the part of the plant above the tie; if girdling goes unnoticed, the part of the plant above the constriction will die.

Grafting.   With this method of plant propagation, a section of one plant (called the *scion*) is inserted into a branch of another plant (the *stock*). Procedural information is on pages 41–44.

Ground bark.   The bark of trees, ground up or shredded for use as a mulch or soil amendment, is known as ground bark. It may have other names in some areas.

Harden off.   This process adapts a plant that has been grown in a greenhouse, indoors, or under protective shelter, to full outdoor exposure. The plant is exposed, over a week or more, to increasing intervals of time outdoors, so that when it is planted out in the garden it can make the transition with a minimum of shock.

Hardy.   This term describes a plant's resistance to, or tolerance of, frost or freezing temperatures (as in "hardy to −20° F."). The word does not mean tough, pest resistant, or disease resistant. A half-hardy plant is hardy in a given situation in normal years, but subject to freezing in coldest winters.

Heading back.   This is a pruning term for cutting a branch back to a side branch or bud to promote more compact growth. See pages 68–69.

Heavy soil.   This rather imprecise term refers to dense soil made up of extremely fine particles packed closely together. The term is used interchangeably with clay and adobe. See page 33.

Heeling in.   This term refers to a means of preventing roots of bareroot plants from drying out before you can set them out in the garden. Simplest is to dig a shallow trench, lay the plant on its side so that roots are in the trench, then cover roots with soil, sawdust, or other material, moistened to keep roots damp.

Herbaceous.   Herbaceous, the opposite of *woody,* describes a plant with soft (non-woody) tissues. In the strictest sense it refers to plants that die to the ground each year and regrow stems the following growing season. In the broadest sense it refers to any non-woody plant—annual, perennial, or bulb.

Honeydew drip.   Aphids, as well as several other sucking insects, secrete a sticky substance called *honeydew;* certain ants and fungi feed on honeydew, adding to the mess. Often honeydew from a tree will drip onto whatever is below: car, patio, or other plants.

Humus.   The soft brown or black substance formed in the last stages of decomposition of animal or vegetable matter is called humus. Common usage has incorrectly applied the word to almost all organic materials that eventually would decompose into humus—sawdust, ground bark, leaf mold, and animal manures, for example.

Hybrid.   See **Plant classification.**

Iron chelate (pronounced *key*-late).   This chemical remedy for plants that show signs of CHLOROSIS is a combination of iron and a complex organic substance that makes the iron readily available to roots.

Lath.   In gardening, this word designates any overhead plant-protecting structure (originally a roof of spaced laths) that reduces the amount of sunlight that shines on plants beneath or protects them from frost.

Layering.   In this method of propagating plants, a branch is rooted while it is still attached to the plant. See page 40.

Leaching.   Think of brewing tea or coffee. When you pour hot water through tea leaves or ground coffee you are *leaching.* You leach soil with water when you want to remove excess salts (see SALINITY). In high-rainfall areas, rain water leaches good as well as bad substances from the soil.

Leader.   In a single-trunked shrub or tree, this is the central, upward-growing stem.

Leaflet.   If a leaf is divided into completely separated divisions, these are called leaflets. They may be arranged like the fingers of a hand (palmate) or like the divisions of a feather (pinnate).

Leaf mold.   This term refers to partially decomposed leaves that can be dug into the soil as an organic amendment. Most familiar is oak leaf mold.

Leaf scar.   This usually rounded or crescent shaped mark on a branch indicates where a leaf stalk once was attached.

Light soil.   The opposite of HEAVY SOIL, this is an imprecise term referring to soil composed of relatively large particles loosely packed together. The term is synonymous with sandy (see page 33).

Mulch.   Any loose, usually organic material placed over the soil, such as ground bark, sawdust, straw, or leaves, is a mulch. The process of applying such materials is called *mulching.* A mulch can do any of these tasks: reduce evaporation of moisture from soil; reduce or prevent weed growth; insulate soil from extreme or rapid changes of temperature; prevent mud from splashing onto foliage and other surfaces; protect falling fruit from injury; or make a garden bed look tidy.

Naturalize.   This means to plant out randomly, without precise pattern, and leave in place to spread at will. Some plants have the capability to naturalize, meaning they can spread or re-seed themselves, growing as wildflowers.

Node.   This joint in a stem is the point where a leaf starts to grow. The part between joints is the internode.

Offset.   In some perennials, a mature plant may send out from its base a short stem, at the end of which develops a small new plant. The new plant is the offset. Familiar examples are hen and chicks *(Echeveria),* hen and chickens *(Sempervivum),* and strawberry. Also see STOLON.

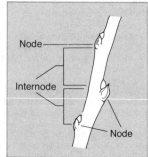

Organic matter.   This term includes any material of organic origin—peat moss, ground bark, compost, and manure, for example—that can be dug into the soil to improve its condition.

Parasite. See **Epiphyte.**

Peat moss. This highly water-retentive, spongy organic soil amendment is the partially decomposed remains of any of several mosses. It is somewhat acid in reaction, adding to soil acidity.

Perennial. A perennial is a non-woody plant that lives for more than two years. Frequently the word is used to mean a plant in which the top growth dies down each winter and regrows the following spring, but some perennials keep their leaves all year.

Perlite. Perlite is a mineral expanded by heating to form white, very lightweight, porous granules useful in container soil mixes for retaining moisture and air.

Petals. See **Flower parts.**

Pinching back. This basic pruning technique is simply using thumb and forefinger to nip off the tips of branches; this forces side growth so that plant will grow to be more compact and dense.

Pistils. See **Flower parts.**

Plant classification. Botanists have classified plants into an orderly, ranked system reflecting similarities among the world's plant life. The plant kingdom is broken down into groups that are less and less inclusive: division, class, order, and then the groups defined below, which are the ones of most significance to gardeners.

Family. Each plant belongs to a family. All members of a particular family share certain characteristics that are not found in other families. Although family names—Rosaceae (rose family), Liliaceae (lily family)—aren't as important to gardeners as are the groups into which the families are divided, sometimes knowing the family name contributes to an understanding of a plant's cultural requirements.

Genus. A plant family is divided into groups of more closely related plants, each group called a genus (the plural is *genera*). Sometimes a family will contain only one genus: the Ginkgoaceae contains only the genus *Ginkgo;* at the other extreme, the composite family (Compositae) contains around 950 genera. The first word in a plant's botanical name is the name of the genus to which the plant belongs: for example, *Ginkgo, Liquidambar, Primula.*

Species. Each genus is subdivided into groups of individuals called species; the second word in a plant's botanical name designates the species. A few genera contain only one species (the genus *Ginkgo* consists only of the species *Ginkgo biloba*), but more often a genus contains two or more species. Each species is a generally distinct entity, reproducing from seed with only a small amount of variation. Species in a genus share many common features but differ in one or more characteristic.

Subspecies, Variety. A third word in a botanical name indicates a subspecies or variety. In the strictest sense, a subspecies is more inclusive than a variety. Subspecies is often used to denote a geographical variant of a species, but in general usage subspecies and variety have become virtually interchangeable. Subspecies or varieties retain most characteristics of their species while differing in some particular way, such as flower color or leaf size. The name may appear in either of two ways: *Juniperus chinensis sargentii* (subspecies), or *Juniperus chinensis* 'San Jose' (a variety).

Horticultural variety (clone or cultivar). These often are of hybrid origin. They are usually listed by genus name followed by cultivar name, as *Rosa* 'Chrysler Imperial'. Some have been found as wild plants but have been perpetuated by cuttings or other means of vegetative propagation.

Hybrid. This is a distinct plant resulting from a cross between two species, subspecies, varieties, cultivars, strains—or any combination of the above—or even between two plants belonging to different genera. Some occur in the wild (such as *Halimiocistus,* a hybrid between a species of *Halimium* and a species of *Cistus*), but more often hybrids are the deliberate product of horticultural experiment.

Strain. Many popular annuals and some perennials are sold as strains, such as State Fair zinnias. Plants in a strain usually share similar growth characteristics but are variable in some way—usually in flower color.

Pleaching. This is a method of training plant growth where branches are interwoven and plaited together to form a hedge or arbor. Subsequent pruning merely keeps a neat, rather formal pattern.

Pollarding. In this pruning style the main limbs of a young tree are drastically cut back to short lengths. Each dormant season following, the growth from these branch stubs is cut back to one or two buds. In time branch ends become large and knobby. The result is a compact, leafy dome during the growing season and a somewhat grotesque branch structure during the dormant months. London plane tree *(Platanus acerifolia)* is most often subjected to this treatment.

Pollination. This occurs when pollen is transferred from stamens to pistils (see FLOWER PARTS for definition of stamens and pistils) for the purpose of setting fruit or seed. Usually pollination is accomplished by natural means—wind, insects, self-pollination—though the gardener can transfer pollen from one flower to another to insure fruit or to attempt a hybrid cross.

Some plants—certain hollies, for example—bear male flowers (stamens only) and female flowers (pistils only) on separate plants; to produce fruit on the female plant, you need to locate a male plant nearby. With some fruit trees you need to plant two varieties in order to get fruit. This may be because a variety will not set fruit using its own pollen, or because its pollen is not ripe at the same time as the pistil is receptive—so you need a different variety that will ripen pollen when the pistil of the first is ready.

Pot bound. See **Root bound.**

Pseudobulb. This thickened, aboveground modified stem, found in some orchids such as *Cymbidium*, serves as a storage organ for nutrients.

Ray flower. See **Composite family.**

Rhizome. This thickened, modified stem grows horizontally along or under the soil surface. It may be long and slender, as in some lawn grasses, or thick and fleshy, as in many irises.

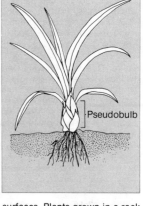

Pseudobulb

Rock garden. Usually a man-made landscape, often on sloping ground, a rock garden contains natural-appearing rock outcrops and rocky soil surfaces. Plants grown in a rock garden are generally low-growing, spreading or mat-forming types that conform to the rocky terrain. A special type of rock garden is the alpine garden, in which plants from high altitudes are grown in a replica of their native setting. Many favorite rock garden plants require fast drainage, full sun, and are somewhat drought tolerant.

Root bound. This condition develops when a plant grows for too long in its container. With no room for additional growth, roots become tangled, matted, and grow in circles. Root bound plants placed in the ground without having roots untangled often never outgrow their choked condition and fail to grow well—or grow at all.

Rootstock. This is the part of a budded or grafted plant (see BUDDING, GRAFTING) that furnishes the root system and sometimes part of the branch structure. UNDERSTOCK has the same meaning.

Runner. In common usage, this imprecise term has come to refer either to OFFSETS or STOLONS. A runner is a slender stem sent out from the bases of certain perennials, at the end of which an OFFSET develops.

Salinity. Gardeners use this word when speaking of an excess of salts in the soil. Frequently a buildup of salts occurs in semiarid regions, resulting from continued light watering with low-quality water containing sodium. In such regions, gardeners must periodically wash (leach) accumulated salts out of the plant root zone. High salinity can do great harm to many plants, causing leaves to scorch and turn yellow, and stunting plant growth.

Scree. These are the fragmented rocks and pebbles found in nature at the base of a cliff or around large rocks in a rocky landscape. Some gardeners create their own artificial scree as a place for growing choice alpine plants. Also see ROCK GARDEN.

Self-branching. This term describes certain annuals that produce numerous side growths and grow compactly without having to be pinched back.

Semidouble flower. This flower form has a few more than the basic minimum number of petals for its kind (see SINGLE FLOWER), but not so many petals that the stamens and pistils are obscured. (*Petals, stamens,* and *pistils* are defined under FLOWER PARTS.)

Sepals. See **Flower parts.**

Single flower. This flower type has the minimum number of petals for its kind, usually 4, 5, or 6 (basic number for roses, for example, is 5).

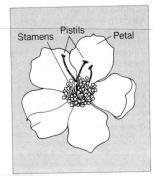

Species. See **Plant classification.**

Sphagnum. Various mosses native to bogs are called sphagnum. Much of the PEAT MOSS sold in the West is composed partly or entirely of sphagnum mosses in a partially decomposed state. These mosses also are collected live and packaged in whole pieces, fresh or dried, and used in planting certain orchids, for lining hanging baskets, and for air layering.

Spike. This is a flowering stem on which flowers are directly attached (without any short stem to each flower) along the upper portion of its length. The flowers open in sequence, beginning at the bottom of the spike. Familiar examples are *Gladiolus* and red hot poker *(Kniphofia)*.

Spore. A spore is a simple type of reproductive cell capable of producing a new plant. Certain kinds of plants (such as algae, fungi, mosses, and ferns) reproduce by spores.

Spur. Some fruit trees, particularly apples and cherries, bear their blossoms on a specialized short twig called a spur.

Spurs. These are short and saclike or long and tubular projections from a flower (the columbine, *Aquilegia,* is a familiar example). Spurs can arise from either sepals or petals (see FLOWER PARTS for *sepal* and *petal* definitions).

Stamens. See **Flower parts.**

Standard. A plant that does not naturally grow as a tree can be trained into a small treelike form, with a single, upright trunk topped by a rounded crown of foliage. The "tree rose" is the most familiar example of a standard.

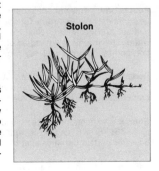

Stolon

Stolon. This is a stem that creeps along the surface of the ground, taking root at intervals and forming new plants where it roots (as opposed to OFFSETS which may form at the ends of RUNNERS). Bermuda and St. Augustine grasses spread by stolons.

Strain. See **Plant classification.**

Stress. Stress refers to the condition or conditions under which a plant is growing with danger to its health. Stress may stem from lack of water, too much heat, wind, or moisture, or low temperatures. The stressful condition varies according to the particular plant and its needs.

Subshrub. This type of plant, usually under 3 feet high and with more or less woody stems, is sometimes grown and used as a perennial, sometimes grown and used as a shrub.

Subspecies. See **Plant classification.**

Sucker. In a grafted or budded plant, sucker growth originates from the ROOTSTOCK rather than from the desired grafted or budded part of the plant. In trees, any strong vertical shoot growing from the main framework of trunk and branches is sometimes called a sucker, although the more proper term for such growth is *watersprout.*

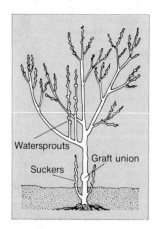

Watersprouts

Suckers

Graft union

Systemic. A systemic is any chemical that is absorbed into a plant's system, either to kill organisms that feed on the plant or to kill the plant itself. There are systemic insecticides, fungicides, and weed killers.

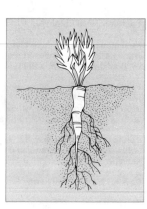

Taproot. This main root grows straight down, like the root of a carrot or dandelion. In dry areas, some plants have very deep taproots to reach a deep water table.

Tender. Tender means the opposite of HARDY. It denotes low tolerance of freezing temperatures.

Tendrils. These twisting, threadlike projections are found on some vines. Tendrils enable vines to cling to supports and climb.

Thinning out. This pruning term means to remove entire branches—large or small—back to the main trunk, a side branch, or the ground. The object is to give the plant a more open structure. Also see page 69.

In growing plants from seed, thinning out means removing excess plants so those remaining are spaced far enough apart to develop well.

Topdress. To topdress means to apply on the surface, usually referring to the spreading of an organic material such as ground bark or manure on the soil as a mulch. Sometimes it refers to application of manure or sewage sludge on a lawn as a low-grade plant food.

Topiary. This is the technique of shaping shrubs and trees into formalized shapes resembling such things as animals and geometrical figures. Sometimes inaccurately called "poodle pruning" which really describes only the sort of topiary work that produces puffs of growth.

Truss. A cluster of flowers, usually rather compact, at the end of a stem, branch, or stalk is called a truss. The most familiar rhododendrons carry their flowers in trusses.

Tuber. This fat underground stem, from which a plant grows, is similar to a RHIZOME but is usually shorter, thicker, and doesn't lengthen greatly as it grows. The world's most famous tuber is the potato.

Tuberous root. This thickened underground food storage structure is actually a root rather than a true tuber, which is a modified stem. Growth buds are in the old stems at the upper end of the root. The dahlia is a familiar example.

Underplant. Underplanting refers to planting one plant beneath another, such as a ground cover under a tree.

Understock. See **Rootstock.**

Variety. See **Plant classification.**

Vermiculite. A mineral (mica) is heated and puffed up to form spongelike, lightweight granules useful in conditioning container soils. Vermiculite granules hold both water and air.

Watersprout. See **Sucker.**

Wettable powder. This finely ground pesticide can be mixed in water and sprayed onto plants. Some kinds also can be dusted on, as described under DUST.

Whorls. Whorls are composed of three or more leaves, branches, or flowers growing in a circle from a joint (node) on a stem or trunk.

Whorls

A guide to understanding botanical names

Botanical names are in Latin, the universal language of scholars at the time plant classification was formalized. The genus name of a plant (see PLANT CLASSIFICATION) usually is a classical word that has a general or indefinite meaning. The species name usually is descriptive (color, form, leaf structure), commemorative (named after a person), or geographical

(signifying the region where the plant grows or was discovered).
The following words occur regularly in the botanical names of plants. All are descriptive adjectives used in the meaning of species, subspecies, and varieties. We have listed all such words as ending in "-us", but the same root word ending in "-a" carries the same meaning.

Color of flowers or foliage
albus—white
argentatus—silvery
aureus—golden
azureus—azure, sky blue
caesius—blue gray
coeruleus—dark blue
candidus—pure white, shiny
canus—ashy gray, hoary
carneus—flesh colored
cereus—waxy
citrinus—yellow
coccineus—scarlet

concolor—one color
croceus—yellow
cruentus—bloody
discolor—two colors, separate colors
glaucus—as though sprinkled with light powder
incanus—gray, hoary
luteus—reddish yellow
purpureus—purple
rubens, ruber—red, ruddy
rufus—ruddy

Form of leaf
acerifolius—maplelike leaves
angustifolius—narrow leaves
aquifolius—sharp leaves
buxifolius—leaves like boxwood
ilicifolius—hollylike leaves

laurifolius—laurel-like leaves
parvifolius—small leaves
populifolius—poplarlike leaves
salicifolius—willowlike leaves

Shape of plants
adpressus—pressing against, hugging
altus—tall
arboreus—treelike
capitatus—headlike
compactus—compact, dense
confertus—crowded, pressed together
contortus—twisted
decumbens—lying down
depressus—pressed down
elegans—elegant; slender, willowy
fastigiatus—branches erect and close together

humifusus—sprawling on the ground
humilis—low, small, humble
impressus—impressed upon
nanus—dwarf
procumbens—trailing
prostratus—prostrate
pumilus—dwarfish, small
pusillus—puny, insignificant
repens—creeping
reptans—creeping
scandens—climbing

Where it came from
The suffix *-ensis* (of a place) is added to place names to specify the habitat where the plant was first discovered.
australis—southern
borealis—northern
campestris—of the field or plains
canadensis—of Canada
canariensis—of the Canary Islands
capensis—of the Cape of Good Hope area

chilensis—of Chile
chinensis—of China
hortensis—of gardens
insularis—of the island
littoralis—of the seashore
montanus—of the mountains
riparius—of river banks
rivalis, rivularis—of brooks
saxatilis—inhabiting rocks

Plant peculiarities
armatus—armed
baccatus—berried, berrylike
barbatus—barbed or bearded
campanulatus—bell or cup shaped
ciliaris—fringed
cordatus—heart shaped
cornutus—horned
crassus—thick, fleshy
decurrens—running down the stem
dendron—tree
diversi—varying
edulis—edible
floridus—free flowering
fruticosus—shrubby
fulgens—shiny
gracilis—slender, thin, small
grandi—large, showy
ifer, iferous—bearing or having. For example, *stoloniferous*, having stolons
laciniatus—fringed or with torn edges
laevigatus—smooth
lobatus—lobed

maculatus—spotted
mollis—soft, soft hairy
mucronatus—pointed
nutans—nodding, swaying
officinalis—medicinal
obtusa—blunt or flattened
oides—like or resembling. For example: *jasminoides,* like a jasmine
patens—open spreading growth
pinnatus—constructed like a feather
plenus—double, full
plumosus—feathery
praecox—precocious
pungens—piercing
radicans—rooting, especially along the stem
reticulatus—veined
retusus—notched at blunt apex
rugosus—wrinkled, rough
saccharatus—sweet, sugary
sagittalis—arrowlike
scabrus—rough feeling
scoparius—broomlike

Index

The index that follows gives page numbers for general garden subjects only. Plant encyclopedia is on pages 161—505.

(Continued on next page)

Photographers

William Aplin: 121 bottom, 124, 148 top. **Diana Bunce:** 145 left. **Ed Carman:** 116. **William Carter:** 151. **Glenn Christiansen:** 128, 132 bottom, 134. **Gerald R. Fredrick:** 114, 150. **Steve W. Marley:** 97, 98, 101, 105, 139 right, 140 top right, 145 right. **Ells Marugg:** 100, 102, 104 left, 106, 109, 112, 131 bottom, 135, 137, 138, 140 top left, 146, 155, front cover. **Don Normark:** 152. **Norman A. Plate:** 104 right, 123, 132 top, 140 bottom, 157, 159. **Bill Ross:** 131 top, 139 left, 143, 153, 158. **Darrow M. Watt:** 121 top. **Peter D. Whiteley:** 148 bottom.